PHILIP'S ROAD

2018 MOTORIST'S BRITAIN & IRELAND

robertharding / Alamy

www.philips-maps.co.uk

First published in 2017 by Philip's
a division of Octopus Publishing Group Ltd
www.octopusbooks.co.uk
Carmelite House, 50 Victoria Embankment
London EC4Y 0DZ
An Hachette UK Company
www.hachette.co.uk

First edition 2017
First impression 2017

ISBN 978-1-84907-460-5

Cartography by Philip's
Copyright © 2017 Philip's

This product includes mapping data licensed from Ordnance Survey®, with the permission of the Controller of Her Majesty's Stationery Office. © Crown copyright 2017. All rights reserved. Licence number 100011710

The map of Ireland on pages XIV-XV is based upon the Crown Copyright and is reproduced with the permission of Land & Property Services under delegated authority from the Controller of Her Majesty's Stationery Office, © Crown Copyright and database right 2017, PMLPA No 100503, and on Ordnance Survey Ireland by permission of the Government © Ordnance Survey Ireland / Government of Ireland Permit number 9075.

Information for National Parks, Areas of Outstanding Natural Beauty, National Trails and Country Parks in Wales supplied by the Countryside Council for Wales.

Information for National Parks, Areas of Outstanding Natural Beauty, National Trails and Country Parks in England supplied by Natural England. Data for Regional Parks, Long Distance Footpaths and Country Parks in Scotland provided by Scottish Natural Heritage.

Gaelic name forms used in the Western Isles provided by Comhairle nan Eilean.

Data for the National Nature Reserves in England provided by Natural England. Data for the National Nature Reserves in Wales provided by Countryside Council for Wales. Darparwyd data'n ymwneud â Gwarchodfeydd Natur Cenedlaethol Cymru gan Gyngor Cefn Gwlad Cymru.

Information on the location of National Nature Reserves in Scotland was provided by Scottish Natural Heritage.

Data for National Scenic Areas in Scotland provided by the Scottish Executive Office. Crown copyright material is reproduced with the permission of the Controller of HMSO and the Queen's Printer for Scotland. Licence number C02W0003960.

Printed in China

*Data from Nielsen Total Consumer Market 2015, Weeks 1–48

CONTENTS

Inside back cover: **County and unitary authority boundaries**

Road map symbols

Symbol	Description
M6	Motorway, toll motorway
4 · 5	Motorway junction – full, restricted access
S · S	Motorway service area – full, restricted access
	Motorway under construction
A453	Primary route – dual, single carriageway
S · S	Service area, roundabout, multi-level junction
4 · 5	Numbered junction – full, restricted access
	Primary route under construction
	Narrow primary route
Derby	Primary destination
A34	A road – dual, single carriageway
	A road under construction, narrow A road
B2135	B road – dual, single carriageway
	B road under construction, narrow B road
	Minor road – over 4 metres, under 4 metres wide
	Minor road with restricted access
2	Distance in miles
	Scenic route
TOLL	Toll, steep gradient – arrow points downhill
	Tunnel
	National trail – England and Wales
	Long distance footpath – Scotland
	Railway with station
	Level crossing, tunnel
	Preserved railway with station
	National boundary
	County / unitary authority boundary
	Car ferry, catamaran
	Passenger ferry, catamaran
	Hovercraft
CALAIS	Ferry destination
Ferry	Car ferry – river crossing
	Principal airport, other airport
	National park
	Area of Outstanding Natural Beauty – England and Wales
	National Scenic Area – Scotland
	forest park / regional park / national forest
	Woodland
	Beach
	Linear antiquity
	Roman road
1066	Hillfort, battlefield – with date
795	Viewpoint, nature reserve, spot height – in metres
	Golf course, youth hostel, sporting venue
	Camp site, caravan site, camping and caravan site
P&R	Shopping village, park and ride
29	Adjoining page number – road maps

Relief

Feet	metres
3000	914
2600	792
2200	671
1800	549
1400	427
1000	305
0	0

Road map scale 1:200 000 • 3·15 miles to 1 inch

0 1 2 3 4 5 6 miles
0 1 2 3 4 5 6 7 8 9 10 km

Parts of Scotland 1:250 000 • 3·94 miles to 1 inch

0 1 2 3 4 5 6 7 8 miles
0 1 2 3 4 5 6 7 8 9 10 11 12 km

Orkney and Shetland Islands 1:340 000, approximately 5.25 miles to 1 inch

Approach map symbols

Symbol	Description
M6	Motorway
	Toll motorway
6 · 5	Motorway junction – full, restricted access
S	Service area
	Under construction
A6	Primary route – dual, single carriageway
S	Service area
	Multi-level junction
	Roundabout
	Under construction
A195	A road – dual, single carriageway
B1288	B road – dual, single carriageway
	Minor road – dual, single carriageway
	Ring road
3	Distance in miles
COSELEY	Railway with station
LOXDALE	Tramway with station
M	Underground or metro station
	Congestion charge area

Town plan symbols

Symbol	Description
	Motorway
	Primary route – dual, single carriageway
	A road – dual, single carriageway
	B road – dual, single carriageway
	Minor through road
	One-way street
	Pedestrian roads
	Shopping streets
	Railway with station
City Hall	Tramway with station
	Bus or railway station building
	Shopping precinct or retail park
	Park
	Building of public interest
	Theatre, cinema
P	Parking, shopmobility
Bank	Underground station
West St	Metro station
H	Hospital, Police station
PO	Post office

Tourist information

Symbol	Description	Symbol	Description	Symbol	Description	Symbol	Description
✝	Abbey, cathedral or priory		Church		House and garden		Safari park
	Ancient monument		Country park England and Wales Scotland		Motor racing circuit		Theme park
	Aquarium		Farm park		Museum		Tourist information centre
	Art gallery		Garden		Picnic area	i	open all year
	Bird collection or aviary		Historic ship		Preserved railway	i	open seasonally
							Zoo
	Castle		House		Race course		
						Roman antiquity	Other place of interest

Motorway service areas

Motorway service area
Kinross
M9
M90
Stirling
M80
M9
Old Inns
Bothwell
M8
Heart of Scotland
Hamilton
M74
Happendon
Abington
A74(M)
Annandale Water
Gretna Green
Todhills
Southwaite
Washington
Durham
A1(M)
M6
Tebay
Killington Lake
Burton-in-Kendal
Scotch Corner
A1(M)
Wetherby
Lancaster
M6
M55
M65
Hartshead Moor
Blackburn with Darwen
Ferrybridge
Charnock Richard
M62
M62
Doncaster North
Birch
Rivington
Woolley Edge
M180
Burtonwood
M1
Blyth
Knutsford
Woodall
M56
Chester
Sandbach
Tibshelf
M1
Trowell
Keele
Stafford
Donington Park
M6
Telford
Norton Canes
Leicester
M54
Hilton Park
Leicester Forest East
Tamworth
Peterborough
Corley
A1(M)
Frankley
M1
M6
Watford Gap
Hopwood Park
Northampton
Warwick
M5
Newport Pagnell
Strensham
M40
M1
Baldock
M11
M50
Cherwell Valley
Ross Spur
A1(M)
Toddington
Birchanger Green
Gloucester
M5
Pont Abraham
Oxford
Swansea
South Mimms
Michaelwood
M25
M25
M4
Cardiff Gate
Magor
Beaconsfield
London Gateway
Sarn Park
Severn View
M4
Membury
Heston
Thurrock
M4
Reading
Cardiff West
Gordano
Leigh Delamere
Chieveley
Medway
M5
Cobham
M3
Fleet
M2
Sedgemoor
M25
Clacket Lane
Maidstone
M23
Stop 24
M20
Bridgwater
Winchester
Pease Pottage
Tiverton
M5
Taunton Deane
Rownhams
M27
M27
Cullompton
Exeter

Restricted motorway junctions

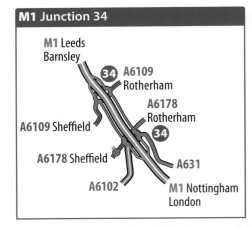

M1 Junction 34

M1 Leeds
Barnsley
34 A6109 Rotherham
A6178 Rotherham
A6109 Sheffield
34
A6178 Sheffield
A631
A6102
M1 Nottingham London

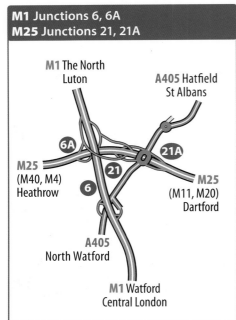

M1 Junctions 6, 6A
M25 Junctions 21, 21A

M1 The North
Luton
A405 Hatfield St Albans
6A
21A
M25 (M40, M4) Heathrow
21
M25 (M11, M20) Dartford
6
A405 North Watford
M1 Watford Central London

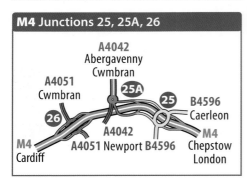

M4 Junctions 25, 25A, 26

A4042 Abergavenny Cwmbran
A4051 Cwmbran
25A
25 B4596 Caerleon
26
A4042
M4 Chepstow London
M4 Cardiff
A4051 Newport B4596

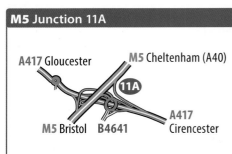

M5 Junction 11A

A417 Gloucester
M5 Cheltenham (A40)
11A
A417 Cirencester
M5 Bristol B4641

M8 Junctions 8, 9 · M73 Junctions 1, 2 · M74 Junctions 2A, 3, 3A, 4

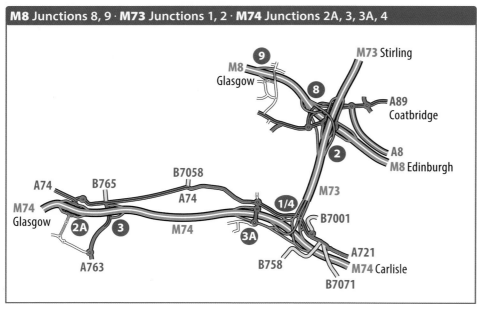

M73 Stirling
M8 9
Glasgow
8
A89 Coatbridge
2
A8 M8 Edinburgh
A74 B765 B7058
M74 Glasgow
A74 1/4 M73 B7001
2A 3 M74 3A B758 B7001
A763
B758 A721 M74 Carlisle
B7071

M1	Northbound	Southbound
2	No exit	No access
4	No exit	No access
6A	No exit. Access from M25 only	No access. Exit to M25 only
7	No exit. Access from A414 only	No access. Exit to A414 only
17	No access. Exit to M45 only	No exit. Access from M45 only
19	No exit to A14	No access from A14
21A	No access	No exit
23A		Exit to A42 only
24A	No exit	No access
35A	No access	No exit
43	No access. Exit to M621 only	No exit. Access from M621 only
48	No exit to A1(M) southbound	

M3	Eastbound	Westbound
8	No exit	No access
10	No access	No exit
13	No access to M27 eastbound	
14	No exit	No access

M4	Eastbound	Westbound
1	Exit to A4 eastbound only	Access from A4 westbound only
2	Access from A4 eastbound only	Access to A4 westbound only
21	No exit	No access
23	No access	No exit
25	No exit	No access
25A	No exit	No access
29	No exit	No access
38		No access
39	No exit or access	No exit
41	No access	No exit
41A	No access	
42	Access from A483 only	Exit to A483 only

M5	Northbound	Southbound
10	No exit	No access
11A	No access from A417 eastbound	No exit to A417 westbound

M6	Northbound	Southbound
3A	No access.	No exit. Access from M6 eastbound only
4A	No exit. Access from M42 southbound only	No access. Exit to M42 only
5	No access	No exit
10A	No access. Exit to M54 only	No exit. Access from M54 only
11A	No exit. Access from M6 Toll only	No access. Exit to M6 Toll only
20	No exit to M56 eastbound	No access from M56 westbound
24	No access	No exit
25	No access	No exit
30	No exit. Access from M61 northbound only	No access. Exit to M61 southbound only
31A	No access	No exit
45	No access	No exit

M6 Toll	Northbound	Southbound
T1		No exit
T2	No exit, no access	No access
T5	No exit	No access
T7	No access	No exit
T8	No access	No exit

M8	Eastbound	Westbound
6	No exit	No access
6A	No exit	No access
7	No Access	No exit
7A	No exit. Access from A725 northbound only	No access. Exit to A725 southbound only
8	No exit to M73 northbound	No access from M73 southbound
9	No exit	No access
13	No exit southbound	Access from M73 southbound only
14	No access	No exit
16	No exit	No access
17	No exit	
18		No exit
19	No exit to A814 eastbound	No access from A814 westbound
20	No exit	No access
21	No access from M74	No exit
22	No exit. Access from M77 only	No access. Exit to M77 only
23	No exit	No access
25	Exit to A739 northbound only. Access from A739 southbound only	
25A	No exit	No access
28	No exit	No access
28A	No exit	No access

M9	Eastbound	Westbound
1A	No exit	No access
2	No access	No exit
3	No access	No exit
6	No access	No exit
8	No exit	No access

M11	Northbound	Southbound
4	No exit	No access
5	No access	No exit
9	No access	No exit
13	No access	No exit
14	No exit to A428 westbound	No exit. Access from A14 westbound only

M20	Eastbound	Westbound
2	No access	No exit
3	No exit	No access. Exit to M26 eastbound only
11A	No access	No exit

M23	Northbound	Southbound
7	No exit to A23 southbound	No access from A23 northbound
10A	No exit	No access

M25	Clockwise	Anticlockwise
5	No exit to M26 eastbound	No access from M26 westbound
19	No access	No exit
21	No exit to M1 southbound. Access from M1 southbound only	No exit to M1 southbound. Access from M1 southbound only
31	No exit	No access

M27	Eastbound	Westbound
10	No exit	No access
12	No access	No exit

M40	Eastbound	Westbound
3	No exit	No access
7	No exit	No access
8	No exit	No access
13	No exit	No access
14	No access	No exit
16	No access	No exit

M42	Northbound	Southbound
1	No exit	No access
7	No access. Exit to M6 northbound only	No exit. Access from M6 northbound only
7A	No access. Exit to M6 southbound only	No exit
8	No exit. Access from M6 southbound only	Exit to M6 northbound only. Access from M6 southbound only

M45	Eastbound	Westbound
M1 J17	Access to M1 southbound only	No access from M1 southbound
With A45	No access	No exit

M48	Eastbound	Westbound
M4 J21	No exit to M4 westbound	No access from M4 eastbound
M4 J23	No access from M4 westbound	No exit to M4 eastbound

M11 Junctions 13, 14

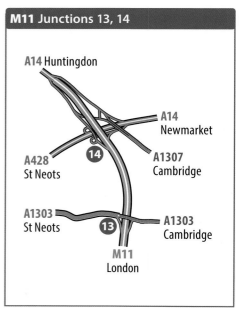

A14 Huntingdon
A14 Newmarket
14
A428 St Neots
A1307 Cambridge
A1303 St Neots
13
A1303 Cambridge
M11 London

M49	Southbound	Northbound
18A	No exit to M5 northbound	No access from M5 southbound

M53	Northbound	Southbound
11	Exit to M56 eastbound only. Access from M56 westbound only	Exit to M56 eastbnd only. Access from M56 westbound only

M56	Eastbound	Westbound
2	No exit	No access
3	No access	No exit
4	No exit	No access
7	No access	
8	No exit or access	No exit
9	No access from M6 northbound	No access to M6 southbound
15	No exit to M53	No access from M53 northbound

M57	Northbound	Southbound
3	No exit	No access
5	No exit	No access

M58	Eastbound	Westbound
1	No exit	No access

M60	Clockwise	Anticlockwise
2	No exit	No access
3	No exit to A34 northbound	No exit to A34 northbound
4	No access from M56	No exit to M56
5	No exit to A5103 southbound	No exit to A5103 northbound
14	No exit	No access
16	No exit	No access
20	No access	No exit
22		No access
25	No access	
26		No exit or access
27	No exit	No access

M61	Northbound	Southbound
2	No access from A580 eastbound	No exit to A580 westbound
3	No access from A580 eastbound. No access from A666 southbound	No exit to A580 westbound
M6 J30	No exit to M6 southbound	No access from M6 northbound

M62	Eastbound	Westbound
23	No access	No exit

M65	Eastbound	Westbound
9	No access	No exit
11	No exit	No access

M66	Northbound	Southbound
1	No access	No exit

M67	Eastbound	Westbound
1A	No access	No exit
2	No exit	No access

M69	Northbound	Southbound
2	No exit	No access

M73	Northbound	Southbound
2	No access from M8 eastbound	No exit to M8 westbound

M74	Northbound	Southbound
3	No access	No exit
3A	No exit	No access
7	No exit	No access
9	No exit or access	No access
10		No exit
11	No exit	No access
12	No access	No exit

M77	Northbound	Southbound
4	No exit	No access
6	No exit	No access
7	No exit	
8	No access	

M80	Northbound	Southbound
4A	No access	No exit
6A	No exit	No access
8	Exit to M876 northbound only. No access	Access from M876 southbound only. No exit

M90	Northbound	Southbound
1	Access from A90 northbound only	No access. Exit to A90 southbound only
2A	No access	No exit
7	No exit	No access
8	No access	No exit
10	No access from A912	No exit to A912

M180	Eastbound	Westbound
1	No access	No exit

M621	Eastbound	Westbound
2A	No exit	No access
4	No exit	
5	No exit	No access
6	No access	No exit

M876	Northbound	Southbound

A1(M)	Northbound	Southbound
2	No access	
3		No access
5	No exit	No exit, no access
14	No exit	No access
40	No access	No access
43	No exit. Access from M1 only	No access. Exit to M1 only
57	No access	No exit
65	No access	No exit

A3(M)	Northbound	Southbound
1	No exit	No access
4	No access	No exit

A38(M) with Victoria Rd, (Park Circus) Birmingham

Northbound	No exit
Southbound	No access

A48(M)	Northbound	Southbound
M4 Junc 29	Exit to M4 eastbound only	Access from M4 westbound only
29A	Access from A48 eastbound only	Exit to A48 westbound only

A57(M)	Eastbound	Westbound
With A5103	No access	No exit
With A34	No access	No exit

A58(M)		Southbound
With Park Lane and Westgate, Leeds		No access

A64(M)		Eastbound	Westbound
With A58 Clay Pit Lane, Leeds		No access from A58	No exit to A58

A74(M)	Northbound	Southbound
18	No access	No exit
22		No exit to A75

A194(M)		Northbound	Southbound
A1(M) J65 Gateshead Western Bypass		Access from A1(M) northbound only	Exit to A1(M) southbound only

M3 Junctions 13, 14 · M27 Junction 4

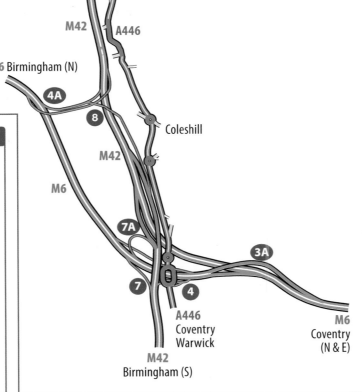

M6 Junctions 3A, 4A · M42 Junctions 7, 7A, 8, 9 · M6 Toll Junctions T1, T2

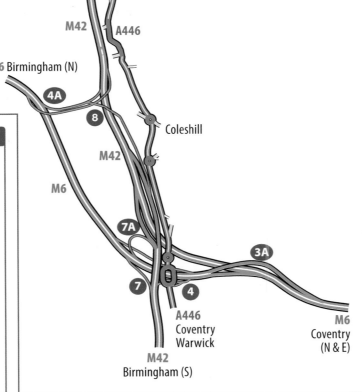

M6 Junction 20 · M56 Junction 9

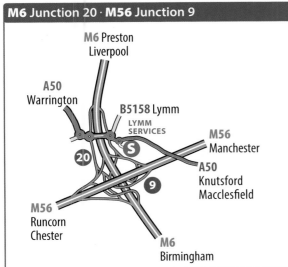

M62 Junctions 32A, 33 · A1(M) Junctions 40, 41

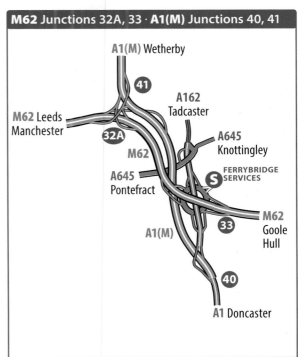

Mobile Layby Cafés – gourmet or gruesome?

Do you drive on by?

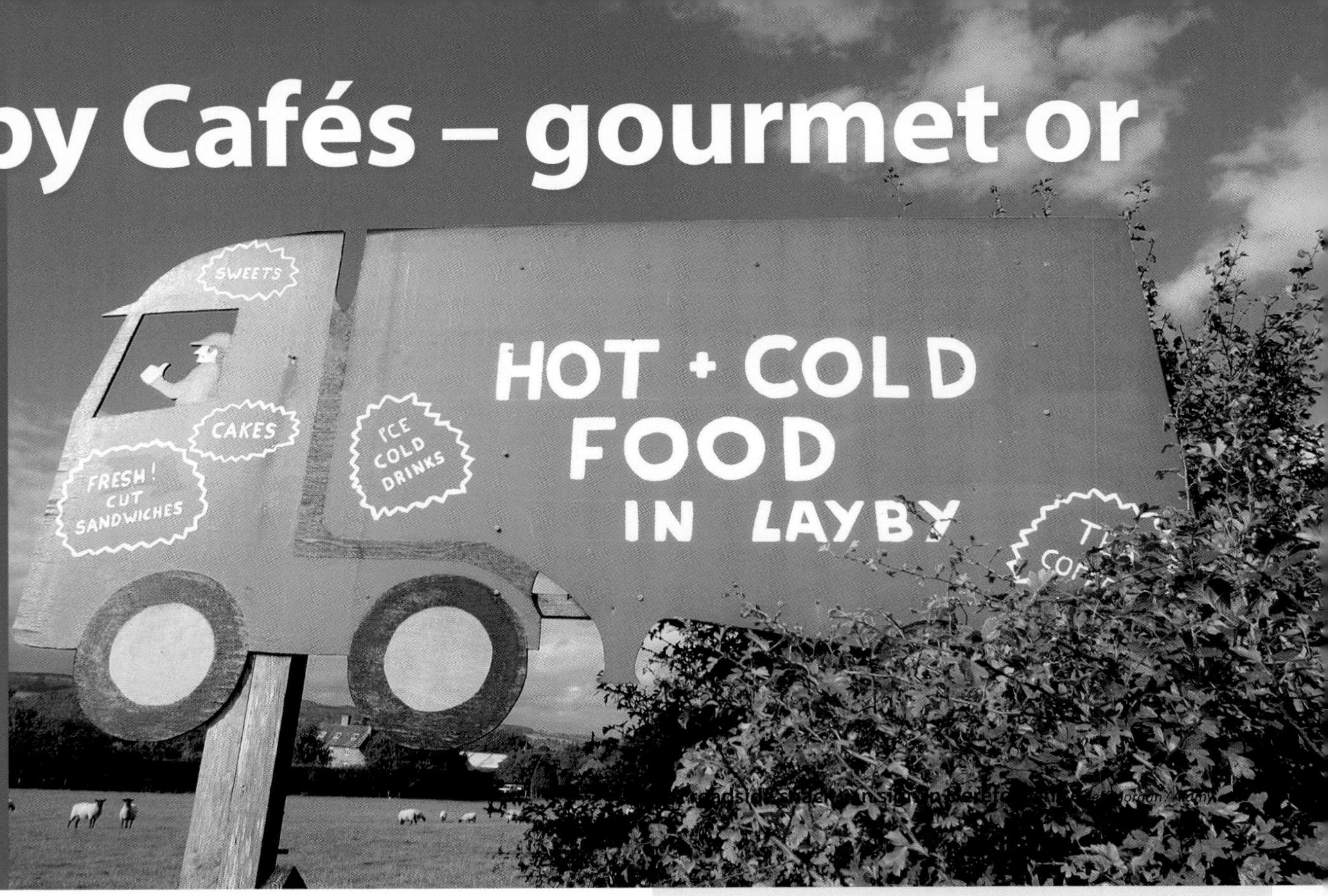

Stephen Mesquita,
Philip's On the Road
Correspondent

Have you ever done this? You're driving along on one of Britain's A-Roads. It's sometime between 6am and 2pm. You're feeling a bit peckish. You see a layby coming up. There's a notice by the road. Something about hot food. There's a van flying a Union Jack. There are a couple of truck drivers there, queueing up. You might even catch a tempting whiff of something frying.

And you drive straight past. Not really for you? You've never eaten in a layby so you'll wait for a place you know and recognise. Or buy a sandwich at the next petrol station.

Well, that's what I've always done. Up until yesterday. That's when I set out, with my trusty accomplice (and Philip's Sales Supremo) Stuart, to see if my lifelong prejudices were justified.

Butty Vans

A quick word about terminology first. We're going to drop the 'Mobile Layby Cafés' and go with 'Butty Vans'. Stuart and I were out to beat The Breakfast Buns from Butty Vans in One Morning Record.

And so it was with some trepidation that we set off from Northampton and headed for our first Butty Van. Here's confession number one: as soon as we'd photographed the bacon roll that we'd ordered, we polished it off.

This was a good start – and in stark contrast to our Motorway Service Area research, where the fare was so unappetising that we tried only a tiny portion of each item and left the rest.

And as the day started, so it went on. Of the eight buns, only one really disappointed. The other seven were tasty, hot, great value and came with friendly chat. Stuart and I polished almost all of them off – and two especially good ones were down the gullets of Philip's intrepid breakfast critics before you could say 'another bacon roll please'.

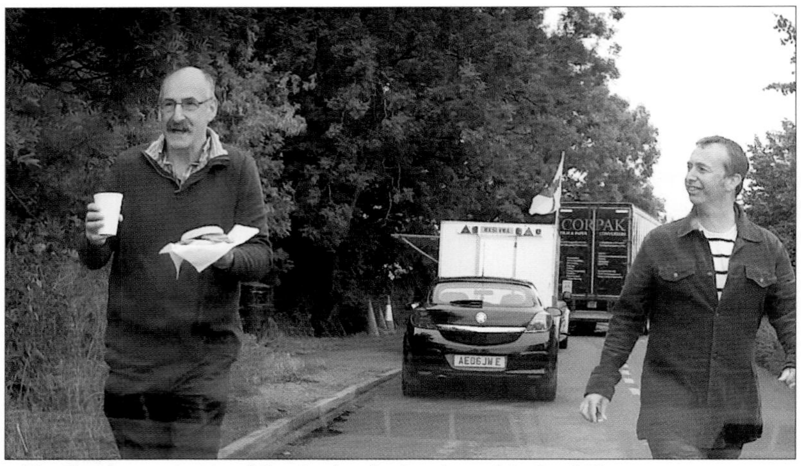

▲ The first bacon butty of the day in a layby alongside the A43

Eight in a Day

Would I recommend eight in a day? As a gastronomic experience, no. It's too much salt intake (my car was littered with empty bottles of water by the end of the day). And I did long for a freshly made flat white by the end of the day.

But a Butty Van breakfast or snack every now and again? Absolutely. Now I've done it once, I'll be very happy to do it again. In fact, I'm rather ashamed I hadn't managed to overcome my prejudices before now.

So to answer my question. Gourmet: no. Gruesome: certainly not. A tasty roadside snack, piping hot, cooked to order and served with a smile – definitely.

I'll have one of those.

Butty Vans vs. Motorway Service Areas – how they compare

If you're expecting Butty Vans to serve up the fare you get at your local deli, you probably don't need to read on. The buns are not made of artisanal sourdough ciabatta. The butter isn't Danish unsalted. The bacon didn't cost £15 a kilo. The eggs probably aren't fresh from the farm that morning. Butty Vans aren't posh.

But the point is this – all the Butty Vans we ate at were owned by people who took great pride in what they did. We met one real foody proprietor who told us he'd been to a burger fair the weekend before and always offered specials ('Codfinger'; 'Blue Burger Special'). All of them were aware that, to compete against the big brands, they had to offer good food at good prices.

The ingredients were perfectly decent. The bacon was almost universally of a better quality than we tasted last year in our Full English Breakfast campaign in Motorway Service Areas. And it was all cooked to order in front of you, which gave it one spectacular advantage over the Motorway Service Areas. It was hot.

And it was a fraction of the price.

The only disappointment was the tea and coffee. But at £0.70–£0.80 a cup, you should know what you're getting and you get what you pay for – although at one Butty Van, the teabags were Yorkshire Tea.

You can compare further in our
Butty Van vs. Motorway Service Area checklist:

	Butty Vans	Motorway Services
Good Value for Money	✔	✗
Proud of what they do	✔	✗
Cooked to Order	✔	rarely
Meal Hot	✔	✗
Quality of ingredients	See above	See above
Quality of hot drinks	✗	✗
Friendly Service	✔	✗
Parking	✔	✔
Easy to find	✗	✔

How to find Butty Vans

Most Butty Vans are either an 'impulse buy' (you see them as you pass by) or have their regular customers who know where they are. But say you are planning a journey and you want to know for sure there's a Butty Van at a point on your route. Then you need the free app from Butty Van Finder (go to buttyvan.com). We don't even need to describe it: these screen grabs say it all.

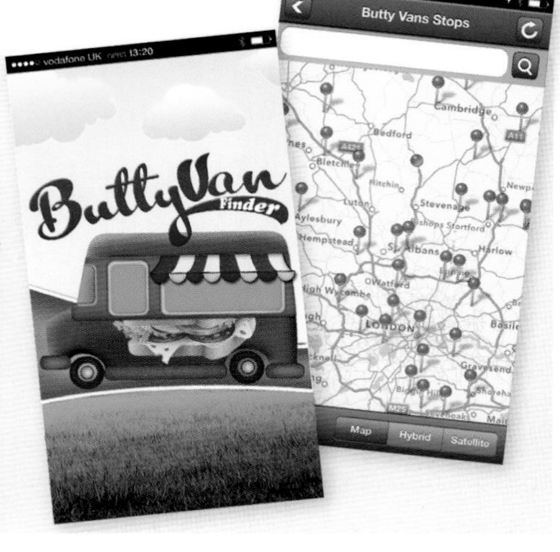

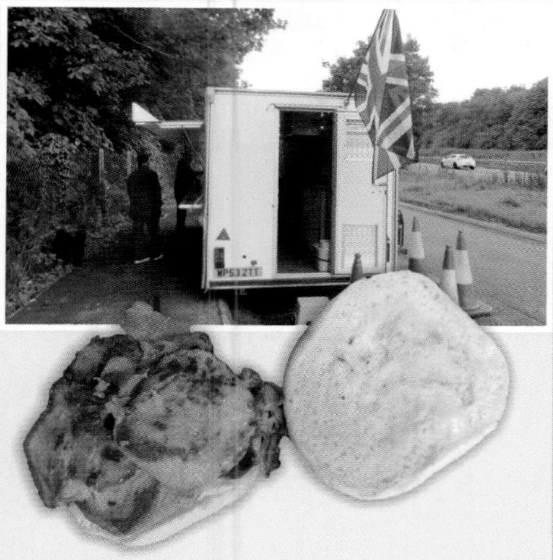

Meal in a Bun One:

Location	A43 West of Northampton
Meal	Bacon roll plus tea
Price	£2.50 plus £0.60

Verdict: Generous helping of tasty bacon, cooked in front of us and piping hot. The tea was wet and warm.

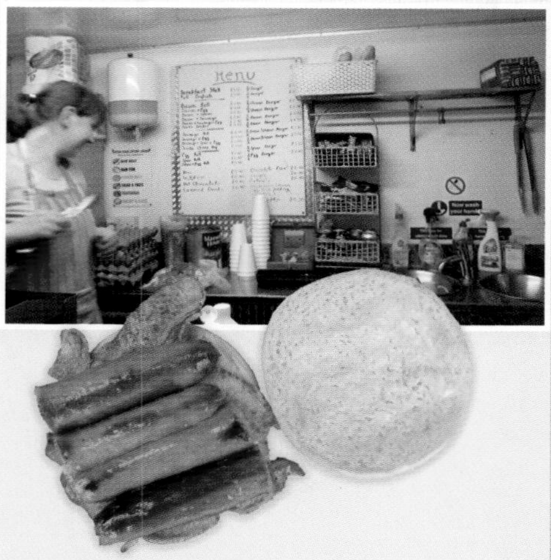

Meal in a Bun Two:

Location	A43 Brackley
Meal	Sausage and Bacon roll plus tea
Price	£3.20 plus £0.50

Verdict: A breakfast on its own served with a smile and lots of chat. The ingredients were nothing special but all tasty.

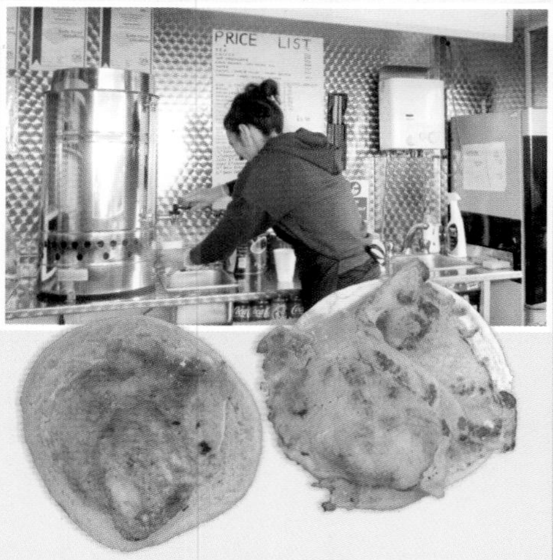

Meal in a Bun Three:

Location	A422 between Buckingham and Milton Keynes
Meal	Bacon and Egg roll plus coffee
Price	£3.00 plus £0.80

Verdict: Another very decent breakfast in a bun, with the egg cooked to order. Yorkshire Tea teabags spurned for instant coffee. Should have had the tea.

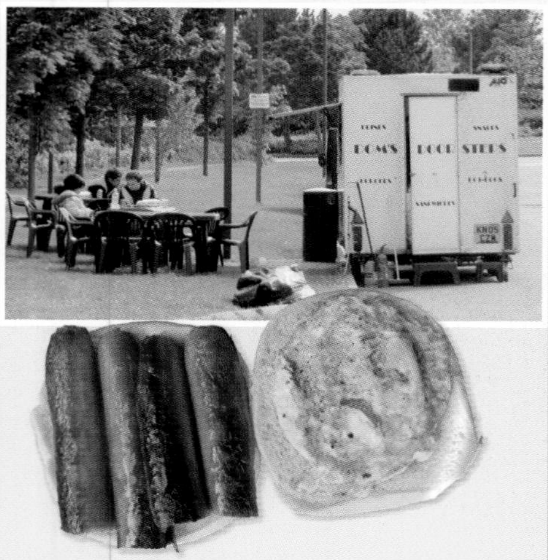

Meal in a Bun Four:

Location:	Harding Road, Milton Keynes
Meal:	Sausage and Egg roll plus tea
Price:	£2.25 plus £0.50

Verdict: Sausage and egg: not expensive ingredients but properly cooked, nice and hot and at a nugatory price.

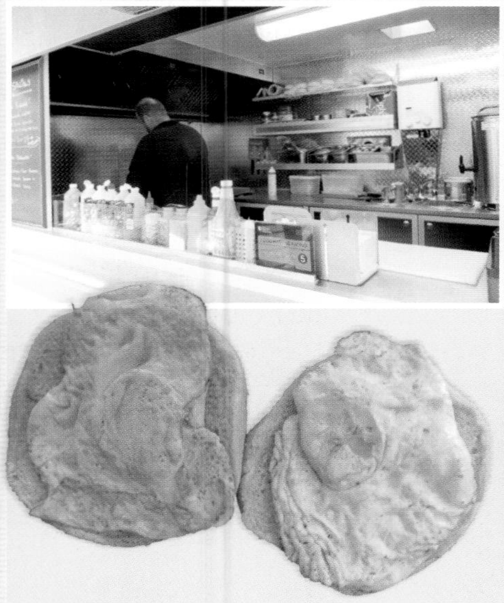

Meal in a Bun Five:

Location	Yardley Road Industrial Estate, Olney
Meal	Double egg roll
Price	£2.50

Verdict: I was stupid. I had a double egg sandwich (which was tasty) but I was rightly berated by Mr Sizzler for not being more adventurous and having one of his speciality burgers or chicken dishes. The things I sacrifice to make these surveys fair.

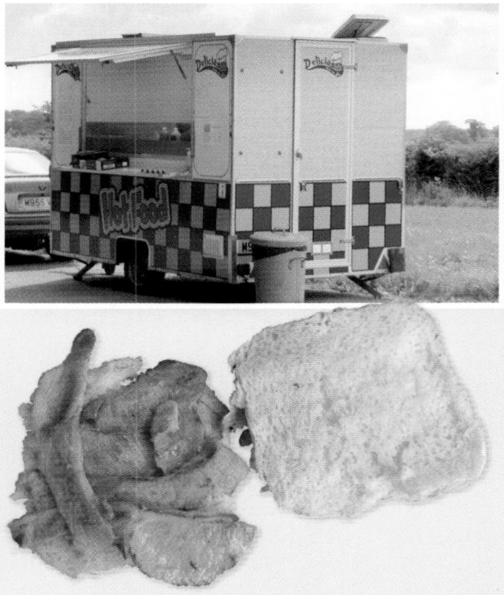

Meal in a Bun Six:

Location	A505 West of Royston
Meal	Bacon Roll
Price	£2.00

Verdict: The best bread (slightly toasted) and loads of decent bacon for £2.00. I rest my case. I should have added: cooked by Italians. They know how to cook, the Italians. Even good old English Bacon butties. Buonissimo!

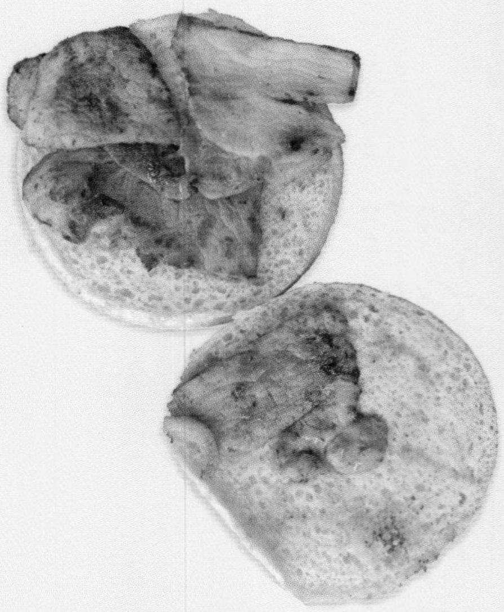

Meal in a Bun Seven:

Location	A505 West of Royston
Meal	Bacon Roll
Price	£2.50

Verdict: A bit disappointing. Bread tough, bacon tough. Our only below par experience of the day.

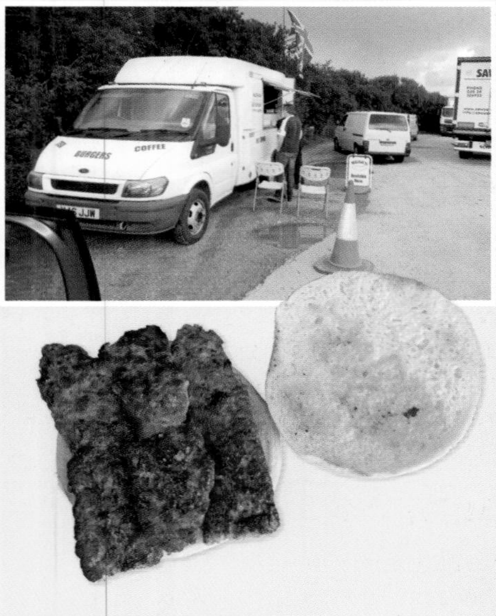

Meal in a Bun Eight:

Location:	A505 East of Royston
Meal:	Sausage roll
Price:	£3.00

Verdict: This café was called Smell the Bacon but the sausages were from Musks of Newmarket. They were delicious! They seemed to disappear remarkably quickly, Stuart.

Butty Vans – what you need to know

- **Layby cafes are licensed by the local authority**, normally annually, to do business in a particular layby.
- **Food Hygiene is an important part of their credibility** – most of them display their certificates prominently.
- **You can't go there for dinner.** Most open early (often around 6am) and shut up around 2pm (sometimes 3pm).
- **They aren't just found in laybys on A Roads.** Some are on industrial estates and business parks.
- **The good ones are there come rain or shine** (bad weather can be good for business) most days of the year.

- **Most of them have a name:** we sampled the fare at *Dom's Doorsteps, Taste Buds Snacks, Sizzlers, Delicias* and *Smell the Bacon*.
- **It's a competitive business** – and their regulars (mostly truck drivers and white van men on A Roads) are discerning customers who expect tasty food at reasonable prices. We heard one van driver say he draws the line at paying £1 for a cup of tea.
- **We were made very welcome**, even though it was obvious we weren't their usual clientele.

Our thanks to all the proprietors who answered our questions about their businesses so openly.

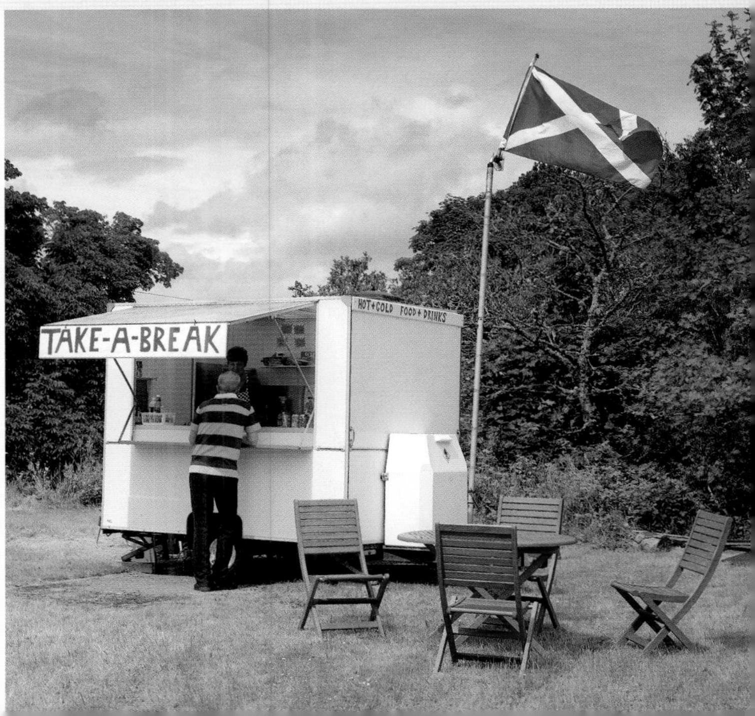

▶ Roadside snack van, Perthshire *Mar Photographics / Alamy*

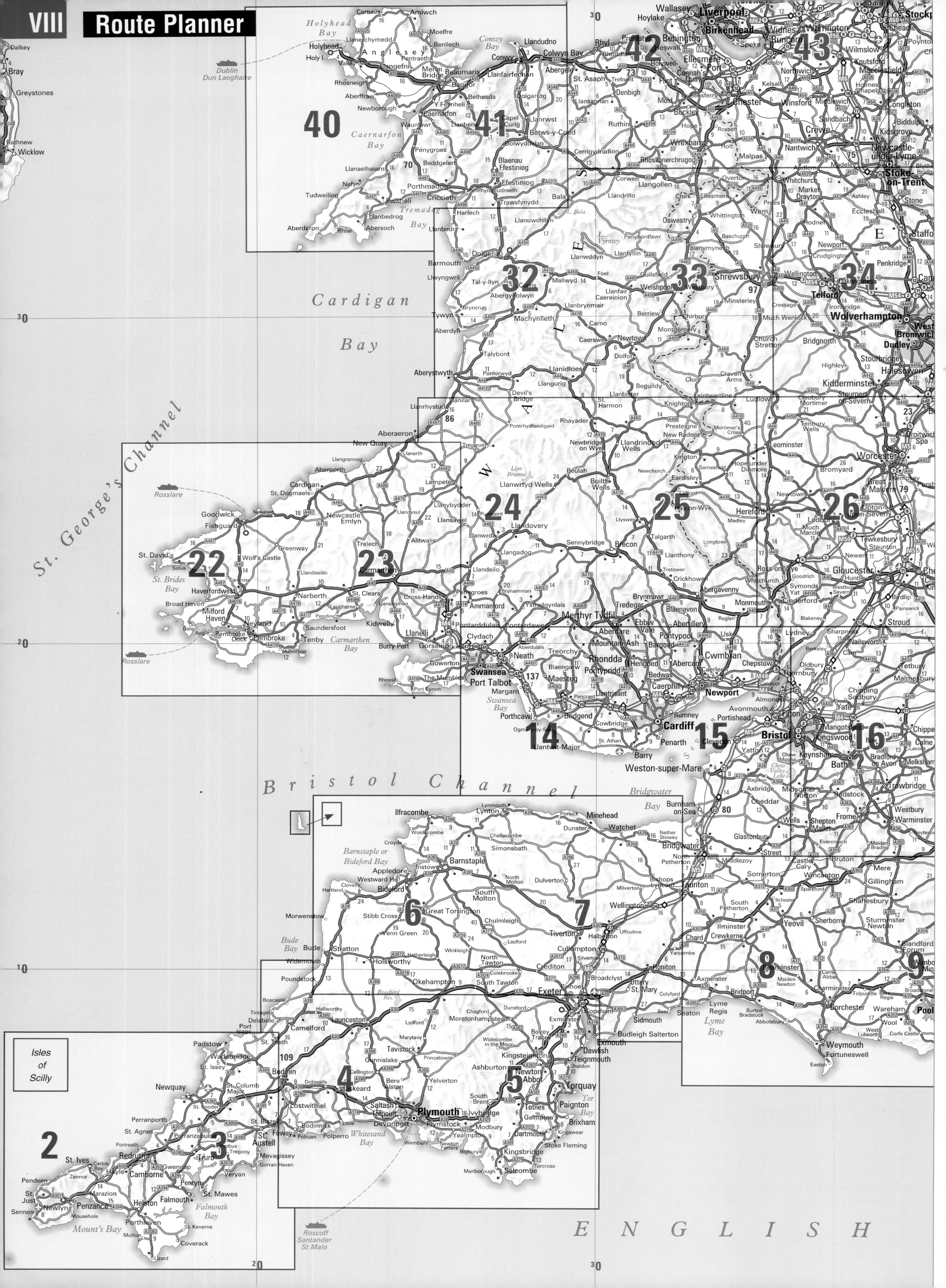
Cardigan
Bay
St. George's Channel
Bristol Channel
ENGLISH
Caernarfon Bay
Tremadog Bay
Carmarthen Bay
Swansea Bay
Bridgwater Bay
Barnstaple or Bideford Bay
Bude Bay
Lyme Bay
Whitsand Bay
Mount's Bay
Falmouth Bay
St. Brides Bay
Isles of Scilly
Anglesey
Holyhead Bay
Conwy Bay
Dublin
Dun Laoghaire
Rosslare
Roscoff
Santander
St Malo
Dalkey
Bray
Greystones
Rathnew
Wicklow
40
41
42
43
32
33
34
22
23
24
25
26
14
15
16
2
3
4
5
6
7
8
9
Holyhead
Bangor
Caernarfon
Llandudno
Colwyn Bay
Conwy
Rhyl
Liverpool
Birkenhead
Chester
Wrexham
Stoke-on-Trent
Crewe
Shrewsbury
Telford
Wolverhampton
Dudley
Aberystwyth
Cardigan
Fishguard
Haverfordwest
Milford Haven
Pembroke
Tenby
Carmarthen
Llanelli
Swansea
Port Talbot
Neath
Merthyr Tydfil
Pontypridd
Caerphilly
Newport
Cardiff
Barry
Bristol
Bath
Gloucester
Hereford
Worcester
Weston-super-Mare
Bridgwater
Taunton
Yeovil
Exeter
Ilfracombe
Barnstaple
Bideford
Plymouth
Torquay
Paignton
Newton Abbot
Bodmin
Newquay
St. Austell
Truro
Falmouth
Penzance
St. Ives
Camborne
Redruth
Launceston
Okehampton
Tiverton
Dorchester
Weymouth
Wales
England

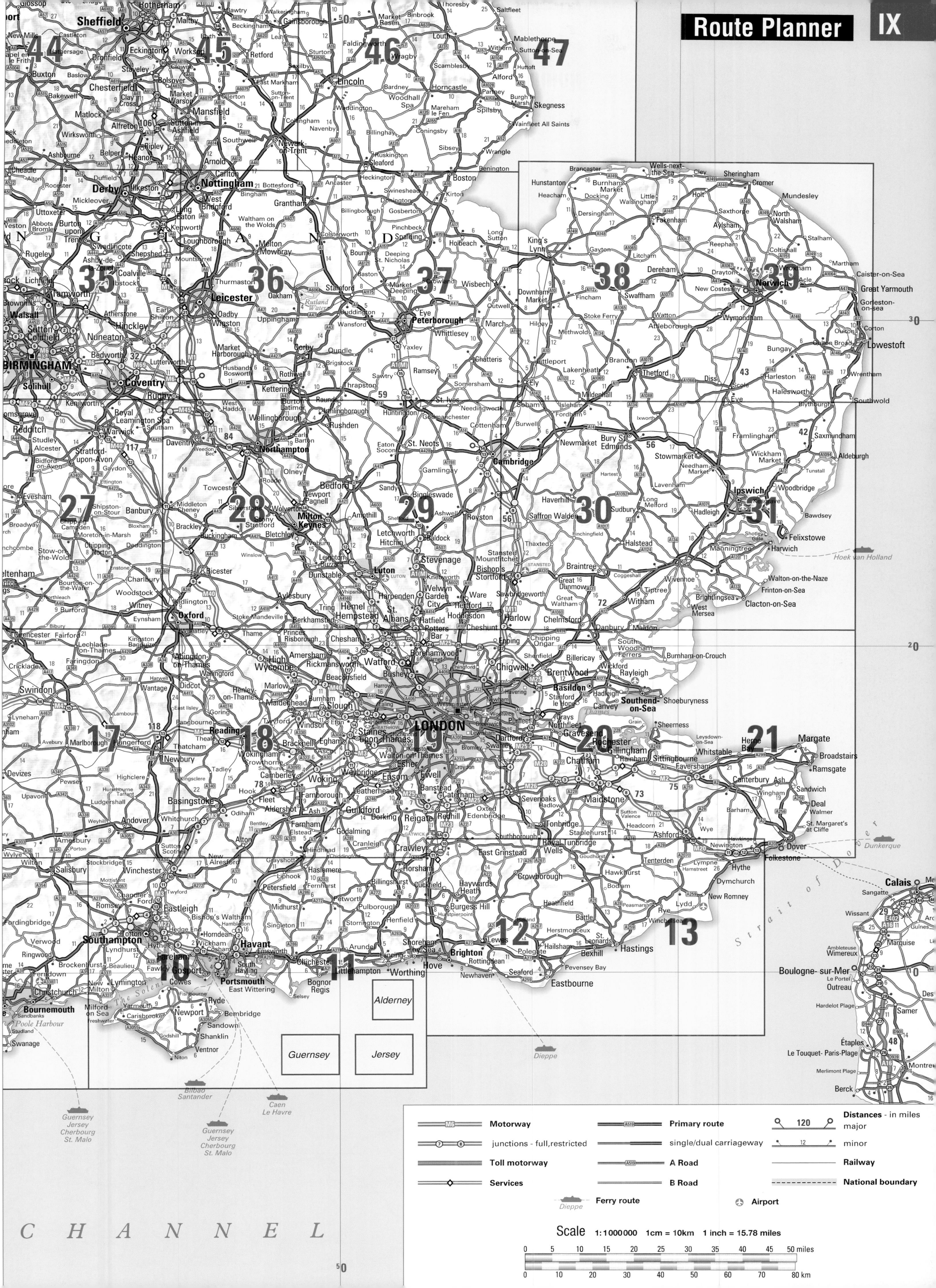

Scale   1:1000000   1cm = 10km   1 inch = 15.78 miles

Distances - in miles

120   major

12   minor

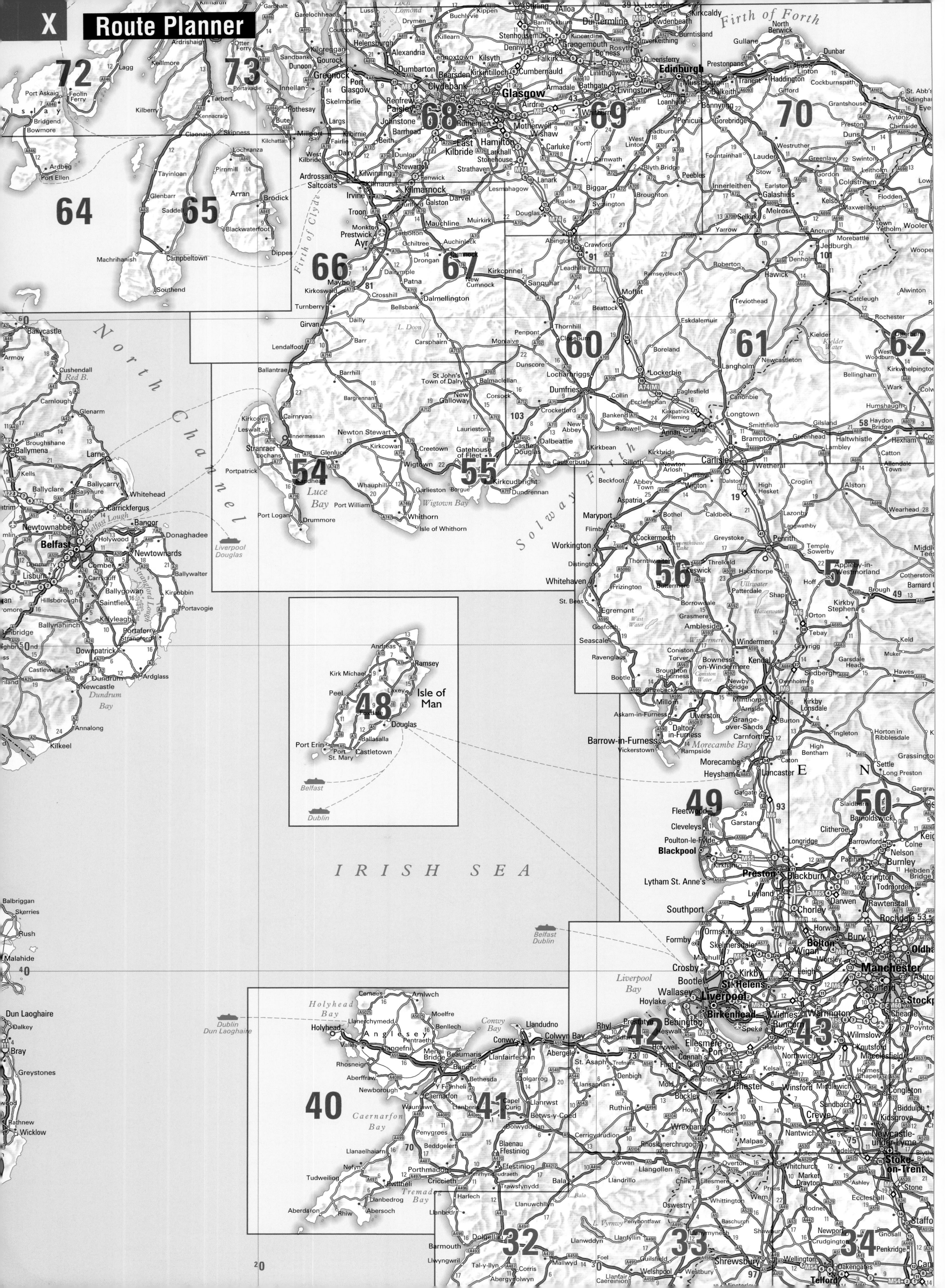

Firth of Forth
North Channel
IRISH SEA
Solway Firth
Firth of Clyde
Isle of Man
Luce Bay
Wigtown Bay
Morecambe Bay
Liverpool Bay
Holyhead Bay
Conwy Bay
Caernarfon Bay
Tremadog Bay
Dundrum Bay
Anglesey
Arran
Islay
Edinburgh
Glasgow
Belfast
Liverpool
Manchester
Carlisle
Dumfries
Blackpool
Preston
Douglas
72
73
68
69
70
64
65
66
67
60
61
62
54
55
56
57
48
49
50
40
41
42
43
32
33
34

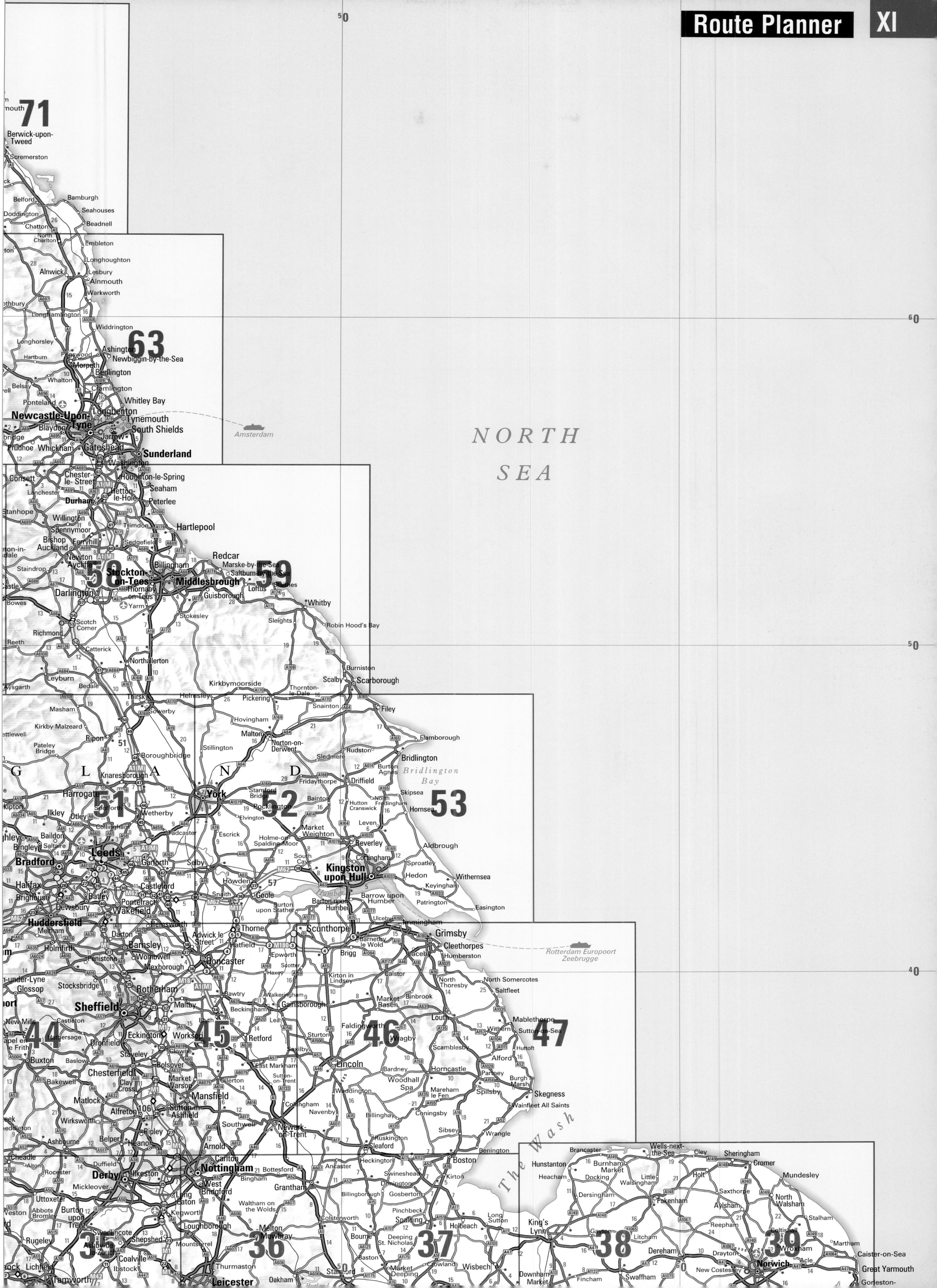
NORTH
SEA
71
63
58
59
51
52
53
44
45
46
47
36
37
38
39
Berwick-upon-Tweed
Scremerston
Bamburgh
Seahouses
Beadnell
Belford
Chatton
Embleton
Longhoughton
Alnwick
Lesbury
Alnmouth
Warkworth
Longframlington
Widdrington
Longhorsley
Ashington
Newbiggin-by-the-Sea
Morpeth
Bedlington
Cramlington
Whitley Bay
Ponteland
Longbenton
Newcastle-Upon-Tyne
Tynemouth
South Shields
Amsterdam
Blaydon
Jarrow
Prudhoe
Whickham
Gateshead
Sunderland
Washington
Consett
Houghton-le-Spring
Seaham
Lanchester
Durham
Peterlee
Stanhope
Willington
Hartlepool
Spennymoor
Trimdon
Bishop Auckland
Ferryhill
Sedgefield
Newton Aycliffe
Redcar
Staindrop
Stockton-on-Tees
Billingham
Marske-by-the-Sea
Saltburn-by-the-Sea
Middlesbrough
Thornaby on Tees
Loftus
Darlington
Guisborough
Yarm
Whitby
Bowes
Stokesley
Scotch Corner
Sleights
Robin Hood's Bay
Richmond
Reeth
Catterick
Northallerton
Burniston
Leyburn
Bedale
Kirkbymoorside
Scalby
Scarborough
Aysgarth
Thirsk
Helmsley
Pickering
Thornton-le-Dale
Snainton
Filey
Masham
Sowerby
Hovingham
Kirkby Malzeard
Malton
Flamborough
Ripon
Norton-on-Derwent
Pateley Bridge
Stillington
Boroughbridge
Rudston
Sledmere
Bridlington
Bridlington Bay
Knaresborough
Burton Agnes
Fridaythorpe
Driffield
Harrogate
York
Stamford Bridge
Skipsea
Ilkley
Otley
Spofforth
Wetherby
Pocklington
Hutton Cranswick
North Frodingham
Hornsea
Elvington
Leven
Baildon
Tadcaster
Escrick
Holme-on-Spalding-Moor
Market Weighton
Beverley
Aldbrough
Bradford
Leeds
Garforth
Selby
Cottingham
Sproatley
Withernsea
Halifax
Castleford
Howden
South Cave
Kingston upon Hull
Hedon
Keyingham
Brighouse
Batley
Pontefract
Snaith
Goole
Humber
Patrington
Dewsbury
Wakefield
Barton upon Humber
Easington
Huddersfield
Hemsworth
Burton upon Stather
Immingham
Thorne
Scunthorpe
Grimsby
Cleethorpes
Holmfirth
Barnsley
Adwick le Street
Hatfield
Barnetby le Wold
Humberston
Rotterdam Europoort
Zeebrugge
Penistone
Wombwell
Doncaster
Epworth
Brigg
Mexborough
Caistor
North Somercotes
Glossop
Stocksbridge
Rotherham
Kirton in Lindsey
North Thoresby
Saltfleet
Sheffield
Maltby
Gainsborough
Market Rasen
Binbrook
Bawtry
Louth
Mablethorpe
Castleton
Eckington
Worksop
Retford
Sturton
Faldingworth
Wragby
Withern
Sutton-on-Sea
Buxton
Dronfield
Staveley
Clowne
Scamblesby
Huttoft
Baslow
Bolsover
East Markham
Saxilby
Lincoln
Alford
Chesterfield
Bakewell
Market Warsop
Ollerton
Bardney
Horncastle
Burgh le Marsh
Clay Cross
Mansfield
Woodhall Spa
Partney
Skegness
Matlock
Sutton-in-Ashfield
Waddington
Mareham le Fen
Spilsby
Wainfleet All Saints
Alfreton
Collingham
Navenby
Coningsby
Wirksworth
Billinghay
Southwell
Sibsey
Ripley
Newark-on-Trent
Wrangle
Ashbourne
Belper
Heanor
Ruskington
Arnold
Sleaford
Benington
The Wash
Cheadle
Duffield
Carlton
Heckington
Boston
Wells-next-the-Sea
Brancaster
Cley
Sheringham
Cromer
Derby
Ilkeston
Nottingham
Bottesford
Ancaster
Swineshead
Kirton
Hunstanton
Burnham Market
Heacham
Docking
Little Walsingham
Holt
Mundesley
Rocester
Mickleover
West Bridgford
Bingham
Grantham
Donington
Dersingham
Fakenham
Saxthorpe
North Walsham
Uttoxeter
Long Eaton
Waltham on the Wolds
Billingborough
Gosberton
Aylsham
Abbots Bromley
Burton upon Trent
Kegworth
Colsterworth
Pinchbeck
Spalding
Long Sutton
Holbeach
King's Lynn
Gayton
Reepham
Stalham
Swadlincote
Loughborough
Melton Mowbray
Bourne
Deeping St. Nicholas
Coltishall
Rugeley
Ashby de la Zouch
Shepshed
Mountsorrel
Litcham
Wroxham
Martham
Lichfield
Coalville
Thurmaston
Baston
Market Deeping
Crowland
Wisbech
Dereham
Drayton
Acle
Caister-on-Sea
Ibstock
Tamworth
Leicester
Oakham
Stamford
Downham Market
Fincham
Swaffham
New Costessey
Norwich
Great Yarmouth
Gorleston-

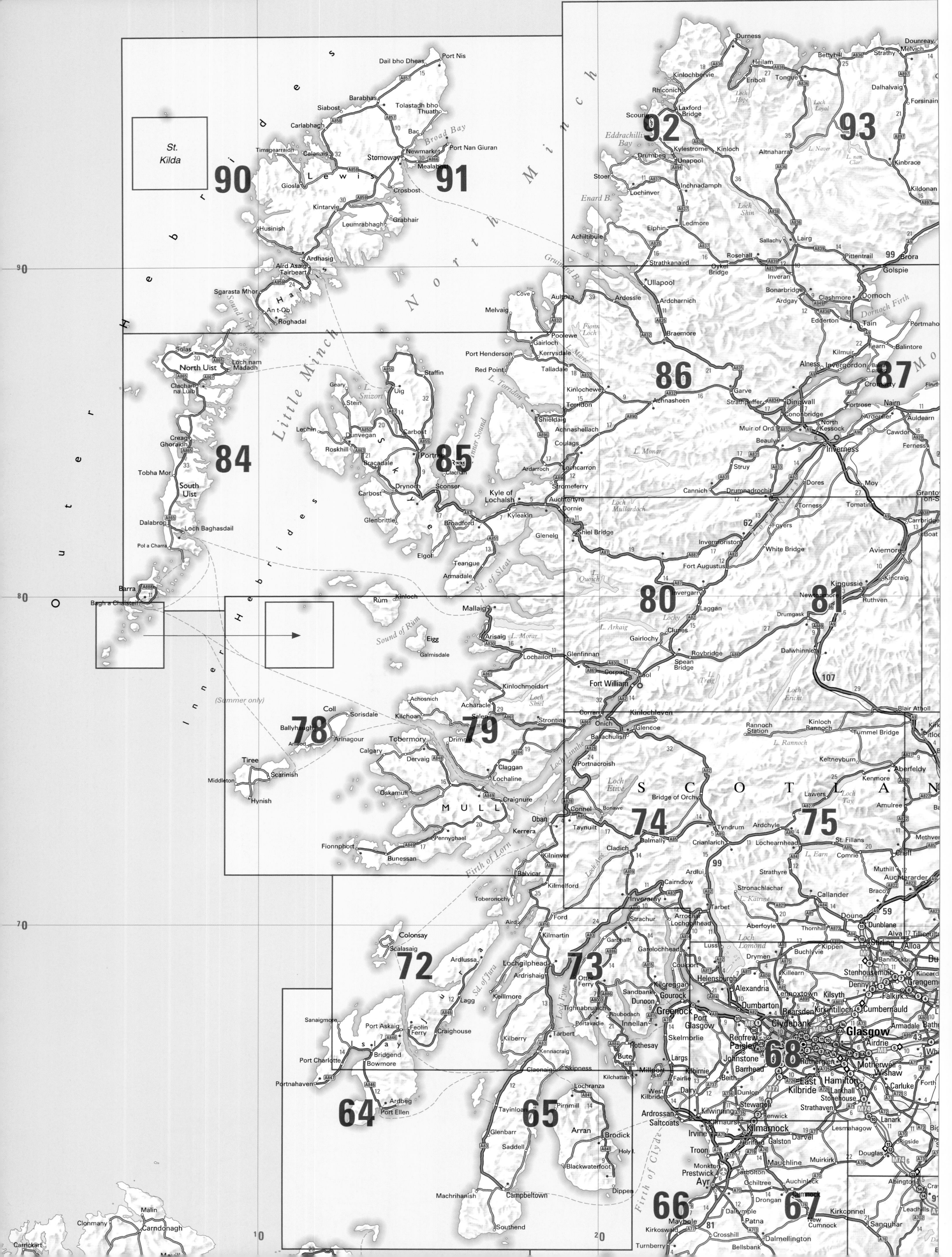
St. Kilda
90
91
92
93
84
85
86
87
80
81
78
79
74
75
72
73
64
65
66
67
68
Outer Hebrides
Inner Hebrides
Little Minch
North Minch
Lewis
Harris
North Uist
South Uist
Skye
MULL
Islay
Jura
Arran
SCOTLAN
Stornoway
Port Nis
Tairbeart
Loch nam Madadh
Lochboisdale
Loch Baghasdail
Barra
Portree
Dunvegan
Kyle of Lochalsh
Mallaig
Rum
Eigg
Coll
Tiree
Tobermory
Oban
Fort William
Inverness
Ullapool
Durness
Thurso
Scourie
Lochinver
Gairloch
Dingwall
Nairn
Kingussie
Aviemore
Pitlochry
Callander
Stirling
Dunblane
Inveraray
Lochgilphead
Campbeltown
Brodick
Greenock
Paisley
Glasgow
Kilmarnock
Ayr
Troon
Irvine
Cumbernauld
Hamilton
Bute
Port Ellen
Bowmore
Firth of Clyde
Firth of Lorn
Dornoch Firth
Sound of Rum
(Summer only)

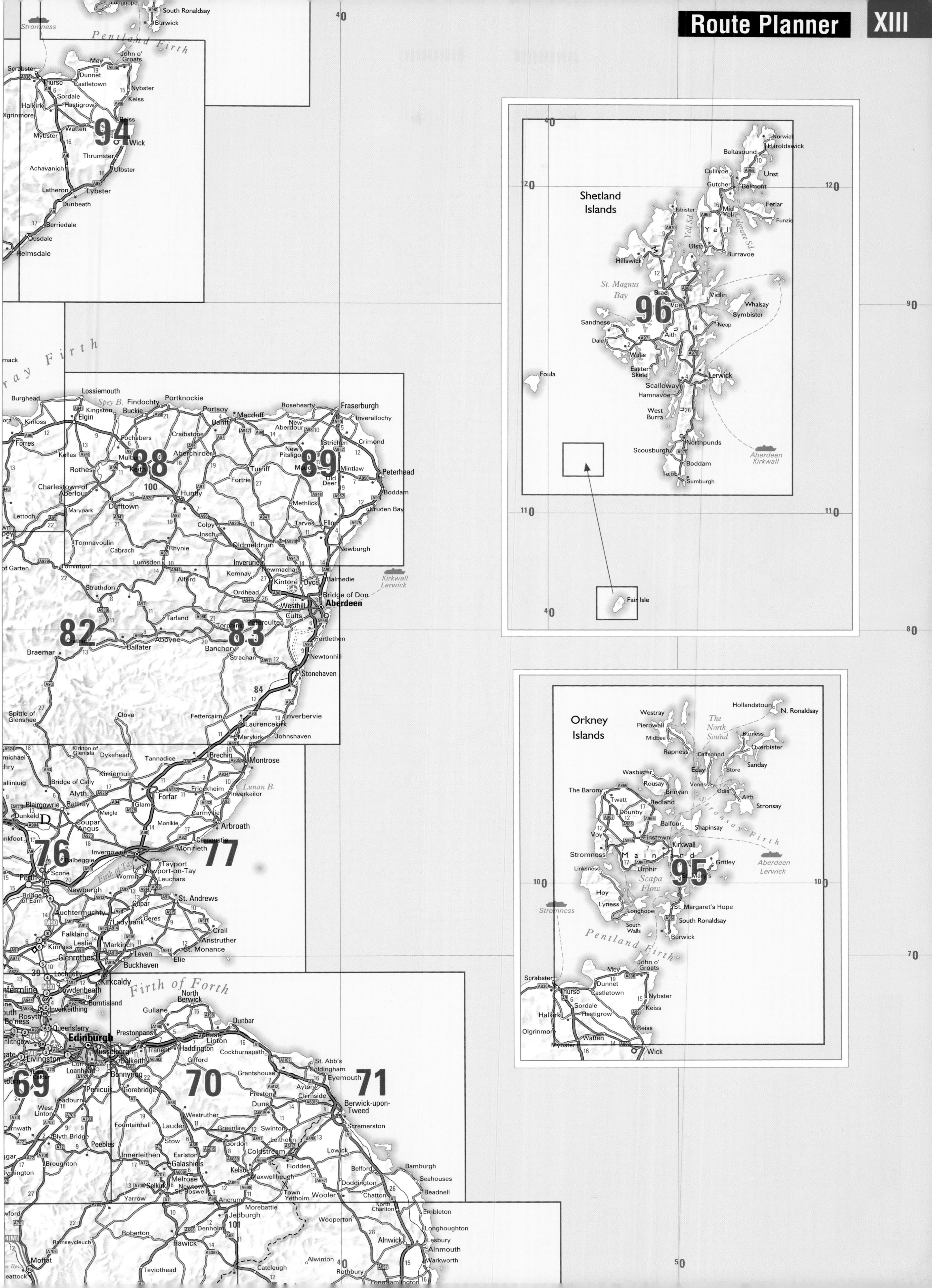
Shetland Islands
96
Orkney Islands
95
94
88
89
82
83
76
77
69
70
71
Pentland Firth
Moray Firth
Firth of Forth
Firth of Tay
St. Magnus Bay
Scapa Flow
Stronsay Firth
The North Sound
Lunan B.
Spey B.
Aberdeen Kirkwall
Aberdeen Lerwick
Kirkwall Lerwick
Stromness
Lerwick
Kirkwall
Thurso
Wick
John o' Groats
Helmsdale
Elgin
Fraserburgh
Peterhead
Aberdeen
Stonehaven
Montrose
Arbroath
Forfar
Perth
St. Andrews
Edinburgh
Dunbar
Berwick-upon-Tweed
Galashiels
Kelso
Jedburgh
Hawick
Alnwick
Fair Isle
Foula

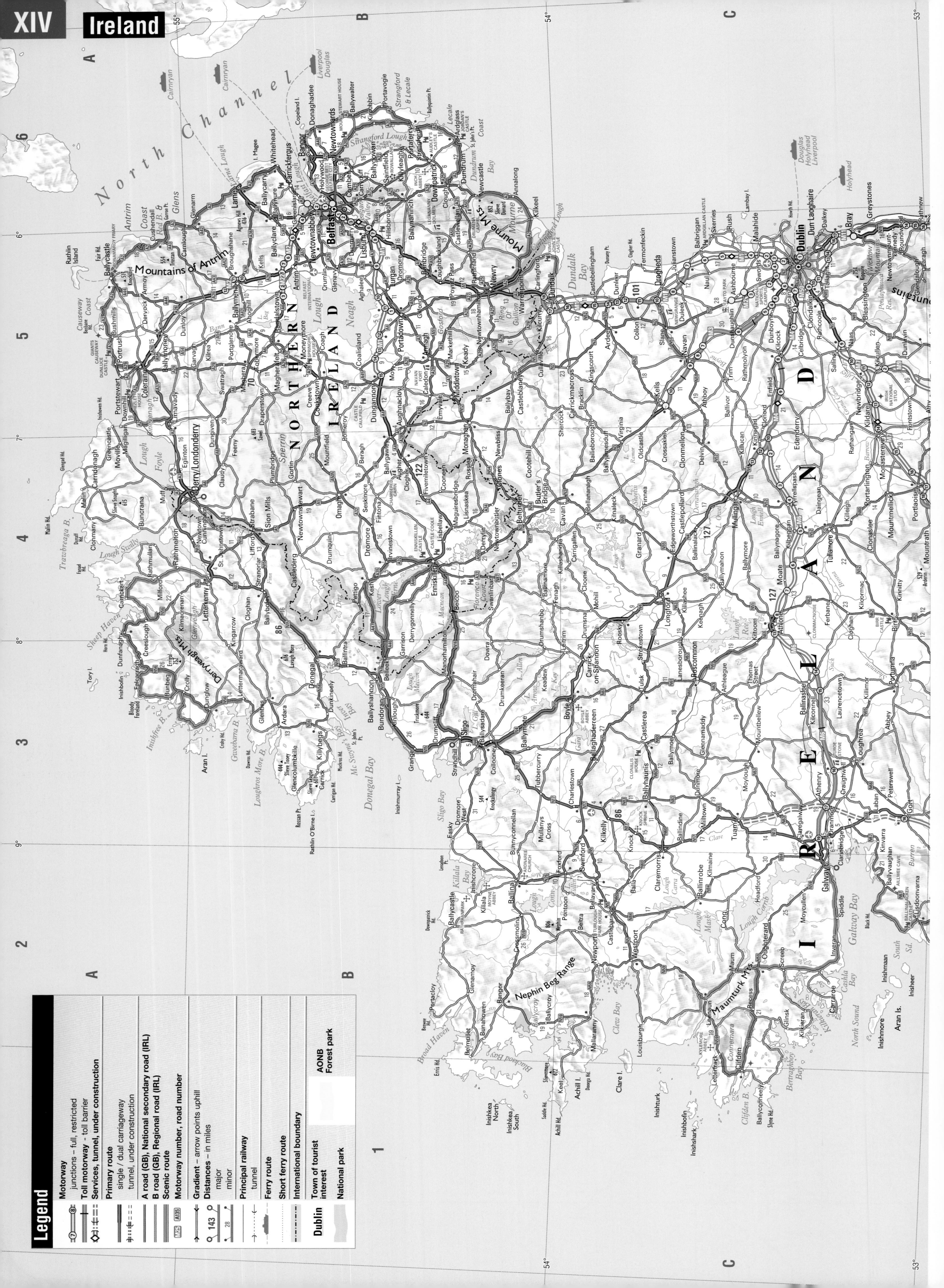
Legend
Motorway
junctions – full, restricted
Toll motorway - toll barrier
Services, tunnel, under construction
Primary route
single / dual carriageway
tunnel, under construction
A road (GB), National secondary road (IRL)
B road (GB), Regional road (IRL)
Scenic route
Motorway number, road number
Gradient – arrow points uphill
Distances – in miles
major
minor
Principal railway
tunnel
Ferry route
Short ferry route
International boundary
Dublin
Town of tourist interest
National park
AONB
Forest park
North Channel
NORTHERN IRELAND
IRELAND
Mountains of Antrim
Mourne Mts.
Derryveagh Mts.
Nephin Beg Range
Maumturk Mts.
Belfast
Derry/Londonderry
Dublin
Dun Laoghaire
Galway
Sligo
Donegal Bay
Galway Bay
Clew Bay
Dundalk Bay
Lough Neagh
Holyhead
Douglas
Liverpool
Cairnryan

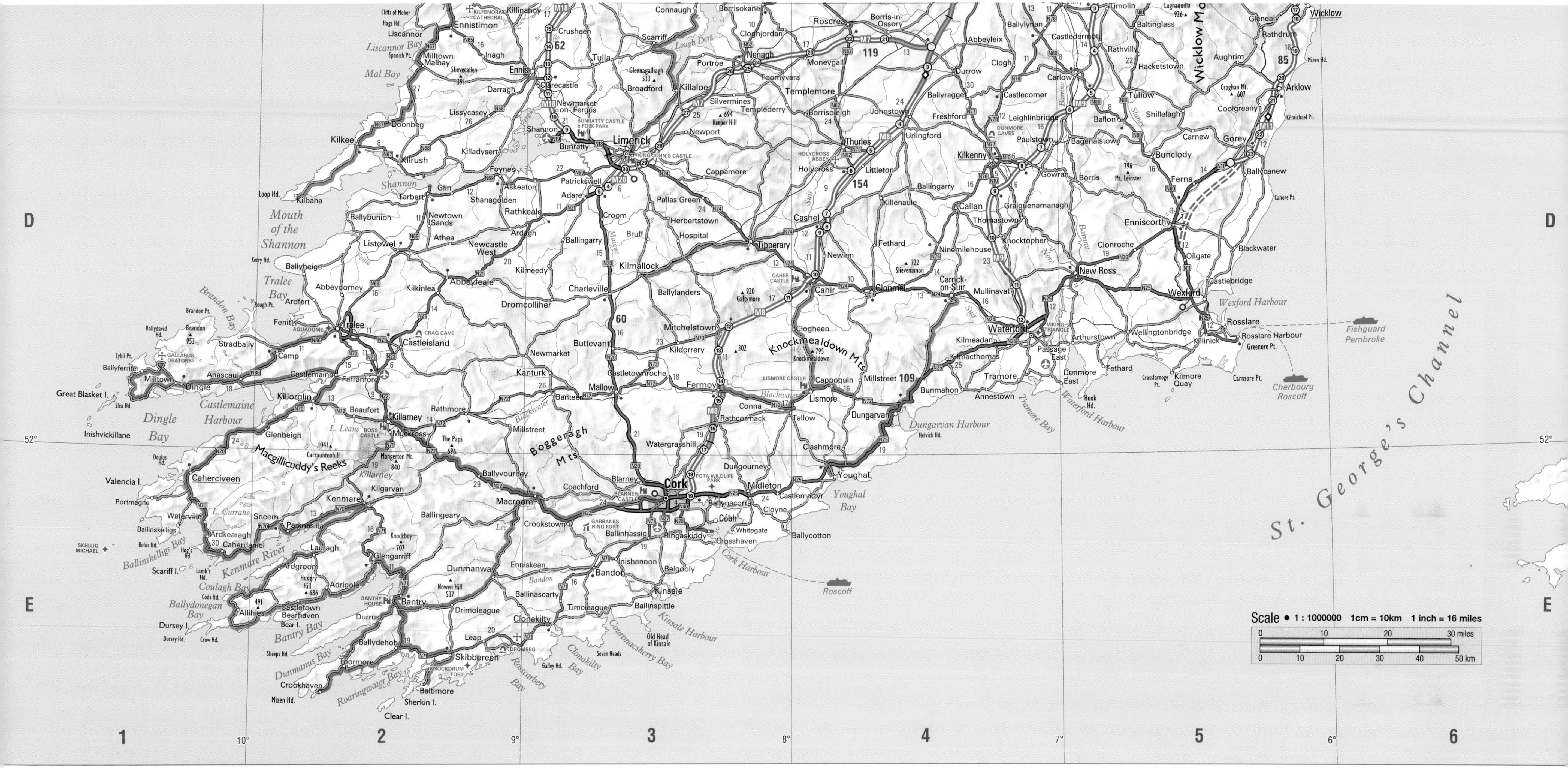

St. George's Channel

Scale ● 1 : 1 000 000 1cm = 10km 1 inch = 16 miles

Distance table

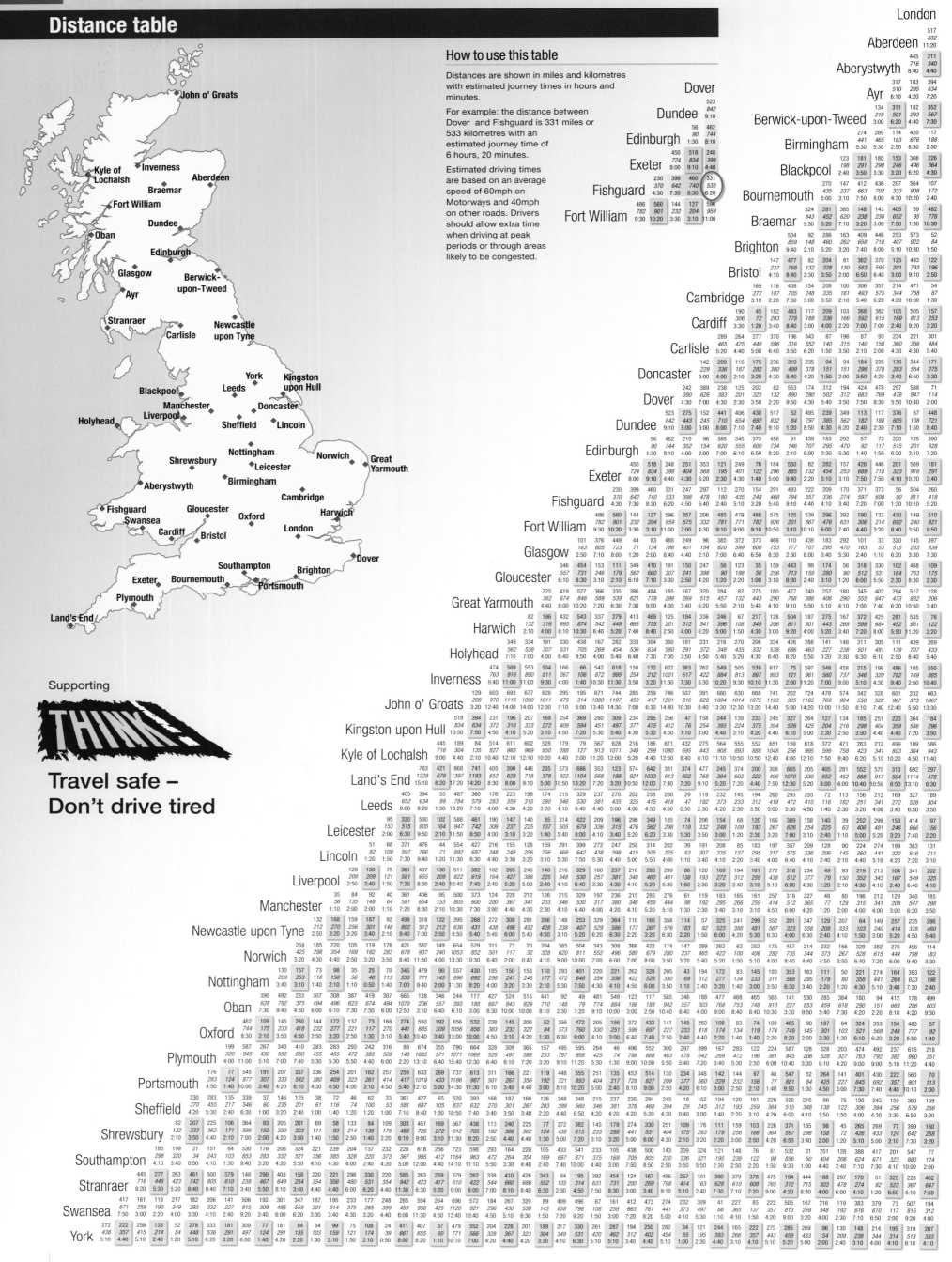

How to use this table

Distances are shown in miles and kilometres with estimated journey times in hours and minutes.

For example: the distance between Dover and Fishguard is 331 miles or 533 kilometres with an estimated journey time of 6 hours, 20 minutes.

Estimated driving times are based on an average speed of 60mph on Motorways and 40mph on other roads. Drivers should allow extra time when driving at peak periods or through areas likely to be congested.

Dover					
Dundee					523 / 842 / 9:10
Edinburgh				56 / 90 / 1:30	462 / 744 / 8:10
Exeter			450 / 724 / 8:00	518 / 834 / 9:10	248 / 399 / 4:40
Fishguard		230 / 370 / 4:30	399 / 642 / 7:30	460 / 740 / 8:30	331 / 533 / 6:20
Fort William	486 / 782 / 9:30	560 / 901 / 10:20	144 / 232 / 3:30	127 / 204 / 3:10	596 / 959 / 11:00

Supporting THINK!

Travel safe – Don't drive tired

Town	Swansea	Stranraer	Southampton	Shrewsbury	Sheffield	Portsmouth	Plymouth	Oxford	Oban	Nottingham	Norwich	Newcastle upon Tyne	Manchester	Liverpool	Lincoln	Leicester	Leeds	Land's End	Kyle of Lochalsh	Kingston upon Hull	John o' Groats	Inverness	Holyhead	Harwich	Great Yarmouth	Gloucester	Glasgow	Fort William	Fishguard	Exeter	Edinburgh	Dundee	Dover	Doncaster	Carlisle	Cardiff	Cambridge	Bristol	Brighton	Braemar	Bournemouth	Blackpool	Birmingham	Berwick-upon-Tweed	Ayr	Aberystwyth	Aberdeen	London
London																																																
Aberdeen																																																517 / 832 / 11:20
Aberystwyth																																															445 / 716 / 8:40	211 / 340 / 4:40
Ayr																																														317 / 510 / 6:10	183 / 295 / 4:20	394 / 634 / 7:20
Berwick-upon-Tweed																																													134 / 216 / 3:00	311 / 501 / 6:20	182 / 293 / 4:40	352 / 567 / 7:30
Birmingham																																												274 / 441 / 5:30	289 / 465 / 5:30	114 / 183 / 2:50	420 / 676 / 8:30	117 / 188 / 2:50
Blackpool																																											123 / 198 / 2:40	181 / 291 / 3:50	180 / 290 / 3:30	153 / 246 / 3:20	308 / 496 / 6:20	226 / 364 / 4:30
Bournemouth																																										270 / 435 / 5:00	147 / 237 / 3:10	412 / 663 / 7:50	436 / 702 / 8:00	207 / 333 / 4:30	564 / 908 / 10:20	107 / 172 / 2:40
Braemar																																									524 / 843 / 9:30	281 / 452 / 5:20	385 / 620 / 7:10	148 / 238 / 3:20	143 / 230 / 3:00	405 / 652 / 7:50	59 / 95 / 1:30	482 / 776 / 10:30
Brighton																																								534 / 859 / 9:40	92 / 148 / 2:10	286 / 460 / 5:20	163 / 262 / 3:20	409 / 658 / 7:40	446 / 718 / 8:00	253 / 407 / 5:10	573 / 922 / 10:30	52 / 84 / 1:50
Bristol																																							147 / 237 / 4:10	477 / 768 / 8:40	82 / 132 / 2:30	204 / 328 / 3:50	81 / 130 / 2:00	362 / 583 / 6:50	370 / 595 / 6:40	125 / 201 / 3:00	493 / 793 / 9:10	122 / 196 / 2:50
Cambridge																																						169 / 272 / 3:10	116 / 187 / 2:20	438 / 705 / 7:50	154 / 248 / 3:00	208 / 335 / 3:50	100 / 161 / 2:10	306 / 493 / 5:40	357 / 575 / 6:20	214 / 344 / 4:20	471 / 758 / 10:00	54 / 87 / 1:30
Cardiff																																					190 / 306 / 3:30	45 / 72 / 1:20	182 / 293 / 3:40	483 / 778 / 8:40	117 / 188 / 3:00	209 / 336 / 4:00	103 / 166 / 2:20	368 / 592 / 7:00	382 / 615 / 7:00	105 / 169 / 2:40	505 / 813 / 9:20	157 / 253 / 3:20
Carlisle																																				289 / 465 / 5:20	264 / 425 / 4:40	277 / 446 / 5:00	370 / 596 / 6:40	196 / 316 / 3:50	343 / 552 / 6:20	87 / 140 / 1:50	196 / 315 / 3:50	87 / 140 / 2:10	93 / 150 / 2:00	224 / 360 / 4:30	221 / 356 / 4:30	301 / 484 / 5:40
Doncaster																																			142 / 229 / 3:00	209 / 336 / 4:00	116 / 187 / 2:10	175 / 282 / 3:20	236 / 380 / 4:30	310 / 499 / 5:40	235 / 378 / 4:20	94 / 151 / 1:50	94 / 151 / 2:00	184 / 296 / 3:50	235 / 378 / 4:20	176 / 283 / 3:40	344 / 554 / 6:50	171 / 275 / 3:30
Dover																																		242 / 390 / 4:30	389 / 626 / 7:00	238 / 383 / 4:30	125 / 201 / 2:30	202 / 325 / 3:50	82 / 132 / 2:20	553 / 890 / 9:50	174 / 280 / 4:30	312 / 502 / 5:40	194 / 312 / 3:50	424 / 683 / 7:50	478 / 769 / 8:30	297 / 478 / 5:50	588 / 947 / 10:40	71 / 114 / 2:00
Dundee																																	523 / 842 / 9:10	275 / 443 / 5:00	152 / 245 / 3:00	441 / 710 / 8:00	406 / 654 / 7:10	430 / 692 / 7:40	517 / 832 / 9:10	52 / 84 / 1:20	495 / 797 / 8:50	239 / 385 / 4:30	349 / 562 / 6:20	113 / 182 / 2:40	117 / 188 / 2:30	376 / 605 / 7:10	67 / 108 / 1:50	448 / 721 / 8:40
Edinburgh																																56 / 90 / 1:30	462 / 744 / 8:10	219 / 352 / 4:00	96 / 154 / 2:00	385 / 620 / 7:00	345 / 555 / 6:10	373 / 600 / 6:50	456 / 734 / 8:20	91 / 146 / 2:10	439 / 707 / 8:00	183 / 295 / 3:30	292 / 470 / 5:30	57 / 92 / 1:40	73 / 117 / 1:50	320 / 515 / 6:20	125 / 201 / 3:10	390 / 628 / 7:20
Exeter																															450 / 724 / 8:00	518 / 834 / 9:10	248 / 399 / 4:40	251 / 404 / 4:30	353 / 568 / 6:20	121 / 195 / 2:30	249 / 401 / 4:30	76 / 122 / 1:40	184 / 296 / 5:00	550 / 885 / 9:40	82 / 132 / 2:20	282 / 454 / 5:10	157 / 253 / 3:10	428 / 689 / 7:50	446 / 718 / 7:50	201 / 323 / 4:10	569 / 916 / 10:20	181 / 291 / 3:40
Fishguard																														230 / 370 / 4:30	399 / 642 / 7:30	460 / 740 / 8:30	331 / 533 / 6:20	247 / 398 / 4:50	297 / 478 / 5:40	112 / 180 / 2:40	270 / 435 / 5:10	154 / 248 / 3:20	291 / 468 / 5:40	493 / 794 / 9:10	222 / 357 / 4:40	209 / 336 / 4:10	170 / 274 / 3:40	371 / 597 / 7:20	373 / 600 / 7:00	56 / 90 / 1:30	504 / 811 / 10:10	260 / 418 / 5:20
Fort William																													486 / 782 / 9:30	560 / 901 / 10:20	144 / 232 / 3:30	127 / 204 / 3:10	596 / 959 / 11:00	357 / 575 / 7:00	206 / 332 / 4:30	485 / 781 / 9:10	479 / 771 / 9:00	486 / 782 / 9:10	575 / 926 / 10:50	125 / 201 / 3:10	539 / 867 / 10:10	296 / 476 / 6:00	392 / 631 / 7:40	190 / 306 / 4:40	133 / 214 / 3:20	430 / 692 / 8:40	149 / 240 / 3:50	510 / 821 / 9:50
Glasgow																												101 / 163 / 2:50	376 / 605 / 7:10	449 / 723 / 8:00	44 / 71 / 1:20	83 / 134 / 2:00	488 / 786 / 8:40	249 / 401 / 4:40	96 / 154 / 2:10	385 / 620 / 7:00	372 / 599 / 6:40	373 / 600 / 6:50	468 / 753 / 8:30	110 / 177 / 2:30	439 / 707 / 8:00	183 / 295 / 3:40	292 / 470 / 5:30	101 / 163 / 2:40	33 / 53 / 1:10	320 / 515 / 6:20	145 / 233 / 3:30	397 / 639 / 7:30
Gloucester																											346 / 557 / 6:10	454 / 731 / 8:30	153 / 246 / 3:10	111 / 179 / 2:10	349 / 562 / 6:10	410 / 660 / 7:10	191 / 307 / 3:30	150 / 241 / 2:50	247 / 398 / 4:20	56 / 90 / 1:20	123 / 198 / 2:20	35 / 56 / 1:00	159 / 256 / 3:10	443 / 713 / 8:00	99 / 159 / 2:40	174 / 280 / 3:10	56 / 90 / 1:20	318 / 512 / 6:00	330 / 531 / 5:50	102 / 164 / 2:30	468 / 753 / 8:30	109 / 175 / 2:30
Great Yarmouth																										225 / 362 / 4:40	419 / 674 / 8:00	527 / 848 / 10:20	366 / 589 / 7:20	335 / 539 / 6:30	386 / 621 / 7:30	484 / 779 / 9:00	185 / 298 / 4:00	167 / 269 / 3:40	320 / 515 / 6:20	284 / 457 / 5:50	82 / 132 / 2:10	275 / 443 / 5:40	180 / 290 / 4:10	477 / 768 / 9:10	240 / 386 / 5:00	252 / 406 / 5:10	180 / 290 / 4:10	345 / 555 / 7:00	402 / 647 / 7:40	294 / 473 / 6:20	517 / 832 / 10:50	128 / 206 / 3:40
Harwich																									82 / 132 / 2:10	196 / 316 / 4:00	432 / 695 / 8:10	543 / 874 / 10:30	337 / 542 / 6:40	279 / 449 / 5:20	413 / 665 / 7:40	469 / 755 / 8:40	125 / 201 / 2:50	194 / 312 / 4:00	336 / 541 / 6:20	246 / 396 / 5:00	67 / 108 / 1:50	217 / 349 / 4:30	128 / 206 / 3:00	504 / 811 / 9:20	187 / 301 / 4:00	275 / 443 / 5:20	167 / 269 / 3:40	372 / 599 / 7:20	425 / 684 / 8:00	281 / 452 / 5:50	535 / 861 / 11:20	76 / 122 / 2:20
Holyhead																								349 / 562 / 7:10	334 / 538 / 7:00	191 / 307 / 4:00	330 / 531 / 6:40	438 / 705 / 8:50	167 / 269 / 4:00	282 / 454 / 5:40	333 / 536 / 6:40	394 / 634 / 7:30	360 / 580 / 7:00	181 / 291 / 3:50	231 / 372 / 4:50	216 / 348 / 5:40	270 / 435 / 5:20	206 / 332 / 4:30	334 / 538 / 6:40	426 / 686 / 8:20	288 / 463 / 5:50	141 / 227 / 3:20	148 / 238 / 3:30	311 / 501 / 6:30	305 / 491 / 6:10	111 / 179 / 2:50	439 / 707 / 8:40	269 / 433 / 5:40
Inverness																							474 / 763 / 9:40	569 / 916 / 11:00	553 / 890 / 11:00	504 / 811 / 9:30	166 / 267 / 4:00	66 / 106 / 1:40	542 / 872 / 10:30	618 / 995 / 11:30	158 / 254 / 3:50	132 / 212 / 3:20	622 / 1001 / 11:30	383 / 617 / 7:30	262 / 422 / 5:30	549 / 884 / 10:20	505 / 813 / 9:30	539 / 867 / 10:10	617 / 993 / 11:30	75 / 121 / 2:00	597 / 961 / 11:20	348 / 560 / 7:00	458 / 737 / 9:00	215 / 346 / 5:10	199 / 320 / 4:30	486 / 782 / 9:40	105 / 169 / 2:50	550 / 885 / 10:40
John o' Groats																						129 / 208 / 3:20	603 / 970 / 12:40	693 / 1116 / 14:00	677 / 1090 / 14:00	628 / 1011 / 12:30	295 / 475 / 7:10	195 / 314 / 5:00	671 / 1080 / 13:40	744 / 1197 / 14:30	285 / 459 / 7:00	259 / 417 / 6:30	746 / 1201 / 14:40	507 / 816 / 10:30	391 / 629 / 8:40	680 / 1094 / 13:30	630 / 1014 / 12:30	668 / 1075 / 13:20	741 / 1193 / 14:40	202 / 325 / 5:00	724 / 1165 / 14:20	478 / 769 / 10:00	574 / 924 / 11:50	342 / 550 / 8:10	328 / 528 / 7:40	601 / 967 / 12:40	232 / 373 / 5:50	663 / 1067 / 13:30
Kingston upon Hull																					518 / 834 / 10:50	394 / 634 / 7:50	231 / 372 / 4:50	196 / 316 / 4:10	207 / 333 / 5:20	169 / 272 / 3:10	254 / 409 / 4:50	369 / 594 / 7:20	280 / 451 / 5:30	309 / 497 / 5:40	234 / 377 / 4:30	295 / 475 / 5:30	256 / 412 / 4:50	47 / 76 / 1:10	158 / 254 / 3:00	244 / 393 / 4:40	139 / 224 / 3:10	233 / 375 / 4:20	245 / 394 / 4:40	327 / 526 / 6:10	264 / 425 / 5:00	127 / 204 / 2:30	134 / 216 / 2:50	185 / 298 / 3:50	251 / 404 / 4:40	223 / 359 / 4:40	364 / 586 / 7:20	184 / 296 / 3:50
Kyle of Lochalsh																				445 / 716 / 9:00	189 / 304 / 4:40	84 / 135 / 2:10	514 / 827 / 10:40	611 / 983 / 12:10	602 / 969 / 12:10	528 / 850 / 10:20	179 / 288 / 4:40	79 / 127 / 2:00	567 / 913 / 11:20	628 / 1011 / 12:00	216 / 348 / 5:20	186 / 299 / 4:40	671 / 1080 / 12:50	432 / 695 / 8:40	275 / 443 / 6:10	564 / 908 / 11:10	555 / 893 / 10:50	552 / 888 / 10:50	651 / 1048 / 12:40	159 / 256 / 4:00	618 / 995 / 12:10	372 / 599 / 7:50	471 / 758 / 9:40	263 / 423 / 6:20	212 / 341 / 5:10	499 / 803 / 10:20	189 / 304 / 4:50	586 / 943 / 11:40
Land's End																			763 / 1228 / 15:10	421 / 678 / 8:20	868 / 1397 / 17:20	741 / 1193 / 14:20	405 / 652 / 8:30	390 / 628 / 8:00	446 / 718 / 9:10	235 / 378 / 5:00	573 / 922 / 10:50	686 / 1104 / 13:20	353 / 568 / 7:20	123 / 198 / 3:20	574 / 924 / 10:50	642 / 1033 / 12:00	381 / 613 / 7:40	374 / 602 / 7:20	477 / 768 / 9:10	245 / 394 / 5:20	374 / 602 / 7:20	200 / 322 / 4:40	308 / 496 / 7:50	665 / 1070 / 12:30	205 / 330 / 5:20	405 / 652 / 8:00	281 / 452 / 6:00	552 / 888 / 10:40	570 / 917 / 10:50	313 / 504 / 6:50	692 / 1114 / 13:10	297 / 478 / 6:30
Leeds																		405 / 652 / 8:00	394 / 634 / 8:20	55 / 89 / 1:30	487 / 784 / 10:20	360 / 579 / 7:10	176 / 283 / 4:00	223 / 359 / 4:30	196 / 315 / 4:20	174 / 280 / 3:20	215 / 346 / 4:10	329 / 530 / 6:40	237 / 381 / 4:40	270 / 435 / 5:00	202 / 325 / 4:00	258 / 415 / 4:50	260 / 418 / 4:50	29 / 47 / 0:50	119 / 192 / 2:30	232 / 373 / 4:20	145 / 233 / 2:50	194 / 312 / 3:50	260 / 419 / 5:00	293 / 472 / 5:30	255 / 410 / 4:50	72 / 116 / 1:40	113 / 182 / 2:30	156 / 251 / 3:20	212 / 341 / 4:00	169 / 272 / 3:40	327 / 526 / 6:50	189 / 304 / 3:50
Leicester																	95 / 153 / 2:00	320 / 515 / 6:30	500 / 805 / 9:50	102 / 164 / 2:10	588 / 947 / 11:50	461 / 742 / 8:50	190 / 306 / 4:00	147 / 237 / 3:10	140 / 225 / 3:20	85 / 137 / 1:40	314 / 505 / 5:40	422 / 679 / 8:00	209 / 336 / 4:10	196 / 315 / 3:40	296 / 476 / 5:20	349 / 562 / 6:20	185 / 298 / 3:30	74 / 119 / 1:30	206 / 332 / 3:50	154 / 248 / 3:00	68 / 109 / 1:20	120 / 193 / 2:30	166 / 267 / 3:20	389 / 626 / 7:00	158 / 254 / 3:10	140 / 225 / 2:40	39 / 63 / 1:10	252 / 406 / 5:00	299 / 481 / 5:20	153 / 246 / 3:20	414 / 666 / 7:40	97 / 156 / 2:20
Lincoln																51 / 82 / 1:20	68 / 109 / 1:50	371 / 597 / 7:30	476 / 766 / 9:40	44 / 71 / 1:20	554 / 892 / 11:30	427 / 687 / 8:30	216 / 348 / 4:40	155 / 249 / 3:30	128 / 206 / 3:20	159 / 256 / 3:10	291 / 468 / 5:30	399 / 642 / 7:50	272 / 438 / 5:30	247 / 398 / 4:40	258 / 415 / 5:00	314 / 505 / 5:50	202 / 325 / 4:00	39 / 63 / 1:10	191 / 307 / 3:40	208 / 335 / 4:10	85 / 137 / 2:20	183 / 295 / 3:40	197 / 317 / 4:00	357 / 575 / 6:40	209 / 336 / 4:10	128 / 206 / 2:40	90 / 145 / 2:10	224 / 360 / 4:40	274 / 441 / 5:10	199 / 320 / 4:20	383 / 616 / 7:20	131 / 211 / 3:10
Liverpool															129 / 208 / 2:50	130 / 209 / 2:40	75 / 121 / 1:50	361 / 581 / 7:20	407 / 655 / 8:30	130 / 209 / 2:40	511 / 822 / 10:40	382 / 615 / 7:40	102 / 164 / 2:40	265 / 427 / 5:20	240 / 386 / 5:00	140 / 225 / 2:40	216 / 348 / 4:10	329 / 530 / 6:40	160 / 257 / 3:30	237 / 381 / 4:30	216 / 348 / 4:10	286 / 460 / 5:20	299 / 481 / 5:30	86 / 138 / 1:50	120 / 193 / 2:30	169 / 272 / 3:20	194 / 312 / 3:40	161 / 259 / 3:10	272 / 438 / 5:10	318 / 512 / 6:00	234 / 377 / 4:30	49 / 79 / 1:20	93 / 150 / 2:10	219 / 352 / 4:30	213 / 343 / 4:10	104 / 167 / 2:40	341 / 549 / 6:40	202 / 325 / 4:10
Manchester														35 / 56 / 1:10	84 / 135 / 2:00	92 / 148 / 2:00	40 / 64 / 1:10	361 / 581 / 7:20	406 / 654 / 8:30	95 / 153 / 2:10	500 / 805 / 10:30	373 / 600 / 7:30	124 / 200 / 3:00	228 / 367 / 4:40	212 / 341 / 4:30	126 / 203 / 2:30	215 / 346 / 4:10	329 / 530 / 6:40	197 / 317 / 4:00	236 / 380 / 4:20	215 / 346 / 4:10	285 / 459 / 5:20	276 / 444 / 5:10	61 / 98 / 1:30	119 / 192 / 2:30	183 / 295 / 3:40	165 / 266 / 3:10	161 / 259 / 3:10	257 / 414 / 4:50	318 / 512 / 6:00	227 / 365 / 4:20	48 / 77 / 1:20	80 / 129 / 2:00	196 / 315 / 4:00	212 / 341 / 4:00	129 / 208 / 3:00	340 / 547 / 6:30	185 / 298 / 3:50
Newcastle upon Tyne													132 / 212 / 2:50	168 / 270 / 3:20	159 / 256 / 3:20	187 / 301 / 3:40	92 / 148 / 2:10	498 / 802 / 9:40	318 / 512 / 7:00	132 / 212 / 2:50	395 / 636 / 8:50	268 / 431 / 5:40	272 / 438 / 5:40	308 / 496 / 6:00	281 / 452 / 5:40	266 / 428 / 4:50	148 / 238 / 3:10	253 / 407 / 5:20	329 / 529 / 6:20	364 / 586 / 6:30	110 / 177 / 2:20	166 / 267 / 3:20	358 / 576 / 6:30	114 / 183 / 2:20	57 / 92 / 1:50	325 / 523 / 6:00	241 / 388 / 4:20	299 / 481 / 5:30	352 / 567 / 6:30	201 / 323 / 4:00	347 / 558 / 6:30	129 / 208 / 2:40	207 / 333 / 4:10	64 / 103 / 1:50	149 / 240 / 3:00	257 / 414 / 5:20	235 / 378 / 4:50	286 / 460 / 5:40
Norwich												264 / 425 / 5:20	185 / 298 / 4:30	220 / 354 / 4:40	105 / 169 / 2:50	119 / 192 / 3:20	176 / 283 / 3:50	421 / 678 / 8:40	582 / 937 / 11:50	149 / 240 / 4:00	654 / 1053 / 13:30	529 / 852 / 10:30	311 / 501 / 6:40	73 / 117 / 2:00	20 / 32 / 0:40	204 / 328 / 4:10	385 / 620 / 9:00	504 / 811 / 10:00	343 / 552 / 7:00	308 / 496 / 6:00	366 / 589 / 7:00	422 / 679 / 8:00	174 / 280 / 3:50	147 / 237 / 3:20	289 / 465 / 5:40	262 / 422 / 5:20	62 / 100 / 1:50	252 / 406 / 5:10	175 / 282 / 4:00	457 / 735 / 8:40	214 / 344 / 4:40	232 / 373 / 4:50	166 / 267 / 3:50	328 / 528 / 6:40	382 / 615 / 7:20	276 / 444 / 6:00	496 / 798 / 9:40	114 / 183 / 3:30
Nottingham											130 / 209 / 3:40	157 / 253 / 3:10	73 / 118 / 1:40	98 / 158 / 2:10	35 / 56 / 1:10	25 / 40 / 0:50	70 / 113 / 1:40	345 / 555 / 7:00	479 / 771 / 9:40	90 / 145 / 2:00	557 / 896 / 11:30	430 / 692 / 8:20	185 / 298 / 4:00	150 / 241 / 3:20	153 / 246 / 3:30	110 / 177 / 2:10	293 / 472 / 5:30	401 / 646 / 7:50	220 / 354 / 4:30	221 / 356 / 4:10	262 / 422 / 4:50	328 / 528 / 6:00	205 / 330 / 3:50	43 / 69 / 1:10	194 / 312 / 3:40	172 / 277 / 3:20	83 / 134 / 1:40	145 / 233 / 3:00	193 / 311 / 3:50	353 / 568 / 6:30	183 / 295 / 3:40	111 / 179 / 2:20	50 / 80 / 1:20	221 / 356 / 4:30	274 / 441 / 5:10	164 / 264 / 3:40	393 / 633 / 7:30	122 / 196 / 2:40
Oban										390 / 628 / 7:30	492 / 792 / 9:40	233 / 375 / 4:50	307 / 494 / 6:00	308 / 496 / 6:10	387 / 623 / 7:30	419 / 674 / 7:50	307 / 494 / 6:00	665 / 1070 / 12:50	128 / 206 / 3:10	346 / 557 / 6:40	244 / 393 / 6:10	117 / 188 / 3:00	427 / 687 / 8:30	524 / 843 / 10:00	515 / 829 / 10:00	441 / 710 / 8:10	92 / 148 / 2:30	49 / 79 / 1:20	481 / 774 / 9:10	549 / 884 / 10:00	123 / 198 / 3:00	117 / 188 / 2:50	585 / 942 / 10:40	346 / 557 / 6:40	188 / 303 / 4:00	477 / 768 / 9:00	468 / 753 / 8:40	465 / 748 / 8:40	565 / 910 / 10:30	141 / 227 / 3:30	530 / 853 / 9:50	285 / 459 / 5:40	384 / 618 / 7:30	180 / 290 / 4:20	94 / 151 / 2:20	412 / 663 / 8:10	178 / 286 / 4:20	499 / 803 / 9:30
Oxford									462 / 744 / 8:30	109 / 175 / 2:10	145 / 233 / 3:50	260 / 418 / 4:50	144 / 232 / 2:50	172 / 277 / 3:20	137 / 221 / 2:50	73 / 117 / 1:30	168 / 270 / 3:10	274 / 441 / 5:40	550 / 885 / 10:40	192 / 309 / 3:40	656 / 1056 / 13:00	532 / 856 / 10:00	238 / 383 / 4:50	145 / 233 / 3:10	200 / 322 / 4:20	52 / 84 / 1:30	356 / 573 / 6:30	472 / 760 / 9:00	205 / 330 / 4:10	156 / 251 / 3:00	372 / 599 / 6:40	433 / 697 / 7:40	141 / 227 / 2:50	145 / 233 / 2:40	260 / 418 / 4:40	108 / 174 / 2:20	83 / 134 / 1:40	74 / 119 / 1:40	108 / 174 / 2:20	465 / 749 / 8:20	90 / 145 / 2:00	187 / 301 / 3:30	64 / 103 / 1:30	324 / 521 / 6:10	353 / 568 / 6:20	154 / 248 / 3:20	483 / 777 / 8:50	57 / 92 / 1:40
Plymouth								199 / 320 / 4:00	587 / 945 / 11:00	267 / 430 / 5:10	343 / 552 / 7:00	410 / 660 / 7:40	283 / 455 / 5:30	283 / 455 / 5:30	293 / 472 / 5:50	242 / 389 / 4:40	316 / 509 / 6:00	89 / 143 / 2:20	674 / 1085 / 13:10	355 / 571 / 6:40	790 / 1271 / 15:40	664 / 1069 / 12:30	328 / 528 / 6:40	309 / 497 / 6:10	365 / 588 / 7:20	157 / 253 / 3:20	495 / 797 / 9:10	595 / 958 / 11:20	264 / 425 / 5:30	46 / 74 / 1:30	496 / 798 / 9:00	552 / 888 / 10:00	300 / 483 / 5:50	297 / 478 / 5:40	399 / 642 / 7:20	167 / 269 / 3:40	293 / 472 / 5:30	122 / 196 / 2:50	224 / 361 / 6:00	587 / 945 / 10:40	128 / 206 / 3:30	328 / 528 / 6:10	203 / 327 / 4:20	474 / 763 / 9:00	492 / 792 / 9:00	237 / 382 / 5:10	615 / 990 / 11:20	218 / 351 / 4:40
Portsmouth							176 / 283 / 4:50	77 / 124 / 1:40	545 / 877 / 10:00	191 / 307 / 3:40	207 / 333 / 4:20	337 / 542 / 6:10	236 / 380 / 4:30	254 / 409 / 4:50	201 / 323 / 4:00	162 / 261 / 3:10	257 / 414 / 4:50	259 / 417 / 5:40	633 / 1019 / 12:10	269 / 433 / 5:00	737 / 1186 / 14:30	613 / 987 / 11:30	311 / 501 / 6:10	166 / 267 / 3:40	221 / 356 / 4:40	119 / 192 / 3:00	448 / 721 / 8:10	555 / 893 / 10:20	251 / 404 / 5:00	135 / 217 / 2:40	453 / 729 / 8:10	514 / 827 / 9:00	130 / 209 / 2:50	234 / 377 / 4:20	348 / 560 / 6:10	142 / 229 / 3:00	144 / 232 / 2:50	97 / 156 / 2:10	48 / 77 / 1:40	547 / 881 / 9:50	52 / 84 / 1:30	264 / 425 / 4:50	141 / 227 / 3:00	401 / 645 / 7:30	430 / 692 / 7:40	222 / 357 / 4:40	560 / 901 / 10:10	70 / 113 / 2:00
Sheffield						230 / 370 / 4:20	283 / 455 / 5:30	135 / 217 / 2:40	339 / 546 / 6:30	37 / 60 / 1:00	146 / 235 / 3:20	125 / 201 / 2:40	38 / 61 / 1:00	72 / 116 / 1:40	46 / 74 / 1:20	62 / 100 / 1:20	33 / 53 / 1:00	361 / 581 / 7:10	427 / 687 / 8:40	65 / 105 / 1:30	520 / 837 / 10:50	393 / 632 / 7:40	168 / 270 / 3:40	187 / 301 / 3:50	166 / 267 / 3:40	126 / 203 / 2:20	248 / 399 / 4:40	348 / 560 / 6:50	215 / 346 / 4:20	237 / 381 / 4:20	235 / 378 / 4:20	291 / 468 / 5:20	245 / 394 / 4:30	18 / 29 / 0:40	152 / 245 / 3:00	194 / 312 / 3:40	120 / 193 / 2:20	161 / 259 / 3:10	226 / 364 / 4:20	320 / 515 / 6:00	216 / 348 / 4:10	86 / 138 / 1:50	76 / 122 / 1:50	190 / 306 / 4:00	245 / 394 / 4:30	159 / 256 / 3:30	360 / 579 / 6:50	159 / 256 / 3:20
Shrewsbury					82 / 132 / 2:10	207 / 333 / 3:50	225 / 362 / 4:40	106 / 171 / 2:10	364 / 586 / 7:00	93 / 150 / 2:00	205 / 330 / 4:20	201 / 323 / 3:50	69 / 111 / 1:40	58 / 93 / 1:50	133 / 214 / 2:50	84 / 135 / 1:40	109 / 175 / 2:20	303 / 488 / 6:10	451 / 726 / 9:00	169 / 272 / 3:10	567 / 912 / 11:30	438 / 705 / 8:20	113 / 182 / 2:50	240 / 386 / 4:40	225 / 362 / 4:40	77 / 124 / 1:30	272 / 438 / 5:00	382 / 615 / 7:20	145 / 233 / 3:10	179 / 288 / 3:20	274 / 441 / 5:00	330 / 531 / 6:00	251 / 404 / 4:30	109 / 175 / 2:10	176 / 283 / 3:20	111 / 179 / 2:20	159 / 256 / 3:00	103 / 166 / 2:50	226 / 364 / 4:20	371 / 597 / 6:50	185 / 298 / 3:40	98 / 158 / 2:00	45 / 72 / 1:20	265 / 426 / 5:10	269 / 433 / 5:00	77 / 124 / 2:10	399 / 642 / 7:30	160 / 258 / 3:20
Southampton				185 / 298 / 4:10	199 / 320 / 3:40	21 / 34 / 0:50	151 / 243 / 4:10	64 / 103 / 1:30	530 / 853 / 9:40	176 / 283 / 3:20	206 / 332 / 4:20	324 / 521 / 5:50	221 / 356 / 4:10	239 / 385 / 4:30	204 / 328 / 4:00	137 / 220 / 2:40	232 / 373 / 4:20	228 / 367 / 5:00	618 / 995 / 12:00	256 / 412 / 4:40	723 / 1164 / 14:10	598 / 963 / 11:10	293 / 472 / 5:50	164 / 264 / 3:30	220 / 354 / 4:40	105 / 169 / 2:40	433 / 697 / 7:40	541 / 871 / 10:00	233 / 375 / 4:40	105 / 169 / 3:00	438 / 705 / 7:50	500 / 805 / 8:50	143 / 230 / 2:50	209 / 336 / 3:50	324 / 521 / 5:50	121 / 195 / 2:30	148 / 238 / 2:50	76 / 122 / 2:20	61 / 98 / 1:50	532 / 856 / 9:30	31 / 50 / 1:00	251 / 404 / 4:40	128 / 206 / 2:40	388 / 624 / 7:10	417 / 671 / 7:30	201 / 323 / 4:10	547 / 880 / 10:00	77 / 124 / 2:00
Stranraer			445 / 716 / 8:20	277 / 446 / 5:30	263 / 423 / 5:20	461 / 742 / 8:40	500 / 805 / 9:40	379 / 610 / 7:10	148 / 238 / 3:40	290 / 467 / 5:50	403 / 649 / 8:10	158 / 254 / 3:40	220 / 354 / 4:40	221 / 356 / 4:40	298 / 480 / 6:00	330 / 531 / 6:20	220 / 354 / 4:40	585 / 942 / 11:30	263 / 423 / 6:30	259 / 417 / 5:20	379 / 610 / 9:00	262 / 422 / 6:00	338 / 544 / 7:00	410 / 660 / 8:10	426 / 686 / 8:40	343 / 552 / 6:30	84 / 135 / 2:30	195 / 314 / 4:50	392 / 631 / 7:50	454 / 731 / 8:30	124 / 200 / 3:00	167 / 269 / 3:40	496 / 798 / 9:10	257 / 414 / 5:10	101 / 163 / 2:40	390 / 628 / 7:30	379 / 610 / 7:10	378 / 608 / 7:20	475 / 765 / 9:00	194 / 312 / 4:20	444 / 715 / 8:30	188 / 303 / 4:00	297 / 478 / 6:00	170 / 274 / 4:10	51 / 82 / 1:20	325 / 523 / 6:50	228 / 367 / 5:10	402 / 647 / 7:50
Swansea		417 / 671 / 7:50	161 / 259 / 3:00	118 / 190 / 2:20	217 / 349 / 4:00	182 / 293 / 3:30	206 / 332 / 4:10	141 / 227 / 2:40	506 / 815 / 9:20	192 / 309 / 3:40	301 / 485 / 6:00	347 / 559 / 6:20	187 / 301 / 3:30	195 / 314 / 3:40	233 / 375 / 4:30	177 / 285 / 3:20	248 / 399 / 4:40	285 / 459 / 6:00	594 / 956 / 11:30	264 / 425 / 4:50	696 / 1120 / 13:40	572 / 921 / 10:40	184 / 296 / 4:50	267 / 430 / 5:10	329 / 530 / 6:30	89 / 143 / 1:50	409 / 658 / 7:20	496 / 798 / 9:20	67 / 108 / 1:50	161 / 259 / 3:00	412 / 663 / 7:20	473 / 761 / 8:20	274 / 441 / 5:00	232 / 373 / 4:10	309 / 497 / 5:30	41 / 66 / 1:10	227 / 365 / 4:10	85 / 137 / 1:50	222 / 357 / 4:20	505 / 813 / 9:00	167 / 269 / 3:20	216 / 348 / 4:00	119 / 192 / 2:30	383 / 616 / 7:10	379 / 610 / 6:50	73 / 117 / 2:00	507 / 816 / 9:20	194 / 312 / 4:00
York	272 / 438 / 5:10	222 / 357 / 4:40	258 / 415 / 5:10	133 / 214 / 2:40	52 / 84 / 1:20	278 / 448 / 5:10	333 / 536 / 6:20	181 / 291 / 3:20	309 / 497 / 6:00	77 / 124 / 1:40	181 / 291 / 4:20	84 / 135 / 2:20	64 / 103 / 1:30	99 / 159 / 2:10	75 / 121 / 1:50	108 / 174 / 2:10	24 / 39 / 0:50	411 / 661 / 8:00	407 / 655 / 8:20	37 / 60 / 1:10	479 / 771 / 10:10	352 / 566 / 7:00	204 / 328 / 4:20	228 / 367 / 4:40	201 / 323 / 4:20	189 / 304 / 3:30	217 / 349 / 4:10	330 / 531 / 6:30	261 / 420 / 5:10	287 / 462 / 5:10	194 / 312 / 3:40	250 / 402 / 4:40	282 / 454 / 5:10	34 / 55 / 1:00	121 / 195 / 2:30	244 / 393 / 4:40	165 / 266 / 3:10	222 / 357 / 4:10	275 / 443 / 5:10	285 / 459 / 5:20	269 / 433 / 5:00	96 / 154 / 2:00	130 / 209 / 2:40	148 / 238 / 3:10	214 / 344 / 4:00	195 / 314 / 4:10	319 / 513 / 6:10	207 / 333 / 4:10

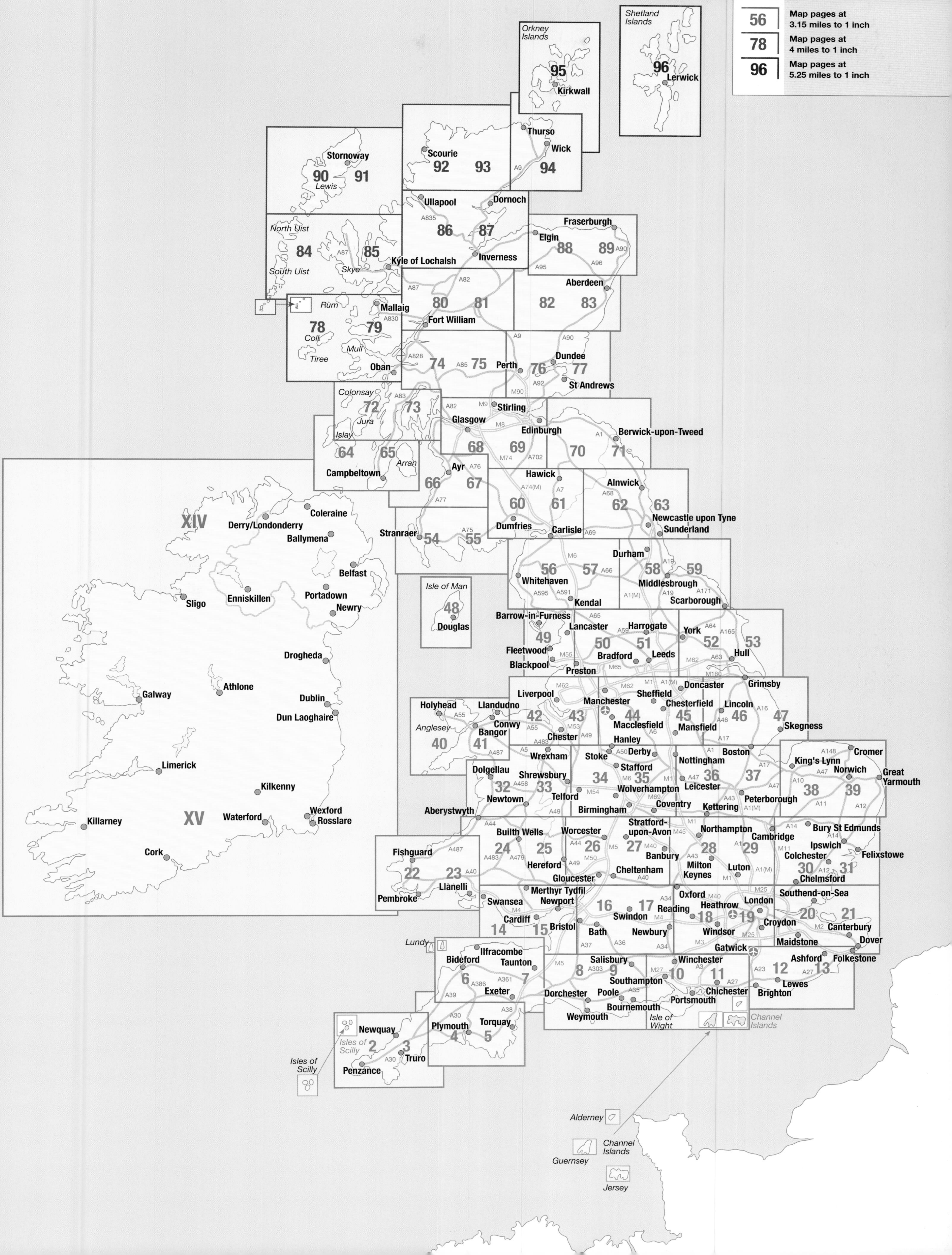

Key to road map pages

56	Map pages at 3.15 miles to 1 inch
78	Map pages at 4 miles to 1 inch
96	Map pages at 5.25 miles to 1 inch

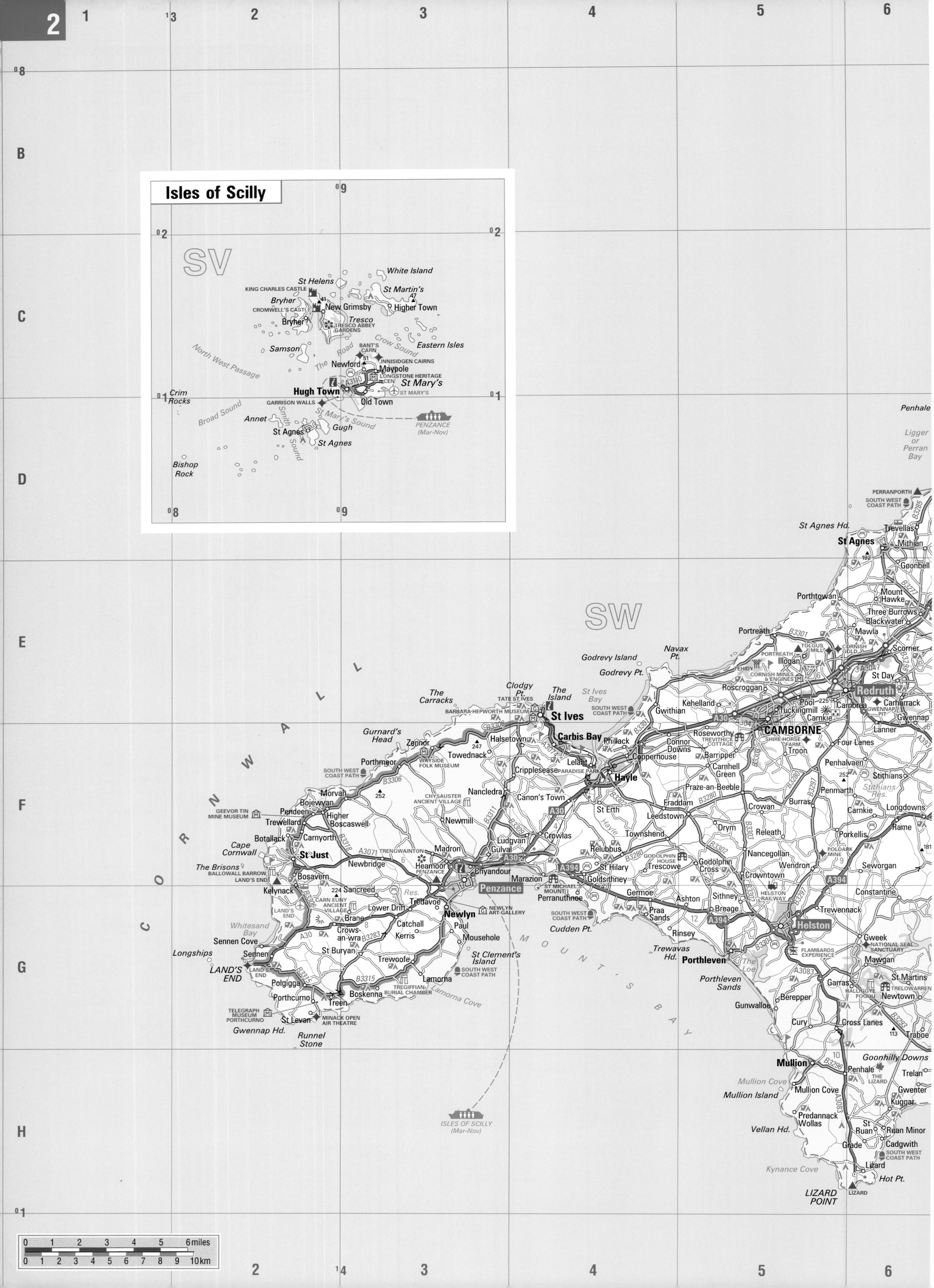

Isles of Scilly

SV

White Island
St Helens
KING CHARLES CASTLE
St Martin's
Bryher
CROMWELL'S CASTLE
New Grimsby
Higher Town
Bryher
Tresco
TRESCO ABBEY GARDENS
Samson
Crow Sound
Eastern Isles
BANT'S CARN
Newford
INNISIDGEN CAIRNS
North West Passage
The Road
Maypole
LONGSTONE HERITAGE CEN
St Mary's
Crim Rocks
Hugh Town
GARRISON WALLS
Old Town
ST MARY'S
Broad Sound
Annet
St Agnes
Gugh
St Mary's Sound
PENZANCE (Mar-Nov)
Penhale
St Agnes
Smith Sound
Bishop Rock
Ligger or Perran Bay

SW

PERRANPORTH
SOUTH WEST COAST PATH
St Agnes Hd.
Trevellas
St Agnes
Mithian
Goonbell
Porthtowan
Mount Hawke
Three Burrows
Blackwater
Mawla
Portreath
PORTREATH
TOLGUS MILLS
CORNISH GOLD J.T.
Scorrier
Godrevy Island
Navax Pt.
TEHIDY
CORNISH MINES & ENGINES
St Day
Godrevy Pt.
Roscroggan
Redruth
The Carracks
Clodgy Pt.
The Island
St Ives Bay
Gwithian
Pool
Carharrack
TATE ST IVES
SOUTH WEST COAST PATH
Kehelland
CAMBORNE
Carnkie
Gwennap
Gurnard's Head
BARBARA HEPWORTH MUSEUM
St Ives
SHIRE HORSE FARM
Roseworthy
Lanner
Zennor
Carbis Bay
Connor Downs
TREVITHICK COTTAGE
Troon
Four Lanes
Porthmeor
Towednack
Halsetown
Phillack
Copperhouse
Barripper
Penhalvaen
SOUTH WEST COAST PATH
247
Carnhell Green
Praze-an-Beeble
Penmarth
Morvah
WAYSIDE FOLK MUSEUM
PARADISE PARK
Hayle
Fraddam
Crowan
Burras
Carnkie
Bojewyan
CHYSAUSTER ANCIENT VILLAGE
Nancledra
Canon's Town
Stithians Res.
Pendeen
Higher Boscaswell
Newmill
St Erth
Leedstown
Drym
Releath
Porkellis
Rame
Longdowns
GEEVOR TIN MINE MUSEUM
252
Ludgvan
Crowlas
Townshend
Nancegollan
POLDARK MINE
Trewellard
Botallack
Carnyorth
Madron
Gulval
Relubbus
GODOLPHIN HOUSE
Godolphin Cross
Wendron
Seworgan
Cape Cornwall
TRENGWAINTON
Godolphin
St Just
Newbridge
Heamoor
PENZANCE
Chyandour
A30
Marazion
Goldsithney
Crowntown
The Brisons
BALLOWALL BARROW
LAND'S END
Bosavern
224
Sancreed
Res.
ST MICHAEL'S MOUNT
Germoe
HELSTON RAILWAY
Constantine
Kelynack
Penzance
Perranuthnoe
Ashton
Sithney
Breage
Trewennack
Lower Drift
Tredavoe
NEWLYN ART GALLERY
SOUTH WEST COAST PATH
Praa Sands
LAND'S END
Brane
Newlyn
Rinsey
A394
Helston
Catchall
Paul
Cudden Pt.
Trewavas Hd.
FLAMBARDS EXPERIENCE
Whitesand Bay
Crows-an-wra
Kerris
Mousehole
Porthleven
The Loe
Gweek
NATIONAL SEAL SANCTUARY
Sennen Cove
St Buryan
Trewoofe
St Clement's Island
Garras
HALLIGGYE FOGOU
Newtown
Longships
Sennen
Lamorna
SOUTH WEST COAST PATH
Porthleven Sands
TRELOWARREN
St Martins
LAND'S END
TREGIFFIAN BURIAL CHAMBER
Lamorna Cove
Berepper
Polgigga
Boskenna
Gunwalloe
Cross Lanes
Porthcurno
Treen
Cury
113
Traboe
TELEGRAPH MUSEUM PORTHCURNO
MINACK OPEN AIR THEATRE
Goonhilly Downs
St Levan
Mullion
Penhale
Trelan
Gwennap Hd.
Runnel Stone
THE LIZARD
Gwenter
Mullion Cove
Kuggar
Mullion Island
Predannack Wollas
St Ruan
Ruan Minor
Vellan Hd.
Grade
Cadgwith
Kynance Cove
Lizard
Hot Pt.
LIZARD POINT

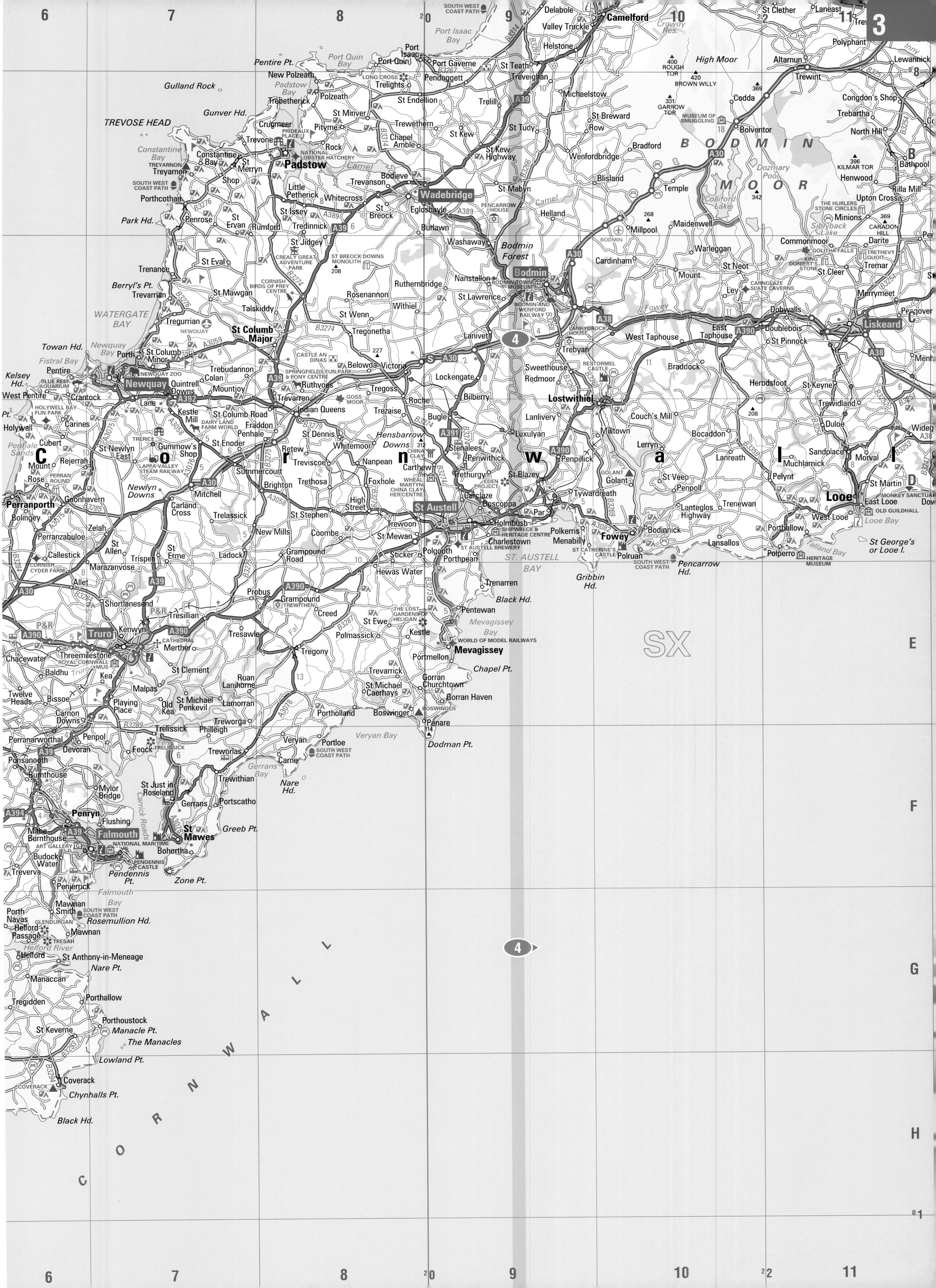
Cornwall
BODMIN MOOR
SX
Camelford
Delabole
Valley Truckle
Helstone
Port Isaac
Port Isaac Bay
Port Quin
Port Quin Bay
Port Gaverne
Pendoggett
Pentire Pt.
New Polzeath
Padstow Bay
Polzeath
Trebetherick
Gulland Rock
Gunver Hd.
TREVOSE HEAD
Constantine Bay
Treyarnon
Padstow
Wadebridge
St Minver
St Endellion
Trelights
St Teath
Treveighan
Michaelstow
Trelill
St Tudy
St Kew
St Kew Highway
St Mabyn
St Breward
Wenfordbridge
Blisland
Bradford
Temple
High Moor
ROUGH TOR
BROWN WILLY
GARROW TOR
Altarnun
Trewint
Codda
Bolventor
Dozmary Pool
Colliford Lake
Congdon's Shop
Trebartha
North Hill
KILMAR TOR
Bathpool
Henwood
Rilla Mill
Upton Cross
Minions
THE HURLERS STONE CIRCLES
CARADON HILL
Darite
Commonmoor
GOLITHA FALLS
TRETHEVY QUOIT
KING DONIERT'S STONE
St Cleer
Tremar
Merrymeet
Siblyback Lake
Laneast
St Clether
Polyphant
Lewannick
Crowdy Res.
MUSEUM OF SMUGGLING
Helland
Millpool
Maidenwell
Warleggan
Cardinham
St Neot
Mount
Ley
CARNGLAZE SLATE CAVERNS
Dobwalls
Doublebois
Liskeard
St Pinnock
East Taphouse
West Taphouse
Braddock
Herodsfoot
St Keyne
Trewidland
Duloe
Sandplace
Muchlarnick
Morval
Widegates
Pelynt
St Martin
Looe
East Looe
West Looe
Looe Bay
St George's or Looe I.
MONKEY SANCTUARY
OLD GUILDHALL
Porthallow
Polperro
HERITAGE MUSEUM
Talland Bay
Lansallos
Trenewan
Lanteglos Highway
Penpoll
St Veep
Lanreath
Bocaddon
Lerryn
Couch's Mill
Milltown
Golant
Bodinnick
Fowey
Polruan
Pencarrow Hd.
SOUTH WEST COAST PATH
ST CATHERINE'S CASTLE
Gribbin Hd.
Polkerris
Menabilly
Tywardreath
Par
Lostwithiel
RESTORMEL CASTLE
Lanlivery
Redmoor
Sweethouse
Trebyan
LANHYDROCK HOUSE
Bodmin
BODMIN TOWN MUSEUM
BODMIN AND WENFORD RAILWAY
Bodmin Forest
Nanstallon
St Lawrence
Lanivet
Washaway
Burlawn
Egloshayle
PENCARROW HOUSE
Ruthernbridge
Rosenannon
Withiel
St Wenn
Tregonetha
Belowda
Victoria
Lockengate
Bilberry
Roche
Bugle
Luxulyan
Penwithick
Stenalees
Tregoss
GOSS MOOR
Trezaise
Hensbarrow Downs
CHINA CLAY
WHEAL MARTYN CHINA CLAY HERITAGE CENTRE
Carthew
Trethurgy
EDEN PROJECT
St Blazey
Penpillick
Carclaze
Boscoppa
Holmbush
St Austell
St Austell Bay
ST AUSTELL BREWERY
SHIPWRECK & HERITAGE CENTRE
Charlestown
Porthpean
Polgooth
Trewoon
St Mewan
Sticker
Hewas Water
Trenarren
Black Hd.
Pentewan
Mevagissey Bay
Mevagissey
WORLD OF MODEL RAILWAYS
Chapel Pt.
Portmellon
Gorran Churchtown
Gorran Haven
Boswinger
Penare
Dodman Pt.
Veryan Bay
Portholland
St Michael Caerhays
Trevarrick
Kestle
Polmassick
St Ewe
THE LOST GARDENS OF HELIGAN
Creed
Grampound
TREWITHEN
Grampound Road
Probus
Tregony
Coombe
St Stephen
High Street
Foxhole
Nanpean
Trethosa
Whitemoor
Treviscoe
St Dennis
Retew
Brighton
New Mills
Ladock
Trelassick
Summercourt
Fraddon
Penhale
Indian Queens
Trevarren
St Columb Road
St Columb Major
Talskiddy
Ruthvoes
SPRINGFIELDS FUN PARK & PONY CENTRE
CASTLE AN DINAS
St Jidgey
St Breock
ST BREOCK DOWNS MONOLITH
Tredinnick
St Issey
Little Petherick
Whitecross
Trevanson
Bodieve
Rock
Pityme
Trewethern
Chapel Amble
Trevone
Crugmeer
PRIDEAUX PLACE
NATIONAL LOBSTER HATCHERY
St Merryn
Shop
Porthcothan
Penrose
St Ervan
Rumford
Park Hd.
St Eval
CREALY GREAT ADVENTURE PARK
CORNISH BIRDS OF PREY CENTRE
Trenance
Berryl's Pt.
Trevarrian
St Mawgan
WATERGATE BAY
Tregurrian
NEWQUAY
Newquay Bay
Towan Hd.
Fistral Bay
Porth
St Columb Minor
NEWQUAY ZOO
Newquay
Kelsey Hd.
Pentire
BLUE REEF AQUARIUM
West Pentire
Crantock
Quintrell Downs
Trebudannon
Colan
Mountjoy
Lane
Kestle Mill
DAIRY LAND FARM WORLD
HOLYWELL BAY FUN PARK
Holywell
Carines
Cubert
Penhale Sands
St Newlyn East
TRERICE
Gummow's Shop
LAPPA VALLEY STEAM RAILWAY
St Enoder
Rejerrah
Mount
Rose
PERRAN ROUND
Newlyn Downs
Mitchell
Carland Cross
Perranporth
Goonhavern
Bolingey
Zelah
Perranzabuloe
St Allen
Trispen
St Erme
Callestick
CORNISH CYDER FARM
Marazanvose
Allet
Shortlanesend
Tresillian
Kenwyn
Truro
CATHEDRAL
Merther
Tresawle
Threemilestone
ROYAL CORNWALL MUS
Chacewater
Baldhu
Kea
St Clement
Malpas
Ruan Lanihorne
Twelve Heads
Bissoe
Playing Place
Old Kea
St Michael Penkevil
Lamorran
Carnon Downs
Treworga
Perranarworthal
Penpol
Devoran
Trelissick
Feock
Philleigh
Treworlas
Veryan
Portloe
Carne
Nare Hd.
Gerrans Bay
Trewithian
Ponsanooth
Burnthouse
Mylor Bridge
St Just in Roseland
Carrick Roads
Gerrans
Portscatho
Penryn
Flushing
Mabe Burnthouse
Falmouth
ART GALLERY
NATIONAL MARITIME
St Mawes
Bohortha
Greeb Pt.
Budock Water
Treverva
PENDENNIS CASTLE
Pendennis Pt.
Zone Pt.
Penjerrick
Falmouth Bay
Mawnan Smith
Porth Navas
GLENDURGAN
Rosemullion Hd.
Helford Passage
Mawnan
TREBAH
Helford River
Helford
St Anthony-in-Meneage
Nare Pt.
Manaccan
Porthallow
Tregidden
Porthoustock
St Keverne
Manacle Pt.
The Manacles
Lowland Pt.
Coverack
COVERACK
Chynhalls Pt.
Black Hd.
C O R N W A L L
A30
A39
A38
A389
A390
A391
A392
A394
A3058
A3059
A3075
A3076
A3078
A3082
B3266
B3267
B3268
B3269
B3274
B3275
B3276
B3287
B3289
B3293
B3294
B3314
P&R
4
6 7 8 9 10 11
A B C D E F G H

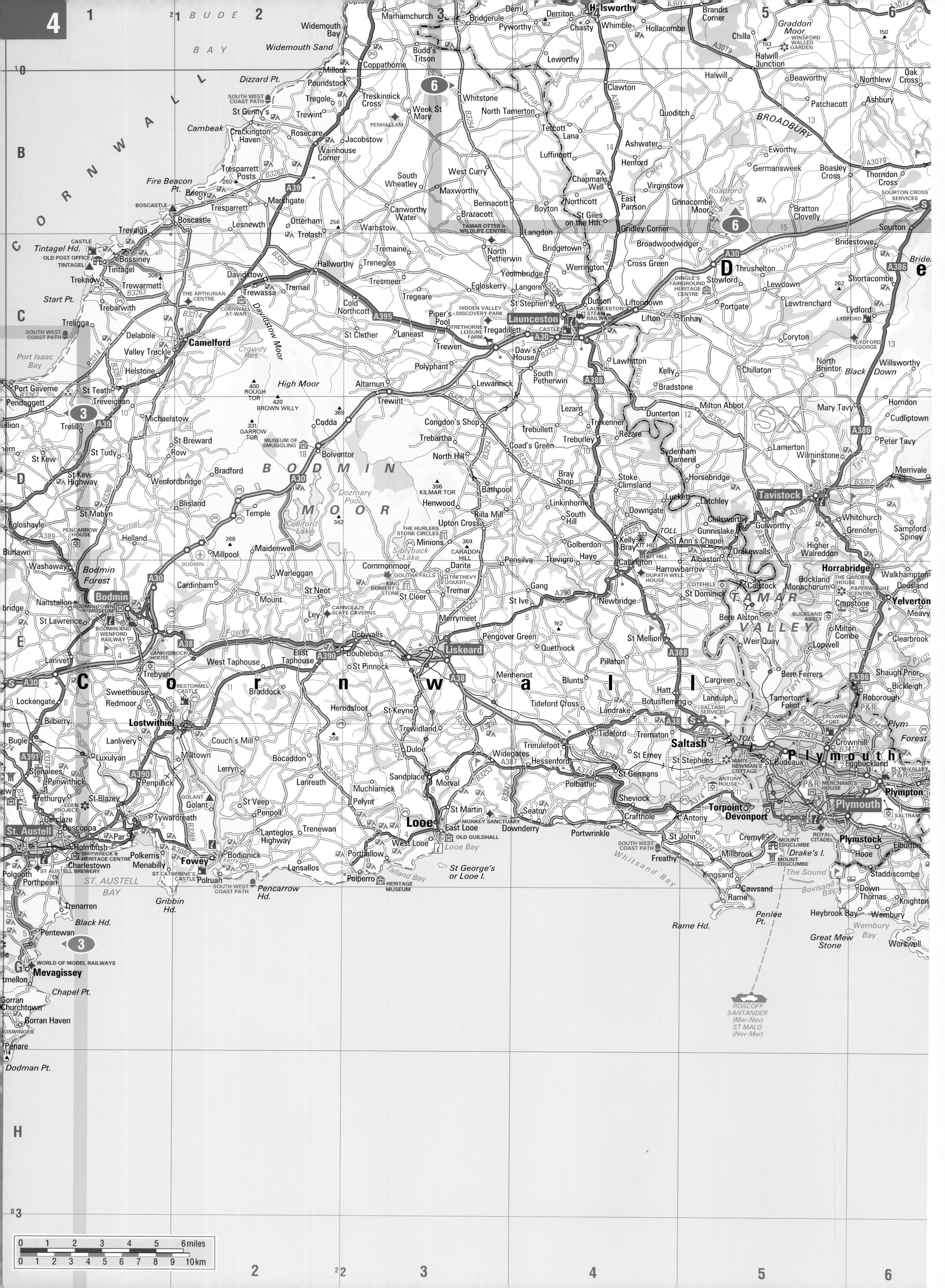
BUDE BAY
Widemouth Bay
Widemouth Sand
Marhamchurch
Bridgerule
Derril
Pyworthy
Derriton
Holsworthy
Chasty
Whimble
Hollacombe
Brandis Corner
Graddon Moor
Chilla
Winsford Walled Garden
Halwill Junction
Budd's Titson
Coppathorne
Millook
Dizzard Pt.
Poundstock
Lewworthy
Halwill
Beaworthy
Northlew
Oak Cross
Whitstone
Clawton
South West Coast Path
St Gennys
Tregole
Treskinnick Cross
Week St Mary
North Tamerton
Quoditch
Patchacott
Ashbury
Broadbury
Trewint
Cambeak
Crackington Haven
Rosecare
Penhallam
Jacobstow
Tetcott
Lana
Wainhouse Corner
Ashwater
Luffincott
Henford
Eworthy
Germansweek
Boasley Cross
Thorndon Cross
Tresparrett Posts
Fire Beacon Pt.
South Wheatley
West Curry
Chapmans Well
Virginstow
Beeny
Maxworthy
Marshgate
Tresparrett
Bennacott
Northcott
East Panson
Grinacombe Moor
Roadford Res.
Bratton Clovelly
Sourton Cross Services
Boscastle
Canworthy Water
Otterham
Brazacott
Boyton
St Giles on the Hth.
Lesnewth
Trevalga
Trelash
Warbstow
Tamar Otter & Wildlife Centre
Langdon
Gridley Corner
Sourton
Castle
Tintagel Hd.
Bossiney
Old Post Office Tintagel
Tintagel
Tremaine
Treneglos
North Petherwin
Bridgetown
Broadwoodwidger
Bridestowe
Cross Green
Thrushelton
Werrington
Yeolmbridge
Hallworthy
Treknow
Trewarmett
Davidstow
Tresmeer
Egloskerry
Langore
Stowford
Lewdown
Dingle's Fairground Heritage Centre
Shortacombe
Start Pt.
The Arthurian Centre
Trewassa
Tremail
Tregeare
Trebarwith
Davidstow Moor
Hidden Valley Discovery Park
St Stephen's
Dutson
Liftondown
Portgate
Lewtrenchard
Lydford
Cornwall at War
Cold Northcott
Launceston Steam Railway
Launceston
Lifton
Tinhay
Piper's Pool
Trelligga
Delabole
St Clether
Laneast
Trethorne Leisure Farm
Tregadillett
Castle
South West Coast Path
Camelford
Crowdy Res.
Trewen
Daw's House
Coryton
Lydford Gorge
Port Isaac Bay
Valley Truckle
Polyphant
Lawhitton
Willsworthy
Helstone
Rough Tor
Brown Willy
High Moor
Altarnun
South Petherwin
Kelly
Chillaton
North Brentor
Black Down
Port Gaverne
St Teath
Lewannick
Bradstone
Pendoggett
Treveighan
Trewint
Lezant
Dunterton
Milton Abbot
Mary Tavy
Horndon
Cudliptown
Trelill
Michaelstow
Garrow Tor
Codda
Congdon's Shop
Trebullett
Trekenner
Museum of Smuggling
Trebartha
Treburley
Rezare
Peter Tavy
St Breward
Row
Bolventor
Coad's Green
Sydenham Damerel
Lamerton
St Kew
St Tudy
North Hill
Wilminstone
St Kew Highway
Bradford
Wenfordbridge
Bodmin Moor
Kilmar Tor
Bray Shop
Horsebridge
Merrivale
Dozmary Pool
Henwood
Bathpool
Stoke Climsland
Lucket
Latchley
Tavistock
Blisland
St Mabyn
Temple
Colliford Lake
Linkinhorne
Downgate
Rilla Mill
South Hill
Chilsworthy
Gulworthy
Whitchurch
Grenofen
Egloshayle
Pencarrow House
Helland
The Hurlers Stone Circles
Upton Cross
Minions
Kelly Bray
Kit Hill
St Ann's Chapel
Gunnislake
Sampford Spiney
Burlawn
Millpool
Maidenwell
Siblyback Lake
Caradon Hill
Golberdon
Haye
Drakewalls
Higher Walreddon
Washaway
Bodmin Forest
Pensilva
Trevigro
Callington
Albaston
Horrabridge
Walkhampton
Warleggan
Commonmoor
Darite
Harrowbarrow
Buckland Monachorum
The Garden House
Paperweight Centre
Dousland
Golitha Falls
Trethevy Quoit
Dupath Well House
Cotehele
Calstock
Cardinham
St Neot
King Doniert's Stone
Tremar
Gang
St Dominick
Tamar Valley
Crapstone
Yelverton
Bodmin
Nanstallon
Mount
St Cleer
St Ive
Newbridge
Bere Alston
Buckland Abbey
Meavy
Bodmin Town Museum
Carnglaze Slate Caverns
Ley
Merrymeet
St Lawrence
Bodmin and Wenford Railway
Fowey
Dobwalls
Pengover Green
Quethiock
St Mellion
Milton Combe
Clearbrook
Weir Quay
Lopwell
Lanhydrock House
East Taphouse
Doublebois
Liskeard
Lanivet
West Taphouse
St Pinnock
Menheniot
Pillaton
Shaugh Prior
Trebyan
Blunts
Cargreen
Bere Ferrers
Bickleigh
Cornwall
Restormel Castle
Braddock
Sweethouse
Redmoor
Tideford Cross
Hatt
Botusfleming
Landulph
Tamerton Foliot
Roborough
Lockengate
Herodsfoot
St Keyne
Landrake
Saltash Services
Crownhill Fort
Lostwithiel
Bilberry
Trewidland
Plym Forest
Bugle
Lanlivery
Couch's Mill
Duloe
Tideford
Trematon
Saltash
Crownhill
Luxulyan
Milltown
Bocaddon
Widegates
Trerulefoot
Hessenford
St Erney
St Stephens
Mary Newman's Cottage
St Budeaux
Plymouth
Eggbuckland
Stenalees
Penwithick
Penpillick
Lerryn
Lanreath
Sandplace
Morval
St Germans
Antony House
Merchant's House
Plympton
Trethurgy
St Blazey
Golant
Muchlarnick
Pelynt
Polbathic
Sheviock
Plym Valley
Carclaze
Eden Project
Tywardreath
St Veep
Penpoll
St Martin
Monkey Sanctuary
Seaton
Crafthole
Antony
Torpoint
Devonport
Saltram
St. Austell
Boscoppa
Par
Lanteglos Highway
Trenewan
Looe
East Looe
Downderry
Portwrinkle
Plymstock
Elburton
Holmbush
Shipwreck & Heritage Centre
Polkerris
Menabilly
Fowey
Bodinnick
West Looe
Old Guildhall
Looe Bay
St John
Cremyll
Mount Edgcumbe
Royal Citadel
Hooe
Charlestown
St Austell Brewery
Polruan
Portballow
St George's or Looe I.
Whitsand Bay
Freathy
Millbrook
Drake's I.
Polgooth
St Catherine's Castle
Lansallos
Talland Bay
Kingsand
The Sound
Staddiscombe
Porthpean
St. Austell Bay
Pencarrow Hd.
Polperro
Heritage Museum
Cawsand
Bovisand Bay
Down Thomas
Gribbin Hd.
Rame
Knighton
Trenarren
Penlee Pt.
Heybrook Bay
Wembury
Black Hd.
Rame Hd.
Wembury Bay
Pentewan
Great Mew Stone
Worswell
World of Model Railways
Mevagissey
Chapel Pt.
Gorran Churchtown
Gorran Haven
Roscoff Santander (Mar-Nov) St Malo (Nov-Mar)
Penare
Dodman Pt.
0 1 2 3 4 5 6 miles
0 1 2 3 4 5 6 7 8 9 10 km

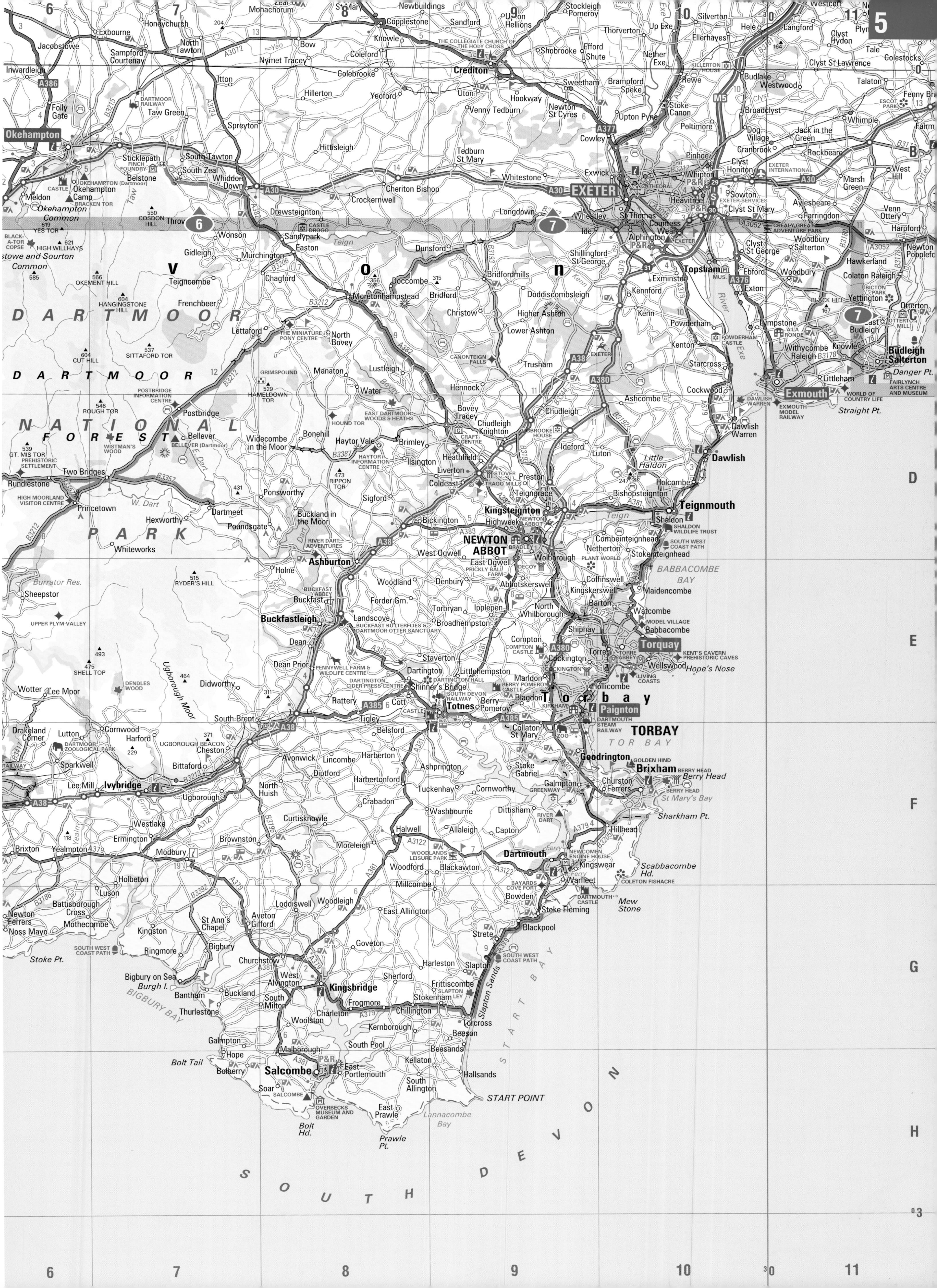

DARTMOOR
DARTMOOR
NATIONAL
FOREST
PARK
Devon
SOUTH DEVON
Okehampton
Okehampton Camp
Okehampton Common
Jacobstowe
Exbourne
Honeychurch
Sampford Courtenay
North Tawton
Inwardleigh
Folly Gate
Taw Green
Sticklepath
South Tawton
South Zeal
Belstone
Whiddon Down
Meldon
Throwleigh
Wonson
Gidleigh
Chagford
Murchington
Easton
Sandypark
Drewsteignton
Castle Drogo
Teigncombe
Frenchbeer
Lettaford
North Bovey
Moretonhampstead
Doccombe
Spreyton
Hittisleigh
Crockernwell
Cheriton Bishop
Tedburn St Mary
Whitestone
Longdown
Dunsford
Bridford
Christow
Bridfordmills
Doddiscombsleigh
Higher Ashton
Lower Ashton
Trusham
Hennock
Canonteign Falls
Bow
Nymet Tracey
Coleford
Colebrooke
Copplestone
Knowle
Crediton
Yeoford
Hillerton
Uton
Venny Tedburn
Hookway
Newbuildings
Sandford
Upton Hellions
Shobrooke
Efford
Shute
Newton St Cyres
Sweetham
Brampford Speke
Stockleigh Pomeroy
Thorverton
Up Exe
Nether Exe
Silverton
Ellerhayes
Killerton House
Rewe
Stoke Canon
Upton Pyne
Cowley
Exwick
EXETER
St Thomas
Alphington
Countess Wear
Ide
Shillingford St George
Heavitree
Pinhoe
Whipton
Sowton
Clyst St Mary
Clyst Honiton
Poltimore
Broadclyst
Budlake
Westwood
Dog Village
Cranbrook
Rockbeare
Jack in the Green
Whimple
Talaton
Clyst Hydon
Clyst St Lawrence
Langford
Hele
Tale
Colestocks
Fenny Bridges
Marsh Green
West Hill
Aylesbeare
Farringdon
Venn Ottery
Harpford
Newton Poppleford
Woodbury Salterton
Clyst St George
Ebford
Woodbury
Hawkerland
Colaton Raleigh
Exton
Topsham
Exminster
Kennford
Kenn
Powderham
Powderham Castle
Kenton
Starcross
Cockwood
Lympstone
Exmouth
Withycombe Raleigh
Budleigh Salterton
East Budleigh
Yettington
Otterton
Littleham
Danger Pt.
Straight Pt.
Dawlish Warren
Dawlish
Ashcombe
Chudleigh
Chudleigh Knighton
Bovey Tracey
Little Haldon
Ideford
Luton
Holcombe
Teignmouth
Shaldon
Bishopsteignton
Teigngrace
Preston
Kingsteignton
Highweek
NEWTON ABBOT
Wolborough
Combeinteignhead
Netherton
Stokeinteignhead
BABBACOMBE BAY
Maidencombe
Coffinswell
Kingskerswell
Abbotskerswell
Barton
Watcombe
Babbacombe
Shiphay
Torre
Torquay
Wellswood
Hope's Nose
Cockington
Compton
Marldon
Collaton St Mary
Paignton
Torbay
TORBAY
TOR BAY
Goodrington
Brixham
Berry Head
Churston Ferrers
St Mary's Bay
Sharkham Pt.
Galmpton
Stoke Gabriel
Hillhead
Kingswear
Dartmouth
Warfleet
Scabbacombe Hd.
Mew Stone
Stoke Fleming
Blackpool
Strete
Slapton
Slapton Sands
START BAY
Torcross
Beeson
Beesands
Hallsands
START POINT
Kellaton
South Allington
East Prawle
Prawle Pt.
Lannacombe Bay
East Portlemouth
Salcombe
Bolt Hd.
Soar
Bolt Tail
Hope
Bolberry
Galmpton
Malborough
South Pool
Kernborough
Chillington
Stokenham
Frittiscombe
Charleton
Frogmore
Kingsbridge
West Alvington
South Milton
Woolston
Thurlestone
Buckland
Bantham
Bigbury on Sea
Burgh I.
BIGBURY BAY
Bigbury
Churchstow
Ringmore
Kingston
St Ann's Chapel
Aveton Gifford
Loddiswell
Woodleigh
East Allington
Goveton
Harleston
Sherford
Stoke Pt.
Noss Mayo
Newton Ferrers
Mothecombe
Battisborough Cross
Holbeton
Luson
Brixton
Yealmpton
Ermington
Modbury
Brownston
Westlake
Ugborough
Ivybridge
Lee Mill
Sparkwell
Cornwood
Harford
Cheston
Bittaford
Lutton
Drakeland Corner
Wotter
Lee Moor
Sheepstor
Burrator Res.
South Brent
Avonwick
Lincombe
Diptford
North Huish
Curtisknowle
Crabadon
Moreleigh
Halwell
Woodford
Blackawton
Millcombe
Harberton
Harbertonford
Tuckenhay
Ashprington
Cornworthy
Washbourne
Dittisham
Allaleigh
Capton
Totnes
Tigley
Belsford
Rattery
Cott
Dartington
Shinner's Bridge
Staverton
Littlehempston
Berry Pomeroy
Blagdon
Didworthy
Ugborough Moor
Dean Prior
Dean
Buckfastleigh
Buckfast
Landscove
Broadhempston
Torbryan
Ipplepen
North Whilborough
Forder Grn.
Woodland
Denbury
East Ogwell
West Ogwell
Ashburton
Holne
Bickington
Liverton
Coldeast
Heathfield
Ilsington
Sigford
Buckland in the Moor
Poundsgate
Dartmeet
Hexworthy
Ponsworthy
Widecombe in the Moor
Bonehill
Haytor Vale
Brimley
Manaton
Lustleigh
Water
Postbridge
Bellever
Two Bridges
Princetown
Rundlestone
Whiteworks
Ryder's Hill
Rippon Tor
Hameldown Tor
Hound Tor
Sittaford Tor
Cut Hill
Hangingstone Hill
Okement Hill
High Willhays
Yes Tor
Cosdon Hill
Rough Tor
Gt. Mis Tor
Shell Top
Upper Plym Valley
Dendles Wood
Sourton Common

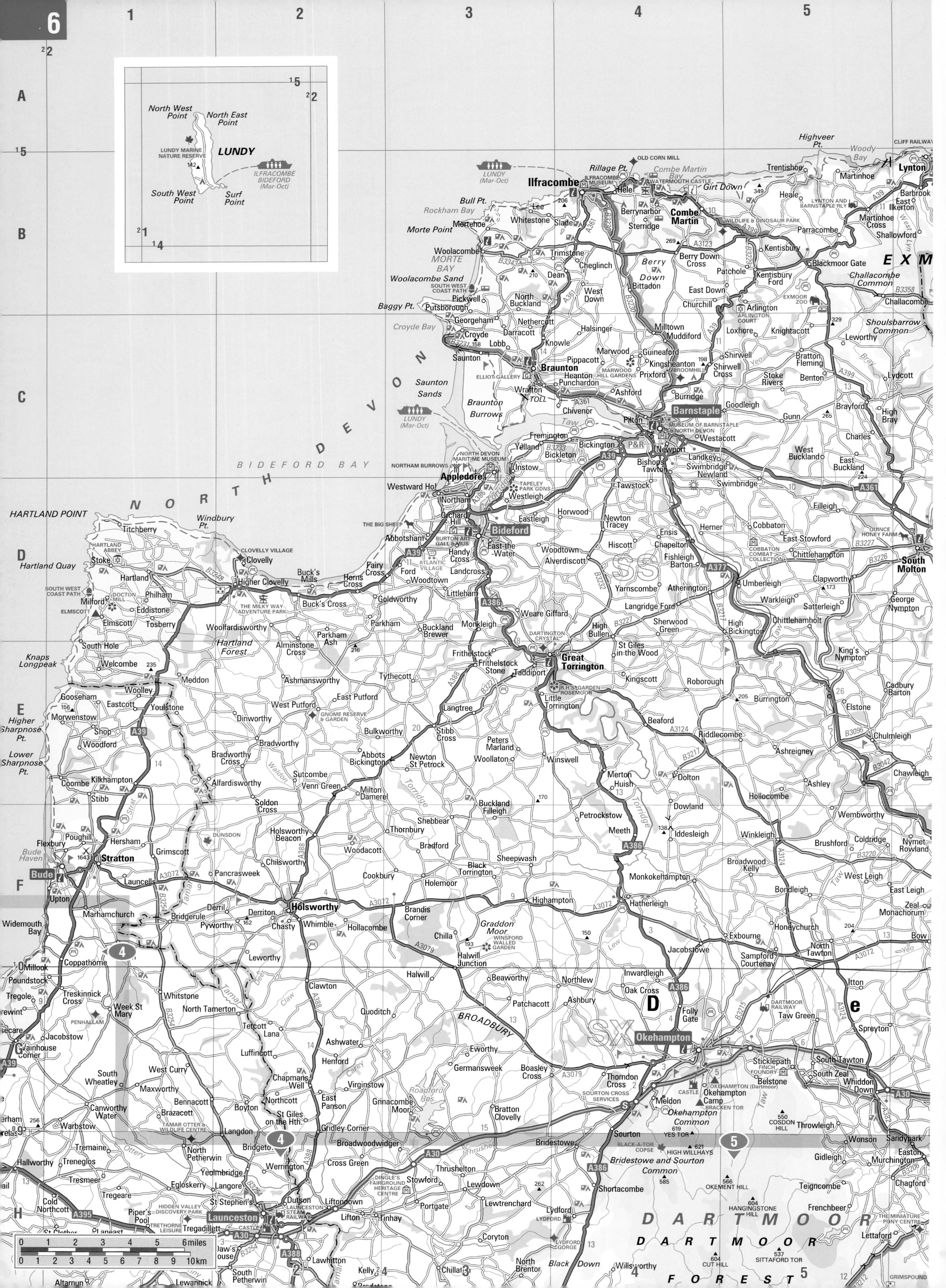
LUNDY
North West Point
North East Point
LUNDY MARINE NATURE RESERVE
South West Point
Surf Point
ILFRACOMBE BIDEFORD (Mar-Oct)
LUNDY (Mar-Oct)
Ilfracombe
Rillage Pt.
OLD CORN MILL
Combe Martin Bay
WATERMOUTH CASTLE
Girt Down
Highveer Pt.
Woody Bay
CLIFF RAILWAY
Lynton
Trentishoe
Martinhoe
Heale
Barbrook
LYNTON AND BARNSTAPLE RLY
East Ilkerton
Martinhoe Cross
Parracombe
Shallowford
Bull Pt.
Rockham Bay
Lee
Whitestone
Slade
Hele
Berrynarbor
Combe Martin
WILDLIFE & DINOSAUR PARK
Sterridge
Mortehoe
Morte Point
Woolacombe
MORTE BAY
Woolacombe Sand
SOUTH WEST COAST PATH
Trimstone
Cheglinch
Dean
Berry Down Cross
Berry Down
Bittadon
Patchole
Kentisbury
Kentisbury Ford
Blackmoor Gate
EXM
Challacombe Common
Challacombe
Baggy Pt.
Putsborough
Pickwell
North Buckland
West Down
East Down
Churchill
Arlington
ARLINGTON COURT
EXMOOR ZOO
Croyde Bay
Georgeham
Croyde
Nethercott
Darracott
Lobb
Saunton
Knowle
Halsinger
Milltown
Muddiford
Loxhore
Knightacott
Shoulsbarrow Common
Lyworthy
Braunton
Pippacott
Heanton Punchardon
Marwood
MARWOOD HILL GARDENS
Guineaford
Kingsheanton
Prixford
BROOMHILL
Shirwell
Shirwell Cross
Bratton Fleming
Benton
Lydcott
Stoke Rivers
ELLIOT GALLERY
Wrafton
TOLL
Chivenor
Ashford
Burridge
Goodleigh
Saunton Sands
Braunton Burrows
Gunn
Brayford
High Bray
Barnstaple
Pilton
MUSEUM OF BARNSTAPLE & NORTH DEVON
Newport
Westacott
Charles
Fremington
Yelland
Bickington
Bickleton
Bishops Tawton
Landkey
Swimbridge Newland
Swimbridge
West Buckland
East Buckland
NORTH DEVON
BIDEFORD BAY
NORTH DEVON MARITIME MUSEUM
NORTHAM BURROWS
Appledore
Instow
TAPELEY PARK GDNS
Westward Ho!
Northam
Westleigh
Tawstock
Eastleigh
Horwood
Newton Tracey
Filleigh
HARTLAND POINT
Windbury Pt.
THE BIG SHEEP
Orchard Hill
Bideford
Abbotsham
BURTON ART GALL & MUS
East-the-Water
Titchberry
HARTLAND ABBEY
CLOVELLY VILLAGE
Clovelly
Hartland Quay
Stoke
Hartland
Higher Clovelly
Buck's Mills
Horns Cross
Fairy Cross
Ford
Handy Cross
ATLANTIC VILLAGE
Landcross
Woodtown
Alverdiscott
Hiscott
Ensis
Chapelton
Herner
Cobbaton
COBBATON COMBAT COLLECTION
East Stowford
QUINCE HONEY FARM
Chittlehampton
South Molton
Fishleigh Barton
SOUTH WEST COAST PATH
DOCTON MILL
Philham
Milford
ELMSCOTT
Elmscott
Eddistone
Tosberry
THE MILKY WAY ADVENTURE PARK
Buck's Cross
Woodtown
Littleham
Goldworthy
Yarnscombe
Atherington
Umberleigh
Clapworthy
Warkleigh
Satterleigh
George Nympton
Langridge Ford
Woolfardisworthy
Parkham
Parkham Ash
Buckland Brewer
Monkleigh
Weare Giffard
High Bullen
Sherwood Green
High Bickington
Chittlehamholt
Hartland Forest
Alminstone Cross
DARTMOOR CRYSTAL
Frithelstock
Great Torrington
St Giles in the Wood
Knaps Longpeak
South Hole
Welcombe
Meddon
Ashmansworthy
Tythecott
Frithelstock Stone
Taddiport
R.H.S. GARDEN ROSEMOOR
Kingscott
Roborough
King's Nympton
Gooseham
Woolley
Eastcott
Youlstone
West Putford
East Putford
GNOME RESERVE & GARDEN
Langtree
Little Torrington
Burrington
Cadbury Barton
Elstone
Higher Sharpnose Pt.
Morwenstow
Shop
Woodford
Dinworthy
Bradworthy
Bulkworthy
Stibb Cross
Peters Marland
Beaford
Riddlecombe
Ashreigney
Chulmleigh
Lower Sharpnose Pt.
Bradworthy Cross
Abbots Bickington
Newton St Petrock
Woollaton
Winswell
Dolton
Chawleigh
Coombe
Kilkhampton
Stibb
Alfardisworthy
Sutcombe
Venn Green
Milton Damerel
Merton
Huish
Ashley
Hollocombe
Soldon Cross
Buckland Filleigh
Petrockstow
Dowland
Wembworthy
Poughill
Flexbury
Hersham
Grimscott
DUNSDON
Holsworthy Beacon
Thornbury
Shebbear
Meeth
Iddesleigh
Winkleigh
Brushford
Coldridge
Nymet Rowland
Bude Haven
Stratton
Chilsworthy
Woodacott
Bradford
Sheepwash
Broadwood Kelly
Bude
Launcells
Pancrasweek
Cookbury
Black Torrington
Monkokehampton
West Leigh
Upton
Holemoor
Bondleigh
East Leigh
Widemouth Bay
Marhamchurch
Derril
Bridgerule
Pyworthy
Derriton
Holsworthy
Chasty
Whimble
Hollacombe
Brandis Corner
Highampton
Hatherleigh
Honeychurch
Zeal Monachorum
Graddon Moor
WINSFORD WALLED GARDEN
Chilla
Halwill Junction
Exbourne
Bow
Coppathorne
Lewortby
Jacobstowe
Sampford Courtenay
North Tawton
Millook
Poundstock
Treskinnick Cross
Whitstone
Halwill
Beaworthy
Northlew
Inwardleigh
Oak Cross
Itton
Tregole
Week St Mary
PENHALLAM
North Tamerton
Clawton
Quoditch
Patchacott
Ashbury
Folly Gate
DARTMOOR RAILWAY
Taw Green
Spreyton
Jacobstow
Tetcott
Lana
BROADBURY
Okehampton
Vainhouse Corner
Luffincott
Ashwater
Eworthy
Germansweek
Henford
Boasley Cross
Thorndon Cross
Sticklepath
FINCH FOUNDRY
South Tawton
South Zeal
Whiddon Down
Belstone
South Wheatley
West Curry
Maxworthy
Chapmans Well
Virginstowe
Grinacombe Moor
SOURTON CROSS SERVICES
OKEHAMPTON (Dartmoor)
Okehampton Camp
Meldon
CASTLE
BRACKEN TOR
Okehampton Common
Bennacott
Brazacott
Canworthy Water
Northcott
Boyton
East Panson
Roadford Res.
Bratton Clovelly
COSDON HILL
Throwleigh
Warbstow
TAMAR OTTER & WILDLIFE CENTRE
Langdon
St Giles on the Hth.
Gridley Corner
Sourton
YES TOR
BLACK-A-TOR COPSE
HIGH WILLHAYS
Tremaine
North Petherwin
Bridgetown
Broadwoodwidger
Bridestowe
Wonson
Sandypark
Hallworthy
Treneglos
Yeolmbridge
Werrington
Cross Green
Thrushelton
Bridestowe and Sourton Common
Gidleigh
Easton
Murchington
Tresmeer
Egloskerry
Langore
DINGLE'S FAIRGROUND HERITAGE CENTRE
Stowford
Lewdown
Shortacombe
OKEMENT HILL
Chagford
Teigncombe
Tregeare
St Stephen's
Dutson
LAUNCESTON STEAM RAILWAY
Liftondown
Portgate
Lewtrenchard
HANGINGSTONE HILL
Cold Northcott
HIDDEN VALLEY DISCOVERY PARK
Piper's Pool
Launceston
Lifton
Tinhay
Lydford
Frenchbeer
TRETHORNE LEISURE
Tregadillett
CASTLE
LYDFORD
DARTMOOR
THE MINIATURE PONY CENTRE
Coryton
LYDFORD GORGE
Lettaford
Lawhitton
DARTMOOR FOREST
North Brentor
Black Down
Willsworthy
CUT HILL
SITTAFORD TOR
South Petherwin
Kelly
Chillaton
Altarnun
Lewannick
GRIMSPOUND
P&R
SS
SX
0 1 2 3 4 5 6 miles
0 1 2 3 4 5 6 7 8 9 10 km

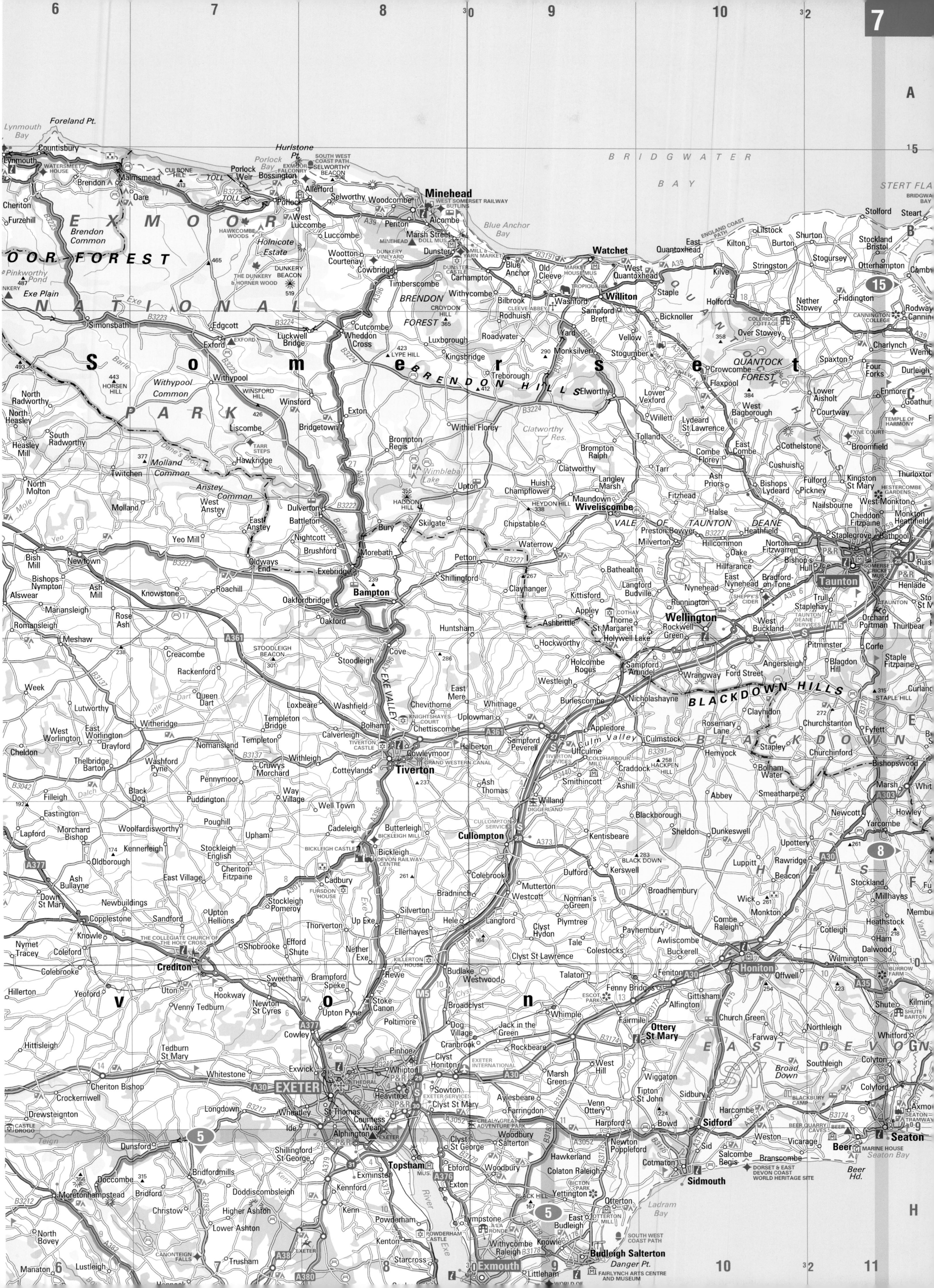
6
7
8
9
10
11
A
B
C
D
E
F
H
Lynmouth Bay
Foreland Pt.
Countisbury
Lynmouth
Watersmeet House
Brendon
Malmsead
Oare
Culbone Hill
Porlock Weir
Porlock
Porlock Bay
Hurlstone Pt.
Bossington
Exmoor Falconry
South West Coast Path
Selworthy Beacon
Allerford
Selworthy
Woodcombe
Minehead
West Somerset Railway
Butlins
Alcombe
Periton
West Luccombe
Luccombe
Hawkcombe Woods
Holnicote Estate
Cheriton
Furzehill
Brendon Common
E X M O O R
Exmoor Forest
Pinkworthy Pond
Exe Plain
N A T I O N A L
P A R K
Simonsbath
Dunkery Beacon
The Dunkery & Horner Wood
Wootton Courtenay
Cowbridge
Dunkery Vineyard
Minehead
Marsh Street
Dunster
Dunster Castle
Mill & Yarn Market
Blue Anchor Bay
Blue Anchor
Carhampton
Timberscombe
Brendon Forest
Croydon Hill
Withycombe
Old Cleeve
Cleeve Abbey
Bilbrook
Rodhuish
Washford
Tropiquaria
Market House Mus
Watchet
Williton
West Quantoxhead
East Quantoxhead
England Coast Path
Staple
Kilve
Lilstock
Kilton
Shurton
Burton
Stogursey
Stockland Bristol
Stringston
Otterhampton
Holford
Nether Stowey
Fiddington
Stolford
Steart
Stert Flats
Bridgwater Bay
B R I D G W A T E R
B A Y
Edgcott
Exford
Luckwell Bridge
Cutcombe
Wheddon Cross
Lype Hill
Luxborough
Roadwater
Sampford Brett
Bicknoller
Yard
Monksilver
Vellow
Stogumber
West Somerset Railway
Coleridge Cottage
Over Stowey
Cannington College
Rodway
Charlynch
Spaxton
Four Forks
Durleigh
Quantock Forest
Crowcombe
Flaxpool
Kingsbridge
Treborough
B R E N D O N   H I L L S
Elworthy
S o m e r s e t
Barle
Horsen Hill
Withypool
Withypool Common
Winsford Hill
Winsford
North Radworthy
North Heasley
South Radworthy
Heasley Mill
Liscombe
Tarr Steps
Hawkridge
Molland Common
Dane's Brook
Exton
Bridgetown
Withiel Florey
Clatworthy Res.
Brompton Regis
Wimbleball Lake
Upton
Brompton Ralph
Clatworthy
Lower Vexford
Willett
Lydeard St Lawrence
Tolland
Combe Florey
East Combe
West Bagborough
Lower Aisholt
Courtway
Enmore
Goathurst
Temple of Harmony
Fyne Court
Broomfield
Cothelstone
Cushuish
Tarr
Ash Priors
Bishops Lydeard
Fulford
Pickney
Kingston St Mary
Hestercombe Gardens
Thurloxton
Twitchen
North Molton
Anstey Common
West Anstey
East Anstey
Molland
Dulverton
Battleton
Haddon Hill
Skilgate
Huish Champflower
Heydon Hill
Maundown
Langley Marsh
Wiveliscombe
Chipstable
Fitzhead
Halse
Vale of Taunton Deane
Preston Bowyer
Milverton
Heathfield
Norton Fitzwarren
Nailsbourne
West Monkton
Cheddon Fitzpaine
Monkton Heathfield
Staplegrove
Bathpool
Yeo
Yeo Mill
Nightcott
Bury
Brushford
Morebath
Waterrow
Petton
Hillcommon
Oake
Bishop's Hull
Hillfarance
Bradford-on-Tone
Taunton
Somerset Cricket Mus
Henlade
Bish Mill
Newtown
Bishops Nympton
Alswear
Ash Mill
Knowstone
Roachill
Oldways End
Exebridge
Bampton
Shillingford
Clayhanger
Bathealton
Langford Budville
Nynehead
East Nynehead
Sheppy's Cider
Trull
Staplehay
Taunton Deane Services
Orchard Portman
Thurlbear
Mariansleigh
Rose Ash
Oakfordbridge
Oakford
Kittisford
Cothay
Appley
Thorne St Margaret
Ashbrittle
Runnington
Wellington
Rockwell Green
West Buckland
Romansleigh
Meshaw
Creacombe
Rackenford
Stoodleigh Beacon
Stoodleigh
Cove
Huntsham
Hockworthy
Holywell Lake
Holcombe Rogus
Sampford Arundel
Wrangway
Ford Street
Angersleigh
Pitminster
Corfe
Blagdon Hill
Staple Fitzpaine
Staple Hill
B L A C K D O W N   H I L L S
Exe Valley
Week
Queen Dart
Lutworthy
Loxbeare
Washfield
East Mere
Chevithorne
Westleigh
Burlescombe
Nicholashayne
Knightshayes Court
Whitnage
Uplowman
Clayhidon
Churchstanton
Fyfett
Rosemary Lane
Appledore
Culmstock
Culm Valley
Hemyock
Stapley
Churchinford
Bishopswood
West Worlington
East Worlington
Drayford
Witheridge
Templeton Bridge
Templeton
Calverleigh
Bolham
Chettiscombe
Tiverton Castle
Cowleymoor
Halberton
Sampford Peverell
Uffculme
Tiverton Services
Coldharbour Mill
Craddock
Hackpen Hill
Bolham Water
Marsh
Cheldon
Thelbridge Barton
Nomansland
Washford Pyne
Withleigh
Cruwys Morchard
Cotteylands
Tiverton
Grand Western Canal
Ash Thomas
Smithincott
Ashill
Abbey
Smeatharpe
Pennymoor
Black Dog
Puddington
Way Village
Well Town
Willand
Diggerland
Filleigh
Dalch
Eastington
Morchard Bishop
Lapford
Woolfardisworthy
Poughill
Upham
Cadeleigh
Butterleigh
Bickleigh Mill
Cullompton Services
Cullompton
Kentisbeare
Blackborough
Sheldon
Dunkeswell
Newcott
Yarcombe
Howley
Kennerleigh
Oldborough
Stockleigh English
Bickleigh Castle
Bickleigh
Devon Railway Centre
Black Down
Kerswell
Dulford
Upottery
Rawridge
Luppitt
Beacon
Ash Bullayne
East Village
Cheriton Fitzpaine
Cadbury
Fursdon House
Colebrook
Mutterton
Westcott
Bradninch
Norman's Green
Broadhembury
Stockland
Millhayes
Down St Mary
Newbuildings
Copplestone
Stockleigh Pomeroy
Silverton
Wick
Monkton
Heathstock
Sandford
Upton Hellions
Thorverton
Up Exe
Hele
Langford
Plymtree
Clyst Hydon
Payhembury
Combe Raleigh
Cotleigh
Knowle
Nymet Tracey
Coleford
The Collegiate Church of the Holy Cross
Shobrooke
Efford Shute
Nether Exe
Ellerhayes
Killerton House
Tale
Colestocks
Awliscombe
Buckerell
Clyst St Lawrence
Dalwood
Wilmington
Burrow Farm
Crediton
Colebrooke
Sweetham
Brampford Speke
Rewe
Budlake
Westwood
Talaton
Feniton
Honiton
Offwell
Hillerton
Yeoford
Uton
Hookway
Venny Tedburn
Newton St Cyres
Stoke Canon
Upton Pyne
Broadclyst
Escot Park
Fenny Bridges
Alfington
Gittisham
Shute
Shute Barton
Kilmington
D e v o n
Poltimore
Whimple
Fairmile
Ottery St Mary
Church Green
Northleigh
Farway
Whitford
Hittisleigh
Cowley
Dog Village
Jack in the Green
Cranbrook
Rockbeare
E A S T   D E V O N
Tedburn St Mary
Pinhoe
Whipton
Clyst Honiton
Exeter International
West Hill
Wiggaton
Broad Down
Southleigh
Colyton
Cheriton Bishop
Whitestone
Exwick
Exeter
Cathedral
Heavitree
Sowton
Exeter Services
Marsh Green
Tipton St John
Sidbury
Colyford
Crockernwell
Longdown
Aylesbeare
Venn Ottery
Blackbury Camp
Drewsteignton
Castle Drogo
Wheatley
St Thomas
Clyst St Mary
Farringdon
Harcombe
Axmouth
Seaton Tramway
Teign
Ide
Countess Wear
Crealy Great Adventure Park
Harpford
Bowd
Sidford
Beer Quarry Caves
Beer
Seaton
Dunsford
Alphington
Clyst St George
Woodbury Salterton
Newton Poppleford
Weston
Vicarage
Marine House
Seaton Bay
Shillingford St George
Topsham
Ebford
Hawkerland
Salcombe Regis
Branscombe
Sid
Cotmaton
Sidmouth
Dorset & East Devon Coast World Heritage Site
Beer Hd.
Doccombe
Bridfordmills
Exminster
Exe
Woodbury
Colaton Raleigh
Bicton Park
Moretonhampstead
Bridford
Doddiscombsleigh
Kenn
Kennford
River
Exton
Yettington
Otterton
Ladram Bay
Christow
Higher Ashton
Kenn
Powderham
Lympstone
A La Ronde
Black Hill
East Budleigh
Otterton Mill
North Bovey
Lower Ashton
Kenton
Powderham Castle
Withycombe Raleigh
Knowle
South West Coast Path
Canonteign Falls
Trusham
Starcross
Exmouth
Budleigh Salterton
Danger Pt.
Manaton
Lustleigh
Littleham
Fairlynch Arts Centre and Museum
M5
A30
A38
A39
A361
A377
A380
A396
A373
A375
A35
A303
A358
A376
A379
A3052
B3224
B3223
B3227
B3137
B3191
B3190
B3188
B3181
B3212
B3174
B3178
B3179
B3180
B3176
B3391
B3440
B3225
B3222
15
8
5

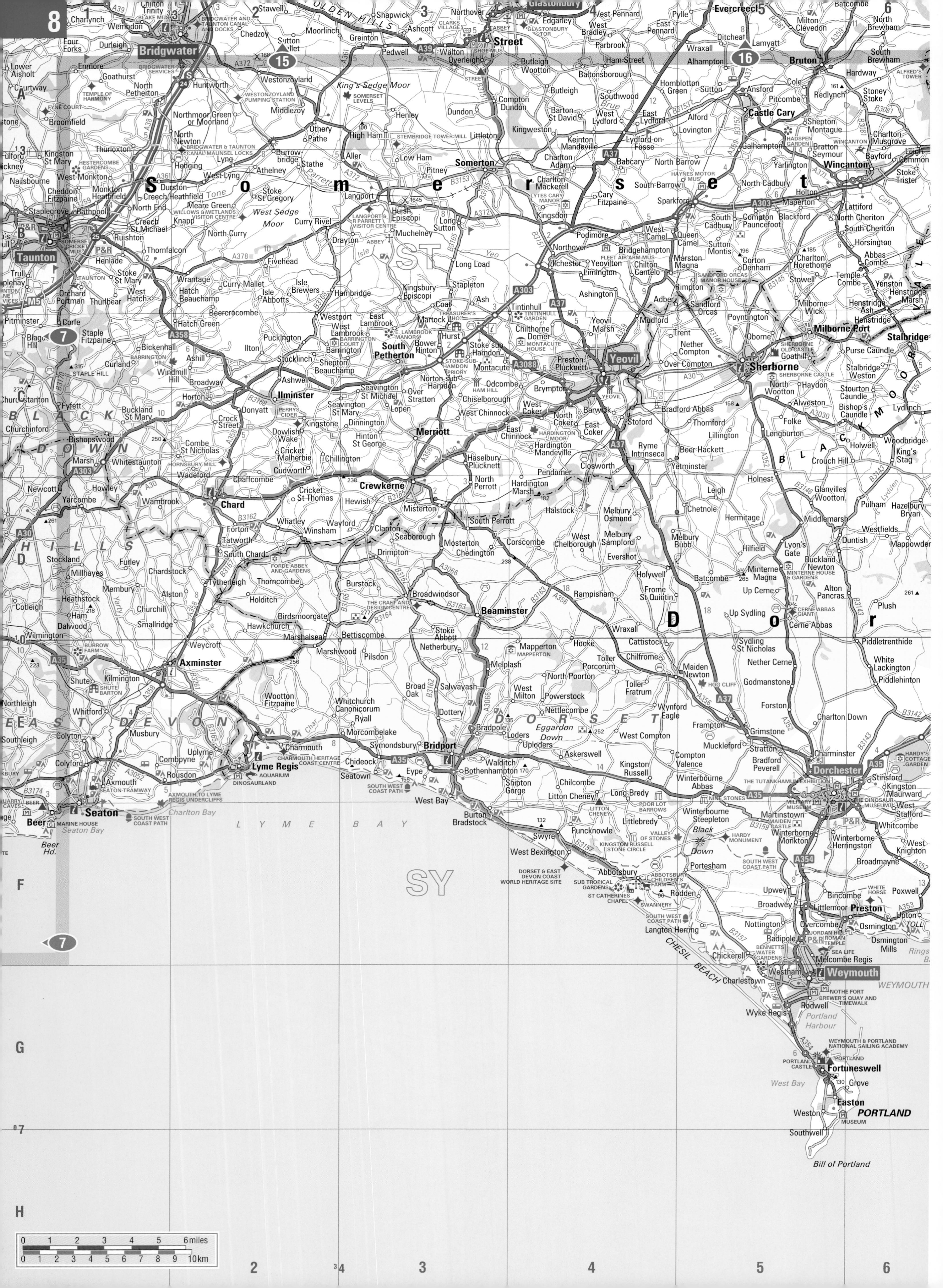
Bridgwater
Glastonbury
Street
Somerton
Langport
Taunton
Wincanton
Castle Cary
Bruton
Sherborne
Yeovil
Ilminster
Crewkerne
Chard
South Petherton
Merriott
Milborne Port
Stalbridge
Axminster
Seaton
Beer
Lyme Regis
Bridport
Beaminster
Dorchester
Weymouth
Fortuneswell
Easton
PORTLAND
Bill of Portland
Chesil Beach
L Y M E   B A Y
Lyme Bay
Charlton Bay
Seaton Bay
Portland Harbour
West Bay
Weymouth Bay
S o m e r s e t
D o r s e t
D O R S E T
E A S T   D E V O N
B L A C K   D O W N   H I L L S
B L A C K M O O R   V A L E
King's Sedge Moor
West Sedge Moor
Eggardon Down
Black Down
ST
SY
15
16
7
0 1 2 3 4 5 6 miles
0 1 2 3 4 5 6 7 8 9 10 km

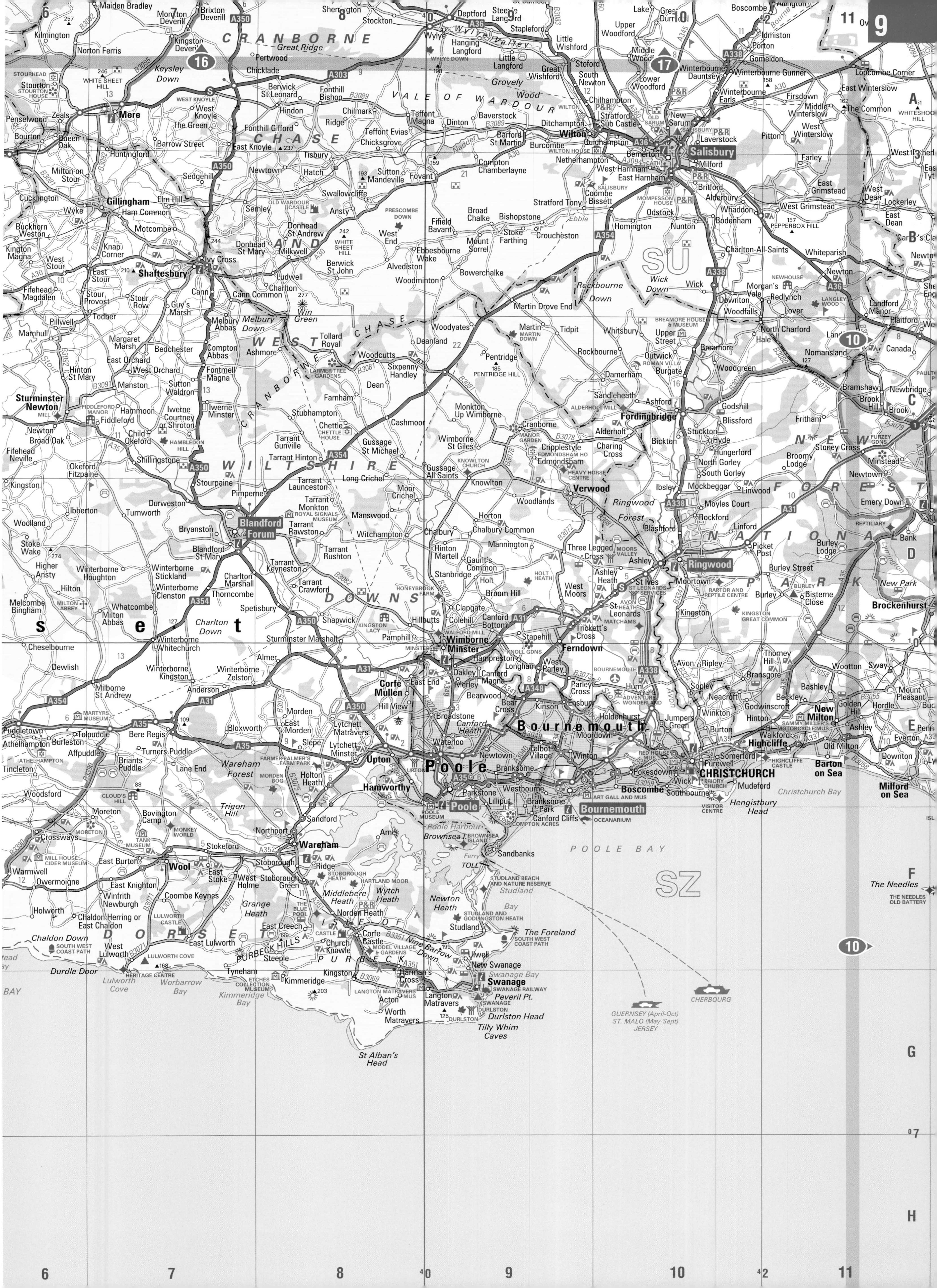
CRANBORNE
Great Ridge
VALE OF WARDOUR
CHASE
AND
WEST CHASE
CRANBORNE CHASE
WILTSHIRE
DOWNS
DORSET
ISLE OF PURBECK
PURBECK HILLS
NEW FOREST NATIONAL PARK
SU
SZ
POOLE BAY
Poole Harbour
Christchurch Bay
Swanage Bay
Worbarrow Bay
Kimmeridge Bay
Studland Bay
Salisbury
Wilton
Mere
Gillingham
Shaftesbury
Sturminster Newton
Blandford Forum
Wimborne Minster
Verwood
Fordingbridge
Ringwood
Ferndown
Bournemouth
Poole
Upton
Hamworthy
Corfe Mullen
Wareham
Wool
Swanage
Corfe Castle
CHRISTCHURCH
Highcliffe
New Milton
Barton on Sea
Milford on Sea
Brockenhurst
Boscombe
Sandbanks
Downton
Alderbury
Whiteparish
Durdle Door
Lulworth Cove
St Alban's Head
Durlston Head
Peveril Pt.
The Foreland
Hengistbury Head
The Needles
GUERNSEY (April-Oct)
ST. MALO (May-Sept)
JERSEY
CHERBOURG
A36
A30
A303
A350
A354
A338
A31
A35
A348
A351
A352
16
17
10
6
7
8
9
10
11
A
B
C
D
E
F
G
H

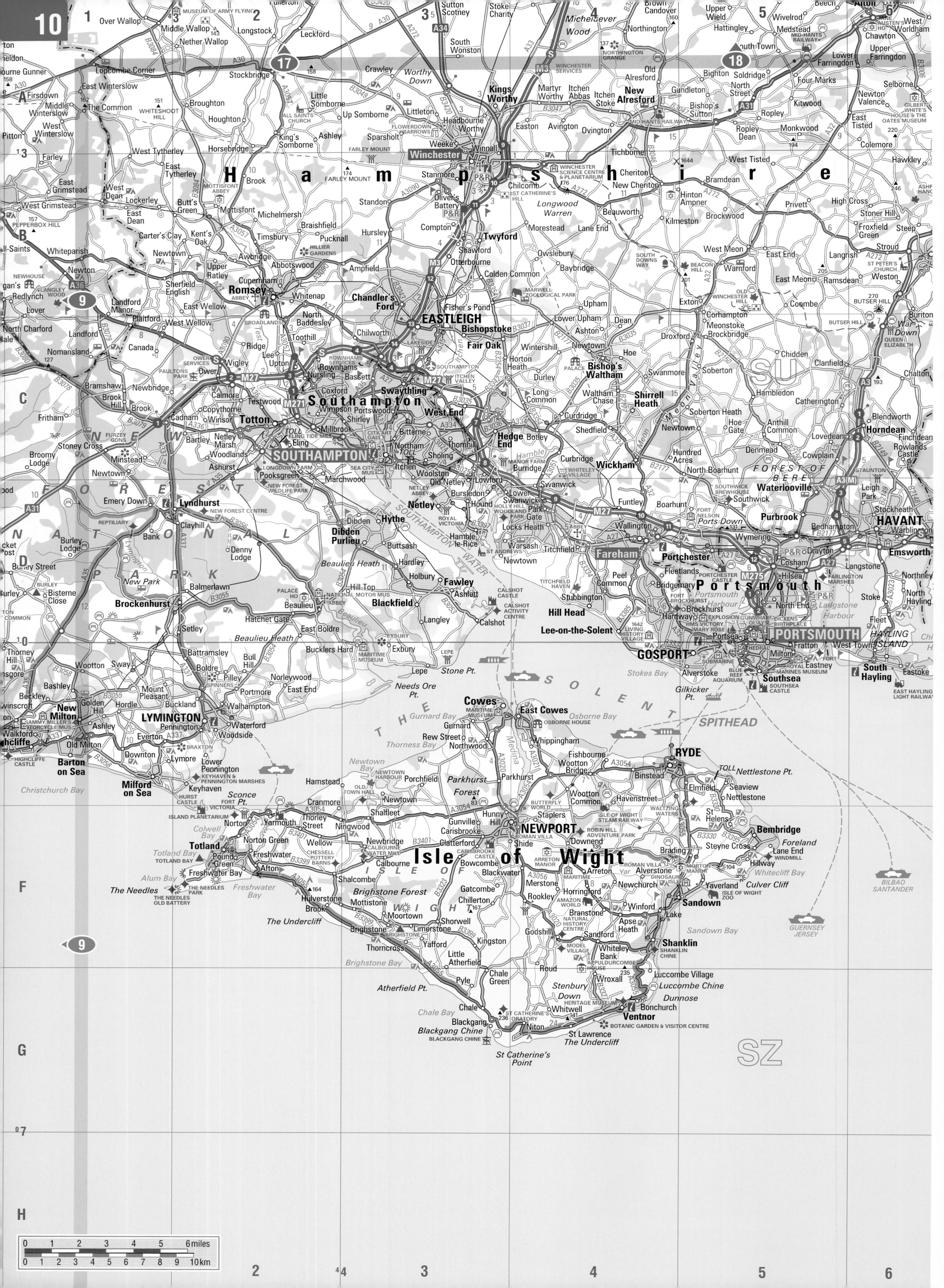
Hampshire
Isle of Wight
New Forest National Park
The Solent
Spithead
Southampton Water
SOUTHAMPTON
Southampton
Winchester
EASTLEIGH
Romsey
Totton
Lyndhurst
Brockenhurst
LYMINGTON
New Milton
Barton on Sea
Milford on Sea
Hythe
Dibden Purlieu
Fawley
Blackfield
Netley
Hedge End
West End
Bishop's Waltham
Fareham
Portchester
Portsmouth
PORTSMOUTH
GOSPORT
Southsea
HAVANT
Waterlooville
Horndean
Emsworth
South Hayling
Hayling Island
Lee-on-the-Solent
Hill Head
Stubbington
Wickham
Twyford
Kings Worthy
New Alresford
Chandler's Ford
Bishopstoke
Fair Oak
Cowes
East Cowes
NEWPORT
RYDE
Bembridge
Sandown
Shanklin
Ventnor
Yarmouth
Totland
Freshwater
The Needles
St Catherine's Point
Needles Ore Pt.
Stone Pt.
Stokes Bay
Gilkicker Pt.
Osborne Bay
Gurnard Bay
Thorness Bay
Newtown Bay
Christchurch Bay
Colwell Bay
Totland Bay
Alum Bay
Freshwater Bay
Brighstone Bay
Chale Bay
Sandown Bay
Whitecliff Bay
Culver Cliff
Foreland
Atherfield Pt.
The Undercliff
Brighstone Forest
Parkhurst Forest
Langstone Harbour
Portsmouth Harbour
Beaulieu
Beaulieu Heath
Exbury
Calshot
Hamble-le-Rice
Titchfield
Forest of Bere
Longwood Warren
Worthy Down
Micheldever Wood
BILBAO SANTANDER
GUERNSEY JERSEY
SZ
17
18
9
A B C D E F G H
1 2 3 4 5 6
0 1 2 3 4 5 6 miles
0 1 2 3 4 5 6 7 8 9 10 km

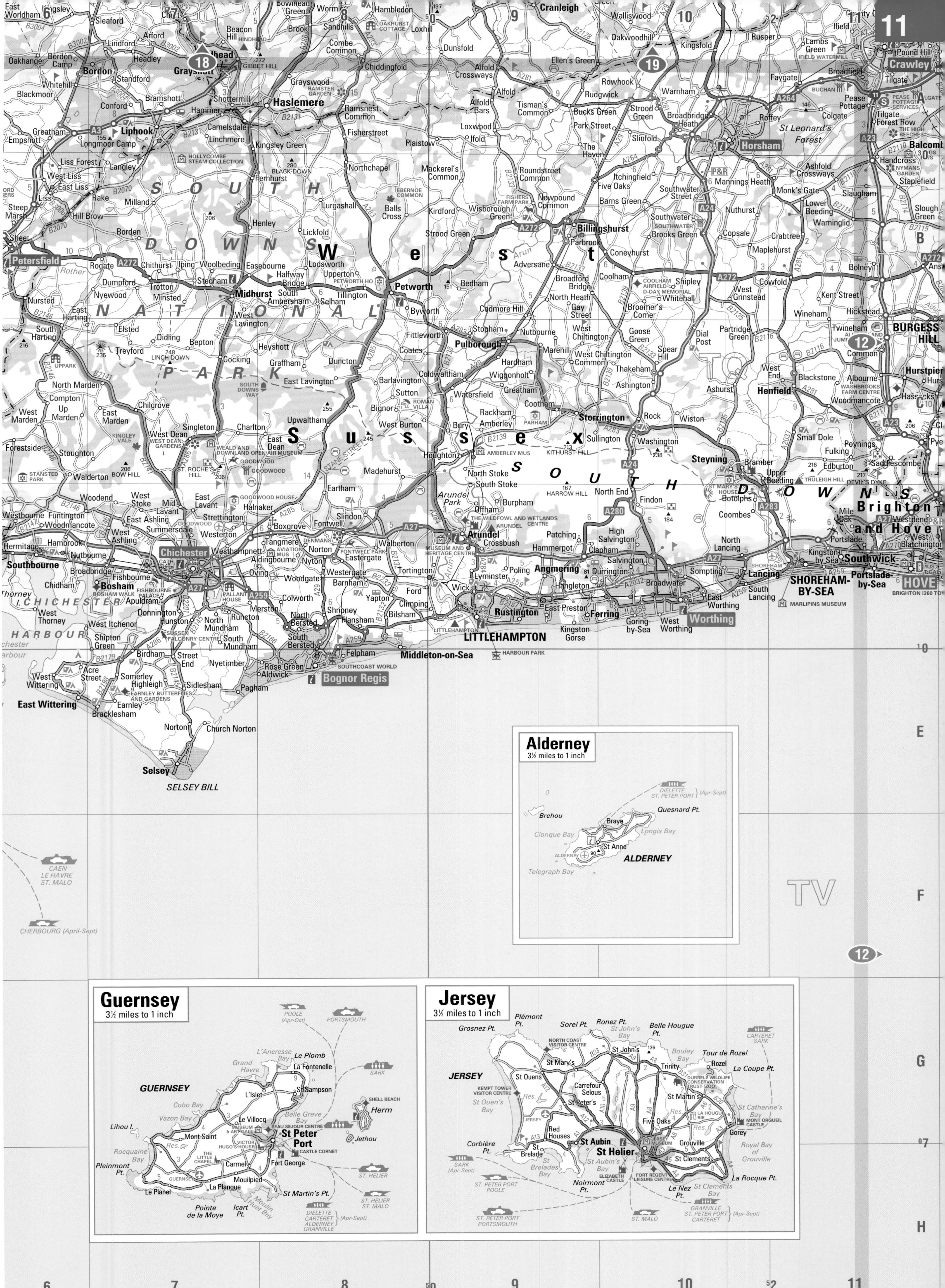
Crawley
Horsham
Haslemere
Liphook
Bordon
Petersfield
Midhurst
Petworth
Pulborough
Billingshurst
Cranleigh
Chichester
Bognor Regis
LITTLEHAMPTON
Arundel
Worthing
Angmering
Rustington
Ferring
Storrington
Steyning
Henfield
Lancing
SHOREHAM-BY-SEA
Southwick
Portslade-by-Sea
HOVE
Brighton and Hove
BURGESS HILL
Hurstpierpoint
Selsey
SELSEY BILL
East Wittering
West Wittering
Bosham
Southbourne
Emsworth
CHICHESTER HARBOUR
Middleton-on-Sea
SOUTHCOAST WORLD
HARBOUR PARK
SOUTH DOWNS NATIONAL PARK
West Sussex
SOUTH DOWNS
TQ
TV
A27
A272
A29
A24
A283
A281
A264
A259
A286
A285
A280
A23
A3
18
19
12
Alderney
3½ miles to 1 inch
ALDERNEY
Brehou
Braye
Quesnard Pt.
Clonque Bay
Longis Bay
St Anne
Telegraph Bay
DIELETTE
ST. PETER PORT
(Apr-Sept)
CAEN
LE HAVRE
ST. MALO
CHERBOURG (April-Sept)
Guernsey
3½ miles to 1 inch
GUERNSEY
POOLE
(Apr-Oct)
PORTSMOUTH
SARK
L'Ancresse Bay
Le Plomb
La Fontenelle
Grand Havre
L'Islet
St Sampson
Cobo Bay
Vazon Bay
Lihou I.
Le Villocq
Belle Greve Bay
St Peter Port
Mont Saint
Rocquaine Bay
Castel
Carmel
Fort George
CASTLE CORNET
Pleinmont Pt.
Le Planel
La Planque
Mouilpied
St Martin's Pt.
Pointe de la Moye
Icart Pt.
Moulin Huet Bay
Herm
SHELL BEACH
Jethou
ST. HELIER
ST. MALO
DIELETTE
CARTERET
ALDERNEY
GRANVILLE
(Apr-Sept)
Jersey
3½ miles to 1 inch
JERSEY
Plémont Pt.
Grosnez Pt.
Sorel Pt.
Ronez Pt.
St John's Bay
Belle Hougue Pt.
NORTH COAST VISITOR CENTRE
St Mary's
St John's
Bouley Bay
Tour de Rozel
Rozel
La Coupe Pt.
Trinity
DURRELL WILDLIFE CONSERVATION TRUST (ZOO)
St Ouens
KEMPT TOWER VISITOR CENTRE
Carrefour Selous
St Ouen's Bay
St Peter's
St Martin's
LA HOUGUE BIE
St Catherine's Bay
MONT ORGUEIL CASTLE
Five Oaks
Gorey
Red Houses
St Aubin
St Helier
Grouville
Royal Bay of Grouville
Corbière Pt.
St Brelade
St Brelade's Bay
St Aubin's Bay
ELIZABETH CASTLE
FORT REGENT LEISURE CENTRE
St Clements
La Rocque Pt.
Noirmont Pt.
Le Nez Pt.
St Clements Bay
SARK
(Apr-Sept)
ST. PETER PORT
POOLE
ST. PETER PORT
PORTSMOUTH
ST. MALO
GRANVILLE
ST. PETER PORT
CARTERET
6
7
8
9
10
11
B
C
D
E
F
G
H

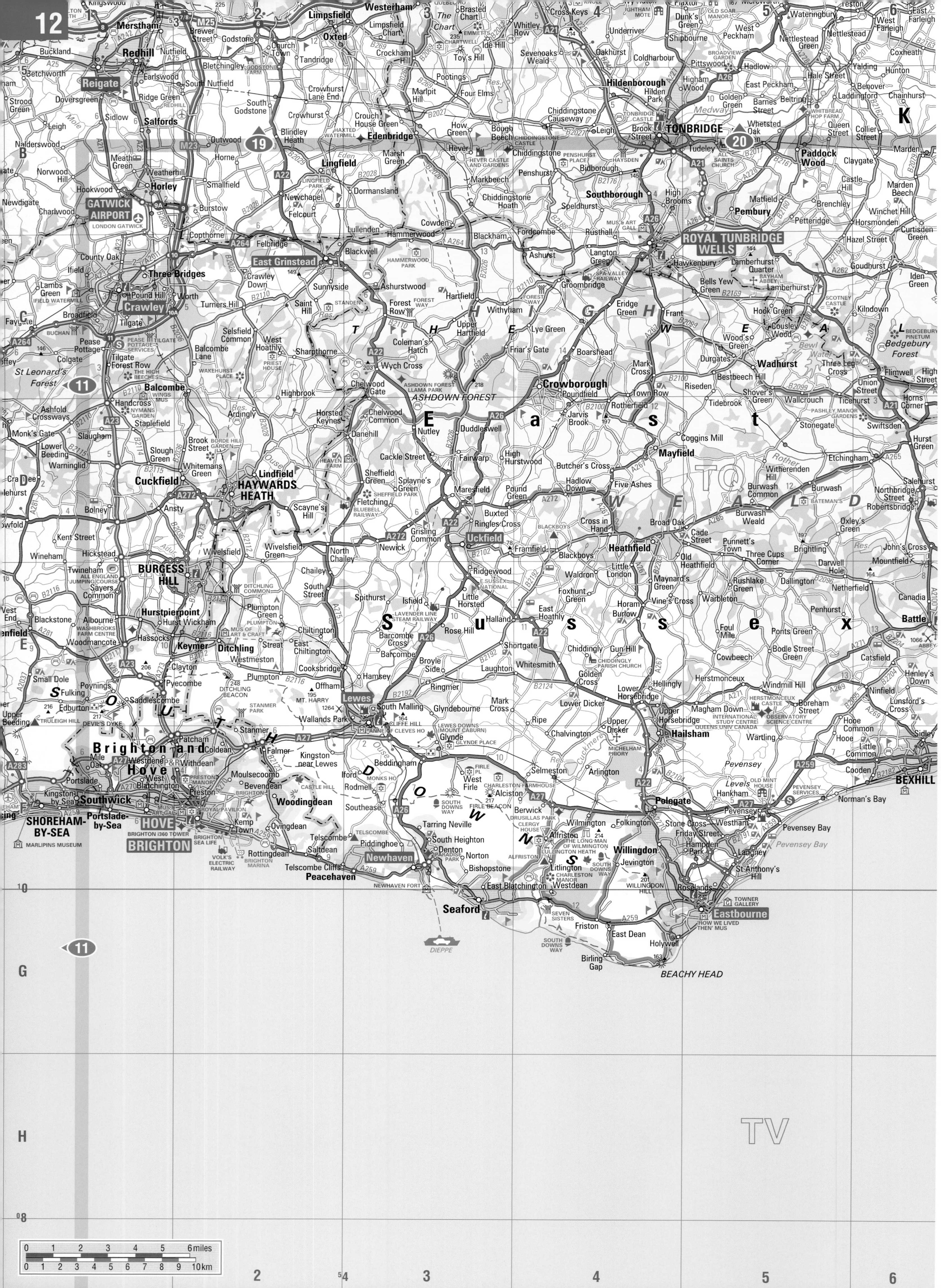
Merstham
Redhill
Reigate
Buckland
Betchworth
Strood Green
Doversgreen
Leigh
Nalderswood
Sidlow
Salfords
Earlswood
Ridge Green
Nutfield
South Nutfield
Bletchingley
Godstone
South Godstone
Brewer Street
Outwood
Horne
Meath Green
Norwood Hill
Hookwood
Horley
Weatherhill
Smallfield
Newdigate
Charlwood
GATWICK AIRPORT
LONDON GATWICK
Burstow
Copthorne
County Oak
Ifield
Lambs Green
Three Bridges
Crawley
Pound Hill
Worth
Broadfield
Faygate
Tilgate
Pease Pottage
Colgate
Tilgate Forest Row
St Leonard's Forest
Balcombe
Handcross
NYMANS GARDEN
Staplefield
Ashfold Crossways
Monk's Gate
Slaugham
Lower Beeding
Warninglid
Cuckfield
Bolney
Ansty
HAYWARDS HEATH
Lindfield
Slough Green
Whitemans Green
Brook Street
Ardingly
Balcombe Lane
Selsfield Common
West Hoathly
Turners Hill
Crawley Down
Felbridge
East Grinstead
Sunnyside
Saint Hill
Sharpthorne
Highbrook
Horsted Keynes
Danehill
Chelwood Gate
Chelwood Common
Wych Cross
Coleman's Hatch
Forest Row
Ashurstwood
Hartfield
Withyham
Upper Hartfield
ASHDOWN FOREST
Nutley
Duddleswell
Fairwarp
Lye Green
Friar's Gate
Crowborough
Poundfield
Jarvis Brook
Rotherfield
Groombridge
Eridge Green
Frant
Mark Cross
Town Row
Boarshead
Mayfield
Coggins Mill
Butcher's Cross
Five Ashes
Hadlow Down
High Hurstwood
Maresfield
Pound Green
Buxted
Uckfield
Framfield
Ringles Cross
Blackboys
Cross in Hand
Heathfield
Broad Oak
Cade Street
Old Heathfield
Waldron
Little London
Punnett's Town
Three Cups Corner
Burwash Weald
Burwash
Burwash Common
Etchingham
Witherenden Hill
Robertsbridge
Northbridge Street
Salehurst
Oxley's Green
John's Cross
Brightling
Darwell Hole
Mountfield
Netherfield
Dallington
Rushlake Green
Warbleton
Vine's Cross
Horam
Burlow
Maynard's Green
Foxhunt Green
Penhurst
Canadia
Battle
Ponts Green
Foul Mile
Bodle Street Green
Cowbeech
Catsfield
Herstmonceux
Windmill Hill
Ninfield
Henley's Down
Lunsford's Cross
Boreham Street
Magham Down
Hailsham
Hellingly
Upper Horsebridge
Lower Horsebridge
Upper Dicker
Lower Dicker
Golden Cross
Chiddingly
Gun Hill
Whitesmith
Laughton
Shortgate
East Hoathly
Halland
Chalvington
Ripe
Mark Cross
Ringmer
Broyle Side
Glyndebourne
Glynde
Lewes
South Malling
Hamsey
Offham
Cooksbridge
Barcombe
Barcombe Cross
Isfield
Little Horsted
Ridgewood
Spithurst
North Chailey
Chailey
South Street
Newick
Grisling Common
Wivelsfield
Wivelsfield Green
Scayne's Hill
Sheffield Green
Splayne's Green
Fletching
Cackle Street
Plumpton Green
Plumpton
Chiltington
East Chiltington
Streat
Westmeston
Ditchling
Keymer
Hassocks
Hurstpierpoint
Hurst Wickham
BURGESS HILL
Sayers Common
Twineham
Hickstead
Wineham
Kent Street
Albourne
Blackstone
Woodmancote
Small Dole
Fulking
Poynings
Edburton
Saddlescombe
Pyecombe
Clayton
Upper Beeding
DEVIL'S DYKE
DITCHLING BEACON
Stanmer
Falmer
Patcham
Coldean
Brighton and Hove
Withdean
Westdene
Mile Oak
Portslade
West Blatchington
Preston
Moulsecoomb
Bevendean
Kingston by Sea
Southwick
SHOREHAM-BY-SEA
Portslade-by-Sea
HOVE
BRIGHTON
Kemp Town
Ovingdean
Woodingdean
Rottingdean
Saltdean
Telscombe
Telscombe Cliffs
Peacehaven
Kingston near Lewes
Iford
Rodmell
Southease
Piddinghoe
Newhaven
Beddingham
Tarring Neville
South Heighton
Denton
Norton
Bishopstone
Seaford
DIEPPE
West Firle
Alciston
Selmeston
Arlington
Berwick
Alfriston
Litlington
Westdean
East Blatchington
Wilmington
Folkington
Willingdon
Jevington
Polegate
Friston
East Dean
Birling Gap
Holywell
BEACHY HEAD
Eastbourne
Roselands
St Anthony's Hill
Hampden Park
Langney
Stone Cross
Westham
Pevensey
Pevensey Bay
Pevensey Levels
Hankham
Wartling
Hooe
Hooe Common
Little Common
Cooden
BEXHILL
Norman's Bay
Sidley
Westerham
Limpsfield
Limpsfield Chart
Oxted
Tandridge
Church Town
Crockham Hill
The Chart
Brasted Chart
Ide Hill
Toy's Hill
Pootings
Four Elms
Marlpit Hill
Crowhurst Lane End
Crowhurst
Crouch House Green
Edenbridge
Blindley Heath
Lingfield
Dormansland
Newchapel
Felcourt
Marsh Green
How Green
Bough Beech
Hever
Chiddingstone
Markbeech
Chiddingstone Hoath
Cowden
Lullenden
Hammerwood
Blackwell
Blackham
Fordcombe
Ashurst
Penshurst
Speldhurst
Rusthall
Langton Green
Southborough
Bidborough
Chiddingstone Causeway
Leigh
Hildenborough
Hilden Park
TONBRIDGE
Brook Street
Tudeley
High Brooms
ROYAL TUNBRIDGE WELLS
Hawkenbury
Bells Yew Green
Lamberhurst
Lamberhurst Quarter
Pembury
Matfield
Brenchley
Petteridge
Horsmonden
Paddock Wood
Whetsted
Capel
Golden Green
East Peckham
Hadlow
Higham Wood
Pittswood
Shipbourne
Dunk's Green
West Peckham
Plaxtol
Underriver
Sevenoaks Weald
Whitley Row
Cross Keys
Oakhurst
Coldharbour
Nettlestead
Nettlestead Green
Wateringbury
West Farleigh
East Farleigh
Teston
Yalding
Hunton
Coxheath
Chainhurst
Laddingford
Benover
Beltring
Barnes Street
Hale Street
Queen Street
Collier Street
Claygate
Marden
Marden Beech
Castle Hill
Winchet Hill
Curtisden Green
Hazel Street
Goudhurst
Kilndown
Iden Green
Bedgebury Forest
Flimwell
Ticehurst
Union Street
Wallcrouch
Shover's Green
Three Leg Cross
Wadhurst
Durgates
Wood's Green
Cousley Wood
Hook Green
Bewl Water
Bestbeech Hill
Riseden
Tidebrook
Stonegate
Swiftsden
Hurst Green
Horns Corner
High Street
T H E H I G H W E A L D
S O U T H D O W N S
E a s t S u s s e x
TQ
TV
K B C D E G H
1 2 3 4 5 6
10 8
0 1 2 3 4 5 6 miles
0 1 2 3 4 5 6 7 8 9 10km

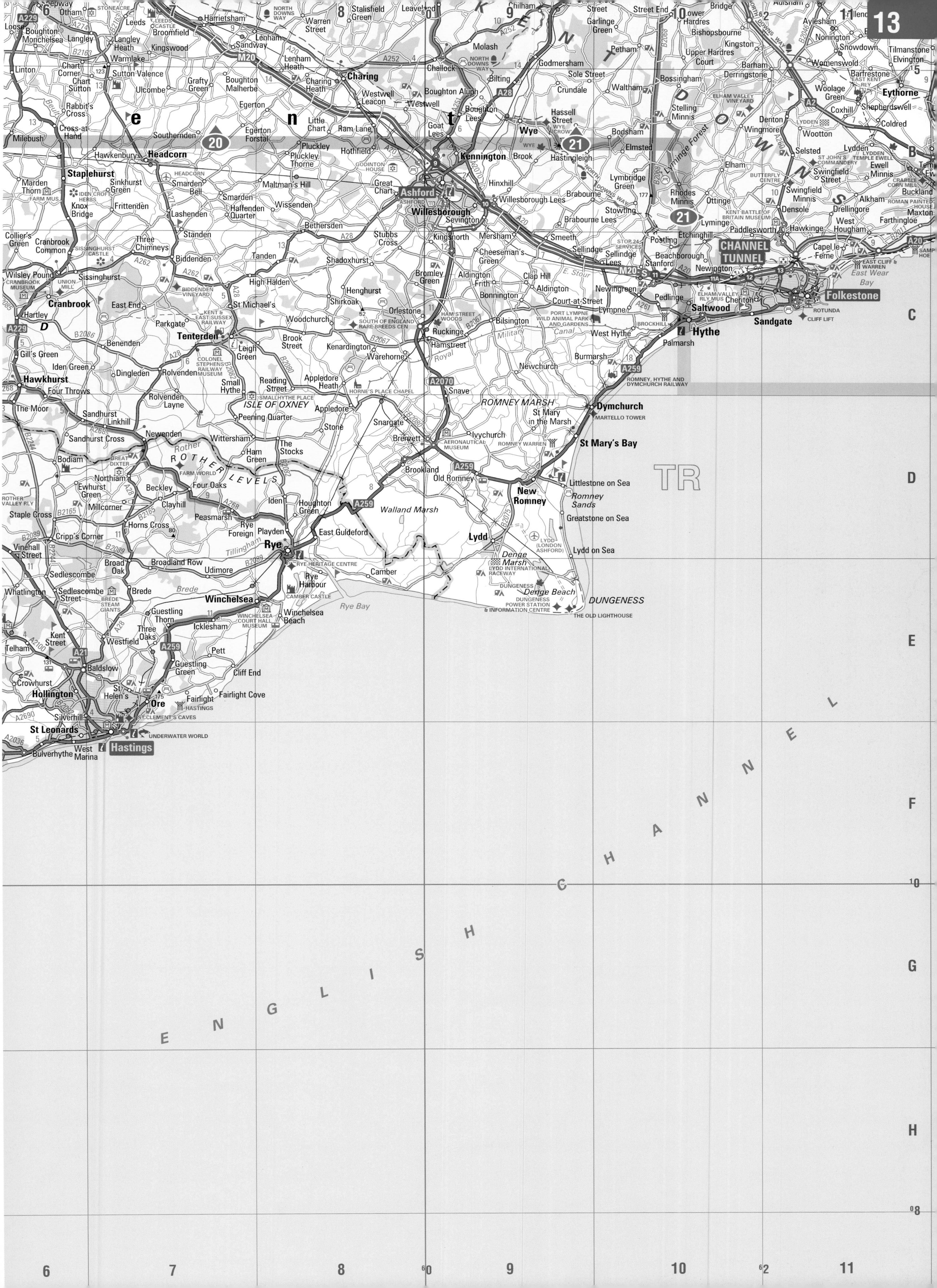
Otham
Leeds
Harrietsham
Broomfield
Lenham
Sandway
Warren Street
Stalisfield Green
Leaveland
Chilham
Street End
Lower Hardres
Bishopsbourne
Bridge
Aylesham
Nonington
Snowdown
Tilmanstone
Elvington
Loose
Boughton Monchelsea
Langley
Langley Heath
Kingswood
Lenham Heath
Charing
Charing Heath
Molash
Challock
Godmersham
Garlinge Green
Petham
Upper Hardres Court
Kingston
Barham
Womenswold
Barfrestone
Linton
Chart Corner
Chart Sutton
Sutton Valence
Warmlake
Ulcombe
Grafty Green
Boughton Malherbe
Westwell Leacon
Westwell
Boughton Aluph
Bilting
Sole Street
Crundale
Waltham
Bossingham
Derringstone
Woolage Green
Eythorne
Rabbit's Cross
Cross-at-Hand
Egerton
Egerton Forstal
Little Chart
Ram Lane
Goat Lees
Boughton Lees
Hassell Street
Wye
Stelling Minnis
Denton
Coxhill
Shepherdswell
Coldred
Milebush
Southernden
Pluckley
Pluckley Thorne
Hothfield
Kennington
Brook
Hastingleigh
Bodsham
Elmsted
Wingmore
Wootton
Lydden
Ewell Minnis
Selsted
Swingfield Street
Swingfield Minnis
Hawkenbury
Headcorn
Staplehurst
Sinkhurst Green
Smarden Bell
Smarden
Haffenden Quarter
Maltman's Hill
Great Chart
Ashford
Willesborough
Sevington
Hinxhill
Willesborough Lees
Brabourne
Lymbridge Green
Stowting
Brabourne Lees
Rhodes Minnis
Ottinge
Lyminge
Elham
Densole
Drellingore
Alkham
Buckland
Maxton
Farthingloe
Hougham
Marden Thorn
Knox Bridge
Frittenden
Lashenden
Wissenden
Standen
Bethersden
Stubbs Cross
Kingsnorth
Mersham
Smeeth
Sellindge
Sellindge Lees
Postling
Etchinghill
Paddlesworth
Hawkinge
Capel le Ferne
Collier's Green
Cranbrook Common
Three Chimneys
Biddenden
Tanden
Shadoxhurst
Cheeseman's Green
Bromley Green
Aldington Frith
Clap Hill
Aldington
Bonnington
Beachborough
Stanford
Newington
CHANNEL TUNNEL
Folkestone
East Wear Bay
Wilsley Pound
Sissinghurst
High Halden
Henghurst
Shirkoak
Orlestone
Court-at-Street
Newingreen
Pedlinge
Lympne
Cheriton
Saltwood
Sandgate
Cranbrook
East End
St Michael's
Woodchurch
Ruckinge
Bilsington
West Hythe
Hythe
Palmarsh
Hartley
Parkgate
Tenterden
Brook Street
Kenardington
Hamstreet
Warehorne
Royal Military Canal
Newchurch
Burmarsh
Gill's Green
Benenden
Leigh Green
Iden Green
Dingleden
Rolvenden
Small Hythe
Reading Street
Appledore Heath
Snave
Hawkhurst
Four Throws
Rolvenden Layne
ISLE OF OXNEY
Appledore
ROMNEY MARSH
St Mary in the Marsh
Dymchurch
The Moor
Sandhurst
Linkhill
Peening Quarter
Stone
Snargate
Brenzett
Ivychurch
St Mary's Bay
Sandhurst Cross
Newenden
Wittersham
Ham Green
The Stocks
Bodiam
ROTHER LEVELS
Brookland
Old Romney
Littlestone on Sea
TR
Northiam
Ewhurst Green
Beckley
Four Oaks
New Romney
Romney Sands
Millcorner
Clayhill
Iden
Houghton Green
Walland Marsh
Greatstone on Sea
Staple Cross
Horns Cross
Peasmarsh
Rye Foreign
Playden
Cripp's Corner
East Guldeford
Lydd
Vinehall Street
Rye
Lydd on Sea
Broad Oak
Broadland Row
Udimore
Denge Marsh
Sedlescombe
Camber
Rye Harbour
Sedlescombe Street
Brede
Winchelsea
Denge Beach
DUNGENESS
Whatlington
Guestling Thorn
Icklesham
Winchelsea Beach
Rye Bay
Kent Street
Three Oaks
Westfield
Telham
Pett
Baldslow
Guestling Green
Cliff End
Crowhurst
Hollington
St Helen's
Ore
Fairlight
Fairlight Cove
Silverhill
St Leonards
Hastings
West Marina
Bulverhythe
ENGLISH CHANNEL
6
7
8
9
10
11
A
B
C
D
E
F
G
H

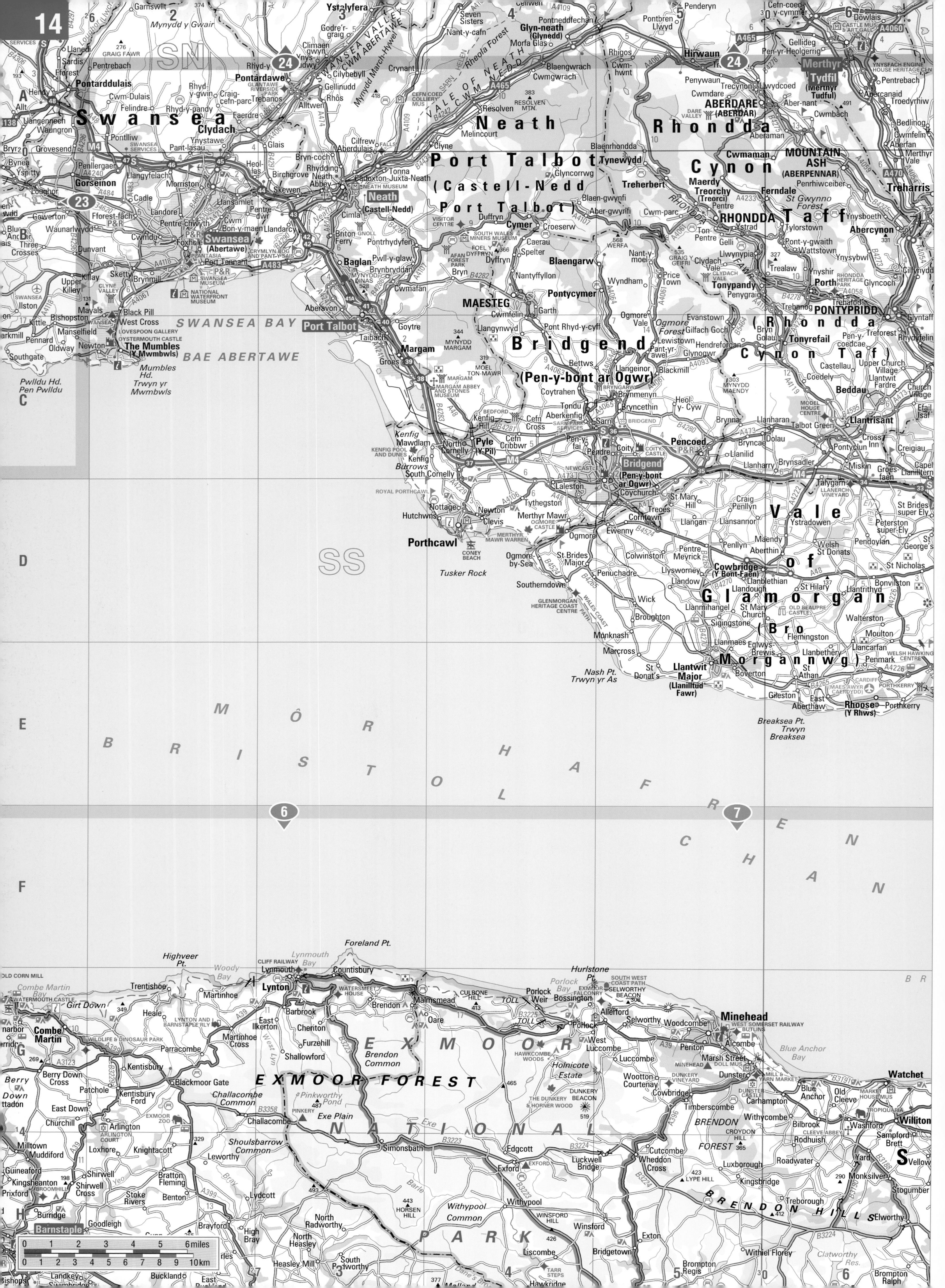
SN
SS
Swansea
Neath
Rhondda
Port Talbot
(Castell-Nedd Port Talbot)
Cynon
Taff
Bridgend
(Pen-y-bont ar Ogwr)
(Rhondda Cynon Taf)
Vale of Glamorgan
(Bro Morgannwg)
SWANSEA BAY
BAE ABERTAWE
MÔR HAFREN
BRISTOL CHANNEL
EXMOOR
EXMOOR FOREST
NATIONAL PARK
BRENDON HILLS
Pontarddulais
Gorseinon
Clydach
Pontardawe
Ystalyfera
Glyn-neath (Glynedd)
Hirwaun
Merthyr Tydfil (Merthyr Tudful)
ABERDARE (ABERDÂR)
MOUNTAIN ASH (ABERPENNAR)
Treharris
Neath
Swansea (Abertawe)
Port Talbot
Margam
Maesteg
Treorchy (Treorci)
RHONDDA
Tonypandy
Porth
PONTYPRIDD
Tonyrefail
Llantrisant
Pencoed
Bridgend (Pen-y-bont ar Ogwr)
Pyle (Y Pîl)
Porthcawl
Cowbridge (Y Bont-Faen)
Llantwit Major (Llanilltud Fawr)
Rhoose (Y Rhws)
The Mumbles (Y Mwmbwls)
Mumbles Hd. Trwyn yr Mwmbwls
Pwlldu Hd. Pen Pwlldu
Tusker Rock
Nash Pt. Trwyn yr As
Breaksea Pt. Trwyn Breaksea
Foreland Pt.
Highveer Pt.
Hurlstone Pt.
Lynmouth
Lynton
Combe Martin
Porlock
Minehead
Dunster
Watchet
Williton
Exford
Simonsbath
Withypool
Barnstaple
Blue Anchor Bay
M4
A48
A465
0 1 2 3 4 5 6 miles
0 1 2 3 4 5 6 7 8 9 10 km

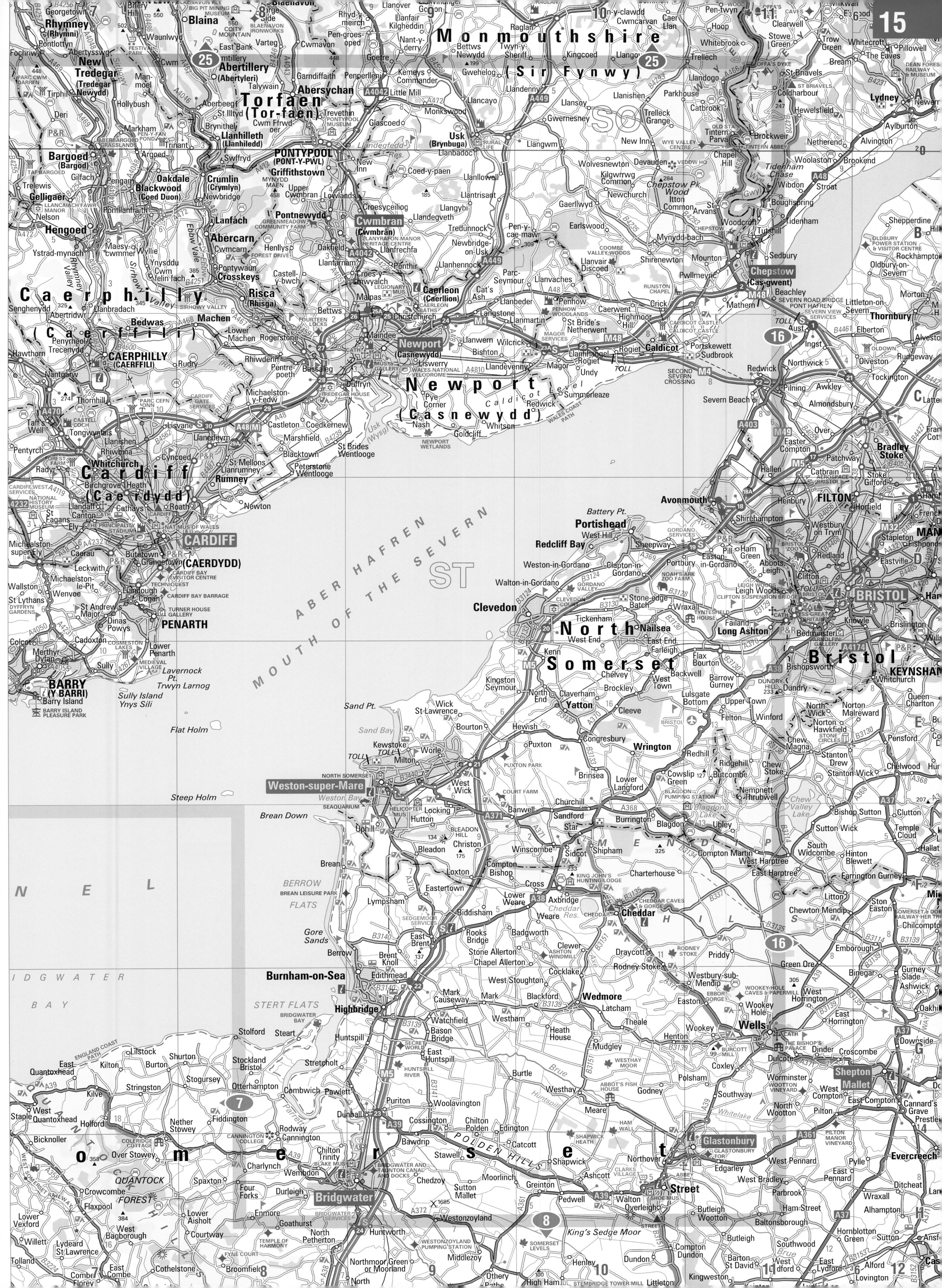
Monmouthshire
(Sir Fynwy)
Torfaen
(Tor-faen)
Caerphilly
(Caerffili)
Newport
(Casnewydd)
Cardiff
(Caerdydd)
North
Somerset
Bristol
ABER HAFREN
MOUTH OF THE SEVERN
ST
SO
Rhymney
(Rhymni)
Georgetown
Blaina
Blaenavon
Llanover
Raglan
Pen-twyn
Clearwell
Stowe
Trow Green
Whitecroft
Pillowell
Pontlottyn
Fochriw
Abertysswg
New Tredegar
(Tredegar Newydd)
Abertillery
(Abertyleri)
Cwm
East Bank
Varteg
Cwmavon
Goetre
Penperlleni
Kemeys Commander
Bettws Newydd
Twyn-y-Sheriff
Kingcoed
Llangoed
Trellech
Whitebrook
Hoop
Bream
The Eaves
St Briavels
Coldharbour
Lydney
Aylburton
Hewelsfield
Tirphil
Manmoel
Talywain
Garndiffaith
Abersychan
Little Mill
Gwehelog
Llandenny
Llanishen
Parkhouse
Llandogo
Catbrook
Trelleck Grange
Deri
Hollybush
Aberbeeg
Llanhilleth
(Llanhiledd)
Brynithel
Cwm Ffrwd-oer
Trevethin
Glascoed
Monkswood
Llancayo
Llansoy
Gwernesney
Usk
(Brynbuga)
Llanbadoc
Llangwm
New Inn
Tintern Parva
Brockweir
Netherend
Alvington
Bargoed
(Bargod)
Argoed
Swffryd
Trinant
Markham
Pontypool
(Pont-y-pŵl)
Griffithstown
New Inn
Coed-y-paen
Llanllowell
Wolvesnewton
Devauden
Kilgwrrwg Common
Chapel Hill
Tidenham Chase
Woolaston
Brookend
Oakdale
Blackwood
(Coed Duon)
Crumlin
(Crymlyn)
Newbridge
Pengam
Gilfach
Trelewis
Gelligaer
Nelson
Hengoed
Ystrad-mynach
Pontllanfraith
Lanfach
Abercarn
Cwmcarn
Upper Cwmbran
Lowlands
Pontnewydd
Cwmbran
(Cwmbrân)
Croesyceiliog
Llandegveth
Llangybi
Llantrisant
Newchurch
Chepstow Pk. Wood
Itton Common
Wibdon
Stroat
Boughspring
Tidenham
Shepperdine
Maesycwmmer
Wyllie
Ynysddu
Cwm felin fach
Pontywaun
Crosskeys
Risca
(Rhisga)
Henllys
Oakfield
Llantarnam
Llanfrechfa
Ponthir
Croes-y-mwyalch
Castell-y-bwch
Tredunnock
Newbridge-on-Usk
Llanhennock
Pen-y-cae-mawr
Gaerllwyd
Earlswood
Llanvair Discoed
Shirenewton
Mounton
Mynydd-bach
St Arvans
Woodcroft
Tutshill
Sedbury
Chepstow
(Cas-gwent)
Pwllmeyric
Beachley
Rockhampton
Oldbury-on-Severn
Morton
Littleton-on-Severn
Thornbury
Caerleon
(Caerllion)
Malpas
Bettws
Christchurch
Parc-Seymour
Cat's Ash
Llanvaches
Llanbeder
Penhow
Caerwent
Crick
Mathern
Senghenydd
Abertridwr
Llanbradach
Bedwas
Machen
Lower Machen
Rogerstone
Maindee
Langstone
Llanmartin
St Bride's Netherwent
Highmoor Hill
Caldicot
Portskewett
Sudbrook
Aust
Ingst
Elberton
Alveston
Penyrheol
Trecenydd
Caerphilly
(Caerffili)
Hawthorn
Rudry
Rhiwderin
Pentre-poeth
Bassaleg
Duffryn
Newport
(Casnewydd)
Liswerry
Llanwern
Bishton
Wilcrick
Llandevenny
Magor
Llanfihangel Rogiet
Rogiet
Undy
Redwick
Northwick
Olveston
Rudgeway
Tockington
Nantgarw
Thornhill
Michaelston-y-Fedw
Castleton
Coedkernew
Pye Corner
Nash
Caldicot Level
Summerleaze
Redwick
Whitson
Goldcliff
Pilning
Awkley
Severn Beach
Almondsbury
Taff's Well
Tongwynlais
Lisvane
Llanishen
Llanedeyrn
Marshfield
St Brides Wentlooge
Easter Compton
Over
Bradley Stoke
Pentyrch
Radyr
Whitchurch
Cyncoed
St Mellons
Llanrumney
Rumney
Blacktown
Peterstone Wentlooge
Hallen
Patchway
Catbrain
Stoke Gifford
Birchgrove
Heath
Llandaff
Canton
St Fagans
Ely
Cathays
Roath
Newton
Avonmouth
Henbury
Filton
Horfield
Battery Pt.
Portishead
Shirehampton
Westbury on Trym
Stapleton
Fishponds
Michaelston-super-Ely
Caerau
Leckwith
Michaelston-le-Pit
Wenvoe
Butetown
Grangetown
CARDIFF
(CAERDYDD)
West Hill
Redcliff Bay
Sheepway
Pill
Ham Green
Easton-in-Gordano
Portbury
Abbots Leigh
Redland
Clifton
Eastville
Weston-in-Gordano
Clapton-in-Gordano
Walton-in-Gordano
Leigh Woods
Wallston
St Lythans
St Andrew's Major
Dinas Powys
Llandough
Cogan
Penarth
Clevedon
Stone-edge Batch
Wraxall
Tickenham
Nailsea
Failand
Long Ashton
Bedminster
Knowle
Brislington
BRISTOL
Cadoxton
Colcot
Merthyr Dyfan
Lower Penarth
Lavernock Pt.
Trwyn Larnog
Kenn
West End
East End
Farleigh
Flax Bourton
Bishopsworth
Keynsham
Barry
(Y Barri)
Barry Island
Sully
Sully Island
Ynys Sili
Kingston Seymour
North End
Chelvey
Brockley
Backwell
West Town
Barrow Gurney
Dundry
Whitchurch
Sand Pt.
Wick St Lawrence
Claverham
Yatton
Cleeve
Lulsgate Bottom
Upper Town
Winford
North Wick
Norton Malreward
Queen Charlton
Flat Holm
Sand Bay
Bourton
Hewish
Congresbury
Felton
Norton Hawkfield
Pensford
Kewstoke
Milton
Worle
Puxton
Wrington
Redhill
Chew Magna
Stanton Drew
Weston-super-Mare
West Wick
Brinsea
Lower Langford
Cowslip Green
Ridgehill
Butcombe
Chew Stoke
Stanton Wick
Chelwood
Steep Holm
Weston Bay
Locking
Hutton
Banwell
Churchill
Nempnett Thrubwell
Bishop Sutton
Clutton
Brean Down
Uphill
Bleadon Hill
Sandford
Star
Burrington
Blagdon
Blagdon Lake
Ubley
Chew Valley Lake
Sutton Wick
Temple Cloud
Christon
Bleadon
Winscombe
Sidcot
Shipham
Compton Martin
West Harptree
East Harptree
South Widcombe
Hinton Blewett
Brean
Loxton
Compton Bishop
Charterhouse
Farrington Gurney
MENDIP
Berrow Flats
Eastertown
Cross
Axbridge
Cheddar Res.
Cheddar
Lower Weare
Weare
Litton
Chewton Mendip
Ston Easton
Lympsham
Biddisham
Badgworth
Gore Sands
East Brent
Rooks Bridge
Stone Allerton
Chapel Allerton
Clewer
Draycott
Rodney Stoke
Priddy
Emborough
Berrow
Brent Knoll
Green Ore
Binegar
Gurney Slade
Ashwick
Burnham-on-Sea
Edithmead
Cocklake
West Stoughton
Westbury-sub-Mendip
Easton
West Horrington
East Horrington
Bridgwater Bay
Stert Flats
Highbridge
Mark Causeway
Mark
Blackford
Wedmore
Latcham
Wookey Hole
Oakhill
Stolford
Steart
Huntspill
Watchfield
Westham
Theale
Wookey
Wells
Downside
Bason Bridge
East Huntspill
Heath House
Henton
Mudgley
Dulcote
Dinder
Croscombe
Lilstock
Kilton
Burton
Shurton
Stockland Bristol
Stretcholt
Burtle
Coxley
Worminster
Shepton Mallet
East Quantoxhead
Stogursey
Otterhampton
Polsham
Stringston
Combwich
Pawlett
Westhay
Southway
West Compton
East Compton
Pilton
Cannard's Grave
Kilve
Puriton
Woolavington
Godney
North Wootton
Prestleigh
Staple
West Quantoxhead
Holford
Fiddington
Nether Stowey
Dunball
Cossington
Chilton Polden
Edington
Meare
Rodway
Cannington
Bawdrip
Catcott
Polden Hills
Glastonbury
Bicknoller
Over Stowey
Chilton Trinity
Charlynch
Wembdon
Stawell
Shapwick
Northover
West Pennard
Pylle
Evercreech
East Pennard
Quantock Forest
Spaxton
Chedzoy
Moorlinch
Ashcott
Edgarley
West Bradley
Crowcombe
Four Forks
Durleigh
Bridgwater
Sutton Mallet
Greinton
Pedwell
Walton
Street
Parbrook
Wraxall
Ditcheat
Flaxpool
Lower Aisholt
Enmore
Westonzoyland
Overleigh
Butleigh Wootton
Ham Street
Baltonsbury
Alhampton
Lower Vexford
West Bagborough
Courtway
Goathurst
North Petherton
Huntworth
King's Sedge Moor
Butleigh
Hornblotton Green
Sutton
Willett
Lydeard St Lawrence
Middlezoy
Compton Dundon
Southwood
Tolland
Combe Florey
East Combe
Cothelstone
Broomfield
Northmoor Green or Moorland
Othery
Henley
Dundon
Barton St David
West Lydford
East Lydford
Alford
Lovington
North
High Ham
Littleton
Kingweston
Bristol Channel
Bridgwater Bay
Gordano Services
Sedgemoor Services
Bridgwater Services
Magor Services
Cardiff Gate Services
Severn View Services
Second Severn Crossing
Severn Road Bridge
Toll
Weston-super-Mare
Newport
Cwmbran
Chepstow
Glastonbury
Shepton Mallet
Bridgwater
CARDIFF
BRISTOL

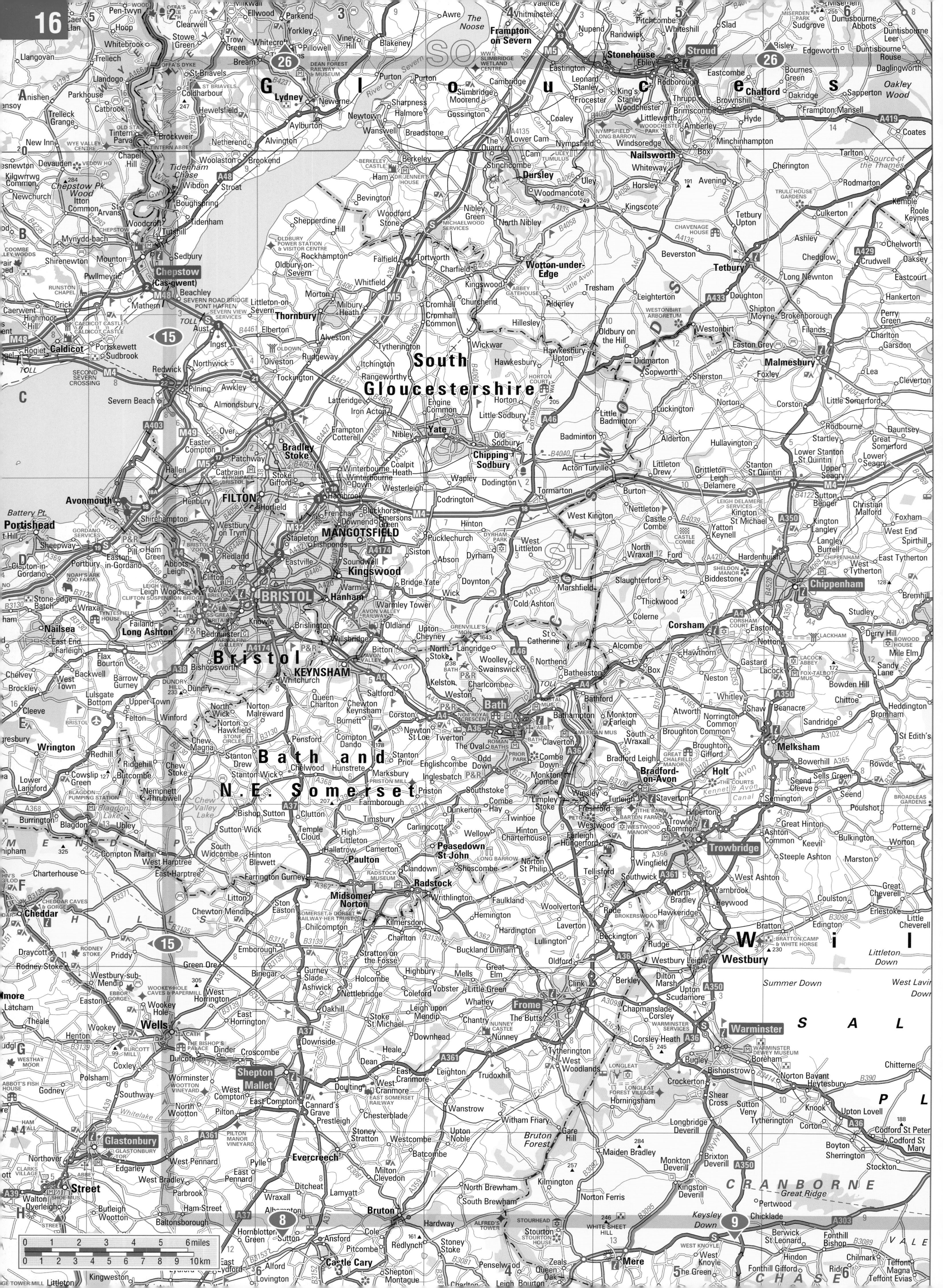
Gloucestershire
South Gloucestershire
Bristol
Bath and N.E. Somerset
Wil
SAL
PL
CRANBORNE
CHASE
MENDIP
HILLS
COTSWOLDS
SO
ST
Stroud
Chepstow (Cas-gwent)
BRISTOL
Bath
Chippenham
Trowbridge
Frome
Warminster
Wells
Shepton Mallet
Glastonbury
Lydney
Thornbury
Dursley
Nailsworth
Stonehouse
Tetbury
Malmesbury
Wotton-under-Edge
Chipping Sodbury
Yate
Bradley Stoke
FILTON
MANGOTSFIELD
Kingswood
Hanham
KEYNSHAM
Portishead
Avonmouth
Nailsea
Long Ashton
Caldicot
Clevedon
Wrington
Cheddar
Street
Evercreech
Bruton
Castle Cary
Midsomer Norton
Radstock
Paulton
Peasedown St John
Bradford-on-Avon
Melksham
Corsham
Westbury
Mere
Holt
Chalford
Frampton on Severn
Oldbury-on-Severn
Severn Beach
Marshfield
Batheaston
Saltford
Chew Magna
Blagdon
Timsbury
Rode
Beckington
Nunney
Longleat
Stourton
Heytesbury
Codford St Peter
Codford St Mary
Tinhead
Kemble
Easton Grey
Sherston
Badminton
Pucklechurch
Dyrham
Wick
Hawkesbury Upton
Chew Valley Lake
Blagdon Lake
Tidenham Chase
Chepstow Pk. Wood
Oakley Wood
Bruton Forest
Great Ridge
Summer Down
Littleton Down
Keysley Down
Source of the Thames
River Severn
Avon
M4
M5
M48
M49
M32
A4
A36
A37
A38
A39
A46
A48
A350
A361
A303
A419
A429
26
15
8
9
0 1 2 3 4 5 6 miles
0 1 2 3 4 5 6 7 8 9 10 km

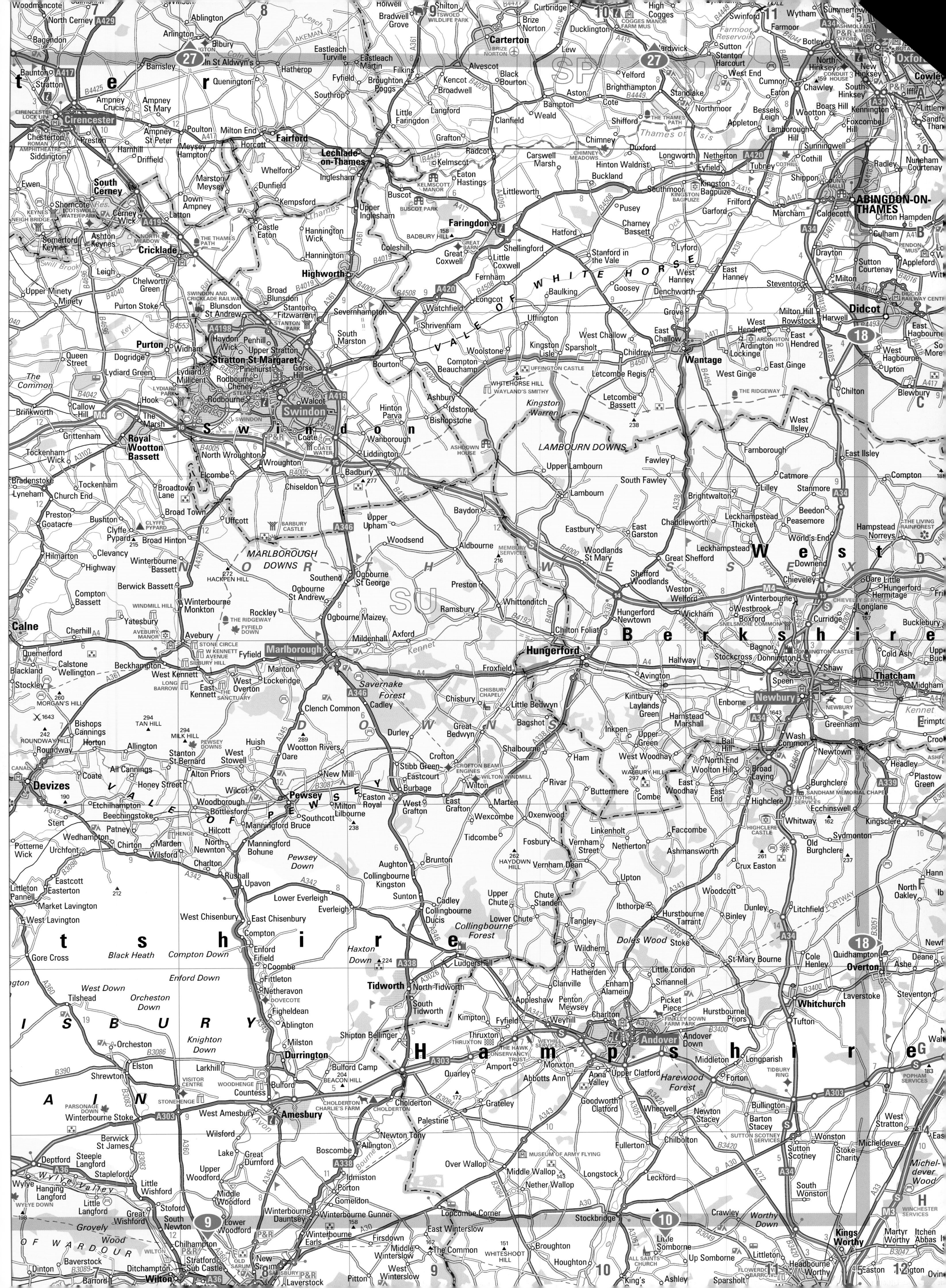

8
9
10
11
SP
SU
27
18
9
10
Woodmancote
North Cerney
Bagendon
Ablington
Arlington
Bibury
Barnsley
Coln St Aldwyn's
Quenington
Hatherop
Eastleach Turville
Eastleach Martin
Holwell
Bradwell Grove
Shilton
COTSWOLD WILDLIFE PARK
Fyfield
Filkins
Broughton Poggs
Southrop
Carterton
BRIZE NORTON
Brize Norton
Curbridge
Alvescot
Kencot
Broadwell
Black Bourton
Ducklington
Lew
COGGES MANOR FARM MUS
High Cogges
Hardwick
Yelford
Brighthampton
Aston
Cote
Standlake
Swinford
Farmoor
Farmoor Reservoir
Sutton
Stanton Harcourt
Wytham
Summertown
ASHMOLEAN
Botley
Oxford
North Hinksey
New Hinksey
Cowley
Iffley
West End
Cumnor
Chawley
South Hinksey
Eaton
Kennington
Boars Hill
Wootton
Bessels Leigh
Northmoor
Appleton
Foxcombe Hill
Lamborough Hill
Sunningwell
Cirencester
Baunton
Stratton
Ampney Crucis
Ampney St Mary
Ampney St Peter
Chesterton
Preston
Siddington
Harnhill
Driffield
Poulton
Meysey Hampton
Milton End
Fairford
Horcott
Lechlade-on-Thames
Little Faringdon
Langford
Clanfield
Grafton
Bampton
Weald
Radcot
Kelmscott
KELMSCOTT MANOR
Eaton Hastings
Shifford
Chimney
Duxford
Thames or Isis
Carswell Marsh
CHIMNEY MEADOWS
Longworth
Hinton Waldrist
Netherton
Fyfield
Tubney
Cothill
Radley
Nuneham Courtenay
South Cerney
Ewen
Shorncote
COTSWOLD WATER PARK
Cerney Wick
Somerford Keynes
Ashton Keynes
Marston Meysey
Whelford
Dunfield
Inglesham
Down Ampney
Latton
Kempsford
Upper Inglesham
Buscot
BUSCOT PARK
Littleworth
Buckland
Southmoor
Kingston Bagpuize
Frilford
Marcham
Shippon
Abingdon-on-Thames
Caldecott
Clifton Hampden
Culham
Cricklade
Castle Eaton
Hannington Wick
Hannington
Coleshill
Faringdon
Badbury Hill
Great Coxwell
Shellingford
Little Coxwell
Hatford
Pusey
Charney Bassett
Garford
Stanford in the Vale
Lyford
Drayton
Sutton Courtenay
Appleford
Leigh
Chelworth Green
Upper Minety
Minety
Purton Stoke
Highworth
Broad Blunsdon
Blunsdon St Andrew
Stanton Fitzwarren
Sevenhampton
Watchfield
Shrivenham
Fernham
Longcot
Baulking
Uffington
West Hanney
East Hanney
Goosey
Denchworth
Grove
Steventon
Milton
Didcot
Harwell
Milton Hill
Rowstock
VALE OF WHITE HORSE
Purton
Widham
Haydon Wick
Penhill
Upper Stratton
Stratton St Margaret
South Marston
Queen Street
Dogridge
Lydiard Millicent
Lydiard Green
Pinehurst
Rodbourne Cheney
Gorse Hill
The Common
Hook
Rodbourne
Swindon
Walcot
Bourton
Woolstone
Compton Beauchamp
Kingston Lisle
Sparsholt
West Challow
East Challow
Childrey
Wantage
West Hendred
East Hendred
Ardington
Locking
East Ginge
West Ginge
East Hagbourne
West Hagbourne
Upton
Chilton
Blewbury
Brinkworth
Callow Hill
The Marsh
Royal Wootton Bassett
Grittenham
Hinton Parva
Ashbury
Idstone
Bishopstone
WHITEHORSE HILL
UFFINGTON CASTLE
WAYLAND'S SMITHY
Kingston Warren
Letcombe Regis
Letcombe Bassett
THE RIDGEWAY
West Ilsley
Swindon
Tockenham Wick
North Wroughton
Wroughton
Coate
COATE WATER
Wanborough
Liddington
ASHDOWN HOUSE
LAMBOURN DOWNS
Farnborough
East Ilsley
Bradenstoke
Lyneham
Tockenham
Church End
Elcombe
Broadtown Lane
Badbury
Chiseldon
Upper Lambourn
Fawley
South Fawley
Lambourn
Catmore
Lilley
Compton
Stanmore
Brightwalton
Preston
Goatacre
Broad Town
Uffcott
Bushton
Clyffe Pypard
Broad Hinton
BARBURY CASTLE
Upper Upham
Baydon
Eastbury
East Garston
Chaddleworth
Leckhampstead Thicket
Beedon
Peasemore
Hampstead Norreys
THE LIVING RAINFOREST
Woodsend
Aldbourne
MEMBURY SERVICES
Woodlands St Mary
Leckhampstead
World's End
Hilmarton
Clevancy
Highway
Winterbourne Bassett
MARLBOROUGH DOWNS
HACKPEN HILL
Great Shefford
Shefford Woodlands
Downend
Chieveley
West
Berwick Bassett
Southend
Ogbourne St George
Ogbourne St Andrew
Preston
Weston
Welford
Oare
Little Hungerford
Hermitage
Compton Bassett
WINDMILL HILL
Winterbourne Monkton
Rockley
Ramsbury
Whittonditch
Hungerford Newtown
Winterbourne
Westbrook
Boxford
Longlane
Calne
Yatesbury
THE RIDGEWAY
FYFIELD DOWN
Ogbourne Maizey
Mildenhall
Axford
Chilton Foliat
Wickham
SNELSMORE COMMON
Curridge
Bucklebury
Cherhill
AVEBURY MANOR
Avebury
STONE CIRCLE
W KENNETT AVENUE
SILBURY HILL
Fyfield
Marlborough
Kennet
Hungerford
Berkshire
Bagnor
DONNINGTON CASTLE
Cold Ash
Quemerford
Calstone Wellington
Blackland
Beckhampton
West Kennett
Manton
Froxfield
Halfway
Stockcross
Donnington
Shaw
Thatcham
Midgham
Stockley
LONG BARROW
East Kennett
West Overton
Lockeridge
Savernake Forest
Avington
Speen
MORGAN'S HILL
THE SANCTUARY
Cadley
CHISBURY CHAPEL
Chisbury
Little Bedwyn
Kintbury
Laylands Green
Enborne
Newbury
Greenham
TAN HILL
Clench Common
Hamstead Marshall
Bishops Cannings
Roundway
Horton
MILK HILL
PEWSEY DOWNS
Allington
Durley
Great Bedwyn
Bagshot
Inkpen
Upper Green
Ball Hill
Wash Common
Newtown
Huish
Wootton Rivers
Stanton St Bernard
West Stowell
Oare
Shalbourne
Crofton
CROFTON BEAM ENGINES
Ham
West Woodhay
North End
Woolton Hill
Broad Laying
Headley
All Cannings
Alton Priors
New Mill
Stibb Green
Eastcourt
WILTON WINDMILL
WALBURY HILL
Devizes
Coate
Honey Street
Wilcot
Pewsey
Burbage
Wilton
Rivar
Combe
East Woodhay
Burghclere
Plastow Green
Woodborough
Bottlesford
Easton Royal
East Grafton
Marten
Buttermere
East End
Highclere
SANDHAM MEMORIAL CHAPEL
TOTHILL SERVICES
Etchilhampton
Beechingstoke
VALE OF PEWSEY
Milton Lilbourne
Southcott
West Grafton
Wexcombe
Oxenwood
Ecchinswell
Kingsclere
Stert
Patney
Manningford Bruce
Tidcombe
Linkenholt
Faccombe
Whitway
HIGHCLERE CASTLE
Sydmonton
Potterne Wick
Wedhampton
Chirton
Marden
North Newnton
Manningford Bohune
Fosbury
Vernham Street
Netherton
Ashmansworth
Old Burghclere
Urchfont
Wilsford
Charlton
Pewsey Down
Aughton
Brunton
HAYDOWN HILL
Vernham Dean
Crux Easton
Eastcott
Easterton
Rushall
Upavon
Collingbourne Kingston
Upton
Littleton Pannell
Market Lavington
Lower Everleigh
Everleigh
Sunton
Cadley
Collingbourne Ducis
Upper Chute
Chute Standen
Woodcott
Ibthorpe
Hurstbourne Tarrant
Dunley
Litchfield
North Oakley
West Lavington
West Chisenbury
East Chisenbury
Collingbourne Forest
Lower Chute
Tangley
Binley
Compton
Haxton Down
Doles Wood
Stoke
Gore Cross
Black Heath
Compton Down
Enford
Fifield
Wiltshire
Ludgershall
Wildhern
St Mary Bourne
Cole Henley
Quidhampton
Overton
Deane
Ashe
Coombe
Enford Down
Hatherden
Little London
Smannell
Fittleton
Netheravon
DOVECOTE
Tidworth
North Tidworth
Clanville
Penton Mewsey
Enham Alamein
West Down
Tilshead
Orcheston Down
Figheldean
South Tidworth
Appleshaw
Picket Piece
Hurstbourne Priors
Whitchurch
Laverstoke
Steventon
Ablington
Kimpton
Fyfield
Weyhill
Charlton
FINKLEY DOWN FARM PARK
Tufton
SALISBURY
Orcheston
Milston
Shipton Bellinger
Thruxton
THRUXTON
THE HAWK CONSERVANCY TRUST
WEYHILL SERVICES
Andover
Andover Down
Knighton Down
Durrington
Hampshire
Elston
Larkhill
Bulford Camp
Quarley
Amport
Monxton
Anna Valley
Upper Clatford
Middleton
Longparish
TIDBURY RING
Shrewton
VISITOR CENTRE
WOODHENGE
BEACON HILL
Abbotts Ann
Harewood Forest
Forton
POPHAM SERVICES
Bulford
Countess
STONEHENGE
CHOLDERTON CHARLIE'S FARM
Cholderton
Grateley
Goodworth Clatford
Wherwell
PARSONAGE DOWN
Winterbourne Stoke
West Amesbury
Amesbury
Palestine
Newton Stacey
Bullington
Barton Stacey
West Stratton
Berwick St James
Wilsford
Newton Tony
Fullerton
Chilbolton
SUTTON SCOTNEY SERVICES
Wonston
Sutton Scotney
Stoke Charity
Micheldever
Deptford
Steeple Langford
Lake
Great Durnford
Boscombe
Allington
MUSEUM OF ARMY FLYING
Over Wallop
Middle Wallop
Longstock
Leckford
Micheldever Wood
Wylye
Stapleford
Upper Woodford
Idmiston
Nether Wallop
Hanging Langford
Little Wishford
Porton
South Wonston
Wylye Valley
WYLYE DOWN
Little Langford
Middle Woodford
Gomeldon
Great Wishford
Stoford
South Newton
Lower Woodford
Winterbourne Dauntsey
Winterbourne Gunner
Lopcombe Corner
Stockbridge
Crawley
Worthy Down
WINCHESTER SERVICES
Kings Worthy
Martyr Worthy
Itchen Abbas
Grovely Wood
VALE OF WARDOUR
Chilhampton
Winterbourne Earls
Firsdown
East Winterslow
Middle Winterslow
The Common
WHITESHOOT HILL
Broughton
Little Somborne
ALL SAINTS CHURCH
Up Somborne
Littleton
Headbourne Worthy
Baverstock
Stratford sub Castle
OLD SARUM
New
West Winterslow
Houghton
Dinton
Barford
Ditchampton
Wilton
Laverstock
Pitton
King's
Ashley
Sparsholt
Easton

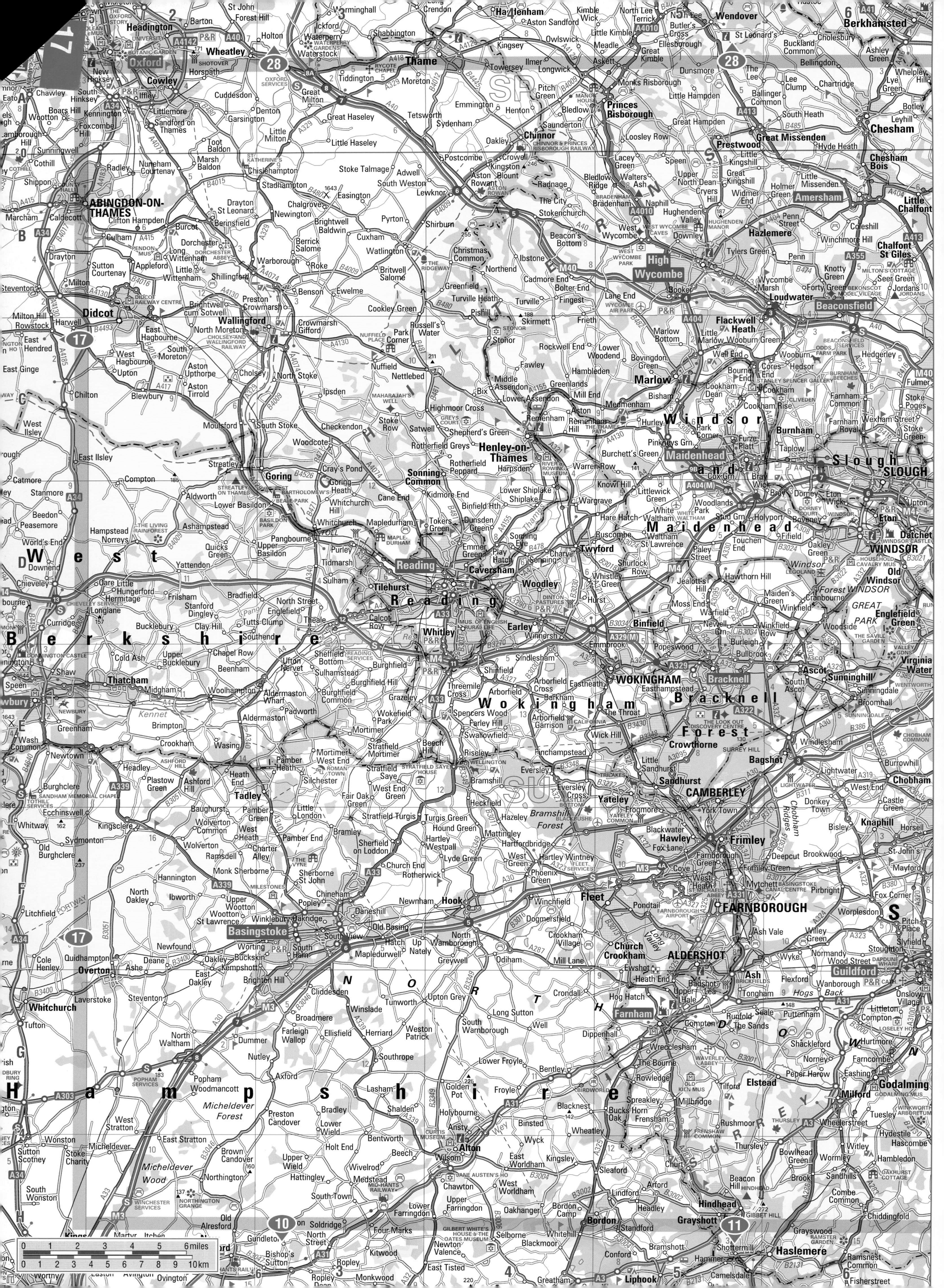
17
28
28
10
11
17
Headington
Oxford
Cowley
Wheatley
Thame
Haddenham
Wendover
Berkhamsted
Princes Risborough
Chinnor
Great Missenden
Chesham
Amersham
ABINGDON-ON-THAMES
Didcot
Wallingford
High Wycombe
Beaconsfield
Marlow
Henley-on-Thames
Maidenhead
Slough
SLOUGH
WINDSOR
Eton
Datchet
Goring
Sonning Common
Reading
Caversham
Woodley
Tilehurst
Twyford
Wokingham
WOKINGHAM
Bracknell
Ascot
Sunninghill
Virginia Water
Thatcham
Newbury
Tadley
Camberley
CAMBERLEY
Sandhurst
Yateley
Frimley
Bagshot
Chobham
Fleet
FARNBOROUGH
ALDERSHOT
Church Crookham
Hook
Basingstoke
Overton
Whitchurch
Odiham
Farnham
Alton
Bordon
Hindhead
Grayshott
Haslemere
Liphook
Godalming
Milford
Guildford
Elstead
Tufton
West Berkshire
Hampshire
Surrey
Windsor and Maidenhead
Wokingham
Bracknell Forest
CHILTERN HILLS
NORTH DOWNS
SP
SU
Micheldever Forest
Micheldever Wood
Bramshill Forest
GREAT PARK
0 1 2 3 4 5 6 miles
0 1 2 3 4 5 6 7 8 9 10 km

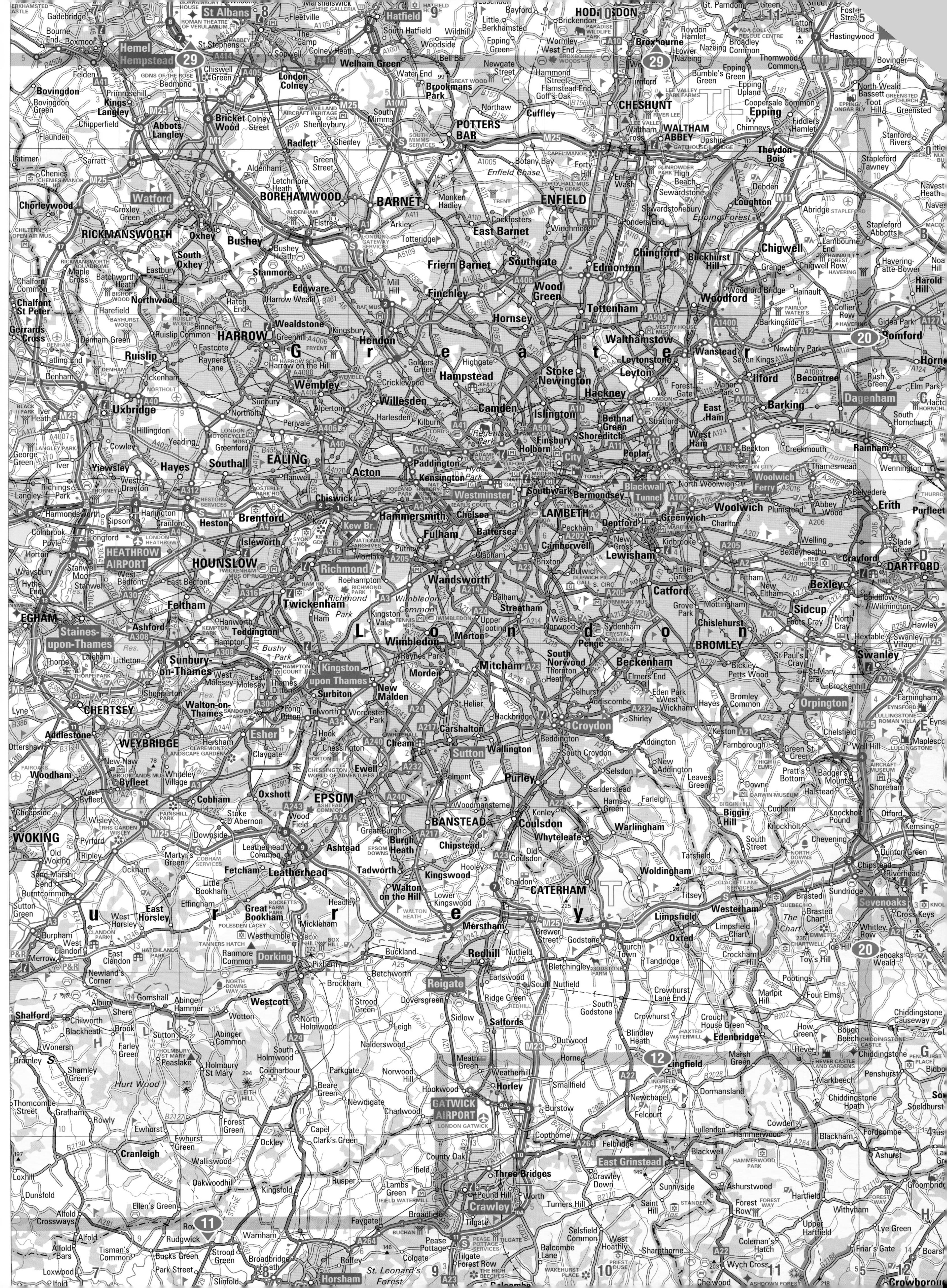

St Albans
Hatfield
Hoddesdon
Hemel Hempstead
29
Welham Green
London Colney
Brookmans Park
Cheshunt
Waltham Abbey
Epping
Potters Bar
Watford
Borehamwood
Barnet
Enfield
Loughton
Rickmansworth
Bushey
East Barnet
Chingford
Chigwell
Stanmore
Edgware
Southgate
Edmonton
Finchley
Wood Green
Woodford
Northwood
Tottenham
Hornsey
Harrow
Walthamstow
Romford
20
Ruislip
Hendon
Greater London
Wembley
Hampstead
Stoke Newington
Ilford
Becontree
Hackney
Leyton
Uxbridge
Willesden
Camden
Islington
Barking
Dagenham
Ealing
Hayes
Southall
Acton
Paddington
Kensington
City
Shoreditch
Rainham
West Ham
Woolwich Ferry
Westminster
Blackwall Tunnel
Hammersmith
Chelsea
Lambeth
Bermondsey
Woolwich
Erith
Brentford
Kew Br.
Fulham
Battersea
Deptford
Greenwich
Heathrow Airport
Hounslow
Richmond
Lewisham
Camberwell
Dartford
Wandsworth
Bexley
Feltham
Twickenham
Catford
Sidcup
Egham
Staines-upon-Thames
Wimbledon
Streatham
Bromley
Swanley
Sunbury-on-Thames
Kingston upon Thames
Mitcham
Beckenham
Chertsey
Surbiton
New Malden
Croydon
Orpington
Weybridge
Esher
Sutton
Purley
Woking
Epsom
Banstead
Coulsdon
Leatherhead
Caterham
Sevenoaks
Dorking
Redhill
Reigate
Edenbridge
Lingfield
12
Gatwick Airport
Horley
Crawley
East Grinstead
11
Horsham
Cranleigh

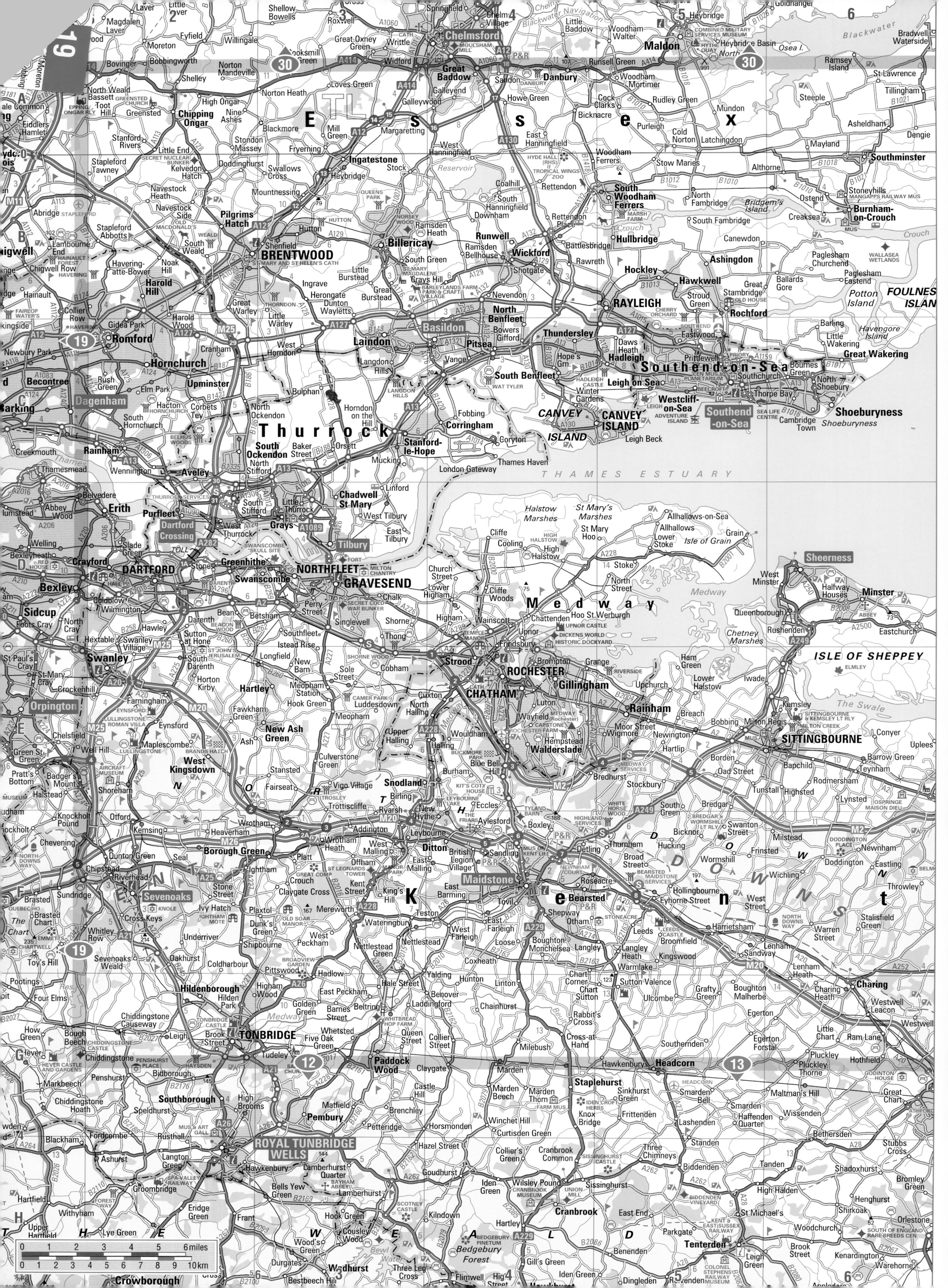
19
30
19
12
13
E s s e x
Thurrock
Medway
K e n t
N O R T H D O W N S
Chelmsford
Great Baddow
Danbury
Maldon
Heybridge
Chipping Ongar
Ingatestone
Billericay
BRENTWOOD
Wickford
South Woodham Ferrers
Burnham-on-Crouch
Southminster
RAYLEIGH
Rochford
Hockley
Basildon
Laindon
Pitsea
Thundersley
Hadleigh
Southend-on-Sea
Leigh on Sea
Westcliff-on-Sea
Shoeburyness
CANVEY ISLAND
Stanford-le-Hope
Corringham
Romford
Hornchurch
Upminster
Dagenham
Barking
Rainham
Aveley
Purfleet
Grays
Tilbury
Erith
Dartford Crossing
DARTFORD
Crayford
Bexley
Sidcup
Swanley
Orpington
NORTHFLEET
GRAVESEND
Swanscombe
Greenhithe
Strood
ROCHESTER
CHATHAM
Gillingham
Rainham
Walderslade
SITTINGBOURNE
Sheerness
Minster
ISLE OF SHEPPEY
Snodland
Ditton
Maidstone
Bearsted
Borough Green
Sevenoaks
Hildenborough
TONBRIDGE
Southborough
ROYAL TUNBRIDGE WELLS
Pembury
Paddock Wood
Staplehurst
Headcorn
Cranbrook
Tenterden
Charing
Wadhurst
Crowborough
THAMES ESTUARY
0 1 2 3 4 5 6 miles
0 1 2 3 4 5 6 7 8 9 10 km

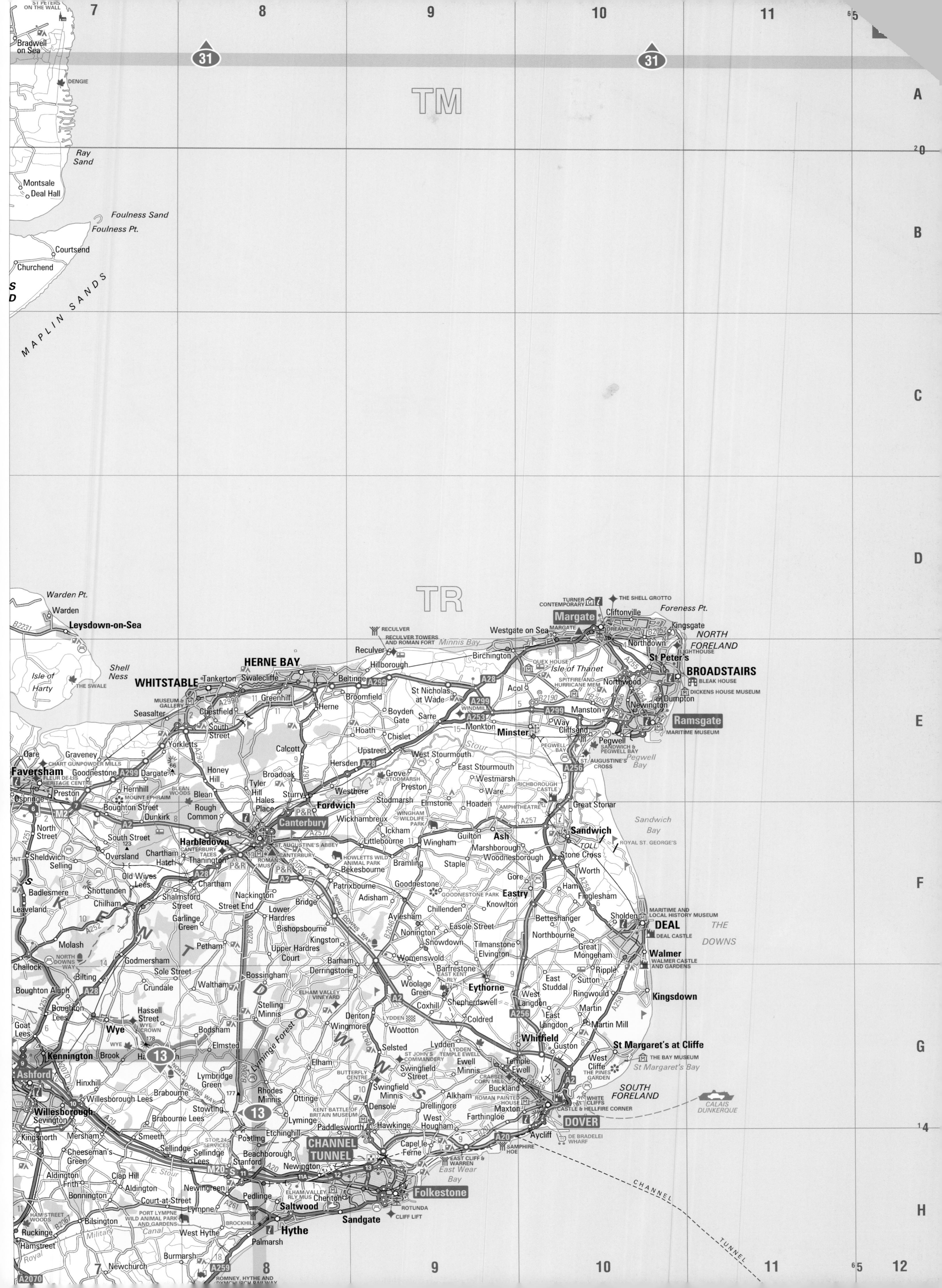

7
8
9
10
11
31
TM
TR
A
B
C
D
E
F
G
H
Bradwell on Sea
DENGIE
Ray Sand
Montsale
Deal Hall
Foulness Sand
Foulness Pt.
Courtsend
Churchend
MAPLIN SANDS
Warden Pt.
Warden
Leysdown-on-Sea
Isle of Harty
Shell Ness
THE SWALE
WHITSTABLE
HERNE BAY
Tankerton
Swalecliffe
Seasalter
Chestfield
Greenhill
Herne
Beltinge
Broomfield
Reculver
RECULVER TOWERS AND ROMAN FORT
Minnis Bay
Hillborough
Birchington
Westgate on Sea
Margate
TURNER CONTEMPORARY
THE SHELL GROTTO
Cliftonville
Foreness Pt.
Kingsgate
NORTH FORELAND
Northdown
St Peter's
BROADSTAIRS
BLEAK HOUSE
DICKENS HOUSE MUSEUM
Dumpton
Newington
Ramsgate
MARITIME MUSEUM
Isle of Thanet
QUEX HOUSE
Acol
Manston
Minster
Monkton
St Nicholas at Wade
Sarre
Boyden Gate
Chislet
Hoath
Calcott
Upstreet
West Stourmouth
East Stourmouth
Westmarsh
Ware
Pegwell
Pegwell Bay
ST. AUGUSTINE'S CROSS
RICHBOROUGH CASTLE
Great Stonar
Sandwich
Sandwich Bay
ROYAL ST. GEORGE'S
Stone Cross
Worth
Ham
Finglesham
Sholden
DEAL
DEAL CASTLE
THE DOWNS
Walmer
WALMER CASTLE AND GARDENS
Kingsdown
Ripple
Sutton
Ringwould
Martin
Martin Mill
St Margaret's at Cliffe
St Margaret's Bay
West Cliffe
SOUTH FORELAND
WHITE CLIFFS
DOVER
CALAIS DUNKERQUE
CHANNEL TUNNEL
Faversham
Graveney
Oare
Goodnestone
Dargate
Hernhill
Preston
Ospringe
Boughton Street
Dunkirk
Yorkletts
South Street
Honey Hill
Blean
Rough Common
Tyler Hill
Hales Place
Sturry
Broadoak
Fordwich
Westbere
Grove
Stodmarsh
Hersden
Canterbury
Harbledown
Thanington
Chartham
Chartham Hatch
Bekesbourne
Patrixbourne
Littlebourne
Ickham
Wickhambreux
Wingham
Elmstone
Hoaden
Ash
Guilton
Marshborough
Woodnesborough
Staple
Bramling
Goodnestone
Gore
Eastry
Knowlton
Chillenden
Adisham
Aylesham
Nonington
Easole Street
Tilmanstone
Elvington
Betteshanger
Northbourne
Great Mongeham
East Studdal
West Langdon
East Langdon
Whitfield
Guston
Eythorne
Barfrestone
Womenswold
Snowdown
Woolage Green
Shepherdswell
Coxhill
Coldred
Lydden
Temple Ewell
Ewell Minnis
Buckland
River
Alkham
Drellingore
Maxton
Farthingloe
Aycliff
West Hougham
Capel le Ferne
Hawkinge
Densole
Swingfield Minnis
Swingfield Street
Selsted
Wootton
Denton
Wingmore
Elham
Lyminge
Ottinge
Etchinghill
Paddlesworth
Postling
Beachborough
Newington
Cheriton
Folkestone
Sandgate
Saltwood
Hythe
Palmarsh
Pedlinge
Lympne
West Hythe
Burmarsh
Newchurch
Stanford
Sellindge
Sellindge Lees
Smeeth
Stowting
Rhodes Minnis
Lymbridge Green
Brabourne
Brabourne Lees
Lyminge Forest
Elmsted
Bodsham
Stelling Minnis
Bossingham
Waltham
Derringstone
Barham
Kingston
Upper Hardres Court
Bishopsbourne
Lower Hardres
Bridge
Nackington
Street End
Petham
Garlinge Green
Shalmsford Street
Old Wives Lees
Shottenden
Chilham
Selling
Sheldwich
Badlesmere
Leaveland
Oversland
North Street
Molash
Godmersham
Sole Street
Crundale
Challock
Bilting
Boughton Aluph
Boughton Lees
Hassell Street
Wye
Brook
Goat Lees
Kennington
Ashford
Hinxhill
Willesborough Lees
Willesborough
Sevington
Mersham
Kingsnorth
Cheeseman's Green
Aldington
Aldington Frith
Clap Hill
Bonnington
Court-at-Street
Bilsington
Ruckinge
Hamstreet
PORT LYMPNE WILD ANIMAL PARK AND GARDENS
KENT
NORTH DOWNS
CHANNEL TUNNEL
13

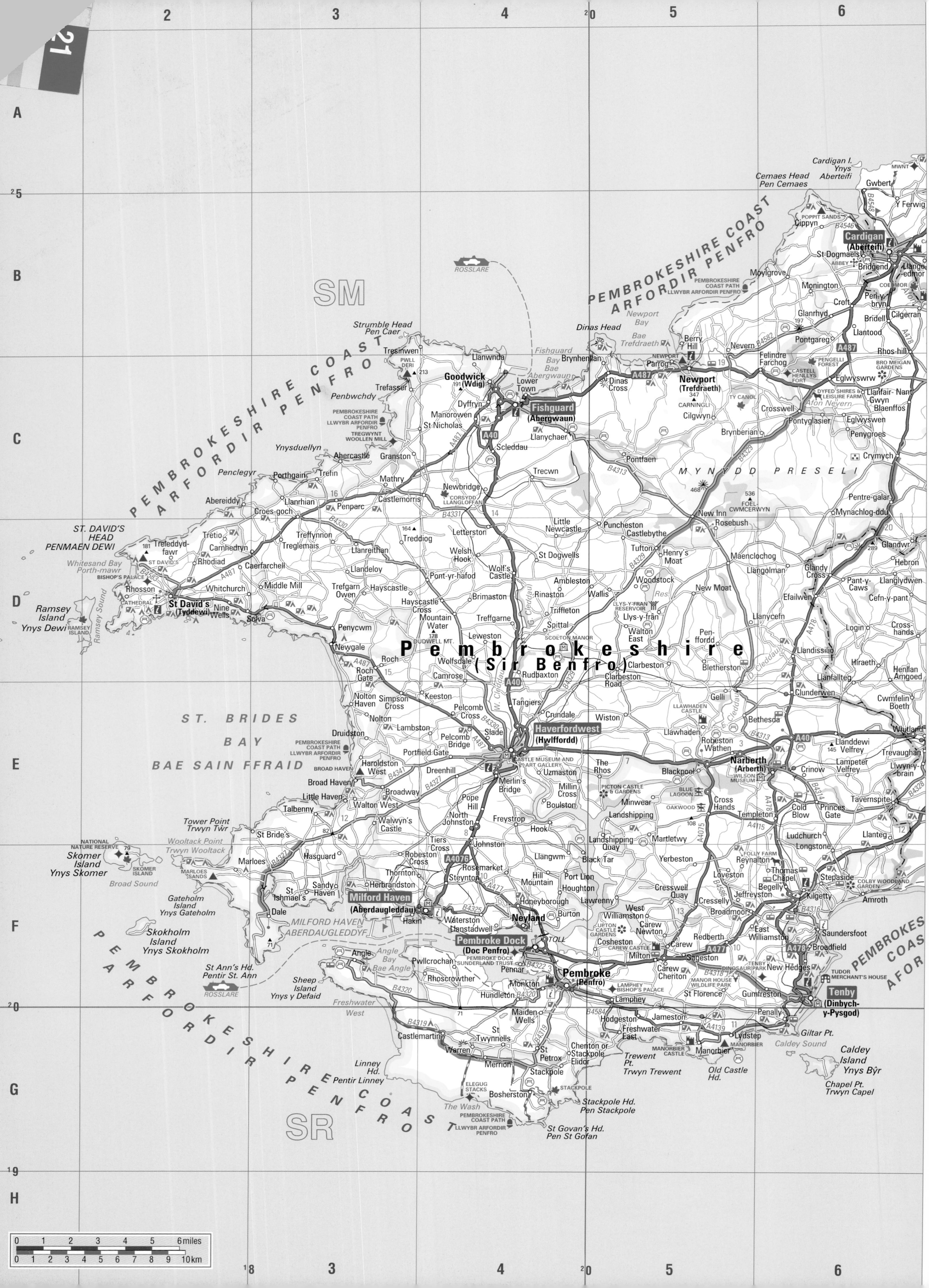
SM
SR
Pembrokeshire
(Sir Benfro)
PEMBROKESHIRE COAST
ARFORDIR PENFRO
ST. BRIDES
BAY
BAE SAIN FFRAID
MYNYDD PRESELI
MILFORD HAVEN
ABERDAUGLEDDYF
ROSSLARE
Fishguard Bay
Bae Abergwaun
Newport Bay
Bae Trefdraeth
Strumble Head
Pen Caer
Dinas Head
Cemaes Head
Pen Cemaes
Cardigan I.
Ynys Aberteifi
ST. DAVID'S HEAD
PENMAEN DEWI
Whitesand Bay
Porth-mawr
Ramsey Island
Ynys Dewi
Ramsey Sound
Skomer Island
Ynys Skomer
Broad Sound
Gateholm Island
Ynys Gateholm
Skokholm Island
Ynys Skokholm
Tower Point
Trwyn Twr
Wooltack Point
Trwyn Woolteck
St Ann's Hd.
Pentir St. Ann
Sheep Island
Ynys y Defaid
Angle Bay
Bae Angle
Freshwater West
Linney Hd.
Pentir Linney
The Wash
Stackpole Hd.
Pen Stackpole
St Govan's Hd.
Pen St Gofan
Trewent Pt.
Trwyn Trewent
Old Castle Hd.
Caldey Sound
Caldey Island
Ynys Bŷr
Giltar Pt.
Chapel Pt.
Trwyn Capel
Cardigan
(Aberteifi)
Fishguard
(Abergwaun)
Haverfordwest
(Hwlffordd)
Milford Haven
(Aberdaugleddau)
Pembroke Dock
(Doc Penfro)
Pembroke
(Penfro)
Tenby
(Dinbych-y-Pysgod)
Newport
(Trefdraeth)
Goodwick
(Wdig)
St David's
(Tyddewi)
Narberth
(Arberth)
Neyland
A40
A487
A477
A478
A4076
Gwbert
Y Ferwig
Cippyn
St Dogmaels
Bridgend
Moylgrove
Monington
Croft
Glanrhyd
Pontgareg
Nevern
Felindre Farchog
Eglwyswrw
Crosswell
Pontyglasier
Brynberian
Crymych
Berry Hill
Parrog
Dinas Cross
Cilgwyn
Llanwnda
Tresinwen
Trefasser
Penbwchdy
Lower Town
Dyffryn
Manorowen
St Nicholas
Llanychaer
Scleddau
Pontfaen
Trecwn
Granston
Abercastle
Trefin
Porthgain
Penclegyr
Mathry
Ynysduellyn
Abereiddy
Llanrhian
Croes-goch
Penparc
Castlemorris
Newbridge
Tretio
Treleddyd-fawr
Carnhedryn
Rhodiad
Caerfarchell
Rhosson
Whitchurch
Middle Mill
Nine Wells
Solva
Treffynnon
Treglemais
Llanreithan
Llandeloy
Treddiog
Letterston
Welsh Hook
Pont-yr-hafod
Wolf's Castle
Hayscastle
Hayscastle Cross
Trefgarn Owen
Mountain Water
Brimaston
Treffgarne
Little Newcastle
Puncheston
Castlebythe
St Dogwells
Ambleston
Rinaston
Wallis
Tufton
Henry's Moat
Woodstock
New Moat
Maenclochog
Llangolman
New Inn
Rosebush
Mynachlog-ddu
Pentre-galar
Glandwr
Hebron
Glandy Cross
Efailwen
Llanycefn
Login
Llandissilio
Llanfallteg
Clunderwen
Penycwm
Newgale
Roch
Roch Gate
Wolfsdale
Camrose
Keeston
Leweston
Rudbaxton
Triffleton
Spittal
Llys-y-frân
Walton East
Clarbeston
Clarbeston Road
Penffordd
Bletherston
Nolton Haven
Nolton
Simpson Cross
Pelcomb Cross
Pelcomb Bridge
Tangiers
Crundale
Wiston
Lambston
Druidston
Portfield Gate
Slade
Llawhaden
Robeston Wathen
Gelli
Bethesda
Haroldston West
Broad Haven
Little Haven
Dreenhill
Merlin's Bridge
Uzmaston
The Rhos
Millin Cross
Boulston
Blackpool
Broadway
Walton West
Talbenny
Pope Hill
North Johnston
Freystrop
Hook
Minwear
Landshipping
Cross Hands
Templeton
St Bride's
Walwyn's Castle
Marloes
Hasguard
Tiers Cross
Johnston
Robeston Cross
Thornton
Rosemarket
Steynton
Llangwm
Black Tar
Landshipping Quay
Martletwy
Yerbeston
Loveston
Reynalton
Dale
St Ishmael's
Sandy Haven
Herbrandston
Hakin
Waterston
Llanstadwell
Hill Mountain
Port Lion
Houghton
Honeyborough
Lawrenny
Cresswell Quay
Cresselly
Jeffreyston
Begelly
Thomas Chapel
Kilgetty
Stepaside
Amroth
Burton
West Williamston
Carew Newton
Cosheston
Milton
Carew
Carew Cheriton
Redberth
Sageston
Broadmoor
East Williamston
Saundersfoot
Broadfield
New Hedges
Angle
Pwllcrochan
Rhoscrowther
Pennar
Monkton
Hundleton
Lamphey
St Florence
Gumfreston
Penally
Maiden Wells
Hodgeston
Jameston
Freshwater East
Lydstep
Manorbier
Castlemartin
St Twynnells
Warren
St Petrox
Merrion
Cheriton or Stackpole Elidor
Stackpole
Bosherston
Whitland
Llanddewi Velfrey
Lampeter Velfrey
Crinow
Cold Blow
Princes Gate
Ludchurch
Longstone
Llanteg
Tavernspite
Llwyn-y-brain
Trevaughan
Cwmfelin Boeth
Henllan Amgoed
Hiraeth
Cross-hands
Cefn-y-pant
Llanglydwen
Pant-y-Caws
Blaenffos
Llanfair-Nant-Gwyn
Eglwyswen
Penygroes
Cilgerran
Rhos-hill
Llantood
Bridell
Pen-y-bryn
Llangoedmor
CARNINGLI
FOEL CWMCERWYN
DUDWELL MT.
PENGELLI FOREST
CASTELL HENLLYS FORT
BRO MEIGAN GARDENS
DYFED SHIRES & LEISURE FARM
POPPIT SANDS
ABBEY
TY CANOL
PWLL DERI
TREGWYNT WOOLLEN MILL
CORSYDD LLANGLOFFAN
LLYS-Y-FRAN RESERVOIR
SCOLTON MANOR
LLAWHADEN CASTLE
CASTLE MUSEUM AND ART GALLERY
PICTON CASTLE & GARDENS
BLUE LAGOON
OAKWOOD
WILSON MUSEUM
FOLLY FARM
COLBY WOODLAND GARDEN
UPTON CASTLE GARDENS
CAREW CASTLE
PEMBROKE DOCK SUNDERLAND TRUST
LAMPHEY BISHOP'S PALACE
MANOR HOUSE WILDLIFE PARK
DINOSAUR PARK
TENBY
TUDOR MERCHANT'S HOUSE
MANORBIER CASTLE
STACKPOLE
ELEGUG STACKS
NATIONAL NATURE RESERVE
SKOMER ISLAND
MARLOES SANDS
BISHOP'S PALACE
CATHEDRAL
TOLL
PEMBROKESHIRE COAST PATH
LLWYBR ARFORDIR PENFRO
0 1 2 3 4 5 6 miles
0 1 2 3 4 5 6 7 8 9 10 km

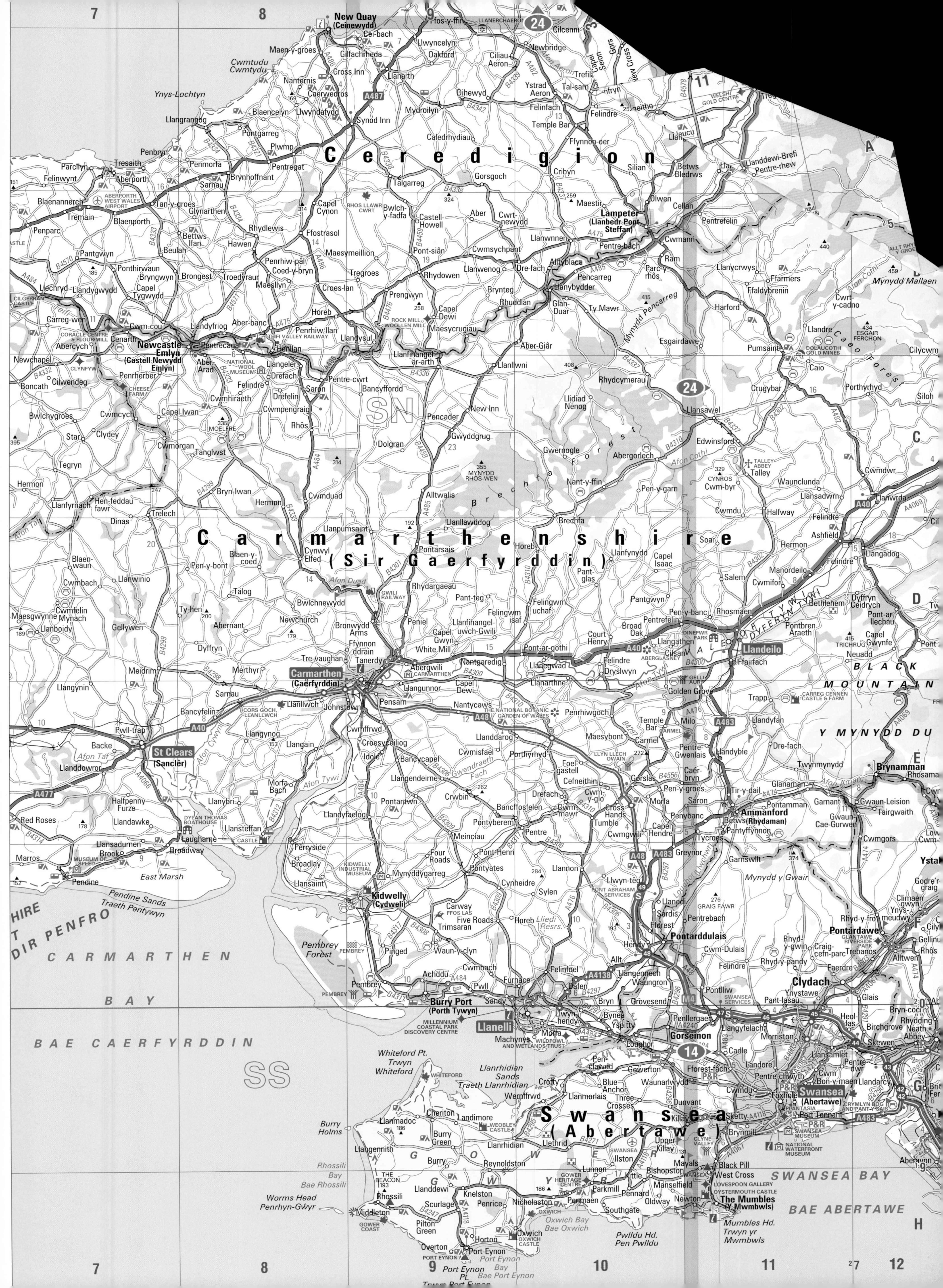
Ceredigion
Carmarthenshire
(Sir Gaerfyrddin)
Swansea
(Abertawe)
New Quay
(Ceinewydd)
Lampeter
(Llanbedr Pont Steffan)
Newcastle Emlyn
(Castell Newydd Emlyn)
Carmarthen
(Caerfyrddin)
St Clears
(Sanclêr)
Llandeilo
Ammanford
(Rhydaman)
Kidwelly
(Cydweli)
Burry Port
(Porth Tywyn)
Llanelli
Pontarddulais
Gorseinon
Pontardawe
Clydach
Brynamman
The Mumbles
(Y Mwmbwls)
Aberporth
Cardigan Bay
CARMARTHEN BAY
BAE CAERFYRDDIN
SWANSEA BAY
BAE ABERTAWE
BLACK MOUNTAIN
Y MYNYDD DU
Brechfa Forest
Caeo Forest
Mynydd Pencarreg
Pembrey Forest
GOWER
Worms Head
Penrhyn-Gŵyr
Rhossili Bay
Bae Rhossili
Oxwich Bay
Bae Oxwich
Port Eynon Bay
Mumbles Hd.
Whiteford Pt.
Llanrhidian Sands
Pendine Sands
Traeth Pentywyn
SN
SS

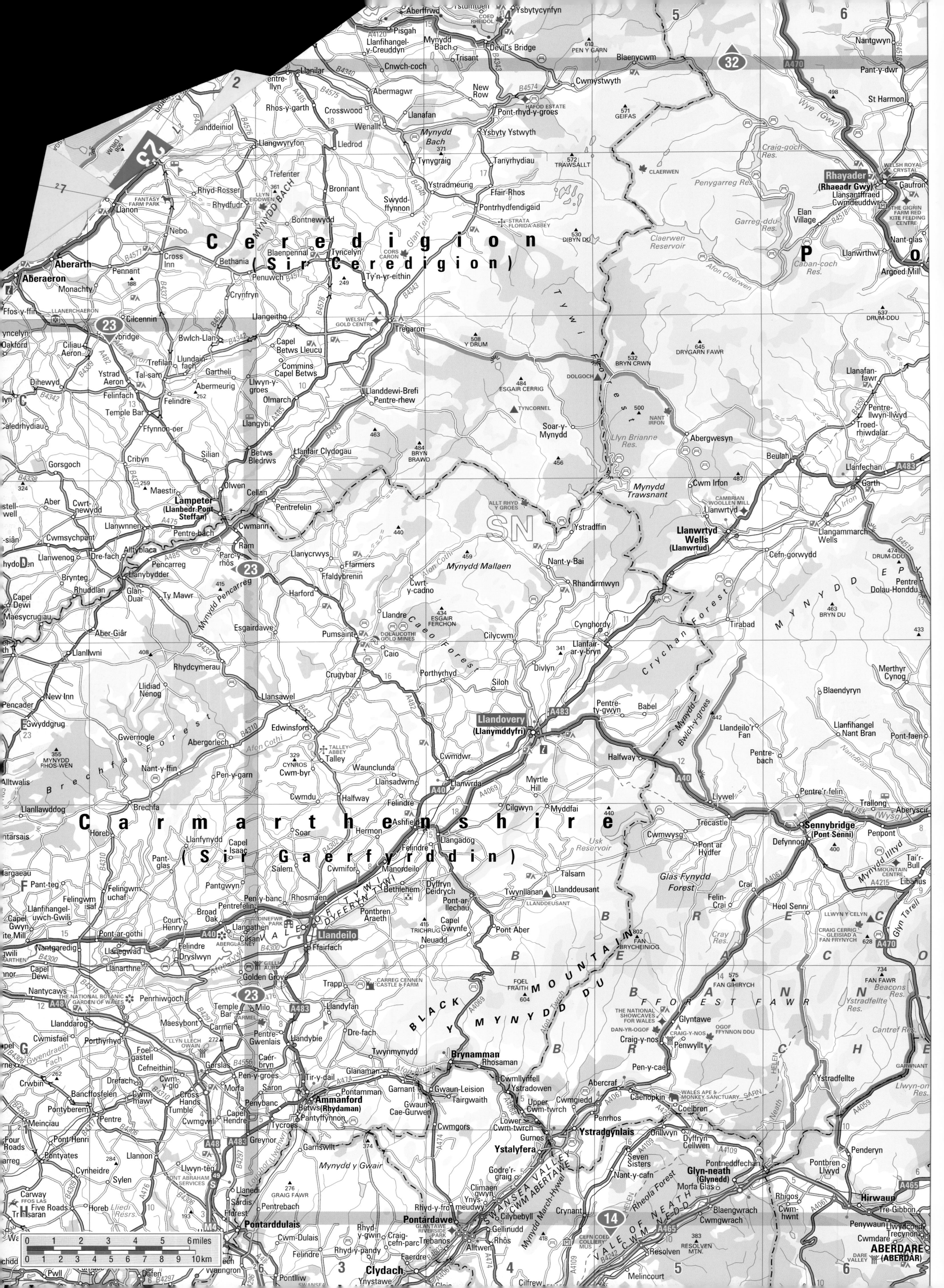

Ceredigion
(Sir Ceredigion)
Carmarthenshire
(Sir Gaerfyrddin)
P
o
SN
Aberffrwd
Ysbyty Cynfyn
Coed Rheidol
Pisgah
Llanfihangel-y-Creuddyn
Mynydd Bach
Trisant
Devil's Bridge
610 Pen y Garn
Blaenycwm
32
A470
Nantgwyn
Pant-y-dwr
St Harmon
498
Wye (Gwy)
Llanilar
B4340
Cnwch-coch
Abermagwr
Cwmystwyth
New Row
Pont-rhyd-y-groes
Hafod Estate
571 Geifas
Rhos-y-garth
Crosswood
Wenallt
Llanafan
Lledrod
Mynydd Bach
371
Ysbyty Ystwyth
Tynygraig
Tanyrhydiau
572 Trawsallt
Claerwen
Craig-goch Res.
Penygarreg Res.
Rhayader
(Rhaeadr Gwy)
Llansantffraed Cwmdeuddwr
Welsh Royal Crystal
Gaufron
Llangwyryfon
Trefenter
Bronnant
Ystradmeurig
Ffair-Rhos
Pontrhydfendigaid
Strata Florida Abbey
Swydd-ffynnon
Llyn Eiddwen
Mynydd Bach
Rhyd-Rosser
Rhydfudr
Fantasy Farm Park
Llanon
Nebo
Bontnewydd
Glan Teifi
530 Dibyn Du
Garreg-ddu Res.
Claerwen Reservoir
Elan Village
The Gigrin Farm Red Kite Feeding Centre
Nant-glas
Llanwrthwl
Caban-coch Res.
Afon Claerwen
Argoed Mill
Aberarth
Aberaeron
Monachty
Pennant
188
Cross Inn
Bethania
Blaenpennal
Tyncelyn
Cors Caron
Penuwch
249
Ty'n-yr-eithin
Tywi Forest
Llannerchaeron
Ffos-y-ffin
Cilcennin
Crynfryn
Llangeitho
Welsh Gold Centre
Tregaron
537 Drum-ddu
23
Ystradaeron
Ciliau Aeron
Oakford
Bwlch-Llan
Capel Betws Lleucu
508 Y Drum
532 Bryn Crwn
645 Drygarn Fawr
Trefilan
Llundain-fach
Commins Capel Betws
Gartheli
Llwyn-y-groes
Dihewyd
Tal-sarn
Abermeurig
252
Olmarch
Llanddewi-Brefi
Pentre-rhew
484 Esgair Cerrig
Dolgoch
Llanafan-fawr
Felinfach
Temple Bar
Felindre
Ffynnon-oer
Llangybi
Tyncornel
500
Nant Irfon
Pentre-llwyn-llwyd
Troed-rhiwdalar
Caledrhydiau
Silian
463
484 Bryn Brawd
Soar-y-Mynydd
Llyn Brianne Res.
Abergwesyn
Gorsgoch
Cribyn
Betws Bledrws
Llanfair Clydogau
456
Beulah
Llanfechan
A483
Garth
324
Maestir
Lampeter
(Llanbedr Pont Steffan)
Olwen
Cellan
Mynydd Trawsnant
Cwm Irfon
487
Cambrian Woollen Mill
Llanwrtyd
Aber
Cwrt-newydd
Pentrefelin
Allt Rhyd y Groes
Irfon
Llanwnnen
Cwmann
Ystradffin
Llanwrtyd Wells
(Llanwrtud)
Llangammarch Wells
Cwmsychpant
Pentre-bach
Ram
440
Llanwenog
Dre-fach
Alltyblaca
Llanybydder
Parc-y-rhôs
Llanycrwys
459
Mynydd Mallaen
Nant-y-Bai
Cefn-gorwydd
474 Drum-ddu
B4519
Pencarreg
Ffarmers
Afon Cothi
Epynt
Pentre Dolau-Honddu
Brynteg
Rhuddlan
Ffaldybrenin
Rhandirmwyn
Glan-Duar
Ty Mawr
415
Mynydd Pencarreg
Harford
Cwrt-y-cadno
Capel Dewi
Maesycrugiau
434 Esgair Ferchon
Cynghordy
Mynydd
Llandre
Caeo Forest
Tirabad
463 Bryn Du
Aber-Giâr
Esgairdawe
Pumsaint
Dolaucothi Gold Mines
Cilycwm
11
Crychan Forest
433
Llanllwni
408
Caio
341
Llanfair-ar-y-bryn
Rhydcymerau
Crugybar
16
Porthyrhyd
Silod
Divlyn
Merthyr Cynog
Lllidiad Nenog
Pentre-ty-gwyn
Babel
Blaendyryn
New Inn
Pencader
Llansawel
Llandovery
(Llanymddyfri)
Mynydd Bwlch-y-groes
442
Llanfihangel Nant Bran
Gwyddgrug
Edwinsford
Llandeilo'r Fan
Pont-faen
Gwernogle
Abergorlech
Afon Cothi
329 Cynros
Talley Abbey
Talley
Cwm-byr
Waunclunda
Cwmdwr
Halfway
Pentre-bach
Brechfa Forest
355 Mynydd Rhos-wen
Nant-y-ffin
Pen-y-garn
Llansadwrn
Llanwrda
Myrtle Hill
A40
Alltwalis
Cwmdu
Halfway
A4069
Llywel
Pentre'r-felin
Trallong
Aberyscir
Llanllawddog
Brechfa
Felindre
Cilgwyn
Myddfai
440
Usk (Wysg)
Horeb
Ashfield
Hermon
Soar
Llangadog
Trecastle
Sennybridge
(Pont Senni)
Defynnog
Penpont
Llanfynydd
Capel Isaac
Felindre
Cwmwysg
Usk Reservoir
Pont ar Hydfer
400
Mynydd Illtyd
Tai'r-Bull
Mountain Centre
Pant-glas
Salem
Cwmifor
Manordeilo
Talsarn
Glas Fynydd Forest
Crai
A4215
Libanus
Pant-teg
Felingwm uchaf
Pantgwyn
Bethlehem
Dyffryn Ceidrych
Twynllanan
Llanddeusant
Felin-Crai
Llanfihangel-uwch-Gwili
Felingwm isaf
Pen-y-banc
Rhosmaen
Tywi
Dyffryn Tywi
Pontbren Araeth
Pont-ar-llechau
Heol Senni
Llwyn y Celyn
Broad Oak
Pentrefelin
Dinefwr Park
Capel Gwynfe
Court Henry
Llangathen
Vale of Tywi
Llandeilo
415 Trichrug
Pont Aber
802 Fan Brycheiniog
Cray Res.
Craig Cerrig Gleisiad a Fan Frynych
628
Glyn Tarell
A470
Capel Gwyn
Pont-ar-gothi
Cilsan
Aberglasney
Felindre
Dryslwyn
Ffairfach
Neuadd
Black Mountain
Y Mynydd Du
Brecon Beacons
Fforest Fawr
Nantgaredig
Llanegwad
B4300
Llanarthne
Afon Tywi
Gelli Aur
Golden Grove
Capel Dewi
Trapp
Carreg Cennen Castle & Farm
Foel Fraith 604
14 575 Fan Gihirych
734 Fan Fawr
Beacons Res.
Nantycaws
The National Botanic Garden of Wales
Penrhiwgoch
A48
A476
Milo
Temple Bar
Llandyfan
A4069
The National Showcaves for Wales
Dan-yr-Ogof
Glyntawe
Ogof Ffynnon Ddu
Ystradfellte Res.
Llanddarog
Maesybont
Carmel
Dre-fach
Craig-y-nos
Penwyllt
Cantref Res.
Cwmisfael
Porthyrhyd
Llyn Llech Owain
Pentre-Gwenlais
Llandybie
Gwendraeth Fach
272
Foel-gastell
Caer-bryn
Twynmynydd
Brynamman
Rhosaman
Cefneithin
Gorslas
Afon Aman
Pen-y-cae
Garwnant
Crwbin
262
Drefach
Cwm-y-glo
Pen-y-groes
Glanaman
Tir-y-dail
Cwmllynfell
Ystradowen
Abercraf
Ystradfellte
Llwyn-on Res.
Bancffosfelen
Cwm-mawr
Morfa
Saron
Pontamman
Garnant
Gwaun-Leision
Tairgwaith
Cwmgiedd
Caehopkin
Wales Ape & Monkey Sanctuary
Sarn Helen
Cross Hands
Tumble
Penybanc
Ammanford
(Rhydaman)
Gwaun-Cae-Gurwen
Upper Cwm-twrch
Coelbren
Neath
Pontyberem
Pentre
Cwmgwili
Capel Hendre
Betws
Pantyffynnon
Tycroes
Cwmgors
Lower Cwm-twrch
Penrhos
Ystradgynlais
Onllwyn
Dyffryn Cellwen
A4059
Meinciau
Greynor
Garnswllt
374
Gurnos
Ystalyfera
Penderyn
Four Roads
Pont-Henri
Pontyates
Llannon
Loughor (Llwchwr)
Mynydd y Gwair
Godre'r-graig
Seven Sisters
Pontneddfechan
Pontbren Llwyd
Cynheidre
Sylen
Llwyn-teg
Pont Abraham Services
Nant-y-cafn
Glyn-neath
(Glynedd)
Carway
Ffos Las
Five Roads
Horeb
Llannedi
Sardis
276 Graig Fawr
Climaen-gwyn
Ynys-meudwy
Swansea Valley
Cwm Abertawe
Rheola Forest
Morfa Glas
Rhigos
Hirwaun
A465
Trimsaran
Lliedi Resrs.
Fforest
Pentrebach
Rhyd-y-fro
Cilybebyll
Crynant
Blaengwrach
Cwmgwrach
Cwm-hwnt
Tre-Gibbon
Pontarddulais
Rhyd-y-gwin
Craig-cefn-parc
Pontardawe
Glantawe Riverside Park
Gellinudd
14
Vale of Neath
Cwm Nedd
Penywaun
Llwydcoed
Trecynon
Cwmdare
193
M4
Cwm-Dulais
Trebanos
Rhôs
Mynydd March-Hywel
418
Cefn Coed Colliery Museum
383 Resolven Mtn.
Aberdare
(Aberdar)
Dare Valley
Felindre
Rhyd-y-pandy
Faerdre
Alltwen
Resolven
Pwll
Dafen
Pontlliw
Clydach
Ynystawe
Cilfrew
Melincourt
0 1 2 3 4 5 6 miles
0 1 2 3 4 5 6 7 8 9 10km
2
3
4
5
6
C
D
E
F
G
H

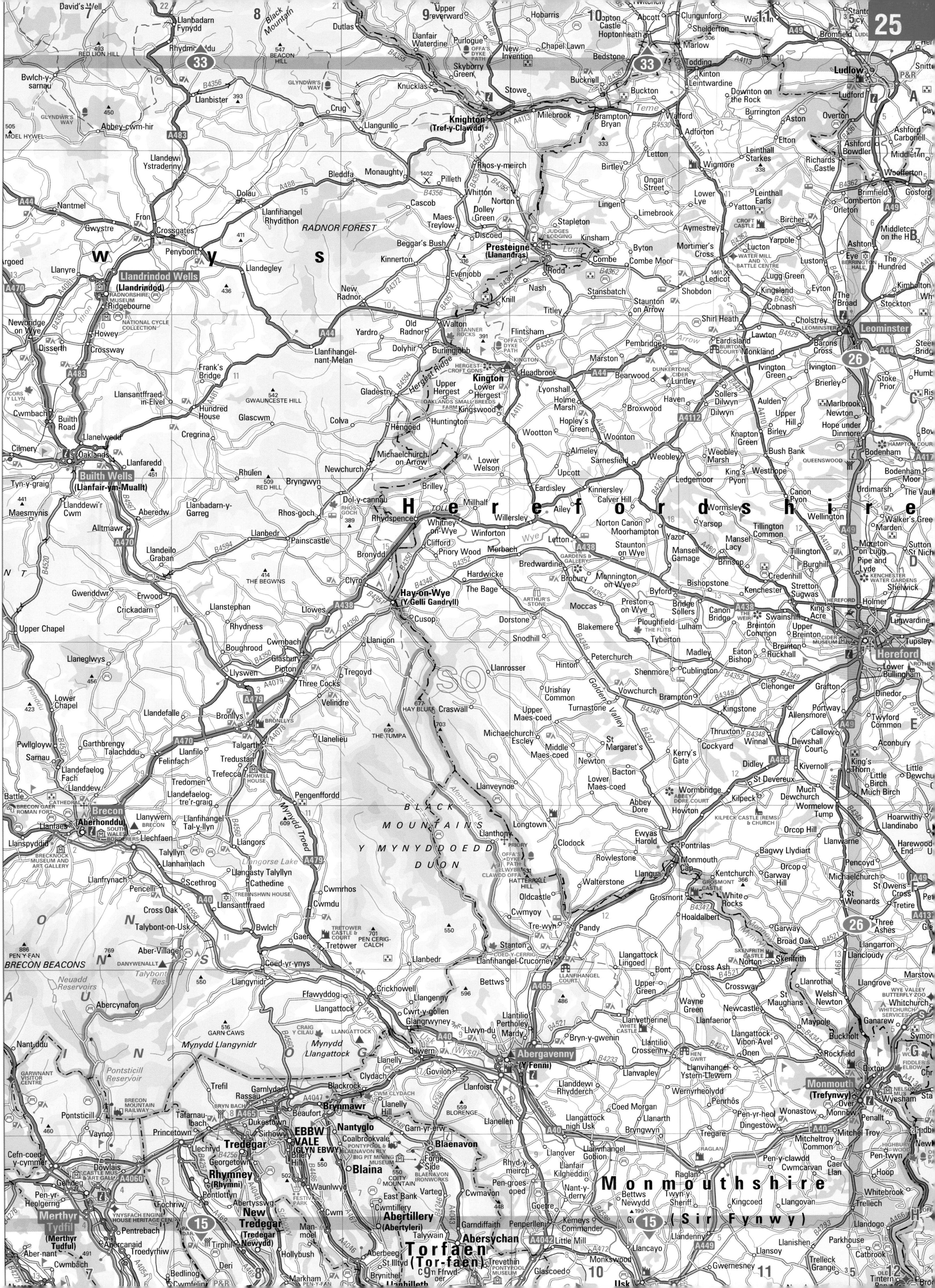
Knighton (Tref-y-Clawdd)
Presteigne (Llanandras)
Llandrindod Wells (Llandrindod)
Builth Wells (Llanfair-ym-Muallt)
Kington
Hay-on-Wye (Y Gelli Gandryll)
Brecon (Aberhonddu)
Abergavenny (Y Fenni)
Monmouth (Trefynwy)
Hereford
Leominster
Ludlow
Herefordshire
Monmouthshire (Sir Fynwy)
Torfaen (Tor-faen)
Merthyr Tydfil (Merthyr Tudful)
Tredegar
Ebbw Vale (Glyn Ebwy)
Brynmawr
Nantyglo
Blaenavon
Blaina
Abertillery (Abertyleri)
Abersychan
New Tredegar (Tredegar Newydd)
Rhymney (Rhymni)
Crickhowell
Talgarth
Bronllys
Glasbury
Llyswen
Erwood
Painscastle
Clyro
Whitney-on-Wye
Eardisley
Weobley
Pembridge
Kingsland
Wigmore
Leintwardine
Brampton Bryan
Bucknell
Stowe
Knucklas
Llangunllo
Bleddfa
Monaughty
Pilleth
Whitton
Norton
Discoed
Kinnerton
New Radnor
Old Radnor
Walton
Evenjobb
Knill
Titley
Staunton on Arrow
Shobdon
Mortimer's Cross
Lucton
Yarpole
Eye
Orleton
Richards Castle
Aymestrey
Lingen
Kinsham
Byton
Combe
Stapleton
Rodd
Nash
Stansbatch
Lyonshall
Almeley
Sarnesfield
Dilwyn
Bodenham
Marden
Wellington
Canon Pyon
King's Pyon
Mansel Lacy
Yazor
Credenhill
Kenchester
Swainshill
Breinton
Madley
Eaton Bishop
Clehonger
Kingstone
Allensmore
Cockyard
Thruxton
Kerry's Gate
Wormbridge
Kilpeck
Much Dewchurch
St Devereux
Pontrilas
Ewyas Harold
Abbey Dore
Bacton
Vowchurch
Peterchurch
Dorstone
Moccas
Bredwardine
Brobury
Staunton on Wye
Letton
Willersley
Winforton
Clifford
Cusop
Llanigon
Craswall
Longtown
Clodock
Llanthony
Cwmyoy
Pandy
Grosmont
Skenfrith
Garway
Llanvetherine
Llantilio Crossenny
Raglan
Dingestow
Mitchel Troy
Penallt
Llanover
Goytre
Usk
Llanfoist
Govilon
Gilwern
Llanelly
Clydach
Bwlch
Llangynidr
Llangattock
Talybont-on-Usk
Llansantffraed
Pencelli
Llanfrynach
Llanfaes
Llanspyddid
Sarnau
Battle
Felinfach
Llanfilo
Trefecca
Llangorse
Talyllyn
Llanhamlach
Cathedine
Scethrog
Tretower
Cwmdu
Llanbedr
Bettws
Llanvihangel Crucorney
Llangattock Lingoed
Cross Ash
Newcastle
Wonastow
Rockfield
Dixton
Cwmcarvan
Trellech
Llandogo
Penyclawdd
Black Mountains
Y Mynyddoedd Duon
Radnor Forest
Brecon Beacons
Mynydd Llangynidr
Mynydd Llangattock
Mynydd Troed
Hergest Ridge
Golden Valley
Llangorse Lake
Pontsticill Reservoir
Talybont Res.
Neuadd Reservoirs
Hay Bluff
The Tumpa
The Begwns
Gwaunceste Hill
Red Hill
Offa's Dyke Path
Glyndŵr's Way
A44
A438
A470
A479
A40
A465
A49
A4113
A483
A488
A481
A4112
A4110
A466
A4042
A4047
A4060
A449
33
15
26

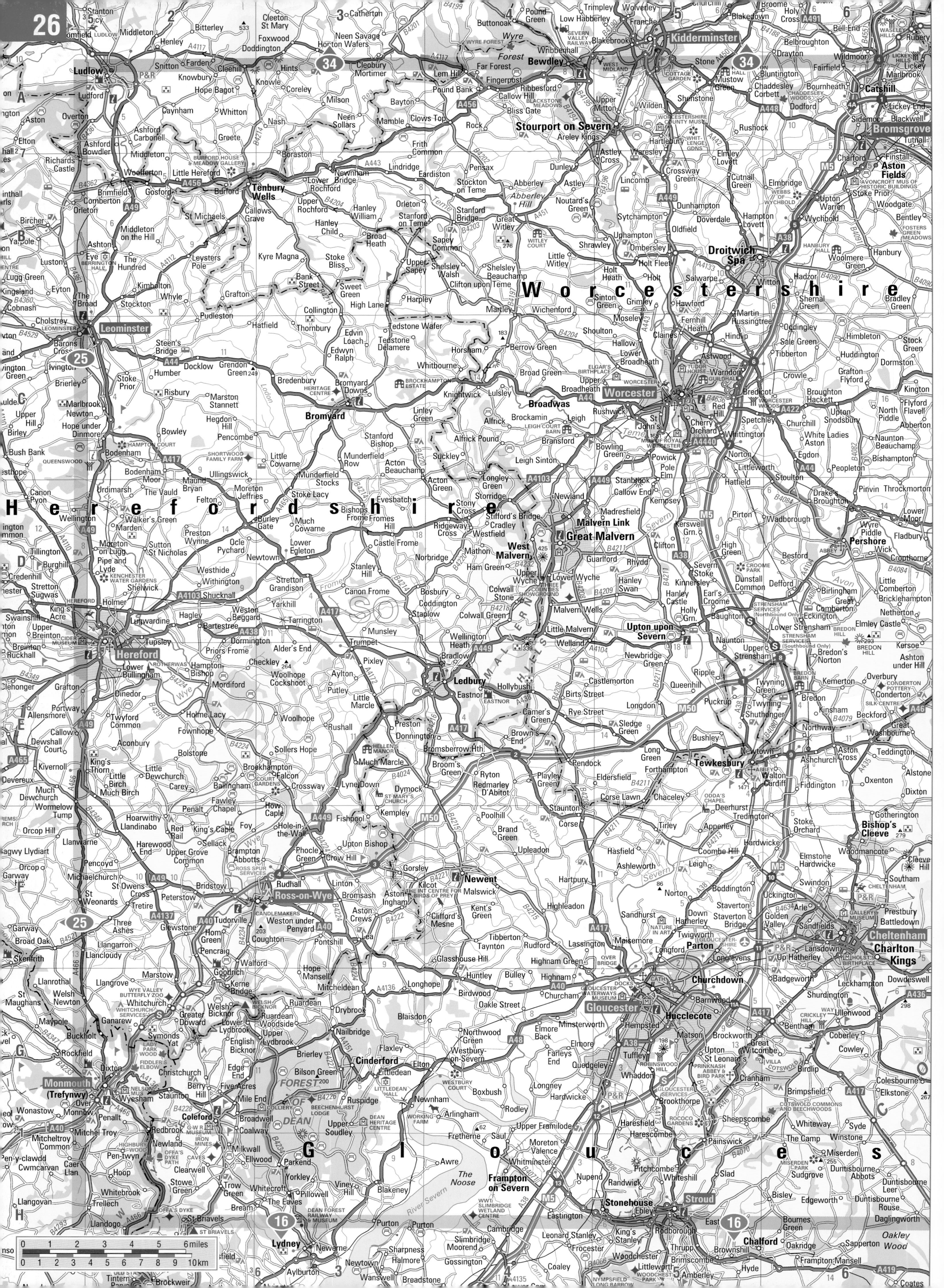
Ludlow
Kidderminster
Bewdley
Stourport on Severn
Bromsgrove
Catshill
Tenbury Wells
Leominster
Droitwich Spa
Worcestershire
Worcester
Bromyard
Herefordshire
Hereford
Great Malvern
Malvern Link
West Malvern
Upton upon Severn
Pershore
Ledbury
Tewkesbury
Newent
Ross-on-Wye
Gloucester
Cheltenham
Charlton Kings
Hucclecote
Churchdown
Bishop's Cleeve
Monmouth
(Trefynwy)
Coleford
Cinderford
Lydney
Stonehouse
Stroud
Chalford
Frampton on Severn
Forest of Dean
Gloucestershire
Wyre Forest
Abberley Hill
Malvern Hills
The Noose
River Severn
Oakley Wood
Teme
Wye
Severn
Leadon
Lugg
Frome
Avon
Tenbury Wells
Broadwas
Parton
Bredon
Cleobury Mortimer
Clee St Margaret
Aston Fields
Hanley Castle
Tupsley
Mordiford
Fownhope
Dymock
Much Marcle
Huntley
Mitcheldean
Drybrook
Whitchurch
Goodrich
Symonds Yat
Rodborough
Painswick
Brockworth
Shurdington
Leckhampton
Hardwicke
Quedgeley
Tuffley
Matson
Hempsted
0 1 2 3 4 5 6 miles
0 1 2 3 4 5 6 7 8 9 10 km
34
25
16

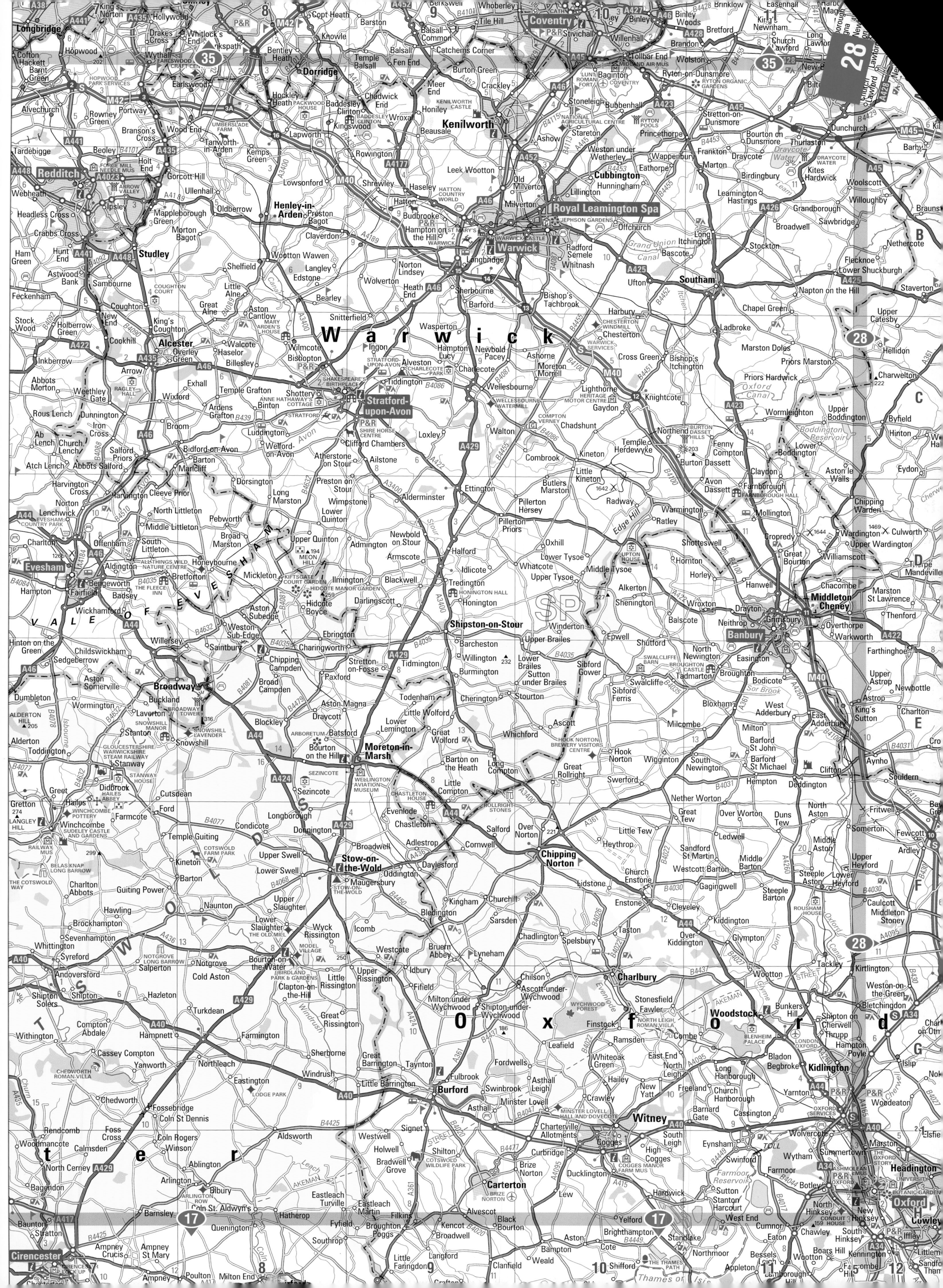
28
Longbridge
King's Norton
Hollywood
Whitlock's End
Drakes Cross
Hopwood
Cofton Hackett
Barnt Green
Wythall
Earlswood
Alvechurch
Rowney Green
Portway
Branson's Cross
Wood End
Tardebigge
Beoley
Holt End
Redditch
Webheath
Headless Cross
Crabbs Cross
Ipsley
Mappleborough Green
Morton Bagot
Ham Green
Hunt End
Studley
Astwood Bank
Sambourne
Feckenham
Coughton
Stock Wood
New End
Holberrow Green
King's Coughton
Cookhill
Alcester
Inkberrow
Arrow
Abbots Morton
Weethley Gate
Rous Lench
Dunnington
Ab Lench
Church Lench
Iron Cross
Salford Priors
Atch Lench
Abbots Salford
Harvington Cross
Harvington
Norton
Lenchwick
Charlton
Offenham
Evesham
Bengeworth
Fairfield
Hampton
Badsey
Wickhamford
Hinton on the Green
Childswickham
Sedgeberrow
Aston Somerville
Dumbleton
Wormington
Alderton
Toddington
Stanton
Snowshill
Stanway
Didbrook
Greet
Hailes
Winchcombe
Gretton
Langley Hill
Farmcote
Ford
Cutsdean
Temple Guiting
Kineton
Barton
Guiting Power
Charlton Abbots
Hawling
Naunton
Brockhampton
Sevenhampton
Whittington
Syreford
Andoversford
Salperton
Shipton
Shipton Solers
Hazleton
Notgrove
Cold Aston
Compton Abdale
Withington
Turkdean
Hampnett
Cassey Compton
Yanworth
Northleach
Chedworth
Fossebridge
Coln St Dennis
Rendcomb
Woodmancote
Calmsden
Foss Cross
Coln Rogers
Winson
North Cerney
Ablington
Arlington
Bibury
Bagendon
Barnsley
Coln St. Aldwyn's
Baunton
Stratton
Cirencester
Ampney Crucis
Ampney St Mary
Quenington
Poulton
Milton End
Hatherop
Southrop
Fyfield
Eastleach Turville
Eastleach Martin
Aldsworth
Sherborne
Windrush
Great Barrington
Little Barrington
Taynton
Burford
Fulbrook
Signet
Westwell
Holwell
Shilton
Bradwell Grove
Kencot
Broadwell
Filkins
Broughton Poggs
Langford
Little Faringdon
Alvescot
Black Bourton
Clanfield
Carterton
Brize Norton
Curbridge
Bampton
Aston
Cote
Weald
Shifford
Yelford
Brighthampton
Standlake
Lew
Ducklington
Witney
Cogges
High Cogges
South Leigh
Hardwick
Northmoor
Stanton Harcourt
Sutton
Eynsham
Swinford
Farmoor
Wytham
West End
Cumnor
Bessels
Appleton
Eaton
Wootton
Boars Hill
Chawley
Botley
North Hinksey
New Hinksey
South Hinksey
Kennington
Iffley
Cowley
Oxford
Headington
Marston
Summertown
Wolvercote
Cassington
Yarnton
Kidlington
Begbroke
Bladon
Long Hanborough
Church Hanborough
Freeland
Barnard Gate
North Leigh
East End
New Yatt
Hailey
Crawley
Minster Lovell
Asthall
Asthall Leigh
Swinbrook
Fordwells
Leafield
Whiteoak Green
Ramsden
Finstock
Combe
Woodstock
Stonesfield
Fawler
Charlbury
Ascott-under-Wychwood
Shipton-under-Wychwood
Milton under Wychwood
Chilson
Lyneham
Bruern Abbey
Idbury
Fifield
Westcote
Icomb
Bledington
Kingham
Churchill
Sarsden
Chadlington
Spelsbury
Taston
Enstone
Church Enstone
Cleveley
Lidstone
Chipping Norton
Over Norton
Salford
Cornwell
Little Rollright
Great Rollright
Swerford
Hook Norton
Wigginton
South Newington
Barford St John
Barford St Michael
Milton
Bloxham
Milcombe
Adderbury
Deddington
Clifton
Hempton
Nether Worton
Over Worton
Great Tew
Little Tew
Duns Tew
Heythrop
Sandford St Martin
Ledwell
Westcott Barton
Middle Barton
Steeple Barton
Gagingwell
Kiddington
Over Kiddington
Glympton
Wootton
Tackley
Kirtlington
Bletchingdon
Weston-on-the-Green
Shipton on Cherwell
Thrupp
Hampton Poyle
Islip
Bunkers Hill
Rousham
Steeple Aston
Middle Aston
North Aston
Lower Heyford
Upper Heyford
Caulcott
Middleton Stoney
Somerton
Fritwell
Fewcott
Ardley
Souldern
Aynho
Charlton
King's Sutton
Astrop
Newbottle
Upper Astrop
Farthinghoe
Warkworth
Overthorpe
Thenford
Marston St Lawrence
Middleton Cheney
Chacombe
Banbury
Grimsbury
Neithrop
Drayton
Wroxton
Balscote
Hanwell
Horley
Hornton
Shotteswell
Warmington
Ratley
Alkerton
Shenington
Epwell
Shutford
North Newington
Broughton
Tadmarton
Swalcliffe
Sibford Ferris
Sibford Gower
Bodicote
Easington
Wardington
Upper Wardington
Williamscott
Cropredy
Great Bourton
Mollington
Claydon
Chipping Warden
Culworth
Edgcote
Eydon
Aston le Walls
Lower Boddington
Upper Boddington
Byfield
Hinton
Wormleighton
Fenny Compton
Burton Dassett
Avon Dassett
Farnborough
Northend
Knightcote
Gaydon
Lighthorne
Chadshunt
Kineton
Little Kineton
Radway
Butlers Marston
Combrook
Temple Herdewycke
Pillerton Hersey
Pillerton Priors
Oxhill
Lower Tysoe
Middle Tysoe
Upper Tysoe
Whatcote
Idlicote
Tredington
Honington
Halford
Ettington
Alderminster
Shipston-on-Stour
Barcheston
Willington
Burmington
Winderton
Upper Brailes
Lower Brailes
Sutton under Brailes
Cherington
Stourton
Whichford
Ascott
Long Compton
Little Compton
Barton on the Heath
Great Wolford
Little Wolford
Todenham
Tidmington
Stretton-on-Fosse
Paxford
Ebrington
Charingworth
Chipping Campden
Broad Campden
Aston Magna
Draycott
Blockley
Batsford
Bourton on the Hill
Moreton-in-Marsh
Sezincote
Longborough
Donnington
Evenlode
Chastleton
Adlestrop
Broadwell
Oddington
Daylesford
Stow-on-the-Wold
Maugersbury
Upper Swell
Lower Swell
Condicote
Upper Slaughter
Lower Slaughter
Wyck Rissington
Bourton-on-the-Water
Little Rissington
Great Rissington
Upper Rissington
Clapton-on-the-Hill
Farmington
Eastington
Broadway
Buckland
Laverton
Willersey
Saintbury
Weston Sub-Edge
Aston Subedge
Mickleton
Hidcote Boyce
Ilmington
Darlingscott
Blackwell
Armscote
Admington
Newbold on Stour
Upper Quinton
Lower Quinton
Wimpstone
Preston on Stour
Atherstone on Stour
Long Marston
Dorsington
Pebworth
Broad Marston
Honeybourne
Bretforton
Aldington
South Littleton
Middle Littleton
North Littleton
Cleeve Prior
Marlcliff
Bidford-on-Avon
Broom
Welford-on-Avon
Luddington
Clifford Chambers
Ailstone
Loxley
Walton
Wellesbourne
Charlecote
Hampton Lucy
Newbold Pacey
Ashorne
Moreton Morrell
Stratford-upon-Avon
Tiddington
Alveston
Shottery
Binton
Temple Grafton
Ardens Grafton
Exhall
Wixford
Haselor
Walcote
Billesley
Bishopton
Wilmcote
Ingon
Snitterfield
Wasperton
Barford
Sherbourne
Bearley
Aston Cantlow
Great Alne
Little Alne
Shelfield
Wootton Wawen
Langley
Edstone
Wolverton
Norton Lindsey
Heath End
Claverdon
Henley-in-Arden
Preston Bagot
Oldberrow
Ullenhall
Gorcott Hill
Tanworth-in-Arden
Kemps Green
Lapworth
Lowsonford
Rowington
Shrewley
Hatton
Haseley
Budbrooke
Hampton on the Hill
Warwick
Longbridge
Leek Wootton
Old Milverton
Milverton
Royal Leamington Spa
Lillington
Cubbington
Hunningham
Offchurch
Radford Semele
Whitnash
Bishop's Tachbrook
Harbury
Chesterton
Ufton
Southam
Long Itchington
Bascote
Stockton
Ladbroke
Bishop's Itchington
Cross Green
Marston Doles
Priors Marston
Priors Hardwick
Napton on the Hill
Chapel Green
Upper Catesby
Hellidon
Charwelton
Staverton
Lower Shuckburgh
Flecknoe
Nethercote
Broadwell
Sawbridge
Grandborough
Willoughby
Woolscott
Kites Hardwick
Birdingbury
Leamington Hastings
Marton
Frankton
Draycote
Thurlaston
Dunchurch
Bourton on Dunsmore
Stretton-on-Dunsmore
Princethorpe
Wappenbury
Eathorpe
Weston under Wetherley
Stareton
Ashow
Stoneleigh
Bubbenhall
Ryton-on-Dunsmore
Baginton
Kenilworth
Crackley
Burton Green
Beausale
Honiley
Wroxall
Meer End
Baddesley Clinton
Kingswood
Chadwick End
Hockley Heath
Dorridge
Bentley Heath
Knowle
Temple Balsall
Balsall
Fen End
Balsall Common
Catchems Corner
Barston
Copt Heath
Berkswell
Tile Hill
Whoberley
Coventry
Stivichall
Willenhall
Binley
Binley Woods
Tollbar End
Brandon
Wolston
Bretford
Brinklow
Easenhall
King's Newnham
Church Lawford
Long Lawford
Warwick
Oxford
Vale of Evesham
Cotswolds

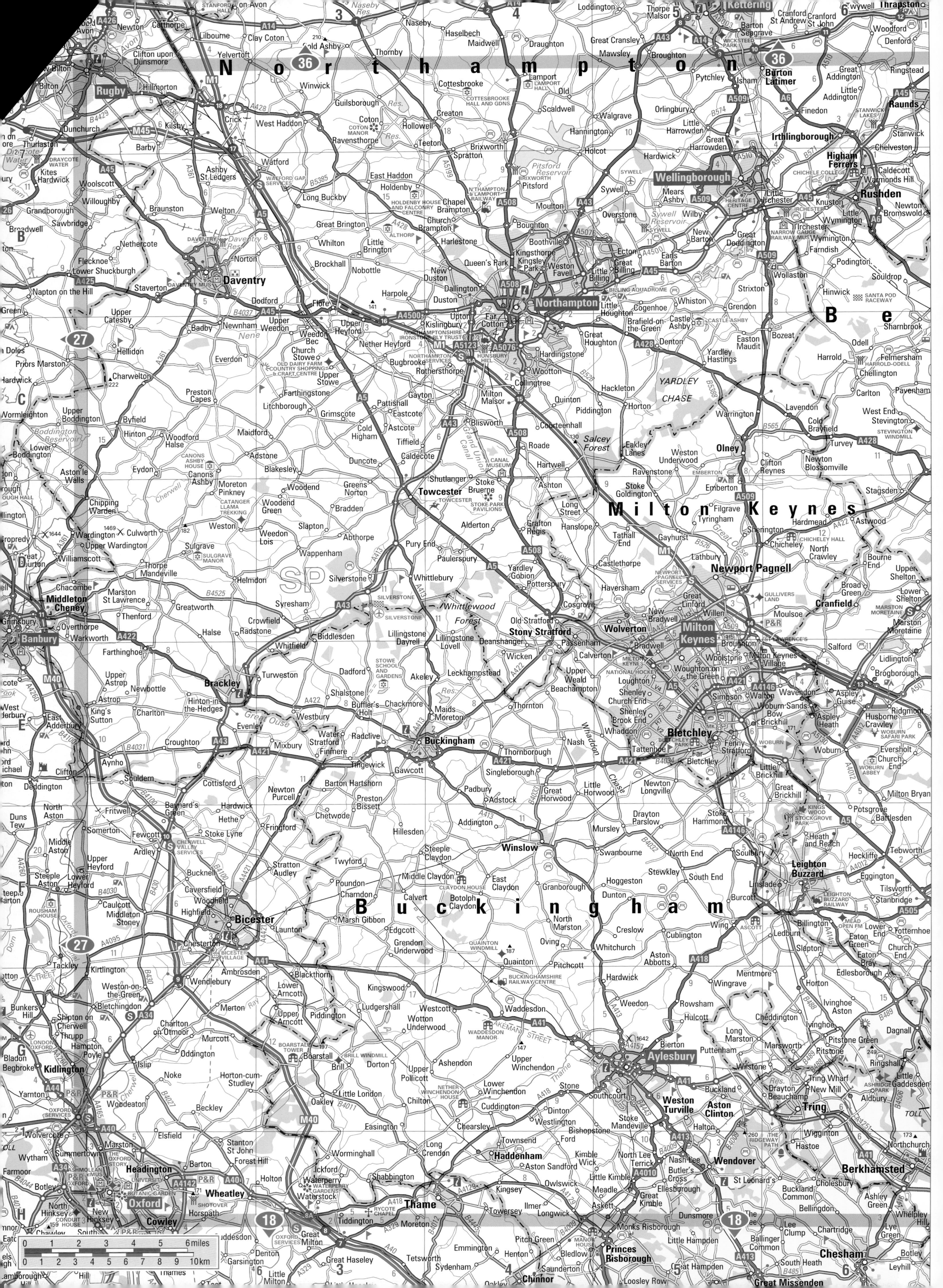
Northampton
Milton Keynes
Buckingham
Kettering
Rugby
Wellingborough
Northampton
Milton Keynes
Banbury
Aylesbury
Oxford
Daventry
Towcester
Brackley
Buckingham
Bicester
Bletchley
Newport Pagnell
Olney
Winslow
Leighton Buzzard
Tring
Thame
Wendover
Berkhamsted
Chesham
Princes Risborough
Kidlington
Rushden
Higham Ferrers
Irthlingborough
Raunds
Burton Latimer
Thrapston
Stony Stratford
Wolverton
Cranfield
Middleton Cheney
Haddenham
Wheatley
Headington
Cowley
Great Missenden
36
27
18
0 1 2 3 4 5 6 miles
0 1 2 3 4 5 6 7 8 9 10km

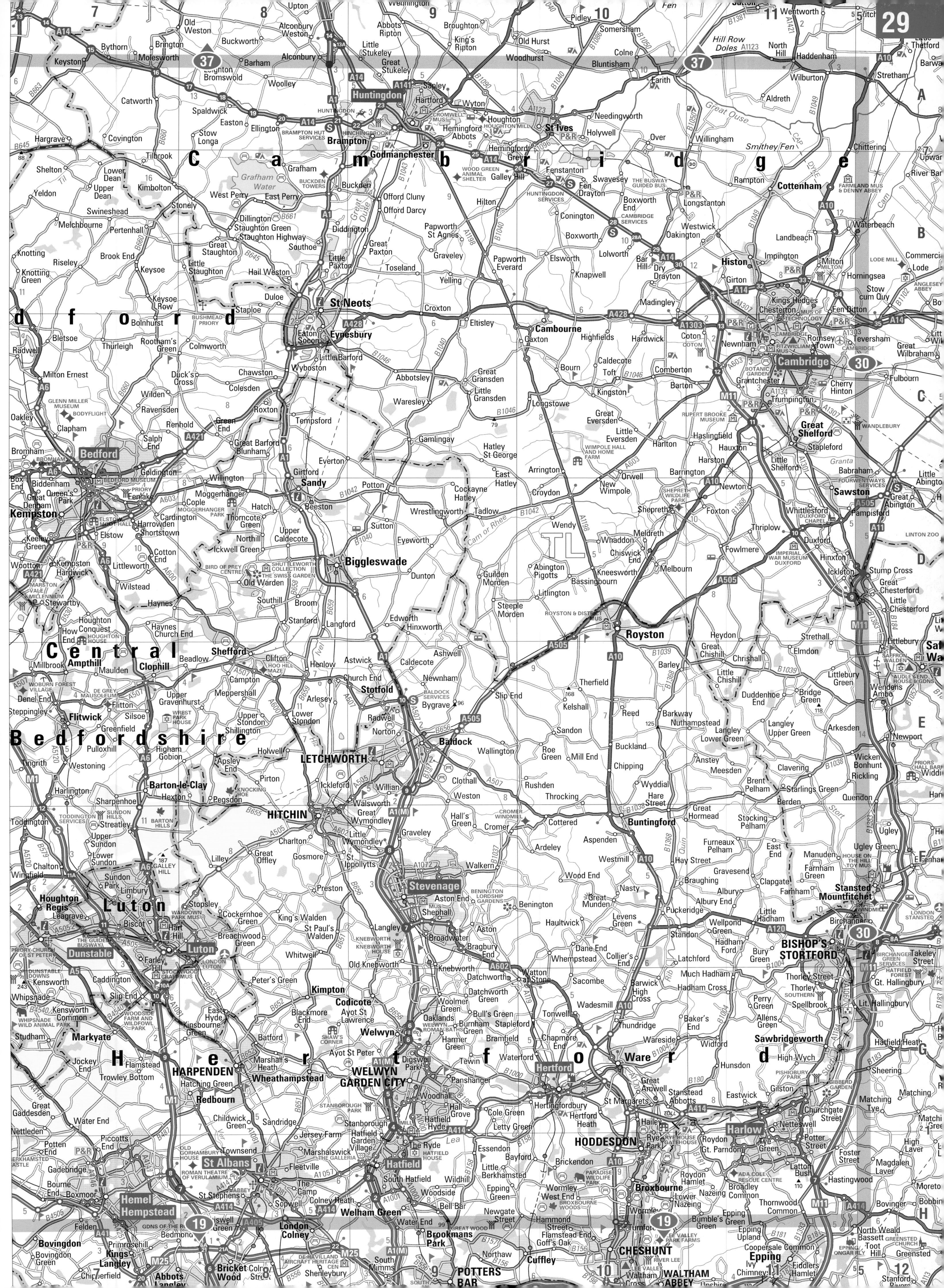
Upton
Wennington
Broughton
Old Hurst
Pidley
Somersham
Fen
Sutton
Wentworth
Old Weston
Alconbury Weston
Abbots Ripton
King's Ripton
Colne
Hill Row
Doles
North Hill
Haddenham
Little Thetford
Bythorn
Brington
Buckworth
Little Stukeley
Great Stukeley
Woodhurst
Bluntisham
Earith
Stretham
Keyston
Molesworth
Barham
Alconbury
Leighton Bromswold
Woolley
Huntingdon
Sapley
Hartford
Wyton
Houghton
Wilburton
Aldreth
Catworth
Spaldwick
Easton
Ellington
Brampton
Needingworth
St Ives
Holywell
Hemingford Abbots
Hemingford Grey
Godmanchester
Great Ouse
Hargrave
Covington
Stow Longa
Tilbrook
Willingham
Over
Smithey Fen
Chittering
Cambridge
Shelton
Lower Dean
Upper Dean
Kimbolton
Grafham
Grafham Water
Buckden
Galley Hill
Fenstanton
Fen Drayton
Swavesey
Rampton
Cottenham
Yeldon
Stonely
West Perry
East Perry
Offord Cluny
Offord Darcy
Hilton
Boxworth End
Longstanton
Swineshead
Melchbourne
Pertenhall
Dillington
Staughton Green
Staughton Highway
Diddington
Papworth St Agnes
Conington
Westwick
Oakington
Waterbeach
Landbeach
Great Staughton
Southoe
Great Paxton
Boxworth
Lolworth
Knotting
Riseley
Brook End
Keysoe
Little Staughton
Hail Weston
Little Paxton
Toseland
Graveley
Papworth Everard
Elsworth
Bar Hill
Dry Drayton
Histon
Impington
Milton
Commercial End
Lode
Horningsea
Stow cum Quy
Knotting Green
Yelling
Knapwell
Girton
Keysoe Row
Duloe
Staploe
St Neots
Croxton
Eltisley
Madingley
Kings Hedges
Chesterton
Fen Ditton
Bolnhurst
Eaton Socon
Eynesbury
Cambourne
Caxton
Highfields
Hardwick
Coton
Newnham
Romsey Town
Teversham
Great Wilbraham
Bletsoe
Radwell
Thurleigh
Roxton's Green
Colmworth
Little Barford
Wyboston
Chawston
Colesden
Duck's Cross
Abbotsley
Great Gransden
Little Gransden
Bourn
Caldecote
Toft
Comberton
Barton
Grantchester
Cherry Hinton
Fulbourn
Milton Ernest
Wilden
Ravensden
Waresley
Longstowe
Kingston
Trumpington
Oakley
Clapham
Roxton
Tempsford
Great Eversden
Little Eversden
Haslingfield
Hauxton
Great Shelford
Stapleford
Bromham
Bedford
Renhold
Salph End
Great Barford
Green End
Blunham
Gamlingay
Hatley St George
Harlton
Harston
Little Shelford
Babraham
Little Abington
Biddenham
Queen's Park
Goldington
Everton
Arrington
Orwell
Barrington
Great Abington
Sawston
Great Denham
Kempston
Willington
Moggerhanger
Cople
Girtford
Sandy
Potton
Cockayne Hatley
East Hatley
Croydon
New Wimpole
Newton
Foxton
Pampisford
Whittlesford
Shepreth
Cardington
Harrowden
Shortstown
Hatch
Thorncote Green
Upper Caldecote
Beeston
Wrestlingworth
Tadlow
Wendy
Whaddon
Meldreth
Thriplow
Duxford
Elstow
Keeley Green
Northill
Ickwell Green
Sutton
Eyeworth
Biggleswade
Dunton
Chiswick End
Melbourn
Fowlmere
Kneesworth
Hinxton
Ickleton
Stump Cross
Great Chesterford
Little Chesterford
Wootton
Kempston Hardwick
Littleworth
Cotton End
Old Warden
Wilstead
Haynes
Southill
Broom
Guilden Morden
Abington Pigotts
Bassingbourn
Litlington
Steeple Morden
Stewartby
Houghton Conquest
Haynes Church End
Stanford
Langford
Edworth
Hinxworth
Royston
Heydon
Strethall
Littlebury
How End
Ampthill
Shefford
Clifton
Henlow
Astwick
Ashwell
Caldecote
Great Chishill
Chrishall
Elmdon
Little Chishill
Barley
Central Bedfordshire
Millbrook
Maulden
Clophill
Beadlow
Campton
Church End
Stotfold
Newnham
Therfield
Littlebury Green
Wendens Ambo
Denel End
Upper Gravenhurst
Meppershall
Arlesey
Radwell
Bygrave
Slip End
Kelshall
Reed
Barkway
Nuthampstead
Duddenhoe End
Bridge Green
Flitwick
Flitton
Silsoe
Upper Stondon
Lower Stondon
Shillington
Norton
Baldock
Sandon
Langley Upper Green
Langley Lower Green
Arkesden
Newport
Steppingley
Greenfield
Pulloxhill
Higham Gobion
Holwell
Letchworth
Wallington
Roe Green
Mill End
Buckland
Anstey
Meesden
Wicken Bonhunt
Rickling
Tingrith
Westoning
Apsley End
Pirton
Ickleford
William
Clothall
Rushden
Chipping
Wyddial
Clavering
Brent Pelham
Starlings Green
Harlington
Barton-le-Clay
Sharpenhoe
Hexton
Pegsdon
Hitchin
Walsworth
Great Wymondley
Little Wymondley
Weston
Throcking
Hare Street
Great Hormead
Stocking Pelham
Berden
Quendon
Toddington
Streatley
Upper Sundon
Lower Sundon
Lilley
Charlton
Great Offley
Gosmore
St Ippollytts
Graveley
Hall's Green
Cromer
Cottered
Buntingford
Aspenden
Westmill
Furneaux Pelham
East End
Ugley
Ugley Green
Wingfield
Chalton
Sundon Park
Limbury
Preston
Walkern
Ardeley
Hay Street
Wood End
Gravesend
Braughing
Manuden
Farnham Green
Clapgate
Farnham
Houghton Regis
Leagrave
Luton
Biscot
Stopsley
Cockernhoe Green
King's Walden
St Paul's Walden
Stevenage
Aston End
Shephall
Benington
Great Munden
Nasty
Albury
Albury End
Stansted Mountfitchet
Dunstable
Hart Hill
Breachwood Green
Langley
Aston
Broadwater
Hault wick
Levens Green
Puckeridge
Standon
Wellpond Green
Little Hadham
Birchanger
Kensworth
Caddington
Farley Hill
Whitwell
Bragbury End
Dane End
Whempstead
Collier's End
Hadham Ford
Bury Green
Bishop's Stortford
Takeley Street
Whipsnade
Slip End
Peter's Green
Kimpton
Old Knebworth
Knebworth
Datchworth
Watton at Stone
Sacombe
Latchford
Much Hadham
Hadham Cross
Thorley Street
Thorley
Gt. Hallingbury
Lit. Hallingbury
Kensworth Common
Markyate
East Hyde
Codicote
Blackmore End
Ayot St Lawrence
Datchworth Green
Woolmer Green
Oaklands
Burnham Green
Bull's Green
Stapleford
Tonwell
Wadesmill
Barwick
High Cross
Perry Green
Spellbrook
Studham
Kinsbourne Green
Batford
Welwyn
Harmer Green
Bramfield
Chapmore End
Thundridge
Baker's End
Allens Green
Sawbridgeworth
Hatfield Heath
Jockey End
Flamstead
Harpenden
Marshall's Heath
Ayot St Peter
Digswell Park
Tewin
Waterford
Hertford
Ware
Wareside
Widford
High Wych
Hertfordshire
Trowley Bottom
Hatching Green
Wheathampstead
Welwyn Garden City
Panshanger
Great Amwell
Hunsdon
Sheering
Great Gaddesden
Redbourn
Woodhall
Hertingfordbury
St Margarets
Stanstead Abbotts
Eastwick
Gilston
Matching Tye
Matching
Water End
Childwick Green
Sandridge
Hatfield Hyde
Hill
Cole Green
Letty Green
Hertford Heath
Hailey
Rye Park
Netteswell
Churchgate Street
Nettleden
Piccotts End
Potten End
Jersey Farm
Stanborough
Hatfield Garden Village
The Ryde
Essendon
Hoddesdon
Roydon
Gt. Parndon
Harlow
Tye Green
Potter Street
Foster Street
High Laver
Townsend
Marshalswick
St Albans
Fleetville
Hatfield
South Hatfield
Bayford
Little Berkhamsted
Brickendon
Roydon Hamlet
Latton Bush
Magdalen Laver
Gadebridge
Bourne End
Boxmoor
The Camp
Colney Heath
Wildhill
Woodside
Epping Green
Wormley
West End
Broxbourne
Lower Nazeing
Nazeing
Broadley Common
Hastingwood
Moreton
Hemel Hempstead
St Stephens
Welham Green
Bell Bar
Newgate Street
Wormley West End
Thornwood Common
Bovinger
Bobbingworth
Felden
Bedmond
London Colney
Water End
Brookmans Park
Hammond Street
Flamstead End
Goff's Oak
Turnford
Bumble's Green
Epping Green
Epping Upland
North Weald Bassett
Toot Hill
Bovingdon
Bovingdon Green
Primrose Hill
Kings Langley
Chipperfield
Abbots Langley
Bricket Wood
Colney Street
Shenley
South Mimms
Potters Bar
Northaw
Cuffley
Cheshunt
Waltham Cross
Waltham Abbey
Coopersale Common
Epping
Ivy Chimneys
Fiddlers Hamlet
Greensted
Stanford Rivers
Theydon Garnon

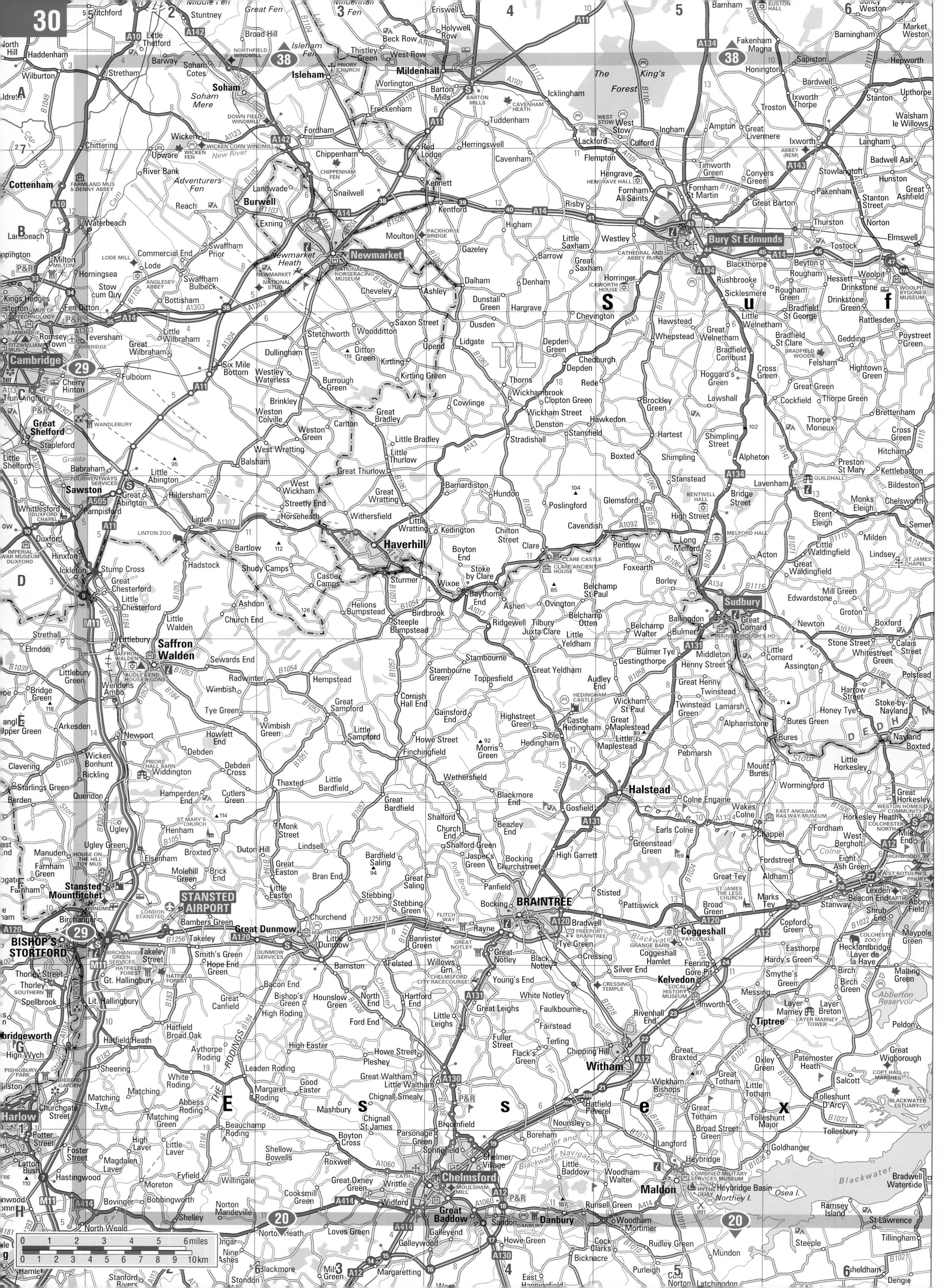

Cambridge
Newmarket
Bury St Edmunds
Sudbury
Haverhill
Saffron Walden
STANSTED AIRPORT
BISHOP'S STORTFORD
Great Dunmow
BRAINTREE
Halstead
Coggeshall
Kelvedon
Witham
Chelmsford
Maldon
Harlow
Tiptree
Mildenhall
Soham
Burwell
Isleham
Sawston
Great Shelford
Cottenham
Waterbeach
Lavenham
Long Melford
Clare
Great Baddow
Danbury
Tollesbury
Colne Engaine
Earls Colne
Castle Hedingham
Finchingfield
Thaxted
Great Bardfield
Stansted Mountfitchet
S u f f
E s s e x
TL
The King's Forest
Blackwater
Abberton Reservoir
Osea I.
Northey I.
38
29
20
A11
A14
A134
A12
A120
A131
A130
A414
M11
0 1 2 3 4 5 6 miles
0 1 2 3 4 5 6 7 8 9 10 km

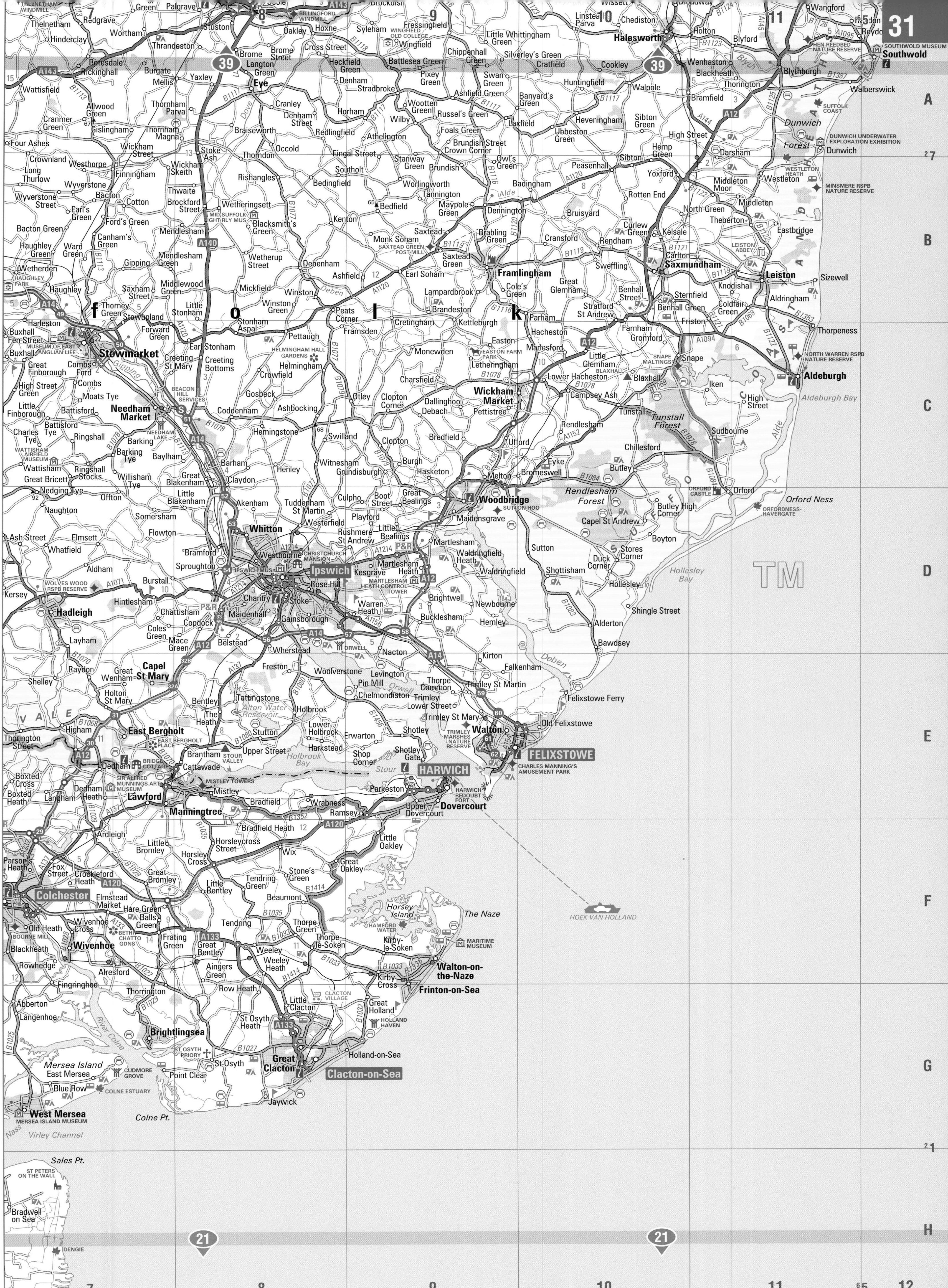
Suffolk
Halesworth
Southwold
Southwold Museum
Wangford
Blyford
Holton
Wenhaston
Blackheath
Blythburgh
Walberswick
Thorington
Bramfield
Walpole
Cookley
Huntingfield
Chediston
Linstead Parva
Heveningham
Sibton Green
Ubbeston Green
High Street
Hemp Green
Darsham
Dunwich
Dunwich Forest
Dunwich Underwater Exploration Exhibition
Suffolk Coast
Westleton
Westleton Heath
Minsmere RSPB Nature Reserve
Middleton Moor
Middleton
Yoxford
Sibton
Peasenhall
Rotten End
Bruisyard
North Green
Theberton
Eastbridge
Curlew Green
Kelsale
Carlton
Saxmundham
Leiston
Leiston Abbey
Sizewell
Knodishall
Aldringham
Sternfield
Benhall Street
Benhall Green
Coldfair Green
Friston
Thorpeness
Aldeburgh
North Warren RSPB Nature Reserve
Snape
Snape Maltings
Farnham
Gromford
Blaxhall
Iken
High Street
Aldeburgh Bay
Tunstall
Tunstall Forest
Sudbourne
Chillesford
Butley
Orford
Orford Castle
Orford Ness
Orfordness-Havergate
Rendlesham
Rendlesham Forest
Eyke
Campsey Ash
Lower Hacheston
Hacheston
Marlesford
Little Glemham
Great Glemham
Stratford St Andrew
Parham
Framlingham
Cole's Green
Cransford
Rendham
Sweffling
Badingham
Dennington
Brabling Green
Saxtead
Saxtead Green
Saxtead Green Post Mill
Earl Soham
Lampardbrook
Brandeston
Kettleburgh
Easton
Easton Farm Park
Letheringham
Wickham Market
Pettistree
Charsfield
Cretingham
Monewden
Dallinghoo
Debach
Bredfield
Ufford
Melton
Bromeswell
Woodbridge
Sutton Hoo
Maidensgrave
Capel St Andrew
Butley High Corner
Boyton
Sutton
Shottisham
Duck Corner
Stores Corner
Hollesley
Hollesley Bay
TM
Shingle Street
Alderton
Bawdsey
Ramsholt
Kirton
Falkenham
Trimley St Martin
Trimley St Mary
Trimley Marshes Nature Reserve
Walton
Felixstowe
Felixstowe Ferry
Old Felixstowe
Charles Manning's Amusement Park
Harwich
Harwich Redoubt Fort
Dovercourt
Upper Dovercourt
Parkeston
Ramsey
Wrabness
Bradfield
Bradfield Heath
Mistley
Mistley Towers
Manningtree
Lawford
Cattawade
Brantham
Stour Valley
Stutton
Holbrook
Lower Holbrook
Holbrook Bay
Harkstead
Erwarton
Shotley
Shotley Gate
Shop Corner
Chelmondiston
Pin Mill
Woolverstone
Freston
Tattingstone
Alton Water Reservoir
Bentley
The Heath
East Bergholt
East Bergholt Place
Bridge Cottage
Dedham
Sir Alfred Munnings Art Museum
Dedham Heath
Higham
Holton St Mary
Capel St Mary
Great Wenham
Raydon
Shelley
Layham
Hadleigh
Kersey
Wolves Wood RSPB Reserve
Aldham
Whatfield
Elmsett
Ash Street
Naughton
Nedging Tye
Offton
Great Bricett
Wattisham
Wattisham Airfield Museum
Ringshall
Ringshall Stocks
Willisham Tye
Barking Tye
Barking
Battisford
Battisford Tye
Charles Tye
Little Finborough
Moats Tye
High Street Green
Great Finborough
Combs
Combs Ford
Buxhall
Buxhall Fen Street
Harleston
Stowmarket
Museum of East Anglian Life
Haughley
Haughley Park
Wetherden
Haughley Green
Ward Green
Canham's Green
Ford's Green
Bacton Green
Wyverstone Street
Earl's Green
Bacton
Cotton
Wyverstone
Long Thurlow
Westhorpe
Crownland
Four Ashes
Cranmer Green
Gislingham
Allwood Green
Wattisfield
Rickinghall
Botesdale
Redgrave
Hinderclay
Thelnetham
Wortham
Palgrave
Stuston
Thrandeston
Burgate
Mellis
Yaxley
Eye
Brome
Brome Street
Langton Green
Oakley
Hoxne
Syleham
Wingfield
Wingfield Old College
Fressingfield
Billingford Windmill
Cross Street
Heckfield Green
Battlesea Green
Pixey Green
Denham
Stradbroke
Chippenhall Green
Little Whittingham Green
Silverley's Green
Cratfield
Swan Green
Ashfield Green
Banyard's Green
Laxfield
Wootten Green
Russel's Green
Foals Green
Wilby
Horham
Denham Street
Cranley
Thornham Parva
Thornham Magna
Wickham Street
Wickham Skeith
Finningham
Stoke Ash
Thorndon
Occold
Braiseworth
Redlingfield
Athelington
Fingal Street
Stanway Green
Brundish
Brundish Street
Crown Corner
Owl's Green
Southolt
Worlingworth
Tannington
Maypole Green
Bedingfield
Bedfield
Rishangles
Thwaite
Brockford Street
Wetheringsett
Mid Suffolk Light Rly Mus
Blacksmith's Green
Mendlesham
Mendlesham Green
Gipping
Saxham Street
Middlewood Green
Thorney Green
Stowupland
Forward Green
Little Stonham
Stonham Aspal
Earl Stonham
Mickfield
Wetherup Street
Debenham
Ashfield
Winston
Winston Green
Kenton
Monk Soham
Peats Corner
Framsden
Pettaugh
Helmingham
Helmingham Hall Gardens
Crowfield
Creeting St Mary
Creeting Bottoms
Gosbeck
Coddenham
Needham Market
Needham Lake
Beacon Hill Services
Otley
Clopton Corner
Clopton
Ashbocking
Hemingstone
Swilland
Witnesham
Grundisburgh
Burgh
Hasketon
Henley
Barham
Claydon
Great Blakenham
Little Blakenham
Baylham
Akenham
Tuddenham St Martin
Culpho
Boot Street
Great Bealings
Little Bealings
Playford
Westerfield
Rushmere St Andrew
Martlesham
Martlesham Heath
Martlesham Heath Control Tower
Kesgrave
Waldringfield Heath
Waldringfield
Brightwell
Newbourne
Hemley
Bucklesham
Warren Heath
Nacton
Levington
Thorpe Common
Trimley Lower Street
Whitton
Westbourne
Christchurch Mansion
Ipswich
Ipswichmus
Rose Hill
Chantry
Stoke
Maidenhall
Gainsborough
Wherstead
Orwell
Bramford
Sproughton
Burstall
Hintlesham
Chattisham
Copdock
Coles Green
Mace Green
Belstead
Somersham
Flowton
Thorington Street
Vale
Boxted Cross
Boxted Heath
Langham
Ardleigh
Little Bromley
Great Bromley
Horsleycross Street
Horsley Cross
Wix
Little Oakley
Great Oakley
Stone's Green
Tendring Green
Little Bentley
Beaumont
Tendring
Thorpe Green
Thorpe-le-Soken
Hamford Water
Horsey Island
The Naze
Kirby-le-Soken
Maritime Museum
Walton-on-the-Naze
Frinton-on-Sea
Kirby Cross
Great Holland
Holland Haven
Clacton Village
Little Clacton
Holland-on-Sea
Great Clacton
Clacton-on-Sea
Jaywick
St Osyth
St Osyth Priory
St Osyth Heath
Point Clear
Brightlingsea
Weeley
Weeley Heath
Aingers Green
Great Bentley
Row Heath
Frating Green
Thorrington
Alresford
Wivenhoe
Wivenhoe Cross
Beth Chatto Gdns
Balls Green
Hare Green
Elmstead Market
Crockleford Heath
Fox Street
Parson's Heath
Colchester
Old Heath
Bourne Mill
Blackheath
Rowhedge
Fingringhoe
Abberton
Langenhoe
River Colne
Mersea Island
East Mersea
Cudmore Grove
Blue Row
Colne Estuary
West Mersea
Mersea Island Museum
Colne Pt.
Virley Channel
Sales Pt.
St Peters on the Wall
Bradwell on Sea
Dengie
Hoek van Holland
Deben
Stour
Gipping
Dove
Alde
Blyth
39
21
A
B
C
D
E
F
G
H
7
8
9
10
11
12

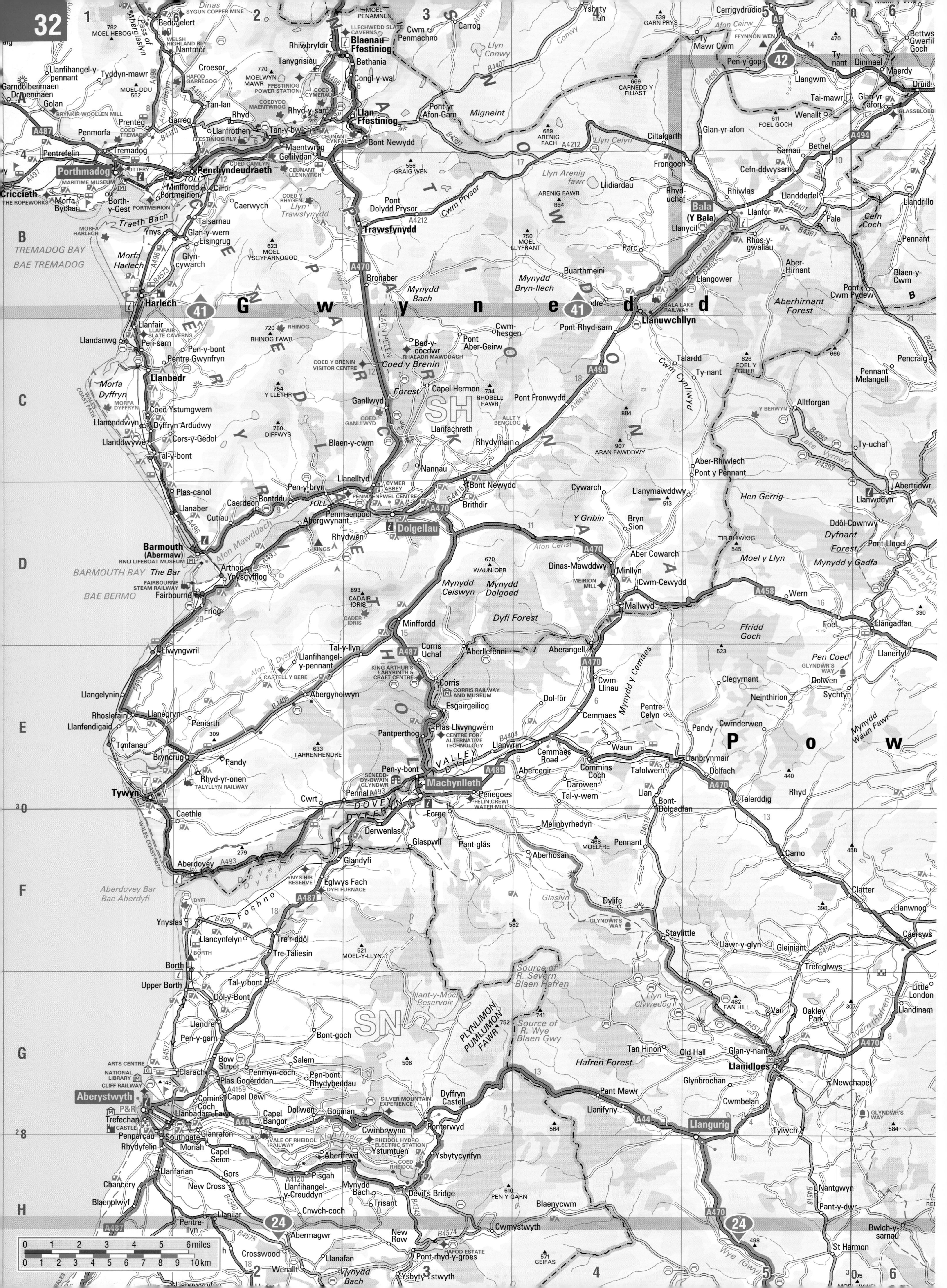
Porthmadog
Criccieth
Penrhyndeudraeth
Blaenau Ffestiniog
Llan-Ffestiniog
Bala (Y Bala)
Trawsfynydd
Harlech
Llanbedr
Llanuwchllyn
Gwynedd
Powys
Barmouth (Abermaw)
Dolgellau
Dinas-Mawddwy
Mallwyd
Machynlleth
Tywyn
Aberdovey
Borth
Aberystwyth
Llanidloes
Llangurig
Caersws
Llanbrynmair
Devil's Bridge
Ponterwyd
TREMADOG BAY
BAE TREMADOG
BARMOUTH BAY
BAE BERMO
Aberdovey Bar
Bae Aberdyfi
Cadair Idris
Plynlimon Pumlumon Fawr
Hafren Forest
Dyfi Forest
Coed y Brenin Forest
Nant-y-Moch Reservoir
Llyn Clywedog
Lake Vyrnwy
Llyn Tegid or Bala Lake
Source of R. Severn Blaen Hafren
Source of R. Wye Blaen Gwy
SH
SN
A470
A487
A493
A494
A458
A489
A44
0 1 2 3 4 5 6 miles
0 1 2 3 4 5 6 7 8 9 10 km

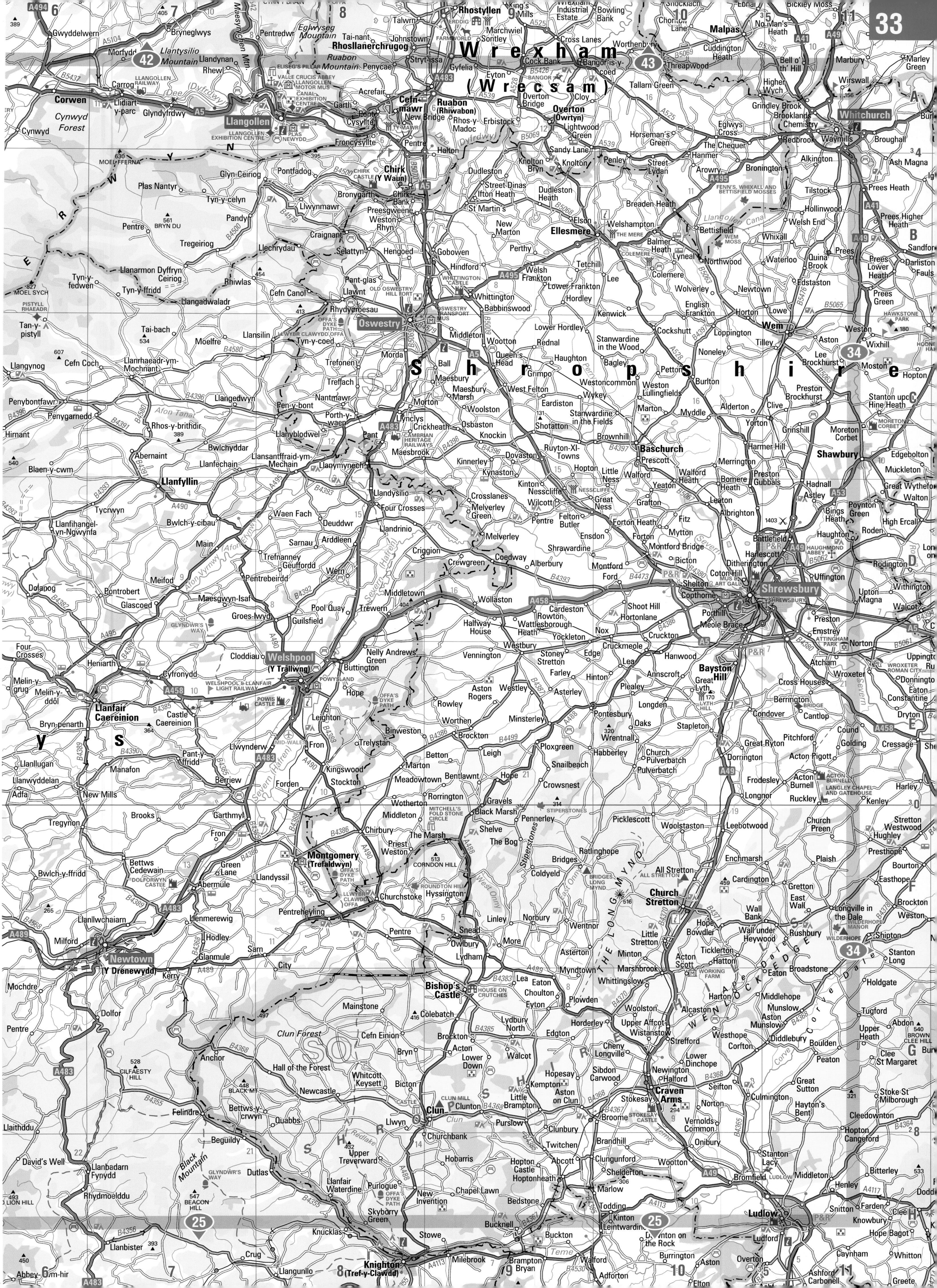
Wrexham
(Wrecsam)
Shropshire
Rhostyllen
Rhosllanerchrugog
Ruabon Mountain
Eglwyseg Mountain
Llantysilio Mountain
Ruabon (Rhiwabon)
Cefn-mawr
Llangollen
Corwen
Cynwyd Forest
Chirk (Y Waun)
Overton (Owrtyn)
Malpas
Whitchurch
Ellesmere
Oswestry
Wem
Shawbury
Baschurch
Shrewsbury
Welshpool (Y Trallwng)
Llanfair Caereinion
Llanfyllin
Newtown (Y Drenewydd)
Montgomery (Trefaldwyn)
Church Stretton
Bishop's Castle
Clun Forest
Clun
Craven Arms
Knighton (Tref-y-Clawdd)
Ludlow
The Long Mynd
Wenlock Edge
Corve Dale
Stiperstones
Bayston Hill
Pontesbury
Minsterley
Churchstoke
Kerry
Llanbister
Beguildy
Llangollen Canal
Offa's Dyke Path
Glyndŵr's Way
Whittington
St Martin's
Gobowen
Llanymynech
Four Crosses
Berriew
Chirbury
Lydham
Leintwardine
Bucknell
Brampton Bryan
Wistanstow
Stokesay Castle
Hopton Castle
Clunbury
Onibury
Bromfield
Acton Burnell
Condover
Atcham
Wroxeter
Haughmond Abbey
Attingham Park
Hawkstone Park
Moreton Corbet
Bettisfield
Hanmer
Penley
Bangor-is-y-coed
Holt
Cross Lanes
Marchwiel
Erddig
Llanrhaeadr-ym-Mochnant
Llangynog
Penybontfawr
Llansantffraid-ym-Mechain
Meifod
Guilsfield
Castle Caereinion
Manafon
Tregynon
Abermule
Dolfor
Felindre
Anchor
Cilfaesty Hill
Beacon Hill
Black Mountain
Corndon Hill
Pennerley
Ratlinghope
Cardington
Longville in the Dale
Rushbury
Munslow
Diddlebury
Culmington
Stanton Lacy
Middleton
Richards Castle

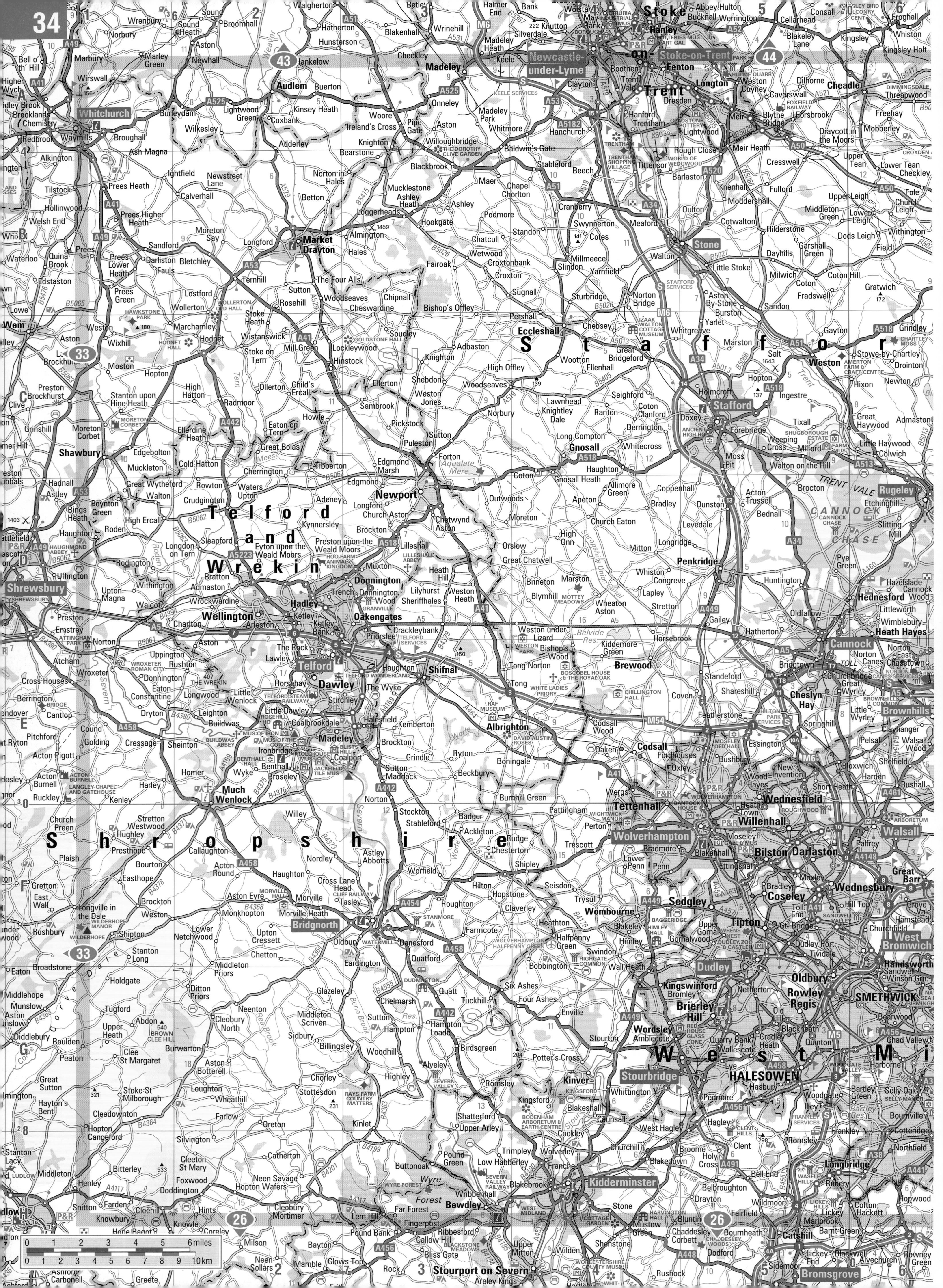
Whitchurch
Audlem
Market Drayton
Newcastle-under-Lyme
Stoke-on-Trent
Hanley
Fenton
Longton
Cheadle
Stone
Eccleshall
Stafford
Rugeley
Cannock
Hednesford
Penkridge
Gnosall
Newport
Shawbury
Wem
Shrewsbury
Wellington
Telford
Hadley
Oakengates
Donnington
Dawley
Madeley
Shifnal
Albrighton
Codsall
Brewood
Much Wenlock
Bridgnorth
Wolverhampton
Wednesfield
Willenhall
Walsall
Bilston
Darlaston
Wednesbury
Sedgley
Tipton
Dudley
Oldbury
Rowley Regis
SMETHWICK
West Bromwich
Kingswinford
Brierley Hill
Stourbridge
HALESOWEN
Kinver
Kidderminster
Bewdley
Stourport on Severn
Cleobury Mortimer
Bromsgrove
Telford and Wrekin
Shropshire
Stafford
West Mi
CANNOCK CHASE
TRENT VALE
M6
M54
M5
A5
A41
A49
A442
A458
A454
A449
A518
A34
A50
A53
A51
A525
Wyre Forest
1 2 3 4 5 6 miles
0 1 2 3 4 5 6 7 8 9 10km

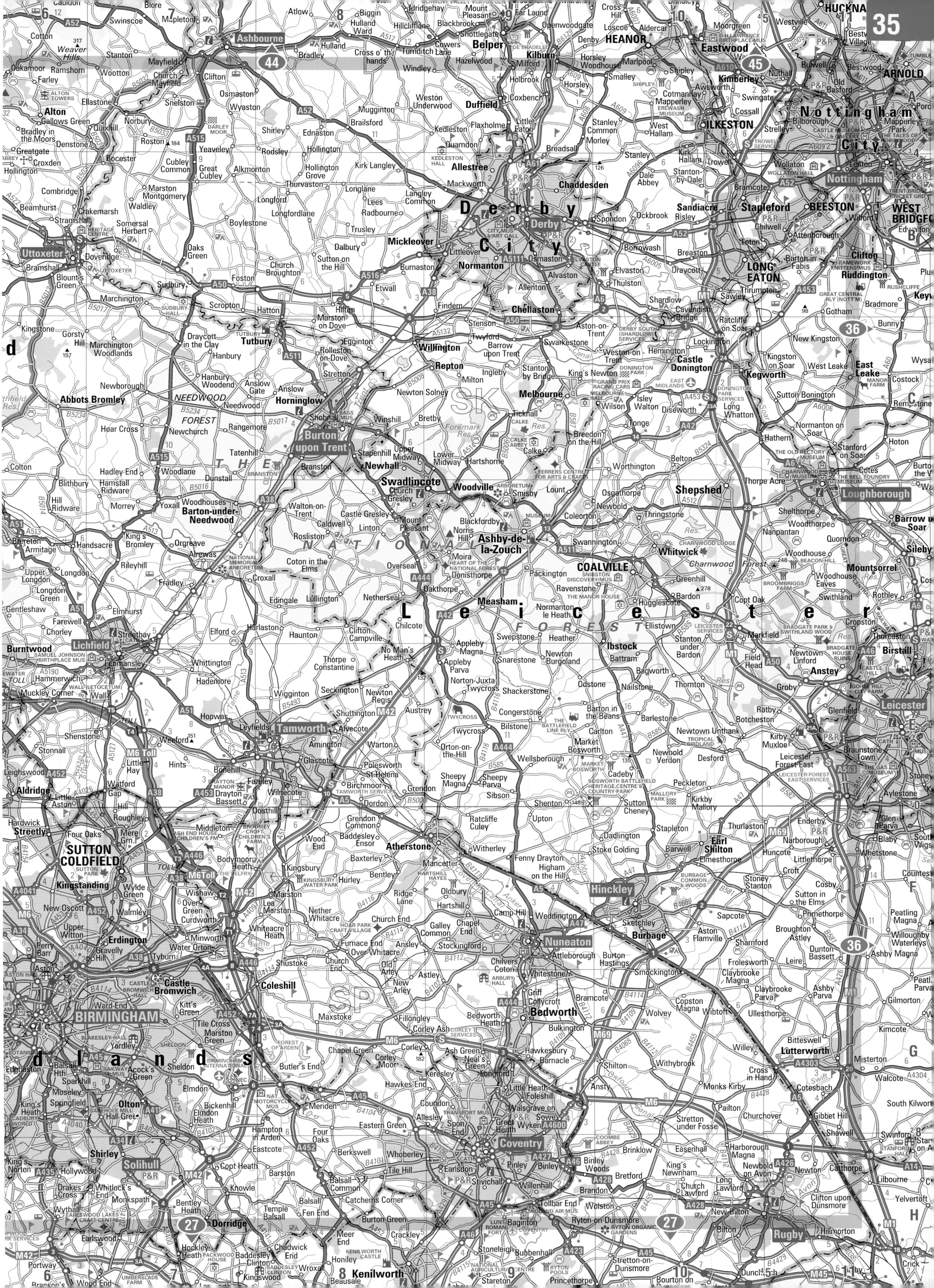
Ashbourne
Uttoxeter
Derby
Derby City
Nottingham
Nottingham City
Burton upon Trent
Loughborough
Lichfield
Tamworth
Leicester
Nuneaton
Hinckley
Coventry
Solihull
Rugby
BIRMINGHAM
SUTTON COLDFIELD
Belper
HEANOR
Eastwood
ILKESTON
Kimberley
ARNOLD
WEST BRIDGFORD
BEESTON
LONG EATON
Stapleford
Sandiacre
Duffield
Allestree
Mickleover
Normanton
Chellaston
Chaddesden
Tutbury
Castle Donington
Kegworth
Melbourne
Swadlincote
Ashby-de-la-Zouch
COALVILLE
Shepshed
Whitwick
Mountsorrel
Birstall
Anstey
Measham
Ibstock
Atherstone
Bedworth
Coleshill
Kenilworth
Lutterworth
Earl Shilton
Burbage
Erdington
Aldridge
Dorridge
Shirley
Castle Bromwich
Leicestershire
NEEDWOOD FOREST
THE NATIONAL FOREST
CHARNWOOD FOREST
44
45
36
27
6
7
8
9
10
11

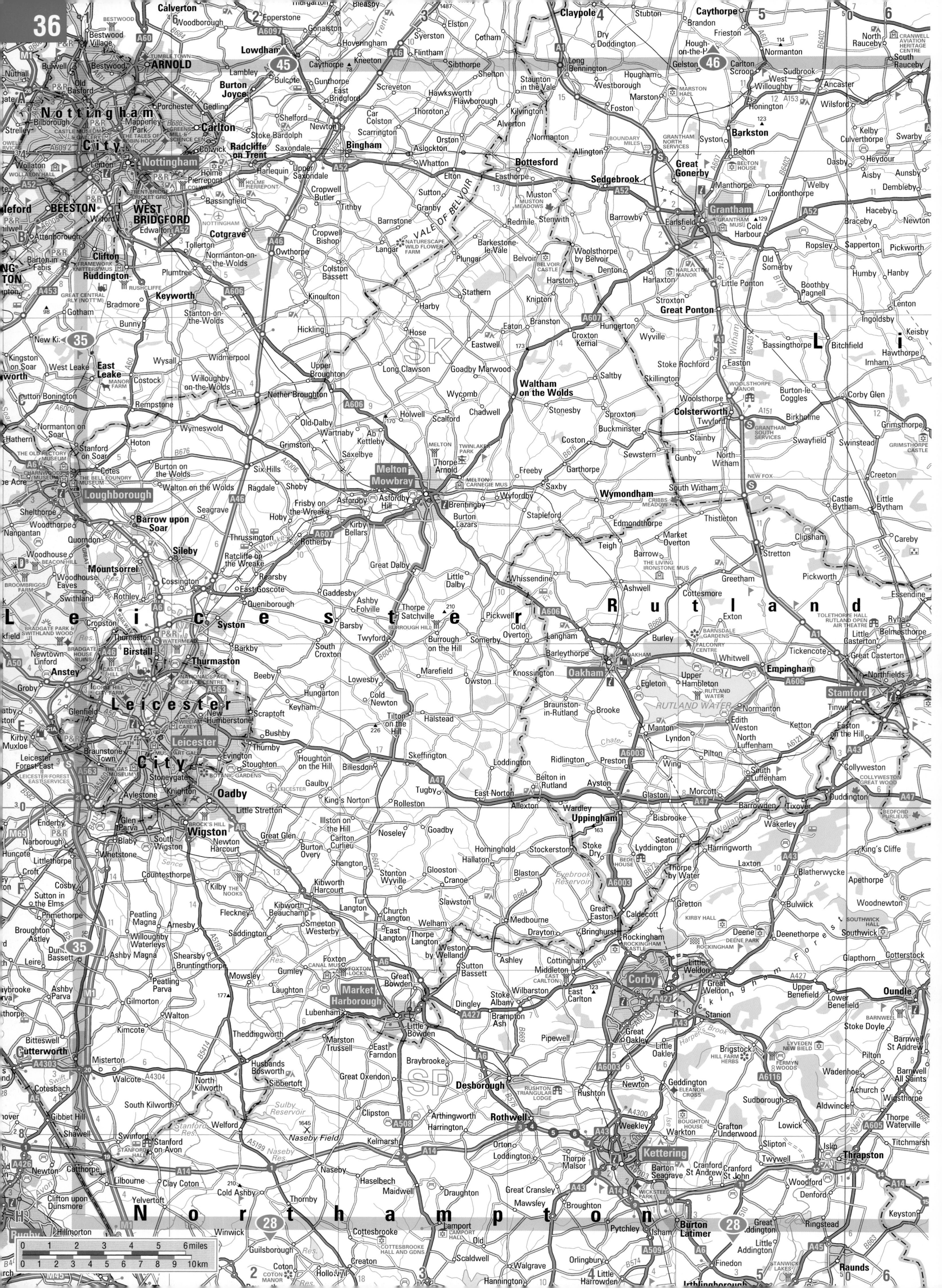

Nottingham
Nottingham City
ARNOLD
Carlton
BEESTON
WEST BRIDGFORD
Radcliffe on Trent
Bingham
Cotgrave
Clifton
Ruddington
Keyworth
Calverton
Lowdham
Burton Joyce
Claypole
Long Bennington
Bottesford
Sedgebrook
Great Gonerby
Grantham
Caythorpe
Barkston
Ancaster
VALE OF BELVOIR
Belvoir
Harlaxton
Great Ponton
Colsterworth
Waltham on the Wolds
Melton Mowbray
Loughborough
East Leake
Barrow upon Soar
Sileby
Mountsorrel
Syston
Birstall
Thurmaston
Leicester
Leicester City
Oadby
Wigston
Anstey
Oakham
Rutland
RUTLAND WATER
Uppingham
Empingham
Stamford
Leicestershire
Lincolnshire
Market Harborough
Lutterworth
Corby
Kettering
Desborough
Rothwell
Burton Latimer
Oundle
Thrapston
Raunds
Northamptonshire
Naseby Field
Rockingham
Rockingham Forest
Welland
SK
SP
0 1 2 3 4 5 6 miles
0 1 2 3 4 5 6 7 8 9 10 km

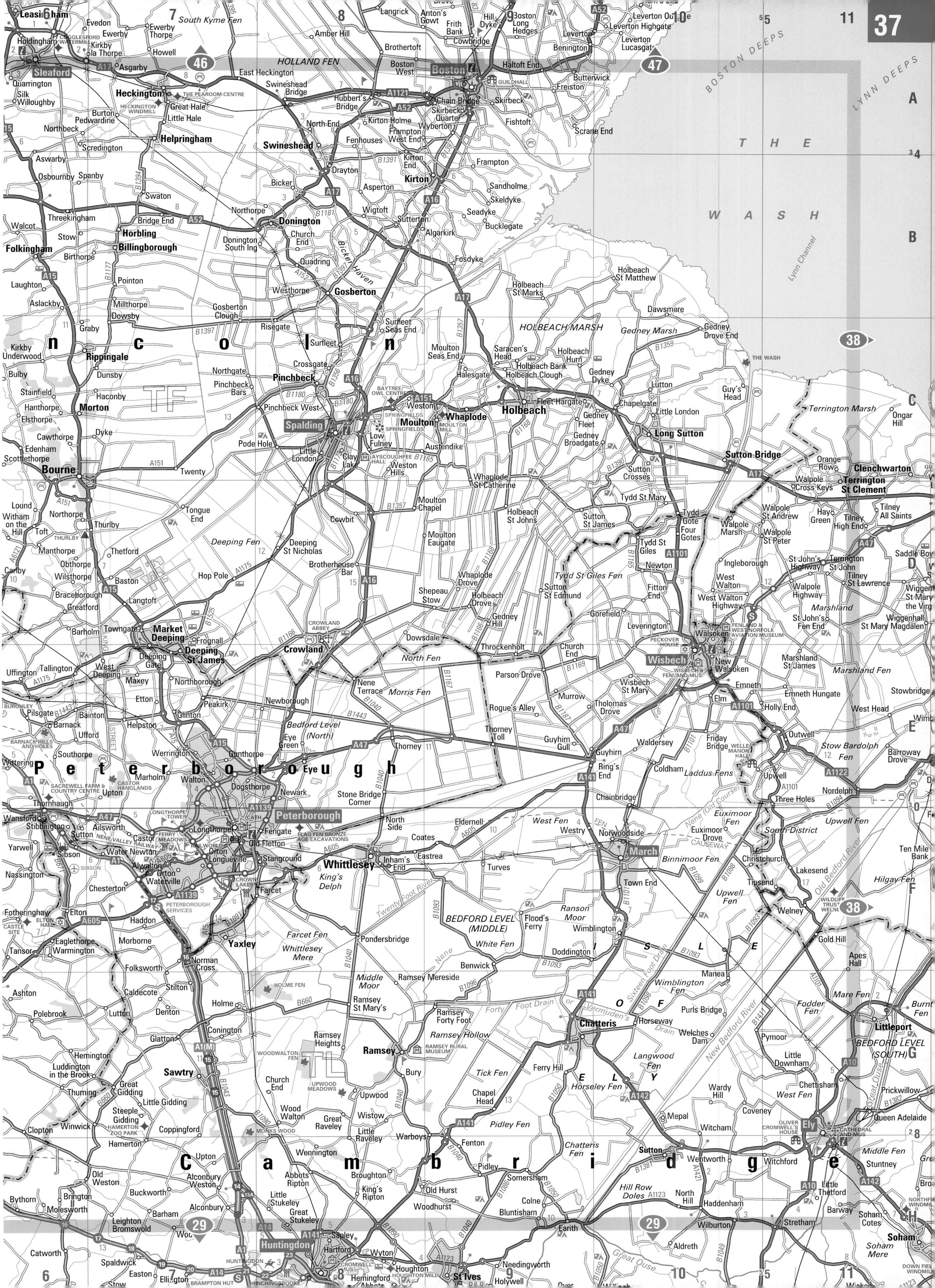
Leasingham
South Kyme Fen
Evedon
Ewerby
Ewerby Thorpe
Holdingham
Kirkby la Thorpe
Howell
Sleaford
Asgarby
Quarrington
Silk Willoughby
Heckington
THE PEAROOM CENTRE
Great Hale
HECKINGTON WINDMILL
Little Hale
Burton Pedwardine
Northbeck
Helpringham
Scredington
Aswarby
Osbournby
Spanby
Swaton
Threekingham
Walcot
Stow
Folkingham
Birthorpe
Horbling
Billingborough
Bridge End
Pointon
Laughton
Aslackby
Millthorpe
Dowsby
Graby
Kirkby Underwood
Rippingale
Dunsby
Bulby
Stainfield
Haconby
Hanthorpe
Morton
Elsthorpe
Dyke
Cawthorpe
Edenham
Scottlethorpe
Bourne
Twenty
Lound
Witham on the Hill
Northorpe
Toft
Thurlby
THURLBY
Manthorpe
Thetford
Obthorpe
Wilsthorpe
Baston
Carlby
Braceborough
Langtoft
Greatford
Barholm
Towngate
Market Deeping
Frognall
Deeping St James
Deeping Gate
Uffington
Tallington
West Deeping
Maxey
Northborough
Etton
BURGHLEY
Pilsgate
Bainton
Barnack
Ufford
BARNACK HILLS AND HOLES
Helpston
Glinton
Peakirk
Wittering
Southorpe
Werrington
Gunthorpe
Marholm
Walton
Dogsthorpe
Eye
Eye Green
SACREWELL FARM & COUNTRY CENTRE
Upton
CASTOR HANGLANDS
Newark
Thornhaugh
Wansford
Stibbington
Sutton
LONGTHORPE TOWER
Longthorpe
Peterborough
Ailsworth
Castor
FERRY MEADOWS
NENE VALLEY RAILWAY
RAILWORLD
Old Fletton
Fengate
FLAG FEN BRONZE AGE EXCAVATIONS
Yarwell
Sibson
Water Newton
Orton Longueville
Stanground
Alwalton
Orton Waterville
Nassington
SIBSON
Chesterton
CROWN LAKES
Farcet
Fotheringhay
Elton
ELTON HALL
CASTLE SITE
PETERBOROUGH SERVICES
Haddon
Yaxley
Eaglethorpe
Warmington
Tansor
Morborne
Norman Cross
Folksworth
Stilton
Caldecote
Ashton
Denton
Polebrook
Lutton
Holme
HOLME FEN
Glatton
Conington
Hemington
Luddington in the Brook
Sawtry
Great Gidding
Thurning
Little Gidding
Steeple Gidding
HAMERTON ZOO PARK
Winwick
Clopton
Coppingford
Hamerton
Upton
Old Weston
Alconbury Weston
Buckworth
Bythorn
Brington
Molesworth
Barham
Alconbury
Leighton Bromswold
Woolley
Catworth
Spaldwick
Easton
Ellington
BRAMPTON HUT
HUNTINGDON
HINCHINGBROOKE
Stow
Cambridge
Peterborough
Lincoln
Amber Hill
Langrick
Anton's Gowt
Frith Bank
Hill Dyke
Boston Long Hedges
Cowbridge
HOLLAND FEN
Brothertoft
East Heckington
Boston West
Boston
GUILDHALL
Haltoft End
Leverton Outgate
Leverton Highgate
Leverton
Leverton Lucasgate
Benington
Butterwick
Freiston
Swineshead Bridge
Hubbert's Bridge
Chain Bridge
Skirbeck
Skirbeck Quarter
Kirton Holme
Wyberton
Fishtoft
Scrane End
North End
Frampton West End
Fenhouses
Swineshead
Kirton End
Frampton
Drayton
Kirton
Sandholme
Bicker
Asperton
Skeldyke
Seadyke
Wigtoft
Sutterton
Northorpe
Donington
Algarkirk
Bucklegate
Church End
Donington South Ing
Bicker Haven
Quadring
Fosdyke
Westhorpe
Gosberton
Gosberton Clough
Risegate
Surfleet
Surfleet Seas End
Holbeach St Matthew
Holbeach St Marks
Dawsmere
HOLBEACH MARSH
Gedney Marsh
Gedney Drove End
Moulton Seas End
Saracen's Head
Holbeach Hurn
Holbeach Bank
Holbeach Clough
Gedney Dyke
Halesgate
Crossgate
Northgate
Pinchbeck
Pinchbeck Bars
BAYTREE OWL CENTRE
Weston
Whaplode
Holbeach
Fleet Hargate
Gedney
Fleet
Gedney Broadgate
Chapelgate
Lutton
Guy's Head
Little London
Long Sutton
Pinchbeck West
SPRINGFIELDS
Spalding
Moulton
MOULTON MILL
Low Fulney
Pode Hole
Little London
Austendike
Clay Lake
AYSCOUGHFEE HALL
Weston Hills
Whaplode St Catherine
Sutton Crosses
Sutton Bridge
Tongue End
Moulton Chapel
Cowbit
Holbeach St Johns
Tydd St Mary
Sutton St James
Tydd Gote
Four Gotes
Tydd St Giles
Newton
Moulton Eaugate
Deeping Fen
Deeping St Nicholas
Hop Pole
Brotherhouse Bar
Whaplode Drove
Tydd St Giles Fen
Sutton St Edmund
Fitton End
Shepeau Stow
Holbeach Drove
Gedney Hill
Gorefield
Leverington
CROWLAND ABBEY
Crowland
Dowsdale
Throckenholt
Church End
PECKOVER HOUSE
Wisbech
WISBECH & FENLAND MUS
North Fen
Parson Drove
Wisbech St Mary
Murrow
Tholomas Drove
Nene Terrace
Morris Fen
Newborough
Rogue's Alley
Bedford Level (North)
Thorney Toll
Thorney
Guyhirn
Guyhirn Gull
Waldersey
Ring's End
Coldham
Friday Bridge
Elm
Emneth
Stone Bridge Corner
Chainbridge
North Side
Eldernell
West Fen
Westry
Norwoodside
Coates
Eastrea
March
Whittlesey
Inham's End
King's Delph
Turves
Binnimoor Fen
Twenty Foot River
Town End
BEDFORD LEVEL (MIDDLE)
Flood's Ferry
Ranson Moor
Wimblington
Pondersbridge
Farcet Fen
Whittlesey Mere
White Fen
Benwick
Doddington
Ramsey Mereside
Middle Moor
Ramsey St Mary's
Ramsey Forty Foot
Forty Foot Drain
Vermuden's Drain
Chatteris
Sixteen Foot Drain
Wimblington Fen
Horseway
Ramsey Hollow
Ramsey Heights
Ramsey
RAMSEY RURAL MUSEUM
WOODWALTON FEN
Bury
Tick Fen
Ferry Hill
Langwood Fen
Church End
Chapel Head
Horseley Fen
UPWOOD MEADOWS
Upwood
Wood Walton
Great Raveley
Little Raveley
Wistow
Warboys
Pidley Fen
MONKS WOOD
Fenton
Chatteris Fen
Wennington
Pidley
Somersham
Abbots Ripton
Broughton
King's Ripton
Old Hurst
Colne
Little Stukeley
Great Stukeley
Woodhurst
Bluntisham
Earith
Huntingdon
Sapley
Hartford
Wyton
CROMWELL MUS
Houghton
HOUGHTON MILL
St Ives
Needingworth
Hemingford Abbots
Holywell
Great Ouse
BOSTON DEEPS
LYNN DEEPS
THE WASH
Lynn Channel
THE WASH
Terrington Marsh
Ongar Hill
Orange Row
Clenchwarton
Walpole Cross Keys
Terrington St Clement
Hay Green
Tilney All Saints
Tilney High End
Walpole St Andrew
Walpole Marsh
Walpole St Peter
Ingleborough
St John's Highway
Terrington St John
Tilney St Lawrence
Saddle Bow
West Walton
Walpole Highway
West Walton Highway
Marshland
Wiggenhall St Mary the Virgin
Wiggenhall St Mary Magdalen
St John's Fen End
FENLAND & WEST NORFOLK AVIATION MUSEUM
Walsoken
New Walsoken
Marshland St James
Marshland Fen
Emneth Hungate
Stowbridge
Holly End
West Head
Outwell
Stow Bardolph Fen
Barroway Drove
WELLE MANOR HALL
Laddus Fens
Upwell
Nordelph
Three Holes
Euximoor Fen
Euximoor Drove
Upwell Fen
South District
Christchurch
Ten Mile Bank
Lakesend
Tipsend
Hilgay Fen
Upwell Fen
Old Bedford River
Welney
WILDLIFE TRUST WELNEY
Gold Hill
ISLE OF ELY
Manea
Apes Hall
Mare Fen
Purls Bridge
Fodder Fen
Welches Dam
Burnt Fen
Littleport
New Bedford River
Pymoor
BEDFORD LEVEL (SOUTH)
Little Downham
Chettisham
Prickwillow
West Fen
Wardy Hill
Coveney
Mepal
Witcham
OLIVER CROMWELL'S HOUSE
Ely
CATHEDRAL AND MUS
Queen Adelaide
Middle Fen
Sutton
Wentworth
Witchford
Stuntney
Hill Row Doles
North Hill
Haddenham
Little Thetford
Barway
Soham Cotes
NORTHFIELD WINDMILL
Wilburton
Stretham
Soham
Aldreth
Soham Mere
DOWN FIELD WINDMILL
THE WASH

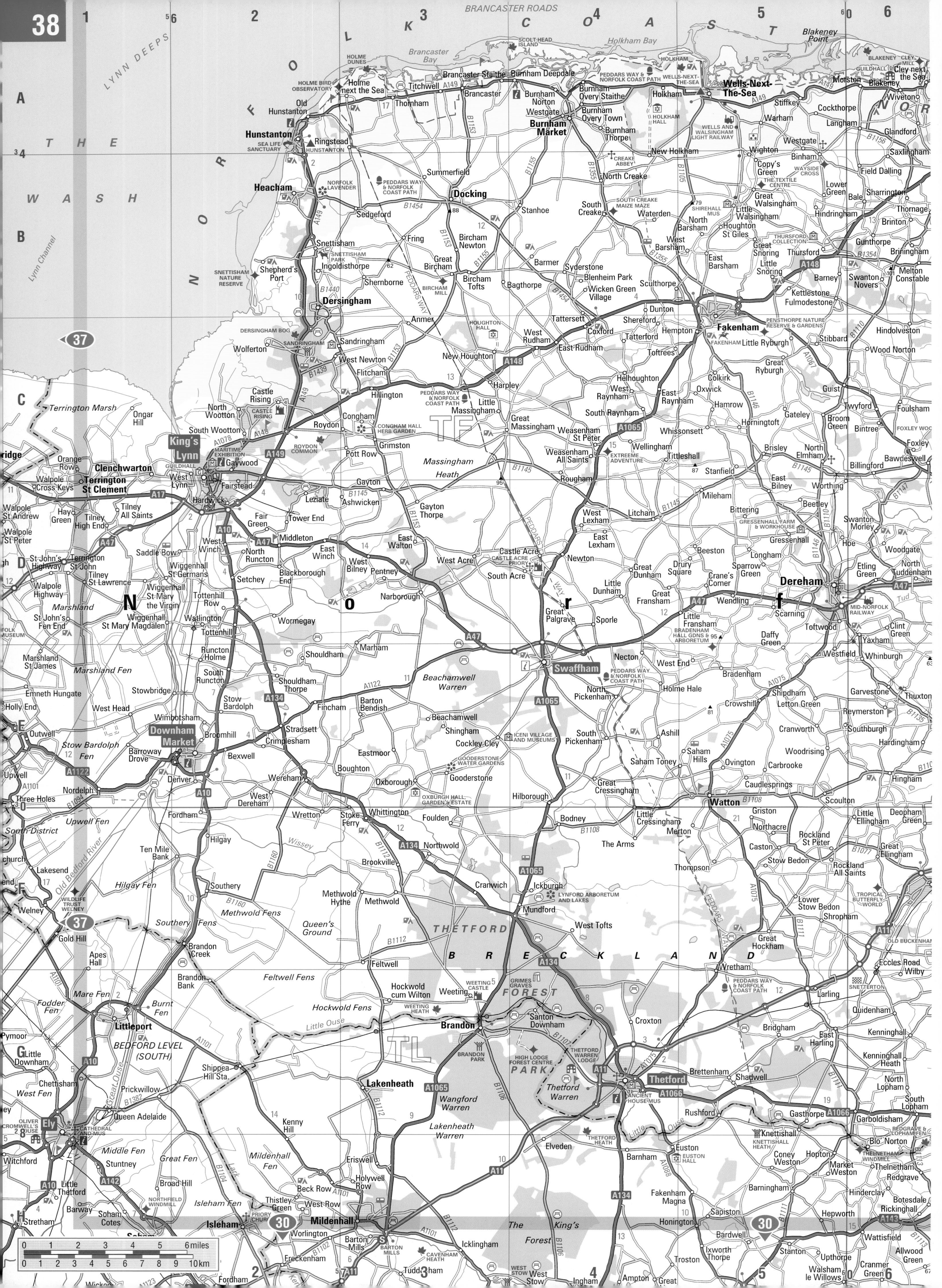
BRANCASTER ROADS
NORFOLK COAST
LYNN DEEPS
THE WASH
Lynn Channel
Holkham Bay
Brancaster Bay
Blakeney Point
Scolt Head Island
Holme Dunes
Holme Bird Observatory
Holme next the Sea
Titchwell
Brancaster
Brancaster Staithe
Burnham Deepdale
Burnham Norton
Burnham Market
Burnham Overy Staithe
Burnham Overy Town
Burnham Thorpe
Westgate
Peddars Way & Norfolk Coast Path
Wells-Next-The-Sea
Holkham
Holkham Hall
Wells and Walsingham Light Railway
Stiffkey
Morston
Blakeney
Cley next the Sea
Wiveton
Cockthorpe
Langham
Glandford
Warham
Saxlingham
Binham
Wighton
Field Dalling
Copy's Green
Wayside Cross
The Textile Centre
Lower Green
Great Walsingham
Little Walsingham
Shirehall Mus
Sharrington
Bale
Thornage
Hindringham
Brinton
Houghton St Giles
Thursford Collection
Thursford
Gunthorpe
Briningham
Great Snoring
Little Snoring
Melton Constable
Swanton Novers
Barney
Kettlestone
Fulmodestone
Old Hunstanton
Hunstanton
Sea Life Sanctuary
Ringstead
Thornham
Docking
Summerfield
Heacham
Norfolk Lavender
Sedgeford
Snettisham
Snettisham Park
Snettisham Nature Reserve
Shepherd's Port
Ingoldisthorpe
Shernborne
Fring
Bircham Newton
Great Bircham
Bircham Mill
Bircham Tofts
Stanhoe
Barmer
Bagthorpe
Syderstone
Blenheim Park
Wicken Green Village
Sculthorpe
North Creake
South Creake
South Creake Maize Maze
Creake Abbey
New Holkham
Waterden
North Barsham
West Barsham
East Barsham
Dersingham
Dersingham Bog
Sandringham
Wolferton
Anmer
Houghton Hall
West Rudham
East Rudham
Tattersett
Coxford
Shereford
Dunton
Hempton
Fakenham
Pensthorpe Nature Reserve & Gardens
Little Ryburgh
Stibbard
Hindolveston
Wood Norton
Great Ryburgh
Tatterford
Toftrees
West Newton
New Houghton
Flitcham
Harpley
Hillington
Castle Rising
North Wootton
South Wootton
Congham
Congham Hall Herb Garden
Little Massingham
Great Massingham
Roydon
Roydon Common
Grimston
Pott Row
Helhoughton
Colkirk
West Raynham
East Raynham
South Raynham
Oxwick
Hamrow
Horningtoft
Whissonsett
Gateley
Guist
Twyford
Foulsham
Broom Green
Bintree
Foxley Wood
Foxley
Bawdeswell
Weasenham St Peter
Weasenham All Saints
Extreeme Adventure
Wellingham
Tittleshall
Stanfield
Brisley
North Elmham
Billingford
Massingham Heath
Rougham
King's Lynn
Maritime Exhibition
Guildhall
Gaywood
West Lynn
Fairstead
Hardwick
Orange Row
Clenchwarton
Terrington St Clement
Walpole Cross Keys
Terrington Marsh
Ongar Hill
Gayton
Leziate
Ashwicken
Gayton Thorpe
Litcham
West Lexham
East Lexham
Mileham
East Bilney
Worthing
Beetley
Bittering
Gressenhall Farm & Workhouse
Gressenhall
Swanton Morley
Hoe
Woodgate
North Tuddenham
Etling Green
Walpole St Andrew
Walpole St Peter
Hay Green
Tilney High End
Tilney All Saints
Fair Green
Tower End
Middleton
West Winch
North Runcton
East Winch
West Bilney
East Walton
Pentney
West Acre
Castle Acre
Castle Acre Priory
South Acre
Newton
Great Dunham
Little Dunham
Beeston
Drury Square
Sparrow Green
Longham
Crane's Corner
Dereham
Mid-Norfolk Railway
Saddle Bow
St John's Highway
Terrington St John
Tilney St Lawrence
Walpole Highway
Wiggenhall St Germans
Wiggenhall St Mary the Virgin
Wiggenhall St Mary Magdalen
Blackborough End
Setchey
Tottenhill Row
Tottenhill
Watlington
Wormegay
Narborough
Great Fransham
Little Fransham
Wendling
Scarning
Toftwood
Great Palgrave
Sporle
Bradenham Hall Gdns & Arboretum
Marshland
St John's Fen End
Marshland St James
Marshland Fen
Runcton Holme
South Runcton
Shouldham
Shouldham Thorpe
Marham
Swaffham
Necton
West End
Bradenham
Daffy Green
Yaxham
Clint Green
Westfield
Whinburgh
Beachamwell Warren
North Pickenham
Holme Hale
Shipdham
Garvestone
Thuxton
Emneth Hungate
Stowbridge
Stow Bardolph
Wimbotsham
West Head
Holly End
Outwell
Downham Market
Broomhill
Fincham
Barton Bendish
Beachamwell
Shingham
Iceni Village and Museums
Cockley Cley
South Pickenham
Ashill
Crowshill
Letton Green
Reymerston
Cranworth
Southburgh
Stow Bardolph Fen
Barroway Drove
Stradsett
Crimplesham
Bexwell
Eastmoor
Gooderstone Water Gardens
Gooderstone
Saham Hills
Saham Toney
Ovington
Carbrooke
Woodrising
Hardingham
Upwell
Nordelph
Denver
Wereham
Boughton
Oxborough
Oxburgh Hall, Garden & Estate
Great Cressingham
Hingham
Caudlesprings
Three Holes
West Dereham
Hilborough
Watton
Scoulton
Fordham
Upwell Fen
South District
Wretton
Stoke Ferry
Whittington
Foulden
Bodney
Little Cressingham
Griston
Little Ellingham
Deopham Green
Northacre
Rockland St Peter
Hilgay
Wissey
Northwold
The Arms
Merton
Caston
Great Ellingham
Ten Mile Bank
Old Bedford River
Brookville
Stow Bedon
Rockland All Saints
Lakesend
Hilgay Fen
Southery
Methwold Hythe
Methwold
Cranwich
Ickburgh
Lynford Arboretum and Lakes
Thompson
Lower Stow Bedon
Tropical Butterfly World
Wildlife Trust Welney
Welney
Methwold Fens
Mundford
Shropham
Southery Fens
Queen's Ground
West Tofts
Gold Hill
Thetford Breckland
Great Hockham
Brandon Creek
Feltwell
Wretham
Eccles Road
Wilby
Old Buckenham
Apes Hall
Feltwell Fens
Grimes Graves
Peddars Way & Norfolk Coast Path
Snetterton
Brandon Bank
Weeting Castle
Hockwold cum Wilton
Weeting
Forest
Larling
Quidenham
Fodder Fen
Mare Fen
Burnt Fen
Hockwold Fens
Weeting Heath
Santon Downham
Croxton
Littleport
Little Ouse
Brandon
Bridgham
East Harling
Kenninghall
Pymoor
Little Downham
Bedford Level (South)
Brandon Park
High Lodge Forest Centre
Thetford Warren Lodge
Kenninghall Heath
Chettisham
Shippea Hill Sta.
Prickwillow
Lakenheath
Park
Thetford Warren
Thetford
Brettenham
Shadwell
North Lopham
West Fen
Great Ouse
Ancient House Mus
South Lopham
Queen Adelaide
Ely
Oliver Cromwell's House
Cathedral and Mus
Kenny Hill
Wangford Warren
Lakenheath Warren
Rushford
Gasthorpe
Garboldisham
Redgrave & Lopham Fen
Witchford
Middle Fen
Great Fen
Stuntney
Mildenhall Fen
Eriswell
Elveden
Thetford Heath
Barnham
Euston
Euston Hall
Knettishall
Knettishall Heath
Blo' Norton
Coney Weston
Hopton
Market Weston
Thelnetham Windmill
Thelnetham
Redgrave
Broad Hill
Little Thetford
Barway
Holywell Row
Beck Row
Northfield Windmill
Isleham Fen
Soham Cotes
Stretham
Thistley Green
West Row
Fakenham Magna
Barningham
Hinderclay
Botesdale
Rickinghall
Sapiston
Hepworth
Isleham
Priory Chur
Mildenhall
Honington
The King's Forest
Worlington
Freckenham
Barton Mills
Icklingham
Bardwell
Wattisfield
Ixworth Thorpe
Stanton
Upthorpe
Allwood Green
Walsham le Willows
Cranmer Green
Cavenham Heath
Tuddenham
West Stow
Ingham
Ampton
Great
Troston
Fordham
A149
A148
A1065
A1078
A17
A47
A10
A134
A1122
A1075
A1066
A11
A1101
A142
A143
A1067
B1153
B1155
B1454
B1355
B1105
B1440
B1439
B1145
B1146
B1110
B1147
B1108
B1112
B1160
B1106
B1107
B1111
B1382
B1104
B1102
B1113
B1354
B1156
A1088
A1122
37
30
TF
TL
0 1 2 3 4 5 6 miles
0 1 2 3 4 5 6 7 8 9 10 km

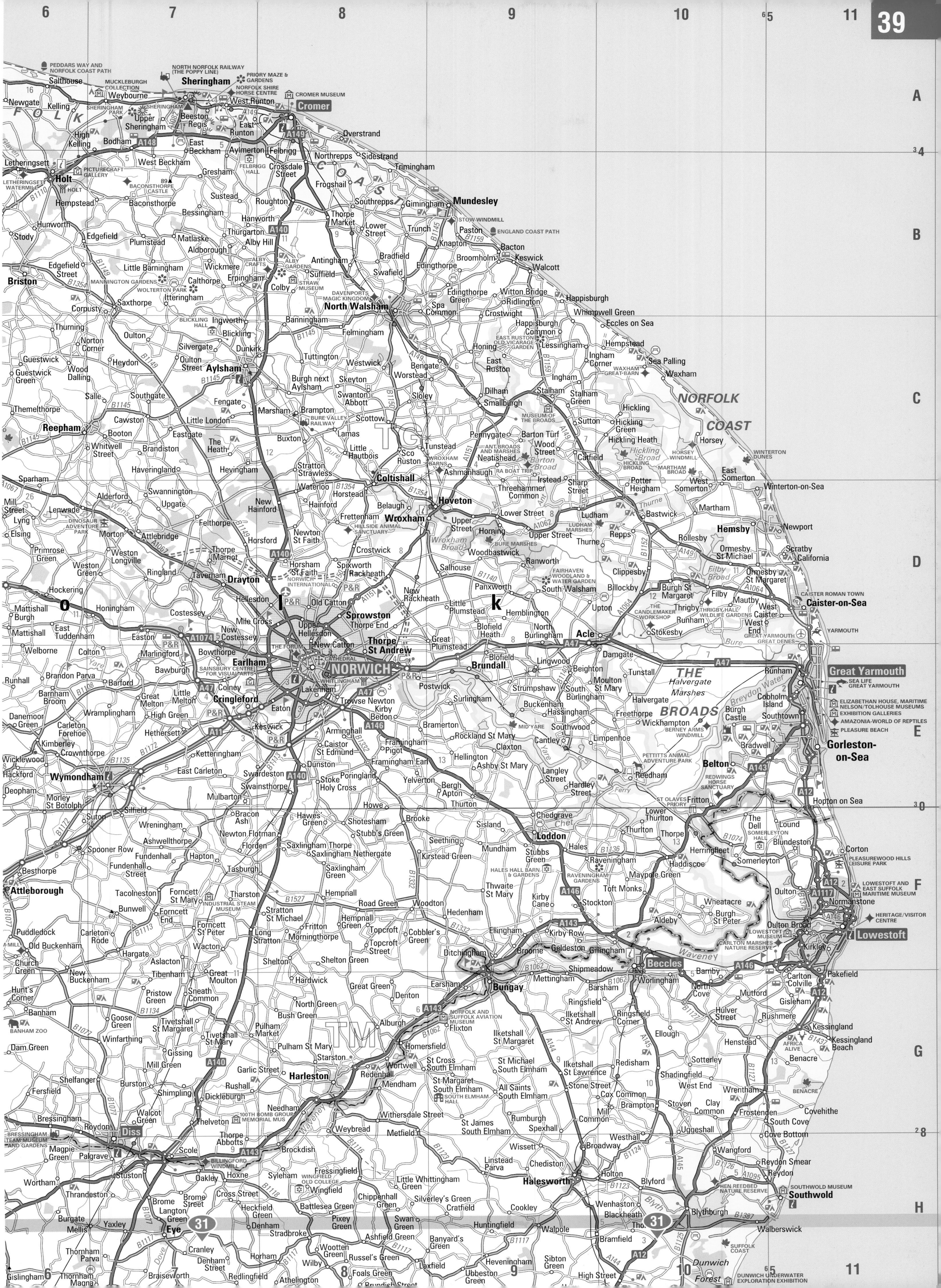
6
7
8
9
10
11
A
B
C
D
E
F
G
H
Sheringham
Cromer
Mundesley
North Walsham
Aylsham
Holt
Reepham
Coltishall
Hoveton
Wroxham
Drayton
Sprowston
Thorpe St Andrew
NORWICH
Earlham
Cringleford
Wymondham
Attleborough
Brundall
Acle
Hemsby
Caister-on-Sea
Great Yarmouth
Gorleston-on-Sea
Belton
Loddon
Beccles
Bungay
Lowestoft
Harleston
Diss
Eye
Halesworth
Southwold
Briston
NORFOLK COAST
THE BROADS
Halvergate Marshes
PEDDARS WAY AND NORFOLK COAST PATH
NORTH NORFOLK RAILWAY (THE POPPY LINE)
PRIORY MAZE & GARDENS
MUCKLEBURGH COLLECTION
NORFOLK SHIRE HORSE CENTRE
CROMER MUSEUM
ENGLAND COAST PATH
STOW WINDMILL
BLICKLING HALL
FELBRIGG HALL
BURE VALLEY RAILWAY
MUSEUM OF THE BROADS
WINTERTON DUNES
HORSEY WINDMILL
BANHAM ZOO
SEA LIFE GREAT YARMOUTH
ELIZABETHAN HOUSE, MARITIME
NELSON/TOLHOUSE MUSEUMS
EXHIBITION GALLERIES
AMAZONIA-WORLD OF REPTILES
PLEASURE BEACH
CAISTER ROMAN TOWN
PLEASUREWOOD HILLS LEISURE PARK
LOWESTOFT AND EAST SUFFOLK MARITIME MUSEUM
HERITAGE/VISITOR CENTRE
NORFOLK AND SUFFOLK AVIATION MUSEUM
100TH BOMB GROUP MEMORIAL MUS
BRESSINGHAM STEAM MUSEUM AND GARDENS
SOUTHWOLD MUSEUM
HEN REEDBED NATURE RESERVE
SUFFOLK COAST
DUNWICH UNDERWATER EXPLORATION EXHIBITION
Dunwich Forest
A140
A149
A148
A1151
A47
A11
A146
A143
A12
A1074
A1062
A1064
A144
A145
A1117
A1095
31
TG
TM

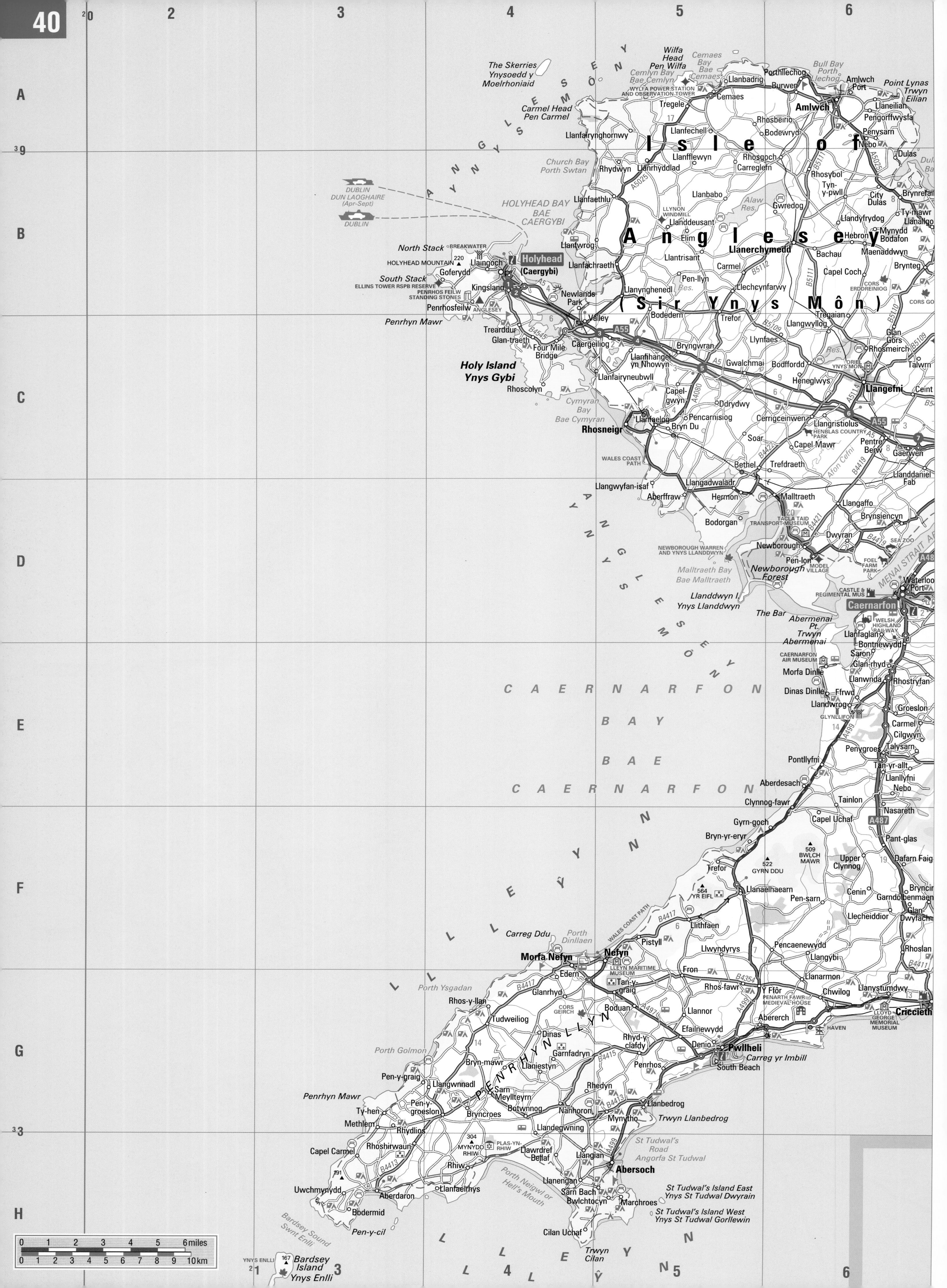
Isle of Anglesey
(Sir Ynys Môn)
ANGLESEY MÔN
CAERNARFON BAY
BAE CAERNARFON
LLEYN LLŶN
PENRHYN LLŶN
The Skerries
Ynysoedd y Moelrhoniaid
Carmel Head
Pen Carmel
Wilfa Head
Pen Wilfa
Cemlyn Bay
Bae Cemlyn
Cemaes Bay
Bae Cemaes
WYLFA POWER STATION AND OBSERVATION TOWER
Bull Bay
Porth Llechog
Point Lynas
Trwyn Eilian
Llanbadrig
Porthllechog
Burwen
Amlwch Port
Amlwch
Cemaes
Tregele
Llanfechell
Llaneilian
Pengorffwysfa
Rhosbeirio
Bodewryd
Penysarn
Nebo
Llanfairynghornwy
Llanfflewyn
Rhosgoch
Carreglefn
Dulas
Church Bay
Porth Swtan
Rhydwyn
Llanrhyddlad
Rhosybol
Tyn-y-pwll
City Dulas
Brynrefail
Ty-mawr
Llanallgo
DUBLIN
DUN LAOGHAIRE (Apr-Sept)
DUBLIN
HOLYHEAD BAY
BAE CAERGYBI
Llanfaethlu
Llanbabo
Alaw Res.
Gwredog
LLYNON WINDMILL
Llanddeusant
Llandyfrydog
Mynydd Bodafon
Hebron
Elim
Llanerchymedd
Maenaddwyn
North Stack
BREAKWATER
HOLYHEAD MOUNTAIN
220
Llaingoch
Holyhead
(Caergybi)
Goferydd
South Stack
ELLINS TOWER RSPB RESERVE
Kingsland
PENRHOS FEILW STANDING STONES
Penrhosfeilw
Llanfwrog
Llanfachraeth
Llantrisant
Carmel
Pen-llyn
Bachau
Capel Coch
Brynteg
Llanynghenedl
Llechcynfarwy
CORS ERDDREINIOG
Newlands Park
Valley
Bodedern
Trefor
Tregaian
CORS GOCH
Penrhyn Mawr
Trearddur
Glan-traeth
Four Mile Bridge
Caergeiliog
Llanfihangel yn Nhowyn
Bryngwran
Llynfaes
Llangwyllog
Res.
Glan Gors
Rhosmeirch
Talwrn
Holy Island
Ynys Gybi
Rhoscolyn
Llanfairyneubwll
Gwalchmai
Bodffordd
ORIEL YNYS MÔN
Heneglwys
Llangefni
Ceint
Cymyran Bay
Bae Cymyran
Capel-gwyn
Ddrydwy
Rhosneigr
Llanfaelog
Pencarnisiog
Bryn Du
Cerrigceinwen
Llangristiolus
HENBLAS COUNTRY PARK
Soar
Capel Mawr
Pentre Berw
Gaerwen
WALES COAST PATH
Bethel
Trefdraeth
Afon Cefni
Llanddaniel Fab
Llangwyfan-isaf
Aberffraw
Llangadwaladr
Hermon
Malltraeth
Llangaffo
Bodorgan
TACLA TAID TRANSPORT MUSEUM
Brynsiencyn
Dwyran
SEA ZOO
NEWBOROUGH WARREN AND YNYS LLANDDWYN
Newborough
Pen-lon
MODEL VILLAGE
FOEL FARM PARK
MENAI STRAIT
Malltraeth Bay
Bae Malltraeth
Newborough Forest
Waterloo Port
CASTLE & REGIMENTAL MUS
Llanddwyn I.
Ynys Llanddwyn
Caernarfon
The Bar
Abermenai Pt.
Trwyn Abermenai
WELSH HIGHLAND RAILWAY
Llanfaglan
Bontnewydd
CAERNARFON AIR MUSEUM
Saron
Glan-rhyd
Morfa Dinlle
Llanwnda
Rhostryfan
Dinas Dinlle
Ffrwd
Llandwrog
Groeslon
GLYNLLIFON
Carmel
Cilgwyn
Penygroes
Talysarn
Pontllyfni
Tan-yr-allt
Llanllyfni
Nebo
Aberdesach
Clynnog-fawr
Tainlon
Nasareth
Capel Uchaf
Gyrn-goch
Bryn-yr-eryr
Pant-glas
509 BWLCH MAWR
522 GYRN DDU
Upper Clynnog
Dafarn Faig
Trefor
564 YR EIFL
Llanaelhaearn
Cenin
Pen-sarn
Bryncir
Garndolbenmaen
Glan-Dwyfach
Llecheiddior
Llithfaen
Carreg Ddu
Porth Dinllaen
Pistyll
Pencaenewydd
Llwyndyrys
Llangybi
Rhoslan
Morfa Nefyn
Nefyn
LLEYN MARITIME MUSEUM
Edern
Fron
Llanarmon
Tan-y-graig
Rhos-fawr
Y Ffôr
Chwilog
Llanystumdwy
Porth Ysgadan
Glanrhyd
PENARTH FAWR MEDIEVAL HOUSE
Criccieth
Rhos-y-llan
CORS GEIRCH
Boduan
Llannor
Abererch
LLOYD GEORGE MEMORIAL MUSEUM
Tudweiliog
Efailnewydd
HAVEN
Dinas
Rhyd-y-clafdy
Denio
Pwllheli
Porth Golmon
Garnfadryn
Carreg yr Imbill
South Beach
Bryn-mawr
Llaniestyn
Penrhos
Pen-y-graig
Llangwnnadl
Rhedyn
Sarn Meyllteyrn
Llanbedrog
Penrhyn Mawr
Ty-hen
Pen-y-groeslon
Bryncroes
Botwnnog
Nanhoron
Mynytho
Trwyn Llanbedrog
Methlem
Rhydlios
Llandegwning
304 MYNYDD RHIW
PLAS-YN-RHIW
St Tudwal's Road
Angorfa St Tudwal
Capel Carmel
Rhoshirwaun
Llawrdref Bellaf
Llangian
Rhiw
Abersoch
191
Uwchmynydd
Aberdaron
Llanfaelrhys
Porth Neigwl or Hell's Mouth
Llanengan
Sarn Bach
St Tudwal's Island East
Ynys St Tudwal Dwyrain
Bodermid
Bwlchtocyn
Marchroes
St Tudwal's Island West
Ynys St Tudwal Gorllewin
Bardsey Sound
Swnt Enlli
Pen-y-cil
Cilan Uchaf
Trwyn Cilan
YNYS ENLLI
167
Bardsey Island
Ynys Enlli
0 1 2 3 4 5 6 miles
0 1 2 3 4 5 6 7 8 9 10 km

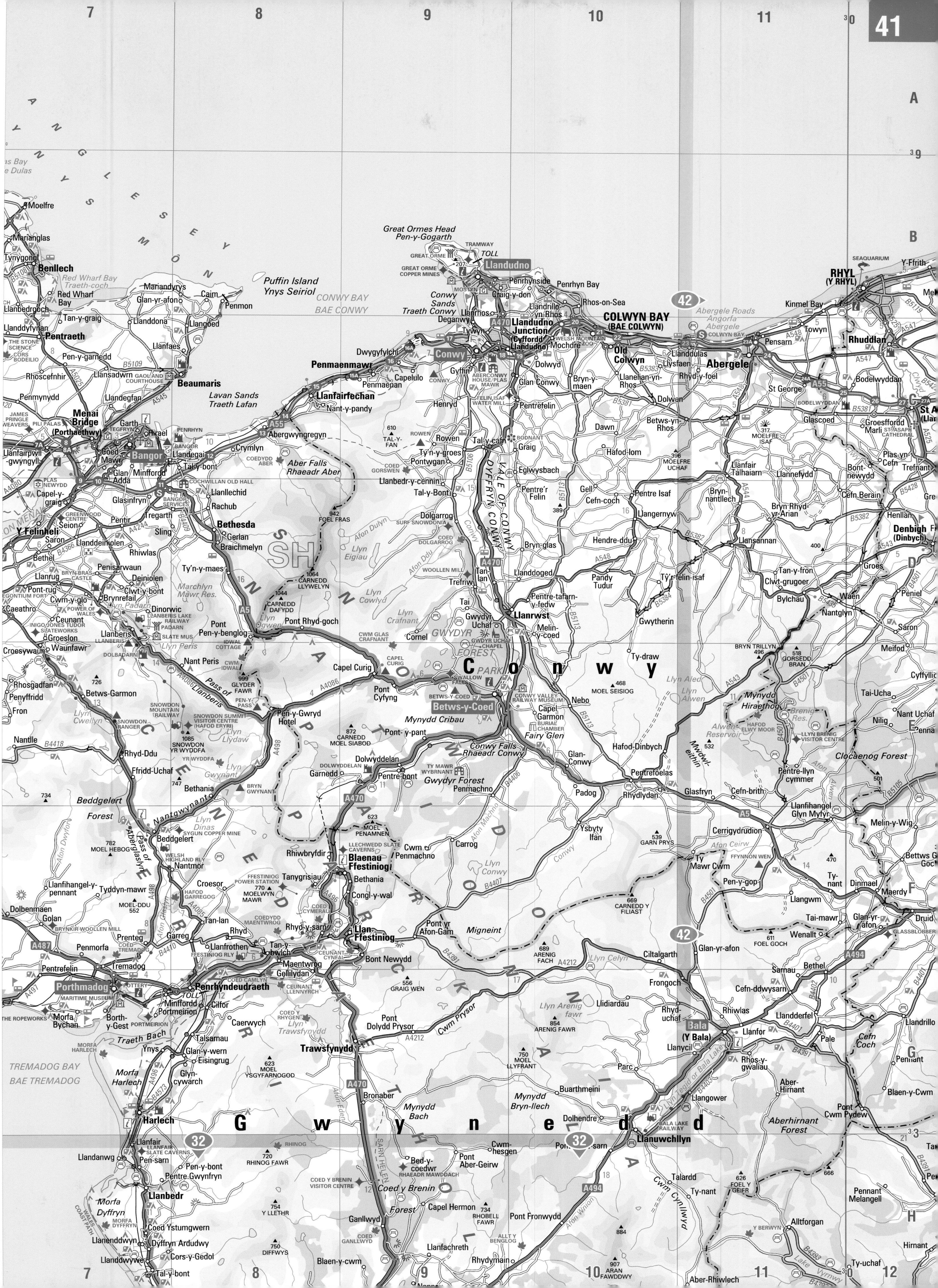

7
8
9
10
11
A
B
C
D
E
F
G
H
ANGLESEY
YNYS MÔN
Moelfre
Marianglas
Tynygongl
Benllech
Red Wharf Bay
Traeth-coch
Red Wharf Bay
Llanbedrgoch
Tan-y-graig
Llanddyfnan
Pentraeth
THE STONE SCIENCE
CORS BODEILIO
Pen-y-garnedd
Rhoscefnhir
Penmynydd
Mariandyrys
Glan-yr-afon
Caim
Penmon
Llanddona
Llangoed
Llanfaes
Llansadwrn
GAOL AND COURTHOUSE
Beaumaris
Llandegfan
Lavan Sands
Traeth Lafan
Puffin Island
Ynys Seiriol
CONWY BAY
BAE CONWY
Menai Bridge
(Porthaethwy)
Garth
Hirael
PENRHYN
TEGFRYN
Bangor
Llandegai
Crymlyn
Llanfairpwll
-gwyngyll
Coed Mawr
Glan Adda
Minffordd
Tal-y-bont
Capel-y-graig
COCHWILLAN OLD HALL
Llanllechid
Rachub
Glasinfryn
Pentir
Tregarth
Bethesda
Gerlan
Braichmelyn
Y Felinheli
Seion
Saron
Llanddeiniolen
Bethel
Sling
Rhiwlas
Llanrug
Penisarwaun
Pont-rug
Deiniolen
Clwt-y-bont
Cwm-y-glo
Brynrefail
Dinorwic
Caeathro
Ceunant
Llanberis
Groeslon
Waunfawr
Croesywaun
Rhosgadfan
Penyffridd
Fron
Betws-Garmon
Nant Peris
Pass of Llanberis
Ty'n-y-maes
Marchlyn Mawr Res.
Llyn Padarn
Llyn Peris
Llyn Ogwen
Pont Rhyd-goch
Pont Pen-y-benglog
GLYDER FAWR
SNOWDON
YR WYDDFA
Llyn Cwellyn
Nantlle
Rhyd-Ddu
Ffridd-Uchaf
Bethania
Beddgelert Forest
Beddgelert
Nantgwynant
Llyn Dinas
Pass of Aberglaslyn
Nantmor
Croesor
Llanfihangel-y-pennant
Tyddyn-mawr
Dolbenmaen
Golan
Prenteg
Garreg
Tan-lan
Penmorfa
Tremadog
Pentrefelin
Porthmadog
Morfa Bychan
Borth-y-Gest
Minffordd
Portmeirion
Penrhyndeudraeth
Cilfor
Talsarnau
Ynys
Glan-y-wern
Eisingrug
Glyn-cywarch
Traeth Bach
TREMADOG BAY
BAE TREMADOG
Morfa Harlech
Harlech
Llanfair
Llandanwg
Pen-sarn
Pen-y-bont
Pentre Gwynfryn
Llanbedr
Morfa Dyffryn
Coed Ystumgwern
Llanenddwyn
Dyffryn Ardudwy
Llanddwywe
Cors-y-Gedol
Tal-y-bont
Great Ormes Head
Pen-y-Gogarth
Llandudno
Penrhynside
Penrhyn Bay
Craig-y-don
Rhos-on-Sea
Llandrillo-yn-Rhos
Conwy Sands
Traeth Conwy
Llanrhos
Deganwy
Tywyn
Llandudno Junction
(Cyffordd Llandudno)
Mochdre
COLWYN BAY
(BAE COLWYN)
Old Colwyn
Llanddulas
Llysfaen
Abergele
Abergele Roads
Angorfa Abergele
Dwygyfylchi
Penmaenmawr
Penmaenan
Capelulo
Conwy
Gyffin
Glan Conwy
Llanfairfechan
Nant-y-pandy
Abergwyngregyn
Aber Falls
Rhaeadr Aber
Henryd
Dolwyd
Bryn-y-maen
Llanelian-yn-Rhos
Dolwen
Pentrefelin
Rowen
Ty'n-y-groes
Pontwgan
Tal-y-cafn
Graig
Dawn
Betws-yn-Rhos
Hafod-lom
Llanbedr-y-cennin
Eglwysbach
Tal-y-Bont
Pentre'r Felin
Gell
Cefn-coch
Pentre Isaf
Dolgarrog
Llyn Eigiau
Llyn Dulyn
FOEL FRAS
CARNEDD LLYWELYN
CARNEDD DAFYDD
Llyn Cowlyd
Llyn Crafnant
Bryn-glas
Llanddoged
Tan-lan
Trefriw
Tai
Gwydyr Uchaf
Llanrwst
Pentre-tafarn-y-fedw
Melin-y-coed
Pandy Tudur
Hendre-ddu
Llangernyw
Cornel
GWYDYR FOREST PARK
Capel Curig
Pont Cyfyng
Betws-y-Coed
Pen-y-Gwryd Hotel
Mynydd Cribau
Pont-y-pant
MOEL SIABOD
Dolwyddelan
Pentre-bont
Garnedd
Gwydyr Forest
Penmachno
Conwy Falls
Rhaeadr Conwy
Capel Garmon
Fairy Glen
Nebo
MOEL SEISIOG
Hafod-Dinbych
Glan-Conwy
Padog
Pentrefoelas
Rhydlydan
Glasfryn
Ysbyty Ifan
GARN PRYS
Ty Mawr Cwm
Pen-y-gop
Ty-draw
Gwytherin
Tŷ'r-felin-isaf
Llyn Aled
Llyn Alwen
Conwy
VALE OF CONWY
DYFFRYN CONWY
Cwm Penmachno
Carrog
MOEL PENAMNEN
Blaenau Ffestiniog
Rhiwbryfdir
Bethania
Tanygrisiau
MOELWYN MAWR
Congl-y-wal
Rhyd-y-sarn
Rhyd
Llan-Ffestiniog
Llanfrothen
Tan-y-bwlch
Maentwrog
Gellilydan
Bont Newydd
Pont yr Afon-Gam
Migneint
Llyn Conwy
CARNEDD Y FILIAST
ARENIG FACH
Llyn Celyn
GRAIG WEN
Pont Dolydd Prysor
Cwm Prysor
Llyn Trawsfynydd
Trawsfynydd
ARENIG FAWR
Llyn Arenig fawr
MOEL LLYFRANT
YSGYFARNOGOD
Bronaber
Mynydd Bach
Mynydd Bryn-llech
Buarthmeini
Dolhendre
Parc
Llidiardau
Frongoch
Ciltalgarth
Glan-yr-afon
Rhyd-uchaf
Bala
(Y Bala)
Llanycil
Llanfor
Llanuwchllyn
Cwm-hesgen
Pont Aber-Geirw
Bed-y-coedwr
RHAEADR MAWDDACH
RHINOG FAWR
Coed y Brenin
Forest
Capel Hermon
RHOBELL FAWR
Pont Fronwydd
Ganllwyd
Llanfachreth
Rhydymain
Blaen-y-cwm
Y LLETHR
DIFFWYS
ARAN FAWDDWY
Aber-Rhiwlech
Talardd
Ty-nant
Cwm Cynllwyd
Llyn Tegid or Bala Lake
Llangower
Gwynedd
Conwy
SNOWDONIA
RHYL
(Y RHYL)
Y-Ffrith
Kinmel Bay
Towyn
Pensarn
Rhuddlan
St George
Bodelwyddan
St Asaph
Glascoed
Groesffordd Marli
Plas-yn-Cefn
Trefnant
Llanfair Talhaiarn
Llannefydd
Bont-newydd
Cefn Berain
Bryn-nantllech
Bryn Rhyd-yr-Arian
Henllan
Denbigh
(Dinbych)
Llansannan
Tan-y-fron
Clwt-grugoer
Groes
Bylchau
Waen
Peniel
Nantglyn
Saron
Meifod
BRYN TRILLYN
GORSEDD BRAN
Cyffylliog
Mynydd Hiraethog
Brenig Res.
Alwen Reservoir
Tai-Ucha
Nant Uchaf
Nilig
Clocaenog Forest
Pentre-llyn cymmer
Cefn-brith
Llanfihangel Glyn Myfyr
Melin-y-Wig
Cerrigydrudion
Afon Ceirw
Betws Gwerfil Goch
Ty-nant
Dinmael
Maerdy
Llangwm
Tai-mawr
Glan-yr-afon
Druid
Wenallt
FOEL GOCH
Bethel
Sarnau
Cefn-ddwysarn
Rhiwlas
Llandderfel
Llandrillo
Pale
Cefn Coch
Penmaen
Rhos-y-gwaliau
Aber-Hirnant
Blaen-y-Cwm
Aberhirnant Forest
Pont Cwm Pydew
FOEL Y GEIFR
Pennant Melangell
Alltforgan
Y BERWYN
Hirnant
Ty-uchaf
Lake Vyrnwy
A5
A55
A470
A494
A487
A498
A4086
A4212
A543
A548
A547
A525
B5113
B4391
42
32

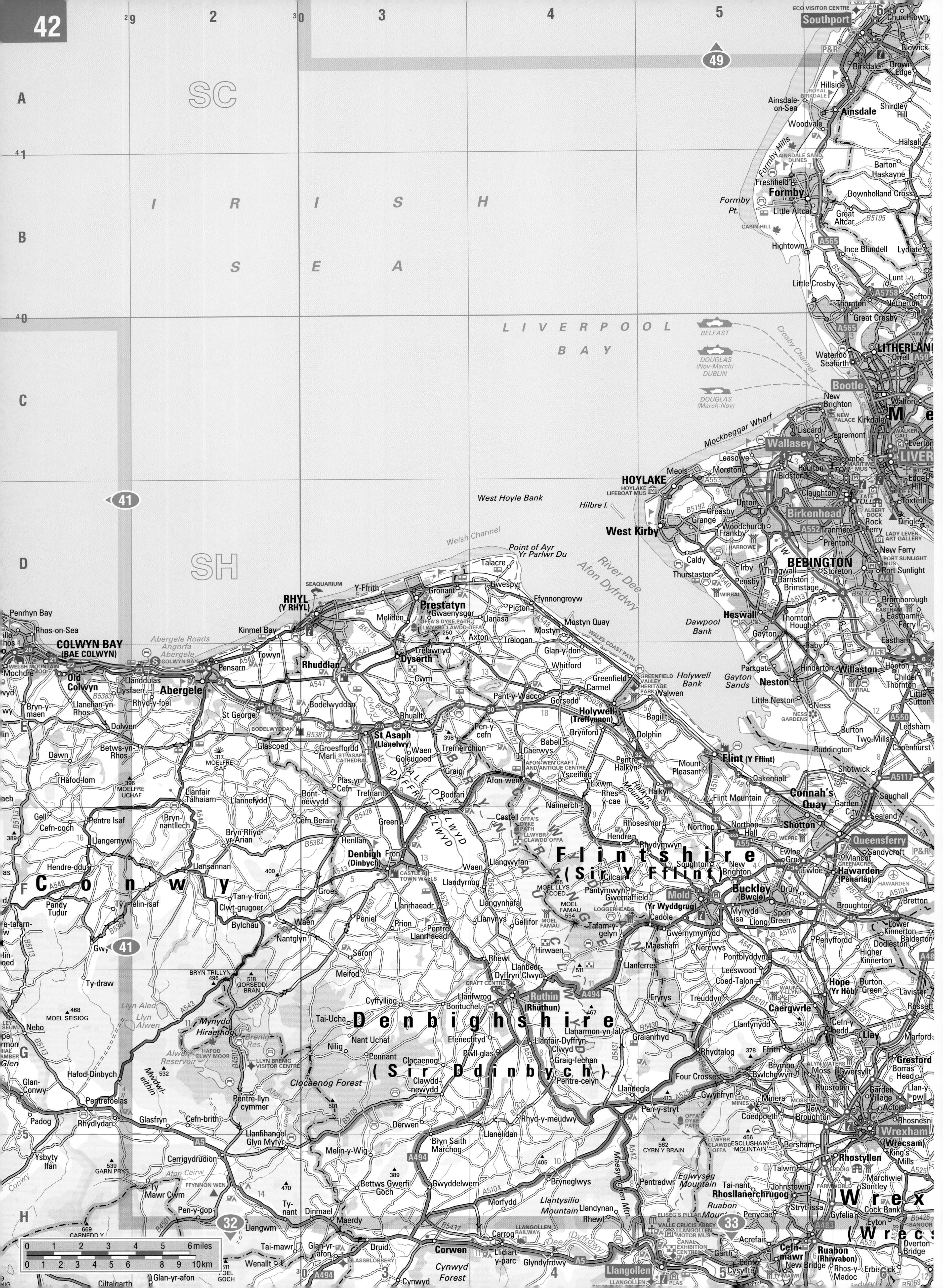

SC
SH
I R I S H
S E A
L I V E R P O O L
B A Y
Southport
Birkdale
Hillside
Ainsdale-on-Sea
Ainsdale
Woodvale
Formby Hills
Formby
Formby Pt.
Little Altcar
Great Altcar
Hightown
Ince Blundell
Little Crosby
Thornton
Great Crosby
Waterloo
Seaforth
LITHERLAND
Bootle
Crosby Channel
New Brighton
Wallasey
Mockbeggar Wharf
Leasowe
Moreton
Meols
HOYLAKE
Hilbre I.
West Hoyle Bank
West Kirby
Birkenhead
Greasby
Upton
Woodchurch
Frankby
Caldy
Irby
Thurstaston
Pensby
Heswall
BEBINGTON
Dawpool Bank
Gayton
Parkgate
Neston
Willaston
Little Neston
Ness
Burton
Welsh Channel
Point of Ayr
Yr Parlwr Du
Talacre
River Dee
Afon Dyfrdwy
Gronant
Prestatyn
Gwaenysgor
Meliden
Llanasa
Picton
Ffynnongroyw
Mostyn Quay
Mostyn
Trelogan
Axton
Glan-y-don
Whitford
Greenfield
Carmel
Holywell
(Treffynnon)
Holywell Bank
Gayton Sands
Bagillt
Flint (Y Fflint)
Connah's Quay
Shotton
Queensferry
Hawarden
(Penarlâg)
Buckley
(Bwcle)
Mold
(Yr Wyddgrug)
Flintshire
(Sir Y Fflint)
RHYL
(Y RHYL)
Kinmel Bay
Towyn
Rhuddlan
Dyserth
Trelawnyd
Abergele Roads
Pensarn
Abergele
Llanddulas
COLWYN BAY
(BAE COLWYN)
Rhos-on-Sea
Penrhyn Bay
Old Colwyn
Mochdre
St George
Bodelwyddan
St Asaph
(Llanelwy)
Denbigh
(Dinbych)
VALE OF CLWYD
DYFFRYN CLWYD
Conwy
Llansannan
Llangernyw
Ruthin
(Rhuthun)
Denbighshire
(Sir Ddinbych)
Clocaenog Forest
Llyn Brenig
Alwen Reservoir
Cerrigydrudion
Corwen
Llangollen
Cefn-mawr
Ruabon
(Rhiwabon)
Wrexham
(Wrecsam)
Caergwrle
Hope
(Yr Hôb)
Gresford
Llandegla
Four Crosses
Rhosllanerchrugog
Eglwyseg Mountain
Ruabon Mountain
Llantysilio Mountain
Gwyddelwern
Bettws Gwerfil Goch
Maerdy
Druid
Cynwyd
Cynwyd Forest
Glyndyfrdwy
Pentrefoelas
Glasfryn
Padog
Ysbyty Ifan
Rhydlydan
Hafod-Dinbych
Nebo
49
41
32
33
0 1 2 3 4 5 6 miles
0 1 2 3 4 5 6 7 8 9 10 km

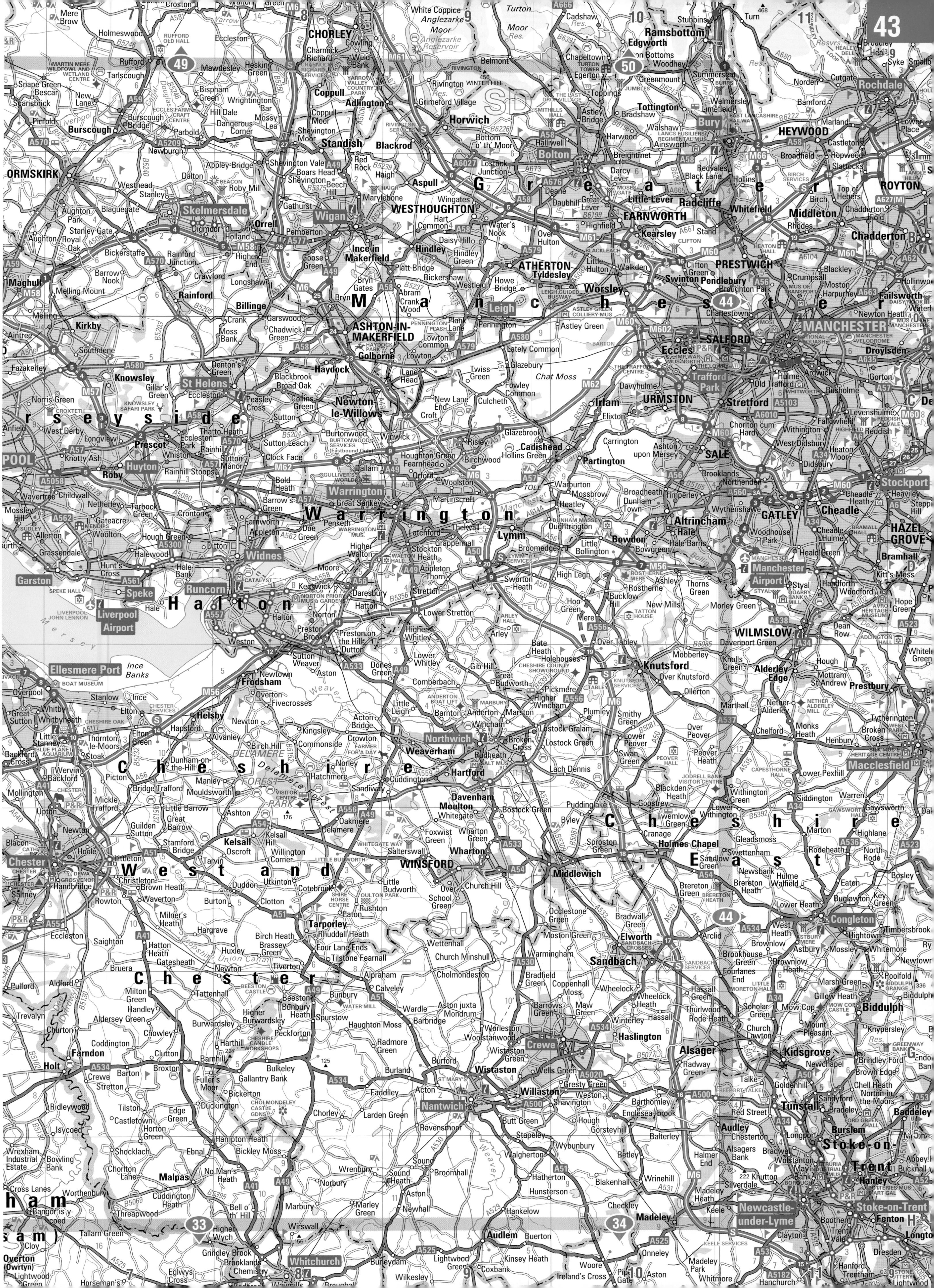

CHORLEY
Ramsbottom
Edgworth
Rochdale
HEYWOOD
ROYTON
ORMSKIRK
Burscough
Skelmersdale
Wigan
Standish
Horwich
Bolton
Bury
WESTHOUGHTON
FARNWORTH
Radcliffe
Whitefield
Middleton
Chadderton
PRESTWICH
ATHERTON
Tyldesley
Worsley
Leigh
Greater Manchester
MANCHESTER
SALFORD
Eccles
Trafford Park
URMSTON
Stretford
Droylsden
Kirkby
Knowsley
St Helens
ASHTON-IN-MAKERFIELD
Golborne
Haydock
Newton-le-Willows
Merseyside
Prescot
Huyton
Warrington
Widnes
Runcorn
Halton
Speke
Garston
Liverpool Airport
Irlam
Cadishead
Partington
SALE
Altrincham
Lymm
Stockport
Cheadle
GATLEY
HAZEL GROVE
Manchester Airport
WILMSLOW
Knutsford
Alderley Edge
Prestbury
Macclesfield
Ellesmere Port
Frodsham
Helsby
Northwich
Weaverham
Hartford
Cheshire West and Chester
Cheshire East
Chester
Kelsall
WINSFORD
Middlewich
Holmes Chapel
Sandbach
Congleton
Biddulph
Tarporley
Crewe
Nantwich
Alsager
Kidsgrove
Tunstall
Burslem
Stoke-on-Trent
Hanley
Newcastle-under-Lyme
Farndon
Holt
Malpas
Audlem
Whitchurch
Madeley
Wrexham
M6
M56
M62
M60
M61
M58
M57
M53
A49
A51
A534
A556
A34
A50

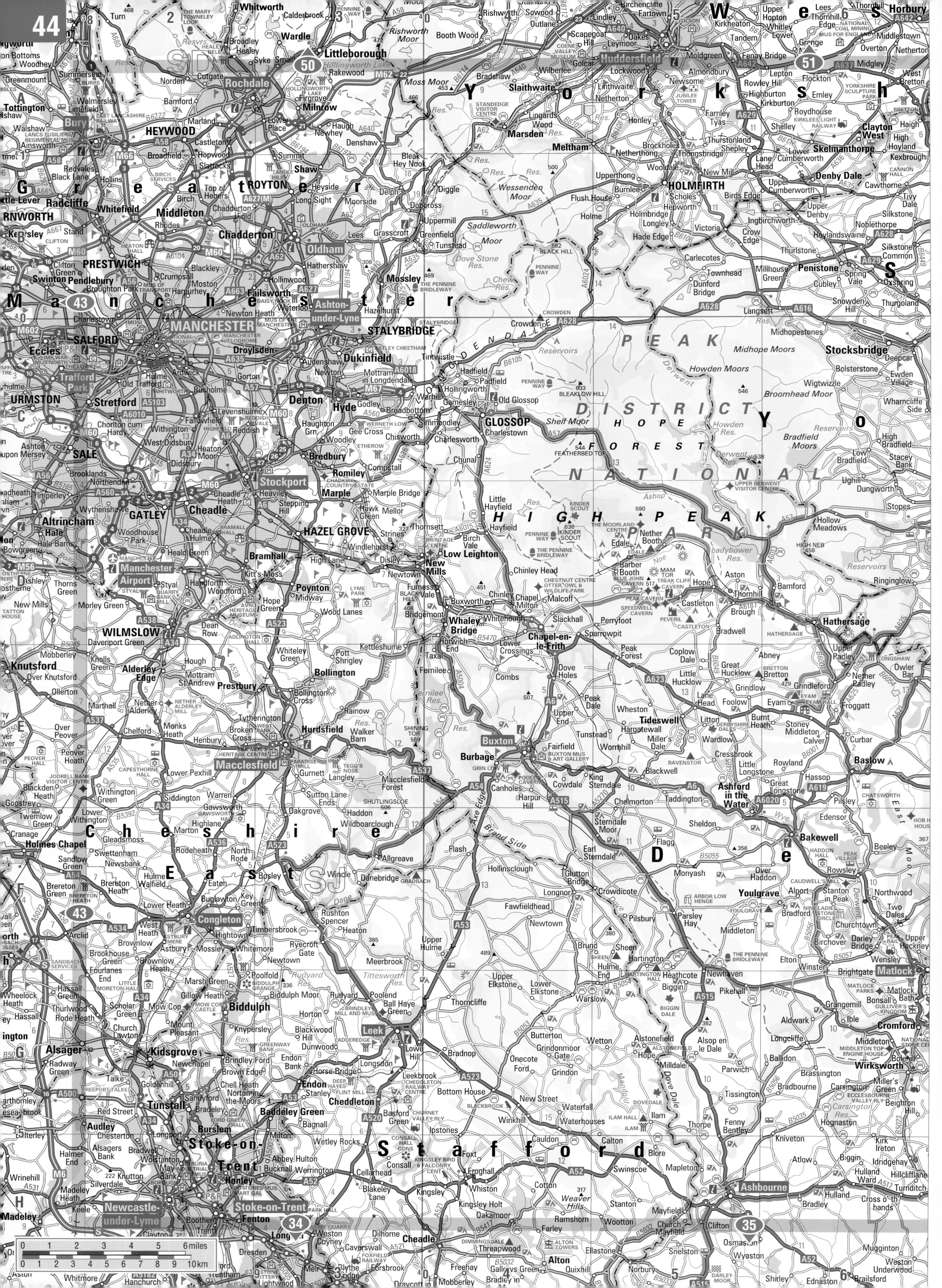
Greater Manchester
West Yorkshire
South Yorkshire
Derbyshire
Cheshire East
Stafford
PEAK DISTRICT NATIONAL PARK
HOPE FOREST
HIGH PEAK
MANCHESTER
SALFORD
Stockport
Oldham
Rochdale
Bury
Huddersfield
HOLMFIRTH
GLOSSOP
Buxton
Macclesfield
Congleton
Leek
Stoke-on-Trent
Newcastle-under-Lyme
Ashbourne
Matlock
Bakewell
Hathersage
Stocksbridge
Penistone
Littleborough
HEYWOOD
ROYTON
Middleton
Chadderton
PRESTWICH
Ashton-under-Lyne
STALYBRIDGE
Dukinfield
Hyde
Denton
URMSTON
Stretford
SALE
Altrincham
GATLEY
Cheadle
HAZEL GROVE
Manchester Airport
WILMSLOW
Knutsford
Alderley Edge
Bollington
Poynton
Marple
Romiley
Bredbury
New Mills
Whaley Bridge
Chapel-en-le-Frith
Tideswell
Baslow
Biddulph
Kidsgrove
Alsager
Tunstall
Burslem
Hanley
Fenton
Cheddleton
Cheadle
Alton
Wirksworth
Cromford
Marsden
Meltham
Slaithwaite
Denby Dale
Skelmanthorpe
Clayton West
0 1 2 3 4 5 6 miles
0 1 2 3 4 5 6 7 8 9 10 km

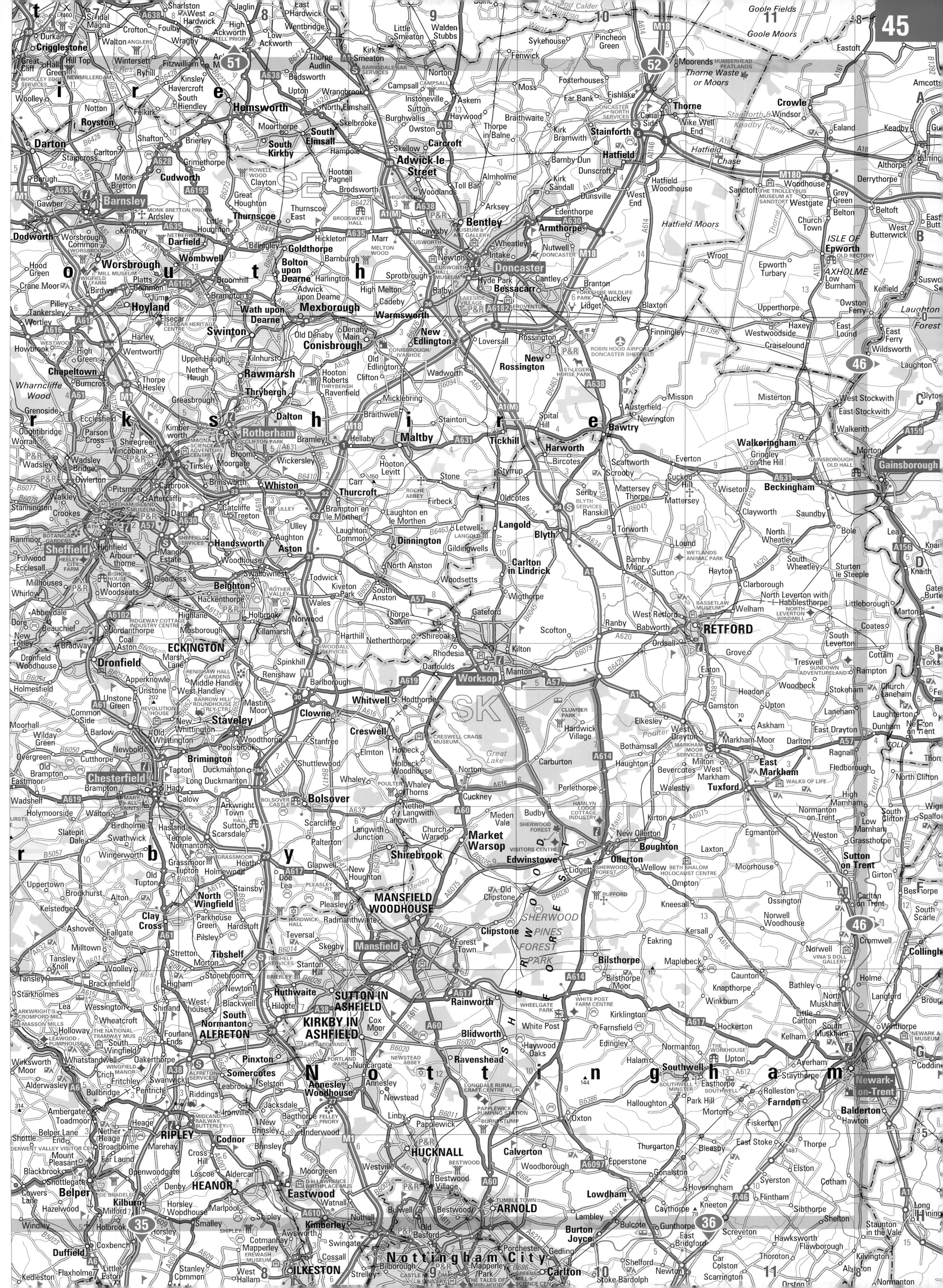

Barnsley
Hemsworth
Royston
Darton
Cudworth
Thurnscoe
Darfield
Wombwell
Worsbrough
Hoyland
Goldthorpe
Bolton upon Dearne
Mexborough
Wath upon Dearne
Swinton
Conisbrough
Rawmarsh
Thrybergh
Rotherham
Chapeltown
Adwick-le-Street
South Elmsall
South Kirkby
Carcroft
Bentley
Doncaster
Armthorpe
Bessacarr
Warmsworth
New Edlington
New Rossington
Stainforth
Hatfield
Thorne
Crowle
Epworth
Isle of Axholme
Maltby
Tickhill
Harworth
Bawtry
Gainsborough
Beckingham
Walkeringham
Sheffield
Handsworth
Aston
Beighton
Dinnington
Langold
Blyth
Carlton in Lindrick
Worksop
Retford
Eckington
Dronfield
Staveley
Chesterfield
Clowne
Creswell
Whitwell
Bolsover
Shirebrook
Market Warsop
Edwinstowe
Ollerton
Boughton
Tuxford
East Markham
Clay Cross
North Wingfield
Tibshelf
Mansfield Woodhouse
Mansfield
Clipstone
Sherwood Forest
Sutton in Ashfield
Kirkby in Ashfield
Huthwaite
South Normanton
Alfreton
Rainworth
Bilsthorpe
Blidworth
Ravenshead
Southwell
Newark-on-Trent
Farndon
Balderton
Ripley
Somercotes
Annesley Woodhouse
Hucknall
Heanor
Belper
Eastwood
Kimberley
Arnold
Calverton
Lowdham
Burton Joyce
Carlton
Nottingham City
Ilkeston
Duffield
Nottingham
Yorkshire
Derbyshire
M1
M18
M180
A1
A1(M)
A57
A60
A614
A617
A631
A638
A46
51
52
46
35
36

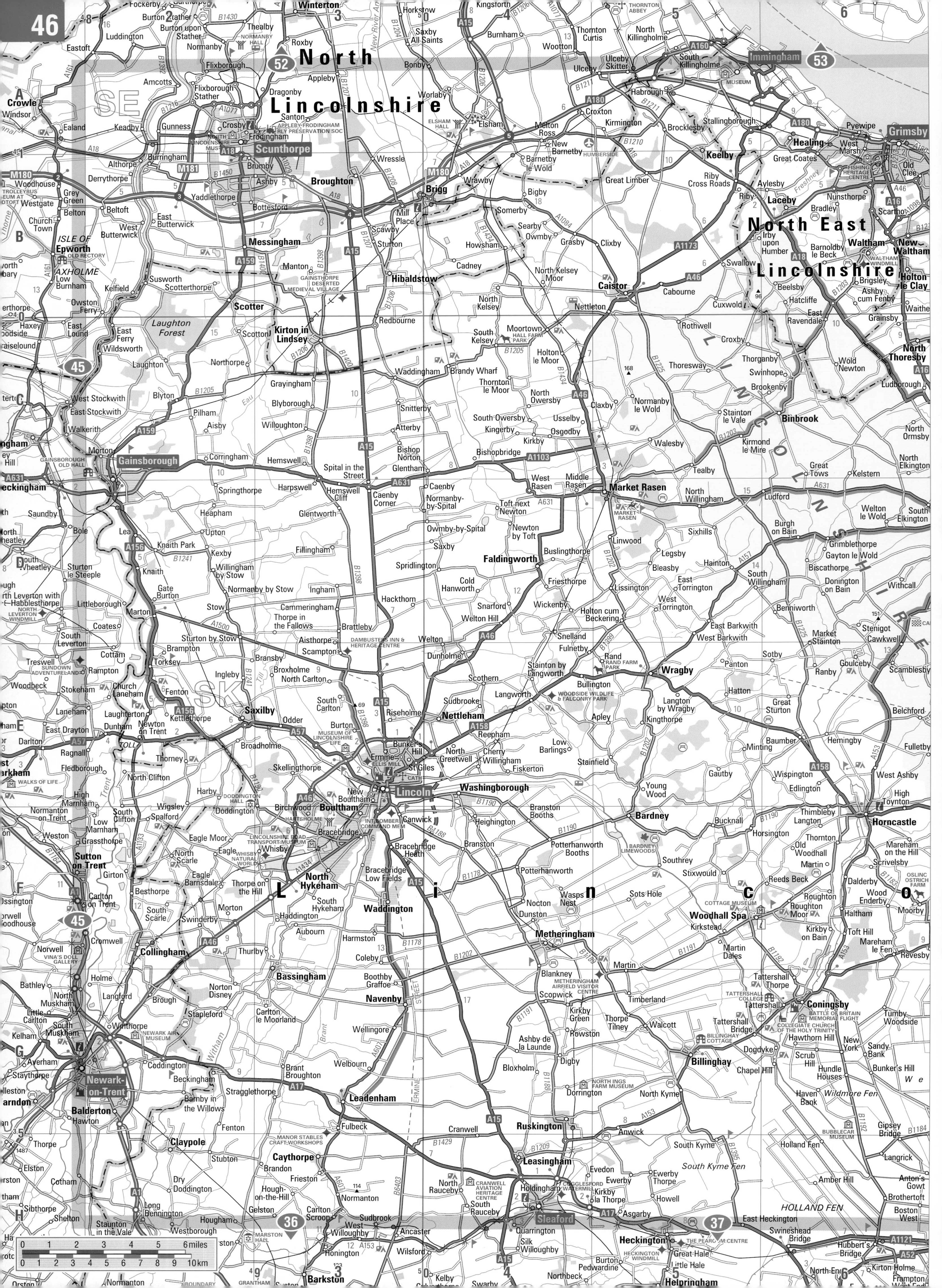
North Lincolnshire
North East Lincolnshire
Lincolnshire
Scunthorpe
Grimsby
Immingham
Brigg
Gainsborough
Market Rasen
Caistor
Lincoln
Horncastle
Woodhall Spa
Coningsby
Sleaford
Newark-on-Trent
Saxilby
Wragby
Nettleham
North Hykeham
Waddington
Metheringham
Ruskington
Leasingham
Billinghay
Heckington
Navenby
Bassingham
Collingham
Leadenham
Caythorpe
Claypole
Messingham
Scotter
Kirton in Lindsey
Hibaldstow
Broughton
Keelby
Laceby
Waltham
Binbrook
Bardney
Washingborough
Faldingworth
Boultham
Balderton
Barkston
52
53
45
36
37
0 1 2 3 4 5 6 miles
0 1 2 3 4 5 6 7 8 9 10 km

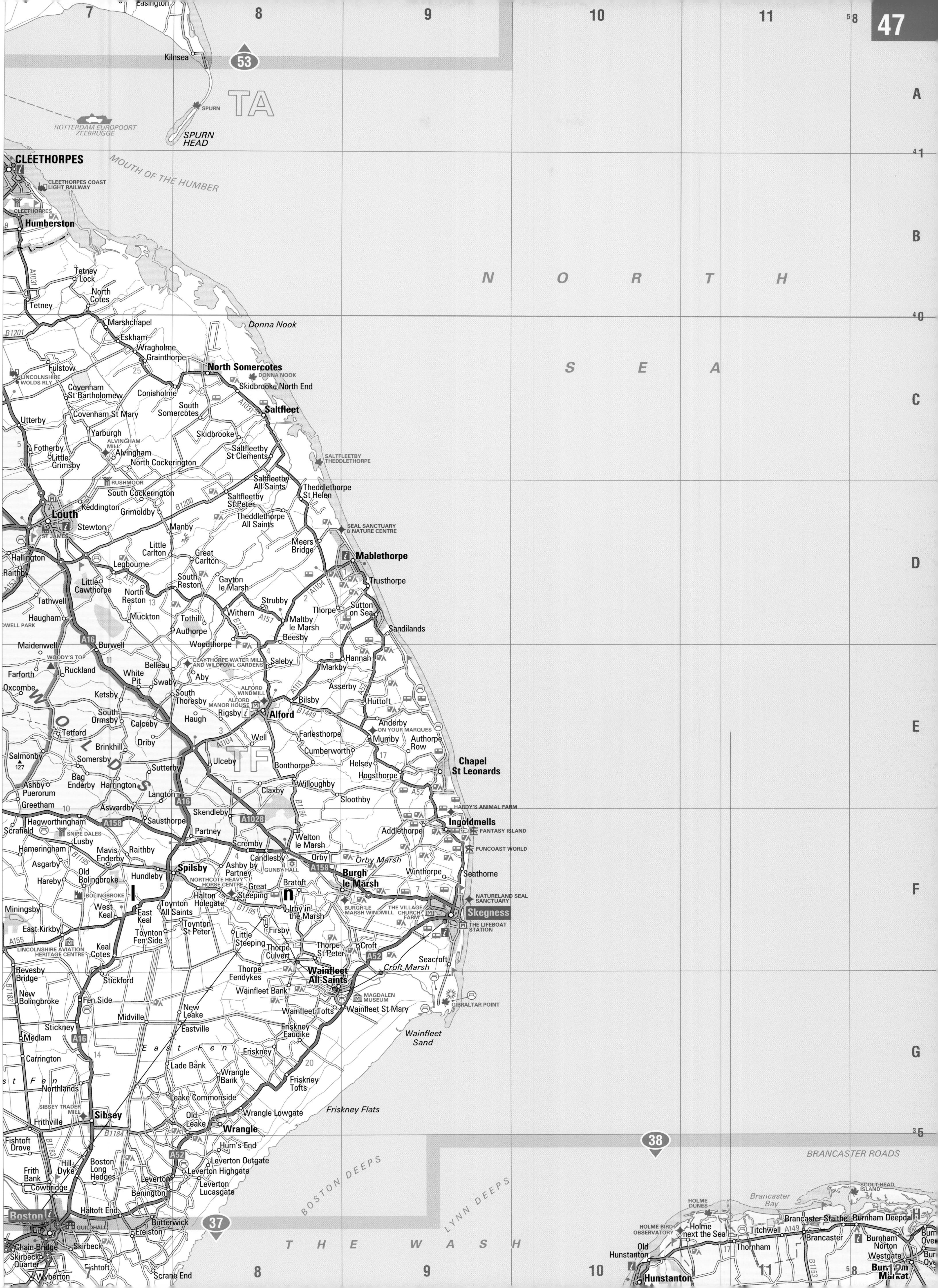

7
8
9
10
11
58
Easington
Kilnsea
53
SPURN
TA
ROTTERDAM EUROPOORT
ZEEBRUGGE
SPURN HEAD
A
CLEETHORPES
CLEETHORPES COAST LIGHT RAILWAY
MOUTH OF THE HUMBER
41
CLEETHORPES
Humberston
B
A1031
Tetney Lock
North Cotes
Tetney
N O R T H
Marshchapel
Donna Nook
40
B1201
Eskham
Wragholme
Grainthorpe
Fulstow
North Somercotes
DONNA NOOK
LINCOLNSHIRE WOLDS RLY
Covenham St Bartholomew
Conisholme
Skidbrooke North End
S E A
Covenham St Mary
South Somercotes
A1031
Saltfleet
C
Utterby
Yarburgh
Skidbrooke
ALVINGHAM MILL
Fotherby
Alvingham
Saltfleetby St Clements
Little Grimsby
North Cockerington
SALTFLEETBY THEDDLETHORPE
RUSHMOOR
Saltfleetby All Saints
Theddlethorpe St Helen
South Cockerington
Louth
Keddington
Grimoldby
B1200
Saltfleetby St Peter
ST JAMES
Stewton
Manby
Theddlethorpe All Saints
SEAL SANCTUARY & NATURE CENTRE
Hallington
Little Carlton
Great Carlton
Meers Bridge
Mablethorpe
Raithby
Legbourne
D
A157
Little Cawthorpe
South Reston
Gayton le Marsh
A1104
Trusthorpe
North Reston
Tathwell
13
Strubby
Sutton on Sea
Haugham
Muckton
Tothill
Withern
A157
Maltby le Marsh
Thorpe
B1373
Authorpe
Sandilands
OWELL PARK
A16
Beesby
Maidenwell
Burwell
Woodthorpe
WOODY'S TOP
11
CLAYTHORPE WATER MILL AND WILDFOWL GARDENS
Saleby
Hannah
Markby
Farforth
Ruckland
Belleau
White Pit
Aby
Oxcombe
Swaby
Asserby
A52
ALFORD WINDMILL
Ketsby
South Thoresby
ALFORD MANOR HOUSE
A1111
Huttoft
Bilsby
South Ormsby
Rigsby
Alford
B1449
Haugh
E
Calceby
Anderby
ON YOUR MARQUES
Tetford
Driby
Farlesthorpe
Mumby
Authorpe Row
Brinkhill
A1104
Cumberworth
Salmonby
Somersby
TF
17
Chapel St Leonards
127
Ulceby
Helsey
Sutterby
Bonthorpe
Bag Enderby
Harrington
Hogsthorpe
Ashby Puerorum
Langton
Willoughby
A52
Claxby
B1196
Sloothby
Greetham
10
A16
HARDY'S ANIMAL FARM
Aswardby
Skendleby
Hagworthingham
A158
A1028
Ingoldmells
Scrafield
SNIPE DALES
Sausthorpe
Partney
Addlethorpe
FANTASY ISLAND
Lusby
Welton le Marsh
Hameringham
Mavis Enderby
Raithby
Scremby
FUNCOAST WORLD
B1195
Asgarby
Candlesby
Orby
Orby Marsh
Old Bolingbroke
Spilsby
Ashby by Partney
GUNBY HALL
A158
Hareby
Hundleby
Burgh le Marsh
Winthorpe
Seathorne
BOLINGBROKE
NORTHCOTE HEAVY HORSE CENTRE
Bratoft
Great Steeping
F
Miningsby
Halton Holegate
7
NATURELAND SEAL SANCTUARY
West Keal
Toynton All Saints
B1195
Irby in the Marsh
BURGH LE MARSH WINDMILL
THE VILLAGE CHURCH FARM
Skegness
East Kirkby
East Keal
Toynton St Peter
THE LIFEBOAT STATION
A155
Toynton Fen Side
Firsby
LINCOLNSHIRE AVIATION HERITAGE CENTRE
Little Steeping
Thorpe St Peter
Croft
Keal Cotes
Thorpe Culvert
A52
Seacroft
Revesby Bridge
Thorpe Fendykes
Wainfleet All Saints
Croft Marsh
Stickford
Wainfleet Bank
MAGDALEN MUSEUM
B1183
Fen Side
New Bolingbroke
New Leake
Wainfleet Tofts
Wainfleet St Mary
GIBRALTAR POINT
Midville
Stickney
Eastville
Friskney Eaudike
Wainfleet Sand
Medlam
A16
14
East Fen
Friskney
G
Carrington
Lade Bank
Wrangle Bank
20
Northlands
st Fen
Friskney Tofts
Leake Commonside
SIBSEY TRADER MILL
Sibsey
Old Leake
Wrangle Lowgate
Friskney Flats
Frithville
Wrangle
B1184
Fishtoft Drove
B1183
38
35
A52
Hurn's End
BRANCASTER ROADS
Hill Dyke
Boston Long Hedges
Leverton Outgate
BOSTON DEEPS
Frith Bank
Leverton Highgate
Cowbridge
Leverton
SCOLT HEAD ISLAND
Benington
Leverton Lucasgate
LYNN DEEPS
HOLME DUNES
Brancaster Bay
Boston
Haltoft End
Brancaster Staithe
Burnham Deepdale
GUILDHALL
Butterwick
37
HOLME BIRD OBSERVATORY
Holme next the Sea
Titchwell
A149
Chain Bridge
Skirbeck
Freiston
Brancaster
Burnham Norton
Skirbeck Quarter
THE WASH
Old Hunstanton
Thornham
17
B1153
Westgate
Wyberton
Fishtoft
Scrane End
Hunstanton
Burnham Market

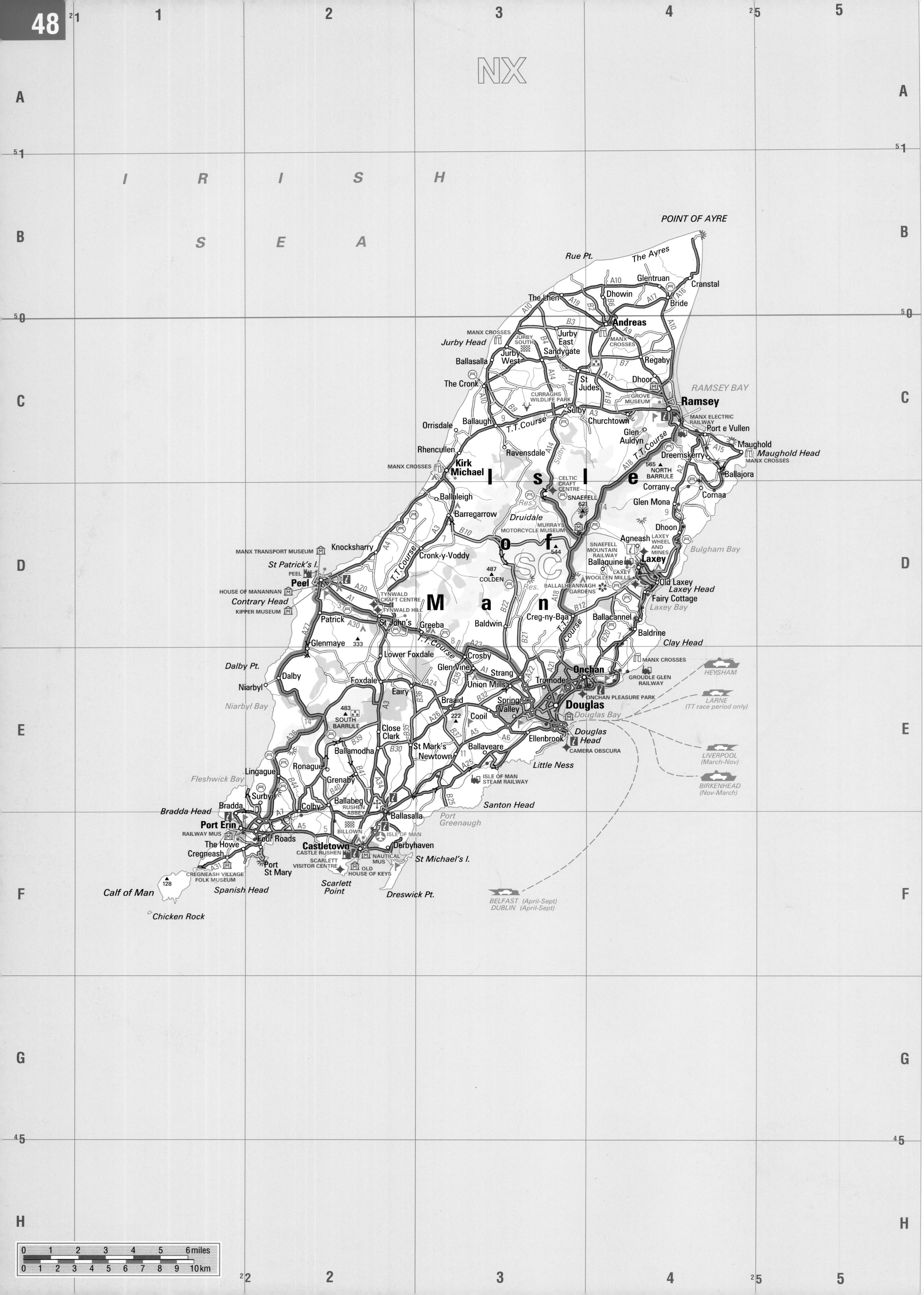
NX
SC
IRISH SEA
Isle of Man
POINT OF AYRE
The Ayres
Rue Pt.
Glentruan
Cranstal
Dhowin
Bride
The Lhen
Andreas
MANX CROSSES
Jurby Head
JURBY SOUTH
Jurby East
Jurby West
Sandygate
Ballasalla
Regaby
The Cronk
St Judes
Dhoor
RAMSEY BAY
CURRAGHS WILDLIFE PARK
GROVE MUSEUM
Ramsey
Sulby
Churchtown
MANX ELECTRIC RAILWAY
Port e Vullen
Orrisdale
Ballaugh
T.T. Course
Glen Auldyn
Maughold
Maughold Head
Rhencullen
Ravensdale
Dreemskerry
Kirk Michael
565 NORTH BARRULE
Ballajora
CELTIC CRAFT CENTRE
SNAEFELL 621
Corrany
Cornaa
Ballaleigh
Glen Mona
Barregarrow
Druidale
MURRAYS MOTORCYCLE MUSEUM
Dhoon
Agneash
LAXEY WHEEL AND MINES
Bulgham Bay
SNAEFELL MOUNTAIN RAILWAY
MANX TRANSPORT MUSEUM
Knockssharry
St Patrick's I.
PEEL
Cronk-y-Voddy
544
Ballaquine
Laxey
LAXEY WOOLLEN MILLS
487 COLDEN
Old Laxey
Laxey Head
Peel
HOUSE OF MANANNAN
BALLALHEANNAGH GARDENS
Fairy Cottage
Laxey Bay
Contrary Head
TYNWALD CRAFT CENTRE
TYNWALD HILL
KIPPER MUSEUM
Patrick
St John's
Greeba
Baldwin
Creg-ny-Baa
Ballacannel
Baldrine
Glenmaye
333
Clay Head
Lower Foxdale
Crosby
Dalby Pt.
Glen Vine
Strang
Onchan
GROUDLE GLEN RAILWAY
HEYSHAM
Dalby
Union Mills
Tromode
Niarbyl
Foxdale
Eairy
ONCHAN PLEASURE PARK
Niarbyl Bay
Braaid
Spring Valley
Douglas
LARNE (TT race period only)
483 SOUTH BARRULE
222
Cooil
Douglas Bay
Close Clark
Ellenbrook
Douglas Head
CAMERA OBSCURA
Ballamodha
St Mark's
Newtown
Ballaveare
LIVERPOOL (March-Nov)
Ronague
Little Ness
Lingague
Fleshwick Bay
Grenaby
ISLE OF MAN STEAM RAILWAY
BIRKENHEAD (Nov-March)
Surby
Bradda
Ballabeg
Colby
RUSHEN ABBEY
Santon Head
Bradda Head
Ballasalla
Port Greenaugh
Port Erin
BILLOWN
RAILWAY MUS
Four Roads
ISLE OF MAN
The Howe
Castletown
Derbyhaven
Cregneash
CASTLE RUSHEN
NAUTICAL MUS
St Michael's I.
Port St Mary
SCARLETT VISITOR CENTRE
OLD HOUSE OF KEYS
CREGNEASH VILLAGE FOLK MUSEUM
128
Calf of Man
Spanish Head
Scarlett Point
Dreswick Pt.
BELFAST (April-Sept)
DUBLIN (April-Sept)
Chicken Rock
0 1 2 3 4 5 6 miles
0 1 2 3 4 5 6 7 8 9 10 km

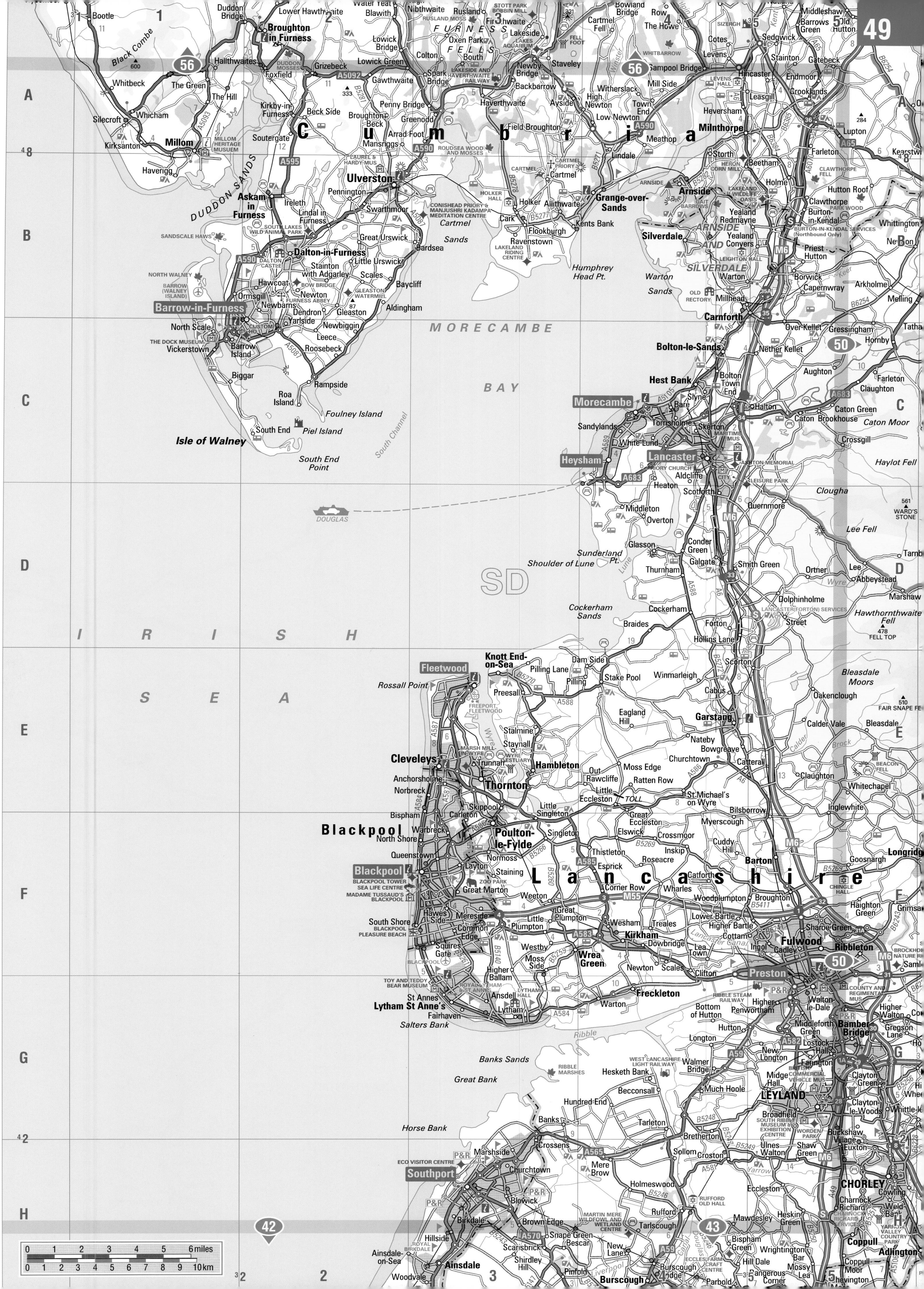
Cumbria
Lancashire
IRISH SEA
MORECAMBE BAY
SD
Bootle
Duddon Bridge
Broughton in Furness
Millom
Silecroft
Kirksanton
Haverigg
Whicham
Whitbeck
Black Combe
Hallthwaites
Foxfield
Grizebeck
Kirkby-in-Furness
Ulverston
Askam in Furness
Dalton-in-Furness
Barrow-in-Furness
Isle of Walney
Vickerstown
North Scale
Roa Island
Piel Island
Foulney Island
Rampside
Biggar
South End
South End Point
Walney Island
DUDDON SANDS
Ireleth
Lindal in Furness
Swarthmoor
Pennington
Great Urswick
Little Urswick
Bardsea
Baycliff
Aldingham
Newbiggin
Gleaston
Roosebeck
Cartmel
Cartmel Sands
Grange-over-Sands
Kents Bank
Flookburgh
Cark
Holker
Allithwaite
Humphrey Head Pt.
Newby Bridge
Staveley
Lindale
Witherslack
Meathop
Milnthorpe
Arnside
Silverdale
Beetham
Storth
Levens
Sedgwick
Heversham
Warton
Warton Sands
Carnforth
Bolton-le-Sands
Hest Bank
Morecambe
Heysham
Lancaster
Sandylands
Bare
Slyne
Torrisholme
Skerton
Halton
Caton
Aldcliffe
Heaton
Scotforth
Middleton
Overton
Glasson
Sunderland Pt.
Shoulder of Lune
Conder Green
Galgate
Thurnham
Cockerham
Cockerham Sands
Forton
Quernmore
Dolphinholme
Hollins Lane
Scorton
Winmarleigh
Cabus
Garstang
Knott End-on-Sea
Fleetwood
Rossall Point
Preesall
Pilling
Stalmine
Hambleton
Cleveleys
Thornton
Anchorsholme
Norbreck
Bispham
Blackpool
Poulton-le-Fylde
Singleton
Staining
Great Marton
South Shore
Kirkham
Wesham
Wrea Green
Freckleton
Lytham St Anne's
Lytham
Ansdell
St Annes
Fairhaven
Salters Bank
Warton
Preston
Fulwood
Ribbleton
Penwortham
Walton-le-Dale
Bamber Bridge
Longton
Hutton
Much Hoole
Walmer Bridge
Hesketh Bank
Banks Sands
Great Bank
Horse Bank
Banks
Crossens
Tarleton
Bretherton
Croston
Leyland
Chorley
Eccleston
Rufford
Mawdesley
Southport
Churchtown
Marshside
Birkdale
Ainsdale
Ainsdale-on-Sea
Woodvale
Scarisbrick
Burscough
Ormskirk
Adlington
Coppull
Euxton
Broughton
Barton
Goosnargh
Longridge
Catterall
Bilsborrow
St Michael's on Wyre
Great Eccleston
Inskip
Elswick
Thistleton
Weeton
Blackpool Tower Sea Life Centre
Madame Tussaud's Blackpool
Blackpool Pleasure Beach
DOUGLAS
Lee Fell
Clougha
Haylot Fell
Bleasdale Moors
Hawthornthwaite Fell
Ward's Stone
Fair Snape Fell
M6
M55
M65
A590
A595
A5087
A683
A6
A588
A585
A583
A584
A59
A565
A570
0 1 2 3 4 5 6 miles
0 1 2 3 4 5 6 7 8 9 10 km

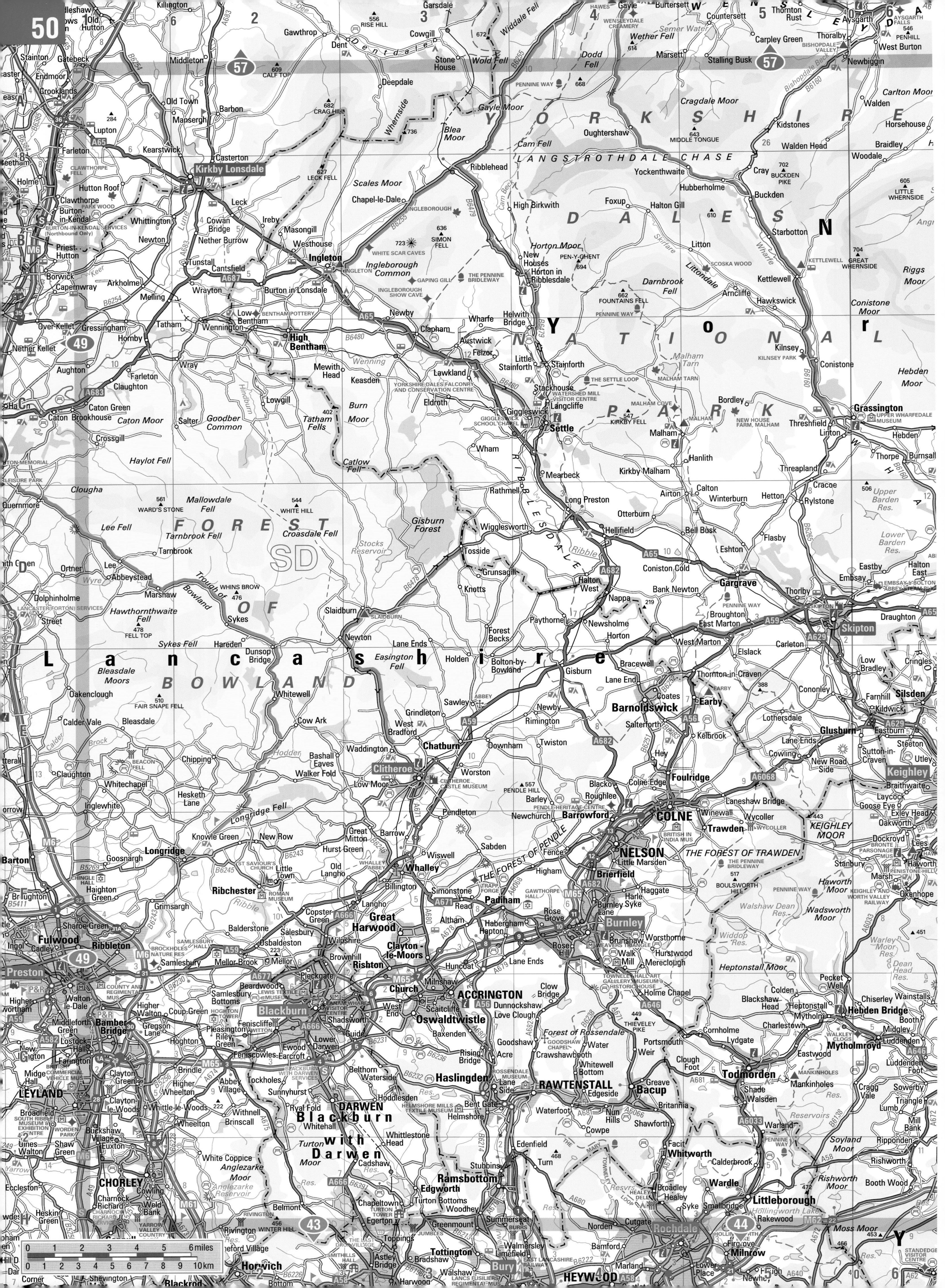
Y O R K S H I R E
D A L E S
N A T I O N A L
P A R K
L a n c a s h i r e
F O R E S T
O F
B O W L A N D
SD
Kirkby Lonsdale
Ingleton
High Bentham
Settle
Giggleswick
Grassington
Skipton
Clitheroe
Barnoldswick
Earby
Foulridge
COLNE
NELSON
Brierfield
Burnley
Padiham
Whalley
Longridge
Ribchester
Preston
Fulwood
Ribbleton
Blackburn
ACCRINGTON
Oswaldtwistle
Great Harwood
Clayton-le-Moors
Rishton
Church
Haslingden
RAWTENSTALL
Bacup
Todmorden
Hebden Bridge
Mytholmroyd
Littleborough
Rochdale
Milnrow
HEYWOOD
Bury
Ramsbottom
Edgworth
Tottington
Horwich
DARWEN
Blackburn with Darwen
CHORLEY
LEYLAND
Bamber Bridge
Walton-le-Dale
Keighley
Silsden
Glusburn
Gargrave
Hellifield
Long Preston
Slaidburn
Dunsop Bridge
Chatburn
Gisburn
Kettlewell
Buckden
Malham
Horton in Ribblesdale
Ribblehead
Dent
Sedbergh
Gawthrop
Garsdale
Hawes
Gayle
Thornton Rust
Aysgarth
West Burton
Newbiggin
Carlton Moor
Kidstones
Horsehouse
Langstrothdale Chase
Yockenthwaite
Hubberholme
Starbotton
Arncliffe
Litton
Halton Gill
Hawkswick
Kilnsey
Conistone
Threshfield
Linton
Hebden
Burnsall
Thorpe
Cracoe
Rylstone
Hetton
Airton
Calton
Winterburn
Otterburn
Kirkby Malham
Hanlith
Stainforth
Langcliffe
Stackhouse
Clapham
Austwick
Lawkland
Eldroth
Wham
Mearbeck
Rathmell
Wigglesworth
Tosside
Halton West
Nappa
Paythorne
Newsholme
Horton
East Marton
West Marton
Broughton
Thorlby
Embsay
Draughton
Carleton
Elslack
Thornton-in-Craven
Cononley
Farnhill
Kildwick
Lothersdale
Sutton-in-Craven
Cowling
Laneshaw Bridge
Trawden
Wycoller
Winewall
Barrowford
Newchurch
Roughlee
Blacko
Barley
Sabden
Pendleton
Worston
Downham
Twiston
Rimington
Newby
Sawley
Grindleton
West Bradford
Waddington
Bashall Eaves
Walker Fold
Low Moor
Hurst Green
Great Mitton
Barrow
Wiswell
Billington
Langho
Old Langho
Simonstone
Read
Altham
Hapton
Habergham
Rose Grove
Worsthorne
Hurstwood
Cliviger
Holme Chapel
Huncoat
Milnshaw
Scaitcliffe
Dunnockshaw
Love Clough
Goodshaw
Crawshawbooth
Water
Weir
Cornholme
Portsmouth
Lydgate
Walsden
Shade
Whitworth
Wardle
Smallbridge
Rakewood
Moss Moor
Stubbins
Edenfield
Helmshore
Waterfoot
Shawforth
Britannia
Hoddlesden
Belthorn
Tockholes
Abbey Village
Whittle-le-Woods
Wheelton
Brinscall
Withnell
Anglezarke Moor
Rivington
Belmont
Chapeltown
Egerton
Turton Bottoms
Greenmount
Summerseat
Walmersley
Samlesbury
Mellor
Mellor Brook
Salesbury
Wilpshire
Osbaldeston
Balderstone
Grimsargh
Haighton Green
Goosnargh
Whitechapel
Chipping
Knowle Green
Hesketh Lane
Inglewhite
Bleasdale
Calder Vale
Oakenclough
Sykes
Hareden
Whitewell
Cow Ark
Newton
Easington Fell
Holden
Bolton-by-Bowland
Forest Becks
Knotts
Grunsagill
Abbeystead
Marshaw
Tarnbrook
Lee
Ortner
Dolphinholme
Quernmore
Clougha
Caton
Caton Green
Brookhouse
Crossgill
Claughton
Farleton
Wray
Hornby
Aughton
Gressingham
Over Kellet
Nether Kellet
Tatham
Wennington
Low Bentham
Burton in Lonsdale
Wrayton
Melling
Arkholme
Cantsfield
Tunstall
Nether Burrow
Cowan Bridge
Leck
Ireby
Masongill
Westhouse
Whittington
Newton
Casterton
Kearstwick
Barbon
Mansergh
Old Town
Middleton
Lupton
Farleton
Holme
Clawthorpe
Burton-in-Kendal
Priest Hutton
Borwick
Capernwray
Hutton Roof
Gatebeck
Endmoor
Crooklands
Stainton
Killington
Old Hutton
Deepdale
Cowgill
Stone House
Chapel-le-Dale
Scales Moor
Whernside
Blea Moor
Gayle Moor
Cam Fell
Oughtershaw
Cragdale Moor
Dodd Fell
Wold Fell
Widdale Fell
Marsett
Stalling Busk
Countersett
Carpley Green
Thoralby
Walden
Walden Head
Woodale
Braidley
Cray
Foxup
High Birkwith
Horton Moor
New Houses
Darnbrook Fell
Fountains Fell
Malham Tarn
Malham Cove
Bordley
Riggs Moor
Conistone Moor
Hebden Moor
Keasden
Mewith Head
Burn Moor
Tatham Fells
Catlow Fell
Gisburn Forest
Stocks Reservoir
Croasdale Fell
White Hill
Mallowdale Fell
Haylot Fell
Goodber Common
Caton Moor
Salter
Lowgill
Tarnbrook Fell
Lee Fell
Trough of Bowland
Hawthornthwaite Fell
Fell Top
Sykes Fell
Bleasdale Moors
Fair Snape Fell
Longridge Fell
Pendle Hill
The Forest of Pendle
Forest of Rossendale
The Forest of Trawden
Keighley Moor
Boulsworth Hill
Heptonstall Moor
Haworth Moor
Wadsworth Moor
Soyland Moor
Rishworth Moor
Turton Moor
Lancaster (Forton) Services
Burton-in-Kendal Services (Northbound Only)
White Scar Caves
Gaping Gill
Ingleborough
Ingleborough Common
Pen-y-ghent
Simon Fell
Calf Top
Crag Hill
Rise Hill
Great Whernside
Buckden Pike
Middle Tongue
Little Whernside
Kilnsey Park
Yorkshire Dales Falconry and Conservation Centre
Watershed Mill Visitor Centre
Clitheroe Castle Museum
Pennine Way
The Pennine Bridleway
Blackburn with Darwen Services
Rossendale Museum
Helmshore Mills Textile Museum
East Lancashire Railway
Keighley and Worth Valley Railway
Bronte Parsonage Museum
Haworth
Oxenhope
Oakworth
Laycock
Braithwaite
Goose Eye
Exley Head
Stanbury
Marsh
M6
M65
M61
M62
A65
A59
A56
A682
A629
A666
A6068
A646
A681
A671
A680
A58
B6478
B6480
B6479
B6160
B6265
B6255
B6254
49
57
43
44
0 1 2 3 4 5 6 miles
0 1 2 3 4 5 6 7 8 9 10 km

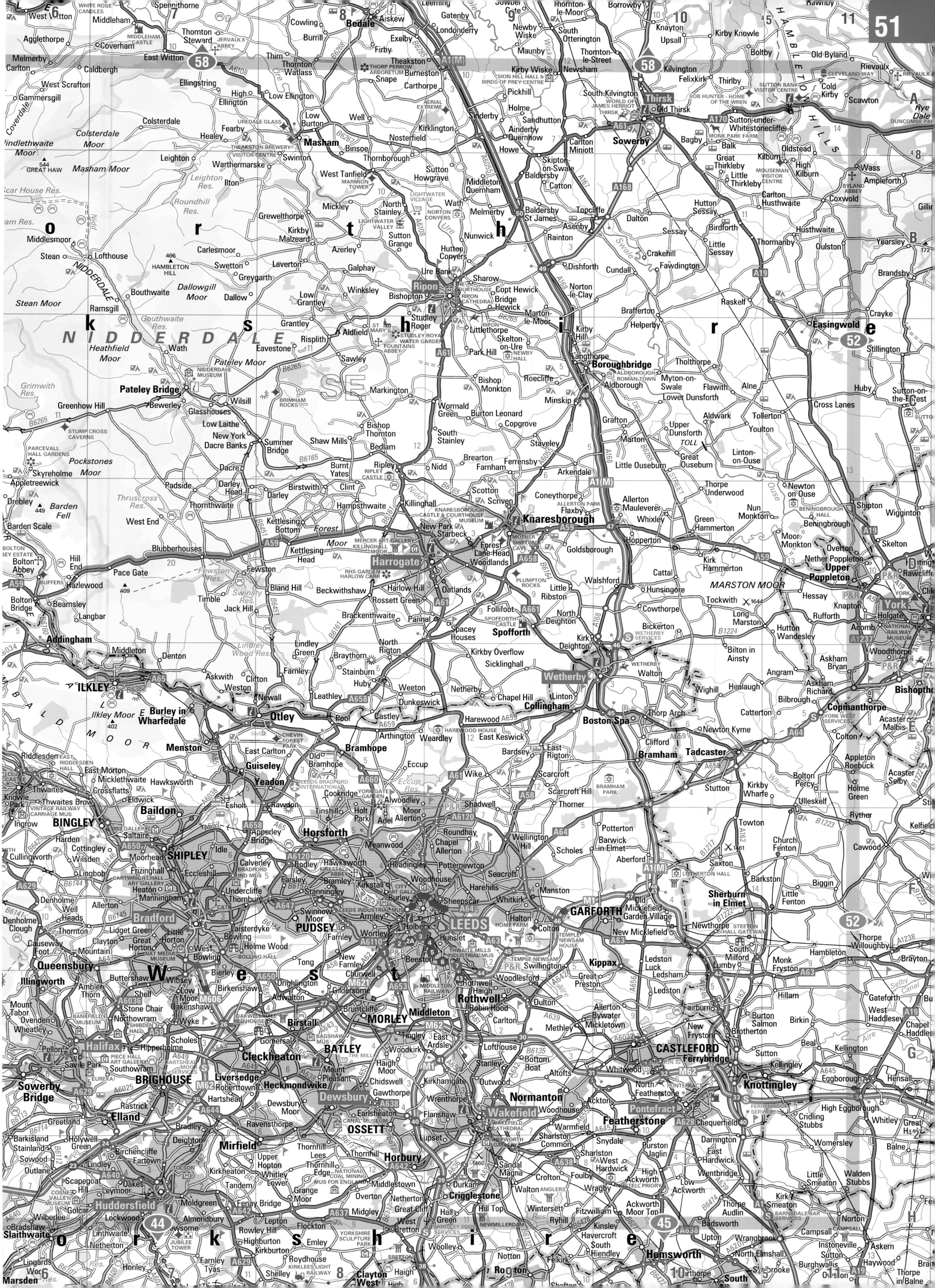
North Yorkshire
West Yorkshire
NIDDERDALE
HAMBLETON HILLS
Bedale
Masham
Thirsk
Sowerby
Ripon
Easingwold
Boroughbridge
Pateley Bridge
Knaresborough
Harrogate
Wetherby
York
Upper Poppleton
Ilkley
Otley
Burley in Wharfedale
Menston
Guiseley
Yeadon
Baildon
Bingley
Shipley
Bradford
Horsforth
Leeds
Pudsey
Garforth
Tadcaster
Boston Spa
Queensbury
Halifax
Brighouse
Cleckheaton
Batley
Morley
Rothwell
Dewsbury
Ossett
Wakefield
Normanton
Castleford
Pontefract
Knottingley
Featherstone
Huddersfield
Elland
Mirfield
Horbury
Hemsworth
Sherburn in Elmet
Selby
MARSTON MOOR
Masham Moor
Ilkley Moor

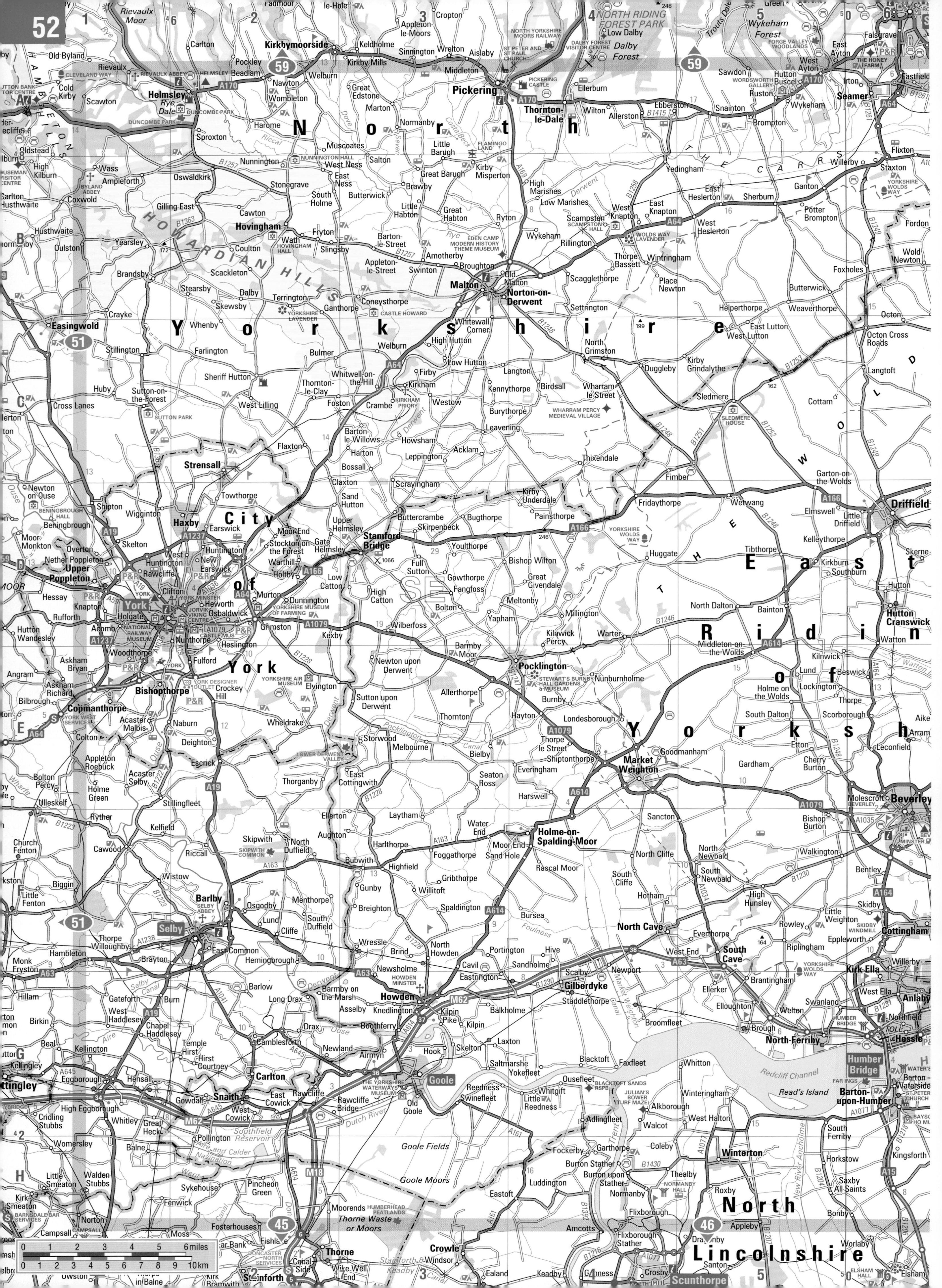
North Yorkshire
City of York
The East Riding of Yorkshire
North Lincolnshire
NORTH RIDING FOREST PARK
Dalby Forest
Wykeham Forest
HOWARDIAN HILLS
THE CARRS
THE WOLDS
HAMBLETON HILLS
Helmsley
Kirkbymoorside
Pickering
Thornton-le-Dale
Malton
Norton-on-Derwent
Easingwold
Hovingham
Strensall
Haxby
York
Upper Poppleton
Stamford Bridge
Bishopthorpe
Copmanthorpe
Pocklington
Market Weighton
Holme-on-Spalding-Moor
Driffield
Beverley
Cottingham
Hessle
Kirk Ella
Anlaby
North Ferriby
Barton-upon-Humber
Humber Bridge
Selby
Barlby
Howden
Goole
Snaith
Carlton
Gilberdyke
North Cave
South Cave
Winterton
Crowle
Thorne
Scunthorpe
Seamer
Hutton Cranswick
Knottingley
Goole Fields
Goole Moors
Thorne Waste or Moors
Redcliff Channel
Read's Island
Selby Canal
Aire and Calder Navigation
Dutch River
Pocklington Canal
Market Weighton Canal
A170
A64
A19
A1079
A166
A614
A63
A163
A1237
M62
M18
A1035
A15
A161
A645
SE
0 1 2 3 4 5 6 miles
0 1 2 3 4 5 6 7 8 9 10 km
59
51
45
46

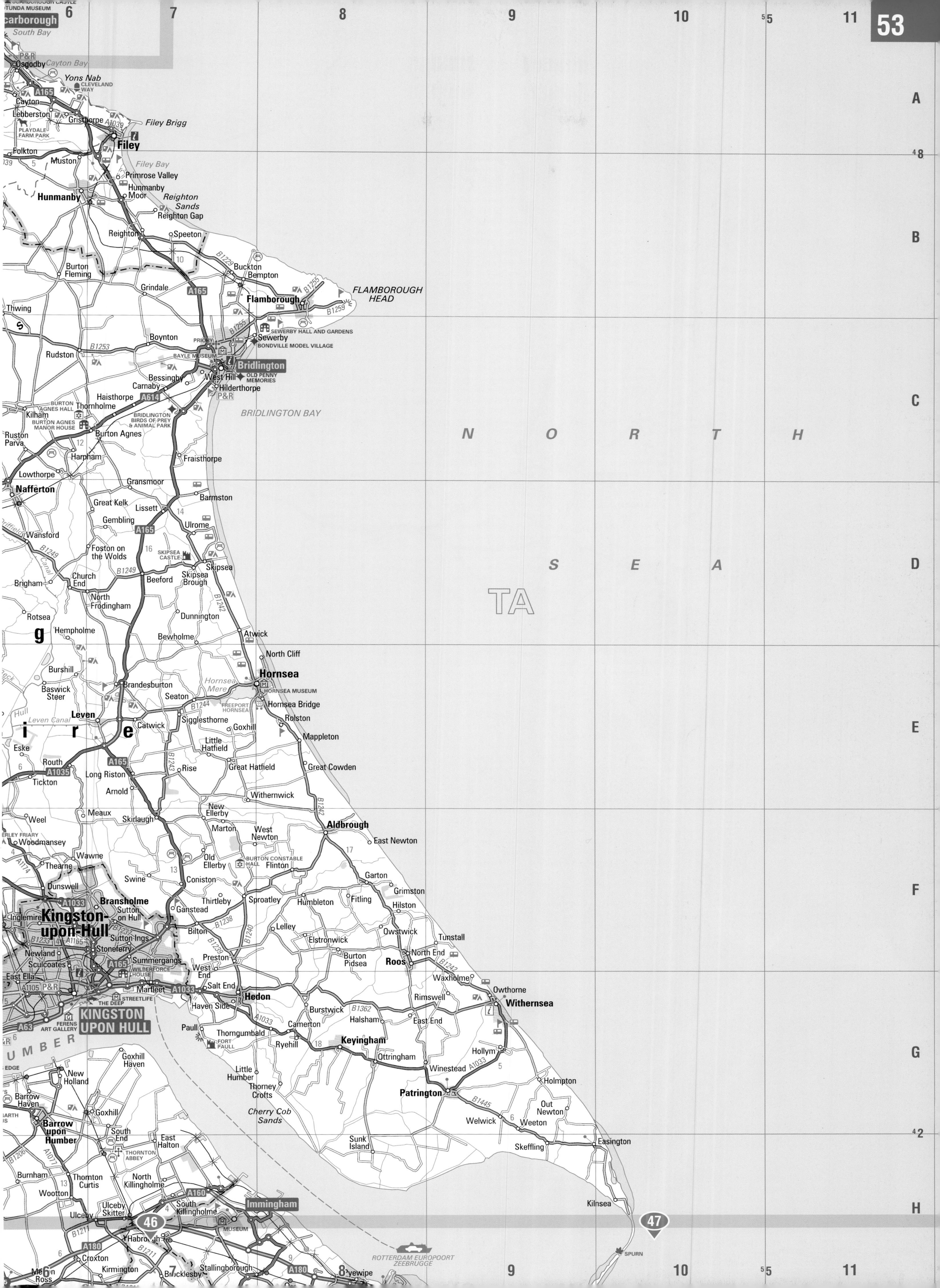
Scarborough
South Bay
Cayton Bay
Osgodby
Yons Nab
CLEVELAND WAY
Cayton
Lebberston
Gristhorpe
PLAYDALE FARM PARK
Filey Brigg
Filey
Folkton
Muston
Filey Bay
Primrose Valley
Hunmanby Moor
Hunmanby
Reighton Sands
Reighton Gap
Reighton
Speeton
Burton Fleming
Buckton
Bempton
Grindale
Flamborough
FLAMBOROUGH HEAD
Thwing
SEWERBY HALL AND GARDENS
Sewerby
BONDVILLE MODEL VILLAGE
Boynton
PRIORY
Rudston
BAYLE MUSEUM
Bridlington
Bessingby
West Hill
OLD PENNY MEMORIES
Carnaby
Hilderthorpe
Haisthorpe
BURTON AGNES HALL
Thornholme
Kilham
BRIDLINGTON BIRDS OF PREY & ANIMAL PARK
BRIDLINGTON BAY
BURTON AGNES MANOR HOUSE
Burton Agnes
Ruston Parva
Harpham
Fraisthorpe
N O R T H
Lowthorpe
Gransmoor
Nafferton
Barmston
Great Kelk
Lissett
Gembling
Ulrome
Wansford
Foston on the Wolds
SKIPSEA CASTLE
Skipsea
Church End
Beeford
Skipsea Brough
S E A
Brigham
North Frodingham
TA
Rotsea
Dunnington
Hempholme
Bewholme
Atwick
North Cliff
Burshill
Hornsea
Brandesburton
Hornsea Mere
HORNSEA MUSEUM
Baswick Steer
Seaton
FREEPORT HORNSEA
Hornsea Bridge
Leven
Leven Canal
Catwick
Sigglesthorne
Rolston
Goxhill
Mappleton
Little Hatfield
Eske
Routh
Tickton
Long Riston
Rise
Great Hatfield
Great Cowden
Arnold
Withernwick
Weel
Meaux
Skirlaugh
New Ellerby
Marton
West Newton
Aldbrough
East Newton
Woodmansey
Wawne
Thearne
Old Ellerby
BURTON CONSTABLE HALL
Flinton
Swine
Coniston
Garton
Dunswell
Grimston
Bransholme
Thirtleby
Sproatley
Humbleton
Fitling
Hilston
Kingston-upon-Hull
Sutton on Hull
Ganstead
Inglemire
Lelley
Owstwick
Sutton Ings
Bilton
Elstronwick
Tunstall
Newland
Stoneferry
Summergangs
Preston
Burton Pidsea
North End
Roos
Sculcoates
WILBERFORCE HOUSE
West End
Waxholme
East Ella
Salt End
Owthorne
Marfleet
Hedon
Rimswell
Withernsea
THE DEEP
STREETLIFE
Haven Side
Burstwick
FERENS ART GALLERY
KINGSTON UPON HULL
Halsham
East End
Camerton
Paull
Thorngumbald
FORT PAULL
Keyingham
Ryehill
HUMBER
Ottringham
Hollym
Goxhill Haven
Little Humber
Winestead
New Holland
Holmpton
Thorney Crofts
Patrington
Barrow Haven
Out Newton
Goxhill
Cherry Cob Sands
Welwick
Weeton
Barrow upon Humber
South End
East Halton
Skeffling
Easington
THORNTON ABBEY
Sunk Island
Burnham
Thornton Curtis
North Killingholme
Wootton
South Killingholme
Immingham
Kilnsea
Ulceby
Ulceby Skitter
MUSEUM
46
47
Habrough
Croxton
ROTTERDAM EUROPOORT ZEEBRUGGE
SPURN
Kirmington
Brocklesby
Stallingborough
Melton Ross
Keelby
Yewipe
A165
A1039
B1229
B1255
B1259
B1256
B1253
A614
B1249
B1242
B1244
B1243
A1035
A1174
A1033
B1237
B1233
A1165
A1105
A63
B1238
B1239
B1240
B1362
B1445
A160
B1206
A1077
B1211
A180
6
7
8
9
10
11
A
B
C
D
E
F
G
H

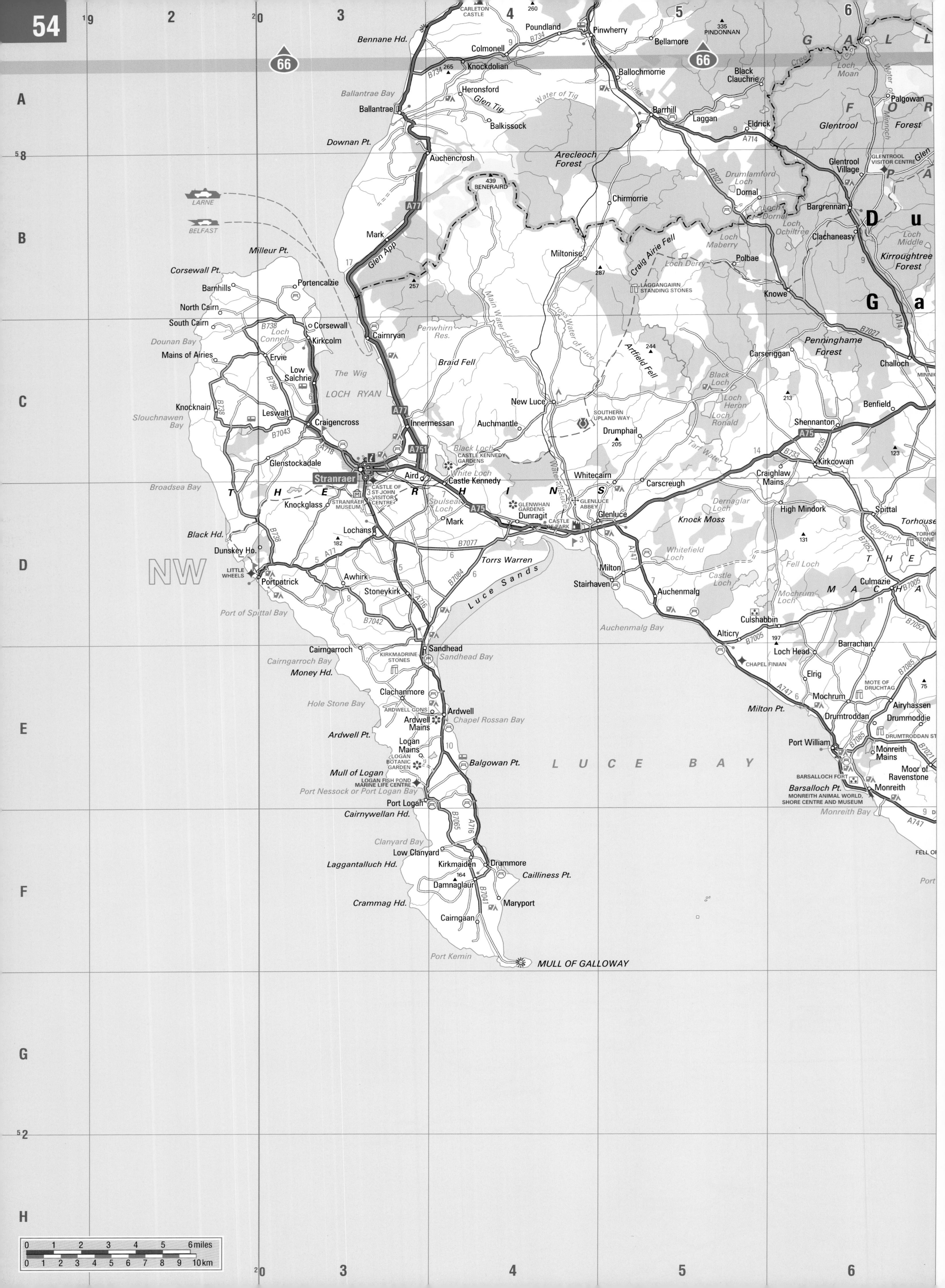

66
Bennane Hd.
CARLETON CASTLE
Poundland
Pinwherry
Bellamore
335 PINDONNAN
Colmonell
Knockdolian
Ballantrae Bay
Heronsford
Glen Tig
Water of Tig
Ballochmorrie
Black Clauchrie
Ballantrae
Balkissock
Barrhill
Laggan
Eldrick
A714
Downan Pt.
Auchencrosh
Arecleoch Forest
Glentrool
Forest
Palgowan
Loch Moan
Glentrool Village
GLENTROOL VISITOR CENTRE
Drumlamford Loch
Dornal
439 BENERAIRD
LARNE
BELFAST
A77
Chirmorrie
Loch Dornal
Bargrennan
Loch Ochiltree
Clachaneasy
Loch Middle
Kirroughtree Forest
Mark
Milleur Pt.
Glen App
Miltonise
Craig Airie Fell
Loch Maberry
Loch Derry
Polbae
Corsewall Pt.
Barnhills
Portencalzie
257
287
LAGGANGAIRN STANDING STONES
Knowe
North Cairn
South Cairn
Corsewall
Loch Connell
Kirkcolm
Dounan Bay
Mains of Airies
Ervie
Cairnryan
Penwhirn Res.
Main Water of Luce
Cross Water of Luce
Artfield Fell
244
Carseriggan
Penninghame Forest
Challoch
Low Salchrie
The Wig
LOCH RYAN
Braid Fell
Black Loch
Loch Heron
Loch Ronald
213
Knocknain
Leswalt
Slouchnawen Bay
Craigencross
Innermessan
New Luce
Auchmantle
SOUTHERN UPLAND WAY
Drumphail
205
Benfield
Shennanton
A75
B733
B735
Kirkcowan
123
Glenstockadale
B7043
A718
A751
Black Loch
CASTLE KENNEDY GARDENS
White Loch
Tarf Water
Stranraer
Aird
Castle Kennedy
Whitecairn
Carscreugh
Craighlaw Mains
Broadsea Bay
T H E R H I N S
CASTLE OF ST JOHN VISITOR CENTRE
STRANRAER MUSEUM
Knockglass
Soulseat Loch
GLENWHAN GARDENS
GLENLUCE ABBEY
Dernaglar Loch
High Mindork
Spittal
Torhouse
Mark
Dunragit
CASTLE OF PARK
Glenluce
Knock Moss
Black Hd.
Lochans
182
B7077
131
Bladnoch
Dunskey Ho.
Torrs Warren
Whitefield Loch
NW
LITTLE WHEELS
Portpatrick
Awhirk
Luce Sands
Milton
Stairhaven
A747
Fell Loch
Castle Loch
Culmazie
Auchenmalg
Mochrum Loch
Stoneykirk
B7084
A716
B7042
Port of Spittal Bay
Auchenmalg Bay
Culshabbin
B7052
Alticry
B7005
197
Barrachan
Loch Head
Cairngarroch
Sandhead
Sandhead Bay
KIRKMADRINE STONES
Cairngarroch Bay
Money Hd.
CHAPEL FINIAN
Elrig
B7085
MOTE OF DRUCHTAG
75
Clachanmore
Hole Stone Bay
ARDWELL GDNS
Ardwell
Ardwell Mains
Chapel Rossan Bay
Mochrum
Airyhassen
Milton Pt.
Drumtroddan
Drummoddie
DRUMTRODDAN ST
Ardwell Pt.
Logan Mains
LOGAN BOTANIC GARDEN
Balgowan Pt.
L U C E B A Y
Port William
Monreith Mains
B7021
Moor of Ravenstone
Mull of Logan
LOGAN FISH POND MARINE LIFE CENTRE
Port Nessock or Port Logan Bay
BARSALLOCH FORT
Barsalloch Pt.
MONREITH ANIMAL WORLD, SHORE CENTRE AND MUSEUM
Monreith
Monreith Bay
Port Logan
Cairnywellan Hd.
B7065
Clanyard Bay
Low Clanyard
Laggantalluch Hd.
Kirkmaiden
Drummore
164
Damnaglaur
Cailliness Pt.
B7041
Maryport
Crammag Hd.
Cairngaan
Port Kemin
MULL OF GALLOWAY
FELL OF
Port
G A L L O R
F O
D u
G a
T H E M A C H A
0 1 2 3 4 5 6 miles
0 1 2 3 4 5 6 7 8 9 10 km

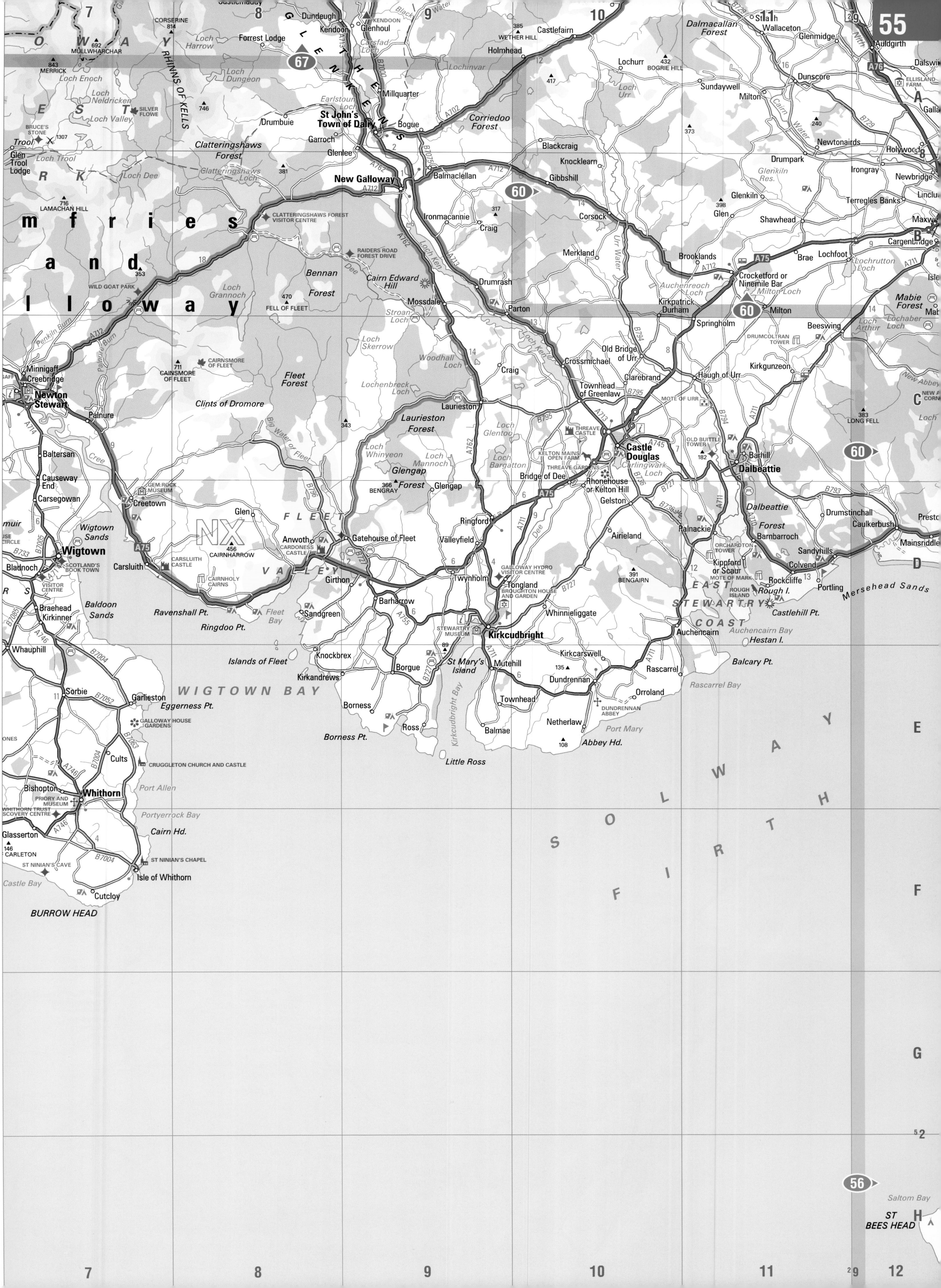
Dumfries and Galloway
NX
SOLWAY FIRTH
WIGTOWN BAY
FLEET VALLEY
EAST STEWARTRY COAST
GLENKENS
RHINNS OF KELLS
Newton Stewart
Wigtown
Whithorn
Isle of Whithorn
Creetown
Gatehouse of Fleet
Kirkcudbright
Castle Douglas
Dalbeattie
New Galloway
St John's Town of Dalry
Carsphairn
Dundeugh
Kendoon
Glenhoul
Forrest Lodge
Castlefairn
Holmhead
Millquarter
Bogue
Drumbuie
Garroch
Glenlee
Balmaclellan
Gibbshill
Corsock
Ironmacannie
Craig
Merkland
Drumrash
Parton
Mossdale
Crossmichael
Townhead of Greenlaw
Clarebrand
Old Bridge of Urr
Haugh of Urr
Laurieston
Glengap
Ringford
Valleyfield
Twynholm
Tongland
Bridge of Dee
Rhonehouse or Kelton Hill
Gelston
Airieland
Whinnieliggate
Kirkcarswell
Rascarrel
Dundrennan
Orroland
Netherlaw
Townhead
Balmae
Mutehill
Borgue
Ross
Borness
Knockbrex
Kirkandrews
Sandgreen
Barharrow
Girthon
Anwoth
Carsluith
Glen
Palnure
Baltersan
Causeway End
Carsegowan
Bladnoch
Braehead
Kirkinner
Whauphill
Sorbie
Garlieston
Cults
Bishopton
Glasserton
Cutcloy
Minnigaff
Creebridge
Glen Trool Lodge
Trool
Lochurr
Dunscore
Sundaywell
Milton
Newtonairds
Drumpark
Irongray
Glenkiln
Glen
Shawhead
Brooklands
Crocketford or Ninemile Bar
Kirkpatrick Durham
Springholm
Milton
Beeswing
Kirkgunzeon
Barhill
Palnackie
Kippford or Scaur
Rockcliffe
Colvend
Sandyhills
Portling
Barnbarroch
Drumstinchall
Caulkerbush
Auchencairn
Auldgirth
Wallaceton
Glenmidge
Holywood
Newbridge
Terregles Banks
Lochfoot
Brae
Cargenbridge
Dalmacallan Forest
Corriedoo Forest
Clatteringshaws Forest
Fleet Forest
Laurieston Forest
Bennan Forest
Glengap Forest
Dalbeattie Forest
Mabie Forest
Clints of Dromore
Cairn Edward Hill
Loch Ken
Loch Skerrow
Woodhall Loch
Lochenbreck Loch
Loch Whinyeon
Loch Mannoch
Loch Grannoch
Loch Dee
Loch Trool
Milton Loch
Auchenreoch Loch
Carlingwark Loch
Loch Arthur
Lochaber Loch
CLATTERINGSHAWS FOREST VISITOR CENTRE
RAIDERS ROAD FOREST DRIVE
WILD GOAT PARK
CAIRNSMORE OF FLEET
GEM ROCK MUSEUM
CARDONESS CASTLE
CARSLUITH CASTLE
CAIRNHOLY CAIRNS
SCOTLAND'S BOOK TOWN
GALLOWAY HOUSE GARDENS
CRUGGLETON CHURCH AND CASTLE
PRIORY AND MUSEUM
WHITHORN TRUST DISCOVERY CENTRE
ST NINIAN'S CAVE
ST NINIAN'S CHAPEL
THREAVE CASTLE
THREAVE GARDENS
KELTON MAINS OPEN FARM
MOTE OF URR
OLD BUITTLE TOWER
ORCHARDTON TOWER
MOTE OF MARK
ROUGH ISLAND
GALLOWAY HYDRO VISITOR CENTRE
BROUGHTON HOUSE AND GARDEN
STEWARTRY MUSEUM
DUNDRENNAN ABBEY
DRUMCOLTRAN TOWER
ELLISLAND FARM
Ravenshall Pt.
Ringdoo Pt.
Fleet Bay
Islands of Fleet
Eggerness Pt.
Port Allen
Portyerrock Bay
Cairn Hd.
Castle Bay
BURROW HEAD
Borness Pt.
Little Ross
St Mary's Isle
Kirkcudbright Bay
Abbey Hd.
Port Mary
Rascarrel Bay
Balcary Pt.
Hestan I.
Auchencairn Bay
Rough I.
Castlehill Pt.
Mersehead Sands
Saltom Bay
ST BEES HEAD
A75
A712
A762
A713
A711
A745
A710
A714
A746
A755
A702
A76
B7000
B7075
B795
B794
B736
B727
B793
B796
B7004
B7052
B7063
B7085
B7005
B733
B729
67
60
56
7
8
9
10
11
12
A
B
C
D
E
F
G
H

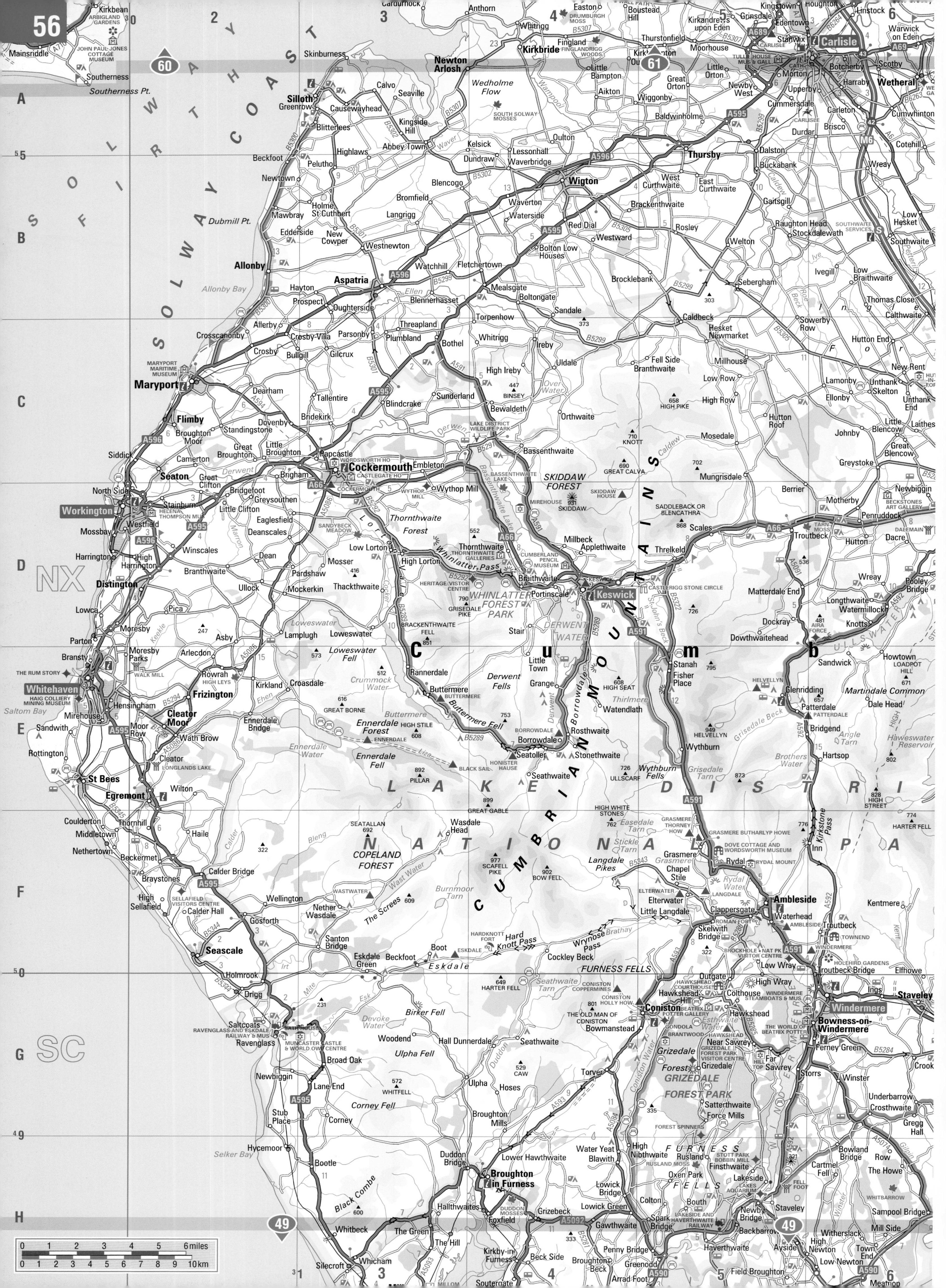
SOLWAY FIRTH
SOLWAY COAST
Kirkbean
Mainsriddle
Southerness
Southerness Pt.
Silloth
Skinburness
Newton Arlosh
Kirkbride
Carlisle
Wetheral
Wedholme Flow
Abbey Town
Wigton
Thursby
Dubmill Pt.
Allonby
Allonby Bay
Aspatria
Maryport
Flimby
Seaton
Workington
Cockermouth
Harrington
Distington
Whitehaven
Saltom Bay
Cleator Moor
Frizington
St Bees
Egremont
Seascale
Keswick
Bassenthwaite
SKIDDAW FOREST
SKIDDAW
Thornthwaite Forest
WHINLATTER FOREST PARK
Derwent Water
Derwent Fells
Loweswater
Loweswater Fell
Buttermere
Ennerdale Forest
Ennerdale Fell
Borrowdale
CUMBRIAN MOUNTAINS
LAKE DISTRICT NATIONAL PARK
Cumbria
GREAT GABLE
SCAFELL PIKE
BOW FELL
HELVELLYN
COPELAND FOREST
Wast Water
The Screes
Grasmere
Rydal
Ambleside
Windermere
Bowness-on-Windermere
Troutbeck
Staveley
Hard Knott Pass
Wrynose Pass
FURNESS FELLS
Eskdale
Coniston
Hawkshead
Grizedale Forest
GRIZEDALE FOREST PARK
Ulpha Fell
Ravenglass
Corney Fell
Black Combe
Broughton in Furness
Selker Bay
Whicham
Silecroft
Newby Bridge
NX
SC

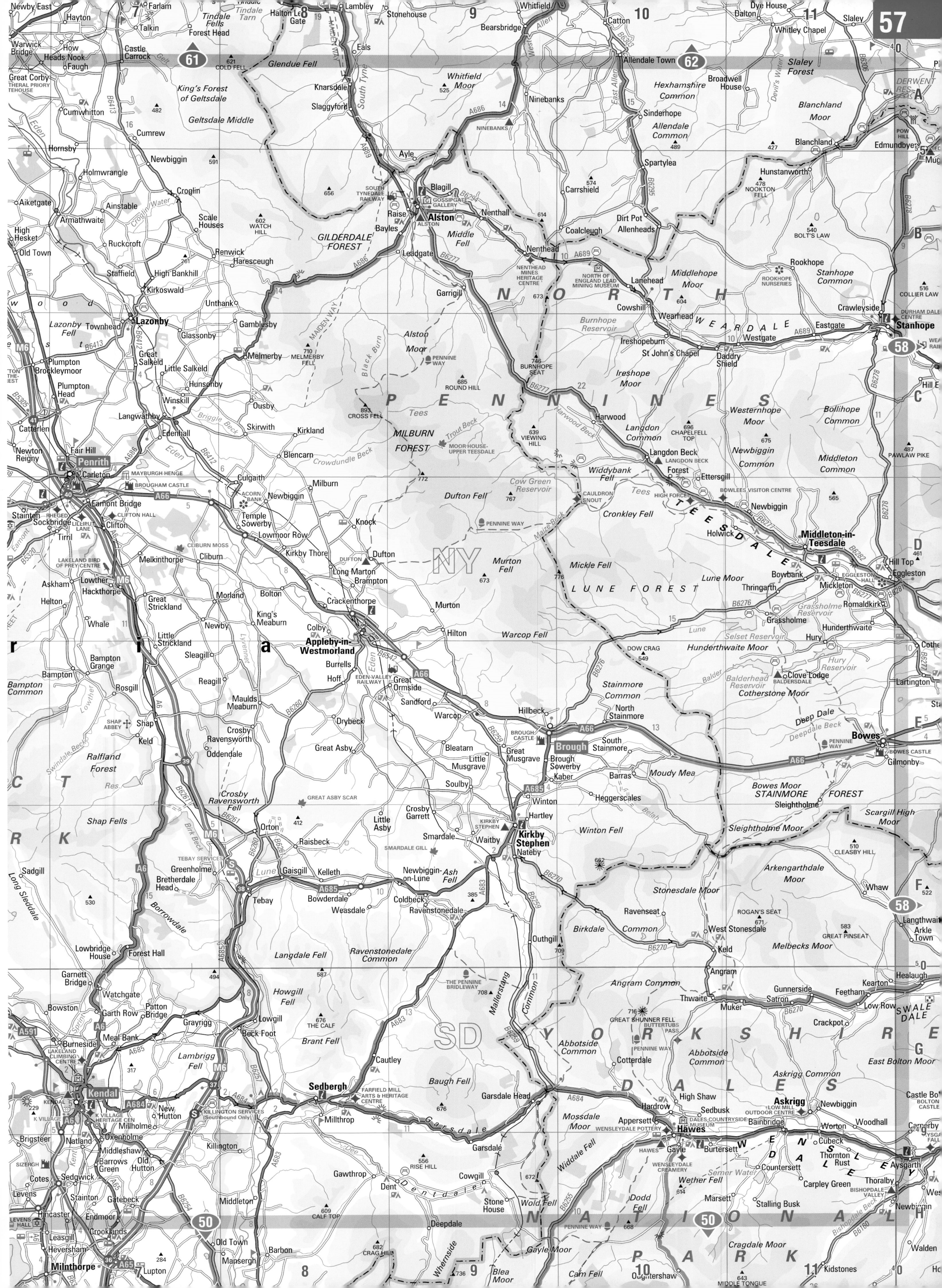
Newby East
Hayton
Farlam
Talkin
Tindale Fells
Forest Head
Halton Lea Gate
Lambley
Stonehouse
Whitfield
Bearsbridge
Catton
Dye House
Dalton
Slaley
Whitley Chapel
Warwick Bridge
How
Heads Nook
Faugh
Castle Carrock
Cold Fell
Glendue Fell
Allendale Town
Slaley Forest
Great Corby
King's Forest of Geltsdale
Whitfield Moor
Knarsdale
Slaggyford
Hexhamshire Common
Broadwell House
Blanchland Moor
Cumwhitton
Geltsdale Middle
Ninebanks
Sinderhope
Allendale Common
Cumrew
Hornsby
Blanchland
Edmundbyers
Newbiggin
Holmwrangle
Ayle
Spartylea
Hunstanworth
Nookton Fell
Croglin
Aiketgate
Ainstable
Armathwaite
Blagill
Alston
Nenthall
Carrshield
South Tynedale Railway
Gossipgate Gallery
Raise
Bayles
Scale Houses
Watch Hill
Dirt Pot
Allenheads
Bolt's Law
High Hesket
Ruckcroft
Gilderdale Forest
Middle Fell
Coalcleugh
Old Town
Renwick
Harescugh
Leadgate
Nenthead
Nenthead Mines Heritage Centre
North of England Lead Mining Museum
Rookhope
Rookhope Nurseries
Stanhope Common
Staffield
High Bankhill
Middlehope Moor
Lanehead
Collier Law
Kirkoswald
Garrigill
NORTH
Cowshill
Crawleyside
Unthank
Wearhead
Weardale
Stanhope
Lazonby
Lazonby Fell
Townhead
Glassonby
Gamblesby
Alston Moor
Burnhope Reservoir
Ireshopeburn
Westgate
Eastgate
Maiden Way
Melmerby Fell
Melmerby
Pennine Way
St John's Chapel
Daddry Shield
Great Salkeld
Little Salkeld
Plumpton
Brockleymoor
Burnhope Seat
Round Hill
Ireshope Moor
Hunsonby
Plumpton Head
Winskill
Ousby
Cross Fell
PENNINES
Harwood
Westernhope Moor
Bollihope Common
Langwathby
Skirwith
Kirkland
Tees
Milburn Forest
Viewing Hill
Langdon Common
Chapelfell Top
Catterlen
Edenhall
Moor House-Upper Teesdale
Blencarn
Crowdundle Beck
Langdon Beck
Newbiggin Common
Middleton Common
Pawlaw Pike
Newton Reigny
Fair Hill
Penrith
Carleton
Mayburgh Henge
Culgaith
Milburn
Widdybank Fell
Forest
Ettersgill
Cow Green Reservoir
Cauldron Snout
High Force
Bowlees Visitor Centre
Newbiggin
Brougham Castle
Acorn Bank
Eamont Bridge
Dufton Fell
Cronkley Fell
Stainton
Rheged
Sockbridge
Lilliput Lane
Clifton Hall
Clifton
Temple Sowerby
Knock
Pennine Way
Teesdale
Tirril
Lowmoor Row
Holwick
Middleton-in-Teesdale
Cliburn Moss
Cliburn
Melkinthorpe
Kirkby Thore
Lakeland Bird of Prey Centre
Dufton
NY
Murton Fell
Mickle Fell
Hill Top
Eggleston
Lowther
Askham
Hackthorpe
Long Marton
Brampton
Lune Forest
Lune Moor
Bowbank
Thringarth
Mickleton
Eggleston Hall
Great Strickland
Morland
Bolton
Crackenthorpe
Murton
Grassholme Reservoir
Grassholme
Romaldkirk
Helton
Whale
King's Meaburn
Newby
Colby
Hilton
Warcop Fell
Selset Reservoir
Hury
Hunderthwaite
Little Strickland
Sleagill
Appleby-in-Westmorland
Dow Crag
Hunderthwaite Moor
Cotherstone
Bampton Grange
Burrells
Hoff
Eden Valley Railway
Great Ormside
Hury Reservoir
Clove Lodge
Baldersdale
Balderhead Reservoir
Cotherstone Moor
Lartington
Bampton
Bampton Common
Rosgill
Reagill
Stainmore Common
Maulds Meaburn
Sandford
Warcop
Hillbeck
North Stainmore
Deep Dale
Deepdale Beck
Shap Abbey
Shap
Keld
Drybeck
Crosby Ravensworth
Brough Castle
Brough
South Stainmore
Bowes
Bowes Castle
Gilmonby
Ralfland Forest
Oddendale
Great Asby
Bleatarn
Little Musgrave
Great Musgrave
Brough Sowerby
Kaber
Barras
Moody Mea
Soulby
Heggerscales
Bowes Moor
Stainmore Forest
Sleightholme
Crosby Ravensworth Fell
Great Asby Scar
Winton
Scargill High Moor
Shap Fells
Orton
Little Asby
Crosby Garrett
Hartley
Kirkby Stephen
Winton Fell
Sleightholme Moor
Raisbeck
Smardale
Waitby
Nateby
Cleasby Hill
Smardale Gill
Tebay Services
Sadgill
Greenholme
Gaisgill
Kelleth
Newbiggin-on-Lune
Ash Fell
Arkengarthdale Moor
Bretherdale Head
Tebay
Bowderdale
Weasdale
Coldbeck
Ravenstonedale
Stonesdale Moor
Whaw
Long Sleddale
Borrowdale
Ravenseat
Rogan's Seat
Langthwaite
Arkle Town
Birkdale
Common
West Stonesdale
Great Pinseat
Keld
Melbecks Moor
Lowbridge House
Forest Hall
Langdale Fell
Ravenstonedale Common
Outhgill
Angram
Garnett Bridge
The Pennine Bridleway
Mallerstang
Angram Common
Kearton
Healaugh
Watchgate
Howgill Fell
Thwaite
Muker
Gunnerside
Satron
Feetham
Low Row
Swale Dale
Bowston
Garth Row
Patton Bridge
Grayrigg
Lowgill
The Calf
Great Shunner Fell
Buttertubs Pass
Crackpot
Meal Bank
Beck Foot
Brant Fell
SD
YORKSHIRE
Burneside
Lakeland Climbing Centre
Lambrigg Fell
Cautley
Abbotside Common
Pennine Way
Cotterdale
East Bolton Moor
Kendal
Sedbergh
Farfield Mill Arts & Heritage Centre
Baugh Fell
Garsdale Head
DALES
Askrigg Common
High Shaw
Askrigg
Low Mill Outdoor Centre
Newbiggin
Castle Bolton
K Village
K Village Heritage Centre
New Hutton
Killington Services (Southbound Only)
Millthrop
Garsdale
Mossdale Moor
Wensleydale Pottery
Hardrow
Appersett
Sedbusk
Dales Countryside Museum
Hawes
Bainbridge
Worton
Woodhall
Carperby
Millholme
Brigsteer
Natland
Oxenholme
Killington
Garsdale
Widdale Fell
Gayle
Burtersett
Wensleydale Creamery
Cubeck
Thornton Rust
Aysgarth
Sizergh
Middleshaw
Barrows Green
Old Hutton
Rise Hill
Semer Water
Countersett
Cotes
Sedgwick
Gawthrop
Cowgill
Dent
Dentdale
Wether Fell
Carpley Green
Thoralby
Levens
Stainton
Gatebeck
Stone House
Marsett
Stalling Busk
Bishopdale Valley
Newbiggin
Hincaster
Levens Hall
Endmoor
Middleton
Calf Top
Dodd Fell
Wold Fell
NATIONAL
Crooklands
Deepdale
Pennine Way
Leasgill
Heversham
Old Town
Barbon
Crag Hill
Whernside
Gayle Moor
PARK
Cragdale Moor
Walden
Milnthorpe
Lupton
Mansergh
Blea Moor
Cam Fell
Oughtershaw
Middle Tongue
Kidstones

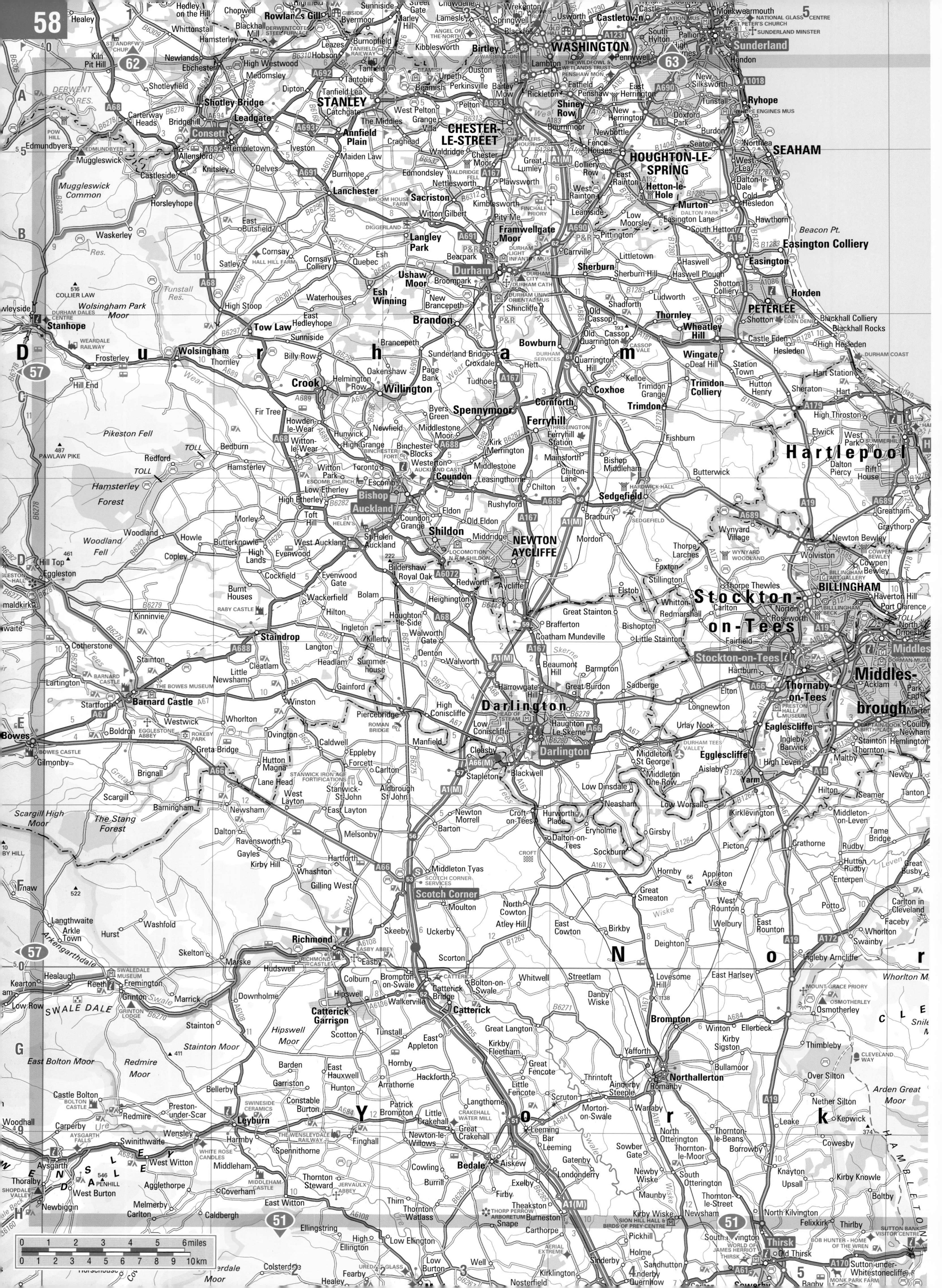

WASHINGTON
Sunderland
STANLEY
CHESTER-LE-STREET
Consett
HOUGHTON-LE-SPRING
SEAHAM
Lanchester
Sacriston
Durham
Easington Colliery
PETERLEE
Stanhope
Wolsingham
Crook
Willington
Spennymoor
Ferryhill
Hartlepool
Bishop Auckland
Shildon
NEWTON AYCLIFFE
Sedgefield
BILLINGHAM
Stockton-on-Tees
Middlesbrough
Thornaby-on-Tees
Darlington
Barnard Castle
Staindrop
Bowes
Yarm
Eaglescliffe
Scotch Corner
Richmond
Catterick Garrison
Catterick
Northallerton
Leyburn
Bedale
Thirsk
Durham
North York
WENSLEYDALE
SWALE DALE
Muggleswick Common
Wolsingham Park Moor
Pikeston Fell
Hamsterley Forest
Woodland Fell
Scargill High Moor
The Stang Forest
Hipswell Moor
Stainton Moor
Redmire Moor
East Bolton Moor
Arden Great Moor
Beacon Pt.
0 1 2 3 4 5 6 miles
0 1 2 3 4 5 6 7 8 9 10 km

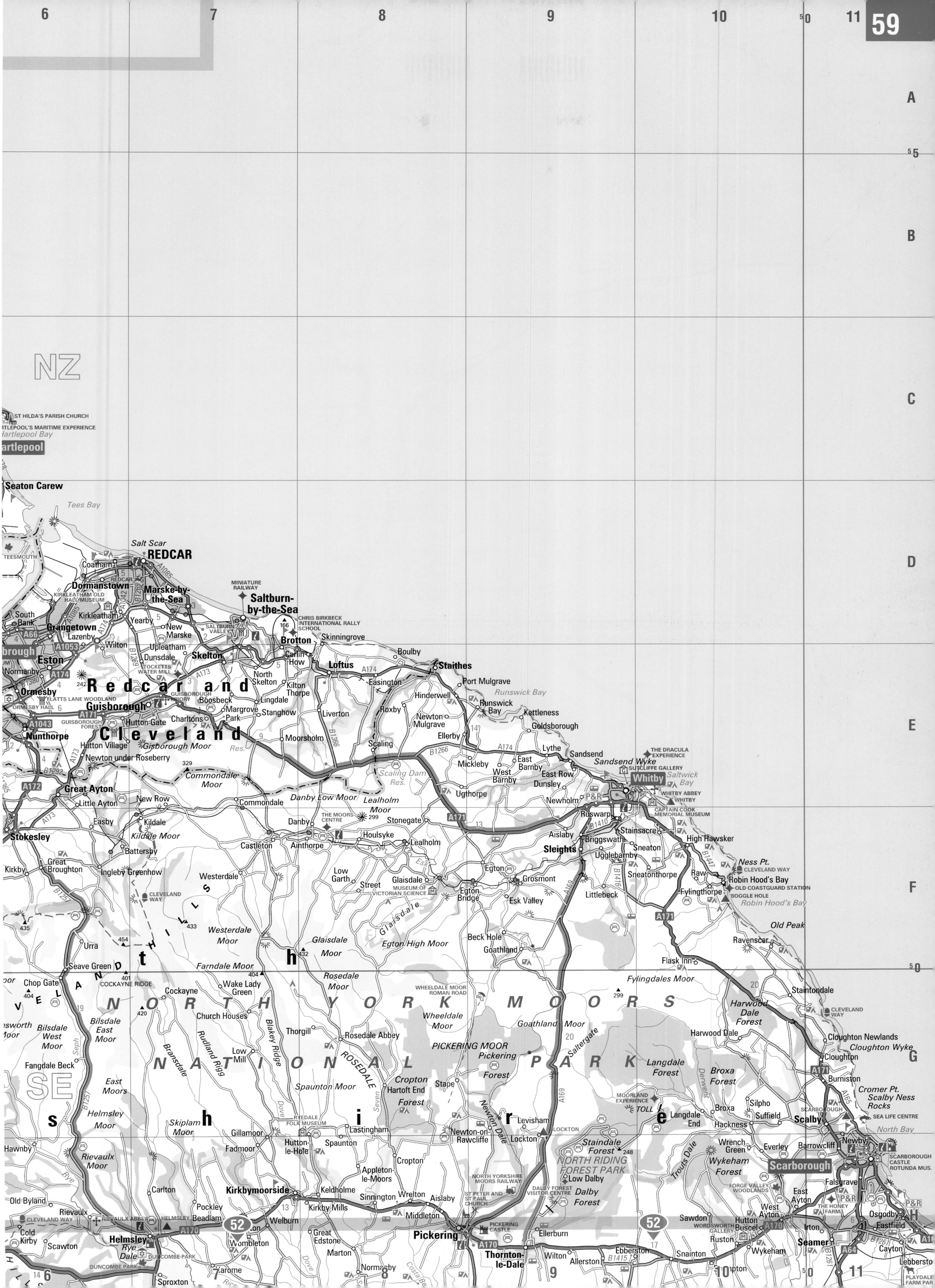

NZ
SE
ST HILDA'S PARISH CHURCH
HARTLEPOOL'S MARITIME EXPERIENCE
Hartlepool Bay
Seaton Carew
Tees Bay
TEESMOUTH
Salt Scar
REDCAR
Coatham
Dormanstown
KIRKLEATHAM OLD HALL MUSEUM
Marske-by-the-Sea
MINIATURE RAILWAY
Saltburn-by-the-Sea
CHRIS BIRKBECK INTERNATIONAL RALLY SCHOOL
South Bank
Grangetown
Kirkleatham
Yearby
New Marske
SALTBURN VALLEY
Lazenby
Wilton
Upleatham
Skelton
Brotton
Skinningrove
Eston
Dunsdale
TOCKETTS WATER MILL
Carlin How
Loftus
Boulby
Staithes
Normanby
North Skelton
Kilton Thorpe
Easington
Port Mulgrave
Ormesby
Redcar and Cleveland
FLATTS LANE WOODLAND
GUISBOROUGH PRIORY
Boosbeck
Lingdale
Hinderwell
Runswick Bay
ORMESBY HALL
Guisborough
Margrove Park
Stanghow
Liverton
Roxby
Newton Mulgrave
Kettleness
GUISBOROUGH FOREST
Hutton Gate
Charltons
Goldsborough
Nunthorpe
Hutton Village
Gisborough Moor
Moorsholm
Scaling
Ellerby
Lythe
Sandsend
Sandsend Wyke
THE DRACULA EXPERIENCE
SUTCLIFFE GALLERY
Newton under Roseberry
Commondale Moor
Scaling Dam Res.
Mickleby
East Barnby
West Barnby
East Row
Dunsley
Whitby
Saltwick Bay
WHITBY ABBEY
Great Ayton
Little Ayton
New Row
Commondale
Danby Low Moor
Lealholm Moor
Ugthorpe
Newholm
CAPTAIN COOK MEMORIAL MUSEUM
Easby
Kildale
THE MOORS CENTRE
Danby
Stonegate
Ruswarp
Stainsacre
High Hawsker
Stokesley
Kildale Moor
Castleton
Ainthorpe
Houlsyke
Lealholm
Aislaby
Sleights
Briggswath
Ugglebarnby
Sneaton
Battersby
Great Broughton
Kirkby
Ingleby Greenhow
Westerdale
Low Garth
Glaisdale
Street
Egton
Grosmont
Littlebeck
Sneatonthorpe
Raw
Ness Pt.
CLEVELAND WAY
Robin Hood's Bay
OLD COASTGUARD STATION
BOGGLE HOLE
Fylingthorpe
MUSEUM OF VICTORIAN SCIENCE
Egton Bridge
Esk Valley
Robin Hood's Bay
Old Peak
Westerdale Moor
Glaisdale Moor
Egton High Moor
Beck Hole
Goathland
Ravenscar
Urra
Seave Green
Farndale Moor
Flask Inn
Chop Gate
COCKAYNE RIDGE
Wake Lady Green
Rosedale Moor
WHEELDALE MOOR ROMAN ROAD
Fylingdales Moor
Staintondale
NORTH YORK MOORS NATIONAL PARK
Cockayne
Harwood Dale Forest
Bilsdale West Moor
Bilsdale East Moor
Church Houses
Wheeldale Moor
Goathland Moor
Harwood Dale
Cloughton Newlands
Cloughton Wyke
Thorgill
Rosedale Abbey
Saltergate
Blakey Ridge
Rudland Rigg
Bransdale
Low Mill
PICKERING MOOR
Pickering Forest
Cloughton
Fangdale Beck
ROSEDALE
Langdale Forest
Broxa Forest
Burniston
East Moors
Cropton Forest
Hartoft End
Stape
Cromer Pt.
Scalby Ness Rocks
Spaunton Moor
MOORLAND EXPERIENCE
Silpho
Suffield
SCALBY
Helmsley Moor
RYEDALE FOLK MUSEUM
Newton Dale
Levisham
Langdale End
Broxa
Hackness
SEA LIFE CENTRE
North Bay
Skiplam Moor
Gillamoor
Lastingham
Newton-on-Rawcliffe
LOCKTON
Lockton
Wrench Green
Everley
Barrowcliff
Newby
Hawnby
Fadmoor
Hutton-le-Hole
Spaunton
Staindale Forest
NORTH RIDING FOREST PARK
Wykeham Forest
Trouts Dale
Scarborough
SCARBOROUGH CASTLE
ROTUNDA MUS.
Rievaulx Moor
Cropton
Appleton-le-Moors
NORTH YORKSHIRE MOORS RAILWAY
Low Dalby
Falsgrave
Carlton
Kirkbymoorside
Keldholme
Sinnington
Wrelton
Aislaby
ST PETER AND ST PAUL CHURCH
DALBY FOREST VISITOR CENTRE
Dalby Forest
FORGE VALLEY WOODLANDS
East Ayton
Old Byland
Rievaulx
Pockley
Beadlam
Kirkby Mills
Middleton
West Ayton
THE HONEY FARM
Osgodby
P&R
CLEVELAND WAY
RIEVAULX ABBEY
HELMSLEY
Welburn
PICKERING CASTLE
Sawdon
Hutton Buscel
Irton
Eastfield
Cold Kirby
Helmsley
Wombleton
Great Edstone
Pickering
Ellerburn
WORDSWORTH GALLERY
Ruston
Seamer
Scawton
Rye Dale
DUNCOMBE PARK
Marton
Thornton-le-Dale
Wilton
Allerston
Ebberston
Snainton
Wykeham
Cayton
Lebberston
DUNCOMBE PARK
Normanby
Sproxton
PLAYDALE FARM PARK
A66
A1053
A174
A171
A1043
A172
A173
A1085
A1042
B1269
B1366
B1266
A174
B1292
B1380
B1257
B1257
A169
B1410
B1416
B1447
A171
A165
A170
A64
B1261
B1415
Esk
Seph
Rye
Dove
Seven
Costa Beck
Derwent
Rye
Riccal
Res.
Dale
166
242
329
299
435
454
433
404
401
404
420
299
248
52
52
6
7
8
9
10
11
A
B
C
D
E
F
G

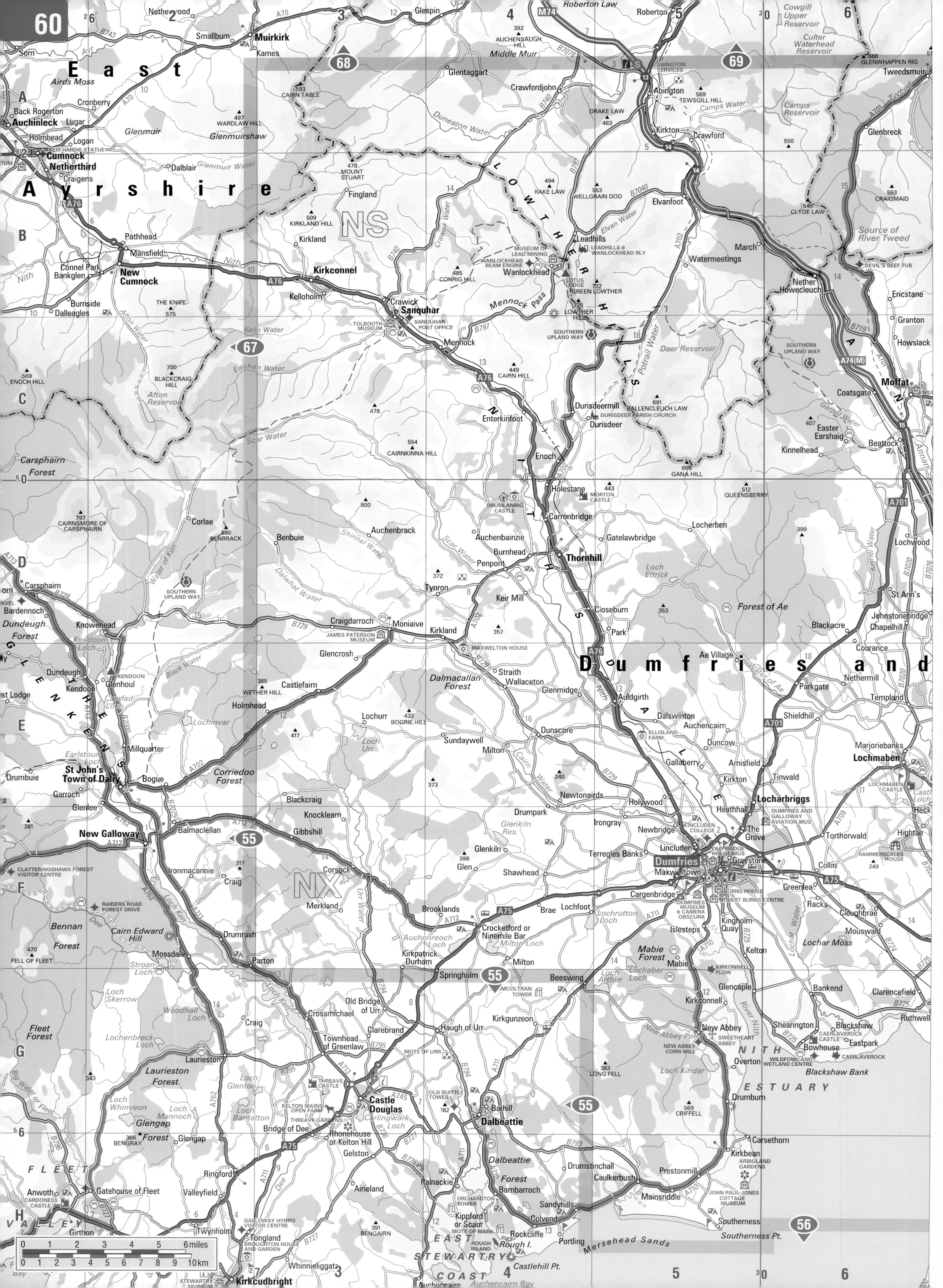
East Ayrshire
Dumfries and
Muirkirk
Netherwood
Smallburn
Kames
Glespin
Roberton Law
Roberton
Cowgill Upper Reservoir
Culter Waterhead Reservoir
392 AUCHENSAUGH HILL
Middle Muir
Glentaggart
ABINGTON SERVICES
Abington
569 TEWSGILL HILL
Camps Water
Camps Reservoir
688 GLENWHAPPEN RIG
Tweedsmuir
Sorn
Airds Moss
593 CAIRN TABLE
Crawfordjohn
DRAKE LAW 483
Back Rogerton
Auchinleck
Cronberry
Lugar
497 WARDLAW HILL
Glenmuir
Glenmuirshaw
Duneaton Water
Kirkton
Crawford
550
Glenbreck
Holmhead
Logan
KEIR HARDIE STATUE
Cumnock
Netherthird
Craigens
Dalblair
Glenmuir Water
478 MOUNT STUART
Fingland
LOWTHER HILLS
494 RAKE LAW
553 WELLGRAIN DOD
Elvanfoot
546 CLYDE LAW
553 CRAIGMAID
NS
509 KIRKLAND HILL
Kirkland
Pathhead
Mansfield
Leadhills
Elvan Water
LEADHILLS & WANLOCKHEAD RLY
March
Source of River Tweed
MUSEUM OF LEAD MINING
WANLOCKHEAD BEAM ENGINE
Wanlockhead
Watermeetings
DEVIL'S BEEF TUB
Connel Park
Bankglen
New Cumnock
Kirkconnel
485 CONRIG HILL
LOTUS LODGE
732 GREEN LOWTHER
Nether Howecleuch
Ericstane
Nith
Kelloholm
Crawick
Sanquhar
Mennock Pass
725 LOWTHER HILL
Granton
Burnside
Dalleagles
THE KNIPE 575
Afton Water
Kello Water
TOLBOOTH MUSEUM
SANQUHAR POST OFFICE
Mennock
SOUTHERN UPLAND WAY
Potrail Water
Daer Reservoir
Howslack
Euchan Water
700 BLACKCRAIG HILL
569 ENOCH HILL
449 CAIRN HILL
691 BALLENCLEUCH LAW
Moffat
Coatsgate
Afton Reservoir
478
Durisdeermill
Enterkinfoot
DURISDEER PARISH CHURCH
Durisdeer
407
Easter Earshaig
Garpol Water
Beattock
Kinnelhead
Scar Water
554 CAIRNKINNA HILL
Carsphairn Forest
Enoch
668 GANA HILL
Holestane
443 MORTON CASTLE
512 QUEENSBERRY
500
DRUMLANRIG CASTLE
797 CAIRNSMORE OF CARSPHAIRN
Corlae
580 BENBRACK
Benbuie
Auchenbrack
Shinnel Water
Auchenbainzie
Carronbridge
Locherben
Gatelawbridge
399
Lochwood
Kinnel Water
Water of Ken
Burnhead
Penpont
Thornhill
Loch Ettrick
372
Tynron
Keir Mill
Carsphairn
Bardennoch
Dundeugh Forest
Knowehead
Kendoon Loch
Dalwhat Water
Craigdarroch
Moniaive
JAMES PATERSON MUSEUM
Kirkland
357
Closeburn
353
Forest of Ae
Park
Blackacre
St Ann's
Johnstonebridge
Chapelhill
Courance
Glencrosh
MAXWELTON HOUSE
Black Water
Dundeugh
KENDOON
Glenhoul
Kendoon
385 WETHER HILL
Castlefairn
Straith
Wallaceton
Dalmacallan Forest
Ae Village
Nethermill
Parkgate
Templand
Glenmidge
Auldgirth
Holmhead
Lochurr
432 BOGRIE HILL
Dalswinton
Auchencairn
Shieldhill
Lochinvar
417
Loch Urr
Sundaywell
Milton
Dunscore
ELLISLAND FARM
Duncow
Marjoriebanks
Lochmaben
Earlstoun Loch
Millquarter
Gallaberry
Amisfield
Tinwald
Drumbuie
St John's Town of Dalry
Bogue
Corriedoo Forest
240
Kirkton
Garroch
Blackcraig
Knocklearn
373
Newtonairds
Holywood
Locharbriggs
Glenlee
Heathhall
DUMFRIES AND GALLOWAY AVIATION MUS
LOCHMABEN CASTLE
381
New Galloway
Balmaclellan
Gibbshill
Drumpark
Glenkiln Res.
Irongray
Newbridge
LINCLUDEN COLLEGE
The Grove
Torthorwald
Hightae
CLATTERINGSHAWS FOREST VISITOR CENTRE
317
Ironmacannie
Craig
Corsock
398 Glen
Glenkiln
Shawhead
Terregles Banks
Lincluden
Dumfries
OLD BRIDGE HOUSE MUS
Greystone
RAMMERSCALES HOUSE
249
Collin
Maxwelltown
NX
Merkland
Urr Water
BURNS HOUSE
ROBERT BURNS CENTRE
Greenlea
RAIDERS ROAD FOREST DRIVE
Brooklands
Brae
Lochfoot
Cargenbridge
DUMFRIES MUSEUM & CAMERA OBSCURA
Racks
Cleughbrae
Bennan Forest
Cairn Edward Hill
Drumrash
Auchenreoch Loch
Crocketford or Ninemile Bar
Lochrutton Loch
Islesteps
Kingholm Quay
Mouswald
Milton Loch
Mabie Forest
Mabie
Kelton
Lochar Moss
Lochar Water
470 FELL OF FLEET
Mossdale
Parton
Kirkpatrick Durham
Milton
Stroan Loch
Loch Arthur
Lochaber Loch
KIRKCONNELL FLOW
Springholm
Beeswing
MCOLTRAN TOWER
Glencaple
Bankend
Clarencefield
Loch Skerrow
Loch Ken
Old Bridge of Urr
Woodhall Loch
Crossmichael
Kirkgunzeon
Kirkconnell
River Nith
Ruthwell
Fleet Forest
Craig
Clarebrand
Haugh of Urr
New Abbey Pow
New Abbey
SWEETHEART ABBEY
NEW ABBEY CORN MILL
Shearington
Blackshaw
CAERLAVEROCK CASTLE
Eastpark
Lochenbreck Loch
Townhead of Greenlaw
MOTE OF URR
Bowhouse
WILDFOWL AND WETLAND CENTRE
CAERLAVEROCK
Laurieston
NITH
Overton
383 LONG FELL
Loch Kindar
Blackshaw Bank
343
Laurieston Forest
Loch Glentoo
THREAVE CASTLE
ESTUARY
Big Water of Fleet
Loch Whinyeon
Loch Mannoch
KELTON MAINS OPEN FARM
THREAVE GARDENS
Castle Douglas
Carlingwark Loch
OLD BUITTLE TOWER
182
Barhill
Dalbeattie
Drumburn
569 CRIFFELL
Loch Bargatton
Glengap Forest
366 BENGRAY
Glengap
Bridge of Dee
Rhonehouse or Kelton Hill
Carsethorn
Gelston
Dalbeattie Forest
Drumstinchall
Kirkbean
ARBIGLAND GARDENS
FLEET
Ringford
Preston Mill
Caulkerbush
Anwoth
CARDONESS CASTLE
Gatehouse of Fleet
Valleyfield
Airieland
Palnackie
Barnbarroch
Mainsriddle
JOHN PAUL JONES COTTAGE MUSEUM
ORCHARDTON TOWER
Sandyhills
VALLEY
GALLOWAY HYDRO VISITOR CENTRE
Twynholm
Kippford or Scaur
MOTE OF MARK
Rockcliffe
Colvend
Southerness
391 BENGAIRN
Girthon
Tongland
BROUGHTON HOUSE AND GARDEN
ROUGH ISLAND
Rough I.
Portling
Mersehead Sands
Southerness Pt.
EAST STEWARTRY COAST
Whinnieliggate
Castlehill Pt.
Kirkcudbright
Auchencairn Bay
0 1 2 3 4 5 6 miles
0 1 2 3 4 5 6 7 8 9 10 km
68
69
67
55
56
M74
A70
A76
A74(M)
A701
A702
A75
A712
A713
A710
A711
A762
B729
B797
B740
B7040
B7078
B725

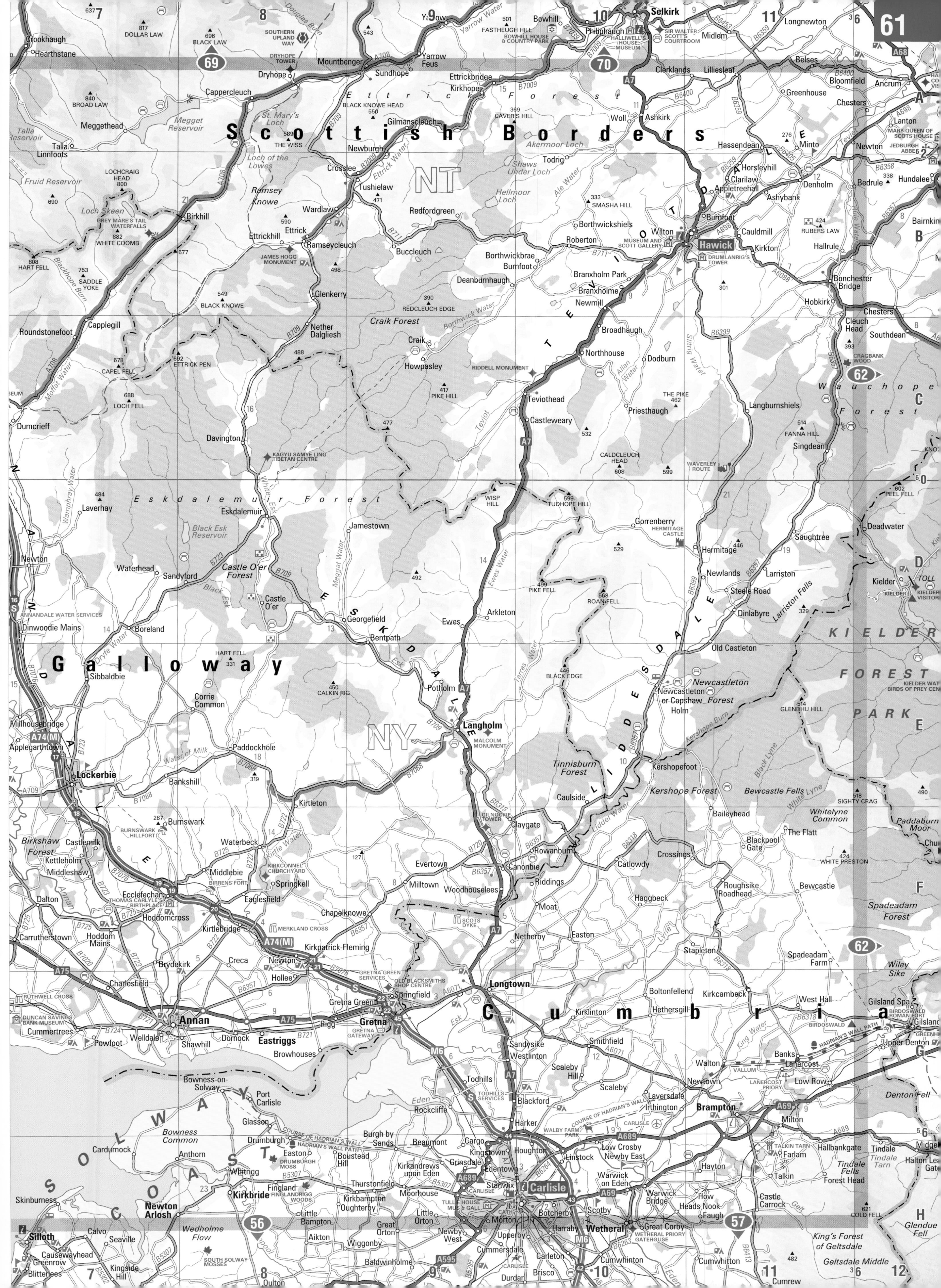
Scottish Borders
Galloway
Cumbria
SOLWAY COAST
Ettrick Forest
Eskdalemuir Forest
Craik Forest
Castle O'er Forest
Wauchope Forest
KIELDER FOREST PARK
Kershope Forest
Newcastleton Forest
Tinnisburn Forest
Spadeadam Forest
Bewcastle Fells
Whitelyne Common
Bowness Common
Wedholme Flow
TEVIOTDALE
ESKDALE
LIDDESDALE
ANNANDALE
NT
NY
69
70
62
56
57
Selkirk
Philiphaugh
HALLIWELL'S HOUSE MUSEUM
SIR WALTER SCOTT'S COURTROOM
Midlem
Longnewton
Yarrow
Yarrow Feus
Bowhill
FASTHEUGH HILL
BOWHILL HOUSE & COUNTRY PARK
Mountbenger
Dryhope
DRYHOPE TOWER
SOUTHERN UPLAND WAY
Sundhope
Ettrickbridge
Kirkhope
Crookhaugh
Hearthstane
DOLLAR LAW
BLACK LAW
BROAD LAW
Cappercleuch
Meggethead
Talla Reservoir
Talla
Linnfoots
Megget Reservoir
St. Mary's Loch
THE WISS
Loch of the Lowes
Fruid Reservoir
LOCHCRAIG HEAD
Loch Skeen
GREY MARE'S TAIL WATERFALLS
WHITE COOMB
HART FELL
SADDLE YOKE
Birkhill
Ramsey Knowe
BLACK KNOWE HEAD
Gilmanscleuch
Newburgh
Crosslee
Tushielaw
Wardlaw
Ettrick
Ettrickhill
Ramseycleuch
JAMES HOGG MONUMENT
Buccleuch
Redfordgreen
CAVER'S HILL
Akermoor Loch
Shaws Under Loch
Hellmoor Loch
Todrig
Woll
Ashkirk
Clerklands
Lilliesleaf
Belses
Bloomfield
Ancrum
Greenhouse
Chesters
Lanton
MARY QUEEN OF SCOTS HOUSE
JEDBURGH ABBEY
Hassendean
Minto
Horsleyhill
Clarilaw
Appletreehall
Denholm
Newton
Bedrule
Hundalee
Ashybank
SMASHA HILL
Borthwickshiels
Burnfoot
Wilton
MUSEUM AND SCOTT GALLERY
Hawick
DRUMLANRIG'S TOWER
Cauldmill
RUBERS LAW
Kirkton
Hallrule
Bairnkine
Roberton
Borthwickbrae
Burnfoot
Deanburnhaugh
Branxholm Park
Branxholme
Newmill
Bonchester Bridge
Hobkirk
Chesters
Cleuch Head
Southdean
CRAGBANK WOOD
REDCLEUCH EDGE
BLACK KNOWE
Glenkerry
Capplegill
Roundstonefoot
Nether Dalgliesh
Craik
Howpasley
RIDDELL MONUMENT
PIKE HILL
CAPEL FELL
ETTRICK PEN
LOCH FELL
Dumcrieff
Davington
KAGYU SAMYE LING TIBETAN CENTRE
Broadhaugh
Northhouse
Dodburn
Teviothead
Castleweary
THE PIKE
Priesthaugh
Langburnshiels
FANNA HILL
Singdean
CALDCLEUCH HEAD
WAVERLEY ROUTE
Laverhay
Eskdalemuir
Black Esk Reservoir
Jamestown
WISP HILL
TUDHOPE HILL
Gorrenberry
HERMITAGE CASTLE
Hermitage
Saughtree
Deadwater
PEEL FELL
Newton
Waterhead
Sandyford
Newlands
Larriston
Kielder
Steele Road
Larriston Fells
Dinlabyre
PIKE FELL
ROAN FELL
Castle O'er
Georgefield
Arkleton
Ewes
ANNANDALE WATER SERVICES
Dinwoodie Mains
Boreland
Bentpath
Old Castleton
HART FELL
Sibbaldbie
CALKIN RIG
BLACK EDGE
Potholm
Newcastleton or Copshaw Holm
GLENDHU HILL
Corrie Common
Millhousebridge
Applegarthtown
Langholm
MALCOLM MONUMENT
Paddockhole
Lockerbie
Bankshill
Kershopefoot
Caulside
Kirtleton
GILNOCKIE TOWER
Claygate
Baileyhead
SIGHTY CRAG
Paddaburn Moor
Burnswark
BURNSWARK HILLFORT
The Flatt
Birkshaw Forest
Castlemilk
Waterbeck
Kettleholm
Middleshaw
Middlebie
Evertown
Rowanburn
Catlowdy
Crossings
Blackpool Gate
WHITE PRESTON
KIRKCONNEL CHURCHYARD
BIRRENS FORT
Springkell
Milltown
Canonbie
Woodhouselees
Riddings
Roughsike
Roadhead
Bewcastle
Ecclefechan
THOMAS CARLYLE'S BIRTHPLACE
Eaglesfield
Dalton
Hoddomcross
Moat
Haggbeck
Chapelknowe
SCOTS DYKE
MERKLAND CROSS
Carrutherstown
Hoddom Mains
Kirtlebridge
Netherby
Easton
Kirkpatrick-Fleming
Stapleton
Spadeadam Farm
Wiley Sike
Brydekirk
Creca
Newton
Hollee
GRETNA GREEN SERVICES
OLD BLACKSMITHS SHOP CENTRE
Charlesfield
Longtown
Boltonfellend
Kirkcambeck
West Hall
Gilsland Spa
BIRDOSWALD ROMAN FORT
Gilsland
RUTHWELL CROSS
DUNCAN SAVINGS BANK MUSEUM
Annan
Gretna Green
Springfield
Gretna
GRETNA GATEWAY
Rigg
Kirklinton
Hethersgill
Cummertrees
Powfoot
Welldale
Shawhill
Dornock
Eastriggs
Browhouses
Sandysike
Westlinton
Smithfield
HADRIAN'S WALL PATH
Upper Denton
Banks
Lanercost
LANERCOST PRIORY
Low Row
Walton
VALLUM
Scaleby Hill
Scaleby
Newtown
Denton Fell
Bowness-on-Solway
Port Carlisle
Todhills
TODHILLS SERVICES
Blackford
Laversdale
Irthington
Brampton
Milton
Rockcliffe
Glasson
COURSE OF HADRIAN'S WALL
Harker
WALBY FARM PARK
CARLISLE
Burgh by Sands
Beaumont
Cargo
Drumburgh
Easton
DRUMBURGH MOSS
Boustead Hill
Kirkandrews upon Eden
Grinsdale
Kingstown
Houghton
Linstock
Low Crosby
Newby East
TALKIN TARN
Farlam
Hallbankgate
Tindale
Midgeholm
Halton Lea Gate
Tindale Fells
Tindale Tarn
Cardurnock
Anthorn
Whitrigg
Edentown
Hayton
Talkin
Forest Head
Warwick on Eden
Skinburness
Kirkbride
Fingland
FINGLANDRIGG WOODS
Thurstonfield
Moorhouse
Stanwix
Carlisle
Warwick Bridge
How
Heads Nook
Castle Carrock
Newton Arlosh
Kirkbampton
Oughterby
Little Bampton
Little Orton
TULLIE HOUSE MUSEUM & GALLERY
Morton
Botcherby
Harraby
Scotby
Wetheral
WETHERAL PRIORY GATEHOUSE
Great Corby
Faugh
COLD FELL
Glendue Fell
Silloth
Calvo
Seaville
Aikton
Great Orton
Newby West
Upperby
Wiggonby
King's Forest of Geltsdale
Causewayhead
Greenrow
Blitterlees
SOUTH SOLWAY MOSSES
Kingside Hill
Baldwinholme
Cummersdale
Carleton
Cumwhinton
Cumwhitton
Geltsdale Middle
Oulton
Durdar
Brisco
Cumrew
A7
A68
A698
A708
A701
A74(M)
A709
A75
A6071
M6
A689
A69
A595
B709
B711
B7009
B6399
B6357
B6318
B7068
B723
B722
B725
B7076
B6357
B5307
B721
B724
B6264
B6263
B6413

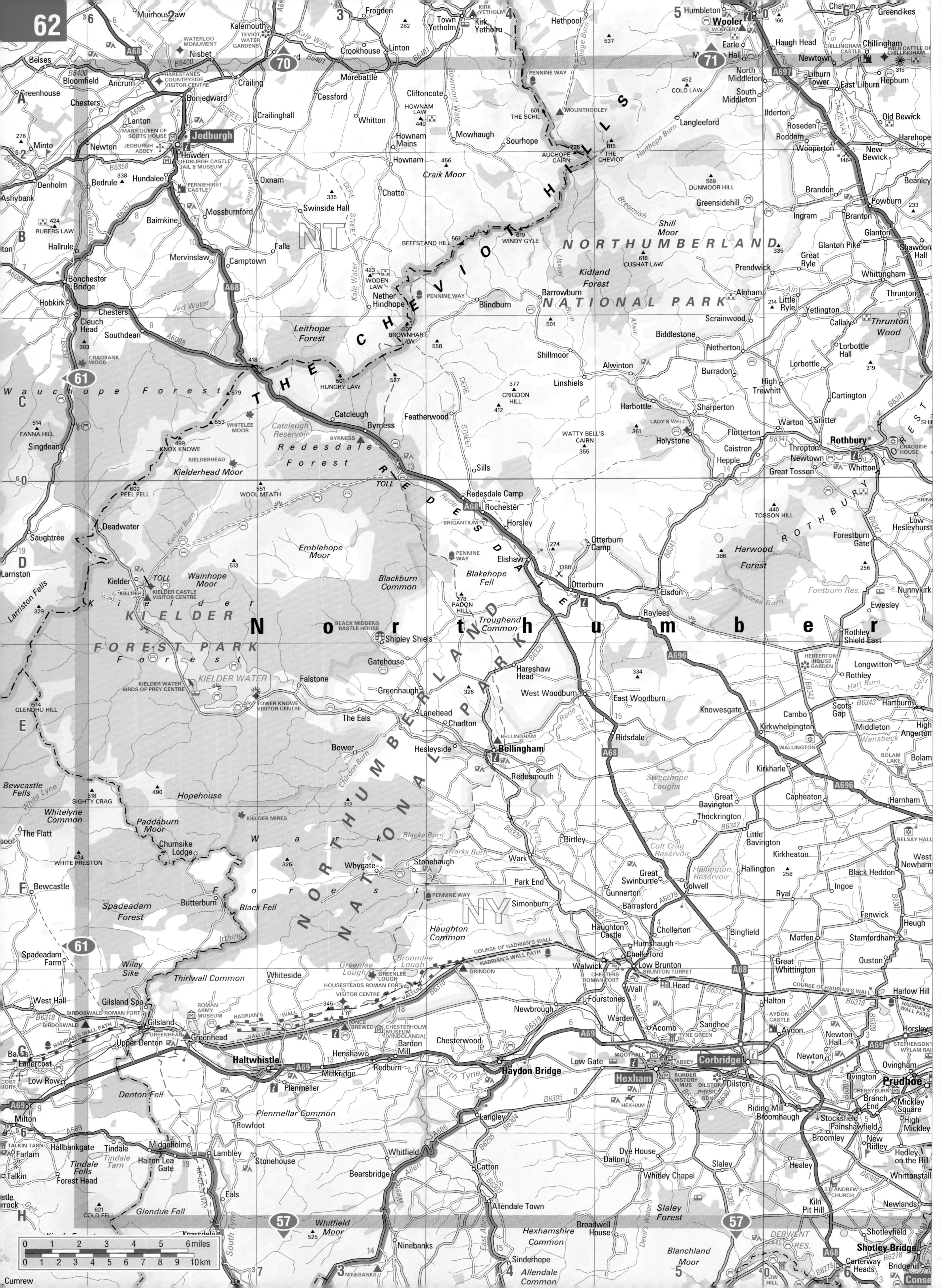

THE CHEVIOT HILLS
NORTHUMBERLAND NATIONAL PARK
Northumber
NORTHUMBERLAND NATIONAL PARK
KIELDER FOREST PARK
Kielder Forest
Redesdale Forest
REDESDALE
Wark Forest
Wauchope Forest
ROTHBURY FOREST
NT
NY
70
71
61
57
Jedburgh
Wooler
Rothbury
Bellingham
Otterburn
Haltwhistle
Haydon Bridge
Hexham
Corbridge
Prudhoe
Greenhead
Gilsland
Kielder
Kielder Water
Byrness
Catcleugh
Rochester
Elsdon
Alwinton
Harbottle
Holystone
Kirk Yetholm
Town Yetholm
Morebattle
Crailing
Ancrum
Denholm
Bonchester Bridge
Chesters
Southdean
Camptown
Oxnam
Hownam
Craik Moor
Windy Gyle
The Cheviot
Auchope Cairn
Cushat Law
Kidland Forest
Shill Moor
Barrowburn
Blindburn
Leithope Forest
Hungry Law
Deadwater
Saughtree
Kielderhead Moor
Peel Fell
Emblehope Moor
Blackburn Common
Blakehope Fell
Troughend Common
Shipley Shiels
Gatehouse
Falstone
Greenhaugh
The Eals
Lanehead
Charlton
Hesleyside
Redesmouth
Hareshaw Head
West Woodburn
East Woodburn
Ridsdale
Sweethope Loughs
Kirkwhelpington
Cambo
Harwood Forest
Fontburn Res.
Wallington
Capheaton
Kirkharle
Great Bavington
Thockrington
Little Bavington
Colt Crag Reservoir
Hallington Reservoir
Birtley
Wark
Stonehaugh
Whygate
Park End
Simonburn
Gunnerton
Barrasford
Chollerton
Humshaugh
Chollerford
Walwick
Wall
Hill Head
Fourstones
Warden
Acomb
Sandhoe
Dilston
Riding Mill
Broomhaugh
Stocksfield
Ovington
Ovingham
Mickley Square
Horsley
Halton
Aydon
Matfen
Stamfordham
Ingoe
Ryal
Bingfield
Great Whittington
Hopehouse
Paddaburn Moor
Churnsike Lodge
Butterburn
Spadeadam Forest
Bewcastle
Bewcastle Fells
Whitelyne Common
The Flatt
Spadeadam Farm
Wiley Sike
Thirlwall Common
Whiteside
Greenlee Lough
Broomlee Lough
Housesteads Roman Fort
Vindolanda
Once Brewed
Bardon Mill
Henshaw
Redburn
Melkridge
Plenmeller
Plenmellar Common
Chesterwood
Newbrough
Low Gate
Langley
Whitfield
Catton
Allendale Town
Allendale Common
Sinderhope
Ninebanks
Whitfield Moor
Hexhamshire Common
Broadwell House
Slaley
Slaley Forest
Whitley Chapel
Dalton
Dye House
Blanchland Moor
Shotley Bridge
Derwent Res.
Lambley
Stonehouse
Bearsbridge
Midgeholme
Halton Lea Gate
Tindale
Tindale Fells
Glendue Fell
Eals
Denton Fell
Upper Denton
Lanercost
Low Row
Milton
Hallbankgate
Farlam
Talkin
Forest Head
Cold Fell
Cumrew
Humbleton
Earle
Haugh Head
Chillingham
Chatton
Newtown
Lilburn Tower
East Lilburn
Hepburn
North Middleton
South Middleton
Ilderton
Roseden
Roddam
Wooperton
New Bewick
Old Bewick
Harehope
Beanley
Brandon
Powburn
Branton
Ingram
Glanton
Glanton Pike
Shawdon Hall
Great Ryle
Little Ryle
Prendwick
Whittingham
Alnham
Thrunton
Thrunton Wood
Yetlington
Callaly
Scrainwood
Biddlestone
Netherton
Lorbottle
Lorbottle Hall
Burradon
High Trewhitt
Cartington
Sharperton
Flotterton
Warton
Snitter
Caistron
Hepple
Thropton
Great Tosson
Tosson Hill
Whitton
Cragside House
Forestburn Gate
Low Hesleyhurst
Ewesley
Nunnykirk
Raylees
Rothley
Longwitton
Hartburn
Scots' Gap
Middleton
Angerton
Bolam
Harnham
Belsay Hall
Black Heddon
Fenwick
Heugh
Ouston
Harlow Hill
Newton
Bywell
Broomley
High Mickley
Hedley on the Hill
Whittonstall
Newlands
Kiln Pit Hill
Carterway Heads
Shotleyfield
Healey
Kalemouth
Nisbet
Belses
Bloomfield
Greenhouse
Lanton
Newton
Minto
Howden
Bedrule
Hundalee
Bairnkine
Mossburnford
Hallrule
Mervinslaw
Falla
Hobkirk
Cleuch Head
Cragbank Wood
Singdean
Fanna Hill
Knox Knowe
Whitelee Moor
Wool Meath
Wainhope Moor
Larriston Fells
Glendhu Hill
Sighty Crag
White Preston
Black Fell
Haughton Common
Haughton Castle
Swinside Hall
Chatto
Nether Hindhope
Woden Law
Featherwood
Crigdon Hill
Watty Bell's Cairn
Sills
Redesdale Camp
Horsley
Elishaw
Otterburn Camp
Linshiels
Shillmoor
Mowhaugh
Sourhope
Cliftoncote
Hownam Mains
Whitton
Cessford
Crookhouse
Linton
Frogden
Langleeford
Hethpool
Mounthooley
The Schil
Cold Law
Dunmoor Hill
Greensidehill
Muirhouselaw
A68
A69
A696
A697
A6088
A698
A686
A689
B6320
B6318
B6341
B6342
Hadrian's Wall
Pennine Way
0 1 2 3 4 5 6 miles
0 1 2 3 4 5 6 7 8 9 10 km

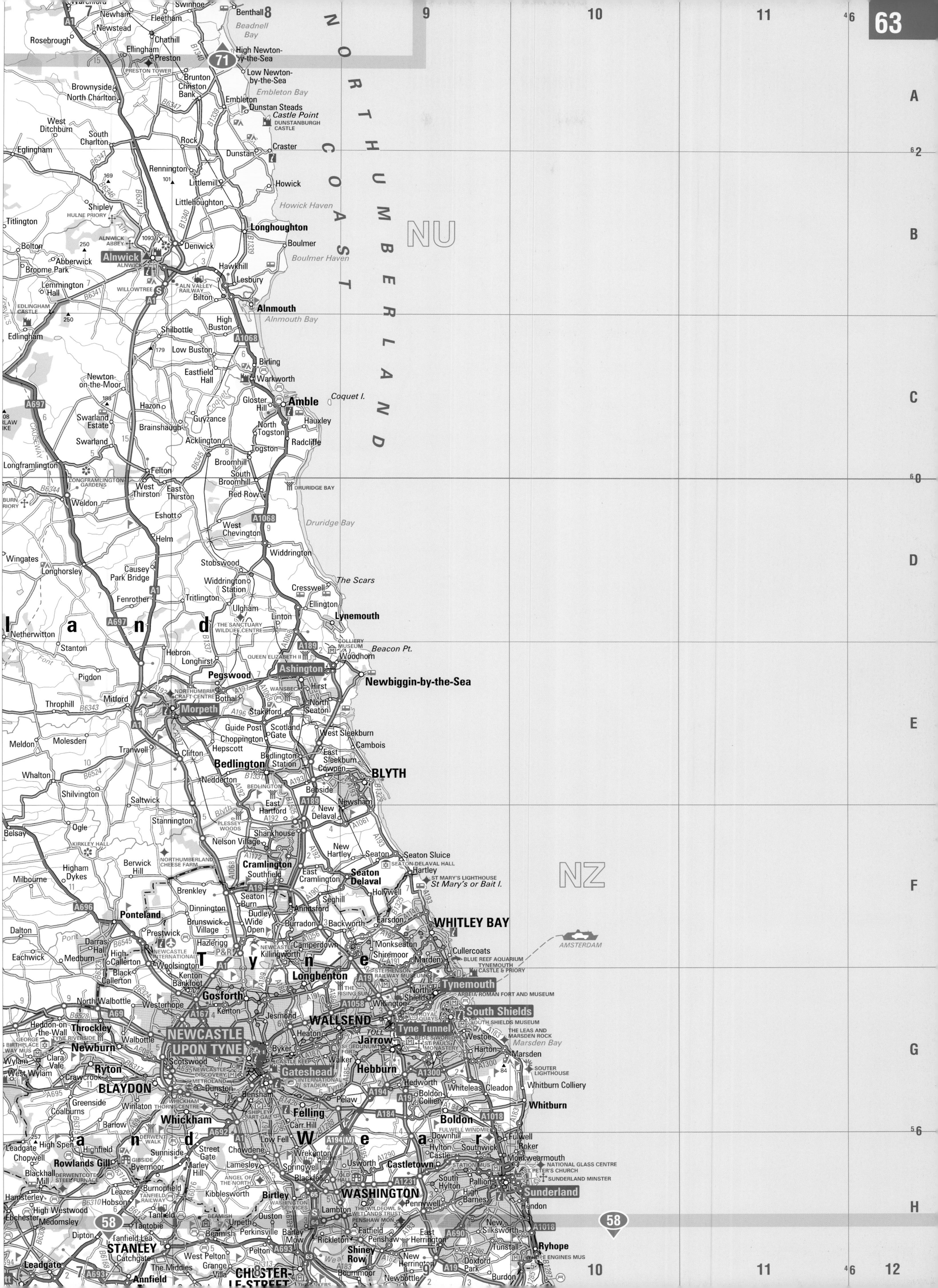
NORTHUMBERLAND COAST
NU
NZ
Newham
Swinhoe
Benthall
Beadnell Bay
Fleetham
Newstead
Rosebrough
Chathill
Ellingham
Preston
PRESTON TOWER
High Newton-by-the-Sea
Low Newton-by-the-Sea
Brunton
Christon Bank
Embleton Bay
Brownyside
North Charlton
Embleton
Dunstan Steads
Castle Point
DUNSTANBURGH CASTLE
West Ditchburn
South Charlton
Rock
Craster
Eglingham
Dunstan
Rennington
Littlemill
Howick
Shipley
HULNE PRIORY
Littlehoughton
Howick Haven
Titlington
Longhoughton
ALNWICK ABBEY
Boulmer
Bolton
Denwick
Boulmer Haven
Abberwick
Alnwick
Hawkhill
Broome Park
Lesbury
Lemmington Hall
WILLOWTREE
ALN VALLEY RAILWAY
Bilton
EDLINGHAM CASTLE
Alnmouth
Alnmouth Bay
Edlingham
High Buston
Shilbottle
Low Buston
Birling
Eastfield Hall
Warkworth
Newton-on-the-Moor
Coquet I.
Gloster Hill
Amble
Hazon
Guyzance
Hauxley
Swarland Estate
Brainshaugh
North Togston
Swarland
Acklington
Radcliffe
Togston
Broomhill
Longframlington
Felton
South Broomhill
LONGFRAMLINGTON GARDENS
West Thirston
East Thirston
DRUIDGE BAY
Red Row
Weldon
Eshott
Druridge Bay
West Chevington
Helm
Widdrington
Wingates
Longhorsley
Causey Park Bridge
Stobswood
Cresswell
The Scars
Widdrington Station
Ellington
Fenrother
Tritlington
Ulgham
Lynemouth
Netherwitton
Linton
THE SANCTUARY WILDLIFE CENTRE
Stanton
COLLIERY MUSEUM
Beacon Pt.
Hebron
Longhirst
QUEEN ELIZABETH II
Woodhorn
Ashington
Pigdon
Pegswood
Newbiggin-by-the-Sea
Hirst
Throphill
Mitford
NORTHUMBRIA CRAFT CENTRE
Bothal
WANSBECK
North Seaton
Morpeth
Stakeford
Guide Post
Scotland Gate
West Sleekburn
Meldon
Molesden
Choppington
Cambois
Hepscott
Tranwell
East Sleekburn
Clifton
Bedlington
Bedlington Station
Cowpen
Whalton
BLYTH
Nedderton
Bebside
Shilvington
BEDLINGTON
Saltwick
East Hartford
New Delaval
Newsham
Stannington
PLESSEY WOODS
Ogle
Shankhouse
Belsay
KIRKLEY HALL
Nelson Village
New Hartley
Seaton Sluice
Berwick Hill
NORTHUMBERLAND CHEESE FARM
Seaton
SEATON DELAVAL HALL
Higham Dykes
Cramlington
Hartley
Milbourne
Southfield
East Cramlington
Seaton Delaval
ST MARY'S LIGHTHOUSE
St Mary's or Bait I.
Brenkley
Holywell
Seaton Burn
Seghill
Dinnington
Annitsford
Ponteland
Dudley
Earsdon
WHITLEY BAY
Dalton
Brunswick Village
Wide Open
Burradon
Backworth
Prestwick
Hazlerigg
AMSTERDAM
Darras Hall
Camperdown
Monkseaton
Eachwick
High Callerton
NEWCASTLE INTERNATIONAL
Killingworth
Shiremoor
Cullercoats
Medburn
Woolsington
Marden
BLUE REEF AQUARIUM
TYNEMOUTH CASTLE & PRIORY
Black Callerton
STEPHENSON RAILWAY MUSEUM
Kenton Bankfoot
Longbenton
Tynemouth
North Walbottle
Westerhope
Gosforth
THE RISING SUN
North Shields
Kenton
ARBEIA ROMAN FORT AND MUSEUM
Willington
Jesmond
WALLSEND
South Shields
Heddon-on-the-Wall
Throckley
SOUTH SHIELDS MUSEUM
NEWCASTLE UPON TYNE
ROYAL QUAYS
Walbottle
Tyne Tunnel
Newburn
Heaton
Jarrow
BEDE'S WORLD
Westoe
THE LEAS AND MARSDEN ROCK
Byker
ST PAUL'S MONASTERY
Marsden Bay
Wylam
Clara Vale
Harton
Marsden
Scotswood
SEGEDUNUM FORT
Ryton
Walker
SOUTER LIGHTHOUSE
West Wylam
Crawcrook
NEWCASTLE DISCOVERY
CASTLE KEEP
Hebburn
Gateshead
Whitburn Colliery
METROLAND
INTERNATIONAL STADIUM
BLAYDON
Dunston
Hedworth
Whiteleas
Cleadon
Greenside
WHICKHAM THORNS CENTRE
Bensham
Boldon Colliery
Whitburn
Coalburns
Winlaton
SHIPLEY ART GALLERY
Pelaw
Felling
Boldon
Barlow
Whickham
Carr Hill
FULWELL WINDMILL
DERWENT WALK
Fulwell
Leadgate
High Spen
Highfield
Low Fell
Downhill
Roker
Street Gate
Hylton Castle
Southwick
Chopwell
Sunniside
Chowdene
Wrekenton
Monkwearmouth
Rowlands Gill
GIBSIDE
Marley Hill
Springwell
Usworth
Castletown
STATION MUS
NATIONAL GLASS CENTRE
Byermoor
Lamesley
ST PETER'S CHURCH
Blackhall Mill
DERWENTCOTE STEEL FURNACE
ANGEL OF THE NORTH
Blackfell
South Hylton
Pallion
SUNDERLAND MINSTER
Burnopfield
Kibblesworth
WASHINGTON
Hamsterley
Leazes
Birtley
High Barnes
Sunderland
TANFIELD RAILWAY
WASHINGTON SERVICES
Lambton
THE WILDFOWL & WETLANDS TRUST
Pennywell
Hendon
High Westwood
Hobson
Ebchester
Medomsley
Tantobie
Tanfield
BEAMISH
Urpeth
Ouston
PENSHAW MON
New Silksworth
Beamish
Perkinsville
Barley Mow
Fatfield
Penshaw
East Herrington
Dipton
Tanfield Lea
Rickleton
Tunstall
Ryhope
STANLEY
West Pelton
Pelton
Shiney Row
New Herrington
Doxford Park
Catchgate
Grange Villa
CHESTER-LE-STREET
Bournmoor
RYHOPE ENGINES MUS
Leadgate
The Middles
Newbottle
Burdon
Annfield
A
B
C
D
E
F
G
H
7
8
9
10
11
12

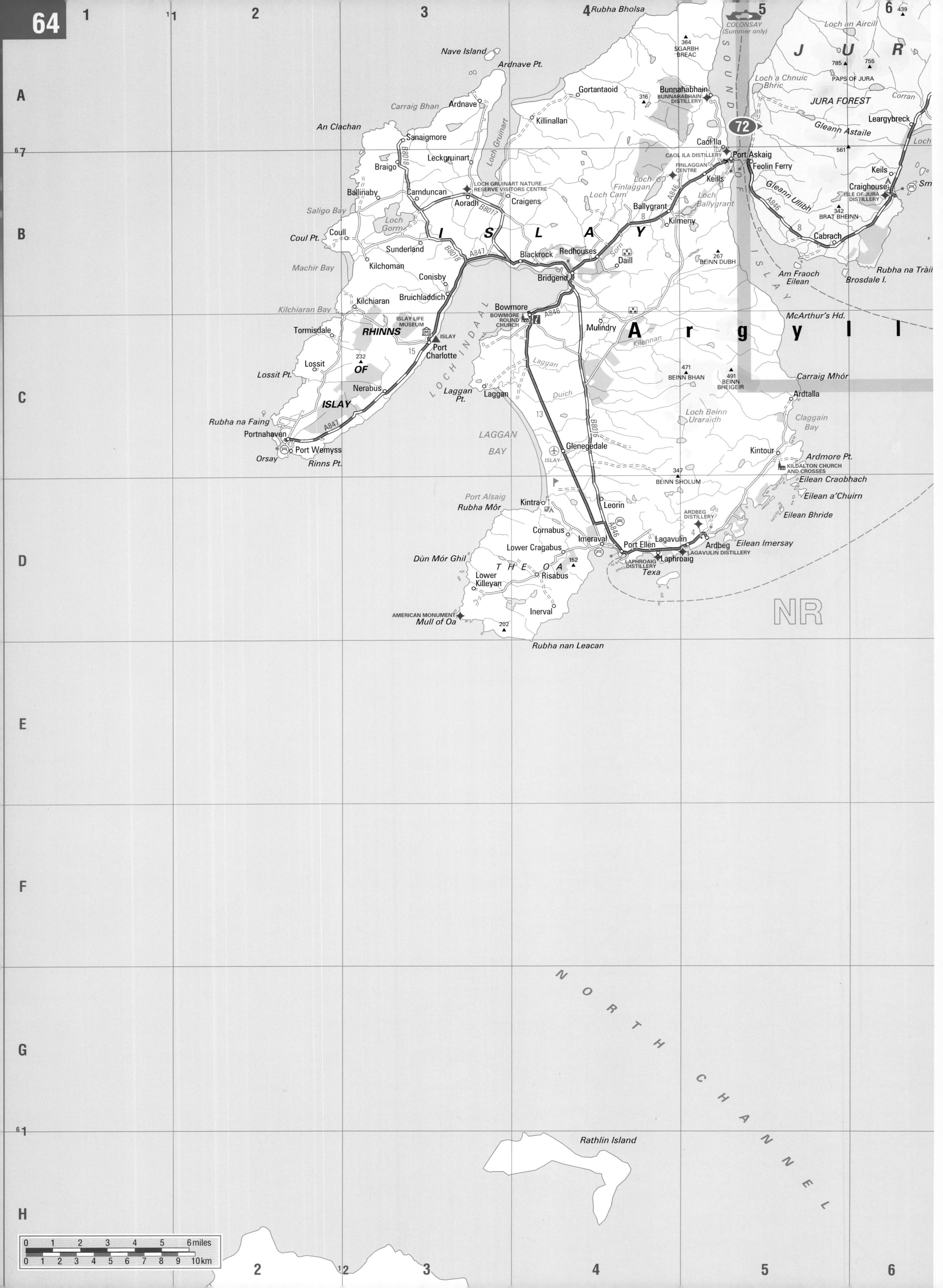
ISLAY
OF
RHINNS
ISLAY
Argyll
JURA
JURA FOREST
PAPS OF JURA
NR
NORTH CHANNEL
SOUND OF ISLAY
COLONSAY (Summer only)
72
Rubha Bholsa
Nave Island
Ardnave Pt.
Ardnave
Carraig Bhan
An Clachan
Sanaigmore
Braigo
Leckgruinart
Loch Gruinart
LOCH GRUINART NATURE RESERVE VISITORS CENTRE
Ballinaby
Carnduncan
Aoradh
Craigens
Saligo Bay
Loch Gorm
Coul Pt.
Coull
Sunderland
Machir Bay
Kilchoman
Conisby
Bruichladdich
Kilchiaran
Kilchiaran Bay
Tormisdale
ISLAY LIFE MUSEUM
ISLAY
Port Charlotte
Lossit
Lossit Pt.
Nerabus
Rubha na Faing
Portnahaven
Port Wemyss
Orsay
Rinns Pt.
Gortantaoid
Killinallan
364 SGARBH BREAC
316
Bunnahabhain
BUNNAHABHAIN DISTILLERY
Caol Ila
CAOL ILA DISTILLERY
Port Askaig
FINLAGGAN CENTRE
Loch Finlaggan
Loch Cam
Keills
Ballygrant
Loch Ballygrant
Kilmeny
Blackrock
Redhouses
Sorn
Daill
Bridgend
267 BEINN DUBH
Bowmore
BOWMORE ROUND CHURCH
LOCH INDAAL
Mulindry
Kilennan
Laggan
Laggan Pt.
Laggan
Duich
471 BEINN BHAN
491 BEINN BHEIGEIR
Loch Beinn Uraraidh
LAGGAN BAY
Glenegedale
ISLAY
347 BEINN SHOLUM
Port Alsaig
Rubha Mór
Kintra
Leorin
Cornabus
Imeraval
Lower Cragabus
Dùn Mór Ghil
THE OA
152
Lower Killeyan
Risabus
Inerval
AMERICAN MONUMENT
Mull of Oa
202
Rubha nan Leacan
Port Ellen
LAPHROAIG DISTILLERY
Laphroaig
Texa
Lagavulin
LAGAVULIN DISTILLERY
ARDBEG DISTILLERY
Ardbeg
Eilean Imersay
Eilean Bhride
Eilean a'Chuirn
Eilean Craobhach
KILDALTON CHURCH AND CROSSES
Ardmore Pt.
Kintour
Claggain Bay
Ardtalla
Carraig Mhór
McArthur's Hd.
Am Fraoch Eilean
Brosdale I.
Rubha na Tràil
Cabrach
342 BRAT BHEINN
ISLE OF JURA DISTILLERY
Craighouse
Keils
Gleann Ullibh
Feolin Ferry
561
Gleann Astaile
Leargybreck
Corran
Loch a Chnuic Bhric
785
755
439
Loch an Aircill
Loch
Sm
A846
A847
B8016
B8017
B8018
13
15
8
4
Rathlin Island
0 1 2 3 4 5 6 miles
0 1 2 3 4 5 6 7 8 9 10 km
1 2 3 4 5 6
A B C D E F G H

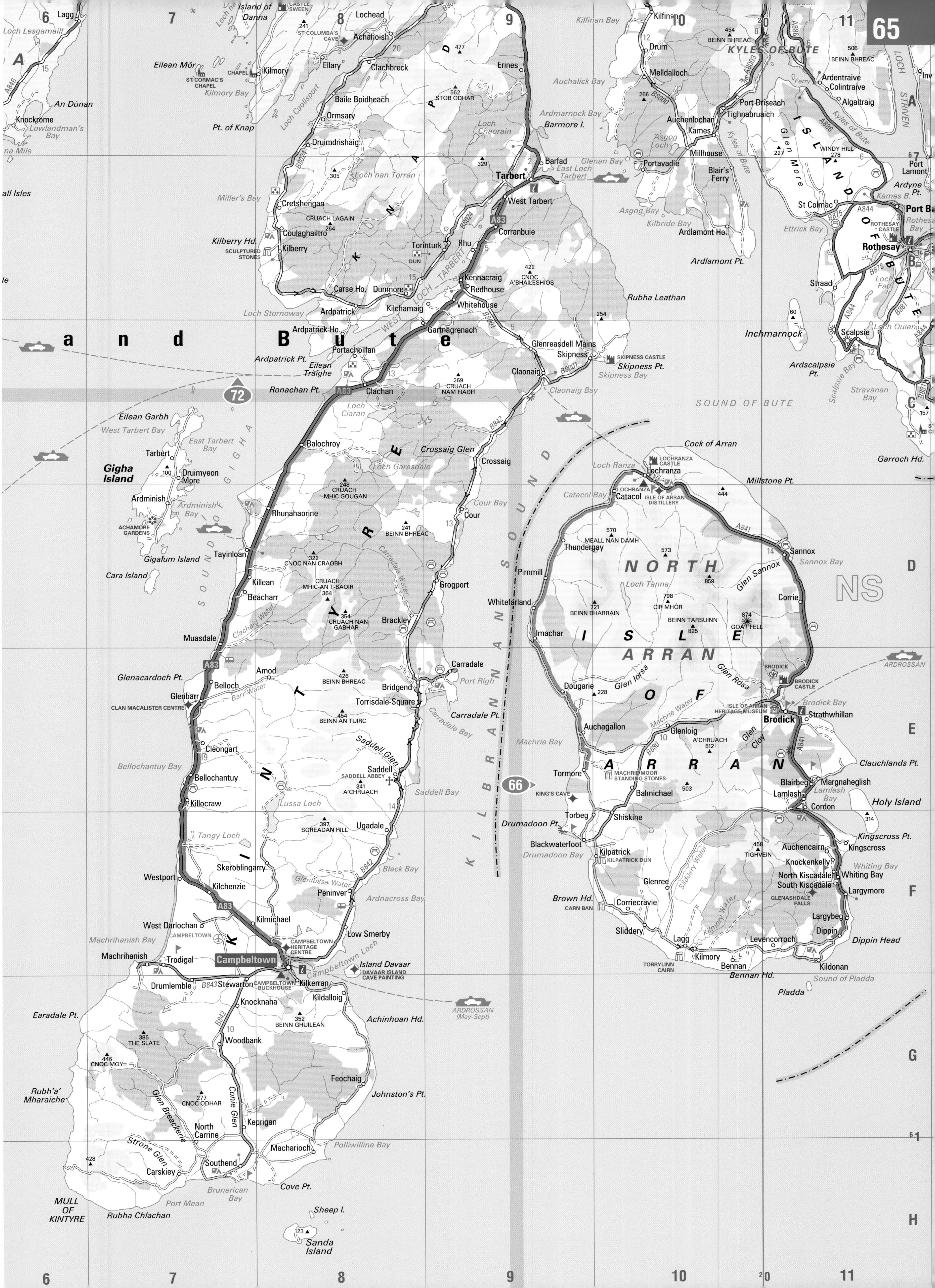

Lagg
Loch Lesgamaill
Island of Danna
Castle Sween
St Columba's Cave
Lochead
Achahoish
Eilean Mòr
St Cormac's Chapel
Chapel
Kilmory
Kilmory Bay
Ellary
Clachbreck
Erines
An Dùnan
Knockrome
Lowlandman's Bay
Baile Boidheach
Loch Caolisport
Ormsary
562 Stob Odhar
Pt. of Knap
Druimdrishaig
Loch Chaorain
Barmore I.
Ardmarnock Bay
Auchalick Bay
Kilfinan Bay
Kilfinan
Drum
Melldalloch
266
Beinn Bhreac 454
Kyles of Bute
Beinn Bhreac 506
Loch Striven
Ardentraive
Colintraive
Port Driseach
Tighnabruaich
Algaltraig
Auchenlochan
Kames
Asgog Loch
Millhouse
Portavadie
Blair's Ferry
Kyles of Bute
Glen More
Island of Bute
Windy Hill 278
227
Port Lamont
Ardyne Pt.
Kames B.
Port Bannatyne
St Colmac
Rothesay Castle
Rothesay Bay
Rothesay
Ettrick Bay
Straad
Loch Fad
Loch Quien
Scalpsie
Scalpsie Bay
Ardscalpsie Pt.
Stravanan Bay
Inchmarnock
60
Ardlamont Ho.
Ardlamont Pt.
Kilbride Bay
Asgog Bay
Barfad
East Loch Tarbert
Glenan Bay
Tarbert
West Tarbert
329
305
Loch nan Torran
Knapdale
Miller's Bay
Cretshengan
Cruach Lagain 264
Coulaghailtro
Kilberry
Kilberry Hd.
Sculptured Stones
Torinturk
Dun
Rhu
Corranbuie
422 Cnoc a'Bhaileshios
Kennacraig
Redhouse
Carse Ho.
Dunmore
West Loch Tarbert
Kilchamaig
Whitehouse
Loch Stornoway
Ardpatrick
Ardpatrick Ho.
Gartnagrenach
Rubha Leathan
254
Argyll and Bute
Portachoillan
Ardpatrick Pt.
Eilean Traighe
Glenreasdell Mains
Skipness
Skipness Castle
Skipness Pt.
Skipness Bay
Claonaig
Claonaig Bay
Ronachan Pt.
Clachan
269 Cruach nam Fiadh
72
Sound of Bute
Eilean Garbh
West Tarbert Bay
East Tarbert Bay
Loch Ciaran
Balochroy
Crossaig Glen
Crossaig
Loch Garasdale
248 Cruach Mhic Gougan
Tarbert
Gigha Island
Druimyeon More
100
Ardminish
Ardminish Bay
Achamore Gardens
Sound of Gigha
Gigalum Island
Cara Island
Rhunahaorine
Cour Bay
Cour
241 Beinn Bhreac
Tayinloan
322 Cnoc nan Craobh
Killean
Beacharr
Cruach Mhic-an t-Saoir 364
354 Cruach nan Gabhar
Carradale Water
Grogport
Brackley
Clachaig Water
Muasdale
Kintyre
Kilbrannan Sound
Cock of Arran
Lochranza Castle
Loch Ranza
Lochranza
Catacol Bay
Catacol
Isle of Arran Distillery
444
Millstone Pt.
Pirnmill
Thundergay
Meall nan Damh 570
573
North
Loch Tanna
859
Glen Sannox
Sannox
Sannox Bay
Corrie
798 Cir Mhòr
721 Beinn Bharrain
Beinn Tarsuinn 825
874 Goat Fell
Whitefarland
Imachar
Isle of Arran
NS
Glenacardoch Pt.
Belloch
Amod
426 Beinn Bhreac
Carradale
Port Righ
Bridgend
Glenbarr
Clan Macalister Centre
Barr Water
Torrisdale-Square
Carradale Pt.
Carradale Bay
454 Beinn an Tuirc
Dougarie
228
Glen Iorsa
Glen Rosa
Brodick
Brodick Castle
Brodick Bay
Isle of Arran Heritage Museum
Strathwhillan
Ardrossan
Cleongart
Bellochantuy Bay
Bellochantuy
Saddell Glen
Saddell
Saddell Abbey
341 A'Chruach
Saddell Bay
Killocraw
Lussa Loch
Machrie Water
Auchagallon
Machrie Bay
Glenloig
A'Chruach 512
Glen Cloy
Tormore
Machrie Moor Standing Stones
503
King's Cave
Balmichael
Clauchlands Pt.
Blairbeg
Margnaheglish
Lamlash
Lamlash Bay
Cordon
Holy Island
314
66
Tangy Loch
397 Sgreadan Hill
Ugadale
Torbeg
Shiskine
Drumadoon Pt.
Blackwaterfoot
Drumadoon Bay
Kilpatrick
Kilpatrick Dun
458 Tighvein
Kingscross Pt.
Kingscross
Auchencairn
Knockenkelly
Whiting Bay
North Kiscadale
South Kiscadale
Largymore
Glenashdale Falls
Westport
Skeroblingarry
Black Bay
Kilchenzie
Glenlussa Water
Peninver
Ardnacross Bay
Sliddery Water
Glenree
Brown Hd.
Carn Ban
Corriecravie
Kilmory Water
Largybeg
Dippin
Dippin Head
West Darlochan
Machrihanish Bay
Campbeltown
Kilmichael
Low Smerby
Campbeltown Heritage Centre
Machrihanish
Trodigal
Campbeltown Loch
Island Davaar
Davaar Island Cave Painting
Sliddery
Lagg
Kilmory
Levencorroch
Bennan
Torrylinn Cairn
Bennan Hd.
Kildonan
Sound of Pladda
Pladda
Drumlemble
Stewarton
Campbeltown Buckhouse
Kilkerran
Kildalloig
Knocknaha
Eararadale Pt.
352 Beinn Ghuilean
Achinhoan Hd.
Ardrossan (May-Sept)
385 The Slate
Woodbank
446 Cnoc Moy
Feochaig
Rubh' a' Mharaiche
Glen Breackerie
277 Cnoc Odhar
Conie Glen
Johnston's Pt.
North Carrine
Keprigan
Strone Glen
Machariroch
Polliwilline Bay
428
Southend
Carskiey
Brunerican Bay
Cove Pt.
Port Mean
Mull of Kintyre
Rubha Chlachan
Sheep I.
123
Sanda Island
A83
A846
A886
A8003
B8000
B8024
B8001
B842
B843
A841
B880
A844
B875
B878
B881
6
7
8
9
10
11
A
B
C
D
E
F
G
H

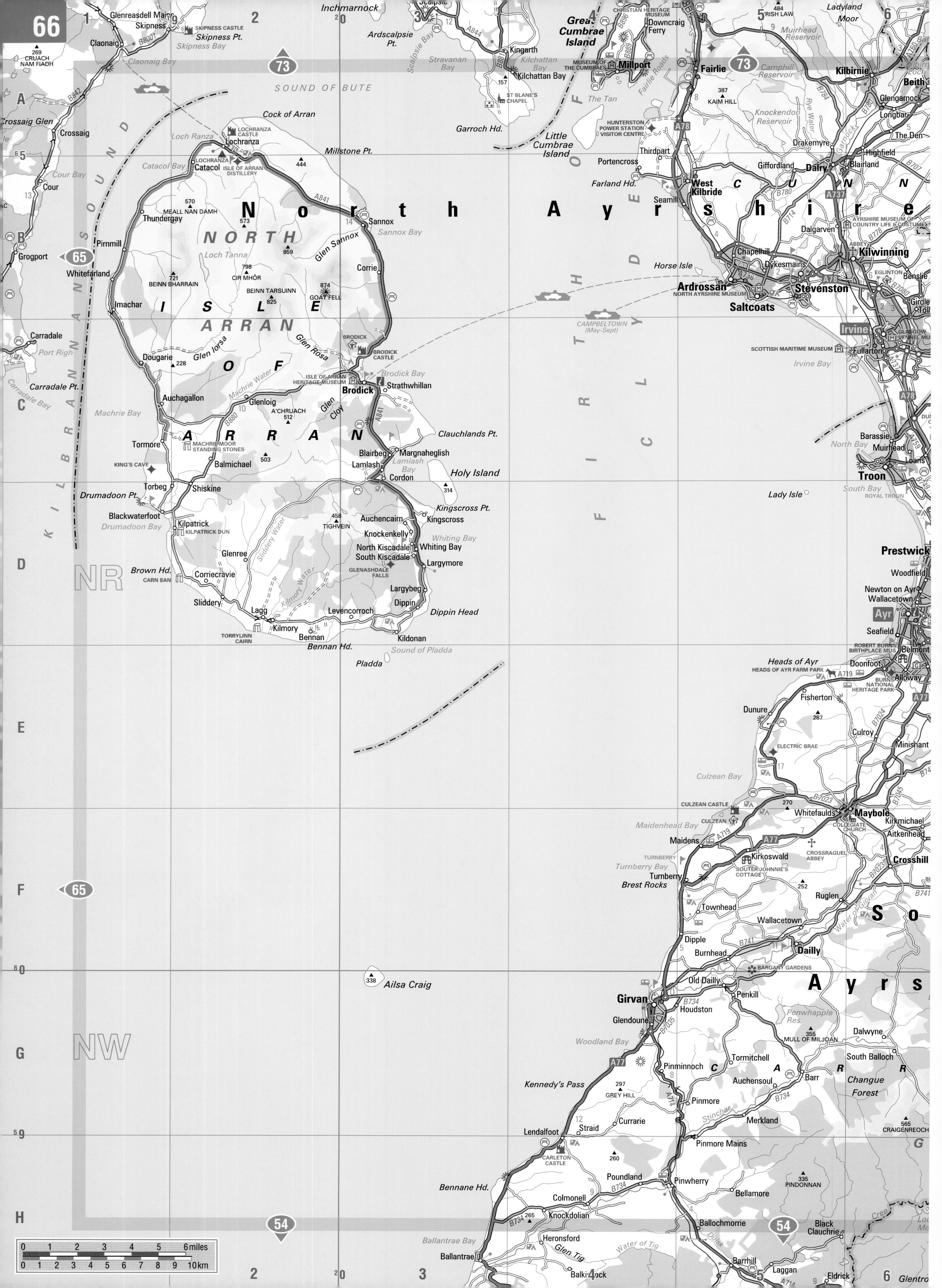
Glenreasdell Mains
Skipness
Skipness Castle
Skipness Pt.
Skipness Bay
Claonaig
Claonaig Bay
B8001
269
CRUACH NAM FIADH
Inchmarnock
Ardscalpsie Pt.
Stravanan Bay
Scalpsie Bay
A844
Kingarth
Kilchattan Bay
157
St Blane's Chapel
B881
Great Cumbrae Island
Christian Heritage Museum
Downcraig Ferry
B896
B899
Museum of the Cumbraes
Millport
Fairlie
Fairlie Roads
73
484
Rish Law
Muirhead Reservoir
Camphill Reservoir
Ladyland Moor
Kilbirnie
Beith
Glengarnock
Longbar
The Den
Highfield
Blairland
Dalry
B784
B780
B707
B714
B778
A737
A760
Sound of Bute
Cock of Arran
Garroch Hd.
The Tan
387
Kaim Hill
Knockendon Reservoir
Rye Water
Hunterston Power Station Visitor Centre
A78
Little Cumbrae Island
Drakemyre
Thirdpart
Portencross
Giffordland
Farland Hd.
West Kilbride
Seamill
Crossaig Glen
Crossaig
B842
Lochranza Castle
Loch Ranza
Lochranza
Millstone Pt.
444
Catacol Bay
Catacol
Isle of Arran Distillery
Cour Bay
Cour
13
A841
570
Meall nan Damh
Thundergay
573
North Ayrshire
North
Sannox
Sannox Bay
14
Pirnmill
Loch Tanna
859
Glen Sannox
Grogport
65
Whitefarland
798
Cir Mhòr
721
Beinn Bharrain
Beinn Tarsuinn
825
874
Goat Fell
Corrie
Isle of Arran
Imachar
Kilbrannan Sound
Firth of Clyde
Horse Isle
Chapelhill
Dykesmains
Dalgarven
Ayrshire Museum of Country Life & Costume
Abbey
Kilwinning
Eglinton
Bensile
Ardrossan
North Ayrshire Museum
A738
Stevenston
Saltcoats
B7080
Girdle Toll
Carradale
Port Righ
Carradale Pt.
Carradale Bay
Dougarie
228
Glen Iorsa
Glen Rosa
Brodick
Brodick Castle
Campbeltown (May-Sept)
Irvine
Glasgow Vennel Museum
Scottish Maritime Museum
Fullarton
Irvine Bay
Isle of Arran Heritage Museum
Brodick Bay
Strathwhillan
Machrie Water
Auchagallon
Glenloig
10
A'Chruach
512
Glen Cloy
Machrie Bay
B880
Machrie Moor Standing Stones
Tormore
Arran
Clauchlands Pt.
A78
Barassie
North Bay
Muirhead
Loans
Troon
A759
Blairbeg
Margnaheglish
Lamlash Bay
Lamlash
503
Balmichael
King's Cave
Cordon
Holy Island
314
Torbeg
Shiskine
Drumadoon Pt.
Lady Isle
South Bay
Royal Troon
Blackwaterfoot
Drumadoon Bay
Kilpatrick
Kilpatrick Dun
458
Tighvein
Auchencairn
Kingscross Pt.
Kingscross
Knockenkelly
Sliddery Water
Whiting Bay
Glenree
North Kiscadale
South Kiscadale
Glenashdale Falls
Largymore
Prestwick
NR
Brown Hd.
Carn Ban
Corriecravie
Kilmory Water
Woodfield
Largybeg
Newton on Ayr
Wallacetown
Sliddery
Dippin
Dippin Head
Ayr
Lagg
Levencorroch
Torrylinn Cairn
Kilmory
Bennan
Bennan Hd.
Kildonan
Sound of Pladda
Pladda
Seafield
Robert Burns Birthplace Mus
Belmont
Heads of Ayr
Heads of Ayr Farm Park
A719
Doonfoot
Alloway
Burns National Heritage Park
Fisherton
A77
Dunure
287
B7024
Culroy
Minishant
Electric Brae
17
Culzean Bay
B7023
Culzean Castle
270
Whitefaulds
Maybole
Collegiate Church
Kirkmichael
Culzean
Maidenhead Bay
Maidens
Aitkenhead
Crossraguel Abbey
Kirkoswald
Turnberry
Turnberry Bay
Souter Johnnie's Cottage
Crosshill
Brest Rocks
252
Ruglen
B741
Townhead
Wallacetown
Water of Girvan
South Ayrshire
Dipple
Burnhead
Dailly
Bargany Gardens
Old Dailly
338
Ailsa Craig
Girvan
Penkill
B734
Houston
Glendoune
Penwhapple Res.
B7035
355
Mull of Miljoan
Dalwyne
NW
Woodland Bay
South Balloch
Tormitchell
Carrick
Pinminnoch
Changue Forest
Barr
Auchensoul
Kennedy's Pass
297
Grey Hill
A714
Pinmore
Stinchar
12
Straid
Currarie
Merkland
565
Craigenreoch
Lendalfoot
Pinmore Mains
Carleton Castle
260
Poundland
335
Pindonnan
Bennane Hd.
Pinwherry
Colmonell
Bellamore
Knockdolian
265
54
Ballochmorrie
Black Clauchrie
Ballantrae Bay
Heronsford
Glen Tig
Water of Tig
Duisk
Ballantrae
Balkissock
Barrhill
Laggan
Eldrick
Glentrool
0 1 2 3 4 5 6 miles
0 1 2 3 4 5 6 7 8 9 10 km

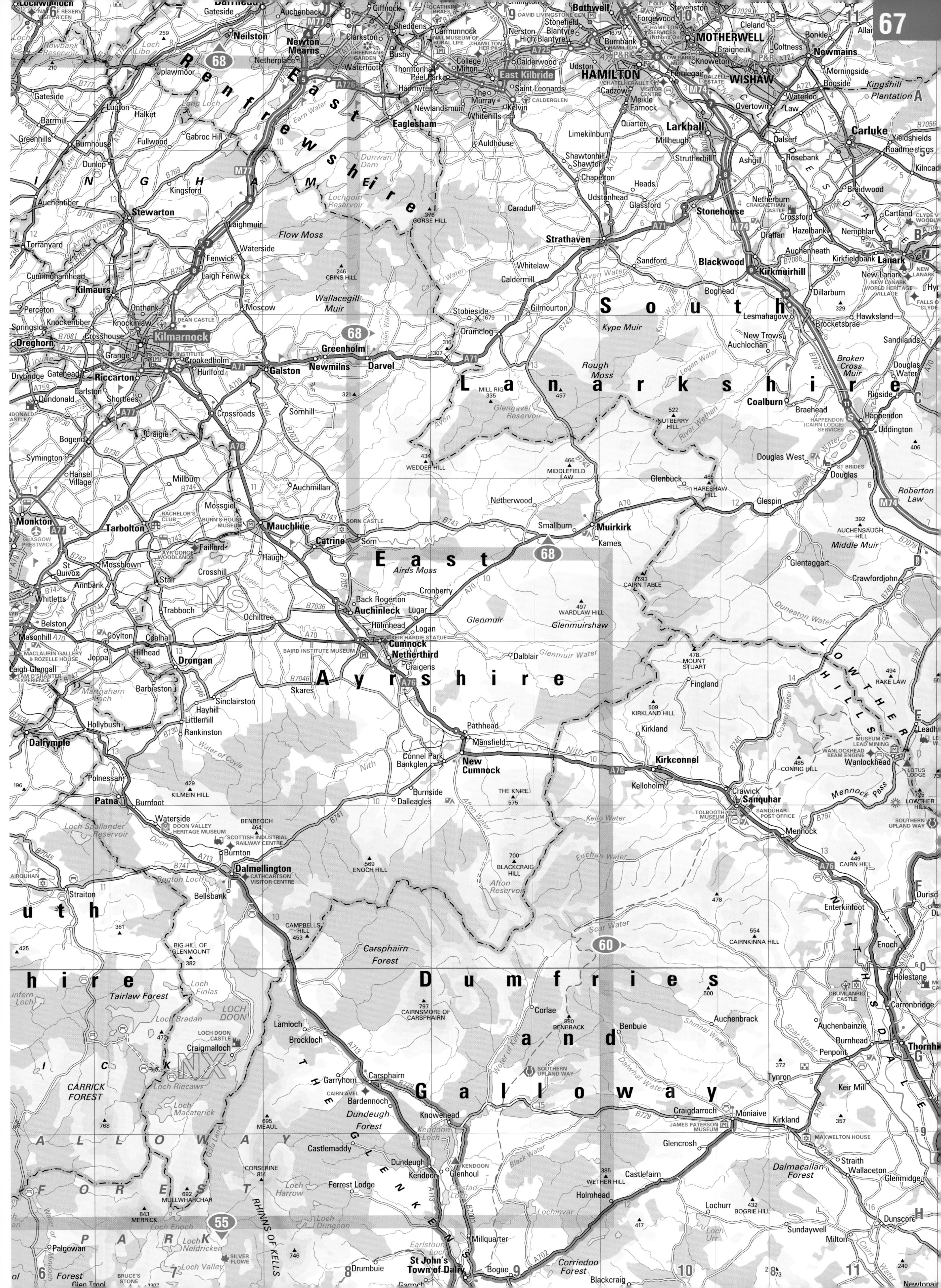
Renfrewshire
East
South
Lanarkshire
East
Ayrshire
Dumfries
and
Galloway
Neilston
Newton Mearns
Clarkston
Busby
East Kilbride
Eaglesham
Bothwell
MOTHERWELL
HAMILTON
WISHAW
Newmains
Larkhall
Carluke
Stonehouse
Strathaven
Lanark
Blackwood
Kirkmuirhill
Lesmahagow
Coalburn
Douglas
Uplawmoor
Stewarton
Kilmaurs
Kilmarnock
Dreghorn
Riccarton
Hurlford
Galston
Newmilns
Darvel
Fenwick
Mauchline
Catrine
Tarbolton
Monkton
Auchinleck
Cumnock
Muirkirk
Drongan
Dalrymple
Patna
Dalmellington
New Cumnock
Kirkconnel
Sanquhar
Wanlockhead
Leadhills
Carsphairn
Moniaive
Penpont
Thornhill
St John's Town of Dalry
Galloway Forest Park
Carsphairn Forest
Lowther Hills
The Glenkens
Nithsdale
Clydesdale
Rhinns of Kells
Afton Reservoir
Loch Doon
Cairn Table
Blackcraig Hill
Cairnsmore of Carsphairn
68
60
55

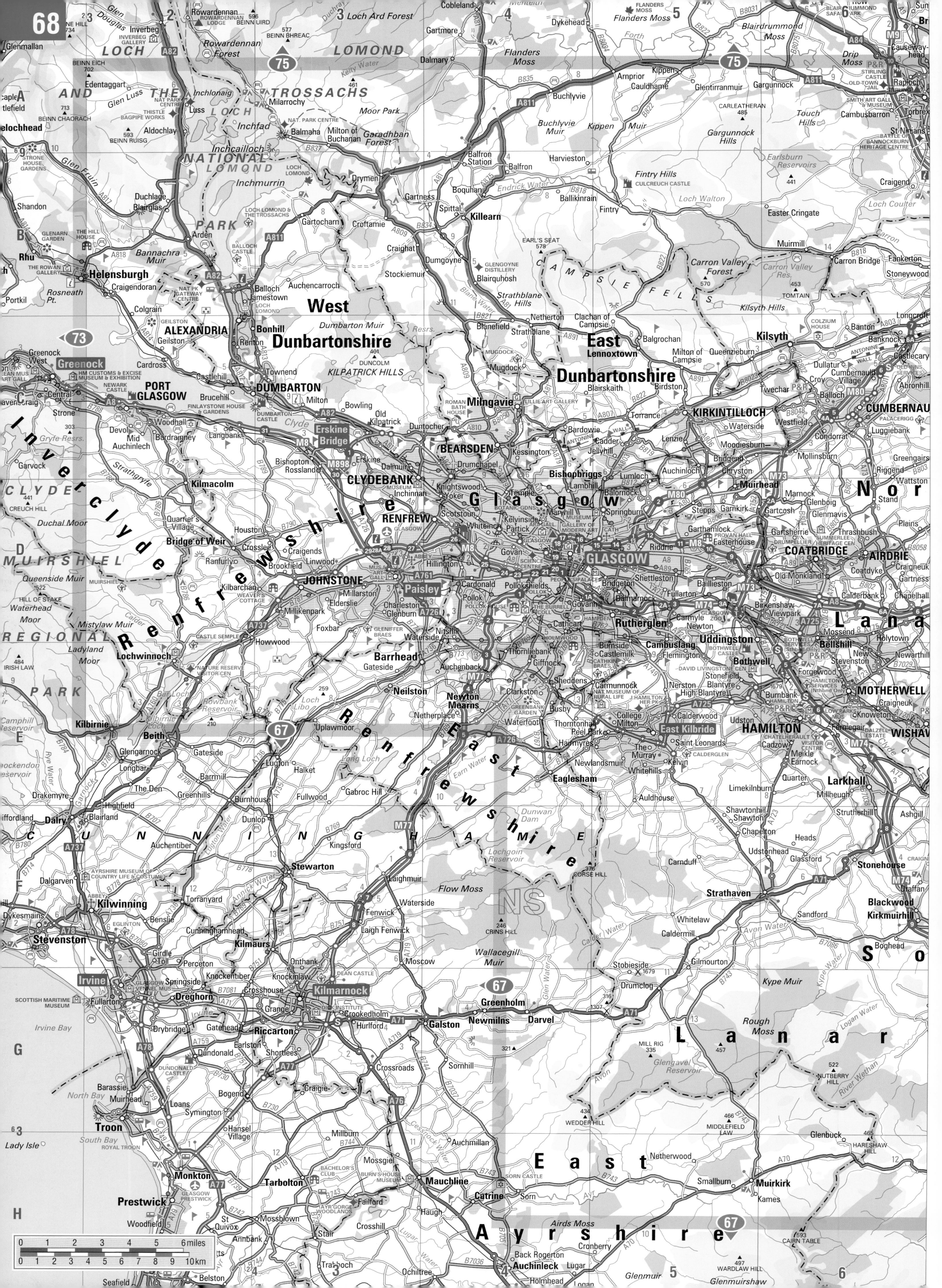

Loch Ard Forest
Rowardennan
Inverbeg
Glen Douglas
Glenmallan
LOCH LOMOND
AND THE TROSSACHS
NATIONAL PARK
Rowardennan Forest
Inchlonaig
Milarrochy
Moor Park
Luss
Glen Luss
Inchfad
Balmaha
Milton of Buchanan
Garadhban Forest
Aldochlay
Inchcailloch
Inchmurrin
Edentaggart
Garelochhead
Shandon
Duchlage
Blairglas
Glen Fruin
Drymen
Gartocharn
Croftamie
Arden
Rhu
Helensburgh
Bannachra Muir
Craigendoran
Rosneath Pt.
Portkil
Balloch
Jamestown
Auchencarroch
Colgrain
ALEXANDRIA
Bonhill
Renton
Geilston
Cardross
Greenock
PORT GLASGOW
Castlehill
Brucehill
DUMBARTON
Milton
Bowling
Old Kilpatrick
Duntocher
Strone
Devol
Mid Auchinlech
Woodhall
Bardrainney
Langbank
Erskine Bridge
Erskine
Bishopton
Rossland
Dalmuir
CLYDEBANK
Garvock
Strathgryfe
Kilmacolm
Inverclyde
Duchal Moor
Quarrier's Village
Houston
Bridge of Weir
Crosslee
Craigends
RENFREW
Ranfurly
Brookfield
Linwood
JOHNSTONE
Kilbarchan
MUIRSHIEL REGIONAL PARK
Queenside Muir
Waterhead Moor
Mistylaw Muir
Ladyland Moor
Lochwinnoch
Howwood
Renfrewshire
Millarston
Elderslie
Millikenpark
Paisley
Charleston
Glenburn
Foxbar
Waterside
Barrhead
Gateside
Neilston
Uplawmoor
Kilbirnie
Beith
Gateside
Lugton
Halket
Long Loch
Glengarnock
Longbar
Barrmill
The Den
Greenhills
Burnhouse
Fullwood
Gabroc Hill
Drakemyre
Highfield
Dalry
Blairland
Dunlop
Auchentiber
Kingsford
CUNNINGHAME
Stewarton
Dalgarven
Kilwinning
Torranyard
Laighmuir
Fenwick
Laigh Fenwick
Waterside
Flow Moss
Bensli
Cunninghamhead
Kilmaurs
Dykesmains
Stevenston
Girdle Toll
Perceton
Springside
Knockentiber
Onthank
Knockinlaw
Irvine
Dreghorn
Crosshouse
Kilmarnock
Fullarton
Grange
Crookedholm
Hurlford
Galston
Newmilns
Greenholm
Darvel
Moscow
Irvine Bay
Drybridge
Gatehead
Riccarton
Dundonald
Earlston
Shortlees
Crossroads
Sornhill
North Bay
Barassie
Muirhead
Loans
Symington
Bogend
Craigie
Troon
Lady Isle
South Bay
Hansel Village
Millburn
Auchmillan
Mossgiel
Monkton
Tarbolton
Mauchline
Catrine
Sorn
Prestwick
Failford
Haugh
Woodfield
St Quivox
Mossblown
Annbank
Stair
Crosshill
Trabboch
Ochiltree
Belston
Seafield
Back Rogerton
Auchinleck
Lugar
Holmhead
Cronberry
Airds Moss
Glenmuir
Glenmuirshaw
Ayrshire
East
Muirkirk
Kames
Smallburn
Netherwood
Glenbuck
Rough Moss
Glengavel Reservoir
Lanark
Kype Muir
Drumclog
Stobieside
Gilmourton
Caldermill
Whitelaw
Sandford
Strathaven
Blackwood
Kirkmuirhill
Boghead
Stonehouse
Glassford
Udstonhead
Chapelton
Shawton
Carnduff
Heads
Ashgill
Larkhall
Millheugh
Strutherhill
Limekilnburn
Quarter
Auldhouse
Eaglesham
Newlandsmuir
Flanders Moss
Dykehead
Gartmore
Dalmary
Blairdrummond Moss
Drip Moss
Causewayhead
Stirling
Arnprior
Kippen
Cauldhame
Glentirranmuir
Gargunnock
Cambusbarron
Touch Hills
Buchlyvie
Buchlyvie Muir
Gargunnock Hills
St. Ninians
Harvieston
Balfron Station
Balfron
Boquhan
Fintry Hills
Ballikinrain
Fintry
Gartness
Spittal
Killearn
Craighat
Dumgoyne
Stockiemuir
Blairquhosh
Strathblane Hills
CAMPSIE FELLS
Carron Valley Forest
Carron Bridge
Fankerton
Stoneywood
Muirmill
Easter Cringate
Craigend
Loch Coulter
Kilsyth Hills
Kilsyth
Banton
Banknock
Castlecary
Netherton
Clachan of Campsie
Balgrochan
Blanefield
Strathblane
Mugdock
Milton of Campsie
Queenzieburn
West Dunbartonshire
Dumbarton Muir
KILPATRICK HILLS
East Dunbartonshire
Lennoxtown
Milngavie
Blairskaith
Birdston
Twechar
Croy
Dullatur
Cumbernauld Village
Abronhill
CUMBERNAULD
Balloch
Torrance
KIRKINTILLOCH
Waterside
Westfield
Condorrat
Luggiebank
BEARSDEN
Bardowie
Cadder
Jellyhill
Kessington
Lenzie
Moodiesburn
Mollinsburn
Drumchapel
Bishopbriggs
Lumloch
Bridgend
Chryston
Auchinloch
Muirhead
Greengairs
Riggend
Knightswood
Yoker
Lambhill
Balornock
Glasgow
Scotstoun
Whiteinch
Maryhill
Springburn
Stepps
Garnkirk
Marnock
Glenboig
Glenmavis
Gartcosh
Kelvinside
Partick
Garthamlock
Easterhouse
Gartsherrie
Thrashbush
Plains
Govan
Riddrie
COATBRIDGE
AIRDRIE
Hillington
GLASGOW
Shettleston
Baillieston
Old Monkland
Coatdyke
Craigneuk
Cardonald
Pollokshields
Bridgeton
Dalmarnock
Fullarton
Pollok
Govanhill
Calderbank
Chapelhall
Rutherglen
Carmyle
Newton
Birkenshaw
Viewpark
Cathcart
Uddingston
Mossend
Holytown
Bellshill
Thornliebank
Giffnock
Burnside
Castlemilk
Cambuslang
Flemington
Bothwell
Newarthill
New Stevenston
Auchenback
Shieldhill
Newton Mearns
Clarkston
Sheddens
Carmunnock
Nerston
High Blantyre
Stonefield
Blantyre
Forgewood
MOTHERWELL
Busby
Netherplace
Waterfoot
Thorntonhall
Peel Park
College
Milton
East Kilbride
Calderwood
Udston
Burnbank
Craigneuk
Knowetop
HAMILTON
WISHAW
Hairmyres
The Murray
Saint Leonards
Kelvin
Whitehills
Cadzow
Meikle Earnock
Ferniegair
East Renfrewshire
Crins Hill
Wallacegill Muir
Corse Hill
Lochgoin Reservoir
Dunwan Dam
Mill Rig
Wedder Hill
Middlefield Law
Nutberry Hill
Hareshaw Hill
Wardlaw Hill
Cairn Table
NS
0 1 2 3 4 5 6 miles
0 1 2 3 4 5 6 7 8 9 10 km

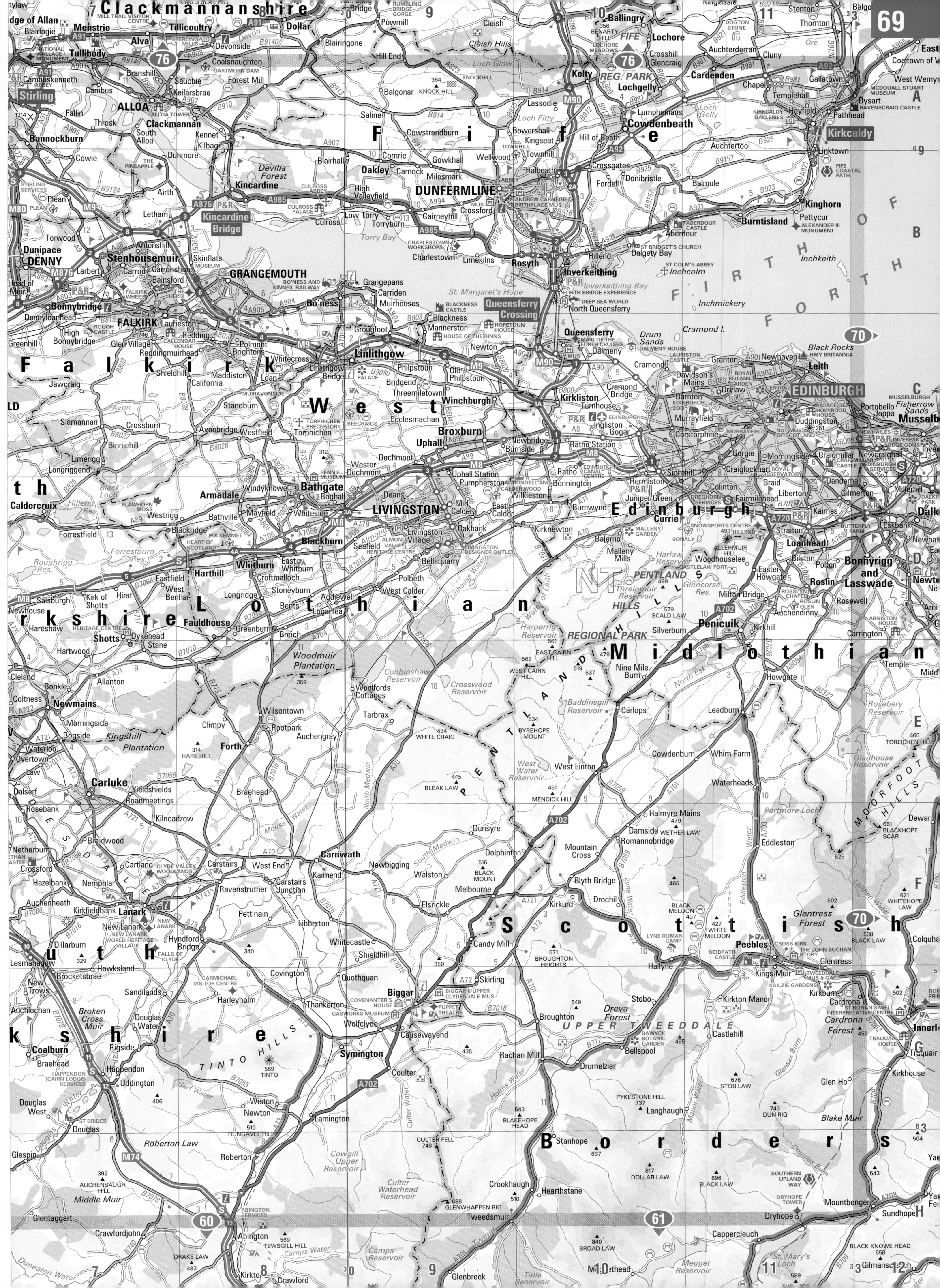
Clackmannanshire
Fife
Falkirk
West Lothian
Edinburgh
Midlothian
Scottish Borders
FIRTH OF FORTH
Stirling
ALLOA
Clackmannan
Kincardine
Kincardine Bridge
GRANGEMOUTH
FALKIRK
DENNY
Stenhousemuir
Bonnybridge
Bo'ness
Linlithgow
DUNFERMLINE
Rosyth
Inverkeithing
Queensferry Crossing
Queensferry
Cowdenbeath
Lochgelly
Kirkcaldy
Burntisland
Kinghorn
Leith
EDINBURGH
Musselburgh
Dalkeith
Bonnyrigg and Lasswade
Loanhead
Penicuik
LIVINGSTON
Bathgate
Armadale
Broxburn
Uphall
Winchburgh
Kirkliston
Whitburn
Blackburn
Fauldhouse
Shotts
Carluke
Lanark
Carnwath
Biggar
Symington
Peebles
West Linton
Carlops
Abington
Crawford
Tweedsmuir
PENTLAND HILLS REGIONAL PARK
PENTLAND HILLS
MOORFOOT HILLS
TINTO HILLS
UPPER TWEEDDALE
76
70
60
61

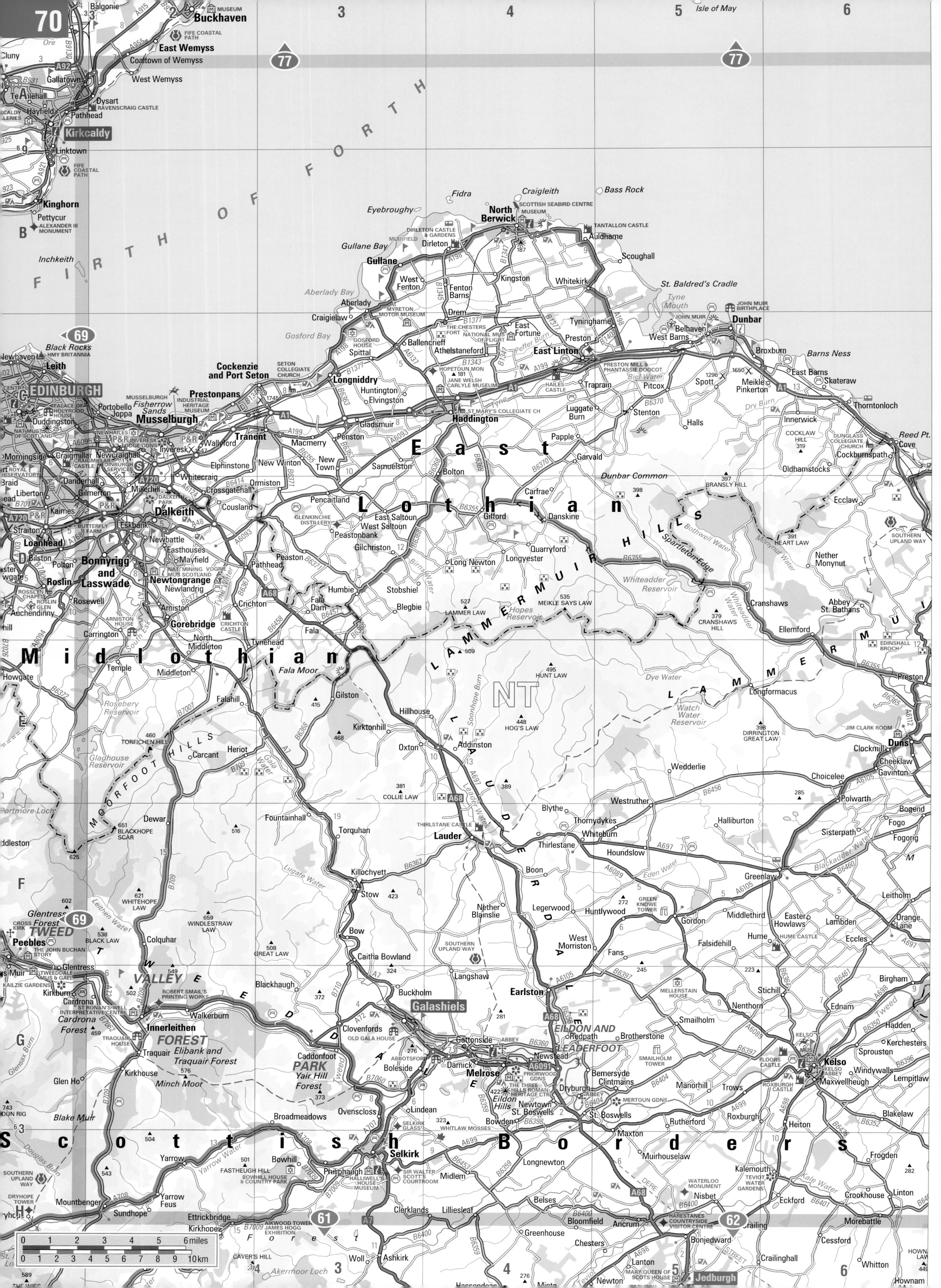
Buckhaven
East Wemyss
Coaltown of Wemyss
West Wemyss
Dysart
Kirkcaldy
Linktown
Kinghorn
Pettycur
Inchkeith
FIRTH OF FORTH
Isle of May
Fidra
Craigleith
Bass Rock
Eyebroughy
North Berwick
SCOTTISH SEABIRD CENTRE
TANTALLON CASTLE
Auldhame
Scoughall
Gullane Bay
Gullane
Dirleton
Kingston
Whitekirk
St. Baldred's Cradle
Aberlady Bay
Aberlady
Craigielaw
Drem
Gosford Bay
Dunbar
Belhaven
West Barns
Tyninghame
East Linton
Athelstaneford
Ballencrieff
Spittal
Black Rocks
Newhaven
Leith
EDINBURGH
Cockenzie and Port Seton
Prestonpans
Longniddry
Musselburgh
Portobello
Joppa
Tranent
Haddington
Gladsmuir
Macmerry
Penston
Traprain
Pitcox
Stenton
Spott
Broxburn
Barns Ness
East Barns
Skateraw
Thorntonlech
Innerwick
Reed Pt.
Cove
Cockburnspath
Oldhamstocks
East Lothian
Dunbar Common
Garvald
Papple
Bolton
Samuelston
Elphinstone
Dalkeith
Pencaitland
East Saltoun
West Saltoun
Gifford
Danskine
Longyester
Long Newton
Humbie
Pathhead
Bonnyrigg and Lasswade
Newtongrange
Loanhead
Roslin
Gorebridge
LAMMERMUIR HILLS
Whiteadder Reservoir
Cranshaws
Abbey St. Bathans
Ellemford
Midlothian
Fala Moor
Temple
Middleton
Hunt Law
Longformacus
Watch Water Reservoir
Duns
Preston
Gilston
Hillhouse
Oxton
Addinston
Heriot
MOORFOOT HILLS
Lauder
THIRLSTANE CASTLE
Blythe
Westruther
Thornydykes
Whiteburn
Thirlestane
Houndslow
Polwarth
Halliburton
Greenlaw
Stow
Fountainhall
Torquhan
Killochyett
Legerwood
Nether Blainslie
Gordon
Westruther
Earlston
Peebles
TWEED
Glentress Forest
Innerleithen
Walkerburn
Traquair
Cardrona
Galashiels
Clovenfords
Melrose
Darnick
Gattonside
Newstead
Eildon Hills
Newtown St. Boswells
St. Boswells
Dryburgh
Smailholm
Kelso
Hume
Eccles
Birgham
Ednam
Stichill
Nenthorn
Selkirk
Philiphaugh
Bowhill
Yarrow
Yarrow Feus
Mountbenger
Scottish Borders
Lilliesleaf
Midlem
Maxton
Rutherford
Roxburgh
Heiton
Ancrum
Nisbet
Eckford
Morebattle
Cessford
Bonjedward
Jedburgh
Ashkirk
Greenhouse
Chesters
Ettrickbridge
Kirkhope
Crailinghall
Whitton
Hownam
0 1 2 3 4 5 6 miles
0 1 2 3 4 5 6 7 8 9 10 km

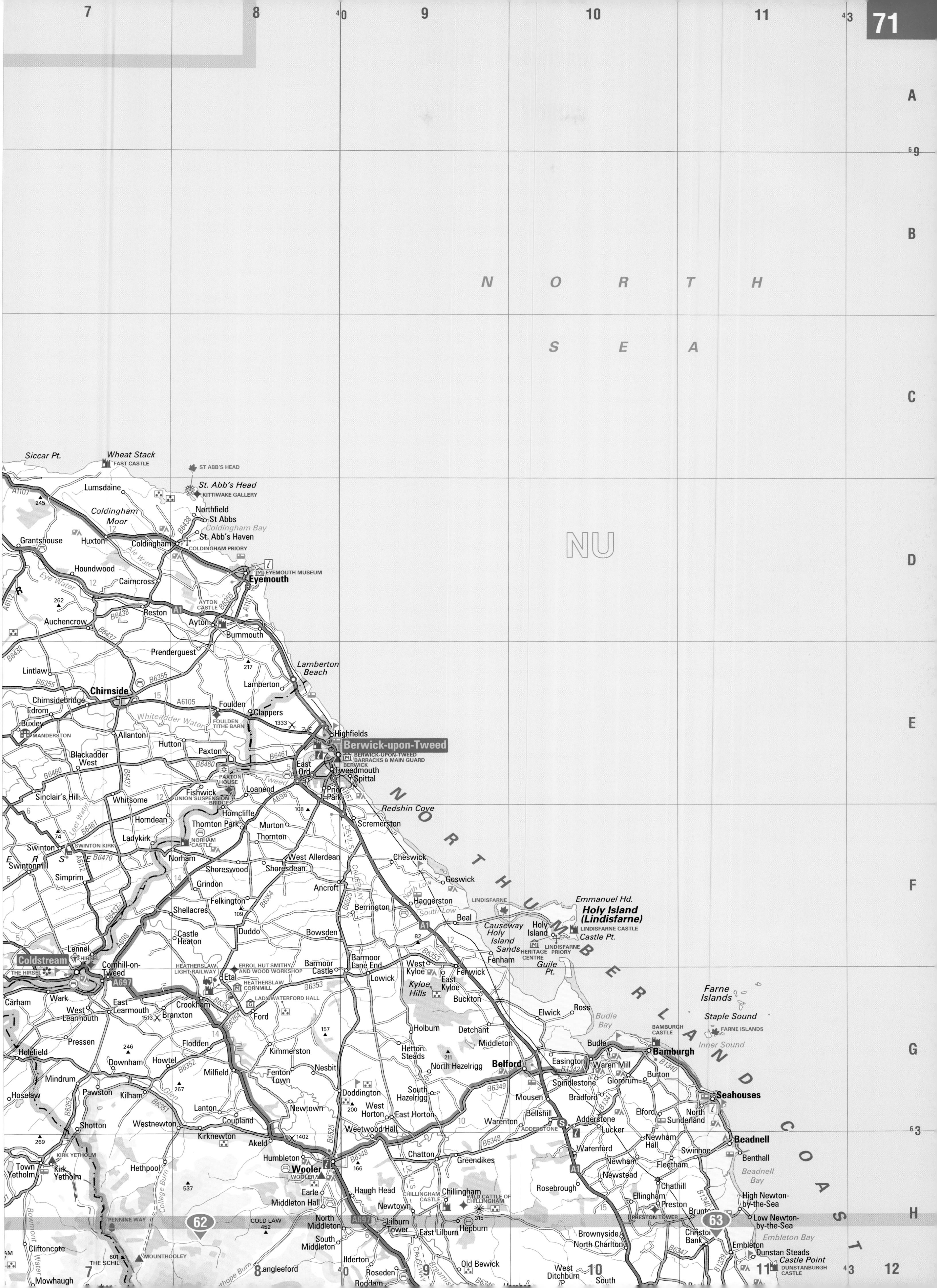
N O R T H
S E A
NU
NORTHUMBERLAND COAST
Siccar Pt.
Wheat Stack
FAST CASTLE
ST ABB'S HEAD
St. Abb's Head
KITTIWAKE GALLERY
Lumsdaine
Coldingham Moor
Northfield
St Abbs
Coldingham Bay
St. Abb's Haven
Grantshouse
Huxton
Coldingham
COLDINGHAM PRIORY
Houndwood
Cairncross
EYEMOUTH MUSEUM
Eyemouth
AYTON CASTLE
Reston
Auchencrow
Ayton
Burnmouth
Prenderguest
Lamberton Beach
Lamberton
Lintlaw
Chirnside
Chirnsidebridge
Edrom
Foulden
FOULDEN TITHE BARN
Clappers
Whiteadder Water
Buxley
MANDERSTON
Allanton
Hutton
Paxton
Highfields
Berwick-upon-Tweed
BERWICK-UPON-TWEED BARRACKS & MAIN GUARD
BERWICK
Tweedmouth
Spittal
East Ord
Blackadder West
PAXTON HOUSE
Sinclair's Hill
Whitsome
Fishwick
UNION SUSPENSION BRIDGE
Loanend
Prior Park
Redshin Cove
Horncliffe
Horndean
Thornton Park
Murton
Scremerston
Ladykirk
Thornton
NORHAM CASTLE
SWINTON KIRK
Swinton
Swintonmill
Norham
West Allerdean
Cheswick
Shoreswood
Shoresdean
Simprim
Grindon
Goswick
Ancroft
Felkington
Haggerston
Berrington
Beal
LINDISFARNE
Emmanuel Hd.
Holy Island (Lindisfarne)
LINDISFARNE CASTLE
Castle Pt.
Holy Island
Causeway
Holy Island Sands
LINDISFARNE PRIORY
HERITAGE CENTRE
Shellacres
Castle Heaton
Duddo
Bowsden
Fenham
Guile Pt.
Lennel
Coldstream
THE HIRSEL
HIRSEL
Cornhill-on-Tweed
HEATHERSLAW LIGHT RAILWAY
ERROL HUT SMITHY AND WOOD WORKSHOP
HEATHERSLAW CORNMILL
Etal
Barmoor Castle
Barmoor Lane End
West Kyloe
Fenwick
Lowick
East Kyloe
Kyloe Hills
Farne Islands
LADY WATERFORD HALL
Buckton
Carham
Wark
West Learmouth
East Learmouth
Crookham
Branxton
Ford
Elwick
Ross
Budle Bay
Staple Sound
FARNE ISLANDS
BAMBURGH CASTLE
Pressen
Flodden
Holburn
Detchant
Inner Sound
Hetton Steads
Middleton
Budle
Bamburgh
Holefield
Downham
Howtel
Kimmerston
North Hazelrigg
Belford
Easington
Waren Mill
Mindrum
Milfield
Fenton Town
Nesbit
Spindlestone
Glororum
Burton
Hoselaw
Pawston
Kilham
Doddington
South Hazelrigg
Mousen
Bradford
Seahouses
West Horton
East Horton
Bellshill
Elford
North Sunderland
Lanton
Newtown
Shotton
Westnewton
Coupland
Weetwood Hall
Warenton
ADDERSTONE
Adderstone
Lucker
Kirknewton
Akeld
Newham Hall
Beadnell
KIRK YETHOLM
Warenford
Swinhoe
Humbleton
Chatton
Greendikes
Newham
Benthall
Town Yetholm
Kirk Yetholm
Hethpool
Wooler
WOOLER
Newstead
Fleetham
Beadnell Bay
Earle
Haugh Head
Chillingham
CHILLINGHAM CASTLE
WILD CATTLE OF CHILLINGHAM
Rosebrough
Chathill
Ellingham
High Newton-by-the-Sea
Middleton Hall
Newtown
Preston
Brunton
PENNINE WAY
COLD LAW
North Middleton
Lilburn Tower
Hepburn
PRESTON TOWER
Low Newton-by-the-Sea
Brownyside
Christon Bank
Embleton Bay
Cliftoncote
North Charlton
Embleton
South Middleton
East Lilburn
Dunstan Steads
Castle Point
THE SCHIL
MOUNTHOOLEY
Ilderton
Old Bewick
West Ditchburn
South
DUNSTANBURGH CASTLE
Langleeford
Roseden
Roddam
Mowhaugh
College Burn
Bowmont Water
A1
A1107
A697
A698
A6105
A6112
B6438
B6437
B6355
B6460
B6461
B6470
B6354
B6353
B6525
B6348
B6349
B6351
B6352
B6364
B1340
B1341
B1342
B6347
62
63

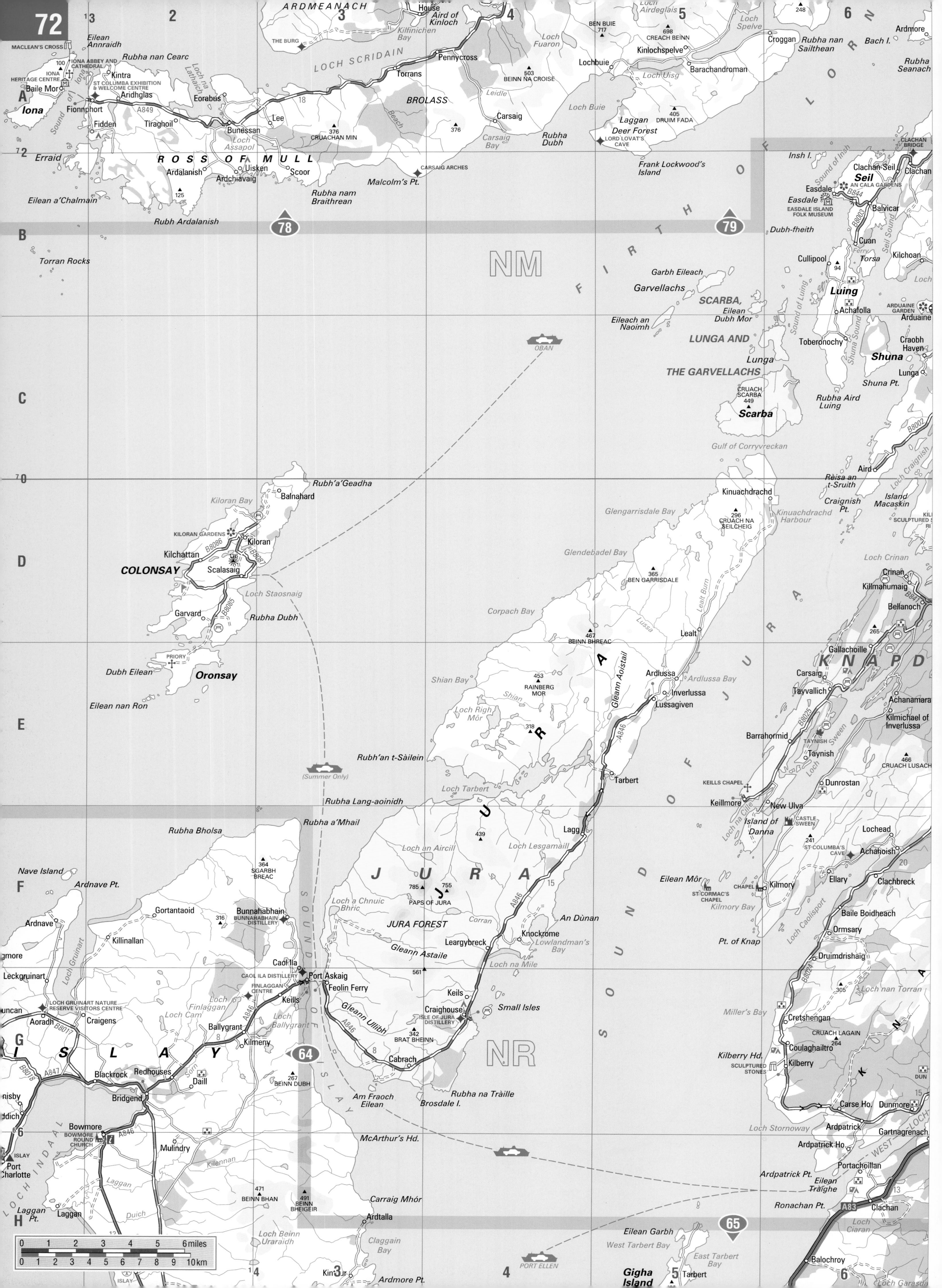
ARDMEANACH
House
Aird of Kinloch
Kilfinichen Bay
THE BURG
LOCH SCRIDAIN
Pennycross
Torrans
Loch Fuaron
BEN BUIE 717
698 CREACH BEINN
Loch Airdeglais
Loch Spelve
Kinlochspelve
Croggan
Rubha nan Sailthean
Bach I.
Ardmore
Rubha Seanach
Lochbuie
Loch Uisg
Barachandroman
503 BEINN NA CROISE
Leidle
BROLASS
Loch Buie
405 DRUIM FADA
Laggan Deer Forest
LORD LOVAT'S CAVE
Carsaig
Carsaig Bay
Rubha Dubh
MACLEAN'S CROSS
Eilean Annraidh
Rubha nan Cearc
100 IONA ABBEY AND CATHEDRAL
IONA HERITAGE CENTRE
Kintra
ST COLUMBA EXHIBITION & WELCOME CENTRE
Baile Mor
Iona
Sound of Iona
Fionnphort
Aridhglas
A849
Loch na Lathaich
Eorabus
Fidden
Tiraghoil
Bunessan
Lee
Loch Assapol
376 CRUACHAN MIN
376
Beach
Erraid
ROSS OF MULL
Ardalanish
Uisken
Scoor
Ardchiavaig
CARSAIG ARCHES
Malcolm's Pt.
125
Eilean a'Chalmain
Rubha nam Braithrean
Rubh Ardalanish
78
79
Frank Lockwood's Island
Insh I.
Sound of Insh
CLACHAN BRIDGE
Clachan-Seil
Clachan
Seil
AN CALA GARDENS
Easdale
Easdale
EASDALE ISLAND FOLK MUSEUM
B844
B8003
Balvicar
Dubh-fheith
Cuan
Ferry
Torsa
Seil Sound
Kilchoan
Torran Rocks
NM
FIRTH OF LORN
Garbh Eileach
Garvellachs
Cullipool
94
Luing
Sound of Luing
ARDUAINE GARDEN
Arduaine
Achafolla
SCARBA, Eilean Dubh Mor
Eileach an Naoimh
OBAN
LUNGA AND THE GARVELLACHS
Lunga
Toberonochy
Craobh Haven
Shuna
Shuna Sound
Lunga
Shuna Pt.
CRUACH SCARBA 449
Scarba
Rubha Aird Luing
B8002
Gulf of Corryvreckan
Aird
Rèisa an t-Sruith
Loch Craignish
Craignish Pt.
Island Macaskin
Rubh'a'Geadha
Balnahard
Kiloran Bay
KILORAN GARDENS
Kiloran
Kilchattan
B8086
B8087
136
Scalasaig
COLONSAY
Loch Staosnaig
Garvard
B8085
Rubha Dubh
PRIORY
Dubh Eilean
Oronsay
Eilean nan Ron
Kinuachdrachd
296 CRUACH NA SEILCHEIG
Kinuachdrachd Harbour
Glengarrisdale Bay
Glendebadel Bay
365 BEN GARRISDALE
Loch Crinan
Crinan
Kilmahumaig
Bellanoch
B841
Lealt Burn
Lussa
Corpach Bay
467 BEINN BHREAC
Lealt
265
Gallachoille
KNAPD
Shian Bay
453 RAINBERG MOR
Shian
Gleann Aoistail
Ardlussa
Ardlussa Bay
Inverlussa
Lussagiven
Carsaig
Tayvallich
Achanamara
Kilmichael of Inverlussa
Loch Righ Mòr
318
A846
B8025
Barrahormid
TAYNISH
Taynish
Loch Sween
466 CRUACH LUSACH
Rubh'an t-Sàilein
(Summer Only)
Tarbert
KEILLS CHAPEL
Dunrostan
Loch Tarbert
Rubha Lang-aoinidh
Keillmore
New Ulva
Rubha a'Mhail
Rubha Bholsa
CASTLE SWEEN
Island of Danna
Loch na Cille
Lagg
439
Loch an Aircill
Loch Lesgamaill
241 ST COLUMBA'S CAVE
Lochhead
Achahoish
364 SGARBH BREAC
Nave Island
Ardnave Pt.
JURA
785
755
PAPS OF JURA
Eilean Mòr
ST CORMAC'S CHAPEL
CHAPEL
Kilmory
Ellary
Clachbreck
Kilmory Bay
Loch a Chnuic Bhric
JURA FOREST
Corran
Gortantaoid
Bunnahabhain
BUNNAHABHAIN DISTILLERY
316
An Dùnan
Baile Boidheach
Ardnave
Killinallan
Knockrome
Leargybreck
Lowlandman's Bay
Gleann Astaile
Pt. of Knap
Ormsary
Loch Caolisport
Loch Gruinart
Caol Ila
Loch na Mile
Druimdrishaig
561
Leckgruinart
CAOL ILA DISTILLERY
Port Askaig
Feolin Ferry
FINLAGGAN CENTRE
Loch Finlaggan
Keills
B8024
305
Loch nan Torran
LOCH GRUINART NATURE RESERVE VISITORS CENTRE
Aoradh
Craigens
Loch Cam
Loch Ballygrant
Gleann Ullibh
Craighouse
ISLE OF JURA DISTILLERY
Small Isles
Miller's Bay
Cretshengan
B8017
Ballygrant
Kilmeny
A846
342 BRAT BHEINN
SOUND OF ISLAY
CRUACH LAGAIN 264
ISLAY
64
NR
Kilberry Hd.
Coulaghailtro
SCULPTURED STONES
Kilberry
A847
Blackrock
Redhouses
Sorn
Daill
267 BEINN DUBH
Cabrach
DUN
Bridgend
Am Fraoch Eilean
Brosdale I.
Rubha na Tràille
Carse Ho.
Dunmore
Bowmore
BOWMORE ROUND CHURCH
A846
Mulindry
Kilennan
McArthur's Hd.
Loch Stornoway
Ardpatrick
Gartnagrenach
Ardpatrick Ho.
WEST LOCH
ISLAY
Port Charlotte
LOCH INDAAL
Laggan
Portachoillan
Ardpatrick Pt.
Eilean Traighe
471 BEINN BHAN
491 BEINN BHEIGEIR
Carraig Mhór
Laggan Pt.
Laggan
Duich
Ronachan Pt.
A83
Clachan
Loch Ciaran
Ardtalla
65
Eilean Garbh
West Tarbert Bay
Loch Beinn Uraraidh
Claggain Bay
East Tarbert Bay
PORT ELLEN
Gigha Island
Tarbert
Balochroy
Ardmore Pt.
0 1 2 3 4 5 6 miles
0 1 2 3 4 5 6 7 8 9 10 km

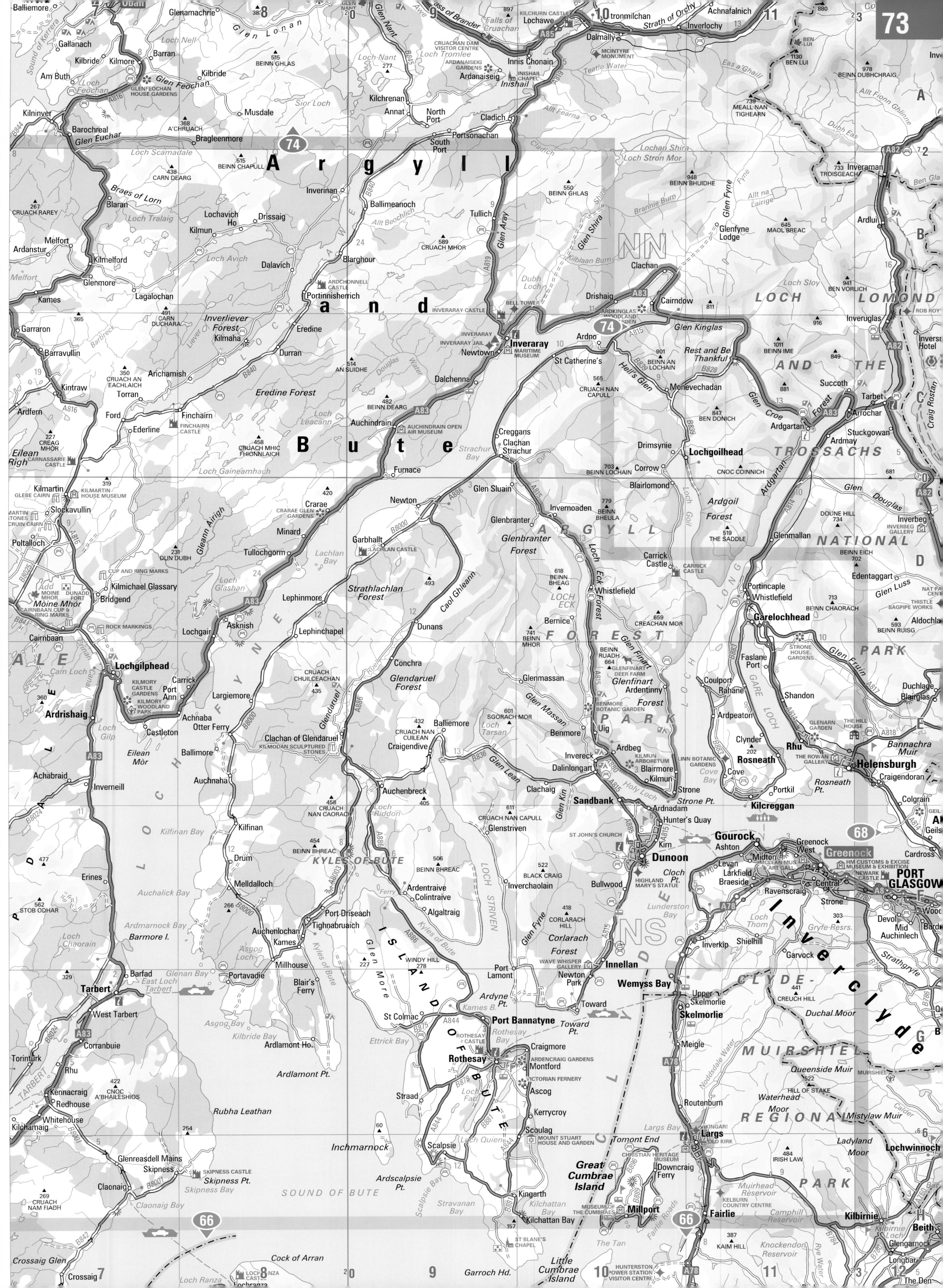
Argyll and Bute
Inverclyde
Loch Lomond and the Trossachs National Park
Muirshiel Regional Park
Argyll Forest Park
Oban
Kilninver
Barochreal
Kilmore
Glen Feochan
Musdale
Bragleenmore
Kilmelford
Glenmore
Melfort
Ardanstur
Kames
Garraron
Barravullin
Kintraw
Ardfern
Torran
Ford
Ederline
Finchairn
Kilmartin
Slockavullin
Poltalloch
Kilmichael Glassary
Bridgend
Cairnbaan
Lochgilphead
Ardrishaig
Castleton
Achnaba
Otter Ferry
Ballimore
Auchnaha
Kilfinan
Drum
Melldalloch
Auchenlochan
Kames
Tighnabruaich
Portavadie
Millhouse
Blair's Ferry
Ardlamont Ho.
Tarbert
West Tarbert
Corranbuie
Rhu
Kennacraig
Redhouse
Whitehouse
Kilchamaig
Glenreasdell Mains
Skipness
Claonaig
Crossaig
Lochawe
Dalmally
Innis Chonain
Ardanaiseig
Kilchrenan
Annat
North Port
Cladich
Portsonachan
South Port
Inverinan
Ballimeanoch
Lochavich Ho
Kilmun
Drissaig
Dalavich
Blarghour
Portinnisherrich
Eredine
Durran
Arichamish
Eredine Forest
Inverliever Forest
Kilmaha
Tullich
Inveraray
Newtown
Dalchenna
Auchindrain
Furnace
Crarae
Minard
Tullochgorm
Lochgair
Asknish
Lephinmore
Lephinchapel
Strachur
Creggans
Clachan
Newton
Garbhallt
Glen Sluain
Strathlachlan Forest
Dunans
Conchra
Glendaruel Forest
Largiemore
Clachan of Glendaruel
Craigendive
Balliemore
Auchenbreck
Glenbranter
Glenbranter Forest
Invernoaden
Whistlefield
Bernice
Glenmassan
Glenfinart
Ardentinny
Benmore
Uig
Invereck
Ardbeg
Dalinlongart
Blairmore
Kilmun
Strone
Sandbank
Clachaig
Glenstriven
Ardnadam
Hunter's Quay
Kirn
Dunoon
Bullwood
Inverchaolain
Corlarach Forest
Innellan
Port Lamont
Toward
Colintraive
Ardentraive
Algaltraig
Kyles of Bute
Island of Bute
Port Bannatyne
St Colmac
Rothesay
Craigmore
Montford
Ascog
Kerrycroy
Scoulag
Straad
Scalpsie
Kingarth
Kilchattan Bay
Inchmarnock
Sound of Bute
Great Cumbrae Island
Millport
Little Cumbrae Island
Clachan
Drishaig
Cairndow
Ardno
St Catherine's
Hell's Glen
Rest and Be Thankful
Monevechadan
Lochgoilhead
Drimsynie
Corrow
Blairlomond
Ardgoil Forest
Carrick Castle
Inverlochy
Tronmilchan
Strath of Orchy
Achnafalnich
Inverarnan
Ardlui
Glenfyne Lodge
Inveruglas
Succoth
Tarbet
Arrochar
Ardgartan
Stuckgowan
Ardmay
Glenmallan
Inverbeg
Edentaggart
Portincaple
Whistlefield
Garelochhead
Faslane Port
Shandon
Coulport
Rahane
Ardpeaton
Clynder
Rosneath
Cove
Kilcreggan
Rhu
Helensburgh
Craigendoran
Colgrain
Portkil
Gourock
Ashton
Greenock
Port Glasgow
Inverkip
Wemyss Bay
Skelmorlie
Meigle
Routenburn
Largs
Fairlie
Kilbirnie
Lochwinnoch
Beith
Cumbrae
Kilchattan Bay
Sound of Bute
Loch Fyne
Loch Eck
Loch Long
Gare Loch
Holy Loch
Loch Striven
Loch Riddon
Loch Gilp
Loch Goil
Loch Awe
Loch Avich
Loch Shira
Loch Sloy
Loch Lomond

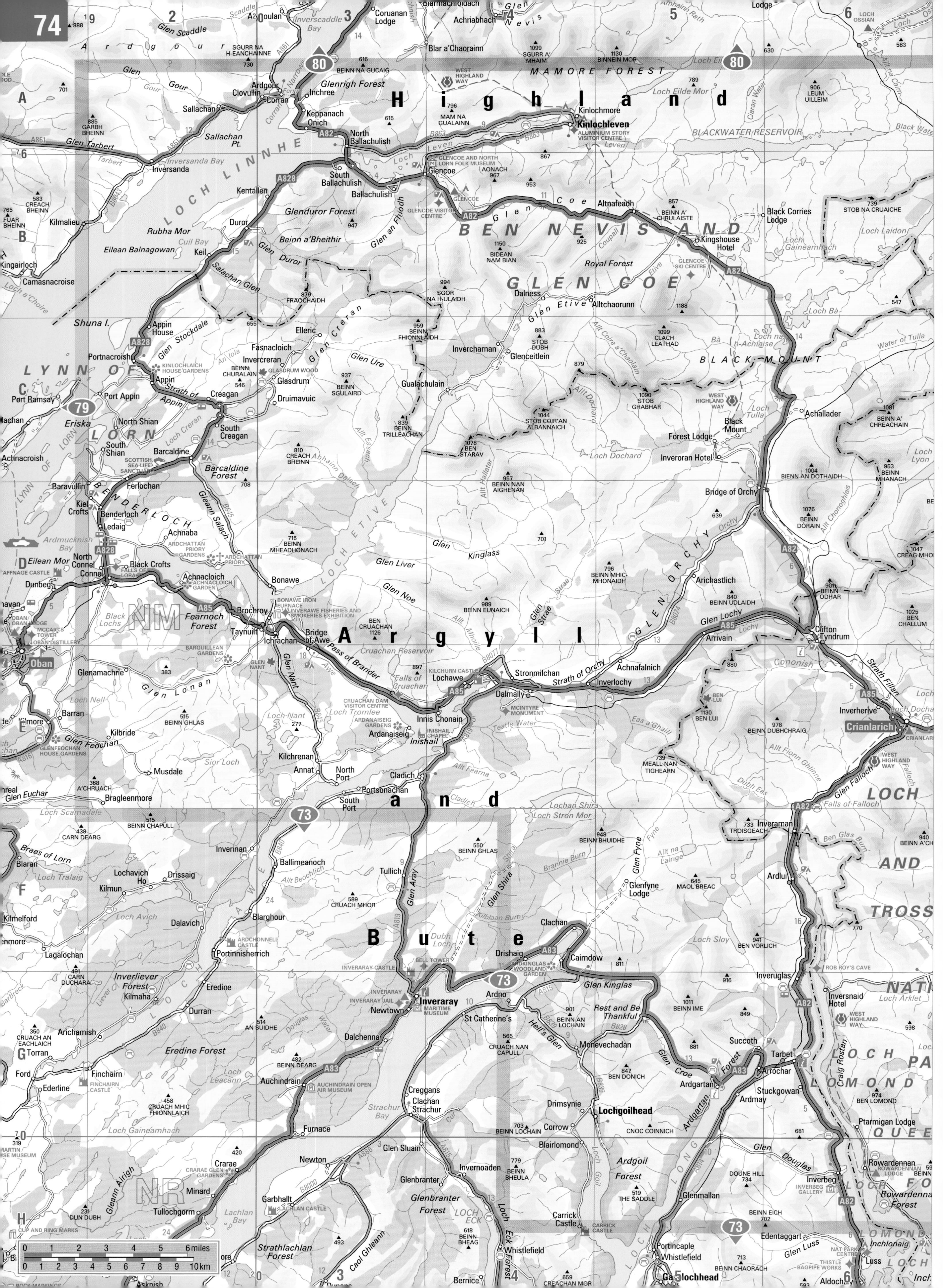
Highland
Argyll and Bute
BEN NEVIS AND GLEN COE
MAMORE FOREST
BLACK MOUNT
LOCH LOMOND AND THE TROSSACHS NATIONAL PARK
BLACKWATER RESERVOIR
LOCH LINNHE
LYNN OF LORN
LYNN OF LORN
Ardgour
Glen Scaddle
Coruanan Lodge
Blar a'Chaorainn
Achriabhach
Glen Nevis
Glen Gour
Glenrigh Forest
Ardgour
Clovullin
Corran
Inchree
Corran Narrows
Keppanach
Onich
Sallachan
Sallachan Pt.
Glen Tarbert
Inversanda
Inversanda Bay
North Ballachulish
South Ballachulish
Ballachulish
Kinlochmore
Kinlochleven
ALUMINIUM STORY VISITOR CENTRE
Loch Leven
Glencoe
GLENCOE AND NORTH LORN FOLK MUSEUM
GLENCOE VISITOR CENTRE
Glen Coe
Altnafeadh
Kingshouse Hotel
GLENCOE SKI CENTRE
Royal Forest
Black Corries Lodge
Loch Laidon
Kentallen
Duror
Glenduror Forest
Glen an Fhiodh
Kilmalieu
Rubha Mor
Cuil Bay
Keil
Eilean Balnagowan
Kingairloch
Camasnacroise
Salachan Glen
Glen Duror
Beinn a'Bheithir
Shuna I.
Appin House
Glen Stockdale
Portnacroish
KINLOCHLAICH HOUSE GARDENS
Appin
Strath of Appin
Port Appin
Port Ramsay
Eriska
North Shian
South Shian
Creagan
South Creagan
Loch Creran
Barcaldine
Barcaldine Forest
SCOTTISH SEA LIFE SANCTUARY
Achnacroish
Baravullin
Ferlochan
Kiel Crofts
Benderloch
Ledaig
Ardmucknish Bay
Achnaba
ARDCHATTAN PRIORY GARDENS
ARDCHATTAN PRIORY
North Connel
Connel
Black Crofts
FALLS OF LORA
Eilean Mor
Dunbeg
Achnacloich
ACHNACLOICH GARDEN
Bonawe
BONAWE IRON FURNACE
INVERAWE FISHERIES AND SMOKERIES EXHIBITION
Brochroy
Fearnoch Forest
Taynuilt
Ichrachan
Bridge of Awe
Pass of Brander
Cruachan Reservoir
Black Lochs
OBAN LODGE
MCCAIG'S TOWER
OBAN DISTILLERY
Oban
BARGUILLEAN GARDENS
GLEN NANT
Glen Nant
Glenamachrie
Glen Lonan
Loch Nell
Barran
Kilmore
Kilbride
Glen Feochan
GLENFEOCHAN HOUSE GARDENS
Musdale
Sior Loch
Glen Euchar
A'CHRUACH
Bragleenmore
Loch Scamadale
Elleric
Glen Creran
Fasnacloich
Invercreran
Glen Ure
GLASDRUM WOOD
Glasdrum
Druimavuic
Gualachulain
Inverchanan
Glenceitlein
Glen Etive
Dalness
Alltchaorunn
Loch Etive
Glen Kinglass
Glen Liver
Glen Noe
Glen Strae
Glen Orchy
Arichastlich
Bridge of Orchy
Inveroran Hotel
Forest Lodge
Loch Tulla
Black Mount
Achallader
Loch Dochard
WEST HIGHLAND WAY
Glen Lochy
Arrivain
Clifton
Tyndrum
Strath Fillan
Inverherive
Crianlarich
Stronmilchan
Strath of Orchy
Achnafalnich
Inverlochy
Lochawe
KILCHURN CASTLE
Falls of Cruachan
Dalmally
MCINTYRE MONUMENT
CRUACHAN DAM VISITOR CENTRE
Loch Tromlee
ARDANAISEIG GARDENS
Ardanaiseig
Innis Chonain
INISHAIL CHAPEL
Inishail
Teatle Water
Eas a'Ghaill
Allt Fionn Ghlinne
Loch Nant
Kilchrenan
Annat
North Port
Cladich
Portsonachan
South Port
Lochan Shira
Loch Stron Mor
Brannie Burn
Glen Fyne
Glenfyne Lodge
Glen Falloch
Falls of Falloch
Inverarnan
Ben Glas Burn
Ardlui
Inverinan
Braes of Lorn
Blaran
Loch Tralaig
Ballimeanoch
Allt Beochlich
Tullich
Glen Aray
Glen Shira
Lochavich Ho
Drissaig
Kilmun
Loch Avich
Dalavich
Blarghour
Kilmelford
Lagalochan
ARDCHONNELL CASTLE
Portinnisherrich
Dubh Loch
INVERARAY CASTLE
BELL TOWER
Drishaig
Clachan
Cairndow
ARDKINGLAS WOODLAND GARDEN
Loch Sloy
Inverliever Forest
Kilmaha
Eredine
Durran
INVERARAY JAIL
Inveraray
Newtown
MARITIME MUSEUM
Ardno
Glen Kinglas
Rest and Be Thankful
Hell's Glen
St Catherine's
Arichamish
Eredine Forest
Torran
Ford
Finchairn
FINCHAIRN CASTLE
Edderline
Dalchenna
Auchindrain
AUCHINDRAIN OPEN AIR MUSEUM
Loch Leacann
Creggans
Clachan Strachur
Strachur Bay
Monevechadan
Glen Croe
Succoth
Ardgartan
Arrochar
Tarbet
Stuckgowan
Ardmay
Inveruglas
ROB ROY'S CAVE
Inversnaid Hotel
Loch Arklet
Drimsynie
Lochgoilhead
Corrow
Blairlomond
Loch Goil
Ardgoil Forest
Loch Long
Glen Douglas
Loch Gaineamhach
Furnace
Glen Sluain
Newton
Craran
CRARAE GLEN GARDENS
Glenbranter
Glenbranter Forest
Invernoaden
Loch Eck
Minard
Garbhallt
LACHLAN CASTLE
Lachlan Bay
Tullochgorm
Strathlachlan Forest
Caol Ghleann
Whistlefield
Carrick Castle
CARRICK CASTLE
Glenmallan
Portincaple
Whistlefield
Garelochhead
Glen Luss
Edentaggart
Inverbeg
INVERBEG GALLERY
Rowardennan
ROWARDENNAN LODGE
Rowardennan Forest
Ptarmigan Lodge
Inchlonaig
Luss
THISTLE BAGPIPE WORKS
Aldochlay
Craig Rostan
CUP AND RING MARKS
DUN DUBH
Glenann Airigh
Bernice
Asknish
SGURR NA H-EANCHAINNE
BEINN NA GUCAIG
SGURR A' MHAIM
BINNEIN MOR
MAM NA GUALAINN
LEUM UILLEIM
AONACH
BEINN A' CHRULAISTE
STOB NA CRUAICHE
BIDEAN NAM BIAN
SGOR NA H-ULAIDH
FRAOCHAIDH
BEINN FHIONNLAIDH
STOB DUBH
CLACH LEATHAD
BEINN CHURALAIN
BEINN SGULAIRD
STOB GHABHAR
STOB COIR'AN ALBANNAICH
BEINN TRILLEACHAN
BEN STARAV
CREACH BHEINN
BEINN NAN AIGHENAN
BEINN MHEADHONACH
BEINN MHIC-MHONAIDH
BEINN EUNAICH
BEN CRUACHAN
BEINN UDLAIDH
BEINN A' CHREACHAIN
BIENN AN DOTHAIDH
BEINN MHANACH
BEINN DORAIN
BEINN ODHAR
CREAG MHOR
BEN CHALLUM
BEN LUI
BEINN DUBHCHRAIG
MEALL NAN TIGHEARN
BEINN BHUIDHE
TROISGEACH
BEINN GHLAS
BEINN CHAPULL
CARN DEARG
CRUACH MHOR
MAOL BREAC
BEN VORLICH
CARN DUCHARA
AN SUIDHE
BEINN AN LOCHAIN
BEINN IME
CRUACH AN EACHLAICH
CRUACH NAN CAPULL
BEINN DEARG
BEN DONICH
CRUACH MHIC FHIONNLAICH
BEINN LOCHAIN
CNOC COINNICH
BEN LOMOND
BEINN BHEULA
DOUNE HILL
THE SADDLE
BEINN EICH
BEINN BHEAG
BEINN CHAORACH
CREACHAN MOR
FUAR BHEINN
CREACH BHEINN
GARBH BHEINN
A861
A82
A828
A85
A83
A819
A815
A886
A814
B863
B8074
B8077
B845
B840
B828
B839
B8000
B8043
80
79
73
NM
NR
0 1 2 3 4 5 6 miles
0 1 2 3 4 5 6 7 8 9 10 km

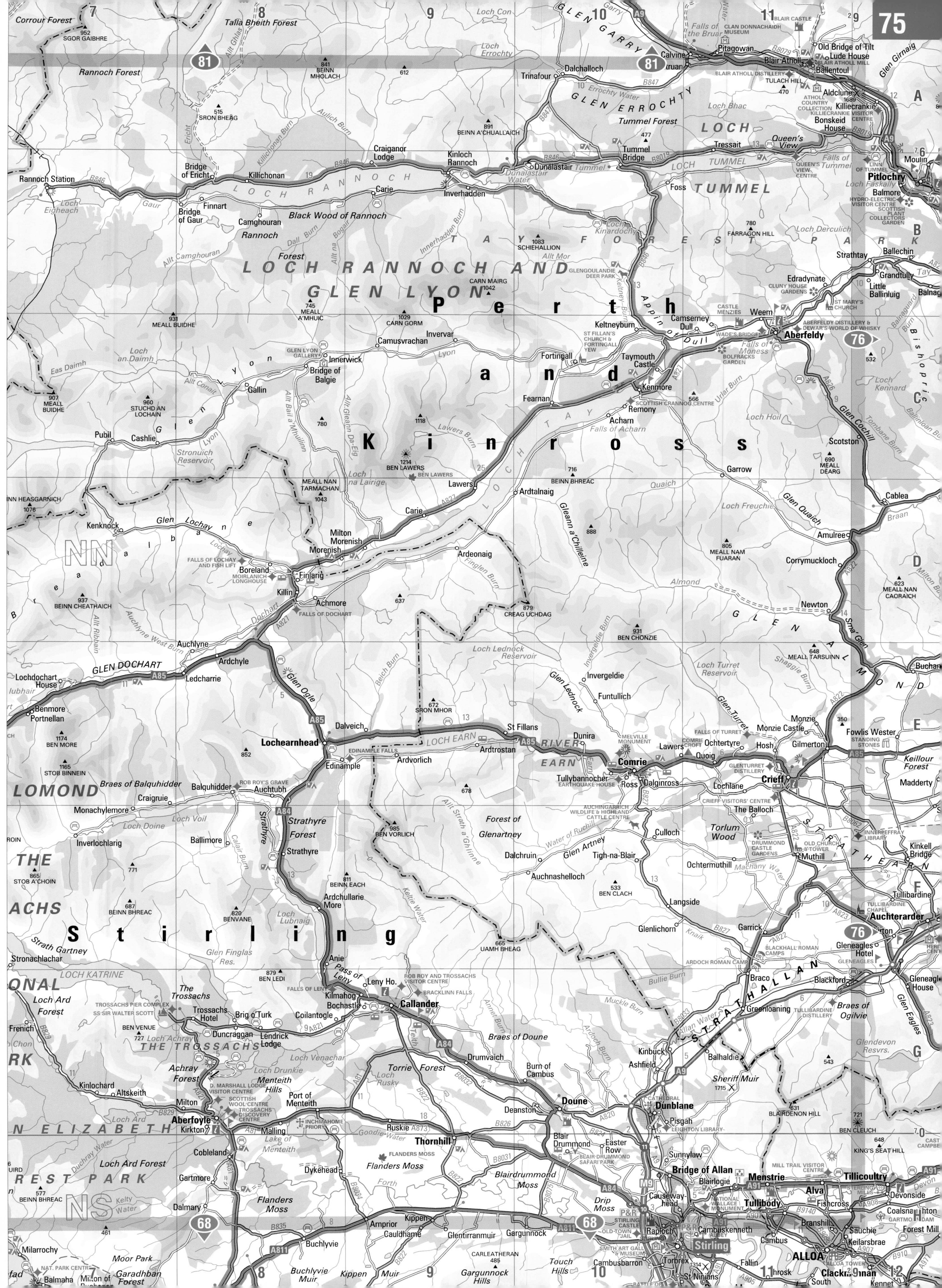
Corrour Forest
Talla Bheith Forest
Rannoch Forest
952 SGOR GAIBHRE
841 BEINN MHOLACH
Loch Con
Loch Errochty
GLEN GARRY
Falls of the Bruar
CLAN DONNACHAIDH MUSEUM
BLAIR CASTLE
Calvine
Pitagowan
Blair Atholl
Old Bridge of Tilt
Lude House
Ballentoul
Glen Girnaig
Dalchalloch
Trinafour
BLAIR ATHOLL DISTILLERY
TULACH HILL
Aldclune
Killiecrankie
KILLIECRANKIE VISITOR CENTRE
ATHOLL COUNTRY COLLECTION
Bonskeid House
GLEN ERROCHTY
Loch Bhac
Tummel Forest
515 SRON BHEAG
891 BEINN A'CHUALLAICH
Craiganor Lodge
Kinloch Rannoch
Tummel Bridge
Tressait
LOCH TUMMEL
Queen's View
QUEEN'S VIEW CENTRE
Falls of Tummel
Moulin
Pitlochry
Loch Faskally
HYDRO-ELECTRIC VISITOR CENTRE
SCOTTISH PLANT COLLECTORS GARDEN
Balmore
Rannoch Station
Loch Eigheach
Bridge of Ericht
Killichonan
Dunalastair
Dunalastair Water
LOCH RANNOCH
Carie
Inverhadden
Foss
Bridge of Gaur
Finnart
Camghouran
Black Wood of Rannoch
Rannoch Forest
Loch Kinardochy
FARRAGON HILL
Loch Derculich
TAY FOREST PARK
1083 SCHIEHALLION
Allt Mor
Strathtay
Ballechin
LOCH RANNOCH AND GLEN LYON
GLENGOULANDIE DEER PARK
Edradynate
Grandtully
CLUNY HOUSE GARDENS
Little Ballinluig
CARN MAIRG 1042
745 MEALL A'MHUIC
1029 CARN GORM
Perth and Kinross
931 MEALL BUIDHE
Keltneyburn
Camserney
Dull
Appin of Dull
Weem
CASTLE MENZIES
Aberfeldy
ABERFELDY DISTILLERY & DEWAR'S WORLD OF WHISKY
WADE'S BRIDGE
Falls of Moness
BOLFRACKS GARDEN
ST MARY'S CHURCH
Invervar
Camusvrachan
GLEN LYON GALLERY
Innerwick
Bridge of Balgie
Loch an Daimh
Eas Daimh
Gallin
Fortingall
ST FILLAN'S CHURCH & FORTINGALL YEW
Taymouth Castle
Kenmore
SCOTTISH CRANNOG CENTRE
Fearnan
Remony
Acharn
Falls of Acharn
Loch Kennard
Glen Cochill
907 MEALL BUIDHE
960 STUCHD AN LOCHAIN
Glen Lyon
Pubil
Cashlie
Stronuich Reservoir
1118
Lawers Burn
LOCH TAY
Loch Hoil
Scotston
1214 BEN LAWERS
BEN LAWERS
690 MEALL DEARG
Garrow
Lawers
716 BEINN BHREAC
Quaich
Loch na Lairige
MEALL NAN TARMACHAN 1043
Ardtalnaig
Gleann a'Chilleine
Loch Freuchie
Glen Quaich
Cablea
INN HEASGARNICH 1076
Kenknock
Glen Lochay
Carie
888
Milton Morenish
Morenish
Ardeonaig
805 MEALL NAN FUARAN
Amulree
Corrymuckloch
NN
Breadalbane
FALLS OF LOCHAY AND FISH LIFT
Boreland
MOIRLANICH LONGHOUSE
Finlarig
Killin
Achmore
FALLS OF DOCHART
Finglen Burn
Almond
623 MEALL NAN CAORAICH
937 BEINN CHEATHAICH
637
879 CREAG UCHDAG
Newton
GLEN ALMOND
Sma' Glen
Auchlyne
Auchlyne West Burn
Dochart
931 BEN CHONZIE
Loch Lednock Reservoir
648 MEALL TARSUINN
Loch Turret Reservoir
Buchanty
Lochdochart House
GLEN DOCHART
Ardchyle
Ledcharrie
Glen Ogle
Invergeldie
Funtullich
Glen Lednock
Glen Turret
Benmore
Portnellan
672 SRON MHOR
Dalveich
St Fillans
Dunira
MELVILLE MONUMENT
FALLS OF TURRET
Monzie
Monzie Castle
Fowlis Wester
Lawers
COMRIE CROFT
Ochtertyre
Hosh
Gilmerton
STANDING STONES
1174 BEN MORE
Lochearnhead
LOCH EARN
RIVER EARN
Comrie
Quoig
GLENTURRET DISTILLERY
Crieff
Keillour Forest
Madderty
852
EDINAMPLE FALLS
Edinample
Ardvorlich
Ardtrostan
Tullybannocher
EARTHQUAKE HOUSE
Ross
Dalginross
Lochlane
1165 STOB BINNEIN
LOMOND
Braes of Balquhidder
ROB ROY'S GRAVE
Balquhidder
Auchtubh
678
AUCHINGARRICH WILDLIFE & HIGHLAND CATTLE CENTRE
CRIEFF VISITORS' CENTRE
The Balloch
Craigruie
Monachylemore
Loch Doine
Loch Voil
Strathyre Forest
Forest of Glenartney
Culloch
Torlum Wood
INNERPEFFRAY LIBRARY
Inverlochlarig
Ballimore
Calair Burn
985 BEN VORLICH
Allt Strath a'Ghlinne
Water of Ruchill
Glen Artney
Dalchruin
Tigh-na-Blair
DRUMMOND CASTLE GARDENS
OLD CHURCH & TOWER
Muthill
Kinkell Bridge
THE
865 STOB A'CHOIN
771
Strathyre
811 BEINN EACH
Auchnashelloch
Ochtermuthill
Machany Water
STRATHEARN
ACHS
687 BEINN BHREAC
820 BENVANE
Ardchullarie More
Keltie Water
533 BEN CLACH
Langside
Tullibardine
TULLIBARDINE CHAPEL
Auchterarder
Loch Lubnaig
Stirling
Strath Gartney
Stronachlachar
Glen Finglas Res.
665 UAMH BHEAG
Glenlichorn
Knaik
Garrick
BLACKHALL ROMAN CAMPS
Gleneagles Hotel
GLENEAGLES
ARDOCH ROMAN CAMP
LOCH KATRINE
879 BEN LEDI
Anie
Pass of Leny
FALLS OF LENY
Leny Ho.
ROB ROY AND TROSSACHS VISITOR CENTRE
BRACKLINN FALLS
Bullie Burn
Braco
Blackford
Gleneagles House
ONAL
The Trossachs
Loch Ard Forest
TROSSACHS PIER COMPLEX
SS SIR WALTER SCOTT
Trossachs Hotel
Brig o'Turk
Kilmahog
Bochastle
Callander
Coilantogle
STRATHALLAN
Muckle Burn
Greenloaning
TULLIBARDINE DISTILLERY
Braes of Ogilvie
Glen Eagles
BEN VENUE
Loch Achray
Duncraggan
Lendrick Lodge
Braes of Doune
Allan Water
Frenich
THE TROSSACHS
Achray Forest
Loch Drunkie
Loch Venachar
Menteith Hills
Torrie Forest
Loch Rusky
Drumvaich
Burn of Cambus
Kinbuck
Ashfield
Balhaldie
Sheriff Muir
1715
Glendevon Resvrs.
543
Kinlochard
Altskeith
D. MARSHALL LODGE VISITOR CENTRE
SCOTTISH WOOL CENTRE
TROSSACHS DISCOVERY CENTRE
Milton
Port of Menteith
Doune
CATHEDRAL
Dunblane
Deanston
Pisgah
631 BLAIRDENON HILL
721 BEN CLEUCH
N ELIZABETH
Aberfoyle
Kirkton
INCHMAHOME PRIORY
Malling
Lake of Menteith
Ruskie
Goodie Water
Thornhill
Blair Drummond
BLAIR DRUMMOND SAFARI PARK
Easter Row
LEIGHTON LIBRARY
648 KING'S SEAT HILL
Duchray Water
Cobleland
Loch Ard Forest
FLANDERS MOSS
Flanders Moss
Dykehead
Blairdrummond Moss
Sunnylaw
Bridge of Allan
Blairlogie
MILL TRAIL VISITOR CENTRE
Menstrie
Tillicoultry
REST PARK
Gartmore
Forth
Drip Moss
Causewayhead
NATIONAL WALLACE MONUMENT
Alva
Tullibody
Fishcross
Devonside
577 BEINN BHREAC
NS
Kelty Water
Dalmary
Flanders Moss
Coalsnaughton
Arnprior
Kippen
Cauldhame
Glentirranmuir
Gargunnock
STIRLING CASTLE
OLD TOWN JAIL
Raploch
Cambuskenneth
Stirling
Branshill
Sauchie
Forest Mill
Cambus
Keilarsbrae
461
Buchlyvie
Milarrochy
Moor Park
CARLEATHERAN 485
SMITH ART GALL. & MUSEUM
Cambusbarron
Touch Hills
Torbrex
St Ninians
Fallin
Throsk
ALLOA
ALLOA TOWER
Clackmannan
Kennet
NAT. PARK CENTRE
Balmaha
Milton of Buchanan
Garadhban Forest
Buchlyvie Muir
Kippen Muir
Gargunnock Hills

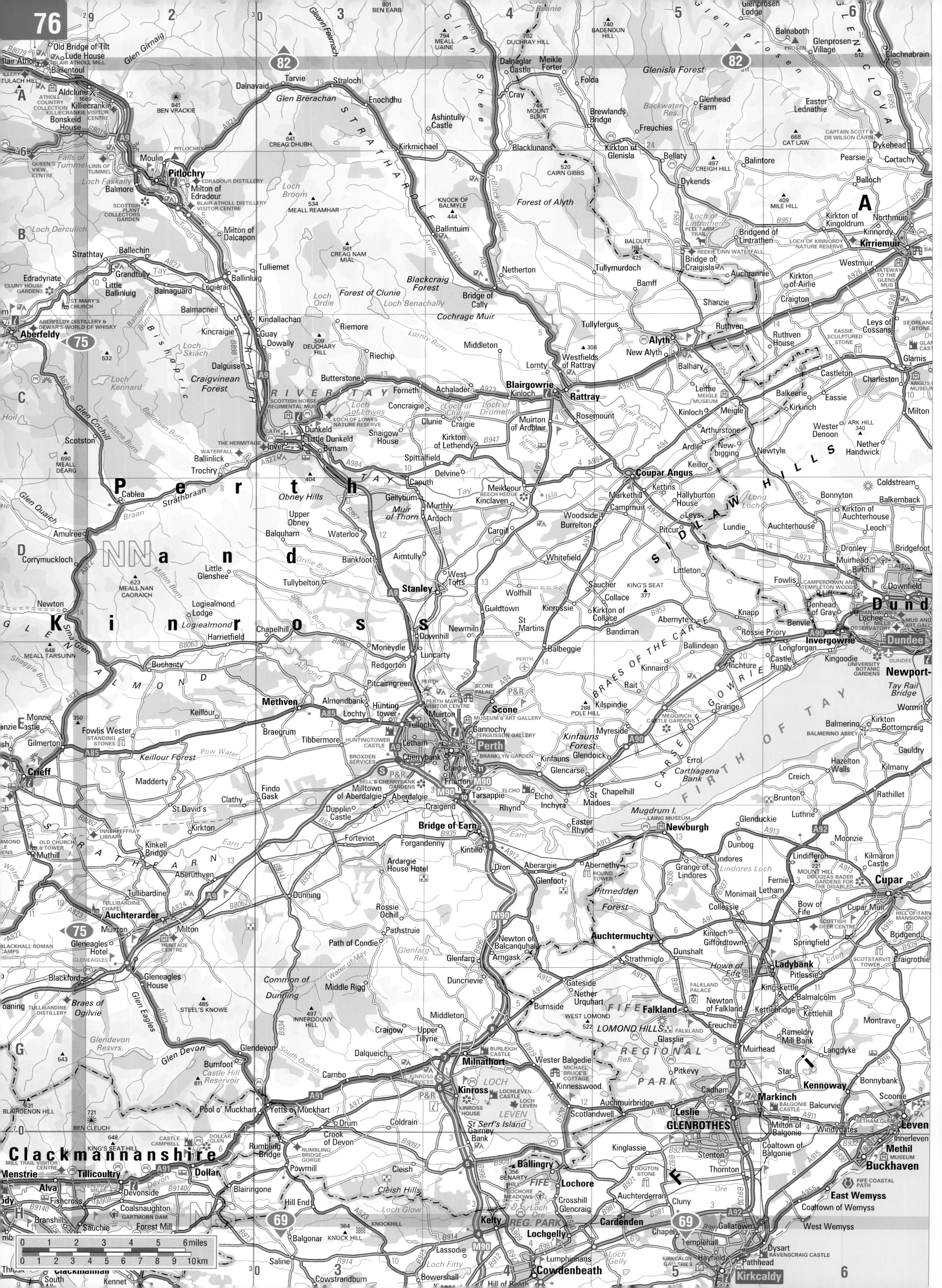
Perth and Kinross
Clackmannanshire
FIFE
Pitlochry
Blair Atholl
Killiecrankie
Aberfeldy
Dunkeld
Birnam
Blairgowrie
Rattray
Alyth
Kirriemuir
Coupar Angus
Meigle
Glamis
Stanley
Perth
Scone
Methven
Crieff
Auchterarder
Bridge of Earn
Newburgh
Auchtermuchty
Ladybank
Cupar
Falkland
Milnathort
Kinross
Glenrothes
Leslie
Markinch
Kennoway
Leven
Methil
Buckhaven
East Wemyss
Kirkcaldy
Cowdenbeath
Lochgelly
Lochore
Ballingry
Kelty
Cardenden
Dollar
Tillicoultry
Alva
Menstrie
Dundee
Invergowrie
Newport-on-Tay
Tay Rail Bridge
FIRTH OF TAY
CARSE OF GOWRIE
BRAES OF THE CARSE
SIDLAW HILLS
LOMOND HILLS REGIONAL PARK
LOCH LEVEN
STRATHARDLE
GLEN ALMOND
STRATHEARN
Forest of Alyth
Glenisla Forest
Forest of Clunie
Craigvinean Forest
Pitmedden Forest
Cleish Hills
Common of Dunning
Ochil Hills
Glen Eagles
Gleneagles
Muthill
Comrie
Kinfauns Forest
Abernethy
Strathmiglo
Freuchie
Kettlebridge
Pitlessie
Springfield
Craigrothie
Kilmany
Balmerino
Wormit
Errol
Longforgan
Inchture
Dunning
Forteviot
Glenfarg
Gleneagles Hotel
Kinross Services
Yetts o' Muckhart
Pool o' Muckhart
Glendevon
Blairingone
Saline
Kirkcaldy
0 1 2 3 4 5 6 miles
0 1 2 3 4 5 6 7 8 9 10 km

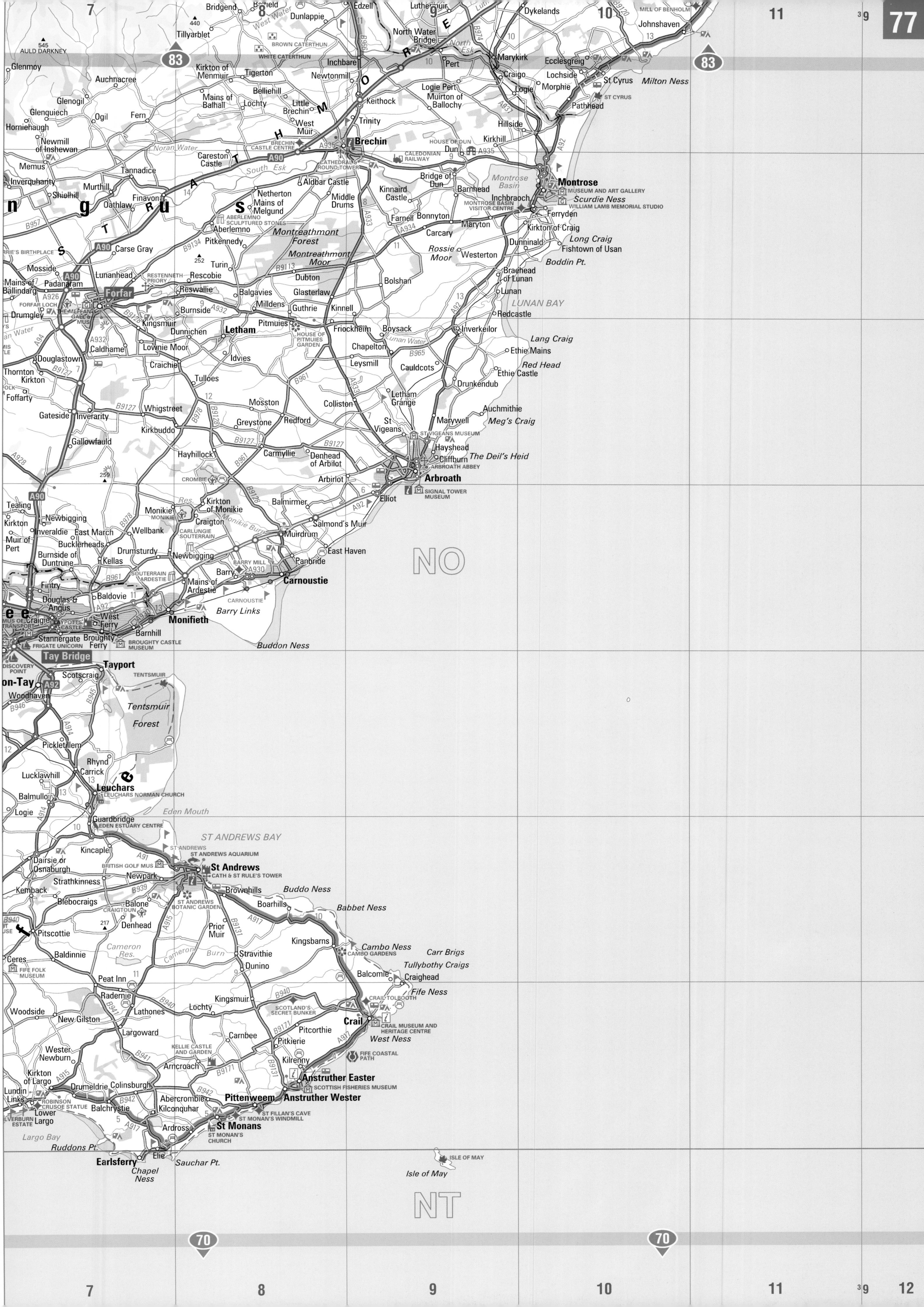
Bridgend
Tillyarblet
Dunlappie
Edzell
North Water Bridge
Dykelands
Johnshaven
MILL OF BENHOLM
AULD DARKNEY
Glenmoy
Auchnacree
Kirkton of Menmuir
Tigerton
Inchbare
Marykirk
Ecclesgreig
St Cyrus
Milton Ness
BROWN CATERTHUN
WHITE CATERTHUN
Newtonmill
Pert
Craigo
Lochside
Morphie
Logie
Pathhead
ST CYRUS
Glenogil
Mains of Balhall
Belliehill
Lochty
Little Brechin
Keithock
Logie Pert
Muirton of Ballochy
Glenquiech
Ogil
Fern
West Muir
Trinity
Hillside
Kirkhill
Hornieháugh
Newmill of Inshewan
Noran Water
BRECHIN CASTLE CENTRE
Brechin
HOUSE OF DUN
Dun
CALEDONIAN RAILWAY
Memus
Careston Castle
Tannadice
South Esk
CATHEDRAL & ROUND TOWER
Aldbar Castle
Bridge of Dun
Montrose Basin
Montrose
MUSEUM AND ART GALLERY
Scurdie Ness
WILLIAM LAMB MEMORIAL STUDIO
Inverquharity
Shielhill
Murthill
Finavon
Oathlaw
Netherton
Mains of Melgund
Middle Drums
Kinnaird Castle
Barnhead
MONTROSE BASIN VISITOR CENTRE
Inchbraoch
Ferryden
ABERLEMNO SCULPTURED STONES
Aberlemno
Farnell
Bonnyton
Maryton
Kirkton of Craig
Montreathmont Forest
Pitkennedy
Carcary
Dunninald
Long Craig
Fishtown of Usan
Carse Gray
Montreathmont Moor
Rossie Moor
Westerton
Boddin Pt.
Mosside
Turin
Braehead of Lunan
Mains of Ballindarg
Padanaram
Lunanhead
RESTENNETH PRIORY
Rescobie
Dubton
Bolshan
Forfar
Reswallie
Balgavies
Glasterlaw
Lunan
FORFAR LOCH
Milldens
Guthrie
Kinnell
LUNAN BAY
Redcastle
Drumgley
Burnside
Kingsmuir
Dunnichen
Letham
Pitmuies
HOUSE OF PITMUIES GARDEN
Friockheim
Boysack
Lunan Water
Inverkeilor
Lang Craig
Caldhame
Lownie Moor
Chapelton
Ethie Mains
Douglastown
Idvies
Leysmill
Cauldcots
Red Head
Ethie Castle
Thornton
Kirkton
Craichie
Tulloes
Drunkendub
Foffarty
Letham Grange
Mosston
Colliston
Auchmithie
Gateside
Inverarity
Whigstreet
Greystone
Redford
St Vigeans
Marywell
Meg's Craig
Kirkbuddo
ST VIGEANS MUSEUM
Gallowfauld
Carmyllie
Denhead of Arbilot
Hayshead
Hayhillock
Cliffburn
The Deil's Heid
ARBROATH ABBEY
CROMBIE
Arbirlot
Arbroath
SIGNAL TOWER MUSEUM
Tealing
Kirkton of Monikie
Balmirmer
Elliot
Newbigging
Monikie
Craigton
Inveraldie
East March
Wellbank
CARLUNGIE SOUTERRAIN
Salmond's Muir
Muirdrum
Muir of Pert
Bucklerheads
Drumsturdy
East Haven
NO
Burnside of Duntrune
Kellas
Newbigging
Panbride
BARRY MILL
Fintry
SOUTERRAIN ARDESTIE
Barry
Carnoustie
Mains of Ardestie
Douglas & Angus
Baldovie
CARNOUSTIE
Barry Links
Craigie
West Ferry
Monifieth
Stannergate
Broughty Ferry
Barnhill
FRIGATE UNICORN
BROUGHTY CASTLE MUSEUM
Buddon Ness
Tay Bridge
Tayport
DISCOVERY POINT
Scotscraig
TENTSMUIR
Woodhaven
Tentsmuir Forest
Pickletillem
Rhynd
Carrick
Lucklawhill
Leuchars
LEUCHARS NORMAN CHURCH
Balmullo
Logie
Eden Mouth
Guardbridge
EDEN ESTUARY CENTRE
ST ANDREWS BAY
Kincaple
ST ANDREWS AQUARIUM
Dairsie or Osnaburgh
BRITISH GOLF MUS
St Andrews
Newpark
CATH & ST RULE'S TOWER
Strathkinness
Kemback
Brownhills
Buddo Ness
Blebocraigs
Balone
ST ANDREWS BOTANIC GARDEN
Boarhills
Babbet Ness
CRAIGTOUN
Denhead
Prior Muir
Pitscottie
Kingsbarns
Cambo Ness
CAMBO GARDENS
Carr Brigs
Cameron Res.
Stravithie
Baldinnie
Dunino
Tullybothy Craigs
Ceres
FIFE FOLK MUSEUM
Balcomie
Craighead
Peat Inn
Fife Ness
CRAIL TOLBOOTH
Radernie
Kingsmuir
Woodside
New Gilston
Lathones
Lochty
SCOTLAND'S SECRET BUNKER
Crail
CRAIL MUSEUM AND HERITAGE CENTRE
Largoward
Carnbee
Pitcorthie
West Ness
Wester Newburn
KELLIE CASTLE AND GARDEN
Pitkierie
FIFE COASTAL PATH
Kirkton of Largo
Arncroach
Kilrenny
Anstruther Easter
Drumeldrie
Colinsburgh
SCOTTISH FISHERIES MUSEUM
Lundin Links
Abercrombie
Pittenweem
Anstruther Wester
ROBINSON CRUSOE STATUE
Balchrystie
Kilconquhar
ST FILLAN'S CAVE
Lower Largo
ST MONAN'S WINDMILL
Ardross
St Monans
ST MONAN'S CHURCH
Largo Bay
Ruddons Pt.
Earlsferry
Elie
Sauchar Pt.
Chapel Ness
ISLE OF MAY
Isle of May
NT

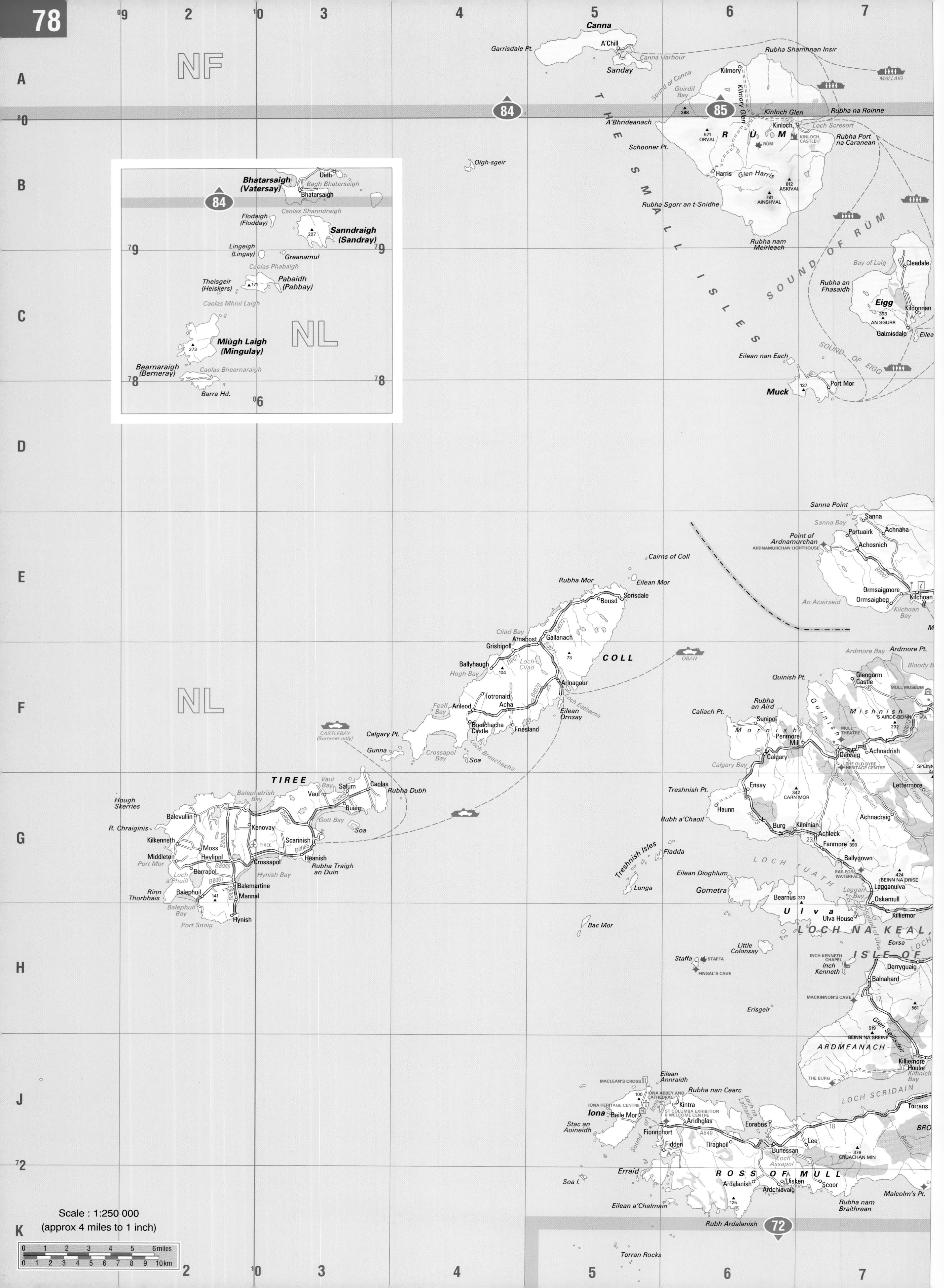

Canna
Garrisdale Pt.
A'Chill
Sanday
Canna Harbour
Rubha Shamhnan Insir
MALLAIG
THE SMALL ISLES
Sound of Canna
Guirdil Bay
Kilmory
Kinloch Glen
Rubha na Roinne
A'Bhrideanach
388
571 ORVAL
RÙM
Kinloch
Loch Scresort
RÙM
KINLOCH CASTLE
Rubha Port na Caranean
Harris
Glen Harris
812
781 ASKIVAL
AINSHVAL
Oigh-sgeir
Rubha Sgorr an t-Snidhe
SOUND OF RÙM
Rubha nam Meirleach
Bay of Laig
Cleadale
Rubha an Fhasaidh
Eigg
393 AN SGURR
Kildonnan
Galmisdale
Eilea
Eilean nan Each
SOUND OF EIGG
Muck
137
Port Mor

Inset box (NL region):

Bhatarsaigh
(Vatersay)
Uidh
Bagh Bhatarsaigh
84
Bhatarsaigh
Caolas Shanndraigh
Flodaigh
(Flodday)
207
Sanndraigh
(Sandray)
Lingeigh
(Lingay)
Greanamul
Caolas Phabaigh
Theisgeir
(Heiskers)
171
Pabaidh
(Pabbay)
Caolas Mhiui Laigh
NL
Miùgh Laigh
(Mingulay)
273
Bearnaraigh
(Berneray)
Caolas Bhearnaraigh
Barra Hd.
06

NL

Sanna Point
Sanna Bay
Sanna
Portuairk
Achnaha
Point of Ardnamurchan
ARDNAMURCHAN LIGHTHOUSE
Achosnich
Ormsaigmore
Kilchoan
An Acairseid
Ormsaigbeg
Kilchoan Bay

Cairns of Coll
Rubha Mor
Eilean Mor
Bousd
Sorisdale
Eilean Mor
Cliad Bay
Amabost
Gallanach
Grishipoll
OBAN
COLL
Ardmore Bay
Ardmore Pt.
Bloody B
Ballyhaugh
104
73
Loch Cliad
Quinish Pt.
Glengorm Castle
MULL MUSEUM
Hogh Bay
Arinagour
Caliach Pt.
Rubha an Aird
Quinish
Mishnish
Feall Bay
Anleod
Totronald
Acha
Loch Eatharna
Sunipol
Penmore Mill
MULL THEATRE
'S AIRDE-BEINN
292
Breachacha Castle
Friesland
Eilean Ornsay
Mornish
Dervaig
Achnadrish
CASTLEBAY
(Summer only)
Calgary Pt.
Gunna
Crossapol Bay
Soa
Loch Breachacha
THE OLD BYRE HERITAGE CENTRE
SPEINN
Calgary Bay
Calgary
Lettermore
TIREE
Vaul Bay
Salum
Caolas
Rubha Dubh
Treshnish Pt.
Ensay
342 CARN MOR
Loch
Hough Skerries
Balephetrish Bay
Vaul
Ruaig
Soa
Gott Bay
Haunn
Rubh a'Chaoil
Burg
Kilninian
Achleck
Achnacraig
R. Chraiginis
Balevullin
Kenovay
Scarinish
B8065
Treshnish Isles
Fladda
Fanmore
390
Kilkenneth
Moss
Heylipol
TIREE
Heanish
Rubha Traigh an Duin
Lunga
Eilean Dioghlum
Ballygown
424 BEINN A DRISE
Middleton
Barrapol
Crossapol
Hynish Bay
Bearnus
313
Lagganulva
Port Mor
Loch a'Phuill
Balemartine
Gometra
Oskamull
Killiemor
Rinn Thorbhais
Balephuil
141
Mannal
Bac Mor
Ulva
ISLE OF
Balephuil Bay
Port Snoig
Hynish
Ulva House
LOCH NA KEAL
Eorsa
Little Colonsay
INCH KENNETH CHAPEL
Loch
Staffa
STAFFA
Inch Kenneth
Derryguaig
Fingal's Cave
Balnahard
MACKINNON'S CAVE
Erisgeir
561
Glen
BEINN NA SREINE
519
ARDMEANACH
Killiemore House
Kilfinich Bay
THE BURG
MACLEAN'S CROSS
Eilean Annraidh
Rubha nan Cearc
LOCH SCRIDAIN
IONA ABBEY AND CATHEDRAL
100
Kintra
Loch na Lathaich
ST COLUMBA EXHIBITION & WELCOME CENTRE
IONA HERITAGE CENTRE
Iona
Baile Mor
Aridhglas
Eorabus
Torrans
Stac an Aoineidh
Fionnphort
A849
Lee
Bunessan
BRO
Fidden
Tiraghoil
376 CRUACHAN MIN
Erraid
Loch Assapol
ROSS OF MULL
Soa I.
Ardalanish
Uisken
Scoor
Eilean a'Chalmain
125
Ardchiavaig
Rubha nam Braithrean
Rubh Ardalanish
72
Torran Rocks
Malcolm's Pt.

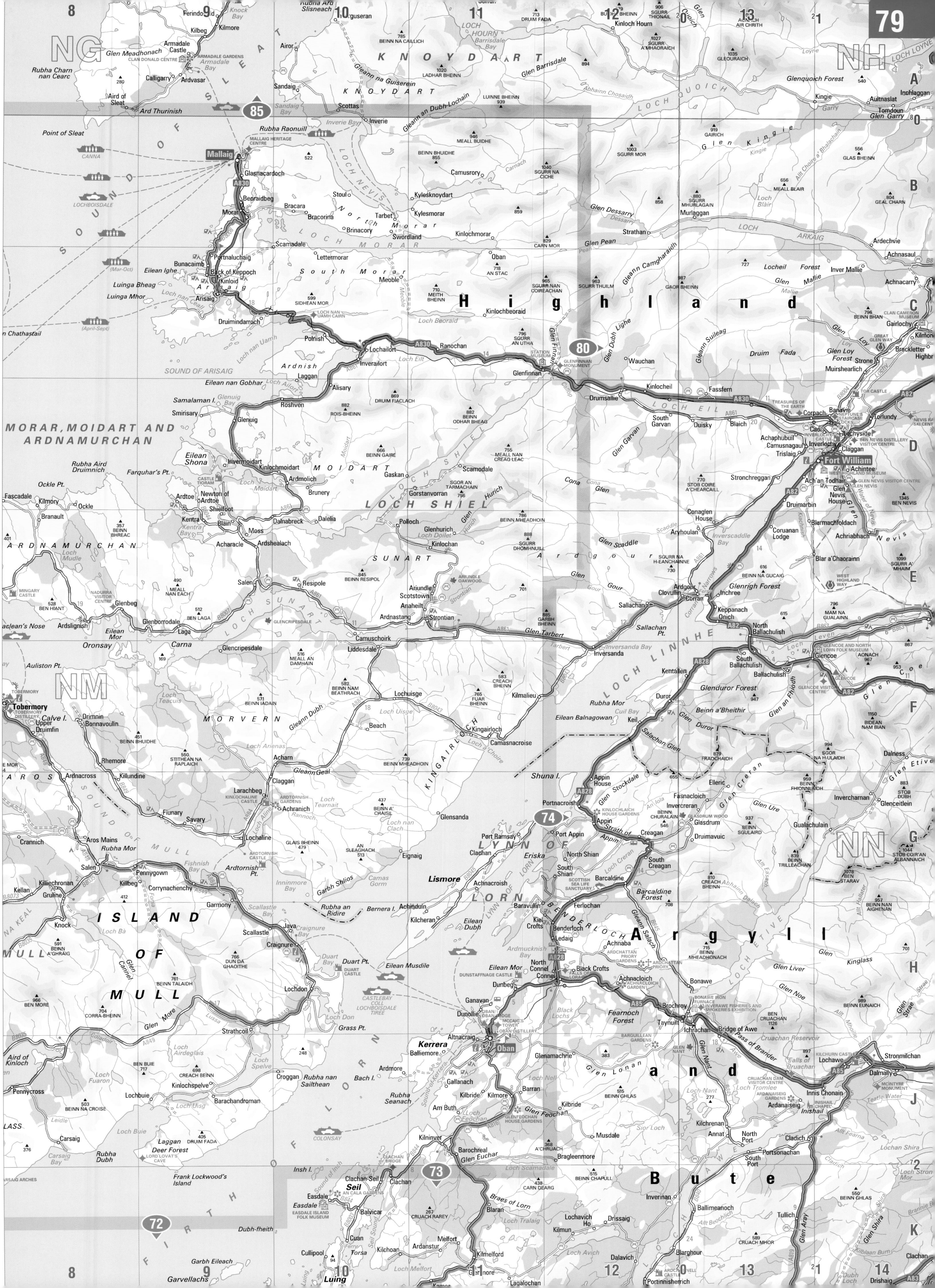

NG
NM
NN
NH
Highland
Argyll and Bute
KNOYDART
MORAR, MOIDART AND ARDNAMURCHAN
ARDNAMURCHAN
MOIDART
SUNART
MORVERN
KINGAIRLOCH
LOCH SHIEL
ISLAND OF MULL
LYNN OF LORN
LORN
BENDERLOCH
SOUND OF SLEAT
SOUND OF ARISAIG
SOUND OF MULL
FIRTH OF LORN
LOCH LINNHE
LOCH EIL
LOCH ARKAIG
LOCH QUOICH
LOCH HOURN
LOCH NEVIS
LOCH MORAR
LOCH SUNART
LOCH ETIVE
LOCH AWE
LOCH LOYNE
Mallaig
Fort William
Oban
Tobermory
Armadale
Ardvasar
Aird of Sleat
Ard Thurinish
Point of Sleat
Inverie
Airor
Sandaig
Scottas
Glasnacardoch
Morar
Arisaig
Kinloid
Back of Keppoch
Portnaluchaig
Bunacaimb
Lochailort
Inverailort
Glenfinnan
Kinlocheil
Fassfern
Corpach
Banavie
Caol
Inverlochy
Glen Nevis House
Achintee
Glencoe
Ballachulish
North Ballachulish
Onich
Corran
Ardgour
Strontian
Salen
Acharacle
Glenborrodale
Kilchoan
Lochaline
Craignure
Salen
Ledaig
Connel
North Connel
Taynuilt
Dalmally
Lochawe
Kilninver
Clachan-Seil
Seil
Easdale
Luing
Lismore
Kerrera
Invergarry
Tomdoun
Kinloch Hourn
Glen Garry
Glen Dessarry
Glen Kingie
Glen Pean
Glen Roy
Glen Coe
Glen Etive
Glen Orchy
Glen Nant
Glen More
Loch Don
Duart Castle
Eilean Musdile
Strathcoil
Lochbuie
Lochdon
Pennycross
Carsaig
Craignure
A830
A82
A861
A828
A85
A816
A849
A884
B8043
B8007
B844
85
80
74
73
72
8 9 10 11 12 13 14
A B C D E F G H J K

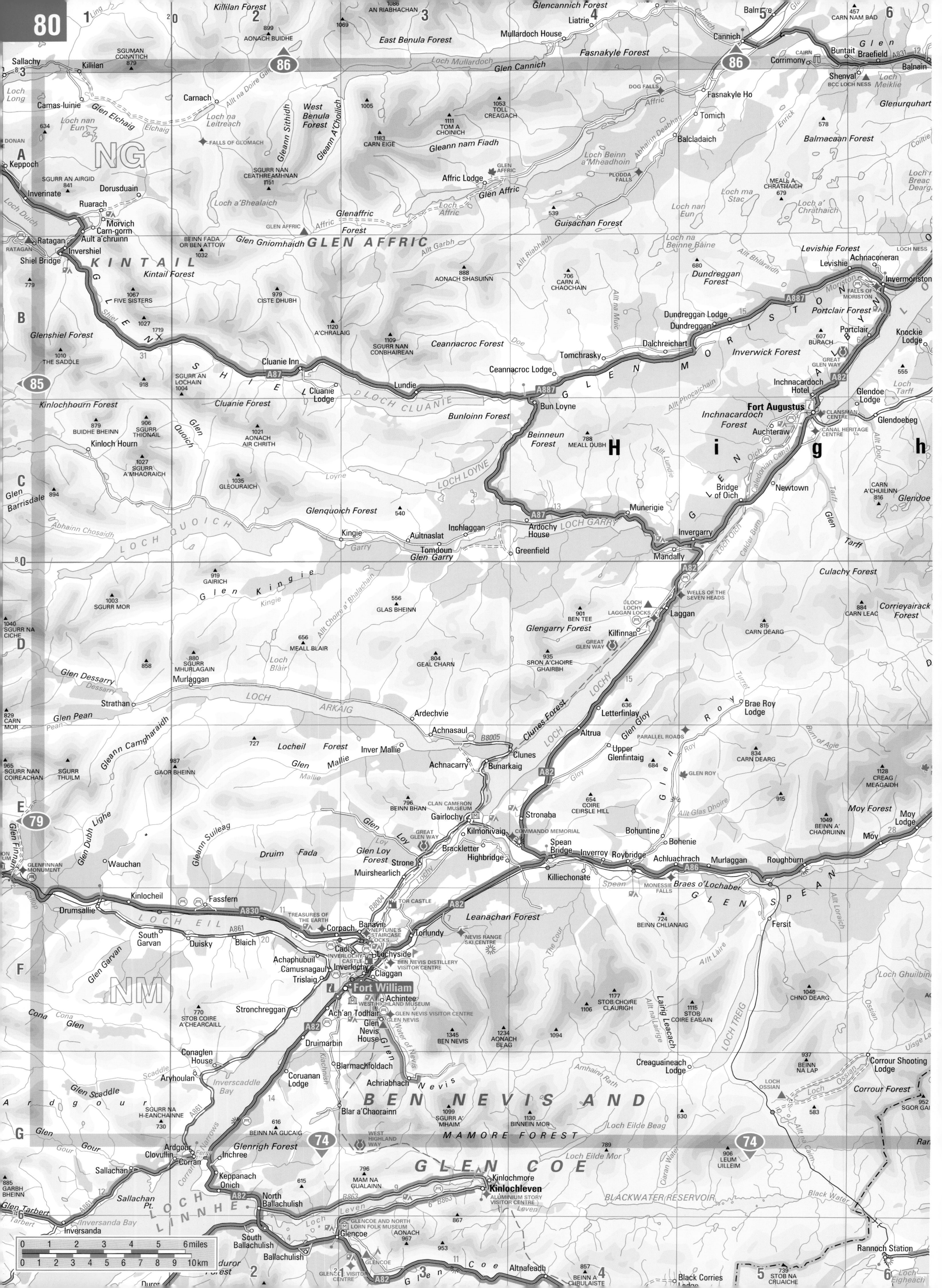
Killilan Forest
1086
AN RIABHACHAN
Glencannich Forest
Liatrie
Balnaire
457
CARN NAM BAD
899
AONACH BUIDHE
1069
East Benula Forest
Mullardoch House
Cannich
SGUMAN COINNTICH
879
Fasnakyle Forest
Glen
Braefield
Buntait
Sallachy
Killilan
86
Loch Mullardoch
Glen Cannich
CAIRN
Corrimony
A831
Balnain
Shenval
BCC LOCH NESS
Loch Meiklie
Loch Long
DOG FALLS
Fasnakyle Ho
Carnach
Glenurquhart
Camas-luinie
Glen Elchaig
Allt na Doire Gaire
West Benula Forest
1005
1053
TOLL CREAGACH
Affric
Tomich
Loch nan Eun
Loch na Leitreach
Elchaig
1111
TOM A CHOINICH
Gleann Sithidh
Gleann A'Choilich
Abhainn Deabhag
578
Balcladaich
Balmacaan Forest
634
DONAN
FALLS OF GLOMACH
1183
CARN EIGE
Gleann nam Fiadh
Enrick
NG
Loch Beinn a'Mheadhoin
Keppoch
SGURR NAN CEATHREAMHNAN
1151
GLEN AFFRIC
PLODDA FALLS
SGURR AN AIRGID
841
Affric Lodge
MEALL A CHRATHAICH
679
Invernate
Dorusduain
Glen Affric
Loch ma Stac
Loch Duich
Ruarach
Loch a'Bhealaich
Loch Affric
Loch nan Eun
Loch a' Chrathaich
Morvich
Carn-gorm
Glenaffric Forest
539
Guisachan Forest
Ault a'chruinn
GLEN AFFRIC
Ratagan
Inverhiel
BEINN FADA OR BEN ATTOW
1032
Glen Gniomhaidh
GLEN AFFRIC
Allt Garbh
Loch na Beinne Baine
Levishie Forest
RATAGAN
Shiel Bridge
KINTAIL
Allt Riabhach
LOCH NESS
Achnaconeran
Levishie
Kintail Forest
888
AONACH SHASUINN
706
CARN A CHAOCHAIN
680
Dundreggan Forest
Allt Bhlaraidh
Invermoriston
779
1067
FIVE SISTERS
979
CISTE DHUBH
Allt na Muic
FALLS OF MORISTON
A887
Portclair Forest
GLEN SHIEL
1027
1719
1120
A'CHRALAIG
Dundreggan Lodge
Dundreggan
Glenshiel Forest
1109
SGURR NAN CONBHAIREAN
Ceannacroc Forest
Doe
Dalchreichart
GLEN MORISTON
607
BURACH
Portclair
Knockie Lodge
1010
THE SADDLE
Inverwick Forest
Tomchrasky
Cluanie Inn
GREAT GLEN WAY
85
SGURR AN LOCHAIN
1004
A87
Ceannacroc Lodge
555
918
Lundie
A887
Inchnacardoch Hotel
Loch Tarff
Cluanie Lodge
LOCH CLUANIE
Allt Phocachain
A82
Glendoe Lodge
Kinlochhourn Forest
Cluanie Forest
Bun Loyne
Fort Augustus
Bunloinn Forest
Inchnacardoch Forest
CLANSMAN CENTRE
879
BUIDHE BHEINN
906
SGURR THIONAIL
Glen Quoich
1021
AONACH AIR CHRITH
Beinneun Forest
788
MEALL DUBH
Highland
CANAL HERITAGE CENTRE
Glendoebeg
Auchteraw
Kinloch Hourn
1027
SGURR A'MHAORAICH
Allt Lundie
Caledonian Canal
Oich
Allt Doe
Loyne
1035
GLEOURAICH
LOCH LOYNE
Bridge of Oich
Newtown
Glen Barrisdale
894
CARN A'CHUILINN
816
Glendoe
Glenquoich Forest
540
Munerigie
Glen Tarff
Abhainn Chosaidh
Kingie
Aultnaslat
Inchlaggan
A87
Ardochy House
LOCH GARRY
Invergarry
LOCH QUOICH
Garry
Tomdoun
Glen Garry
Greenfield
Mandally
Loch Oich
Calder Burn
919
GAIRICH
A82
Culachy Forest
Glen Kingie
Kingie
Allt Choire a' Bhalachain
556
GLAS BHEINN
WELLS OF THE SEVEN HEADS
1003
SGURR MOR
901
BEN TEE
LOCH LOCHY LAGGAN LOCKS
Laggan
884
CARN LEAC
Corrieyairack Forest
1040
SGURR NA CICHE
656
MEALL BLAIR
Glengarry Forest
Kilfinnan
815
CARN DEARG
GREAT GLEN WAY
Loch Blair
880
SGURR MHURLAGAIN
858
804
GEAL CHARN
935
SRON A'CHOIRE GHAIRBH
Glen Dessarry
Dessarry
Murlaggan
LOCH LOCHY
Turret
Strathan
LOCH ARKAIG
636
Brae Roy Lodge
829
CARN MOR
Glen Pean
Pean
Ardechvie
Letterfinlay
Glen Gloy
Glen Roy
Gleann Camgharaidh
Achnasaul
Clunes Forest
Altrua
PARALLEL ROADS
Burn of Agie
727
Locheil Forest
B8005
Upper Glenfintaig
987
GAOR BHEINN
Inver Mallie
Clunes
834
CARN DEARG
965
SGURR NAN COIREACHAN
SGURR THUILM
Glen Mallie
Achnacarry
Bunarkaig
684
1128
CREAG MEAGAIDH
A82
Gloy
GLEN ROY
654
COIRE CEIRSLE HILL
915
Moy Forest
796
BEINN BHAN
CLAN CAMERON MUSEUM
Stronaba
1049
BEINN A' CHAORUINN
Moy Lodge
79
Glen Dubh Lighe
Glen Loy
Gairlochy
Allt Glas Dhoire
Gleann Suileag
GREAT GLEN WAY
Kilmonivaig
COMMANDO MEMORIAL
Bohuntine
Moy
Bohenie
Glen Finnan
Druim Fada
Glen Loy Forest
Brackletter
Spean Bridge
Inverroy
Roybridge
Achluachrach
Murlaggan
Roughburn
Wauchan
Highbridge
A86
GLENFINNAN MONUMENT
Strone
Muirshearlich
Killiechonate
Spean
MONESSIE FALLS
Braes o'Lochaber
GLEN SPEAN
Allt Loraich
Kinlocheil
Fassfern
TOR CASTLE
Drumsallie
A830
LOCH EIL
TREASURES OF THE EARTH
B8004
A82
Leanachan Forest
Fersit
South Garvan
A861
Corpach
Banavie
NEPTUNE'S STAIRCASE LOCKS
Torlundy
Duisky
Blaich
Caol
NEVIS RANGE SKI CENTRE
The Cour
724
BEINN CHLIANAIG
Allt Laire
INVERLOCHY CASTLE
Lochyside
Glen Garvan
Achaphubuil
BEN NEVIS DISTILLERY VISITOR CENTRE
Camusnagaul
Inverlochy
Claggan
Loch Ghuilbinn
Trislaig
Fort William
NM
Achintee
WEST HIGHLAND MUSEUM
1177
STOB CHOIRE CLAURIGH
1046
CHNO DEARG
Cona Glen
770
STOB COIRE A'CHEARCAILL
Stronchreggan
Ach'an Todhair
GLEN NEVIS VISITOR CENTRE
Glen Nevis House
1106
Allt na Lairige
Lairig Leacach
1115
STOB COIRE EASAIN
Ossian
A82
Water of Nevis
Glen Nevis
1345
BEN NEVIS
1234
AONACH BEAG
1094
LOCH TREIG
Conaglen House
Druimarbin
Blarmachfoldach
937
BEINN NA LAP
Uisge Labhair
Scaddle
Aryhoulan
Inverscaddle Bay
Amhainn Rath
Creaguaineach Lodge
Corrour Shooting Lodge
Coruanan Lodge
Kiachnish
Achriabhach
Glen Scaddle
Ardgour
BEN NEVIS AND
LOCH OSSIAN
Loch Ossian
Corrour Forest
SGURR NA H-EANCHAINNE
730
1099
SGURR A' MHAIM
1130
BINNEIN MOR
630
952
SGOR GAIBHRE
583
Blar a'Chaorainn
Glen Gour
Gour
616
BEINN NA GUCAIG
MAMORE FOREST
Loch Eilde Beag
Ardgour
Corran Narrows
Glenrigh Forest
74
WEST HIGHLAND WAY
789
906
LEUM UILLEIM
Clovullin
Corran
Inchree
Loch Eilde Mor
GLEN COE
796
MAM NA GUALAINN
Ciaran Water
Allt na Cairn
Sallachan
Keppanach
615
Kinlochmore
885
GARBH BHEINN
Onich
Kinlochleven
ALUMINIUM STORY VISITOR CENTRE
Sallachan Pt.
North Ballachulish
B863
BLACKWATER RESERVOIR
Black Water
Glen Tarbert
LOCH LINNHE
Leven
A861
Tarbert
Inversanda Bay
Inversanda
GLENCOE AND NORTH LORN FOLK MUSEUM
867
South Ballachulish
Glencoe
AONACH
967
953
Ballachulish
GLENCOE
Rannoch Station
Glen Coe
Altnafeadh
857
BEINN A' CHRULAISTE
Black Corries Lodge
739
STOB NA CRUAICHE
Loch Eigheach
GLENCOE VISITOR CENTRE
A82
0 1 2 3 4 5 6 miles
0 1 2 3 4 5 6 7 8 9 10km

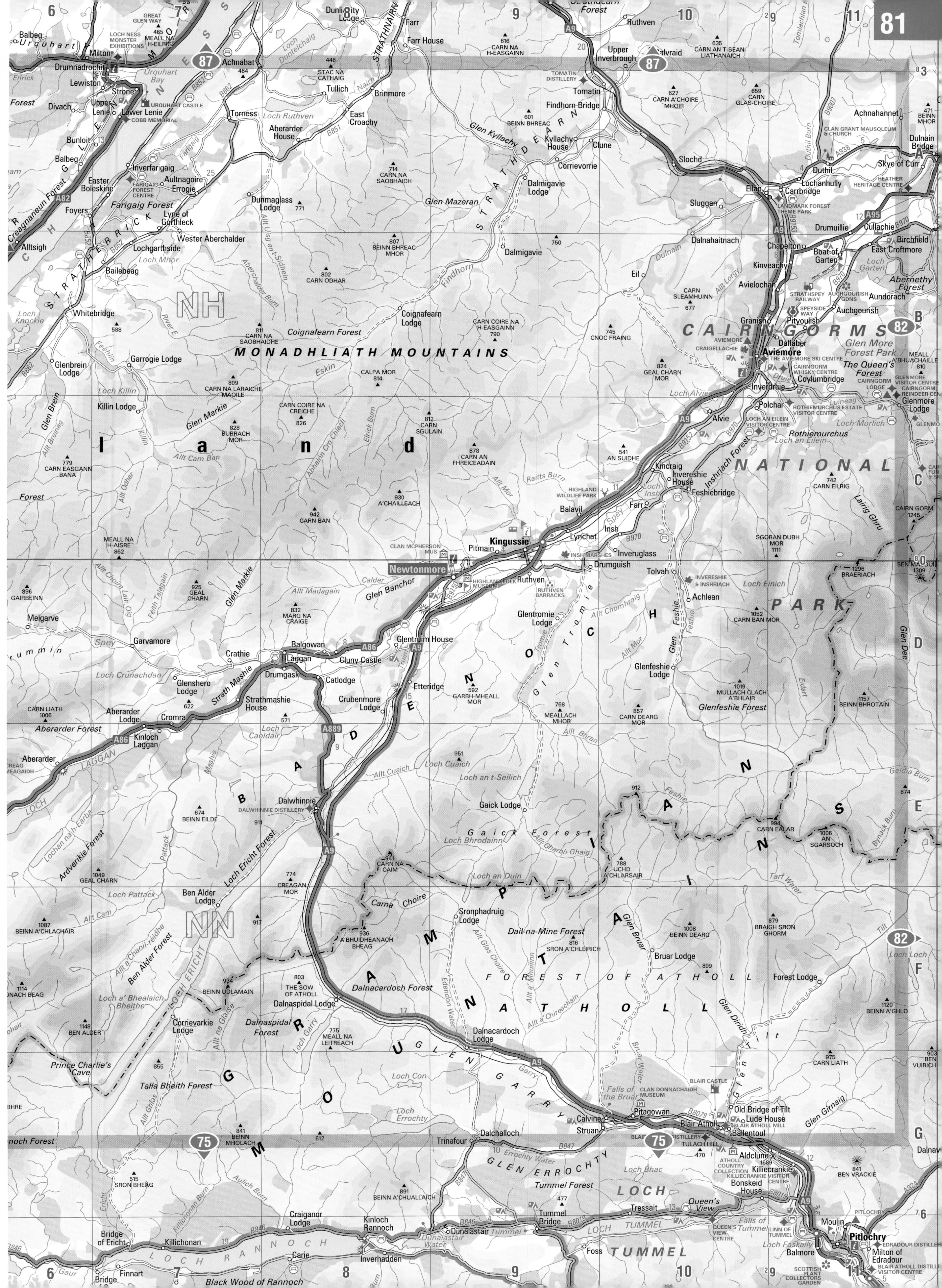
MONADHLIATH MOUNTAINS
CAIRNGORMS NATIONAL PARK
GRAMPIAN MOUNTAINS
FOREST OF ATHOLL
LOCH NESS
NH
NN
Highland
Drumnadrochit
Lewiston
Milton
Strone
Urquhart Bay
URQUHART CASTLE
Lower Lenie
COBB MEMORIAL
Divach
Bunloit
Balbeg
Achnabat
Torness
Loch Ruthven
Aberarder House
East Croachy
Brinmore
Tullich
STAC NA CATHAIG
Farr
Farr House
Dunlichity Lodge
STRATHNAIRN
Loch Duntelchaig
CARN NA H-EASGAINN
Ruthven
Upper Inverbrough
Tomatin
TOMATIN DISTILLERY
Findhorn Bridge
CARN A'CHOIRE MHOIR
CARN GLAS-CHOIRE
CARN AN T-SEAN-LIATHANAICH
Slochd
Glen Kyllachy
Kyllachy House
Clune
Corrievorrie
STRATHDEARN
BEINN BHREAC
Dalmigavie Lodge
Dalmigavie
Glen Mazeran
CARN NA SAOBHAIDH
Inverfarigaig
Aultnagoire
Errogie
Farigaig Forest
FARIGAIG FOREST CENTRE
Foyers
Boleskine
Easter Boleskine
Lyne of Gorthleck
Wester Aberchalder
Lochgarthside
Loch Mhor
Bailebeag
Dunmaglass Lodge
STRATHERRICK
Creagnaneun Forest
Alltsigh
Whitebridge
Loch Knockie
Glenbrein Lodge
Garrogie Lodge
Loch Killin
Killin Lodge
Glen Markie
Coignafearn Forest
Coignafearn Lodge
CARN NA SAOBHAIDHE
CARN COIRE NA H-EASGAINN
BEINN BHREAC MHOR
CARN ODHAR
CALPA MOR
CARN NA LARAICHE MAOILE
CARN COIRE NA CREICHE
BURRACH MOR
CARN SGULAIN
CARN AN FHREICEADAIN
CARN EASGANN BANA
A'CHAILLEACH
CARN BAN
MEALL NA H-AISRE
GAIRBEINN
GEAL CHARN
MARG NA CRAIGE
CNOC FRAING
GEAL CHARN MOR
AN SUIDHE
CARN SLEAMHUINN
Sluggan
Dalnahaitnach
Eil
Carrbridge
LANDMARK FOREST THEME PARK
Ellan
Duthil
Lochanhully
HEATHER HERITAGE CENTRE
Achnahannet
CLAN GRANT MAUSOLEUM & CHURCH
Dulnain Bridge
Skye of Curr
Drumuillie
Cullachie
Birchfield
East Croftmore
Chapelton
Boat of Garten
Kinveachy
Avielochan
Loch Garten
Abernethy Forest
STRATHSPEY RAILWAY
AUCHGOURISH GDNS
Aundorach
Auchgourish
Granish
SPEYSIDE WAY
Pityoulish
Dalfaber
Aviemore
CRAIGELLACHIE
THE AVIEMORE SKI CENTRE
CAIRNGORM WHISKY CENTRE
Coylumbridge
Glen More Forest Park
The Queen's Forest
GLENMORE VISITOR CENTRE
CAIRNGORM REINDEER CENTRE
Glenmore Lodge
Inverdruie
Polchar
ROTHIEMURCHUS ESTATE VISITOR CENTRE
Loch Morlich
LOCH AN EILEIN VISITOR CENTRE
Loch an Eilein
Rothiemurchus
Loch Alvie
Alvie
Inshriach Forest
Kincraig
Invereshie House
Feshiebridge
HIGHLAND WILDLIFE PARK
Loch Insh
Balavil
Farr
Insh
Lynchat
Kingussie
Pitmain
CLAN MCPHERSON MUS
Newtonmore
HIGHLAND FOLK MUSEUM
Ruthven
RUTHVEN BARRACKS
INSH MARSHES
Inveruglass
Drumguish
Tolvah
INVERESHIE & INSHRIACH
Loch Einich
Achlean
SGORAN DUBH MOR
CARN EILRIG
CAIRN GORM
Lairig Ghru
BRAERIACH
BEN MACDUI
CARN BAN MOR
Glen Feshie
Glenfeshie Lodge
MULLACH CLACH A'BHLAIR
Glenfeshie Forest
BEINN BHROTAIN
Glen Dee
Eidart
Glen Banchor
Calder
Allt Madagain
Melgarve
Garvamore
Spey
Crathie
Balgowan
Laggan
Cluny Castle
Glentruim House
Catlodge
Drumgask
Loch Crunachdan
Glenshero Lodge
Strath Mashie
Strathmashie House
Crubenmore Lodge
Etteridge
GARBH-MHEALL MOR
Glentromie Lodge
Glen Tromie
MEALLACH MHOR
CARN DEARG MOR
CARN LIATH
Aberarder Lodge
Aberarder Forest
Cromra
Kinloch Laggan
Aberarder
CREAG MEAGAIDH
LOCH LAGGAN
Loch Caoldair
Loch Cuaich
Loch an t-Seilich
Allt Cuaich
Dalwhinnie
DALWHINNIE DISTILLERY
BEINN EILDE
Gaick Lodge
Gaick Forest
Loch Bhrodainn
CARN NA CAIM
UCHD A'CHLARSAIR
CARN EALAR
AN SGARSOCH
Tarf Water
Geldie Burn
Loch Ericht Forest
Ardverikie Forest
Lochan na h-Earba
Pattack
GEAL CHARN
CREAGAN MOR
Loch Pattack
Ben Alder Lodge
Loch an Duin
Cama' Choire
Sronphadruig Lodge
Dail-na-Mine Forest
SRON A'CHLEIRICH
Glen Bruar
Bruar Lodge
BEINN DEARG
BRAIGH SRON GHORM
Tilt
BEINN A'CHLACHAIR
Ben Alder Forest
A'BHUIDHEANACH BHEAG
LOCH ERICHT
BEINN UDLAMAIN
THE SOW OF ATHOLL
Dalnaspidal Lodge
Dalnacardoch Forest
Forest Lodge
BEINN A'GHLO
Loch a' Bhealaich Bheithe
BEN ALDER
Corrievarkie Lodge
Dalnaspidal Forest
Loch Garry
MEALL NA LEITREACH
Dalnacardoch Lodge
Edendon Water
Glen Diridh
CARN LIATH
Prince Charlie's Cave
Talla Bheith Forest
GLEN GARRY
Loch Con
Falls of the Bruar
CLAN DONNACHAIDH MUSEUM
BLAIR CASTLE
Loch Errochty
Calvine
Struan
Pitagowan
Old Bridge of Tilt
Lude House
BLAIR ATHOLL MILL
Blair Atholl
Glen Girnaig
BEINN MHOLACH
Trinafour
Dalchalloch
TULACH HILL
Bellentoul
Aldclune
Killiecrankie
KILLIECRANKIE VISITOR CENTRE
ATHOLL COUNTRY COLLECTION
BEN VRACKIE
GLEN ERROCHTY
Errochty Water
Tummel Forest
Loch Bhac
Bonskeid House
SRON BHEAG
BEINN A'CHUALLAICH
Tressait
Queen's View
QUEEN'S VIEW CENTRE
Falls of Tummel
LINN OF TUMMEL
Pitlochry
Moulin
Craiganor Lodge
Kinloch Rannoch
Dunalastair
Tummel Bridge
LOCH TUMMEL
Bridge of Ericht
Killichonan
LOCH RANNOCH
Carie
Inverhadden
Dunalastair Water
Foss
Loch Faskally
Balmore
Milton of Edradour
EDRADOUR DISTILLERY
BLAIR ATHOLL DISTILLERY VISITOR CENTRE
SCOTTISH PLANT COLLECTORS GARDEN
Finnart
Bridge of Gaur
Black Wood of Rannoch
A9
A86
A82
A889
A95
A938
B970
B9152
B846
B847
B8019
B8079
B851
B852
B862
87
82
75

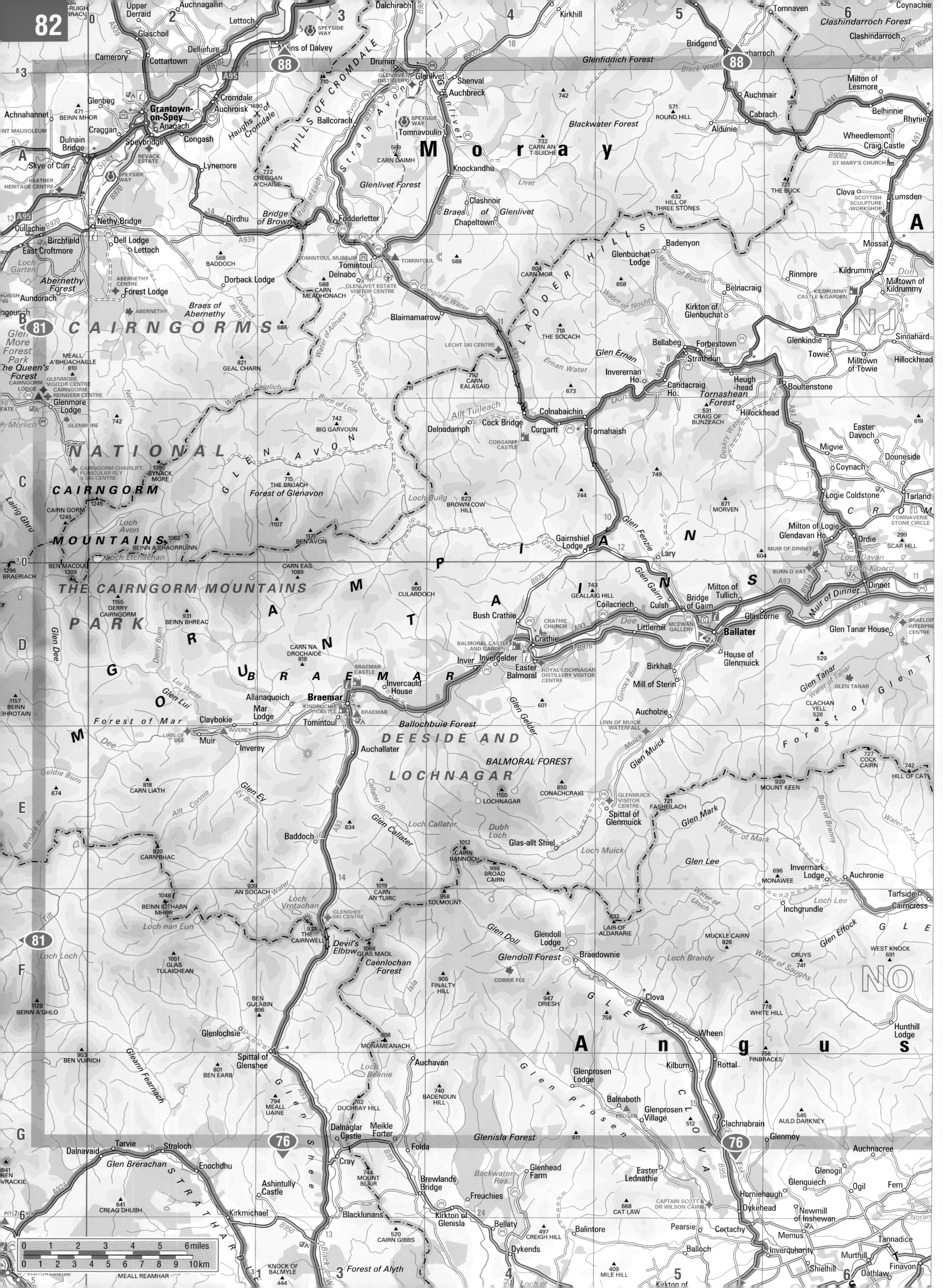
Upper Derraid
Auchnagallin
Lettoch
Glaschoil
Dellefure
Mains of Dalvey
Camerory
Cottartown
Drumin
Glenlivet
Shenval
Auchbreck
Dalchirach
Kirkhill
Tomnaven
Coynachie
Clashindarroch Forest
Clashindarroch
Bridgend
Glenfiddich Forest
Milton of Lesmore
Auchmair
Cabrach
Belhinnie
Rhynie
Aldunie
Wheedlemont
Craig Castle
St Mary's Church
Glenbeg
Grantown-on-Spey
Cromdale
Auchroisk
Haughs of Cromdale
Hills of Cromdale
Ballcorach
Tomnavoulin
Strath Avon
Speyside Way
Achnahannet
Beinn Mhor
Craggan
Anagach
Congash
Speybridge
Dulnain Bridge
Revack Estate
Skye of Curr
Heather Heritage Centre
Lynemore
Creggan A'Chaise
Carn Daimh
Moray
Carn an t-Suidhe
Knockandhu
Blackwater Forest
Round Hill
Glenlivet Forest
Clashnoir
Braes of Glenlivet
Chapeltown
Hill of Three Stones
The Buck
Clova
Scottish Sculpture Workshop
Lumsden
Nethy Bridge
Dirdhu
Bridge of Brown
Fodderletter
Cullachie
Birchfield
East Croftmore
Dell Lodge
Lettoch
Baddoch
Tomintoul Museum
Tomintoul
Delnabo
Glenlivet Estate Visitor Centre
Carn Meadhonach
Dorback Lodge
Abernethy Forest
Audorach
Abernethy Centre
Forest Lodge
Braes of Abernethy
Carn Mor
Ladder Hills
Glenbuchat Lodge
Badenyon
Water of Buchat
Belnacraig
Kirkton of Glenbuchat
Mossat
Rinmore
Kildrummy
Kildrummy Castle & Garden
Milltown of Kildrummy
Blairnamarrow
Conglass Water
Water of Nochty
Cairngorms
Glen More Forest Park
The Queen's Forest
Meall a'Bhuachaille
Geal Charn
The Socach
Lecht Ski Centre
Bellabeg
Forbestown
Strathdon
Glenkindie
Towie
Milltown of Towie
Sinnahard
Hillockhead
Glenmore Visitor Centre
Cairngorm Reindeer Centre
Glenmore Lodge
Carn Ealasaid
Glen Ernan
Ernan Water
Inverernan Ho.
Candacraig Ho.
Heugh-head
Boultenstone
Tornashean Forest
Glenmore
Big Garvoun
Allt Tuileach
Delnadamph
Cock Bridge
Colnabaichin
Corgarff
Corgarff Castle
Tornahaish
Craig of Bunzeach
Hillockhead
Easter Davoch
Migvie
Coynach
Douneside
National
Cairngorm Chairlift, Funicular Rly & Ski Centre
Bynack More
Glen Avon
The Bruach
Forest of Glenavon
Loch Builg
Brown Cow Hill
Cairngorm
Cairn Gorm
Loch Avon
Mountains
Ben Avon
Beinn a'Chaorruinn
Gairnshiel Lodge
Glen Fenzie
Lary
Morven
Logie Coldstone
Tarland
Tomnaverie Stone Circle
Milton of Logie
Glendavan Ho.
Ordie
Scar Hill
Muir of Dinnet
Loch Davan
Loch Kinord
Burn o Vat
Dinnet
Ben Macdui
Loch Etchachan
Braeriach
The Cairngorm Mountains
Carn Eas
Culardoch
Grampian Mountains
Gealaig Hill
Glen Gairn
Milton of Tullich
Bridge of Gairn
Coilacriech
Culsh
Derry Cairngorm
Beinn Bhreac
Park
Bush Crathie
Crathie Church
Crathie
Littlemill
McEwan Gallery
Ballater
Glascorrie
Glen Tanar House
Braeloine Interpretive Centre
Glen Dee
Derry Burn
Carn na Drochaide
Balmoral Castle and Gardens
Inver
Invergelder
Easter Balmoral
Royal Lochnagar Distillery Visitor Centre
Birkhall
House of Glenmuick
Mill of Sterin
Glen Tanar
Beinn Bhrotain
Lui Water
Glen Lui
Allanaquoich
Braemar
Braemar Castle
Invercauld House
Kindrochit Castle
Mar Lodge
Claybokie
Forest of Mar
Tomintoul
Inverey
Linn of Dee
Muir
Ballochbuie Forest
Deeside and Lochnagar
Auchallater
Glen Gelder
Aucholzie
Linn of Muick Waterfall
Clachan Yell
Forest of Glen Tanar
Balmoral Forest
Glen Muick
Cock Cairn
Hill of Cat
Mount Keen
Geldie Burn
Carn Liath
Glen Ey
Allt Connie
Lochnagar
Conachcraig
Glenmuick Visitor Centre
Spittal of Glenmuick
Fasheilach
Glen Mark
Water of Mark
Burn of Branny
Water of Tarf
Bynack Burn
Callater Burn
Glen Callater
Loch Callater
Dubh Loch
Glas-allt Shiel
Loch Muick
Baddoch
Carn Bhac
Cairn Bannoch
Broad Cairn
Glen Lee
Monawee
Invermark Lodge
Auchronie
Tarfside
Cairncross
An Socach
Clunie Water
Loch Vrotachan
Carn an Tuirc
Tolmount
Water of Unich
Loch Lee
Inchgrundle
Beinn Iutharn Mhor
Glenshee Ski Centre
Loch nan Eun
The Cairnwell
Devil's Elbow
Glas Maol
Lair of Aldararie
Glen Doll
Glendoll Lodge
Muckle Cairn
Glen Effock
West Knock
Loch Loch
Glas Tulaichean
Caenlochan Forest
Glendoll Forest
Braedownie
Loch Brandy
Cruys
Water of Saughs
Corrie Fee
Finalty Hill
Driesh
Clova
Glen Clova
Beinn a'Ghlo
Ben Gulabin
Isla
White Hill
Glenlochsie
Monamenach
Wheen
Hunthill Lodge
Ben Vuirich
Gleann Fearnach
Ben Earb
Spittal of Glenshee
Auchavan
Loch Beanie
Angus
Kilburn
Rottal
Finbracks
Glenprosen Lodge
Glen Prosen
Meall Uaine
Badendun Hill
Duchray Hill
Balnaboth
Prosen
Glenprosen Village
Clachnabrain
Auld Darkney
Glenmoy
Dalnaglar Castle
Meikle Forter
Folda
Glenisla Forest
Dalnavaid
Tarvie
Straloch
Enochdhu
Glen Brerachan
Strathardle
Ben Vrackie
Cray
Mount Blair
Glen Shee
Brewlands Bridge
Backwater Res.
Glenhead Farm
Easter Lednathie
Auchnacree
Glenogil
Glenquiech
Ogil
Fern
Ashintully Castle
Freuchies
Creag Dhubh
Kirkmichael
Blacklunans
Kirkton of Glenisla
Captain Scott & Dr Wilson Cairn
Cat Law
Hornieshaugh
Dykehead
Newmill of Inshewan
Noran
Bellaty
Creigh Hill
Balintore
Pearsie
Cortachy
Memus
Tannadice
Cairn Gibbs
Dykends
Balloch
Inverquharity
Murthill
Finavon
Meall Reamhar
Knock of Balmyle
Forest of Alyth
Mile Hill
Shielhill
Oathlaw
Kirkton of
Loch of
NJ
NO
0 1 2 3 4 5 6 miles
0 1 2 3 4 5 6 7 8 9 10 km

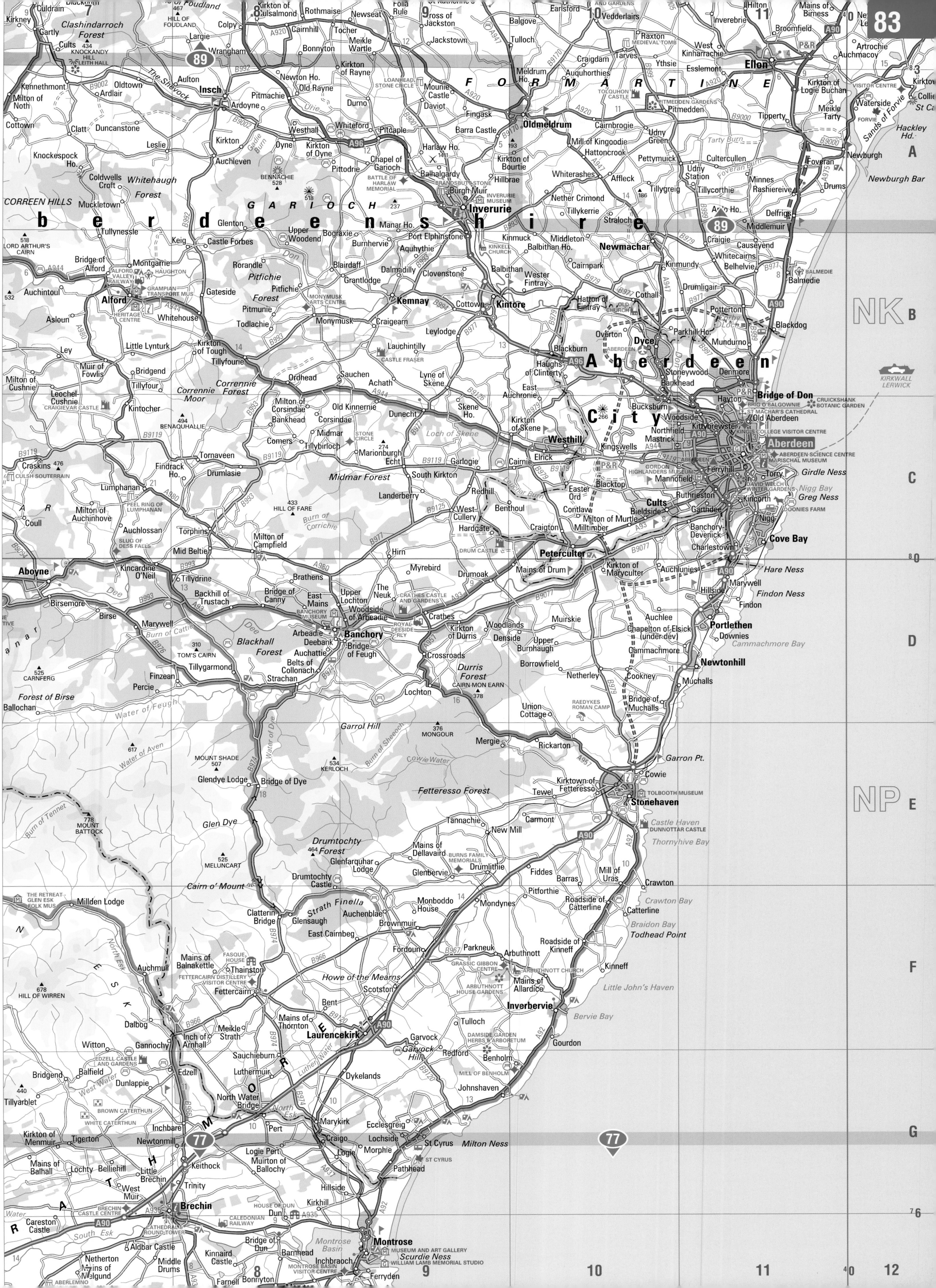
Aberdeenshire
Aberdeen City
FORMARTINE
GARIOCH
MEARNS
Aberdeen
Bridge of Don
Old Aberdeen
Dyce
Bucksburn
Westhill
Cults
Bieldside
Peterculter
Kingswells
Torry
Nigg
Cove Bay
Portlethen
Newtonhill
Muchalls
Stonehaven
Cowie
Inverbervie
Gourdon
Johnshaven
St Cyrus
Montrose
Ferryden
Brechin
Edzell
Laurencekirk
Fettercairn
Auchenblae
Fordoun
Drumlithie
Glenbervie
Banchory
Crathes
Aboyne
Kincardine O'Neil
Torphins
Lumphanan
Alford
Kemnay
Kintore
Inverurie
Insch
Oldmeldrum
Newmachar
Ellon
Newburgh
Balmedie
Blackdog
Potterton
Pitmedden
Udny Green
Tarves
Kirkton of Skene
Echt
Drumoak
Durris
Maryculter
Stoneywood
Bankhead
Woodside
Kittybrewster
Mastrick
Northfield
Ferryhill
Mannofield
Garthdee
Kincorth
Hazlehead
Blacktop
Milltimber
Newton of Murtle
Craigton
Charlestown
Findon
Hillside
Marywell
Girdle Ness
Greg Ness
Hare Ness
Findon Ness
Cammachmore Bay
Garron Pt.
Castle Haven
Dunnottar Castle
Thornyhive Bay
Crawton
Crawton Bay
Braidon Bay
Todhead Point
Catterline
Kinneff
Little John's Haven
Bervie Bay
Milton Ness
Scurdie Ness
Montrose Basin
Newburgh Bar
Sands of Forvie
Hackley Hd.
Kirkwall
Lerwick
Bennachie
Hill of Fare
Midmar Forest
Durris Forest
Fetteresso Forest
Drumtochty Forest
Blackhall Forest
Forest of Birse
Glen Dye
Cairn o' Mount
Strath Finella
Howe of the Mearns
Garvock Hill
Correen Hills
Whitehaugh Forest
Pitfichie Forest
Correnie Forest
Clashindarroch Forest
Mount Battock
Mount Shade
Kerloch
Mongour
Cairn-mon Earn
Clochnaben
Loch of Skene
Castle Fraser
Drum Castle
Crathes Castle and Gardens
Craigievar Castle
Fasque House
Arbuthnott House Gardens
Brechin Castle Centre
Edzell Castle and Gardens
Museum and Art Gallery
William Lamb Memorial Studio
Montrose Basin Visitor Centre
Tolbooth Museum
Aberdeen Science Centre
Marischal Museum
Gordon Highlanders Museum
King's College Visitor Centre
St Machar's Cathedral
Brig o' Balgownie
Cruickshank Botanic Garden
David Welch Winter Gardens
Doonies Farm
Grampian Transport Mus
Alford Valley Railway
Royal Deeside Rly
Caledonian Railway
Grassic Gibbon Centre
Arbuthnott Church
Burns Family Memorials
Fettercairn Distillery Visitor Centre
Raedykes Roman Camp
A90
A96
A93
A92
A944
A980
A947
A920
A975
A957
A937
A935
B9077
B979
B977
B9119
B993
B974
B966
89
77
NK
NP
A
B
C
D
E
F
G
7
8
9
10
11
12

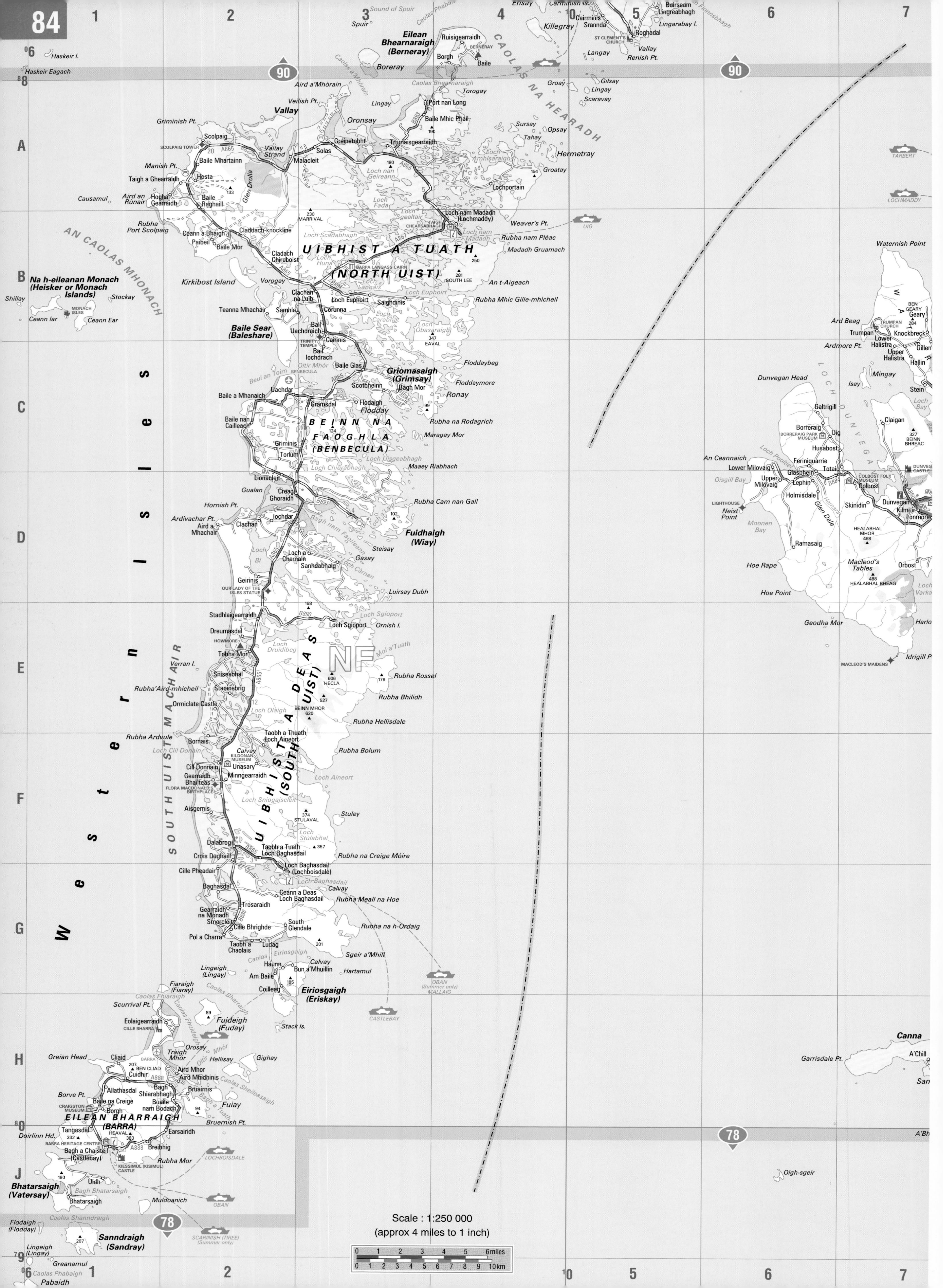
Sound of Spuir
Spuir
Eilean Bhearnaraigh (Berneray)
Ruisigearraidh
Borgh
Baile
Boreray
Caolas Bhearnaraigh
CAOLAS NA HEARADH
Killegray
Cairminis
Srannda
ST CLEMENT'S CHURCH
Roghadal
Lingarabay I.
Langay
Vallay
Renish Pt.
Haskeir I.
Haskeir Eagach
90
Aird a'Mhòrain
Torogay
Groay
Gilsay
Lingay
Scaravay
Veilish Pt.
Vallay
Lingay
Port nan Long
Oronsay
Baile Mhic Phàil
Sursay
Tahay
Opsay
Griminish Pt.
Scolpaig
SCOLPAIG TOWER
Greinetobht
Trumaisgearraidh
Solas
Vallay Strand
Malacleit
Baile Mhartainn
Manish Pt.
Taigh a Ghearraidh
Hosta
Aird an Rùnair
Hogha Gearraidh
Baile Raghaill
Glen Drolla
Causamul
Loch nan Geireann
Hermetray
Groatay
Lochportain
Loch Fada
MARRIVAL
Loch Sgealtair
Loch nam Madadh (Lochmaddy)
TAIGH CHEARSABHAGH
Weaver's Pt.
UIG
Rubha Port Scolpaig
AN CAOLAS MHONACH
Ceann a Bhaigh
Paibeil
Baile Mor
Claddach-knockline
Loch Scadabhagh
UIBHIST A TUATH (NORTH UIST)
Rubha nam Plèac
Madadh Gruamach
Cladach Chireboist
Loch Hunda
BARPA LANGASS CAIRN
SOUTH LEE
Na h-eileanan Monach (Heisker or Monach Islands)
Kirkibost Island
Vorogay
An t-Aigeach
Shillay
Stockay
MONACH ISLES
Ceann Iar
Ceann Ear
Clachan na Luib
Loch Euphoirt
Saighdinis
Rubha Mhic Gille-mhicheil
Teanna Mhachair
Samhla
Corùnna
Baile Sear (Baleshare)
Bail Uachdraich
Cairinis
TRINITY TEMPLE
EAVAL
Bail Iochdrach
Oitir Mhòr
Baile Glas
Floddaybeg
Beul an Toim
BENBECULA
Griomasaigh (Grimsay)
Floddaymore
Scotbheinn
Bagh Mor
Ronay
Baile a Mhanaich
Uachdar
Gramsdal
Flodaigh
Flodday
Baile nan Cailleach
BEINN NA FAOGHLA (BENBECULA)
Rubha na Rodagrich
Maragay Mor
Griminis
Torlum
Loch Uisgeabhagh
Loch Chiurabhagh
Maaey Riabhach
Lionacleit
Gualan
Creag Ghoraidh
Rubha Cam nan Gall
Hornish Pt.
Ardivachar Pt.
Aird a Mhachair
Clachan
Iochdar
Fuidhaigh (Wiay)
Loch Bi
Loch a Charnain
Steisay
Gasay
Sanndabhaig
Geirinis
OUR LADY OF THE ISLES STATUE
Luirsay Dubh
Stadhlaigearraidh
Loch Sgioport
Ornish I.
Dreumasdal
HOWMORE
Tobha Mor
Loch Druidibeg
Mol a'Tuath
Verran I.
NF
Sniseabhal
HECLA
Rubha Rossel
Rubha'Aird-mhicheil
Staoinebrig
Rubha Bhilidh
SOUTH UIST MACHAIR
Ormiclate Castle
Loch Olaigh
BEINN MHOR
Rubha Hellisdale
UIBHIST A DEAS (SOUTH UIST)
Rubha Ardvule
Taobh a Thuath Loch Aineort
Bornais
Loch Cill Donnain
Calvay
KILDONAN MUSEUM
Rubha Bolum
Cill Donnain
Unasary
Gearraidh Bhailteas
Minngearraidh
FLORA MACDONALD'S BIRTHPLACE
Loch Aineort
Aisgernis
Loch Sniogaiscleit
Stuley
STULAVAL
Western Isles
Dalabrog
Loch Stulabhal
Crois Dughaill
Taobh a Tuath Loch Baghasdail
Rubha na Creige Móire
Cille Pheadair
Loch Baghasdail (Lochboisdale)
Calvay
Baghasdal
Ceann a Deas Loch Baghasdail
Rubha Meall na Hoe
Trosaraidh
Gearraidh na Monadh
Smercleit
Cille Bhrighde
South Glendale
Rubha na h-Ordaig
Pol a Charra
Taobh a Chaolais
Ludag
Sgeir a'Mhill
Caolas Eiriosgaigh
Lingeigh (Lingay)
Haunn
Bun a'Mhuillin
Calvay
Hartamul
Am Baile
Coilleag
Eiriosgaigh (Eriskay)
OBAN (Summer only) MALLAIG
CASTLEBAY
Fiaraigh (Fiaray)
Caolas Fhiaraigh
Scurrival Pt.
Fuideigh (Fuday)
Eolaigearraidh
CILLE BHARRA
Stack Is.
Orosay
Greian Head
Cliaid
BEN CLIAD
Traigh Mhor
Hellisay
Gighay
Cuidhir
Aird Mhor
Aird Mhidhinis
Caolas Sheileasaigh
Borve Pt.
Allathasdal
Bagh Shiarabhagh
Bruairnis
Baile na Creige
Buaile nam Bodach
CRAIGSTON MUSEUM
Borgh
Fuiay
EILEAN BHARRAIGH (BARRA)
Bruernish Pt.
Doirlinn Hd.
Tangasdal
HEAVAL
Earsairidh
BARRA HERITAGE CENTRE
Breibhig
Bagh a Chaisteil (Castlebay)
Rubha Mor
LOCHBOISDALE
KIESSIMUL (KISIMUL) CASTLE
Uidh
Bhatarsaigh (Vatersay)
Bagh Bhatarsaigh
Bhatarsaigh
Muldoanich
OBAN
Flodaigh (Flodday)
Caolas Shanndraigh
78
SCARINISH (TIREE) (Summer only)
Sanndraigh (Sandray)
Lingeigh (Lingay)
Greanamul
Caolas Phabaigh
Pabaidh
Scale : 1:250 000
(approx 4 miles to 1 inch)
miles
km
TARBERT
LOCHMADDY
Waternish Point
Ard Beag
Trumpan
TRUMPAN CHURCH
BEN GEARY
Geary
Knockbreck
Gillen
Lower Halistra
Upper Halistra
Ardmore Pt.
Hallin
Dunvegan Head
Isay
Mingay
Stein
LOCH DUNVEGAN
Galtrigill
Claigan
Borreraig
BORRERAIG PARK MUSEUM
Uig
BEINN BHREAC
Husabost
An Ceannaich
Feriniquarrie
Lower Milovaig
Upper Milovaig
Glasphein
Totaig
Oisgill Bay
Lephin
COLBOST FOLK MUSEUM
Colbost
LIGHTHOUSE
Neist Point
Holmisdale
Glen Dale
Skinidin
Dunvegan
Kilmuir
Lonmore
Moonen Bay
Ramasaig
HEALABHAL MHOR
Hoe Rape
Macleod's Tables
HEALABHAL BHEAG
Orbost
Hoe Point
Geodha Mor
MACLEOD'S MAIDENS
Idrigill Pt.
Canna
A'Chill
Garrisdale Pt.
Oigh-sgeir
A'Bh

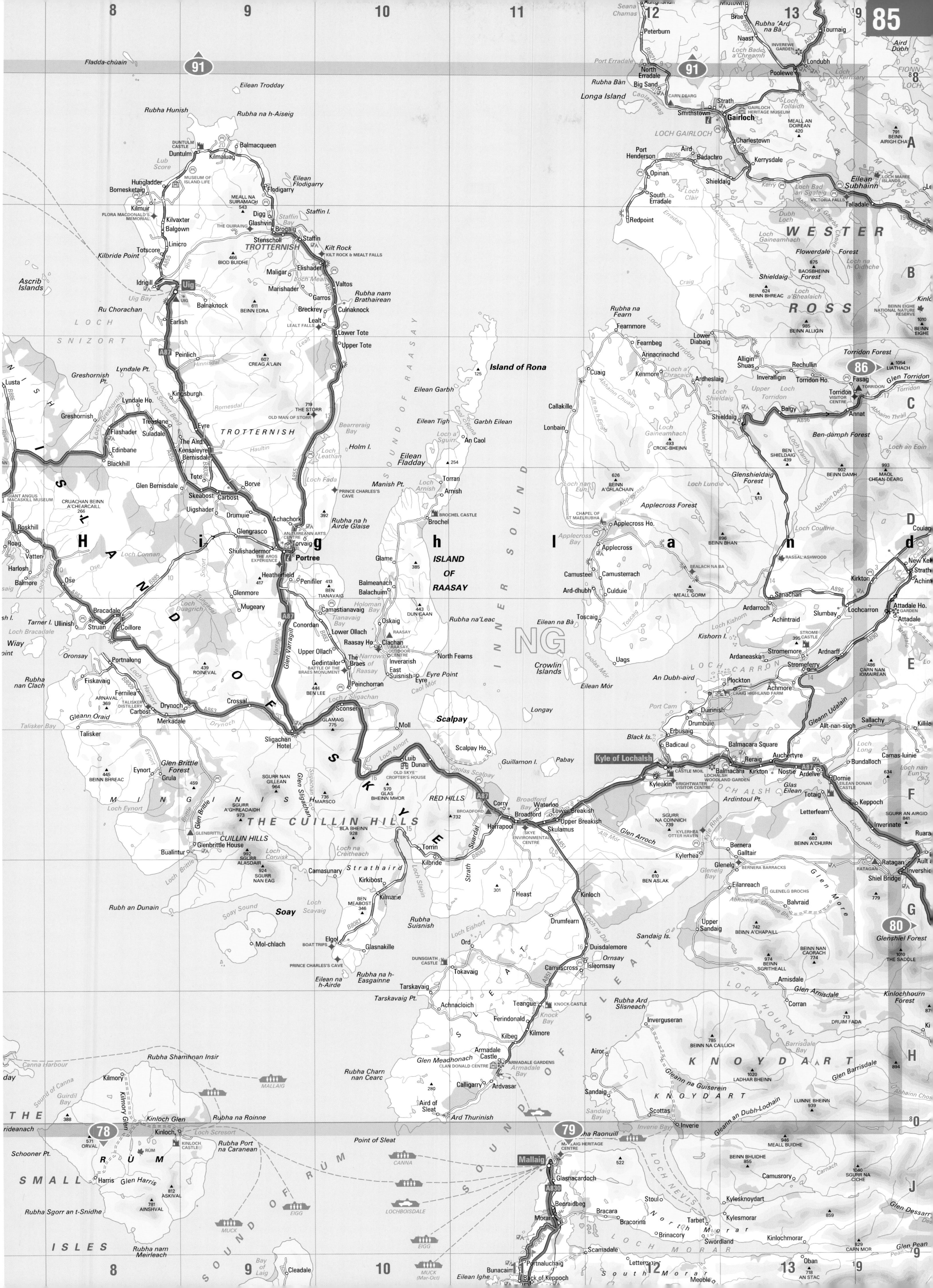
ISLE OF SKYE
TROTTERNISH
Portree
Uig
Dunvegan
THE CUILLIN HILLS
CUILLIN HILLS
ISLAND OF RAASAY
Island of Rona
Scalpay
Soay
RÙM
SMALL ISLES
SLEAT
SOUND OF SLEAT
INNER SOUND
SOUND OF RAASAY
SOUND OF RÙM
Kyle of Lochalsh
Mallaig
Gairloch
Broadford
Kyleakin
Plockton
Lochcarron
Applecross
Torridon
WESTER ROSS
KNOYDART
LOCH HOURN
LOCH ALSH
LOCH CARRON
LOCH TORRIDON
LOCH GAIRLOCH
Armadale Castle
Elgol
Glenelg
Inverie
Morar
NG
91
86
80
79
78

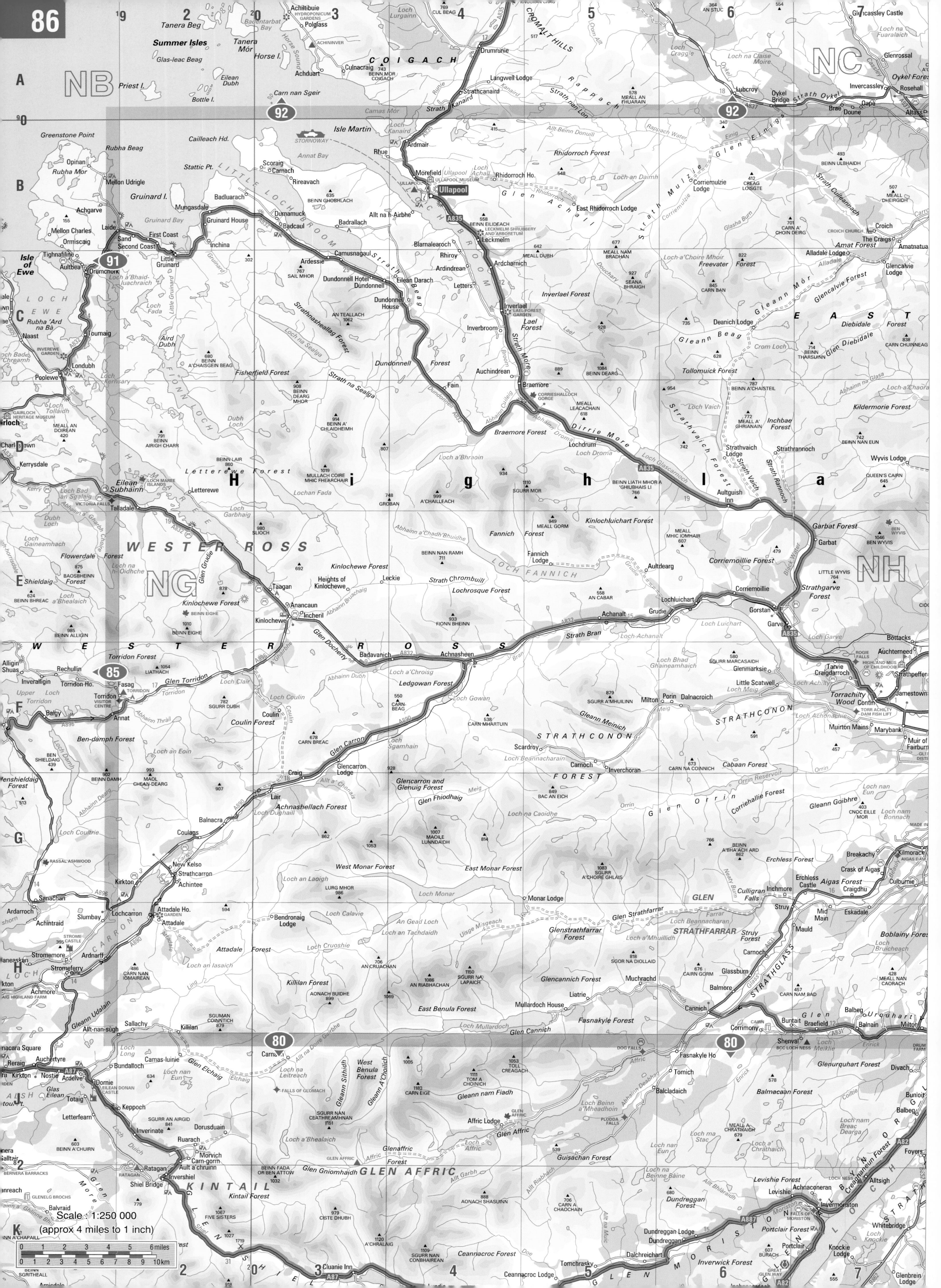
NB
NC
NG
NH
Summer Isles
Tanera Beg
Tanera Mór
Horse I.
Glas-leac Beag
Eilean Dubh
Priest I.
Bottle I.
Achiltibuie
Polglass
Achduart
Culnacraig
COIGACH
CROMALT HILLS
Drumrunie
Langwell Lodge
Strathcanaird
Strath Kanaird
Rappach
Strath nan Lon
Loch Craggie
Lubcroy
Oykel Bridge
Strath Oykel
Glencassley Castle
Glenrossal
Invercassley
Rosehall
Brae
Doune
Oape
Altass
Carn nan Sgeir
Isle Martin
Cailleach Hd.
Greenstone Point
Rubha Beag
Opinan
Rubha Mor
Mellon Udrigle
Stattic Pt.
Gruinard I.
Gruinard Bay
Scoraig
Carnach
Rireavach
Annat Bay
LITTLE LOCH BROOM
Ardmair
Rhue
Morefield
Ullapool
Rhidorroch Forest
Rhidorroch Ho.
East Rhidorroch Lodge
Glen Achall
Strath Mulzie
Corriemulzie Lodge
Glen Einig
Strath Cuileannach
Croich
The Craigs
Amatnatua
Amat Forest
Alladale Lodge
Glencalvie Lodge
Glencalvie Forest
Badluarach
Mungasdale
Gruinard House
Durnamuck
Badcaul
Badrallach
Allt na h-Airbhe
LOCH BROOM
Leckmelm
Achgarve
Mellon Charles
Ormiscaig
Laide
Sand
Second Coast
First Coast
Inchina
Little Gruinard
Isle of Ewe
Tighnafiline
Aultbea
Drumchork
LOCH EWE
Rubha 'Ard na Bà
Naast
Tournaig
Inverewe Garden
Londubh
Poolewe
Camusnagaul
Strath Beag
Ardessie
Dundonnell Hotel
Dundonnell
Eilean Darach
Dundonnell House
Blarnalearoch
Rhiroy
Ardindrean
Letters
Ardcharnich
Inverlael
Inverlael Forest
Lael Forest
Inverbroom
Strath More
Auchindrean
Braemore
Fain
Dundonnell Forest
Strathnasheallag Forest
Fisherfield Forest
Strath na Sealga
Fionn Loch
Dubh Loch
Freevater Forest
Deanich Lodge
Gleann Mór
Gleann Beag
Diebidale
Glen Diebidale
Tollomuick Forest
Strathvaich Forest
Inchbae Forest
Kildermorie Forest
Wyvis Lodge
Braemore Forest
Dirrie More
Lochdrum
Loch Droma
Loch Glascarnoch
Strathvaich Lodge
Strath Vaich
Strath Rannoch
Strathrannoch
Aultguish Inn
Garbat Forest
Garbat
Letterewe Forest
Highland
Loch Maree
Eilean Subhainn
Letterewe
Talladale
Kerrysdale
Gairloch
Charlestown
Loch Bad an Sgalaig
Victoria Falls
Kinlochluichart Forest
Fannich Forest
Fannich Lodge
Loch Fannich
Aultdearg
Corriemoillie Forest
Corriemoillie
Strathgarve Forest
Lochluichart
Gorstan
Garve
Loch Garve
WESTER ROSS
Flowerdale Forest
Shieldaig
Baosbheinn Forest
Glen Grudie
Kinlochewe Forest
Kinlochewe
Taagan
Anancaun
Incheril
Heights of Kinlochewe
Leckie
Strath Chrombuill
Lochrosque Forest
Kinlochewe Forest
Glen Docherty
Badavanich
Achnasheen
Achanalt
Grudie
Strath Bran
Loch Luichart
Bottacks
Auchterneed
Strathpeffer
Tarvie
Craigdarroch
Jamestown
Torrachilty Wood
Contin
Marybank
Muirton Mains
Muir of Fairburn
Torridon Forest
Alligin Shuas
Rechullin
Inveralligin
Torridon Ho.
Fasag
Torridon
Annat
Balgy
Glen Torridon
Loch Clair
Loch Coulin
Coulin
Coulin Forest
Ledgowan Forest
Loch Gowan
Loch Bhad Ghaineamhaich
Glenmarksie
Little Scatwell
Milton
Porin
Dalnacroich
Strathconon
Gleann Meinich
Scardroy
Carnoch
Inverchoran
Cabaan Forest
Ben-damph Forest
Bendamph Forest
Loch an Eoin
Glen Carron
Craig
Glencarron Lodge
Glencarron and Glenuig Forest
Glen Fhiodhaig
Lair
Achnashellach Forest
Loch Dughaill
Balnacra
Coulags
Loch na Caoidhe
Glen Orrin
Orrin Reservoir
Corriehallie Forest
Gleann Goibhre
Loch Coultrie
Rassal Ashwood
New Kelso
Strathcarron
Achintee
Kirkton
West Monar Forest
East Monar Forest
Loch an Laoigh
Loch Monar
Monar Lodge
Erchless Forest
Breakachy
Kilmorack
Crask of Aigas
Aigas Forest
Erchless Castle
Inchmore
Culburnie
Culligran Falls
Glen Strathfarrar
Struy
Craigdhu
Mid Main
Eskadale
Sanachan
Ardarroch
Achintraid
Slumbay
Lochcarron
Attadale Ho.
Attadale
Bendronaig Lodge
Loch Calavie
Uisge Misgeach
Glenstrathfarrar Forest
STRATHFARRAR
Struy Forest
Mauld
Boblainy Forest
Stromemore
Ardnarff
Loch Cruoshie
Attadale Forest
Stromeferry
Achmore
Killilan Forest
Glencannich Forest
Muchrachd
Glassburn
Balmore
Strathglass
Cannich
Gleann Udalain
Sallachy
Killilan
East Benula Forest
Mullardoch House
Liatrie
Fasnakyle Forest
Corrimony
Buntait
Glen Urquhart
Balbeg
Balnain
Milton
Alltnan-sugh
Loch Mullardoch
Glen Cannich
Loch Long
Camas-luinie
Bundalloch
Auchertyre
Reraig
Kirkton
Nostie
Ardelve
Dornie
Eilean Donan Castle
Glen Elchaig
Loch nan Eun
Carnach
West Benula Forest
Gleann Sithidh
Glenn A'Choilich
Gleann nam Fiadh
Dog Falls
Fasnakyle Ho
Tomich
Balcladaich
Shenval
Glenurquhart Forest
Divach
Balmacaan Forest
Bunloit
Balbeg
Loch Alsh
Eilean Totaig
Keppoch
Letterfearn
Inverinate
Dorusduain
Ruarach
Morvich
Carn-gorm
Ault a'chruinn
Ratagan
Invershiel
Shiel Bridge
Affric Lodge
Glen Affric
Plodda Falls
Loch Beinn a'Mheadhoin
Loch ma Stac
Loch nan Eun
Guisachan Forest
Glenaffric Forest
GLEN AFFRIC
Glen Gniomhaidh
KINTAIL
Kintail Forest
GLEN SHIEL
Glenelg Brochs
Balvraid
Levishie Forest
Levishie
Achnaconeran
Invermoriston
Dundreggan Forest
Dundreggan Lodge
Dundreggan
GLEN MORISTON
Portclair Forest
Portclair
Inverwick Forest
Dalchreichart
Tomchrasky
Ceannacroc Forest
Ceannacroc Lodge
Cluanie Inn
Creag nan Eun Forest
Alltsigh
Whitebridge
Knockie Lodge
Glenbrein Lodge
Foyers
LOCH NESS
Scale : 1:250 000
(approx 4 miles to 1 inch)
6 miles
10 km

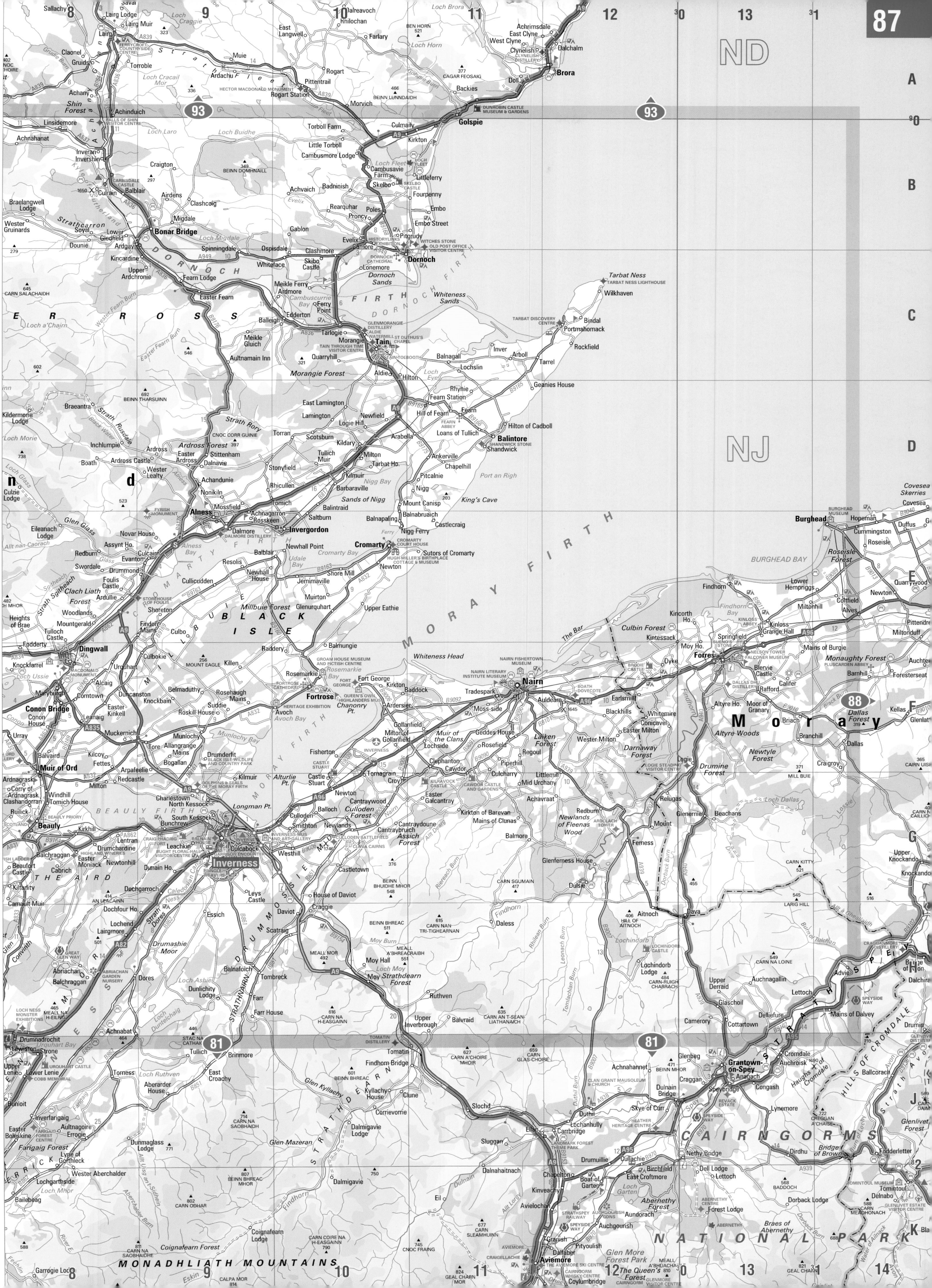
ND
NJ
A
B
C
D
E
F
G
H
J
K
Lairg
Brora
Golspie
Dornoch
Bonar Bridge
Ardgay
Dornoch Firth
Tain
Tarbat Ness
Portmahomack
Balintore
Alness
Invergordon
Cromarty
Cromarty Firth
Moray Firth
Dingwall
Conon Bridge
Muir of Ord
Beauly
Beauly Firth
Inverness
Fortrose
Black Isle
Nairn
Forres
Burghead
Burghead Bay
Moray
Grantown-on-Spey
Carrbridge
Aviemore
Cairngorms National Park
Monadhliath Mountains
Strathdearn
Strathnairn
Ross
The Aird
Culloden Forest
Culbin Forest
Darnaway Forest
Shin Forest
Morangie Forest
Millbuie Forest
Abernethy Forest
Glen More Forest Park
Hills of Cromdale
Strath Spey
Tomatin
Drumnadrochit
Dores
Foyers
Nethy Bridge
Boat of Garten
Dulnain Bridge
Tomintoul
Dallas
Kinloss
Fort George
Ardersier
Cawdor
Croy
Tornagrain
Dalcross
Kessock
Evanton
Culcairn
Muir of Ord

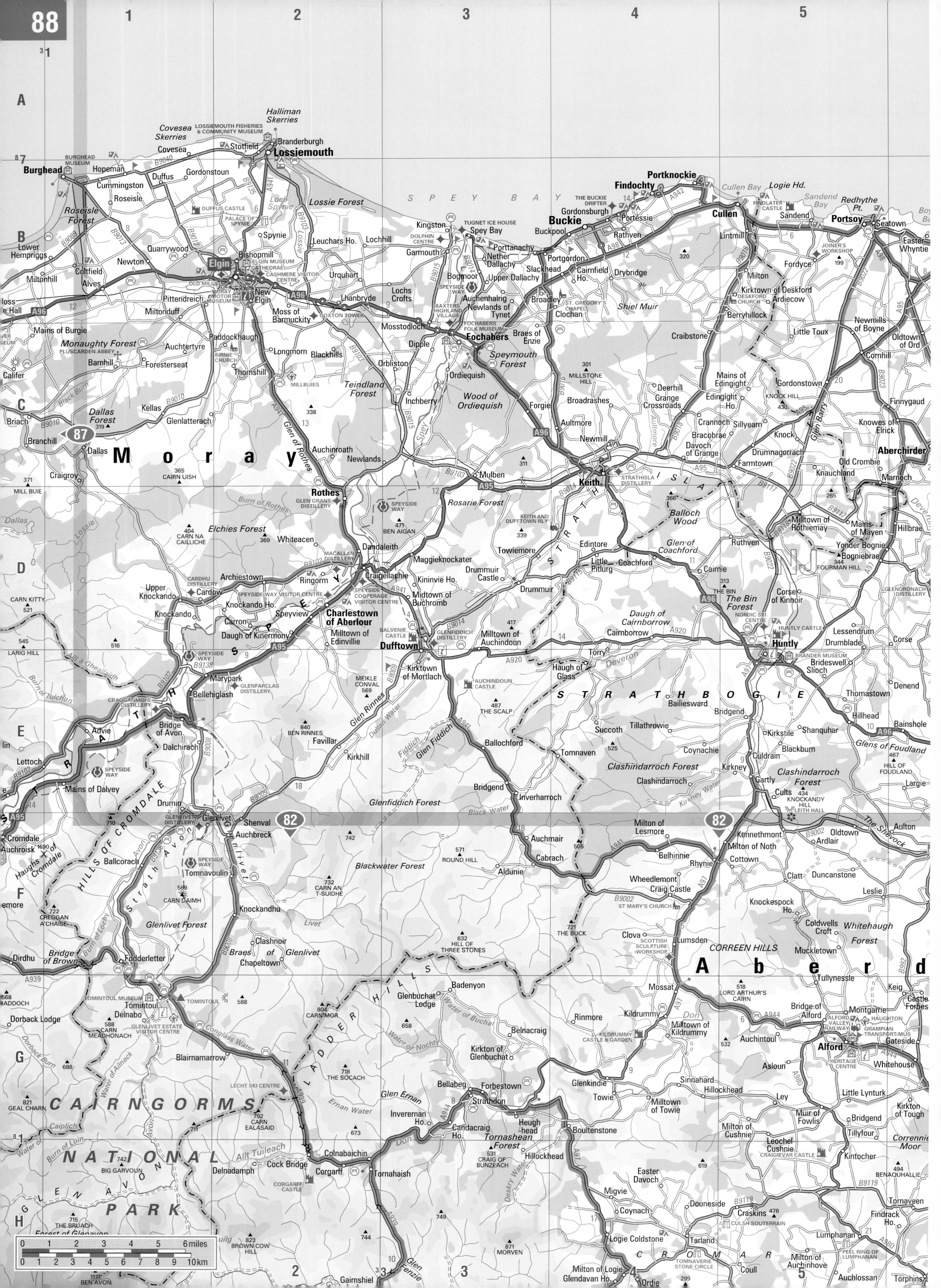
Halliman Skerries
Covesea Skerries
LOSSIEMOUTH FISHERIES & COMMUNITY MUSEUM
Branderburgh
Lossiemouth
Covesea
Stotfield
Burghead
Hopeman
Duffus
Gordonstoun
Cummingston
Roseisle
Roseisle Forest
DUFFUS CASTLE
PALACE OF SPYNIE
Spynie
Loch Spynie
Lossie Forest
SPEY BAY
Lower Hempriggs
Quarrywood
Bishopmill
Elgin
ELGIN MUSEUM
CATHEDRAL
CASHMERE VISITOR CENTRE
Newton
Miltonhill
Coltfield
Alves
OLD MILLS
MORAY MOTOR MUSEUM
New Elgin
Pittendreich
Miltonduff
Moss of Barmuckity
COXTON TOWER
Lhanbryde
Urquhart
Leuchars Ho.
Lochhill
Lochs
Crofts
Kingston
DOLPHIN CENTRE
Garmouth
TUGNET ICE HOUSE
Spey Bay
Porttanachy
Nether Dallachy
Upper Dallachy
Bogmoor
SPEYSIDE WAY
Auchenhalrig
Newlands of Tynet
BAXTERS HIGHLAND VILLAGE
Mosstodloch
FOCHABERS FOLK MUSEUM
Fochabers
Dipple
Braes of Enzie
Speymouth Forest
Slackhead
Portgordon
Buckpool
Buckie
THE BUCKIE DRIFTER
Gordonsburgh
Portessie
Findochty
Portknockie
Rathven
Cullen Bay
Logie Hd.
Cullen
FINDLATER CASTLE
Sandend
Sandend Bay
Redhythe Pt.
Portsoy
Seatown
Easter Whyntie
Cairnfield Ho.
Drybridge
Broadley
ST. GREGORY'S CHAPEL
Clochan
Shiel Muir
Lintmill
Milton
Kirktown of Deskford
DESKFORD CHURCH
Ardiecow
Berryhillock
Fordyce
JOINER'S WORKSHOP
Craibstone
Little Toux
Newmills of Boyne
Oldtown of Ord
Cornhill
Mains of Burgie
Monaughty Forest
PLUSCARDEN ABBEY
Barnhill
Califer
Auchtertyre
Paddockhaugh
Foresterseat
BIRNIE CHURCH
Thomshill
Longmorn
Blackhills
MILLBUIES
Orbliston
Teindland Forest
Ordiequish
Inchberry
Wood of Ordiequish
Forgie
MILLSTONE HILL
Deerhill
Grange Crossroads
Mains of Edingight
Edingight Ho.
KNOCK HILL
Gordonstown
Finnygaud
Broadrashes
Aultmore
Newmill
Crannoch
Bracobrae
Davoch of Grange
Sillyearn
Knock
Glen Barry
Knowes of Elrick
Aberchirder
Drumnagorrach
Farmtown
Old Crombie
Knauchland
Marnoch
Briach
Branchill
Dallas Forest
Kellas
Glenlatterach
Glen of Rothes
Auchinroath
Newlands
Dallas
Moray
Craigroy
MILL BUIE
CAIRN UISH
Rothes
GLEN GRANT DISTILLERY
Mulben
SPEYSIDE WAY
BEN AIGAN
Rosarie Forest
Keith
STRATHISLA DISTILLERY
ISLA
Balloch Wood
KEITH AND DUFFTOWN RLY
Burn of Rothes
Elchies Forest
CARN NA CAILLICHE
Whiteacen
Dandaleith
Maggieknockater
Towiemore
Edintore
Little Pitlurg
Coachford
Glen of Coachford
Cairnie
Ruthven
Milltown of Rothiemay
Mains of Mayen
Hillbrae
Yonder Bognie
Bogniebrae
FOURMAN HILL
Archiestown
CARDHU DISTILLERY
MACALLAN DISTILLERY
Craigellachie
Kininvie Ho.
Drummuir Castle
Drummuir
STRATH ISLA
THE BIN
The Bin Forest
Corse of Kinnoir
GLENDRONACH DISTILLERY
Upper Knockando
Cardow
SPEYSIDE WAY VISITOR CENTRE
Ringorm
SPEYSIDE COOPERAGE VISITOR CENTRE
Midtown of Buchromb
CARN KITTY
Knockando Ho.
Knockando
Carron
Speyview
Charlestown of Aberlour
Daugh of Kinermony
Milltown of Edinvillie
BALVENIE CASTLE
Dufftown
GLENFIDDICH DISTILLERY
Milltown of Auchindoun
Daugh of Cairnborrow
Cairnborrow
NORDIC SKI CENTRE
HUNTLY CASTLE
Huntly
Lessendrum
Drumblade
Corse
LARIG HILL
SPEY
Marypark
GLENFARCLAS DISTILLERY
Kirktown of Mortlach
Torry
Haugh of Glass
Deveron
BRANDER MUSEUM
Brideswell
Slioch
CRAGGANMORE DISTILLERY
Bellehiglash
MEIKLE CONVAL
AUCHINDOUN CASTLE
THE SCALP
STRATHBOGIE
Bailiesward
Bridgend
Thomastown
Denend
Hillhead
Advie
Bridge of Avon
BEN RINNES
Glen Rinnes
Succoth
Tillathrowie
Kirkstile
Shanquhar
Bainshole
Dalchirach
Favillar
Dullan Water
Glen Fiddich
Ballochford
Coynachie
Blackburn
Glens of Foudland
HILL OF FOUDLAND
Lettoch
STRATH
Kirkhill
Tomnaven
Clashindarroch Forest
Culdrain
Clashindarroch Forest
Largie
SPEYSIDE WAY
Mains of Dalvey
HILLS OF CROMDALE
Clashindarroch
Kirkney
Gartly
Cults
KNOCKANDY HILL
LEITH HALL
Drumin
Bridgend
Inverharroch
Kirkney Water
Glenfiddich Forest
Black Water
GLENLIVET DISTILLERY
Glenlivet
Shenval
Auchbreck
Milton of Lesmore
Kennethmont
Oldtown
Aulton
The Shevock
Cromdale
Auchroisk
Haughs of Cromdale
Auchmair
Ardlair
Milton of North
Rhynie
Cottown
Belhinnie
Ballcorach
ROUND HILL
Cabrach
Aldunie
SPEYSIDE WAY
Tomnavoulin
Strath Avon
Blackwater Forest
CARN AN T-SUIDHE
Livet
Wheedlemont
Craig Castle
Clatt
Duncanstone
Leslie
CARN DAIMH
Knockandhu
ST MARY'S CHURCH
Knockespock Ho.
CREGGAN A'CHAISE
Glenlivet Forest
THE BUCK
Clova
SCOTTISH SCULPTURE WORKSHOP
Lumsden
CORREEN HILLS
Coldwells Croft
Whitehaugh Forest
Clashnoir
Braes of Glenlivet
Chapeltown
HILL OF THREE STONES
Muckletown
Dirdhu
Bridge of Brown
Burn of Lochy
Fodderletter
Aberd
LADDER HILLS
Badenyon
Mossat
LORD ARTHUR'S CAIRN
Tullynessle
Keig
DADDOCH
Dorback Lodge
TOMINTOUL MUSEUM
Tomintoul
Delnabo
CARN MEADHONACH
GLENLIVET ESTATE VISITOR CENTRE
CARN MOR
Glenbuchat Lodge
Water of Buchat
Rinmore
Kildrummy
Don
Milltown of Kildrummy
KILDRUMMY CASTLE & GARDEN
Bridge of Alford
Montgarrie
Castle Forbes
ALFORD VALLEY RAILWAY
HAUGHTON
GRAMPIAN TRANSPORT MUS
Alford
Gateside
HERITAGE CENTRE
Whitehouse
Dorback Burn
Water of Ailnack
Conglass Water
Blairnamarrow
Water of Nochty
Kirkton of Glenbuchat
Belnacraig
Auchintoul
Asloun
THE SOCACH
LECHT SKI CENTRE
Glenkindie
Towie
Sinnahard
Hillockhead
Ley
Little Lynturk
Kirkton of Tough
GEAL CHARN
CAIRNGORMS
Glen Ernan
Ernan Water
Bellabeg
Forbestown
Strathdon
Inverernan Ho.
CARN EALASAID
Candacraig Ho.
Heugh-head
Tornashean Forest
Boultenstone
Milltown of Towie
Muir of Fowlis
Bridgend
Tillyfour
Milton of Cushnie
Leochel-Cushnie
CRAIGIEVAR CASTLE
Kintocher
Corrennie Moor
NATIONAL
Caiplich
Burn of Loin
Allt Tuileach
Colnabaichin
Cock Bridge
Corgarff
CORGARFF CASTLE
Tornahaish
CRAIG OF BUNZEACH
Hillockhead
Deskry Water
Delnadamph
BIG GARVOUN
GLEN AVON
PARK
Easter Davoch
Migvie
Coynach
Douneside
Craskins
CULSH SOUTERRAIN
BENAQUHALLIE
Tornaveen
Findrack Ho.
Lumphanan
PEEL RING OF LUMPHANAN
THE BRUACH
Forest of Glenavon
BROWN COW HILL
MORVEN
Logie Coldstone
Tarland
CROMAR
TOMNAVERIE STONE CIRCLE
Milton of Auchinhove
Milton of Logie
Glendavan Ho.
Coull
Auchlossan
Torphins
BEN AVON
Gairnshiel
Glen Fenzie
Ordie
miles
km

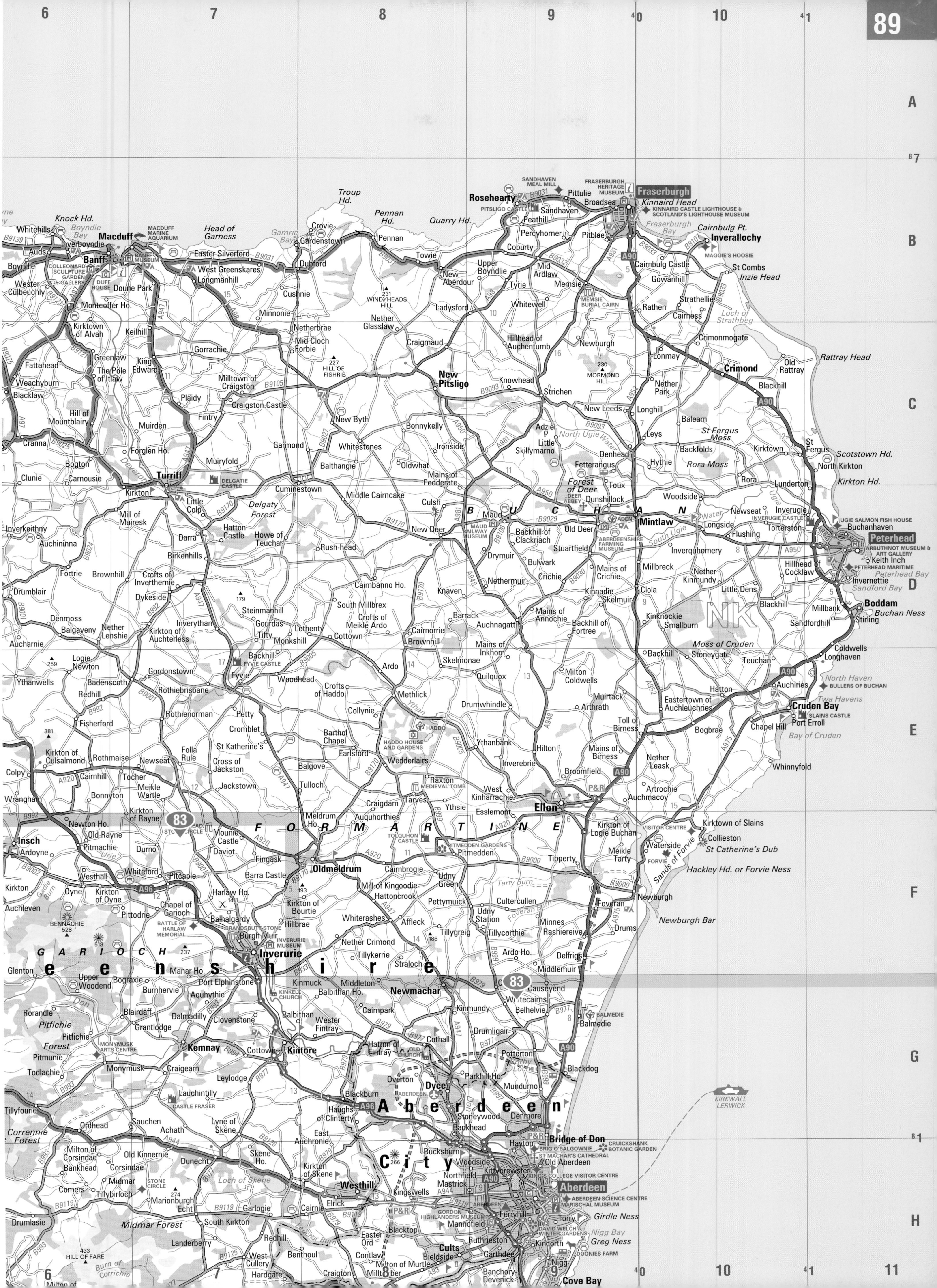
Fraserburgh
Kinnaird Head
Rosehearty
Sandhaven
Pittulie
Inverallochy
Cairnbulg Castle
Troup Hd.
Pennan Hd.
Quarry Hd.
Knock Hd.
Macduff
Banff
Whitehills
Gardenstown
Crovie
Pennan
New Aberdour
Rathen
Crimond
Rattray Head
Strichen
New Pitsligo
New Byth
Turriff
Delgaty Forest
Cuminestown
New Deer
Maud
Mintlaw
Longside
St Fergus
Peterhead
Buchanhaven
Boddam
Buchan Ness
Fyvie
Methlick
Tarves
Ellon
Cruden Bay
Port Erroll
Bay of Cruden
Hatton
Collieston
Newburgh
Sands of Forvie
Oldmeldrum
Inverurie
Insch
Kemnay
Kintore
Newmachar
Balmedie
Dyce
Westhill
Bridge of Don
Aberdeen
Cults
Torry
Girdle Ness
Cove Bay
Bennachie
B U C H A N
F O R M A R T I N E
G A R I O C H
Aberdeenshire
Aberdeen City
Kirkwall
Lerwick
A90
A96
A947
A948
A98
A952
A950
A920
NK

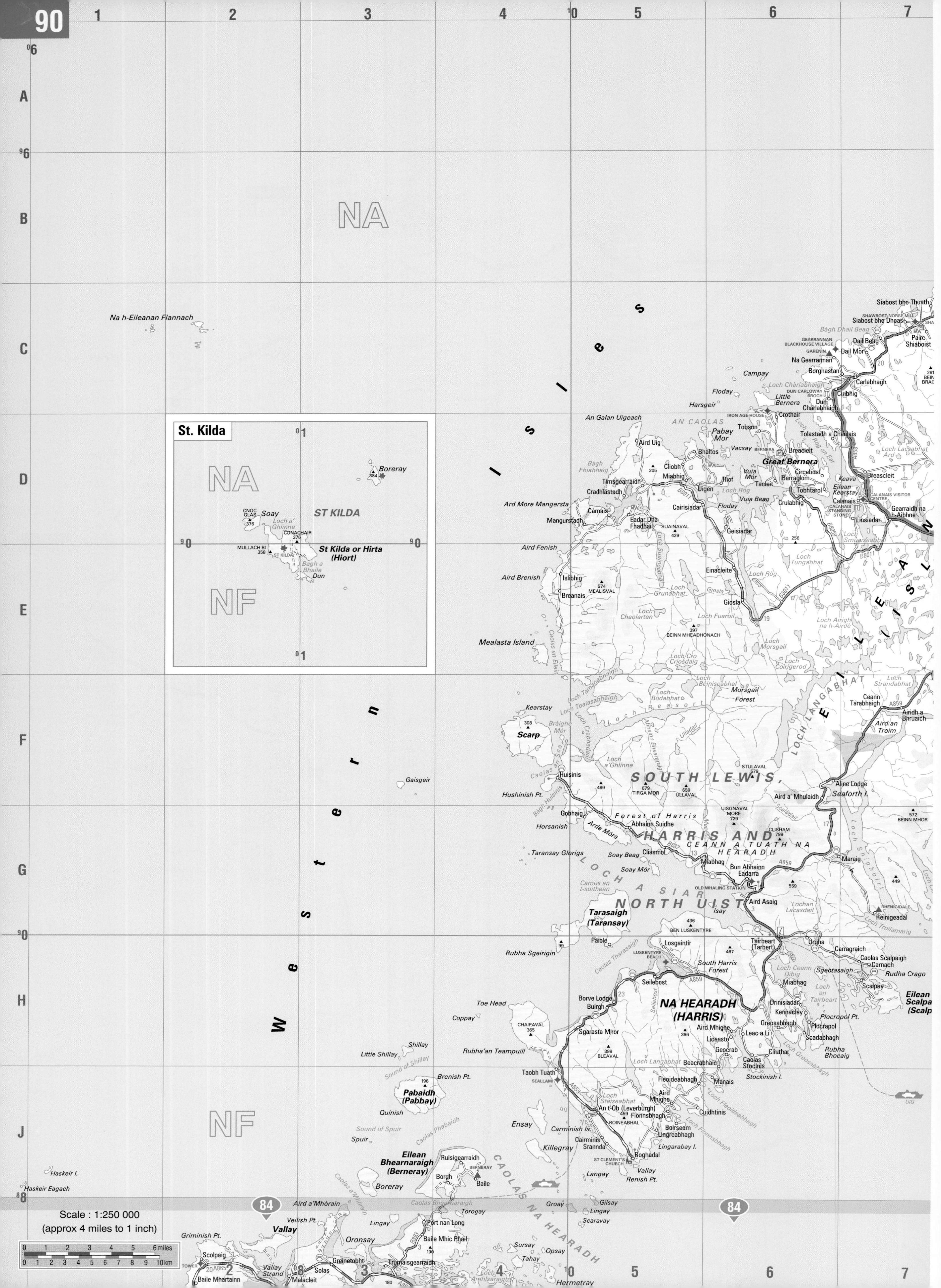

St. Kilda

NA

NF

ST KILDA

Boreray
384

CNOC
GLAS
376   Soay
Loch a'
Ghlinne

CONACHAIR
376

MULLACH BI
358   ST KILDA

St Kilda or Hirta
(Hiort)

Bagh a
Bhaile
Dun

NA

I s l e s

NF

W e s t e r n

Na h-Eileanan Flannach

Gaisgeir

Kearstay

Bràighe
Mòr
308

Scarp

Huisinis

Hushinish Pt.

489

Gobhaig

Horsanish

Taransay Glorigs

Camus an
t-suithean

**Tarasaigh
(Taransay)**

Rubha Sgeirigin

Paible
99

Toe Head

Coppay

Little Shillay   Shillay
Sound of Shillay
196
Brenish Pt.

**Pabaidh
(Pabbay)**
Quinish

Spuir   Sound of Spuir

NF

Haskeir I.

Haskeir Eagach

**Eilean
Bhearnaraigh
(Berneray)**

Ruisigearraidh
Borgh   Baile
Boreray

Aird a'Mhòrain   Torogay   Groay   Gilsay
Veilish Pt.   Lingay   Scaravay
Griminish Pt.   Port nan Long
Scolpaig   Oronsay   Baile Mhic Phail   Sursay   Tahay
Baile Mhartainn   Greinetobht   190   Opsay   Hermetray
TOWER   2 0 A865   Malacleit   Lingay
Valley Strand   8   Solas   3   Hornish   4   Loch   5

Siabost bho Thuath
SHAWBOST, NORSE MILL   Siabost bho Dheas
Bàgh Dhail Beag
GEARRANNAN   Dail Beag
BLACKHOUSE VILLAGE   Pairc Shiaboist
GARENIN   Dail Mòr
Na Gearrannan
Campay   Borghastan   Carlabhagh   20   261
Loch Chàrlabhaigh   BEINN
Floday   Little   DUN CARLOWAY   Ciribhig   BRAC
Harsgeir   Bernera   BROCH   Crothair
IRON AGE HOUSE   Tobson
An Galan Uigeach   Pabay   Loch Ròg an Ear   Tolastadh a Chaolais
Aird Uig   Mòr   Vacsay   BERNERA   Breacleit   Loch Lacasbhat
Bhaltos   **Great Bernera**   Àrd
Cliobh   205   Miabhig   Riof   Circebost   Keava   Breascleit
Timsgearraidh   Vuia   Barraglom   Eilean
Ard More Mangersta   Cradhlastadh   Mòr   Tobhtarol   Kearstay
Càrnais   Vuia Beag   Crulabhig   CALANAIS VISITOR   Gearraidh na h-Aibhne
Mangurstadh   Eadar Dha   Floday   Uigen   CENTRE   Linsiadar
Fhadhail   SUAINAVAL   Geisiadar   CALANAIS   B8011
429   STANDING   Loch   Gearraidh na h-Aibhne
Aird Fenish   256   STONES   Smuaisebhat
Aird Brenish   Einacleite   Loch Ròg
Islibhig   574   Loch   Loch   L E W I S
Breanais   MEALISVAL   Grunabhat   Tungabhat
397   Giosla   B8011
BEINN MHEADHONACH   Loch   Loch Airigh
Loch   Morsgail   na h-Airdé
Mealasta Island   Chaolartan   19
Loch/Cro   Loch
Criosdaig   Coirigerod   Loch
Strandabhat
Loch   Strandabhat
Loch Tamhnabhaigh   Bòdabhat   Beiniseabhal   A859
Morsgail   Ceann
Loch Tealasabhaigh   Forest   Tarabhaigh
Loch   Reasort   Airidh a
Loch Crabhadail   Bhruaich
308   Aird an
Troim
STULAVAL   A859
679   STULAVAL   579   Aline Lodge
TIRGA MÒR   659   Seaforth I.
489   ULLAVAL   Aird a' Mhulaidh   17
Loch   UISGNAVAL   572
g'Ghlinne   **SOUTH LEWIS,**   MORE   BEINN MHOR
729
Forest of Harris   CUISHAM   Maraig
Arda Mòra   Abhainn Suidhe   799   559   449
Soay Beag   Cliasmol   **HARRIS AND**
Soay Mòr   Miabhag   Bun Abhainn   CEANN A TUATH NA
13   Eadarra   HEARADH
OLD WHALING STATION   Aird Asaig   3   RHENIGIDALE
NORTH UIST   436   Isay   'Lochan   Reinigeadal
BEN LUSKENTYRE   Lacasdail   Loch Trollamarig
Tarasaigh   Losgaintir   A859   Urgha
(Taransay)   467   Tàirbeart   Carragraich
South Harris   **(Tarbert)**   Caolas Scalpaigh   Carnach
Caolas Tharasaigh   Forest   Loch Ceann   Sgeotasaigh   Rubha Crago
LUSKENTYRE   Dibig   Miabhag   Scalpay   Scalpay
BEACH   A859   Drinisiadar   Loch an   **Eilean
Seilebost   23   Kennacley   Tairbeart   Scalpa
NA HEARADH   Greosabhagh   (Scalp
Borve Lodge   **(HARRIS)**   Aird Mhighe   Leac a Li   Plocropol Pt.
Buirgh   386   Plocrapol   Rubha
CHAIPAVAL   Sgarasta Mhor   Geocrab   Scadabhagh   Bhocaig
365   Liceasto   Cliuthar   Caolas Stocinis
Rubha'an Teampuill   398   Beacrabhaic
BLEAVAL   Manais   Stockinish I.
Taobh Tuath   Loch Langabhat   Fleoideabhagh
SEALLAM!   Aird   UIG
An t-Ob (Leverburgh)   Mhighe   Loch Fleoideabhagh
Ensay   459   Fionnsbhagh   Cuidhtinis
Carminish Is.   ROINEABHAL   Boirseam
Cairinis   Srannda   Lingreabhagh   Loch Fiannsbhagh
Killegray   Lingarabay I.
ST CLEMENT'S   Roghadal
Langay   CHURCH   Valley
Renish Pt.

Loch   Loch Langabhat   Loch   Siophoirt

C A O L A S   N A   H E A R A D H

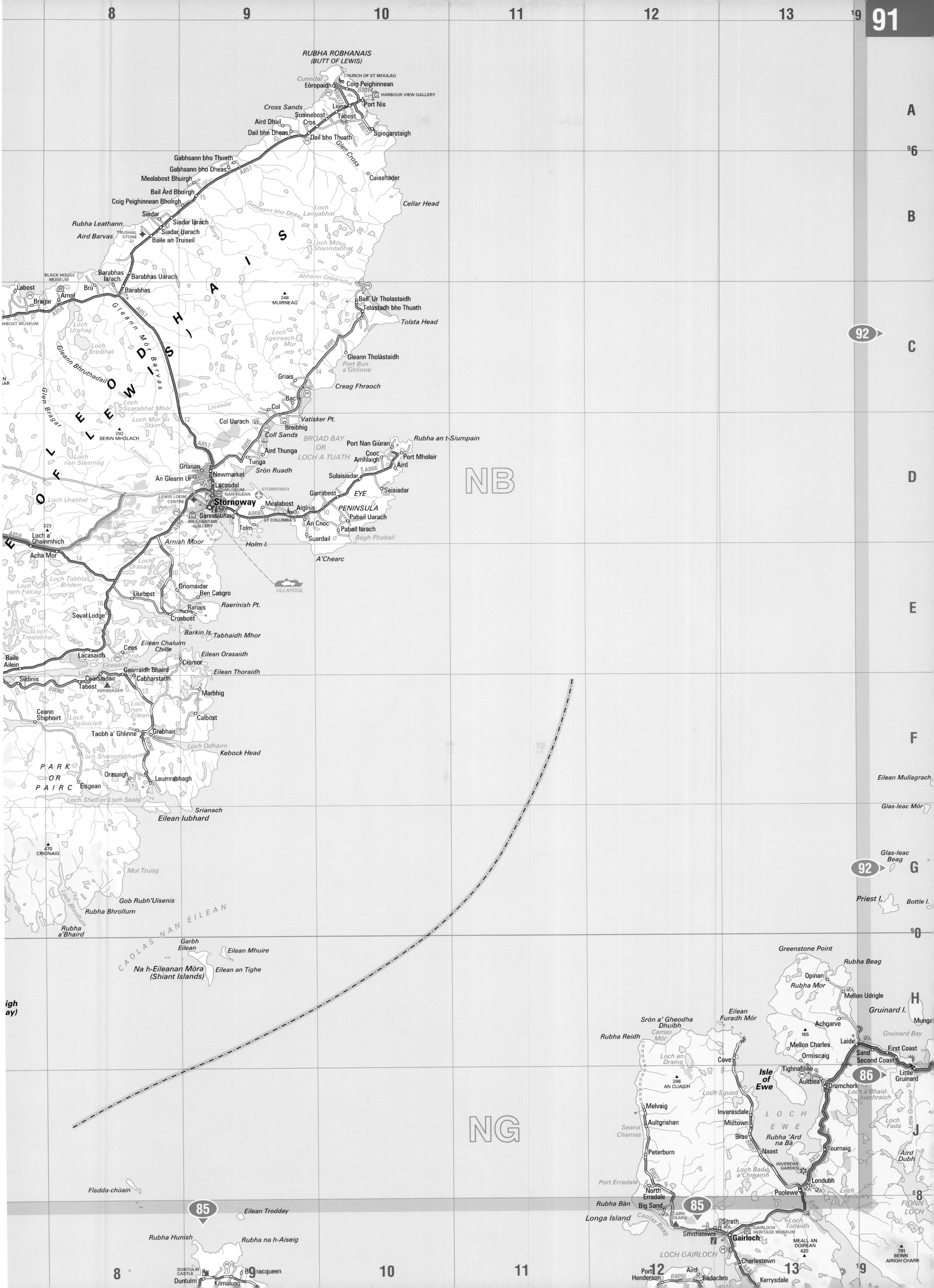

A
B
C
D
E
F
G
H
J

92
92
85
85
86

RUBHA ROBHANAIS
(BUTT OF LEWIS)

CHURCH OF ST MOULAG
Cunndal
Eòropaidh
Coig Peighinnean
B8014
HARBOUR VIEW GALLERY
Cross Sands
Suaineabost
Port Nis
Lional
Aird Dhail
Cros
Tàbost
Dail bho Dheas
Dail bho Thuath
Sgiogarstaigh

Gabhsann bho Thuath
Gabhsann bho Dheas
A857
Mealabost Bhuirgh
Bail Àrd Bhuirgh
Cuiashader
Coig Peighinnean Bhuirgh
Loch
Langabhat
Cellar Head
Siadar
Rubha Leathann
Siadar Ìarach
Siadar Uarach
Aird Barvas
TRUSHAL STONE
Baile an Truiseil

Loch Mòr
Shanndabhat
Barabhas
BLACK HOUSE MUSEUM
Barabhas Ìarach
Barabhas Uarach
Labost
Brù
Arnol
Bragar
Abhainn Ghearadha
Bail' Ur Tholastaidh
Tolastadh bho Thuath
248 MUIRNEAG
Tolsta Head
WBOST MUSEUM

A858
Loch
Urghag
Loch
Breibhat
Gleann Bhruthadail
Glen Bragar
Loch
Sgeireach
Mor
Gleann Mòr Barvas
Grais
Gleann Tholàstaidh
Port Bun
a'Ghlinne
Griais
Creag Fhraoch
Loch
Scarabhat Mhòr
292 BEINN MHOLACH
Loch Mòr an
Stàirr
Lacasdal
Col
Col Uarach
Vatisker Pt.
A857
Breibhig
Loch
nan Stearnag
Coll Sands
BROAD BAY
OR
LOCH A TUATH
Port Nan Giùran
Rubha an t-Siumpain
Grianan
An Gleann Ur
Newmarket
Aird Thunga
Cnoc
Amhlaigh
NB
Loch Urabhal
Lacasdal
LEWIS LOOM
CENTRE
MUSEUM
NAN EILEAN
Tunga
Srón Ruadh
Port Mholair
Aird
A866
223
Loch a'
Ghainmhich
STORNOWAY
Sulaisiadar
Seisiadar
Acha Mor
14
Sanndabhaig
Mealabost
Garrabost
EYE
Ghoil
AN LANNTAIR
GALLERY
St COLUMBA'S
Aiginis
PENINSULA
Arnish Moor
Tolm
Pabail Uarach
A866
Loch
Orasaigh
Holm I.
An Cnoc
Pabail Ìarach
Loch Tobhta
Bridein
Griomsidar
Suardail
Bàgh Phabail
Ben Casgro
A'Chearc
Loch
nam Falcag
Liurbost
Raerinish Pt.
ULLAPOOL
B8060
Ranais
Soval Lodge
Crosbost
Tabhaidh Mhor
Barkin Is.
Loch
Trealabhal
Lacasaidh
Ceos
Eilean Chaluim
Chille
Eilean Orasaidh
Baile
Ailein
Gearraidh Bhaird
Cromor
Eilean Thoraidh
Sildinis
Cearsiadar
Cabharstadh
B8060
Tabost
KERSHADER
Marbhig
13
Ceann
Shiphoirt
Loch
Sgibacleit
Calbost
Loch
Nan
Eilean
Taobh a' Ghlinne
Grabhair
Loch Odhairn
Kebock Head
PARK
OR
PAIRC
Leumrabhagh
Eisgean
Orasaigh
Loch Shanndabhat
Eilean Mullagrach
Loch Shell or Loch Seal
Srianach
Glas-leac Mór
Eilean Iubhard
470
CRIONAIG
Glas-leac
Beag
Mol Truisg
Loch Bronllum
Gob Rubh'Uisenis
Priest I.
Bottle I.
Rubha Bhrollum
Rubha
a'Bhaird
CAOLAS NAN EILEAN
Greenstone Point
Garbh
Eilean
Rubha Beag
Na h-Eileanan Mòra
(Shiant Islands)
Eilean Mhuire
Opinan
Rubha Mór
Eilean an Tighe
Mellon Udrigle
Sròn a' Gheodha
Dhuibh
Eilean
Furadh Mór
NG
Gruinard I.
igh
ay)
Rubha Reidh
Camas
Mór
Gruinard Bay
Achgarve
Munga
Loch an
Draing
155
Mellon Charles
Laide
First Coast
Cove
Ormiscaig
Sand
Second Coast
Isle of Ewe
86
296
AN CUAIDH
Tighnafiline
Little Guinard
Aultbea
Drumchork
Melvaig
Inverasdale
Aultgrishan
Midtown
LOCH
EWE
Rubha 'Ard
na Bà
Seana
Chamas
Brae
Tournaig
Naast
Peterburn
INVEREWE
GARDEN
Port Erradale
Londubh
NB
Rubha Bàn
North
Erradale
Big Sand
85
CAIRN DEARG
Poolewe
Fladda-chùain
Longa Island
Eilean Trodday
Rubha Hunish
Rubha na h-Aiseig
DUNTULM
CASTLE
Macqueen
Duntulm
Kilmaluag
Port
Henderson
Aird
Badachro
Kerrysdale
Smithstown
GAIRLOCH
HERITAGE MUSEUM
Gairloch
MEALL AN
DOIREAN
420
791
BEINN
AIRIGH CHARR
Charlestown
LOCH GAIRLOCH
Strath
Aird
Dubh
FIONN
LOCH
B8056
B8021

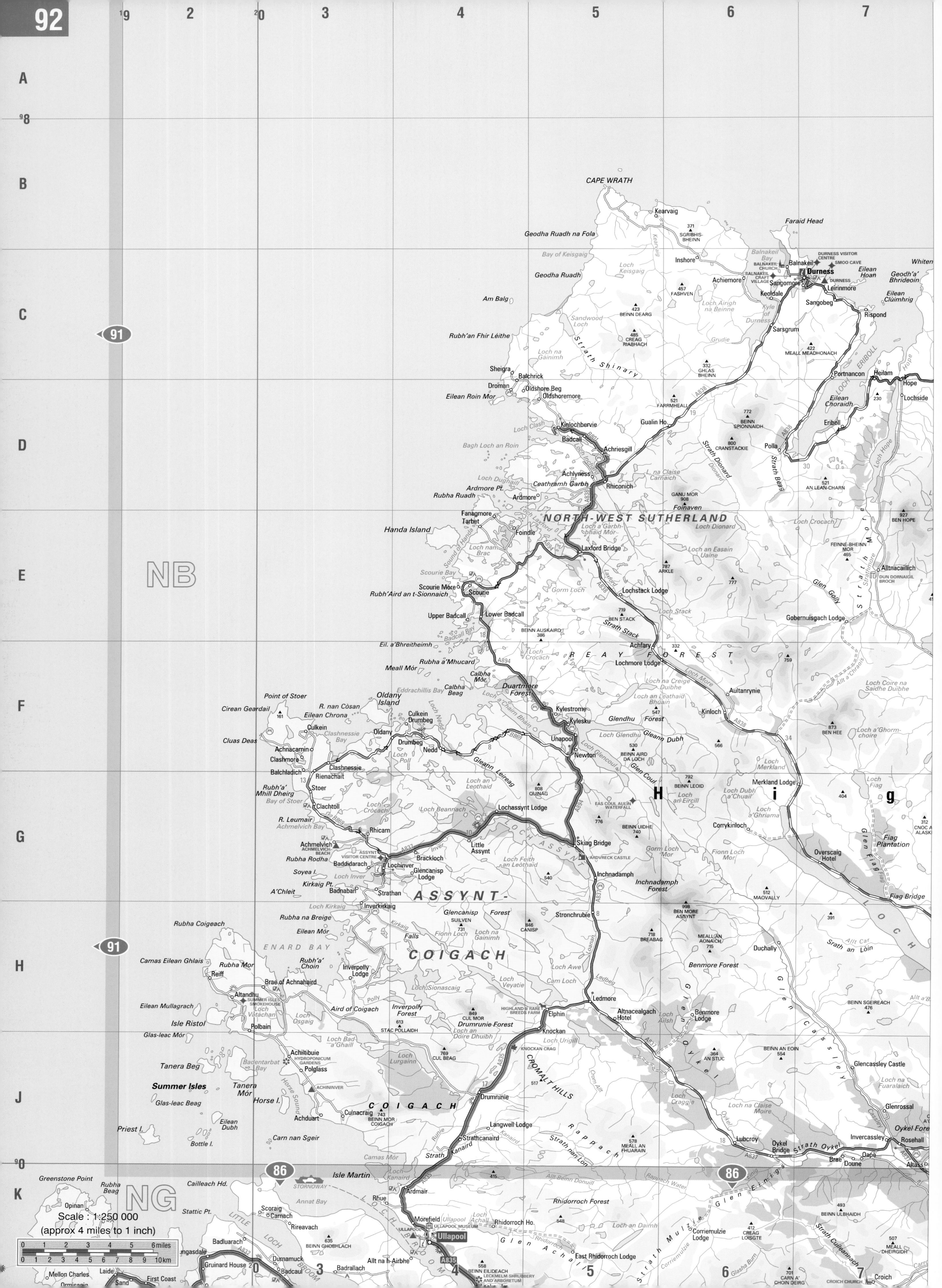
CAPE WRATH
Kearvaig
Faraid Head
Geodha Ruadh na Fola
Bay of Keisgaig
Inshore
Balnakeil
Durness
DURNESS VISITOR CENTRE
SMOO CAVE
Geodha Ruadh
Achiemore
Sangomore
Leirinmore
Keoldale
Sangobeg
Rispond
Eilean Hoan
Geodh'a' Bhrideoin
Eilean Clùimhrig
Am Balg
Sandwood Loch
Strath Shinary
Sarsgrum
Rubh'an Fhir Lèithe
Sheigra
Balchrick
Droman
Oldshore Beg
Oldshoremore
Eilean Roin Mor
Portnancon
Heilam
Hope
Lochside
Eilean Choraidh
LOCH ERIBOLL
Eriboll
Kinlochbervie
Badcall
Achriesgill
Gualin Ho.
Bagh Loch an Roin
Polla
Strath Dionard
Strath Beag
Achlyness
Ceathramh Garbh
Rhiconich
Ardmore Pt.
Rubha Ruadh
Ardmore
Foinaven
AN LEAN-CHARN
BEN HOPE
NORTH-WEST SUTHERLAND
Fanagmore
Tarbet
Handa Island
Foindle
Loch Dionard
Laxford Bridge
Scourie Bay
Scourie More
Scourie
Rubh'Aird an t-Sionnaich
ARKLE
Lochstack Lodge
Alltnacaillich
Glen Golly
Upper Badcall
Lower Badcall
BEN STACK
Strath Stack
Gobernuisgach Lodge
Eil. a'Bhreitheimh
Achfary
REAY FOREST
Rubha a'Mhucard
Lochmore Lodge
Meall Mór
Calbha Mór
Calbha Beag
Eddrachillis Bay
Duartmore Forest
Point of Stoer
Oldany Island
Aultanrynie
Cirean Geardail
R. nan Còsan
Eilean Chrona
Kylestrome
Kylesku
Kinloch
BEN HEE
Culkein
Culkein Drumbeg
Oldany
Glendhu Forest
Cluas Deas
Achnacarnin
Drumbeg
Nedd
Unapool
Clashmore
Clashnessie
Newton
Balchladich
Rienachait
Gleann Leireag
Stoer
QUINAG
BEINN LEOID
Merkland Lodge
Rubh'a' Mhill Dheirg
Bay of Stoer
Clachtoll
Lochassynt Lodge
EAS COUL AULIN WATERFALL
Corrykinloch
R. Leumair
Achmelvich Bay
Rhicarn
LOCH ASSYNT
Flag Plantation
Achmelvich
Little Assynt
Skiag Bridge
Overscaig Hotel
Rubha Rodha
ASSYNT VISITOR CENTRE
Brackloch
ARDVRECK CASTLE
Baddidarach
Soyea I.
Lochinver
Glencanisp Lodge
Inchnadamph
Kirkaig Pt.
Badnaban
A'Chleit
Strathan
Inchnadamph Forest
ASSYNT-
Inverkirkaig
BEN MORE ASSYNT
MAOVALLY
Fiag Bridge
Rubha Coigeach
Rubha na Breige
Glencanisp Forest
SUILVEN
Stronchrubie
Eilean Mór
Fionn Loch
CANISP
BREABAG
ENARD BAY
Falls
COIGACH
Duchally
Camas Eilean Ghlais
Rubha Mor
Rubh'a' Choin
Inverpolly Lodge
Benmore Forest
Reiff
Brae of Achnahaird
Loch Veyatie
Altandhu
SUMMER ISLES SMOKEHOUSE
Loch Sionascaig
Cam Loch
Ledmore
Eilean Mullagrach
Aird of Coigach
Inverpolly Forest
Altnacealgach Hotel
Benmore Lodge
Isle Ristol
CUL MOR
Drumrunie Forest
HIGHLAND & RARE BREEDS FARM
Elphin
Polbain
STAC POLLAIDH
Knockan
Glas-leac Mór
KNOCKAN CRAG
Achiltibuie
HYDROPONICUM GARDENS
CUL BEAG
AN STUC
BEINN AN EOIN
Tanera Beg
Badentarbat Bay
Loch Lurgainn
CROMALT HILLS
Glencassley Castle
Polglass
Summer Isles
Tanera Mór
ACHININVER
Horse I.
Drumrunie
Glas-leac Beag
COIGACH
BEINN MOR COIGACH
Culnacraig
Glenrossal
Achduart
Eilean Dubh
Langwell Lodge
Oykel Forest
Priest I.
Carn nan Sgeir
Strathcanaird
Strath Kanaird
MEALL AN FHUARAIN
Lubcroy
Oykel Bridge
Strath Oykel
Invercassley
Rosehall
Bottle I.
Camas Mór
Strath nan Lon
Brae
Doune
Altass
Greenstone Point
Cailleach Hd.
Isle Martin
STORNOWAY
Rappach Water
Glen Einig
Rubha Beag
Ardmair
Rhue
Rhidorroch Forest
Opinan
Scale : 1:250 000
(approx 4 miles to 1 inch)
Static Pt.
Scoraig
Carnach
Annat Bay
Morefield
ULLAPOOL MUSEUM
Rhidorroch Ho.
Loch an Daimh
Strath Mulzie
Corriemulzie Lodge
CREAG LOISGTE
Strath Cuileannach
Rireavach
BEINN GHOBHLACH
Ullapool
Glen Achall
Badluarach
LITTLE LOCH BROOM
Dundonnell
Allt na h-Airbhe
East Rhidorroch Lodge
BEINN EILIDEACH
LECKMELM SHRUBBERY AND ARBORETUM
Gruinard House
Badcaul
Badrallach
Mellon Charles
Laide
Sand
First Coast
CARN A' CHOIN DEIRG
CROICH CHURCH
Croich
NB
NG
91
86

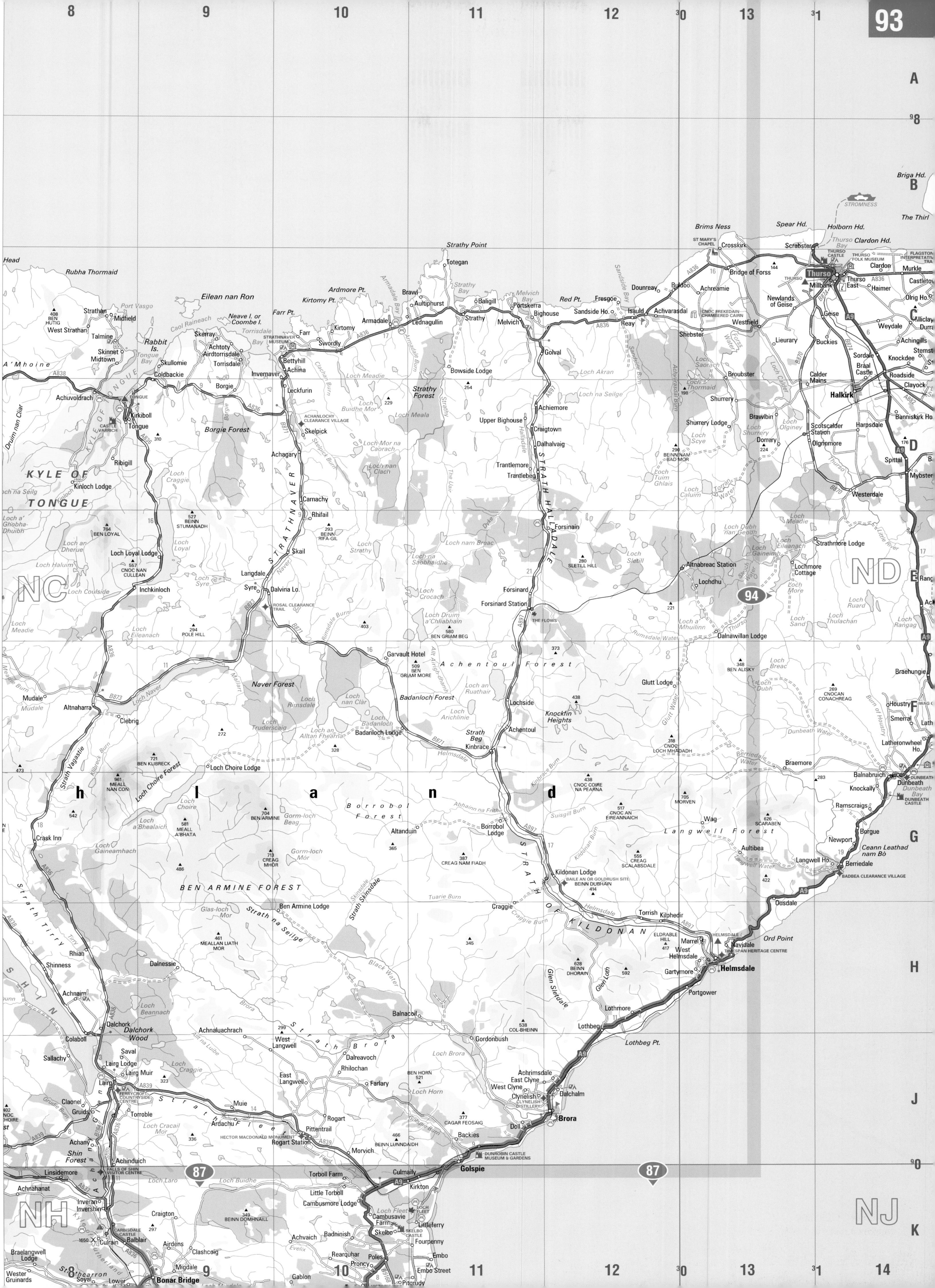

8
9
10
11
12
13
14
A
B
C
D
E
F
G
H
J
K
NC
ND
NH
NJ
94
87
KYLE OF TONGUE
Highland
Briga Hd.
STROMNESS
The Thirl
Brims Ness
Spear Hd.
Holborn Hd.
Thurso Bay
Clardon Hd.
Strathy Point
Head
Rubha Thormaid
Eilean nan Ron
Ardmore Pt.
Kirtomy Pt.
Farr Pt.
Neave I. or Coombe I.
Rabbit Is.
Port Vasgo
Caol Raineach
Torrisdale Bay
Tongue Bay
Armadale Bay
Strathy Bay
Melvich Bay
Red Pt.
Sandside Bay
A'Mhoine
Strathan
Midfield
West Strathan
Talmine
Skinnet
Midtown
Skerray
Achtoty
Airdtorrisdale
Torrisdale
Skullomie
Coldbackie
Borgie
Invernaver
Bettyhill
Achina
STRATHNAVER MUSEUM
Farr
Swordly
Kirtomy
Armadale
Lednagullin
Brawl
Aultiphurst
Totegan
Strathy
Baligill
Portskerra
Melvich
Bighouse
Golval
Fresgoe
Sandside Ho.
Dounreay
Isauld
Reay
Achvarasdal
Buldoo
Achreamie
Crosskirk
ST MARY'S CHAPEL
Bridge of Forss
Shebster
Westfield
Scrabster
THURSO CASTLE
THURSO FOLK MUSEUM
Thurso
Thurso East
Millbank
Newlands of Geise
Geise
Lieurary
Buckies
Clardon
Haimer
Murkle
Castletown
Olrig Ho.
Weydale
Achingills
Sordale
Braal Castle
Knockdee
Calder Mains
Halkirk
Roadside
Clayock
Bannisk irk Ho.
Harpsdale
Scotscalder Station
Olgrinmore
Spittal
Mybster
Westerdale
Strathmore Lodge
Lochmore Cottage
Altnabreac Station
Lochdhu
Dalnawillan Lodge
Glutt Lodge
Braehungie
Houstry
Smerral
Latheronwheel Ho.
Braemore
Balnabruich
Dunbeath
DUNBEATH CASTLE
Knockally
Ramscraigs
Newport
Borgue
Ceann Leathad nam Bò
Langwell Ho.
Berriedale
BADBEA CLEARANCE VILLAGE
Ousdale
Ord Point
Navidale
TIMESPAN HERITAGE CENTRE
Helmsdale
West Helmsdale
Marrel
Gartymore
Portgower
Lothmore
Lothbeg
Lothbeg Pt.
Kilphedir
Torrish
Kildonan Lodge
BAILE AN OR GOLDRUSH SITE
Craggie
STRATH OF KILDONAN
Achiemore
Upper Bighouse
Craigtown
Dalhalvaig
Trantlemore
Trantlebeg
STRATH HALLADALE
Forsinain
Forsinard
Forsinard Station
THE FLOWS
Lochside
Achentoul
Achentoul Forest
Knockfin Heights
Kinbrace
Strath Beg
Borrobol Lodge
Borrobol Forest
Altanduin
Langwell Forest
Wag
MORVEN
Garvault Hotel
Badanloch Forest
Badanloch Lodge
Bowside Lodge
Strathy Forest
Achanlochy Clearance Village
Skelpick
Achagary
Carnachy
Rhifail
Skail
STRATHNAVER
Langdale
Syre
Dalvina Lo.
ROSAL CLEARANCE TRAIL
Naver Forest
Achuvoldrach
Tongue
Kirkiboll
CASTLE VARRICH
Ribigill
Kinloch Lodge
Borgie Forest
Loch Loyal Lodge
Inchkinloch
Mudale
Altnaharra
Clebrig
Loch Choire Lodge
Loch Choire Forest
Crask Inn
Strath Vagastie
BEN ARMINE FOREST
Ben Armine Lodge
Strath na Seilge
Strath Skinsdale
Dalnessie
Rhian
Shinness
Achnairn
Dalchork
Dalchork Wood
Colaboll
Sallachy
Lairg Lodge
Lairg Muir
Lairg
FERRYCROFT COUNTRYSIDE CENTRE
Saval
Achnaluachrach
West Langwell
Balnacoil
Strath Brora
Dalreavoch
Rhilochan
East Langwell
Farlary
Gordonbush
Loch Brora
Achrimsdale
East Clyne
West Clyne
Clynelish
CLYNELISH DISTILLERY
Dalchalm
Brora
Doll
Backies
DUNROBIN CASTLE MUSEUM & GARDENS
Golspie
Muie
Strath Fleet
Ardachu
Rogart
Pittentrail
Rogart Station
HECTOR MACDONALD MONUMENT
Morvich
Torroble
Claonel
Gruids
Achany
Shin Forest
Achinduich
Linsidemore
FALLS OF SHIN VISITOR CENTRE
Achnahanat
Inveran
Invershin
CARBISDALE CASTLE
Culrain
Balblair
Craigton
Airdens
Clashcoig
Braelangwell Lodge
Wester Gruinards
Soyal
Lower
Migdale
Bonar Bridge
Torboll Farm
Little Torboll
Cambusmore Lodge
Culmaily
Kirkton
Loch Fleet
Cambusavie Farm
Skelbo
SKELBO CASTLE
Littleferry
Fourpenny
Badninish
Achvaich
Rearquhar
Embo
Embo Street
Poles
Proncy
Gablon
Pitgrudy
764 BEN LOYAL
408 BEN HUTIG
557 CNOC NAN CULLEAN
527 BEINN STUMANADH
293 BEINN RIFA-GIL
294 POLE HILL
721 BEN KLIBRECK
961 MEALL NAN CON
704 BEN ARMINE
581 MEALL A'BHATA
713 CREAG MHOR
461 MEALLAN LIATH MOR
509 BEN GRIAM MORE
580 BEN GRIAM BEG
280 SLETILL HILL
387 CREAG NAM FIADH
414 BEINN DUBHAIN
438 CNOC COIRE NA FEARNA
517 CNOC AN EIREANNAICH
318 CNOC LOCH MHADADH
348 BEN ALISKY
269 CNOCAN CONACHREAG
626 SCARABEN
555 CREAG SCALABSDALE
417 ELDRABLE HILL
628 BEINN DHORAIN
538 COL-BHEINN
521 BEN HORN
377 CAGAR FEOSAIG
466 BEINN LUNNDAIDH
349 BEINN DOMHNAILL
290 BEINN NAM BAD MOR
CNOC FREKEDAIN CHAMBERED CAIRN
A836
A838
A897
A9
A882
B871
B873
B874
B870
A839

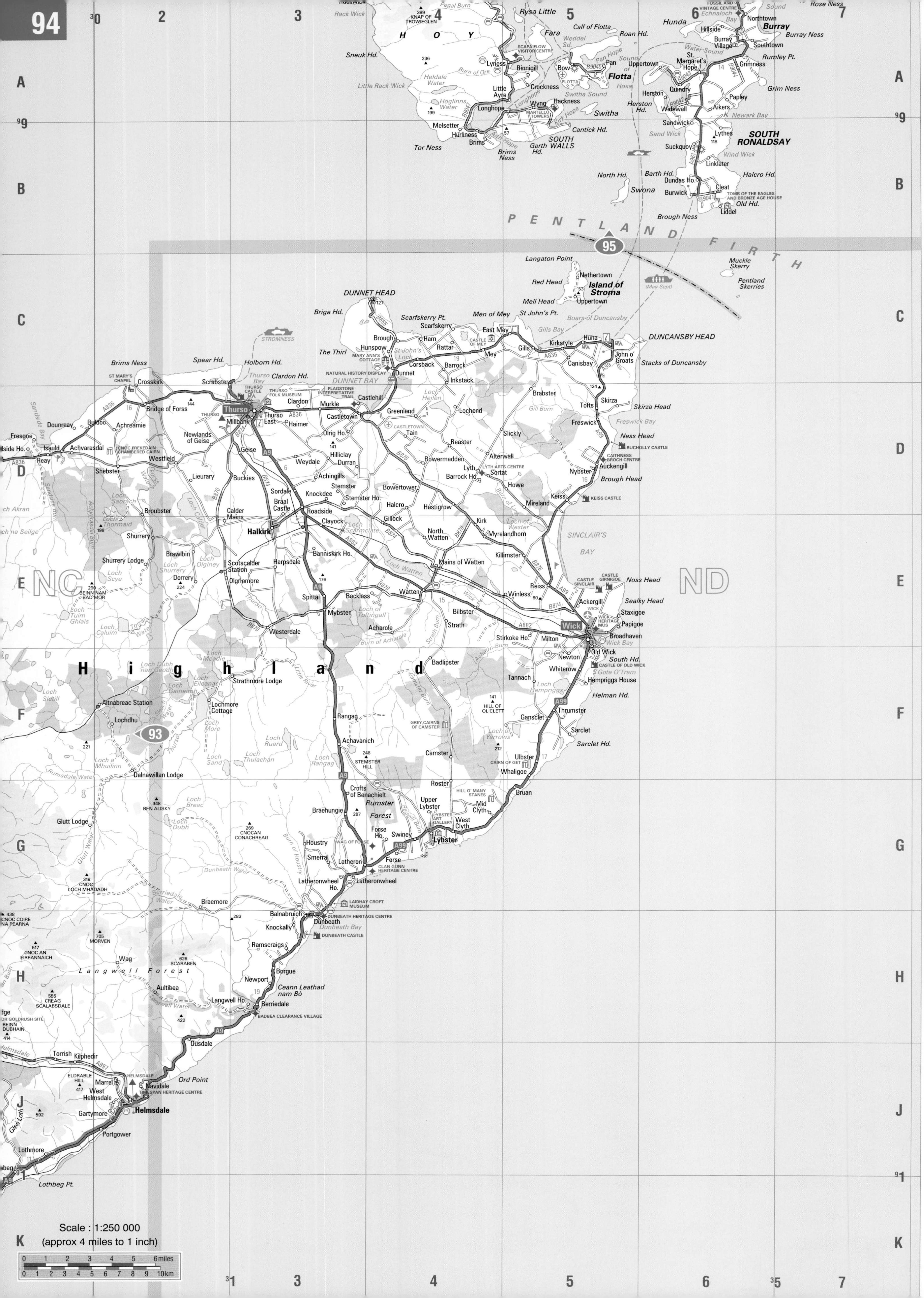
HOY
Rysa Little
Fara
Calf of Flotta
Roan Hd.
Hunda
Burray
Burray Ness
Northtown
Southtown
Rose Ness
Rack Wick
Pegal Burn
KNAP OF TROWIEGLEN
Sneuk Hd.
SCAPA FLOW VISITOR CENTRE
Lyness
Rinnigill
Bow
Pan
Flotta
Uppertown
St. Margaret's Hope
Grimness
Rumley Pt.
Heldale Water
Burn of Ore
Little Rack Wick
Little Ayre
Crockness
Swithа Sound
Hoxa
Herston
Quindry
Papley
Grim Ness
Hoglinns Water
Longhope
Wyng
Hackness
Herston Hd.
Widewall
Aikers
MARTELLO TOWERS
Switha
Melsetter
Hurliness
Brims
Cantick Hd.
Sandwick
Newark Bay
Sand Wick
Lythes
SOUTH RONALDSAY
Tor Ness
Brims Ness
SOUTH WALLS
Garth Hd.
Suckquoy
Wind Wick
Linklater
North Hd.
Barth Hd.
Halcro Hd.
Swona
Dundas Ho.
Burwick
Cleat
TOMB OF THE EAGLES AND BRONZE AGE HOUSE
Old Hd.
Liddel
Brough Ness
PENTLAND FIRTH
95
Langaton Point
Nethertown
Red Head
Island of Stroma
Mell Head
Uppertown
Muckle Skerry
Pentland Skerries
(May-Sept)
DUNNET HEAD
Briga Hd.
Scarfskerry Pt.
Men of Mey
St John's Pt.
Boars of Duncansby
Scarfskerry
East Mey
Gills Bay
Huna
DUNCANSBY HEAD
Brough
Ham
Rattar
CASTLE OF MEY
Mey
Gills
Kirkstyle
John o' Groats
STROMNESS
The Thirl
Hunspow
St John's Loch
MARY ANN'S COTTAGE
Corsback
Barrock
Canisbay
Stacks of Duncansby
Brims Ness
Spear Hd.
Holborn Hd.
Thurso Bay
Clardon Hd.
NATURAL HISTORY DISPLAY
Dunnet
Dunnet Bay
Inkstack
ST MARY'S CHAPEL
Crosskirk
Scrabster
THURSO CASTLE
THURSO FOLK MUSEUM
FLAGSTONE INTERPRETATIVE TRAIL
Castlehill
Brabster
Tofts
Skirza
Skirza Head
Bridge of Forss
Thurso
Clardon
Murkle
Castletown
Greenland
Loch Heilen
Lochend
Gill Burn
Freswick
Freswick Bay
Dounreay
Buldoo
Achreamie
Thurso East
Haimer
Millbank
Newlands of Geise
Olrig Ho.
CASTLETOWN
Tain
Slickly
Ness Head
BUCHOLLY CASTLE
Fresgoe
Isauld
Achvarasdal
CNOC FREKEDAIN CHAMBERED CAIRN
Geise
Hilliclay
Durran
Reaster
Alterwall
CAITHNESS BROCH CENTRE
Reay
Westfield
Weydale
Bowermadden
Lyth
LYTH ARTS CENTRE
Sortat
Barrock Ho.
Nybster
Auckengill
Brough Head
Shebster
Lieurary
Buckies
Achingills
Stemster
Bowertower
Howe
Keiss
KEISS CASTLE
Loch Saorach
Broubster
Loch Calder
Sordale
Knockdee
Stemster Ho.
Mireland
Calder Mains
Braal Castle
Roadside
Halcro
Hastigrow
Loch Thormaid
Clayock
Gillock
Kirk
Loch of Wester
Halkirk
Loch Scarmclate
North Watten
Myrelandhorn
SINCLAIR'S BAY
Shurrery
Brawlbin
Loch Olginey
Scotscalder Station
Harpsdale
Banniskirk Ho.
Killimster
Shurrery Lodge
Loch Shurrery
Loch Scye
Dorrery
Olgrinmore
Loch Watten
Mains of Watten
CASTLE SINCLAIR
CASTLE GIRNIGOE
Noss Head
NC
ND
BEINN NAM BAD MOR
Spittal
Backlass
Watten
Winless
Reiss
Ackergill
Sealky Head
Loch Tuim Ghlais
Mybster
Loch of Toftingall
Bilbster
Staxigoe
Papigoe
Loch Caluim
Westerdale
Acharole
Strath
Stirkoke Ho.
Milton
Wick
WICK HERITAGE MUS
Broadhaven
Wick Bay
Newton
Old Wick
South Hd.
CASTLE OF OLD WICK
Gote O'Tram
Loch Meadie
Loch Dubh nan Geodh
Highland
Little River
Badlipster
Whiterow
Hempriggs House
Tannach
Loch Hempriggs
Loch Eileanach
Strathmore Lodge
Loch Sietill
Loch Gaineimh
Altnabreac Station
Lochmore Cottage
HILL OF OLICLETT
Helman Hd.
Lochdhu
93
Rangag
GREY CAIRNS OF CAMSTER
Gansclet
Thrumster
Loch More
Loch Ruard
Achavanich
Loch of Yarrows
Sarclet
Sarclet Hd.
Loch a' Mhuilinn
Loch Thulachan
Loch Sand
Loch Rangag
STEMSTER HILL
Camster
CAIRN OF GET
Ulbster
Whaligoe
Rumsdale Water
Dalnawillan Lodge
Roster
Crofts of Benachielt
HILL O' MANY STANES
Bruan
BEN ALISKY
Loch Breac
Rumster Forest
Upper Lybster
Mid Clyth
Glutt Lodge
Loch Dubh
Braehungie
LYBSTER ART GALLERY
West Clyth
CNOCAN CONACHREAG
Forse Ho.
Swiney
Lybster
Glutt Water
Burn of Houstry
Houstry
WAG OF FORSE
Smerral
Latheron
Forse
CLAN GUNN HERITAGE CENTRE
Dunbeath Water
CNOC LOCH MHADAIDH
Latheronwheel Ho.
Latheronwheel
LAIDHAY CROFT MUSEUM
Berriedale Water
Braemore
Balnabruich
DUNBEATH HERITAGE CENTRE
Dunbeath
CNOC COIRE NA PEARNA
Knockally
Dunbeath Bay
DUNBEATH CASTLE
MORVEN
Ramscraigs
CNOC AN EIREANNAICH
Wag
SCARABEN
Langwell Forest
Borgue
Newport
Ceann Leathad nam Bò
CREAG SCALABSDALE
Aultibea
Langwell Water
Langwell Ho.
Berriedale
BADBEA CLEARANCE VILLAGE
BEINN DUBHAIN
Ousdale
Torrish
Kilphedir
EALDRABLE HILL
HELMSDALE
Navidale
TIMESPAN HERITAGE CENTRE
Ord Point
West Helmsdale
Marrel
Helmsdale
Gartymore
Glen Loth
Portgower
Lothmore
Lothbeg Pt.
A9
A99
A836
A882
B870
B874
B876
B855
A961
B9044
B9045
B9043
B9041

Scale : 1:250 000
(approx 4 miles to 1 inch)

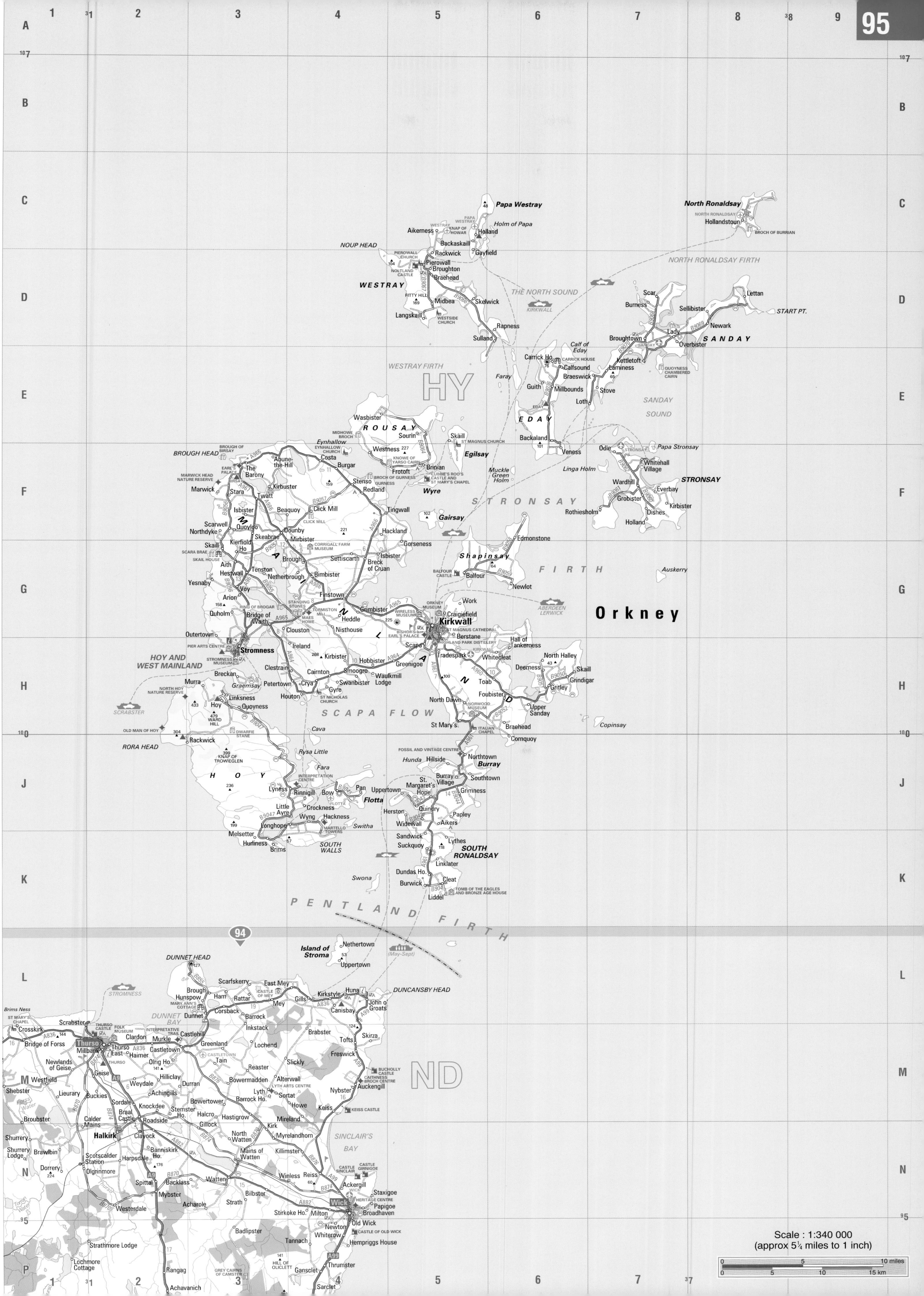
Orkney
HY
ND
Papa Westray
North Ronaldsay
Hollandstoun
Holm of Papa
Aikerness
Holland
Backaskaill
Rackwick
Gayfield
NOUP HEAD
Pierowall
Broughton
Braehead
WESTRAY
Midbea
Skelwick
Langskaill
Rapness
Sulland
THE NORTH SOUND
NORTH RONALDSAY FIRTH
Scar
Burness
Lettan
START PT.
Sellibister
Newark
Lady
Broughtown
Overbister
SANDAY
Calf of Eday
Carrick Ho.
Calfsound
Kettletoft
Lamness
Braeswick
Stove
Guith
Millbounds
Loth
WESTRAY FIRTH
Faray
EDAY
SANDAY SOUND
Backaland
Veness
Papa Stronsay
Whitehall Village
STRONSAY
Wardhill
Everbay
Grobister
Kirbister
Dishes
Rothiesholm
Holland
Wasbister
ROUSAY
Sourin
Westness
Skaill
Egilsay
Eynhallow
Costa
Burgar
BROUGH HEAD
Abune-the-Hill
The Barony
Twatt
Frotoft
Brinian
Wyre
Stenso
Redland
Marwick
Stara
Kirbuster
Muckle Green Holm
Linga Holm
STRONSAY
Isbister
Beaquoy
Click Mill
Tingwall
Gairsay
Scarwell
Northdyke
Quoyloo
Dounby
Hackland
Skaill
Kierfiold Ho
Skeabrae
Mirbister
Gorseness
Edmonstone
Brough
Settiscarth
Isbister
Shapinsay
Aith
Tenston
Netherbrough
Breck of Cruan
FIRTH
Auskerry
Hestwall
Bimbister
Balfour
Yesnaby
Voy
Newlot
Arion
Finstown
Work
Quholm
Bridge of Waith
Grimbister
Craigiefield
Kirkwall
Heddle
ABERDEEN LERWICK
Clouston
Nisthouse
Berstane
Outertown
Hall of Tankerness
Stromness
Ireland
Scapa
Kirbister
HOY AND WEST MAINLAND
Tradespark
Whitecleat
North Halley
Skaill
Hobbister
Greenigoe
Deerness
Grindigar
Clestrain
Cairnton
Smoogro
Waulkmill Lodge
Toab
Breckan
Graemsay
Murra
Petertown
Crya
Swanbister
Gyre
Gritley
Foubister
Houton
Linksness
Hoy
Quoyness
North Dawn
SCAPA FLOW
Upper Sanday
SCRABSTER
Ward Hill
St Mary's
Braehead
Copinsay
Cava
Cornquoy
OLD MAN OF HOY
RORA HEAD
Rackwick
Rysa Little
Northtown
Hunda
Hillside
Burray
Fara
HOY
Southtown
Burray Village
Pan
Uppertown
St. Margaret's Hope
Lyness
Rinnigill
Bow
Flotta
Grimness
Little Ayre
Crockness
Herston
Quinery
Papley
Wyng
Hackness
Widewall
Aikers
Longhope
Switha
Melsetter
Sandwick
Lythes
Hurliness
Suckquoy
SOUTH RONALDSAY
Brims
SOUTH WALLS
Linklater
Swona
Dundas Ho.
Cleat
Burwick
Liddel
PENTLAND FIRTH
94
Nethertown
Island of Stroma
Uppertown
DUNNET HEAD
Scarfskerry
East Mey
DUNCANSBY HEAD
STROMNESS
Brough
Ham
Kirkstyle
Huna
Hunspow
Rattar
Mey
Gills
John o' Groats
Brims Ness
Dunnet
Corsback
Canisbay
Scrabster
DUNNET BAY
Barrock
Crosskirk
Castlehill
Inkstack
Brabster
Tofts
Skirza
Thurso
Clardon
Murkle
Greenland
Bridge of Forss
Millbank
Hamer
Castletown
Lochend
Freswick
Thurso East
Newlands of Geise
Tain
Olrig Ho
Reaster
Slickly
Geise
Hillclay
Westfield
Weydale
Durran
Bowermadden
Alterwall
Nybster
Auckengill
Shebster
Lieurary
Buckies
Achingills
Lyth
Sortat
Sordale
Barrock Ho.
Knockdee
Bowertower
Howe
Keiss
Broubster
Calder Mains
Braal Castle
Roadside
Stemster Ho.
Halcro
Hastigrow
Mireland
Gillock
Halkirk
Kirk
Shurrery
Clayock
North Watten
Myrelandhorn
SINCLAIR'S BAY
Shurrery Lodge
Brawlbin
Scotscalder Station
Banniskirk Ho.
Mains of Watten
Killimster
Harpsdale
Dorrery
Olgrinmore
Backlass
Watten
Winless
Reiss
Ackergill
Spittal
Staxigoe
Mybster
Bilbster
Wick
Papigoe
Acharole
Strath
Westerdale
Stirkoke Ho.
Milton
Broadhaven
Old Wick
Newton
Badlipster
Whiterow
Strathmore Lodge
Tannach
Hempriggs House
Lochmore Cottage
Thrumster
Rangag
Gansclet
Achavanich
Sarclet
Scale : 1:340 000
(approx 5¼ miles to 1 inch)
0 5 10 miles
0 5 10 15 km

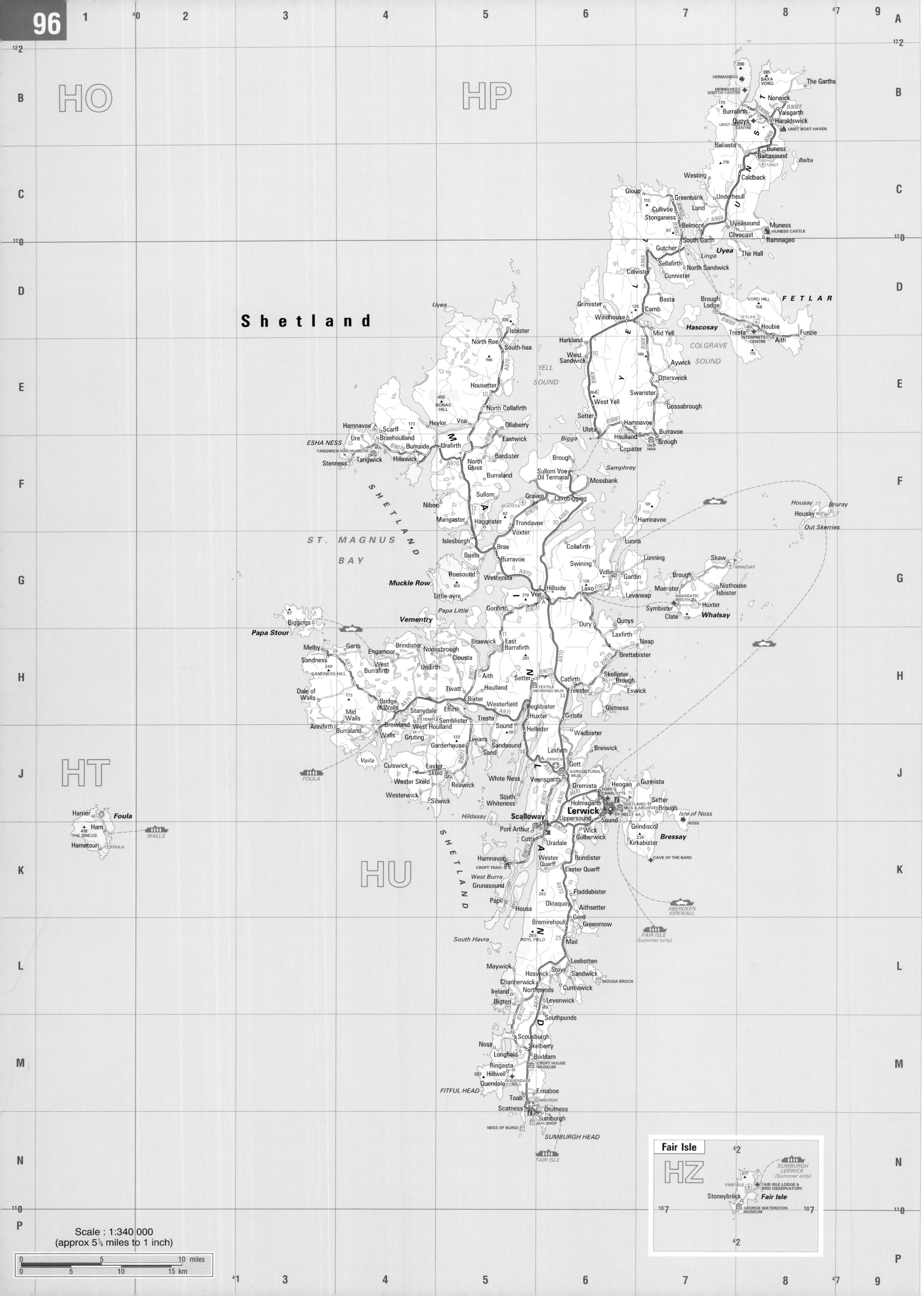
Shetland
HO
HP
HT
HU
HZ
Fair Isle
Scale : 1:340 000
(approx 5¼ miles to 1 inch)
0 5 10 miles
0 5 10 15 km
Hermaness
Hermaness Visitor Centre
Saxa Vord
The Garths
Norwick
Valsgarth
Burrafirth
Haroldswick
Quoys
Unst Heritage Centre
Unst Boat Haven
Baliasta
Buness
Baltasound
Balta
Unst
Westing
Caldback
Gloup
Greenbank
Underhoull
Cullivoe
Lund
Stonganess
Belmont
Uyeasound
Muness
Muness Castle
Clivocast
Ramnageo
South Garth
Gutcher
Uyea
Linga
The Hall
Sellafirth
North Sandwick
Colvister
Cunnister
Basta
Brough Lodge
Vord Hill
Fetlar
Grimister
Windhouse
Camb
Mid Yell
Hascosay
Houbie
Funzie
Tresta
Aith
Interpretative Centre
Harkland
West Sandwick
Colgrave Sound
Aywick
Yell Sound
Otterswick
Yell
Swarister
West Yell
Gossabrough
Setter
Hamnavoe
Ulsta
Burravoe
Houlland
Brough
Old Haa
Copister
Bigga
Samphrey
Uyea
Isbister
North Roe
South-haa
Housetter
Ronas Hill
North Collafirth
Heylor
Voe
Ollaberry
Hamnavoe
Scarff
Eastwick
Esha Ness
Ure
Braehoulland
Burnside
Urafirth
Tangwick Haa Museum
Tangwick
Hillswick
Stenness
Bardister
North Gluss
Burraland
Brough
Sullom Voe Oil Terminal
Mossbank
Sullom
Graven
Laxobigging
Scatsta
Nibon
Mangaster
Haggrister
Trondavoe
Voxter
Hamnavoe
Housay
Bruray
Out Skerries
Shetland
St. Magnus Bay
Islesburgh
Brae
Lunna
Busta
Burravoe
Collafirth
Lunning
Skaw
Whalsay
Swining
Vidlin
Gardin
Brough
Roesound
Wethersta
Muckle Row
Hillside
Laxo
Levaneap
Marrister
Nisthouse
Isbister
Little-ayre
Voe
Symbister
Hanseatic Booth
Huxter
Clate
Whalsay
Papa Little
Gonfirth
Vementry
Dury
Quoys
Biggings
Papa Stour
Laxfirth
Neap
Melby
Garth
Brindister
Noonsbrough
Braewick
East Burrafirth
Brettabister
Sandness
Engamoor
Clousta
West Burrafirth
Unifirth
Aith
Setter
Catfirth
Skellister
Brough
Sandness Hill
Textile Working Mus
Freester
Eswick
Twatt
Houlland
Dale of Walls
Bixter
Westerfield
Bridge of Walls
Stanydale
Effirth
Tresta
Girlsta
Gletness
Mid Walls
Temple
Semblister
Weisdale
Huxter
Annifirth
Burraland
Browland
West Houlland
Sound
Hellister
Wadbister
Walls
Gruting
Garderhouse
Leeans
Sandsound
Breiwick
Sand
Laxfirth
Vaila
Culswick
Easter Skeld
Gott
Foula
Wester Skeld
Reawick
White Ness
Veensgarth
Agricultural Mus
Gremista
Heogan
Gunnista
Westerwick
Silwick
South Whiteness
Fort Charlotte
Holmsgarth
Setter
Brough
Harrier
Foula
Lerwick
Shetland Mus & Archives
Up Helly Aa
Isle of Noss
Noss
Hildasay
Scalloway
Uppersound
Sound
Ham
The Sneug
Hametoun
Walls
Port Arthur
Cutts
Wick
Gulberwick
Grindiscol
Bressay
Kirkabister
Uradale
Hamnavoe
Wester Quarff
Brindister
Cave of the Bard
Croft Trail
West Burra
Easter Quarff
Grunasound
Fladdabister
Papil
Houss
Okraquoy
Aithsetter
Aberdeen Kirkwall
Bremirehoull
Gord
Greenmow
Royl Field
Mail
Fair Isle (Summer only)
South Havra
Leebotten
Maywick
Hoswick
Stove
Sandwick
Channerwick
Ireland
Northpunds
Cumliewick
Mousa Broch
Bigton
Levenwick
Southpunds
Scousburgh
Noss
Skelberry
Longfield
Boddam
Croft House Museum
Ringasta
Hillwell
Quendale
Quendale Mill
Fitful Head
Exnaboe
Toab
Sumburgh
Scatness
Grutness
Sumburgh
Jarlshof
Ness of Burgi
Sumburgh Head
Fair Isle
Sumburgh Lerwick (Summer only)
Fair Isle Lodge & Bird Observatory
Stoneybreck
Fair Isle
George Waterston Museum

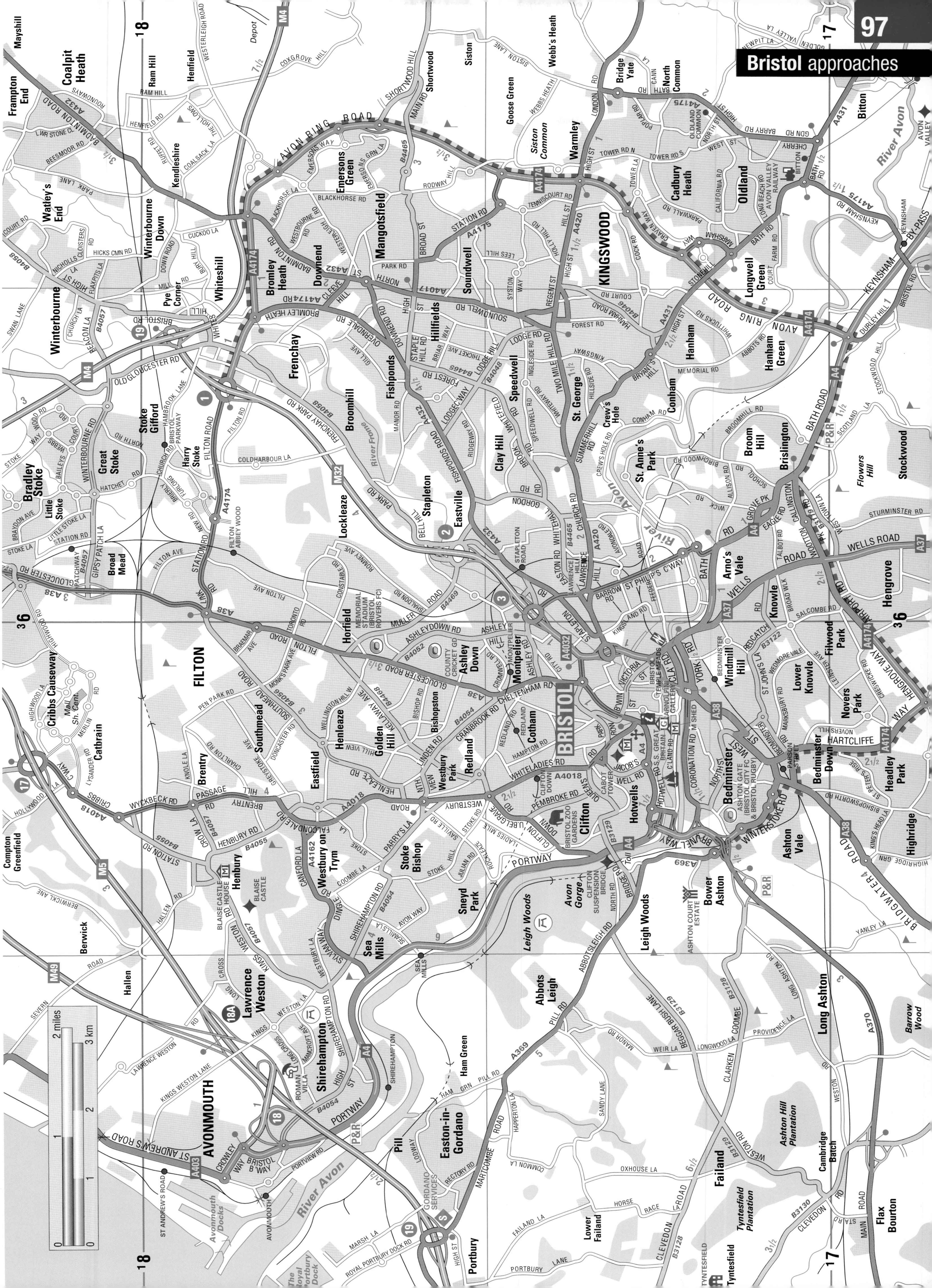
BRISTOL
AVONMOUTH
FILTON
KINGSWOOD
Mayshill
Coalpit Heath
Frampton End
Winterbourne
Watley's End
Winterbourne Down
Whiteshill
Kendleshire
Pye Corner
Ram Hill
Henfield
Bromley Heath
Downend
Mangotsfield
Emersons Green
Shortwood
Siston
Webb's Heath
Goose Green
Siston Common
Warmley
Bridge Yate
North Common
Bitton
Cadbury Heath
Oldland
Soundwell
Frenchay
Hillfields
Fishponds
Speedwell
St. George
Two Mile Hill
Longwell Green
Hanham
Hanham Green
Conham
Crew's Hole
St. Anne's Park
Broom Hill
Brislington
Stockwood
Flowers Hill
Broomhill
Stoke Gifford
Great Stoke
Bradley Stoke
Little Stoke
Harry Stoke
Broad Mead
Lockleaze
Stapleton
Eastville
Clay Hill
Horfield
Ashley Down
Montpelier
Bishopston
Redland
Cotham
Golden Hill
Henleaze
Westbury Park
Southmead
Brentry
Eastfield
Clifton
Hotwells
Westbury on Trym
Stoke Bishop
Sneyd Park
Sea Mills
Henbury
Cribbs Causeway
Cathbrain
Compton Greenfield
Berwick
Hallen
Lawrence Weston
Shirehampton
Pill
Easton-in-Gordano
Ham Green
Abbots Leigh
Leigh Woods
Avon Gorge
Clifton Suspension Bridge
Bedminster
Windmill Hill
Knowle
Arno's Vale
Hengrove
Filwood Park
Lower Knowle
Novers Park
Bedminster Down
Headley Park
Highridge
Ashton Vale
Bower Ashton
Long Ashton
Barrow Wood
Ashton Hill Plantation
Cambridge Batch
Failand
Lower Failand
Tyntesfield
Tyntesfield Plantation
Flax Bourton
Portbury
Avonmouth Docks
The Royal Portbury Dock
River Avon
River Frome
Avon Ring Road
M4
M5
M32
M49
A4
A38
A37
A4174
A432
A420
A431
A369
A370
A403
A4018
A4162
Bristol Parkway
Temple Meads
Gordano Services
Memorial Stadium (Bristol Rovers FC)
County Cricket Gd
Ashton Gate (Bristol City FC & Bristol Rugby)
Bristol Zoo Gardens
Blaise Castle
Mall Sh. Cent.
Bath Road
Wells Road
Gloucester Road
Portway
Hartcliffe Way
Bridgwater Road
Keynsham By-Pass
18
17
36
2 miles
3 km

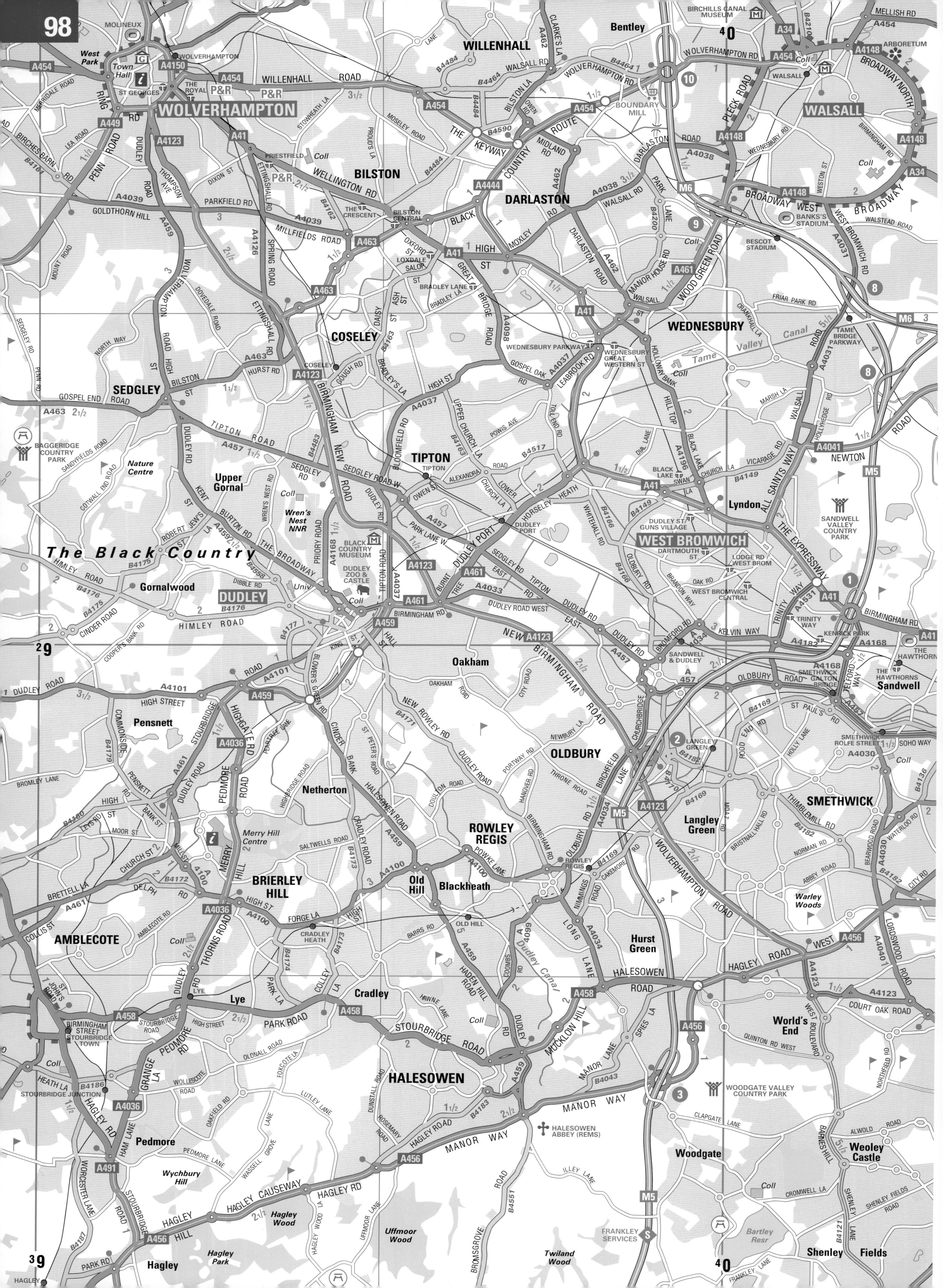
WOLVERHAMPTON
WILLENHALL
Bentley
BIRCHILLS CANAL MUSEUM
WALSALL
ARBORETUM
BILSTON
DARLASTON
WEDNESBURY
COSELEY
SEDGLEY
TIPTON
Upper Gornal
Wren's Nest NNR
BLACK COUNTRY MUSEUM
DUDLEY ZOO & CASTLE
The Black Country
Gornalwood
DUDLEY
WEST BROMWICH
Lyndon
NEWTON
SANDWELL VALLEY COUNTRY PARK
Oakham
OLDBURY
Sandwell
SMETHWICK
Langley Green
Pensnett
Netherton
ROWLEY REGIS
Merry Hill Centre
BRIERLEY HILL
Old Hill
Blackheath
AMBLECOTE
Hurst Green
Warley Woods
Lye
Cradley
World's End
HALESOWEN
Pedmore
Woodgate
WOODGATE VALLEY COUNTRY PARK
Weoley Castle
Wychbury Hill
Hagley Wood
Uffmoor Wood
Twiland Wood
Hagley Park
Hagley
HALESOWEN ABBEY (REMS)
FRANKLEY SERVICES
Bartley Resr
Shenley Fields
BAGGERIDGE COUNTRY PARK
Nature Centre
BESCOT STADIUM
BANKS'S STADIUM
MOLINEUX
West Park
M6
M5
A41
A4123
A459
A456
A458
A461
A463
A4036
A4100
A4101
A457
A4041
A4031
A4148
A454
A34
A462
A4038
A4037
A4033
A4034
A4168
A4182
A4030
A4040
A491
39
29
40

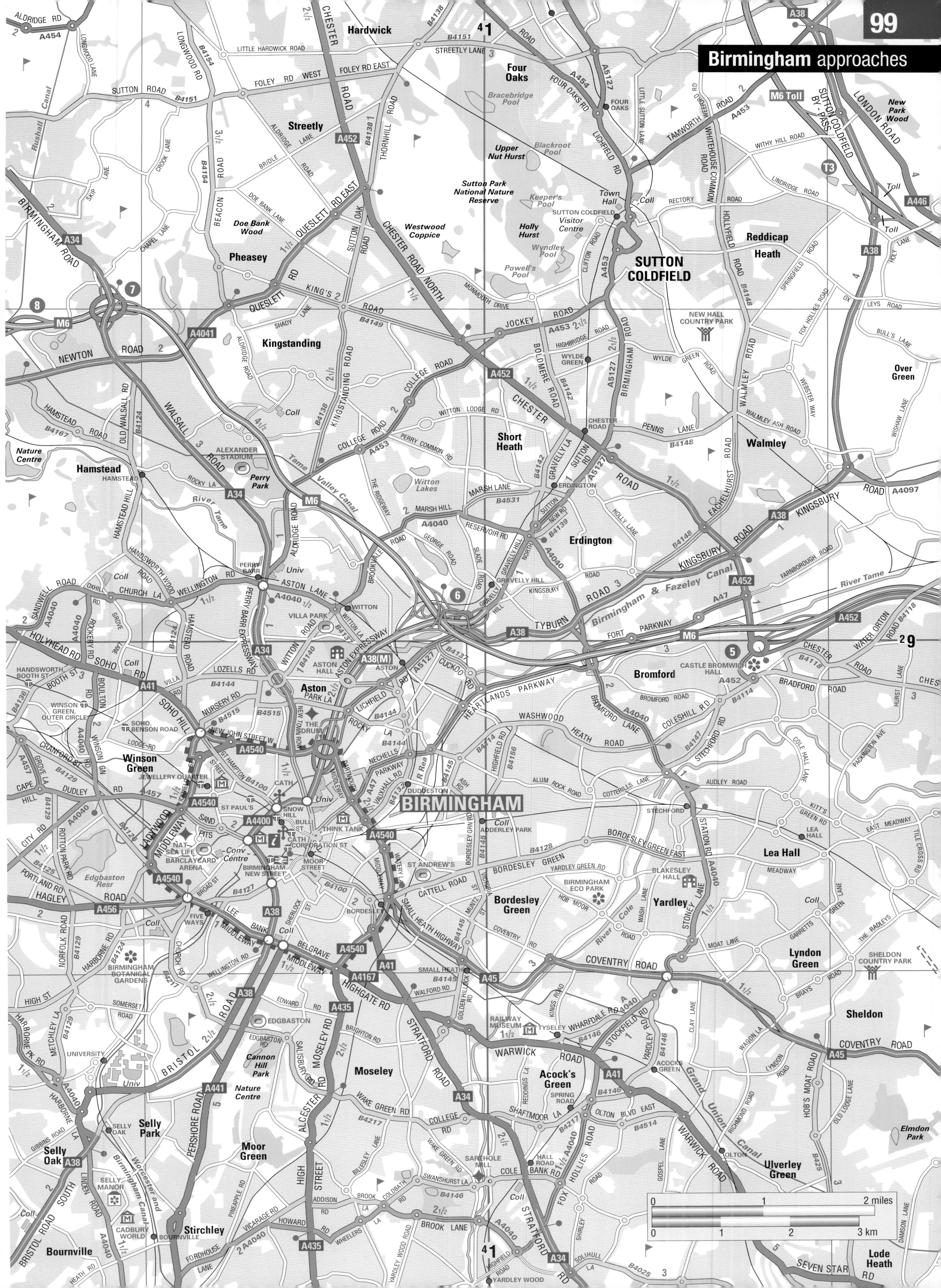
Hardwick
Four Oaks
Bracebridge Pool
Blackroot Pool
Upper Nut Hurst
Sutton Park National Nature Reserve
Keeper's Pool
Holly Hurst
Wyndley Pool
Powell's Pool
Westwood Coppice
Streetly
Doe Bank Wood
Pheasey
SUTTON COLDFIELD
SUTTON COLDFIELD Visitor Centre
Town Hall
Reddicap Heath
New Park Wood
NEW HALL COUNTRY PARK
Over Green
Walmley
Kingstanding
Short Heath
Hamstead
Nature Centre
ALEXANDER STADIUM
Perry Park
Witton Lakes
Erdington
Tame Valley Canal
River Tame
Birmingham & Fazeley Canal
Bromford
CASTLE BROMWICH HALL
Aston
ASTON HALL
VILLA PARK
Winson Green
JEWELLERY QUARTER
BIRMINGHAM
THINK TANK
NAT SEA LIFE
BARCLAYCARD ARENA
Conv Centre
Edgbaston Resr
BIRMINGHAM NEW STREET
MOOR STREET
ST ANDREW'S
Bordesley Green
BIRMINGHAM ECO PARK
Yardley
BLAKESLEY HALL
Lea Hall
Lyndon Green
SHELDON COUNTRY PARK
Sheldon
BIRMINGHAM BOTANICAL GARDENS
EDGBASTON
Cannon Hill Park
Nature Centre
Moseley
RAILWAY MUSEUM
TYSELEY
Acock's Green
Selly Park
Selly Oak
Moor Green
SAREHOLE MILL
Ulverley Green
Elmdon Park
SELLY MANOR
CADBURY WORLD
Stirchley
Bournville
Lode Heath
Grand Union Canal
Worcester and Birmingham Canal
M6
M6 Toll
A38(M)
0 1 2 miles
0 1 2 3 km

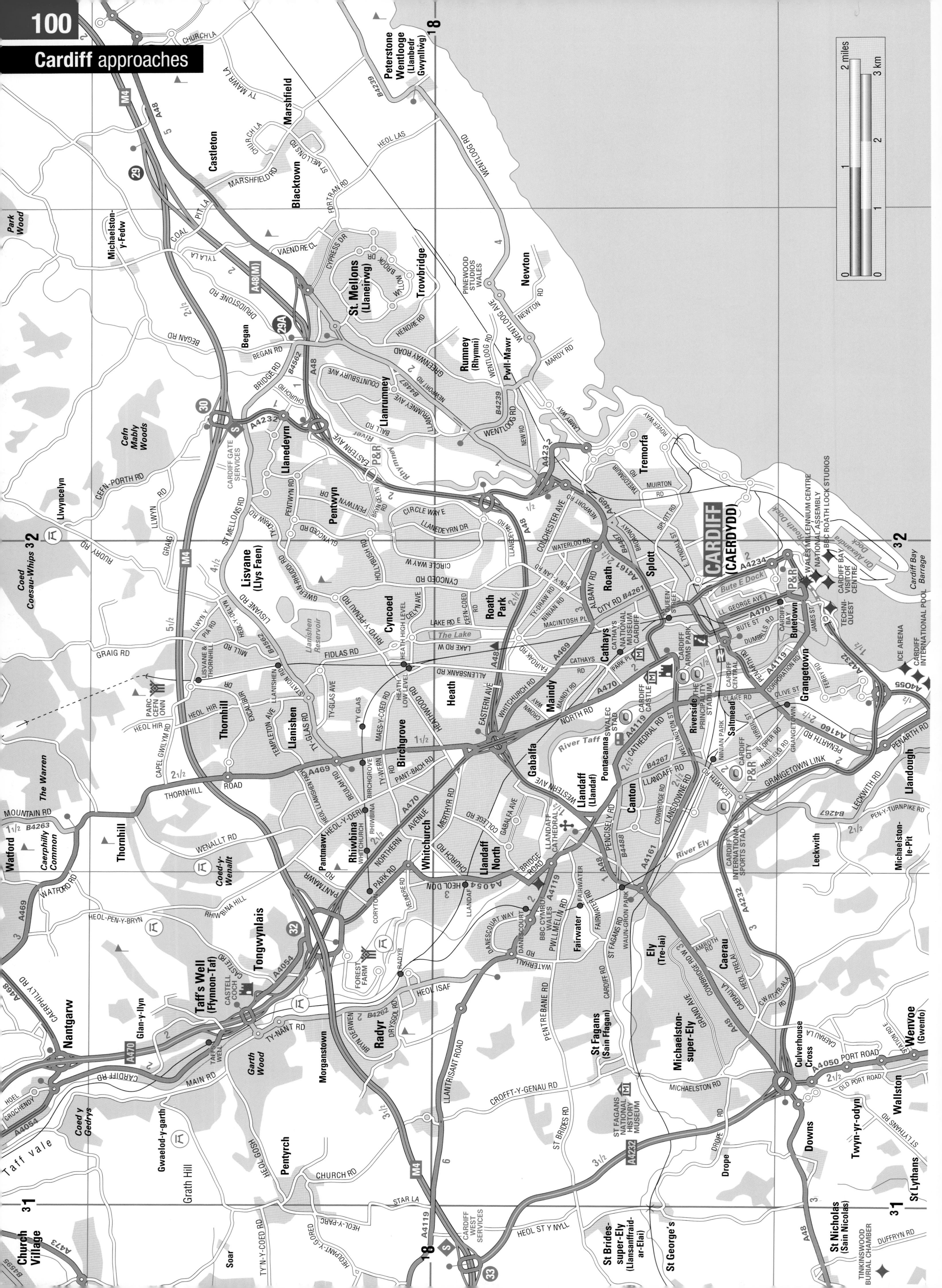
CARDIFF
(CAERDYDD)
Peterstone Wentlooge (Llanbedr Gwynllŵg)
Marshfield
Castleton
Blacktown
Michaelston-y-Fedw
Park Wood
St. Mellons (Llaneirwg)
Trowbridge
Newton
Began
Rumney (Rhymni)
Pwll-Mawr
Llanrumney
Llanedeyrn
Tremorfa
Cefn Mably Woods
Pentwyn
Llwyncelyn
Lisvane (Llys Faen)
Cyncoed
Roath Park
Roath
Splott
Coed Coesau-Whips
Llanishen Reservoir
The Lake
Cathays
Butetown
Heath
Llanishen
Thornhill
Maindy
Gabalfa
Birchgrove
Riverside
Saltmead
Grangetown
Llandough
Pontcanna
Canton
Llandaff (Llandaf)
Llandaff North
Whitchurch
Rhiwbina
Pantmawr
The Warren
Caerphilly Common
Watford
Coed-y-Wenallt
Tongwynlais
Taff's Well (Ffynnon-Taf)
Castell Coch
Nantgarw
Glan-y-llyn
Radyr
Morganstown
Garth Wood
Fairwater
Ely (Tre-lai)
Caerau
Leckwith
Michaelston-le-Pit
St Fagans (Sain Ffagan)
Michaelston-super-Ely
Culverhouse Cross
Wenvoe (Gwenfô)
Wallston
Twyn-yr-odyn
Downs
Drope
St Fagans National History Museum
Coed y Gedrys
Gwaelod-y-garth
Pentyrch
Graig Hill
Taff vale
Church Village
Soar
St Brides-super-Ely (Llansanffraid-ar-Elai)
St George's
St Nicholas (Sain Nicolas)
St Lythans
Tinkinswood Burial Chamber
Cardiff West Services
Cardiff Gate Services
Pinewood Studios Wales
Wales Millennium Centre
National Assembly
BBC Roath Lock Studios
Cardiff Bay Visitor Centre
Techniquest
Ice Arena
Cardiff International Pool
Cardiff Bay Barrage
Bute E Dock
Roath Dock
Qn Alexandra Dock
Cardiff Castle
National Museum Cardiff
Principality Stadium
Cardiff Arms Park
SWALEC Stad
Cardiff City Stad
Cardiff International Sports Stad
Llandaff Cathedral
BBC Cymru Wales
Parc Cefn Onn
Forest Farm
River Taff
River Ely
Rhymney River
M4
A48(M)
A48
A4232
A469
A470
A4119
A4054
A4050
A4160
A4055
A4161
A4234
2 miles
3 km
18
31
32

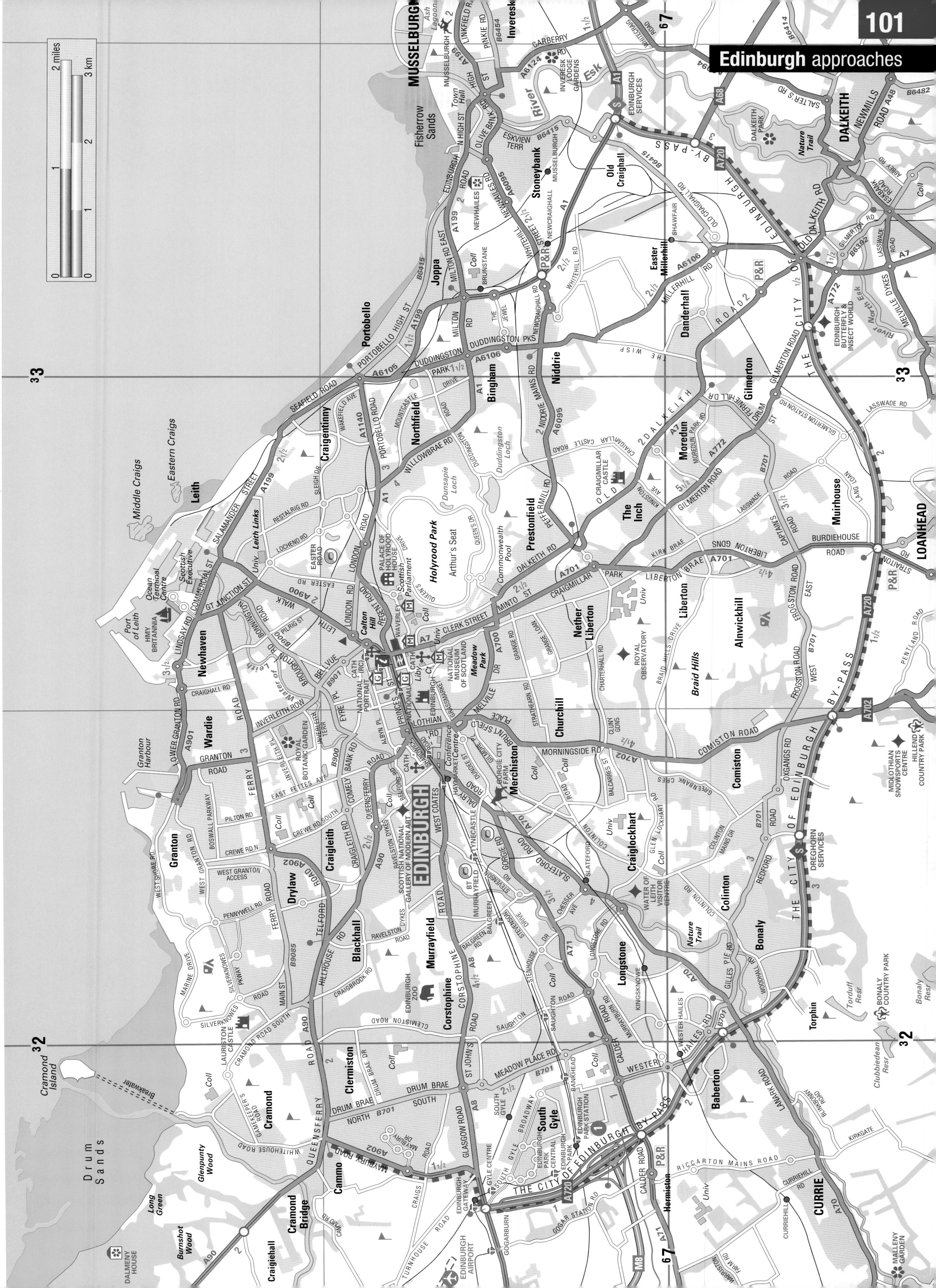
EDINBURGH
Leith
Newhaven
Granton
Wardie
Portobello
Joppa
Musselburgh
Fisherrow Sands
Craigentinny
Northfield
Bingham
Niddrie
Stoneybank
Old Craighall
Dalkeith
Loanhead
Danderhall
Gilmerton
Moredun
The Inch
Prestonfield
Holyrood Park
Arthur's Seat
Duddingston Loch
Dunsapie Loch
Calton Hill
Meadow Park
Nether Liberton
Liberton
Alnwickhill
Braid Hills
Muirhouse
Churchill
Merchiston
Comiston
Craiglockhart
Colinton
Bonaly
Longstone
Murrayfield
Corstophine
Blackhall
Craigleith
Drylaw
Clermiston
Cramond
Cramond Island
Cramond Bridge
Cammo
Craigiehall
Drum Sands
Long Green
Burnshot Wood
Glenpunty Wood
South Gyle
Baberton
Hermiston
Currie
Torphin
Middle Craigs
Eastern Craigs
Granton Harbour
Port of Leith
HMY BRITANNIA
Ocean Terminal Centre
Scottish Executive
ROYAL BOTANIC GARDEN
EDINBURGH ZOO
ROYAL OBSERVATORY
PALACE OF HOLYROOD HOUSE
Scottish Parliament
NATIONAL MUSEUM OF SCOTLAND
SCOTTISH NATIONAL GALLERY OF MODERN ART
GORGIE CITY FARM
WATER OF LEITH VISITOR CENTRE
CRAIGMILLAR CASTLE
LAURISTON CASTLE
DALMENY HOUSE
EDINBURGH AIRPORT
EDINBURGH BUTTERFLY & INSECT WORLD
MIDLOTHIAN SNOWSPORTS CENTRE
HILLEND COUNTRY PARK
BONALY COUNTRY PARK
MALLENY GARDEN
DALKEITH PARK
INVERESK LODGE GARDENS
EDINBURGH SERVICES
DREGHORN SERVICES
THE CITY OF EDINBURGH BY-PASS
A1
A7
A8
A70
A71
A90
A199
A702
A720
A772
M8
33
32
67
0
1
2 miles
3 km

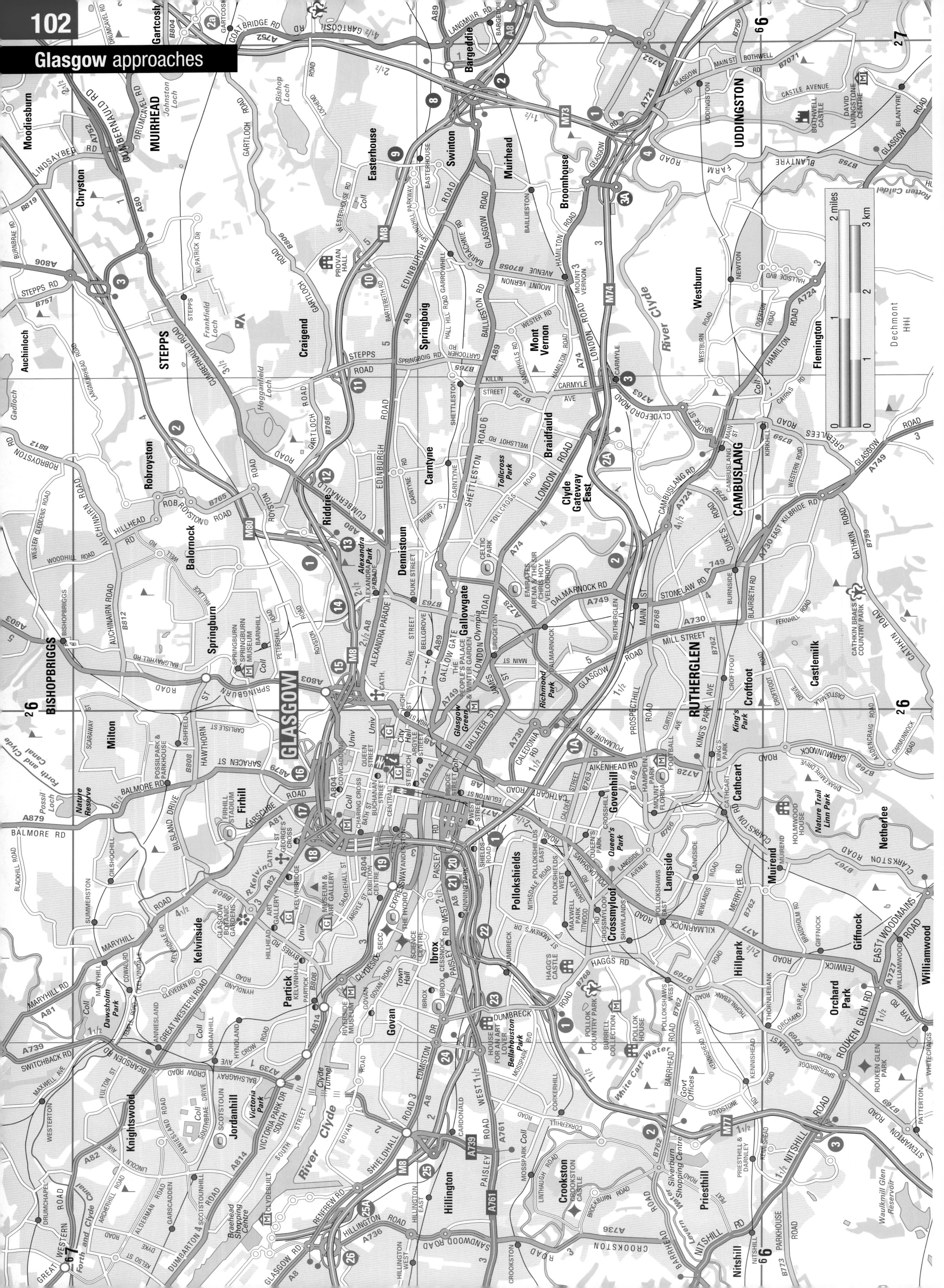
GLASGOW
Gartcosh
Muirhead
Moodiesburn
Chryston
Bargeddie
Easterhouse
Swinton
Muirhead
Broomhouse
Uddingston
Bothwell Castle
David Livingstone Centre
Stepps
Auchinloch
Craigend
Springboig
Mont Vernon
Westburn
Flemington
Dechmont Hill
Robroyston
Riddrie
Carntyne
Braidfauld
Tollcross Park
Clyde Gateway East
Cambuslang
Balornock
Dennistoun
Alexandra Park
Gallowgate
Celtic Park
Emirates Arena & the Sir Chris Hoy Velodrome
Springburn
Springburn Museum
Bishopbriggs
Rutherglen
Castlemilk
Cathkin Braes Country Park
Croftfoot
King's Park
Milton
Glasgow Green
The People's Palace & Winter Garden
Richmond Park
Possilpark & Parkhouse
Nature Reserve
Possil Loch
Forth and Clyde Canal
Firhill
Firhill Stadium
Govanhill
Cathcart
Nature Trail Linn Park
Holmwood House
Netherlee
St George's Cross
Pollokshields
Queen's Park
Langside
Muirend
Kelvinside
Glasgow Botanic Gardens
Art Gallery
Museum & Art Gallery
Exhibition Centre
SECC
The Hydro
Science Centre
Crosshill
Crossmyloof
Shawlands
Mount Florida
Hampden Park
Pollokshaws East
Partick
Dawsholm Park
Ibrox
Town Hall
Govan
Riverside Museum
Haggs Castle
Pollok Country Park
Burrell Collection
Pollok House
Hillpark
Giffnock
Orchard Park
Williamwood
Dumbreck
House for an Art Lover
Bellahouston Park
White Cart Water
Rouken Glen Park
Knightswood
Jordanhill
Victoria Park
Scotstoun
Clyde Tunnel
River Clyde
Hillington
Crookston
Crookston Castle
Silverburn Shopping Centre
Priesthill
Nitshill
Braehead Shopping Centre
Waulkmill Glen Reservoir
Govt Offices
M8
M73
M74
M77
M80
A8
A80
A730
A749
A739
A761
A77
A727
A736
A814
A803
A879
26
27
66
67
2 miles
3 km

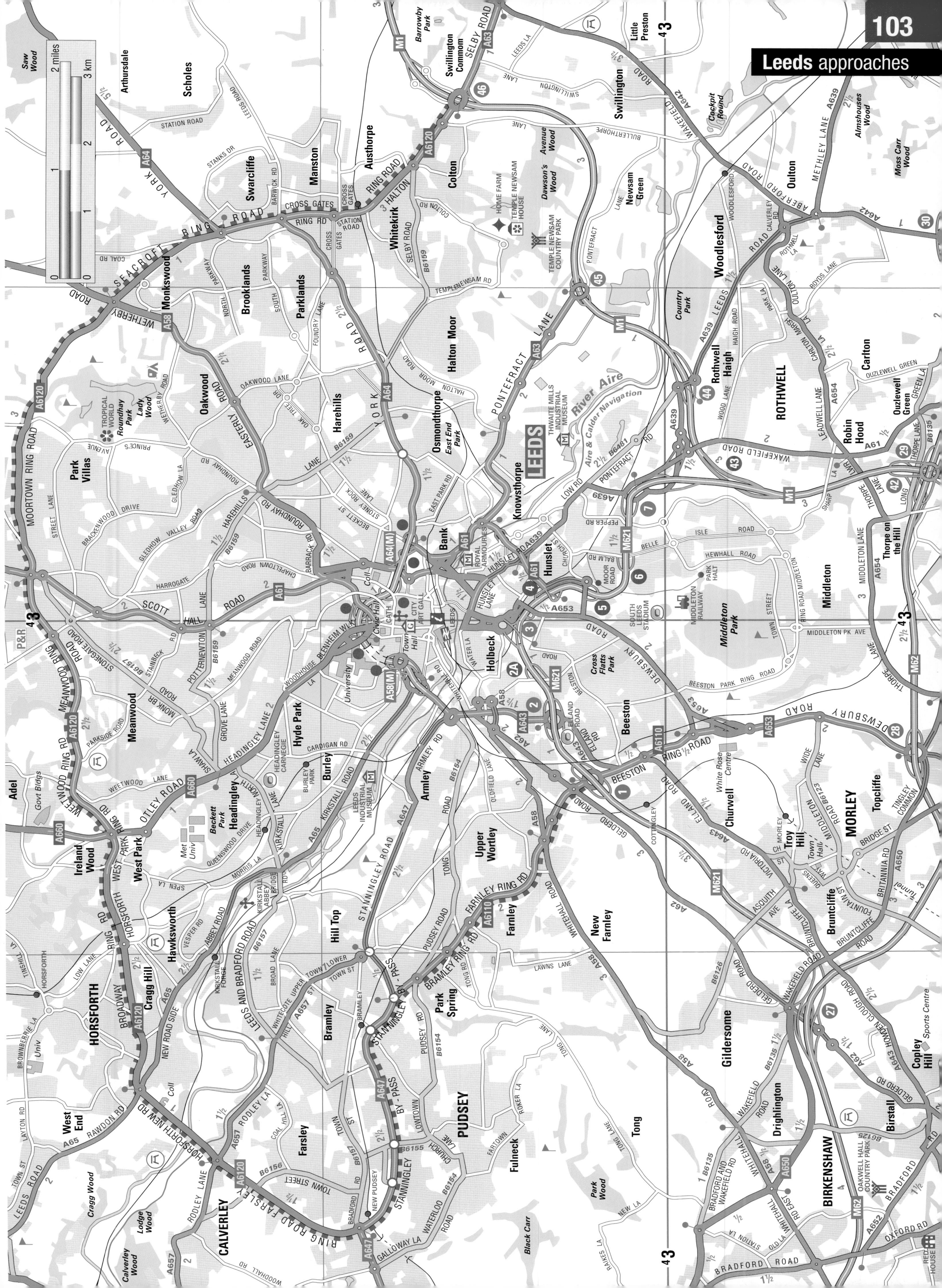
0 1 2 3 km
0 1 2 miles
LEEDS
Saw Wood
Arthursdale
Scholes
Swarcliffe
Manston
Austhorpe
Colton
Whitekirk
Barrowby Park
Swillington Common
Little Preston
Swillington
Cockpit Round
Almshouses Wood
Moss Carr Wood
Oulton
Woodlesford
Newsam Green
Dawson's Wood
Avenue Wood
HOME FARM
TEMPLE NEWSAM HOUSE
TEMPLE NEWSAM COUNTRY PARK
Monkswood
Brooklands
Parklands
Halton Moor
Country Park
Rothwell Haigh
ROTHWELL
Carlton
Oulton Green
Robin Hood
Oakwood
Harehills
Osmondthorpe
East End Park
THWAITE MILLS INDUSTRIAL MUSEUM
River Aire
Aire & Calder Navigation
Knowsthorpe
TROPICAL WORLD
Roundhay Park
Lady Wood
Park Villas
Bank
ROYAL ARMOURIES
Hunslet
Middleton
Thorpe on the Hill
Middleton Park
MIDDLETON RAILWAY
PARK HALT
SOUTH LEEDS STADIUM
Holbeck
Cross Flatts Park
Beeston
University
Civic Hall
CITY ART GALL
Town Hall
Hyde Park
Burley
HEADINGLEY CARNEGIE
BURLEY PARK
LEEDS INDUSTRIAL MUSEUM
Armley
Meanwood
Adel
Govt Bldgs
Headingley
Beckett Park
Met Univ
Ireland Wood
West Park
Hawksworth
KIRKSTALL ABBEY
KIRKSTALL FORGE
Hill Top
Upper Wortley
Farnley
New Farnley
Churwell
White Rose Centre
Troy Hill
MORLEY
Topcliffe
TINGLEY COMMON
Bruntcliffe
Gildersome
Drighlington
Copley Hill
Birstall
BIRKENSHAW
OAKWELL HALL COUNTRY PARK
RED HOUSE
Cragg Hill
HORSFORTH
Bramley
Park Spring
PUDSEY
Farsley
West End
Cragg Wood
Lodge Wood
Calverley Wood
CALVERLEY
NEW PUDSEY
Tong
Fulneck
Park Wood
Black Carr
YORK ROAD
RING ROAD
SEACROFT
WETHERBY ROAD
CROSS GATES
SELBY ROAD
LEEDS LA
SWILLINGTON LANE
BULLERTHORPE LANE
WAKEFIELD ROAD
ABERFORD ROAD
METHLEY LANE
PONTEFRACT LANE
OAKWOOD LANE
HALTON MOOR ROAD
TEMPLENEWSAM RD
MOORTOWN RING ROAD
STREET LANE
SCOTT HALL ROAD
HARROGATE RD
CHAPELTOWN ROAD
MEANWOOD RING ROAD
OTLEY ROAD
HEADINGLEY LANE
KIRKSTALL ROAD
STANNINGLEY ROAD
DEWSBURY ROAD
BEESTON RING ROAD
BEESTON PARK RING ROAD
MIDDLETON LANE
MIDDLETON PK AVE
GELDERD ROAD
ELLAND ROAD
FARNLEY RING RD
BRAMLEY RING RD
STANNINGLEY BY-PASS
TOWN STREET
RODLEY LANE
HORSFORTH NEW RD
RING ROAD FARSLEY
LEEDS ROAD
BRADFORD ROAD
OXFORD RD
NEW LA
TONG LANE
WHITEHALL ROAD
BRADFORD AND WAKEFIELD RD
M1
M62
M621
A64(M)
A58(M)
A64
A63
A61
A58
A639
A642
A6120
A660
A65
A647
A657
A62
A643
A653
A654
A650
A652
A110
A6110
B6159
B6157
B6154
B6155
B6156
B6135
B6126
B6123
B6481
B6125
43
46
45
44
43
42
30
29
28
27
7
6
5
4
3
2A
2
1

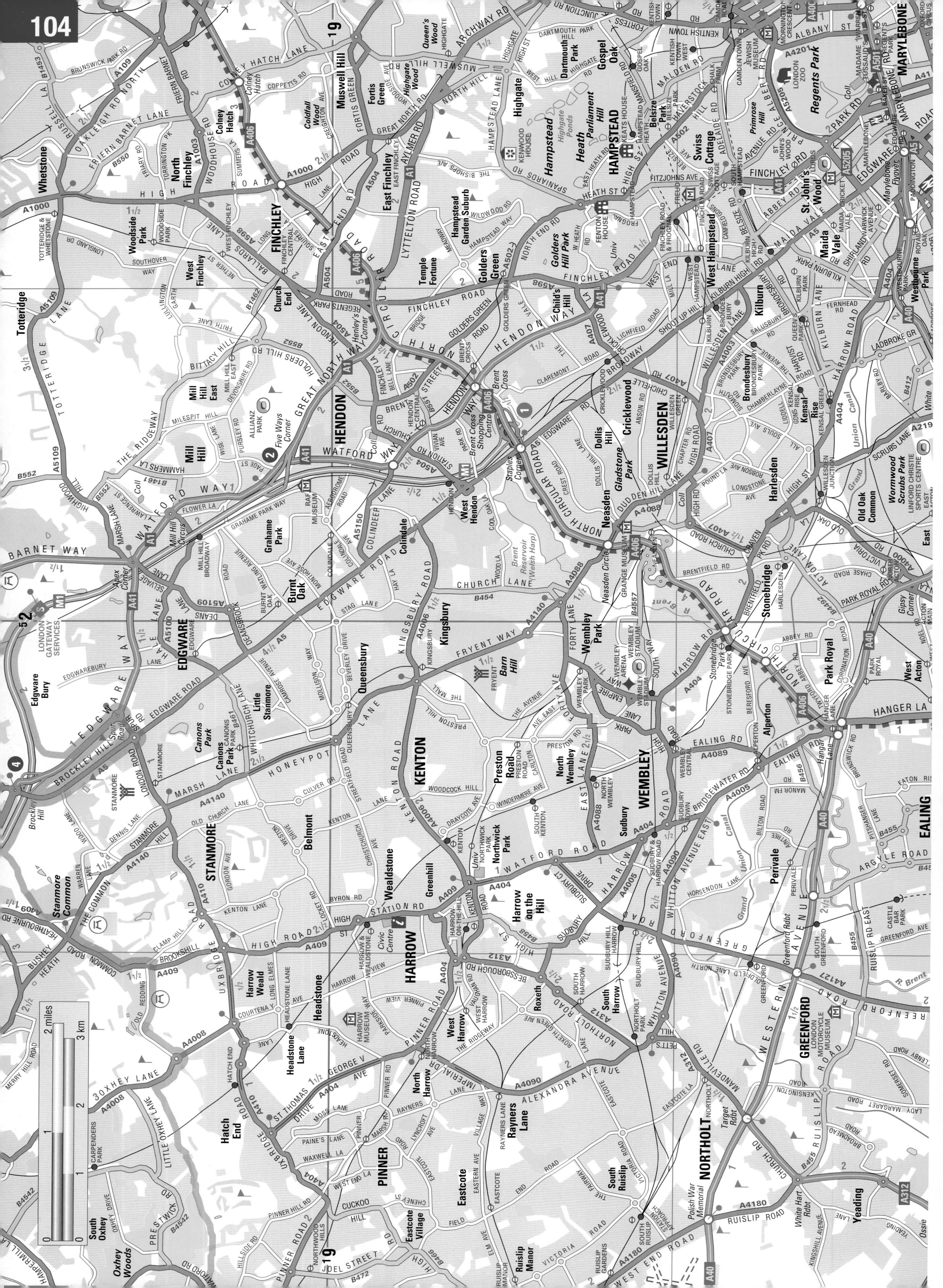
Whetstone
North Finchley
Colney Hatch
Muswell Hill
Fortis Green
East Finchley
Highgate
Hampstead Heath
HAMPSTEAD
Parliament Hill
Gospel Oak
Dartmouth Park
Belsize Park
Swiss Cottage
Primrose Hill
Regents Park
MARYLEBONE
St. John's Wood
Maida Vale
Kilburn
West Hampstead
Golders Hill Park
Golders Green
Temple Fortune
Hampstead Garden Suburb
FINCHLEY
Woodside Park
West Finchley
Church End
Totteridge
Mill Hill
Mill Hill East
HENDON
Childs Hill
Cricklewood
Dollis Hill
Gladstone Park
WILLESDEN
Brondesbury
Kensal Rise
Harlesden
Neasden
Colindale
West Hendon
Grahame Park
Burnt Oak
EDGWARE
Edgware Bury
Kingsbury
Queensbury
Barn Hill
Wembley Park
WEMBLEY
North Wembley
Stonebridge
Park Royal
Alperton
West Acton
Old Oak Common
Wormwood Scrubs Park
EALING
Perivale
GREENFORD
NORTHOLT
Yeading
Sudbury
Preston Road
KENTON
Northwick Park
HARROW
Harrow on the Hill
Wealdstone
Greenhill
STANMORE
Stanmore Common
Canons Park
Little Stanmore
Belmont
Headstone
Harrow Weald
Headstone Lane
Hatch End
PINNER
North Harrow
West Harrow
Rayners Lane
South Harrow
Roxeth
Eastcote
Eastcote Village
Ruislip Manor
South Ruislip
South Oxhey
Oxhey Woods
Brockley Hill
Five Ways Corner
Apex Corner
Henley's Corner
Mill Hill Circus
Brent Cross
Staples Corner
Neasden Circle
Target Rdbt
White Hart Rdbt
Greenford Rdbt
Polish War Memorial
LONDON GATEWAY SERVICES
2 miles
3 km

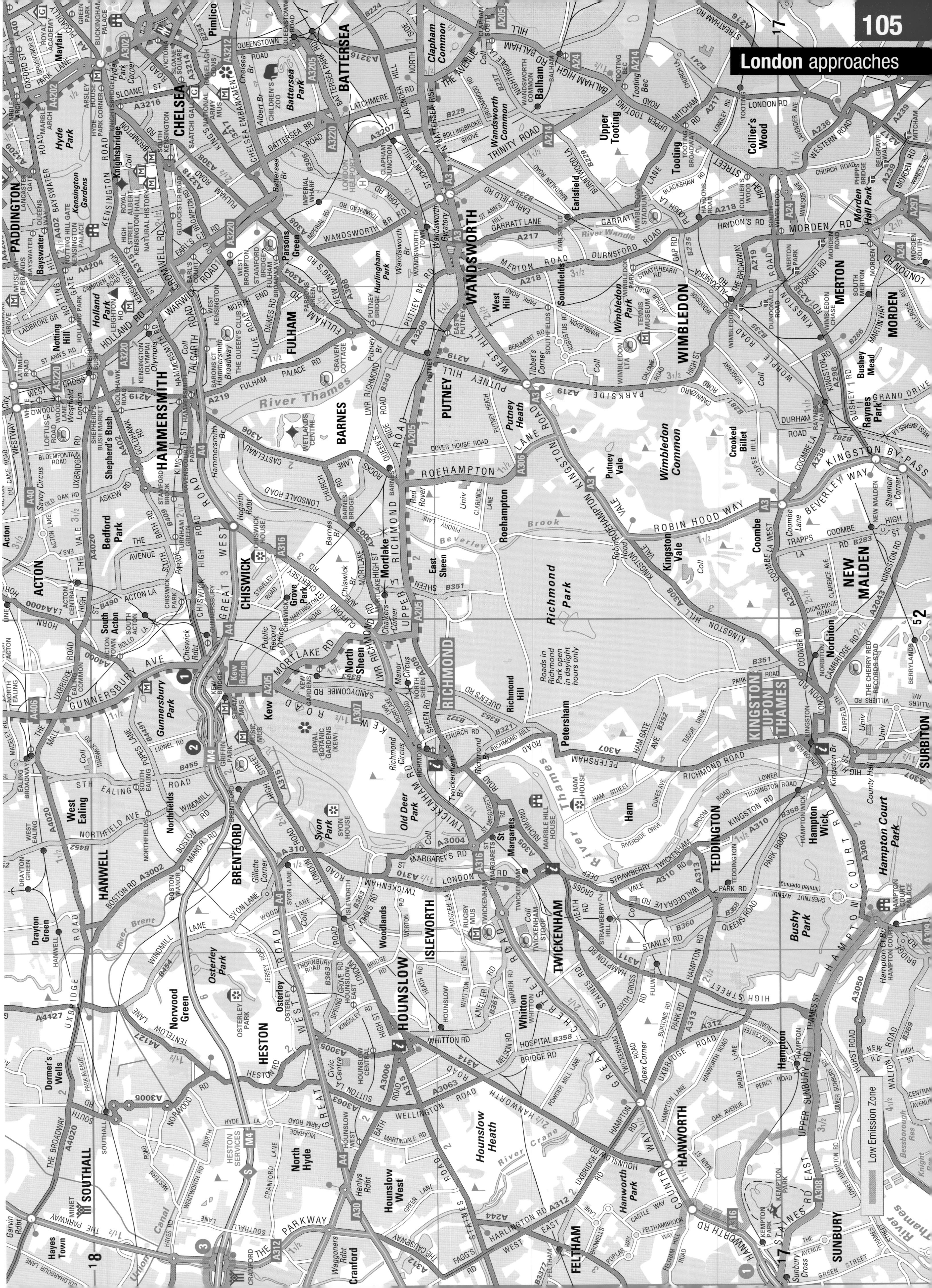
PADDINGTON
Bayswater
Hyde Park
Kensington Gardens
Mayfair
Pimlico
CHELSEA
Knightsbridge
BATTERSEA
Battersea Park
Clapham Common
Balham
Upper Tooting
Tooting
Collier's Wood
Notting Hill
Holland Park
FULHAM
Parsons Green
Hurlingham Park
WANDSWORTH
Wandsworth Common
Earlsfield
Southfields
West Hill
Wimbledon Park
WIMBLEDON
Morden Hall Park
MERTON
MORDEN
Bushey Mead
Raynes Park
HAMMERSMITH
Shepherd's Bush
BARNES
PUTNEY
Putney Heath
Wimbledon Common
Putney Vale
Crooked Billet
Roehampton
Acton
ACTON
South Acton
Bedford Park
CHISWICK
East Sheen
Mortlake
Kingston Vale
Coombe
NEW MALDEN
Richmond Park
Norbiton
RICHMOND
Kew
Richmond Hill
Petersham
KINGSTON UPON THAMES
SURBITON
Gunnersbury Park
West Ealing
HANWELL
BRENTFORD
Syon Park
Old Deer Park
Ham
TEDDINGTON
Hampton Wick
Hampton Court Park
ISLEWORTH
TWICKENHAM
St Margarets
Bushy Park
Drayton Green
Osterley Park
Norwood Green
HESTON
HOUNSLOW
Whitton
Hampton
Dormer's Wells
SOUTHALL
North Hyde
Hounslow Heath
Hounslow West
Hanworth Park
HANWORTH
Hayes Town
Cranford
FELTHAM
SUNBURY
River Thames
Low Emission Zone

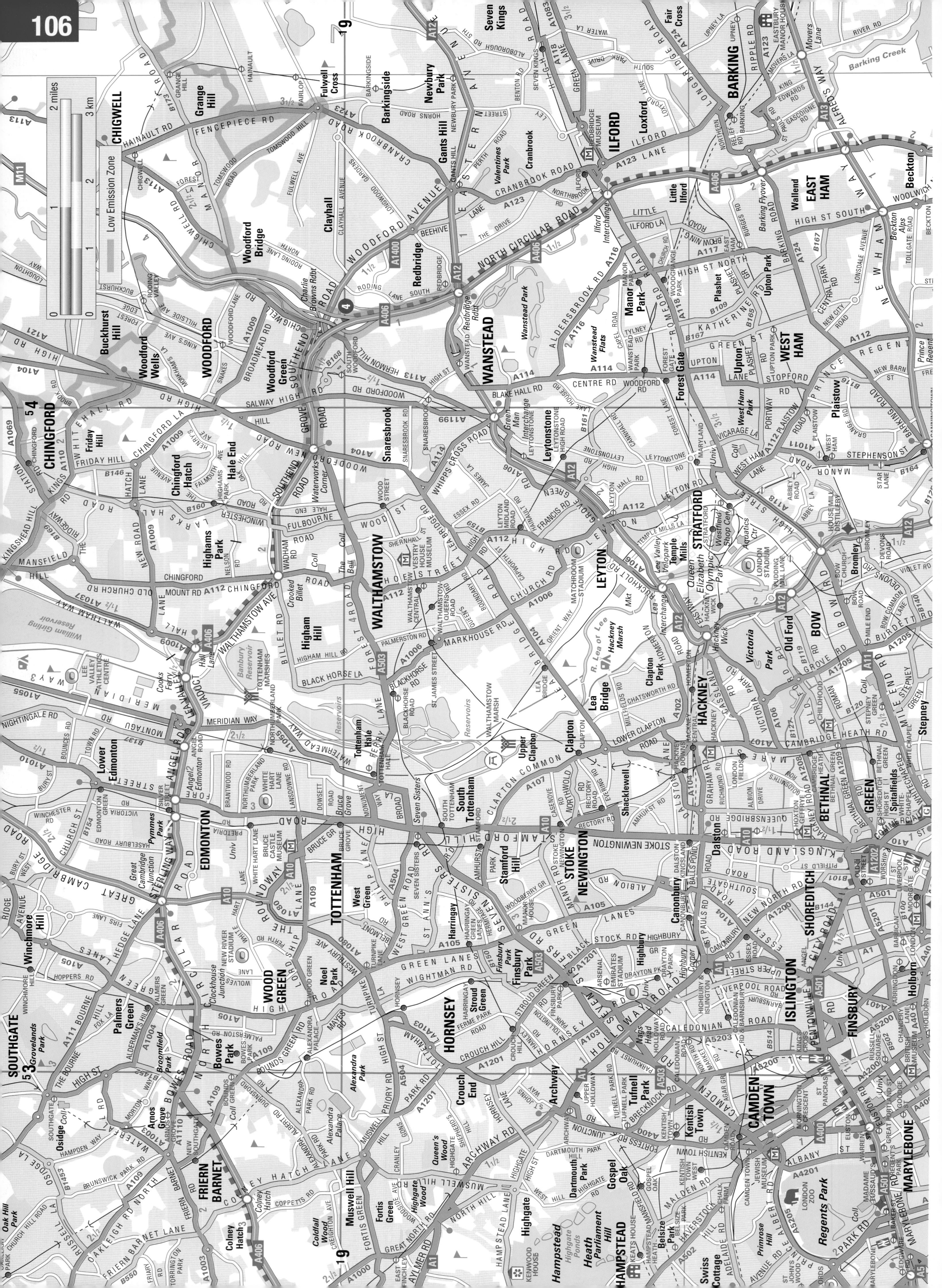
CHIGWELL
Grange Hill
Fulwell Cross
Barkingside
Newbury Park
Seven Kings
Fair Cross
BARKING
Gants Hill
Cranbrook
ILFORD
Loxford
Little Ilford
Clayhall
Redbridge
Woodford Bridge
Valentines Park
Wanstead Park
WANSTEAD
Manor Park
EAST HAM
Wallend
Beckton
Upton Park
Plashet
Buckhurst Hill
Woodford Wells
WOODFORD
Woodford Green
Forest Gate
Upton
WEST HAM
Plaistow
West Ham Park
CHINGFORD
Friday Hill
Chingford Hatch
Hale End
Snaresbrook
Leytonstone
Highams Park
WALTHAMSTOW
Crooked Billet
Higham Hill
LEYTON
STRATFORD
Temple Mills
Queen Elizabeth Olympic Park
Bromley
BOW
Old Ford
Victoria Park
Hackney Marsh
Clapton Park
Lea Bridge
Clapton
Upper Clapton
HACKNEY
William Girling Reservoir
Banbury Reservoir
Tottenham Hale
Lower Edmonton
EDMONTON
Pymmes Park
South Tottenham
Seven Sisters
Stamford Hill
STOKE NEWINGTON
Shacklewell
Dalston
BETHNAL GREEN
Stepney
TOTTENHAM
West Green
Harringay
Finsbury Park
Highbury
Canonbury
SHOREDITCH
ISLINGTON
FINSBURY
Holborn
Winchmore Hill
WOOD GREEN
Noel Park
HORNSEY
Stroud Green
Palmers Green
SOUTHGATE
Grovelands Park
Bowes Park
Crouch End
Archway
Tufnell Park
Kentish Town
CAMDEN TOWN
Arnos Grove
Osidge
Alexandra Park
Alexandra Palace
Queen's Wood
Highgate Wood
Muswell Hill
Fortis Green
Highgate
Dartmouth Park
Gospel Oak
FRIERN BARNET
Colney Hatch
Coldfall Wood
Hampstead Heath
Parliament Hill
HAMPSTEAD
Belsize Park
Swiss Cottage
Primrose Hill
Regents Park
MARYLEBONE
Low Emission Zone
2 miles
3 km
NORTH CIRCULAR ROAD
EASTERN AVENUE

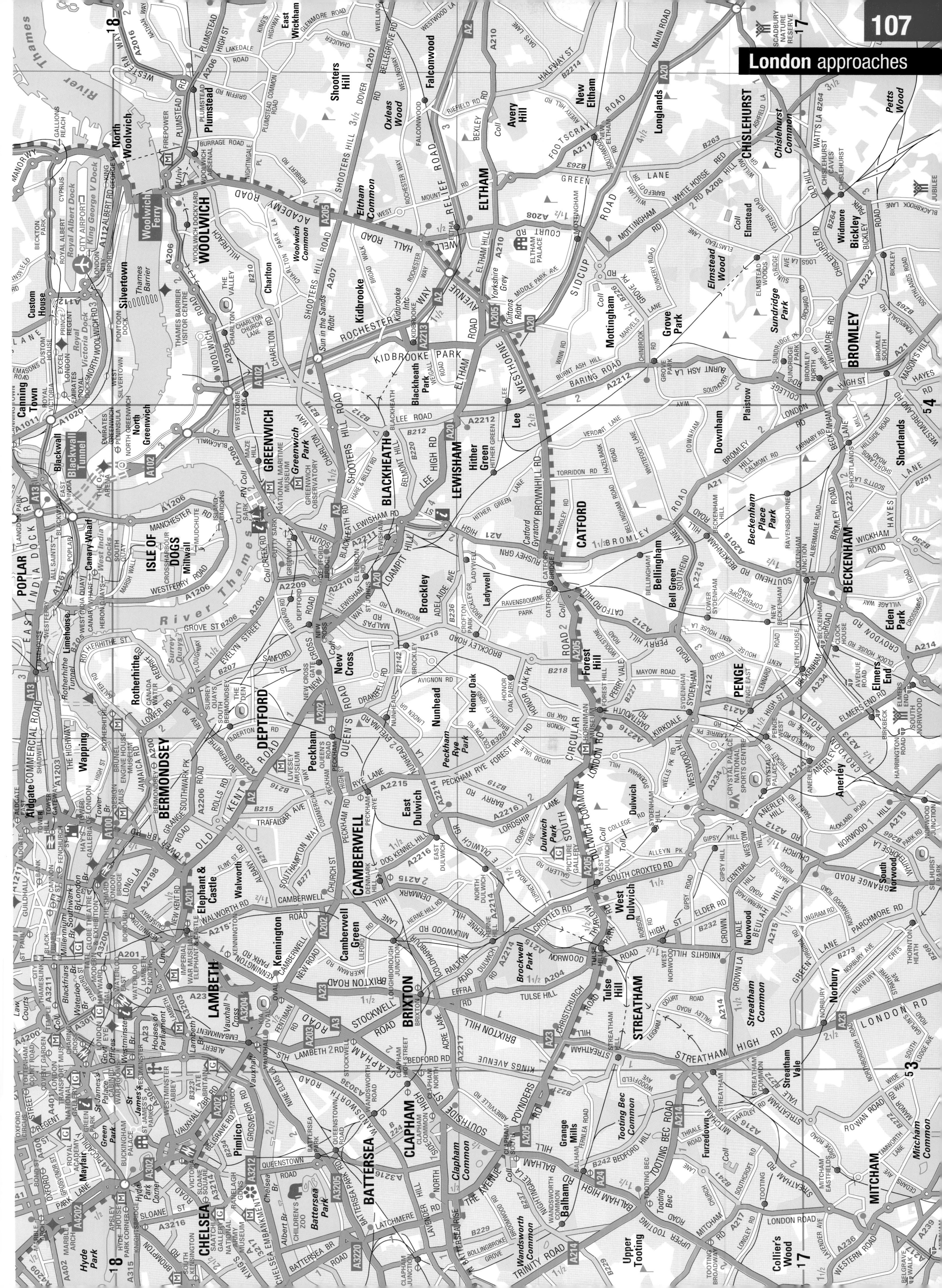
River Thames
North Woolwich
Plumstead
Shooters Hill
Falconwood
East Wickham
Oxleas Wood
Eltham Common
Woolwich Common
WOOLWICH
Woolwich Ferry
Silvertown
Thames Barrier
Charlton
Kidbrooke
ELTHAM
Avery Hill
New Eltham
Longlands
CHISLEHURST
Chislehurst Common
Petts Wood
SIDCUP
Mottingham
Grove Park
Elmstead Wood
Sundridge Park
BROMLEY
Bickley
Widmore
Custom House
Canning Town
Blackwall
Blackwall Tunnel
North Greenwich
GREENWICH
Greenwich Park
Blackheath Park
BLACKHEATH
LEWISHAM
Hither Green
Lee
CATFORD
Downham
Plaistow
Shortlands
POPLAR
Canary Wharf
ISLE OF DOGS
Millwall
Limehouse
Rotherhithe
Surrey Quays
DEPTFORD
Brockley
Ladywell
Bellingham
Bell Green
Beckenham Place Park
BECKENHAM
Eden Park
Elmers End
New Cross
Nunhead
Honor Oak
Forest Hill
PENGE
Peckham Rye Park
Peckham
Wapping
BERMONDSEY
Aldgate
East Dulwich
Dulwich
Dulwich Park
Anerley
CAMBERWELL
Elephant & Castle
Walworth
West Dulwich
South Norwood
Kennington
Camberwell Green
Brockwell Park
LAMBETH
BRIXTON
Tulse Hill
STREATHAM
Streatham Common
Norbury
Streatham Vale
Vauxhall Cross
Mayfair
Green Park
Pimlico
CLAPHAM
Clapham Common
BATTERSEA
Battersea Park
Grange Mills
Tooting Bec Common
Furzedown
MITCHAM
Mitcham Common
Hyde Park
CHELSEA
Wandsworth Common
Balham
Tooting Bec
Upper Tooting
Collier's Wood

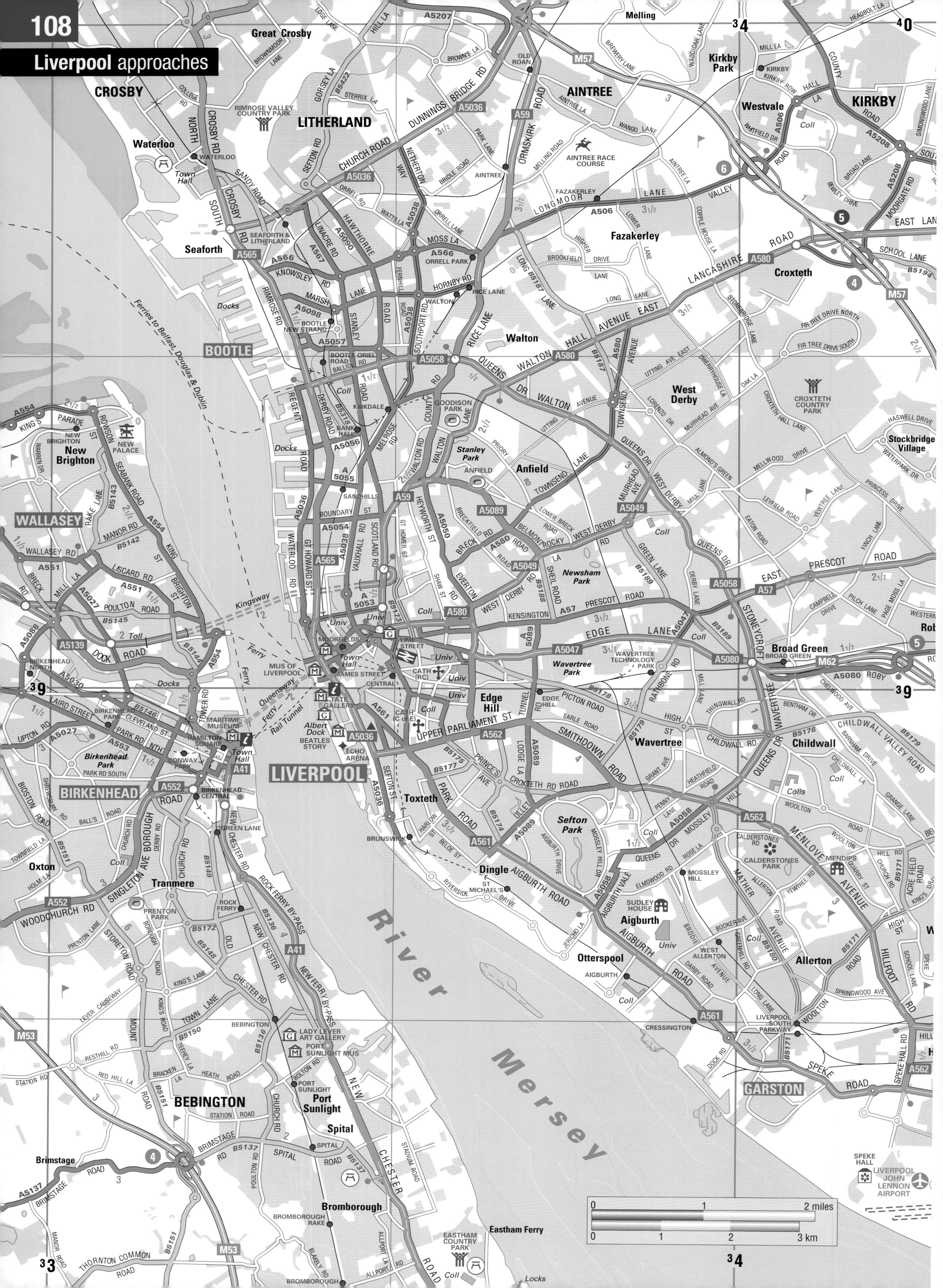
Great Crosby
CROSBY
Waterloo
Seaforth
LITHERLAND
AINTREE
AINTREE RACE COURSE
Melling
Kirkby Park
KIRKBY
Westvale
Fazakerley
Croxteth
Walton
West Derby
CROXTETH COUNTRY PARK
Stockbridge Village
BOOTLE
Anfield
Stanley Park
Newsham Park
Broad Green
Wavertree Park
Wavertree
Childwall
Edge Hill
LIVERPOOL
Toxteth
Sefton Park
Dingle
Aigburth
Otterspool
Allerton
GARSTON
SPEKE HALL
LIVERPOOL JOHN LENNON AIRPORT
New Brighton
WALLASEY
BIRKENHEAD
Birkenhead Park
Oxton
Tranmere
BEBINGTON
Port Sunlight
Spital
Brimstage
Bromborough
Eastham Ferry
EASTHAM COUNTRY PARK
River Mersey
Ferries to Belfast, Douglas & Dublin
Kingsway
Queensway
Rail Tunnel
0 1 2 miles
0 1 2 3 km

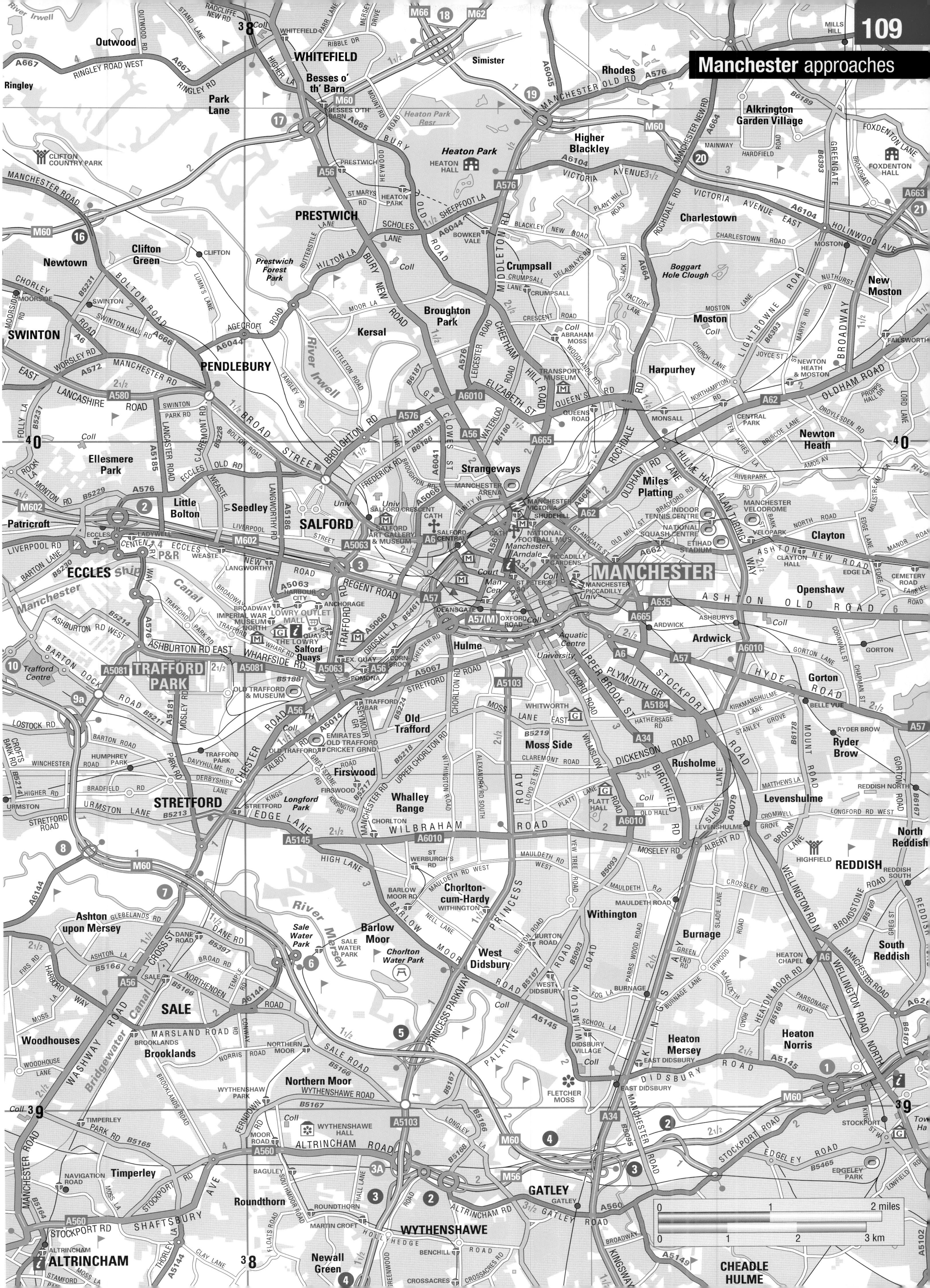
Outwood
Ringley
WHITEFIELD
Besses o' th' Barn
Simister
Rhodes
Park Lane
Heaton Park
Higher Blackley
Alkrington Garden Village
CLIFTON COUNTRY PARK
FOXDENTON HALL
PRESTWICH
Charlestown
Newtown
Clifton Green
Prestwich Forest Park
Crumpsall
Boggart Hole Clough
New Moston
SWINTON
Kersal
Broughton Park
Moston
PENDLEBURY
River Irwell
Harpurhey
Ellesmere Park
Strangeways
Newton Heath
Little Bolton
Seedley
SALFORD
Miles Platting
Clayton
Patricroft
ECCLES
MANCHESTER
Openshaw
Manchester Ship Canal
Hulme
Ardwick
TRAFFORD PARK
Salford Quays
Gorton
Old Trafford
Moss Side
Rusholme
Ryder Brow
Firswood
Whalley Range
Longford Park
STRETFORD
Levenshulme
North Reddish
REDDISH
Chorlton-cum-Hardy
Ashton upon Mersey
Barlow Moor
Withington
Burnage
South Reddish
Sale Water Park
River Mersey
West Didsbury
SALE
Woodhouses
Brooklands
Heaton Mersey
Heaton Norris
Northern Moor
FLETCHER MOSS
WYTHENSHAWE HALL
Timperley
GATLEY
Roundthorn
WYTHENSHAWE
ALTRINCHAM
Newall Green
CHEADLE HULME
0 1 2 miles
0 1 2 3 km

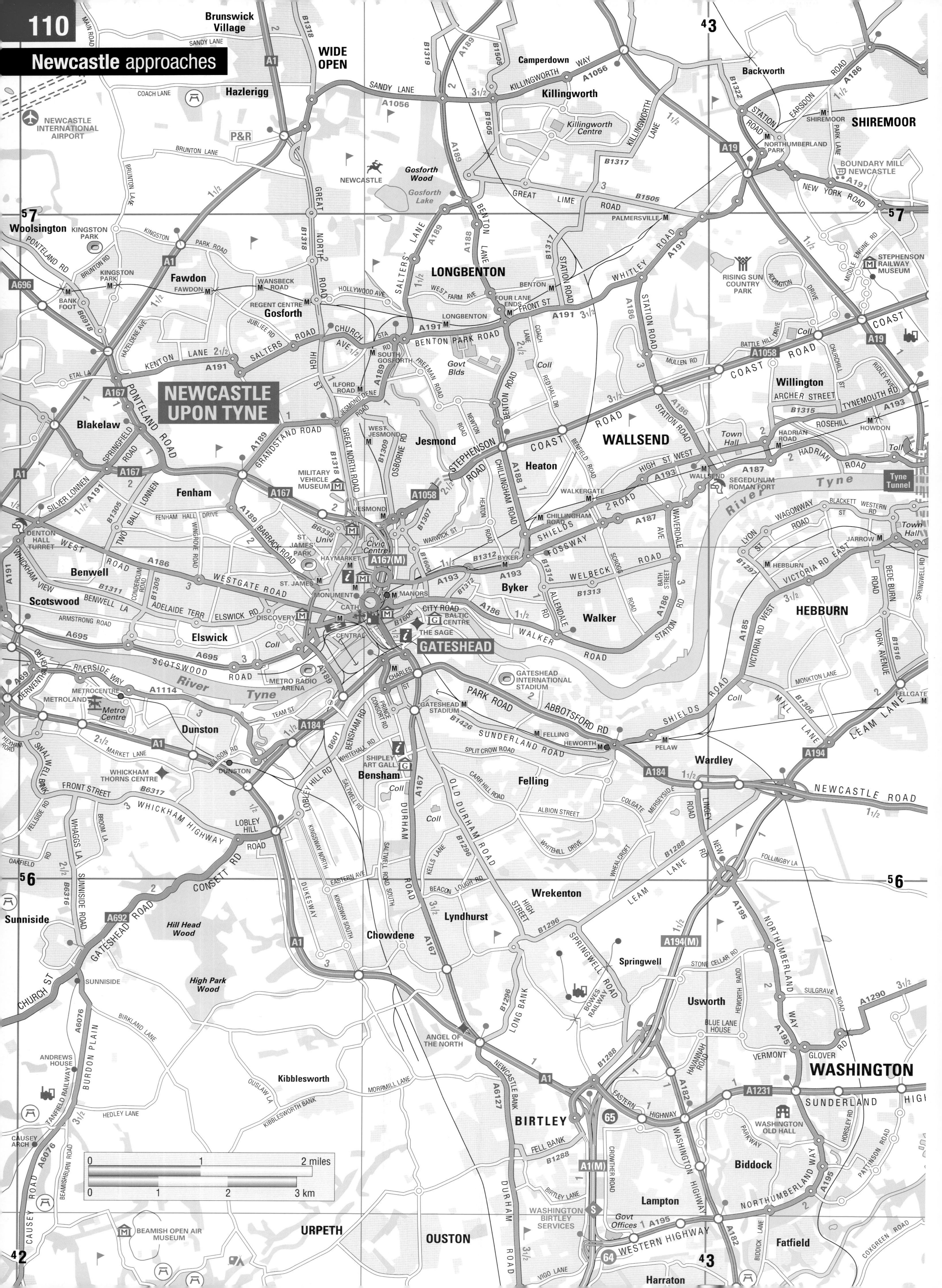
Brunswick Village
WIDE OPEN
Hazlerigg
NEWCASTLE INTERNATIONAL AIRPORT
Camperdown
Killingworth
Killingworth Centre
Backworth
SHIREMOOR
NORTHUMBERLAND PARK
BOUNDARY MILL NEWCASTLE
NEWCASTLE
Gosforth Wood
Gosforth Lake
PALMERSVILLE
Woolsington
KINGSTON PARK
Fawdon
LONGBENTON
RISING SUN COUNTRY PARK
STEPHENSON RAILWAY MUSEUM
Gosforth
SOUTH GOSFORTH
Govt Blds
NEWCASTLE UPON TYNE
Willington
Blakelaw
Jesmond
WALLSEND
Heaton
HOWDON
Fenham
MILITARY VEHICLE MUSEUM
SEGEDUNUM ROMAN FORT
Tyne Tunnel
River Tyne
DENTON HALL TURRET
Civic Centre
HAYMARKET
Benwell
Byker
HEBBURN
Scotswood
MONUMENT
MANORS
Walker
DISCOVERY
BALTIC CENTRE
Elswick
CENTRAL
THE SAGE
GATESHEAD
METRO RADIO ARENA
GATESHEAD INTERNATIONAL STADIUM
METROCENTRE
METROLAND
Metro Centre
Dunston
GATESHEAD STADIUM
FELLING
HEWORTH
PELAW
Wardley
SHIPLEY ART GALL.
Bensham
WHICKHAM THORNS CENTRE
Felling
LOBLEY HILL
Wrekenton
Sunniside
Hill Head Wood
Lyndhurst
Chowdene
Springwell
High Park Wood
SUNNISIDE
BOWES RAILWAY
Usworth
BLUE LANE HOUSE
ANGEL OF THE NORTH
VERMONT
WASHINGTON
ANDREWS HOUSE
Kibblesworth
BIRTLEY
WASHINGTON OLD HALL
CAUSEY ARCH
Biddock
Lampton
WASHINGTON BIRTLEY SERVICES
Govt Offices
BEAMISH OPEN AIR MUSEUM
URPETH
OUSTON
Fatfield
Harraton
0 1 2 miles
0 1 2 3 km

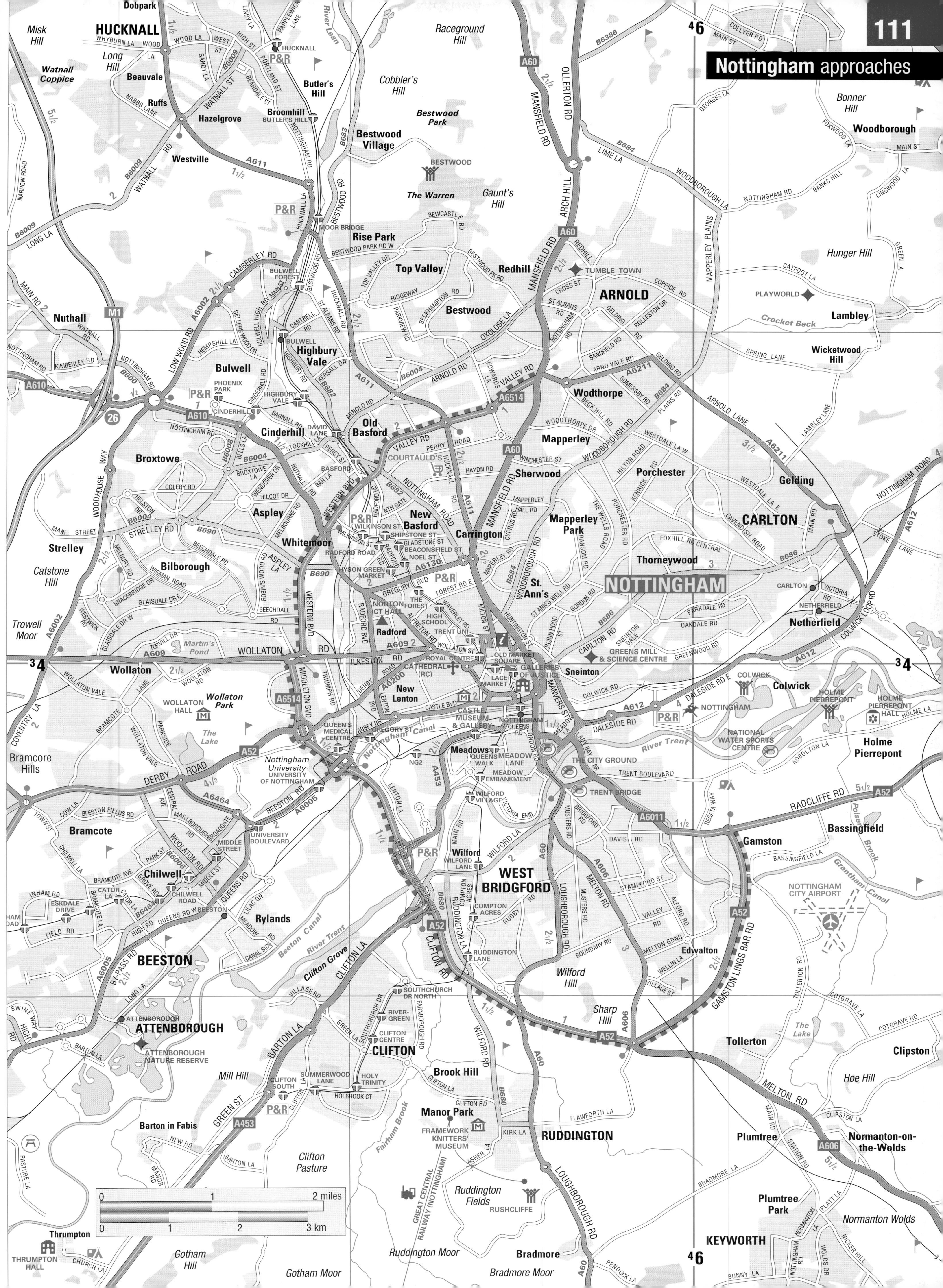
NOTTINGHAM
HUCKNALL
Hucknall
Dobpark
Misk Hill
Long Hill
Watnall Coppice
Beauvale
Ruffs
Hazelgrove
Westville
Broomhill
Butler's Hill
Raceground Hill
Cobbler's Hill
Bestwood Park
Bestwood Village
Bestwood
The Warren
Gaunt's Hill
Rise Park
Top Valley
Redhill
Tumble Town
ARNOLD
Bonner Hill
Woodborough
Hunger Hill
Playworld
Lambley
Crocket Beck
Wicketwood Hill
Nuthall
Bulwell
Highbury Vale
Cinderhill
Old Basford
Wodthorpe
Mapperley
Sherwood
Porchester
Gelding
Broxtowe
Aspley
New Basford
Carrington
Mapperley Park
CARLTON
Strelley
Whitemoor
Thorneywood
Catstone Hill
Bilborough
St. Ann's
Trowell Moor
Radford
Netherfield
Wollaton
Wollaton Park
Wollaton Hall
The Lake
Sneinton
Greens Mill & Science Centre
Colwick
Holme Pierrepont
Holme Pierrepont Hall
New Lenton
Castle Museum & Gallery
Galleries of Justice
Old Market Square
Lace Market
Royal Centre
Cathedral (RC)
Bramcore Hills
Nottingham University
University of Nottingham
Queen's Medical Centre
Nottingham Canal
Meadows
River Trent
The City Ground
Trent Bridge
National Water Sports Centre
Bramcote
Chilwell
Wilford
West Bridgford
Gamston
Bassingfield
Nottingham City Airport
Grantham Canal
Rylands
Beeston Canal
Clifton Grove
BEESTON
Compton Acres
Edwalton
Wilford Hill
Sharp Hill
ATTENBOROUGH
Attenborough Nature Reserve
CLIFTON
Tollerton
The Lake
Clipston
Hoe Hill
Mill Hill
Brook Hill
Manor Park
Framework Knitters' Museum
Barton in Fabis
Clifton Pasture
RUDDINGTON
Plumtree
Normanton-on-the-Wolds
Fairham Brook
Great Central Railway (Nottingham)
Ruddington Fields
Rushcliffe
Plumtree Park
Normanton Wolds
Thrumpton
Thrumpton Hall
Gotham Hill
Ruddington Moor
Bradmore
KEYWORTH
Gotham Moor
Bradmore Moor
M1
A60
A610
A611
A6002
A6514
A609
A52
A6005
A6464
A453
A606
A612
A6211
A6011
0
1
2 miles
0
1
2
3 km

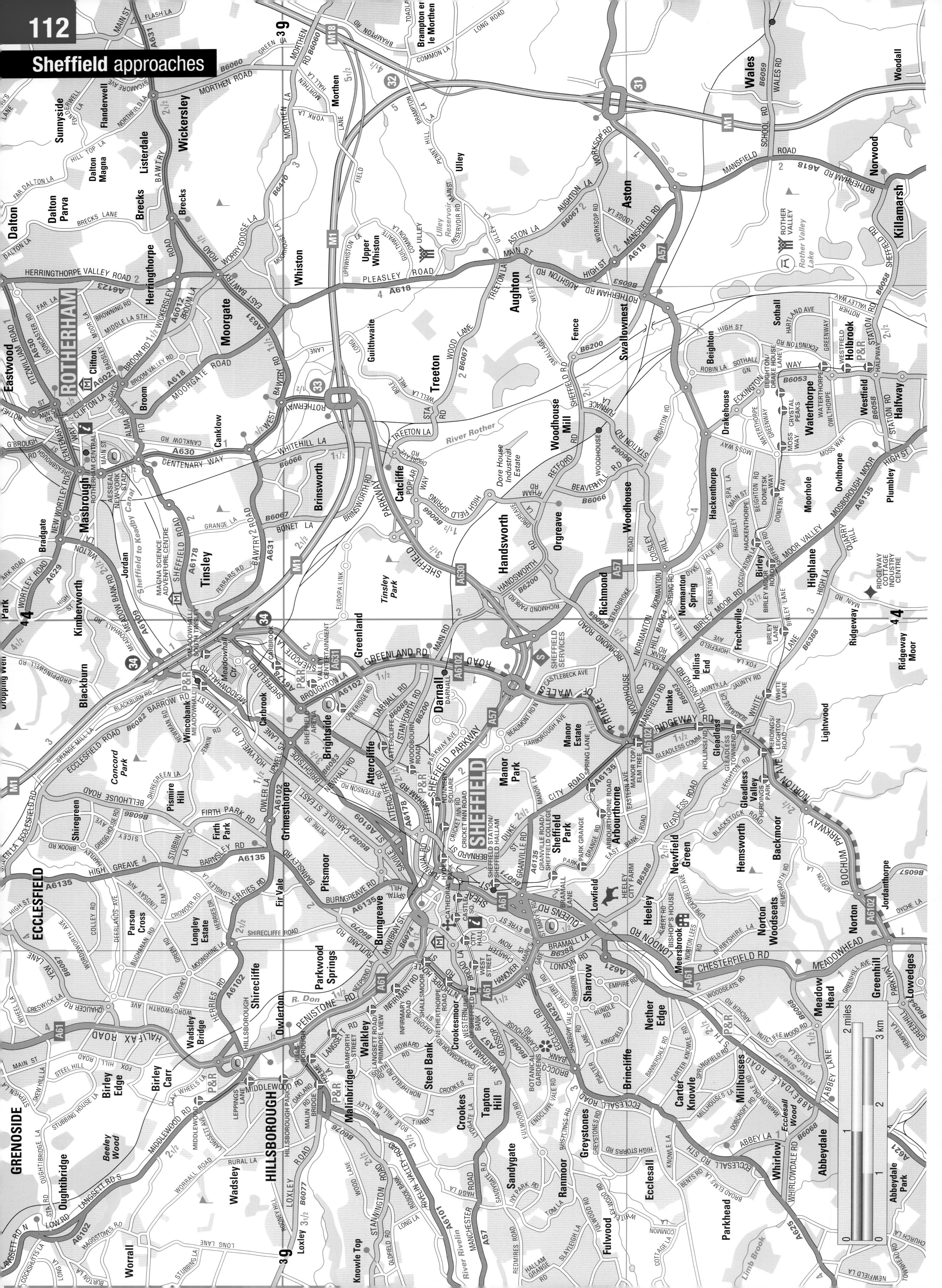
ROTHERHAM
SHEFFIELD
ECCLESFIELD
GRENOSIDE
HILLSBOROUGH
Wickersley
Moorgate
Herringthorpe
Brecks
Listerdale
Flanderwell
Sunnyside
Dalton
Dalton Parva
Dalton Magna
Whiston
Upper Whiston
Morthen
Ulley
Aston
Aughton
Treeton
Swallownest
Fence
Guilthwaite
Wales
Woodall
Norwood
Killamarsh
Beighton
Sothall
Holbrook
Halfway
Westfield
Waterthorpe
Drakehouse
Hackenthorpe
Moorhole
Owlthorpe
Plumbley
Woodhouse
Woodhouse Mill
Orgreave
Handsworth
Catcliffe
Brinsworth
Canklow
Broom
Clifton
Eastwood
Masbrough
Bradgate
Kimberworth
Jordan
Tinsley
Tinsley Park
Greenland
Darnall
Richmond
Normanton Spring
Frecheville
Birley
Highlane
Ridgeway
Ridgeway Moor
Hollins End
Intake
Gleadless
Gleadless Townend
Gleadless Valley
Lightwood
Manor Estate
Manor Park
Arbourthorne
Sheffield Park
Attercliffe
Brightside
Carbrook
Wincobank
Blackburn
Shiregreen
Pismire Hill
Firth Park
Grimesthorpe
Pitsmoor
Fir Vale
Parson Cross
Longley Estate
Shirecliffe
Parkwood Springs
Burngreave
Owlerton
Wadsley Bridge
Birley Carr
Birley Edge
Wadsley
Worrall
Oughtibridge
Loxley
Malin Bridge
Walkley
Steel Bank
Crookesmoor
Crookes
Tapton Hill
Sandygate
Ranmoor
Fulwood
Greystones
Ecclesall
Brincliffe
Nether Edge
Sharrow
Carter Knowle
Millhouses
Abbeydale
Abbeydale Park
Whirlow
Parkhead
Heeley
Lowfield
Newfield Green
Meersbrook
Norton
Norton Woodseats
Hemsworth
Backmoor
Jordanthorpe
Meadow Head
Greenhill
Lowedges
Knowle Top
Rother Valley Lake
Ulley Reservoir
River Rother
River Sheaf
R. Don
River Rivelin
Limb Brook
Ecclesall Wood
Beeley Wood
Concord Park
Meadowhall
Sheffield Arena
Dore House Industrial Estate
Sheffield Services
Magna Science Adventure Centre
Ridgeway Cottage Industry Centre
Botanical Gardens
Heeley City Farm
Bishop's House
2 miles
3 km

Bath

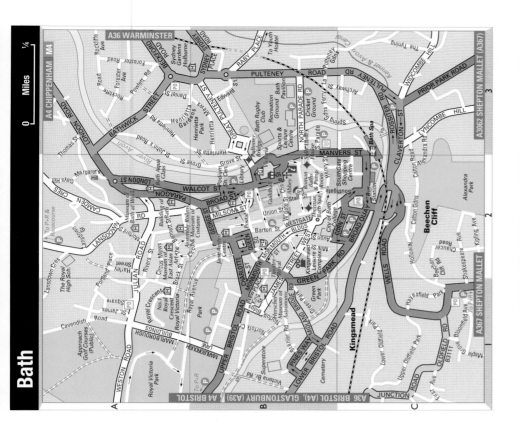

Blackpool

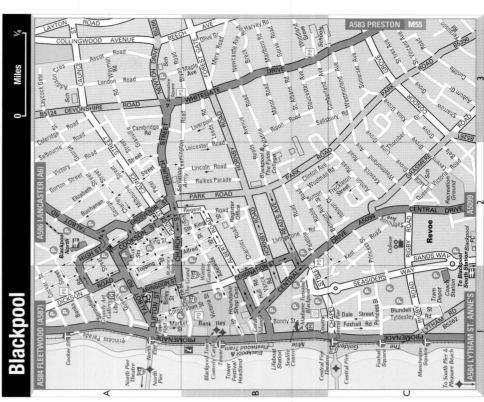

Aberdeen

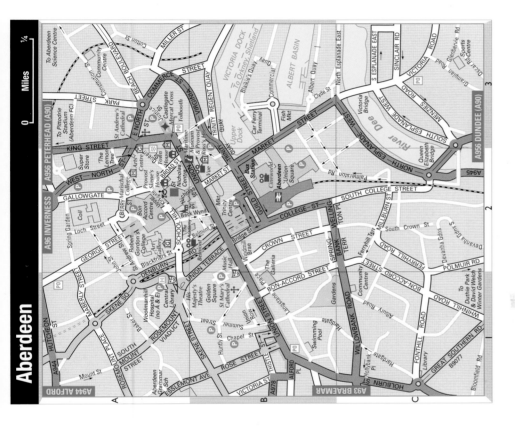

Town plan symbols

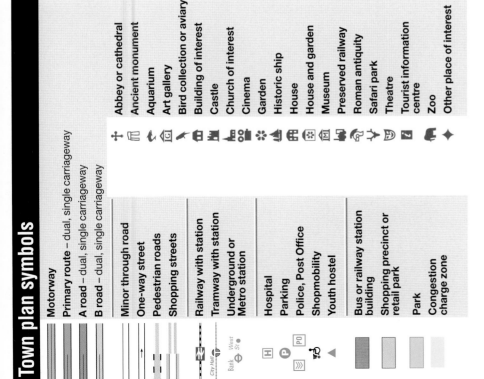

Motorway
Primary route – dual, single carriageway
A road – dual, single carriageway
B road – dual, single carriageway
Minor through road
One-way street
Pedestrian roads
Shopping streets
Railway with station
Tramway with station
Underground or Metro station
Hospital
Parking
Police, Post Office
Shopmobility
Youth hostel
Bus or railway station building
Shopping precinct or retail park
Park
Congestion charge zone

Abbey or cathedral
Ancient monument
Aquarium
Art gallery
Bird collection or aviary
Building of interest
Castle
Church of interest
Cinema
Garden
Historic ship
House
House and garden
Museum
Preserved railway
Roman antiquity
Safari park
Theatre
Tourist information centre
Zoo
Other place of interest

Birmingham

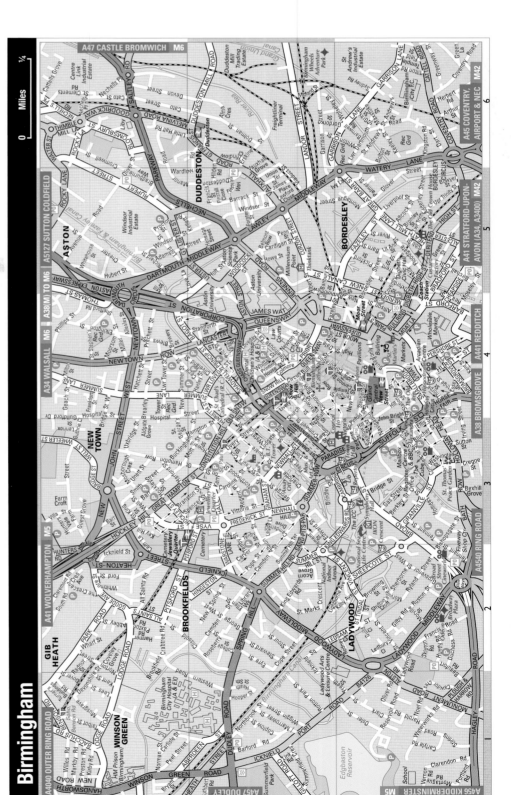

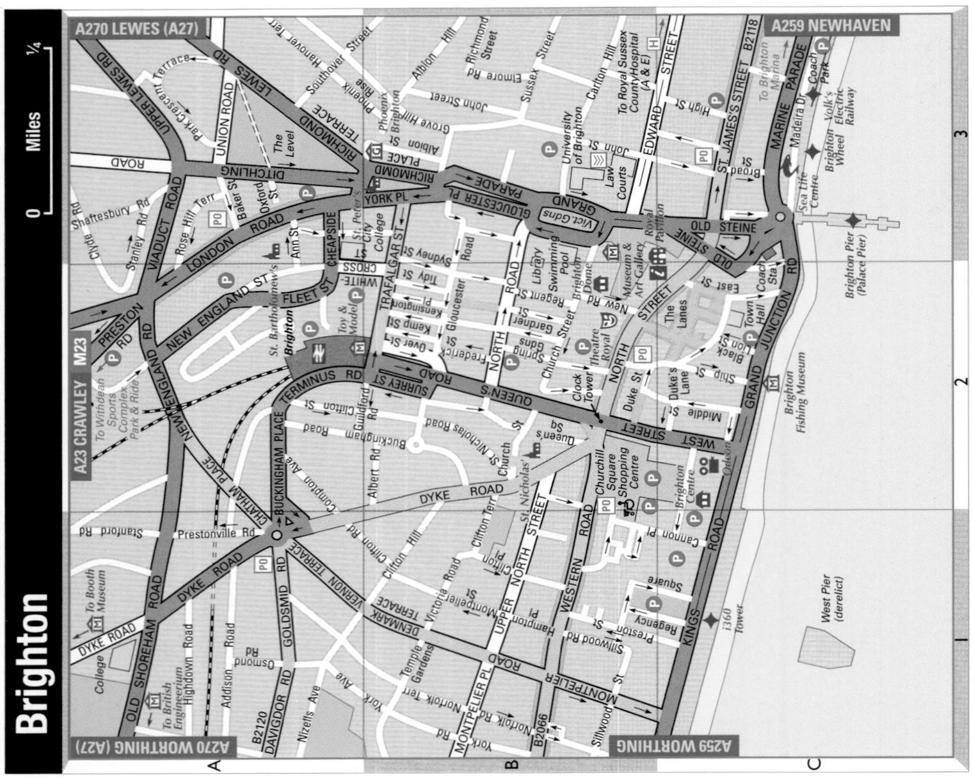
Brighton
A270 LEWES (A27)
A259 NEWHAVEN
A23 CRAWLEY
M23
A270 WORTHING (A27)
A259 WORTHING
Miles

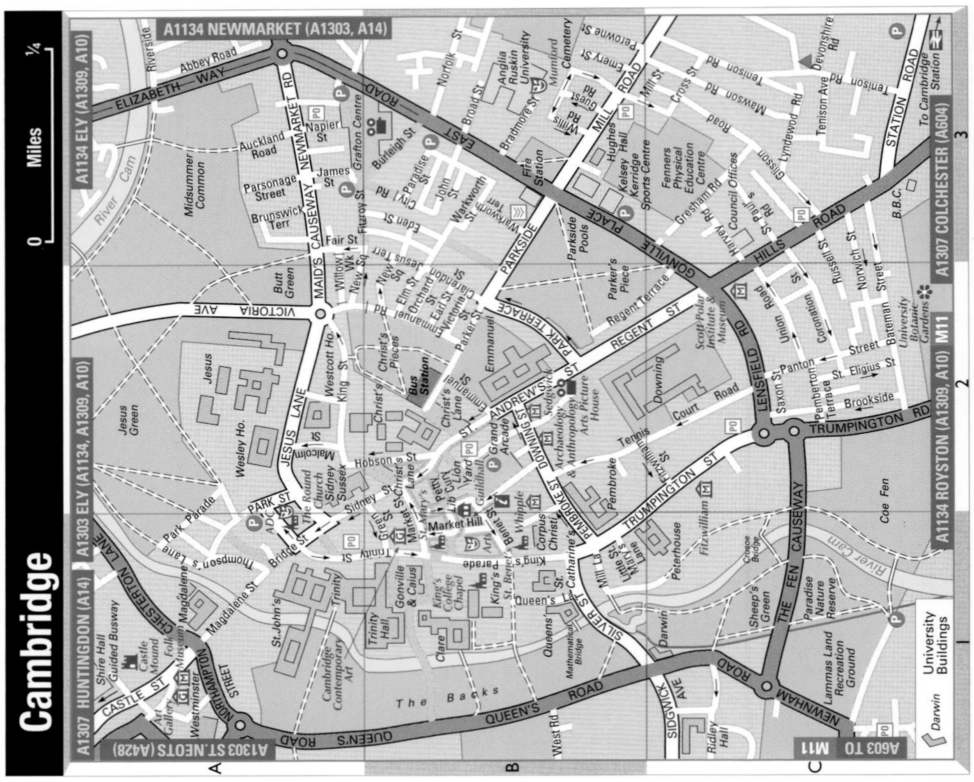
Cambridge
A1134 NEWMARKET (A1303, A14)
A1134 ELY (A1309, A10)
A1303 ELY (A1134, A1309, A10)
A1307 HUNTINGDON (A14)
A1303 ST.NEOTS (A428)
A603 TO M11
A1134 ROYSTON (A1309, A10) M11
A1307 COLCHESTER (A604)
Miles

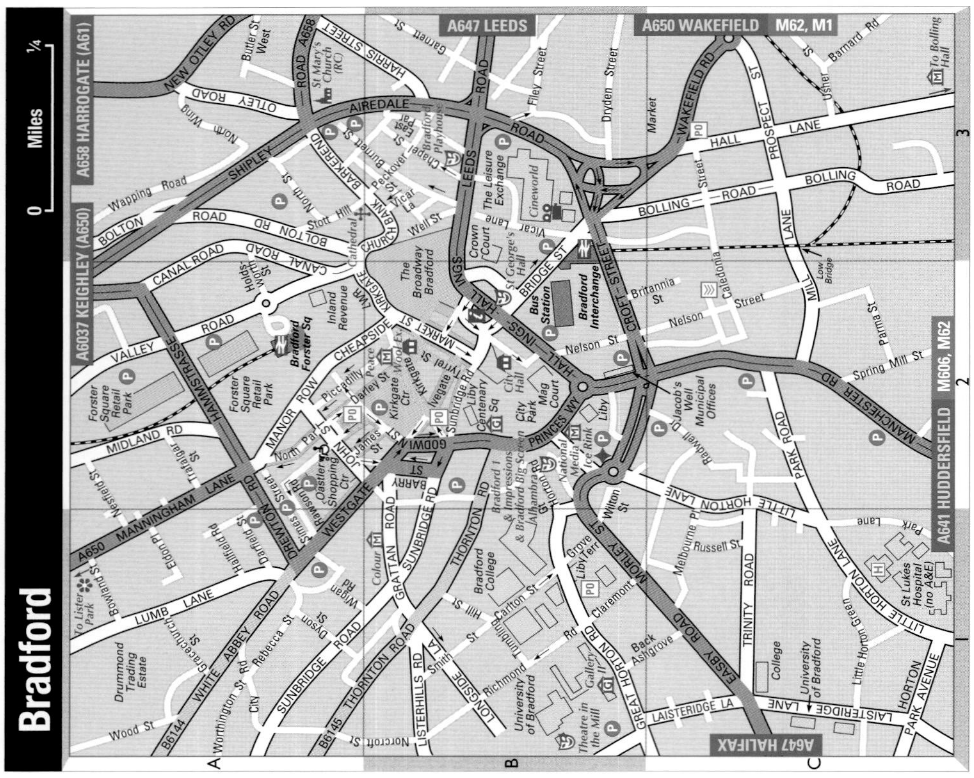
Bradford
A647 LEEDS
A650 WAKEFIELD M62, M1
A658 HARROGATE (A61)
A6037 KEIGHLEY (A650)
M606, M62
A641 HUDDERSFIELD
A647 HALIFAX
Miles

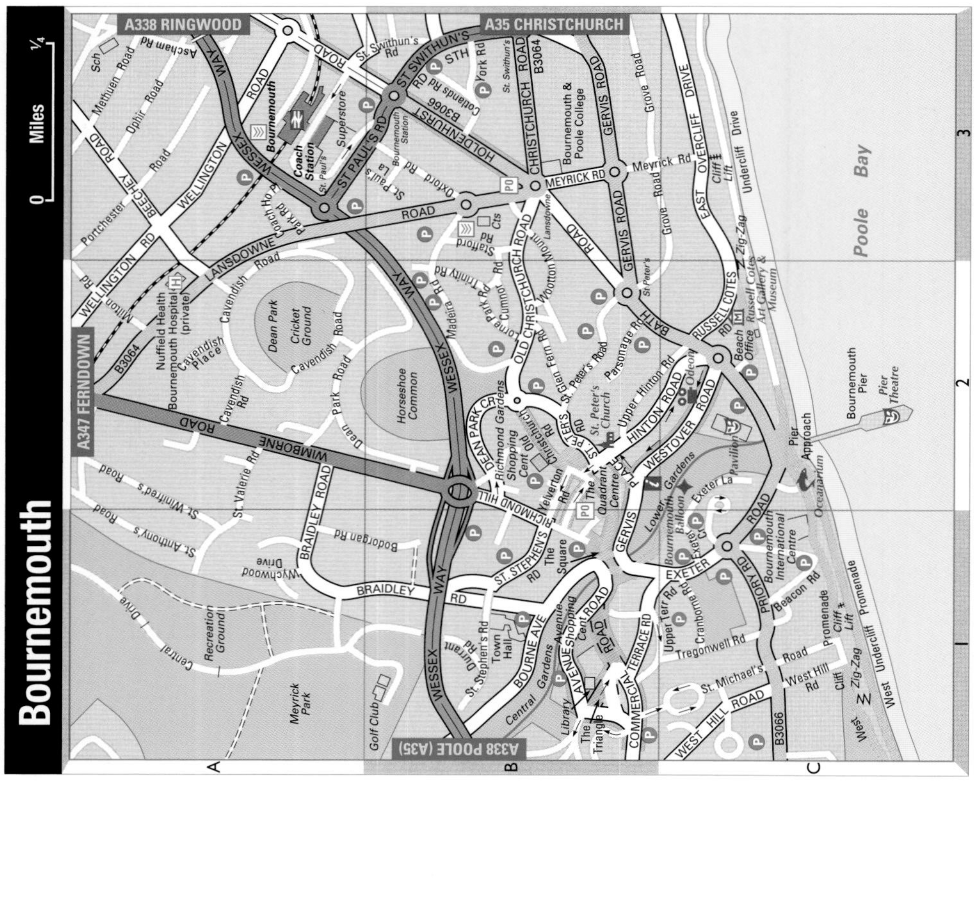
Bournemouth
A338 RINGWOOD
A35 CHRISTCHURCH
A347 FERNDOWN
A338 POOLE (A35)
Poole Bay
Miles

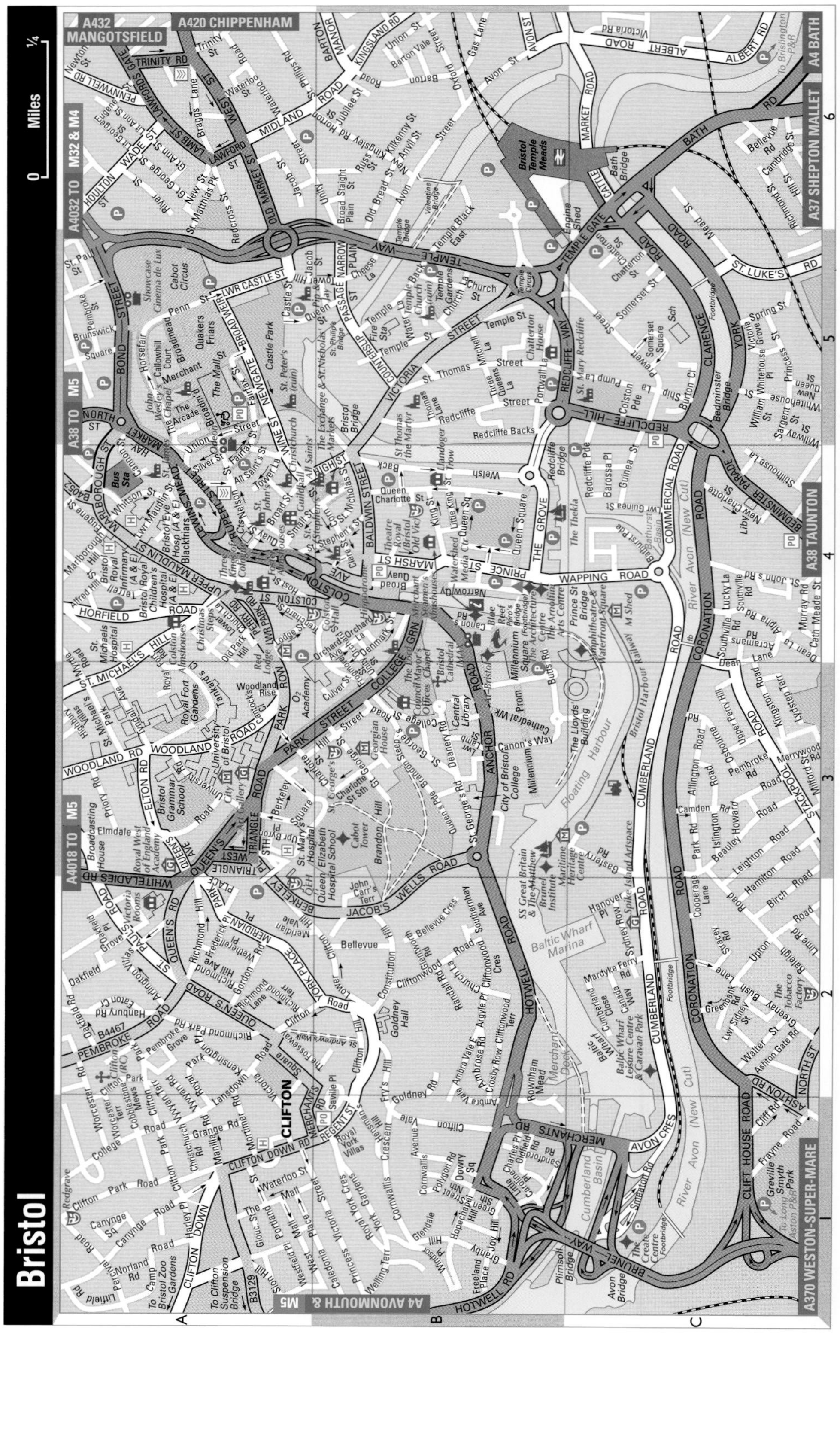
Bristol
A432 MANGOTSFIELD
A420 CHIPPENHAM
A4032 TO M32 & M4
A38 TO M5
A4018 TO M5
A4 AVONMOUTH & M5
A370 WESTON-SUPER-MARE
A38 TAUNTON
A37 SHEPTON MALLET
A4 BATH
Miles

Canterbury page 21 • **Cardiff** page 15 • **Cheltenham** page 26 • **Chester** page 43 • **Chichester** page 11 • **Colchester** page 31

115

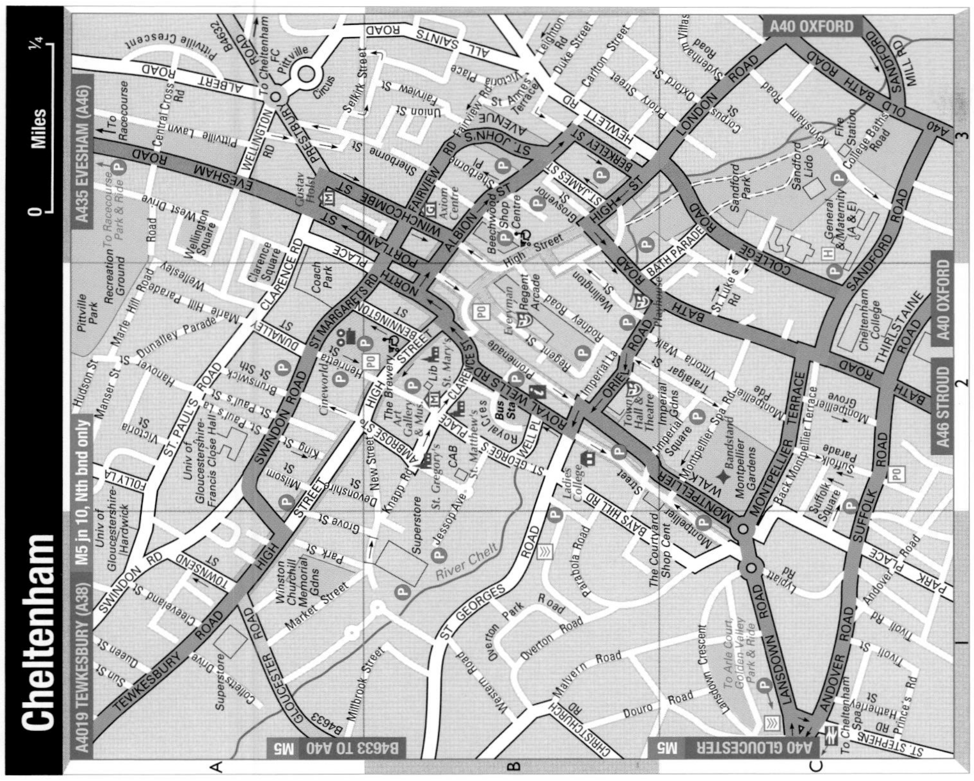

Cheltenham

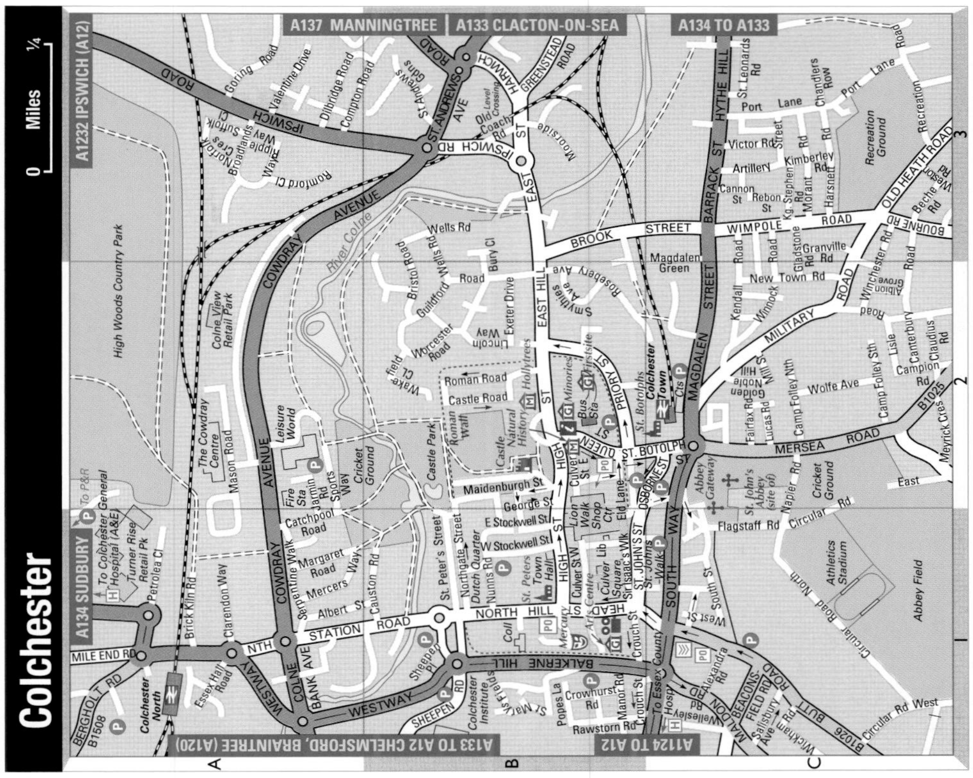

Colchester

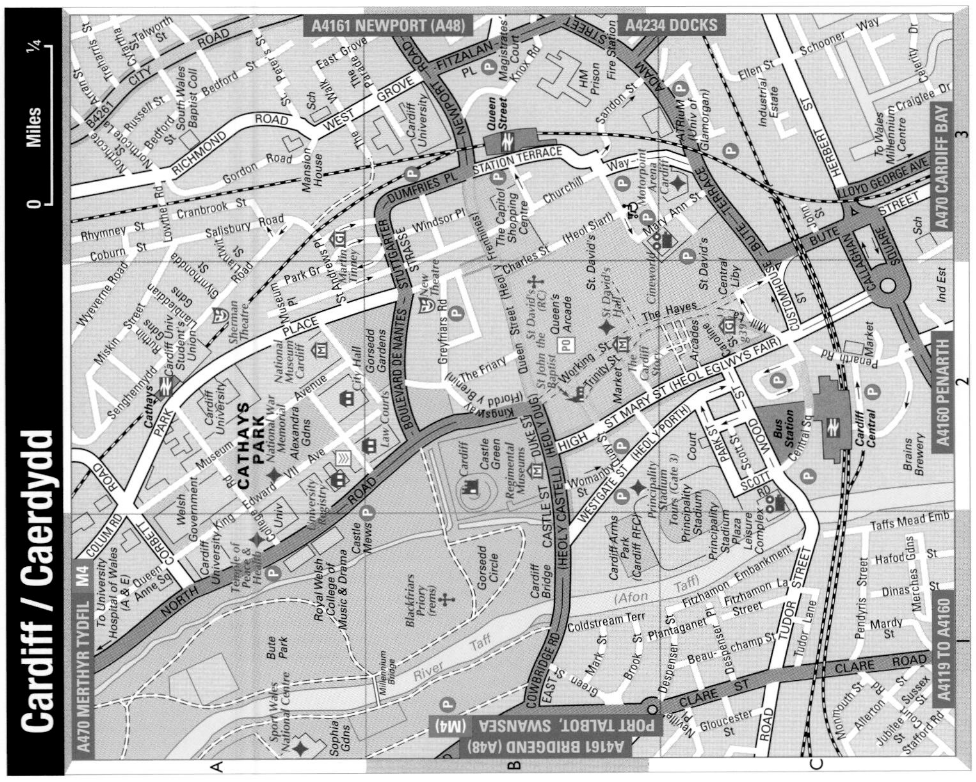

Cardiff / Caerdydd

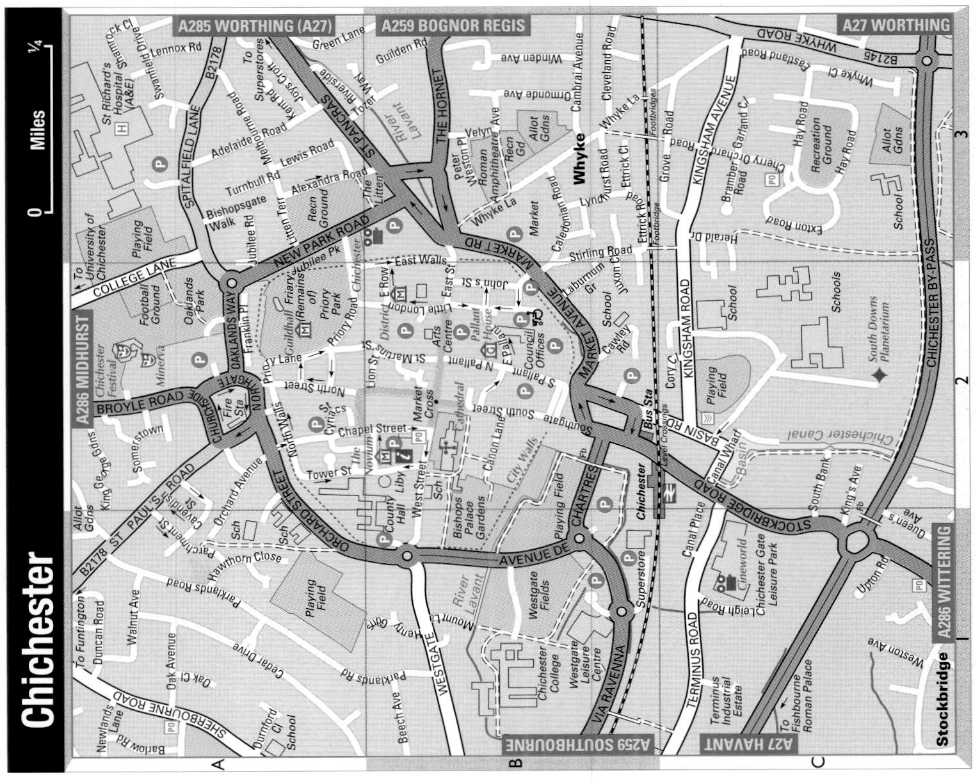

Chichester

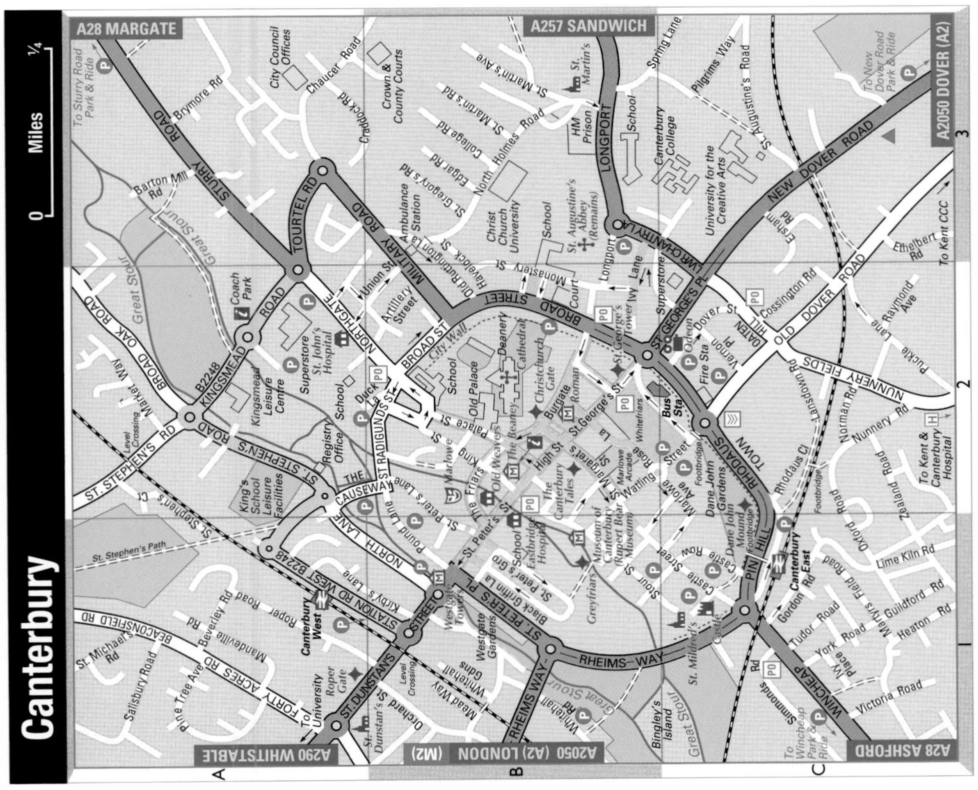

Canterbury

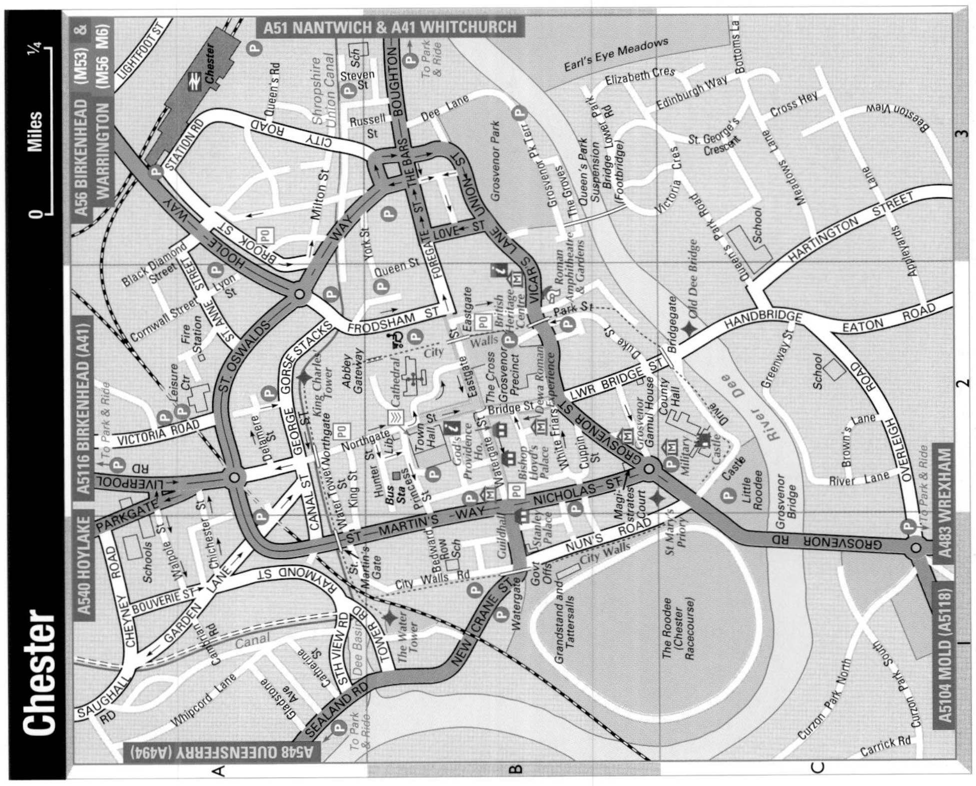

Chester

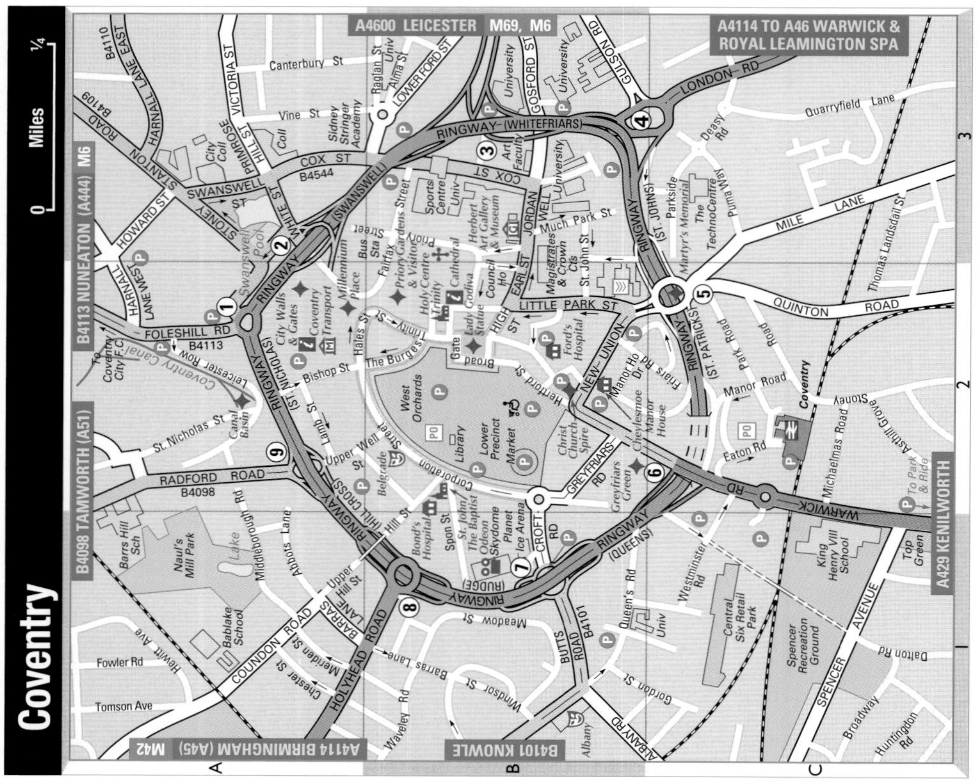
Coventry
A4600 LEICESTER M69, M6
A4114 TO A46 WARWICK & ROYAL LEAMINGTON SPA
A429 KENILWORTH
B4101 KNOWLE
A4114 BIRMINGHAM (A45) M42
B4098 TAMWORTH (A51)
B4113 NUNEATON (A444) M6
Miles

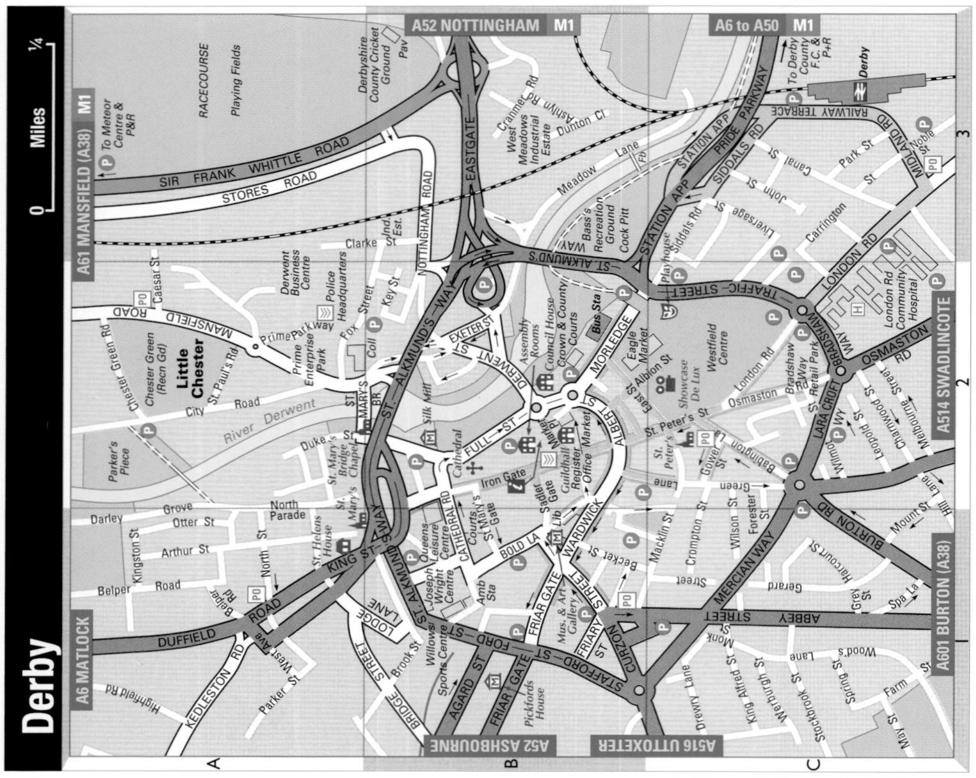
Derby
A52 NOTTINGHAM M1
A6 to A50 M1
A514 SWADLINCOTE
A601 BURTON (A38)
A516 UTTOXETER
A52 ASHBOURNE
A6 MATLOCK
A61 MANSFIELD (A38) M1
Miles

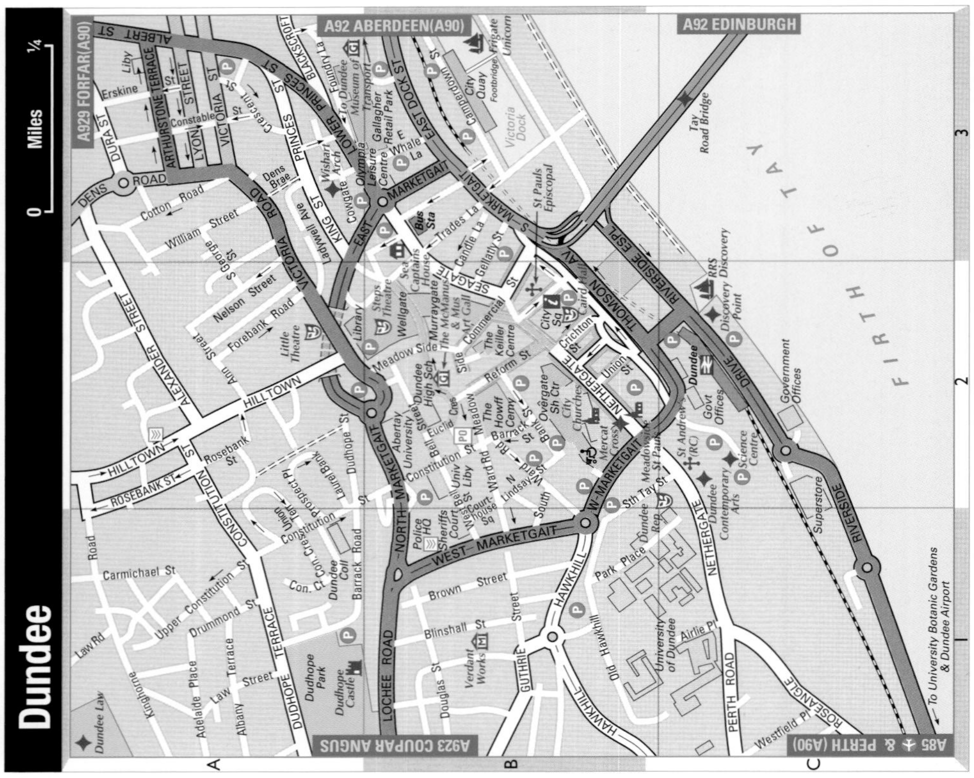
Dundee
A92 ABERDEEN (A90)
A92 EDINBURGH
A85 & PERTH (A90)
A923 COUPAR ANGUS
A929 FORFAR (A90)
FIRTH OF TAY
Miles

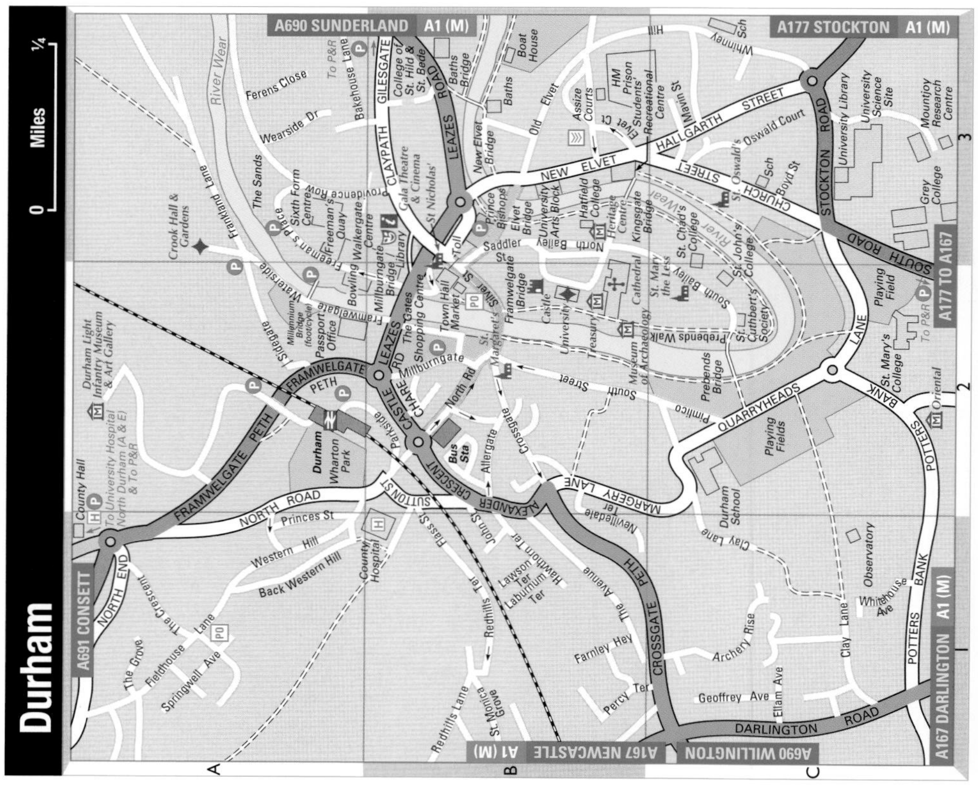
Durham
A690 SUNDERLAND A1 (M)
A177 STOCKTON A1 (M)
A177 TO A167
A167 DARLINGTON A1 (M)
A690 WILLINGTON A167 NEWCASTLE A1 (M)
A691 CONSETT
Miles

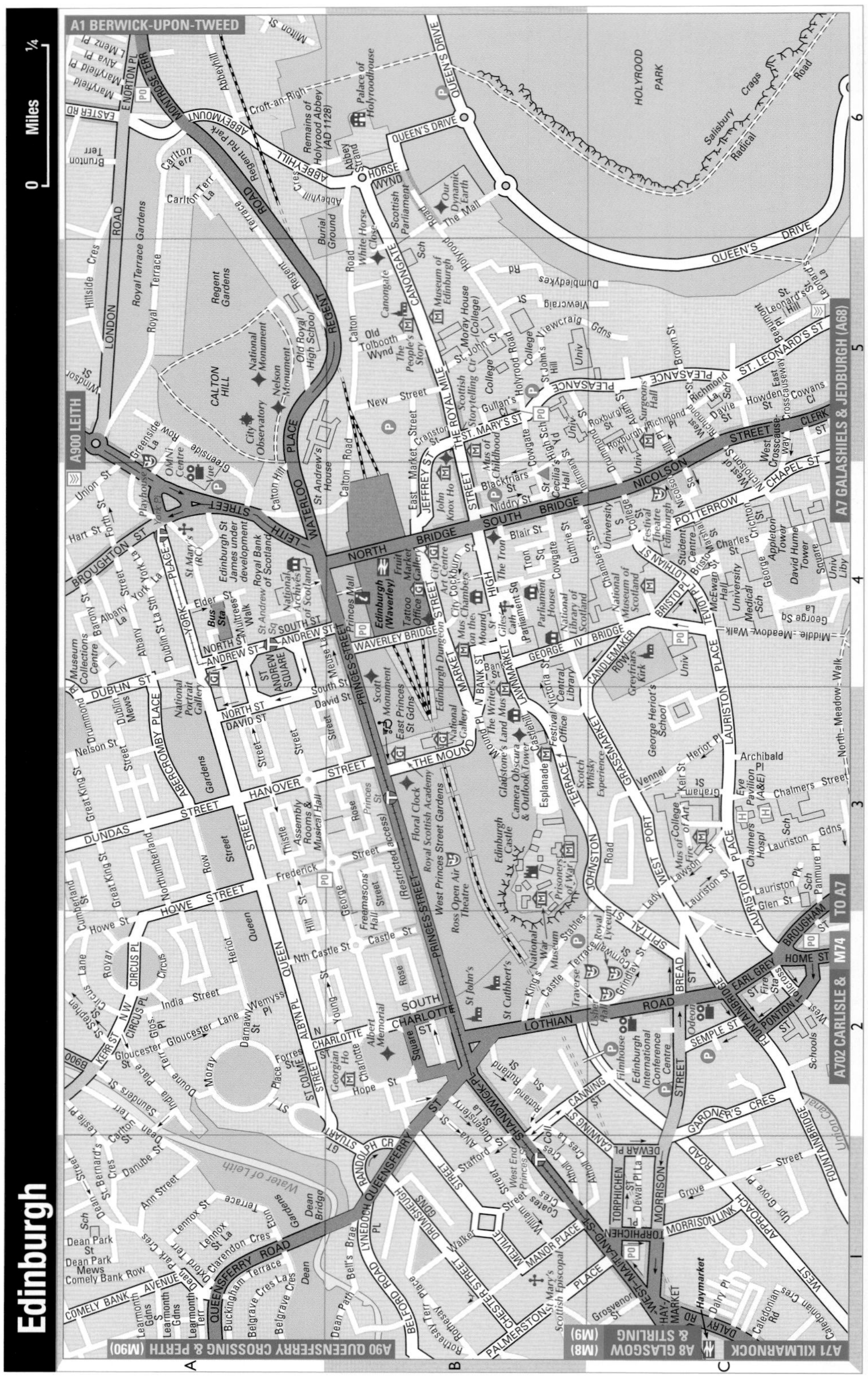
Edinburgh
A1 BERWICK-UPON-TWEED
A7 GALASHIELS & JEDBURGH (A68)
A702 CARLISLE & M74 TO A7
A71 KILMARNOCK
A8 GLASGOW (M8) & STIRLING (M9)
A90 QUEENSFERRY CROSSING & PERTH (M90)
A900 LEITH
HOLYROOD PARK
Miles

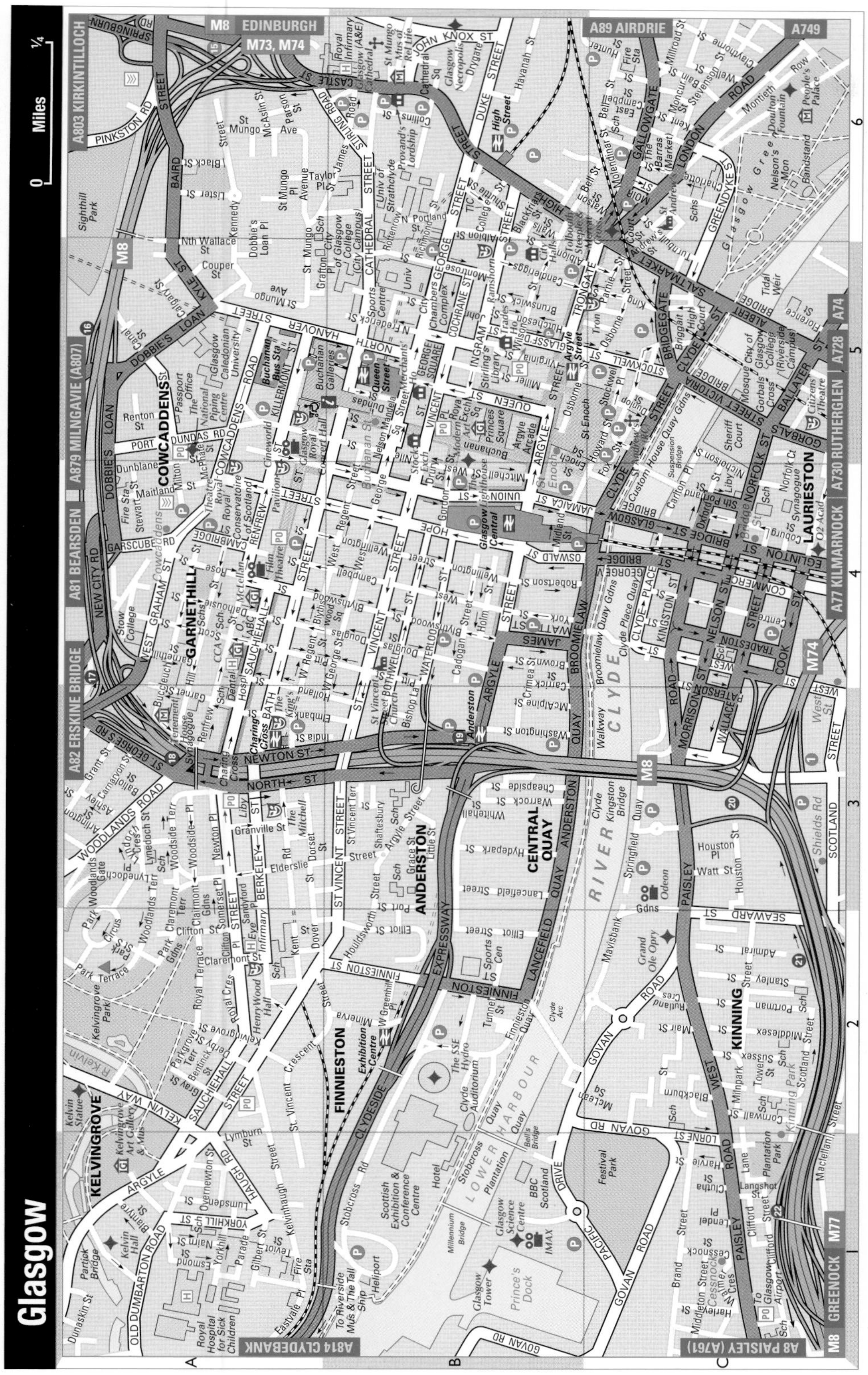
Exeter
0 Miles ¼
B3183 TIVERTON (A396)
B3212
A377 BARNSTAPLE
B3183 HONITON (A30), TAUNTON (M5)
B3212 OKEHAMPTON (A30)
A377 PLYMOUTH (A38)
A3015 EXMOUTH (A376)
St David's
Polsloe Park
Mount Radford
Friars' Green
St Thomas

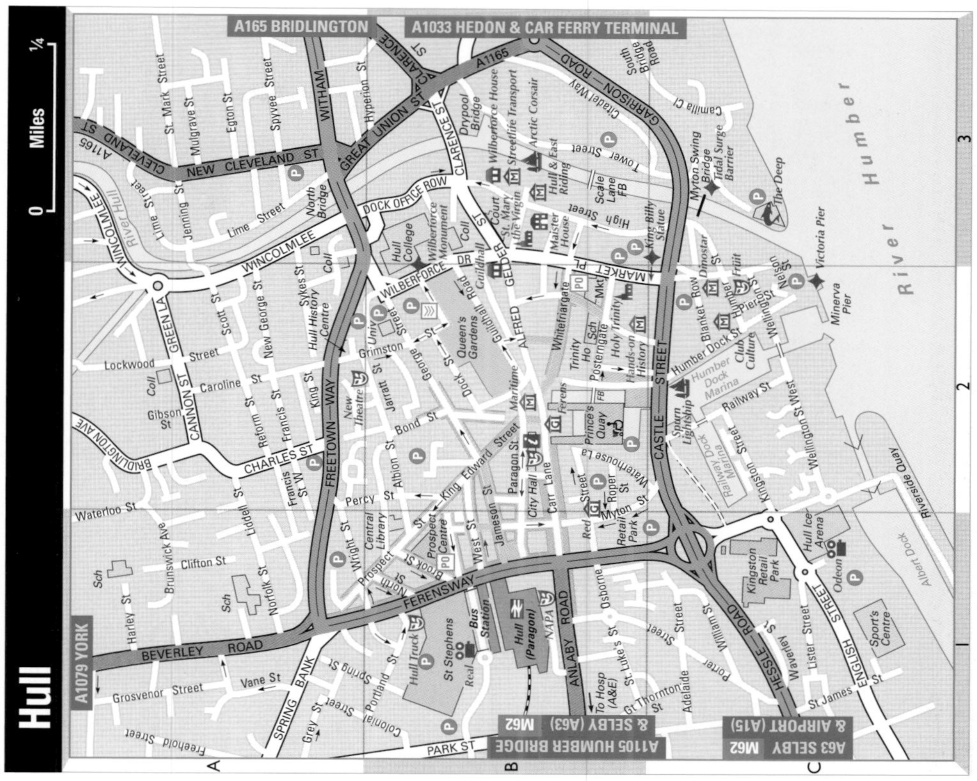
Glasgow
0 Miles ¼
A82 ERSKINE BRIDGE
A81 BEARSDEN
A879 MILNGAVIE (A807)
A803 KIRKINTILLOCH
M8 EDINBURGH
A814 CLYDEBANK
A8 PAISLEY (A761)
M8 GREENOCK M77
A77 KILMARNOCK
A730 RUTHERGLEN
A728
A74
A89 AIRDRIE
A749
KELVINGROVE
GARNETHILL
COWCADDENS
FINNIESTON
ANDERSTON
CENTRAL QUAY
KINNING
LAURIESTON
RIVER CLYDE

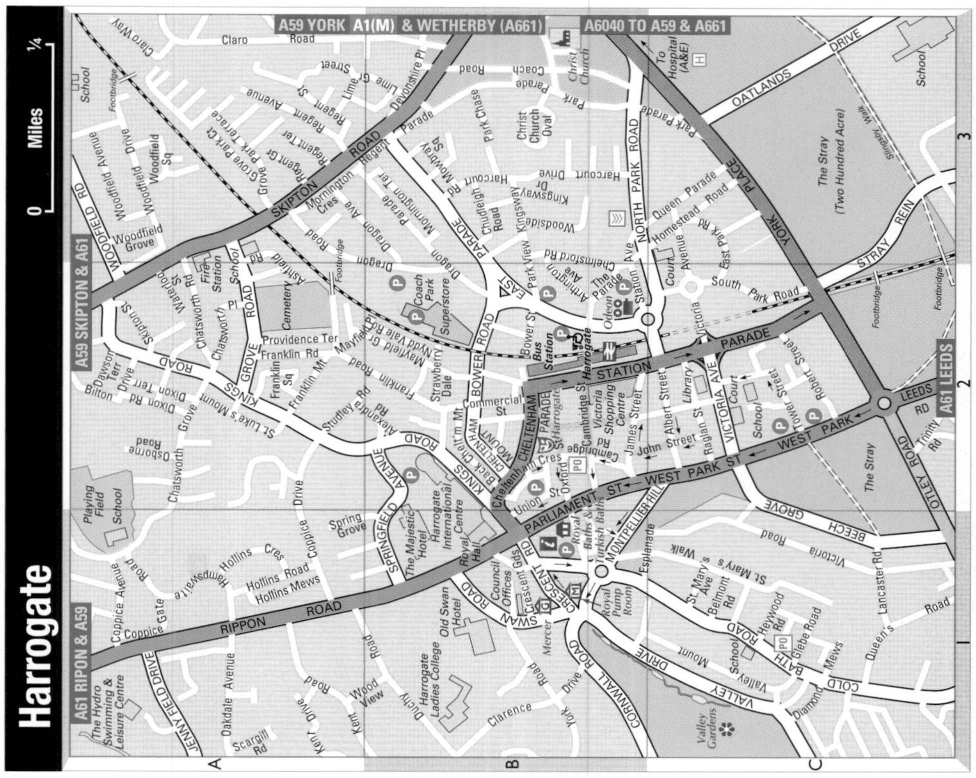
Gloucester
0 Miles ¼
A38 CHELTENHAM (A40) & M5
A417 ROSS-ON-WYE (A40)
A4302 TO A38
A430 TO A38 BRISTOL M5

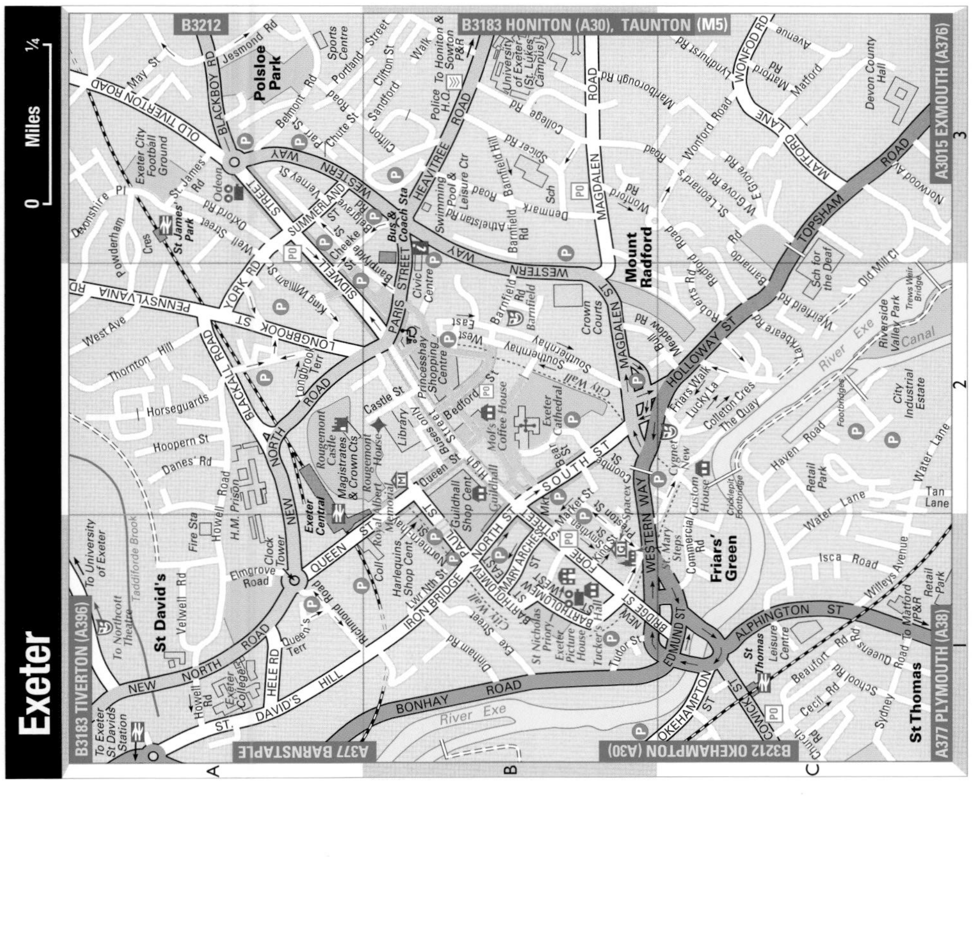
Harrogate
0 Miles ¼
A61 RIPON & A59
A59 SKIPTON & A61
A59 YORK A1(M) & WETHERBY (A661)
A6040 TO A59 & A661
A61 LEEDS
The Stray (Two Hundred Acre)

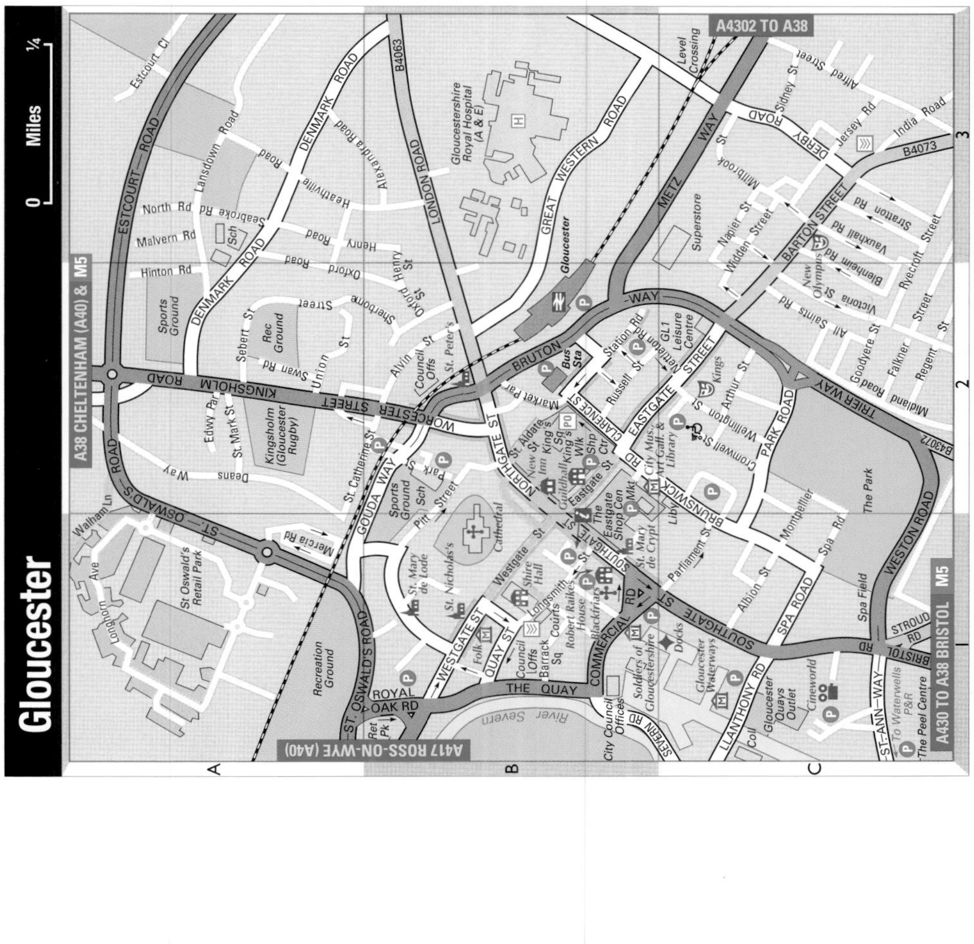
Hull
0 Miles ¼
A1079 YORK
A165 BRIDLINGTON
A1033 HEDON & CAR FERRY TERMINAL
A1105 HUMBER BRIDGE & SELBY (A63) M62
A63 SELBY & AIRPORT (A15) M62
River Humber

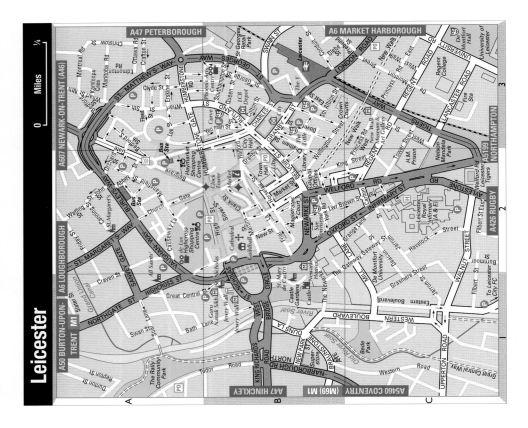
Leicester
A47 PETERBOROUGH
A6 MARKET HARBOROUGH
A607 NEWARK-ON-TRENT (A46)
A6 LOUGHBOROUGH
A50 BURTON-UPON-TRENT M1
A47 HINCKLEY
A5460 COVENTRY (M69) M1
A426 RUGBY
A5199 NORTHAMPTON

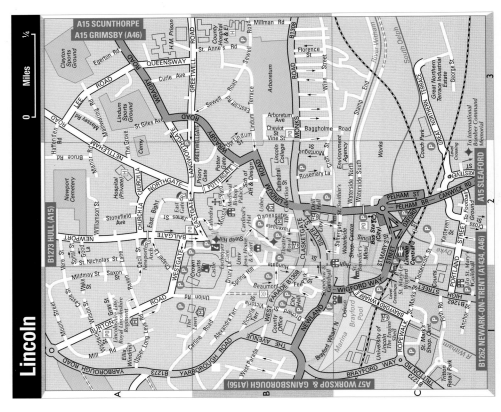
Lincoln
A15 SCUNTHORPE
A15 GRIMSBY (A46)
B1273 HULL (A15)
A57 WORKSOP & GAINSBOROUGH (A156)
B1262 NEWARK-ON-TRENT (A1434, A46)
A15 SLEAFORD

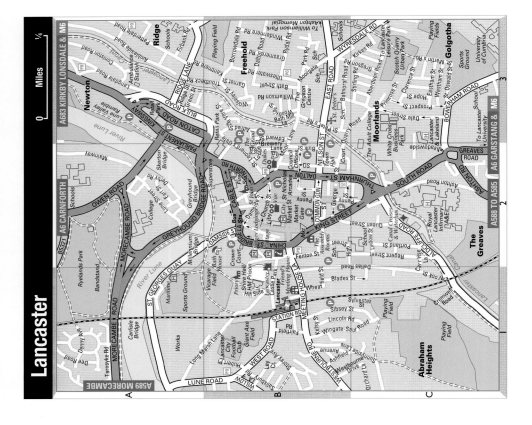
Lancaster
A683 KIRKBY LONSDALE & M6
A6 CARNFORTH
A589 MORECAMBE
A588 TO A585
A6 GARSTANG & M6

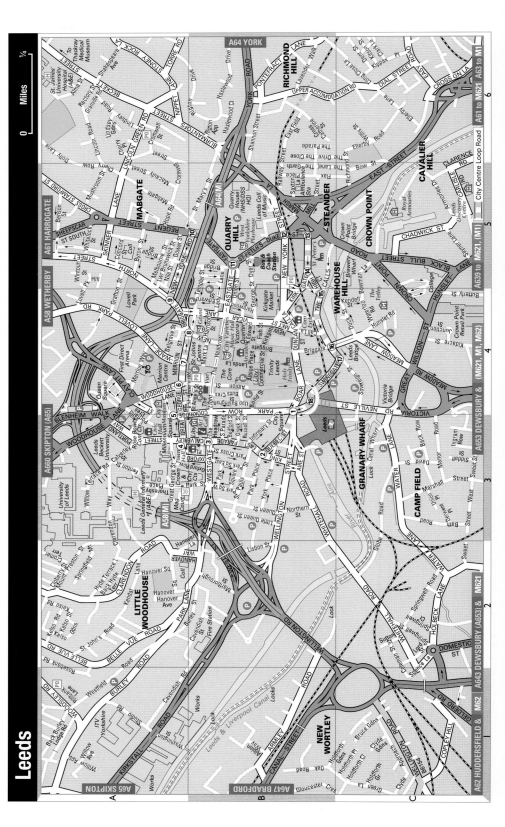
Ipswich
A1214 WOODBRIDGE, LOWESTOFT (A12)
A1071 WOODBRIDGE (A1214)
A1156 FELIXSTOWE (A14)
A1156 NORWICH (A14, A140)
A1214 COLCHESTER (A12)
A137 MANNINGTREE

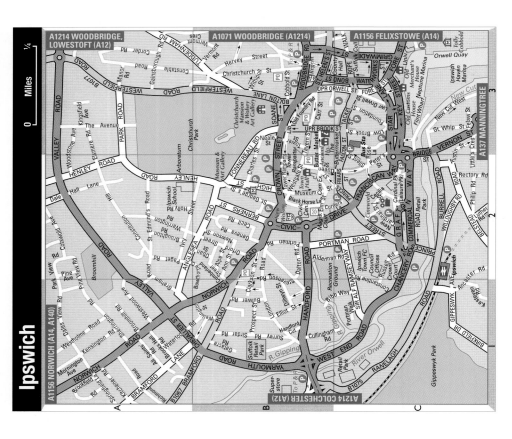
Leeds
A64 YORK
A61 HARROGATE
A58 WETHERBY
A660 SKIPTON (A65)
A65 SKIPTON
A647 BRADFORD
A62 HUDDERSFIELD & M62
A643 DEWSBURY (A653) & M621
A653 DEWSBURY & (M621, M1, M62)
A639 to M621, M1
A61 to M621
A63 to M1

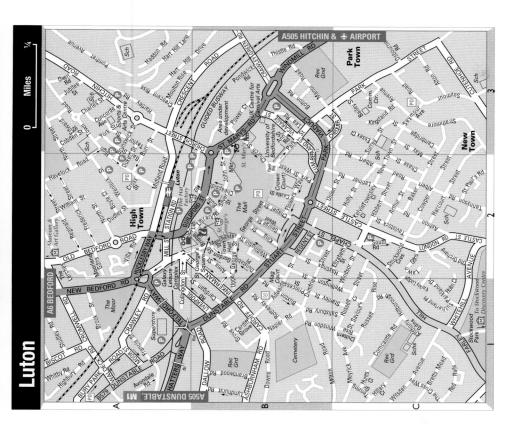
Luton
A505 HITCHIN & AIRPORT
A6 BEDFORD
A505 DUNSTABLE M1
Miles

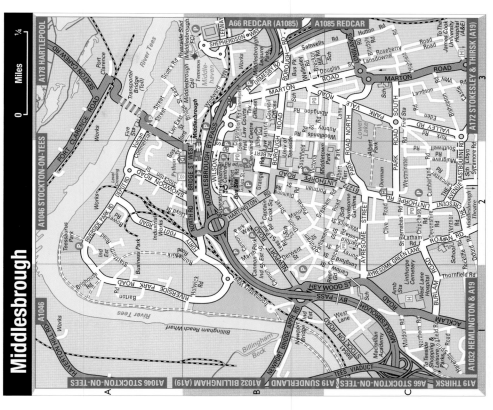
Middlesbrough
A66 REDCAR (A1085)
A1085 REDCAR
A178 HARTLEPOOL
A1046 STOCKTON-ON-TEES
A172 STOKESLEY & THIRSK (A19)
A1032 HEMLINGTON & A19
A19 THIRSK A66 STOCKTON-ON-TEES A19 SUNDERLAND A1032 BILLINGHAM (A19) A1046 STOCKTON-ON-TEES
Miles

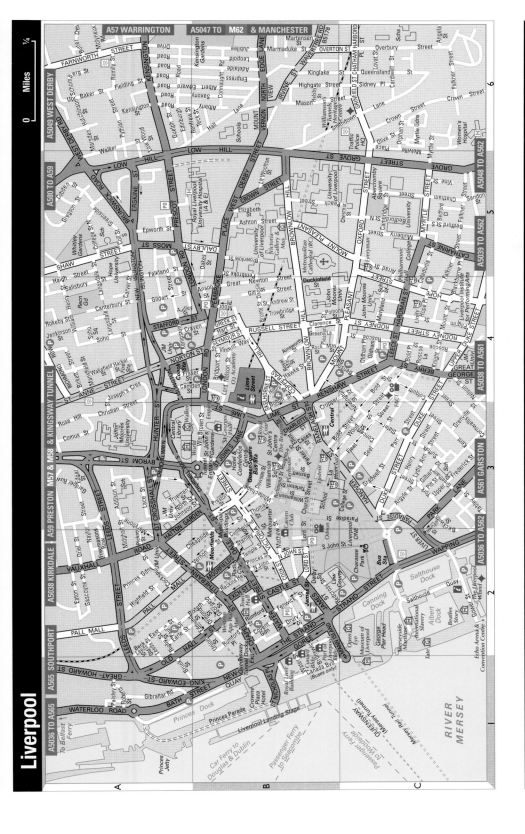
Liverpool
A57 WARRINGTON
A5047 TO M62 & MANCHESTER
A5036 TO A565
A565 SOUTHPORT
A5038 KIRKDALE
A59 PRESTON M57 & M58 & KINGSWAY TUNNEL
A580 TO A59
A5049 WEST DERBY
A5048 TO A562
A5039 TO A562
A5038 TO A561
A561 GARSTON
A5036 TO A562
RIVER MERSEY
Miles

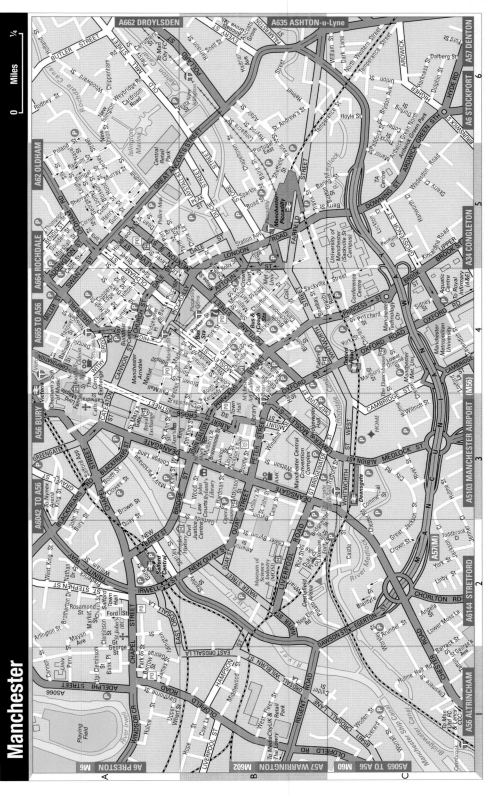
Manchester
A662 DROYLSDEN
A635 ASHTON-u-Lyne
A56 ALTRINCHAM
A6144 STRETFORD
A5103 MANCHESTER AIRPORT (M56)
A34 CONGLETON
A6 STOCKPORT
A57 DENTON
A6042 TO A56
A56 BURY
A665 TO A56
A664 ROCHDALE
A62 OLDHAM
A6 PRESTON M6
M602 A57 WARRINGTON M60 A5065 TO A56
Miles

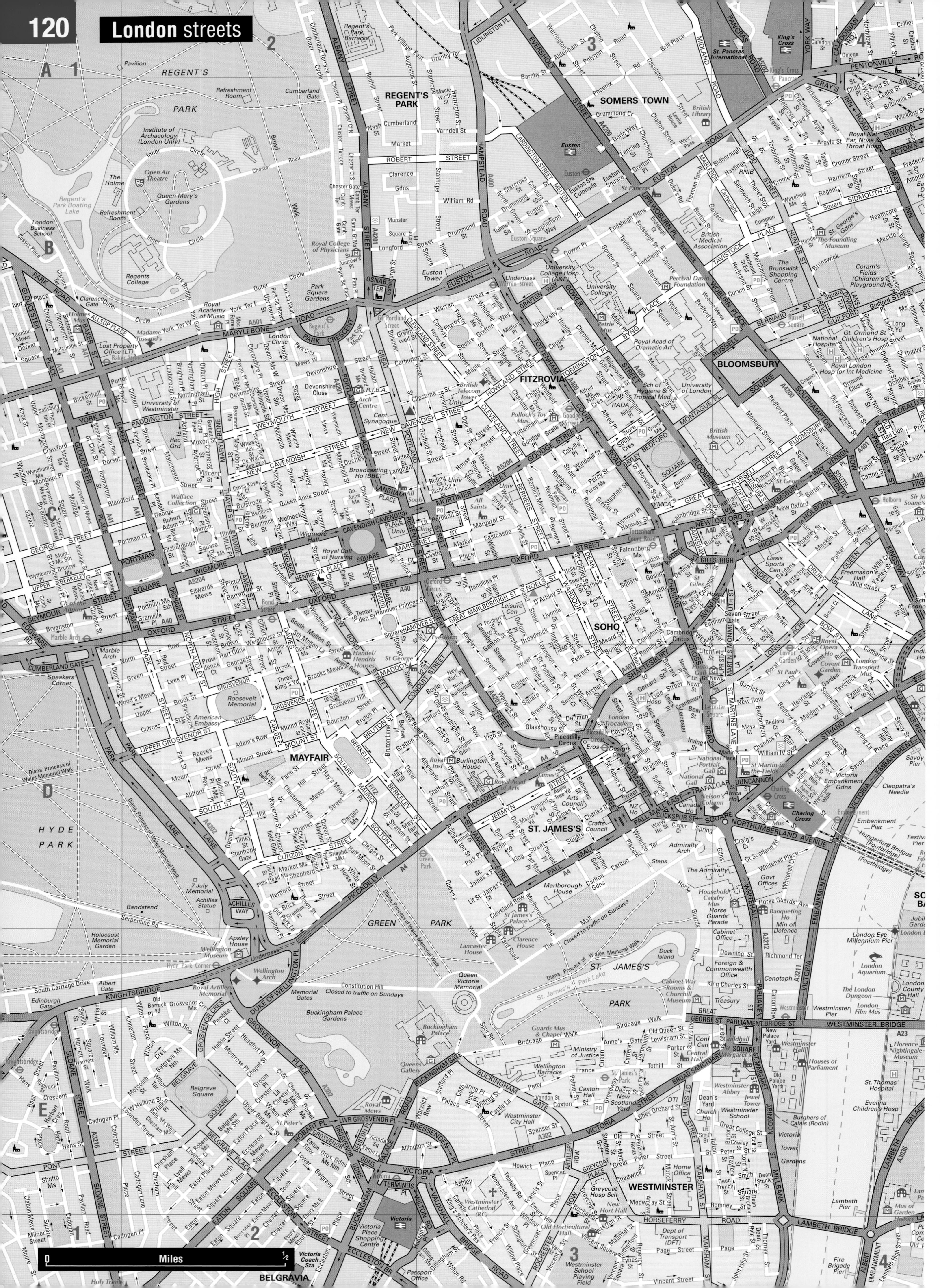
REGENT'S PARK
SOMERS TOWN
REGENT'S PARK
BLOOMSBURY
FITZROVIA
SOHO
MAYFAIR
ST. JAMES'S
WESTMINSTER
HYDE PARK
GREEN PARK
ST. JAMES'S PARK
BELGRAVIA
Euston
St. Pancras International
King's Cross St Pancras
British Library
British Museum
University College
University of London
Regent's Park Boating Lake
Queen Mary's Gardens
Open Air Theatre
London Business School
Madame Tussaud's
Wallace Collection
Marble Arch
Speakers Corner
Hyde Park Corner
Wellington Arch
Apsley House
Buckingham Palace
Buckingham Palace Gardens
Queen Victoria Memorial
Clarence House
Piccadilly Circus
Trafalgar Square
National Gallery
Nelson's Column
Charing Cross
Houses of Parliament
Westminster Abbey
Westminster Bridge
Westminster Cathedral (RC)
Victoria
Lambeth Bridge
London Eye Millennium Pier
London Aquarium
Cleopatra's Needle
Embankment
Horse Guards Parade
Downing St
Tate
Oxford Circus
Cambridge Circus
Covent Garden
Royal Opera Ho
0 Miles 1/2

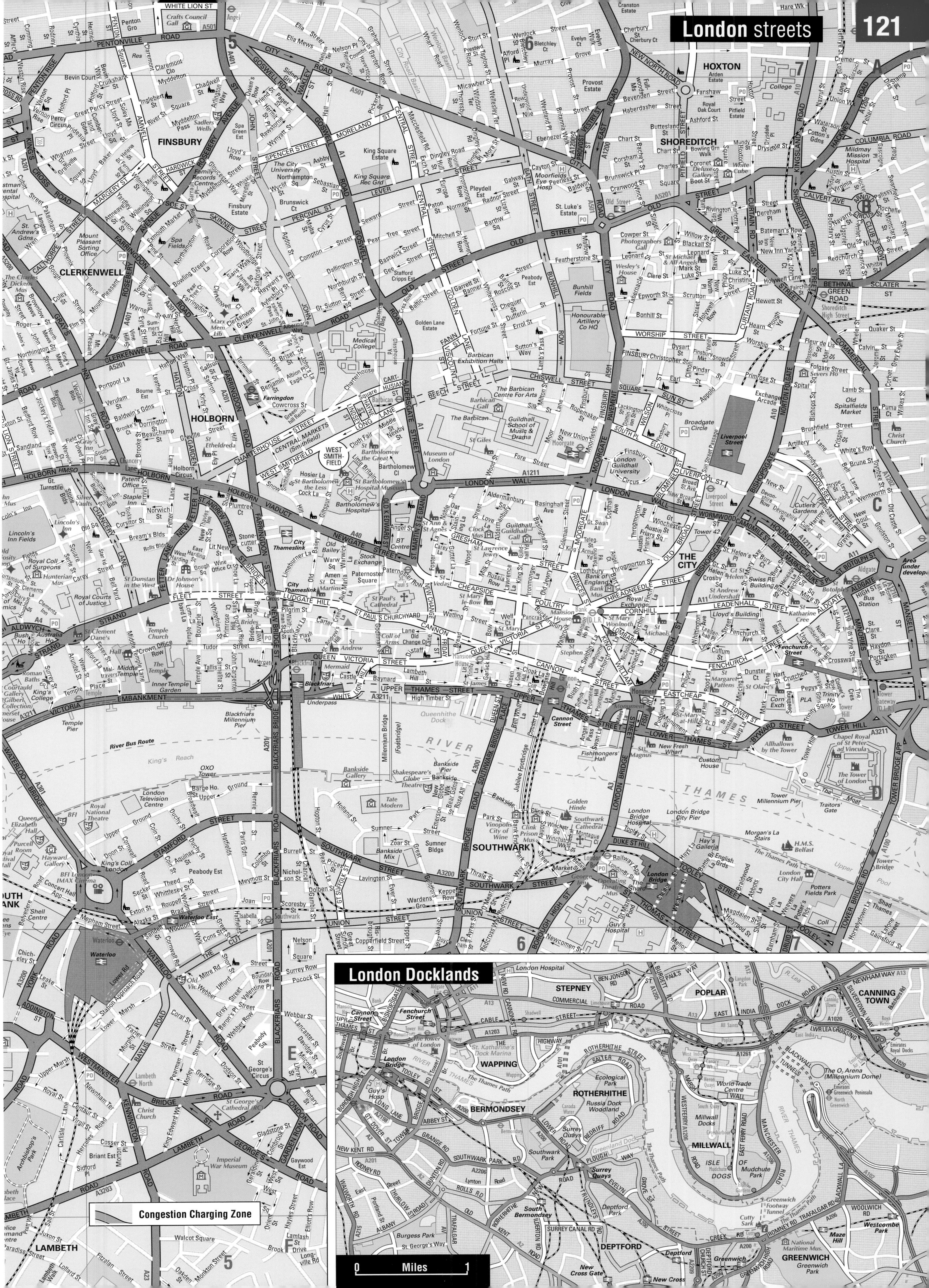

London Docklands

Congestion Charging Zone

0 — Miles — 1

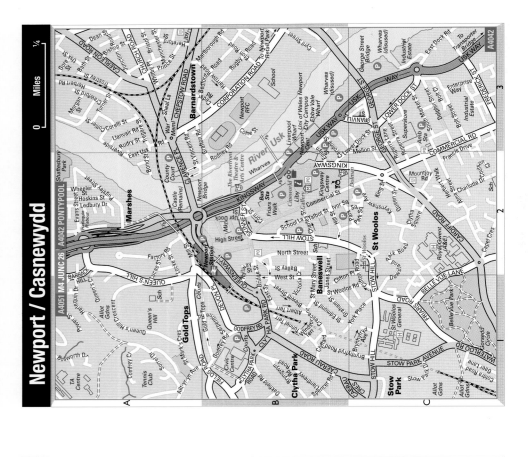

Newport / Casnewydd

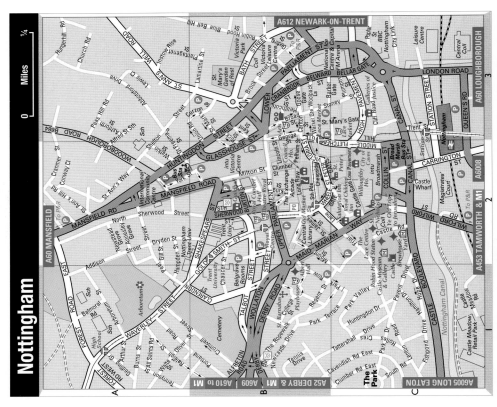

Nottingham

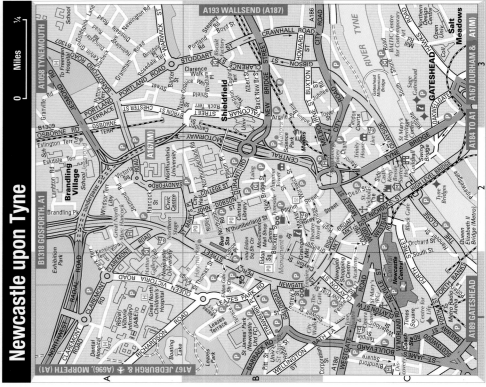

Newcastle upon Tyne

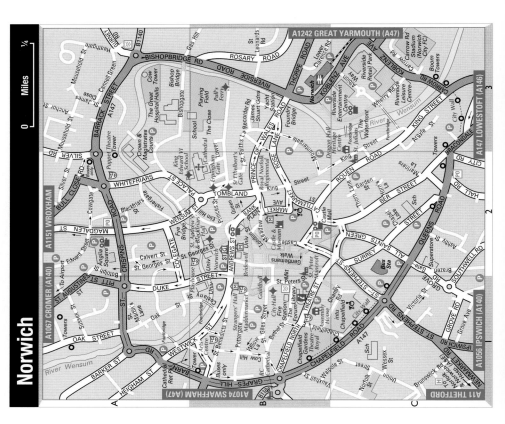

Norwich

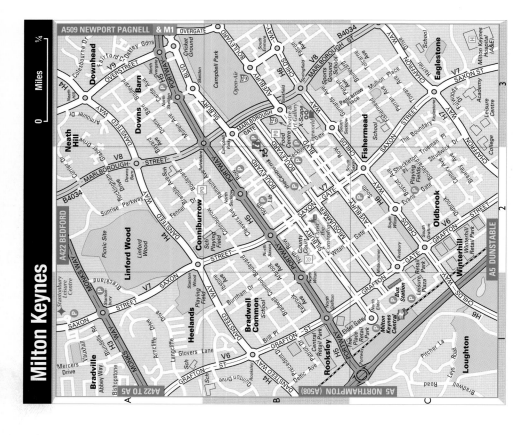

Milton Keynes

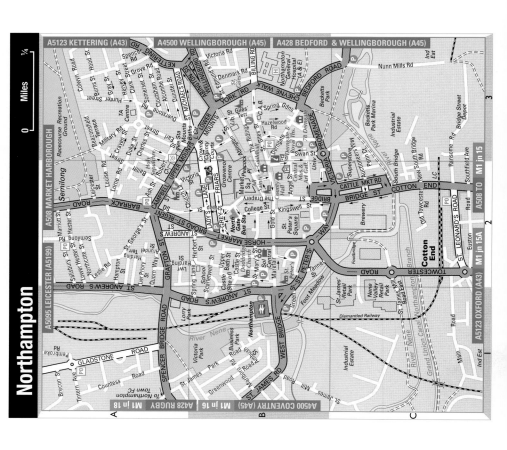

Northampton

Oxford page 28 • **Peterborough** page 37 • **Plymouth** page 4 • **Poole** page 9 • **Portsmouth** page 10 • **Preston** page 49

123

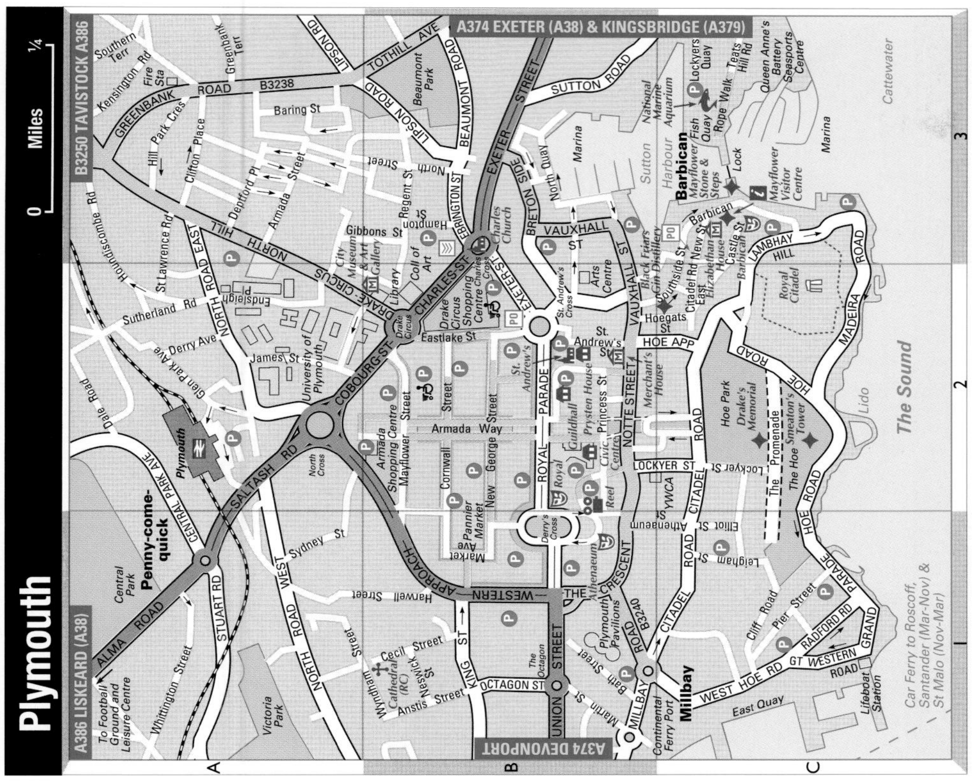

Plymouth

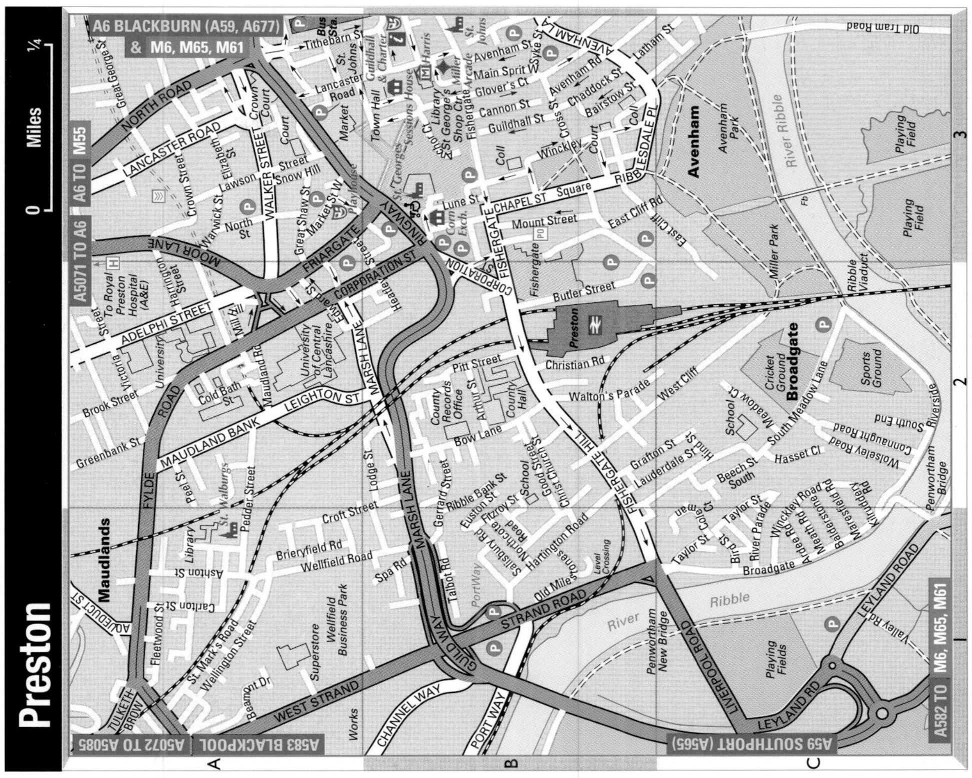

Preston

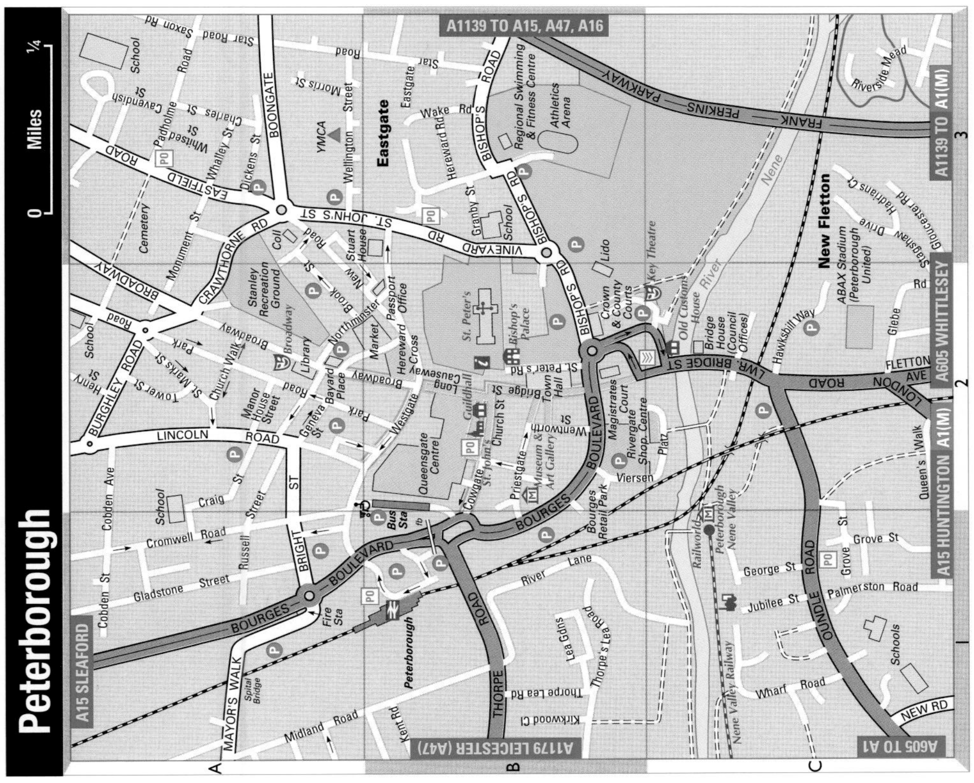

Peterborough

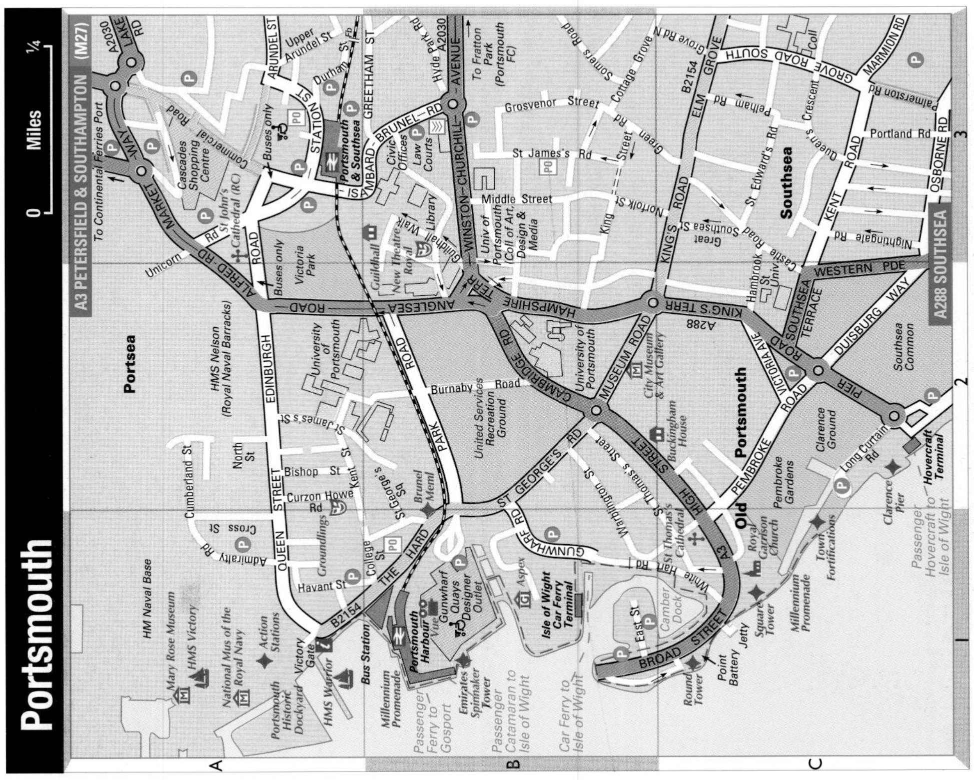

Portsmouth

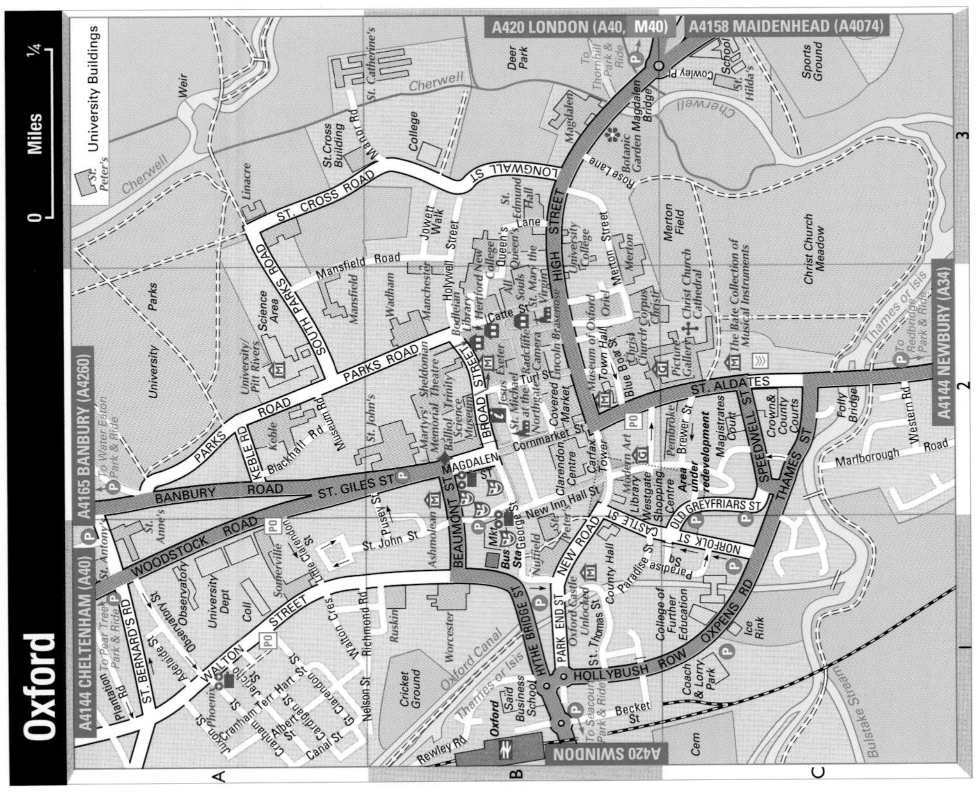

Oxford

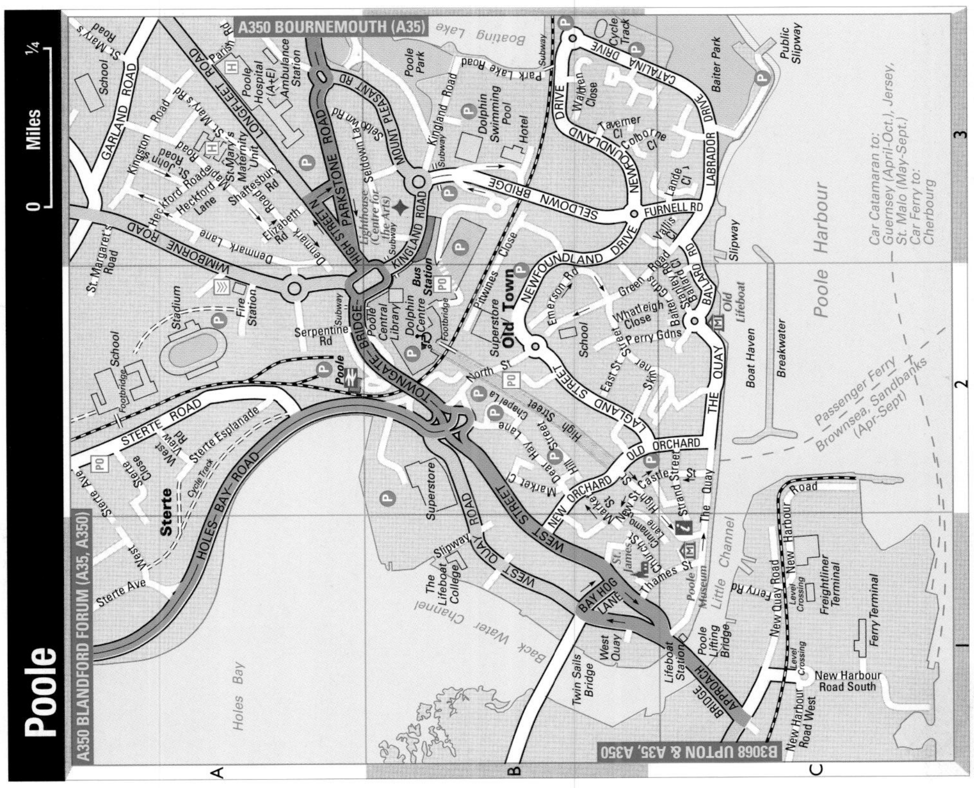

Poole

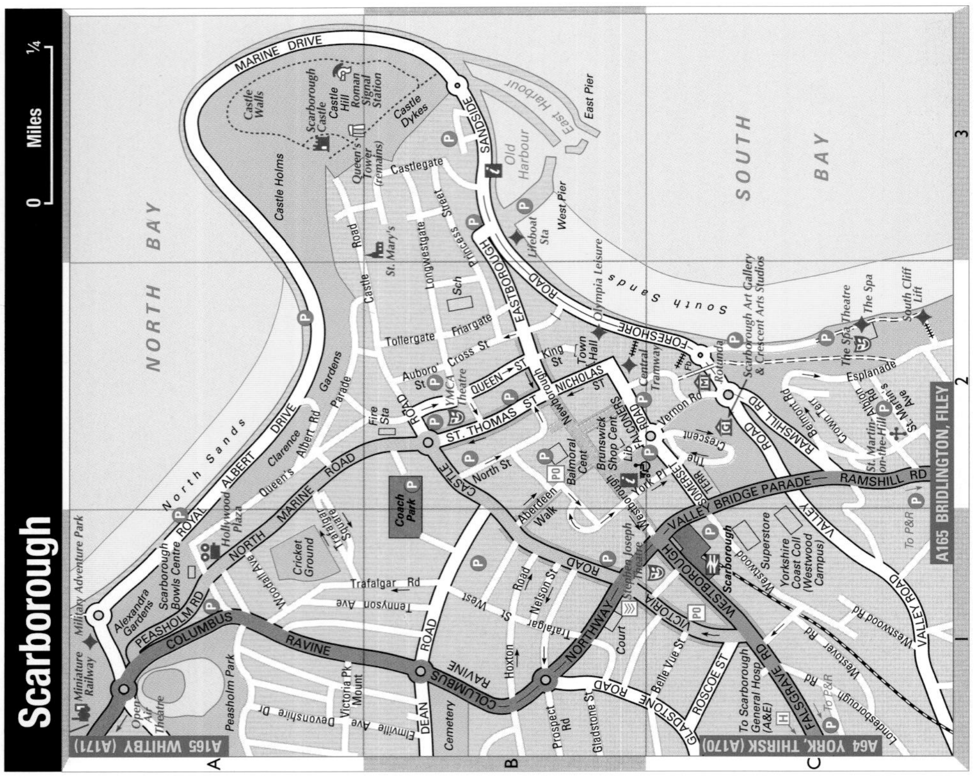
Scarborough
A165 BRIDLINGTON, FILEY
A64 YORK, THIRSK (A170)
A165 WHITBY (A171)

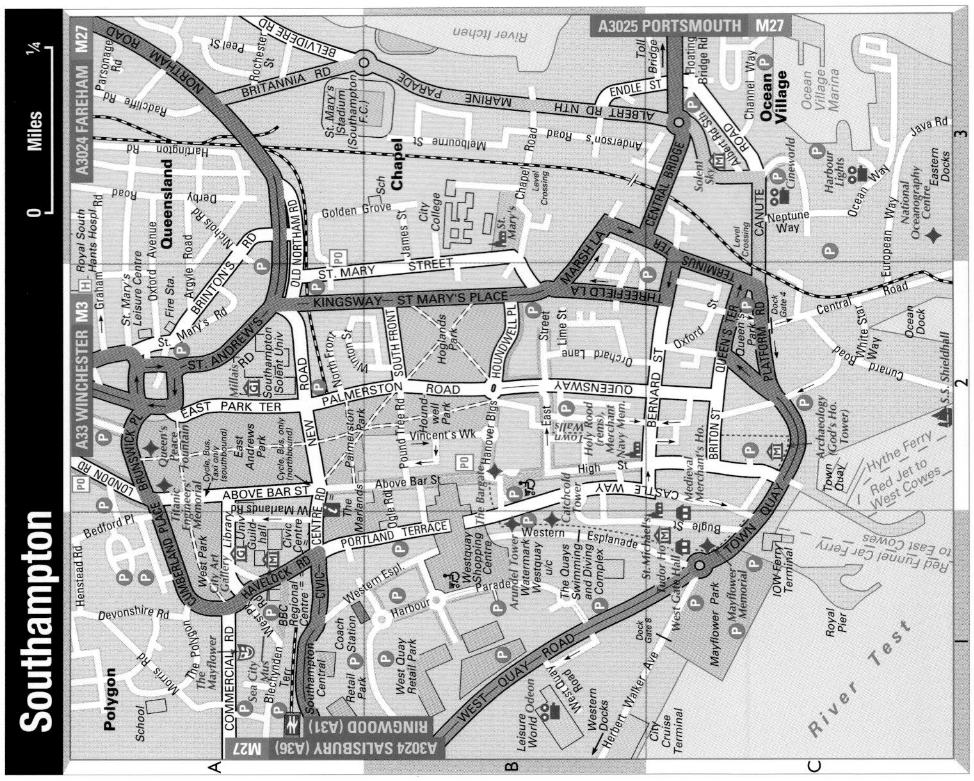
Southampton
A3025 PORTSMOUTH M27
A3024 SALISBURY (A36) RINGWOOD (A31) M27

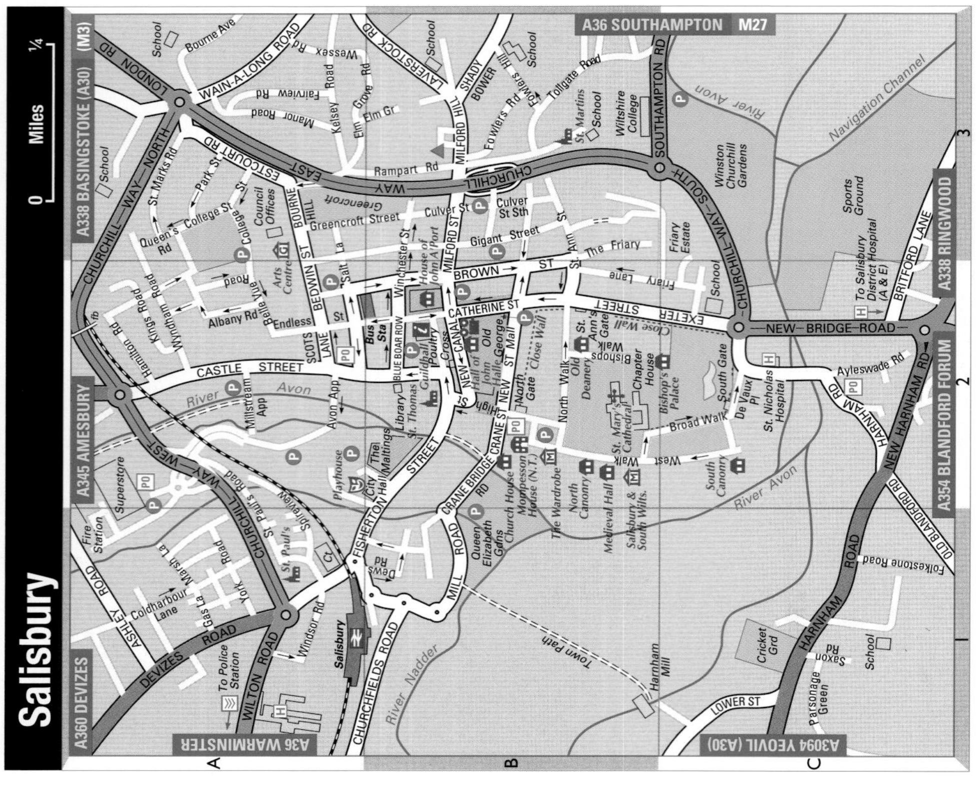
Salisbury
A36 SOUTHAMPTON M27
A338 RINGWOOD
A354 BLANDFORD FORUM
A3094 YEOVIL (A30)
A36 WARMINSTER
A360 DEVIZES
A345 AMESBURY
A338 BASINGSTOKE (A30) (M3)

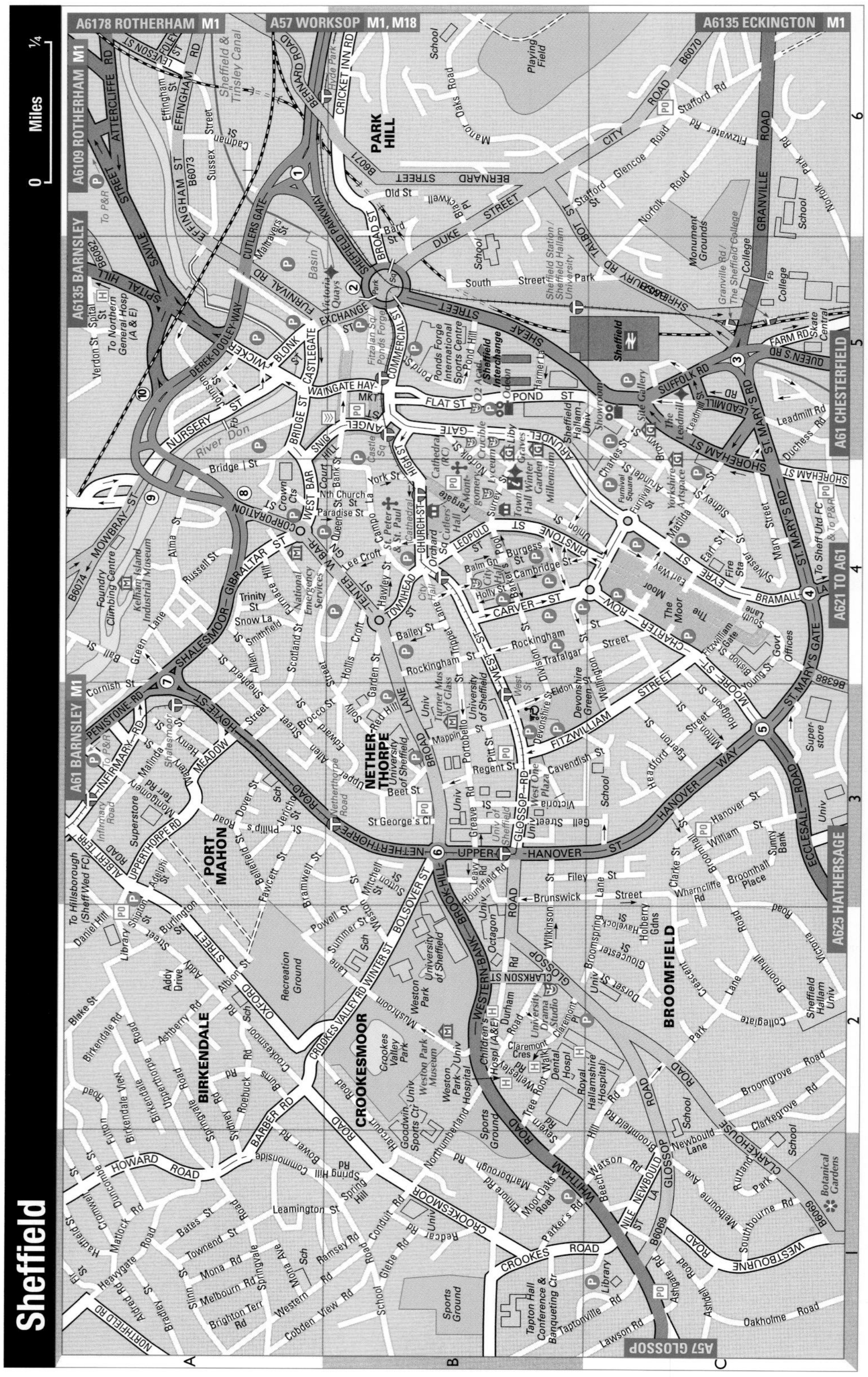
Sheffield
A6178 ROTHERHAM M1
A57 WORKSOP M1, M18
A6135 ECKINGTON M1
A61 CHESTERFIELD
A621 TO A61
A625 HATHERSAGE
A57 GLOSSOP
A61 BARNSLEY M1
A6135 BARNSLEY
A6109 ROTHERHAM M1

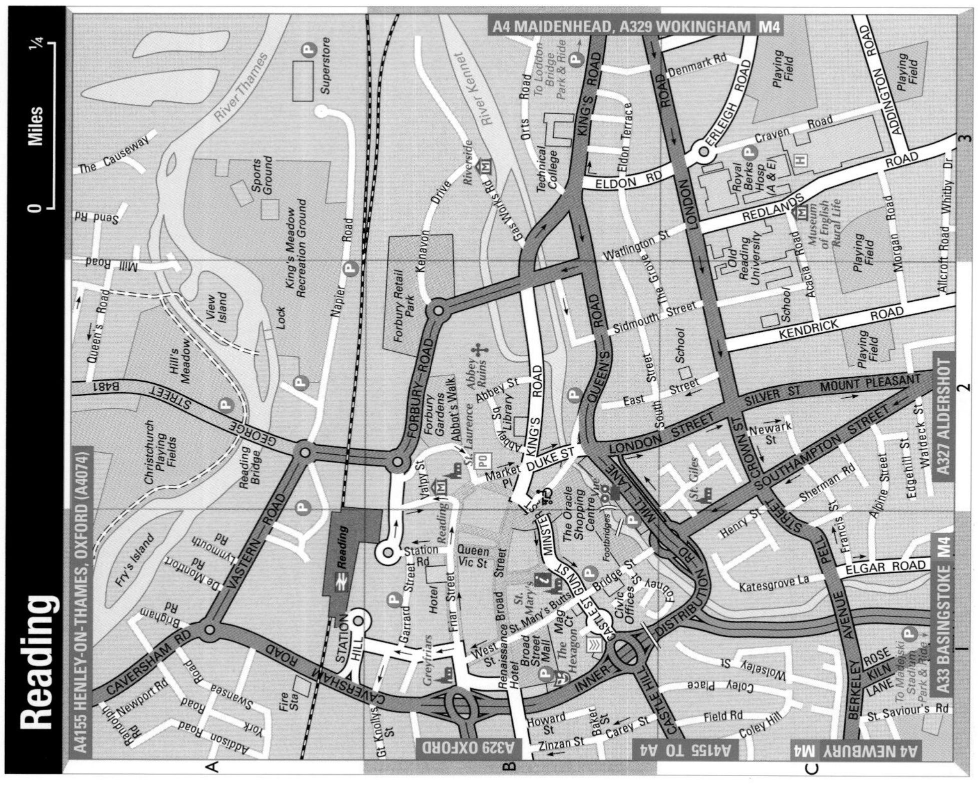
Reading
A4 MAIDENHEAD, A329 WOKINGHAM M4
A327 ALDERSHOT
A33 BASINGSTOKE M4
A4 NEWBURY M4
A4155 TO A4
A329 OXFORD
A4155 HENLEY-ON-THAMES, OXFORD (A4074)

Southend-on-Sea page 20 • **Stoke-on-Trent (Hanley)** page 44 • **Stratford-upon-Avon** page 27 • **Sunderland** page 63 • **Swansea** page 14 • **Swindon** page 17

125

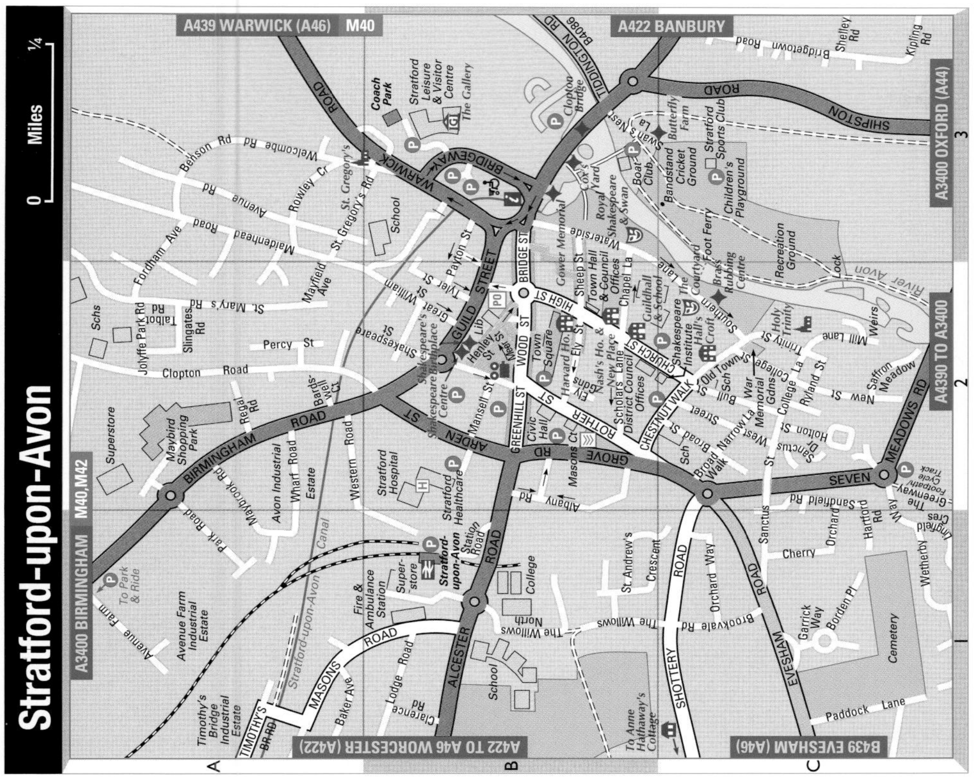

Stratford-upon-Avon

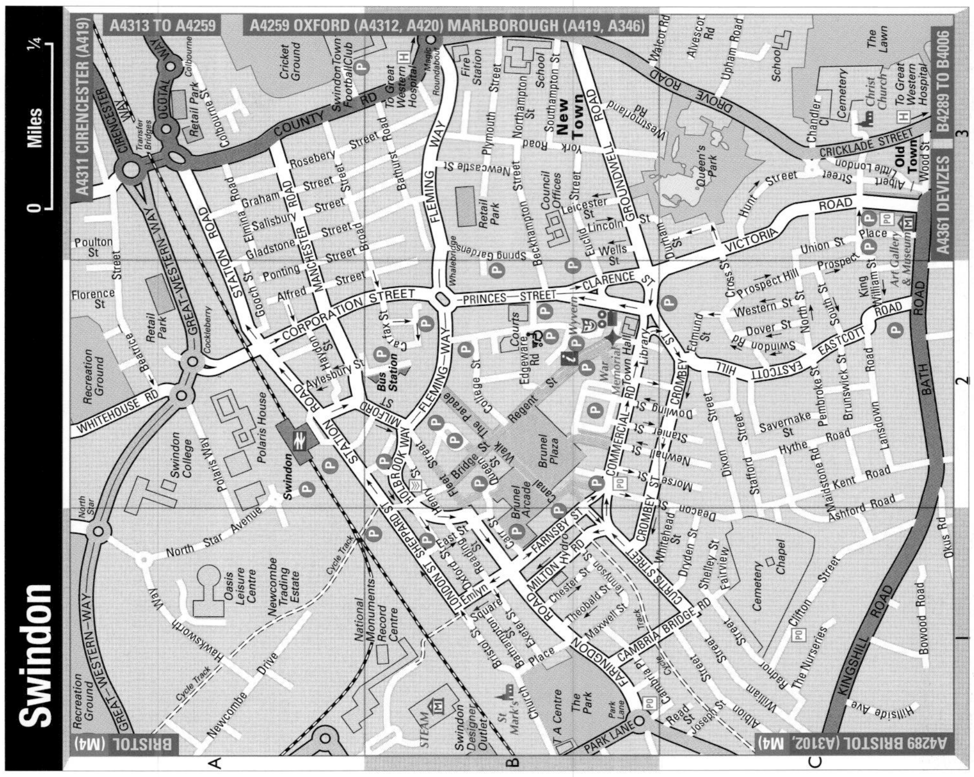

Swindon

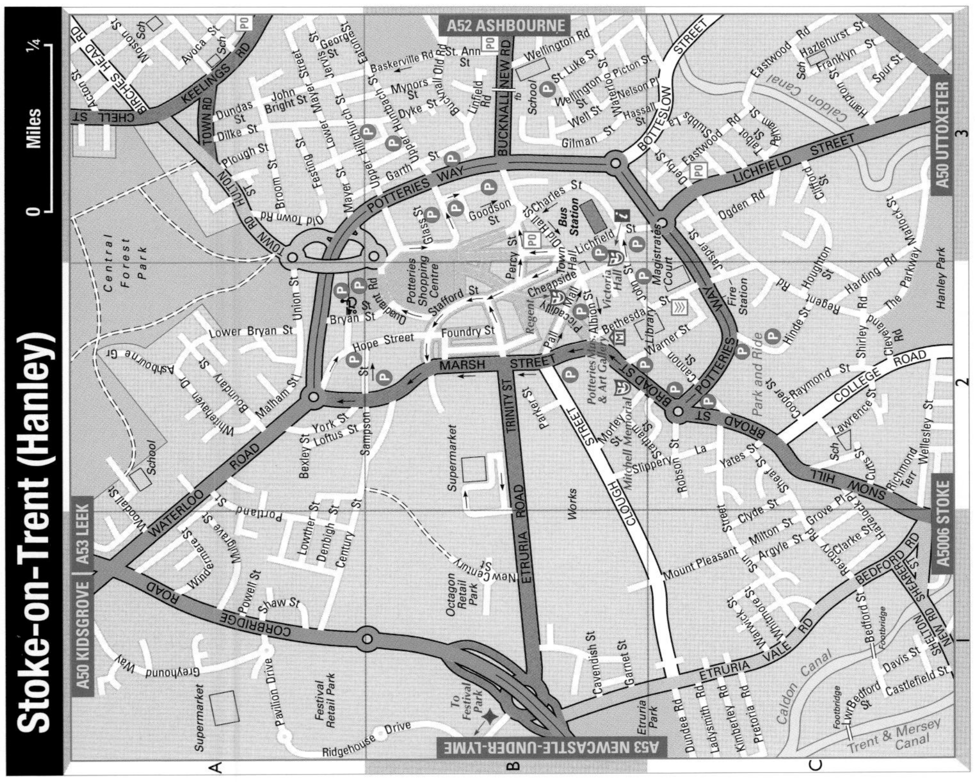

Stoke-on-Trent (Hanley)

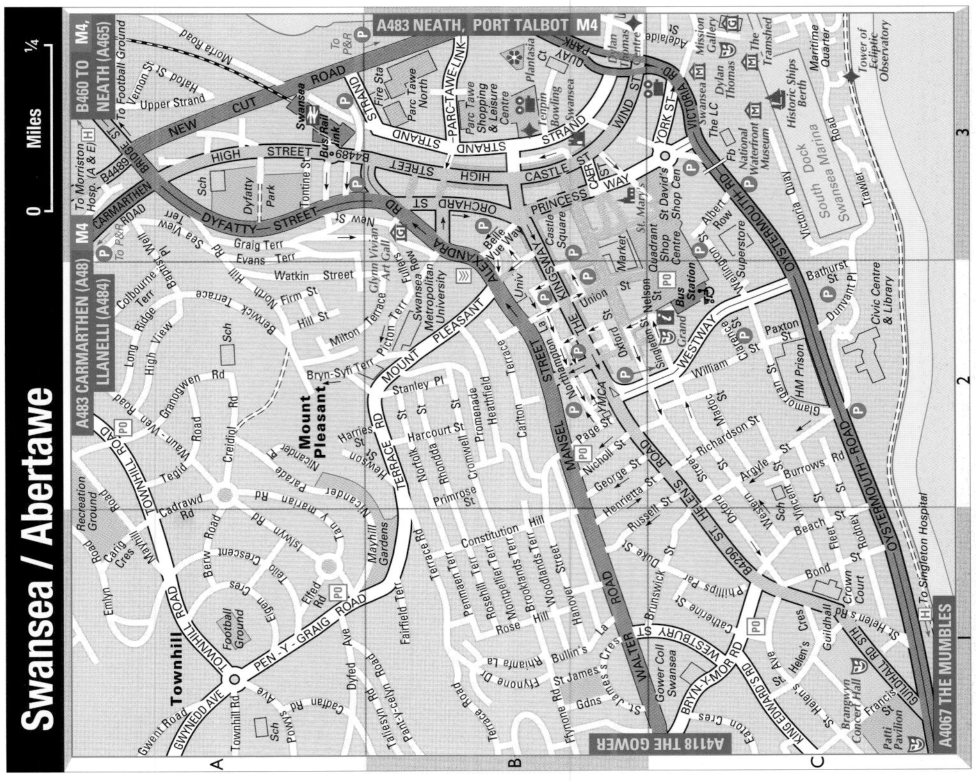

Swansea / Abertawe

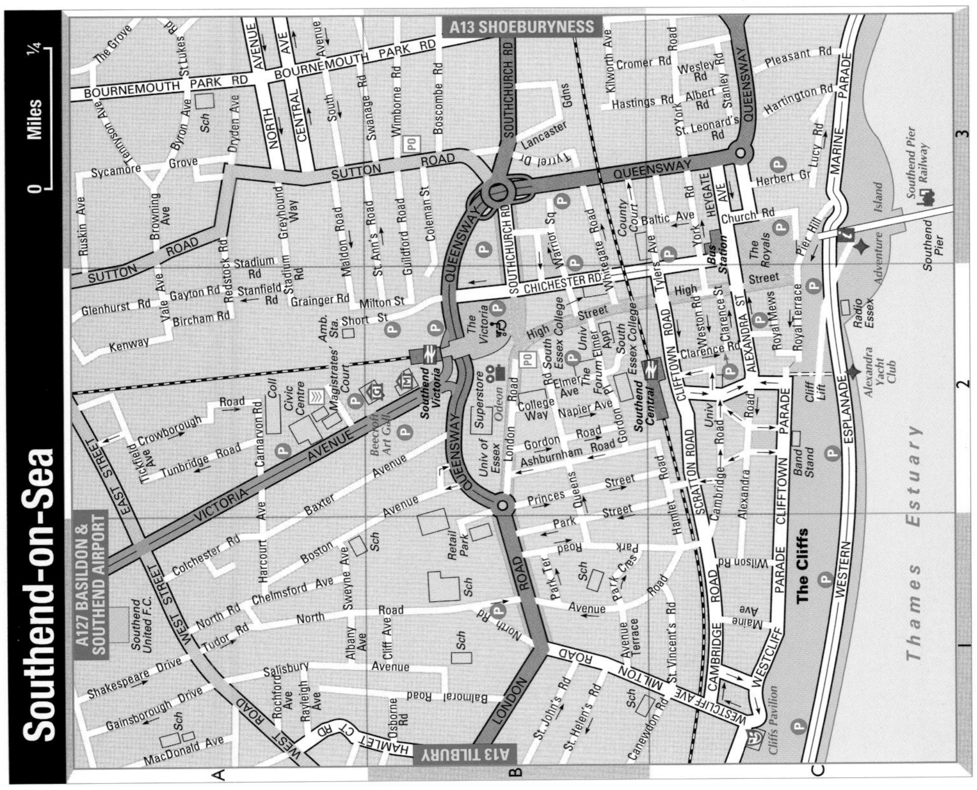

Southend-on-Sea

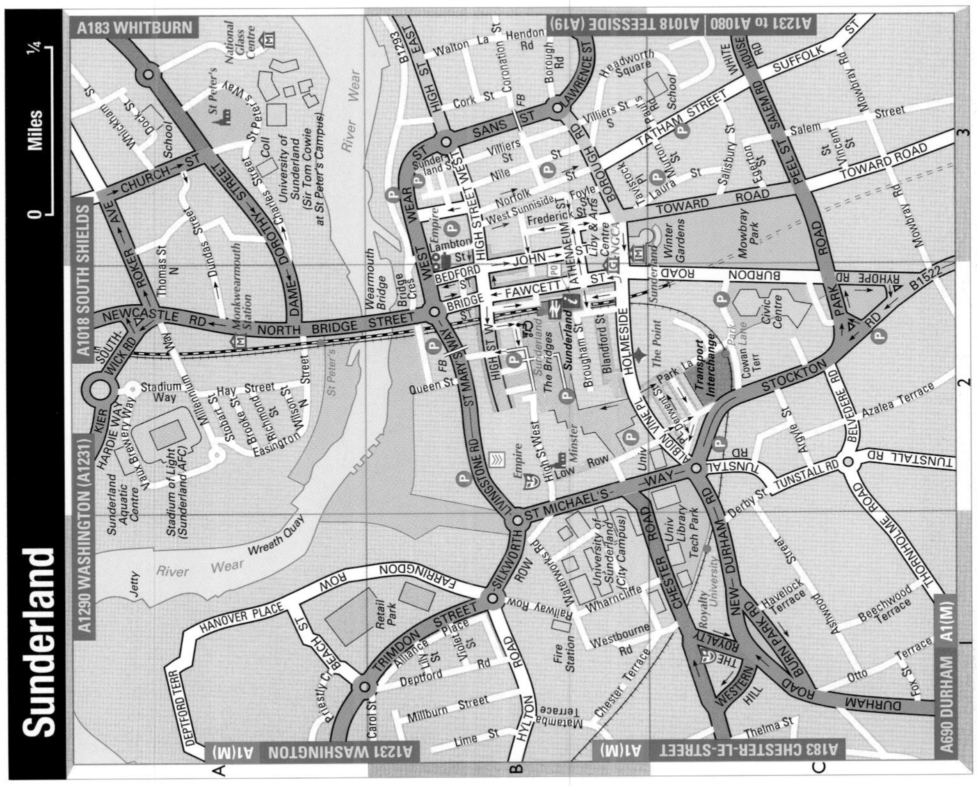

Sunderland

Winchester

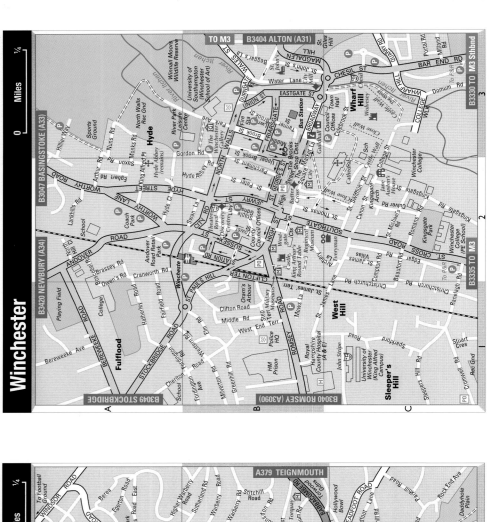

York

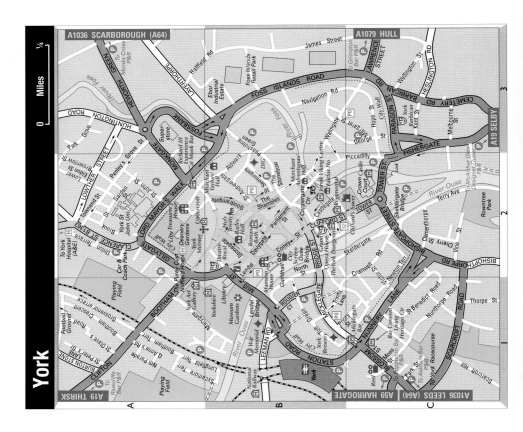

Torquay

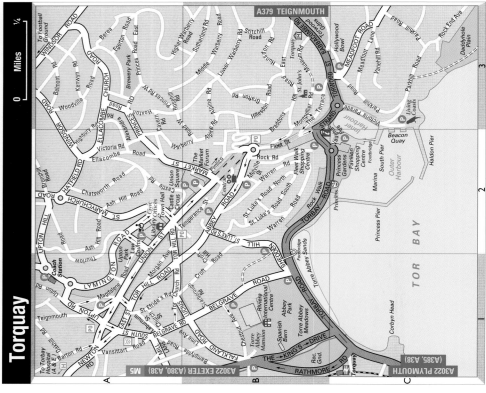

Worcester

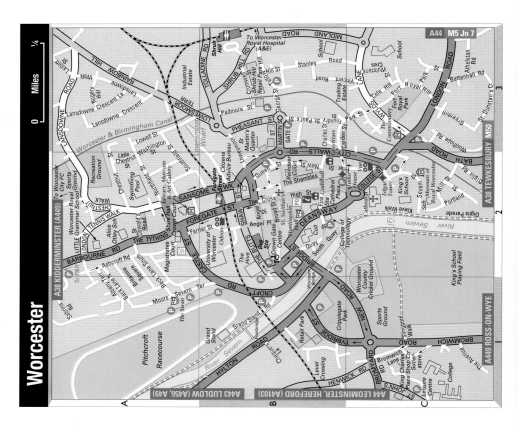

Telford

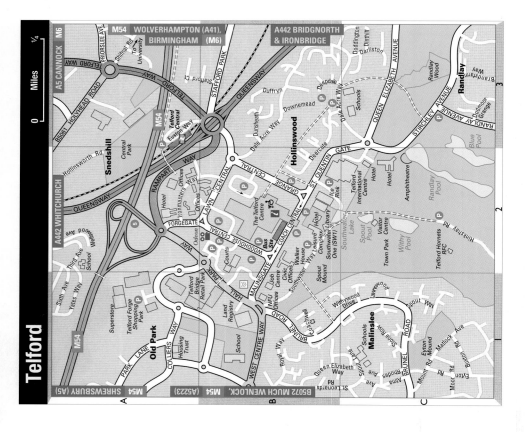

Windsor

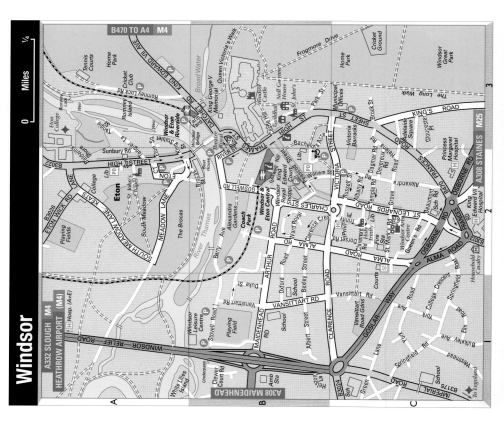

Royal Cr . . . B2
Royal Wells Rd . . . B2
St George's Pl . . . B2
St Georges Rd . . . B1
St Gregory's . . . B2
St James St . . . B3
St John's Ave . . . B2
St Luke's Rd . . . C2
St Margarets Rd . . . A2
St Mary's . . . B2
St Matthew's . . . B2
St Paul's La . . . A2
St Paul's Rd . . . A2
St Paul's St . . . A2
St Stephen's Rd . . . C1
Sandford Lido . . . C3
Sandford Mill Rd . . . C3
Sandford Park . . . C3
Sandford Rd . . . C2
Selkirk St . . . A3
Sherborne Pl . . . B3
Sherborne St . . . B3
Suffolk Pde . . . C2
Suffolk Rd . . . C1
Suffolk Sq . . . C1
Sun St . . . A1
Swindon Rd . . . B2
Sydenham Villas Rd . . . C3
Tewkesbury Rd . . . A1
The Courtyard . . . B1
Thirlstaine Rd . . . C2
Tivoli Rd . . . C1
Tivoli St . . . C1
Town Hall & Theatre . . . B2
Townsend St . . . A1
Trafalgar St . . . C2
Union St . . . B3
University of Gloucestershire (Francis Cl Hall) . . . A2
University of Gloucestershire (Hardwick) . . . A1
Victoria Pl . . . B3
Victoria St . . . A2
Vittoria Walk . . . C2
Wel Pl . . . B2
Wellesley Rd . . . A2
Wellington Rd . . . A3
Wellington Sq . . . A3
Wellington St . . . B2
West Drive . . . A3
Western Rd . . . B1
Winchcombe St . . . B3
Winston Churchill Meml Gardens . . . A1

Chester 115

Abbey Gateway . . . A2
Appleyards La . . . C3
Bars,The . . . B3
Bedward Row . . . B1
Beeston View . . . C3
Bishop Lloyd's Palace . . . B2
Black Diamond St . . . A2
Bottoms La . . . C3
Boughton . . . B3
Bouverie St . . . A1
Bridge St . . . B2
Bridgegate . . . C2
British Heritage Centre . . . B2
Brook St . . . A3
Brown's La . . . C2
Bus Station . . . B2
Cambrian Rd . . . A1
Canal St . . . A2
Carrick Rd . . . C1
Castle . . . C2
Castle Dr . . . C2
Cathedral . . . B2
Catherine St . . . A1
Chester . . . A3
Cheyney Rd . . . A1
Chichester St . . . A1
City Rd . . . A3
City Walls . . . B1/B2
City Walls Rd . . . B1
Cornwall St . . . A2
County Hall . . . C2
Cross Hey . . . C3
Cross,The . . . B2
Cuppin St . . . B2
Curzon Park N . . . C1
Curzon Park S . . . C1
Dee Basin . . . A1
Dee La . . . B3
Delamere St . . . A2
Dewa Roman Experience . . . B2
Duke St . . . B2
Eastgate . . . B2
Eastgate St . . . B2
Eaton Rd . . . C2
Edinburgh Way . . . C3
Elizabeth Cr . . . B3
Fire Station . . . A2
Foregate St . . . B2
Frodsham St . . . B2
Gamul House . . . B2
Garden La . . . A1
George St . . . A2
Gladstone Ave . . . A1
God's Providence House . . . B2
Gorse Stacks . . . A2
Greenway St . . . C2
Grosvenor Bridge . . . C1
Grosvenor Mus . . . B2
Grosvenor Park . . . B3
Grosvenor Pk Terr . . . C1
Grosvenor Prec . . . B2
Grosvenor St . . . B2
Groves Rd . . . B3
Groves,The . . . B3
Guildhall Mus . . . B1
Handbridge . . . C2
Hartington St . . . C3
Hoole Way . . . A2
Hunter St . . . B2
Information Ctr . . . B2
King Charles' Tower . . . A2
King St . . . A2
Leisure Centre . . . A2
Library . . . B2
Lightfoot St . . . A3
Little Roodee . . . C2
Liverpool Rd . . . A2
Love St . . . B3
Lower Bridge St . . . B2
Lower Park Rd . . . B3
Lyon St . . . A2
Magistrates Court . . . B2
Meadows La . . . C3
Meadows,The . . . B3
Military Mus . . . C2
Milton St . . . A3
New Crane St . . . B1
Nicholas St . . . B2
Northgate . . . A2
Northgate St . . . A2
Nun's Rd . . . B1
Old Dee Bridge . . . C2
Overleigh Rd . . . C2
Park St . . . B2
Police Station . . . B2
Post Office . . . A2/A3/B2
Princess St . . . B2
Queen St . . . B2
Queen's Park Rd . . . C3
Queen's Rd . . . A3
Race Course . . . B1
Raymond St . . . A1
River La . . . C2
Roman Amphitheatre & Gardens . . . B2
Roodee (Chester Racecourse),The . . . B1
Russell St . . . A3
St Anne St . . . A2
St George's Cr . . . C3
St Martin's Gate . . . A1
St Martin's Way . . . B1
St Mary's Priory . . . B2
St Oswalds Way . . . A2
Saughall Rd . . . A1
Sealand Rd . . . A1
South View Rd . . . A1
Stanley Palace . . . B1
Station Rd . . . A3
Steven St . . . A3
Tower Rd . . . B1
Town Hall . . . B2
Union St . . . B3
Vicar's La . . . B2
Victoria Cr . . . C3
Victoria Rd . . . A2
Walpole St . . . A1
Water Tower St . . . A1
Water Tower,The . . . B1
Watergate . . . B1
Watergate St . . . B2
Whipcord La . . . A1
White Friars . . . B2
York St . . . B3

Chichester 115

Adelaide Rd . . . A3
Alexandra Rd . . . A3
Arts Centre . . . B2
Ave de Chartres . . . B1/B2
Barlow Rd . . . A1
Basin Rd . . . C2
Beech Ave . . . B1
Bishops Palace Gardens . . . B2
Bishopsgate Walk . . . A3
Bramber Rd . . . C3
Broyle Rd . . . A2
Bus Station . . . B2
Caledonian Rd . . . B3
Cambrai Ave . . . B3
Canal Pl . . . C1
Canal Wharf . . . C2
Canon La . . . B2
Cathedral . . . B2
Cavendish St . . . A1
Cawley Rd . . . B2
Cedar Dr . . . A1
Chapel St . . . A2
Cherry Orchard Rd . . . C3
Chichester . . . B2
Chichester By-Pass . . . C2/C3
Chichester Coll . . . B1
Chichester Cinema . . . B3
Chichester Festival . . . A2
Chichester Gate Leisure Pk . . . C1
Churchside . . . A2
Cineworld . . . C1
City Walls . . . B2
Cleveland Rd . . . B3
College La . . . A2
Cory Cl . . . C2
Council Offices . . . B2
County Hall . . . B2
District . . . B2
Duncan Rd . . . A1
Durnford Cl . . . A1
East Pallant . . . B2
East Row . . . B2
East St . . . B2
East Walls . . . B3
Eastland Rd . . . C3
Ettrick Cl . . . B3
Ettrick Rd . . . B3
Exton Rd . . . C3
Fire Station . . . A2
Football Ground . . . A2
Franklin Pl . . . A2
Friary (Rems of) . . . A2
Garland Cl . . . C3
Green La . . . A3
Grove Rd . . . C3
Guilden Rd . . . B3
Guildhall . . . A2
Hawthorn Cl . . . A1
Hay Rd . . . C3
Henty Gdns . . . B1
Herald Dr . . . C3
Hornet,The . . . B3
Information Ctr . . . B2
John's St . . . B2
Joys Croft . . . A3
Jubilee Pk . . . A3
Jubilee Rd . . . A3
Juxon Cl . . . B1
Kent Rd . . . A3
King George Gdns . . . A2
King's Ave . . . C2
Kingsham Ave . . . C3
Kingsham Rd . . . C2
Laburnum Gr . . . B2
Leigh Rd . . . C1
Lennox Rd . . . A3
Lewis Rd . . . A3
Library . . . B2
Lion St . . . B2
Litten Terr . . . A3
Litten,The . . . A3
Little London . . . B2
Lyndhurst Rd . . . B3
Market . . . B3
Market Ave . . . B2
Market Cross . . . B2
Market Rd . . . B3
Melbourne Rd . . . A3
Minerva . . . A2
Mount La . . . B1
New Park Rd . . . A3
Newlands La . . . A1
North Pallant . . . B2
North St . . . A2
North Walls . . . A2
Northgate . . . A2
Novium,The . . . B2
Oak Ave . . . A1
Oak Cl . . . A1
Oaklands Park . . . A2
Oaklands Way . . . A2
Orchard Ave . . . A1
Orchard St . . . A1
Ormonde Ave . . . B3
Pallant House . . . B2
Parchment St . . . A1
Parklands Rd . . . A1/B1
Peter Weston Pl . . . B3
Police Station . . . C2
Post Office . . . A1/B2/C3
Priory La . . . A2
Priory Park . . . A2
Priory Rd . . . A2
Queen's Ave . . . C1
Riverside . . . A3
Roman Amphitheatre . . . B3
St Cyriacs . . . A2
St Martins' St . . . B2
St Pancras . . . A3
St Paul's Rd . . . A2
St Richard's Hospital (A&E) . . . A3
Shamrock Cl . . . A3
Sherbourne Rd . . . A1
Somerstown . . . A2
South Bank . . . C2
South Downs Planetarium . . . C2
South Pallant . . . B2
South St . . . B2
Southgate . . . B2
Spitalfield La . . . A3
Stirling Rd . . . B3
Stockbridge Rd . . . C1/C2
Swanfield Dr . . . A3
Terminus Ind Est . . . C1
Tower St . . . A2
Tozer Way . . . A3
Turnbull Rd . . . A3
Upton Rd . . . C1
Velyn Ave . . . B3
Via Ravenna . . . B1
Walnut Ave . . . A1
West St . . . B2
Westgate . . . B1
Westgate Fields . . . B1
Westgate L Ctr . . . B1
Weston Ave . . . C1
Whyke Cl . . . C3
Whyke La . . . B3
Whyke Rd . . . C3
Winden Ave . . . B3

Colchester 115

Abbey Gateway . . . C2
Albert St . . . A1
Albion Grove . . . C2
Alexandra Rd . . . C1
Artillery St . . . C3
Arts Centre . . . B1
Balkerne Hill . . . B1
Barrack St . . . C3
Beaconsfield Rd . . . C1
Beche Rd . . . C3
Bergholt Rd . . . A1
Bourne Rd . . . C3
Brick Kiln Rd . . . A1
Bristol Rd . . . B2
Broadlands Way . . . A3
Brook St . . . B3
Bury Cl . . . B2
Bus Sta . . . B2
Butt Rd . . . C1
Camp Folley North . . . C2
Camp Folley South . . . C2
Campion Rd . . . C2
Cannon St . . . C3
Canterbury Rd . . . C2
Castle . . . B2
Castle Park . . . B2
Castle Rd . . . B2
Catchpool Rd . . . A1
Causton Rd . . . B1
Chandlers Row . . . C3
Circular Rd East . . . C2
Circular Rd North . . . C1
Circular Rd West . . . C1
Clarendon Way . . . A1
Claudius Rd . . . C2
Colchester . . . A1
Colchester Camp Abbey Field . . . C1
Colchester Inst . . . B1
Colchester Town . . . C2
Colne Bank Ave . . . A1
Colne View Ret Pk . . . A2
Compton Rd . . . A3
Cowdray Ave . . . A1/A2
Cowdray Ctr,The . . . A2
Crouch St . . . B1
Crowhurst Rd . . . B1
Culver Sq Sh Ctr . . . B1
Culver St East . . . B2
Culver St West . . . B1
Dilbridge Rd . . . A3
East Hill . . . B2
East St . . . B3
East Stockwell St . . . B1
Eld La . . . B1
Essex Hall Rd . . . A1
Exeter Dr . . . B2
Fairfax Rd . . . C2
Fire Station . . . A2
Firstsite . . . B2
Flagstaff Rd . . . C1
George St . . . B2
Gladstone Rd . . . C2
Golden Noble Hill . . . C2
Goring Rd . . . A3
Granville Rd . . . C3
Greenstead Rd . . . B3
Guildford Rd . . . B2
Harsnett Rd . . . C3
Harwich Rd . . . B3
Head St . . . B1
High St . . . B1/B2
High Woods Country Park . . . A2
Hollytrees . . . B2
Hythe Hill . . . C3
Information Ctr . . . B2
Ipswich Rd . . . A3
Jarmin Rd . . . A2
Kendall Rd . . . C2
Kimberley Rd . . . C3
King Stephen Rd . . . C3
Leisure World . . . A2
Library . . . B1
Lincoln Way . . . B2
Lion Walk Sh Ctr . . . B1
Lisle Rd . . . C2
Lucas Rd . . . C2
Magdalen Green . . . C3
Magdalen St . . . C2
Maidenburgh St . . . B2
Maldon Rd . . . C1
Manor Rd . . . B1
Margaret Rd . . . A1
Mason Rd . . . A2
Mercers Way . . . A1
Mercury . . . B1
Mersea Rd . . . C2
Meyrick Cr . . . C2
Mile End Rd . . . A1
Military Rd . . . C2
Mill St . . . C2
Minories . . . B2
Moorside . . . B3
Morant Rd . . . C3
Napier Rd . . . C2
Natural History . . . B2
New Town Rd . . . C2
Norfolk Cr . . . A3
North Hill . . . B1
North Station Rd . . . A1
Northgate St . . . B1
Nunns Rd . . . B1
Odeon . . . B1
Old Coach Rd . . . B3
Old Heath Rd . . . C3
Osborne St . . . B2
Petrolea Cl . . . A1
Police Station . . . C1
Popes La . . . B1
Port La . . . C3
Post Office . . . B2/C1
Priory St . . . B2
Queen St . . . B2
Rawstorn Rd . . . B1
Rebon St . . . C3
Recreation Rd . . . C3
Ripple Way . . . A3
Roman Rd . . . B2
Roman Wall . . . B2
Romford Cl . . . A3
Rosebery Ave . . . B2
St Andrews Ave . . . B3
St Andrews Gdns . . . B3
St Botolph St . . . B2
St Botolphs . . . B2
St John's Abbey (site of) . . . C2
St John's St . . . B1
St Johns Walk Shopping Centre . . . B1
St Leonards Rd . . . C3
St Marys Fields . . . B1
St Peter's St . . . B1
St Peters . . . B1
Salisbury Ave . . . C1
Serpentine Walk . . . A1
Sheepen Pl . . . B1
Sheepen Rd . . . B1
Sir Isaac's Walk . . . B1
Smythies Ave . . . B2
South St . . . C1
South Way . . . C1
Sports Way . . . A2
Suffolk Cl . . . A3
Town Hall . . . B1
Turner Rise Ret Pk . . . A1
Valentine Dr . . . A3
Victor Rd . . . C3
Wakefield Cl . . . B2
Wellesley Rd . . . C1
Wells Rd . . . B2/B3
West St . . . C1
West Stockwell St . . . B1
Weston Rd . . . C3
Westway . . . A1
Wickham Rd . . . C1
Wimpole Rd . . . C3
Winchester Rd . . . C2
Winnock Rd . . . C2
Wolfe Ave . . . C2
Worcester Rd . . . B2

Coventry 116

Abbots La . . . A1
Albany . . . B1
Albany Rd . . . B1
Alma St . . . B3
Art Faculty . . . B3
Asthill Grove . . . C2
Bablake School . . . A1
Barras La . . . A1/B1
Barrs Hill School . . . A1
Belgrade . . . B2
Bishop St . . . A2
Bond's Hospital . . . B1
Broad Gate . . . B2
Broadway . . . C1
Burges,The . . . B2
Bus Station . . . A3
Butts Radial . . . B1
Canal Basin . . . A2
Canterbury St . . . A3
Cathedral . . . B3
Central Six Ret Pk . . . C1
Chester St . . . A1
Cheylesmore Manor House . . . B2
Christ Church Spire . . . B2
City College . . . A3
City Walls & Gates . . . A2
Corporation St . . . B2
Council House . . . B2
Coundon Rd . . . A1
Coventry Sta . . . C2
Coventry Transport Museum . . . A2
Cox St . . . A3
Croft Rd . . . B1
Dalton Rd . . . C1
Deasy Rd . . . C3
Earl St . . . B2
Eaton Rd . . . C2
Fairfax St . . . B2
Foleshill Rd . . . A2
Ford's Hospital . . . B2
Fowler Rd . . . A1
Friars Rd . . . C2
Gordon St . . . C1
Gosford St . . . B3
Greyfriars Gn . . . B2
Greyfriars Rd . . . B2
Gulson Rd . . . B3
Hales St . . . A2
Harnall Lane East . . . A3
Harnall Lane West . . . A2
Herbert Art Gallery & Museum . . . B3
Hertford St . . . B2
Hewitt Ave . . . A1
High St . . . B2
Hill St . . . B1
Holy Trinity . . . B2
Holyhead Rd . . . A1
Howard St . . . A3
Huntingdon Rd . . . C1
Information Ctr . . . B2
Jordan Well . . . B3
King Henry VIII School . . . C1
Lady Godiva Statue . . . B2
Lamb St . . . A2
Leicester Row . . . A2
Library . . . B2
Little Park St . . . B2
London Rd . . . C3
Lower Ford St . . . B3
Lower Precinct Shop Ctr . . . B2
Magistrates & Crown Courts . . . B2
Manor House Drive . . . B2
Manor Rd . . . C2
Market . . . B2
Martyr's Meml . . . C2
Meadow St . . . B1
Meriden St . . . A1
Michaelmas Rd . . . C2
Middleborough Rd . . . A1
Mile La . . . C3
Millennium Pl . . . A2
Much Park St . . . B3
Naul's Mill Park . . . A1
New Union . . . B2
Odeon . . . B1
Park Rd . . . C2
Parkside . . . C3
Planet Ice Arena . . . B1
Post Office . . . B2/C2
Primrose Hill St . . . A3
Priory Gardens & Visitor Centre . . . B2
Priory St . . . B3
Puma Way . . . C3
Quarryfield La . . . C3
Queen's Rd . . . B1
Quinton Rd . . . C2
Radford Rd . . . A2
Raglan St . . . B3
Ringway (Hill Cross) . . . A1
Ringway (Queens) . . . B1
Ringway (Rudge) . . . B1
Ringway (St Johns) . . . B3
Ringway (St Nicholas) . . . A2
Ringway (St Patricks) . . . C2
Ringway (Swanswell) . . . A2
Ringway (Whitefriars) . . . B3
St John St . . . B2
St John the Baptist . . . B2
St Nicholas St . . . A2
Sidney Stringer Academy . . . A3
Skydome . . . B1
Spencer Ave . . . C1
Spencer Rec Gnd . . . C1
Spon St . . . B1
Sports Centre . . . B3
Stoney Rd . . . C2
Stoney Stanton Rd . . . A3
Swanswell Pool . . . A3
Technocentre,The . . . C3
Thomas Landsdail St . . . C2
Tomson Ave . . . A1
Top Green . . . C1
Trinity St . . . B2
University . . . B3
Univ Sports Ctr . . . B3
Upper Hill St . . . A1
Upper Well St . . . A2
Victoria St . . . A3
Vine St . . . A3
Warwick Rd . . . C2
Waveley Rd . . . B1
West Orchards Shopping Ctr . . . B2
Westminster Rd . . . C1
White St . . . A3
Windsor St . . . B1

Derby 116

Abbey St . . . C1
Agard St . . . B1
Albert St . . . B2
Albion St . . . B2
Ambulance Sta . . . B1
Arthur St . . . A1
Ashlyn Rd . . . B3
Assembly Rooms . . . B2
Babington La . . . C2
Becket St . . . B1
Belper Rd . . . A1
Bold La . . . B1
Bradshaw Way . . . C2
Bradshaw Way Retail Park . . . C2
Bridge St . . . B1
Brook St . . . B1
Burton Rd . . . C1
Bus Station . . . B2
Caesar St . . . A2
Canal St . . . C3
Carrington St . . . C3
Cathedral . . . B2
Cathedral Rd . . . B1
Charnwood St . . . C2
Chester Green Rd . . . A2
City Rd . . . A2
Clarke St . . . A3
Cock Pitt . . . B3
Council House . . . B2
Courts . . . B1
Cranmer Rd . . . B3
Crompton St . . . C1
Crown & County Courts . . . B2
Curzon St . . . B1
Darley Grove . . . A1
Derby . . . C3
Derbyshire County Cricket Ground . . . B3
Derwent Bsns Ctr . . . A2
Derwent St . . . B2
Drewry La . . . C1
Duffield Rd . . . A1
Duke St . . . A2
Dunton Cl . . . B3
Eagle Market . . . C2
East St . . . B2
Eastgate . . . B3
Exeter St . . . B2
Farm St . . . C1
Ford St . . . B1
Forester St . . . C1
Fox St . . . A2
Friar Gate . . . B1
Friary St . . . B1
Full St . . . B2
Gerard St . . . C1
Gower St . . . C2
Green La . . . C2
Grey St . . . C1
Guildhall . . . B2
Harcourt St . . . C1
Highfield Rd . . . A1
Hill La . . . C2
Information Ctr . . . B2
Iron Gate . . . B2
John St . . . C3
Joseph Wright Ctr . . . B1
Kedleston Rd . . . A1
Key St . . . B2
King Alfred St . . . C1
King St . . . A1
Kingston St . . . A1
Lara Croft Way . . . C2
Leopold St . . . C2
Library . . . B1
Liversage St . . . C3
Lodge La . . . B1
London Rd . . . C2
London Rd Com Hosp . . . C2
Macklin St . . . C1
Mansfield Rd . . . A2
Market . . . B2
Market Pl . . . B2
May St . . . C1
Meadow La . . . B3
Melbourne St . . . C2
Mercian Way . . . C1
Midland Rd . . . C3
Monk St . . . C1
Morledge . . . B2
Mount St . . . C1
Museum & Art Gallery . . . B1
Noble St . . . C3
North Parade . . . A1
North St . . . A1
Nottingham Rd . . . A3
Osmaston Rd . . . C2
Otter St . . . A1
Park St . . . C3
Parker St . . . A1
Pickfords Ho . . . B1
Playhouse . . . C2
Police HQ . . . A2
Police Station . . . B2
Post Office . . . A1/A2/B1/C2/C3
Pride Parkway . . . C3
Prime Enterprise Park . . . A2
Prime Parkway . . . A2
Queens Leisure Ctr . . . B1
Racecourse . . . A3
Railway Terr . . . C3
Register Office . . . B2
Sadler Gate . . . B1
St Alkmund's Way . . . B1/B2
St Helens House . . . A1
St Mary's . . . A1
St Mary's Bridge . . . A2
St Mary's Bridge Chapel . . . A2
St Mary's Gate . . . B1
St Paul's Rd . . . A2
St Peter's . . . C2
St Peter's St . . . C2
Showcase De Lux . . . C2
Siddals Rd . . . C3
Silk Mill . . . B2
Sir Frank Whittle Rd . . . A3
Spa La . . . C1
Spring St . . . C1
Stafford St . . . B1
Station Approach . . . C3
Stockbrook St . . . C1
Stores Rd . . . A3
Traffic St . . . C2
Wardwick . . . B1
Werburgh St . . . C1
West Ave . . . A1
West Meadows Industrial Estate . . . B3
Westfield Centre . . . C2
Wharf Rd . . . A2
Wilmot St . . . C2
Wilson St . . . C1
Wood's La . . . C1

Dundee 116

Abertay University . . . B2
Adelaide Pl . . . A1
Airlie Pl . . . C1
Albany Terr . . . A1
Albert St . . . A3
Alexander St . . . A2
Ann St . . . A2
Arthurstone Terr . . . A3
Bank St . . . B2
Barrack Rd . . . A1
Barrack St . . . B2
Bell St . . . B2
Blackscroft . . . A3
Blinshall St . . . B1
Brown St . . . B1
Bus Station . . . B3
Caird Hall . . . B2
Camperdown St . . . B3
Candle La . . . B3
Carmichael St . . . A1
City Churches . . . B2
City Quay . . . B3
City Sq . . . B2
Commercial St . . . B2
Constable St . . . A3
Constitution Cres . . . A1
Constitution Ct . . . A1
Constitution St . . . A1/B2
Cotton Rd . . . A3
Courthouse Sq . . . B1
Cowgate . . . A3
Crescent St . . . A3
Crichton St . . . B2
Dens Brae . . . A3
Dens Rd . . . A3
Discovery Point . . . C2
Douglas St . . . B1
Drummond St . . . A1
Dudhope Castle . . . A1
Dudhope St . . . A2
Dudhope Terr . . . A1
Dundee . . . C2
Dundee Contemporary Arts . . . C2
Dundee High School . . . B2
Dundee Law . . . A1
Dundee Repertory . . . C2
Dunhope Park . . . A1
Dura St . . . A3
East Dock St . . . B3
East Marketgait . . . B3
East Whale La . . . B3
Erskine St . . . A3
Euclid Cr . . . B2
Forebank Rd . . . A2
Foundry La . . . A3
Frigate Unicorn . . . B3
Gallagher Ret Pk . . . B3
Gellatly St . . . B3
Government Offices . . . C2
Guthrie St . . . B1
Hawkhill . . . B1
Hilltown . . . A2
Howff Cemetery, The . . . B2
Information Ctr . . . B2
Keiller Sh Ctr . . . B2
Keiller Ctr,The . . . B2
King St . . . A3
Kinghorne Rd . . . A1
Ladywell Ave . . . A3
Laurel Bank . . . A2
Law Rd . . . A1
Law St . . . A1
Library . . . A2/A3
Library and Steps Theatre . . . A2
Little Theatre . . . A2
Lochee Rd . . . B1
Lower Princes St . . . A3
Lyon St . . . A3
McManus Mus & Art Gallery,The . . . B2
Meadow Side . . . B2
Meadowside St Pauls . . . B2
Mercat Cross . . . B2
Murraygate . . . B2
Nelson St . . . A2
Nethergate . . . B2/C1
North Lindsay St . . . B2
North Marketgait . . . B2
Old Hawkhill . . . B1
Olympia L Ctr . . . B3
Overgate Sh Ctr . . . B2
Park Pl . . . B1
Perth Rd . . . C1
Police Sta . . . A2/B1
Post Office . . . B2
Princes St . . . A3
Prospect Pl . . . A2
Reform St . . . B2
Riverside Dr . . . C2
Riverside Esplanade . . . C2
Roseangle . . . C1
Rosebank St . . . A2
RRS Discovery . . . C2
St Andrew's . . . C2
St Pauls Episcopal . . . B3
Science Centre . . . C2
Seagate . . . B2
Sheriffs Court . . . B1
Shopmobility . . . B2
South George St . . . A2
South Marketgait . . . B3
South Tay St . . . B2
South Ward Rd . . . B2
Tay Road Bridge . . . C3
Thomson Ave . . . B2
Trades La . . . B3
Union St . . . B2
Union Terr . . . A1
University Library . . . B2
Univ of Dundee . . . B1
Upper Constitution St . . . A1
Verdant Works . . . B1
Victoria Dock . . . B3
Victoria Rd . . . A2
Victoria St . . . A3
Ward Rd . . . B1
Wellgate . . . B2
West Bell St . . . B1
West Marketgait . . . B1/B2
Westfield Pl . . . C1
William St . . . A3
Wishart Arch . . . A3

Durham 116

Alexander Cr . . . B2
Allergate . . . B2
Archery Rise . . . C1
Assize Courts . . . B3
Avenue,The . . . B1
Back Western Hill . . . A1
Bakehouse La . . . A3
Baths . . . B3
Baths Bridge . . . B3
Boat House . . . B3
Bowling . . . A2
Boyd St . . . C3
Bus Station . . . B2
Castle . . . B2
Castle Chare . . . B2
Cathedral . . . B2
Church St . . . C3
Clay La . . . C1
Claypath . . . B3
College of St Hild & St Bede . . . B3
County Hall . . . A1
County Hospital . . . B1
Crescent,The . . . A1
Crook Hall & Gardens . . . A3
Crossgate . . . B2
Crossgate Peth . . . C1
Darlington Rd . . . C1
Durham . . . A2
Durham Light Infantry Museum & Arts Gallery . . . A2
Durham School . . . C2
Ellam Ave . . . C1
Elvet Bridge . . . B3
Elvet Court . . . B3
Farnley Hey . . . B1
Ferens Cl . . . A3
Fieldhouse La . . . A1
Flass St . . . B1
Framewelgate Bridge . . . B2
Framwelgate . . . A2
Framwelgate Peth . . . A2
Framwelgate Waterside . . . A2
Frankland La . . . A3
Freeman's Pl . . . A3
Freeman's Quay Leisure Centre . . . A3
Gala Theatre & Cinema . . . B3
Gates Sh Ctr,The . . . B2
Geoffrey Ave . . . C1
Gilesgate . . . B3
Grey College . . . C3
Grove,The . . . A1
Hallgarth St . . . C3
Hatfield College . . . B3
Hawthorn Terr . . . B1
Heritage Centre . . . B3
HM Prison . . . B3
Information Ctr . . . B3
John St . . . B1
Kingsgate Bridge . . . B3
Laburnum Terr . . . B1
Lawson Terr . . . B1
Leazes Rd . . . B2/B3
Library . . . B2
Margery La . . . B2
Market . . . B2
Mavin St . . . C3
Millburngate . . . B2
Millburngate Bridge . . . B2
Millennium Bridge (foot/cycle) . . . A2
Mountjoy Research Centre . . . C3
Museum of Archaeology . . . B2
Neville Dale Terr . . . B1
New Elvet . . . B3
New Elvet Bridge . . . B3
North Bailey . . . B3
North End . . . A1
North Rd . . . A1/B2
Observatory . . . C1
Old Elvet . . . B3
Oriental Mus . . . C2
Oswald Court . . . C3
Parkside . . . B2
Passport Office . . . A2
Percy Terr . . . B1
Pimlico . . . C2
Police Station . . . B3
Post Office . . . A1/B2
Potters Bank . . . C1/C2
Prebends Bridge . . . C2
Prebends Walk . . . C2
Prince Bishops Shopping Centre . . . B3
Princes St . . . A1
Providence Row . . . A3
Quarryheads La . . . C2
Redhills La . . . B1
Redhills Terr . . . B1
Saddler St . . . B3
St Chad's College . . . C3
St Cuthbert's Society . . . C2
St John's College . . . C2
St Margaret's . . . B2
St Mary the Less . . . C2
St Mary's College . . . C2
St Monica Grove . . . B1
St Nicholas' . . . B3
St Oswald's . . . C3
Sands,The . . . A3
Sidegate . . . A2
Silver St . . . B2
Sixth Form College . . . A3
South Bailey . . . C2
South Rd . . . C3
South St . . . B2
Springwell Ave . . . A1
Stockton Rd . . . C3
Students' Rec Ctr . . . B3
Sutton St . . . B2
Town Hall . . . B2
Treasury Mus . . . B2
University . . . B2
Univ Arts Block . . . B3
University Library . . . C3
Univ Science Site . . . C3
Walkergate Centre . . . A3
Wearside Dr . . . A3
Western Hill . . . A1
Wharton Park . . . A2
Whinney Hill . . . C3
Whitehouse Ave . . . C1

Edinburgh 116

Abbey Strand . . . B6
Abbeyhill . . . A6
Abbeyhill Cr . . . B6
Abbeymount . . . A6
Abercromby Pl . . . A3
Adam St . . . C5
Albany La . . . A4
Albany St . . . A4
Albert Meml . . . B2
Albyn Pl . . . A2
Alva Pl . . . A6
Alva St . . . B1
Ann St . . . A1
Appleton Tower . . . C4
Archibald Pl . . . C3
Assembly Rooms & Musical Hall . . . A3
Atholl Cr . . . B1
Atholl Crescent La . . . C1
Bank St . . . B4
Barony St . . . A4
Beaumont Pl . . . C5
Belford Rd . . . B1
Belgrave Cr . . . A1
Belgrave Cres La . . . A1
Bell's Brae . . . B1
Blackfriars St . . . B4
Blair St . . . B4
Bread St . . . C2
Bristo Pl . . . C4
Bristo St . . . C4
Brougham St . . . C2
Broughton St . . . A4
Brown St . . . C5
Brunton Terr . . . A6
Buckingham Terr . . . A1
Burial Ground . . . A6
Bus Station . . . A4
Caledonian Cr . . . C1
Caledonian Rd . . . C1
Calton Hill . . . A4
Calton Hill . . . A5
Calton Rd . . . B4
Camera Obscura & Outlook Tower . . . B3
Candlemaker Row . . . C4
Canning St . . . C2
Canongate . . . B5
Canongate . . . B5
Carlton St . . . A1
Carlton Terr . . . A6
Carlton Terrace La . . . A6
Castle St . . . B2
Castle Terr . . . B2
Castlehill . . . B3
Central Library . . . B4
Chalmers Hosp . . . C3
Chalmers St . . . C3
Chambers St . . . C4
Chapel St . . . C4
Charles St . . . C4
Charlotte Sq . . . B2
Chester St . . . B1
Circus La . . . A2
Circus Place . . . A2
City Art Centre . . . B4
City Chambers . . . B4
City Observatory . . . A5
Clarendon Cr . . . A1
Clerk St . . . C5
Coates Cr . . . B1
Cockburn St . . . B4
College of Art . . . C3
Comely Bank Ave . . . A1
Comely Bank Row . . . A1
Cornwall St . . . C2
Cowans Cl . . . C5
Cowgate . . . B4
Cranston St . . . B5
Crichton St . . . C4
Croft-An-Righ . . . A6
Cumberland St . . . A2
Dalry Pl . . . C1
Dalry Rd . . . C1
Danube St . . . A1
Darnawy St . . . A2
David Hume Tower . . . C4
Davie St . . . C5
Dean Bridge . . . A1
Dean Gdns . . . A1
Dean Park Cr . . . A1
Dean Park Mews . . . A1
Dean Park St . . . A1
Dean Path . . . B1
Dean St . . . A1
Dean Terr . . . A1
Dewar Pl . . . C1
Dewar Place La . . . C1
Doune Terr . . . A2
Drummond Pl . . . A3
Drummond St . . . C5
Drumsheugh Gdns . . . B1
Dublin Mews . . . A3
Dublin St . . . A4
Dublin St La South . . . A4
Dumbiedykes Rd . . . B5
Dundas St . . . A3
Earl Grey St . . . C2
East Crosscauseway . . . C5
East Market St . . . B4
East Norton Pl . . . A6
East Princes St Gdns . . . B3
Easter Rd . . . A6
Edinburgh (Waverley) . . . B4
Edinburgh Castle . . . B3
Edinburgh Dungeon . . . B4
Edinburgh Int Conference Ctr . . . C2
Elder St . . . A4
Esplanade . . . B3
Eton Terr . . . A1
Eye Pavilion . . . C3
Festival Office . . . B3
Festival Theatre Edinburgh . . . C4
Filmhouse . . . C2
Fire Station . . . C2
Floral Clock . . . B3
Forres St . . . A2
Forth St . . . A4
Fountainbridge . . . C2
Frederick St . . . A3
Freemasons' Hall . . . B3
Fruit Market . . . B4
Gardner's Cr . . . C2
George Heriot's School . . . C3
George IV Bridge . . . B4
George Sq . . . C4
George Sq La . . . C4
George St . . . B3
Georgian House . . . B2
Gladstone's Land . . . B3
Glen St . . . C3
Gloucester La . . . A2
Gloucester Pl . . . A2
Gloucester St . . . A2
Graham St . . . C3
Grassmarket . . . C3
Great King St . . . A3
Great Stuart . . . B1
Greenside La . . . A5
Greenside Row . . . A5
Greyfriars Kirk . . . C4
Grindlay St . . . C2
Grosvenor St . . . C1
Grove St . . . C1
Gullan's Cl . . . B5
Guthrie St . . . B4
Hanover St . . . A3
Hart St . . . A4
Haymarket . . . C1
Haymarket Sta . . . C1
Heriot Pl . . . C3
Heriot Row . . . A2
High School Yard . . . B5
High St . . . B4
Hill Pl . . . C5
Hill St . . . A2
Hillside Cr . . . A5
Holyrood Park . . . C6
Holyrood Rd . . . B5
Home St . . . C2
Hope St . . . B2
Horse Wynd . . . B6
Howden St . . . C5
Howe St . . . A2
India Pl . . . A2
India St . . . A2
Infirmary St . . . B4
Information Ctr . . . B4
Jeffrey St . . . B4
John Knox Ho . . . B4
Johnston Terr . . . C3
Keir St . . . C3
Kerr St . . . A2
King's Stables Rd . . . B2
Lady Lawson St . . . C3
Lauriston Gdns . . . C3
Lauriston Park . . . C3
Lauriston Pl . . . C3
Lauriston St . . . C3
Lawnmarket . . . B3
Learmonth Gdns . . . A1
Learmonth Terr . . . A1

Leith St A4
Lennox St A1
Lennox St La A1
Leslie Pl A2
London Rd A5
Lothian Rd B2
Lothian St C4
Lower Menz Pl A6
Lynedoch Pl B1
Mall,The B6
Manor Pl B1
Market St B4
Marshall St C4
Maryfield A6
Maryfield Pl A6
McEwan Hall C4
Medical School C4
Melville St B1
Meuse La B4
Middle Mdw Walk C4
Milton St A6
Montrose Terr A6
Moray Ho (Coll) B5
Moray Place A2
Morrison Link C1
Morrison St C1
Mound Pl B3
Mound,The B3
Multrees Walk A4
Museum Collections Centre A4
Museum of Childhood B5
Museum of Edinburgh B5
Museum of Fire C3
Museum on the Mound B4
National Archives of Scotland A4
National Museum of Scotland C4
National Gallery B3
National Library of Scotland B4
National Monument ✦ A5
National Portrait Gallery B4
Nelson Monument ✦ A5
Nelson St A3
New St B5
Nicolson Sq C4
Nicolson St C4
Niddry St B4
North Bank St B3
North Bridge B4
North Castle St A2
North Charlotte St A2
North Mdw Walk C3
North St Andrew St A4
North St David St A3
North West Cir Pl A2
Northumberland St A3
Odeon C2
Old Royal High School A5
Old Tolbooth Wynd B5
OMNi Centre ✦ A4
Our Dynamic Earth ✦ B6
Oxford Terr A1
Palace of Holyroodhouse B6
Palmerston Pl B1
Panmure Pl C3
Parliament Ho B4
Parliament Sq B4
People's Story, The B5
Playhouse Theatre A4
Pleasance C5
Police Station A4
Ponton St C2
Post Office A3/B4/B5/C1/C2/C4
Potterrow C4
Princes Mall B4
Princes St B3
Princes St B3
Prisoners of War B3
Queen St A2
Queen Street Gdns A3
Queen's Dr B6/C6
Queensferry Rd A1
Queensferry St B1
Queensferry St La B2
Radical Rd C6
Randolph Cr B1
Regent Gdns A5
Regent Rd B5
Regent Rd Park A6
Regent Terr A5
Holyrood Abbey, remains of (AD 1128) A6
Richmond La C5
Richmond Pl C5
Rose St B2
Ross Open Air Theatre B3
Rothesay Pl B1
Rothesay Terr B1
Roxburgh Pl C5
Roxburgh St C5
Royal Bank of Scotland A4
Royal Circus A2
Royal Lyceum C2
Royal Mile,The B5
Royal Scottish Academy B3
Royal Terr A5
Royal Terr Gdns A5
Rutland Sq B2
Rutland St B2
St Andrew Sq A4
St Andrew Sq A4
St Andrew's House A4
St Bernard's Cr A1
St Cecilia's Hall B4
St Colme St A2
St Cuthbert's B2
St Giles' ✝ B4
St John St B5
St John's B2
St John's Hill B5
St Leonard's Hill C5
St Leonard's La C5
St Leonard's St C5
St Mary's
St Mary's Scottish Episcopal ✝ B1
St Mary's St B5
St Stephen St A2
Salisbury Crags C6
Saunders St A2
Scotch Whisky Experience ✦ B3
Scott Monument ✦ B4
Scottish Parliament B6
Scottish Storytelling Centre ✦ B5
Semple St C2
Shandwick Pl B2
South Bridge B4
South Charlotte St B2
South College St C4
South Learmonth Gdns A1
South St Andrew Street A4
South St David Street A3
Spittal St C2
Stafford St B1
Student Centre C4
Surgeons' Hall C5
Tattoo Office B4
Teviot Pl C4
Thistle St A3
Torphichen Pl C1
Torphichen St C1
Traverse Theatre B2
Tron Sq B4
Tron,The ✦ B4
Union St A4
University C4
University Library C4
Upper Grove Pl C1
Usher Hall C2
Vennel C3
Victoria St B3
Viewcraig Gdns B5
Viewcraig St B5
Vue A4
Walker St B1
Waterloo Pl A4
Waverley Bridge B4
Wemyss Pl A2
West Approach Rd C1
West Crosscauseway C5
West End Princess St B1
West Maitland St C1
West of Nicholson St C4
West Port C3
West Princes Street Gdns B3
West Richmond St C5
West Tollcross C2
White Horse Cl ✦ B5
William St B1
Windsor St A5
Writer's Museum, The B4
York La A4
York Pl A4
York Pl A4
Young St B2

Exeter 117

Alphington St C1
Athelstan Rd B3
Bampfylde St B2
Barnardo Rd C3
Barnfield Hill B3
Barnfield Rd B2/B3
Barnfield Theatre B2
Bartholomew St East B1
Bartholomew St West B1
Bear St B2
Beaufort Rd C1
Bedford St B2
Belgrave Rd A3
Belmont Rd A3
Blackall Rd A2
Blackboy Rd A3
Bonhay Rd B1
Bull Meadow Rd C2
Bus & Coach Sta B3
Castle St B2
Cecil Rd C1
Cheeke St A3
Church Rd C1
Chute St A3
City Industrial Estate C2
City Wall B1/B2
Civic Centre B2
Clifton Rd B3
Clifton St B3
Clock Tower A1
College Rd B3
Colleton Cr C2
Commercial Rd C1
Coombe St B2
Cowick St C1
Crown Courts B2
Custom House C2
Cygnet New Theatre C2
Danes' Rd A2
Denmark Rd B3
Devon County Hall C3
Devonshire Pl A3
Dinham Rd B1
East Grove Rd C3
Edmund St C1
Elmgrove Rd A1
Exe St B1
Exeter Cathedral ✝ B2
Exeter Central Station A1
Exeter City Football Ground A3
Exeter College A1
Exeter Picture House B1
Fire Station A1
Fore St B1
Friars Walk C2
Guildhall B2
Guildhall Sh Ctr B2
Harlequins Sh Ctr B1
Haven Rd C2
Heavitree Rd B3
Hele Rd A1
High St B2
HM Prison A2
Holloway St C2
Hoopern St A2
Horseguards A2
Howell Rd A1
Information Ctr B3
Iron Bridge B1
Isca Rd C1
Jesmond Rd A3
King St B1
King William St A2
Larkbeare Rd C2
Leisure Centre C1
Library B2
Longbrook St A2
Longbrook Terr A2
Lower North St B1
Lucky La C2
Lyndhurst Rd C3
Magdalen Rd B3
Magdalen St B2
Magistrates & Crown Courts A2
Market B2
Market St B2
Marlborough Rd C3
Mary Arches St B1
Matford Ave C3
Matford La C3
Matford Rd C3
May St A3
Mol's Coffee House B2
New Bridge St B1
New North Rd A1/A2
North St B1
Northernhay St B1
Norwood Ave C3
Odeon A3
Okehampton St C1
Old Mill Cl C2
Old Tiverton Rd A3
Oxford Rd A3
Paris St B2
Parr St A3
Paul St B1
Pennsylvania Rd A2
Police HQ B3
Portland Street A3
Post Office A3/B2/B3/C1
Powderham Cr A3
Preston St B1
Princesshay Shopping Centre B2
Quay,The C2
Queen St A1
Queen's Terr A1
Queens Rd C1
Radford Rd C2
Richmond Rd A1
Roberts Rd C2
Rougemont Castle A2
Rougemont House ✦ B2
Royal Albert Memorial Mus B2
St David's Hill A1
St James' Park Station A3
St James' Rd A3
St Leonard's Rd C3
St Mary Steps C1
St Nicholas Priory B1
St Thomas Sta C1
Sandford Walk B3
School for the Deaf C2
School Rd C1
Sidwell St A2
Smythen St B1
South St B2
Southernhay East B2
Southernhay West B2
Spacex Gallery B1
Spicer Rd B3
Sports Centre A3
Summerland St A3
Swimming Pool & Leisure Centre B3
Sydney Rd C1
Tan La C2
Thornton Hill A2
Topsham Rd C3
Tucker's Hall B1
Tudor St B1
Univ of Exeter (St Luke's Campus) B3
Velwell Rd A1
Verney St A3
Water La C1/C2
Weirfield Rd C2
Well St A3
West Ave A2
West Grove Rd C3
Western Way A3/B1/B2
Willeys Ave C1
Wonford Rd B3/C3
York Rd A2

Glasgow 117

Admiral St C2
Albert Bridge C5
Albion St B5
Anderston B3
Anderston Quay B3
Argyle Arcade B5
Argyle St A1/A2/B3/B4/B5
Argyle Street B5
Arlington St A3
Arts Centre B3
Ashley St A3
Bain St C6
Baird St A6
Baliol St A3
Ballater St C5
Barras (Mkt),The C6
Bath St A3
BBC Scotland B1
Bell St C6
Bell's Bridge B1
Bentinck St A2
Berkeley St A3
Bishop La B3
Black St A6
Blackburn St C2
Blackfriars St B6
Blantyre St A1
Blythswood Sq A4
Blythswood St B4
Bothwell St B4
Brand St C1
Breadalbane St A2
Bridge St C4
Bridge St C4
Bridgegate C5
Briggait C5
Broomielaw B4
Broomielaw Quay Gdns B3
Brown St B4
Brunswick St B5
Buccleuch St A3
Buchanan Bus Sta A5
Buchanan Galleries A5
Buchanan St B5
Buchanan St B5
Cadogan St B4
Caledonian Univ A5
Calgary St A5
Cambridge St A4
Canal St A5
Candleriggs B5
Carlton Pl C4
Carnarvon St A3
Carrick St B4
Castle St B6
Cathedral Sq B6
Cathedral St B5
Centre for Contemporary Arts A4
Centre St C4
Cessnock C1
Cessnock St C1
Charing Cross A3
Charlotte St C6
Cheapside St B3
Cineworld A5
Citizens' Theatre C5
City Chambers Complex B5
City Halls B5
City of Glasgow Coll (City Campus) B5
City of Glasgow Coll (Riverside Campus) C5
Clairmont Gdns A2
Claremont St A2
Claremont Terr A2
Claythorne St C6
Cleveland St A3
Clifford La C1
Clifford St C1
Clifton Pl A2
Clifton St A2
Clutha St C1
Clyde Arc B2
Clyde Auditorium B2
Clyde Pl C4
Clyde Place Quay C4
Clyde St C5
Clyde Walkway C3
Clydeside Expressway B2
Coburg St C4
Cochrane St B5
College St B6
Collins St B6
Commerce St C4
Cook St C4
Cornwall St C2
Couper St A5
Cowcaddens A4
Cowcaddens Rd A4
Crimea St B3
Custom House Quay Gdns C4
Dalhousie St A4
Dental Hospital A4
Derby St A2
Dobbie's Loan A4/A5
Dobbie's Loan Pl A5
Dorset St A3
Douglas St B4
Doulton Fountain ✦ C6
Dover St A2
Drury St B4
Drygate B6
Duke St B6
Dunaskin St A1
Dunblane St A4
Dundas St B5
Dunlop St C5
East Campbell St C6
Eastvale Pl A1
Eglinton St C4
Elderslie St A3
Elliot St B2
Elmbank St A3
Esmond St A1
Exhibition Ctr B2
Eye Infirmary A2
Festival Park C1
Film Theatre A4
Finnieston Quay B2
Finnieston St B2
Fire Station C6
Florence St C5
Fox St C5
Gallowgate C6
Garnet St A3
Garnethill St A4
Garscube Rd A4
George Sq B5
George St B5
George V Bridge C4
Gilbert St A1
Glasgow Bridge C4
Glasgow Cathedral ✝ B6
Glasgow Central B4
Glasgow Green C6
Glasgow Necropolis ✦ B6
Glasgow Royal Concert Hall A5
Glasgow Science Centre ✦ B1
Glasgow Tower ✦ B1
Glassford St B5
Glebe St A6
Gorbals Cross C5
Gorbals St C5
Gordon St B4
Govan Rd B1/C1/C2
Grace St B3
Grafton Pl A5
Grand Ole Opry ✦ C2
Grant St A3
Granville St A3
Gray St A2
Greendyke St C6
Grey Eagle St B7
Harley St C1
Harvie St C1
Haugh Rd A1
Havanah St B6
Heliport B1
Henry Wood Hall A2
High Court C5
High St B6
High Street B6
Hill St A3
Holland St A3
Holm St B4
Hope St A5
Houldsworth St B2
Houston Pl C3
Houston St C3
Howard St C5
Hunter St C6
Hutcheson St B5
Hydepark St B3
Imax Cinema B1
India St A3
Information Ctr B5
Ingram St B5
Jamaica St B4
James Watt St B4
John Knox St B6
John St B5
Kelvin Hall ✦ A1
Kelvin Statue ✦ A2
Kelvin Way A2
Kelvingrove Art Gallery & Mus A1
Kelvingrove Park A2
Kelvingrove St A2
Kelvinhaugh St A1
Kennedy St A6
Kent Rd A2
Killermont St A5
King St B5
King's,The A3
Kingston Bridge C3
Kingston St C4
Kinning Park C2
Kyle St A5
Lancefield Quay B2
Lancefield St B3
Langshot St C1
Lendel Pl C1
Lighthouse,The ✦ B4
Lister St A6
Little St B3
London Rd C6
Lorne St C1
Lower Harbour B1
Lumsden St A1
Lymburn St A1
Lyndoch Cr A3
Lynedoch Pl A3
Lynedoch St A3
Maclellan St C1
Mair St C2
Maitland St A4
Mansell St C7
Mavisbank Gdns C2
Mcalpine St B3
Mcaslin St A6
McLean Sq C2
McLellan Gallery A4
McPhater St A4
Merchants' Ho B5
Middlesex St C2
Middleton St C1
Midland St B4
Miller St B5
Millennium Bridge B1
Millroad St C6
Milnpark St C2
Milton St A4
Minerva St B2
Mitchell Lby,The A3
Mitchell St West B4
Mitchell Theatre, The A3
Modern Art Gallery B5
Moir St C6
Molendinar St C6
Moncur St C6
Montieth Row C6
Montrose St B5
Morrison St C3
Mosque C5
Nairn St A1
National Piping Centre,The ✦ A5
Nelson Mandela Square B5
Nelson St C4
Nelson's Monument C6
New City Rd A4
Newton Pl A3
Newton St A3
Nicholson St C4
Nile St B5
Norfolk Court C4
Norfolk St C4
North Frederick St B5
North Hanover St B5
North Portland St B6
North St A3
North Wallace St A5
O2 ABC A4
O2 Academy ✦ C4
Odeon C3
Old Dumbarton Rd A1
Osborne St B5/C5
Oswald St B4
Overnewton St A1
Oxford St C4
Pacific Dr B1
Paisley Rd C3
Paisley Rd West C1
Park Circus A2
Park Gdns A2
Park St South A2
Park Terr A2
Parkgrove Terr A2
Parnie St C5
Parson St A6
Partick Bridge A1
Passport Office A5
Pavilion Theatre A4
Pembroke St A3
People's Pal C6
Pinkston Rd A6
Pitt St A4/B4
Plantation Park C1
Plantation Quay B1
Police Station A4/A6
Port Dundas Rd A5
Port St B2
Portman St C2
Prince's Dock B1
Princes Sq B5
Provand's Lordship B6
Queen St B5
Queen Street B5
Ramshorn B5
Renfrew St A3/A4
Renton St A5
Richmond St B5
Robertson St B4
Rose St A4
Rottenrow B5
Royal Concert Hall A5
Royal Conservatoire of Scotland A4
Royal Crescent A2
Royal Exchange Sq B5
Royal Highland Fusiliers Mus A3
Royal Hospital For Sick Children A1
Royal Infirmary B6
Royal Terr A2
Rutland Crescent C2
St Andrew's C6
St Andrew's (RC) ✝ C5
St Andrew's St C5
St Enoch B5
St Enoch Shopping Ctr B5
St Enoch Sq B4
St George's Rd A3
St James Rd B6
St Kent St C6
St Mungo Ave A5/A6
St Mungo Museum of Religious Life B6
St Mungo Pl A6
St Vincent Cr A2
St Vincent Pl B5
St Vincent St B3/B4
St Vincent Street Church B4
St Vincent Terr B3
Saltmarket C5
Sandyford Pl A3
Sauchiehall St A2/A4
School of Art A4
Sclater St B7
Scotland St C2
Scott St A4
Scottish Exhibition & Conference Ctr B1
Seaward St C2
Shaftesbury St B3
Sheriff Court C5
Shields Rd C3
Shopmobility A5
Shuttle St B6
Sighthill Park A6
Somerset Pl A2
South Portland St C4
Springburn Rd A6
Springfield Quay C3
SSE Hydro The B2
Stanley St C2
Stevenson St C6
Stewart St A4
Stirling Rd B6
Stirling's Library B5
Stobcross Quay B1
Stobcross Rd B1
Stock Exchange B5
Stockwell Pl C5
Stockwell St B5
Stow College A4
Sussex St C2
Synagogues A3/C4
Taylor Pl A6
Tenement Ho A3
Teviot St A1
Theatre Royal A4
Tolbooth Steeple & Mercat Cross ✦ C6
Tower St C2
Trades House B5
Tradeston St C4
Transport Mus A1
Tron C5
Trongate B5
Tunnel St B2
Turnbull St C5
Union St B4
Univ of Strathclyde B6
Victoria Bridge C5
Virginia St B5
Wallace St C3
Walls St B6
Walmer Cr C1
Warrock St B3
Washington St B3
Waterloo St B4
Watson St B6
Watt St C3
Wellington St B4
West Campbell St B4
West George St B4
West Graham St A4
West Greenhill Pl B2
West Regent St A4
West Regent St B4
West St C4
West St C4
Whitehall St B3
Wilkes St C7
Wilson St B5
Woodlands Gate A3
Woodlands Rd A3
Woodlands Terr A2
Woodside Pl A3
Woodside Terr A3
York St B4
Yorkhill Pde A1
Yorkhill St A1

Gloucester 117

Albion St C1
Alexandra Rd B3
Alfred St C3
All Saints Rd C2
Alvin St B2
Arthur St C2
Barrack Square B1
Barton St C2
Blackfriars ✝ B1
Blenheim Rd C2
Bristol Rd C1
Brunswick Rd C2
Bruton Way B2
Bus Station B2
Cineworld C1
City Council Offices B1
City Mus, Art Gallery & Library B2
Clarence St B2
Commercial Rd B1
Council Offices B1
Courts B1
Cromwell St C2
Deans Way A2
Denmark Rd A3
Derby Rd C3
Docks ✦ C1
Eastgate St B2
Eastgate,The B1
Edwy Pde A2
Estcourt Cl A3
Estcourt Rd A3
Falkner St C2
Folk Museum B1
GL1 Leisure Ctr C2
Gloucester Cathedral ✝ B1
Gloucester Quays Outlet C1
Gloucester Sta B2
Gloucester Waterways C1
Gloucestershire Royal Hospital (A&E) B3
Goodyere St C2
Gouda Way A1
Great Western Rd B3
Guildhall B2
Heathville Rd A3
Henry Rd B3
Henry St B2
Hinton Rd A2
India Rd C3
Information Ctr B1
Jersey Rd C3
King's C2
King's Walk Shopping Ctr B2
Kingsholm (Gloucester Rugby) A2
Kingsholm Rd A2
Lansdown Rd A3
Library C2
Llanthony Rd C1
London Rd B3
Longhorn Ave A1
Longsmith St B1
Malvern Rd A3
Market B2
Market Pde B2
Mercia Rd A1
Metz Way C3
Midland Rd C2
Millbrook St C3
Montpellier C1
Napier St C3
Nettleton Rd C2
New Inn B2
New Olympus C3
North Rd A3
Northgate St B2
Oxford Rd A2
Oxford St B2
Park & Ride Gloucester A1
Park Rd C2
Park St B2
Park,The C2
Parliament St C1
Peel Centre,The C1
Pitt St B1
Police Sta B1/C3
Post Office B2
Quay St B1
Quay,The B1
Recreation Gd A1/A2
Regent St C2
Robert Raikes House B1
Royal Oak Rd B1
Russell St B2
Ryecroft St C2
St Aldate St B2
St Ann Way C1
St Catherine St A2
St Mark St A2
St Mary de Crypt B1
St Mary de Lode B1
St Nicholas's B1
St Oswald's Rd A1
St Oswald's Ret Pk A1
St Peter's B2
Seabroke Rd A3
Sebert St A2
Severn Rd C1
Sherborne St B2
Shire Hall B1
Sidney St C3
Soldiers of Gloucestershire B1
Southgate St B1/C1
Spa Field C1
Spa Rd C1
Sports Ground A2/B2
Station Rd B2
Stratton Rd C3
Stroud Rd C1
Superstore A1
Swan Rd A2
Trier Way C1/C2
Union St A2
Vauxhall Rd C3
Victoria St C2
Walham Lane A1
Wellington St C2
Westgate Retail Pk B1
Westgate St B1
Weston Rd C1
Widden St C2
Worcester St B2

Harrogate 117

Albert St C2
Alexandra Rd B2
Arthington Ave B2
Ashfield Rd A2
Back Cheltenham Mount B2
Beech Grove C1
Belmont Rd C1
Bilton Dr A2
Bower Rd B2
Bower St B2
Bus Station B2
Cambridge Rd B2
Cambridge St B2
Cemetery A2
Chatsworth Grove A2
Chatsworth Pl A2
Chatsworth Rd A2
Chelmsford Rd B3
Cheltenham Cr B2
Cheltenham Mt B2
Cheltenham Pde B2
Christ Church B3
Christ Church Oval B3
Chudleigh Rd B3
Clarence Dr B1
Claro Rd A3
Claro Way A3
Coach Park B2
Coach Rd B3
Cold Bath Rd C1
Commercial St B2
Coppice Ave A1
Coppice Dr A1
Coppice Gate A1
Cornwall Rd B1
Council Offices B1
Court C3
Crescent Gdns B1
Crescent Rd B1
Dawson Terr A2
Devonshire Pl B3
Diamond Mews C1
Dixon Rd A2
Dixon Terr A2
Dragon Ave B3
Dragon Parade B2
Dragon Rd B2
Duchy Rd B1
East Parade B2
East Park Rd C3
Esplanade B1
Fire Station A2
Franklin Mount A2
Franklin Rd B2
Franklin Square A2
Glebe Rd C1
Grove Park Ct A3
Grove Park Terr A3
Grove Rd A2
Hampswaite Rd A1
Harcourt Dr B3
Harcourt Rd B3
Harrogate B2
Harrogate International Ctr B1
Harrogate Ladies College B1
Harrogate Theatre B2
Heywood Rd C1
Hollins Cr A1
Hollins Mews A1
Hollins Rd A1
Homestead Rd C3
Hydro Leisure Centre,The A1
Information Ctr B1
James St B2
Jenny Field Dr A1
John St B2
Kent Dr A1
Kent Rd A1
Kings Rd A2
Kingsway B3
Kingsway Dr B3
Lancaster Rd C1
Leeds Rd C2
Lime Grove B3
Lime St A3
Mayfield Grove B2
Mayfield Pl A2
Mercer B1
Montpellier Hill B1
Mornington Crescent A3
Mornington Terr B3
Mowbray Sq B3
North Park Rd B3
Nydd Vale Rd B2
Oakdale Ave A1
Oatlands Dr C3
Odeon B2
Osborne Rd A2
Otley Rd C2
Oxford St B2
Parade,The B2
Park Chase B3
Park Parade B3
Park View B2
Parliament St B1
Police Station B3
Post Office B2/C1
Providence Terr A2
Queen Parade C3
Queen's Rd C1
Raglan St C2
Regent Ave A3
Regent Grove A3
Regent Parade A3
Regent St A3
Regent Terr A3
Rippon Rd A1
Robert St C2
Royal Baths & Turkish Baths B1
Royal Pump Room B1
St Luke's Mount A2
St Mary's Ave C1
St Mary's Walk C1
Scargill Rd A1
Skipton Rd A3
Skipton St A2
Slingsby Walk C3
South Park Rd C2
Spring Grove A1
Springfield Ave B1
Station Ave B2
Station Parade B2
Strawberry Dale B2
Stray Rein C3
Stray,The C2/C3
Studley Rd A2
Superstore B2
Swan Rd B1
Tower St C2
Trinity Rd C2
Union St B2
Valley Dr C1
Valley Gardens C1
Valley Mount C1
Victoria Ave C2
Victoria Rd C1
Victoria Sh Ctr B2
Waterloo St A2
West Park C2
West Park St C2
Wood View A1
Woodfield Ave A3
Woodfield Dr A3
Woodfield Grove A3
Woodfield Rd A3
Woodfield Square A3
Woodside B3
York Pl C3
York Rd B1

Hull 117

Adelaide St C1
Albert Dock C1
Albion St B2
Alfred Gelder St B2
Anlaby Rd B1
Arctic Corsair ✦ B3
Beverley Rd A1
Blanket Row C2
Bond St B2
Bridlington Ave A2
Brook St B1
Brunswick Ave A1
Bus Station B1
Camilla Cl C3
Cannon St A2
Caroline St A2
Carr La B2
Castle St C2
Central Library B1
Charles St A2
Citadel Way B3
City Hall B2
City Hall Theatre B2
Clarence St B3
Cleveland St A3
Clifton St A1
Club Culture C2
Colonial St B1
Court B2
Deep,The C3
Dinostar C2
Dock Office Row B3
Dock St B2
Drypool Bridge B3
Egton St A3
English St C1
Ferens Gallery B2
Ferensway B1
Francis St A2
Francis St West A2
Freehold St A1
Freetown Way A2
Früit Theatre C2
Garrison Rd B3
George St B2
Gibson St A2
Great Thornton St B1
Great Union St A3
Green La A2
Grey St A1
Grimston St B2
Grosvenor St A1
Guildhall B2
Guildhall Rd B2
Hands-on History B2
Harley St A1
Hessle Rd C1
High St B3
Holy Trinity B2
Hull (Paragon) Station B1
Hull & East Riding Museum B3
Hull Ice Arena C1
Hull College B3
Hull History Ctr A2
Hull Truck Theatre B1
Humber Dock Marina C2
Humber Dock St C2
Humber St C2
Hyperion St A3
Information Ctr B2
Jameson St B1
Jarratt St B2
Jenning St A3
King Billy Statue ✦ C2
King Edward St B2
King St A2
Kingston Retail Pk C1
Kingston St C2
Liddell St A1
Lime St A3
Lister St C1
Lockwood St A2
Maister House B3
Maritime Mus B2
Market B2
Market Place B2
Minerva Pier C2
Mulgrave St A3
Myton Swing Bridge C3
Myton St B1
NAPA (Northern Acad of Performing Arts) B1
Nelson St C2
New Cleveland St A3
New George St A2
New Theatre A2
Norfolk St A1
North Bridge A3
North St B1
Odeon C1
Old Harbour C3
Osborne St B1
Paragon St B2
Park St B1
Percy St A2
Pier St C2
Police Station B2
Porter St C1
Portland St B1
Post Office B1/B2
Posterngate B2
Prince's Quay B2
Prospect Centre B1
Prospect St B1
Queen's Gdns B2
Railway Dock Marina C2
Railway St C2
Real B1
Red Gallery B1
Reform St A2
Retail Park B1
Riverside Quay C2
Roper St B2
St James St C1
St Luke's St B1
St Mark St A3
St Mary the Virgin B3
St Stephens Shopping Ctr B1
Scale Lane Footbridge B3
Scott St A2
South Bridge Rd B3
Sport's Centre C1
Spring Bank A1
Spring St B1
Spurn Lightship C2
Spyvee St A3
Streetlife Transport Museum B3
Sykes St A2
Tidal Surge Barrier ✦ C3
Tower St B3
Trinity House B2
University B2
Vane St A1
Victoria Pier C2
Waterhouse La B2
Waterloo St A1
Waverley St C1
Wellington St C2
Wellington St West C2
West St B1
Whitefriargate B2
Wilberforce Dr B2
Wilberforce House B3
Wilberforce Monument ✦ B3
William St C1
Wincolmlee A3
Witham A3
Wright St A1

132 London • Luton • Manchester

Police Station
✉ A4/A6/B4
Pomona St B4
Port of Liverpool
Building 🏛 B2
Post Office ✉ A2/A4/
A5/B2/B3/B4/C4
Pownall St C2
Prescot St A5
Preston St B3
Princes Dock A1
Princes Gdns A2
Princes Jetty A1
Princes Parade B1
Princes St B2
Pythian St A6
Queen Sq Bus Sta B3
Queensland St C6
Queensway Tunnel
(Docks exit) B1
Queensway Tunnel
(Entrance) B3
Radio City B2
Ranelagh St B3
Redcross St B2
Renfrew St B6
Renshaw St B4
Richmond Row A4
Richmond St B3
Rigby St A2
Roberts St A1
Rock St B4
Rodney St C4
Rokeby St A4
Romily St A6
Roscoe La C4
Roscoe St C4
Rose Hill A3
Royal Ct Theatre 🎭 B3
Royal Liver
Building 🏛 B1
Royal Liverpool
Hospital (A&E) ⊞ B5
Royal Mail St B4
Rumford Place B2
Rumford St B2
Russell St B4
St Andrew St B4
St Anne St A4
St Georges Hall 🏛 B3
St John's Centre B3
St John's Gdns B3
St John's La B3
St Joseph's Cr A4
St Minishull St B5
St Nicholas Place B1
St Paul's Sq A2
St Vincent Way B4
Salisbury St A4
Salthouse Dock C2
Salthouse Quay C2
Sandon St C5
Saxony Rd B6
Schomberg St A6
School La B2
Seel St C3
Seymour St B4
Shaw St A5
Shopmobility C2
Sidney Place C6
Sir Thomas St B3
Skelhorne St B4
Slater St C3
Smithdown La B6
Soho Sq A4
Soho St A4
South John St B2
Springfield A4
Stafford St A4
Standish St A3
Stanley St B2
Strand St C2
Strand, The B2
Suffolk St C3
Tabley St C3
Tarleton St B3
Tate Gallery 🏛 C2
Teck St B6
Temple St B2
Tithebarn St B2
Town Hall 🏛 B2
Traffic Police
Headquarters ✉ C6
Trowbridge St B4
Trueman St A3
Union St B2
Unity Theatre 🎭 C4
University C5
Univ of Liverpool B5
Upper Baker St A6
Upper Duke St C4
Upper Frederick St C3
Vauxhall Rd A2
Vernon St B2
Victoria Gallery &
Museum 🏛 B5
Victoria St B2
Vine St C5
Wakefield St A4
Walker Art
Gallery 🏛 A3
Walker St A6
Wapping C2
Water St B1/B2
Waterloo Rd A1
Wavertree Rd B6
West Derby Rd A6
West Derby St B5
Western Approaches
War Museum 🏛 B2
Whitechapel B3
Whitley Gdns A5
William Brown St B3
William Henry St A4
Williamson Sq B3
Williamson St B3
Williamson's Tunnels
Heritage Ctr ✦ C6
Women's Hosp ⊞ C6
Wood St B3
World Museum,
Liverpool 🏛 A3
York St C3

London 120

Abbey Orchard St E3
Abchurch La D6
Abingdon St E4
Achilles Way D2
Acton St B4
Addington St E4
Air St D3
Albany St B2
Albemarle St D3
Albert Emb F4
Aldenham St A3
Aldersgate St C6
Aldford St D2
Aldgate ⊖ C7
Aldgate High St C7
Aldwych C4
Allsop Pl B1
Amwell St B5
Andrew Borde St C3
Angel ⊖ A5
Appold St C7
Argyle Sq B4
Argyle St B4
Argyll St C3
Arnold Circus B7
Artillery La C7
Artillery Row E3
Association of
Photographers
Gallery 🏛 B6
Baker St ⊖ B1
Baker St B1
Baldwin's Gdns C5
Baltic St B6
Bank ⊖ C6
Bank Museum 🏛 C6
Bank of England C6
Bankside D6
Bankside
Gallery 🏛 D5
Banner St B6
Barbican ⇌⊖ C6
Barbican Centre
for Arts, The C6
Barbican
Gallery 🏛 C6
Basil St E1
Bastwick St B6
Bateman's Row B7
Bath St B6
Bayley St C3
Baylis Rd E5
Beak St D3
Bedford Row C4
Bedford Sq C3
Bedford St D4
Bedford Way B3
Beech St C6
Belgrave Pl E2
Belgrave Sq E2
Bell La C7
Belvedere Rd E4
Berkeley Sq D2
Berkeley St D2
Bernard St B4
Berners Pl C3
Berners St C3
Berwick St C3
Bethnal Green Rd B7
Bevenden St B6
Bevis Marks C7
BFI (British Film
Institute) 🎦 D4
BFI London IMAX
Cinema 🎦 D5
Bidborough St B4
Binney St C2
Birdcage Walk E3
Bishopsgate C7
Blackfriars ⇌⊖ D5
Blackfriars Bridge D5
Blackfriars Rd E5
Blandford St C1
Blomfield St C6
Bloomsbury St C3
Bloomsbury Way C4
Bolton St D2
Bond St ⊖ C2
Borough High St E6
Boswell St C4
Bow St C4
Bowling Green La B5
Brad St D5
Bressenden Pl E3
Brewer St D3
Brick St D2
Bridge St E4
Britannia Walk B6
British Film Institute
(BFI) 🎦 D4
British Library 🏛 B3
British Museum 🏛 C4
Britton St B5
Broad Sanctuary E3
Broadway E3
Brook Dr F5
Brook St D2
Brunswick Pl B6
Brunswick Shopping
Centre, The B4
Brunswick Sq B4
Brushfield St C7
Bruton St D2
Bryanston St C1
BT Centre C6
Buckingham Gate E3
Buckingham Pal 🏛 E3
Buckingham Palace
Rd F2
Bunhill Row B6
Byward St D7
Cabinet War Rooms
& Churchill
Museum 🏛 E3
Cadogan La E2
Cadogan Pl E1
Cadogan Sq F1
Caledonian Rd A4
Calshot St A4
Calthorpe St B4
Calvert Ave B7
Cambridge Circus C3
Camomile St C7
Cannon St D6
Cannon St ⇌⊖ D6
Carey St C4
Carlisle La E4
Carlisle Pl E3
Carlton House Terr D3
Carmelite St D5
Carnaby St C3
Carter La C5
Carthusian St C6
Cartwright Gdns B4
Castle Baynard St D5
Cavendish Pl C2
Cavendish Sq C2
Caxton Hall E3
Caxton St E3
Central St B6
Chalton St B3
Chancery Lane ⊖ C5
Chapel St E2
Charing Cross
⇌⊖ D4
Charing Cross Rd C3
Charles II St D3
Charles Sq B6
Charles St D2
Charlotte Rd B7
Charlotte St C3
Chart St B6
Charterhouse Sq C5
Charterhouse St C5
Cheapside C6
Chenies St C3
Chesham St E2
Chester Sq F2
Chesterfield Hill D2
Chiltern St C2
Chiswell St C6
City Garden Row A5
City Rd B6
City Thameslink ⇌ C5
City Univ, The B5
Claremont Sq A5
Clarges St D2
Clerkenwell Cl B5
Clerkenwell Green B5
Clerkenwell Rd B5
Cleveland St C3
Clifford St D3
Clink Prison
Museum 🏛 D6
Clock Museum 🏛 C6
Club Row B7
Cockspur St D3
Coleman St C6
Columbia Rd B7
Commercial St C7
Compton St B5
Conduit St D2
Constitution Hill E2
Copperfield St E5
Coptic St C4
Cornhill C6
Cornwall Rd D5
Coronet St B7
Courtauld Gallery
🏛 D4
Covent Garden ⊖ D4
Covent Garden ✦ D4
Cowcross St C5
Cowper St B6
Cranbourn St D3
Craven St D4
Crawford St C1
Creechurch La C7
Cremer St A7
Cromer St B4
Cumberland Gate D1
Cumberland Terr A2
Curtain Rd B7
Curzon St D2
Cut, The E5
D'arblay St C3
Davies St C2
Dean St C3
Deluxe Gallery 🏛 B7
Denmark St C3
Dering St C2
Devonshire St C2
Diana, Princess of
Wales Meml Wlk E3
Dingley Rd B6
Dorset St C1
Doughty St B4
Dover St D2
Downing St E4
Druid St E7
Drummond St B3
Drury La C4
Drysdale St B7
Duchess St C2
Dufferin St B6
Duke of Wellington
Place E2
Duke St C2
Duke St D3
Duke St Hill D6
Duke's Pl C7
Duncannon St D4
East Rd B6
Eastcastle St C3
Eastcheap D7
Eastman Dental
Hospital ⊞ B4
Eaton Pl E2
Eaton Sq E2
Eccleston St E2
Edgware Rd C1
Eldon St C6
Embankment ⊖ D4
Endell St C4
Endsleigh Pl B3
Euston ⇌⊖ B3
Euston Rd B3
Euston Square ⊖ B3
Evelina Children's
Hospital E4
Eversholt St A3
Exmouth Market B5
Fann St B6
Farringdon ⇌⊖ C5
Farringdon Rd C5
Farringdon St C5
Featherstone St B6
Fenchurch St D7
Fenchurch St ⇌ D7
Fetter La C5
Finsbury Circus C6
Finsbury
Pavement C6
Finsbury Sq B6
Fitzalan St F5
Fitzmaurice Pl D2
Fleet St C5
Floral St D4
Florence Nightingale
Museum 🏛 E4
Folgate St C7
Foot Hospital ⊞ B3
Fore St C6
Foster La C6
Francis St F3
Frazier St E5
Freemason's Hall C4
Friday St C6
Gainsford St E7
Garden Row E5
Gee St B6
George St C1
Gerrard St D3
Giltspur St C5
Glasshouse St D3
Gloucester Pl C1
Golden Hinde ⛴ D6
Golden La B6
Golden Sq D3
Goodge St ⊖ C3
Goodge St C3
Gordon Sq B3
Goswell Rd B5
Gough St B4
Goulston St C7
Gower St B3
Gracechurch St D6
Grafton Way B3
Gray's Inn Rd B4
Great College St E4
Great Cumberland
Pl C1
Great Eastern St B7
Great Guildford St D6
Great Marlborough
St C3
Great Ormond St B4
Great Ormond Street
Children's Hospital
⊞ B4
Great Percy St B4
Great Peter St E3
Great Portland St
⊖ B2
Great Portland St C2
Great Queen St C4
Great Russell St C3
Great Scotland Yd D4
Great Smith St E3
Great Suffolk St D5
Great Titchfield St C3
Great Tower St D7
Great Windmill St D3
Greek St C3
Green Park ⊖ D3
Green St D2
Greencoat Pl E3
Gresham St C6
Greville St B4/C5
Greycoat Hosp Sch E3
Greycoat Pl E3
Grosvenor Cres E2
Grosvenor Gdns E2
Grosvenor Pl E2
Grosvenor Sq D2
Grosvenor St D2
Guards Museum
and Chapel 🏛 E3
Guildhall
Art Gallery 🏛 C6
Guilford St B4
Guy's Hospital ⊞ D6
Haberdasher St B6
Hackney Rd B7
Half Moon St D2
Halkin St E2
Hall St B5
Hallam St C2
Hampstead Rd B3
Hanover Sq C2
Hans Cres E1
Hanway St C3
Hardwick St B5
Harley St C2
Harrison St B4
Hastings St B4
Hatfields D5
Hay's Galleria D7
Hay's Mews D2
Hayles St F5
Haymarket D3
Hayne St C5
Hayward Gallery
🏛 D4
Helmet Row B6
Herbrand St B4
Hercules Rd E4
Hertford St D2
High Holborn C4
Hill St D2
HMS Belfast ⛴ D7
Hobart Pl E2
Holborn ⊖ C4
Holborn C5
Holborn Viaduct C5
Holland St D5
Holmes Mus 🏛 B1
Holywell La B7
Horse Guards' Rd D3
Houndsditch C7
Houses of
Parliament 🏛 E4
Howland St C3
Hoxton Sq B7
Hoxton St B7
Hunter St B4
Hunterian Mus 🏛 C4
Hyde Park D1
Hyde Park Cnr ⊖ E2
Imperial War
Museum 🏛 E5
Inner Circle B2
Inst of Archaeology
(London Univ) B2
Ironmonger Row B6
James St C2
James St D4
Jermyn St D3
Jockey's Fields C4
John Carpenter St D5
John St B4
Judd St B4
Kennington Rd E5
King Charles St E4
King St D3
King St D4
King William St C6
King's Coll London D5
King's Cross ⇌ A4
King's Cross Rd B4
King's Cross St
Pancras ⊖ A4
King's Rd E2
Kingley St C3
Kingsland Rd B7
Kingsway C4
Kinnerton St E2
Knightsbridge ⊖ E1
Lamb St C7
Lamb's Conduit St C4
Lambeth Bridge F4
Lambeth High St F4
Lambeth North ⊖ E5
Lambeth Palace 🏛 E4
Lambeth Pal Rd E4
Lambeth Rd E5
Lambeth Walk F4
Lancaster Pl D4
Langham Pl C2
Leadenhall St C7
Leake St E4
Leather La C5
Leicester Sq ⊖ D3
Leicester St D3
Leonard St B6
Lever St B6
Lexington St D3
Lidlington Pl A3
Lime St D7
Lincoln's Inn
Fields C4
Lindsey St C5
Lisle St D3
Liverpool St C7
Liverpool St ⇌⊖ C7
Lloyd Baker St B5
Lloyd Sq B5
Lombard St C6
London
Aquarium ✦ E4
London Bridge
⇌⊖ D6
London Bridge
Hospital ⊞ D6
London City Hall
🏛 D7
London Dungeon,
The 🏛 E4
London Film
Museum ✦ E4
London Guildhall
University C6
London Rd E5
London Transport
Museum 🏛 D4
London Wall C6
London-Eye ✦ E4
Long Acre D4
Long La C5
Longford St B2
Lower Belgrave St E2
Lower Grosvenor
Pl E2
Lower Marsh E5
Lower Thames St D6
Lowndes St E2
Ludgate Circus C5
Ludgate Hill C5
Luxborough St C2
Lyall St E2
Macclesfield Rd B6
Madame
Tussaud's ✦ B2
Maddox St D2
Malet St C3
Mall, The E3
Manchester Sq C2
Manchester St C2
Mandeville Pl C2
Mansell St D7
Mansion House 🏛 C6
Mansion House ⊖ D6
Maple St C3
Marble Arch ⊖ C1
Marble Arch D1
Marchmont St B4
Margaret St C3
Margery St B5
Mark La D7
Marlborough Rd D3
Marshall St C3
Marsham St E3
Marylebone High
St C2
Marylebone La C2
Marylebone Rd B2
Marylebone St C2
Mecklenburgh Sq B4
Middle Temple La C5
Middlesex St
(Petticoat La) C7
Midland Rd A3
Minories C7
Monck St E3
Monmouth St C4
Montagu Pl C1
Montagu Sq C1
Montagu St C4
Montague Pl C3
Monument ⊖ D6
Monument St D6
Monument, The ✦ D6
Moor La C6
Moorfields C6
Moorfields Eye
Hospital ⊞ B6
Moorgate C6
Moorgate ⇌⊖ C6
Moreland St B5
Morley St E5
Mortimer St C3
Mount Pleasant B5
Mount St D2
Murray Gr A6
Museum of Garden
History 🏛 E4
Mus of London 🏛 C6
Museum St C4
Myddelton Sq B5
Myddelton St B5
National Gallery 🏛 D3
National Hosp ⊞ B4
National Portrait
Gallery 🏛 D3
Neal St C4
Nelson's
Column ✦ D4
New Bond St C2/D2
New Bridge St C5
New Cavendish St C2
New Change C6
New Fetter La C5
New Inn Yard B7
New North Rd A6
New Oxford St C3
New Scotland Yard E3
New Sq C4
Newgate St C5
Newton St C4
Nile St B6
Noble St C6
Noel St C3
North Audley St D2
North Cres C3
North Row D2
Northampton Sq B5
Northington St B4
Northumberland
Ave D4
Norton Folgate C7
Nottingham Pl C2
Obstetric Hosp ⊞ B3
Old Bailey C5
Old Broad St C6
Old Compton St C3
Old County Hall E4
Old Gloucester St C4
Old King Edward St C6
Old Nichol St B7
Old Paradise St F4
Old Spitalfields
Market C7
Old St B6
Old St ⇌⊖ B6
Old Vic 🎭 E5
Open Air Theatre 🎭 B2
Operating Theatre
Museum 🏛 D6
Orange St D3
Orchard St C2
Ossulston St A3
Outer Circle B1
Oxford Circus ⊖ C3
Oxford St C2/C3
Paddington St C2
Palace St E3
Pall Mall D3
Pall Mall East D3
Pancras Rd A4
Panton St D3
Paris Gdn D5
Park Cres B2
Park La D2
Park Rd B1
Park St D2
Park St D6
Parker St C4
Parliament Sq E4
Parliament St E4
Paternoster Sq C5
Paul St B6
Pear Tree St B5
Penton Rise B4
Penton St A5
Pentonville Rd A4/A5
Percival St B5
Petticoat La
(Middlesex St) C7
Petty France E3
Phoenix Pl B4
Phoenix Rd A3
Photo Gallery 🏛 D3
Piccadilly D2
Piccadilly Cir ⊖ D3
Pitfield St B7
Pollock's Toy
Museum 🏛 C3
Polygon Rd A3
Pont St E1
Portland Pl C2
Portman Mews C2
Portman Sq C2
Portman St C1
Portugal St C4
Poultry C6
Primrose St C7
Princes St C6
Procter St C4
Provost St B6
Quaker St B7
Queen Anne St C2
Queen Elizabeth
Hall 🎭 D4
Queen Sq B4
Queen St D6
Queen Street Pl D6
Queen Victoria St D5
Queens Gallery 🏛 E3
Radnor St B6
Rathbone Pl C3
Rawstorne St B5
Red Lion Sq C4
Red Lion St C4
Redchurch St B7
Redcross Way D6
Regency St F3
Regent Sq B4
Regent St C3
Regent's Park B2
Richmond Terr E4
Ridgmount St C3
Rivington St B7
Robert St B2
Rochester Row F3
Ropemaker St C6
Rosebery Ave B5
Roupell St D5
Royal Academy of
Arts 🏛 D3
Royal Academy of
Dramatic Art B3
Royal Academy of
Music B2
Royal Artillery
Memorial ✦ E2
Royal College of
Nursing C2
Royal College of
Surgeons C4
Royal Festival
Hall 🎭 D4
Royal London Hosp
for Integrated
Medicine C4
Royal National
Theatre 🎭 D5
Royal National
Throat, Nose and
Ear Hospital ⊞ B4
Royal Opera Ho 🎭 D4
Russell Sq B3
Russell Square ⊖ B4
Sackville St D3
Sadlers Wells 🎭 B5
Saffron Hill C5
St Alban's St D3
St Andrew St C5
St Bartholomew's
Hospital ⊞ C5
St Botolph St C7
St Bride St C5
St George's Circus E5
St George's Rd E5
St Giles High St C3
St James's Pal 🏛 D3
St James's Park ⊖ E3
St James's St D3
St John St B5
St Margaret St E4
St Mark's Hosp ⊞ B5
St Martin's La D4
St Martin's Le
Grand C6
St Mary Axe C7
St Pancras Int ⇌ A4
St Paul's ⊖ C6
St Paul's Cath ✝ C6
St Paul's
Churchyard C5
St Peter's Hosp ⊞ D4
St Thomas St D6
St Thomas' Hosp ⊞ E4
Savile Row D3
Savoy Pl D4
Savoy St D4
School of Hygiene &
Tropical Medicine C3
Scrutton St B7
Sekforde St B5
Serpentine Rd D1
Seven Dials C4
Seward St B5
Seymour St C1
Shad Thames D7
Shaftesbury Ave D3
Shakespeare's
Globe Theatre 🎭 D6
Shepherd Market D2
Sherwood St D3
Shoe La C5
Shoreditch High St B7
Shoreditch
High St ⊖ B7
Shorts Gdns C4
Sidmouth St B4
Silk St C6
Sir John Soane's
Museum 🏛 C4
Skinner St B5
Sloane St E1
Snow Hill C5
Soho Sq C3
Somerset Ho 🏛 D4
South Audley St D2
South Carriage Dr E1
South Molton St C2
South Pl C6
South St D2
Southampton Row C4
Southampton St D4
Southwark ⊖ D5
Southwark Bridge D6
Southwark Bridge
Rd D6
Southwark
Cathedral ✝ D6
Southwark St D6
Speakers' Corner D1
Spencer St B5
Spital Sq C7
Stamford St D5
Stanhope St B3
Stephenson Way B3
Stock Exchange C5
Stoney St D6
Strand C5
Stratton St D2
Sumner St D5
Sutton's Way B6
Swanfield St B7
Swinton St B4
Tabernacle St B6
Tate Modern 🏛 D6
Tavistock Pl B4
Tavistock Sq B3
Tea & Coffee
Museum 🏛 D6
Temple ⊖ D5
Temple Ave D5
Temple Pl D4
Terminus Pl E2
Thayer St C2
Theobald's Rd C4
Thorney St F4
Threadneedle St C6
Throgmorton St C6
Tonbridge St B4
Tooley St D7
Torrington Pl B3
Tothill St E3
Tottenham Ct Rd B3
Tottenham Court Rd
⊖ C3
Tottenham St C3
Tower Bridge ✦ D7
Tower Bridge App D7
Tower Bridge Rd E7
Tower Hill D7
Tower Hill ⊖ D7
Tower of London,
The 🏛 D7
Toynbee St C7
Trafalgar Square D3
Trinity Sq D7
Trocadero Centre D3
Tudor St D5
Turnmill St C5
Ufford St E5
Union St D5
Univ Coll Hosp ⊞ B3
Univ of London C3
University of
Westminster C2
University St B3
Upper Belgrave St E2
Upper Berkeley St C1
Upper Brook St D2
Upper Grosvenor
St D2
Upper Ground D5
Upper Montague
St C1
Upper St Martin's
La D4
Upper Thames St D6
Upper Wimpole St C2
Upper Woburn Pl B3
Vere St C2
Vernon Pl C4
Vestry St B6
Victoria ⇌⊖ E2
Victoria Emb D4
Victoria Pl Sh Ctr F2
Victoria St E3
Villiers St D4
Vincent Sq F3
Vinopolis City
of Wine 🏛 D6
Virginia Rd B7
Wakley St B5
Walbrook C6
Wallace
Collection 🏛 C2
Wardour St C3/D3
Warner St B5
Warren St ⊖ B3
Warren St B3
Waterloo ⇌⊖ E5
Waterloo Bridge D4
Waterloo East ⇌ D5
Waterloo Rd E5
Watling St C6
Webber St E5
Welbeck St C2
Wellington Arch ✦ E2
Wellington Mus 🏛 E2
Wells St C3
Wenlock St A6
Wentworth St C7
West Smithfield C5
West Sq E5
Westminster ⊖ E4
Westminster
Abbey ✝ E4
Westminster
Bridge E4
Westminster Bridge
Rd E5
Westminster
Cathedral (RC) ✝ E3
Westminster
City Hall E3
Westminster Hall
🏛 E4
Weymouth St C2
Wharf Rd A6
Wharton St B4
Whitcomb St D3
White Cube 🏛 B7
White Lion Hill D5
White Lion St A5
Whitecross St B6
Whitefriars St C5
Whitehall D4
Whitehall Pl D4
Wigmore Hall C2
Wigmore St C2
William IV St D4
Wilmington Sq B5
Wilson St C6
Wilton Cres E2
Wimpole St C2
Windmill Walk D5
Woburn Pl B4
Woburn Sq B3
Women's Hosp ⊞ C3
Wood St C6
Woodbridge St B5
Wootton St D5
Wormwood St C7
Worship St B6
Wren St B4
Wynyatt St B5
York Rd E4
York St C1
York Terrace East B2
York Terrace West B2
York Way A4

Luton 119

Adelaide St B1
Albert Rd C2
Alma St B2
Alton Rd C3
Anthony Gdns C1
Arthur St C2
Ashburnham Rd B1
Ashton Rd C2
Avondale Rd A1
Back St A2
Bailey St C3
Baker St C2
Biscot Rd A1
Bolton Rd B3
Boyle Cl A2
Brantwood Rd B1
Bretts Mead C1
Bridge St B2
Brook St A1
Brunswick St A3
Burr St A3
Bury Park Rd A1
Bute St B2
Buxton Rd B2
Cambridge St C3
Cardiff Grove B1
Cardiff Rd B1
Cardigan St A2
Castle St B2/C2
Chapel St C2
Charles St A3
Chase St C2
Cheapside B2
Chequer St C3
Chiltern Rise C1
Church St B2/B3
Cinema 🎦 A2
Cobden St A3
Collingdon St A1
Community Centre C3
Concorde Ave A3
Corncastle Rd C1
Cowper St C2
Crawley Green Rd B3
Crawley Rd A1
Crescent Rd A3
Crescent Rise A3
Cromwell Rd A1
Cross St A2
Cross Way, The C1
Crown Court B2
Cumberland St B2
Cutenhoe Rd C3
Dallow Rd B1
Downs Rd B1
Dudley St A2
Duke St A2
Dumfries St B1
Dunstable Place B2
Dunstable Rd A1/B1
Edward St A3
Elizabeth St C2
Essex Cl C3
Farley Hill C1
Farley Lodge C1
Flowers Way B2
Francis St A1
Frederick St A2
Galaxy L Complex A2
George St B2
George St West B2
Gordon St B2
Grove Rd B1
Guildford St A2
Haddon Rd A3
Harcourt St C2
Hart Hill Drive A3
Hart Hill Lane A3
Hartley Rd A3
Hastings St B2
Hat Factory, The 🎭 B2
Hatters Way A1
Havelock Rd A2
Hibbert St C2
High Town Rd A3
Highbury Rd A1
Hightown Com
Sports & Arts Ctr A3
Hillary Cres C1
Hillborough Rd C1
Hitchin Rd A3
Holly St C2
Holm C1
Hucklesby Way A2
Hunts Cl C1
Information Ctr ℹ B2
Inkerman St A2
John St B2
Jubilee St A3
Kelvin Cl C2
King St B2
Kingsland Rd C3
Larches, The A2
Latimer Rd C2
Lawn Gdns C2
Lea Rd B3
Library B2
Library Rd B2
Liverpool Rd B1
London Rd C2
Luton Station ⇌ A2
Lyndhurst Rd B1
Magistrates Court B2
Mall, The B2
Manchester St B2
Manor Rd B3
May St C3
Meyrick Ave C1
Midland Rd A2
Mill St A2
Milton Rd B1
Moor St A1
Moor, The A1
Moorland Gdns A2
Moulton Rise A3
Museum &
Art Gallery 🏛🏛 A2
Napier Rd B1
New Bedford Rd A1
New Town St C2
North St A3
Old Bedford Rd A2
Old Orchard C2
Osbourne Rd C3
Oxen Rd A3
Park Sq B2
Park St B3/C3
Park St West B2
Park Viaduct B3
Parkland Drive C1
Police Station ✉ B1
Pomfret Ave A3
Pondwicks Rd B3
Post Office
✉ A1/A2/B2/C3
Power Court B3
Princess St B1
Red Rails C1
Regent St B2
Reginald St A2
Rothesay Rd B1
Russell Rise C1
Russell St C1
St Ann's Rd B3
St George's 🎭 B2
St George's Sq B2
St Mary's ⛪ B3
St Marys Rd B3
St Paul's Rd C2
St Saviour's Cres C1
Salisbury Rd B1
Seymour Ave C3
Seymour Rd C3
Silver St B2
South Rd C2
Stanley St B1
Station Rd A2
Stockwood Cres C2
Stockwood Park C1
Strathmore Ave C2
Stuart St B2
Studley Rd A1
Surrey St C3
Sutherland Place C1
Tavistock St C2
Taylor St A3
Telford Way A1
Tennyson Rd C2
Tenzing Grove C1
Thistle Rd B3
Town Hall B2
Townsley Close C2
UK Centre for
Carnival Arts ✦ B3
Union St B2
University of
Bedfordshire B3
Upper George St B2
Vicarage St B3
Villa Rd A2
Waldeck Rd A1
Wellington St B1/B2
Wenlock St A2
Whitby Rd A1
Whitehill Ave C1
William St A2
Wilsden Ave C1
Windmill Rd B3
Windsor St C2
Winsdon Rd B1
York St A3

Manchester 119

Adair St B6
Addington St A5
Adelphi St A1
Albert Sq B3
Albion St C3
AMC Great
Northern 🎦 B3
Ancoats Gr B6
Ancoats Gr North B6
Angela St C2
Aquatic Centre C4
Ardwick Gn North C5
Ardwick Gn Park C5
Ardwick Gn South C5
Arlington St A2
Artillery St B3
Arundel St C2
Atherton St B2
Atkinson St B3
Aytoun St B4
Back Piccadilly A4
Baird St B5
Balloon St A4
Bank Pl A1
Baring St B5
Barrack St C1
Barrow St A1
Bendix St A5
Bengal St A5
Berry St C5
Blackfriars Rd A3
Blackfriars St A3
Blantyre St C2
Bloom St B4
Blossom St A5
Boad St B5
Bombay St B4
Booth St A3
Booth St B4
Bootle St B3
Brazennose St B3
Brewer St A5
Bridge St A3
Bridgewater Hall B3
Bridgewater Pl A4
Bridgewater St B2
Brook St C4
Brotherton Dr A2
Brown St A3
Brown St B4
Brunswick St C6
Brydon Ave C6
Buddhist Centre A4
Bury St A2
Bus & Coach Sta B4
Bus Station B4
Butler St A6
Buxton St C5
Byrom St B3
Cable St A5
Calder St B1
Cambridge St C3/C4
Camp St B3
Canal St B4
Cannon St A1
Cannon St A4
Cardroom Rd A6
Carruthers St A6
Castle St C2
Castlefield Arena B2
Cateaton St A3
Cathedral ✝ A3
Cathedral St A3
Cavendish St C4
Central Retail Pk A5
Chapel St A1/A3
Chapeltown St B5

Charles St C4
Charlotte St B4
Chatham St B4
Cheapside A3
Chepstow St B3
Chester Rd C1/C2
Chester St C4
Chetham's Sch of Music A3
China La B5
Chippenham Rd A6
Chorlton Rd C2
Chorlton St B4
Church St A2
Church St A4
City Park A4
City Rd C3
Civil Justice Ctr B2
Cleminson St A2
Clowes St A3
College Land A3
Collier St B2
Commercial St C3
Conference Ctr C4
Cooper St B4
Copperas St A4
Corn Exchange, The A4
Cornbrook 🚋 C1
Cornell St A5
Corporation St A4
Cotter St C6
Cotton St A5
Cow La B1
Cross St B3
Crown Court B4
Crown St C2
Dalberg St C6
Dale St A4/B5
Dancehouse, The 🎭 C4
Dantzic St A4
Dark La C6
Dawson St C2
Dean St A5
Deansgate A3/B3
Deansgate Castlefield 🚋 C3
Deansgate Sta ⇌ C3
Dolphin St C6
Downing St C5
Ducie St B5
Duke Pl B2
Duke St B2
Durling St C6
East Ordsall La A2/B1
Edge St A4
Egerton St C2
Ellesmere St C1
Everard St C1
Every St B6
Fairfield St B5
Faulkner St B4
Fennel St A3
Ford St A2
Ford St C6
Fountain St B4
Frederick St A2
Gartside St B2
Gaythorne St A1
George Leigh St A5
George St A1
George St B4
Gore St A2
Goulden St A5
Granby Row B4
Gravel St A3
Great Ancoats St A5
Great Bridgewater St B3
Great George St A1
Great Jackson St C2
Great Marlborough St C4
Greengate A3
Grosvenor St C5
Gun St A5
Hadrian Ave B6
Hall St B3
Hampson St B1
Hanover St A4
Hanworth Cl C5
Hardman St B3
Harkness St C6
Harrison St B6
Hart St B4
Helmet St B6
Henry St A5
Heyrod St B6
High St A4
Higher Ardwick C6
Hilton St A4/A5
Holland St A6
HOME ✦ C3
Hood St A5
Hope St B1
Hope St B4
Houldsworth St A5
Hoyle St C6
Hulme Hall Rd C1
Hulme St A1
Hulme St C3
Hyde Rd C6
Information Ctr ⓘ B4
Irwell St A2
Islington St A2
Jackson Cr C2
Jackson's Row B3
James St A1
Jenner Cl C2
Jersey St A5
John Dalton St B3
John Ryland's Library ⌂ B3
John St A2
Kennedy St B3
Kincardine Rd C5
King St A3
King St West A3
Law Courts B3
Laystall St B5
Lever St A5
Library B3
Linby St C2
Little Lever St A4
Liverpool Rd B2
Liverpool St B1
Lloyd St B3
Lockton Cl C5
London Rd B5
Long Millgate A3
Longacre St B6
Loom St A5
Lower Byrom St B2
Lower Mosley St B3
Lower Moss La C2
Lower Ormond St C4
Loxford La C4
Luna St A5
Major St B4
Manchester Arndale A4
Manchester Art Gallery 🏛 B4
Manchester Central Convention Complex B3
Manchester Metropolitan University B4/C4
Manchester Piccadilly Sta ⇌ B5
Manchester Technology Ctr C4
Mancunian Way C3
Manor St C5
Marble St A4
Market St A2
Market St A4
Market St 🚋 A4
Marsden St A3
Marshall St A5
Mayan Ave A2
Medlock St C3
Middlewood St B1
Miller St A4
Minshull St B4
Mosley St A4
Mount St B3
Mulberry St B3
Murray St A5
Museum of Science & Industry (MOSI) 🏛 B2
Nathan Dr A2
National Football Mus 🏛 A4
Naval St A5
New Bailey St A2
New Elm Rd B2
New Islington A6
New Islington Station 🚋 B6
New Quay St B2
New Union St A6
Newgate St A4
Newton St A5
Nicholas St B4
North Western St C6
Oak St A4
Odeon 🎥 A4
Old Mill St A6
Oldfield Rd A1/C1
Oldham Rd A5
Oldham St A4
Opera House 🎭 B3
Ordsall La C1
Oxford Rd C4
Oxford Rd ⇌ C4
Oxford St B4
Paddock St C6
Palace Theatre 🎭 B4
Pall Mall A3
Palmerston St B6
Park St A1
Parker St B4
Peak St B5
Penfield Cl C5
Peoples' History Museum 🏛 B2
Peru St A1
Peter St B3
Piccadilly A4
Piccadilly 🚋 B5
Piccadilly Gdns 🚋 B4
Piercy St A6
Poland St A5
Police Museum 🏛 A5
Police Sta ⊠ B3/B5
Pollard St B6
Port St A5
Portland St B4
Portugal St East B5
Post Office ✉ A1/A2/A4/A5/B3/B4
Potato Wharf B2
Princess St B3/C4
Pritchard St C4
Quay St A2
Quay St B2
Queen St B3
Radium St A5
Redhill St A5
Regent Rd B1
Retail Park A5
Rice St B2
Richmond St B4
River St C3
Roby St B5
Rodney St A6
Roman Fort ⌂ B2
Rosamond St A2
Royal Exchange 🎭 A3
Sackville St B4
St Andrew's St B6
St Ann St A3
St Ann's ⛪ A3
St George's Ave C1
St James St B4
St John St B3
St John's Cathedral (RC) ✝ A2
St Mary's ⛪ B3
St Mary's Gate A3
St Mary's Parsonage A3
St Peter's Sq 🚋 B3
St Stephen St A2
Salford Approach A3
Salford Central ⇌ A2
Sheffield St B5
Shepley St B5
Sherratt St A5
Shopmobility A4
Shudehill A4
Shudehill 🚋 A4
Sidney St C4
Silk St A5
Silver St B4
Skerry Cl C5
Snell St B6
South King St B3
Sparkle St B5
Spear St A4
Spring Gdns A4
Stanley St A2/B2
Station Approach B5
Store St B5
Swan St A4
Tariff St B5
Tatton St C1
Temperance St B6/C6
Thirsk St C6
Thomas St A4
Thompson St A5
Tib La B3
Tib St A4
Town Hall (Manchester) B3
Town Hall (Salford) A2
Trafford St C3
Travis St B5
Trinity Way A2
Turner St A4
Union St C6
Univ of Manchester (Sackville St Campus) C5
Univ of Salford A1
Upper Brook St C5
Upper Cleminson St A1
Upper Wharf St A1
Vesta St B6
Victoria 🚋 A4
Victoria Station ⇌ A4
Wadesdon Rd C5
Water St B2
Watson St B3
West Fleet St B1
West King St A2
West Mosley St B4
Weybridge Rd A6
Whitworth St B4
Whitworth St West C3
Wilburn St B1
William St A2
William St C6
Wilmott St C3
Windmill St B3
Windsor Cr A1
Withy Gr A4
Woden St C1
Wood St B3
Woodward St A6
Worrall St C1
Worsley St C2
York St B4
York St C2
York St C4

Middlesbrough 119

Abingdon Rd C3
Acklam Rd C1
Albert Park C3
Albert Rd B2
Albert Terr C2
Ambulance Sta C1
Aubrey St C3
Avenue, The C2
Ayresome Gdns C2
Ayresome Gn La C1
Ayresome St C2
Barton Rd A1
Bilsdale Rd C3
Bishopton Rd C3
Borough Rd B2/B3
Bowes Rd A2
Breckon Hill Rd B3
Bridge St East B3
Bridge St West B2
Brighouse Rd A1
Burlam Rd C1
Bus Station B2
Cannon Park B1
Cannon Park Way B2
Cannon St B1
Captain Cook Sq B2
Carlow St C1
Castle Way C3
Chipchase Rd C2
Cineworld 🎥 B3
Cleveland Centre B2
Clive Rd C2
Commercial St A2
Corporation Rd B2
Costa St C2
Council Offices B3
Crescent Rd C2
Crescent, The C2
Cumberland Rd C2
Depot Rd A2
Derwent St B2
Devonshire Rd C2
Diamond Rd B2
Dorman Mus 🏛 C2
Douglas St B3
Eastbourne Rd C2
Eden Rd C3
Fire Sta A3
Forty Foot Rd A2
Gilkes St B2
Gosford St A2
Grange Rd B2
Gresham Rd B2
Harehills Rd C1
Harford St C2
Hartington Rd B2
Haverton Hill Rd A1
Hey Wood St B1
Highfield Rd C3
Hillstreet Centre B2
Holwick Rd B1
Hutton Rd C3
Ironmasters Way B1
Lambton Rd C3
Lancaster Rd C2
Lansdowne Rd C3
Latham Rd C2
Law Courts B2/B3
Lees Rd B2
Leeway B3
Library B2/C2
Linthorpe Cemetery C1
Linthorpe Rd B2
Lloyd St B2
Longford St C2
Longlands Rd C3
Lower East St A3
Lower Lake C3
Macmillan Acad C1
Maldon Rd C1
Manor St B2
Marsh St B2
Marton Rd B3
Middlehaven B3
Middlesbrough By-Pass B2/C1
Middlesbrough College B3
Middlesbrough Leisure Park B3
Middlesbrough Station ⇌ B2
Middletown Park C2
MIMA 🏛 B3
Mulgrave Rd C2
Newport Bridge B1
Newport Bridge Approach Rd B1
Newport Rd B2
North Ormesby Rd B3
North Rd B2
Northern Rd C1
Outram St B2
Oxford Rd C2
Park La C2
Park Rd North C2
Park Rd South C2
Park Vale Rd C3
Parliament Rd B1
Police Station ⊠ A2
Port Clarence Rd A3
Portman St B2
Post Office ✉ B3/C1/C2
Princes Rd B2
Python 🏛 A2
Riverside Park Rd A1
Riverside Stadium (Middlesbrough FC) B3
Rockliffe Rd C2
Romaldkirk Rd B1
Roman Rd C2
Roseberry Rd C3
St Barnabas' Rd C2
St Paul's Rd B2
Saltwells Rd B3
Scott's Rd A3
Seaton Carew Rd A3
Shepherdson Way B3
Shopmobility B2
Snowdon Rd A2
South West Ironmasters Park B1
Southfield Rd B2
Southwell Rd C2
Springfield Rd C1
Startforth Rd A2
Stockton Rd C1
Stockton St A2
Superstore B2
Surrey St C2
Sycamore Rd C2
Tax Offices B3
Tees Viaduct C1
Teessaurus Park A2
Teesside Tertiary College C3
Temenos ✦ B3
Thornfield Rd C1
Town Hall B2
Transporter Bridge (Toll) A3
Union St B2
Univ of Teesside B2
Upper Lake C2
Valley Rd C3
Ventnor Rd C2
Victoria Rd B2
Vulcan St A2
Warwick St C2
Wellesley Rd B3
West La B1
West La Hosp Ⓗ C1
Westminster Rd C2
Wilson St B2
Windward Way B3
Woodlands Rd B2
York Rd C3

Milton Keynes 122

Abbey Way A1
Arbrook Ave B1
Armourer Dr A3
Arncliffe Dr A1
Avebury ⟳ C2
Avebury Blvd C2
Bankfield ⟳ B3
Bayard Ave A2
Belvedere ⟳ A2
Bishopstone A1
Blundells Rd A1
Boundary, The C3
Boycott Ave C2
Bradwell Common Boulevard B1
Bradwell Rd C1
Bramble Ave A2
Brearley Ave C2
Breckland A1
Brill Place B1
Burnham Dr B1
Bus Station C1
Campbell Park ⟳ B3
Cantle Ave A3
Central Retail Park C1
Century Ave C2
Chaffron Way C3
Childs Way C1
Christ the Cornerstone ⛪ B2
Cineworld 🎥 B2
Civic Offices B2
Cleavers Ave B2
Colesbourne Dr A3
Conniburrow Blvd B2
County Court B2
Currier Dr A2
Dansteed Way A2/A3/B1
Deltic Ave B1
Downs Barn ⟳ A2
Downs Barn Blvd A3
Eaglestone ⟳ C3
Eelbrook Ave B1
Elder Gate B1
Evans Gate C2
Fairford Cr A3
Falcon Ave B3
Fennel Dr A2
Fishermead Blvd C3
Food Centre B3
Fulwoods Dr C3
Glazier Dr A2
Glovers La A1
Grafton Gate C1
Grafton St A1/C2
Gurnards Ave B3
Harrier Dr C3
Ibstone Ave B1
Information Ctr ⓘ B2
Langcliffe Dr A1
Leisure Centre C3
Leisure Plaza C1
Leys Rd C1
Library B2
Linford Wood A2
Marlborough Gate B3
Marlborough St A2/B3
Mercers Dr A1
Midsummer ⟳ C2
Midsummer Boulevard B2
Milton Keynes Central ⇌ C1
Milton Keynes Hospital (A&E) C3
Monks Way A1
Mullen Ave A3
Mullion Pl C3
Neath Hill ⟳ A3
North Elder ⟳ C1
North Grafton ⟳ B1
North Overgate ⟳ A3
North Row B2
North Saxon ⟳ B2
North Secklow ⟳ B2
North Skeldon ⟳ A3
North Witan ⟳ B1
Oakley Gdns A3
Oldbrook Blvd C2
Open-Air Theatre 🎭 B3
Overgate A3
Overstreet A3
Patriot Dr B1
Pencarrow Pl B3
Penryn Ave B3
Perran Ave C3
Pitcher La C1
Pl Retail Pk, The C1
Police Station ⊠ B2
Portway B2
Post Office ✉ A2/B2/B3
Precedent Dr B1
Quinton Dr B1
Ramsons Ave B2
Retail Park C2
Rockingham Dr A2
Rooksley ⟳ B1
Saxon Gate B2
Saxon St A1/C3
Secklow Gate B2
Shackleton Pl C2
Shopmobility B2
Silbury Blvd B2
Skeldon ⟳ A3
South Enmore B3
South Grafton ⟳ C2
South Row C2
South Saxon ⟳ C2
South Secklow ⟳ B3
South Witan ⟳ C2
Springfield ⟳ B3
Stanton Wood ⟳ A1
Stantonbury ⟳ A1
Stantonbury Leisure Centre ✦ A1
Strudwick Dr C2
Sunrise Parkway A2
Theatre & Art Gallery 🎭 B3
theCentre:mk B2
Tolcarne Ave C3
Tourist Information Centre ⓘ B3
Towan Ave C3
Trueman Pl C2
Vauxhall A1
Winterhill Retail Pk C2
Witan Gate B2
X-Scape B3

Newcastle upon Tyne 122

Albert St B3
Argyle St B3
Back New Bridge St B3
BALTIC Centre for Contemporary Art 🏛 C3
Barker St A3
Barrack Rd B1
Bath La B1
Bessie Surtees House ✦ C2
Bigg Market C2
Biscuit Factory 🏛 B3
Black Gate ⌂ C2
Blackett St B2
Blandford Sq C1
Boating Lake A1
Boyd St B3
Brandling Park A2
Bus Station B2
Buxton St B3
Byron St A3
Camden St B2
Castle Keep 🏰 C2
Central Ⓜ C1
Central Library B2
Central Motorway B2
Chester St A3
City Hall B2
City Rd B3/C3
City Walls ✦ C1
Civic Centre A2
Claremont Rd A1
Clarence St B3
Clarence Walk B3
Clayton St C1/B1
Clayton St West C1
Close, The C2
Coach Station C1
College St B2
Collingwood St C2
Copland Terr B3
Coppice Way B3
Corporation St B1
Courts C3
Crawhall Rd B3
Dean St C2
Dental Hospital A1
Dinsdale Pl A3
Dinsdale Rd A3
Discovery 🏛 C1
Doncaster Rd A3
Durant Rd B2
Eldon Sq B1
Eldon Gdn Sh Ctr B1
Ellison Pl B2
Empire 🎥 B1
Eskdale Terr A2
Eslington Terr A2
Exhibition Park A1
Falconar St B3
Fenkle St C1
Forth Banks C1
Forth St C1
Gallowgate B1
Gate, The ✦ B1
Gateshead Millennium Bridge C3
Gibson St B3
Goldspink La A3
Grainger Market B2
Grainger St B2
Grantham Rd A3
Granville Rd A3
Great North Children's Hosp A1
Great North Mus:Hancock 🏛 A2
Grey St B2
Groat Market C2
Guildhall ⌂ C2
Hancock St A2
Hanover St C2
Hatton Gallery 🏛 A1
Hawks Rd C3
Haymarket Ⓜ B2
Heber St B1
Helmsley Rd A3
High Bridge B2
High Level Bridge C2
Hillgate C3
Howard St B3
Hutton Terr A3
Information Ctr ⓘ C3
intu Eldon Sq Shopping Centre B2
Jesmond Ⓜ A2
Jesmond Rd A2/A3
John Dobson St B2
John George Joicey Museum 🏛 C2
Jubilee Rd B3
Kelvin Gr A3
Kensington Terr A2
Laing Gallery 🏛 B2
Lambton Rd A2
Leazes Cr B1
Leazes La B1
Leazes Park B1
Leazes Park Rd B1
Leazes Terr B1
Library A2
Live 🎭 C2
Low Friar St C1
Manor Chare C2
Manors Ⓜ B2
Manors Station ⇌ B2
Market St B2
Melbourne St B2
Mill Rd C3
Monument Ⓜ B2
Monument Mall Shopping Centre B2
Morpeth St A2
Mosley St C2
Napier St A3
New Bridge St B2/B3
Newcastle Central Station ⇌ C1
Newcastle Univ A1
Newgate Sh Ctr C1
Newgate St B1
Newington Rd A3
Northern Design Centre C3
Northern Stage Theatre 🎭 A2
Northumberland Rd B2
Northumberland St B2
Northumbria Univ A2
Northwest Radial Rd A1
O2 Academy ✦ C1
Oakwellgate C3
Open Univ C3
Orchard St C2
Osborne Rd A2
Osborne Terr A3
Pandon C3
Pandon Bank B3
Park Terr A1
Percy St B1
Pilgrim St B2
Pipewellgate C2
Pitt St B1
Plummer Tower 🏛 A2
Police Station ⊠ B1
Portland Rd A3/B3
Portland Terr A3
Post Office ✉ B1/B2
Pottery La C1
Prudhoe Pl B1
Prudhoe St B1
Quayside C2
Queen Elizabeth II Bridge C2
Queen Victoria Rd A1
Richardson Rd A1
Ridley Pl B2
Rock Terr B3
Rosedale Terr A3
Royal Victoria Infirmary Ⓗ A1
Sage Gateshead ✦ C3
St Andrew's St B1
St James Ⓜ B1
St James' Blvd C1
St James' Park (Newcastle Utd FC) B1
St Mary's Heritage Centre ✦ C3
St Mary's (RC) ✝ C1
St Mary's Place B2
St Nicholas ✝ C2
St Nicholas St C2
St Thomas' St B1
Sandyford Rd A2/A3
Science Park B2
Shield St B3
Shieldfield B3
Shopmobility B1
Side, The C2
Simpson Terr B3
South Shore Rd C3
South St C1
Starbeck Ave A3
Stepney Rd B3
Stoddart St B3
Stowell St B1
Strawberry Pl B1
Swing Bridge C2
Temple St C1
Terrace Pl B1
Theatre Royal 🎭 B2
Times Sq C1
Tower St B3
Trinity House C2
Tyne Bridge C2
Tyne Bridges ✦ C2
Tyne Theatre & Opera House 🎭 C1
Tyneside 🎥 B2
Victoria Sq A2
Warwick St A3
Waterloo St C1
Wellington St B1
Westgate Rd C1/C2
Windsor Terr A2
Worswick St B2
Wretham Pl B3

Newport
Casnewydd 122

Albert Terr B1
Allt-yr-Yn Ave A1
Alma St C2
Ambulance Sta C3
Bailey St B2
Barrack Hill A2
Bath St A3
Bedford Rd B3
Belle Vue La C1
Belle Vue Park C1
Bishop St A3
Blewitt St B1
Bolt Cl C3
Bolt St C3
Bond St A2
Bosworth Dr A1
Bridge St B1
Bristol St A3
Bryngwyn Rd B1
Brynhyfryd Ave C1
Brynhyfryd Rd C1
Bus Station B2
Caerau Cres C1
Caerau Rd B1
Caerleon Rd A3
Capel Cres C2
Cardiff Rd C2
Caroline St B3
Castle (Remains) A2
Cedar Rd B3
Charles St B2
Charlotte Dr C2
Chepstow Rd A3
Church Rd A3
Cineworld 🎥 B2
Civic Centre B1
Clarence Pl A2
Clifton Pl B1
Clifton Rd C1
Clyffard Cres B1
Clytha Park Rd B1
Clytha Sq C2
Coldra Rd C1
Collier St A3
Colne St B3
Comfrey Cl A1
Commercial Rd C3
Commercial St B2
Corelli St A3
Corn St B2
Corporation Rd B3
Coulson Cl C2
County Court A2
Courts A1
Courts B1
Crawford St A3
Cyril St B3
Dean St A3
Devon Pl B1
Dewsland Park Rd C2
Dolman 🎭 B2
Dolphin St C3
East Dock Rd C3
East St B1
East Usk Rd A3
Ebbw Vale Wharf B3
Emlyn St B2
Enterprise Way C3
Eton Rd B3
Evans St A2
Factory Rd A2
Fields Rd B1
Francis Dr C2
Frederick St C3
Friars Rd C1
Friars Walk B2
Gaer La C1
George St C3
George St Bridge C3
Godfrey Rd B1
Gold Tops B1
Gore St A3
Gorsedd Circle C1
Grafton Rd A3
Graham St B1
Granville St C3
Harlequin Dr A1
Harrow Rd B3
Herbert Rd A3
Herbert Walk C2
Hereford St A3
High St B2
Hill St B2
Hoskins St A2
Information Ctr ⓘ B2
Ivor Sq B2
Jones St B1
Junction Rd A3
Keynshaw Ave C2
King St C2
Kingsway B2
Kingsway Centre B2
Ledbury Dr A2
Library A3
Library, Museum & Art Gallery 🏛 B2
Liverpool Wharf B3
Llanthewy Rd B1
Llanvair Rd A3
Locke St A2
Lower Dock St C3
Lucas St A2
Manchester St A3
Market B2
Marlborough Rd B3
Mellon St C3
Mill St A2
Morgan St A3
Mountjoy Rd C2
Newport Bridge A2
Newport Ctr B2
Newport RFC B3
Newport Sta ⇌ B2
North St B2
Oakfield Rd B1
Park Sq C2
Police Sta ⊠ A3/C2
Post Office ✉ B2/C3
Power St A1
Prince St A3
Pugsley St A2
Queen St C2
Queen's Cl A1
Queen's Hill A1
Queen's Hill Cres A1
Queensway B2
Railway St B2
Riverfront Theatre & Arts Ctr, The 🎭 B2
Riverside A3
Rodney Rd B2
Royal Gwent (A&E) Ⓗ C2
Rudry St A3
Rugby Rd B3
Ruperra La C3
Ruperra St C3
St Edmund St B1
St Mark's Cres A1
St Mary St B1
St Vincent Rd A3
St Woolos ✝ C2
St Woolos General (no A&E) Ⓗ C1
St Woolos Rd B1
School La B2
Serpentine Rd B1
Shaftesbury Park A2
Sheaf La A3
Skinner St B2
Sorrel Dr A1
South Market St C3
Spencer Rd B1
Stow Hill B2/C1/C2
Stow Park Ave C1
Stow Park Dr C1
TA Centre A1
Talbot St B2
Tennis Club A1
Tregare St A3
Trostrey St A3
Tunnel Terr B1
Turner St A3
Univ of Wales Newport City Campus B3
Upper Dock St B2
Usk St A3
Usk Way B3/C3
Victoria Cr B1
War Memorial A3
Waterloo Rd C1
West St B1
Wharves B2
Wheeler St A2
Whitby Pl A3
Windsor Terr B1
York Pl C1

Northampton 122

78 Derngate ⌂ B3
Abington Sq B3
Abington St B3
Alcombe St A3
All Saints' ⛪ B2
Ambush St B1
Angel St B2
Arundel St A2
Ash St A2
Auctioneers Way C2
Bailiff St A2
Barrack Rd A2
Beaconsfield Terr A3
Becketts Park C3
Becketts Park Marina C3
Bedford Rd B3
Billing Rd B3
Brecon St A1
Brewery C2
Bridge St C2
Broad St B2
Burns St A3
Bus Station B2
Campbell St A2
Castle (Site of) B2
Castle St B2
Cattle Market Rd C2
Central Museum & Art Gallery 🏛 B2
Charles St A3
Cheyne Walk B3
Church La A2
Clare St A3
Cloutsham St A3
College St B2
Colwyn Rd A3
Cotton End C2
Countess Rd A1
County Hall ⌂ B2
Court A2
Craven St A3
Crown & County Courts B3
Denmark Rd B3
Derngate B3
Derngate & Royal Theatres 🎭 B3
Doddridge Church ⛪ B2
Drapery, The B2
Duke St A3
Dunster St A3
Earl St A3
Euston Rd C2
Fire Station A3
Foot Meadow B2
Gladstone Rd A1
Gold St B2
Grafton St A2
Gray St A3
Green St B1
Greenwood Rd B1
Greyfriars B2
Grosvenor Centre B2
Grove Rd A3
Guildhall ⌂ B2
Hampton St A2
Harding Terr A2
Hazelwood Rd B3
Herbert St B2
Hervey St A3
Hester St A2
Holy Sepulchre ⛪ A2
Hood St A3
Horse Market B2
Hunter St A3
Information Ctr ⓘ B1
Kettering Rd A3
Kingswell St B2
Lady's La B2
Leicester St A2
Leslie Rd A2
Library B3
Lorne Rd A2
Lorry Park A1
Louise Rd A2
Lower Harding St A2
Lower Hester St A2
Lower Mounts B3
Lower Priory St A2
Main Rd C1
Marefair B2
Market Sq B2
Marlboro Rd B1
Marriott St A2
Military Rd A3
Mounts Baths L Ctr A3
Nene Valley Ret Pk C1
New South Bridge Rd C2
Northampton General Hospital (A&E) Ⓗ B3
Northampton Station ⇌ B1
Northcote St A2
Nunn Mills Rd C3
Old Towcester Rd C2
Overstone Rd A3
Peacock Pl B2
Pembroke Rd A1
Penn Court C2
Police Station ⊠ B3
Post Office ✉ A1/A2/B3/C2
Quorn Way A2
Ransome Rd C3
Regent Sq A2
Ridings, The B3
Robert St A2
St Andrew's Rd B1
St Andrew's St A2
St Edmund's Rd B3
St George's St A2
St Giles ⛪ B3
St Giles St B3
St Giles' Terr B3
St James Park Rd B1
St James Rd B1
St James Retail Pk C1
St James' Mill Rd B1
St James' Mill Rd East C1
St Leonard's Rd C2
St Mary's St B2
St Michael's Rd A3
St Peter's ⛪ B2
St Peter's Sq Sh Prec B2
St Peter's Way B2
Salisbury St A2
Scarletwell St B2
Semilong Rd A2
Sheep St B2
Sol Central (Leisure Ctr) B2
Somerset St A3
South Bridge C2
Southfield Ave C2
Spencer Bridge Rd A1
Spencer Rd A3
Spring Gdns B3
Spring La B2
Swan St B3
TA Centre A3
Tanner St B2
Tintern Ave A1
Towcester Rd C2
Upper Bath St B2
Upper Mounts A2
Victoria Park A1
Victoria Prom B2
Victoria Rd B3
Victoria St A2
Wellingborough Rd B3
West Bridge B1
York Rd B3

Norwich 122

Albion Way C3
All Saints Green C2
Anchor St A3
Anglia Sq A2
Argyle St C3
Arts Centre 🎭 B1
Ashby St C2
Assembly Ho ⌂ B1
Bank Plain B2
Barker St A1
Barn Rd A1
Barrack St A3
Ber St C2
Bethel St B1
Bishop Bridge A3
Bishopbridge Rd A3
Bishopgate A3
Blackfriars St A2
Botolph St A2
Bracondale C3
Brazen Gate C2
Bridewell 🏛 B2
Brunswick Rd C1
Bull Close Rd A2
Bus Station C2
Calvert St A2
Cannell Green A3
Carrow Rd C3
Castle & Mus 🏰🏛 B2
Castle Mall B2
Castle Meadow B2
Cathedral ✝ B2
Cath Retail Park A1
Cattlemarket St B2
Chantry Rd C1
Chapel Loke C2
Chapelfield East B1
Chapelfield Gdns B1
Chapelfield North B1
Chapelfield Rd B1
City Hall ✦ B1
City Rd C2
City Wall C1/C3
Close, The B3
Colegate A2
Coslany St B1
Cow Hill B1
Cow Tower A3
Cowgate A2
Crown & Magistrates' Courts A2
Dragon Hall Heritage Centre ⌂ C3
Duke St A1
Edward St A2
Elm Hill B2
Erpingham Gate ✦ B2
Fire Station B1
Fishergate A2
Forum, The B1
Foundry Bridge B3
Fye Bridge A2
Garden St C2
Gas Hill B3
Gentlemans Walk B2
Grapes Hill B1
Great Hospital Halls, The A3
Grove Ave C1
Grove Rd C1
Guildhall ✦ B1
Gurney Rd A3
Hall Rd C2
Heathgate A3
Heigham St A1
Horn's La C2
Information Ctr ⓘ B1
intu Chapelfield C1
Ipswich Rd C1
James Stuart Gdns B3
King Edward VI School ✦ B2
King St B2
King St C3
Koblenz Ave C3
Library B1
London St B2
Lower Cl B3
Lower Clarence Rd B3
Maddermarket 🎭 B1
Magdalen St A2
Mariners La C2
Market B2
Market Ave B2
Mountergate B3
Mousehold St A3
Newmarket Rd C1
Norfolk St C1

134 Nottingham • Oxford • Peterborough • Plymouth • Poole • Portsmouth • Preston • Reading • Salisbury

Norwich City FC C3
Norwich Gallery B2
Norwich Station B3
Oak St A1
Palace St A2
Pitt St A1
Playhouse B2
Police Station A3
Post Office A2/B2/C2
Pottergate B1
Prince of Wales Rd B2
Princes St B2
Pull's Ferry B3
Puppet Theatre A2
Queen St B2
Queens Rd C2
RC Cathedral B1
Recorder Rd B3
Riverside Entertainment Ctr C3
Riverside L Ctr C3
Riverside Rd B3
Riverside Retail Pk C3
Rosary Rd B3
Rose La B2
Rouen Rd C2
Royal Norfolk Regimental Museum B2
St Andrews St B2
St Augustines St A1
St Benedicts St B1
St Ethelbert's Gate B2
St Faiths La B3
St Georges St A2
St Giles St B1
St James Cl A3
St Julians C2
St Leonards Rd B3
St Martin's La A1
St Peter Mancroft B2
St Peters St B1
St Stephens Rd C1
St Stephens St C1
Shopmobility C1
Silver Rd A2
Silver St A2
Southwell Rd C2
St. Andrew's & Blackfriars' Hall B2
Strangers' Hall B1
Superstore C2
Surrey St C2
Sussex St A1
Theatre Royal B1
Theatre St B1
Thorn La C2
Thorpe Rd B3
Tombland B2
Union St C1
Vauxhall St B1
Victoria St C1
Walpole St B1
Waterfront, The C3
Wensum St A2
Wessex St C1
Westwick St A1
Wherry Rd C3
Whitefriars A2
Willow La B1
Yacht Station B3

Nottingham 122

Abbotsford Dr A3
Addison St A1
Albert Hall B1
Alfred St South A3
Alfreton Rd B1
All Saints Rd A1
Annesley Gr A2
Arboretum A1
Arboretum St A1
Arthur St A1
Arts Theatre B3
Ashforth St A3
Balmoral Rd A1
Barker Gate B3
Bath St B3
BBC Nottingham C3
Belgrave Rooms B1
Bellar Gate B3
Belward St B3
Blue Bell Hill Rd B3
Brewhouse Yd C2
Broad Marsh Bus Station C2
Broad St B3
Brook St B3
Burns St A1
Burton St B2
Bus Station A2
Canal St C2
Carlton St B3
Carrington St C2
Castle C2
Castle Blvd C1
Castle Gate C2
Castle Meadow Rd C1
Castle Mdw Ret Pk C1
Castle Museum & Gallery C2
Castle Rd C2
Castle Wharf C2
Cavendish Rd East C1
Cemetery B1
Chaucer St B1
Cheapside B2
Church Rd A3
City Link C3
City of Caves C2
Clarendon St B1
Cliff Rd C3
Clumber Rd East C1
Clumber St B2
College St B1
Collin St C2
Conway Cl A2
Council House B2
Cranbrook St B3
Cranmer St A2
Cromwell St B1
Curzon St B3
Derby Rd B1
Dryden St A2
Exchange Ctr, The B2
Fishpond Dr C1
Fletcher Gate B3
Forest Rd East A1
Forest Rd West A1
Friar La C2
Galleries of Justice C3
Gedling Gr A1
Gedling St B3
George St B3
Gill St A2
Glasshouse St B2
Goldsmith St B2
Goose Gate B3
Great Freeman St A2
Guildhall B2
Hamilton Dr C1
Hampden St A1
Heathcote St B3
High Pavement C3
High School A1
Holles Cr C1
Hope Dr C1
Hungerhill Rd A3
Huntingdon Dr C1
Huntingdon St A2
Information Ctr B2
Instow Rise A3
Int Com Ctr A2
intu Broadmarsh C2
intu Victoria Ctr B2
Kent St B3
King St B2
Lace Centre, The C2
Lace Market B3
Lace Market Theatre C3
Lamartine St B3
Leisure Ctr C3
Lenton Rd C1
Lewis Cl A3
Lincoln St B2
London Rd C3
Long Row B2
Low Pavement C2
Lower Parliament St B3
Magistrates' Court C2
Maid Marian Way B2
Mansfield Rd A2/B2
Middle Hill C2
Milton St B2
Mount St B2
National Ice Ctr C3
Newcastle Dr B1
Newstead Gr A2
North Sherwood St A2
Nottingham Arena C3
Nottingham Sta C3
Nottingham Trent University A2/B2
Old Mkt Square B2
Oliver St A1
Park Dr C1
Park Row C1
Park Terr B1
Park Valley C1
Park, The C1
Peas Hill Rd A3
Peel St A1
Pelham St B2
Peveril Dr C1
Plantagenet St A3
Playhouse Theatre B1
Plumptre St C3
Police Sta B1/B2
Poplar St C3
Portland Rd B1
Post Office B2
Queen's Rd C3
Raleigh St A1
Regent St B1
Rick St B3
Robin Hood St B3
Robin Hood Statue C2
Ropewalk, The B1
Royal Centre B2
Royal Children Inn C2
Royal Concert Hall B2
St Ann's Hill Rd A2
St Ann's Way A2
St Ann's Well Rd A3
St Barnabas B1
St James' St B2
St Mark's St B3
St Mary's Garden of Rest B3
St Mary's Gate B3
St Nicholas C2
St Peter's C2
St Peter's Gate B2
Salutation Inn C2
Shakespeare St B2
Shelton St A2
Shopmobility A2
South Pde B2
South Rd C1
South Sherwood St B2
Station St C3
Station Street C3
Stoney St B3
Talbot St B1
Tattershall Dr C1
Tennis Dr B1
Tennyson St A1
Theatre Royal B2
Trent St C3
Trent University B2
Union Rd B3
Upper Parliament St B2
Victoria L Ctr B3
Victoria Park B3
Victoria St B2
Walter St A1
Warser Gate B3
Watkin St A2
Waverley St A1
Wheeler Gate B2
Wilford Rd C2
Wilford St C2
Willoughby Ho C2
Wollaton St B1
Woodborough Rd A2
Woolpack La B3
Ye Old Trip to Jerusalem C2
York St A2

Oxford 123

Adelaide St A1
Albert St A1
All Souls (Coll) B2
Ashmolean Mus B2
Balliol (Coll) B2
Banbury Rd A2
Bate Collection of Musical Instruments C2
Beaumont St B1
Becket St B1
Blackhall Rd A2
Blue Boar St B2
Bodleian Liby B2
Botanic Garden B3
Brasenose (Coll) B2
Brewer St C2
Broad St B2
Burton-Taylor Theatre B2
Bus Station B1
Canal St A1
Cardigan St A1
Carfax Tower B2
Castle B1
Castle St B1
Catte St B2
Cemetery C1
Christ Church (Coll) B2
Christ Church Cathedral C2
Christ Church Meadow C2
Clarendon Centre B2
Coach & Lorry Pk C1
College B3
Coll of Further Ed C1
Cornmarket St B2
Corpus Christi (Coll) B2
County Hall B1
Covered Market B2
Cowley Pl C3
Cranham St A1
Cranham Terr A1
Cricket Ground B1
Crown & County Courts C2
Deer Park B3
Exeter (Coll) B2
Folly Bridge C2
George St B1
Great Clarendon St A1
Hart St A1
Hertford (Coll) B2
High St B3
Hollybush Row B1
Holywell St B2
Hythe Bridge St B1
Ice Rink C1
Information Ctr B2
Jericho St A1
Jesus (Coll) B2
Jowett Walk B3
Juxon St A1
Keble (Coll) A2
Keble Rd A2
Library B2
Linacre (Coll) A3
Lincoln (Coll) B2
Little Clarendon St A1
Longwall St B3
Magdalen (Coll) B3
Magdalen Bridge B2
Magdalen St B2
Magistrate's Court C2
Manchester (Coll) B2
Manor Rd B3
Mansfield (Coll) A2
Mansfield Rd A3
Market B1
Marlborough Rd C2
Martyrs' Meml B2
Merton (Coll) B3
Merton Field B3
Merton St B2
Museum of Modern Art B2
Mus of Oxford B2
Museum Rd A2
New College (Coll) B3
New Inn Hall St B2
New Rd B1
New Theatre B2
Norfolk St C1
Nuffield (Coll) B1
Observatory A1
Observatory St A1
Odeon B1/B2
Old Fire Station B1
Old Greyfriars St C2
Oriel (Coll) B2
Oxford Station B1
Oxford University Research Centres A1
Oxpens Rd C1
Paradise Sq C1
Paradise St B1
Park End St B1
Parks Rd A2/B2
Pembroke (Coll) C2
Phoenix A1
Picture Gallery C2
Plantation Rd A1
Playhouse B2
Police Station C2
Post Office A1/B2
Pusey St B1
Queen's (Coll) B3
Queen's La B3
Radcliffe Camera B2
Rewley Rd B1
Richmond Rd A1
Rose La B3
Ruskin (Coll) B1
Said Bsns School B1
St Aldates C2
St Anne's (Coll) A1
St Antony's (Coll) A1
St Bernard's Rd A1
St Catherine's (Coll) B3
St Cross Building A3
St Cross Rd A3
St Edmund Hall (Coll) B3
St Giles St A2
St Hilda's (Coll) C3
St John St B2
St John's (Coll) B2
St Mary the Virgin B2
St Michael at the Northgate B2
St Peter's (Coll) B1
St Thomas St B1
Science Area A2
Science Mus B2
Sheldonian Theatre B2
Somerville (Coll) A1
South Parks Rd A2
Speedwell St C2
Sports Ground C3
Thames St C2
Town Hall B2
Trinity (Coll) B2
Turl St B2
Univ Coll (Coll) B3
Univ Mus & Pitt Rivers Mus A2
University Parks A2
Wadham (Coll) B2
Walton Cr A1
Walton St A1
Western Rd C2
Westgate Sh Ctr B2
Woodstock Rd A1
Worcester (Coll) B1

Peterborough 123

ABAX Stadium (Peterborough United) C2
Athletics Arena B3
Bishop's Palace B2
Bishop's Rd B2/B3
Boongate A3
Bourges Bvd A1
Bourges Ret Pk B1/B2
Bridge House (Council Offices) C2
Bridge St B2
Bright St A1
Broadway A2
Broadway A2
Brook St A2
Burghley Rd A2
Bus Station B2
Cavendish St A3
Charles St A3
Church St B2
Church Walk A2
Cobden Ave A1
Cobden St A1
Cowgate B2
Craig St A2
Crawthorne Rd A2
Cromwell Rd A1
Dickens St A3
Eastfield Rd A3
Eastgate B3
Fire Station A1
Fletton Ave C2
Frank Perkins Parkway C3
Geneva St A2
George St C1
Gladstone St A1
Glebe Rd C2
Gloucester Rd C3
Granby St B3
Grove St C1
Guildhall B2
Hadrians Ct C3
Hawksbill Way C2
Henry St A2
Hereward Cross (shopping) B2
Hereward Rd B3
Information Ctr B2
Jubilee St C1
Kent Rd B1
Key Theatre C2
Kirkwood Cl B1
Lea Gdns B1
Library A2
Lincoln Rd A2
London Rd C2
Long Causeway B2
Lower Bridge St C2
Magistrates Court B2
Manor House St A2
Mayor's Walk A1
Midland Rd A1
Monument St A2
Morris St A3
Museum & Art Gallery B2
Nene Valley Railway C1
New Rd A2
New Rd C1
Northminster A2
Old Customs House C2
Oundle Rd C1
Padholme Rd A3
Palmerston Rd C1
Park Rd A2
Passport Office B2
Peterborough Nene Valley C1
Peterborough Station B1
Police Station B2
Post Office A3/B1/B2/B3/C1
Priestgate B2
Queen's Walk C2
Queensgate Ctr B2
Railworld C1
Regional Swimming & Fitness Centre B3
River La B1
Rivergate Sh Ctr B2
Riverside Mead C3
Russell St A1
St John's B2
St John's St A3
St Marks St A2
St Peter's B2
St Peter's Rd B2
Saxon Rd A3
Spital Bridge A1
Stagshaw Dr C3
Star Rd B3
Thorpe Lea Rd B1
Thorpe Rd B1
Thorpe's Lea Rd B1
Tower St A2
Town Hall B2
Viersen Platz B2
Vineyard Rd B3
Wake Rd B3
Wellington St A3
Wentworth St B2
Westgate B2
Whalley St A3
Wharf Rd C1
Whitsed St A3
YMCA A3

Plymouth 123

Alma Rd A1
Anstis St B1
Armada Shop Ctr B2
Armada St A3
Armada Way B2
Arts Centre B2
Athenaeum B1
Athenaeum St C1
Barbican C3
Barbican C3
Baring St A3
Bath St B1
Beaumont Park B3
Beaumont Rd B3
Black Friars Gin Distillery C2
Breton Side B3
Castle St C3
Cathedral (RC) B1
Cecil St B1
Central Park A1
Central Park Ave A2
Charles Church B3
Charles Cross B3
Charles St B2
Citadel Rd C2
Citadel Rd East C2
City Museum & Art Gallery B2
Civic Centre B2
Cliff Rd C1
Clifton Pl A3
Cobourg St A2
College of Art B2
Continental Ferry Port B1
Cornwall St B2
Crescent, The B1
Dale Rd A2
Deptford Pl A3
Derry Ave A2
Derry's Cross B1
Drake Circus B2
Drake Cir Sh Ctr B2
Drake's Meml C2
Eastlake St B2
Ebrington St B3
Elizabethan Ho C3
Elliot St C1
Endsleigh Pl A2
Exeter St B3
Fire Station A3
Fish Quay C3
Gibbons St A3
Glen Park Ave A2
Grand Parade C1
Great Western Rd C1
Greenbank Rd A3
Greenbank Terr A3
Guildhall B2
Hampton St B3
Harwell St B1
Hill Park Cr A3
Hoe Approach B2
Hoe Rd C2
Hoe, The C2
Hoegate St C2
Houndiscombe Rd A2
Information Ctr C3
James St A2
Kensington Rd A3
King St B1
Lambhay Hill C3
Leigham St C1
Library B2
Lipson Rd A3/B3
Lockyer St C2
Lockyers Quay C3
Madeira Rd C2
Marina B3
Market Ave B1
Martin St B1
Mayflower St B2
Mayflower Stone & Steps C3
Mayflower Visitor Centre C3
Merchant's Ho B2
Millbay Rd B1
National Marine Aquarium C3
Neswick St B1
New George St B2
New St C3
North Cross A2
North Hill A3
North Quay B2
North Rd East A2
North Rd West A1
North St B3
Notte St B2
Octagon, The B1
Octagon St B1
Pannier Market B1
Pennycomequick A1
Pier St C1
Plymouth Pavilions B1
Plymouth Sta A2
Police Station B3
Post Office C2
Princess St B2
Promenade, The C2
Prysten House B2
Queen Anne's Battery Seasports Centre C3
Radford Rd C1
Reel B2
Regent St B3
Rope Walk C3
Royal Citadel C2
Royal Pde B2
Royal Theatre B2
St Andrew's B2
St Andrew's Cross B2
St Andrew's St B2
St Lawrence Rd A2
Saltash Rd A2
Shopmobility B2
Smeaton's Tower C2
Southern Terr A3
Southside St C2
Stuart Rd A1
Sutherland Rd A2
Sutton Rd B3
Sydney St A1
Teats Hill Rd C3
Tothill Ave B3
Union St B1
Univ of Plymouth A2
Vauxhall St B2/3
Victoria Park A1
West Hoe Rd C1
Western Approach B1
Whittington St A1
Wyndham St B1
YMCA B2
YWCA C2

Poole 123

Ambulance Sta A3
Baiater Gdns C2
Baiter Park C3
Ballard Cl C2
Ballard Rd C2
Bay Hog La B1
Bridge Approach C1
Bus Station B2
Castle St B2
Catalina Dr B3
Chapel La B2
Church St B1
Cinnamon La B1
Colborne Cl B3
Dear Hay La B2
Denmark La A3
Denmark Rd A3
Dolphin Ctr B2
East St B2
Elizabeth Rd A3
Emerson Rd B2
Ferry Rd C1
Ferry Terminal C1
Fire Station A2
Freightliner Terminal C1
Furnell Rd B3
Garland Rd A3
Green Rd B2
Heckford La A3
Heckford Rd A3
High St B2
High St North A3
Hill St B2
Holes Bay Rd A1
Hospital (A&E) A3
Information Ctr C2
Kingland Rd B3
Kingston Rd A3
Labrador Dr C3
Lagland St B2
Lander Cl C3
Lifeboat Coll, The B2
Lighthouse – Poole Ctr for the Arts B3
Longfleet Rd A3
Maple Rd A3
Market Cl B2
Market St B2
Mount Pleasant Rd B3
New Harbour Rd C1
New Harbour Rd South C1
New Harbour Rd West C1
New Orchard B1
New Quay Rd C1
New St B2
Newfoundland Dr B2
North St B2
Old Lifeboat C2
Old Orchard B2
Parish Rd A3
Park Lake Rd B3
Parkstone Rd A3
Perry Gdns B2
Pitwines Cl B2
Police Station A2
Poole Central Liby B2
Poole Lifting Bridge C1
Poole Park B2
Poole Station A2
Poole Museum C1
Post Office A2/B2
Quay, The C2
St John's Rd A3
St Margaret's Rd A2
St Mary's Maternity Unit A3
St Mary's Rd A3
Seldown Bridge B3
Seldown La B3
Seldown Rd B3
Serpentine Rd A2
Shaftesbury Rd A3
Skinner St B2
Slipway B1
Stanley Rd C2
Sterte Ave A2
Sterte Ave West A1
Sterte Cl A2
Sterte Esplanade A2
Sterte Rd A2
Strand St C2
Swimming Pool B3
Taverner Cl B3
Thames St B1
Towngate Bridge B2
Twin Sails Bridge B1
Vallis Cl C3
Waldren Cl B3
West Quay B1
West Quay Rd B1
West St B1
West View Rd A2
Whatleigh Cl B2
Wimborne Rd A3

Portsmouth 123

Action Stations C1
Admiralty Rd A1
Alfred Rd A2
Anglesea Rd B2
Arundel St B3
Aspex B1
Bishop St A2
Broad St C1
Buckingham Ho C2
Burnaby Rd B2
Bus Station B1
Camber Dock C1
Cambridge Rd B2
Car Ferry to Isle of Wight B1
Cascades Sh Ctr A3
Castle Rd C3
City Museum & Art Gallery B2
Civic Offices B3
Clarence Pier C2
College St B1
Commercial Rd A3
Cottage Gr B3
Cross St A1
Cumberland St A2
Duisburg Way C2
Durham St A3
East St B1
Edinburgh Rd A2
Elm Gr C3
Emirates Spinnaker Tower B1
Great Southsea St C3
Green Rd B3
Greetham St B3
Grosvenor St B3
Groundlings A2
Grove Rd North C3
Grove Rd South C3
Guildhall B3
Guildhall Walk B3
Gunwharf Quays Designer Outlet B1
Gunwharf Rd B1
Hambrook St C2
Hampshire Terr B2
Hanover St A1
Hard, The B1
High St C2
HM Naval Base A1
HMS Nelson (Royal Naval Barracks) A2
HMS Victory A1
HMS Warrior A1
Hovercraft Terminal C2
Hyde Park Rd B3
Information Ctr A1/B3
Isambard Brunel Rd B3
Isle of Wight Car Ferry Terminal B1
Kent Rd C3
Kent St A2
King St B3
King's Rd C3
King's Terr C2
Lake Rd A3
Law Courts B3
Library B3
Long Curtain Rd C2
Market Way A3
Marmion Rd C3
Mary Rose Museum A1
Middle St B3
Millennium Promenade B1/C1
Museum Rd B2
National Museum of the Royal Navy A1
Naval Rec Gd C2
Nightingale Rd C3
Norfolk St B3
North St A2
Osborne Rd C3
Park Rd B2
Passenger Catamaran to Isle of Wight B1
Passenger Ferry to Gosport B1
Pelham Rd C3
Pembroke Gdns C2
Pier Rd C2
Point Battery C1
Police Station B3
Portsmouth & Southsea A3
Portsmouth Harbour B1
Portsmouth Historic Dockyard A1
Post Office A3/B1/B3
Queen St A1
Queen's Cr C3
Round Tower C1
Royal Garrison Church C1
St Edward's Rd C3
St George's Rd B2
St George's Sq B1
St George's Way B2
St James's Rd B3
St James's St A2
St John's Cathedral (RC) A3
St Thomas's Cathedral C1
St Thomas's St B2
Shopmobility A3/B1
Somers Rd B3
Southsea Common C2
Southsea Terr C2
Square Tower C1
Station St A3
Town Fortifications C1
Unicorn Rd A2
United Services Rec Gd B2
University of Portsmouth A2/B2
Univ of Portsmouth – Coll of Art, Design & Media B3
Upper Arundel St A3
Victoria Ave C2
Victoria Park A2
Victory Gate A1
Vue B1
Warblington St B1
Western Pde C2
White Hart Rd C1
Winston Churchill Ave B3

Preston 123

Adelphi St A2
Anchor Ct B3
Aqueduct St A1
Ardee Rd C1
Arthur St B2
Ashton St A1
Avenham La B3
Avenham Park C3
Avenham Rd B3
Avenham St B3
Bairstow St B3
Balderstone Rd C1
Beamont Dr A1
Beech St South C2
Bird St C1
Bow La B2
Brieryfield Rd A1
Broadgate C1
Brook St A2
Bus Station A3
Butler St B2
Cannon St B3
Carlton St A1
Chaddock St B3
Channel Way B1
Chapel St B3
Christ Church St B2
Christian Rd B2
Cold Bath St A2
Coleman Ct C1
Connaught Rd C2
Corn Exchange B3
Corporation St A2/B2
County Hall B2
County Records Office B2
Court A3
Court B3
Cricket Ground C2
Croft St A1
Cross St B3
Crown Court A3
Crown St A3
East Cliff C3
East Cliff Rd B3
Edward St A2
Elizabeth St A3
Euston St B1
Fishergate B2/B3
Fishergate Hill B2
Fishergate Sh Ctr B2
Fitzroy St B1
Fleetwood St A1
Friargate A3
Fylde Rd A1/A2
Gerrard St B2
Glover's Ct B3
Good St B2
Grafton St B2
Great George St A3
Great Shaw St A3
Greenbank St A2
Guild Way B1
Guildhall & Charter B3
Guildhall St B3
Harrington St A2
Harris Museum B3
Hartington Rd B1
Hasset Cl C2
Heatley St B2
Hind St C2
Information Ctr B3
Kilruddery Rd C1
Lancaster Rd A3/B3
Latham St B3
Lauderdale St C2
Lawson St A3
Leighton St A2
Leyland Rd C1
Library A1
Library B3
Liverpool Rd C1
Lodge St B2
Lune St B3
Main Sprit West B3
Maresfield Rd C1
Market St West A3
Marsh La B1/B2
Maudland Bank A2
Maudland Rd A2
Meadow Ct C2
Meath Rd C1
Mill Hill A2
Miller Arcade B3
Miller Park C3
Moor La A3
Mount St B3
North Rd A3
North St A3
Northcote Rd B1
Old Milestones B1
Old Tram Rd C3
Pedder St A1/A2
Peel St A2
Penwortham Bridge C2
Penwortham New Bridge C1
Pitt St B2
Playhouse A3
Police Station A3
Port Way B1
Post Office B3
Preston Station B2
Ribble Bank St B2
Ribble Viaduct C2
Ribblesdale Pl B3
Ringway B3
River Parade C1
Riverside C2
St George's Shopping Ctr B3
St Georges B3
St Johns B3
St Johns Sh Ctr A3
St Mark's Rd A1
St Walburges A1
Salisbury Rd B1
Sessions House B3
Snow Hill A3
South End C2
South Meadow La C2
Spa Rd B1
Sports Ground C2
Strand Rd B1
Syke St B3
Talbot Rd B1
Taylor St C1
Tithebarn St A3
Town Hall B3
Tulketh Brow A1
University of Central Lancashire A2
Valley Rd C1
Victoria St A2
Walker St A3
Walton's Parade B2
Warwick St A3
Wellfield Bsns Pk A1
Wellfield Rd A1
Wellington St A1
West Cliff C2
West Strand A1
Winckley Rd C1
Winckley Square B3
Wolseley Rd C2

Reading 124

Abbey Ruins B2
Abbey Sq B2
Abbey St B2
Abbot's Walk B2
Acacia Rd C2
Addington Rd C3
Addison Rd A1
Allcroft Rd C3
Alpine St C2
Baker St B1
Berkeley Ave C1
Bridge St B1
Brigham Rd A1
Broad St B1
Broad Street Mall B1
Carey St B1
Castle Hill C1
Castle St B1
Causeway, The A3
Caversham Rd A1
Christchurch Playing Fields A2
Civic Offices B1
Coley Hill C1
Coley Pl C1
Craven Rd C3
Crown St C2
De Montfort Rd A1
Denmark Rd C3
Duke St B2
East St B2
Edgehill St C2
Eldon Rd B3
Eldon Terr B3
Elgar Rd C1
Erleigh Rd C3
Field Rd C1
Fire Station A1
Fobney St B1
Forbury Gdns B2
Forbury Rd B2
Forbury Retail Pk B2
Francis St C1
Friar St B1
Garrard St B1
Gas Works Rd B3
George St A2
Great Knollys St B1
Greyfriars B1
Grove, The B2
Gun St B1
Henry St C1
Hexagon Theatre, The B1
Hill's Meadow A2
Howard St B1
Information Ctr B1
Inner Distribution Rd B1
Katesgrove La C1
Kenavon Dr B2
Kendrick Rd C2
King's Mdw Rec Gd A2
King's Rd B2
Library B2
London Rd C3
London St B2
Lynmouth Rd A1
Magistrate's Court B1
Market Pl B2
Mill La B2
Mill Rd A2
Minster St B1
Morgan Rd C3
Mount Pleasant C2
Museum of English Rural Life C3
Napier Rd A2
Newark St C2
Newport Rd A1
Old Reading Univ C3
Oracle Sh Ctr, The B1
Orts Rd B3
Pell St C1
Police Station B1
Post Office B2
Queen Victoria St B1
Queen's Rd A2
Queen's Rd B2
Randolph Rd A1
Reading Bridge A2
Reading Station A1
Redlands Rd C3
Renaissance Hotel B1
Riverside Mus B3
Rose Kiln La C1
Royal Berks Hospital (A&E) C3
St Giles C2
St Laurence B2
St Mary's B1
St Mary's Butts B1
St Saviour's Rd C1
Send Rd A3
Sherman Rd C2
Sidmouth St B2
Silver St C2
South St B2
Southampton St C2
Station Hill A1
Station Rd B1
Superstore A3
Swansea Rd A1
Technical College B3
Valpy St B2
Vastern Rd A1
Vue B2
Waldeck St C2
Watlington St B3
West St B1
Whitby Dr C3
Wolseley St C1
York Rd A1
Zinzan St B1

Salisbury 124

Albany Rd A2
Arts Centre A3
Ashley Rd A1
Avon Approach A2
Ayleswade Rd C2
Bedwin St A2
Belle Vue A2
Bishop's Palace C2
Bishops Walk B2
Blue Boar Row B2
Bourne Ave A3
Bourne Hill A3
Britford La C2
Broad Walk C2
Brown St B2
Bus Station B2
Castle St A2
Catherine St B2
Chapter House B2
Church House B2
Churchfields Rd B1
Churchill Way East B3
Churchill Way North A3
Churchill Way South C2
Churchill Way West A1
City Hall B2
Close Wall B2
Coldharbour La A1
College St A3
Council Offices A3
Court A1
Crane Bridge Rd B2
Crane St B2
Cricket Ground C1
Culver St South B3
De Vaux Pl C2
Devizes Rd A1
Dews Rd B1
Elm Grove B3
Elm Grove Rd A3
Endless St A2
Estcourt Rd A3
Exeter St C2
Fairview Rd A3
Fire Station A1
Fisherton St A1
Folkestone Rd C1
Fowlers Hill B3
Fowlers Rd B3
Friary Estate C3
Friary La B2
Friary, The B3
Gas La A1
Gigant St B3
Greencroft B3
Greencroft St A3
Guildhall B2
Hall of John Halle B2
Hamilton Rd A2
Harnham Mill B1
Harnham Rd C1/C2

Scarborough • Sheffield • Southampton • Southend-on-Sea • Stoke-on-Trent • Stratford-upon-Avon • Sunderland 135

High St B2
Hospital A1
House of John A'Port B2
Information Ctr B2
Kelsey Rd A3
King's Rd A2
Laverstock Rd B3
Library B2
London Rd A3
Lower St C1
Maltings,The B2
Manor Rd A3
Marsh La B2
Medieval Hall B2
Milford Hill B3
Milford St B3
Mill Rd B1
Millstream App A2
Mompesson House (NT) B2
New Bridge Rd C2
New Canal B2
New Harnham Rd C2
New St B2
North Canonry B2
North Gate B2
North Walk B2
Old Blandford Rd C1
Old Deanery B2
Old George Hall B2
Park St A3
Parsonage Green C1
Playhouse Theatre A2
Post Office A2/B2/C2
Poultry Cross B2
Queen Elizabeth Gdns B1
Queen's Rd A3
Rampart Rd B3
St Ann St B2
St Ann's Gate B2
St Marks Rd A3
St Martins B3
St Mary's Cath B2
St Nicholas Hospital C2
St Paul's A1
St Paul's Rd A1
St Thomas B2
Salisbury & South Wiltshire Mus B2
Salisbury Sta A1
Salt La A3
Saxon Rd C1
Scots La A2
Shady Bower B3
South Canonry C2
South Gate C2
Southampton Rd B2
Spire View A1
Sports Ground C3
Tollgate Rd B3
Town Path B1
Wain-a-Long Rd A3
Wardrobe,The B2
Wessex Rd A3
West Walk C2
Wilton Rd A1
Wiltshire College B3
Winchester St B3
Windsor Rd A1
Winston Churchill Gdns C3
Wyndham Rd A2
YHA B3
York Rd A1

Scarborough 124

Aberdeen Walk B2
Albert Rd A2
Albion Rd C2
Alexandra Gardens A1
Auborough St B2
Balmoral Ctr B2
Belle Vue St C1
Belmont Rd C2
Brunswick Shop Ctr B2
Castle Dykes B3
Castle Hill A3
Castle Holms A3
Castle Rd B2
Castle Walls A3
Castlegate B3
Cemetery B1
Central Tramway B2
Clarence Gardens A2
Coach Park B1
Columbus Ravine A1
Court B1
Crescent,The C2
Cricket Ground A1
Cross St B2
Crown Terr C2
Dean Rd B1
Devonshire Dr A1
East Harbour B3
East Pier B3
Eastborough B2
Elmville Ave B1
Esplanade C2
Falconers Rd B2
Falsgrave Rd C1
Fire Station B2
Foreshore Rd B2
Friargate B2
Gladstone Rd B1
Gladstone St B1
Hollywood Plaza A1
Hoxton Rd B1
Information Ctr B2/B3
King St B2
Library B2
Lifeboat Station B3
Londesborough Rd C1
Longwestgate B3
Marine Dr A3
Military Adventure Park A1
Miniature Railway A1
Nelson St B1
Newborough B2
Nicolas St B2
North Marine Rd A1
North St B2
Northway B1
Old Harbour B3
Olympia Leisure B2
Peasholm Park A1
Peasholm Rd A1
Police Station B1
Post Office B2/C1
Princess St B3
Prospect Rd B1
Queen St B2
Queen's Parade A2
Queen's Tower (Remains) A3
Ramshill Rd C2
Roman Signal Station A3
Roscoe St C1
Rotunda Mus C2
Royal Albert Dr A2
St Martin-on-the-Hill C2
St Martin's Ave C2
St Mary's B3
St Thomas St B2
Sandside B3
Scarborough B1
Scarborough Art Gallery and Cres Art Studios C2
Scarborough Bowls Centre A1
Scarborough Castle A3
Shopmobility C2
Somerset Terr C2
South Cliff Lift C2
Spa Theatre, The C2
Spa,The C2
Stephen Joseph Theatre B1
Tennyson Ave B1
Tollergate B2
Town Hall B2
Trafalgar Rd B1
Trafalgar Square A1
Trafalgar St West B1
Valley Bridge Par C2
Valley Rd C1
Vernon Rd C2
Victoria Pk Mount A1
Victoria Rd B1
West Pier B3
Westborough C1
Westover Rd C1
Westwood C1
Woodall Ave A1
YMCA Theatre B2
York Pl B2
Yorkshire Coast College (Westwood Campus) C1

Sheffield 124

Addy Dr A2
Addy St A2
Adelphi St A3
Albert Terrace Rd A3
Albion St A2
Aldred Rd A1
Allen St A4
Alma St A4
Angel St B5
Arundel Gate B5
Arundel St C4
Ashberry Rd A2
Ashdell Rd C1
Ashgate Rd C1
Athletics Centre C2
Attercliffe Rd A6
Bailey St B4
Ball St A4
Balm Green B4
Bank St B4
Barber Rd A2
Bard St B5
Barker's Pool B4
Bates St A1
Beech Hill Rd C1
Beet St B3
Bellefield St A3
Bernard Rd A6
Bernard St B6
Birkendale A2
Birkendale Rd A2
Birkendale View A1
Bishop St C4
Blackwell Pl B6
Blake St A2
Blonk St A5
Bolsover St B2
Botanical Gdns C1
Bower Rd A1
Bradley St A1
Bramall La C4
Bramwell St A3
Bridge St A4/A5
Brighton Terr Rd A1
Broad La B3
Broad St B6
Brocco St A3
Brook Hill B3
Broomfield Rd C1
Broomgrove Rd C2
Broomhall Pl C3
Broomhall Rd C2
Broomhall St C3
Broomspring La C2
Brown St C5
Brunswick St B3
Burgess St B4
Burlington St A2
Burns Rd A2
Cadman St A6
Cambridge St B4
Campo La B4
Carver St B4
Castle Square B5
Castlegate A5
Cathedral B4
Cathedral (RC) B4
Cavendish St B3
Charles St C4
Charter Row C4
Children's Hospital (A&E) B2
Church St B4
City Hall B4
City Hall B4
City Rd C6
Claremont Cr B2
Claremont Pl B2
Clarke St C3
Clarkegrove Rd C2
Clarkehouse Rd C1
Clarkson St B2
Cobden View Rd A1
Collegiate Cr C2
Commercial St B5
Commonside A1
Conduit Rd B1
Cornish St A3
Corporation St A4
Court B4
Cricket Inn Rd B6
Cromwell St A1
Crookes Rd B1
Crookes Valley Pk B2
Crookes Valley Rd B2
Crookesmoor Rd A2
Crown Court A4
Crucible Theatre B5
Cutlers' Hall B4
Cutlers Gate A6
Daniel Hill A2
Dental Hospital B2
Derek Dooley Way A5
Devonshire Green B3
Devonshire St B3
Division St B4
Dorset St C2
Dover St A3
Duchess Rd C5
Duke St B5
Duncombe St A1
Durham Rd B2
Earl St C4
Earl Way C4
Ecclesall Rd C3
Edward St B3
Effingham Rd A6
Effingham St A6
Egerton St C3
Eldon St B3
Elmore Rd B1
Exchange St B5
Eyre St C4
Fargate B4
Farm Rd C5
Fawcett St A3
Filey St B3
Fir St A1
Fire Station C4
Fitzalan Sq/Ponds Forge B5
Fitzwater Rd C6
Fitzwilliam Gate C4
Fitzwilliam St B3
Flat St B5
Foley St A6
Foundry Climbing Centre A4
Fulton Rd A1
Furnace Hill A4
Furnival Rd A5
Furnival Sq C4
Furnival St C4
Garden St B3
Gell St B3
Gibraltar St A4
Glebe Rd B1
Glencoe Rd C6
Glossop Rd B2/B3/C1
Gloucester St C2
Government Offices C4
Granville Rd C6
Granville Rd / The Sheffield Coll C5
Graves Gallery B5
Greave Rd B3
Green La A4
Hadfield St A1
Hanover St C3
Hanover Way C3
Harcourt Rd B1
Harmer La B5
Havelock St C2
Hawley St B4
Haymarket B5
Headford St C3
Heavygate Rd A1
Henry St A3
High St B4
Hodgson St C3
Holberry Gdns C2
Hollis Croft B4
Holly St B4
Hounsfield Rd B3
Howard Rd A1
Hoyle St A3
Hyde Park A6
Infirmary Rd A3
Infirmary Rd A3
Information Ctr B4
Jericho St A3
Johnson St A5
Kelham Island Ind Mus A4
Lawson Rd C1
Leadmill Rd C5
Leadmill St C5
Leadmill,The C5
Leamington St A1
Leavy Rd B3
Lee Croft B4
Leopold St B4
Leveson St A6
Library A2/B5/C1
Lyceum Theatre B5
Malinda St A3
Maltravers St A5
Manor Oaks Rd B6
Mappin St B3
Marlborough Rd B1
Mary St C4
Matilda St C4
Matlock Rd A1
Meadow St A3
Melbourn Rd A1
Melbourne Ave C1
Millennium Galleries B5
Milton St C3
Mitchell St B3
Mona Ave A1
Mona Rd A1
Montgomery Terrace Rd A3
Montgomery Theatre B4
Monument Grounds C6
Moor Oaks Rd B1
Moor,The C4
Moor,The C4
Moore St C3
Mowbray St A4
Mushroom La B2
National Emergency Service A4
Netherthorpe Rd B3
Netherthorpe Rd B3
Newbould La C1
Nile St C1
Norfolk Park Rd C6
Norfolk Rd C6
Norfolk St B4
North Church St B4
Northfield Rd A1
Northumberland Rd B1
Nursery St A5
O2 Academy B5
Oakholme Rd C1
Octagon B2
Odeon B5
Old St B6
Orchard Square B4
Oxford St A2
Paradise St B4
Park La C2
Park Sq B5
Parker's Rd B1
Pearson Building (Univ) C2
Penistone Rd A3
Pinstone St B4
Pitt St B3
Police Station B5
Pond Hill B5
Pond St B5
Ponds Forge Int Sports Ctr B5
Portobello St B3
Post Office A2/B3/B4/B5/C1/C3/C4/C6
Powell St A2
Queen St B4
Queen's Rd C5
Ramsey Rd B1
Red Hill B3
Redcar Rd B1
Regent St B3
Rockingham St B4
Roebuck Rd A2
Royal Hallamshire Hospital C2
Russell St A4
Rutland Park C1
St George's Cl B3
St Mary's Gate C3
St Mary's Rd C4/C5
St Peter & St Paul Cathedral B4
St Philip's Rd A3
Savile St A5
School Rd B1
Scotland St A4
Severn Rd B1
Shalesmoor A4
Shalesmoor A3
Sheaf St B5
Sheffield Hallam University B5
Sheffield Ice Sports Centre – Skate Central C5
Sheffield Interchange B5
Sheffield Parkway A6
Sheffield Sta C5
Sheffield Station/ Sheffield Hallam University C5
Sheffield Univ B2
Shepherd St A3
Shipton St A2
Shopmobility B3
Shoreham St C4
Showroom C5
Shrewsbury Rd C5
Sidney St C4
Site Gallery C5
Slinn St A1
Smithfield A4
Snig Hill A5
Snow La A4
Solly St B3
South La C4
South Street Park B5
Southbourne Rd C1
Spital Hill A5
Spital St A5
Spring Hill B1
Spring Hill Rd B1
Springvale Rd A1
Stafford Rd C6
Stafford St B6
Suffolk Rd C5
Summer St B2
Sunny Bank C3
Superstore A3/C3
Surrey St B4
Sussex St A6
Sutton St B3
Sydney Rd A2
Sylvester St C4
Talbot St B5
Tapton Hall Conference & Banqueting Ctr B1
Taptonville Rd B1
Tenter St B4
Town Hall B4
Townend St A1
Townhead St B4
Trafalgar St B4
Tree Root Walk B2
Trinity St A4
Trippet La B4
Turner Museum of Glass B3
Union St B4
University Drama Studio B2
University of Sheffield B3
Upper Allen St A3
Upper Hanover St B3
Upperthorpe Rd A2/A3
Verdon St A5
Victoria Quays B5
Victoria Rd C2
Victoria St B3
Waingate B5
Watery St A3
Watson Rd C1
Wellesley Rd B2
Wellington St C3
West Bar A4
West Bar Green A4
West One Plaza B3
West St B3
West St B3
Westbourne Rd C1
Western Bank B2
Western Rd A1
Weston Park B2
Weston Park Hospital B2
Weston Pk Mus B2
Weston St B2
Wharncliffe Rd C3
Whitham Rd B1
Wicker A5
Wilkinson St B2
William St C3
Winter Garden B4
Winter St B2
York St B4
Yorkshire Artspace C5
Young St C4

Southampton 124

Above Bar St A2
Albert Rd North B3
Albert Rd South C3
Anderson's Rd B3
Archaeology Museum (God's House Tower) C2
Argyle Rd A2
Arundel Tower B1
Bargate,The B2
BBC Regional Ctr A1
Bedford Pl A1
Belvidere Rd A3
Bernard St C2
Blechynden Terr A1
Brinton's Rd A2
bristol B3
Britannia Rd A3
Briton St C2
Brunswick Pl A1
Bugle St C1
Canute Rd C3
Castle Way C2
Catchcold Tower B1
Central Bridge C3
Central Rd C2
Channel Way C3
Chapel Rd B3
Cineworld C3
City Art Gallery A1
City College B3
City Cruise Terminal C1
Civic Centre A1
Civic Centre Rd A1
Coach Station B1
Commercial Rd A1
Cumberland Pl A1
Cunard Rd C2
Derby Rd A3
Devonshire Rd A1
Dock Gate 4 C2
Dock Gate 8 B1
East Andrews Park A2
East Park Terr A2
East St B2
Endle St B3
European Way C2
Fire Station A2
Floating Bridge Rd C3
Golden Gr A3
Graham Rd A2
Guildhall A1
Hanover Bldgs B2
Harbour Lights C3
Harbour Parade B1
Hartington Rd A3
Havelock Rd A1
Henstead Rd A1
Herbert Walker Ave B1
High St B2
Hoglands Park B2
Holy Rood (Rems), Merchant Navy Memorial B2
Houndwell Park B2
Houndwell Pl B2
Hythe Ferry C2
Information Ctr A1
Isle of Wight Ferry Terminal C1
James St B3
Java Rd C3
Kingsway A2
Leisure World B1
Library A1
Lime St B2
London Rd A2
Marine Pde B3
Marlands Shopping Centre,The A1
Marsh La B2
Mayflower Memorial C1
Mayflower Park C1
Mayflower Theatre, The A1
Medieval Merchant's House C1
Melbourne St B3
Millais A2
Morris Rd A1
National Oceanography Centre C3
Neptune Way C3
New Rd A2
Nichols Rd A3
North Front A2
Northam Rd A3
Ocean Dock C2
Ocean Village Marina C3
Ocean Way C3
Odeon B1
Ogle Rd B1
Old Northam Rd A2
Orchard La B2
Oxford Ave A2
Oxford St C2
Palmerston Park A2
Palmerston Rd A2
Parsonage Rd A3
Peel St A3
Platform Rd C2
Polygon,The A1
Portland Terr B1
Post Office A2/A3/B2
Pound Tree Rd B2
Quays Swimming & Diving Complex, The B1
Queen's Park C2
Queen's Peace Fountain A2
Queen's Terr C2
Queensway B2
Radcliffe Rd A3
Rochester St A3
Royal Pier C1
Royal South Hants Hospital A2
St Andrew's Rd A2
St Mary St A2
St Mary's L Ctr A2
St Mary's Pl B2
St Mary's Rd A2
St Mary's Stadium (Southampton FC) A3
St Michael's C1
Sea City Mus A1
Solent Sky C3
South Front B2
Southampton Central Sta A1
Southampton Solent University A2
SS Shieldhall C2
Terminus Terr C2
Threefield La B2
Titanic Engineers' Memorial A2
Town Quay C1
Town Walls B2
Tudor House C1
Vincent's Walk B2
West Gate Hall C1
West Marlands Rd A1
West Park A1
West Park Rd A1
West Quay Rd B1
West Quay Retail Park B1
Western Esplanade B1
Westquay Shop Ctr B1
White Star Way C2
Winton St A2

Southend-on-Sea 125

Adventure Island C3
Albany Ave A1
Albert Rd C3
Alexandra Rd C2
Alexandra St C2
Alexandra Yacht Club C2
Ashburnham Rd B2
Ave Rd B1
Avenue Terr B1
Balmoral Rd B1
Baltic Ave B3
Baxter Ave A2/B2
Beecroft Art Gallery B2
Bircham Rd A2
Boscombe Rd B3
Boston Ave A1/B2
Bournemouth Park Rd A3
Browning Ave A3
Bus Station C3
Byron Ave A3
Cambridge Rd C1/C2
Canewdon Rd B1
Carnarvon Rd A2
Central Ave A3
Chelmsford Ave A1
Chichester Rd B2
Church Rd C3
Civic Centre A2
Clarence Rd C2
Clarence St C2
Cliff Ave B1
Cliffs Pavilion C1
Clifftown Parade C2
Clifftown Rd C2
Colchester Rd A1
Coleman St B3
College Way B2
County Court B3
Cromer Rd B3
Crowborough Rd A2
Dryden Ave A3
East St A2
Elmer App B2
Elmer Ave B2
Forum,The B2
Gainsborough Dr A1
Gayton Rd A2
Glenhurst Rd A2
Gordon Pl B2
Gordon Rd B2
Grainger Rd A2
Greyhound Way A3
Grove,The A3
Guildford Rd B3
Hamlet Ct Rd B1
Hamlet Rd C1
Harcourt Ave A1
Hartington Rd C3
Hastings Rd B3
Herbert Gr C3
Heygate Ave C3
High St B2/C2
Information Ctr C3
Kenway A2
Kilworth Ave B3
Lancaster Gdns B3
London Rd B1
Lucy Rd C3
MacDonald Ave A1
Magistrates' Court A2
Maine Ave C1
Maldon Rd A2
Marine Parade C3
Marine Rd C1
Milton Rd B1
Milton St B2
Napier Ave B2
North Ave A3
North Rd A1/B1
Odeon B2
Osborne Rd B1
Park Cres B1
Park Rd B1
Park St B1
Park Terr B1
Pier Hill C3
Pleasant Rd C3
Police Station A2
Post Office B2/B3
Princes St B2
Queens Rd B2
Queensway B2/B3/C3
Radio Essex C2
Rayleigh Ave A1
Redstock Rd A2
Rochford Ave A1
Royal Mews C2
Royal Terr C2
Royals Sh Ctr,The C3
Ruskin Ave A3
St Ann's Rd B3
St Helen's Rd B1
St John's Rd B1
St Leonard's Rd C3
St Lukes Rd A3
St Vincent's Rd C1
Salisbury Ave A1/B1
Scratton Rd C2
Shakespeare Dr A1
Shopmobility B2
Short St A2
South Ave A3
South Essex Coll B2
Southchurch Rd B3
Southend Central B2
Southend Pier Railway C3
Southend United FC A1
Southend Victoria B2
Stadium Rd A2
Stanfield Rd A2
Stanley Rd C3
Sutton Rd A3/B3
Swanage Rd B3
Sweyne Ave A1
Sycamore Gr A3
Tennyson Ave A3
Tickfield Ave A2
Tudor Rd A1
Tunbridge Rd A2
Tylers Ave B3
Tyrrel Dr B3
Univ of Essex B2/C2
Vale Ave A2
Victoria Ave A2
Victoria Shopping Centre,The B2
Warrior Sq B3
Wesley Rd C3
West Rd A1
West St A1
Westcliff Ave C1
Westcliff Parade C1
Western Esplanade C1
Weston Rd C2
Whitegate Rd B3
Wilson Rd C1
Wimborne Rd B3
York Rd C3

Stoke-on-Trent (Hanley) 125

Acton St A3
Albion St B2
Argyle St C1
Ashbourne Gr A2
Avoca St A3
Baskerville Rd B3
Bedford Rd C1
Bedford St C1
Bethesda St B2
Bexley St A2
Birches Head Rd A3
Botteslow St C3
Boundary St A2
Broad St C2
Broom St A3
Bryan St A2
Bucknall New Rd B3
Bucknall Old Rd B3
Bus Station B3
Cannon St C2
Castlefield St C1
Cavendish St B1
Central Forest Pk A2
Charles St B3
Cheapside B2
Chell St A3
Clarke St C1
Cleveland Rd C2
Clifford St C3
Clough St B2
Clyde St C1
College Rd C2
Cooper St C2
Corbridge Rd A1
Cutts St C2
Davis St C1
Denbigh St A1
Derby St C3
Dilke St A3
Dundas St A3
Dundee Rd C1
Dyke St B3
Eastwood Rd C3
Eaton St A3
Etruria Park B1
Etruria Rd B1
Etruria Vale Rd C1
Festing St A3
Festival Retail Pk A1
Fire Station C2
Foundry St B2
Franklyn St C3
Garnet St B1
Garth St B3
George St A3
Gilman St B3
Glass St B3
Goodson St B3
Greyhound Way A1
Grove Pl C1
Hampton St C3
Hanley Park C2
Hanley Park C2
Harding Rd C2
Hassall St B3
Havelock Pl C1
Hazlehurst St C3
Hinde St C2
Hope St B2
Houghton St C2
Hulton St A3
Information Ctr B3
Jasper St C2
Jervis St A3
John Bright St A3
John St B2
Keelings Rd A3
Kimberley Rd C1
Ladysmith Rd C1
Lawrence St C2
Leek Rd C3
Library C2
Lichfield St C3
Linfield Rd B3
Loftus St A2
Lower Bedford St C1
Lower Bryan St A2
Lower Mayer St A3
Lowther St A1
Magistrates Court C2
Malham St A2
Marsh St B2
Matlock St C3
Mayer St A3
Milton St C1
Mitchell Memorial Theatre B2
Morley St B2
Moston St A3
Mount Pleasant C1
Mulgrave St A1
Mynors St B3
Nelson Pl B3
New Century St B1
Octagon Retail Pk B1
Ogden Rd C3
Old Hall St B3
Old Town Rd A3
Pall Mall B2
Palmerston St C3
Park and Ride C2
Parker St B2
Parkway,The C2
Pavilion Dr A1
Pelham St C3
Percy St B2
Piccadilly B2
Picton St B3
Plough St A3
Police Station C2
Portland St A1
Post Office A3/B3/C3
Potteries Museum & Art Gallery B2
Potteries Sh Ctr B2
Potteries Way C2
Powell St A1
Pretoria Rd C1
Quadrant Rd B2
Ranelagh St C2
Raymond St C2
Rectory Rd C1
Regent Rd C2
Regent Theatre B2
Richmond Terr C2
Ridgehouse Dr A1
Robson St C2
St Ann St B3
St Luke St B3
Sampson St B2
Shaw St A1
Sheaf St C2
Shearer St C1
Shelton New Rd C1
Shirley Rd C2
Slippery La B2
Snow Hill C2
Spur St C3
Stafford St B2
Statham St B2
Stubbs La C3
Sun St C1
Supermarket A1/B2
Talbot St C3
Town Hall B2
Town Rd A3
Trinity St B2
Union St A2
Upper Hillchurch St A3
Upper Huntbach St B3
Victoria Hall Theatre B3
Warner St C2
Warwick St C1
Waterloo Rd A1
Waterloo St B3
Well St B3
Wellesley St C2
Wellington Rd B3
Wellington St B3
Whitehaven Dr A2
Whitmore St C1
Windermere St A1
Woodall St A1
Yates St C2
York St A2

Stratford-upon-Avon 125

Albany Rd B1
Alcester Rd B1
Ambulance Sta B1
Arden St B2
Avenue Farm A1
Ave Farm Ind Est A1
Avenue Rd A3
Avon Industrial Est A2
Baker Ave A1
Bandstand C3
Benson Rd A3
Birmingham Rd A2
Boat Club B3
Borden Pl C1
Brass Rubbing Centre C2
Bridge St B2
Bridgetown Rd C3
Bridgeway B3
Broad St C2
Broad Walk C2
Brookvale Rd C1
Bull St C2
Butterfly Farm C3
Cemetery C1
Chapel La B2
Cherry Orchard C1
Chestnut Walk B2
Children's Playground C3
Church St C2
Civic Hall B2
Clarence Rd B1
Clopton Bridge B3
Clopton Rd A2
College B1
College La C2
College St C2
Community Sports Centre B1
Council Offices (District) B2
Courtyard,The C2
Cox's Yard B3
Cricket Ground C3
Ely Gdns B2
Ely St B2
Evesham Rd C1
Fire Station B1
Foot Ferry C3
Fordham Ave A2
Gallery,The B3
Garrick Way C1
Gower Meml B3
Great William St B2
Greenhill St B2
Greenway,The C2
Grove Rd B2
Guild St B2
Guildhall & School B2
Hall's Croft C2
Harvard House B2
Henley St B2
High St B2
Holton St C2
Holy Trinity C2
Information Ctr B3
Jolyffe Park Rd A2
Kipling Rd C3
Library B2
Lodge Rd B1
Maidenhead Rd A3
Mansell St B2
Masons Court B2
Masons Rd A1
Maybird Shopping Park A2
Maybrook Rd A1
Mayfield Ave A2
Meer St B2
Mill La C2
Moat House Hotel B3
Narrow La C2
Nash's House & New Place B2
New St C2
Old Town C2
Orchard Way C1
Paddock La C1
Park Rd A1
Payton St B2
Percy St A2
Police Station B2
Post Office B2
Recreation Gd C2
Regal Road A2
Rother St B2
Rowley Cr A3
Royal Shakespeare Theatre B3
Ryland St C2
Saffron Meadow C2
St Andrew's Cr B1
St Gregory's A3
St Gregory's Rd A3
St Mary's Rd A2
Sanctus Dr C2
Sanctus St C1
Sandfield Rd C2
Scholars La B2
Seven Meadows Rd C2
Shakespeare Centre B2
Shakespeare Inst C2
Shakespeare St B2
Shakespeare's Birthplace B2
Sheep St B2
Shelley Rd C3
Shipston Rd C3
Shottery Rd C1
Slingates Rd A2
Southern La C2
Station Rd B1
Stratford Healthcare B2
Stratford Hosp B2
Stratford Leisure & Visitor Centre B3
Stratford Sports Club B1
Stratford-upon-Avon Station B1
Swan Theatre B3
Swan's Nest La B3
Talbot Rd A2
Tiddington Rd B3
Timothy's Bridge Industrial Estate A1
Timothy's Bridge Rd A1
Town Hall & Council Offices B2
Town Sq B2
Trinity St C2
Tyler St B2
War Meml Gdns B3
Warwick Rd B3
Waterside B3
Welcombe Rd A3
West St C2
Western Rd A2
Wharf Rd A2
Willows North, The B1
Willows,The B1
Wood St B2

Sunderland 125

Albion Pl C2
Alliance Pl B1
Argyle St C2
Ashwood St C1
Athenaeum St B2
Azalea Terr C2
Beach St A1
Bedford St B2
Beechwood Terr C1
Belvedere Rd C2
Blandford St B2
Borough Rd B3
Bridge Cr B2
Bridge St B2
Bridges,The B2
Brooke St A2
Brougham St B2
Burdon Rd C2
Burn Park C1
Burn Park Rd C1
Burn Pk Tech Pk C1
Carol St B1
Charles St A3
Chester Rd C1
Chester Terr B1
Church St A3
Civic Centre C2
Cork St B3
Coronation St B3
Cowan Terr C2
Dame Dorothy St A2
Deptford Rd B1
Deptford Terr A1
Derby St C2
Derwent St C2
Dock St A3
Dundas St A2
Durham Rd C1
Easington St A2
Egerton St C3
Empire B3
Empire Theatre B2
Farringdon Row B1
Fawcett St B2
Fire Station B1
Fox St C1
Foyle St B3
Frederick St B3
Hanover Pl A1
Havelock Terr C1
Hay St A2
Headworth Sq B3
Hendon Rd B3
High St East B3
High St West B2/B3
Holmeside B2
Hylton Rd B1
Information Ctr B2
John St B3
Kier Hardie Way A2
Lambton St B3
Laura St C3
Lawrence St B3
Library & Arts Ctr B3
Lily St B1
Lime St B1
Livingstone Rd B2
Low Row B2

Matamba Terr B1
Millburn St B1
Millennium Way A2
Minster B2
Monkwearmouth Sta Mus A2
Mowbray Park C3
Mowbray Rd C3
Murton St C3
National Glass Centre A3
New Durham Rd C1
Newcastle Rd A2
Nile St B3
Norfolk St B3
North Bridge St A2
Northern Gallery for Contemporary Art B3
Otto Terr C1
Park La C2
Park Lane C2
Park Rd C2
Paul's Rd B3
Peel St C3
Police Station B2
Priestly Cr A1
Queen St B2
Railway Row B1
Retail Park B1
Richmond St A2
Roker Ave A2
Royalty Theatre C1
Royalty,The C1
Ryhope Rd C2
St Mary's Way B2
St Michael's Way B2
St Peter's A3
St Peter's A2
St Peter's Way A3
St Vincent St C3
Salem Rd C3
Salem St C3
Salisbury St C3
Sans St B3
Shopmobility B2
Silkworth Row B1
Southwick Rd A2
Stadium of Light (Sunderland AFC) A2
Stadium Way A2
Stobart St A2
Stockton Rd C2
Suffolk St C3
Sunderland A2
Sunderland Aquatic Centre A2
Sunderland Museum B3
Sunderland St B3
Sunderland Sta B2
Tatham St C3
Tavistock Pl B3
Thelma St C1
Thomas St North A2
Thornholme Rd C1
Toward Rd C3
Transport Interchange C2
Trimdon St Way B1
Tunstall Rd C2
University C1
University Library C1
Univ of Sunderland (City Campus) B1
Univ of Sunderland (Sir Tom Cowie at St Peter's Campus) A3
Vaux Brewery Way A2
Villiers St B3
Villiers St South B3
Vine Pl C2
Violet St B1
Walton La B3
Waterworks Rd B1
Wearmouth Bridge B2
West Sunniside B3
West Wear St B3
Westbourne Rd B1
Western Hill C1
Wharncliffe B1
Whickham St A3
White House Rd C3
Wilson St North A2
Winter Gdns C3
Wreath Quay A1

Swansea
Abertawe 125

Adelaide St C3
Albert Row C3
Alexandra Rd B3
Argyle St C1
Baptist Well Pl A2
Beach St C1
Belle Vue Way B3
Berw Rd A1
Berwick Terr A2
Bond St C1
Brangwyn Concert Hall C1
Bridge St A3
Brooklands Terr B1
Brunswick St C1
Bryn-Syfi Terr A2
Bryn-y-Mor Rd C1
Bullins La B1
Burrows Rd C1
Bus Station C2
Bus/Rail link A3
Cadfan Rd A1
Cadrawd Rd A1
Caer St B3
Carig Cr A1
Carlton Terr B2
Carmarthen Rd A3
Castle Square B3
Castle St B3
Catherine St C1
Cinema C3
Civic Ctr & Library C2
Clarence St C2
Colbourne Terr A2
Constitution Hill B1
Court B3
Creidiol Rd A2
Cromwell St B2
Crown Courts C1
Duke St B1
Dunvant Pl C2
Dyfatty Park A3
Dyfatty St A3
Dyfed Ave A1
Dylan Thomas Centre B3
Dylan Thomas Theatre C3
Eaton Cr C1
Eigen Cr A1
Elfed Rd A1
Emlyn Rd A1
Evans Terr A3
Fairfield Terr B1
Ffynone Dr B1
Ffynone Rd B1
Fire Station B3
Firm St A2
Fleet St C1
Francis St C1
Fullers Row B2
George St B2
Glamorgan St C2
Glynn Vivian Art Gallery B3
Gower College Swansea C1
Graig Terr A3
Grand Theatre C2
Granogwen Rd A2
Guildhall C1
Guildhall Rd South C1
Gwent Rd A1
Gwynedd Ave A1
Hafod St A3
Hanover St B1
Harcourt St B2
Harries St A2
Heathfield B2
Henrietta St B2
Hewson St B2
High St A3/B3
High View A2
Hill St A2
Historic Ships Berth C3
HM Prison C2
Information Ctr C2
Islwyn Rd A1
King Edward's Rd C1
Kingsway,The B2
LC,The C3
Long Ridge A2
Madoc St C2
Mansel St B2
Maritime Quarter C3
Market B3
Mayhill Gdns B1
Mayhill Rd A1
Milton Terr A2
Mission Gallery C3
Montpellier Terr B1
Morfa Rd A3
Mount Pleasant B2
National Waterfront Museum C3
Nelson St C2
New Cut Rd A3
New St A3
Nicander Pde A2
Nicander Pl A2
Nicholl St B2
Norfolk St B2
North Hill Rd A2
Northampton La B2
Orchard St B3
Oxford St B2
Oystermouth Rd C1
Page St B2
Pant-y-Celyn Rd B1
Parc Tawe Link B3
Parc Tawe North B3
Parc Tawe Shopping & Leisure Centre B3
Patti Pavilion C1
Paxton St C2
Pen-y-Graig Rd A1
Penmaen Terr B1
Phillips Pde C1
Picton Terr B2
Plantasia B3
Police Station B2
Post Office A1/A2/C1/C2
Powys Ave A1
Primrose St B2
Princess Way B3
Promenade B2
Pryder Gdns A1
Quadrant Shop Ctr C2
Quay Park B3
Rhianfa La B1
Rhondda St B2
Richardson St C2
Rodney St C1
Rose Hill B1
Rosehill Terr B1
Russell St B1
St David's Shop Ctr C3
St Helen's Ave C1
St Helen's Cr C1
St Helen's Rd C1
St James Gdns B1
St James's Cr B1
St Mary's B3
Sea View Terr A3
Singleton St C2
South Dock C3
Stanley Pl B2
Strand B3
Swansea Castle B3
Swansea Metropolitan University B2
Swansea Mus C3
Swansea Sta A3
Taliesyn Rd B1
Tan y Marian Rd A1
Tegid Rd A2
Teilo Cr A1
Tenpin Bowling B3
Terrace Rd B1/B2
Tontine St A3
Tower of Ecliptic Observatory C3
Townhill Rd A1
Tramshed,The C3
Trawler Rd C3
Union St B2
Upper Strand A3
Vernon St A3
Victoria Quay C3
Victoria Rd B3
Vincent St C1
Walter Rd B1
Watkin St A2
Waun-Wen Rd A2
Wellington St C2
Westbury St C1
Western St C1
Westway C2
William St C2
Wind St B3
Woodlands Terr B1
YMCA B2
York St C3

Swindon 125

Albert St C3
Albion St C1
Alfred St A2
Alvescot Rd C3
Art Gallery & Museum C3
Ashford Rd C1
Aylesbury St A2
Bath Rd C2
Bathampton St B1
Bathurst Rd B3
Beatrice St A2
Beckhampton St B3
Bowood Rd C1
Bristol St B1
Broad St A3
Brunel Arcade B2
Brunel Plaza B2
Brunswick St C2
Bus Station B2
Cambria Bridge Rd B1
Cambria Place B1
Canal Walk B2
Carfax St B2
Carr St B1
Cemetery C1/C3
Chandler Cl C3
Chapel C1
Chester St B1
Christ Church C3
Church Place B1
Cirencester Way A3
Clarence St B2
Clifton St C1
Cockleberry A2
Colbourne A3
Colbourne St A3
College St B2
Commercial Rd B2
Corporation St A2
Council Offices B3
County Rd A3
Courts B2
Cricket Ground A3
Cricklade Street C3
Crombey St B1/C2
Cross St C2
Curtis St B1
Deacon St C1
Designer Outlet (Great Western) B1
Dixon St C2
Dover St C2
Dowling St C2
Drove Rd C3
Dryden St C1
Durham St C3
East St B1
Eastcott Hill C2
Eastcott Rd C2
Edgeware Rd B2
Edmund St C2
Elmina Rd A3
Emlyn Square B1
Euclid St B3
Exeter St B1
Fairview C1
Faringdon Rd B1
Farnsby St B1
Fire Station B3
Fleet St B2
Fleming Way B2/B3
Florence St A2
Gladstone St A3
Gooch St A2
Graham St A3
Great Western Way A1/A2
Groundwell Rd B3
Hawksworth Way A1
Haydon St A2
Henry St B2
Hillside Ave C1
Holbrook Way B2
Hunt St C3
Hydro B1
Hythe Rd C2
Information Ctr B2
Joseph St C1
Kent Rd C2
King William St C2
Kingshill Rd C1
Lansdown Rd C2
Lawn,The C3
Leicester St B3
Library B2
Lincoln St B3
Little London C3
London St B1
Magic A3
Maidstone Rd C2
Manchester Rd A3
Maxwell St B1
Milford St B2
Milton Rd B1
Morse St C2
National Monuments Record Centre B1
Newcastle St B3
Newcombe Drive A1
Newcombe Trading Estate A1
Newhall St C2
North St C2
North Star A1
North Star Ave A1
Northampton St B3
Nurseries,The C1
Oasis Leisure Ctr A1
Ocotal Way A3
Okus Rd C1
Old Town C3
Oxford St B1
Parade,The B2
Park Lane B1
Park Lane B1
Park,The B1
Pembroke St C2
Plymouth St B3
Polaris House A2
Polaris Way A2
Police Station B2
Ponting St A2
Post Office B1/B2/C1/C3
Poulton St A3
Princes St B2
Prospect Hill C2
Prospect Place C2
Queen St B2
Queen's Park C3
Radnor St C1
Read St C1
Reading St B1
Regent St B2
Retail Park A2/A3/B3
Rosebery St A3
St Mark's B1
Salisbury St A3
Savernake St C2
Shelley St C1
Sheppard St B1
South St C2
Southampton St B3
Spring Gardens B3
Stafford Street C2
Stanier St C2
Station Road A2
STEAM B1
Swindon College A2
Swindon Rd C2
Swindon Sta A2
Swindon Town Football Club A3
T A Centre B1
Tennyson St B1
Theobald St B1
Town Hall B2
Transfer Bridges A3
Union St C2
Upham Rd C3
Victoria Rd C3
Walcot Rd B3
War Memorial B2
Wells St B3
Western St C2
Westmorland Rd B3
Whalebridge B2
Whitehead St C1
Whitehouse Rd A2
William St C1
Wood St C3
Wyvern Theatre & Arts Centre B2
York Rd B3

Telford 126

Alma Ave C1
Amphitheatre C2
Bowling Alley B2
Brandsfarm Way C3
Brunel Rd B1
Bus Station B2
Buxton Rd C1
Central Park A2
Civic Offices B2
Coach Central B2
Coachwell Cl B1
Colliers Way A1
Courts B2
Dale Acre Way B3
Darliston C3
Deepdale B3
Deercote B2
Dinthill C3
Doddington C3
Dodmoor Grange C3
Downemead B3
Duffryn B3
Dunsheath B3
Euston Way A3
Eyton Mound C1
Eyton Rd C1
Forgegate A2
Grange Central B2
Hall Park Way B1
Hinkshay Rd C2
Hollinsworth Rd A2
Holyhead Rd A3
Housing Trust A1
Ice Rink B2
Information Ctr B2
Ironmasters Way A2
Job Centre B1
Land Registry B1
Lawn Central B2
Lawnswood C1
Library B2
Malinsgate B1
Matlock Ave C1
Moor Rd C1
Mount Rd C1
NFU Offices B1
Odeon B2
Park Lane A1
Police Station B1
Priorslee Ave A3
Queen Elizabeth Ave C3
Queen Elizabeth Way B1
Queensway A2/B3
Rampart Way A2
Randlay Ave C3
Randlay Wood C3
Rhodes Ave C1
Royal Way B1
St Leonards Rd B1
St Quentin Gate B2
Shifnal Rd A3
Sixth Ave A1
Southwater One (SW1) B2
Southwater Way B1
Spout Lane C1
Spout Mound B1
Spout Way C1
Stafford Court B3
Stafford Park B3
Stirchley Ave C3
Stone Row C1
Telford Bridge Retail Park A1
Telford Central Station A3
Telford Ctr,The B2
Telford Forge Shopping Park A1
Telford Hornets RFC C2
Telford Int Ctr C2
Telford Way A3
Third Ave A2
Town Park C2
Town Park Visitor Centre B2
Walker House B2
Wellswood Ave A2
West Centre Way B1
Withywood Drive C1
Woodhouse Central B2
Yates Way A1

Torquay 126

Abbey Rd B2
Alexandra Rd A2
Alpine Rd B3
Ash Hill Rd A2
Babbacombe Rd B3
Bampfylde Rd B1
Barton Rd A1
Beacon Quay C2
Belgrave Rd A1/B1
Belmont Rd A3
Berea Rd A3
Braddons Hill Rd East B3
Brewery Park A3
Bronshill Rd A2
Castle Circus A2
Castle Rd A2
Cavern Rd A3
Central B2
Chatsworth Rd A2
Chestnut Ave B1
Church St A1
Civic Offices A2
Coach Station A1
Corbyn Head C1
Croft Hill B1
Croft Rd B1
Daddyhole Plain C3
East St A1
Egerton Rd A3
Ellacombe Church Rd A3
Ellacombe Rd A2
Falkland Rd B1
Fleet St B2
Fleet Walk Sh Ctr B2
Grafton Rd B3
Haldon Pier C2
Hatfield Rd A2
Highbury Rd A2
Higher Warberry Rd A3
Hillesdon Rd B3
Hollywood Bowl C3
Hoxton Rd A3
Hunsdon Rd B3
Information Ctr B2
Inner Harbour C3
Kenwyn Rd A3
King's Drive,The B1
Laburnum St A1
Law Courts A2
Library A2
Lime Ave B1
Living Coasts C3
Lower Warberry Rd B3
Lucius St B1
Lymington Rd A1
Magdalene Rd A1
Marina C2
Market Forum,The B2
Market St B2
Meadfoot Lane C3
Meadfoot Rd C3
Melville St B2
Middle Warberry Rd B3
Mill Lane A1
Montpellier Rd B3
Morgan Ave A1
Museum Rd B3
Newton Rd A1
Oakhill Rd A1
Outer Harbour C2
Parkhill Rd C3
Pavilion Sh Ctr C2
Pimlico B2
Police Station A1
Post Office A1/B2
Princes Rd A3
Princes Rd East A3
Princes Rd West A3
Princess Gdns C2
Princess Pier C2
Princess Theatre C2
Rathmore Rd B1
Recreation Grd B1
Riviera Int Ctr B1
Rock End Ave C3
Rock Rd B2
Rock Walk B2
Rosehill Rd A3
St Efride's Rd A1
St John's B3
St Luke's Rd B2
St Luke's Rd North B2
St Luke's Rd South B2
St Marychurch Rd A2
Scarborough Rd B1
Shedden Hill B2
South Pier C2
South St A1
Spanish Barn B1
Stitchill Rd B3
Strand B3
Sutherland Rd B3
Teignmouth Rd A1
Temperance St B2
Terrace,The B3
Thurlow Rd A1
Tor Bay B1
Tor Church Rd A1
Tor Hill Rd A1
Torbay Rd B2
Torquay Mus B3
Torquay Station C1
Torre Abbey Mansion B1
Torre Abbey Meadows B1
Torre Abbey Sands B1
Torwood Gdns B3
Torwood St C3
Town Hall A2
Union Square A2
Union St A1
Upton Hill A2
Upton Park A1
Upton Rd A1
Vanehill Rd C3
Vansittart Rd A1
Vaughan Parade C2
Victoria Parade C3
Victoria Rd A2
Warberry Rd West B2
Warren Rd B2
Windsor Rd A2/A3
Woodville Rd A3

Winchester 126

Andover Rd A2
Andover Rd Ret Pk A2
Archery La C2
Arthur Rd A2
Bar End Rd C3
Beaufort Rd C2
Beggar's La B3
Bereweeke Ave A1
Bereweeke Rd A1
Boscobel Rd A2
Brassey Rd A2
Broadway B3
Brooks Sh Ctr,The B3
Bus Station B3
Butter Cross B2
Canon St C2
Castle Wall C2/C3
Castle, King Arthur's Round Table B2
Cathedral C2
Cheriton Rd A1
Chesil St C3
Chesil Theatre C3
Christchurch Rd C1
City Mill B3
City Museum B2
City Rd B2
Clifton Rd B1
Clifton Terr B2
Close Wall C2/C3
Coach Park A2
Colebrook St C3
College St C2
College Walk C3
Compton Rd C2
Council Offices C3
County Council Offices B2
Cranworth Rd A2
Cromwell Rd C1
Culver Rd C2
Domum Rd C3
Durngate Pl B3
Eastgate St B3
Edgar Rd C2
Egbert Rd A2
Elm Rd B1
Everyman C2
Fairfield Rd A1
Fire Station B3
Fordington Ave B1
Fordington Rd A1
Friarsgate B3
Gordon Rd B3
Greenhill Rd B1
Guildhall B3
Hatherley Rd A1
High St B2
Hillier Way A3
HM Prison B1
Hyde Abbey (Remains) A2
Hyde Abbey Rd B2
Hyde Cl A2
Hyde St A2
Information Ctr B3
Jane Austen's House C2
Jewry St B2
John Stripe Theatre C1
King Alfred Pl A2
Kingsgate Arch C2
Kingsgate Park C2
Kingsgate Rd C2
Kingsgate St C2
Lankhills Rd A2
Law Courts B2
Library B2
Lower Brook St B3
Magdalen Hill B3
Market La B2
Mews La B1
Middle Brook St B3
Middle Rd B1
Military Museums B2
Milland Rd C3
Milverton Rd B1
Monks Rd A3
North Hill Cl A2
North Walls B2
North Walls Recreation Gnd A3
Nuns Rd A3
Oram's Arbour B1
Owen's Rd A2
Parchment St B2
Park & Ride C3
Park Ave B3
Playing Field A1
Police HQ B1
Police Station B3
Portal Rd C3
Post Office B2/C1
Quarry Rd C3
Ranelagh Rd C1
Regiment Mus B2
River Park L Ctr B3
Romans' Rd C2
Romsey Rd B1
Royal Hampshire County Hospital (A&E) B1
St Cross Rd C2
St George's St B2
St Giles Hill C3
St James Villas C2
St James' La B1
St James' Terr B1
St John's B3
St John's St B3
St Michael's Rd C2
St Paul's Hill B1
St Peter St B2
St Swithun St C2
St Thomas St C2
Saxon Rd A2
School of Art B3
Sleepers Hill Rd C1
Southgate St B2
Sparkford Rd C1
Square,The B2
Staple Gdns B2
Station Rd B2
Step Terr B1
Stockbridge Rd A1
Stuart Cres C1
Sussex St B2
Swan Lane B2
Tanner St B3
Theatre Royal B2
Tower St B2
Town Hall C3
Union St B3
Univ of Southampton (Winchester School of Art) B3
University of Winchester (King Alfred Campus) C1
Upper Brook St B2
Wales St B3
Water Lane B3
Weirs,The C3
West End Terr B1
Western Rd B1
Westgate B2
Wharf Hill C3
Winchester Coll C2
Winchester Gallery, The B3
Winchester Sta A2
Winnall Moors Wildlife Reserve A3
Wolvesey Castle C3
Worthy Lane A2
Worthy Rd A2

Windsor 126

Adelaide Sq C3
Albany Rd C2
Albert St B1
Alexandra Gdns B2
Alexandra Rd C2
Alma Rd B2
Ambulance Sta B1
Arthur Rd B2
Bachelors Acre B3
Barry Ave B2
Beaumont Rd C2
Bexley St B1
Boat House B2
Brocas St B2
Brocas,The A2
Brook St C3
Bulkeley Ave C1
Castle Hill B3
Charles St B2
Claremont Rd C2
Clarence Cr B2
Clarence Rd B1
Clewer Court Rd B1
Coach Park B2
College Cr C1
Courts C2
Cricket Club A3
Cricket Ground C3
Dagmar Rd C2
Datchet Rd B3
Devereux Rd C2
Dorset Rd C2
Duke St B1
Elm Rd C1
Eton College A3
Eton Ct A2
Eton Sq A2
Eton Wick Rd A2
Farm Yard B3
Fire Station C2
Frances Rd C2
Frogmore Dr B3
Gloucester Pl C3
Goslar Way C1
Goswell Hill B2
Goswell Rd B2
Green La C1
Grove Rd C2
Guildhall B3
Helena Rd C2
Helston La B1
High St A2/B3
Holy Trinity C2
Home Pk,The A3/C3
Hosp (Private) C2
Household Cavalry C2
Imperial Rd C1
Information Ctr B2/B3
Keats La A2
King Edward Ct B2
King Edward VII Ave A3
King Edward VII Hospital C2
King George V Memorial B3
King Stable St A2
King's Rd C3
Library C2
Long Walk,The C3
Maidenhead Rd B1
Meadow La A2
Municipal Offices C3
Nell Gwynne's House B3
Osborne Rd C2
Oxford Rd B1
Park St B3
Peascod St B2
Police Station C2
Post Office A2
Princess Margaret Hospital C3
Queen Victoria's Walk B3
Queen's Rd C2
River St B2
Romney Island A3
Romney Lock A3
Romney Lock Rd A3
Russell St C2
St John's B3
St John's Chapel A2
St Leonards Rd C2
St Mark's Rd C2
Sheet St C3
South Meadow A2
South Meadow La A2
Springfield Rd C1
Stovell Rd B1
Sunbury Rd A3
Tangier La A2
Tangier St A3
Temple Rd C2
Thames St B3
Theatre Royal B3
Trinity Pl C2
Vansittart Rd B1/C1
Vansittart Rd Gdns C1
Victoria Barracks C2
Victoria St C2
Ward Royal B2
Westmead C1
White Lilies Island A1
William St B2
Windsor & Eton Central B2
Windsor & Eton Riverside A3
Windsor Arts Centre C2
Windsor Bridge B3
Windsor Castle B3
Windsor Great Pk C3
Windsor L Ctr B1
Windsor Relief Rd A1
Windsor Royal Sh B2
York Ave C1
York Rd C1

Worcester 126

Albany Terr A1
Alice Otley School A2
Angel Pl B2
Angel St B2
Ashcroft Rd A2
Athelstan Rd C3
Avenue,The C1
Back Lane North A1
Back Lane South A1
Barbourne Rd A2
Bath Rd C2
Battenhall Rd C3
Bridge St B2
Britannia Sq A1
Broad St B2
Bromwich La C1
Bromwich Rd C1
Bromyard Rd C1
Bus Station B2
Butts,The B2
Carden St B3
Castle St A2
Cathedral C2
Cathedral Plaza B2
Charles St B3
Chequers La B1
Chestnut St A2
Chestnut Walk A2
Citizens' Advice Bureau B2
City Walls Rd B2
Cole Hill C3
Coll of Technology B2
College St C2
Commandery, The C3
Cripplegate Park B1
Croft Rd B1
Cromwell St B3
Cross,The B2
Crown Gate Ctr B2
Deansway B2
Diglis Pde C2
Diglis Rd C2
Edgar Tower C2
Farrier St A2
Fire Station B2
Foregate St B2
Foregate Street B2
Fort Royal Hill C3
Fort Royal Park C3
Foundry St B3
Friar St C2
George St B3
Grand Stand Rd B1
Greenhill C3
Greyfriars B2
Guildhall B2
Henwick Rd B1
High St B2
Hill St B3
Hive,The B2
Huntingdon Hall B2
Hylton Rd B1
Information Ctr B2
King Charles Place Shopping Centre C1
King's School C2
King's School Playing Field C2
Kleve Walk C2
Lansdowne Cr A3
Lansdowne Rd A3
Lansdowne Walk A3
Laslett St A3
Leisure Centre A3
Library, Museum & Art Gallery A2
Little Chestnut St A2
Little London A2
London Rd C3
Lowell St A3
Lowesmoor B2
Lowesmoor Terr A3
Lowesmoor Wharf A3
Magistrates Court A2
Midland Rd B3
Mill St C2
Moors Severn Terr A1
Museum of Royal Worcester C2
New Rd C1
New St B2
Northfield St A2
Odeon B2
Padmore St B3
Park St C3
Pheasant St B3
Pitchcroft Racecourse A1
Police Station A2
Portland St C2
Post Office B2
Quay St B2
Queen St B2
Rainbow Hill A3
Recreation Gd A2
Reindeer Court B2
Rogers Hill A3
Sabrina Rd A1
St Dunstan's Cr C3
St John's C1
St Martin's Gate B3
St Martin's Quarter B3
St Oswald's Rd A2
St Paul's St B3
St Swithin's Church B2
St Wulstans Cr C3
Sansome Walk A2
Severn St C2
Shambles,The B2
Shaw St B2
Shire Hall Crown Court A2
Shrub Hill B3
Shrub Hill Rd B3
Shrub Hill Ret Pk B3
Slingpool Walk C1
South Quay B2
Southfield St A2
Sports Ground A2/C1
Stanley Rd B3
Swan,The A1
Swimming Pool A2
Tallow Hill B3
Tennis Walk A2
Tolladine Rd B3
Tudor House B2
Tybridge St B1
Tything,The A2
Univ of Worcester B2
Vincent Rd B3
Vue C2
Washington St A3
Woolhope Rd C3
Worcester Bridge B2
Worcester County Cricket Ground C1
Worcester Royal Grammar School A2
Wylds La C3

York 126

Aldwark B2
Barbican Rd C3
Bar Convent Living Heritage Ctr C1
Barley Hall B2
Bishopgate St C2
Bishopthorpe Rd C2
Blossom St C1
Bootham A1
Bootham Cr A1
Bootham Terr A1
Bridge St B2
Brook St A2
Brownlow St A2
Burton Stone La A1
Castle Museum C2
Castlegate B2
Cemetery Rd C3
Cherry St C2
City Screen B2
City Wall A2/B1/C3
Clarence St A2
Clementhorpe C2
Clifford St B2
Clifford's Tower B2
Clifton A1
Coach park A2
Coney St B2
Coppergate Ctr B2
Cromwell Rd C2
Crown Court C2
Davygate B2
Deanery Gdns A2
DIG B2
Ebor Industrial Est B3
Fairfax House B2
Fishergate C3
Foss Islands Rd B3
Foss Islands Ret Pk B3
Fossbank A3
Garden St A2
George St C3
Gillygate A2
Goodramgate B2
Grand Opera Ho B2
Grosvenor Terr A1
Guildhall B2
Hallfield Rd A3
Heslington Rd C3
Heworth Green A3
Holy Trinity B2
Hope St C3
Huntington Rd A3
Information Ctr B2
James St B3
Jorvik Viking Centre B2
Kent St C3
Lawrence St C3
Layerthorpe A3
Leeman Rd B1
Lendal B2
Lendal Bridge B1
Library A2/B1
Longfield Terr A1
Lord Mayor's Walk A2
Lower Eldon St A2
Lowther St A2
Mansion House B2
Margaret St C3
Marygate A1
Melbourne St C3
Merchant Adventurers' Hall B2
Merchant Taylors' Hall B2
Micklegate B1
Micklegate Bar C1
Monkgate A2
Moss St C1
Museum Gdns B1
Museum St B1
National Railway Museum B1
Navigation Rd B3
Newton Terr C2
North Parade A1
North St B2
Nunnery La C1
Nunthorpe Rd C1
Ouse Bridge B2
Paragon St C3
Park Gr A3
Park St C1
Parliament St B2
Peasholme Green B3
Penley's Grove St A2
Piccadilly B2
Police Station B2
Post Office B1/B2/C3
Priory St B1
Purey Cust Nuffield Hospital,The A2
Queen Anne's Rd A1
Reel C1
Regimental Museum B2
Richard III Experience at Monk Bar A2
Roman Bath B2
Rowntree Park C2
St Andrewgate B2
St Benedict Rd C1
St John St A2
St Olave's Rd A1
St Peter's Gr A1
St Saviourgate B2
Scarcroft Hill C1
Scarcroft Rd C1
Shambles,The B2
Shopmobility B2
Skeldergate C2
Skeldergate Bridge C2
Station Rd B1
Stonebow,The B2
Stonegate B2
Superstore A3
Sycamore Terr A1
Terry Ave C2
Theatre Royal B2
Thorpe St C1
Toft Green B1
Tower St C2
Townend St A2
Treasurer's Ho A2
Trinity La B1
Undercroft Mus A2
Union Terr A2
Victor St C2
Vine St C2
Walmgate B3
War Memorial B1
Wellington St C3
York Art Gallery A1
York Barbican C3
York Brewery B1
York Dungeon, The B2

Index to road maps of Britain

How to use the index

Example **Thornton-le-Beans** N Yorks **58 G4**

- grid square
- page number
- county or unitary authority

Abbreviations used in the index

Aberdeen	**Aberdeen City**	Dumfries	**Dumfries and Galloway**
Aberds	**Aberdeenshire**	Dundee	**Dundee City**
Ald	**Alderney**	Durham	**Durham**
Anglesey	**Isle of Anglesey**	E Ayrs	**East Ayrshire**
Angus	**Angus**	E Dunb	**East Dunbartonshire**
Argyll	**Argyll and Bute**	E Loth	**East Lothian**
Bath	**Bath and North East Somerset**	E Renf	**East Renfrewshire**
Bedford	**Bedford**	E Sus	**East Sussex**
Bl Gwent	**Blaenau Gwent**	E Yorks	**East Riding of Yorkshire**
Blackburn	**Blackburn with Darwen**	Edin	**City of Edinburgh**
Blackpool	**Blackpool**	Essex	**Essex**
Bmouth	**Bournemouth**	Falk	**Falkirk**
Borders	**Scottish Borders**	Fife	**Fife**
Brack	**Bracknell**	Flint	**Flintshire**
Bridgend	**Bridgend**	Glasgow	**City of Glasgow**
Brighton	**City of Brighton and Hove**	Glos	**Gloucestershire**
Bristol	**City and County of Bristol**	Gtr Man	**Greater Manchester**
		Guern	**Guernsey**
Bucks	**Buckinghamshire**	Gwyn	**Gwynedd**
C Beds	**Central Bedfordshire**	Halton	**Halton**
Caerph	**Caerphilly**	Hants	**Hampshire**
Cambs	**Cambridgeshire**	Hereford	**Herefordshire**
Cardiff	**Cardiff**	Herts	**Hertfordshire**
Carms	**Carmarthenshire**	Highld	**Highland**
Ceredig	**Ceredigion**	Hrtlpl	**Hartlepool**
Ches E	**Cheshire East**	Hull	**Hull**
Ches W	**Cheshire West and Chester**	IoM	**Isle of Man**
Clack	**Clackmannanshire**	IoW	**Isle of Wight**
Conwy	**Conwy**	Invclyd	**Inverclyde**
Corn	**Cornwall**	Jersey	**Jersey**
Cumb	**Cumbria**	Kent	**Kent**
Darl	**Darlington**	Lancs	**Lancashire**
Denb	**Denbighshire**	Leicester	**City of Leicester**
Derby	**City of Derby**	Leics	**Leicestershire**
Derbys	**Derbyshire**	Lincs	**Lincolnshire**
Devon	**Devon**	London	**Greater London**
Dorset	**Dorset**	Luton	**Luton**
		M Keynes	**Milton Keynes**
		M Tydf	**Merthyr Tydfil**
Mbro	**Middlesbrough**	Poole	**Poole**
Medway	**Medway**	Powys	**Powys**
Mers	**Merseyside**	Ptsmth	**Portsmouth**
Midloth	**Midlothian**	Reading	**Reading**
Mon	**Monmouthshire**	Redcar	**Redcar and Cleveland**
Moray	**Moray**	Renfs	**Renfrewshire**
N Ayrs	**North Ayrshire**	Rhondda	**Rhondda Cynon Taff**
N Lincs	**North Lincolnshire**	Rutland	**Rutland**
N Lanark	**North Lanarkshire**	S Ayrs	**South Ayrshire**
N Som	**North Somerset**	S Glos	**South Gloucestershire**
N Yorks	**North Yorkshire**	S Lanark	**South Lanarkshire**
NE Lincs	**North East Lincolnshire**	S Yorks	**South Yorkshire**
Norf	**Norfolk**	Scilly	**Scilly**
Newport	**City and County of Newport**	Shetland	**Shetland**
Northants	**Northamptonshire**	Shrops	**Shropshire**
Northumb	**Northumberland**	Slough	**Slough**
Nottingham	**City of Nottingham**	Som	**Somerset**
Notts	**Nottinghamshire**	Soton	**Southampton**
Orkney	**Orkney**	Staffs	**Staffordshire**
Oxon	**Oxfordshire**	Stirling	**Stirling**
Pboro	**Peterborough**	Stockton	**Stockton-on-Tees**
Pembs	**Pembrokeshire**	Stoke	**Stoke-on-Trent**
Perth	**Perth and Kinross**	Suff	**Suffolk**
Plym	**Plymouth**	Sur	**Surrey**
Swansea	**Swansea**		
Swindon	**Swindon**		
T&W	**Tyne and Wear**		
Telford	**Telford and Wrekin**		
Thurrock	**Thurrock**		
Torbay	**Torbay**		
Torf	**Torfaen**		
V Glam	**The Vale of Glamorgan**		
W Berks	**West Berkshire**		
W Dunb	**West Dunbartonshire**		
W Isles	**Western Isles**		
W Loth	**West Lothian**		
W Mid	**West Midlands**		
W Sus	**West Sussex**		
W Yorks	**West Yorkshire**		
Warks	**Warwickshire**		
Warr	**Warrington**		
Wilts	**Wiltshire**		
Windsor	**Windsor and Maidenhead**		
Wokingham	**Wokingham**		
Worcs	**Worcestershire**		
Wrex	**Wrexham**		
York	**City of York**		

Austrey Warks 35 E8
Austwick N Yorks 50 C3
Authorpe Lincs 47 D8
Authorpe Row Lincs 47 E9
Avebury Wilts 17 E8
Aveley Thurrock 20 C2
Avening Glos 16 B5
Averham Notts 45 G11
Aveton Gifford Devon 5 G7
Avielochan Highld 81 B11
Aviemore Highld 81 B10
Avington Hants 10 A4
Avington W Berks 17 E10
Avoch Highld 87 F10
Avon Hants 9 E10
Avon Dassett Warks 27 D11
Avonbridge Falk 69 C8
Avonmouth Bristol 15 D11
Avonwick Devon 5 F8
Awbridge Hants 10 B2
Awhirk Dumfries 54 D3
Awkley S Glos 16 C2
Awliscombe Devon 7 F10
Awre Glos 26 H4
Awsworth Notts 35 A10
Axbridge Som 15 F10
Axford Hants 18 G3
Axford Wilts 17 D9
Axminster Devon 8 E1
Axmouth Devon 8 E1
Axton Flint 42 D4
Aycliff Kent 21 G10
Aycliffe Durham 58 D3
Aydon Northumb 62 G6
Aylburton Glos 16 A3
Ayle Northumb 57 B9
Aylesbeare Devon 7 G9
Aylesbury Bucks 28 G5
Aylesby NE Lincs 46 B6
Aylesford Kent 20 F4
Aylesham Kent 21 F9
Aylestone Leicester 36 E1
Aylmerton Norf 39 B7
Aylsham Norf 39 C7
Aylton Hereford 26 E3
Aymestrey Hereford 25 B11
Aynho Northants 28 E2
Ayot St Lawrence Herts 29 G8
Ayot St Peter Herts 29 G9
Ayr S Ayrs 66 D6
Aysgarth N Yorks 58 H1
Ayside Cumb 49 A3
Ayston Rutland 36 E4
Aythorpe Roding Essex 30 G2
Ayton Borders 71 D8
Aywick Shetland 96 E7
Azerley N Yorks 51 B8

B

Babbacombe Torbay 5 E10
Babbinswood Shrops 33 B9
Babcary Som 8 B4
Babel Carms 24 E5
Babell Flint 42 E4
Babraham Cambs 30 C2
Babworth Notts 45 D10
Bac W Isles 91 C9
Bachau Anglesey 40 B6
Back of Keppoch Highld 79 C9
Back Rogerton E Ayrs 67 D8
Backaland Orkney 95 E6
Backaskaill Orkney 95 C5
Backbarrow Cumb 49 A3
Backe Carms 23 E7
Backfolds Aberds 89 C10
Backford Ches W 43 E7
Backford Cross Ches W 43 E6
Backhill Aberds 89 E10
Backhill Aberds 89 E7
Backhill of Clackriach Aberds 89 D9
Backhill of Fortree Aberds 89 D9
Backhill of Trustach Aberds 83 D8
Backies Highld 93 J11
Backlass Highld 94 E4
Backwell N Som 15 E10
Backworth T&W 63 F9
Bacon End Essex 30 G3
Baconsthorpe Norf 39 B7
Bacton Hereford 25 E10
Bacton Norf 39 B9
Bacton Suff 31 B7
Bacton Green Suff 31 B7
Bacup Lancs 50 G4
Badachro Highld 85 A12
Badanloch Lodge Highld 93 F10
Badavanich Highld 86 F4
Badbury Swindon 17 C8
Badby Northants 28 C2
Badcall Highld 92 D5
Badcaul Highld 86 B3
Baddeley Green Stoke 44 G3
Baddesley Clinton Warks 27 A9
Baddesley Ensor Warks 35 F8
Baddidarach Highld 92 G3
Baddoch Aberds 82 E3
Baddock Highld 87 F10
Badenscoth Aberds 89 E7
Badenyon Aberds 82 B5
Badger Shrops 34 F3
Badger's Mount Kent 19 E11
Badgeworth Glos 26 G6
Badgworth Som 15 F9
Badicaul Highld 85 F12
Badingham Suff 31 B10
Badlesmere Kent 21 F7
Badlipster Highld 94 F4
Badluarach Highld 86 B2
Badminton S Glos 16 C5
Badnaban Highld 92 G3
Badninish Highld 87 B10
Badrallach Highld 86 B3
Badsey Worcs 27 D7
Badshot Lea Sur 18 G5
Badsworth W Yorks 45 A8
Badwell Ash Suff 30 B6
Bae Colwyn = Colwyn Bay Conwy 41 C10
Bag Enderby Lincs 47 E7
Bagby N Yorks 51 A10
Bagendon Glos 27 H7
Bagh a Chaisteil = Castlebay W Isles 84 J1
Bagh Mor W Isles 84 C3
Bagh Shiarabhagh W Isles 84 H2
Baghasdal W Isles 84 G2
Bagillt Flint 42 E5
Baginton Warks 27 A10
Baglan Neath 14 B3
Bagley Shrops 33 C10
Bagnall Staffs 44 G3
Bagnor W Berks 17 E11
Bagshot Sur 18 E6
Bagshot Wilts 17 E10
Bagthorpe Norf 38 B3
Bagthorpe Notts 45 G8
Bagworth Leics 35 E10
Bagwy Llydiart Hereford 25 F11
Bail àrd Bhuirgh W Isles 91 B9
Bail' lochdrach W Isles 84 C3
Bail Uachdraich W Isles 84 B3
Bail' Ur Tholastaidh W Isles 91 C10
Baildon W Yorks 51 F7
Baile W Isles 90 J4
Baile a Mhanaich W Isles 84 C2
Baile Ailein W Isles 91 E7
Baile an Truiseil W Isles 91 B8
Baile Boidheach Argyll 72 F6
Baile Glas W Isles 84 C3
Baile Mhartainn W Isles 84 A2
Baile Mhic Phail W Isles 84 A3
Baile Mor Argyll 78 J5
Baile Mor W Isles 84 B2
Baile na Creige W Isles 84 H1
Baile nan Cailleach W Isles 84 C2
Baile Raghaill W Isles 84 A2
Bailebeag Highld 81 B7
Baileyhead Cumb 61 F11
Bailiesward Aberds 88 E4
Baillieston Glasgow 68 D5
Bainbridge N Yorks 57 G11
Bainsford Falk 69 B7
Bainshole Aberds 88 E6
Bainton E Yorks 52 D5
Bainton Pboro 37 E6
Bairnkine Borders 62 B2
Baker Street Thurrock 20 C3
Baker's End Herts 29 G10
Bakewell Derbys 44 F6
Bala = Y Bala Gwyn 32 B5
Balachuirn Highld 85 D10
Balavil Highld 81 C9
Balbeg Highld 81 A6
Balbeg Highld 86 H7
Balbeggie Perth 76 E4
Balbithan Aberds 83 B9
Balbithan Ho. Aberds 83 B10
Balblair Highld 87 B8
Balblair Highld 87 E10
Balby S Yorks 45 B9
Balchladich Highld 92 F3
Balchraggan Highld 87 G8
Balchraggan Highld 87 H8
Balchrick Highld 92 D4
Balchrystie Fife 77 G7
Balcladaich Highld 80 A4
Balcombe W Sus 12 C2
Balcombe Lane W Sus 12 C2
Balcomie Fife 77 F9
Balcurvie Fife 76 G6
Baldersby N Yorks 51 B9
Baldersby St James N Yorks 51 B9
Balderstone Lancs 50 F2
Balderton Ches W 42 F6
Balderton Notts 46 G2
Baldhu Corn 3 E6
Baldinnie Fife 77 F7
Baldock Herts 29 E9
Baldovie Dundee 77 D7
Baldrine IoM 48 D4
Baldslow E Sus 13 E6
Baldwin IoM 48 D3
Baldwinholme Cumb 56 A5
Baldwin's Gate Staffs 34 A3
Bale Norf 38 B6
Balearn Aberds 89 C10
Balemartine Argyll 78 G2
Balephuil Argyll 78 G2
Balerno Edin 69 D10
Balevullin Argyll 78 G2
Balfield Angus 83 G7
Balfour Orkney 95 G5
Balfron Stirling 68 B4
Balfron Station Stirling 68 B4
Balgaveny Aberds 89 D6
Balgavies Angus 77 B8
Balgonar Fife 69 A9
Balgove Aberds 89 E8
Balgowan Highld 81 D8
Balgown Highld 85 B8
Balgrochan E Dunb 68 C5
Balgy Highld 85 C13
Balhaldie Stirling 75 G11
Balhalgardy Aberds 83 A9
Balham London 19 D9
Balhary Perth 76 C5
Baliasta Shetland 96 C8
Baligill Highld 93 C11
Balintore Angus 76 B5
Balintore Highld 87 D11
Balintraid Highld 87 D10
Balk N Yorks 51 A10
Balkeerie Angus 76 C6
Balkemback Angus 76 D6
Balkholme E Yorks 52 G3
Balkissock S Ayrs 54 A4
Ball Shrops 33 C9
Ball Haye Green Staffs 44 G3
Ball Hill Hants 17 E11
Ballabeg IoM 48 E2
Ballacannel IoM 48 D4
Ballachulish Highld 74 B3
Ballajora IoM 48 C4
Ballaleigh IoM 48 D3
Ballamodha IoM 48 E2
Ballantrae S Ayrs 54 A3
Ballaquine IoM 48 D4
Ballards Gore Essex 20 B6
Ballasalla IoM 48 C3
Ballasalla IoM 48 E2
Ballater Aberds 82 D5
Ballaugh IoM 48 C3
Ballaveare IoM 48 E3
Ballcorach Moray 82 A3
Ballechin Perth 76 B2
Balleigh Highld 87 C10
Ballencrieff E Loth 70 C3
Ballentoul Perth 81 G10
Ballidon Derbys 44 G6
Balliemore Argyll 73 E9
Balliemore Argyll 79 J11
Ballikinrain Stirling 68 B4
Ballimeanoch Argyll 73 B9
Ballimore Argyll 73 E8
Ballimore Stirling 75 F8
Ballinaby Argyll 64 B3
Ballindean Perth 76 E5
Ballingdon Suff 30 D5
Ballinger Common Bucks 18 A6
Ballingham Hereford 26 E2
Ballingry Fife 76 H4
Ballinlick Perth 76 C2
Ballinluig Perth 76 B2
Ballintuim Perth 76 B4
Balloch Angus 76 B6
Balloch Highld 87 G10
Balloch N Lanark 68 C6
Balloch W Dunb 68 B2
Ballochan Aberds 83 D7
Ballochford Moray 88 E3
Ballochmorrie S Ayrs 54 A5
Balls Cross W Sus 11 B8
Balls Green Essex 31 F7
Ballygown Argyll 78 G7
Ballygrant Argyll 64 B4
Ballyhaugh Argyll 78 F4
Balmacara Highld 85 F13
Balmacara Square Highld 85 F13
Balmaclellan Dumfries 55 B9
Balmacneil Perth 76 B2
Balmacqueen Highld 85 A9
Balmae Dumfries 55 E9
Balmaha Stirling 68 A3
Balmalcolm Fife 76 G6
Balmeanach Highld 85 D10
Balmedie Aberds 83 B11
Balmer Heath Shrops 33 B10
Balmerino Fife 76 E6
Balmerlawn Hants 10 D2
Balmichael N Ayrs 66 C2
Balmirmer Angus 77 D8
Balmore Highld 85 D7
Balmore Highld 86 H6
Balmore Highld 87 G11
Balmore Perth 76 B2
Balmule Fife 69 B11
Balmullo Fife 77 E7
Balmungie Highld 87 F10
Balnaboth Angus 82 G5
Balnabruaich Highld 87 E10
Balnabruich Highld 94 H3
Balnacoil Highld 93 H11
Balnacra Highld 86 G2
Balnafoich Highld 87 H9
Balnagall Highld 87 C11
Balnaguard Perth 76 B2
Balnahard Argyll 72 D3
Balnahard Argyll 78 H7
Balnain Highld 86 H7
Balnakeil Highld 92 C6
Balnaknock Highld 85 B9
Balnapaling Highld 87 E10
Balne N Yorks 52 H1
Balochroy Argyll 65 C8
Balone Fife 77 F7
Balornock Glasgow 68 D5
Balquharn Perth 76 D3
Balquhidder Stirling 75 E8
Balsall W Mid 35 H8
Balsall Common W Mid 35 H8
Balsall Hth. W Mid 35 G6
Balscott Oxon 27 D10
Balsham Cambs 30 C2
Baltasound Shetland 96 C8
Balterley Staffs 43 G10
Baltersan Dumfries 55 C7
Balthangie Aberds 89 C8
Baltonsborough Som 8 A4
Balvaird Highld 87 F8
Balvicar Argyll 72 B6
Balvraid Highld 85 G13
Balvraid Highld 87 H11
Bamber Bridge Lancs 50 G1
Bambers Green Essex 30 F2
Bamburgh Northumb 71 G10
Bamff Perth 76 B5
Bamford Derbys 44 D6
Bamford Gtr Man 44 A2
Bampton Cumb 57 E7
Bampton Devon 7 D8
Bampton Oxon 17 A10
Bampton Grange Cumb 57 E7
Banavie Highld 80 F3
Banbury Oxon 27 D11
Bancffosfelen Carms 23 E9
Banchory Aberds 83 D8
Banchory-Devenick Aberds 83 C11
Bancycapel Carms 23 E9
Bancyfelin Carms 23 E8
Bancyffordd Carms 23 C9
Bandirran Perth 76 D5
Banff Aberds 89 B6
Bangor Gwyn 41 C7
Bangor-is-y-coed Wrex 43 H6
Banham Norf 39 G6
Bank Hants 10 D1
Bank Newton N Yorks 50 D5
Bank Street Worcs 26 B3
Bankend Dumfries 60 G6
Bankfoot Perth 76 D3
Bankglen E Ayrs 67 E9
Bankhead Aberdeen 83 B10
Bankhead Aberds 83 C8
Banknock Falk 68 C6
Banks Cumb 61 G11
Banks Lancs 49 G3
Bankshill Dumfries 61 E7
Banningham Norf 39 C8
Banniskirk Ho. Highld 94 E3
Bannister Green Essex 30 F3
Bannockburn Stirling 69 A7
Banstead Sur 19 F9
Bantham Devon 5 G7
Banton N Lanark 68 C6
Banwell N Som 15 F9
Banyard's Green Suff 31 A9
Bapchild Kent 20 E6
Bar Hill Cambs 29 B10
Barabhas W Isles 91 C8
Barabhas Iarach W Isles 91 C8
Barabhas Uarach W Isles 91 B8
Barachandroman Argyll 79 J9
Barassie S Ayrs 66 C6
Baravullin Argyll 79 H11
Barbaraville Highld 87 D10
Barber Booth Derbys 44 D5
Barbieston S Ayrs 67 E7
Barbon Cumb 50 A2
Barbridge Ches E 43 G9
Barbrook Devon 6 B6
Barby Northants 28 A2
Barcaldine Argyll 74 C2
Barcheston Warks 27 E9
Barcombe E Sus 12 E3
Barcombe Cross E Sus 12 E3
Barden N Yorks 58 G2
Barden Scale N Yorks 51 D6
Bardennoch Dumfries 67 G8
Bardfield Saling Essex 30 F3
Bardister Shetland 96 F5
Bardney Lincs 46 F5
Bardon Leics 35 D10
Bardon Mill Northumb 62 G3
Bardowie E Dunb 68 C4
Bardrainney Invclyd 68 C2
Bardsea Cumb 49 B3
Bardsey W Yorks 51 E9
Bardwell Suff 30 A6
Bare Lancs 49 C4
Barfad Argyll 73 G7
Barford Norf 39 E7
Barford Warks 27 B9
Barford St John Oxon 27 E11
Barford St Martin Wilts 9 A9
Barford St Michael Oxon 27 E11
Barfrestone Kent 21 F9
Bargod = Bargoed Caerph 15 B7
Bargoed = Bargod Caerph 15 B7
Bargrennan Dumfries 54 B6
Barham Cambs 37 H7
Barham Kent 21 F9
Barham Suff 31 C8
Barharrow Dumfries 55 D9
Barhill Dumfries 55 C11
Barholm Lincs 37 D6
Barkby Leics 36 E2
Barkestone-le-Vale Leics 36 B3
Barkham Wokingham 18 E4
Barking London 19 C11
Barking Suff 31 C7
Barking Tye Suff 31 C7
Barkingside London 19 C11
Barkisland W Yorks 51 H6
Barkston Lincs 36 A5
Barkston N Yorks 51 F10
Barkway Herts 29 E10
Barlaston Staffs 34 B4
Barlavington W Sus 11 C8
Barlborough Derbys 45 E8
Barlby N Yorks 52 F2
Barlestone Leics 35 E10
Barley Herts 29 E10
Barley Lancs 50 E4
Barley Mow T&W 58 A3
Barleythorpe Rutland 36 E4
Barling Essex 20 C6
Barlow Derbys 45 E7
Barlow N Yorks 52 G2
Barlow T&W 63 G7
Barmby Moor E Yorks 52 E3
Barmby on the Marsh E Yorks 52 G2
Barmer Norf 38 B4
Barmoor Castle Northumb 71 G8
Barmoor Lane End Northumb 71 G9
Barmouth = Abermaw Gwyn 32 D2
Barmpton Darl 58 E4
Barmston E Yorks 53 D7
Barnack Pboro 37 E6
Barnacle Warks 35 G9
Barnard Castle Durham 58 E1
Barnard Gate Oxon 27 G11
Barnardiston Suff 30 D4
Barnbarroch Dumfries 55 D11
Barnburgh S Yorks 45 B8
Barnby Suff 39 G10
Barnby Dun S Yorks 45 B10
Barnby in the Willows Notts 46 G2
Barnby Moor Notts 45 D10
Barnes Street Kent 20 G3
Barnet London 19 B9
Barnetby le Wold N Lincs 46 B4
Barney Norf 38 B5
Barnham Suff 38 H4
Barnham W Sus 11 D8
Barnham Broom Norf 39 E6
Barnhead Angus 77 B9
Barnhill Ches W 43 G7
Barnhill Dundee 77 D7
Barnhill Moray 88 C1
Barnhills Dumfries 54 B2
Barningham Durham 58 E1
Barningham Suff 38 H5
Barnoldby le Beck NE Lincs 46 B6
Barnoldswick Lancs 50 E4
Barns Green W Sus 11 B10
Barnsley Glos 27 H7
Barnsley S Yorks 45 B7
Barnstaple Devon 6 C4
Barnston Essex 30 G3
Barnston Mers 42 D5
Barnstone Notts 36 B3
Barnt Green Worcs 27 A7
Barnton Ches W 43 E9
Barnton Edin 69 C10
Barnwell All Saints Northants 36 G6
Barnwell St Andrew Northants 36 G6
Barnwood Glos 26 G5
Barochreal Argyll 79 J11
Barons Cross Hereford 25 C11
Barr S Ayrs 66 G5
Barra Castle Aberds 83 A9
Barrachan Dumfries 54 E6
Barrack Aberds 89 D8
Barraglom W Isles 90 D6
Barrahormid Argyll 72 E6
Barran Argyll 79 J11
Barrapol Argyll 78 G2
Barras Aberds 83 E10
Barras Cumb 57 E10
Barrasford Northumb 62 F5
Barravullin Argyll 73 C7
Barregarrow IoM 48 D3
Barrhead E Renf 68 E3
Barrhill S Ayrs 54 A5
Barrington Cambs 29 D10
Barrington Som 8 C2
Barripper Corn 2 F5
Barrmill N Ayrs 67 A6
Barrock Highld 94 C4
Barrock Ho. Highld 94 D4
Barrow Lancs 50 F3
Barrow Rutland 36 D4
Barrow Suff 30 B4
Barrow Green Kent 20 E6
Barrow Gurney N Som 15 E11
Barrow Haven N Lincs 53 G6
Barrow-in-Furness Cumb 49 C2
Barrow Island Cumb 49 C1
Barrow Nook Lancs 43 B7
Barrow Street Wilts 9 A7
Barrow upon Humber N Lincs 53 G6
Barrow upon Soar Leics 36 D1
Barrow upon Trent Derbys 35 C9
Barroway Drove Norf 38 E1
Barrowburn Northumb 62 B4
Barrowby Lincs 36 B4
Barrowcliff N Yorks 59 H11
Barrowden Rutland 36 E5
Barrowford Lancs 50 F4
Barrows Green Ches E 43 G9
Barrows Green Cumb 57 H7
Barrow's Green Mers 43 D8
Barry Angus 77 D8
Barry = Y Barri V Glam 15 E7
Barry Island V Glam 15 E7
Barsby Leics 36 D2
Barsham Suff 39 G9
Barston W Mid 35 H8
Bartestree Hereford 26 D2
Barthol Chapel Aberds 89 E8
Barthomley Ches E 43 G10
Bartley Hants 10 C2
Bartley Green W Mid 34 G6
Bartlow Cambs 30 D2
Barton Cambs 29 C11
Barton Ches W 43 G7
Barton Glos 27 F8
Barton Lancs 42 B6
Barton Lancs 49 F5
Barton N Yorks 58 F3
Barton Oxon 28 H2
Barton Torbay 5 E10
Barton Warks 27 C8
Barton Bendish Norf 38 E3
Barton Hartshorn Bucks 28 E3
Barton in Fabis Notts 35 B11
Barton in the Beans Leics 35 E9
Barton-le-Clay C Beds 29 E7
Barton-le-Street N Yorks 52 B3
Barton-le-Willows N Yorks 52 C3
Barton Mills Suff 30 A4
Barton on Sea Hants 9 E11
Barton on the Heath Warks 27 E9
Barton St David Som 8 A4
Barton Seagrave Northants 36 H4
Barton Stacey Hants 17 G11
Barton Turf Norf 39 C9
Barton-under-Needwood Staffs 35 D7
Barton-upon-Humber N Lincs 52 G6
Barton Waterside N Lincs 52 G6
Barugh S Yorks 45 B7
Barway Cambs 37 H11
Barwell Leics 35 F10
Barwick Herts 29 G10
Barwick Som 8 C4
Barwick in Elmet W Yorks 51 F9
Baschurch Shrops 33 C10
Bascote Warks 27 B11
Basford Green Staffs 44 G3
Bashall Eaves Lancs 50 E2
Bashley Hants 9 E11
Basildon Essex 20 C4
Basingstoke Hants 18 F3
Baslow Derbys 44 E6
Bason Bridge Som 15 G9
Bassaleg Newport 15 C8
Bassenthwaite Cumb 56 C4
Bassett Soton 10 C3
Bassingbourn Cambs 29 D10
Bassingfield Notts 36 B2
Bassingham Lincs 46 F3
Bassingthorpe Lincs 36 C5
Basta Shetland 96 D7
Baston Lincs 37 D7
Bastwick Norf 39 D10
Baswick Steer E Yorks 53 E6
Batchworth Heath Herts 19 B7
Batcombe Dorset 8 D5
Batcombe Som 16 H3
Bate Heath Ches E 43 E9
Batford Herts 29 G8
Bath Bath 16 E4
Bathampton Bath 16 E4
Bathealton Som 7 D9
Batheaston Bath 16 E4
Bathford Bath 16 E4
Bathgate W Loth 69 D8
Bathley Notts 45 G11
Bathpool Corn 4 D3
Bathpool Som 8 B1
Bathville W Loth 69 D8
Batley W Yorks 51 G8
Batsford Glos 27 E8
Battersby N Yorks 59 F6
Battersea London 19 D9
Battisborough Cross Devon 5 G6
Battisford Suff 31 C7
Battisford Tye Suff 31 C7
Battle E Sus 12 E6
Battle Powys 25 E7
Battledown Glos 26 F6
Battlefield Shrops 33 D11
Battlesbridge Essex 20 B4
Battlesden C Beds 28 F6
Battlesea Green Suff 39 H8
Battleton Som 7 D8
Battram Leics 35 E10
Battramsley Hants 10 E2
Baughton Worcs 26 D5
Baughurst Hants 18 F2
Baulking Oxon 17 B10
Baumber Lincs 46 E6
Baunton Glos 17 A7
Baverstock Wilts 9 A9
Bawburgh Norf 39 E7
Bawdeswell Norf 38 C6
Bawdrip Som 15 H9
Bawdsey Suff 31 D10
Bawtry S Yorks 45 C10
Baxenden Lancs 50 G3
Baxterley Warks 35 F8
Baybridge Hants 10 B4
Baycliff Cumb 49 B2
Baydon Wilts 17 D9
Bayford Herts 29 H10
Bayford Som 8 B6
Bayles Cumb 57 B9
Baylham Suff 31 C8
Baynard's Green Oxon 28 F2
Bayston Hill Shrops 33 E10
Baythorn End Essex 30 D4
Bayton Worcs 26 A3
Beach Highld 79 F10
Beachampton Bucks 28 E4
Beachamwell Norf 38 E3
Beachans Moray 87 G13
Beacharr Argyll 65 D7
Beachborough Kent 21 H8
Beachley Glos 16 B2
Beacon Devon 7 F10
Beacon End Essex 30 F6
Beacon Hill Sur 18 H5
Beacon's Bottom Bucks 18 B4
Beaconsfield Bucks 18 C6
Beacrabhaic W Isles 90 H6
Beadlam N Yorks 52 A2
Beadlow C Beds 29 E8
Beadnell Northumb 71 H11
Beaford Devon 6 E4
Beal N Yorks 51 G11
Beal Northumb 71 F9
Beamhurst Staffs 35 B6
Beaminster Dorset 8 D3
Beamish Durham 58 A3
Beamsley N Yorks 51 D6
Bean Kent 20 D2
Beanacre Wilts 16 E6
Beanley Northumb 62 B6
Beaquoy Orkney 95 F4
Bear Cross Bmouth 9 E9
Beardwood Blackburn 50 G2
Beare Green Sur 19 G8
Bearley Warks 27 B8
Bearnus Argyll 78 G6
Bearpark Durham 58 B3
Bearsbridge Northumb 62 H3
Bearsden E Dunb 68 C4
Bearsted Kent 20 F4
Bearstone Shrops 34 B3
Bearwood Hereford 25 C10
Bearwood Poole 9 E9
Bearwood W Mid 34 G6
Beattock Dumfries 60 C6
Beauchamp Roding Essex 30 G2
Beauchief S Yorks 45 D7
Beaufort Bl Gwent 25 G8
Beaufort Castle Highld 87 G8
Beaulieu Hants 10 D2
Beauly Highld 87 G8
Beaumaris Anglesey 41 C8
Beaumont Cumb 61 H9
Beaumont Essex 31 F8
Beaumont Hill Darl 58 E3
Beausale Warks 27 A9
Beauworth Hants 10 B4
Beaworthy Devon 6 G3
Beazley End Essex 30 F4
Bebington Mers 42 D6
Bebside Northumb 63 E8
Beccles Suff 39 F10
Becconsall Lancs 49 G4
Beck Foot Cumb 57 G8
Beck Hole N Yorks 59 F9
Beck Row Suff 38 H2
Beck Side Cumb 49 A2
Beckbury Shrops 34 E3
Beckenham London 19 E10
Beckermet Cumb 56 F2
Beckfoot Cumb 56 B2
Beckfoot Cumb 56 F3
Beckford Worcs 26 E6
Beckhampton Wilts 17 E7
Beckingham Lincs 46 G2
Beckingham Notts 45 D11
Beckington Som 16 F5
Beckley E Sus 13 D7
Beckley Hants 9 E11
Beckley Oxon 28 G2
Beckton London 19 C11
Beckwithshaw N Yorks 51 D8
Becontree London 19 C11
Bed-y-coedwr Gwyn 32 C3
Bedale N Yorks 58 H3
Bedburn Durham 58 C2
Bedchester Dorset 9 C7
Beddau Rhondda 14 C6
Beddgelert Gwyn 41 F7
Beddingham E Sus 12 F3
Beddington London 19 E10
Bedfield Suff 31 B9
Bedford Bedford 29 C7
Bedham W Sus 11 B9
Bedhampton Hants 10 D6
Bedingfield Suff 31 B8
Bedlam N Yorks 51 C8
Bedlington Northumb 63 E8
Bedlington Station Northumb 63 E8
Bedlinog M Tydf 14 A6
Bedminster Bristol 16 D2
Bedmond Herts 19 A7
Bednall Staffs 34 D5
Bedrule Borders 62 B2
Bedstone Shrops 33 H9
Bedwas Caerph 15 C7
Bedworth Warks 35 G9
Bedworth Heath Warks 35 G9
Beeby Leics 36 E2
Beech Hants 18 H3
Beech Staffs 34 B4
Beech Hill Gtr Man 43 B8
Beech Hill W Berks 18 E3
Beechingstoke Wilts 17 F7
Beedon W Berks 17 D11
Beeford E Yorks 53 D7
Beeley Derbys 44 F6
Beelsby NE Lincs 46 B6
Beenham W Berks 18 E2
Beeny Corn 4 B2
Beer Devon 7 H11
Beer Hackett Dorset 8 C4
Beercrocombe Som 8 B2
Beesands Devon 5 G9
Beesby Lincs 47 D8
Beeson Devon 5 G9
Beeston C Beds 29 D8
Beeston Ches W 43 G8
Beeston Norf 38 D5
Beeston Notts 35 B11
Beeston W Yorks 51 F8
Beeston Regis Norf 39 A7
Beeswing Dumfries 55 C11
Beetham Cumb 49 B4
Beetley Norf 38 D5
Begbroke Oxon 27 G11
Begelly Pembs 22 F6
Beggar's Bush Powys 25 B9
Beguildy Powys 33 H7
Beighton Norf 39 E9
Beighton S Yorks 45 D8
Beighton Hill Derbys 44 G6
Beith N Ayrs 66 A6
Bekesbourne Kent 21 F8
Belaugh Norf 39 D8
Belbroughton Worcs 34 H5
Belchamp Otten Essex 30 D5
Belchamp St Paul Essex 30 D4
Belchamp Walter Essex 30 D5
Belchford Lincs 46 E6
Belford Northumb 71 G10
Belhaven E Loth 70 C5
Belhelvie Aberds 83 B11
Belhinnie Aberds 82 A6
Bell Bar Herts 29 H9
Bell Busk N Yorks 50 D5
Bell End Worcs 34 H5
Bell o' th' Hill Ches W 43 H8
Bellabeg Aberds 82 B5
Bellamore S Ayrs 66 H5
Bellanoch Argyll 72 D6
Bellaty Angus 76 B5
Belleau Lincs 47 E8
Bellehiglash Moray 88 E1
Bellerby N Yorks 58 G2
Bellever Devon 5 D7
Belliehill Angus 77 A8
Bellingdon Bucks 28 H6
Bellingham Northumb 62 E4
Belloch Argyll 65 E7
Bellochantuy Argyll 65 E7
Bells Yew Green E Sus 12 C5
Bellsbank E Ayrs 67 F7
Bellshill N Lanark 68 D6
Bellshill Northumb 71 G10
Bellspool Borders 69 G10
Bellsquarry W Loth 69 D9
Belmaduthy Highld 87 F9
Belmesthorpe Rutland 36 D6
Belmont Blackburn 50 H2
Belmont London 19 E9
Belmont S Ayrs 66 D6
Belmont Shetland 96 C7
Belnacraig Aberds 82 B5
Belowda Corn 3 C8
Belper Derbys 45 H7
Belper Lane End Derbys 45 H7
Belsay Northumb 63 F7
Belses Borders 70 H4
Belsford Devon 5 F8
Belstead Suff 31 D8
Belston S Ayrs 67 D6
Belstone Devon 6 G5
Belthorn Blackburn 50 G3
Beltinge Kent 21 E8
Beltoft N Lincs 46 B2
Belton Leics 35 C10
Belton Lincs 36 B5
Belton N Lincs 45 B11
Belton Norf 39 E10
Belton in Rutland Rutland 36 E4
Beltring Kent 20 G3
Belts of Collonach Aberds 83 D8
Belvedere London 19 D11
Belvoir Leics 36 B4
Bembridge IoW 10 F5
Bemersyde Borders 70 G4
Bemerton Wilts 9 A10
Bempton E Yorks 53 B7
Ben Alder Lodge Highld 81 F7
Ben Armine Lodge Highld 93 H10
Ben Casgro W Isles 91 E9
Benacre Suff 39 G11
Benbuie Dumfries 60 D3
Benderloch Argyll 74 D2
Bendronaig Lodge Highld 86 H3
Benenden Kent 13 C7
Benfield Dumfries 54 C6
Bengate Norf 39 C9
Bengeworth Worcs 27 D7
Benhall Green Suff 31 B10
Benhall Street Suff 31 B10
Benholm Aberds 83 G10
Beningbrough N Yorks 51 D11
Benington Herts 29 F9
Benington Lincs 47 H7
Benllech Anglesey 41 B7
Benmore Argyll 73 E10
Benmore Stirling 75 E7
Benmore Lodge Highld 92 H6
Bennacott Corn 6 G1
Bennan N Ayrs 66 D2
Benniworth Lincs 46 D6
Benover Kent 20 G4
Bensham T&W 63 G8
Benslie N Ayrs 66 B6
Benson Oxon 18 B3
Bent Aberds 83 F8
Bent Gate Lancs 50 G3
Benthall Northumb 71 H11
Benthall Shrops 34 E2
Bentham Glos 26 G6
Benthoul Aberdeen 83 C10
Bentlawnt Shrops 33 E9
Bentley E Yorks 52 F6
Bentley Hants 18 G4
Bentley S Yorks 45 B9
Bentley Suff 31 E8
Bentley Warks 35 F8
Bentley Worcs 26 B6
Bentley Heath W Mid 35 H7
Benton Devon 6 C5
Bentpath Dumfries 61 D9
Bents W Loth 69 D8
Bentworth Hants 18 G3
Benvie Dundee 76 D6
Benwick Cambs 37 F9
Beoley Worcs 27 B7
Beoraidbeg Highld 79 B9
Bepton W Sus 11 C7
Berden Essex 29 F11
Bere Alston Devon 4 E5
Bere Ferrers Devon 4 E5
Bere Regis Dorset 9 E7
Berepper Corn 2 G5
Bergh Apton Norf 39 E9
Berinsfield Oxon 18 B2
Berkeley Glos 16 B3
Berkhamsted Herts 28 H6
Berkley Som 16 G5
Berkswell W Mid 35 H8
Bermondsey London 19 D10
Bernera Highld 85 F13
Bernice Argyll 73 D10
Bernisdale Highld 85 C9
Berrick Salome Oxon 18 B3
Berriedale Highld 94 H3
Berrier Cumb 56 D5
Berriew Powys 33 E7
Berrington Northumb 71 F9
Berrington Shrops 33 E11
Berrow Som 15 F9
Berrow Green Worcs 26 C4
Berry Down Cross Devon 6 B4
Berry Hill Glos 26 G2
Berry Hill Pembs 22 B5
Berry Pomeroy Devon 5 E9
Berryhillock Moray 88 B5
Berrynarbor Devon 6 B4
Bersham Wrex 42 H6
Berstane Orkney 95 G5
Berwick E Sus 12 F4
Berwick Bassett Wilts 17 D7
Berwick Hill Northumb 63 F7
Berwick St James Wilts 17 H7
Berwick St John Wilts 9 B8
Berwick St Leonard Wilts 9 A8
Berwick-upon-Tweed Northumb 71 E8
Bescar Lancs 43 A6
Besford Worcs 26 D6
Bessacarr S Yorks 45 B10
Bessels Leigh Oxon 17 A11
Bessingby E Yorks 53 C7
Bessingham Norf 39 B7
Bestbeech Hill E Sus 12 C5
Besthorpe Norf 39 F6
Besthorpe Notts 46 F2
Bestwood Nottingham 36 A1
Bestwood Village Notts 45 H9
Beswick E Yorks 52 E6
Betchworth Sur 19 G9
Bethania Ceredig 24 B2
Bethania Gwyn 41 E8
Bethania Gwyn 41 F9
Bethel Anglesey 40 C5
Bethel Gwyn 32 B5
Bethel Gwyn 41 D7
Bethersden Kent 13 B8
Bethesda Gwyn 41 D8
Bethesda Pembs 22 E5
Bethlehem Carms 24 F3
Bethnal Green London 19 C10
Betley Staffs 43 H10
Betsham Kent 20 D3
Betteshanger Kent 21 F10
Bettiscombe Dorset 8 E2
Bettisfield Wrex 33 B10
Betton Shrops 33 E9
Betton Shrops 34 B2
Bettws Bridgend 14 C5
Bettws Mon 25 G9
Bettws Newport 15 B8
Bettws Cedewain Powys 33 F7
Bettws Gwerfil Goch Denb 42 H3
Bettws Ifan Ceredig 23 B8
Bettws Newydd Mon 25 H10
Bettws-y-crwyn Shrops 33 G8
Bettyhill Highld 93 C10
Betws Carms 24 G3
Betws Bledrws Ceredig 23 A10
Betws-Garmon Gwyn 41 E7
Betws-y-Coed Conwy 41 E9
Betws-yn-Rhos Conwy 42 E2
Beulah Ceredig 23 B7
Beulah Powys 24 C6
Bevendean Brighton 12 F2
Bevercotes Notts 45 E10
Beverley E Yorks 52 F6
Beverston Glos 16 B5
Bevington Glos 16 B3
Bewaldeth Cumb 56 C4
Bewcastle Cumb 61 F11
Bewdley Worcs 34 H3
Bewerley N Yorks 51 C7
Bewholme E Yorks 53 D7
Bexhill E Sus 12 F6
Bexley London 19 D11
Bexleyheath London 19 D11
Bexwell Norf 38 E2
Beyton Suff 30 B6
Bhaltos W Isles 90 D5
Bhatarsaigh W Isles 84 J1
Bibury Glos 27 H8
Bicester Oxon 28 F2
Bickenhall Som 8 C1
Bickenhill W Mid 35 G7
Bicker Lincs 37 B8
Bickershaw Gtr Man 43 B9
Bickerstaffe Lancs 43 B7
Bickerton Ches E 43 G8
Bickerton N Yorks 51 D10
Bickington Devon 5 D8
Bickington Devon 6 C4
Bickleigh Devon 4 E6
Bickleigh Devon 7 F8
Bickleton Devon 6 C4
Bickley London 19 E11
Bickley Moss Ches W 43 H8
Bicknacre Essex 20 A4
Bicknoller Som 7 C10
Bicknor Kent 20 F5
Bickton Hants 9 C10
Bicton Shrops 33 D10
Bicton Shrops 33 G8
Bidborough Kent 12 B4
Biddenden Kent 13 C7
Biddenham Bedford 29 D7
Biddestone Wilts 16 D5
Biddisham Som 15 F9
Biddlesden Bucks 28 D3
Biddlestone Northumb 62 C5
Biddulph Staffs 44 G2
Biddulph Moor Staffs 44 G3
Bideford Devon 6 D3
Bidford-on-Avon Warks 27 C8
Bidston Mers 42 C5
Bielby E Yorks 52 E3
Bieldside Aberdeen 83 C10
Bierley IoW 10 G4
Bierley W Yorks 51 F7
Bierton Bucks 28 G5
Big Sand Highld 85 A12
Bigbury Devon 5 G7
Bigbury on Sea Devon 5 G7
Bigby Lincs 46 B4
Biggar Cumb 49 C1
Biggar S Lanark 69 G9
Biggin Derbys 44 G5
Biggin Derbys 44 H6
Biggin N Yorks 51 F11
Biggin Hill London 19 F11
Biggings Shetland 96 G3
Biggleswade C Beds 29 D8
Bighouse Highld 93 C11
Bighton Hants 10 A5
Bignor W Sus 11 C8
Bigton Shetland 96 L5
Bilberry Corn 3 C9
Bilborough Nottingham 35 A11
Bilbrook Som 7 B9
Bilbrough N Yorks 51 E11
Bilbster Highld 94 E4
Bildershaw Durham 58 D3
Bildeston Suff 30 D6
Billericay Essex 20 B3
Billesdon Leics 36 E3
Billesley Warks 27 C8
Billingborough Lincs 37 B7
Billinge Mers 43 B8
Billingford Norf 38 C6
Billingham Stockton 58 D5
Billinghay Lincs 46 G5
Billingley S Yorks 45 B8
Billingshurst W Sus 11 B9
Billingsley Shrops 34 G3
Billington C Beds 28 F6
Billington Lancs 50 F3
Billockby Norf 39 D10
Billy Row Durham 58 C2
Bilsborrow Lancs 49 F5
Bilsby Lincs 47 E8
Bilsham W Sus 11 D8
Bilsington Kent 13 C9
Bilson Green Glos 26 G3
Bilsthorpe Notts 45 F10
Bilsthorpe Moor Notts 45 G10
Bilston Midloth 69 D11
Bilston W Mid 34 F5
Bilstone Leics 35 E9
Bilting Kent 21 G7
Bilton E Yorks 53 F7
Bilton Northumb 63 B8
Bilton Warks 27 A11
Bilton in Ainsty N Yorks 51 E10
Bimbister Orkney 95 G4
Binbrook Lincs 46 C6
Binchester Blocks Durham 58 C3
Bincombe Dorset 8 F5
Bindal Highld 87 C12
Binegar Som 16 G3
Binfield Brack 18 D5
Binfield Hth. Oxon 18 D4
Bingfield Northumb 62 F5
Bingham Notts 36 B3
Bingley W Yorks 51 F7
Bings Heath Shrops 33 D11
Binham Norf 38 B5
Binley Hants 17 F11
Binley W Mid 35 H9
Binley Woods Warks 35 H9
Binniehill Falk 69 C7
Binsoe N Yorks 51 B8
Binstead IoW 10 E4
Binsted Hants 18 G4
Binton Warks 27 C8
Bintree Norf 38 C6
Binweston Shrops 33 E9
Birch Essex 30 G6
Birch Gtr Man 44 B2
Birch Green Essex 30 G6
Birch Heath Ches W 43 F8
Birch Hill Ches W 43 E8
Birch Vale Derbys 44 D4
Bircham Newton Norf 38 B3
Bircham Tofts Norf 38 B3
Birchanger Essex 30 F2
Birchencliffe W Yorks 51 H7
Bircher Hereford 25 B11
Birchgrove Cardiff 15 D7
Birchgrove Swansea 14 B3
Birchington Kent 21 E9
Birchmoor Warks 35 E8
Birchover Derbys 44 F6
Birchwood Lincs 46 F3
Birchwood Warr 43 C9
Bircotes Notts 45 C10
Birdbrook Essex 30 D4
Birdforth N Yorks 51 B10
Birdham W Sus 11 E7
Birdholme Derbys 45 F7
Birdingbury Warks 27 B11
Birdlip Glos 26 G6
Birds Edge W Yorks 44 B6
Birdsall N Yorks 52 C4
Birdsgreen Shrops 34 G3
Birdsmoor Gate Dorset 8 D2
Birdston E Dunb 68 C5
Birdwell S Yorks 45 B7
Birdwood Glos 26 G4
Birgham Borders 70 G6
Birkby N Yorks 58 F4
Birkdale Mers 49 H3
Birkenhead Mers 42 D6
Birkenhills Aberds 89 D7
Birkenshaw N Lanark 68 D5
Birkenshaw W Yorks 51 G8
Birkhall Aberds 82 D5
Birkhill Angus 76 D6
Birkhill Borders 61 B8
Birkholme Lincs 36 C5
Birkin N Yorks 51 G11
Birley Hereford 25 C11
Birling Kent 20 E3
Birling Northumb 63 C8
Birling Gap E Sus 12 G4
Birlingham Worcs 26 D6
Birmingham W Mid 35 G6
Birnam Perth 76 C3
Birse Aberds 83 D7
Birsemore Aberds 83 D7
Birstall Leics 36 E1
Birstall W Yorks 51 G8
Birstwith N Yorks 51 D8
Birthorpe Lincs 37 B7
Birtley Hereford 25 B10
Birtley Northumb 62 F4
Birtley T&W 63 H8
Birts Street Worcs 26 E4
Bisbrooke Rutland 36 F4
Biscathorpe Lincs 46 D6
Biscot Luton 29 F7
Bish Mill Devon 7 D6
Bisham Windsor 18 C5
Bishampton Worcs 26 C6
Bishop Auckland Durham 58 D3
Bishop Burton E Yorks 52 F5
Bishop Middleham Durham 58 C4
Bishop Monkton N Yorks 51 C9
Bishop Norton Lincs 46 C3
Bishop Sutton Bath 16 F2
Bishop Thornton N Yorks 51 C8
Bishop Wilton E Yorks 52 D3
Bishopbridge Lincs 46 C4
Bishopbriggs E Dunb 68 D5
Bishopmill Moray 88 B2
Bishops Cannings Wilts 17 E7
Bishop's Castle Shrops 33 G9
Bishop's Caundle Dorset 8 C5
Bishop's Cleeve Glos 26 F6
Bishops Frome Hereford 26 D3
Bishop's Green Essex 30 G3
Bishop's Hull Som 7 D11
Bishop's Itchington Warks 27 C10
Bishops Lydeard Som 7 D10
Bishops Nympton Devon 7 D6
Bishop's Offley Staffs 34 C3
Bishop'S Stortford Herts 29 F11
Bishop's Sutton Hants 10 A5
Bishop's Tachbrook Warks 27 B10
Bishops Tawton Devon 6 C4
Bishop's Waltham Hants 10 C4
Bishop's Wood Staffs 34 E4
Bishopsbourne Kent 21 F8
Bishopsteignton Devon 5 D10
Bishopstoke Hants 10 C3
Bishopston Swansea 23 H10
Bishopstone Bucks 28 G5
Bishopstone E Sus 12 F3
Bishopstone Hereford 25 D11
Bishopstone Swindon 17 C9
Bishopstone Wilts 9 B9
Bishopstrow Wilts 16 G5
Bishopswood Som 8 C1
Bishopsworth Bristol 16 E2
Bishopthorpe York 52 E1
Bishopton Darl 58 D4
Bishopton Dumfries 55 E7
Bishopton N Yorks 51 B9
Bishopton Renfs 68 C3
Bishopton Warks 27 C8
Bishton Newport 15 C9
Bisley Glos 26 H6
Bisley Sur 18 F6
Bispham Blackpool 49 E3
Bispham Green Lancs 43 A7
Bissoe Corn 3 E6
Bisterne Close Hants 9 D11
Bitchfield Lincs 36 C5
Bittadon Devon 6 B4
Bittaford Devon 5 F7
Bittering Norf 38 D5
Bitterley Shrops 34 H1
Bitterne Soton 10 C3
Bitteswell Leics 35 G11
Bitton S Glos 16 E3
Bix Oxon 18 C4
Bixter Shetland 96 H5
Blaby Leics 36 F1
Black Bourton Oxon 17 A9
Black Callerton T&W 63 G7
Black Clauchrie S Ayrs 54 A5
Black Corries Lodge Highld 74 B5
Black Crofts Argyll 74 D2
Black Dog Devon 7 F7
Black Heddon Northumb 62 F6
Black Lane Gtr Man 43 B10
Black Marsh Shrops 33 F9
Black Mount Argyll 74 C5
Black Notley Essex 30 F4
Black Pill Swansea 14 B2
Black Tar Pembs 22 F4
Black Torrington Devon 6 F3
Blackacre Dumfries 60 D6
Blackadder West Borders 71 E7
Blackawton Devon 5 F9
Blackborough Devon 7 F9
Blackborough End Norf 38 D2
Blackboys E Sus 12 D4
Blackbrook Derbys 45 H7
Blackbrook Mers 43 C8
Blackbrook Staffs 34 B3
Blackburn Aberds 83 B10
Blackburn Aberds 88 E5
Blackburn Blackburn 50 G2
Blackburn W Loth 69 D8
Blackcraig Dumfries 60 E3
Blackden Heath Ches E 43 E10
Blackdog Aberds 83 B11
Blackfell T&W 63 H8
Blackfield Hants 10 D3
Blackford Cumb 61 G9
Blackford Perth 75 G11
Blackford Som 8 B5
Blackford Som 15 G10
Blackfordby Leics 35 D9
Blackgang IoW 10 G3
Blackhall Colliery Durham 58 C5
Blackhall Mill T&W 63 H7
Blackhall Rocks Durham 58 C5
Blackham E Sus 12 C3
Blackhaugh Borders 70 G3
Blackheath Essex 31 F7
Blackheath Suff 31 A11
Blackheath Sur 19 G7
Blackheath W Mid 34 G5
Blackhill Aberds 89 C10
Blackhill Aberds 89 D10
Blackhill Highld 85 C8
Blackhills Highld 87 F12
Blackhills Moray 88 C2
Blackhorse S Glos 16 D3
Blackland Wilts 17 E7
Blacklaw Aberds 89 C6
Blackley Gtr Man 44 B2
Blacklunans Perth 76 A4
Blackmill Bridgend 14 C5
Blackmoor Hants 11 A6
Blackmoor Gate Devon 6 B5
Blackmore Essex 20 A3
Blackmore End Essex 30 E4
Blackmore End Herts 29 G8
Blackness Falk 69 C9
Blacknest Hants 18 G4
Blacko Lancs 50 E4
Blackpool Blackpool 49 F3
Blackpool Devon 5 G9
Blackpool Pembs 22 E5
Blackpool Gate Cumb 61 F11
Blackridge W Loth 69 D7
Blackrock Argyll 64 B4
Blackrock Mon 25 G9
Blackrod Gtr Man 43 A9
Blackshaw Dumfries 60 G6
Blackshaw Head W Yorks 50 G5
Blacksmith's Green Suff 31 B8
Blackstone W Sus 11 C11
Blackthorn Oxon 28 G3
Blackthorpe Suff 30 B6
Blacktoft E Yorks 52 G4
Blacktop Aberdeen 83 C10
Blacktown Newport 15 C8
Blackwall Tunnel London 19 C10
Blackwater Corn 2 E6
Blackwater Hants 18 F5
Blackwater IoW 10 F4
Blackwaterfoot N Ayrs 66 D1
Blackwell Darl 58 E3
Blackwell Derbys 44 E5
Blackwell Derbys 45 G8
Blackwell W Sus 12 C2
Blackwell Warks 27 D9
Blackwell Worcs 26 A6
Blackwood = Coed Duon Caerph 15 B7
Blackwood S Lanark 68 F6
Blackwood Hill Staffs 44 G3
Blacon Ches W 43 F6
Bladnoch Dumfries 55 D7
Bladon Oxon 27 G11
Blaen-gwynfi Neath 14 B4
Blaen-waun Carms 23 D7
Blaen-y-coed Carms 23 D8
Blaen-y-Cwm Denb 32 B6
Blaen-y-cwm Gwyn 32 C3
Blaen-y-cwm Powys 33 C6
Blaenannerch Ceredig 23 B7
Blaenau Ffestiniog Gwyn 41 F9
Blaenavon Torf 25 H9
Blaencelyn Ceredig 23 A8
Blaendyryn Powys 24 E6
Blaenffos Pembs 22 C6
Blaengarw Bridgend 14 B5
Blaengwrach Neath 24 H5
Blaenpennal Ceredig 24 B3
Blaenplwyf Ceredig 32 H1
Blaenporth Ceredig 23 B7
Blaenrhondda Rhondda 14 A5
Blaenycwm Ceredig 32 H4
Blagdon N Som 15 F11
Blagdon Torbay 5 E9
Blagdon Hill Som 7 E11
Blagill Cumb 57 B9
Blaguegate Lancs 43 B7
Blaich Highld 80 F2
Blain Highld 79 E9
Blaina Bl Gwent 25 H9
Blair Atholl Perth 81 G10
Blair Drummond Stirling 75 H10
Blairbeg N Ayrs 66 C3
Blairdaff Aberds 83 B8
Blairglas Argyll 68 B2
Blairgowrie Perth 76 C4
Blairhall Fife 69 B9
Blairingone Perth 76 H2
Blairland N Ayrs 66 B6
Blairlogie Stirling 75 H11
Blairlomond Argyll 74 H4
Blairmore Argyll 73 E10
Blairnamarrow Moray 82 B4
Blairquhosh Stirling 68 B4
Blair's Ferry Argyll 73 G8
Blairskaith E Dunb 68 C4
Blaisdon Glos 26 G4
Blakebrook Worcs 34 H4
Blakedown Worcs 34 H4
Blakelaw Borders 70 G6
Blakeley Staffs 34 F4
Blakeley Lane Staffs 44 H3
Blakemere Hereford 25 D10
Blakeney Glos 26 H3
Blakeney Norf 38 A6
Blakenhall Ches E 43 H10
Blakenhall W Mid 34 F5
Blakeshall Worcs 34 G4
Blakesley Northants 28 C3
Blanchland Northumb 57 A11
Bland Hill N Yorks 51 D8
Blandford Forum Dorset 9 D7
Blandford St Mary Dorset 9 D7
Blanefield Stirling 68 C4
Blankney Lincs 46 F4
Blantyre S Lanark 68 E5
Blar a'Chaorainn Highld 80 G3
Blaran Argyll 73 B7
Blarghour Argyll 73 B8
Blarmachfoldach Highld 80 G2
Blarnalearoch Highld 86 B4
Blashford Hants 9 D10
Blaston Leics 36 F4
Blatherwycke Northants 36 F5
Blawith Cumb 56 H4
Blaxhall Suff 31 C10
Blaxton S Yorks 45 B10
Blaydon T&W 63 G7
Bleadon N Som 15 F9
Bleak Hey Nook Gtr Man 44 B4
Blean Kent 21 E8
Bleasby Lincs 46 D5
Bleasby Notts 45 H11
Bleasdale Lancs 50 E1
Bleatarn Cumb 57 E9
Blebocraigs Fife 77 F7
Bleddfa Powys 25 B9
Bledington Glos 27 F9
Bledlow Bucks 18 A4
Bledlow Ridge Bucks 18 B4
Blegbie E Loth 70 D3
Blencarn Cumb 57 C8
Blencogo Cumb 56 B3
Blendworth Hants 10 C6
Blenheim Park Norf 38 B4
Blennerhasset Cumb 56 B3
Blervie Castle Moray 87 F13
Bletchingdon Oxon 28 G2
Bletchingley Sur 19 F10
Bletchley M Keynes 28 E5
Bletchley Shrops 34 B2
Bletherston Pembs 22 D5
Bletsoe Bedford 29 C7
Blewbury Oxon 18 C2
Blickling Norf 39 C7
Blidworth Notts 45 G9
Blindburn Northumb 62 B4
Blindcrake Cumb 56 C3
Blindley Heath Sur 19 G10
Blisland Corn 4 D2
Bliss Gate Worcs 26 A4
Blissford Hants 9 C10
Blisworth Northants 28 C4
Blithbury Staffs 35 C6
Blitterlees Cumb 56 A3
Blo' Norton Norf 38 H6
Blockley Glos 27 E8
Blofield Norf 39 E9
Blofield Heath Norf 39 D9
Bloomfield Borders 61 A11
Blore Staffs 44 H5
Blount's Green Staffs 35 B6
Blowick Mers 49 H3
Bloxham Oxon 27 E11
Bloxholm Lincs 46 G4
Bloxwich W Mid 34 E5
Bloxworth Dorset 9 E7
Blubberhouses N Yorks 51 D7
Blue Anchor Som 7 B9
Blue Anchor Swansea 23 G10
Blue Row Essex 31 G7
Blundeston Suff 39 F11
Blunham C Beds 29 C8
Blunsdon St Andrew Swindon 17 C8
Bluntington Worcs 26 A5
Bluntisham Cambs 29 A10
Blunts Corn 4 E4
Blyborough Lincs 46 C3
Blyford Suff 39 H10
Blymhill Staffs 34 D4
Blyth Northumb 63 E9
Blyth Notts 45 D10
Blyth Bridge Borders 69 F10
Blythburgh Suff 39 H10
Blythe Borders 70 F4
Blythe Bridge Staffs 34 A5
Blyton Lincs 46 C2
Boarhills Fife 77 F8
Boarhunt Hants 10 D5
Boars Head Gtr Man 43 B8
Boars Hill Oxon 17 A11
Boarshead E Sus 12 C4
Boarstall Bucks 28 G3
Boasley Cross Devon 6 G3
Boat of Garten Highld 81 B11
Boath Highld 87 D8
Bobbing Kent 20 E5
Bobbington Staffs 34 F4
Bobbingworth Essex 30 H2
Bocaddon Corn 4 F2
Bochastle Stirling 75 G9
Bocking Essex 30 F4
Bocking Churchstreet Essex 30 F4
Boddam Aberds 89 D11
Boddam Shetland 96 M5
Boddington Glos 26 F5
Bodedern Anglesey 40 B5
Bodelwyddan Denb 42 E3
Bodenham Hereford 26 C2
Bodenham Wilts 9 B10
Bodenham Moor Hereford 26 C2
Bodermid Gwyn 40 H3
Bodewryd Anglesey 40 A5
Bodfari Denb 42 E3
Bodffordd Anglesey 40 C6
Bodham Norf 39 A7
Bodiam E Sus 13 D6
Bodicote Oxon 27 E11
Bodieve Corn 3 B8
Bodinnick Corn 4 F2
Bodle Street Green E Sus 12 E5
Bodmin Corn 4 E1
Bodney Norf 38 F4
Bodorgan Anglesey 40 D5
Bodsham Kent 21 G8
Boduan Gwyn 40 G5
Bodymoor Heath Warks 35 F7
Bogallan Highld 87 F9
Bogbrae Aberds 89 E10
Bogend Borders 70 F6
Bogend S Ayrs 67 C6
Boghall W Loth 69 D8
Boghead S Lanark 68 F6
Bogmoor Moray 88 B3
Bogniebrae Aberds 88 D5
Bognor Regis W Sus 11 E8
Bograxie Aberds 83 B9
Bogside N Lanark 69 E7
Bogton Aberds 89 C6
Bogue Dumfries 55 A9
Bohenie Highld 80 E4
Bohortha Corn 3 F7
Bohuntine Highld 80 E4
Boirseam W Isles 90 J5
Bojewyan Corn 2 F2
Bolam Durham 58 D2
Bolam Northumb 62 E6
Bolberry Devon 5 H7
Bold Heath Mers 43 D8
Boldon T&W 63 G9
Boldon Colliery T&W 63 G9
Boldre Hants 10 E2
Boldron Durham 58 E1
Bole Notts 45 D11
Bolehill Derbys 44 G6
Boleside Borders 70 G3
Bolham Devon 7 E8
Bolham Water Devon 7 E10
Bolingey Corn 3 D6
Bollington Ches E 44 E3
Bollington Cross Ches E 44 E3
Bolney W Sus 12 D1
Bolnhurst Bedford 29 C7
Bolshan Angus 77 B9
Bolsover Derbys 45 E8
Bolsterstone S Yorks 44 C6
Bolstone Hereford 26 E2
Boltby N Yorks 58 H5
Bolter End Bucks 18 B4
Bolton Cumb 57 D8
Bolton E Loth 70 C4
Bolton E Yorks 52 D3
Bolton Gtr Man 43 B10
Bolton Northumb 63 B7
Bolton Abbey N Yorks 51 D6
Bolton Bridge N Yorks 51 D6
Bolton-by-Bowland Lancs 50 E3
Bolton-le-Sands Lancs 49 C4
Bolton Low Houses Cumb 56 B4
Bolton-on-Swale N Yorks 58 G3
Bolton Percy N Yorks 51 E11
Bolton Town End Lancs 49 C4
Bolton upon Dearne S Yorks 45 B8
Boltonfellend Cumb 61 G10
Boltongate Cumb 56 B4
Bolventor Corn 4 D2
Bomere Heath Shrops 33 D10
Bon-y-maen Swansea 14 B2
Bonar Bridge Highld 87 B9
Bonawe Argyll 74 D3
Bonby N Lincs 52 H6
Boncath Pembs 23 C7
Bonchester Bridge Borders 61 B11
Bonchurch IoW 10 G4
Bondleigh Devon 6 F5
Bonehill Devon 5 D8
Bonehill Staffs 35 E7
Bo'ness Falk 69 B8
Bonhill W Dunb 68 C2
Boningale Shrops 34 E4
Bonjedward Borders 62 A2
Bonkle N Lanark 69 E7
Bonnavoulin Highld 79 F8
Bonnington Edin 69 D10
Bonnington Kent 13 C9
Bonnybank Fife 76 G6
Bonnybridge Falk 69 B7
Bonnykelly Aberds 89 C8
Bonnyrigg and Lasswade Midloth 70 D2
Bonnyton Aberds 89 E6
Bonnyton Angus 76 D6
Bonnyton Angus 77 B9
Bonsall Derbys 44 G6
Bonskeid House Perth 75 A11
Bont Mon 25 G10
Bont-Dolgadfan Powys 32 E4
Bont-goch Ceredig 32 G2
Bont-newydd Conwy 42 E3
Bont Newydd Gwyn 32 C3
Bont Newydd Gwyn 41 F9
Bontddu Gwyn 32 D2
Bonthorpe Lincs 47 E8
Bontnewydd Ceredig 24 B3
Bontnewydd Gwyn 40 E6
Bontuchel Denb 42 G3
Bonvilston V Glam 14 D6
Booker Bucks 18 B5
Boon Borders 70 F4
Boosbeck Redcar 59 E7
Boot Cumb 56 F3
Boot Street Suff 31 D9
Booth W Yorks 50 G6
Booth Wood W Yorks 50 H6
Boothby Graffoe Lincs 46 G3
Boothby Pagnell Lincs 36 B5
Boothen Stoke 34 A4
Boothferry E Yorks 52 G3
Boothville Northants 28 B4
Bootle Cumb 56 H3
Bootle Mers 42 C6
Booton Norf 39 C7
Boquhan Stirling 68 B4
Boraston Shrops 26 A3
Borden Kent 20 E5
Borden W Sus 11 B7
Bordley N Yorks 50 C5
Bordon Hants 18 H5
Bordon Camp Hants 18 H4
Boreham Essex 30 H4
Boreham Wilts 16 G5
Boreham Street E Sus 12 E5
Borehamwood Herts 19 B8
Boreland Dumfries 61 D7
Boreland Stirling 75 D8
Borgh W Isles 84 H1
Borgh W Isles 90 J4
Borghastan W Isles 90 C7
Borgie Highld 93 D9
Borgue Dumfries 55 E9
Borgue Highld 94 H3
Borley Essex 30 D5
Bornais W Isles 84 F2
Bornesketaig Highld 85 A8
Borness Dumfries 55 E9
Borough Green Kent 20 F3
Boroughbridge N Yorks 51 C9
Borras Head Wrex 42 G6
Borreraig Highld 84 C6
Borrobol Lodge Highld 93 G11
Borrowash Derbys 35 B10
Borrowby N Yorks 58 H5
Borrowdale Cumb 56 E4
Borrowfield Aberds 83 D10
Borth Ceredig 32 F2
Borth-y-Gest Gwyn 41 G7
Borthwickbrae Borders 61 B10
Borthwickshiels Borders 61 B10
Borve Highld 85 D9
Borve Lodge W Isles 90 H5
Borwick Lancs 49 B5
Bosavern Corn 2 F2
Bosbury Hereford 26 D3
Boscastle Corn 4 B2
Boscombe Bmouth 9 E10
Boscombe Wilts 17 H9
Boscoppa Corn 3 D9
Bosham W Sus 11 D7
Bosherston Pembs 22 G4
Boskenna Corn 2 G3
Bosley Ches E 44 F3
Bossall N Yorks 52 C3
Bossiney Corn 4 C1
Bossingham Kent 21 G8
Bossington Som 7 B7
Bostock Green Ches W 43 F9
Boston Lincs 37 A9
Boston Long Hedges Lincs 47 H7
Boston Spa W Yorks 51 E10
Boston West Lincs 46 H6
Boswinger Corn 3 E8
Botallack Corn 2 F2
Botany Bay London 19 B9
Botcherby Cumb 61 H10
Botcheston Leics 35 E10
Botesdale Suff 38 H6
Bothal Northumb 63 E8
Bothamsall Notts 45 E10
Bothel Cumb 56 C3
Bothenhampton Dorset 8 E3
Bothwell S Lanark 68 E6
Botley Bucks 18 A6
Botley Hants 10 C4
Botley Oxon 27 H11
Botolph Claydon Bucks 28 F4
Botolphs W Sus 11 D10
Bottacks Highld 86 E7
Bottesford Leics 36 B4
Bottesford N Lincs 46 B2
Bottisham Cambs 30 B2
Bottlesford Wilts 17 F8
Bottom Boat W Yorks 51 G9
Bottom House Staffs 44 G4
Bottom o' th' Moor Gtr Man 43 A9
Bottom of Hutton Lancs 49 G4
Bottomcraig Fife 76 E6
Botusfleming Corn 4 E5
Botwnnog Gwyn 40 G4
Bough Beech Kent 19 G11
Boughrood Powys 25 E8
Boughspring Glos 16 B2
Boughton Norf 38 E2
Boughton Northants 28 B4
Boughton Notts 45 F10
Boughton Aluph Kent 21 G7
Boughton Lees Kent 21 G7
Boughton Malherbe Kent 20 G5
Boughton Monchelsea Kent 20 F4
Boughton Street Kent 21 F7
Boulby Redcar 59 E8
Boulden Shrops 33 G11
Boulmer Northumb 63 B8
Boulston Pembs 22 E4
Boultenstone Aberds 82 B6
Boultham Lincs 46 F3
Bourn Cambs 29 C10
Bourne Lincs 37 C6
Bourne End Bucks 18 C5
Bourne End C Beds 28 D6
Bourne End Herts 29 H7
Bournemouth Bmouth 9 E9
Bournes Green Glos 16 A6
Bournes Green Southend 20 C6
Bournheath Worcs 26 A6
Bournmoor Durham 58 A4
Bournville W Mid 34 G6
Bourton Dorset 9 A6
Bourton N Som 15 E9
Bourton Oxon 17 C9
Bourton Shrops 34 F1
Bourton on Dunsmore Warks 27 A11
Bourton on the Hill Glos 27 E8
Bourton-on-the-Water Glos 27 F8
Bousd Argyll 78 E5
Boustead Hill Cumb 61 H8
Bouth Cumb 56 H5
Bouthwaite N Yorks 51 B7
Boveney Bucks 18 D6
Boverton V Glam 14 E5
Bovey Tracey Devon 5 D9
Bovingdon Herts 19 A7
Bovingdon Green Bucks 18 C5
Bovingdon Green Herts 19 A7
Bovinger Essex 30 H2
Bovington Camp Dorset 9 F7
Bow Borders 70 F3
Bow Devon 6 F6
Bow Orkney 95 J4
Bow Brickhill M Keynes 28 E6
Bow of Fife Fife 76 F6
Bow Street Ceredig 32 G2
Bowbank Durham 57 D11
Bowburn Durham 58 C4
Bowcombe IoW 10 F3
Bowd Devon 7 G10
Bowden Borders 70 G4
Bowden Devon 5 G9
Bowden Hill Wilts 16 E6

Column 1

Easterton Wilts 17 F7
Easterton Som 15 F9
Eastertown of
Auchleuchries
Aberds 89 E10
Eastfield N Lanark 69 D7
Eastfield S Ayrs 52 A6
Eastfield Hall
Northumb 63 C8
Eastgate Durham 57 C11
Eastgate Norf 39 C7
Eastham Mers 42 D6
Eastham Ferry
Mers 42 D6
Easthampstead
Brack 18 E5
Eastheath
Wokingham 18 E5
Easthope Shrops 34 F1
Easthorpe Essex 30 F6
Easthorpe Leics 36 B4
Easthorpe Notts 45 G11
Easthouses Midloth 70 D2
Eastington Devon 6 D3
Eastington Glos 26 H4
Eastington Glos 27 G8
Eastleach Martin
Glos 27 H9
Eastleach Turville
Glos 27 H8
Eastleigh Devon 6 D3
Eastleigh Hants 10 C3
Eastling Kent 20 F6
Eastmoor Derbys 45 E7
Eastmoor Norf 38 E3
Eastney Ptsmth 10 E5
Eastnor Hereford 26 E4
Eastoft N Lincs 52 A4
Eastoke Hants 10 E6
Easton Cambs 29 A8
Easton Cumb 61 H10
Easton Cumb 61 G8
Easton Devon 5 C8
Easton Dorset 8 G5
Easton Hants 10 A4
Easton Lincs 36 C5
Easton Norf 39 D7
Easton Som 15 G11
Easton Suff 31 C9
Easton Wilts 16 D5
Easton Grey Wilts 16 C5
Easton-in-
Gordano N Som 15 D11
Easton Maudit
Northants 28 C5
Easton on the
Hill Northants 36 E6
Easton Royal Wilts 17 E9
Eastrea Cambs 37 F8
Eastriggs Dumfries 61 G8
Eastrington E Yorks 52 G3
Eastry Kent 21 F10
Eastville Bristol 16 D3
Eastville Lincs 47 G8
Eastwell Leics 36 C3
Eastwick Herts 29 G11
Eastwick Shetland 96 F5
Eastwood Notts 45 H8
Eastwood Southend 20 C5
Eastwood W Yorks 50 G5
Eastthorpe W Yorks 51 G8
Eaton Ches E 44 F2
Eaton Ches W 43 F8
Eaton Leics 36 C3
Eaton Norf 39 E8
Eaton Notts 45 E11
Eaton Oxon 17 A11
Eaton Shrops 33 G9
Eaton Shrops 33 G11
Eaton Bishop
Hereford 25 E11
Eaton Bray C Beds 28 F6
Eaton Constantine
Shrops 34 E1
Eaton Green C Beds 28 F6
Eaton Hastings
Oxon 17 B9
Eaton on Tern
Shrops 34 C2
Eaton Socon Cambs 29 C8
Eavestone N Yorks 51 C8
Ebberston N Yorks 52 A4
Ebbesbourne
Wake Wilts 9 B8
Ebbw Vale =
Glyn Ebwy Bl Gwent 25 H8
Ebchester Durham 63 H7
Ebford Devon 5 C10
Ebley Glos 26 H5
Ebnal Ches W 43 H7
Ebrington Glos 27 D8
Ecchinswell Hants 17 F11
Ecclaw Borders 70 D6
Ecclefechan
Dumfries 61 F7
Eccles Borders 70 F6
Eccles Gtr Man 43 C10
Eccles Kent 20 E4
Eccles on Sea
Norf 39 C10
Eccles Road Norf 38 F6
Ecclesall S Yorks 45 D7
Ecclesfield S Yorks 45 C7
Ecclesgreig Aberds 83 G9
Eccleshall Staffs 34 C4
Eccleshill W Yorks 51 F7
Ecclesmachan
W Loth 69 C9
Eccleston Ches W 43 F7
Eccleston Lancs 49 H5
Eccleston Mers 43 C7
Eccleston Park
Mers 43 C7
Eccup W Yorks 51 E8
Echt Aberds 83 C9
Eckford Borders 70 H6
Eckington Derbys 45 E8
Eckington Worcs 26 D6
Ecton Northants 28 B5
Edale Derbys 44 D5
Edburton W Sus 11 D11
Edderside Cumb 56 B2
Edderton Highld 87 C10
Eddistone Devon 6 D1
Eddleston Borders 69 F11
Eden Park London 19 E10
Edenbridge Kent 19 G11
Edenfield Lancs 50 H3
Edenhall Cumb 57 C7
Edenham Lincs 37 C6
Edensor Derbys 44 F6
Edentaggart Argyll 68 A2
Edenthorpe
S Yorks 45 B10
Edentown Cumb 61 H9
Ederline Argyll 73 C7
Edern Gwyn 40 G4
Edgarley Som 15 H11
Edgbaston W Mid 35 G6
Edgcott Bucks 28 F3
Edgcott Som 7 C7
Edge Shrops 33 E9
Edge End Glos 26 G2
Edge Green Ches W 43 G7
Edge Hill Mers 42 C6
Edgebolton Shrops 34 C1
Edgefield Norf 39 B6
Edgefield Street
Norf 39 B6
Edgeside Lancs 50 G4
Edgeworth Glos 26 H6
Edgmond Telford 34 D3
Edgmond Marsh
Telford 34 C3
Edgton Shrops 33 G9
Edgware London 19 B9
Edgworth Blackburn 50 H3
Edinample Stirling 75 E8
Edinbane Highld 85 C8
Edinburgh Edin 69 C11
Edingale Staffs 35 D8
Edingight Ho.
Moray 88 C5
Edingley Notts 45 G10
Edingthorpe Norf 39 B9
Edingthorpe
Green Norf 39 B9
Edington Som 15 H9
Edington Wilts 16 F6
Edintore Moray 88 D4
Edith Weston
Rutland 36 E5
Edithmead Som 15 G9
Edlesborough
Bucks 28 G6
Edlingham
Northumb 63 C7
Edlington Lincs 46 E6
Edmondsham Dorset 9 C9
Edmondsley Durham 58 B3
Edmondthorpe
Leics 36 D4
Edmonstone Orkney 95 F6
Edmonton London 19 B10
Edmundbyers
Durham 58 A1
Ednam Borders 70 G6
Ednaston Derbys 35 A8

Column 2

Edradynate Perth 75 B11
Edrom Borders 71 E7
Edstaston Shrops 33 B11
Edstone Warks 27 B8
Edvin Loach
Hereford 26 C3
Edwalton Notts 36 B1
Edwardstone Suff 30 D6
Edwinsford Carms 24 E3
Edwinstowe Notts 45 F10
Edworth C Beds 29 D9
Edwyn Ralph
Hereford 26 C3
Edzell Angus 83 G7
Efail Isaf Rhondda 14 C6
Efailnewydd Gwyn 40 G5
Efailwen Carms 22 D6
Efenechtyd Denb 42 G4
Effingham Sur 19 F8
Effirth Shetland 96 H5
Efford Devon 7 F7
Egdon Worcs 26 C6
Egerton Gtr Man 43 A10
Egerton Kent 20 G6
Egerton Forstal
Kent 20 G5
Eggborough N Yorks 52 G1
Eggbuckland Plym 4 F6
Eggington C Beds 28 F6
Egginton Derbys 35 C8
Egglescliffe
Stockton 58 E5
Eggleston Durham 57 D11
Egham Sur 19 D7
Egleton Rutland 36 E4
Eglingham Northumb 63 B7
Egloscrow Corn 3 B8
Egloshayle Corn 3 B8
Egloskerry Corn 4 C3
Eglwys-Brewis
V Glam 14 E6
Eglwys Cross Wrex 33 A10
Eglwys Fach
Ceredig 32 F2
Eglwysbach Conwy 41 C10
Eglwyswrw Pembs 22 C6
Eglwys-Brewis
Egmanton Notts 45 F11
Egremont Cumb 56 E2
Egremont Mers 42 C6
Egton N Yorks 59 F9
Egton Bridge
N Yorks 59 F9
Eight Ash Green
Essex 30 F6
Eignaig Highld 79 G10
Eil Highld 81 B10
Eilanreach Highld 85 G13
Eilean Darach
Highld 86 C4
Eileanach Lodge
Highld 87 E8
Einacleite W Isles 90 E6
Eisgean W Isles 91 F8
Eisingrug Gwyn 41 G8
Elan Village Powys 24 B6
Elberton S Glos 16 C3
Elburton Plym 4 F6
Elcho Perth 76 E4
Elcombe Swindon 17 C8
Eldernell Cambs 37 F9
Eldersfield Worcs 26 E5
Eldersie Renfs 68 D3
Eldon Durham 58 D3
Eldrick S Ayrs 54 A5
Eldwick W Yorks 51 E7
Elfhowe Cumb 57 G6
Elford Northumb 71 G10
Elford Staffs 35 D7
Elgin Moray 88 B2
Elgol Highld 85 G10
Elham Kent 21 G8
Elie Fife 77 G7
Elim Anglesey 40 B5
Eling Hants 10 C2
Elishader Highld 85 B10
Elishaw Northumb 62 D4
Elkesley Notts 45 E10
Elkstone Glos 26 G6
Ellan Highld 81 A10
Elland W Yorks 51 G7
Ellary Argyll 72 F6
Ellastone Staffs 35 A7
Ellemford Borders 70 D6
Ellenbrook IoM 48 E3
Ellenhall Staffs 34 C4
Ellen's Green Sur 19 H7
Ellerbeck N Yorks 58 G5
Ellerburn N Yorks 52 A4
Ellerby N Yorks 59 E8
Ellerdine Heath
Telford 34 C2
Elleray Dumfries 54 A5
Ellerhayes Devon 7 F8
Elleric Argyll 74 C3
Ellerker E Yorks 52 G5
Ellerton E Yorks 52 E3
Ellerton Shrops 34 C3
Ellesborough Bucks 28 H5
Ellesmere Shrops 33 B10
Ellesmere Port
Ches W 43 E7
Ellingham Norf 39 F9
Ellingham
Northumb 71 H10
Ellingstring N Yorks 51 A7
Ellington Cambs 29 A8
Ellington Northumb 63 D8
Elliot Angus 77 D9
Ellisfield Hants 18 G3
Ellistown Leics 35 D10
Ellon Aberds 89 E9
Ellonby Cumb 56 C6
Ellough Suff 39 G10
Elloughton E Yorks 52 G5
Ellwood Glos 26 H2
Elm Cambs 37 E10
Elm Hill Dorset 9 B7
Elm Park London 20 C2
Elmbridge Worcs 26 B6
Elmdon Essex 29 E11
Elmdon W Mid 35 G7
Elmdon Heath
W Mid 35 G7
Elmers End London 19 E10
Elmesthorpe Leics 35 F10
Elmfield IoW 10 E5
Elmhurst Staffs 35 D7
Elmley Castle
Worcs 26 D6
Elmley Lovett
Worcs 26 B5
Elmore Glos 26 G4
Elmore Back Glos 26 G4
Elmscott Devon 6 D1
Elmsett Suff 31 D7
Elmstead Market
Essex 31 F7
Elmsted Kent 21 G8
Elmstone Kent 21 E9
Elmstone
Hardwicke Glos 26 F6
Elmswell E Yorks 52 D5
Elmswell Suff 30 B6
Elmton Derbys 45 E9
Elphin Highld 92 H5
Elphinstone E Loth 70 C2
Elrick Aberds 83 C10
Elrig Dumfries 54 E6
Elsdon Northumb 62 D5
Elsecar S Yorks 45 C7
Elsenham Essex 30 F2
Elsfield Oxon 28 G2
Elsham N Lincs 46 A4
Elsing Norf 39 D6
Elslack N Yorks 50 E5
Elson Shrops 33 B9
Elsrickle S Lanark 69 F9
Elstead Sur 18 G6
Elsted W Sus 11 C7
Elsthorpe Lincs 37 C6
Elston Notts 45 H11
Elston Wilts 17 G7
Elstone Devon 6 E5
Elstow Bedford 29 D7
Elstree Herts 19 B8
Elstronwick E Yorks 53 F8
Elswick Lancs 49 F4
Elsworth Cambs 29 B10
Elterwater Cumb 56 F5
Eltham London 19 D11
Eltisley Cambs 29 C9
Elton Cambs 37 F6
Elton Ches W 43 E7
Elton Derbys 44 F6
Elton Glos 26 G4
Elton Hereford 25 A11
Elton Notts 36 B3
Elton Stockton 58 E5
Elton Green Ches W 43 E7
Elvanfoot S Lanark 60 B5
Elvaston Derbys 35 B10
Elveden Suff 38 H4
Elvingston E Loth 70 C3
Elvington Kent 21 F9
Elvington York 52 E2
Elwick Hrtlpl 58 C5
Elwick Northumb 71 G10
Elworth Ches E 43 F10
Elworthy Som 7 C9
Elworthy Som 7 C9
Ely Cambs 37 G11

Column 3

Ely Cardiff 15 D7
Emberton M Keynes 28 D5
Embleton Cumb 56 C3
Embleton Northumb 63 A8
Embo Highld 87 B11
Embo Street Highld 87 B11
Emborough Som 16 F3
Embsay N Yorks 50 D6
Emery Down Hants 10 D1
Emersons Green
S Glos 16 D3
Emley W Yorks 44 A6
Emley Moor
W Yorks 44 A6
Emmbrook
Wokingham 18 E4
Emmer Green
Reading 18 D4
Emmington Oxon 18 A4
Emneth Norf 37 E11
Emneth Hungate
Norf 37 E11
Empingham Rutland 36 E5
Empshott Hants 18 H4
Emstrey Shrops 33 D11
Emsworth Hants 10 D6
Enborne W Berks 17 E11
Enchmarsh Shrops 33 F11
Enderby Leics 35 F11
Endmoor Cumb 49 A5
Endon Staffs 44 G3
Endon Bank Staffs 44 G3
Enfield London 19 B10
Enfield Wash
London 19 B10
Enford Wilts 17 F8
Engamoor Shetland 96 H4
Engine Common
S Glos 16 C3
Englefield W Berks 18 D3
Englefield Green
Sur 18 D6
Engleseabrook
Ches E 43 G10
English Bicknor
Glos 26 G2
English Frankton
Shrops 33 C10
Englishcombe Bath 16 E4
Enham Alamein
Hants 17 G10
Enmore Som 7 C11
Ennerdale Bridge
Cumb 56 E2
Enoch Dumfries 60 C4
Enochdhu Perth 76 A3
Ensay Argyll 78 G6
Ensbury Bmouth 9 E9
Ensdon Shrops 33 D10
Ensis Devon 6 D4
Enstone Oxon 27 F10
Enterkinfoot
Dumfries 60 C4
Enterpen N Yorks 58 F5
Enville Staffs 34 G4
Eolaigearraidh
W Isles 84 H2
Eorabus Argyll 78 J6
Eoropaidh W Isles 91 A10
Epperstone Notts 45 H10
Epping Essex 19 A11
Epping Green
Essex 19 A11
Epping Green
Herts 29 H9
Epping Upland
Essex 19 A11
Eppleby N Yorks 58 E2
Eppleworth E Yorks 52 F6
Epsom Sur 19 E9
Epwell Oxon 27 D10
Epworth N Lincs 45 B11
Epworth Turbary
N Lincs 45 B11
Erbistock Wrex 33 A9
Erbusaig Highld 85 F12
Erchless Castle
Highld 86 G7
Erdington W Mid 35 F7
Eredine Argyll 73 C8
Eriboll Highld 92 D7
Ericstane Dumfries 60 B6
Eridge Green E Sus 12 C4
Erines Argyll 73 F7
Eriswell Suff 38 H3
Erith London 20 D2
Erlestoke Wilts 16 F6
Ermine Lincs 46 E3
Ermington Devon 5 F7
Ernington Norf 39 D7
Errogie Highld 81 A7
Errol Perth 76 E5
Erskine Renfs 68 C3
Erskine Bridge
Renfs 68 C3
Ervie Dumfries 54 C3
Erwarton Suff 31 E9
Erwood Powys 25 D7
Eryholme N Yorks 58 F4
Eryrys Denb 42 G5
Escomb Durham 58 D2
Escrick N Yorks 52 E2
Esgairdawe Carms 24 D3
Esgairgeiliog Powys 32 E3
Esh Durham 58 B2
Esh Winning
Durham 58 B2
Esher Sur 19 E8
Esholt W Yorks 51 E7
Eshott Northumb 63 D8
Eshton N Yorks 50 D5
Esk Valley N Yorks 59 F9
Eskadale Highld 86 H7
Eskbank Midloth 70 D2
Eskdale Green
Cumb 56 F3
Eskdalemuir
Dumfries 61 D8
Eske E Yorks 53 E6
Eskham Lincs 47 C7
Esprick Lancs 49 F4
Essendine Rutland 36 D6
Essendon Herts 29 H9
Essich Highld 87 H9
Essington Staffs 34 E5
Esslemont Aberds 89 E9
Eston Redcar 59 E6
Eswick Shetland 96 H6
Etal Northumb 71 G8
Etchilhampton
Wilts 17 E7
Etchingham E Sus 12 D6
Etchinghill Kent 21 H8
Etchinghill Staffs 34 D6
Etherley Dene
Durham 58 D2
Ethie Castle
Angus 77 C9
Ethie Mains Angus 77 C9
Etling Green Norf 38 D6
Eton Windsor 18 D6
Eton Wick Windsor 18 D6
Etteridge Highld 81 D8
Ettersgill Durham 57 D10
Ettingshall W Mid 34 F5
Ettington Warks 27 D9
Etton E Yorks 52 E5
Etton Pboro 37 E7
Ettrick Borders 61 B8
Ettrickbridge
Borders 61 A9
Ettrickhill Borders 61 B8
Etwall Derbys 35 B8
Euston Suff 38 H4
Euximoor Drove
Cambs 37 F10
Euxton Lancs 50 H1
Evanstown
Bridgend 14 C5
Evanton Highld 87 E9
Evedon Lincs 46 H4
Evelix Highld 87 B10
Evenjobb Powys 25 B9
Evenley Northants 28 E2
Evenlode Glos 27 F9
Evenwood Durham 58 D2
Evenwood Gate
Durham 58 D2
Everbay Orkney 95 F7
Evercreech Som 16 H3
Everdon Northants 28 C2
Everingham E Yorks 52 E4
Everleigh Wilts 17 F9
Everley N Yorks 52 A5
Eversholt C Beds 28 E6
Evershot Dorset 8 D4
Eversley Hants 18 E4
Eversley Cross
Hants 18 E4
Everthorpe E Yorks 52 F5
Everton C Beds 29 C9
Everton Hants 10 E1
Everton Mers 42 C6
Everton Notts 45 C10
Evertown Dumfries 61 F9
Evesbatch Hereford 26 D3
Evesham Worcs 27 D7
Evington Leicester 36 E2
Ewden Village
S Yorks 44 C6
Ewell Sur 19 E9
Ewell Minnis Kent 21 G9
Ewelme Oxon 18 B3
Ewen Glos 17 B7
Ewenny V Glam 14 D5
Ewerby Lincs 46 H5
Ewerby Thorpe
Lincs 46 H5

Column 4

Ewes Dumfries 61 D9
Ewesley Northumb 62 D6
Ewhurst Sur 19 G7
Ewhurst Green
E Sus 13 D6
Ewhurst Green Sur 19 H7
Ewloe Flint 42 F6
Ewloe Grn. Flint 42 F5
Ewood Blackburn 50 G2
Eworthy Devon 6 G3
Ewshot Hants 18 G5
Ewyas Harold
Hereford 25 F10
Exbourne Devon 6 F5
Exbury Hants 10 D3
Exebridge Devon 7 D8
Exelby N Yorks 58 H4
Exeter Devon 7 G8
Exford Som 7 C7
Exhall Warks 27 C8
Exley Head W Yorks 50 F6
Exminster Devon 5 C10
Exmouth Devon 5 C11
Exnaboe Shetland 96 M5
Exning Suff 30 B3
Exton Devon 5 C10
Exton Hants 10 B5
Exton Rutland 36 D5
Exton Som 7 C8
Exwick Devon 5 C10
Eyam Derbys 44 E6
Eydon Northants 28 C2
Eye Hereford 25 B11
Eye Pboro 37 E8
Eye Suff 31 A8
Eye Green Pboro 37 E8
Eyemouth Borders 71 D8
Eyeworth C Beds 29 D9
Eyhorne Street
Kent 20 F5
Eyke Suff 31 C10
Eynesbury Cambs 29 C8
Eynort Highld 85 E8
Eynsford Kent 20 E2
Eynsham Oxon 27 H11
Eype Dorset 8 E3
Eyre Highld 85 C9
Eyre Highld 85 D10
Eythorne Kent 21 G9
Eyton Hereford 25 B11
Eyton Shrops 33 G9
Eyton Wrex 33 A9
Eyton upon the
Weald Moors
Telford 34 D2

F

Faccombe Hants 17 F10
Faceby N Yorks 58 F5
Facit Lancs 50 H4
Faddiley Ches E 43 G8
Fadmoor N Yorks 59 H7
Faerdre Swansea 14 A2
Failand N Som 15 D11
Failford S Ayrs 67 D7
Failsworth Gtr Man 44 B2
Fain Highld 86 D4
Fair Green Norf 38 D2
Fair Hill Cumb 57 C7
Fair Oak Hants 10 C3
Fair Oak Green
Hants 18 E3
Fairbourne Gwyn 32 D2
Fairburn N Yorks 51 G10
Fairfield Derbys 44 E4
Fairfield Stockton 58 E5
Fairfield Worcs 27 D7
Fairfield Worcs 34 H5
Fairford Glos 17 A8
Fairhaven Lancs 49 G3
Fairlie N Ayrs 73 H11
Fairlight E Sus 13 E7
Fairlight Cove E Sus 13 E7
Fairmile Devon 7 G9
Fairmilehead Edin 69 D11
Fairoak Staffs 34 B3
Fairseat Kent 20 E3
Fairstead Essex 30 G4
Fairstead Norf 38 D2
Fairwarp E Sus 12 D3
Fairy Cottage IoM 48 D4
Fairy Cross Devon 6 D3
Fakenham Norf 38 C5
Fakenham Magna
Suff 38 H5
Fala Midloth 70 D3
Fala Dam Midloth 70 D3
Falahill Borders 70 E2
Falcon Hereford 26 E3
Faldingworth Lincs 46 D4
Falfield S Glos 16 B3
Falkenham Suff 31 E9
Falkirk Falk 69 C7
Falkland Fife 76 G5
Fallgate Derbys 45 F7
Fallin Stirling 69 B7
Fallowfield Gtr Man 44 C2
Falls of Blarghour
Argyll 73 B8
Falmer E Sus 12 F2
Falmouth Corn 3 F7
Falsgrave N Yorks 59 H11
Falstone Northumb 62 E3
Fanagmore Highld 92 E4
Fangdale Beck
N Yorks 59 G6
Fangfoss E Yorks 52 D3
Fankerton Falk 68 B6
Fanmore Argyll 78 G7
Fannich Lodge
Highld 86 E5
Fans Borders 70 F5
Far Bank S Yorks 45 A10
Far Bletchley
M Keynes 28 E5
Far Cotton
Northants 28 C4
Far Forest Worcs 26 A4
Far Laund Derbys 45 H7
Far Sawrey Cumb 56 G5
Farcet Cambs 37 F8
Farden Shrops 34 H1
Fareham Hants 10 D4
Farewell Staffs 35 D6
Farforth Lincs 47 E7
Faringdon Oxon 17 B9
Farington Lancs 49 G5
Farlam Cumb 61 H11
Farleigh N Som 15 E10
Farleigh Sur 19 E10
Farleigh
Hungerford Som 16 F5
Farleigh Wallop
Hants 18 G3
Farlesthorpe Lincs 47 E8
Farleton Cumb 49 A5
Farleton Lancs 49 C5
Farley Shrops 33 E9
Farley Staffs 35 A7
Farley Wilts 9 B11
Farley Green Sur 19 G7
Farley Hill Luton 29 F7
Farley Hill
Wokingham 18 E4
Farleys End Glos 26 G4
Farlington N Yorks 52 C2
Farlow Shrops 34 G2
Farmborough Bath 16 E3
Farmcote Glos 27 F7
Farmcote Shrops 34 F3
Farmington Glos 27 G8
Farmoor Oxon 27 H11
Farmtown Moray 88 C5
Farnborough Hants 18 F5
Farnborough
London 19 E11
Farnborough
W Berks 17 C11
Farnborough
Warks 27 D11
Farnborough
Green Hants 18 F5
Farncombe Sur 18 G6
Farndish Bedford 28 B6
Farndon Ches W 43 G7
Farndon Notts 45 G11
Farnell Angus 77 B9
Farnham Dorset 9 C8
Farnham Essex 29 F11
Farnham N Yorks 51 C9
Farnham Suff 31 B10
Farnham Sur 18 G5
Farnham Common
Bucks 18 C6
Farnham Green
Essex 29 F11
Farnham Royal
Bucks 18 C6
Farnhill N Yorks 50 E6
Farningham Kent 20 E2
Farnley N Yorks 51 E8
Farnley W Yorks 51 F8
Farnley Tyas
W Yorks 44 A5
Farnsfield Notts 45 G10
Farnworth Gtr Man 43 B10

Column 5

Farnworth Halton 43 D8
Farr Highld 81 A10
Farr Highld 87 H9
Farr Highld 93 C10
Farr House Highld 81 A9
Farringdon Devon 7 G9
Farrington
Gurney Bath 16 F3
Farsley W Yorks 51 F8
Farthinghoe
Northants 28 E2
Farthingloe Kent 21 G9
Farthingstone
Northants 28 C3
Fartown W Yorks 51 H7
Farway Devon 7 G10
Fasag Highld 85 C13
Fascadale Highld 79 E8
Faslane Port
Argyll 73 E11
Fasnacloich Argyll 74 C3
Fasnakyle Ho
Highld 80 A5
Fassfern Highld 80 F2
Fatfield T&W 58 A4
Fattahead Aberds 89 C6
Faugh Cumb 57 A7
Fauldhouse W Loth 69 D8
Faulkbourne Essex 30 G4
Faulkland Som 16 F4
Fauls Shrops 34 B1
Faversham Kent 21 E7
Favillar Moray 88 E2
Fawdington
N Yorks 51 B10
Fawfieldhead
Staffs 44 F4
Fawkham Green
Kent 20 E2
Fawler Oxon 27 G10
Fawley Bucks 18 C4
Fawley Hants 10 D3
Fawley W Berks 17 C10
Fawley Chapel
Hereford 26 F2
Faxfleet E Yorks 52 G4
Faygate W Sus 11 A11
Fazakerley Mers 42 C6
Fazeley Staffs 35 E8
Fearby N Yorks 51 A7
Fearn Highld 87 D11
Fearn Lodge Highld 87 C9
Fearn Station
Highld 87 D11
Fearnan Perth 75 C10
Fearnbeg Highld 85 C12
Fearnhead Warr 43 C9
Fearnmore Highld 85 B12
Featherstone
Staffs 34 E5
Featherstone
W Yorks 51 G10
Featherwood
Northumb 62 C4
Feckenham Worcs 27 B7
Feering Essex 30 F5
Feetham N Yorks 57 G11
Feizor N Yorks 50 C3
Felbridge Sur 12 C2
Felbrigg Norf 39 B8
Felcourt Sur 12 B2
Felden Herts 19 A7
Felin-Crai Powys 24 F5
Felindre Carms 23 C8
Felindre Carms 23 C10
Felindre Carms 23 D10
Felindre Carms 24 E3
Felindre Ceredig 23 A10
Felindre Powys 33 G7
Felindre Swansea 14 A2
Felindre Farchog
Pembs 22 C6
Felinfach Ceredig 23 A10
Felinfach Powys 25 E7
Felinfoel Carms 23 F10
Felingwm isaf
Carms 23 D10
Felingwm uchaf
Carms 23 D10
Felixkirk N Yorks 51 A10
Felixstowe Suff 31 E9
Felixstowe Ferry
Suff 31 E10
Felkington
Northumb 71 F8
Felkirk W Yorks 45 A7
Fell Side Cumb 56 C5
Felling T&W 63 G8
Felmersham
Bedford 28 C6
Felmingham Norf 39 C8
Felpham W Sus 11 E8
Felsham Suff 30 C6
Felsted Essex 30 F3
Feltham London 19 D8
Felthorpe Norf 39 D7
Felton Hereford 26 D2
Felton N Som 15 E11
Felton Northumb 63 C7
Felton Butler
Shrops 33 D9
Feltwell Norf 38 F3
Fen Ditton Cambs 29 B11
Fen Drayton Cambs 29 B10
Fen End W Mid 35 H8
Fen Side Lincs 47 G7
Fenay Bridge
W Yorks 51 H7
Fence Lancs 50 F4
Fence Houses T&W 58 A4
Fengate Norf 39 C7
Fengate Pboro 37 F8
Fenham Northumb 71 F9
Fenhouses Lincs 46 H6
Feniscliffe
Blackburn 50 G2
Feniscowles
Blackburn 50 G2
Feniton Devon 7 G10
Fenlake Bedford 29 D7
Fenny Bentley
Derbys 44 G5
Fenny Bridges
Devon 7 G10
Fenny Compton
Warks 27 C11
Fenny Drayton
Leics 35 F9
Fenny Stratford
M Keynes 28 E5
Fenrother Northumb 63 D7
Fenstanton Cambs 29 B10
Fenton Cambs 37 H9
Fenton Lincs 46 E2
Fenton Lincs 46 G2
Fenton Stoke 34 A4
Fenton Barns E Loth 70 B4
Fenton Town
Northumb 71 G8
Fenwick E Ayrs 67 B7
Fenwick Northumb 63 F7
Fenwick Northumb 71 F9
Fenwick S Yorks 52 H1
Feochaig Argyll 65 G8
Feock Corn 3 F7
Feolin Ferry Argyll 72 G3
Ferindonald
Highld 85 H11
Feriniquarrie
Highld 84 C6
Ferlochan Argyll 74 C2
Fern Angus 77 A7
Ferndale Rhondda 14 B6
Ferndown Dorset 9 D9
Ferness Highld 87 G12
Ferney Green
Cumb 56 G6
Fernham Oxon 17 B9
Fernhill Heath
Worcs 26 C5
Fernhurst W Sus 11 B7
Fernie Fife 76 F6
Ferniegair S Lanark 68 E6
Fernilee Derbys 44 E4
Ferrensby N Yorks 51 C9
Ferrindonald
Highld 85 H11
Ferring W Sus 11 D9
Ferry Hill Cambs 37 G9
Ferry Point Highld 87 C10
Ferrybridge
W Yorks 51 G10
Ferryden Angus 77 B10
Ferryhill Aberdeen 83 C11
Ferryhill Durham 58 C3
Ferryhill Station
Durham 58 C4
Ferryside Carms 23 E8
Fersfield Norf 39 G6
Fersit Highld 80 F5
Ferwig Ceredig 22 B6
Feshiebridge
Highld 81 C10
Fetcham Sur 19 F8
Fetterangus
Aberds 89 C9
Fettercairn Aberds 83 F8
Fettes Highld 87 F8
Fewcott Oxon 28 F2
Fewston N Yorks 51 D7
Ffair-Rhos Ceredig 24 B4
Ffairfach Carms 24 F3
Ffaldybrenin Carms 24 D3

Column 6

Ffarmers Carms 24 D3
Ffawyddog Powys 25 G9
Fforest Carms 23 F10
Fforest-fâch
Swansea 14 B2
Ffos-y-ffin Ceredig 23 A9
Ffostrasol Ceredig 23 B8
Ffridd-Uchaf Gwyn 41 E7
Ffrith Flint 42 G5
Ffrwd Gwyn 40 E6
Ffynnon ddrain
Carms 23 D9
Ffynnon-oer
Ceredig 23 A10
Ffynnongroyw
Flint 42 D4
Fiddes Aberds 83 E10
Fiddington Glos 26 E6
Fiddington Som 7 B11
Fiddleford Dorset 9 C7
Fiddlers Hamlet
Essex 19 A11
Field Staffs 34 B6
Field Broughton
Cumb 49 A3
Field Dalling Norf 38 B6
Field Head Leics 35 E10
Fifehead
Magdalen Dorset 9 B6
Fifehead Neville
Dorset 9 C6
Fifield Oxon 27 G9
Fifield Wilts 17 F8
Fifield Windsor 18 D6
Fifield Bavant Wilts 9 B9
Figheldean Wilts 17 G8
Filands Wilts 16 C6
Filby Norf 39 D10
Filey N Yorks 53 A7
Filgrave M Keynes 28 D5
Filkins Oxon 17 A9
Filleigh Devon 6 D5
Filleigh Devon 7 E6
Fillingham Lincs 46 D3
Fillongley Warks 35 G8
Filton S Glos 16 D3
Fimber E Yorks 52 C4
Finavon Angus 77 B7
Finchairn Argyll 73 C8
Fincham Norf 38 E2
Finchampstead
Wokingham 18 E4
Finchdean Hants 10 C6
Finchingfield Essex 30 E3
Finchley London 19 B9
Findern Derbys 35 B9
Findhorn Moray 87 E13
Findhorn Bridge
Highld 81 A10
Findo Gask Perth 76 E3
Findochty Moray 88 B4
Findon Aberds 83 D11
Findon W Sus 11 D10
Findrack Ho.
Aberds 83 C8
Finedon Northants 28 A6
Fingal Street Suff 31 B9
Fingask Aberds 83 A9
Fingerpost Worcs 26 A4
Fingest Bucks 18 B4
Finghall N Yorks 58 H2
Fingland Cumb 61 H8
Fingland Dumfries 60 B3
Finglesham Kent 21 F10
Fingringhoe Essex 31 F7
Finlarig Stirling 75 D8
Finmere Oxon 28 E3
Finnart Perth 75 B8
Finningham Suff 31 B7
Finningley S Yorks 45 C11
Finnygaud Aberds 88 C6
Finsbury London 19 C10
Finstall Worcs 26 B6
Finsthwaite Cumb 56 H5
Finstock Oxon 27 G10
Finstown Orkney 95 G4
Fintry Aberds 89 C7
Fintry Dundee 77 D7
Fintry Stirling 68 B5
Finzean Aberds 83 D8
Fionnphort Argyll 78 J6
Fionnsbhagh
W Isles 90 J5
Fir Tree Durham 58 C2
Firbeck S Yorks 45 D9
Firby N Yorks 52 C3
Firby N Yorks 58 H3
Firgrove Gtr Man 44 A3
Firsby Lincs 47 F8
Firsdown Wilts 9 A11
First Coast Highld 86 B2
Fishbourne IoW 10 E4
Fishbourne W Sus 11 D7
Fishburn Durham 58 C4
Fishcross Clack 75 H11
Fisher Place Cumb 56 E5
Fisher's Pond Hants 10 B3
Fisherford Aberds 89 E6
Fisher's Row Lancs 49 E4
Fisherstreet W Sus 11 A8
Fisherton Highld 87 F10
Fisherton S Ayrs 66 E5
Fishguard =
Abergwaun Pembs 22 C4
Fishlake S Yorks 45 A10
Fishleigh Barton
Devon 6 D4
Fishponds Bristol 16 D3
Fishpool Glos 26 F3
Fishtoft Lincs 47 H7
Fishtoft Drove
Lincs 47 H7
Fishtown of Usan
Angus 77 B10
Fishwick Blackburn 50 G1
Fiskavaig Highld 85 E8
Fiskerton Lincs 46 E4
Fiskerton Notts 45 G11
Fittleton Wilts 17 G8
Fittleworth W Sus 11 C9
Fitton End Cambs 37 D10
Fitz Shrops 33 D10
Fitzhead Som 7 D10
Fitzwilliam W Yorks 51 H10
Fiunary Highld 79 G9
Five Acres Glos 26 G2
Five Ashes E Sus 12 D4
Five Oaks Jersey 11
Five Oaks W Sus 11 B9
Five Roads Carms 23 F9
Fivecrosses Ches W 43 E8
Fivehead Som 8 B2
Flack's Green Essex 30 G4
Flackwell Heath
Bucks 18 C5
Fladbury Worcs 26 D6
Fladdabister
Shetland 96 K6
Flagg Derbys 44 F5
Flamborough
E Yorks 53 B8
Flamstead Herts 29 G7
Flamstead End
Herts 19 A10
Flansham W Sus 11 D8
Flanshaw W Yorks 51 G9
Flasby N Yorks 50 D5
Flash Staffs 44 F4
Flashader Highld 85 C8
Flask Inn N Yorks 59 F10
Flaunden Herts 19 A7
Flawborough Notts 36 A3
Flawith N Yorks 51 C10
Flax Bourton N Som 15 E11
Flaxby N Yorks 51 C9
Flaxholme Derbys 45 H7
Flaxley Glos 26 G3
Flaxpool Som 7 C10
Flaxton N Yorks 52 C2
Fleck Shetland 96 M5
Fleckney Leics 36 F2
Flecknoe Warks 28 B2
Fledborough Notts 46 E2
Fleet Hants 10 D6
Fleet Hants 18 F5
Fleet Lincs 37 C9
Fleet Hargate Lincs 37 C9
Fleetham Northumb 71 H10
Fleetlands Hants 10 D4
Fleetville Herts 29 H8
Fleetwood Lancs 49 E3
Flemingston V Glam 14 D6
Flemington S Lanark 68 D5
Flers Essex 30 F5
Fletchertown Cumb 56 B4
Fletching E Sus 12 D3
Flexbury Corn 6 F1
Flexford Sur 18 G6
Flimby Cumb 56 C2
Flimwell E Sus 12 C6
Flint = Y Fflint
Flint 42 E5
Flint Mountain Flint 42 E5
Flintham Notts 36 A3

Column 7

Flinton E Yorks 53 F8
Flintsham Hereford 25 C10
Flitcham Norf 38 C3
Flitton C Beds 29 E7
Flitwick C Beds 29 E7
Flixborough
N Lincs 52 H4
Flixborough
Stather N Lincs 46 A2
Flixton Gtr Man 43 C10
Flixton N Yorks 52 B6
Flixton Suff 39 G9
Flockton W Yorks 44 A6
Flodaigh W Isles 84 C3
Flodden Northumb 71 G8
Flodigarry Highld 85 A9
Flood's Ferry
Cambs 37 F9
Flookburgh Cumb 49 B3
Florden Norf 39 F7
Flore Northants 28 B3
Flotterton
Northumb 62 C5
Flowton Suff 31 D7
Flush House
W Yorks 44 B5
Flushing Aberds 89 D10
Flushing Corn 3 F7
Flyford Flavell
Worcs 26 C6
Foals Green Suff 31 A9
Fobbing Thurrock 20 C4
Fochabers Moray 88 C3
Fochriw Caerph 25 H7
Fockerby N Lincs 52 H4
Fodderletter Moray 82 A3
Fodderty Highld 87 F8
Foel Powys 32 D5
Foel-gastell Carms 23 E10
Foffarty Angus 77 C7
Foggathorpe
E Yorks 52 F3
Fogo Borders 70 F6
Fogorig Borders 70 F6
Foindle Highld 92 E4
Folda Angus 76 A4
Foleshill W Mid 35 G9
Folke Dorset 8 C5
Folkestone Kent 21 H9
Folkingham Lincs 36 B6
Folkington E Sus 12 F4
Folksworth Cambs 37 G7
Folkton N Yorks 52 B6
Folla Rule Aberds 89 E7
Follifoot N Yorks 51 D9
Folly Gate Devon 6 G4
Fonthill Bishop
Wilts 9 A8
Fonthill Gifford
Wilts 9 A8
Fontmell Magna
Dorset 9 C7
Fontwell W Sus 11 D8
Foolow Derbys 44 E5
Foots Cray London 19 D11
Forbestown Aberds 82 B5
Force Mills Cumb 56 G5
Forcett N Yorks 58 E2
Ford Argyll 73 C7
Ford Bucks 28 H4
Ford Devon 6 D3
Ford Glos 27 F7
Ford Northumb 71 G8
Ford Shrops 33 D10
Ford Staffs 44 G4
Ford Wilts 16 D5
Ford W Sus 11 D8
Ford End Essex 30 G3
Ford Street Som 7 E10
Fordcombe Kent 12 B4
Fordell Fife 69 B10
Forden Powys 33 E8
Forder Grn. Devon 5 E8
Fordham Cambs 30 A2
Fordham Essex 30 F6
Fordham Norf 38 F2
Fordhouses W Mid 34 E5
Fordingbridge
Hants 9 C10
Fordon E Yorks 52 B6
Fordoun Aberds 83 F9
Ford's Green Suff 31 B7
Fordstreet Essex 30 F6
Fordwells Oxon 27 G10
Fordwich Kent 21 F8
Fordyce Aberds 88 B5
Forebridge Staffs 34 C5
Foreland Ho. Argyll 64 A3
Foremark Derbys 35 C9
Forest Durham 57 C10
Forest Gate
London 19 C11
Forest Green Sur 19 G8
Forest Hall Cumb 57 F7
Forest Head Cumb 61 H11
Forest Hill Oxon 28 H2
Forest Lane Head
N Yorks 51 D9
Forest Lodge
Argyll 74 B4
Forest Lodge
Highld 82 D2
Forest Lodge Perth 75 A11
Forest Mill Clack 69 A8
Forest Row E Sus 12 C3
Forest Town Notts 45 F9
Forestburn Gate
Northumb 62 D6
Foresterseat Moray 88 C1
Forestside W Sus 11 C6
Forfar Angus 77 B7
Forgandenny Perth 76 F3
Forge Powys 32 F3
Forge Side Torf 25 H9
Forgewood
N Lanark 68 E6
Forgie Moray 88 C3
Forglen Ho. Aberds 89 C6
Formby Mers 42 B5
Forncett End Norf 39 F7
Forncett St Mary
Norf 39 F7
Forncett St Peter
Norf 39 F7
Forneth Perth 76 C3
Fornham All
Saints Suff 30 B5
Fornham St Martin
Suff 30 B5
Forres Moray 87 F13
Forrest Lodge
Dumfries 55 A8
Forsbrook Staffs 34 A5
Forse Highld 94 G4
Forse Ho. Highld 94 G4
Forsinain Highld 93 E12
Forsinard Highld 93 E11
Forsinard Station
Highld 93 E11
Forston Dorset 8 E5
Fort Augustus
Highld 80 C5
Fort George Guern 11
Fort George Highld 87 F10
Fort William Highld 80 F3
Forteviot Perth 76 F3
Forth S Lanark 69 E8
Forth Road
Bridge Edin 69 B10
Forthampton Glos 26 E5
Fortingall Perth 75 C10
Forton Hants 17 G11
Forton Lancs 49 D4
Forton Shrops 33 D10
Forton Som 8 D2
Forton Staffs 34 C3
Forton Heath
Shrops 33 D10
Fortrie Aberds 89 D6
Fortrose Highld 87 F10
Fortuneswell
Dorset 8 G5
Forty Green Bucks 18 B6
Forty Hill London 19 B10
Forward Green
Suff 31 C7
Fosbury Wilts 17 F10
Fosdyke Lincs 37 B9
Foss Perth 75 B10
Foss Cross Glos 27 H7
Fossebridge Glos 27 G7
Foster Street
Essex 29 H11
Fosterhouses
S Yorks 45 A10
Foston Derbys 35 B7
Foston Lincs 36 A4
Foston N Yorks 52 C2
Foston on the
Wolds E Yorks 53 D7
Fotherby Lincs 47 C7
Fotheringhay
Northants 37 F6
Foubister Orkney 95 H6
Foul Mile E Sus 12 E5
Foulby W Yorks 51 H9
Foulden Borders 71 E8
Foulden Norf 38 F3
Foulis Castle Highld 87 E8
Foulridge Lancs 50 E4
Foulsham Norf 38 C6
Fountainhall
Borders 70 F3
Four Ashes Staffs 34 G4
Four Ashes Suff 31 A7
Four Crosses Powys 33 D7

Column 8

Four Crosses Powys 33 E6
Four Crosses Wrex 42 G5
Four Elms Kent 19 G11
Four Forks Som 7 C11
Four Gotes Cambs 37 D10
Four Lane Ends
Ches W 43 F8
Four Mile Bridge
Anglesey 40 C4
Four Oaks E Sus 13 D7
Four Oaks W Mid 35 F7
Four Oaks W Mid 35 G8
Four Roads Carms 23 F9
Four Roads IoM 48 F2
Four Throws Kent 12 D6
Fourlane Ends
Derbys 45 G7
Fourlanes End
Ches E 44 G2
Fourpenny Highld 87 B11
Fourstones
Northumb 62 G4
Fovant Wilts 9 B9
Foveran Aberds 89 F9
Fowey Corn 4 F2
Fowley Common
Warr 43 C9
Fowlis Angus 76 D6
Fowlis Wester Perth 76 E2
Fowlmere Cambs 29 D11
Fownhope Hereford 26 E2
Fox Corner Sur 18 F6
Fox Lane Hants 18 F5
Fox Street Essex 31 F7
Foxbar Renfs 68 D3
Foxcombe Hill
Oxon 17 A11
Foxdale IoM 48 E2
Foxearth Essex 30 D5
Foxfield Cumb 56 H4
Foxham Wilts 16 D6
Foxhole Corn 3 D8
Foxhole Swansea 14 B2
Foxholes N Yorks 52 B6
Foxhunt Green
E Sus 12 E4
Foxley Norf 38 C6
Foxley Wilts 16 C5
Foxt Staffs 44 H4
Foxton Cambs 29 D11
Foxton Durham 58 D4
Foxton Leics 36 F3
Foxup N Yorks 50 B4
Foxwist Green
Ches W 43 F9
Foxwood Shrops 34 H2
Foy Hereford 26 F2
Foyers Highld 81 A6
Foynesfield Highld 87 F11
Fraddam Corn 2 F4
Fraddon Corn 3 D8
Fradley Staffs 35 D7
Fradswell Staffs 34 B5
Fraisthorpe E Yorks 53 C7
Framfield E Sus 12 D3
Framingham Earl
Norf 39 E8
Framingham Pigot
Norf 39 E8
Framlingham Suff 31 B9
Frampton Dorset 8 E5
Frampton Lincs 37 B9
Frampton
Cotterell S Glos 16 C3
Frampton Mansell
Glos 16 A6
Frampton on
Severn Glos 26 H4
Frampton West
End Lincs 37 A8
Framsden Suff 31 C8
Framwellgate
Moor Durham 58 B3
Franche Worcs 34 H4
Frankby Mers 42 D5
Frankley Worcs 34 G5
Frank's Bridge
Powys 25 C8
Frankton Warks 27 A11
Frant E Sus 12 C4
Fraserburgh
Aberds 89 B9
Frating Green
Essex 31 F7
Fratton Ptsmth 10 E5
Freathy Corn 4 F4
Freckenham Suff 30 A3
Freckleton Lancs 49 G4
Freeby Leics 36 C4
Freeland Oxon 27 G11
Freester Shetland 96 H6
Freethorpe Norf 39 E10
Freiston Lincs 47 H7
Fremington Devon 6 C4
Fremington N Yorks 58 G1
French Street
Kent 19 F11
Frenchay S Glos 16 D3
Frenchbeer Devon 5 C7
Frenich Stirling 75 G7
Frensham Sur 18 G5
Fresgoe Highld 93 C12
Freshfield Mers 42 B5
Freshford Bath 16 E4
Freshwater IoW 10 F1
Freshwater Bay
IoW 10 F1
Freshwater East
Pembs 22 G5
Fressingfield Suff 39 H8
Freston Suff 31 E8
Freswick Highld 94 D5
Fretherne Glos 26 H4
Frettenham Norf 39 D8
Freuchie Fife 76 G5
Freuchies Angus 82 G4
Freystrop Pembs 22 E4
Friar's Gate E Sus 12 C3
Friarton Perth 76 E4
Friday Bridge
Cambs 37 E10
Friday Street
E Yorks 12 F5
Friern Barnet
London 19 B9
Friesland Argyll 78 F4
Friesthorpe Lincs 46 D4
Frieston Lincs 46 H3
Frieth Bucks 18 B4
Frilford Oxon 17 B11
Frilsham W Berks 18 D2
Frimley Sur 18 F5
Frimley Green Sur 18 F5
Frindsbury Medway 20 E4
Fring Norf 38 B3
Fringford Oxon 28 F3
Frinsted Kent 20 F5
Frinton-on-Sea
Essex 31 F9
Friockheim Angus 77 C8
Friog Gwyn 32 D2
Frisby on the
Wreake Leics 36 D2
Friskney Lincs 47 G8
Friskney Eaudike
Lincs 47 G8
Friskney Tofts Lincs 47 G8
Friston E Sus 12 G4
Friston Suff 31 B11
Fritchley Derbys 45 G7
Frith Bank Lincs 47 H7
Frith Common
Worcs 26 B3
Fritham Hants 10 C1
Frithelstock Devon 6 E3
Frithelstock Stone
Devon 6 E3
Frithville Lincs 47 G7
Frittenden Kent 13 B7
Frittiscombe Devon 5 G9
Fritton Norf 39 E8
Fritton Norf 39 E10
Fritwell Oxon 28 F2
Frizinghall W Yorks 51 F7
Frizington Cumb 56 E2
Frocester Glos 16 A4
Frodesley Shrops 33 E11
Frodingham N Lincs 46 A2
Frodsham Ches W 43 E8
Frogden Borders 70 H6
Froggatt Derbys 44 E6
Froghall Staffs 44 H4
Frogmore Devon 5 G8
Frogmore Hants 18 F5
Frognall Lincs 37 D7
Frogpool Corn 3 E6
Frogshall Norf 39 B8
Frolesworth Leics 35 F11
Frome Som 16 G4
Frome St Quintin
Dorset 8 D4
Fromes Hill
Hereford 26 D3
Fron Denb 42 F3
Fron Gwyn 40 F5
Fron Gwyn 40 G6
Fron Powys 25 A7
Fron Powys 33 E7
Fron Powys 33 E8
Froncysyllte Wrex 33 A8
Frongoch Gwyn 32 B5
Frostenden Suff 39 G10
Frosterley Durham 58 C1
Frotoft Orkney 95 F5
Froxfield Wilts 17 E9
Froxfield Green
Hants 10 B6
Froyle Hants 18 G4
Fryerning Essex 20 A3
Fryton N Yorks 52 B2
Fulbeck Lincs 46 G3
Fulbourn Cambs 30 C2
Fulbrook Oxon 27 G9
Fulford Som 7 D11
Fulford Staffs 34 B5
Fulford York 52 E2
Fulham London 19 D9
Fulking W Sus 11 C11
Full Sutton E Yorks 52 D3
Fullarton Glasgow 68 D5
Fullarton N Ayrs 66 C6
Fuller Street Essex 30 G4
Fuller's Moor
Ches W 43 G7
Fullerton Hants 17 H10
Fulletby Lincs 46 E6
Fulford Wilts 17 H7
Fullwood E Ayrs 67 A7
Fulmer Bucks 18 C6
Fulmodestone Norf 38 B5
Fulnetby Lincs 46 E4
Fulstow Lincs 47 C7
Fulwell T&W 63 H9
Fulwood Lancs 49 F5
Fulwood S Yorks 45 D7
Fundenhall Norf 39 F7
Fundenhall Street
Norf 39 F7
Funtington W Sus 11 D6
Funtley Hants 10 D4
Funtullich Perth 75 E10
Funzie Shetland 96 D8
Furley Devon 8 D1
Furnace Argyll 73 C9
Furnace Carms 23 F10
Furnace End Warks 35 F8
Furneux Pelham
Herts 29 F11
Furze Platt Windsor 18 C5
Furzehill Devon 7 B6
Fylingthorpe
N Yorks 59 F10
Fyvie Aberds 89 E7

Column 9

Frostenden Suff 39 G10

G

Gabhsann bho
Dheas W Isles 91 B9
Gabhsann bho
Thuath W Isles 91 B9
Gablon Highld 87 B10
Gabroc Hill E Ayrs 67 A7
Gaddesby Leics 36 D2
Gadebridge Herts 29 H7
Gaer Powys 25 F8
Gaerllwyd Mon 15 B10
Gaerwen Anglesey 40 C6
Gagingwell Oxon 27 F11
Gaick Lodge Highld 81 E9
Gailey Staffs 34 D5
Gainford Durham 58 E2
Gainsborough Lincs 46 C2
Gainsborough Suff 31 D8
Gainsford End
Essex 30 E4
Gairloch Highld 85 A13
Gairlochy Highld 80 E3
Gairney Bank Perth 76 H4
Gairnshiel Lodge
Aberds 82 C4
Gaisgill Cumb 57 F8
Gaitsgill Cumb 56 B5
Galachoilie Argyll 73 E6
Galashiels Borders 70 G3
Galgate Lancs 49 D4
Galhampton Som 8 B5
Gallaberry Dumfries 60 E5
Gallachoille Argyll 72 E6
Gallanach Argyll 78 F6
Gallanach Argyll 79 J11
Gallantry Bank
Ches E 43 G8
Gallatown Fife 69 A11
Galley Common
Warks 35 F9
Galley Hill Cambs 29 B10
Galleyend Essex 20 A4
Galleywood Essex 20 A4
Gallin Perth 75 C8
Gallowfauld Angus 77 C7
Gallows Green
Staffs 35 A6
Galltair Highld 85 F13
Galmisdale Highld 78 C7
Galmpton Devon 5 G7
Galmpton Torbay 5 F9
Galphay N Yorks 51 B8
Galston E Ayrs 67 C8
Galtrigill Highld 84 C6
Gamblesby Cumb 57 C8
Gamesley Derbys 44 C4
Gamlingay Cambs 29 C9
Gammersgill
N Yorks 58 H1
Gamston Notts 45 E11
Ganarew Hereford 26 G2
Ganavan Argyll 79 H11
Gang Corn 4 E4
Ganllwyd Gwyn 32 C3
Gannochy Angus 83 F7
Gannochy Perth 76 E4
Gansclet Highld 94 F5
Ganstead E Yorks 53 F7
Ganthorpe N Yorks 52 B2
Ganton N Yorks 52 B5
Garbat Highld 86 E7
Garbhallt Argyll 73 D9
Garboldisham Norf 38 G6
Garden City Flint 42 F6
Garden Village
W Yorks 51 F10
Garden Village
Wrex 42 G6
Gardenhouse
Shetland 96 H5
Garderhouse
Shetland 96 J5
Gardham E Yorks 52 E5
Gardin Shetland 96 G6
Gare Hill Som 16 G5
Garelochhead
Argyll 73 D11
Garford Oxon 17 B11
Garforth W Yorks 51 F10
Gargrave N Yorks 50 D5
Gargunnock Stirling 68 A5
Garlic Street Norf 39 G8
Garlieston Dumfries 55 E7
Garlinge Green
Kent 21 F8
Garlogie Aberds 83 C9
Garmond Aberds 89 C8
Garmony Argyll 79 G9
Garmouth Moray 88 B3
Garn-yr-erw Torf 25 G9
Garnant Carms 24 G3
Garndiffaith Torf 25 H9
Garndolbenmaen
Gwyn 40 F6
Garnedd Conwy 41 E9
Garnett Bridge
Cumb 57 G7
Garnfadryn Gwyn 40 G4
Garnkirk N Lanark 68 D5
Garnlydan Bl Gwent 25 G8
Garnswllt Swansea 23 G11
Garrabost W Isles 91 D10
Garraron Argyll 73 C7
Garras Corn 2 G6
Garreg Gwyn 41 F8
Garrick Perth 75 F11
Garrigill Cumb 57 B9
Garriston N Yorks 58 G2
Garroch Dumfries 55 A8
Garrogie Lodge
Highld 81 B7
Garros Highld 85 B9
Garrow Perth 75 C11
Garryhorn Dumfries 55 A8
Garsdale Cumb 57 H9
Garsdale Head
Cumb 57 G9
Garsdon Wilts 16 C6
Garshall Green
Staffs 34 B5
Garsington Oxon 18 A2
Garstang Lancs 49 E4
Garston Mers 43 D7
Garswood Mers 43 C8
Gartcosh N Lanark 68 D5
Garth Bridgend 14 B4
Garth Gwyn 41 C7
Garth Powys 24 D6
Garth Shetland 96 H4
Garth Wrex 33 A8
Garth Row Cumb 57 G7
Garthamlock
Glasgow 68 D5
Garthbrengy Powys 25 E7
Garthdee Aberdeen 83 C11
Gartheli Ceredig 23 A10
Garthmyl Powys 33 F7
Garthorpe Leics 36 C4
Garthorpe N Lincs 52 H4
Gartly Aberds 88 E5
Gartmore Stirling 75 H8
Gartnagrenach
Argyll 72 H6
Gartness N Lanark 68 D6
Gartness Stirling 68 B4
Gartocharn
W Dunb 68 B3
Garton E Yorks 53 F8
Garton-on-the-
Wolds E Yorks 52 D5
Gartsherrie
N Lanark 68 D6
Gartymore Highld 93 H13
Garvald E Loth 70 C4
Garvamore Highld 81 D7
Garvard Argyll 72 D2
Garvault Hotel
Highld 93 F10
Garve Highld 86 E6
Garvestone Norf 38 E6
Garvock Aberds 83 F9
Garvock Involyd 73 F11
Garway Hereford 25 F11
Garway Hill
Hereford 25 F11
Gaskan Highld 79 D10
Gastard Wilts 16 E5
Gasthorpe Norf 38 G5
Gatcombe IoW 10 F3
Gate Burton Lincs 46 D2
Gate Helmsley
N Yorks 52 D2
Gateacre Mers 43 D7
Gatebeck Cumb 57 H7
Gateford Notts 45 D9
Gateforth N Yorks 52 G1
Gatehead E Ayrs 67 C6
Gatehouse
Northumb 62 E3
Gatehouse of
Fleet Dumfries 55 D9
Gatelawbridge
Dumfries 60 D5
Gateley Norf 38 C5
Gatenby N Yorks 58 H4
Gateshead T&W 63 G8
Gatesheath Ches W 43 F7
Gateside Aberds 83 B8
Gateside Angus 77 C7
Gateside E Renf 68 E3
Gateside Fife 76 G4
Gateside N Ayrs 67 A6
Gathurst Gtr Man 43 B8
Gatley Gtr Man 44 D2
Gattonside Borders 70 G4
Gatwick Airport
W Sus 12 B1
Gaufron Powys 24 B6
Gaulby Leics 36 E2
Gauldry Fife 76 E6
Gaunt's Common
Dorset 9 D9
Gautby Lincs 46 E5
Gavinton Borders 70 E6
Gawber S Yorks 45 B7
Gawcott Bucks 28 E3
Gawsworth Ches E 44 F2
Gawthorpe W Yorks 51 G8
Gawthrop Cumb 57 H8
Gawthwaite Cumb 56 H4
Gay Street W Sus 11 B9
Gaydon Warks 27 C10
Gayhurst M Keynes 28 D5
Gayle N Yorks 57 H10
Gayles N Yorks 58 F2
Gayton Mers 42 D5
Gayton Norf 38 D3
Gayton Northants 28 C4
Gayton Staffs 34 C5
Gayton le Marsh
Lincs 47 D8
Gayton le Wold
Lincs 46 D6
Gayton Thorpe
Norf 38 D3
Gaywood Norf 38 C2
Gazeley Suff 30 B4
Geanies House
Highld 87 D11
Gearraidh
Bhaird W Isles 91 F8
Gearraidh na
h-Aibhne W Isles 90 D7
Gearraidh na
Monadh W Isles 84 G2
Geary Highld 84 B7
Geddes House
Highld 87 F11
Gedding Suff 30 C6
Geddington
Northants 36 G4
Gedling Notts 36 A2
Gedney Lincs 37 C10
Gedney Broadgate
Lincs 37 C10
Gedney Drove
End Lincs 37 C11
Gedney Dyke Lincs 37 C10
Gedney Hill Lincs 37 D9
Gee Cross Gtr Man 44 C3
Geilston Argyll 68 C2
Geirinis W Isles 84 D2
Geise Highld 94 D3
Geisiadar W Isles 90 D6
Geldeston Norf 39 F9
Gell Conwy 41 D10
Gelli Pembs 22 E5
Gelli Rhondda 14 B5
Gellideg M Tydf 25 H7
Gellifor Denb 42 F4
Gelligaer Caerph 15 B7
Gellilydan Gwyn 41 G8
Gellinudd Neath 14 A3
Gellyburn Perth 76 D3
Gellywen Carms 23 D7
Gelston Dumfries 55 D10
Gelston Lincs 36 A5
Gembling E Yorks 53 D7
Gentleshaw Staffs 35 D6
Geocrab W Isles 90 H6
George Green
Bucks 18 C6
George Nympton
Devon 6 D6
Georgefield
Dumfries 61 D8
Georgeham Devon 6 C3
Georgetown
Bl Gwent 25 H8

Column 10

Gerlan Gwyn 41 D8
Germansweek Devon 6 G3
Germoe Corn 2 G4
Gerrans Corn 3 F7
Gerrards Cross
Bucks 18 C6
Gestingthorpe
Essex 30 E5
Geuffordd Powys 33 D8
Gib Hill Ches W 43 E9
Gibbet Hill Warks 35 H11
Gibbshill Dumfries 60 F3
Gidea Park London 20 C2
Gidleigh Devon 5 C7
Giffnock E Renf 68 E4
Gifford E Loth 70 D4
Giffordland N Ayrs 66 B5
Giffordtown Fife 76 F5
Giggleswick N Yorks 50 C4
Gilberdyke E Yorks 52 G4
Gilchriston E Loth 70 D3
Gilcrux Cumb 56 C3
Gildersome W Yorks 51 G8
Gildingwells
S Yorks 45 D9
Gileston V Glam 14 E6
Gilfach Caerph 15 B7
Gilfach Goch
Rhondda 14 C5
Gilfachrheda
Ceredig 23 A8
Gillamoor N Yorks 59 H7
Gillar's Green Mers 43 C7
Gillen Highld 84 C7
Gilling East N Yorks 52 B2
Gilling West
N Yorks 58 F2
Gillingham Dorset 9 B7
Gillingham Medway 20 E4
Gillingham Norf 39 F10
Gillock Highld 94 E4
Gillow Heath Staffs 44 G2
Gills Highld 94 C5
Gill's Green Kent 13 C6
Gilmanscleuch
Borders 61 A9
Gilmerton Edin 69 D11
Gilmerton Perth 75 E11
Gilmonby Durham 57 E11
Gilmorton Leics 35 G11
Gilmourton
S Lanark 68 F5
Gilsland Northumb 62 G2
Gilsland Spa Cumb 62 G2
Gilston Borders 70 E3
Gilston Herts 29 G11
Gilwern Mon 25 G9
Gimingham Norf 39 B8
Giosla W Isles 90 E6
Gipping Suff 31 B7
Gipsey Bridge Lincs 46 H6
Girdle Toll N Ayrs 66 B6
Girlsta Shetland 96 H6
Girsby N Yorks 58 F4
Girtford C Beds 29 D8
Girthon Dumfries 55 D9
Girton Cambs 29 B11
Girton Notts 46 F2
Girvan S Ayrs 66 G4
Gisburn Lancs 50 E4
Gisleham Suff 39 G11
Gislingham Suff 31 A7
Gissing Norf 39 G7
Gittisham Devon 7 G10
Gladestry Powys 25 C9
Gladsmuir E Loth 70 C3
Glais Swansea 14 A3
Glaisdale N Yorks 59 F8
Glame Highld 85 D10
Glamis Angus 76 C6
Glan Adda Gwyn 41 C7
Glan Conwy Conwy 41 D10
Glan-Conwy
Conwy 41 E10
Glan-Duar Carms 23 B10
Glan-Dwyfach
Gwyn 40 F6
Glan Gors Anglesey 40 C6
Glan-rhyd Gwyn 40 E6
Glan-traeth
Anglesey 40 C4
Glan-y-don Flint 42 E4
Glan-y-nant Powys 32 G5
Glan-y-wern Gwyn 41 G8
Glan-yr-afon
Anglesey 41 B8
Glan-yr-afon Gwyn 32 A5
Glan-yr-afon Gwyn 32 A6
Glanaman Carms 24 G3
Glandford Norf 38 A6
Glandwr Pembs 22 D6
Glandy Cross
Carms 22 D6
Glandyfi Ceredig 32 F3
Glangrwyney Powys 25 G9
Glanmule Powys 33 F7
Glanrafon Ceredig 32 G2
Glanrhyd Gwyn 40 G4
Glanrhyd Pembs 22 B6
Glanton Northumb 62 B6
Glanton Pike
Northumb 62 B6
Glanvilles
Wootton Dorset 8 D5
Glapthorn
Northants 36 F6
Glapwell Derbys 45 F8
Glas-allt Shiel
Aberds 82 E4
Glasbren S Lanark 69 G7
Glaschoil Highld 87 H13
Glascoed Denb 42 E2
Glascoed Mon 15 A9
Glascoed Powys 33 D7
Glascorrie Aberds 82 D5
Glascote Staffs 35 E8
Glascwm Powys 25 C8
Glasdrum Argyll 74 C3
Glasfryn Conwy 42 G2
Glasgow Glasgow 68 D4
Glashvin Highld 85 B9
Glasinfryn Gwyn 41 D7
Glasnacardoch
Highld 79 B9
Glasnakille Highld 85 G10
Glasphein Highld 84 D6
Glaspwll Powys 32 F4
Glassburn Highld 86 H6
Glasserton Dumfries 54 F6
Glassford S Lanark 68 F6
Glasshouse Hill
Glos 26 F4
Glasshouses
N Yorks 51 C7
Glasslie Fife 76 G5
Glasson Cumb 61 G8
Glasson Lancs 49 D4
Glassonby Cumb 57 C7
Glasterlaw Angus 77 B8
Glaston Rutland 36 E4
Glastonbury Som 15 H11
Glatton Cambs 37 G7
Glazebrook Warr 43 C9
Glazebury Warr 43 C9
Glazeley Shrops 34 G3
Gleadless S Yorks 45 D7
Gleadsmoss Ches E 44 F2
Gleann
Tholàstaidh
W Isles 91 C10
Gleaston Cumb 49 B2
Gleiniant Powys 32 F5
Glemsford Suff 30 D5
Glen Dumfries 55 D9
Glen Dumfries 60 F5
Glen Auldyn IoM 48 C4
Glen Bernisdale
Highld 85 D9
Glen Ho. Borders 69 G11
Glen Mona IoM 48 D4
Glen Nevis House
Highld 80 F3
Glen Parva Leics 36 F1
Glen Sluain Argyll 73 D9
Glen Tanar House
Aberds 82 D6
Glen Trool Lodge
Dumfries 55 A7
Glen Vine IoM 48 E3
Glenamachrie
Argyll 74 E2
Glenbarr Argyll 65 E7
Glenbeg Highld 79 E8
Glenbeg Highld 82 A2
Glenbervie Aberds 83 E9
Glenboig N Lanark 68 D6
Glenborrodale
Highld 79 E9
Glenbranter Argyll 73 D10
Glenbreck Borders 60 A6
Glenbrein Lodge
Highld 80 B6
Glenbrittle House
Highld 85 F9
Glenbuchat Lodge
Aberds 82 B5
Glenbuck E Ayrs 68 H6
Glenburn Renfs 68 D3
Glencalvie Lodge
Highld 86 C7
Glencanisp
Lodge Highld 92 G4
Glencaple Dumfries 60 G5
Glencarron
Lodge Highld 86 F3
Glencarse Perth 76 E4
Glencassley
Castle Highld 92 J7
Glenceitlin Highld 74 B3
Glencoe Highld 74 B3
Glencraig Fife 76 H4
Glencripesdale
Highld 79 F9
Glencrosh Dumfries 60 E3
Glendavan Ho.
Aberds 82 C6
Glendevon Perth 76 G2
Glendoe Lodge
Highld 80 C6
Glendoebeg Highld 80 C6
Glendoick Perth 76 E5
Glendoll Lodge
Angus 82 F4
Glenduckie Fife 76 F5
Glendye Lodge
Aberds 83 E8
Gleneagles Hotel
Perth 76 F2
Gleneagles House
Perth 76 G2
Glenegedale Argyll 64 C4
Glenelg Highld 85 G13
Glenernie Moray 87 G13
Glenfarg Perth 76 F4
Glenfarquhar
Lodge Aberds 83 E9
Glenferness
House Highld 87 G12
Glenfeshie
Lodge Highld 81 D10
Glenfield Leics 35 E11
Glenfinnan Highld 79 C11
Glenfoot Perth 76 F4
Glenfyne Lodge
Argyll 74 F5
Glengap Dumfries 55 D9
Glengarnock
N Ayrs 66 A6
Glengorm Castle
Argyll 78 F7
Glengrasco Highld 85 D9
Glenhead Farm
Angus 82 G4

Column 11

Frostenden

Glenhoul Dumfries 55 A9
Glenhurich Highld 79 E11
Glenkerry Borders 61 B8
Glenkiln Dumfries 60 F4
Glenkindie Aberds 82 B6
Glenlatterach
Moray 88 C1
Glenlee Dumfries 55 A9
Glenlichorn Perth 75 F11
Glenlivet Moray 82 A3
Glenlochsie Perth 76 A3
Glenloig N Ayrs 66 C2
Glenluce Dumfries 54 D4
Glenmallan Argyll 73 D11
Glenmarksie Highld 86 F6
Glenmassan Argyll 73 E10
Glenmavis N Lanark 68 D6
Glenmaye IoM 48 E2
Glenmidge Dumfries 60 E4
Glenmore Argyll 73 B7
Glenmore Highld 85 D9
Glenmore Lodge
Highld 81 B11
Glenmoy Angus 77 A7
Glenogil Angus 77 A7
Glenprosen
Lodge Angus 82 G5
Glenprosen
Village Angus 82 G6
Glenquiech Angus 77 A7
Glenreasdell
Mains Argyll 73 H7
Glenree N Ayrs 66 D2
Glenridding Cumb 56 E6
Glenrossal Highld 92 J7
Glenrothes Fife 76 G5
Glensanda Highld 79 G11
Glensaugh Aberds 83 F8
Glenshero Lodge
Highld 81 D7
Glenstockadale
Dumfries 54 C3
Glenstriven Argyll 73 F9
Glentaggart
S Lanark 60 A3
Glentham Lincs 46 C4
Glentirranmuir
Stirling 68 A5
Glenton Aberds 83 A8
Glentress Borders 69 G11
Glentromie
Lodge Highld 81 D9
Glentrool Village
Dumfries 54 B6
Glentruim House
Highld 81 D8
Glentworth Lincs 46 D3
Glenuig Highld 79 D9
Glenurquhart
Highld 87 E10
Glespin S Lanark 60 A3
Gletness Shetland 96 H6
Glewstone Hereford 26 F2
Glinton Pboro 37 E7
Glororum Northumb 71 G10
Glossop Derbys 44 C4
Gloster Hill
Northumb 63 C8
Gloucester Glos 26 G5
Gloup Shetland 96 C7
Glusburn N Yorks 50 E6
Glutt Lodge Highld 93 F12
Glutton Bridge
Staffs 44 F4
Glympton Oxon 27 F11
Glyn-Ceiriog Wrex 33 B8
Glyn-cywarch
Gwyn 41 G8
Glyn Ebwy =
Ebbw Vale
Bl Gwent 25 H8
Glyn-neath =
Glynedd Neath 24 H5
Glynarthen Ceredig 23 B8
Glynbrochan Powys 32 G5
Glyncoch Rhondda 14 B6
Glyncorrwg Neath 14 B4
Glynde E Sus 12 F3
Glyndebourne
E Sus 12 E3
Glyndyfrdwy Denb 33 A7
Glynedd =
Glyn-neath Neath 24 H5
Glynogwr Bridgend 14 C5
Glyntaff Rhondda 14 C6
Glyntawe Powys 24 G5

Glenhurich Highld 79 E11
Glenkerry Borders 61 B8
Glenkiln Dumfries 60 F4
Glenkindie Aberds 82 B6
Glenlatterach Moray 88 C1
Glenlee Dumfries 55 A9
Glenlichorn Perth 75 F10
Glenlivet Moray 82 A3
Glenlochsie Perth 82 F2
Glenloig N Ayrs 66 C2
Glenluce Dumfries 54 D5
Glenmallan Argyll 74 H5
Glenmarksie Highld 86 F6
Glenmassan Argyll 73 E10
Glenmavis N Lanark 68 D6
Glenmaye IoM 48 E2
Glenmidge Dumfries 60 E4
Glenmore Argyll 73 B7
Glenmore Highld 85 D9
Glenmore Lodge Highld 82 C1
Glenmoy Angus 77 A7
Glenogil Angus 77 A7
Glenprosen Lodge Angus 82 G4
Glenprosen Village Angus 82 G5
Glenquiech Angus 77 A7
Glenreasdell Mains Argyll 73 H7
Glenree N Ayrs 66 D2
Glenridding Cumb 56 E5
Glenrossal Highld 92 J7
Glenrothes Fife 76 G5
Glensanda Highld 79 G11
Glensaugh Aberds 83 F8
Glenshero Lodge Highld 81 D7
Glenstockadale Dumfries 54 C3
Glenstriven Argyll 73 F9
Glentaggart S Lanark 69 H7
Glentham Lincs 46 C4
Glentirranmuir Stirling 68 A5
Glenton Aberds 83 A8
Glentress Borders 69 G11
Glentromie Lodge Highld 81 D9
Glentrool Village Dumfries 54 B6
Glentruan IoM 48 B4
Glentruim House Highld 81 D8
Glentworth Lincs 46 D3
Glenuig Highld 79 D9
Glenurquhart Highld 87 E10
Glespin S Lanark 69 H7
Gletness Shetland 96 H6
Glewstone Hereford 26 F2
Glinton Pboro 37 E7
Glooston Leics 36 F3
Glororum Northumb 71 G10
Glossop Derbys 44 C4
Gloster Hill Northumb 63 C8
Gloucester Glos 26 G5
Gloup Shetland 96 C7
Glusburn N Yorks 50 E6
Glutt Lodge Highld 93 F12
Glutton Bridge Staffs 44 F4
Glympton Oxon 27 F11
Glyn-Ceiriog Wrex 33 B8
Glyn-cywarch Gwyn 41 G8
Glyn Ebwy = Ebbw Vale Bl Gwent 25 H8
Glyn-neath = Glynedd Neath 24 H5
Glynarthen Ceredig 23 B8
Glynbrochan Powys 32 G5
Glyncoch Rhondda 14 B6
Glyncorrwg Neath 14 B4
Glynde E Sus 12 F3
Glyndebourne E Sus 12 E3
Glyndyfrdwy Denb 33 A7
Glynedd = Glyn-neath Neath 24 H5
Glynogwr Bridgend 14 C5
Glyntaff Rhondda 14 C6
Glyntawe Powys 24 G5
Gnosall Staffs 34 C4
Gnosall Heath Staffs 34 C4
Goadby Leics 36 F3
Goadby Marwood Leics 36 C3
Goat Lees Kent 21 G7
Goatacre Wilts 17 D7
Goathill Dorset 8 C5
Goathland N Yorks 59 F9
Goathurst Som 8 A1
Gobernuisgach Lodge Highld 92 E7
Gobhaig W Isles 90 G5
Gobowen Shrops 33 B9
Godalming Sur 18 G6
Godley Gtr Man 44 C3
Godmanchester Cambs 29 A9
Godmanstone Dorset 8 E5
Godmersham Kent 21 F7
Godney Som 15 G10
Godolphin Cross Corn 2 F5
Godre'r-graig Neath 24 H4
Godshill Hants 9 C10
Godshill IoW 10 F4
Godstone Sur 19 F10
Godwinscroft Hants 9 E10
Goetre Mon 25 H10
Goferydd Anglesey 40 B4
Goff's Oak Herts 19 A10
Gogar Edin 69 C10
Goginan Ceredig 32 G2
Golan Gwyn 41 F7
Golant Corn 4 F2
Golberdon Corn 4 D4
Golborne Gtr Man 43 C9
Golcar W Yorks 51 H7
Gold Hill Norf 37 F11
Goldcliff Newport 15 C9
Golden Cross E Sus 12 E4
Golden Green Kent 20 G3
Golden Grove Carms 23 E10
Golden Hill Hants 10 E1
Golden Pot Hants 18 G4
Golden Valley Glos 26 F6
Goldenhill Stoke 44 G2
Golders Green London 19 C9
Goldhanger Essex 30 H6
Golding Shrops 33 E11
Goldington Bedford 29 C7
Goldsborough N Yorks 51 D9
Goldsborough N Yorks 59 E9
Goldsithney Corn 2 F4
Goldsworthy Devon 6 D2
Goldthorpe S Yorks 45 B8
Gollanfield Highld 87 F11
Golspie Highld 93 J11
Golval Highld 93 C11
Gomeldon Wilts 17 H8
Gomersal W Yorks 51 G8
Gomshall Sur 19 G7
Gonalston Notts 45 H10
Gonfirth Shetland 96 G5
Good Easter Essex 30 G3
Gooderstone Norf 38 E3
Goodleigh Devon 6 C5
Goodmanham E Yorks 52 E4
Goodnestone Kent 21 E7
Goodnestone Kent 21 F9
Goodrich Hereford 26 G2
Goodrington Torbay 5 F9
Goodshaw Lancs 50 G4
Goodwick = Wdig Pembs 22 C4
Goodworth Clatford Hants 17 G10
Goole E Yorks 52 G3
Goonbell Corn 2 E6
Goonhavern Corn 3 D6
Goose Eye W Yorks 50 E6
Goose Green Gtr Man 43 B8
Goose Green Norf 39 G7
Goose Green W Sus 11 C10
Gooseham Corn 6 E1
Goosey Oxon 17 B10
Goosnargh Lancs 50 F1
Goostrey Ches E 43 E10
Gorcott Hill Warks 27 B7
Gord Shetland 96 L6
Gordon Borders 70 F5
Gordonbush Highld 93 J11
Gordonsburgh Moray 88 B4
Gordonstoun Moray 88 B1
Gordonstown Aberds 88 C5
Gordonstown Aberds 89 E7
Gore Kent 21 F10
Gore Cross Wilts 17 F7
Gore Pit Essex 30 G5
Gorebridge Midloth 70 D2
Gorefield Cambs 37 D10
Gorey Jersey 11
Gorgie Edin 69 C11
Goring Oxon 18 C3
Goring-by-Sea W Sus 11 D10
Goring Heath Oxon 18 D3
Gorleston-on-Sea Norf 39 E11
Gornalwood W Mid 34 F5
Gorrachie Aberds 89 C7
Gorran Churchtown Corn 3 E8
Gorran Haven Corn 3 E9
Gorrenberry Borders 61 D10
Gors Ceredig 32 H2
Gorse Hill Swindon 17 C8
Gorsedd Flint 42 E4
Gorseinon Swansea 23 G10
Gorseness Orkney 95 G5
Gorsgoch Ceredig 23 A9
Gorslas Carms 23 E10
Gorsley Glos 26 F3
Gorstan Highld 86 E6
Gorstanvorran Highld 79 D11
Gorsteyhill Staffs 43 G10
Gorsty Hill Staffs 35 C7
Gortantaoid Argyll 64 A4
Gorton Gtr Man 44 C2
Gosbeck Suff 31 C8
Gosberton Lincs 37 B8
Gosberton Clough Lincs 37 C7
Gosfield Essex 30 F4
Gosford Hereford 26 B2
Gosforth Cumb 56 F2
Gosforth T&W 63 G8
Gosmore Herts 29 F8
Gosport Hants 10 E5
Gossabrough Shetland 96 E7
Gossington Glos 16 A4
Goswick Northumb 71 F9
Gotham Notts 35 B11
Gotherington Glos 26 F6
Gott Shetland 96 J6
Goudhurst Kent 12 C6
Goulceby Lincs 46 E6
Gourdas Aberds 89 D7
Gourdon Aberds 83 F10
Gourock Invclyd 73 F11
Govan Glasgow 68 D4
Govanhill Glasgow 68 D4
Goveton Devon 5 G8
Govilon Mon 25 G9
Gowanhill Aberds 89 B10
Gowdall E Yorks 52 G2
Gowerton Swansea 23 G10
Gowkhall Fife 69 B9
Gowthorpe E Yorks 52 D3
Goxhill E Yorks 53 E7
Goxhill N Lincs 53 G7
Goxhill Haven N Lincs 53 G7
Goytre Neath 14 C3
Grabhair W Isles 91 F8
Graby Lincs 37 C6
Grade Corn 2 H6
Graffham W Sus 11 C8
Grafham Cambs 29 B8
Grafham Sur 19 G7
Grafton Hereford 25 E11
Grafton N Yorks 51 C10
Grafton Oxon 17 A9
Grafton Shrops 33 D10
Grafton Worcs 26 B2
Grafton Flyford Worcs 26 C6
Grafton Regis Northants 28 D4
Grafton Underwood Northants 36 G5
Grafty Green Kent 20 G5
Graianrhyd Denb 42 G5
Graig Conwy 41 C10
Graig Denb 42 E3
Graig-fechan Denb 42 G4
Grain Medway 20 D5
Grainsby Lincs 46 C6
Grainthorpe Lincs 47 C7
Grampound Corn 3 E8
Grampound Road Corn 3 D8
Gramsdal W Isles 84 C3
Granborough Bucks 28 F4
Granby Notts 36 B3
Grandborough Warks 27 B11
Grandtully Perth 76 B2
Grange Cumb 56 E4
Grange E Ayrs 67 C7
Grange Medway 20 E4
Grange Mers 42 D5
Grange Perth 76 E5
Grange Crossroads Moray 88 C4
Grange Hall Moray 87 E13
Grange Hill Essex 19 B11
Grange Moor W Yorks 51 H8
Grange of Lindores Fife 76 F5
Grange-over-Sands Cumb 49 B4
Grange Villa Durham 58 A3
Grangemill Derbys 44 G6
Grangemouth Falk 69 B8
Grangepans Falk 69 B9
Grangetown Cardiff 15 D7
Grangetown Redcar 59 D6
Granish Highld 81 B11
Gransmoor E Yorks 53 D7
Granston Pembs 22 C3
Grantchester Cambs 29 C11
Grantham Lincs 36 B5
Grantley N Yorks 51 C8
Grantlodge Aberds 83 B9
Granton Dumfries 60 C6
Granton Edin 69 C11
Grantown-on-Spey Highld 82 A2
Grantshouse Borders 71 D7
Grappenhall Warr 43 D9
Grasby Lincs 46 B4
Grasmere Cumb 56 F5
Grasscroft Gtr Man 44 B3
Grassendale Mers 43 D6
Grassholme Durham 57 D11
Grassington N Yorks 50 C6
Grassmoor Derbys 45 F8
Grassthorpe Notts 45 F11
Grateley Hants 17 G9
Gratwich Staffs 34 B6
Graveley Cambs 29 B9
Graveley Herts 29 F9
Gravelly Hill W Mid 35 F7
Gravels Shrops 33 E9
Graven Shetland 96 F6
Graveney Kent 21 E7
Gravesend Herts 29 F11
Gravesend Kent 20 D3
Grayingham Lincs 46 C3
Grayrigg Cumb 57 G7
Grays Thurrock 20 D3
Grayshott Hants 18 H5
Grayswood Sur 11 A8
Graythorp Hrtlpl 58 D6
Grazeley Wokingham 18 E3
Greasbrough S Yorks 45 C8
Greasby Mers 42 D5
Great Abington Cambs 30 D2
Great Addington Northants 28 A6
Great Alne Warks 27 C8
Great Altcar Lancs 42 B6
Great Amwell Herts 29 G10
Great Asby Cumb 57 E8
Great Ashfield Suff 30 B6
Great Ayton N Yorks 59 E6
Great Baddow Essex 20 A4
Great Bardfield Essex 30 E3
Great Barford Bedford 29 C8
Great Barr W Mid 34 F6
Great Barrington Glos 27 G9
Great Barrow Ches W 43 F7
Great Barton Suff 30 B5
Great Barugh N Yorks 52 B3
Great Bavington Northumb 62 E5
Great Bealings Suff 31 D9
Great Bedwyn Wilts 17 E9
Great Bentley Essex 31 F8
Great Billing Northants 28 B5
Great Bircham Norf 38 B3
Great Blakenham Suff 31 C8
Great Blencow Cumb 56 C6
Great Bolas Telford 34 C2
Great Bookham Sur 19 F8
Great Bourton Oxon 27 D11
Great Bowden Leics 36 G3
Great Bradley Suff 30 C3
Great Braxted Essex 30 G5
Great Bricett Suff 31 C7
Great Brickhill Bucks 28 E6
Great Bridge W Mid 34 F5
Great Bridgeford Staffs 34 C4
Great Brington Northants 28 B3
Great Bromley Essex 31 F7
Great Broughton Cumb 56 C2
Great Broughton N Yorks 59 F6
Great Budworth Ches W 43 E9
Great Burdon Darl 58 E4
Great Burgh Sur 19 F9
Great Burstead Essex 20 B3
Great Busby N Yorks 58 F6
Great Canfield Essex 30 G2
Great Carlton Lincs 47 D8
Great Casterton Rutland 36 E6
Great Chart Kent 13 B8
Great Chatwell Staffs 34 D3
Great Chesterford Essex 30 D2
Great Cheverell Wilts 16 F6
Great Chishill Cambs 29 E11
Great Clacton Essex 31 G8
Great Cliff W Yorks 51 H9
Great Clifton Cumb 56 D2
Great Coates NE Lincs 46 B6
Great Comberton Worcs 26 D6
Great Corby Cumb 56 A6
Great Cornard Suff 30 D5
Great Cowden E Yorks 53 E8
Great Coxwell Oxon 17 B9
Great Crakehall N Yorks 58 G3
Great Cransley Northants 36 H4
Great Cressingham Norf 38 E4
Great Crosby Mers 42 C6
Great Cubley Derbys 35 B7
Great Dalby Leics 36 D3
Great Denham Bedford 29 D7
Great Doddington Northants 28 B5
Great Dunham Norf 38 D4
Great Dunmow Essex 30 F3
Great Durnford Wilts 17 H8
Great Easton Essex 30 F3
Great Easton Leics 36 F4
Great Eccleston Lancs 49 E4
Great Edstone N Yorks 52 A3
Great Ellingham Norf 38 F6
Great Elm Som 16 G4
Great Eversden Cambs 29 C10
Great Fencote N Yorks 58 G3
Great Finborough Suff 31 C7
Great Fransham Norf 38 D4
Great Gaddesden Herts 29 G7
Great Gidding Cambs 37 G7
Great Givendale E Yorks 52 D4
Great Glemham Suff 31 B10
Great Glen Leics 36 F2
Great Gonerby Lincs 36 B4
Great Gransden Cambs 29 C9
Great Green Norf 39 G8
Great Green Suff 30 C6
Great Habton N Yorks 52 B3
Great Hale Lincs 37 A7
Great Hallingbury Essex 30 G2
Great Hampden Bucks 18 A5
Great Harrowden Northants 28 A5
Great Harwood Lancs 50 F3
Great Haseley Oxon 18 A3
Great Hatfield E Yorks 53 E7
Great Haywood Staffs 34 C6
Great Heath W Mid 35 G9
Great Heck N Yorks 52 G1
Great Henny Essex 30 E5
Great Hinton Wilts 16 F6
Great Hockham Norf 38 F5
Great Holland Essex 31 G9
Great Horkesley Essex 30 E6
Great Hormead Herts 29 F10
Great Horton W Yorks 51 F7
Great Horwood Bucks 28 E4
Great Houghton Northants 28 C4
Great Houghton S Yorks 45 B8
Great Hucklow Derbys 44 E5
Great Kelk E Yorks 53 D7
Great Kimble Bucks 28 H5
Great Kingshill Bucks 18 B5
Great Langton N Yorks 58 G3
Great Leighs Essex 30 G4
Great Lever Gtr Man 43 B10
Great Limber Lincs 46 B5
Great Linford M Keynes 28 D5
Great Livermere Suff 30 A5
Great Longstone Derbys 44 E6
Great Lumley Durham 58 B3
Great Lyth Shrops 33 E10
Great Malvern Worcs 26 D4
Great Maplestead Essex 30 E5
Great Marton Blackpool 49 F3
Great Massingham Norf 38 C3
Great Melton Norf 39 E7
Great Milton Oxon 18 A3
Great Missenden Bucks 18 A5
Great Mitton Lancs 50 F3
Great Mongeham Kent 21 F10
Great Moulton Norf 39 F7
Great Munden Herts 29 F10
Great Musgrave Cumb 57 E9
Great Ness Shrops 33 D9
Great Notley Essex 30 F4
Great Oakley Essex 31 F8
Great Oakley Northants 36 G4
Great Offley Herts 29 F8
Great Ormside Cumb 57 E9
Great Orton Cumb 56 A5
Great Ouseburn N Yorks 51 C10
Great Oxendon Northants 36 G3
Great Oxney Green Essex 30 H3
Great Palgrave Norf 38 D4
Great Parndon Essex 29 H11
Great Paxton Cambs 29 B9
Great Plumpton Lancs 49 F3
Great Plumstead Norf 39 D9
Great Ponton Lincs 36 B5
Great Preston W Yorks 51 G10
Great Raveley Cambs 37 G8
Great Rissington Glos 27 G8
Great Rollright Oxon 27 E10
Great Ryburgh Norf 38 C5
Great Ryle Northumb 62 B6
Great Ryton Shrops 33 E10
Great Saling Essex 30 F4
Great Salkeld Cumb 57 C7
Great Sampford Essex 30 E3
Great Sankey Warr 43 D8
Great Saxham Suff 30 B4
Great Shefford W Berks 17 D10
Great Shelford Cambs 29 C11
Great Smeaton N Yorks 58 F4
Great Snoring Norf 38 B5
Great Somerford Wilts 16 C6
Great Stainton Darl 58 D4
Great Stambridge Essex 20 B5
Great Staughton Cambs 29 B8
Great Steeping Lincs 47 F8
Great Stonar Kent 21 F10
Great Strickland Cumb 57 D7
Great Stukeley Cambs 29 A9
Great Sturton Lincs 46 E6
Great Sutton Ches W 43 E6
Great Sutton Shrops 33 G11
Great Swinburne Northumb 62 F5
Great Tew Oxon 27 F10
Great Tey Essex 30 F5
Great Thurkleby N Yorks 51 B10
Great Thurlow Suff 30 C3
Great Torrington Devon 6 E3
Great Tosson Northumb 62 C6
Great Totham Essex 30 G5
Great Totham Essex 30 G5
Great Tows Lincs 46 C6
Great Urswick Cumb 49 B2
Great Wakering Essex 20 C6
Great Waldingfield Suff 30 D6
Great Walsingham Norf 38 B5
Great Waltham Essex 30 G3
Great Warley Essex 20 B2
Great Washbourne Glos 26 E6
Great Weldon Northants 36 G5
Great Welnetham Suff 30 C5
Great Wenham Suff 31 E7
Great Whittington Northumb 62 F6
Great Wigborough Essex 30 G6
Great Wilbraham Cambs 30 C2
Great Wishford Wilts 17 H7
Great Witcombe Glos 26 G6
Great Witley Worcs 26 B4
Great Wolford Warks 27 E9
Great Wratting Suff 30 D3
Great Wymondley Herts 29 F9
Great Wyrley Staffs 34 E5
Great Wytheford Shrops 34 D1
Great Yarmouth Norf 39 E11
Great Yeldham Essex 30 E4
Greater Doward Hereford 26 G2
Greatford Lincs 37 D6
Greatgate Staffs 35 A6
Greatham Hants 11 A6
Greatham Hrtlpl 58 D5
Greatham W Sus 11 C9
Greatstone on Sea Kent 13 D9
Greatworth Northants 28 D2
Greave Lancs 50 G4
Greeba IoM 48 D3
Green Denb 42 F3
Green End Bedford 29 C8
Green Hammerton N Yorks 51 D10
Green Lane Powys 33 F7
Green Ore Som 16 F2
Green St Green London 19 E11
Green Street Herts 19 B8
Greenbank Shetland 96 C7
Greenburn W Loth 69 D8
Greendikes Northumb 71 H9
Greenfield C Beds 29 E7
Greenfield Flint 42 E4
Greenfield Gtr Man 44 B3
Greenfield Highld 80 C4
Greenfield Oxon 18 B4
Greenford London 19 C8
Greengairs N Lanark 68 C6
Greenham W Berks 17 E11
Greenhaugh Northumb 62 E3
Greenhead Northumb 62 G2
Greenhill Falk 69 C7
Greenhill Kent 21 E8
Greenhill Leics 35 D10
Greenhill London 19 C8
Greenhills N Ayrs 67 A6
Greenhithe Kent 20 D2
Greenholm E Ayrs 67 C8
Greenholme Cumb 57 F7
Greenhouse Borders 61 A11
Greenhow Hill N Yorks 51 C7
Greenigoe Orkney 95 H5
Greenland Highld 94 D4
Greenlands Bucks 18 C4
Greenlaw Aberds 89 C6
Greenlaw Borders 70 F6
Greenlea Dumfries 60 F6
Greenloaning Perth 75 G11
Greenmount Gtr Man 43 A10
Greenmow Shetland 96 L6
Greenock Invclyd 73 F11
Greenock West Invclyd 73 F11
Greenodd Cumb 49 A3
Greenrow Cumb 56 A3
Greens Norton Northants 28 D3
Greenside T&W 63 G7
Greensidehill Northumb 62 B5
Greenstead Green Essex 30 F5
Greensted Essex 20 A2
Greenwich London 19 D10
Greet Glos 27 E7
Greete Shrops 26 A2
Greetham Lincs 47 E7
Greetham Rutland 36 D5
Greetland W Yorks 51 G6
Gregg Hall Cumb 56 G6
Gregson Lane Lancs 50 G1
Greinetobht W Isles 84 A3
Greinton Som 15 H10
Gremista Shetland 96 J6
Grenaby IoM 48 E2
Grendon Northants 28 B5
Grendon Warks 35 E8
Grendon Common Warks 35 F8
Grendon Green Hereford 26 C2
Grendon Underwood Bucks 28 F3
Grenofen Devon 4 D5
Grenoside S Yorks 45 C7
Greosabhagh W Isles 90 H6
Gresford Wrex 42 G6
Gresham Norf 39 B7
Greshornish Highld 85 C8
Gressenhall Norf 38 D5
Gressingham Lancs 50 C1
Gresty Green Ches E 43 G10
Greta Bridge Durham 58 E1
Gretna Dumfries 61 G9
Gretna Green Dumfries 61 G9
Gretton Glos 27 E7
Gretton Northants 36 F4
Gretton Shrops 33 F11
Grewelthorpe N Yorks 51 B8
Grey Green N Lincs 45 B11
Greygarth N Yorks 51 B7
Greynor Carms 23 F10
Greysouthen Cumb 56 D2
Greystoke Cumb 56 C6
Greystone Angus 77 C8
Greystone Dumfries 60 F5
Greywell Hants 18 F4
Griais W Isles 91 C9
Grianan W Isles 91 D9
Gribthorpe E Yorks 52 F3
Gridley Corner Devon 6 G2
Griff Warks 35 G9
Griffithstown Torf 15 B8
Grimbister Orkney 95 G4
Grimblethorpe Lincs 46 D6
Grimeford Village Lancs 43 A9
Grimethorpe S Yorks 45 B8
Griminis W Isles 84 C2
Grimister Shetland 96 D6
Grimley Worcs 26 B5
Grimness Orkney 95 J5
Grimoldby Lincs 47 D7
Grimpo Shrops 33 C9
Grimsargh Lancs 50 F1
Grimsbury Oxon 27 D11
Grimsby NE Lincs 46 A6
Grimscote Northants 28 C3
Grimscott Corn 6 F1
Grimsthorpe Lincs 36 C6
Grimston E Yorks 53 F8
Grimston Leics 36 C2
Grimston Norf 38 C3
Grimston York 52 D2
Grimstone Dorset 8 E5
Grinacombe Moor Devon 6 G3
Grindale E Yorks 53 B7
Grindigar Orkney 95 H6
Grindiscol Shetland 96 K6
Grindle Shrops 34 E3
Grindleford Derbys 44 E6
Grindleton Lancs 50 E3
Grindley Staffs 34 C6
Grindley Brook Shrops 33 A11
Grindlow Derbys 44 E5
Grindon Northumb 71 F8
Grindon Staffs 44 G4
Grindonmoor Gate Staffs 44 G4
Gringley on the Hill Notts 45 C11
Grinsdale Cumb 61 H9
Grinshill Shrops 33 C11
Grinton N Yorks 58 G1
Griomsidar W Isles 91 E8
Grishipoll Argyll 78 F4
Grisling Common E Sus 12 D3
Gristhorpe N Yorks 53 A6
Griston Norf 38 F5
Gritley Orkney 95 H6
Grittenham Wilts 17 C7
Grittleton Wilts 16 C5
Grizebeck Cumb 49 A2
Grizedale Cumb 56 G5
Grobister Orkney 95 F7
Groby Leics 35 E11
Groes Conwy 42 F3
Groes Neath 14 C3
Groes-faen Rhondda 14 C6
Groes-lwyd Powys 33 D8
Groesffordd Marli Denb 42 E3
Groeslon Gwyn 40 E6
Groeslon Gwyn 41 D7
Grogport Argyll 65 D9
Gromford Suff 31 C10
Gronant Flint 42 D3
Groombridge E Sus 12 C4
Grosmont Mon 25 F11
Grosmont N Yorks 59 F9
Groton Suff 30 D6
Grougfoot Falk 69 C9
Grouville Jersey 11
Grove Dorset 8 G6
Grove Kent 21 E9
Grove Notts 45 E11
Grove Oxon 17 B11
Grove Park London 19 D11
Grove Vale W Mid 34 F6
Grovesend Swansea 23 F10
Grudie Highld 86 E6
Gruids Highld 93 J8
Gruinard House Highld 86 B2
Grula Highld 85 F8
Gruline Argyll 79 G8
Grunasound Shetland 96 K5
Grundisburgh Suff 31 C9
Grunsagill Lancs 50 D3
Gruting Shetland 96 J4
Grutness Shetland 96 N6
Gualachulain Highld 74 C4
Gualin Ho. Highld 92 D6
Guardbridge Fife 77 F7
Guarlford Worcs 26 D5
Guay Perth 76 C3
Guestling Green E Sus 13 E7
Guestling Thorn E Sus 13 E7
Guestwick Norf 39 C6
Guestwick Green Norf 39 C6
Guide Blackburn 50 G3
Guide Post Northumb 63 E8
Guilden Morden Cambs 29 D9
Guilden Sutton Ches W 43 F7
Guildford Sur 18 G6
Guildtown Perth 76 D4
Guilsborough Northants 28 A3
Guilsfield Powys 33 D8
Guilton Kent 21 F9
Guineaford Devon 6 C4
Guisborough Redcar 59 E7
Guiseley W Yorks 51 E7
Guist Norf 38 C5
Guith Orkney 95 E6
Guiting Power Glos 27 F7
Gulberwick Shetland 96 K6
Gullane E Loth 70 B3
Gulval Corn 2 F3
Gulworthy Devon 4 D5
Gumfreston Pembs 22 F6
Gumley Leics 36 F2
Gummow's Shop Corn 3 D7
Gun Hill E Sus 12 E4
Gunby E Yorks 52 F3
Gunby Lincs 36 C5
Gundleton Hants 10 A5
Gunn Devon 6 C5
Gunnerside N Yorks 57 G11
Gunnerton Northumb 62 F5
Gunness N Lincs 46 A2
Gunnislake Corn 4 D5
Gunnista Shetland 96 J7
Gunthorpe Norf 38 B6
Gunthorpe Notts 36 A2
Gunthorpe Pboro 37 E7
Gunville IoW 10 F3
Gunwalloe Corn 2 G5
Gurnard IoW 10 E3
Gurnett Ches E 44 E3
Gurney Slade Som 16 G3
Gurnos Powys 24 H4
Gussage All Saints Dorset 9 C9
Gussage St Michael Dorset 9 C8
Guston Kent 21 G10
Gutcher Shetland 96 D7
Guthrie Angus 77 B8
Guyhirn Cambs 37 E9
Guyhirn Gull Cambs 37 E9
Guy's Head Lincs 37 C10
Guy's Marsh Dorset 9 B7
Guyzance Northumb 63 C8
Gwaenysgor Flint 42 D3
Gwalchmai Anglesey 40 C5
Gwaun-Cae-Gurwen Neath 24 G4
Gwaun-Leision Neath 24 G4
Gwbert Ceredig 22 B6
Gweek Corn 2 G6
Gwehelog Mon 15 A9
Gwenddwr Powys 25 D7
Gwennap Corn 2 F6
Gwenter Corn 2 H6
Gwernaffield Flint 42 F5
Gwernesney Mon 15 A10
Gwernogle Carms 23 C10
Gwernymynydd Flint 42 F5
Gwersyllt Wrex 42 G6
Gwespyr Flint 42 D4
Gwithian Corn 2 E4
Gwredog Anglesey 40 B6
Gwyddelwern Denb 42 H3
Gwyddgrug Carms 23 C9
Gwydyr Uchaf Conwy 41 D9
Gwynfryn Wrex 42 G5
Gwystre Powys 25 B7
Gwytherin Conwy 41 D10
Gyfelia Wrex 42 H6
Gyffin Conwy 41 C9
Gyre Orkney 95 H4
Gyrn-goch Gwyn 40 F6

H

Habberley Shrops 33 E9
Habergham Lancs 50 F4
Habrough NE Lincs 46 A5
Haceby Lincs 36 B6
Hacheston Suff 31 C10
Hackbridge London 19 E9
Hackenthorpe S Yorks 45 D8
Hackford Norf 39 E6
Hackforth N Yorks 58 G3
Hackland Orkney 95 F4
Hackleton Northants 28 C5
Hackness N Yorks 59 G10
Hackness Orkney 95 J4
Hackney London 19 C10
Hackthorn Lincs 46 D3
Hackthorpe Cumb 57 D7
Haconby Lincs 37 C7
Hacton London 20 C2
Hadden Borders 70 G6
Haddenham Bucks 28 H4
Haddenham Cambs 37 H10
Haddington E Loth 70 C4
Haddington Lincs 46 F3
Haddiscoe Norf 39 F10
Haddon Cambs 37 F7
Haddon Ches E 44 F3
Hade Edge W Yorks 44 B5
Hademore Staffs 35 E7
Hadfield Derbys 44 C4
Hadham Cross Herts 29 G11
Hadham Ford Herts 29 F11
Hadleigh Essex 20 C5
Hadleigh Suff 31 D7
Hadley Telford 34 D2
Hadley End Staffs 35 C7
Hadlow Kent 20 G3
Hadlow Down E Sus 12 D4
Hadnall Shrops 33 D11
Hadstock Essex 30 D2
Hady Derbys 45 E7
Hadzor Worcs 26 B6
Haffenden Quarter Kent 13 B7
Hafod-Dinbych Conwy 41 E10
Hafod-lom Conwy 41 C10
Haggate Lancs 50 F4
Haggbeck Cumb 61 F10
Haggerston Northumb 71 F9
Haggrister Shetland 96 F5
Hagley Hereford 26 D2
Hagley Worcs 34 G5
Hagworthingham Lincs 47 F7
Haigh Gtr Man 43 B9
Haigh S Yorks 44 A6
Haigh Moor W Yorks 51 G8
Haighton Green Lancs 50 F1
Hail Weston Cambs 29 B8
Haile Cumb 56 F2
Hailes Glos 27 E7
Hailey Herts 29 G10
Hailey Oxon 27 G10
Hailsham E Sus 12 F4
Haimer Highld 94 D3
Hainault London 19 B11
Hainford Norf 39 D8
Hainton Lincs 46 D5
Hairmyres S Lanark 68 E5
Haisthorpe E Yorks 53 C7
Hakin Pembs 22 F3
Halam Notts 45 G10
Halbeath Fife 69 B10
Halberton Devon 7 E9
Halcro Highld 94 D4
Hale Gtr Man 43 D10
Hale Halton 43 D7
Hale Hants 9 C10
Hale Bank Halton 43 D7
Hale Street Kent 20 G3
Halebarns Gtr Man 43 D10
Hales Norf 39 F9
Hales Staffs 34 B3
Hales Place Kent 21 F8
Halesfield Telford 34 E3
Halesgate Lincs 37 C9
Halesowen W Mid 34 G5
Halesworth Suff 39 H9
Halewood Mers 43 D7
Halford Shrops 33 G10
Halford Warks 27 D9
Halfpenny Furze Carms 23 E7
Halfpenny Green Staffs 34 F4
Halfway Carms 24 E3
Halfway Carms 24 E5
Halfway W Berks 17 E11
Halfway Bridge W Sus 11 B8
Halfway House Shrops 33 D9
Halfway Houses Kent 20 D6
Halifax W Yorks 51 G6
Halket E Ayrs 67 A7
Halkirk Highld 94 E3
Halkyn Flint 42 E5
Hall Dunnerdale Cumb 56 G4
Hall Green W Mid 35 G7
Hall Green W Yorks 51 H9
Hall Grove Herts 29 G9
Hall of Tankerness Orkney 95 H6
Hall of the Forest Shrops 33 G8
Halland E Sus 12 E3
Hallaton Leics 36 F3
Hallatrow Bath 16 F3
Hallbankgate Cumb 61 H11
Hallen S Glos 15 C11
Halliburton Borders 70 F5
Hallin Highld 84 C7
Halling Medway 20 E4
Hallington Lincs 47 D7
Hallington Northumb 62 F5
Halliwell Gtr Man 43 A10
Halloughton Notts 45 G10
Hallow Worcs 26 C5
Hallrule Borders 61 B11
Halls E Loth 70 C5
Hall's Green Herts 29 F9
Hallsands Devon 5 H9
Hallthwaites Cumb 56 H3
Hallworthy Corn 4 C2
Hallyburton House Perth 76 D5
Hallyne Borders 69 F10
Halmer End Staffs 43 H10
Halmore Glos 16 A3
Halmyre Mains Borders 69 F10
Halnaker W Sus 11 D8
Halsall Lancs 42 A6
Halse Northants 28 D2
Halse Som 7 D10
Halsetown Corn 2 F4
Halsham E Yorks 53 G8
Halsinger Devon 6 C4
Halstead Essex 30 E5
Halstead Kent 19 E11
Halstead Leics 36 E3
Halstock Dorset 8 D4
Haltham Lincs 46 F6
Haltoft End Lincs 47 H7
Halton Bucks 28 G5
Halton Halton 43 D8
Halton Lancs 49 C5
Halton Northumb 62 G5
Halton W Yorks 51 F9
Halton Wrex 33 B9
Halton East N Yorks 50 D6
Halton Gill N Yorks 50 B4
Halton Holegate Lincs 47 F8
Halton Lea Gate Northumb 62 H2
Halton West N Yorks 50 D4
Haltwhistle Northumb 62 G3
Halvergate Norf 39 E10
Halwell Devon 5 F8
Halwill Devon 6 G3
Halwill Junction Devon 6 F3
Ham Devon 7 F11
Ham Glos 16 B3
Ham Highld 94 C4
Ham Kent 21 F10
Ham London 19 D8
Ham Shetland 96 K1
Ham Wilts 17 E10
Ham Common Dorset 9 B7
Ham Green Hereford 26 D4
Ham Green Kent 13 D7
Ham Green Kent 20 E5
Ham Green N Som 15 D11
Ham Green Worcs 27 B7
Ham Street Som 8 A4
Hamble-le-Rice Hants 10 D3
Hambleden Bucks 18 C4
Hambledon Hants 10 C5
Hambledon Sur 18 H6
Hambleton Lancs 49 E3
Hambleton N Yorks 52 F1
Hambridge Som 8 B2
Hambrook S Glos 16 D3
Hambrook W Sus 11 D6
Hameringham Lincs 47 F7
Hamerton Cambs 37 H7
Hametoun Shetland 96 K1
Hamilton S Lanark 68 E6
Hammer W Sus 11 A7
Hammerpot W Sus 11 D9
Hammersmith London 19 D9
Hammerwich Staffs 35 E6
Hammerwood E Sus 12 C3
Hammond Street Herts 19 A10
Hammoon Dorset 9 C7
Hamnavoe Shetland 96 E4
Hamnavoe Shetland 96 E6
Hamnavoe Shetland 96 F6
Hamnavoe Shetland 96 K5
Hampden Park E Sus 12 F5
Hamperden End Essex 30 E2
Hampnett Glos 27 G7
Hampole S Yorks 45 A9
Hampreston Dorset 9 E9
Hampstead London 19 C9
Hampstead Norreys W Berks 18 D2
Hampsthwaite N Yorks 51 D8
Hampton London 19 E8
Hampton Shrops 34 G3
Hampton Worcs 27 D7
Hampton Bishop Hereford 26 E2
Hampton Heath Ches W 43 H7
Hampton in Arden W Mid 35 G8
Hampton Loade Shrops 34 G3
Hampton Lovett Worcs 26 B5
Hampton Lucy Warks 27 C9
Hampton on the Hill Warks 27 B9
Hampton Poyle Oxon 28 G2
Hamrow Norf 38 C5
Hamsey E Sus 12 E3
Hamsey Green London 19 F10
Hamstall Ridware Staffs 35 D7
Hamstead IoW 10 E3
Hamstead W Mid 34 F6
Hamstead Marshall W Berks 17 E11
Hamsterley Durham 58 C2
Hamsterley Durham 63 H7
Hamstreet Kent 13 C9
Hamworthy Poole 9 E8
Hanbury Staffs 35 C7
Hanbury Worcs 26 B6
Hanbury Woodend Staffs 35 C7
Hanby Lincs 36 B6
Hanchurch Staffs 34 A4
Handbridge Ches W 43 F7
Handcross W Sus 12 D1
Handforth Ches E 44 D2
Handley Ches W 43 G7
Handsacre Staffs 35 D6
Handsworth S Yorks 45 D8
Handsworth W Mid 34 F6
Handy Cross Devon 6 D3
Hanford Stoke 34 A4
Hanging Langford Wilts 17 H7
Hangleton W Sus 11 D9
Hanham S Glos 16 D3
Hankelow Ches E 43 H9
Hankerton Wilts 16 B6
Hankham E Sus 12 F5
Hanley Stoke 44 H2
Hanley Castle Worcs 26 D5
Hanley Child Worcs 26 B3
Hanley Swan Worcs 26 D5
Hanley William Worcs 26 B3
Hanlith N Yorks 50 C5
Hanmer Wrex 33 B10
Hannah Lincs 47 E9
Hannington Hants 18 F2
Hannington Northants 28 A5
Hannington Swindon 17 B8
Hannington Wick Swindon 17 B8
Hansel Village S Ayrs 67 C6
Hanslope M Keynes 28 D5
Hanthorpe Lincs 37 C6
Hanwell London 19 C8
Hanwell Oxon 27 D11
Hanwood Shrops 33 E10
Hanworth London 19 D8
Hanworth Norf 39 B7
Happendon S Lanark 69 G7
Happisburgh Norf 39 B9
Happisburgh Common Norf 39 C9
Hapsford Ches W 43 E7
Hapton Lancs 50 F3
Hapton Norf 39 F7
Harberton Devon 5 F8
Harbertonford Devon 5 F8
Harbledown Kent 21 F8
Harborne W Mid 34 G6
Harborough Magna Warks 35 H10
Harbottle Northumb 62 C5
Harbury Warks 27 C10
Harby Leics 36 B3
Harby Notts 46 E2
Harcombe Devon 7 G10
Harden W Mid 34 E6
Harden W Yorks 51 F6
Hardenhuish Wilts 16 D6
Hardgate Aberds 83 C9
Hardham W Sus 11 C9
Hardingham Norf 38 E6
Hardingstone Northants 28 C4
Hardington Som 16 F4
Hardington Mandeville Som 8 C4
Hardington Marsh Som 8 D4
Hardley Hants 10 D3
Hardley Street Norf 39 E9
Hardmead M Keynes 28 D6
Hardrow N Yorks 57 G10
Hardstoft Derbys 45 F8
Hardway Hants 10 D5
Hardway Som 8 A6
Hardwick Bucks 28 G5
Hardwick Cambs 29 C10
Hardwick Norf 38 D2
Hardwick Norf 39 G8
Hardwick Northants 28 B5
Hardwick Notts 45 E10
Hardwick Oxon 27 H10
Hardwick Oxon 28 F2
Hardwick W Mid 35 F6
Hardwicke Glos 26 F6
Hardwicke Glos 26 G4
Hardwicke Hereford 25 D9
Hardy's Green Essex 30 F6
Hare Green Essex 31 F7
Hare Hatch Wokingham 18 D5
Hare Street Herts 29 F10
Hareby Lincs 47 F7
Hareden Lancs 50 D2
Harefield London 19 B7
Harehills W Yorks 51 F9
Harehope Northumb 62 A6
Harescеugh Cumb 57 B8
Harescombe Glos 26 G5
Haresfield Glos 26 G5
Hareshaw N Lanark 69 D7
Hareshaw Head Northumb 62 E4
Harewood W Yorks 51 E9
Harewood End Hereford 26 F2
Harford Carms 24 D3
Harford Devon 5 F7
Hargate Norf 39 F7
Hargatewall Derbys 44 E5
Hargrave Ches W 43 F7
Hargrave Northants 29 A7
Hargrave Suff 30 C4
Harker Cumb 61 G9
Harkland Shetland 96 E6
Harkstead Suff 31 E8
Harlaston Staffs 35 D8
Harlaw Ho. Aberds 83 A9
Harlaxton Lincs 36 B4
Harle Syke Lancs 50 F4
Harlech Gwyn 41 G7
Harlequin Notts 36 B2
Harlescott Shrops 33 D11
Harlesden London 19 C9
Harleston Devon 5 G8
Harleston Norf 39 G8
Harleston Suff 31 C7
Harlestone Northants 28 B4
Harley S Yorks 45 C7
Harley Shrops 34 E1
Harleyholm S Lanark 69 G8
Harlington C Beds 29 E7
Harlington London 19 D7
Harlington S Yorks 45 B8
Harlosh Highld 85 D7
Harlow Essex 29 G11
Harlow Hill N Yorks 51 D8
Harlow Hill Northumb 62 G6
Harlthorpe E Yorks 52 F3
Harlton Cambs 29 C10
Harman's Cross Dorset 9 F8
Harmby N Yorks 58 H2
Harmer Green Herts 29 G9
Harmer Hill Shrops 33 C10
Harmondsworth London 19 D7
Harmston Lincs 46 F3
Harnham Northumb 62 F6
Harnhill Glos 17 A7
Harold Hill London 20 B2
Harold Wood London 20 B2
Haroldston West Pembs 22 E3
Haroldswick Shetland 96 B8
Harome N Yorks 52 A2
Harpenden Herts 29 G8
Harpford Devon 7 G9
Harpham E Yorks 53 C6
Harpley Norf 38 C3
Harpley Worcs 26 B3
Harpole Northants 28 B3
Harpsdale Highld 94 E3
Harpsden Oxon 18 C4
Harpswell Lincs 46 D3
Harpur Hill Derbys 44 E4
Harpurhey Gtr Man 44 B2
Harraby Cumb 56 A6
Harrapool Highld 85 F11
Harrier Shetland 96 J1
Harrietfield Perth 76 E2
Harrietsham Kent 20 F5
Harrington Cumb 56 D1
Harrington Lincs 47 E7
Harrington Northants 36 G3
Harringworth Northants 36 F5
Harris Highld 78 B6
Harrogate N Yorks 51 D9
Harrold Bedford 28 C6
Harrow London 19 C8
Harrow on the Hill London 19 C8
Harrow Street Suff 30 E6
Harrow Weald London 19 B8
Harrowbarrow Corn 4 E4
Harrowden Bedford 29 D7
Harrowgate Hill Darl 58 E3
Harston Cambs 29 C11
Harston Leics 36 B4
Harswell E Yorks 52 E4
Hart Hrtlpl 58 C5
Hart Common Gtr Man 43 B9
Hart Hill Luton 29 F8
Hart Station Hrtlpl 58 C5
Hartburn Northumb 62 E6
Hartburn Stockton 58 E5
Hartest Suff 30 C5
Hartfield E Sus 12 C3
Hartford Cambs 29 A9
Hartford Ches W 43 E9
Hartford End Essex 30 G3
Hartfordbridge Hants 18 F4
Hartforth N Yorks 58 F2
Harthill Ches W 43 G8
Harthill N Lanark 69 D8
Harthill S Yorks 45 D8
Hartington Derbys 44 F5
Hartland Devon 6 D1
Hartlebury Worcs 26 A5
Hartlepool Hrtlpl 58 C6
Hartley Cumb 57 F9
Hartley Kent 13 C6
Hartley Kent 20 E3
Hartley Northumb 63 F9
Hartley Westpall Hants 18 F3
Hartley Wintney Hants 18 F4
Hartlip Kent 20 E5
Hartoft End N Yorks 59 G8
Harton N Yorks 52 C3
Harton Shrops 33 G10
Harton T&W 63 G9
Hartpury Glos 26 F4
Hartshead W Yorks 51 G7
Hartshill Warks 35 F9
Hartshorne Derbys 35 C9
Hartsop Cumb 56 E6
Hartwell Northants 28 C4
Hartwood N Lanark 69 E7
Harvieston Stirling 68 B4
Harvington Worcs 27 D7
Harvington Cross Worcs 27 D7
Harwell Oxon 17 C11
Harwich Essex 31 E9
Harwood Durham 57 C10
Harwood Gtr Man 43 A10
Harwood Dale N Yorks 59 G10
Harworth Notts 45 C10
Hasbury W Mid 34 G5
Hascombe Sur 18 G6
Haselbech Northants 36 H3
Haselbury Plucknett Som 8 C3
Haseley Warks 27 B9
Haselor Warks 27 C8
Hasfield Glos 26 F5
Hasguard Pembs 22 F3
Haskayne Lancs 42 B6
Hasketon Suff 31 C9
Hasland Derbys 45 F7
Haslemere Sur 11 A8
Haslingden Lancs 50 G3
Haslingfield Cambs 29 C11
Haslington Ches E 43 G10
Hassall Ches E 43 G10
Hassall Green Ches E 43 G10
Hassell Street Kent 21 G7
Hassendean Borders 61 A11
Hassingham Norf 39 E9
Hassocks W Sus 12 E1
Hassop Derbys 44 E6
Hastigrow Highld 94 D4
Hastingleigh Kent 13 B9
Hastings E Sus 13 F7
Hastingwood Essex 29 H11
Hastoe Herts 28 H6
Haswell Durham 58 B4
Haswell Plough Durham 58 B4
Hatch C Beds 29 D8
Hatch Hants 18 F3
Hatch Wilts 9 B8
Hatch Beauchamp Som 8 B2
Hatch End London 19 B8
Hatch Green Som 8 C2
Hatchet Gate Hants 10 D2
Hatching Green Herts 29 G8
Hatchmere Ches W 43 E8
Hatcliffe NE Lincs 46 B6
Hatfield Hereford 26 C2
Hatfield Herts 29 H9
Hatfield S Yorks 45 B10
Hatfield Worcs 26 C5
Hatfield Broad Oak Essex 30 G2
Hatfield Garden Village Herts 29 H9
Hatfield Heath Essex 30 G2
Hatfield Hyde Herts 29 G9
Hatfield Peverel Essex 30 G4
Hatfield Woodhouse S Yorks 45 B10
Hatford Oxon 17 B10
Hatherden Hants 17 F10
Hatherleigh Devon 6 F4
Hathern Leics 35 C10
Hatherop Glos 27 H8
Hathersage Derbys 44 D6
Hathershaw Gtr Man 44 B3
Hatherton Ches E 43 H9
Hatherton Staffs 34 D5
Hatley St George Cambs 29 C9
Hatt Corn 4 E4
Hattingley Hants 18 H3
Hatton Aberds 89 E10
Hatton Derbys 35 C8
Hatton Lincs 46 E5
Hatton Shrops 33 F10
Hatton Warks 27 B9
Hatton Warr 43 D8
Hatton Castle Aberds 89 D7
Hatton Heath Ches W 43 F7
Hatton of Fintray Aberds 83 B10
Hattoncrook Aberds 89 F8
Haugh E Ayrs 67 D7
Haugh Gtr Man 44 A3
Haugh Lincs 47 E8
Haugh Head Northumb 71 H9
Haugh of Glass Moray 88 E4
Haugh of Urr Dumfries 55 C11
Haugham Lincs 47 D7
Haughley Suff 31 B7
Haughley Green Suff 31 B7
Haughs of Clinterty Aberdeen 83 B10
Haughton Notts 45 E10
Haughton Shrops 33 C9
Haughton Shrops 34 D1
Haughton Shrops 34 E3
Haughton Shrops 34 F2
Haughton Staffs 34 C4
Haughton Castle Northumb 62 F5
Haughton Green Gtr Man 44 C3
Haughton Moss Ches E 43 G8
Haultwick Herts 29 F10
Haunn Argyll 78 G6
Haunn W Isles 84 G2
Haunton Staffs 35 D8
Hauxley Northumb 63 C8
Hauxton Cambs 29 C11
Havant Hants 10 D6
Haven Hereford 25 C11
Haven Bank Lincs 46 G6
Haven Side E Yorks 53 G7
Havenstreet IoW 10 E4
Havercroft W Yorks 45 A7
Haverfordwest = Hwlffordd Pembs 22 E4
Haverhill Suff 30 D3
Haverigg Cumb 49 B1
Havering-atte-Bower London 20 B2
Haveringland Norf 39 C7
Haversham M Keynes 28 D5
Haverthwaite Cumb 49 A3
Haverton Hill Stockton 58 D5
Hawarden = Penarlâg Flint 42 F6
Hawcoat Cumb 49 B2
Hawen Ceredig 23 B8
Hawes N Yorks 57 H10
Hawes' Green Norf 39 F8
Hawes Side Blackpool 49 F3
Hawford Worcs 26 B5
Hawick Borders 61 B11
Hawk Green Gtr Man 44 D3
Hawkchurch Devon 8 D2
Hawkedon Suff 30 C4
Hawkenbury Kent 12 C4
Hawkenbury Kent 13 B7
Hawkeridge Wilts 16 F5
Hawkerland Devon 7 H9
Hawkes End W Mid 35 G9
Hawkesbury S Glos 16 C4
Hawkesbury Warks 35 G9
Hawkesbury Upton S Glos 16 C4
Hawkhill Northumb 63 B8
Hawkhurst Kent 13 C6
Hawkinge Kent 21 H9
Hawkley Hants 10 B6
Hawkridge Som 7 C7
Hawkshead Cumb 56 G5
Hawkshead Hill Cumb 56 G5
Hawksland S Lanark 69 G7
Hawkswick N Yorks 50 B5
Hawksworth Notts 36 A3
Hawksworth W Yorks 51 E7
Hawksworth W Yorks 51 F8
Hawkwell Essex 20 B5
Hawley Hants 18 F5
Hawley Kent 20 D2
Hawling Glos 27 F7
Hawnby N Yorks 59 H6
Haworth W Yorks 50 F6
Hawstead Suff 30 C5
Hawthorn Durham 58 B5
Hawthorn Rhondda 15 C7
Hawthorn Wilts 16 E5
Hawthorn Hill Brack 18 D5
Hawthorn Hill Lincs 46 G6
Hawthorpe Lincs 36 C6
Hawton Notts 45 G11
Haxby York 52 D2
Haxey N Lincs 45 C11
Hay Green Norf 37 D11
Hay-on-Wye = Y Gelli Gandryll Powys 25 D9
Hay Street Herts 29 F10
Haydock Mers 43 C8
Haydon Dorset 8 C5
Haydon Bridge Northumb 62 G4
Haydon Wick Swindon 17 C8
Haye Corn 4 E4
Hayes London 19 C8
Hayes London 19 E11
Hayfield Derbys 44 D4
Hayfield Fife 69 A11
Hayhill E Ayrs 67 E7
Hayhillock Angus 77 C8
Hayle Corn 2 F4
Haynes C Beds 29 D7
Haynes Church End C Beds 29 D7
Hayscastle Pembs 22 D3
Hayscastle Cross Pembs 22 D4
Hayshead Angus 77 C9
Hayton Aberdeen 83 C11
Hayton Cumb 56 B3
Hayton Cumb 61 H11
Hayton E Yorks 52 E4
Hayton Notts 45 D11
Hayton's Bent Shrops 33 G11
Haytor Vale Devon 5 D8
Haywards Heath W Sus 12 D2
Haywood S Yorks 45 A9
Haywood Oaks Notts 45 G10
Hazel Grove Gtr Man 44 D3
Hazel Street Kent 12 C5
Hazelbank S Lanark 69 F7
Hazelbury Bryan Dorset 8 D6
Hazeley Hants 18 F4
Hazelhurst Gtr Man 44 B3
Hazelslade Staffs 34 D6
Hazelton Glos 27 G7
Hazelton Walls Fife 76 E6
Hazelwood Derbys 45 H7
Hazlemere Bucks 18 B5
Hazlerigg T&W 63 F8
Hazlewood N Yorks 51 D6
Hazon Northumb 63 C7
Heacham Norf 38 B2
Head of Muir Falk 69 B7
Headbourne Worthy Hants 10 A3
Headbrook Hereford 25 C10
Headcorn Kent 13 B7
Headingley W Yorks 51 F8
Headington Oxon 28 H2
Headlam Durham 58 E2
Headless Cross Worcs 27 B7
Headley Hants 18 E2
Headley Hants 18 H5
Headley Sur 19 F9
Headon Notts 45 E11
Heads S Lanark 68 F6
Heads Nook Cumb 61 H10
Heage Derbys 45 G7
Healaugh N Yorks 51 E10
Healaugh N Yorks 58 G1
Heald Green Gtr Man 44 D2
Heale Devon 6 B5
Heale Som 16 G3
Healey Gtr Man 50 H4
Healey N Yorks 51 A7
Healey Northumb 62 H6
Healing NE Lincs 46 A6
Heamoor Corn 2 F3
Heanish Argyll 78 G3
Heanor Derbys 45 H8
Heanton Punchardon Devon 6 C4
Heapham Lincs 46 D2
Hearthstane Borders 69 H10
Heasley Mill Devon 7 C6
Heast Highld 85 G11
Heath Cardiff 15 D7
Heath Derbys 45 F8
Heath and Reach C Beds 28 F6
Heath End Hants 18 E2
Heath End Sur 18 G5
Heath End Warks 27 B9
Heath Hayes Staffs 34 D6
Heath Hill Shrops 34 D3
Heath House Som 15 G10
Heath Town W Mid 34 F5
Heathcote Derbys 44 F5
Heather Leics 35 D9
Heatherfield Highld 85 D9
Heathfield Devon 5 D9
Heathfield E Sus 12 D4
Heathfield Som 7 D10
Heathhall Dumfries 60 F5
Heathrow Airport London 19 D7
Heathstock Devon 8 D1
Heathton Shrops 34 F4
Heatley Warr 43 D10
Heaton Lancs 49 C4
Heaton Staffs 44 F3
Heaton T&W 63 G8
Heaton W Yorks 51 F7
Heaton Moor Gtr Man 44 C2
Heaverham Kent 20 F2
Heaviley Gtr Man 44 D3
Heavitree Devon 7 G8
Hebburn T&W 63 G9
Hebden N Yorks 50 C6
Hebden Bridge W Yorks 50 G5
Hebron Anglesey 40 B6
Hebron Carms 22 D6
Hebron Northumb 63 E7
Heck Dumfries 60 E6
Heckfield Hants 18 E4
Heckfield Green Suff 39 H7
Heckfordbridge Essex 30 F6
Heckington Lincs 37 A7
Heckmondwike W Yorks 51 G8
Heddington Wilts 16 E6
Heddle Orkney 95 G4
Heddon-on-the-Wall Northumb 63 G7
Hedenham Norf 39 F9
Hedge End Hants 10 C3
Hedgerley Bucks 18 C6
Hedging Som 8 B2
Hedley on the Hill Northumb 62 H6
Hednesford Staffs 34 D6
Hedon E Yorks 53 G7
Hedsor Bucks 18 C6
Hedworth T&W 63 G9
Hegdon Hill Hereford 26 C2
Heggerscales Cumb 57 E10
Heglibister Shetland 96 H5
Heighington Darl 58 D3
Heighington Lincs 46 F4
Heights of Brae Highld 87 E8
Heights of Kinlochewe Highld 86 E3
Heilam Highld 92 C7
Heiton Borders 70 G6
Hele Devon 6 B4
Hele Devon 7 F8
Helensburgh Argyll 73 E11
Helford Corn 3 G6
Helford Passage Corn 3 G6
Helhoughton Norf 38 C4
Helions Bumpstead Essex 30 D3
Hellaby S Yorks 45 C9
Helland Corn 4 D1
Hellesdon Norf 39 D8
Hellidon Northants 28 C2
Hellifield N Yorks 50 D4
Hellingly E Sus 12 E4
Hellington Norf 39 E9
Hellister Shetland 96 J5
Helm Northumb 63 D7
Helmdon Northants 28 D2
Helmingham Suff 31 C8
Helmington Row Durham 58 C2
Helmsdale Highld 93 H13
Helmshore Lancs 50 G3
Helmsley N Yorks 52 A2
Helperby N Yorks 51 C10
Helperthorpe N Yorks 52 B5
Helpringham Lincs 37 A7
Helpston Pboro 37 E7
Helsby Ches W 43 E7
Helsey Lincs 47 E9
Helston Corn 2 G5
Helstone Corn 4 C1
Helton Cumb 57 D7
Helwith Bridge N Yorks 50 C4
Hemblington Norf 39 D9
Hemel Hempstead Herts 29 H7
Hemingbrough N Yorks 52 F2
Hemingby Lincs 46 E6
Hemingford Abbots Cambs 29 A9
Hemingford Grey Cambs 29 A9
Hemingstone Suff 31 C8
Hemington Leics 35 C10
Hemington Northants 37 G6
Hemington Som 16 F4
Hemley Suff 31 D9
Hemlington Mbro 58 E6
Hemp Green Suff 31 B10
Hempholme E Yorks 53 D6
Hempnall Norf 39 F8
Hempnall Green Norf 39 F8
Hempriggs House Highld 94 F5
Hempstead Essex 30 E3
Hempstead Medway 20 E4
Hempstead Norf 39 B7
Hempstead Norf 39 C10
Hempsted Glos 26 G5
Hempton Norf 38 C5
Hempton Oxon 27 E11
Hemsby Norf 39 D10
Hemswell Lincs 46 C3
Hemswell Cliff Lincs 46 D3
Hemsworth W Yorks 45 A8
Hemyock Devon 7 E10
Hen-feddau fawr Pembs 23 C7
Henbury Bristol 16 D2
Henbury Ches E 44 E2
Hendon London 19 C9
Hendon T&W 63 H10
Hendre Flint 42 F4
Hendre-ddu Conwy 41 D10
Hendreforgan Rhondda 14 C5
Hendy Carms 23 F10
Heneglwys Anglesey 40 C6
Henfield W Sus 11 C11
Henford Devon 6 G2
Henghurst Kent 13 C8
Hengoed Caerph 15 B7
Hengoed Powys 25 C9
Hengoed Shrops 33 B8
Hengrave Suff 30 B5
Henham Essex 30 F2
Heniarth Powys 33 E7
Henlade Som 8 B1
Henley Shrops 33 H11
Henley Som 8 A3
Henley Suff 31 C8
Henley W Sus 11 B7
Henley-in-Arden Warks 27 B8
Henley-on-Thames Oxon 18 C4
Henley's Down E Sus 12 E6
Henllan Ceredig 23 B8
Henllan Denb 42 F3
Henllan Amgoed Carms 22 D6
Henllys Torf 15 B8
Henlow C Beds 29 E8
Hennock Devon 5 C9
Henny Street Essex 30 E5
Henryd Conwy 41 C9
Henry's Moat Pembs 22 D5
Hensall N Yorks 52 G1
Henshaw Northumb 62 G3
Hensingham Cumb 56 E1
Henstead Suff 39 G10
Henstridge Som 8 C6
Henstridge Ash Som 8 B6
Henstridge Marsh Som 8 B6
Henton Oxon 18 A4
Henton Som 15 G10
Henwood Corn 4 D3
Heogan Shetland 96 J6
Heol-las Swansea 14 B2
Heol Senni Powys 24 F6
Heol-y-Cyw Bridgend 14 C5
Hepburn Northumb 62 A6
Hepple Northumb 62 C5
Hepscott Northumb 63 E8
Heptonstall W Yorks 50 G5
Hepworth Suff 30 A6
Hepworth W Yorks 44 B5
Herbrandston Pembs 22 F3
Hereford Hereford 26 D2
Heriot Borders 70 E2
Hermiston Edin 69 C10
Hermitage Borders 61 D11
Hermitage Dorset 8 D5
Hermitage W Berks 18 D2
Hermitage W Sus 11 D6
Hermon Anglesey 40 D5
Hermon Carms 23 C8
Hermon Carms 24 F3
Hermon Pembs 23 C7
Herne Kent 21 E8
Herne Bay Kent 21 E8
Herner Devon 6 D4
Hernhill Kent 21 E7
Herodsfoot Corn 4 E3
Herongate Essex 20 B3
Heronsford S Ayrs 54 A4
Herriard Hants 18 G3
Herringfleet Suff 39 F10
Herringswell Suff 30 A4
Hersden Kent 21 E9
Hersham Corn 6 F1
Hersham Sur 19 E8
Herstmonceux E Sus 12 E5
Herston Orkney 95 J5
Hertford Herts 29 G10
Hertford Heath Herts 29 G10
Hertingfordbury Herts 29 G10
Hesket Newmarket Cumb 56 C5
Hesketh Bank Lancs 49 G4
Hesketh Lane Lancs 50 E2
Heskin Green Lancs 49 H5
Hesleden Durham 58 C5
Hesleyside Northumb 62 E4
Heslington York 52 D2
Hessay York 51 D11
Hessenford Corn 4 F4
Hessett Suff 30 B6
Hessle E Yorks 52 G6
Hest Bank Lancs 49 C4
Heston London 19 D8
Hestwall Orkney 95 G3
Heswall Mers 42 D5
Hethe Oxon 28 F2
Hethersett Norf 39 E7
Hethersgill Cumb 61 G10
Hethpool Northumb 71 H7
Hett Durham 58 C3
Hetton N Yorks 50 D5
Hetton-le-Hole T&W 58 B4
Hetton Steads Northumb 71 G9
Heugh Northumb 62 F6
Heugh-head Aberds 82 B5
Heveningham Suff 31 A10
Hever Kent 12 B3
Heversham Cumb 49 A4
Hevingham Norf 39 C7
Hewas Water Corn 3 E8
Hewelsfield Glos 16 A2
Hewish N Som 15 E10
Hewish Som 8 D3
Heworth York 52 D2
Hexham Northumb 62 G5
Hextable Kent 20 D2
Hexton Herts 29 E8
Hexworthy Devon 5 D7
Hey Lancs 50 E4
Heybridge Essex 20 B3
Heybridge Essex 30 H5
Heybridge Basin Essex 30 H5
Heybrook Bay Devon 4 G6
Heydon Cambs 29 D11

Kinlocheil Highld 80 F1
Kinlochewe Highld 86 E3
Kinlochleven Highld 74 A4
Kinlochmoidart Highld 79 D10
Kinlochmorar Highld 79 B11
Kinlochmore Highld 74 A4
Kinlochspelve Argyll 79 J9
Kinloid Highld 79 C9
Kinloss Moray 87 E13
Kinmel Bay Conwy 42 D2
Kinmuck Aberds 83 B10
Kinmundy Aberds 83 B10
Kinnadie Aberds 89 D9
Kinnaird Perth 76 E5
Kinnaird Castle Angus 77 B9
Kinneff Aberds 83 F10
Kinnelhead Dumfries 60 C6
Kinnell Angus 77 B9
Kinnerley Shrops 33 C9
Kinnersley Hereford 25 D10
Kinnersley Worcs 26 D5
Kinnerton Powys 25 B9
Kinnesswood Perth 76 G4
Kinninvie Durham 58 D1
Kinnordy Angus 76 B6
Kinoulton Notts 36 B2
Kinross Perth 76 G4
Kinrossie Perth 76 D5
Kinsbourne Green Herts 29 G8
Kinsey Heath Ches E 34 A2
Kinsham Hereford 25 B10
Kinsham Worcs 26 E6
Kinsley W Yorks 45 A8
Kinson Bmouth 9 E9
Kintbury W Berks 17 E10
Kintessack Moray 87 E12
Kintillo Perth 76 F4
Kintocher Aberds 83 C7
Kinton Hereford 25 A11
Kinton Shrops 33 D9
Kintore Aberds 83 B9
Kintour Argyll 64 C5
Kintra Argyll 64 D4
Kintra Argyll 78 J6
Kintraw Argyll 73 C7
Kinuachdrachd Argyll 72 D6
Kinveachy Highld 81 B11
Kinver Staffs 34 G4
Kippax W Yorks 51 F10
Kippen Stirling 68 A5
Kippford or Scaur Dumfries 55 D11
Kirbister Orkney 95 F7
Kirbister Orkney 95 H4
Kirbuster Orkney 95 F3
Kirby Bedon Norf 39 E8
Kirby Bellars Leics 36 D3
Kirby Cane Norf 39 F9
Kirby Cross Essex 31 F9
Kirby Grindalythe N Yorks 52 C5
Kirby Hill N Yorks 51 C9
Kirby Hill N Yorks 58 F2
Kirby Knowle N Yorks 58 H5
Kirby-le-Soken Essex 31 F9
Kirby Misperton N Yorks 52 B3
Kirby Muxloe Leics 35 E11
Kirby Row Norf 39 F9
Kirby Sigston N Yorks 58 G5
Kirby Underdale E Yorks 52 D4
Kirby Wiske N Yorks 51 A9
Kirdford W Sus 11 B9
Kirk Highld 94 E4
Kirk Bramwith S Yorks 45 A10
Kirk Deighton N Yorks 51 D9
Kirk Ella E Yorks 52 G6
Kirk Hallam Derbys 35 A10
Kirk Hammerton N Yorks 51 D10
Kirk Ireton Derbys 44 G6
Kirk Langley Derbys 35 B8
Kirk Merrington Durham 58 C3
Kirk Michael IoM 48 C3
Kirk of Shotts N Lanark 69 D7
Kirk Sandall S Yorks 45 B10
Kirk Smeaton N Yorks 51 H11
Kirk Yetholm Borders 71 H7
Kirkabister Shetland 96 K6
Kirkandrews Dumfries 55 E9
Kirkandrews upon Eden Cumb 61 H9
Kirkbampton Cumb 61 H9
Kirkbean Dumfries 60 H5
Kirkbride Cumb 61 H8
Kirkbuddo Angus 77 C8
Kirkburn Borders 69 G11
Kirkburn E Yorks 52 D5
Kirkburton W Yorks 44 A5
Kirkby Lincs 46 C4
Kirkby Mers 43 C7
Kirkby N Yorks 59 F6
Kirkby Fleetham N Yorks 58 G3
Kirkby Green Lincs 46 G4
Kirkby In Ashfield Notts 45 G9
Kirkby-in-Furness Cumb 49 A2
Kirkby la Thorpe Lincs 46 H5
Kirkby Lonsdale Cumb 50 B2
Kirkby Malham N Yorks 50 C4
Kirkby Mallory Leics 35 E10
Kirkby Malzeard N Yorks 51 B8
Kirkby Mills N Yorks 59 H8
Kirkby on Bain Lincs 46 F6
Kirkby Overflow N Yorks 51 E9
Kirkby Stephen Cumb 57 F9
Kirkby Thore Cumb 57 D8
Kirkby Underwood Lincs 37 C6
Kirkby Wharfe N Yorks 51 E11
Kirkbymoorside N Yorks 59 H7
Kirkcaldy Fife 69 A11
Kirkcambeck Cumb 61 G11
Kirkcarswell Dumfries 55 E10
Kirkcolm Dumfries 54 C3
Kirkconnel Dumfries 60 B3
Kirkconnell Dumfries 60 G5
Kirkcowan Dumfries 54 C6
Kirkcudbright Dumfries 55 D9
Kirkdale Mers 42 C6
Kirkfieldbank S Lanark 69 F7
Kirkgunzeon Dumfries 55 C11
Kirkham Lancs 49 F4
Kirkham N Yorks 52 C3
Kirkhamgate W Yorks 51 G8
Kirkharle Northumb 62 E6
Kirkheaton Northumb 62 F6
Kirkheaton W Yorks 51 H7
Kirkhill Angus 77 A9
Kirkhill Highld 87 G8
Kirkhill Midloth 69 D11
Kirkhill Moray 88 E2
Kirkhope Borders 61 A9
Kirkhouse Borders 70 G2
Kirkiboll Highld 93 D8
Kirkibost Highld 85 G10
Kirkinch Angus 76 C6
Kirkinner Dumfries 55 D7
Kirkintilloch E Dunb 68 C5
Kirkland Cumb 56 E2
Kirkland Cumb 57 C8
Kirkland Dumfries 60 D4
Kirkland Dumfries 60 B3
Kirkleatham Redcar 59 D6
Kirklevington Stockton 58 F5
Kirkley Suff 39 F11
Kirklington N Yorks 51 A9
Kirklington Notts 45 G10
Kirklinton Cumb 61 G10
Kirkliston Edin 69 C10
Kirkmaiden Dumfries 54 F4
Kirkmichael Perth 76 B3
Kirkmichael S Ayrs 66 F6
Kirkmuirhill S Lanark 68 F6
Kirknewton Northumb 71 G8
Kirknewton W Loth 69 D10
Kirkney Aberds 88 E5
Kirkoswald Cumb 57 B7
Kirkoswald S Ayrs 66 F5
Kirkpatrick Durham Dumfries 60 F3
Kirkpatrick-Fleming Dumfries 61 F8
Kirksanton Cumb 49 A1
Kirkstall W Yorks 51 F8
Kirkstead Lincs 46 F5
Kirkstile Aberds 88 E5
Kirkstyle Highld 94 C5
Kirkton Aberds 83 A8
Kirkton Aberds 89 D6
Kirkton Angus 77 C7
Kirkton Angus 77 D7
Kirkton Borders 61 B11
Kirkton Dumfries 60 E5
Kirkton Fife 76 E6
Kirkton Highld 85 F13
Kirkton Highld 86 G2
Kirkton Highld 87 B10
Kirkton Highld 87 F10
Kirkton Perth 76 F2
Kirkton S Lanark 60 A5
Kirkton Stirling 75 G8
Kirkton Manor Borders 69 G11
Kirkton of Airlie Angus 76 B6
Kirkton of Auchterhouse Angus 76 D6
Kirkton of Auchterless Aberds 89 D7
Kirkton of Barevan Highld 87 G11
Kirkton of Bourtie Aberds 89 F8
Kirkton of Collace Perth 76 D4
Kirkton of Craig Angus 77 B10
Kirkton of Culsalmond Aberds 89 E6
Kirkton of Durris Aberds 83 D9
Kirkton of Glenbuchat Aberds 82 B5
Kirkton of Glenisla Angus 76 A5
Kirkton of Kingoldrum Angus 76 B6
Kirkton of Largo Fife 77 G7
Kirkton of Lethendy Perth 76 C4
Kirkton of Logie Buchan Aberds 89 F9
Kirkton of Maryculter Aberds 83 D10
Kirkton of Menmuir Angus 77 A8
Kirkton of Monikie Angus 77 D8
Kirkton of Oyne Aberds 83 A8
Kirkton of Rayne Aberds 83 A8
Kirkton of Skene Aberds 83 C10
Kirkton of Tough Aberds 83 B8
Kirktonhill Borders 70 E3
Kirktown Aberds 89 C10
Kirktown of Alvah Aberds 89 B6
Kirktown of Deskford Moray 88 B5
Kirktown of Fetteresso Aberds 83 E10
Kirktown of Mortlach Moray 88 E3
Kirktown of Slains Aberds 89 F10
Kirkurd Borders 69 F10
Kirkwall Orkney 95 G5
Kirkwhelpington Northumb 62 E5
Kirmington N Lincs 46 A5
Kirmond le Mire Lincs 46 C5
Kirn Argyll 73 F10
Kirriemuir Angus 76 B6
Kirstead Green Norf 39 F8
Kirtlebridge Dumfries 61 F8
Kirtleton Dumfries 61 E8
Kirtling Cambs 30 C3
Kirtling Green Cambs 30 C3
Kirtlington Oxon 27 G11
Kirtomy Highld 93 C10
Kirton Lincs 37 B9
Kirton Notts 45 F10
Kirton Suff 31 E9
Kirton End Lincs 37 A8
Kirton Holme Lincs 37 A8
Kirton in Lindsey N Lincs 46 C3
Kislingbury Northants 28 C3
Kites Hardwick Warks 27 B11
Kittisford Som 7 D9
Kittle Swansea 23 H10
Kitt's Green W Mid 35 G7
Kitt's Moss Gtr Man 44 D2
Kittybrewster Aberdeen 83 C11
Kitwood Hants 10 A5
Kivernoll Hereford 25 E11
Kiveton Park S Yorks 45 D8
Knaith Lincs 46 D2
Knaith Park Lincs 46 D2
Knap Corner Dorset 9 B7
Knaphill Sur 18 F6
Knapp Perth 76 D5
Knapp Som 8 B2
Knapthorpe Notts 45 G11
Knapton Norf 39 B9
Knapton York 52 D1
Knapton Green Hereford 25 C11
Knapwell Cambs 29 B10
Knaresborough N Yorks 51 D9
Knarsdale Northumb 57 A8
Knauchland Moray 88 C5
Knaven Aberds 89 D8
Knayton N Yorks 58 H5
Knebworth Herts 29 F9
Knedlington E Yorks 52 G3
Kneesall Notts 45 F11
Kneesworth Cambs 29 D10
Kneeton Notts 45 H11
Knelston Swansea 23 H9
Knenhall Staffs 34 B5
Knettishall Suff 38 G5
Knightacott Devon 6 C5
Knightcote Warks 27 C10
Knightley Dale Staffs 34 C4
Knighton Devon 4 G6
Knighton Leicester 36 E1
Knighton = Tref-y-Clawdd Powys 25 A9
Knighton Staffs 34 A3
Knighton Staffs 34 C3
Knightswood Glasgow 68 D4
Knightwick Worcs 26 C4
Knill Hereford 25 B9
Knipton Leics 36 B4
Knitsley Durham 58 B2
Kniveton Derbys 44 G6
Knock Argyll 79 H8
Knock Cumb 57 D8
Knock Moray 88 C5
Knockally Highld 94 H3
Knockan Highld 92 H5
Knockandhu Moray 82 A4
Knockando Moray 88 D1
Knockando Ho. Moray 88 D2
Knockbain Highld 87 F9
Knockbreck Highld 84 B7
Knockbrex Dumfries 55 E8
Knockdee Highld 94 D3
Knockdolian S Ayrs 66 H4
Knockenkelly N Ayrs 66 D3
Knockentiber E Ayrs 67 C6
Knockespock Ho. Aberds 83 A7
Knockfarrel Highld 87 F8
Knockglass Dumfries 54 D3
Knockholt Kent 19 F11
Knockholt Pound Kent 19 F11
Knockie Lodge Highld 80 B6
Knockin Shrops 33 C9
Knockinlaw E Ayrs 67 C7
Knocklearn Dumfries 60 F3
Knocknaha Argyll 65 G7
Knocknain Dumfries 54 C2
Knockrome Argyll 72 F4
Knocksharry IoM 48 D2
Knodishall Suff 31 B11
Knolls Green Ches E 44 E2
Knolton Wrex 33 B9
Knolton Bryn Wrex 33 B9
Knook Wilts 16 G6
Knossington Leics 36 E4
Knott End-on-Sea Lancs 49 E3
Knotting Bedford 29 B7
Knotting Green Bedford 29 B7
Knottingley W Yorks 51 G11
Knotts Cumb 56 D6
Knotts Lancs 50 D3
Knotty Ash Mers 43 C7
Knotty Green Bucks 18 B6
Knowbury Shrops 26 A2
Knowe Dumfries 54 B6
Knowehead Dumfries 67 G9
Knowes of Elrick Aberds 88 C6
Knowesgate Northumb 62 E5
Knoweton N Lanark 68 E6
Knowhead Aberds 89 C9
Knowl Hill Windsor 18 D5
Knowle Bristol 16 D3
Knowle Devon 6 C3
Knowle Devon 7 F9
Knowle Devon 7 H9
Knowle Shrops 26 A2
Knowle W Mid 35 H7
Knowle Green Lancs 50 F2
Knowle Park W Yorks 51 E6
Knowlton Dorset 9 C9
Knowlton Kent 21 F9
Knowsley Mers 43 C7
Knowstone Devon 7 D7
Knox Bridge Kent 13 B6
Knucklas Powys 25 A9
Knuston Northants 28 B6
Knutsford Ches E 43 E10
Knutton Staffs 44 H2
Knypersley Staffs 44 G2
Kuggar Corn 2 H6
Kyle of Lochalsh Highld 85 F12
Kyleakin Highld 85 F12
Kylerhea Highld 85 F12
Kylesknoydart Highld 79 B11
Kylesku Highld 92 F5
Kylesmorar Highld 79 B11
Kylestrome Highld 92 F5
Kyllachy House Highld 81 A9
Kynaston Shrops 33 C9
Kynnersley Telford 34 D2
Kyre Magna Worcs 26 B3

L

La Fontenelle Guern 11
La Planque Guern 11
Labost W Isles 91 C7
Lacasaidh W Isles 91 E8
Lacasdal W Isles 91 D9
Laceby NE Lincs 46 B6
Lacey Green Bucks 18 B5
Lach Dennis Ches W 43 E10
Lackford Suff 30 A4
Lacock Wilts 16 E6
Ladbroke Warks 27 C11
Laddingford Kent 20 G3
Lade Bank Lincs 47 G7
Ladock Corn 3 D7
Lady Orkney 95 D7
Ladybank Fife 76 F6
Ladykirk Borders 71 F7
Ladysford Aberds 89 B9
Laga Highld 79 E9
Lagalochan Argyll 73 B7
Lagavulin Argyll 64 D5
Lagg Argyll 72 F4
Lagg N Ayrs 66 D2
Laggan Argyll 64 C3
Laggan Highld 79 D10
Laggan Highld 80 D4
Laggan Highld 81 D8
Laggan S Ayrs 54 A5
Lagganulva Argyll 78 G7
Laide Highld 91 H13
Laigh Fenwick E Ayrs 67 B7
Laigh Glengall S Ayrs 66 E6
Laighmuir E Ayrs 67 B7
Laindon Essex 20 C3
Lair Highld 86 G3
Lairg Highld 93 J8
Lairg Lodge Highld 93 J8
Lairg Muir Highld 93 J8
Lairgmore Highld 87 H8
Laisterdyke W Yorks 51 F7
Laithes Cumb 56 C6
Lake IoW 10 F4
Lake Wilts 17 H8
Lakenham Norf 39 E8
Lakenheath Suff 38 G3
Lakesend Norf 37 F11
Lakeside Cumb 56 H5
Laleham Sur 19 E7
Laleston Bridgend 14 D4
Lamarsh Essex 30 E5
Lamas Norf 39 C8
Lambden Borders 70 F6
Lamberhurst Kent 12 C5
Lamberhurst Quarter Kent 12 C5
Lamberton Borders 71 E8
Lambeth London 19 D10
Lambhill Glasgow 68 D4
Lambley Northumb 62 H2
Lambley Notts 45 H10
Lamborough Hill Oxon 17 A11
Lambourn W Berks 17 D10
Lambourne End Essex 19 B11
Lambs Green W Sus 19 H9
Lambston Pembs 22 E4
Lambton T&W 58 A3
Lamerton Devon 4 D5
Lamesley T&W 63 H8
Laminess Orkney 95 E7
Lamington Highld 87 D10
Lamington S Lanark 69 G8
Lamlash N Ayrs 66 C3
Lamloch Dumfries 67 G8
Lamonby Cumb 56 C6
Lamorna Corn 2 G3
Lamorran Corn 3 E7
Lampardbrook Suff 31 B9
Lampeter = Llanbedr Pont Steffan Ceredig 23 B10
Lampeter Velfrey Pembs 22 E6
Lamphey Pembs 22 F5
Lamplugh Cumb 56 D2
Lamport Northants 28 A4
Lamyatt Som 8 A5
Lana Devon 6 G2
Lanark S Lanark 69 F7
Lancaster Lancs 49 C4
Lanchester Durham 58 B2
Lancing W Sus 11 D10
Landbeach Cambs 29 B11
Landcross Devon 6 D3
Landerberry Aberds 83 C9
Landford Wilts 10 C1
Landford Manor Wilts 10 B1
Landimore Swansea 23 G9
Landkey Devon 6 C4
Landore Swansea 14 B2
Landrake Corn 4 E4
Landscove Devon 5 E8
Landshipping Pembs 22 E5
Landshipping Quay Pembs 22 E5
Landulph Corn 4 E5
Landwade Suff 30 B3
Lane Corn 3 C7
Lane End Bucks 18 B5
Lane End Cumb 56 G3
Lane End Dorset 9 E7
Lane End Hants 10 B4
Lane End IoW 10 F5
Lane End Lancs 50 E4
Lane Ends Lancs 50 D3
Lane Ends Lancs 50 F3
Lane Ends N Yorks 50 E5
Lane Head Derbys 44 E5
Lane Head Durham 58 E2
Lane Head Gtr Man 43 C9
Lane Head W Yorks 44 B5
Lane Side Lancs 50 G3
Laneast Corn 4 C3
Laneham Notts 46 E2
Lanehead Durham 57 B10
Lanehead Northumb 62 E3
Lanercost Cumb 61 G11
Laneshaw Bridge Lancs 50 E5
Lanfach Caerph 15 B8
Langar Notts 36 B3
Langbank Renfs 68 C2
Langbar N Yorks 51 D6
Langburnshiels Borders 61 C11
Langcliffe N Yorks 50 C4
Langdale Highld 93 E9
Langdale End N Yorks 59 G10
Langdon Corn 4 C4
Langdon Beck Durham 57 C10
Langdon Hills Essex 20 C3
Langdyke Fife 76 G6
Langenhoe Essex 31 G7
Langford C Beds 29 D8
Langford Devon 7 F9
Langford Essex 30 H5
Langford Notts 46 G2
Langford Oxon 17 A9
Langford Budville Som 7 D10
Langham Essex 31 E7
Langham Norf 38 A6
Langham Rutland 36 D4
Langham Suff 30 B6
Langhaugh Borders 69 G11
Langho Lancs 50 F3
Langholm Dumfries 61 E9
Langleeford Northumb 62 A5
Langley Ches E 44 E3
Langley Hants 10 D3
Langley Herts 29 F9
Langley Kent 20 F5
Langley Northumb 62 G4
Langley Slough 19 D7
Langley W Sus 11 B7
Langley Warks 27 B8
Langley Burrell Wilts 16 D6
Langley Common Derbys 35 B8
Langley Heath Kent 20 F5
Langley Lower Green Essex 29 E11
Langley Marsh Som 7 D9
Langley Park Durham 58 B3
Langley Street Norf 39 E9
Langley Upper Green Essex 29 E11
Langney E Sus 12 F5
Langold Notts 45 D9
Langore Corn 4 C4
Langport Som 8 B3
Langrick Lincs 46 H6
Langridge Bath 16 E4
Langridge Ford Devon 6 D4
Langrigg Cumb 56 B3
Langrish Hants 10 B6
Langsett S Yorks 44 B6
Langshaw Borders 70 G4
Langside Perth 75 F10
Langskaill Orkney 95 D5
Langstone Hants 10 D6
Langstone Newport 15 B9
Langthorne N Yorks 58 G3
Langthorpe N Yorks 51 C9
Langthwaite N Yorks 58 F1
Langtoft E Yorks 52 C6
Langtoft Lincs 37 D7
Langton Durham 58 E2
Langton Lincs 46 F6
Langton Lincs 47 E7
Langton N Yorks 52 C3
Langton by Wragby Lincs 46 E5
Langton Green Kent 12 C4
Langton Green Suff 31 A8
Langton Herring Dorset 8 F5
Langton Matravers Dorset 9 G9
Langtree Devon 6 E3
Langwathby Cumb 57 C7
Langwell Ho. Highld 94 H3
Langwell Lodge Highld 92 J4
Langwith Derbys 45 F9
Langwith Junction Derbys 45 F9
Langworth Lincs 46 E4
Lanivet Corn 3 C9
Lanlivery Corn 4 F1
Lanner Corn 2 F6
Lanreath Corn 4 F2
Lansallos Corn 4 F2
Lansdown Glos 26 F6
Lanteglos Highway Corn 4 F2
Lanton Borders 62 A2
Lanton Northumb 71 G8
Lapford Devon 7 F6
Laphroaig Argyll 64 D4
Lapley Staffs 34 D4
Lapworth Warks 27 A8
Larachbeg Highld 79 G9
Larbert Falk 69 B7
Larden Green Ches E 43 G8
Largie Aberds 88 E6
Largiemore Argyll 73 E8
Largoward Fife 77 G7
Largs N Ayrs 73 H11
Largybeg N Ayrs 66 D3
Largymore N Ayrs 66 D3
Larkfield Involyd 73 F11
Larkhall S Lanark 68 E6
Larkhill Wilts 17 G8
Larling Norf 38 G5
Larriston Borders 61 D11
Lartington Durham 58 E1
Lary Aberds 82 C5
Lasham Hants 18 G3
Lashenden Kent 13 B7
Lassington Glos 26 F4
Lassodie Fife 69 A10
Lastingham N Yorks 59 G8
Latcham Som 15 G10
Latchford Herts 29 F10
Latchford Warr 43 D9
Latchingdon Essex 20 A5
Latchley Corn 4 D5
Lately Common Warr 43 C9
Lathbury M Keynes 28 D5
Latheron Highld 94 G3
Latheronwheel Highld 94 G3
Latheronwheel Ho. Highld 94 G3
Lathones Fife 77 G7
Latimer Bucks 19 B7
Latteridge S Glos 16 C3
Lattiford Som 8 B5
Latton Wilts 17 B7
Latton Bush Essex 29 H11
Lauchintilly Aberds 83 B9
Lauder Borders 70 F4
Laugharne Carms 23 E8
Laughterton Lincs 46 E2
Laughton E Sus 12 E4
Laughton Leics 36 G2
Laughton Lincs 37 B6
Laughton Lincs 46 C2
Laughton Common S Yorks 45 D9
Laughton en le Morthen S Yorks 45 D9
Launcells Corn 4 A3
Launceston Corn 4 C4
Launton Oxon 28 F3
Laurencekirk Aberds 83 F9
Laurieston Dumfries 55 C9
Laurieston Falk 69 C8
Lavendon M Keynes 28 C6
Lavenham Suff 30 D6
Laverhay Dumfries 61 D7
Laversdale Cumb 61 G10
Laverstock Wilts 9 A10
Laverstoke Hants 17 G11
Laverton Glos 27 E7
Laverton N Yorks 51 B8
Laverton Som 16 F4
Lavister Wrex 42 G6
Law S Lanark 69 E7
Lawers Perth 75 D9
Lawers Perth 75 E10
Lawford Essex 31 E7
Lawhitton Corn 4 C4
Lawkland N Yorks 50 C3
Lawley Telford 34 E2
Lawnhead Staffs 34 C4
Lawrenny Pembs 22 F5
Lawshall Suff 30 C5
Lawton Hereford 25 C11
Laxey IoM 48 D4
Laxfield Suff 31 A9
Laxfirth Shetland 96 H6
Laxfirth Shetland 96 J6
Laxford Bridge Highld 92 E5
Laxo Shetland 96 G6
Laxobigging Shetland 96 F6
Laxton E Yorks 52 G3
Laxton Northants 36 F5
Laxton Notts 45 F11
Laycock W Yorks 50 E6
Layer Breton Essex 30 G6
Layer de la Haye Essex 30 F6
Layer Marney Essex 30 G6
Layham Suff 31 D7
Laylands Green W Berks 17 E10
Laytham E Yorks 52 F3
Layton Blackpool 49 F3
Lazenby Redcar 59 D6
Lazonby Cumb 57 C7
Le Planel Guern 11
Le Skerne Haughton Darl 58 E4
Le Villocq Guern 11
Lea Derbys 45 G7
Lea Hereford 26 F3
Lea Lincs 46 D2
Lea Shrops 33 E10
Lea Shrops 33 G9
Lea Wilts 16 C6
Lea Marston Warks 35 F8
Lea Town Lancs 49 F4
Leabrooks Derbys 45 G8
Leac a Li W Isles 90 H6
Leachkin Highld 87 G9
Leadburn Midloth 69 E11
Leaden Roding Essex 30 G2
Leadenham Lincs 46 G3
Leadgate Cumb 57 B9
Leadgate Durham 58 A2
Leadgate T&W 63 H7
Leadhills S Lanark 60 B4
Leafield Oxon 27 G10
Leagrave Luton 29 F7
Leake N Yorks 58 G5
Leake Commonside Lincs 47 G7
Lealholm N Yorks 59 F8
Lealt Argyll 72 D5
Lealt Highld 85 B10
Leamington Hastings Warks 27 B11
Leamonsley Staffs 35 E7
Leamside Durham 58 B4
Leanaig Highld 87 F8
Leargybreck Argyll 72 F4
Leasgill Cumb 49 A4
Leasingham Lincs 46 H4
Leasingthorne Durham 58 D3
Leasowe Mers 42 C5
Leatherhead Sur 19 F8
Leatherhead Common Sur 19 F8
Leathley N Yorks 51 E8
Leaton Shrops 33 D10
Leaveland Kent 21 F7
Leavening N Yorks 52 C3
Leaves Green London 19 E11
Leazes Durham 63 H7
Lebberston N Yorks 53 A6
Lechlade-on-Thames Glos 17 B9
Leck Lancs 50 B2
Leckford Hants 17 H10
Leckfurin Highld 93 D10
Leckgruinart Argyll 64 B3
Leckhampstead Bucks 28 E4
Leckhampstead W Berks 17 D11
Leckhampstead Thicket W Berks 17 D11
Leckhampton Glos 26 G6
Leckie Highld 86 E3
Leckmelm Highld 86 B4
Leckwith V Glam 15 D7
Leconfield E Yorks 52 E6
Ledaig Argyll 74 D2
Ledburn Bucks 28 F6
Ledbury Hereford 26 E4
Ledcharrie Stirling 75 E8
Ledgemoor Hereford 25 C11
Ledicot Hereford 25 B11
Ledmore Highld 92 H5
Lednagullin Highld 93 C10
Ledsham Ches W 42 E6
Ledsham W Yorks 51 G10
Ledston W Yorks 51 G10
Ledston Luck W Yorks 51 F10
Ledwell Oxon 27 F11
Lee Argyll 78 J7
Lee Devon 6 B3
Lee Hants 10 C2
Lee Lancs 50 D1
Lee Shrops 33 B10
Lee Brockhurst Shrops 33 C11
Lee Clump Bucks 18 A6
Lee Mill Devon 5 F7
Lee Moor Devon 5 E6
Lee-on-the-Solent Hants 10 D4
Leeans Shetland 96 J5
Leebotten Shetland 96 L6
Leebotwood Shrops 33 F10
Leece Cumb 49 C2
Leechpool Pembs 22 E4
Leeds Kent 20 F5
Leeds W Yorks 51 F8
Leedstown Corn 2 F5
Leek Staffs 44 G3
Leek Wootton Warks 27 B9
Leekbrook Staffs 44 G3
Leeming N Yorks 58 H3
Leeming Bar N Yorks 58 G3
Lees Derbys 35 B8
Lees Gtr Man 44 B3
Lees W Yorks 50 F6
Leeswood Flint 42 G5
Legbourne Lincs 47 D7
Legerwood Borders 70 F4
Legsby Lincs 46 D5
Leicester Leicester 36 E1
Leicester Forest East Leics 35 E11
Leigh Dorset 8 D5
Leigh Glos 26 F5
Leigh Gtr Man 43 C9
Leigh Kent 20 G2
Leigh Shrops 33 E9
Leigh Sur 19 G9
Leigh Wilts 17 B7
Leigh Worcs 26 C4
Leigh Beck Essex 20 C5
Leigh Common Som 8 B6
Leigh Delamere Wilts 16 D5
Leigh Green Kent 13 C8
Leigh on Sea Southend 20 C5
Leigh Park Hants 10 D6
Leigh Sinton Worcs 26 C4
Leigh upon Mendip Som 16 G3
Leigh Woods N Som 16 D2
Leighswood W Mid 35 E6
Leighterton Glos 16 B5
Leighton N Yorks 51 B7
Leighton Powys 33 E8
Leighton Shrops 34 E2
Leighton Som 16 G4
Leighton Bromswold Cambs 37 H7
Leighton Buzzard C Beds 28 F6
Leinthall Earls Hereford 25 B11
Leinthall Starkes Hereford 25 B11
Leintwardine Hereford 25 A11
Leire Leics 35 F11
Leirinmore Highld 92 C7
Leiston Suff 31 B11
Leitfie Perth 76 C5
Leith Edin 69 C11
Leitholm Borders 70 F6
Lelant Corn 2 F4
Lelley E Yorks 53 F8
Lem Hill Worcs 26 A4
Lemmington Hall Northumb 63 B7
Lempitlaw Borders 70 G6
Lenchwick Worcs 27 D7
Lendalfoot S Ayrs 66 H4
Lendrick Lodge Stirling 75 G8
Lenham Kent 20 F5
Lenham Heath Kent 20 G6
Lennel Borders 71 F7
Lennoxtown E Dunb 68 C5
Lenton Lincs 36 B6
Lenton Nottingham 36 B1
Lentran Highld 87 G8
Lenwade Norf 39 D6
Leny Ho. Stirling 75 G9
Lenzie E Dunb 68 C5
Leoch Angus 76 D6
Leochel-Cushnie Aberds 83 B7
Leominster Hereford 25 C11
Leonard Stanley Glos 16 A5
Leorin Argyll 64 D4
Lepe Hants 10 E3
Lephin Highld 84 D6
Lephinchapel Argyll 73 D8
Lephinmore Argyll 73 D8
Leppington N Yorks 52 C3
Lepton W Yorks 51 H8
Lerryn Corn 4 F2
Lerwick Shetland 96 J6
Lesbury Northumb 63 B8
Leslie Aberds 83 A7
Leslie Fife 76 G5
Lesmahagow S Lanark 69 G7
Lesnewth Corn 4 B2
Lessendrum Aberds 88 D5
Lessingham Norf 39 C9
Lessonhall Cumb 56 A4
Leswalt Dumfries 54 C3
Letchmore Heath Herts 19 B8
Letchworth Herts 29 E9
Letcombe Bassett Oxon 17 C10
Letcombe Regis Oxon 17 C10
Letham Angus 77 C8
Letham Falk 69 B7
Letham Fife 76 F6
Letham Perth 76 E3
Letham Grange Angus 77 C9
Lethenty Aberds 89 D8
Letheringham Suff 31 C9
Letheringsett Norf 39 B6
Lettaford Devon 5 C8
Lettan Orkney 95 D8
Letterewe Highld 86 D2
Letterfearn Highld 85 F13
Letterfinlay Highld 80 D4
Lettermorar Highld 79 C10
Lettermore Argyll 78 G7
Letters Highld 86 C4
Letterston Pembs 22 D4
Lettoch Highld 82 B2
Lettoch Highld 87 H13
Letton Hereford 25 A10
Letton Hereford 25 D10
Letton Green Norf 38 E5
Letty Green Herts 29 G9
Letwell S Yorks 45 D9
Leuchars Fife 77 E7
Leuchars Ho. Moray 88 B2
Leumrabhagh W Isles 91 F8
Levan Invclyd 73 F11
Levaneap Shetland 96 G6
Levedale Staffs 34 D4
Leven E Yorks 53 E7
Leven Fife 76 G6
Levencorroch N Ayrs 66 D3
Levens Cumb 57 H6
Levens Green Herts 29 F10
Levenshulme Gtr Man 44 C2
Levenwick Shetland 96 L6
Leverburgh = An t-Ob W Isles 90 J5
Leverington Cambs 37 D10
Leverton Lincs 47 H8
Leverton Highgate Lincs 47 H8
Leverton Lucasgate Lincs 47 H8
Leverton Outgate Lincs 47 H8
Levington Suff 31 E9
Levisham N Yorks 59 G9
Levishie Highld 80 B6
Lew Oxon 27 H10
Lewannick Corn 4 C3
Lewdown Devon 4 C5
Lewes E Sus 12 E3
Leweston Pembs 22 D4
Lewisham London 19 D10
Lewiston Highld 81 A7
Lewistown Bridgend 14 C5
Lewknor Oxon 18 B4
Leworthy Devon 6 C5
Leworthy Devon 6 F2
Lewtrenchard Devon 4 C5
Lexden Essex 30 F6
Ley Aberds 83 B7
Ley Corn 4 E2
Leybourne Kent 20 F3
Leyburn N Yorks 58 G2
Leyfields Staffs 35 E8
Leyhill Bucks 18 A6
Leyland Lancs 49 G5
Leylodge Aberds 83 C9
Leymoor W Yorks 51 H7
Leys Aberds 89 C10
Leys Perth 76 D5
Leys Castle Highld 87 G9
Leys of Cossans Angus 76 C6
Leysdown-on-Sea Kent 21 D7
Leysmill Angus 77 C9
Leysters Pole Hereford 26 B2
Leyton London 19 C10
Leytonstone London 19 C10
Lezant Corn 4 D4
Leziate Norf 38 D2
Lhanbryde Moray 88 B2
Liatrie Highld 86 H5
Libanus Powys 24 F6
Libberton S Lanark 69 F8
Liberton Edin 69 D11
Liceasto W Isles 90 H6
Lichfield Staffs 35 E7
Lickey Worcs 34 H5
Lickey End Worcs 26 A6
Lickfold W Sus 11 B8
Liddel Orkney 95 K5
Liddesdale Highld 79 F10
Liddington Swindon 17 C9
Lidgate Suff 30 C4
Lidget S Yorks 45 B10
Lidget Green W Yorks 51 F7
Lidgett Notts 45 F10
Lidlington C Beds 28 E6
Lidstone Oxon 27 F10
Lieurary Highld 94 D2
Liff Angus 76 D6
Lifton Devon 4 C4
Liftondown Devon 4 C4
Lighthorne Warks 27 C10
Lightwater Sur 18 E6
Lightwood Stoke 34 A5
Lightwood Green Ches E 34 A2
Lightwood Green Wrex 33 A9
Lilbourne Northants 36 H1
Lilburn Tower Northumb 62 A6
Lilleshall Telford 34 D3
Lilley Herts 29 F8
Lilley W Berks 17 D11
Lilliesleaf Borders 61 A11
Lillingstone Dayrell Bucks 28 E4
Lillingstone Lovell Bucks 28 D4
Lillington Dorset 8 C5
Lillington Warks 27 B10
Lilliput Poole 9 E9
Lilstock Som 7 B10
Lilyhurst Shrops 34 D3
Limbury Luton 29 F7
Limebrook Hereford 25 B10
Limefield Gtr Man 44 A2
Limekilnburn S Lanark 68 E6
Limekilns Fife 69 B9
Limerigg Falk 69 C7
Limerstone IoW 10 F3
Limington Som 8 B4
Limpenhoe Norf 39 E9
Limpley Stoke Wilts 16 E4
Limpsfield Sur 19 F11
Limpsfield Chart Sur 19 F11
Linby Notts 45 G9
Linchmere W Sus 11 A7
Lincluden Dumfries 60 F5
Lincoln Lincs 46 E3
Lincomb Worcs 26 B5
Lincombe Devon 5 F8
Lindal in Furness Cumb 49 B2
Lindale Cumb 49 A4
Lindean Borders 70 G3
Lindfield W Sus 12 D2
Lindford Hants 18 H5
Lindifferon Fife 76 F6
Lindley W Yorks 51 H7
Lindley Green N Yorks 51 E8
Lindores Fife 76 F5
Lindridge Worcs 26 B3
Lindsell Essex 30 F3
Lindsey Suff 30 D6
Linford Hants 9 D10
Linford Thurrock 20 D3
Lingague IoM 48 E2
Lingards Wood W Yorks 44 A4
Lingbob W Yorks 51 F6
Lingdale Redcar 59 E7
Lingen Hereford 25 B10
Lingfield Sur 12 B2
Lingreabhagh W Isles 90 J5
Lingwood Norf 39 E9
Linicro Highld 85 B8
Linkenholt Hants 17 F10
Linkhill Kent 13 D7
Linkinhorne Corn 4 D4
Linklater Orkney 95 K5
Linksness Orkney 95 H3
Linktown Fife 69 A11
Linley Shrops 33 F9
Linley Green Hereford 26 C3
Linlithgow W Loth 69 C9
Linlithgow Bridge W Loth 69 C8
Linshiels Northumb 62 C4
Linsiadar W Isles 90 D7
Linsidemore Highld 87 B8
Linslade C Beds 28 F6
Linstead Parva Suff 39 H9
Linstock Cumb 61 H10
Linthwaite W Yorks 44 A5
Lintlaw Borders 71 E7
Lintmill Moray 88 B5
Linton Borders 70 H6
Linton Cambs 30 D2
Linton Derbys 35 D8
Linton Hereford 26 F3
Linton Kent 20 G4
Linton N Yorks 50 C5
Linton Northumb 63 D8
Linton W Yorks 51 E9
Linton-on-Ouse N Yorks 51 C10
Linwood Hants 9 D10
Linwood Lincs 46 D5
Linwood Renfs 68 D3
Lionacleit W Isles 84 D2
Lional W Isles 91 A10
Liphook Hants 11 A7
Liscard Mers 42 C6
Liscombe Som 7 C7
Liskeard Corn 4 E3
L'Islet Guern 11
Liss Hants 11 B6
Liss Forest Hants 11 B6
Lissett E Yorks 53 D7
Lissington Lincs 46 D5
Lisvane Cardiff 15 C7
Liswerry Newport 15 C9
Litcham Norf 38 D4
Litchborough Northants 28 C3
Litchfield Hants 17 F11
Litherland Mers 42 C6
Litlington Cambs 29 D10
Litlington E Sus 12 F4
Little Abington Cambs 30 D2
Little Addington Northants 28 A6
Little Alne Warks 27 B8
Little Altcar Mers 42 B6
Little Asby Cumb 57 F8
Little Assynt Highld 92 G4
Little Aston Staffs 35 E6
Little Atherfield IoW 10 F3
Little Ayre Orkney 95 J4
Little-ayre Shetland 96 G5
Little Ayton N Yorks 59 E6
Little Baddow Essex 30 H4
Little Badminton S Glos 16 C5
Little Ballinluig Perth 76 B2
Little Bampton Cumb 61 H8
Little Bardfield Essex 30 E3
Little Barford Bedford 29 C8
Little Barningham Norf 39 B7
Little Barrington Glos 27 G9
Little Barrow Ches W 43 E7
Little Barugh N Yorks 52 B3
Little Bavington Northumb 62 F5
Little Bealings Suff 31 D9
Little Bedwyn Wilts 17 E9
Little Bentley Essex 31 F8
Little Berkhamsted Herts 29 H9
Little Billing Northants 28 B5
Little Birch Hereford 26 E2
Little Blakenham Suff 31 D8
Little Blencow Cumb 56 C6
Little Bollington Ches E 43 D10
Little Bookham Sur 19 F8
Little Bowden Leics 36 G3
Little Bradley Suff 30 C3
Little Brampton Shrops 33 G9
Little Brechin Angus 77 A8
Little Brickhill M Keynes 28 E6
Little Brington Northants 28 B4
Little Bromley Essex 31 F7
Little Broughton Cumb 56 C2
Little Budworth Ches W 43 F8
Little Burstead Essex 20 B3
Little Bytham Lincs 36 D6
Little Carlton Lincs 47 D7
Little Carlton Notts 45 G11
Little Casterton Rutland 36 E6
Little Cawthorpe Lincs 47 D7
Little Chalfont Bucks 18 B6
Little Chart Kent 20 G6
Little Chesterford Essex 30 D2
Little Cheverell Wilts 16 F6
Little Chishill Cambs 29 E11
Little Clacton Essex 31 G8
Little Clifton Cumb 56 D2
Little Colp Aberds 89 D7
Little Comberton Worcs 26 D6
Little Common E Sus 12 F6
Little Compton Warks 27 E9
Little Cornard Suff 30 E5
Little Cowarne Hereford 26 C3
Little Coxwell Oxon 17 B9
Little Crakehall N Yorks 58 G3
Little Cressingham Norf 38 F4
Little Crosby Mers 42 B6
Little Dalby Leics 36 D3
Little Dawley Telford 34 E2
Little Dens Aberds 89 D10
Little Dewchurch Hereford 26 E2
Little Downham Cambs 37 G11
Little Driffield E Yorks 52 D6
Little Dunham Norf 38 D4
Little Dunkeld Perth 76 C3
Little Dunmow Essex 30 F3
Little Easton Essex 30 F3
Little Eaton Derbys 35 A9
Little Eccleston Lancs 49 E4
Little Ellingham Norf 38 F6
Little End Essex 20 A2
Little Eversden Cambs 29 C10
Little Faringdon Oxon 17 A9
Little Fencote N Yorks 58 G3
Little Fenton N Yorks 51 F11
Little Finborough Suff 31 C7
Little Fransham Norf 38 D5
Little Gaddesden Herts 28 G6
Little Gidding Cambs 37 G7
Little Glemham Suff 31 C10
Little Glenshee Perth 76 D2
Little Gransden Cambs 29 C9
Little Green Som 16 G4
Little Grimsby Lincs 47 C7
Little Gruinard Highld 86 C2
Little Habton N Yorks 52 B3
Little Hadham Herts 29 F11
Little Hale Lincs 37 A7
Little Hallingbury Essex 29 G11
Little Hampden Bucks 18 A5
Little Harrowden Northants 28 A5
Little Haseley Oxon 18 A3
Little Hatfield E Yorks 53 E7
Little Hautbois Norf 39 C8
Little Haven Pembs 22 E3
Little Hay Staffs 35 E7
Little Hayfield Derbys 44 D4
Little Haywood Staffs 34 C6
Little Heath W Mid 35 G9
Little Hereford Hereford 26 B2
Little Horkesley Essex 30 E6
Little Horsted E Sus 12 E3
Little Horton W Yorks 51 F7
Little Horwood Bucks 28 E4
Little Houghton Northants 28 C5
Little Houghton S Yorks 45 B8
Little Hucklow Derbys 44 E5
Little Hulton Gtr Man 43 B10
Little Humber E Yorks 53 G7
Little Hungerford W Berks 18 D2
Little Irchester Northants 28 B6
Little Kimble Bucks 28 H5
Little Kineton Warks 27 C10
Little Kingshill Bucks 18 B5
Little Langdale Cumb 56 F5
Little Langford Wilts 17 H7
Little Laver Essex 30 H2
Little Leigh Ches W 43 E9
Little Leighs Essex 30 G4
Little Lever Gtr Man 43 B10
Little London Bucks 28 G3
Little London E Sus 12 E4
Little London Hants 17 G10
Little London Hants 18 F3
Little London Lincs 37 C10
Little London Lincs 37 C8
Little London Norf 39 C7
Little London Powys 32 G6
Little Longstone Derbys 44 E5
Little Lynturk Aberds 83 B7
Little Malvern Worcs 26 D4
Little Maplestead Essex 30 E5
Little Marcle Hereford 26 E3
Little Marlow Bucks 18 C5
Little Marsden Lancs 50 F4
Little Massingham Norf 38 C3
Little Melton Norf 39 E7
Little Mill Mon 15 A9
Little Milton Oxon 18 A3
Little Missenden Bucks 18 B6
Little Musgrave Cumb 57 E9
Little Ness Shrops 33 D10
Little Neston Ches W 42 E5
Little Newcastle Pembs 22 D4
Little Newsham Durham 58 E2
Little Oakley Essex 31 F9
Little Oakley Northants 36 G4
Little Orton Cumb 61 H9
Little Ouseburn N Yorks 51 C10
Little Paxton Cambs 29 B8
Little Petherick Corn 3 B8
Little Pitlurg Moray 88 D4
Little Plumpton Lancs 49 F3
Little Plumstead Norf 39 D9
Little Ponton Lincs 36 B5
Little Raveley Cambs 37 H8
Little Reedness E Yorks 52 G4
Little Ribston N Yorks 51 D9
Little Rissington Glos 27 G8
Little Ryburgh Norf 38 C5
Little Ryle Northumb 62 B6
Little Salkeld Cumb 57 C7
Little Sampford Essex 30 E3
Little Sandhurst Brack 18 E5
Little Saxham Suff 30 B4
Little Scatwell Highld 86 F6
Little Sessay N Yorks 51 B10
Little Shelford Cambs 29 C11
Little Singleton Lancs 49 F3
Little Skillymarno Aberds 89 C9
Little Smeaton N Yorks 51 H11
Little Snoring Norf 38 B5
Little Sodbury S Glos 16 C4
Little Somborne Hants 10 A2
Little Somerford Wilts 16 C6
Little Stainforth N Yorks 50 C4
Little Stainton Darl 58 D4
Little Stanney Ches W 43 E7
Little Staughton Bedford 29 B8
Little Steeping Lincs 47 F8
Little Stoke Staffs 34 B5
Little Stonham Suff 31 B8
Little Stretton Leics 36 E2
Little Stretton Shrops 33 F10
Little Strickland Cumb 57 E7
Little Stukeley Cambs 37 H8
Little Sutton Ches W 42 E6
Little Tew Oxon 27 F10
Little Thetford Cambs 37 H11
Little Thirkleby N Yorks 51 B10
Little Thurlow Suff 30 C3
Little Thurrock Thurrock 20 D3
Little Torboll Highld 87 B10
Little Torrington Devon 6 E3
Little Totham Essex 30 G5
Little Toux Aberds 88 C5
Little Town Cumb 56 E4
Little Town Lancs 50 F2
Little Urswick Cumb 49 B2
Little Wakering Essex 20 C6
Little Walden Essex 30 D2
Little Waldingfield Suff 30 D6
Little Walsingham Norf 38 B5
Little Waltham Essex 30 G4
Little Warley Essex 20 B3
Little Weighton E Yorks 52 F5
Little Weldon Northants 36 G5
Little Welnetham Suff 30 B5
Little Wenlock Telford 34 E2
Little Whittingham Green Suff 39 H8
Little Wilbraham Cambs 30 C2
Little Wishford Wilts 17 H7
Little Witley Worcs 26 B4
Little Wittenham Oxon 18 B2
Little Wolford Warks 27 E9
Little Wratting Suff 30 D3
Little Wymington Bedford 28 B6
Little Wymondley Herts 29 F9
Little Wyrley Staffs 34 E6
Little Yeldham Essex 30 E4
Littlebeck N Yorks 59 F9
Littleborough Gtr Man 50 H5
Littleborough Notts 46 D2
Littlebourne Kent 21 F9
Littlebredy Dorset 8 F4
Littlebury Essex 30 E2
Littlebury Green Essex 29 E11
Littledean Glos 26 G3
Littleferry Highld 87 B11
Littleham Devon 5 C11
Littleham Devon 6 D3
Littlehampton W Sus 11 D9
Littlehempston Devon 5 E9
Littlehoughton Northumb 63 B8
Littlemill Aberds 82 D5
Littlemill E Ayrs 67 E7
Littlemill Highld 87 F12
Littlemill Northumb 63 B8
Littlemoor Dorset 8 F5
Littlemore Oxon 18 A2
Littleover Derby 35 B9
Littleport Cambs 38 G1
Littlestone on Sea Kent 13 D9
Littlethorpe Leics 35 F11
Littlethorpe N Yorks 51 C9
Littleton Ches W 43 F7
Littleton Hants 10 A3
Littleton Perth 76 D5
Littleton Som 8 A3
Littleton Sur 18 G6
Littleton Sur 19 E7
Littleton Drew Wilts 16 C5
Littleton-on-Severn S Glos 16 C2
Littleton Pannell Wilts 17 F7
Littletown Durham 58 B4
Littlewick Green Windsor 18 D5
Littleworth Bedford 29 D7
Littleworth Glos 16 A5
Littleworth Oxon 17 B10
Littleworth Staffs 34 D6
Littleworth Worcs 26 C5
Litton Derbys 44 E5
Litton N Yorks 50 B5
Litton Som 16 F2
Litton Cheney Dorset 8 E4
Liurbost W Isles 91 E8
Liverpool Mers 42 C6
Liverpool Airport Mers 43 D7
Liversedge W Yorks 51 G8
Liverton Devon 5 D9
Liverton Redcar 59 E8
Livingston W Loth 69 D9
Livingston Village W Loth 69 D9
Lixwm Flint 42 E4
Lizard Corn 2 H6
Llaingoch Anglesey 40 B4
Llaithddu Powys 33 G6
Llan Powys 32 E4
Llan Ffestiniog Gwyn 41 F9
Llan-y-pwll Wrex 42 G6
Llanaber Gwyn 32 D2
Llanaelhaearn Gwyn 40 F5
Llanafan Ceredig 24 A3
Llanafan-fawr Powys 24 C6
Llanallgo Anglesey 40 B6
Llanandras = Presteigne Powys 25 B10
Llanarmon Gwyn 40 G6
Llanarmon Dyffryn Ceiriog Wrex 33 B7
Llanarmon-yn-Ial Denb 42 G4
Llanarth Ceredig 23 A9
Llanarth Mon 25 G10
Llanarthne Carms 23 D10
Llanasa Flint 42 D4
Llanbabo Anglesey 40 B5
Llanbadarn Fawr Ceredig 32 G2
Llanbadarn Fynydd Powys 33 H7
Llanbadarn-y-Garreg Powys 25 D8
Llanbadoc Mon 15 A9
Llanbadrig Anglesey 40 A5
Llanbeder Newport 15 B9
Llanbedr Gwyn 32 C1
Llanbedr Powys 25 D8
Llanbedr Powys 25 F9
Llanbedr-Dyffryn-Clwyd Denb 42 G4
Llanbedr Pont Steffan = Lampeter Ceredig 23 B10
Llanbedr-y-cennin Conwy 41 D9
Llanbedrgoch Anglesey 41 B7
Llanbedrog Gwyn 40 G5
Llanberis Gwyn 41 D7
Llanbethêry V Glam 14 E6
Llanbister Powys 25 A8
Llanblethian V Glam 14 D5
Llanboidy Carms 23 D7
Llanbradach Caerph 15 B7
Llanbrynmair Powys 32 E4
Llancarfan V Glam 14 D6
Llancayo Mon 15 A9
Llancloudy Hereford 25 F11
Llancynfelyn Ceredig 32 F2
Llandaff Cardiff 15 D7
Llandanwg Gwyn 32 C1
Llandarcy Neath 14 B3
Llandawke Carms 23 E7
Llanddaniel Fab Anglesey 40 C6
Llanddarog Carms 23 E10
Llanddeiniol Ceredig 24 A2
Llanddeiniolen Gwyn 41 D7
Llandderfel Gwyn 32 B5
Llanddeusant Anglesey 40 B5
Llanddeusant Carms 24 F4
Llanddew Powys 25 E7
Llanddewi Swansea 23 H9
Llanddewi-Brefi Ceredig 24 C3
Llanddewi Rhydderch Mon 25 G10
Llanddewi Velfrey Pembs 22 E6
Llanddewi'r Cwm Powys 25 D7
Llanddoged Conwy 41 D10
Llanddona Anglesey 41 C7
Llanddowror Carms 23 E7
Llanddulas Conwy 42 E2
Llanddwywe Gwyn 32 C2
Llanddyfynan Anglesey 41 C7
Llandefaelog Fach Powys 25 E7
Llandefaelog-tre'r-graig Powys 25 F8
Llandefalle Powys 25 E8
Llandegai Gwyn 41 C7
Llandegfan Anglesey 41 C7
Llandegla Denb 42 G4
Llandegley Powys 25 B8
Llandegveth Mon 15 B9
Llandegwning Gwyn 40 G4
Llandeilo Carms 24 F3
Llandeilo Graban Powys 25 D7
Llandeilo'r Fan Powys 24 E5
Llandeloy Pembs 22 D3
Llandenny Mon 15 A10
Llandevenny Mon 15 C10
Llandewednock Corn 2 H6
Llandewi Ystradenny Powys 25 B8
Llandinabo Hereford 26 F2
Llandinam Powys 32 G6
Llandissilio Pembs 22 D6
Llandogo Mon 15 A11
Llandough V Glam 14 D5
Llandough V Glam 15 D7
Llandovery = Llanymddyfri Carms 24 E4
Llandow V Glam 14 D5
Llandre Carms 24 D3
Llandre Ceredig 32 G2
Llandrillo Denb 32 B6
Llandrillo-yn-Rhos Conwy 41 B10
Llandrindod = Llandrindod Wells Powys 25 B7
Llandrindod Wells = Llandrindod Powys 25 B7
Llandrinio Powys 33 D8
Llandudno Conwy 41 B9
Llandudno Junction = Cyffordd Llandudno Conwy 41 C9
Llandwrog Gwyn 40 E6
Llandybie Carms 24 G3
Llandyfaelog Carms 23 E9
Llandyfan Carms 24 G3
Llandyfriog Ceredig 23 B8
Llandyfrydog Anglesey 40 B6
Llandygwydd Ceredig 23 B7
Llandynan Denb 42 H4
Llandyrnog Denb 42 F4
Llandysilio Powys 33 D8
Llandyssil Powys 33 F7
Llandysul Ceredig 23 B9
Llanedeyrn Cardiff 15 C8
Llanedi Carms 23 F10
Llaneglwys Powys 25 E7
Llanegryn Gwyn 32 E1
Llanegwad Carms 23 D10
Llaneilian Anglesey 40 A6
Llanelian-yn-Rhos Conwy 41 C10
Llanelidan Denb 42 G4
Llanelieu Powys 25 E8
Llanellen Mon 25 G10
Llanelli Carms 23 G10
Llanelltyd Gwyn 32 D3
Llanelly Mon 25 G9
Llanelly Hill Mon 25 G9
Llanelwedd Powys 25 C7
Llanelwy = St Asaph Denb 42 E3
Llanenddwyn Gwyn 32 C1
Llanengan Gwyn 40 H4
Llanerchymedd Anglesey 40 B6
Llanerfyl Powys 33 E6
Llanfachraeth Anglesey 40 B5
Llanfachreth Gwyn 32 C3
Llanfaelog Anglesey 40 C5
Llanfaelrhys Gwyn 40 H4
Llanfaenor Mon 25 G11
Llanfaes Anglesey 41 C8
Llanfaes Powys 25 F7
Llanfaethlu Anglesey 40 B5
Llanfaglan Gwyn 40 D6
Llanfair Gwyn 32 C1
Llanfair-ar-y-bryn Carms 24 E5
Llanfair Caereinion Powys 33 E7
Llanfair Clydogau Ceredig 24 C3
Llanfair-Dyffryn-Clwyd Denb 42 G4
Llanfair Kilgheddin Mon 25 H10
Llanfair-Nant-Gwyn Pembs 22 C6
Llanfair Talhaiarn Conwy 42 E2
Llanfair Waterdine Shrops 33 H8
Llanfair-ym-Muallt = Builth Wells Powys 25 C7
Llanfairfechan Conwy 41 C8
Llanfairpwll-gwyngyll Anglesey 41 C7
Llanfairyneubwll Anglesey 40 C5
Llanfairynghornwy Anglesey 40 A5
Llanfallteg Carms 22 E6
Llanfaredd Powys 25 C7
Llanfarian Ceredig 32 H1
Llanfechain Powys 33 C7
Llanfechan Powys 24 C6
Llanfechell Anglesey 40 A5
Llanfendigaid Gwyn 32 E1
Llanferres Denb 42 F4
Llanfflewyn Anglesey 40 B5
Llanfihangel-ar-arth Carms 23 C9
Llanfihangel-Crucorney Mon 25 F10
Llanfihangel Glyn Myfyr Conwy 42 H2
Llanfihangel Nant Bran Powys 24 E6
Llanfihangel-nant-Melan Powys 25 C8
Llanfihangel Rhydithon Powys 25 B8
Llanfihangel Rogiet Mon 15 C10
Llanfihangel Tal-y-llyn Powys 25 F8
Llanfihangel-uwch-Gwili Carms 23 D9
Llanfihangel-y-Creuddyn Ceredig 32 H2
Llanfihangel-y-pennant Gwyn 32 E2
Llanfihangel-y-pennant Gwyn 41 F7
Llanfihangel-y-traethau Gwyn 41 G7
Llanfihangel-yn-Ngwynfa Powys 33 D6
Llanfihangel yn Nhowyn Anglesey 40 C5
Llanfilo Powys 25 E8
Llanfoist Mon 25 G9
Llanfor Gwyn 32 B5
Llanfrechfa Torf 15 B9
Llanfrothen Gwyn 41 F8
Llanfrynach Powys 25 F7
Llanfwrog Anglesey 40 B5
Llanfwrog Denb 42 G4
Llanfyllin Powys 33 D7
Llanfynydd Carms 23 D10
Llanfynydd Flint 42 G5
Llanfyrnach Pembs 23 C7
Llangadfan Powys 32 D6
Llangadog Carms 24 F4
Llangadwaladr Anglesey 40 D5
Llangadwaladr Powys 33 B7
Llangaffo Anglesey 40 D6
Llangain Carms 23 E8
Llangammarch Wells Powys 24 D6
Llangan V Glam 14 D5
Llangarron Hereford 26 F2
Llangasty Talyllyn Powys 25 F8
Llangathen Carms 23 D10
Llangattock Powys 25 G9
Llangattock Lingoed Mon 25 F10
Llangattock nigh Usk Mon 25 H10
Llangattock-Vibon-Avel Mon 25 G11
Llangedwyn Powys 33 C7
Llangefni Anglesey 40 C6
Llangeinor Bridgend 14 C5
Llangeitho Ceredig 24 C3
Llangeler Carms 23 C8
Llangelynin Gwyn 32 E1
Llangendeirne Carms 23 E9
Llangennech Carms 23 F10
Llangennith Swansea 23 G9
Llangenny Powys 25 G9
Llangernyw Conwy 41 D10
Llangian Gwyn 40 H4
Llanglydwen Carms 22 D6
Llangoed Anglesey 41 C8
Llangoedmor Ceredig 22 B6
Llangollen Denb 33 A8
Llangolman Pembs 22 D6
Llangors Powys 25 F8
Llangovan Mon 25 H11
Llangower Gwyn 32 B5
Llangrannog Ceredig 23 A8
Llangristiolus Anglesey 40 C6
Llangrove Hereford 26 G2
Llangua Mon 25 F10
Llangunllo Powys 25 A9
Llangunnor Carms 23 E9
Llangurig Powys 32 H5
Llangwm Conwy 32 A5
Llangwm Mon 15 A10
Llangwm Pembs 22 F4
Llangwnnadl Gwyn 40 G4
Llangwyfan Denb 42 F4
Llangwyfan-isaf Anglesey 40 D5
Llangwyllog Anglesey 40 C6
Llangwyryfon Ceredig 24 A2
Llangybi Ceredig 24 C3
Llangybi Gwyn 40 F6
Llangybi Mon 15 B9
Llangyfelach Swansea 14 B2
Llangynhafal Denb 42 F4
Llangynidr Powys 25 G8
Llangynin Carms 23 E7
Llangynog Carms 23 E8
Llangynog Powys 33 C6
Llangynwyd Bridgend 14 C4
Llanhamlach Powys 25 F7
Llanharan Rhondda 14 C6
Llanharry Rhondda 14 C6
Llanhennock Mon 15 B9
Llanhiledd = Llanhilleth Bl Gwent 15 A8
Llanhilleth = Llanhiledd Bl Gwent 15 A8
Llanidloes Powys 32 G5
Llaniestyn Gwyn 40 G4
Llanifyny Powys 32 G4
Llanigon Powys 25 E9
Llanilar Ceredig 24 A3
Llanilid Rhondda 14 C5
Llanilltud Fawr = Llantwit Major V Glam 14 E5
Llanishen Cardiff 15 C7
Llanishen Mon 15 A10
Llanllawddog Carms 23 D9
Llanllechid Gwyn 41 D8
Llanllowell Mon 15 B9
Llanllugan Powys 33 E6
Llanllwch Carms 23 E8
Llanllwchaiarn Powys 33 F7
Llanllwni Carms 23 C9
Llanllyfni Gwyn 40 E6
Llanmadoc Swansea 23 G9
Llanmaes V Glam 14 E5
Llanmartin Newport 15 C9
Llanmihangel V Glam 14 D5
Llanmorlais Swansea 23 G10
Llannefydd Conwy 42 E2
Llannon Carms 23 F10
Llannor Gwyn 40 G5
Llanon Ceredig 24 B2
Llanover Mon 25 H10
Llanpumsaint Carms 23 D9
Llanreithan Pembs 22 D3
Llanrhaeadr Denb 42 F3
Llanrhaeadr-ym-Mochnant Powys 33 C7
Llanrhian Pembs 22 C3
Llanrhidian Swansea 23 G9
Llanrhos Conwy 41 B9
Llanrhyddlad Anglesey 40 B5
Llanrhystud Ceredig 24 B2
Llanrosser Hereford 25 E9
Llanrothal Hereford 25 G11
Llanrug Gwyn 41 D7
Llanrumney Cardiff 15 C8
Llanrwst Conwy 41 D10
Llansadurnen Carms 23 E7
Llansadwrn Anglesey 41 C7
Llansadwrn Carms 24 E3
Llansaint Carms 23 F8
Llansamlet Swansea 14 B2
Llansannan Conwy 42 F2
Llansannor V Glam 14 D5
Llansantffraed Ceredig 24 B2
Llansantffraed Powys 25 F8
Llansantffraed Cwmdeuddwr Powys 24 B6
Llansantffraed-in-Elvel Powys 25 C7
Llansantffraid-ym-Mechain Powys 33 C8
Llansawel Carms 24 E3
Llansilin Powys 33 C8
Llansoy Mon 15 A10
Llanspyddid Powys 25 F7
Llanstadwell Pembs 22 F4
Llansteffan Carms 23 E8
Llanstephan Powys 25 D8
Llantarnam Torf 15 B9
Llanteg Pembs 22 E6
Llanthony Mon 25 F9
Llantilio Crossenny Mon 25 G10
Llantilio Pertholey Mon 25 G10
Llantood Pembs 22 B6
Llantrisant Anglesey 40 B5
Llantrisant Mon 15 B9
Llantrisant Rhondda 14 C6
Llantrithyd V Glam 14 D6
Llantwit Fardre Rhondda 14 C6
Llantwit Major = Llanilltud Fawr V Glam 14 E5
Llanuwchllyn Gwyn 41 G10
Llanvaches Newport 15 B10

Llanvair Discoed Mon 15 B10
Llanvapley Mon 25 G10
Llanvetherine Mon 25 G10
Llanveynoe Hereford 25 E10
Llanvihangel Gobion Mon 25 H10
Llanvihangel-Ystern-Llewern Mon 25 G11
Llanwarne Hereford 26 F2
Llanwddyn Powys 32 D6
Llanwenog Ceredig 23 B9
Llanwern Newport 15 C9
Llanwinio Carms 23 D7
Llanwnda Gwyn 40 E6
Llanwnda Pembs 22 C4
Llanwnnen Ceredig 23 B10
Llanwnog Powys 32 F6
Llanwrda Carms 24 E4
Llanwrin Powys 32 E3
Llanwrthwl Powys 24 B6
Llanwrtud = Llanwrtyd Wells Powys 24 D5
Llanwrtyd Powys 24 D5
Llanwrtyd Wells = Llanwrtud Powys 24 D5
Llanwyddelan Powys 33 E6
Llanyblodwel Shrops 33 C8
Llanybri Carms 23 E8
Llanybydder Carms 23 B10
Llanycefn Pembs 22 D5
Llanychaer Pembs 22 C4
Llanycil Gwyn 32 B5
Llanycrwys Carms 24 D3
Llanymawddwy Gwyn 32 D5
Llanymddyfri = Llandovery Carms 24 E4
Llanymynech Powys 33 C8
Llanynghenedl Anglesey 40 B5
Llanynys Denb 42 F4
Llanyre Powys 25 B7
Llanystumdwy Gwyn 40 G6
Llanywern Powys 25 F8
Llawhaden Pembs 22 E5
Llawnt Shrops 33 B8
Llawr Dref Gwyn 40 H4
Llawryglyn Powys 32 F5
Llay Wrex 42 G6
Llechcynfarwy Anglesey 40 B5
Llecheiddior Gwyn 40 F6
Llechfaen Powys 25 F7
Llechryd Caerph 25 H8
Llechryd Ceredig 23 B7
Llechrydau Powys 33 B8
Lledrod Ceredig 24 A3
Llenmerewig Powys 33 F7
Llethrid Swansea 23 G10
Llidiad Nenog Carms 23 C10
Llidiardau Gwyn 41 G10
Llidiart-y-parc Denb 33 A7
Llithfaen Gwyn 40 F5
Llong Flint 42 F5
Llowes Powys 25 D8
Llundain-fach Ceredig 23 A10
Llwydcoed Rhondda 14 A5
Llwyn Shrops 33 G8
Llwyn-du Mon 25 G9
Llwyn-hendy Carms 23 G10
Llwyn-têg Carms 23 F10
Llwyn-y-brain Carms 22 E6
Llwyn-y-groes Ceredig 23 A10
Llwyncelyn Ceredig 23 A9
Llwyndafydd Ceredig 23 A8
Llwynderw Powys 33 E8
Llwyndyrys Gwyn 40 F5
Llwyngwril Gwyn 32 E1
Llwynmawr Wrex 33 B8
Llwynypia Rhondda 14 B5
Llynclys Shrops 33 C8
Llynfaes Anglesey 40 C6
Llys-y-frân Pembs 22 D5
Llysfaen Conwy 41 C10
Llyswen Powys 25 E8
Llysworney V Glam 14 D5
Llywel Powys 24 E5
Loan Falk 69 C8
Loanend Northumb 71 E8
Loanhead Midloth 69 D11
Loans S Ayrs 66 C6
Loans of Tullich Highld 87 D11
Lobb Devon 6 C3
Loch a Charnain W Isles 84 D3
Loch a' Ghainmhich W Isles 91 E7
Loch Baghasdail = Lochboisdale W Isles 84 G2
Loch Choire Lodge Highld 93 F9
Loch Euphoirt W Isles 84 B3
Loch Head Dumfries 54 E6
Loch Loyal Lodge Highld 93 E9
Loch nam Madadh = Lochmaddy W Isles 84 B4
Loch Sgioport W Isles 84 E3
Lochailort Highld 79 C10
Lochaline Highld 79 G9
Lochanhully Highld 81 A11
Lochans Dumfries 54 D3
Locharbriggs Dumfries 60 E5
Lochassynt Lodge Highld 92 G4
Lochavich Ho Argyll 73 B8
Lochawe Argyll 74 E4
Lochboisdale = Loch Baghasdail W Isles 84 G2
Lochbuie Argyll 79 J9
Lochcarron Highld 85 E13
Lochdhu Highld 93 E13
Lochdochart House Stirling 75 E7
Lochdon Argyll 79 H10
Lochdrum Highld 86 D5
Lochead Argyll 72 F6
Lochearnhead Stirling 75 E8
Lochee Dundee 76 D6
Lochend Highld 87 H8
Lochend Highld 94 D4
Locherben Dumfries 60 D5
Lochfoot Dumfries 60 F4
Lochgair Argyll 73 D8
Lochgarthside Highld 81 B7
Lochgelly Fife 69 A10
Lochgilphead Argyll 73 E7
Lochgoilhead Argyll 74 G5
Lochhill Moray 88 B2
Lochindorb Lodge Highld 87 H12
Lochinver Highld 92 G3
Lochlane Perth 75 E11
Lochluichart Highld 86 E6
Lochmaben Dumfries 60 E6
Lochmaddy = Loch nam Madadh W Isles 84 B4
Lochmore Cottage Highld 94 F2
Lochmore Lodge Highld 92 F5
Lochore Fife 76 H4
Lochportain W Isles 84 A4
Lochranza N Ayrs 66 A2
Lochs Crofts Moray 88 B3
Lochside Aberds 77 A10
Lochside Highld 87 F11
Lochside Highld 92 D7
Lochside Highld 93 F11
Lochslin Highld 87 C11
Lochstack Lodge Highld 92 E5
Lochton Aberds 83 D9
Lochty Angus 77 A8
Lochty Fife 77 G8
Lochty Perth 76 E3
Lochuisge Highld 79 F10
Lochurr Dumfries 60 E3
Lochwinnoch Renfs 68 E2
Lochwood Dumfries 60 D6
Lochyside Highld 80 F3
Lockengate Corn 3 C9
Lockerbie Dumfries 61 E7
Lockeridge Wilts 17 E8
Lockerley Hants 10 B1
Locking N Som 15 F9
Lockinge Oxon 17 C11
Lockington E Yorks 52 E5
Lockington Leics 35 C10
Lockleywood Shrops 34 C2
Locks Heath Hants 10 D4
Lockton N Yorks 59 G9
Lockwood W Yorks 51 H7
Loddington Leics 36 E3
Loddington Northants 36 H4
Loddiswell Devon 5 G8
Loddon Norf 39 F9
Lode Cambs 30 B2
Loders Dorset 8 E3
Lodsworth W Sus 11 B8
Lofthouse N Yorks 51 B7
Lofthouse W Yorks 51 G9
Loftus Redcar 59 E8
Logan E Ayrs 67 D8
Logan Mains Dumfries 54 E3
Loganlea W Loth 69 D8
Loggerheads Staffs 34 B3
Logie Angus 77 A9
Logie Fife 77 E7
Logie Moray 87 F13
Logie Coldstone Aberds 82 C6
Logie Hill Highld 87 D10
Logie Newton Aberds 89 E6
Logie Pert Angus 77 A9
Logiealmond Lodge Perth 76 D2
Logierait Perth 76 B2
Login Carms 22 D6
Lolworth Cambs 29 B10
Lonbain Highld 85 C11
Londesborough E Yorks 52 E4
London Colney Herts 19 A8
Londonderry N Yorks 58 H4
Londonthorpe Lincs 36 B5
Londubh Highld 91 J13
Lonemore Highld 87 C10
Long Ashton N Som 15 D11
Long Bennington Lincs 36 A4
Long Bredy Dorset 8 E4
Long Buckby Northants 28 B3
Long Clawson Leics 36 C3
Long Common Hants 10 C4
Long Compton Staffs 34 C4
Long Compton Warks 27 E9
Long Crendon Bucks 28 H3
Long Crichel Dorset 9 C8
Long Ditton Sur 19 E8
Long Drax N Yorks 52 G2
Long Duckmanton Derbys 45 E8
Long Eaton Derbys 35 B10
Long Green Worcs 26 E5
Long Hanborough Oxon 27 G11
Long Itchington Warks 27 B11
Long Lawford Warks 35 H10
Long Load Som 8 B3
Long Marston Herts 28 G5
Long Marston N Yorks 51 D11
Long Marston Warks 27 D8
Long Marton Cumb 57 D8
Long Melford Suff 30 D5
Long Newnton Glos 16 B6
Long Newton E Loth 70 D4
Long Preston N Yorks 50 D4
Long Riston E Yorks 53 E7
Long Sight Gtr Man 44 B3
Long Stratton Norf 39 F7
Long Street M Keynes 28 D4
Long Sutton Hants 18 G4
Long Sutton Lincs 37 C10
Long Sutton Som 8 B3
Long Thurlow Suff 31 B7
Long Whatton Leics 35 C10
Long Wittenham Oxon 18 B2
Longbar N Ayrs 66 A6
Longbenton T&W 63 G8
Longborough Glos 27 F8
Longbridge W Mid 34 H6
Longbridge Warks 27 B9
Longbridge Deverill Wilts 16 G5
Longburton Dorset 8 C5
Longcliffe Derbys 44 G6
Longcot Oxon 17 B9
Longcroft Falk 68 C6
Longden Shrops 33 E10
Longdon Staffs 35 D6
Longdon Worcs 26 E5
Longdon Green Staffs 35 D6
Longdon on Tern Telford 34 D2
Longdown Devon 7 G7
Longdowns Corn 2 F6
Longfield Kent 20 E3
Longfield Shetland 96 M5
Longford Derbys 35 B8
Longford Glos 26 F5
Longford London 19 D7
Longford Shrops 34 B2
Longford Telford 34 D3
Longford W Mid 35 G9
Longfordlane Derbys 35 B8
Longforgan Perth 76 E6
Longformacus Borders 70 E5
Longframlington Northumb 63 C7
Longham Dorset 9 E9
Longham Norf 38 D5
Longhaven Aberds 89 E11
Longhill Aberds 89 C9
Longhirst Northumb 63 E8
Longhope Glos 26 G3
Longhope Orkney 95 J4
Longhorsley Northumb 63 D7
Longhoughton Northumb 63 B8
Longlane Derbys 35 B8
Longlane W Berks 17 D11
Longlevens Glos 26 F5
Longley W Yorks 44 B5
Longley Green Worcs 26 C4
Longmanhill Aberds 89 B7
Longmoor Camp Hants 11 A6
Longmorn Moray 88 C2
Longnewton Borders 70 H4
Longnewton Stockton 58 E4
Longney Glos 26 G4
Longniddry E Loth 70 C3
Longnor Shrops 33 E10
Longnor Staffs 44 F4
Longparish Hants 17 G11
Longport Stoke 44 H2
Longridge Lancs 50 F2
Longridge Staffs 34 D5
Longridge W Loth 69 D8
Longriggend N Lanark 69 C7
Longsdon Staffs 44 G3
Longshaw Gtr Man 43 B8
Longside Aberds 89 D10
Longstanton Cambs 29 B10
Longstock Hants 17 H10
Longstone Pembs 22 F6
Longstowe Cambs 29 C10
Longthorpe Pboro 37 F7
Longthwaite Cumb 56 D6
Longton Lancs 49 G4
Longton Stoke 34 A5
Longtown Cumb 61 G9
Longtown Hereford 25 F10
Longview Mers 43 C7
Longville in the Dale Shrops 33 F11
Longwick Bucks 28 H4
Longwitton Northumb 62 E6
Longwood Shrops 34 E2
Longworth Oxon 17 B10
Longyester E Loth 70 D4
Lonmay Aberds 89 C10
Lonmore Highld 84 D7
Looe Corn 4 F3
Loose Kent 20 F4
Loosley Row Bucks 18 A5
Lopcombe Corner Wilts 17 H9
Lopen Som 8 C3
Loppington Shrops 33 C10
Lopwell Devon 4 E5
Lorbottle Northumb 62 C6
Lorbottle Hall Northumb 62 C6
Lornty Perth 76 C4
Loscoe Derbys 45 H8
Losgaintir W Isles 90 H5
Lossiemouth Moray 88 A2
Lossit Argyll 64 C2
Lostford Shrops 34 B2
Lostock Gralam Ches W 43 E9
Lostock Green Ches W 43 E9
Lostock Hall Lancs 49 G5
Lostock Junction Gtr Man 43 B9
Lostwithiel Corn 4 F2
Loth Orkney 95 E7
Lothbeg Highld 93 H12
Lothersdale N Yorks 50 E5
Lothmore Highld 93 H12
Loudwater Bucks 18 B6
Loughborough Leics 35 D11
Loughor Swansea 23 G10
Loughton Essex 19 B11
Loughton M Keynes 28 E5
Loughton Shrops 34 G2
Lound Lincs 37 D6
Lound Notts 45 D10
Lound Suff 39 F11
Lount Leics 35 D9
Louth Lincs 47 D7
Love Clough Lancs 50 G4
Lovedean Hants 10 C5
Lover Wilts 9 B11
Loversall S Yorks 45 C9
Loves Green Essex 20 A3
Lovesome Hill N Yorks 58 G4
Loveston Pembs 22 F5
Lovington Som 8 A4
Low Ackworth W Yorks 51 H10
Low Barlings Lincs 46 E4
Low Bentham N Yorks 50 C2
Low Bradfield S Yorks 44 C6
Low Bradley N Yorks 50 E6
Low Braithwaite Cumb 56 B6
Low Brunton Northumb 62 F5
Low Burnham N Lincs 45 B11
Low Burton N Yorks 51 A8
Low Buston Northumb 63 C8
Low Catton E Yorks 52 D3
Low Clanyard Dumfries 54 F4
Low Coniscliffe Darl 58 E3
Low Crosby Cumb 61 H10
Low Dalby N Yorks 59 H9
Low Dinsdale Darl 58 E4
Low Ellington N Yorks 51 A8
Low Etherley Durham 58 D2
Low Fell T&W 63 H8
Low Fulney Lincs 37 C8
Low Garth N Yorks 59 F8
Low Gate Northumb 62 G5
Low Grantley N Yorks 51 B8
Low Habberley Worcs 34 H4
Low Ham Som 8 B3
Low Hesket Cumb 57 B6
Low Hesleyhurst Northumb 62 D6
Low Hutton N Yorks 52 C3
Low Laithe N Yorks 51 C7
Low Leighton Derbys 44 D4
Low Lorton Cumb 56 D3
Low Marishes N Yorks 52 B4
Low Marnham Notts 46 F2
Low Mill N Yorks 59 G7
Low Moor Lancs 50 E3
Low Moor W Yorks 51 G7
Low Moorsley T&W 58 B4
Low Newton Cumb 49 A4
Low Newton-by-the-Sea Northumb 63 A8
Low Row Cumb 56 C5
Low Row Cumb 61 G11
Low Row N Yorks 57 G11
Low Salchrie Dumfries 54 C3
Low Smerby Argyll 65 F8
Low Torry Fife 69 B9
Low Worsall N Yorks 58 F4
Low Wray Cumb 56 F5
Lowbridge House Cumb 57 F7
Lowca Cumb 56 D1
Lowdham Notts 45 H10
Lowe Shrops 33 B11
Lowe Hill Staffs 44 G3
Lower Aisholt Som 7 C11
Lower Arncott Oxon 28 G3
Lower Ashton Devon 5 C9
Lower Assendon Oxon 18 C4
Lower Badcall Highld 92 E4
Lower Bartle Lancs 49 F4
Lower Basildon W Berks 18 D3
Lower Beeding W Sus 11 B11
Lower Benefield Northants 36 G5
Lower Boddington Northants 27 C11
Lower Brailes Warks 27 E10
Lower Breakish Highld 85 F11
Lower Broadheath Worcs 26 C5
Lower Bullingham Hereford 26 E2
Lower Cam Glos 16 A4
Lower Chapel Powys 25 E7
Lower Chute Wilts 17 F10
Lower Cragabus Argyll 64 D4
Lower Crossings Derbys 44 D4
Lower Cumberworth W Yorks 44 B6
Lower Cwm-twrch Powys 24 G4
Lower Darwen Blackburn 50 G2
Lower Dean Bedford 29 B7
Lower Diabaig Highld 85 B12
Lower Dicker E Sus 12 E4
Lower Dinchope Shrops 33 G10
Lower Down Shrops 33 G9
Lower Drift Corn 2 G3
Lower Dunsforth N Yorks 51 C10
Lower Egleton Hereford 26 D3
Lower Elkstone Staffs 44 G4
Lower End C Beds 28 F6
Lower Everleigh Wilts 17 F8
Lower Farringdon Hants 18 H4
Lower Foxdale IoM 48 E2
Lower Frankton Shrops 33 B9
Lower Froyle Hants 18 G4
Lower Gledfield Highld 87 B8
Lower Green Norf 38 B5
Lower Hacheston Suff 31 C10
Lower Halistra Highld 84 C7
Lower Halstow Kent 20 E5
Lower Hardres Kent 21 F8
Lower Hawthwaite Cumb 56 H4
Lower Heath Ches E 44 F2
Lower Hempriggs Moray 87 E14
Lower Hergest Hereford 25 C9
Lower Heyford Oxon 27 F11
Lower Higham Kent 20 D4
Lower Holbrook Suff 31 E8
Lower Hordley Shrops 33 C9
Lower Horsebridge E Sus 12 E4
Lower Killeyan Argyll 64 D3
Lower Kingswood Sur 19 F9
Lower Kinnerton Ches W 42 F6
Lower Langford N Som 15 E10
Lower Largo Fife 77 G7
Lower Leigh Staffs 34 B6
Lower Lemington Glos 27 E9
Lower Lenie Highld 81 A7
Lower Lydbrook Glos 26 G2
Lower Lye Hereford 25 B11
Lower Machen Newport 15 C8
Lower Maes-coed Hereford 25 E10
Lower Mayland Essex 20 A6
Lower Midway Derbys 35 C9
Lower Milovaig Highld 84 C6
Lower Moor Worcs 26 D6
Lower Nazeing Essex 29 H10
Lower Netchwood Shrops 34 F2
Lower Ollach Highld 85 E10
Lower Penarth V Glam 15 D7
Lower Penn Staffs 34 F4
Lower Pennington Hants 10 E2
Lower Peover Ches W 43 E10
Lower Pexhill Ches E 44 E2
Lower Place Gtr Man 44 A3
Lower Quinton Warks 27 D8
Lower Rochford Worcs 26 B3
Lower Seagry Wilts 16 C6
Lower Shelton C Beds 28 D6
Lower Shiplake Oxon 18 D4
Lower Shuckburgh Warks 27 B11
Lower Slaughter Glos 27 F8
Lower Stanton St Quintin Wilts 16 C6
Lower Stoke Medway 20 D5
Lower Stondon C Beds 29 E8
Lower Stow Bedon Norf 38 F5
Lower Street Norf 39 B8
Lower Street Norf 39 D9
Lower Strensham Worcs 26 D6
Lower Stretton Warr 43 D9
Lower Sundon C Beds 29 F7
Lower Swanwick Hants 10 D3
Lower Swell Glos 27 F8
Lower Tean Staffs 34 B6
Lower Thurlton Norf 39 F10
Lower Tote Highld 85 B10
Lower Town Pembs 22 C4
Lower Tysoe Warks 27 D10
Lower Upham Hants 10 C4
Lower Vexford Som 7 C10
Lower Weare Som 15 F10
Lower Welson Hereford 25 C9
Lower Whitley Ches W 43 E9
Lower Wield Hants 18 G3
Lower Winchendon Bucks 28 G4
Lower Withington Ches E 44 F2
Lower Woodend Bucks 18 C5
Lower Woodford Wilts 9 A10
Lower Wyche Worcs 26 D4
Lowesby Leics 36 E3
Lowestoft Suff 39 F11
Loweswater Cumb 56 D3
Lowford Hants 10 C3
Lowgill Cumb 57 G8
Lowgill Lancs 50 C2
Lowick Northants 36 G5
Lowick Northumb 71 G9
Lowick Bridge Cumb 56 H4
Lowick Green Cumb 56 H4
Lowlands Torf 15 B8
Lowmoor Row Cumb 57 D8
Lownie Moor Angus 77 C7
Lowsonford Warks 27 B8
Lowther Cumb 57 D7
Lowthorpe E Yorks 52 C6
Lowton Gtr Man 43 C9
Lowton Common Gtr Man 43 C9
Loxbeare Devon 7 E8
Loxhill Sur 19 H7
Loxhore Devon 6 C5
Loxley Warks 27 C9
Loxton N Som 15 F9
Loxwood W Sus 11 A9
Lubcroy Highld 92 J6
Lubenham Leics 36 G3
Luccombe Som 7 B8
Luccombe Village IoW 10 G4
Lucker Northumb 71 G10
Luckett Corn 4 D4
Luckington Wilts 16 C5
Lucklawhill Fife 77 E7
Luckwell Bridge Som 7 C8
Lucton Hereford 25 B11
Ludag W Isles 84 G2
Ludborough Lincs 46 C6
Ludchurch Pembs 22 E6
Luddenden W Yorks 50 G6
Luddenden Foot W Yorks 50 G6
Luddesdown Kent 20 E3
Luddington N Lincs 52 H4
Luddington Warks 27 C8
Luddington in the Brook Northants 37 G7
Lude House Perth 81 G10
Ludford Lincs 46 D6
Ludford Shrops 26 A2
Ludgershall Bucks 28 G3
Ludgershall Wilts 17 F9
Ludgvan Corn 2 F4
Ludham Norf 39 D9
Ludlow Shrops 26 A2
Ludwell Wilts 9 B8
Ludworth Durham 58 B4
Luffincott Devon 6 G2
Lugar E Ayrs 67 D8
Lugg Green Hereford 25 B11
Luggate Burn E Loth 70 C5
Luggiebank N Lanark 68 C6
Lugton E Ayrs 67 A7
Lugwardine Hereford 26 D2
Luib Highld 85 F10
Lulham Hereford 25 D11
Lullenden Sur 12 B3
Lullington Derbys 35 D8
Lullington Som 16 F4
Lulsgate Bottom N Som 15 E11
Lulsley Worcs 26 C4
Lumb W Yorks 50 G6
Lumby N Yorks 51 F10
Lumloch E Dunb 68 D5
Lumphanan Aberds 83 C7
Lumphinnans Fife 69 A10
Lumsdaine Borders 71 D7
Lumsden Aberds 82 A6
Lunan Angus 77 B9
Lunanhead Angus 77 B7
Luncarty Perth 76 E3
Lund E Yorks 52 E5
Lund N Yorks 52 F2
Lund Shetland 96 C7
Lunderton Aberds 89 D11
Lundie Angus 76 D5
Lundie Highld 80 B3
Lundin Links Fife 77 G7
Lunga Argyll 72 C6
Lunna Shetland 96 G6
Lunning Shetland 96 G7
Lunnon Swansea 23 H10
Lunsford's Cross E Sus 12 E6
Lunt Mers 42 B6
Luntley Hereford 25 C10
Luppitt Devon 7 F10
Lupset W Yorks 51 H9
Lupton Cumb 50 A1
Lurgashall W Sus 11 B8
Lusby Lincs 47 F7
Luson Devon 5 G7
Luss Argyll 68 A2
Lussagiven Argyll 72 E5
Lusta Highld 85 C7
Lustleigh Devon 5 C8
Luston Hereford 25 B11
Luthermuir Aberds 83 G8
Luthrie Fife 76 F6
Luton Devon 5 D10
Luton Luton 29 F7
Luton Medway 20 E4
Lutterworth Leics 35 G11
Lutton Devon 5 F6
Lutton Lincs 37 C10
Lutton Northants 37 G7
Lutworthy Devon 7 E6
Luxborough Som 7 C8
Luxulyan Corn 4 F1
Lybster Highld 94 G4
Lydbury North Shrops 33 G9
Lydcott Devon 6 C5
Lydd Kent 13 D9
Lydd on Sea Kent 13 D9
Lydden Kent 21 G9
Lyddington Rutland 36 F4
Lyde Green Hants 18 F4
Lydeard St Lawrence Som 7 C10
Lydford Devon 4 C6
Lydford-on-Fosse Som 8 A4
Lydgate W Yorks 50 G5
Lydham Shrops 33 F9
Lydiard Green Wilts 17 C7
Lydiard Millicent Wilts 17 C7
Lydiate Mers 42 B6
Lydlinch Dorset 8 C6
Lydney Glos 16 A3
Lydstep Pembs 22 G5
Lye W Mid 34 G5
Lye Green Bucks 18 A6
Lye Green E Sus 12 C4
Lyford Oxon 17 B10
Lymbridge Green Kent 13 B10
Lyme Regis Dorset 8 E2
Lyminge Kent 21 G8
Lymington Hants 10 E2
Lyminster W Sus 11 D9
Lymm Warr 43 D9
Lymore Hants 10 E1
Lympne Kent 13 C10
Lympsham Som 15 F9
Lympstone Devon 5 C10
Lynchat Highld 81 C9
Lyndale Ho. Highld 85 C8
Lyndhurst Hants 10 D2
Lyndon Rutland 36 E5
Lyne Sur 19 E7
Lyne Down Hereford 26 E3
Lyne of Gorthleck Highld 81 A7
Lyne of Skene Aberds 83 B9
Lyneal Shrops 33 B10
Lyneham Oxon 27 F9
Lyneham Wilts 17 D7
Lynemore Highld 82 A2
Lynemouth Northumb 63 D8
Lyness Orkney 95 J4
Lyng Norf 39 D6
Lyng Som 8 B2
Lynmouth Devon 7 B6
Lynsted Kent 20 E6
Lynton Devon 6 B6
Lyon's Gate Dorset 8 D5
Lyonshall Hereford 25 C10
Lytchett Matravers Dorset 9 E8
Lytchett Minster Dorset 9 E8
Lyth Highld 94 D4
Lytham Lancs 49 G3
Lytham St Anne's Lancs 49 G3
Lythe N Yorks 59 E9
Lythes Orkney 95 K5

M

Mabe Burnthouse Corn 3 F6
Mabie Dumfries 60 F5
Mablethorpe Lincs 47 D9
Macclesfield Ches E 44 E3
Macclesfield Forest Ches E 44 E3
Macduff Aberds 89 B7
Mace Green Suff 31 D8
Macharioch Argyll 65 H8
Machen Caerph 15 C8
Machrihanish Argyll 65 F7
Machynlleth Powys 32 E3
Machynys Carms 23 G10
Mackerel's Common W Sus 11 B9
Mackworth Derbys 35 B9
Macmerry E Loth 70 C3
Madderty Perth 76 E2
Maddiston Falk 69 C8
Madehurst W Sus 11 C8
Madeley Staffs 34 A3
Madeley Telford 34 E2
Madeley Heath Staffs 43 H10
Madeley Park Staffs 34 A3
Madingley Cambs 29 B10
Madley Hereford 25 E11
Madresfield Worcs 26 D5
Madron Corn 2 F3
Maen-y-groes Ceredig 23 A8
Maenaddwyn Anglesey 40 B6
Maenclochog Pembs 22 D5
Maendy V Glam 14 D6
Maentwrog Gwyn 41 F8
Maer Staffs 34 B3
Maerdy Conwy 32 A6
Maerdy Rhondda 14 B5
Maes-Treylow Powys 25 B9
Maesbrook Shrops 33 C8
Maesbury Shrops 33 C9
Maesbury Marsh Shrops 33 C9
Maesgwyn-Isaf Powys 33 D7
Maesgwynne Carms 23 D7
Maeshafn Denb 42 F5
Maesllyn Ceredig 23 B8
Maesmynis Powys 25 D7
Maesteg Bridgend 14 B4
Maestir Ceredig 23 B10
Maesy cwmmer Caerph 15 B7
Maesybont Carms 23 E10
Maesycrugiau Carms 23 B9
Maesymeillion Ceredig 23 B9
Magdalen Laver Essex 20 A2
Maggieknockater Moray 88 D3
Magham Down E Sus 12 E5
Maghull Mers 43 B6
Magor Mon 15 C10
Magpie Green Suff 39 H6
Maiden Bradley Wilts 16 H5
Maiden Law Durham 58 B2
Maiden Newton Dorset 8 E4
Maiden Wells Pembs 22 G4
Maidencombe Torbay 5 E10
Maidenhall Suff 31 D8
Maidenhead Windsor 18 C5
Maidens S Ayrs 66 F5
Maiden's Green Brack 18 D5
Maidensgrave Suff 31 D9
Maidenwell Corn 4 D2
Maidenwell Lincs 47 E7
Maidford Northants 28 C3
Maids Moreton Bucks 28 E4
Maidstone Kent 20 F4
Maidwell Northants 36 H3
Mail Shetland 96 L6
Main Powys 33 D7
Maindee Newport 15 C9
Mains of Airies Dumfries 54 C2
Mains of Allardice Aberds 83 F10
Mains of Annochie Aberds 89 D9
Mains of Ardestie Angus 77 D8
Mains of Balhall Angus 77 A8
Mains of Ballindarg Angus 77 B7
Mains of Balnakettle Aberds 83 F8
Mains of Birness Aberds 89 E9
Mains of Burgie Moray 87 F13
Mains of Clunas Highld 87 G11
Mains of Crichie Aberds 89 D9
Mains of Dalvey Highld 87 H14
Mains of Dellavaird Aberds 83 E9
Mains of Drum Aberds 83 D10
Mains of Edingight Moray 88 C5
Mains of Fedderate Aberds 89 D8
Mains of Inkhorn Aberds 89 E9
Mains of Mayen Moray 88 D5
Mains of Melgund Angus 77 B8
Mains of Thornton Aberds 83 F8
Mains of Watten Highld 94 E4
Mainsforth Durham 58 C4
Mainsriddle Dumfries 60 H5
Mainstone Shrops 33 G8
Maisemore Glos 26 F5
Malcoff Derbys 44 D4
Maldon Essex 30 H5
Malham N Yorks 50 C5
Maligar Highld 85 B9
Mallaig Highld 79 B9
Malleny Mills Edin 69 D10
Malling Stirling 75 G8
Malltraeth Anglesey 40 D6
Mallwyd Gwyn 32 D4
Malmesbury Wilts 16 C6
Malmsmead Devon 7 B6
Malpas Ches W 43 H7
Malpas Corn 3 E7
Malpas Newport 15 B9
Malswick Glos 26 F4
Maltby S Yorks 45 C9
Maltby Stockton 58 E5
Maltby le Marsh Lincs 47 D8
Malting Green Essex 30 F6
Maltman's Hill Kent 13 B8
Malton N Yorks 52 B3
Malvern Link Worcs 26 D4
Malvern Wells Worcs 26 D4
Mamble Worcs 26 A3
Man-moel Caerph 15 A7
Manaccan Corn 3 G6
Manafon Powys 33 E7
Manais W Isles 90 J6
Manar Ho. Aberds 83 A9
Manaton Devon 5 C8
Manby Lincs 47 D7
Mancetter Warks 35 F9
Manchester Gtr Man 44 C2
Manchester Airport Gtr Man 44 D2
Mancot Flint 42 F6
Mandally Highld 80 C4
Manea Cambs 37 G10
Manfield N Yorks 58 E3
Mangaster Shetland 96 F5
Mangotsfield S Glos 16 D3
Mangurstadh W Isles 90 D5
Mankinholes W Yorks 50 G5
Manley Ches W 43 E8
Mannal Argyll 78 G2
Mannerston W Loth 69 C9
Manningford Bohune Wilts 17 F8
Manningford Bruce Wilts 17 F8
Manningham W Yorks 51 F7
Mannings Heath W Sus 11 B11
Mannington Dorset 9 D9
Manningtree Essex 31 E7
Mannofield Aberdeen 83 C11
Manor London 19 C11
Manor Estate S Yorks 45 D7
Manorbier Pembs 22 G5
Manordeilo Carms 24 F3
Manorhill Borders 70 G5
Manorowen Pembs 22 C4
Mansel Lacy Hereford 25 D11
Manselfield Swansea 23 H10
Mansell Gamage Hereford 25 D10
Mansergh Cumb 50 A2
Mansfield E Ayrs 67 E9
Mansfield Notts 45 F9
Mansfield Woodhouse Notts 45 F9
Mansriggs Cumb 49 A2
Manston Dorset 9 C7
Manston Kent 21 E10
Manston W Yorks 51 F9
Manswood Dorset 9 D8
Manthorpe Lincs 36 B5
Manthorpe Lincs 37 D6
Manton N Lincs 46 B3
Manton Notts 45 E9
Manton Rutland 36 E4
Manton Wilts 17 E8
Manuden Essex 29 F11
Maperton Som 8 B5
Maple Cross Herts 19 B7
Maplebeck Notts 45 F11
Mapledurham Oxon 18 D3
Mapledurwell Hants 18 F3
Maplehurst W Sus 11 B10
Maplescombe Kent 20 E2
Mapleton Derbys 44 H5
Mapperley Derbys 35 A10
Mapperley Park Nottingham 36 A1
Mapperton Dorset 8 E4
Mappleborough Green Warks 27 B7
Mappleton E Yorks 53 E8
Mappowder Dorset 8 D6
Mar Lodge Aberds 82 D2
Maraig W Isles 90 G7
Marazanvose Corn 3 D7
Marazion Corn 2 F4
Marbhig W Isles 91 F9
Marbury Ches E 43 H8
March Cambs 37 F10
March S Lanark 60 B5
Marcham Oxon 17 B11
Marchamley Shrops 34 C1
Marchington Staffs 35 B7
Marchington Woodlands Staffs 35 C7
Marchroes Gwyn 40 H5
Marchwiel Wrex 42 H6
Marchwood Hants 10 C2
Marcross V Glam 14 E5
Marden Hereford 26 D2
Marden Kent 12 B6
Marden T&W 63 F9
Marden Wilts 17 F7
Marden Beech Kent 12 B6
Marden Thorn Kent 13 B6
Mardy Mon 25 G10
Marefield Leics 36 E3
Mareham le Fen Lincs 46 F6
Mareham on the Hill Lincs 46 F6
Marehay Derbys 45 H7
Marehill W Sus 11 C9
Maresfield E Sus 12 D3
Marfleet Hull 53 G7
Marford Wrex 42 G6
Margam Neath 14 C3
Margaret Marsh Dorset 9 C7
Margaret Roding Essex 30 G2
Margaretting Essex 20 A3
Margate Kent 21 D10
Margnaheglish N Ayrs 66 C3
Margrove Park Redcar 59 E7
Marham Norf 38 D3
Marhamchurch Corn 4 A3
Marholm Pboro 37 E7
Mariandyrys Anglesey 41 B8
Marianglas Anglesey 41 B7
Mariansleigh Devon 7 D6
Marionburgh Aberds 83 C9
Marishader Highld 85 B9
Marjoriebanks Dumfries 60 E6
Mark Dumfries 54 D4
Mark S Ayrs 54 B3
Mark Som 15 G9
Mark Causeway Som 15 G9
Mark Cross E Sus 12 C4
Mark Cross E Sus 12 E3
Markbeech Kent 12 B3
Markby Lincs 47 E8
Market Bosworth Leics 35 E10
Market Deeping Lincs 37 E7
Market Drayton Shrops 34 B2
Market Harborough Leics 36 G3
Market Lavington Wilts 17 F7
Market Overton Rutland 36 D4
Market Rasen Lincs 46 D5
Market Stainton Lincs 46 E6
Market Warsop Notts 45 F9
Market Weighton E Yorks 52 E4
Market Weston Suff 38 H5
Markethill Perth 76 D5
Markfield Leics 35 D10
Markham Caerph 15 A7
Markham Moor Notts 45 E11
Markinch Fife 76 G5
Markington N Yorks 51 C8
Marks Tey Essex 30 F6
Marksbury Bath 16 E3
Markyate Herts 29 G7
Marland Gtr Man 44 A2
Marlborough Wilts 17 E8
Marlbrook Hereford 26 C2
Marlbrook Worcs 26 A6
Marlcliff Warks 27 C7
Marldon Devon 5 E9
Marlesford Suff 31 C10
Marley Green Ches E 43 H8
Marley Hill T&W 63 H8
Marley Mount Hants 10 E1
Marlingford Norf 39 E7
Marloes Pembs 22 F2
Marlow Bucks 18 C5
Marlow Hereford 33 H10
Marlow Bottom Bucks 18 C5
Marlpit Hill Kent 19 G11
Marlpool Derbys 45 H8
Marnhull Dorset 9 C6
Marnoch Aberds 88 C5
Marnock N Lanark 68 D6
Marple Gtr Man 44 D3
Marple Bridge Gtr Man 44 D3
Marr S Yorks 45 B9
Marrel Highld 93 H13
Marrick N Yorks 58 G1
Marrister Shetland 96 G7
Marros Carms 23 F7
Marsden T&W 63 G9
Marsden W Yorks 44 A4
Marsett N Yorks 57 H11
Marsh Devon 8 C1
Marsh W Yorks 50 F6
Marsh Baldon Oxon 18 B2
Marsh Gibbon Bucks 28 F3
Marsh Green Devon 7 G9
Marsh Green Kent 12 B3
Marsh Green Staffs 44 G2
Marsh Lane Derbys 45 E8
Marsh Street Som 7 B8
Marshall's Heath Herts 29 G8
Marshalsea Dorset 8 D2
Marshalswick Herts 29 H8
Marsham Norf 39 C7
Marshaw Lancs 50 D1
Marshborough Kent 21 F10
Marshbrook Shrops 33 G10
Marshchapel Lincs 47 C7
Marshfield Newport 15 C8
Marshfield S Glos 16 D4
Marshgate Corn 4 B2
Marshland St James Norf 37 E11
Marshside Mers 49 H3
Marshwood Dorset 8 E2
Marske N Yorks 58 F2
Marske-by-the-Sea Redcar 59 D7
Marston Ches W 43 E9
Marston Hereford 25 C10
Marston Lincs 36 A4
Marston Oxon 28 H2
Marston Staffs 34 C5
Marston Staffs 34 D4
Marston Warks 35 F8
Marston Wilts 16 F6
Marston Doles Warks 27 C11
Marston Green W Mid 35 G7
Marston Magna Som 8 B4
Marston Meysey Wilts 17 B8
Marston Montgomery Derbys 35 B7
Marston Moretaine C Beds 28 D6
Marston on Dove Derbys 35 C8
Marston St Lawrence Northants 28 D2
Marston Stannett Hereford 26 C2
Marston Trussell Northants 36 G2
Marstow Hereford 26 G2
Marsworth Bucks 28 G6
Marten Wilts 17 F9
Marthall Ches E 44 E2
Martham Norf 39 D10
Martin Hants 9 C9
Martin Kent 21 G10
Martin Lincs 46 F6
Martin Lincs 46 G5
Martin Dales Lincs 46 F5
Martin Drove End Hants 9 B9
Martin Hussingtree Worcs 26 B5
Martin Mill Kent 21 G10
Martinhoe Devon 6 B5
Martinhoe Cross Devon 6 B5
Martinscroft Warr 43 D9
Martinstown Dorset 8 F5
Martlesham Suff 31 D9
Martlesham Heath Suff 31 D9
Martletwy Pembs 22 E5
Martley Worcs 26 C4
Martock Som 8 C3
Marton Ches E 44 F2
Marton E Yorks 53 F7
Marton Lincs 46 D2
Marton Mbro 58 E6
Marton N Yorks 51 C10
Marton N Yorks 52 A3
Marton Shrops 33 C10
Marton Shrops 33 E8
Marton Warks 27 B11
Marton-le-Moor N Yorks 51 B9
Martyr Worthy Hants 10 A4
Martyr's Green Sur 19 F7
Marwick Orkney 95 F3
Marwood Devon 6 C4
Mary Tavy Devon 4 D6
Marybank Highld 86 F7
Maryburgh Highld 87 F8
Maryhill Glasgow 68 D4
Marykirk Aberds 83 G8
Marylebone Gtr Man 43 B8
Marypark Moray 88 E1
Maryport Cumb 56 C2
Maryport Dumfries 54 F4
Maryton Angus 77 B9
Marywell Aberds 83 D7
Marywell Aberds 83 D11
Marywell Angus 77 C9
Masham N Yorks 51 A8
Mashbury Essex 30 G3
Masongill N Yorks 50 B2
Masonhill S Ayrs 67 D6
Mastin Moor Derbys 45 E8
Mastrick Aberdeen 83 C10
Matching Essex 30 G2
Matching Green Essex 30 G2
Matching Tye Essex 30 G2
Matfen Northumb 62 F6
Matfield Kent 12 B5
Mathern Mon 15 B11
Mathon Hereford 26 D4
Mathry Pembs 22 C3
Matlaske Norf 39 B7
Matlock Derbys 44 F6
Matlock Bath Derbys 44 G6
Matson Glos 26 G5
Matterdale End Cumb 56 D5
Mattersey Notts 45 D10
Mattersey Thorpe Notts 45 D10
Mattingley Hants 18 F4
Mattishall Norf 39 D6
Mattishall Burgh Norf 39 D6
Mauchline E Ayrs 67 D7
Maud Aberds 89 D9
Maugersbury Glos 27 F9
Maughold IoM 48 C4
Mauld Highld 86 H7
Maulden C Beds 29 E7
Maulds Meaburn Cumb 57 E8
Maunby N Yorks 58 H4
Maund Bryan Hereford 26 C2
Maundown Som 7 D9
Mautby Norf 39 D10
Mavis Enderby Lincs 47 F7
Maw Green Ches E 43 G10
Mawbray Cumb 56 B2
Mawdesley Lancs 43 A7
Mawdlam Bridgend 14 C4
Mawgan Corn 2 G6
Mawla Corn 2 E6
Mawnan Corn 3 G6
Mawnan Smith Corn 3 G6
Mawsley Northants 36 H4
Maxey Pboro 37 E7
Maxstoke Warks 35 G8
Maxton Borders 70 G5
Maxton Kent 21 G10
Maxwellheugh Borders 70 G6
Maxwelltown Dumfries 60 F5
Maxworthy Corn 6 G1
May Bank Staffs 44 H2
Mayals Swansea 14 B2
Maybole S Ayrs 66 F6
Mayfield E Sus 12 D4
Mayfield Midloth 70 D2
Mayfield Staffs 44 H5
Mayfield W Loth 69 D8
Mayford Sur 19 F7
Mayland Essex 20 A6
Maynard's Green E Sus 12 E4
Maypole Mon 25 G11
Maypole Scilly 2 C3
Maypole Green Essex 30 F6
Maypole Green Norf 39 F10
Maypole Green Suff 31 B9
Maywick Shetland 96 L5
Meadle Bucks 28 H5
Meadowtown Shrops 33 E9
Meaford Staffs 34 B4
Meal Bank Cumb 57 G7
Mealabost W Isles 91 D9
Mealabost Bhuirgh W Isles 91 B9
Mealsgate Cumb 56 B4
Meanwood W Yorks 51 F8
Mearbeck N Yorks 50 C4
Meare Som 15 G10
Meare Green Som 8 B2
Mears Ashby Northants 28 B5
Measham Leics 35 D9
Meath Green Sur 12 B1
Meathop Cumb 49 A4
Meaux E Yorks 53 F6
Meavy Devon 4 E6
Medbourne Leics 36 F3
Medburn Northumb 63 F7
Meddon Devon 6 E1
Meden Vale Notts 45 F9
Medlam Lincs 47 G7
Medmenham Bucks 18 C5
Medomsley Durham 58 A2
Medstead Hants 18 H3
Meer End W Mid 27 A9
Meerbrook Staffs 44 F3
Meers Bridge Lincs 47 D8
Meesden Herts 29 E11
Meeth Devon 6 F4
Meggethead Borders 61 A7
Meidrim Carms 23 D7
Meifod Denb 42 G3
Meifod Powys 33 D7
Meigle N Ayrs 73 G10
Meigle Perth 76 C5
Meikle Earnock S Lanark 68 E6
Meikle Ferry Highld 87 C10
Meikle Forter Angus 76 A4
Meikle Gluich Highld 87 C9
Meikle Pinkerton E Loth 70 C6
Meikle Strath Aberds 83 F8
Meikle Tarty Aberds 89 F9
Meikle Wartle Aberds 89 E7
Meikleour Perth 76 D4
Meinciau Carms 23 E9
Meir Stoke 34 A5
Meir Heath Staffs 34 A5
Melbourn Cambs 29 D10
Melbourne Derbys 35 C9
Melbourne E Yorks 52 E3
Melbourne S Lanark 69 F9
Melbury Abbas Dorset 9 B7
Melbury Bubb Dorset 8 D4
Melbury Osmond Dorset 8 D4
Melbury Sampford Dorset 8 D4
Melby Shetland 96 H3
Melchbourne Bedford 29 B7
Melcombe Bingham Dorset 9 D6
Melcombe Regis Dorset 8 F5
Meldon Devon 6 G4
Meldon Northumb 63 E7
Meldreth Cambs 29 D10
Meldrum Ho. Aberds 89 F8
Melfort Argyll 73 B7
Melgarve Highld 81 D6
Meliden Denb 42 D3
Melin-y-coed Conwy 41 D10
Melin-y-ddôl Powys 33 E6
Melin-y-grug Powys 33 E6
Melin-y-Wig Denb 42 H3
Melinbyrhedyn Powys 32 F4
Melincourt Neath 14 A4
Melkinthorpe Cumb 57 D7
Melkridge Northumb 62 G3
Melksham Wilts 16 E6
Melldalloch Argyll 73 F8
Melling Lancs 50 B1
Melling Mers 43 B6
Melling Mount Mers 43 B7
Mellis Suff 31 A8
Mellon Charles Highld 91 H13
Mellon Udrigle Highld 91 H13
Mellor Gtr Man 44 D3
Mellor Lancs 50 F2
Mellor Brook Lancs 50 F2
Mells Som 16 G4
Melmerby Cumb 57 C8
Melmerby N Yorks 51 B9
Melmerby N Yorks 58 H1
Melplash Dorset 8 E3
Melrose Borders 70 G4
Melsetter Orkney 95 K3
Melsonby N Yorks 58 F2
Meltham W Yorks 44 A5
Melton Suff 31 C9
Melton Constable Norf 38 B6
Melton Mowbray Leics 36 D3
Melton Ross N Lincs 46 A4
Meltonby E Yorks 52 D3
Melvaig Highld 91 J12
Melverley Shrops 33 D9
Melverley Green Shrops 33 D9
Melvich Highld 93 C11
Membury Devon 8 D1
Memsie Aberds 89 B9
Memus Angus 77 B7
Menabilly Corn 4 F1
Menai Bridge = Porthaethwy Anglesey 41 C7
Mendham Suff 39 G8
Mendlesham Suff 31 B8
Mendlesham Green Suff 31 B7
Menheniot Corn 4 E3
Mennock Dumfries 60 C4
Menston W Yorks 51 E7
Menstrie Clack 75 H11
Menthorpe N Yorks 52 F2
Mentmore Bucks 28 G6
Meoble Highld 79 C10
Meole Brace Shrops 33 D10
Meols Mers 42 C5
Meonstoke Hants 10 C5
Meopham Kent 20 E3
Meopham Station Kent 20 E3
Mepal Cambs 37 G10
Meppershall C Beds 29 E8
Merbach Hereford 25 D10
Mere Ches E 43 D10
Mere Wilts 9 A7
Mere Brow Lancs 49 H4
Mere Green W Mid 35 F7
Mereclough Lancs 50 F4
Mereside Blackpool 49 F3
Mereworth Kent 20 F3
Mergie Aberds 83 E9
Meriden W Mid 35 G8
Merkadale Highld 85 E8
Merkland Dumfries 60 F3
Merkland S Ayrs 66 G5
Merkland Lodge Highld 92 G7
Merley Poole 9 E9
Merlin's Bridge Pembs 22 E4
Merrington Shrops 33 C10
Merrion Pembs 22 G4
Merriott Som 8 C3
Merrivale Devon 4 D6
Merrow Sur 19 F7
Merrymeet Corn 4 E3
Mersham Kent 13 C9
Merstham Sur 19 F9
Merston W Sus 11 D7
Merstone IoW 10 F4
Merther Corn 3 E7
Merthyr Carms 23 D8
Merthyr Cynog Powys 24 E6
Merthyr-Dyfan V Glam 15 E7
Merthyr Mawr Bridgend 14 D4
Merthyr Tudful = Merthyr Tydfil M Tydf 25 H7
Merthyr Tydfil = Merthyr Tudful M Tydf 25 H7
Merthyr Vale M Tydf 14 B6
Merton Devon 6 E4
Merton London 19 D9
Merton Norf 38 F5
Merton Oxon 28 G2
Mervinslaw Borders 62 B2
Meshaw Devon 7 E6
Messing Essex 30 G5
Messingham N Lincs 46 B2
Metfield Suff 39 G8
Metheringham Lincs 46 F4
Methil Fife 76 H6
Methlem Gwyn 40 G3
Methley W Yorks 51 G9
Methlick Aberds 89 E8
Methven Perth 76 E3
Methwold Norf 38 F3
Methwold Hythe Norf 38 F3
Mettingham Suff 39 G9
Mevagissey Corn 3 E9
Mewith Head N Yorks 50 C3
Mexborough S Yorks 45 B8
Mey Highld 94 C4
Meysey Hampton Glos 17 B8
Miabhag W Isles 90 G5
Miabhag W Isles 90 H6
Miabhig W Isles 90 D5
Michaelchurch Hereford 26 F2
Michaelchurch Escley Hereford 25 E10
Michaelchurch on Arrow Powys 25 C9
Michaelston-le-Pit V Glam 15 D7
Michaelston-y-Fedw Newport 15 C8
Michaelstow Corn 4 D1
Michealston-super-Ely Cardiff 15 D7
Micheldever Hants 18 H2
Michelmersh Hants 10 B2
Mickfield Suff 31 B8
Mickle Trafford Ches W 43 F7
Micklebring S Yorks 45 C9
Mickleby N Yorks 59 E9
Mickleham Sur 19 F8
Mickleover Derby 35 B9
Micklethwaite W Yorks 51 E6
Mickleton Durham 57 D11
Mickleton Glos 27 D8
Mickletown W Yorks 51 G9
Mickley N Yorks 51 B8
Mickley Square Northumb 62 G6
Mid Ardlaw Aberds 89 B9
Mid Auchinlech Involyd 68 C2
Mid Beltie Aberds 83 C8
Mid Calder W Loth 69 D9
Mid Cloch Forbie Aberds 89 C7
Mid Clyth Highld 94 G4
Mid Lavant W Sus 11 D7
Mid Main Highld 86 H7
Mid Urchany Highld 87 G11
Mid Walls Shetland 96 H4
Mid Yell Shetland 96 D7
Midbea Orkney 95 D5
Middle Assendon Oxon 18 C4
Middle Aston Oxon 27 F11
Middle Barton Oxon 27 F11
Middle Cairncake Aberds 89 D8
Middle Claydon Bucks 28 F4
Middle Drums Angus 77 B8
Middle Handley Derbys 45 E8
Middle Littleton Worcs 27 D7
Middle Maes-coed Hereford 25 E10
Middle Mill Pembs 22 D3
Middle Rasen Lincs 46 D4
Middle Rigg Perth 76 G3
Middle Tysoe Warks 27 D10
Middle Wallop Hants 17 H9
Middle Winterslow Wilts 9 A11
Middle Woodford Wilts 17 H8
Middlebie Dumfries 61 F8
Middleforth Green Lancs 49 G5
Middleham N Yorks 58 H2
Middlehope Shrops 33 G10
Middlemarsh Dorset 8 D5
Middlemuir Aberds 89 F9
Middlesbrough Mbro 58 D5
Middleshaw Cumb 57 H7
Middleshaw Dumfries 61 F7
Middlesmoor N Yorks 51 B6
Middlestone Durham 58 C3
Middlestone Moor Durham 58 C3
Middlestown W Yorks 51 H8
Middlethird Borders 70 F5
Middleton Aberds 83 B10
Middleton Argyll 78 G2
Middleton Cumb 57 H8
Middleton Derbys 44 F5
Middleton Derbys 44 G6
Middleton Essex 30 D5
Middleton Gtr Man 44 B2
Middleton Hants 17 G11
Middleton Hereford 26 B2
Middleton Lancs 49 D4
Middleton Midloth 70 E2
Middleton N Yorks 51 E7
Middleton N Yorks 59 H8
Middleton Norf 38 D2
Middleton Northants 36 G4
Middleton Northumb 62 E6
Middleton Northumb 71 G10
Middleton Perth 76 C4
Middleton Perth 76 G4
Middleton Shrops 26 A2
Middleton Shrops 33 F8
Middleton Shrops 33 C9
Middleton Suff 31 B11
Middleton Swansea 23 H9
Middleton W Yorks 51 G8
Middleton Warks 35 F7
Middleton Cheney Northants 27 D11
Middleton Green Staffs 34 B5
Middleton Hall Northumb 71 H8
Middleton-in-Teesdale Durham 57 D11
Middleton Moor Suff 31 B11
Middleton-on-Leven N Yorks 58 F5
Middleton-on-Sea W Sus 11 D8
Middleton on the Hill Hereford 26 B2
Middleton-on-the-Wolds E Yorks 52 E5
Middleton One Row Darl 58 E4
Middleton Priors Shrops 34 F2
Middleton Quernham N Yorks 51 B9
Middleton St George Darl 58 E4
Middleton Scriven Shrops 34 G2
Middleton Stoney Oxon 28 F2
Middleton Tyas N Yorks 58 F3
Middletown Cumb 56 F1
Middletown Powys 33 D9
Middlewich Ches E 43 F9
Middlewood Green Suff 31 B7
Middlezoy Som 8 A2
Middridge Durham 58 D3
Midfield Highld 93 C8
Midge Hall Lancs 49 G5
Midgeholme Cumb 62 H2
Midgham W Berks 18 E2
Midgley W Yorks 44 A6
Midgley W Yorks 50 G6
Midhopestones S Yorks 44 C6
Midhurst W Sus 11 B7
Midlem Borders 70 H4
Midmar Aberds 83 C8
Midsomer Norton Bath 16 F3
Midton Involyd 73 F11
Midtown Highld 91 J13
Midtown Highld 93 C8
Midtown of Buchromb Moray 88 D3
Midville Lincs 47 G7
Midway Ches E 44 D3
Migdale Highld 87 B9
Migvie Aberds 82 C6
Milarrochy Stirling 68 A3
Milborne Port Som 8 C5
Milborne St Andrew Dorset 9 E7
Milborne Wick Som 8 B5
Milbourne Northumb 63 F7
Milburn Cumb 57 D8
Milbury Heath S Glos 16 B3
Milcombe Oxon 27 E11
Milden Suff 30 D6
Mildenhall Suff 30 A4
Mildenhall Wilts 17 E9
Mile Cross Norf 39 D8
Mile Elm Wilts 16 E6
Mile End Essex 30 F6
Mile End Glos 26 G2
Mile Oak Brighton 11 D11
Milebrook Powys 25 A10
Milebush Kent 20 G4
Mileham Norf 38 D5
Milesmark Fife 69 B9
Milfield Northumb 71 G8
Milford Derbys 45 H7
Milford Devon 6 D1
Milford Powys 33 F6
Milford Staffs 34 C5
Milford Sur 18 G6
Milford Wilts 9 B10
Milford Haven = Aberdaugleddau Pembs 22 F4
Milford on Sea Hants 10 E1
Milkwall Glos 26 H2
Milkwell Wilts 9 B8
Mill Bank W Yorks 50 G6
Mill Common Suff 39 G10
Mill End Bucks 18 C4
Mill End Herts 29 E10
Mill Green Essex 20 A3
Mill Green Norf 39 G7
Mill Green Suff 30 D6
Mill Hill London 19 B9
Mill Lane Hants 18 F4
Mill of Kingoodie Aberds 89 F8
Mill of Muiresk Aberds 89 D6
Mill of Sterin Aberds 82 D5
Mill of Uras Aberds 83 E10
Mill Place N Lincs 46 B3
Mill Side Cumb 49 A4
Mill Street Norf 39 D6
Millarston Renfs 68 D3
Millbank Aberds 89 D11
Millbank Highld 94 D3
Millbeck Cumb 56 D4
Millbounds Orkney 95 E6
Millbreck Aberds 89 D10
Millbridge Sur 18 G5
Millbrook C Beds 29 E7
Millbrook Corn 4 F5
Millbrook Soton 10 C2
Millburn S Ayrs 67 D7
Millcombe Devon 5 G9
Millcorner E Sus 13 D7
Milldale Staffs 44 G5
Millden Lodge Angus 83 F7
Milldens Angus 77 B8
Millerhill Midloth 70 D2
Miller's Dale Derbys 44 E5
Miller's Green Derbys 44 G6
Millgreen Shrops 34 C2
Millhalf Hereford 25 D9
Millhayes Devon 7 F11
Millhead Lancs 49 B4
Millheugh S Lanark 68 E6
Millholme Cumb 57 G7
Millhouse Argyll 73 F8
Millhouse Cumb 56 C5
Millhouse Green S Yorks 44 B6
Millhousebridge Dumfries 61 E7
Millhouses S Yorks 45 D7
Millikenpark Renfs 68 D3
Millin Cross Pembs 22 E4
Millington E Yorks 52 D4
Millmeece Staffs 34 B4
Millom Cumb 49 A1
Millook Corn 4 B2
Millpool Corn 4 D2
Millport N Ayrs 66 A4
Millquarter Dumfries 55 A9
Millthorpe Lincs 37 B7
Millthrop Cumb 57 G8
Milltimber Aberdeen 83 C10
Milltown Corn 4 F2
Milltown Derbys 45 F7
Milltown Devon 6 C4
Milltown Dumfries 61 F9
Milltown of Aberdalgie Perth 76 E3
Milltown of Auchindoun Moray 88 D3
Milltown of Craigston Aberds 89 C7
Milltown of Edinvillie Moray 88 D2
Milltown of Kildrummy Aberds 82 B6
Milltown of Rothiemay Moray 88 D5
Milltown of Towie Aberds 82 B6
Milnathort Perth 76 G4
Milner's Heath Ches W 43 F7
Milngavie E Dunb 68 C4
Milnrow Gtr Man 44 A3
Milnshaw Lancs 50 G3
Milnthorpe Cumb 49 A4
Milo Carms 23 E10
Milson Shrops 26 A3
Milstead Kent 20 F6
Milston Wilts 17 G8
Milton Angus 76 C6
Milton Cambs 29 B11
Milton Cumb 61 G11
Milton Derbys 35 C9
Milton Dumfries 54 D5
Milton Dumfries 60 E4
Milton Dumfries 60 F4
Milton Highld 86 F6
Milton Highld 86 H7
Milton Highld 87 D10
Milton Highld 87 G8
Milton Highld 94 E5
Milton Moray 88 B5
Milton N Som 15 E9
Milton Notts 45 E11
Milton Oxon 17 B11
Milton Oxon 27 E11
Milton Pembs 22 F5
Milton Perth 76 F2
Milton Ptsmth 10 E5
Milton Stirling 75 G8
Milton Stoke 44 G3
Milton W Dunb 68 C3
Milton Abbas Dorset 9 D7
Milton Abbot Devon 4 D5
Milton Bridge Midloth 69 D11
Milton Bryan C Beds 28 E6
Milton Clevedon Som 16 H3
Milton Coldwells Aberds 89 E9
Milton Combe Devon 4 E5
Milton Damerel Devon 6 E2
Milton End Glos 17 A8
Milton Ernest Bedford 29 C7
Milton Green Ches W 43 G7
Milton Hill Oxon 17 B11
Milton Keynes M Keynes 28 E5
Milton Keynes Village M Keynes 28 E5
Milton Lilbourne Wilts 17 E8
Milton Malsor Northants 28 C4
Milton Morenish Perth 75 D9
Milton of Auchinhove Aberds 83 C7
Milton of Balgonie Fife 76 G6
Milton of Buchanan Stirling 68 A3
Milton of Campfield Aberds 83 C8
Milton of Campsie E Dunb 68 C5
Milton of Corsindae Aberds 83 C8
Milton of Cushnie Aberds 83 B7
Milton of Dalcapon Perth 76 B2
Milton of Edradour Perth 76 B2
Milton of Gollanfield Highld 87 F10
Milton of Lesmore Aberds 82 A6
Milton of Logie Aberds 82 C6
Milton of Murtle Aberdeen 83 C10
Milton of Noth Aberds 83 A7
Milton of Tullich Aberds 82 D5
Milton on Stour Dorset 9 B6
Milton Regis Kent 20 E6
Milton under Wychwood Oxon 27 G9
Miltonduff Moray 88 B1
Miltonhill Moray 87 E13
Miltonise Dumfries 54 B4
Milverton Som 7 D10
Milverton Warks 27 B10
Milwich Staffs 34 B5
Minard Argyll 73 D8
Minchinhampton Glos 16 A5
Mindrum Northumb 71 G7
Minehead Som 7 B8
Minera Wrex 42 G5
Minety Wilts 17 B7
Minffordd Gwyn 32 B2
Minffordd Gwyn 41 C7
Minffordd Gwyn 41 G7
Miningsby Lincs 47 F7
Minions Corn 4 D3
Minishant S Ayrs 66 E6
Minllyn Gwyn 32 D4
Minnes Aberds 89 F9
Minngearraidh W Isles 84 F2
Minnigaff Dumfries 55 C7
Minnonie Aberds 89 B7
Minskip N Yorks 51 C9
Minstead Hants 10 C1
Minsted W Sus 11 B7
Minster Kent 20 D6
Minster Kent 21 E10
Minster Lovell Oxon 27 G10
Minsterley Shrops 33 E9
Minsterworth Glos 26 G4
Minterne Magna Dorset 8 D5
Minting Lincs 46 E5
Mintlaw Aberds 89 D10
Minto Borders 61 A11
Minton Shrops 33 F10
Minwear Pembs 22 E5
Minworth W Mid 35 F7
Mirbister Orkney 95 F4
Mirehouse Cumb 56 E1
Mireland Highld 94 D5
Mirfield W Yorks 51 H8
Miserden Glos 26 H6
Miskin Rhondda 14 C6
Misson Notts 45 C10
Misterton Leics 36 G1
Misterton Notts 45 C11
Misterton Som 8 D3
Mistley Essex 31 E8
Mitcham London 19 E9
Mitchel Troy Mon 25 G11
Mitcheldean Glos 26 G3
Mitchell Corn 3 D7
Mitcheltroy Common Mon 25 H11
Mitford Northumb 63 E7
Mithian Corn 2 D6
Mitton Staffs 34 D4
Mixbury Oxon 28 E3
Moat Cumb 61 F10
Moats Tye Suff 31 C7
Mobberley Ches E 44 E2
Mobberley Staffs 34 A6
Moccas Hereford 25 D10
Mochdre Conwy 41 C10
Mochdre Powys 33 G6
Mochrum Dumfries 54 E6
Mockbeggar Hants 9 D10
Mockerkin Cumb 56 D2
Modbury Devon 5 F7
Moddershall Staffs 34 B5
Moelfre Anglesey 41 B7
Moelfre Powys 33 C7
Moffat Dumfries 60 C6
Moggerhanger C Beds 29 D8
Moira Leics 35 D9
Mol-chlach Highld 85 G9
Molash Kent 21 F7
Mold = Yr Wyddgrug Flint 42 F5
Moldgreen W Yorks 51 H7

Molehill Green Essex 30 F2
Molescroft E Yorks 52 E6
Molesden Northumb 63 E7
Molesworth Cambs 37 H6
Moll Highld 85 E10
Molland Devon 7 D7
Mollington Ches W 43 E6
Mollington Oxon 27 D11
Mollinsburn N Lanark 68 C6
Monachty Ceredig 24 B2
Monachylemore Stirling 75 F7
Monar Lodge Highld 86 G5
Monaughty Powys 25 B9
Monboddo House Aberds 83 F9
Mondynes Aberds 83 F9
Monevechadan Argyll 74 G4
Monewden Suff 31 C9
Moneydie Perth 76 E3
Moniaive Dumfries 60 D3
Monifieth Angus 77 D7
Monikie Angus 77 D7
Monimail Fife 76 F5
Monington Pembs 22 B6
Monk Bretton S Yorks 45 B7
Monk Fryston N Yorks 51 G11
Monk Sherborne Hants 18 F3
Monk Soham Suff 31 B9
Monk Street Essex 30 F3
Monken Hadley London 19 B9
Monkhopton Shrops 34 F2
Monkland Hereford 25 C11
Monkleigh Devon 6 D3
Monknash V Glam 14 D5
Monkokehampton Devon 6 F4
Monks Eleigh Suff 30 D6
Monk's Gate W Sus 11 B11
Monks Heath Ches E 44 E2
Monks Kirby Warks 35 G10
Monks Risborough Bucks 18 A5
Monkseaton T&W 63 F9
Monkshill Aberds 89 D7
Monksilver Som 7 C9
Monkspath W Mid 35 H7
Monkswood Mon 15 A9
Monkton Devon 7 F10
Monkton Kent 21 E9
Monkton Pembs 22 F4
Monkton S Ayrs 67 D6
Monkton Combe Bath 16 E4
Monkton Deverill Wilts 16 H5
Monkton Farleigh Wilts 16 E5
Monkton Heathfield Som 8 B1
Monkton Up Wimborne Dorset 9 C9
Monkwearmouth T&W 63 H9
Monkwood Hants 10 A5
Monmouth = Trefynwy Mon 26 G2
Monmouth Cap Mon 25 F10
Monnington on Wye Hereford 25 D10
Monreith Dumfries 54 E6
Monreith Mains Dumfries 54 E6
Mont Saint Guern 11
Montacute Som 8 C3
Montcoffer Ho. Aberds 89 B6
Montford Argyll 73 G10
Montford Shrops 33 D10
Montford Bridge Shrops 33 D10
Montgarrie Aberds 83 B7
Montgomery = Trefaldwyn Powys 33 F8
Montrave Fife 76 G6
Montrose Angus 77 B10
Montsale Essex 21 B7
Monxton Hants 17 G10
Monyash Derbys 44 F5
Monymusk Aberds 83 B8
Monzie Perth 75 E11
Monzie Castle Perth 75 E11
Moodiesburn N Lanark 68 C5
Moonzie Fife 76 F6
Moor Allerton W Yorks 51 F8
Moor Crichel Dorset 9 D8
Moor End E Yorks 52 F4
Moor End York 52 D2
Moor Monkton N Yorks 51 D11
Moor of Granary Moray 87 F13
Moor of Ravenstone Dumfries 54 E6
Moor Row Cumb 56 E2
Moor Street Kent 20 E5
Moorby Lincs 46 F6
Moordown Bmouth 9 E9
Moore Halton 43 D8
Moorend Glos 16 A4
Moorends S Yorks 52 H2
Moorgate S Yorks 45 C8
Moorgreen Notts 45 H8
Moorhall Derbys 45 E7
Moorhampton Hereford 25 D10
Moorhead W Yorks 51 F7
Moorhouse Cumb 61 H9
Moorhouse Notts 45 F11
Moorlinch Som 15 H9
Moorsholm Redcar 59 E7
Moorside Gtr Man 44 B3
Moorthorpe W Yorks 45 A8
Moortown Hants 9 D10
Moortown IoW 10 F3
Moortown Lincs 46 C4
Morangie Highld 87 C10
Morar Highld 79 B9
Morborne Cambs 37 F7
Morchard Bishop Devon 7 F6
Morcombelake Dorset 8 E3
Morcott Rutland 36 E5
Morda Shrops 33 C8
Morden Dorset 9 E8
Morden London 19 E9
Mordiford Hereford 26 E2
Mordon Durham 58 D4
More Shrops 33 F9
Morebath Devon 7 D8
Morebattle Borders 62 A3
Morecambe Lancs 49 C4
Morefield Highld 86 B4
Moreleigh Devon 5 F8
Morenish Perth 75 D8
Moresby Cumb 56 D1
Moresby Parks Cumb 56 E1
Morestead Hants 10 B4
Moreton Dorset 9 F7
Moreton Essex 30 H2
Moreton Mers 42 C5
Moreton Oxon 18 A3
Moreton Staffs 34 D3
Moreton Corbet Shrops 34 C1
Moreton-in-Marsh Glos 27 E9
Moreton Jeffries Hereford 26 D3
Moreton Morrell Warks 27 C10
Moreton on Lugg Hereford 26 D2
Moreton Pinkney Northants 28 D2
Moreton Say Shrops 34 B2
Moreton Valence Glos 26 H4
Moretonhampstead Devon 5 C8
Morfa Carms 23 E10
Morfa Carms 23 G10
Morfa Bach Carms 23 E8
Morfa Bychan Gwyn 41 G7
Morfa Dinlle Gwyn 40 E6
Morfa Glas Neath 24 H5
Morfa Nefyn Gwyn 40 F4
Morfydd Denb 42 H4
Morgan's Vale Wilts 9 B10
Moriah Ceredig 32 H2
Morland Cumb 57 D7
Morley Derbys 35 A9
Morley Durham 58 D2
Morley W Yorks 51 G8
Morley Green Ches E 44 D2
Morley St Botolph Norf 39 F6
Morningside Edin 69 C11
Morningside N Lanark 69 E7
Morningthorpe Norf 39 F8
Morpeth Northumb 63 E8
Morphie Aberds 77 A10
Morrey Staffs 35 D7
Morris Green Essex 30 E4
Morriston Swansea 14 B2
Morston Norf 38 A6
Mortehoe Devon 6 B3
Mortimer W Berks 18 E3
Mortimer West End Hants 18 E3
Mortimer's Cross Hereford 25 B11
Mortlake London 19 D9
Morton Cumb 56 A5
Morton Derbys 45 F8
Morton Lincs 37 C6
Morton Lincs 46 C2
Morton Lincs 46 F2
Morton Norf 39 D7
Morton Notts 45 G11
Morton S Glos 16 B3
Morton Shrops 33 C8
Morton Bagot Warks 27 B8
Morton-on-Swale N Yorks 58 G4
Morvah Corn 2 F3
Morval Corn 4 F3
Morvich Highld 80 A1
Morvich Highld 93 J10
Morville Shrops 34 F2
Morville Heath Shrops 34 F2
Morwenstow Corn 6 E1
Mosborough S Yorks 45 D8
Moscow E Ayrs 67 B7
Mosedale Cumb 56 C5
Moseley W Mid 34 F5
Moseley W Mid 35 G6
Moseley Worcs 26 C5
Moss Argyll 78 G2
Moss Highld 79 E9
Moss S Yorks 45 A9
Moss Wrex 42 G6
Moss Bank Mers 43 C8
Moss Edge Lancs 49 E4
Moss End Brack 18 D5
Moss of Barmuckity Moray 88 B2
Moss Pit Staffs 34 C5
Moss-side Highld 87 F11
Moss Side Lancs 49 F3
Mossat Aberds 82 B6
Mossbank Shetland 96 F6
Mossbay Cumb 56 D1
Mossblown S Ayrs 67 D7
Mossbrow Gtr Man 43 D10
Mossburnford Borders 62 B2
Mossdale Dumfries 55 B9
Mossend N Lanark 68 D6
Mosser Cumb 56 D3
Mossfield Highld 87 D9
Mossgiel E Ayrs 67 D7
Mosside Angus 77 B7
Mossley Ches E 44 F2
Mossley Gtr Man 44 B3
Mossley Hill Mers 43 D6
Mosstodloch Moray 88 C3
Mosston Angus 77 C8
Mossy Lea Lancs 43 A8
Mosterton Dorset 8 D3
Moston Gtr Man 44 B2
Moston Shrops 34 C1
Moston Green Ches E 43 F10
Mostyn Flint 42 D4
Mostyn Quay Flint 42 D4
Motcombe Dorset 9 B7
Mothecombe Devon 5 G7
Motherby Cumb 56 D6
Motherwell N Lanark 68 E6
Mottingham London 19 D11
Mottisfont Hants 10 B2
Mottistone IoW 10 F3
Mottram in Longdendale Gtr Man 44 C3
Mottram St Andrew Ches E 44 E2
Mouilpied Guern 11
Mouldsworth Ches W 43 E8
Moulin Perth 76 B2
Moulsecoomb Brighton 12 F2
Moulsford Oxon 18 C2
Moulsoe M Keynes 28 D6
Moulton Ches W 43 F9
Moulton Lincs 37 C9
Moulton N Yorks 58 F3
Moulton Northants 28 B4
Moulton Suff 30 B3
Moulton V Glam 14 D6
Moulton Chapel Lincs 37 D8
Moulton Eaugate Lincs 37 D9
Moulton St Mary Norf 39 E9
Moulton Seas End Lincs 37 C9
Mounie Castle Aberds 83 A9
Mount Corn 3 D6
Mount Corn 4 E2
Mount Highld 87 G12
Mount Bures Essex 30 E6
Mount Canisp Highld 87 D10
Mount Hawke Corn 2 E6
Mount Pleasant Ches E 44 G2
Mount Pleasant Derbys 35 D8
Mount Pleasant Derbys 45 H7
Mount Pleasant Flint 42 E5
Mount Pleasant Hants 10 E1
Mount Pleasant W Yorks 51 G8
Mount Sorrel Wilts 9 B9
Mount Tabor W Yorks 51 G6
Mountain W Yorks 51 F6
Mountain Ash = Aberpennar Rhondda 14 B6
Mountain Cross Borders 69 F10
Mountain Water Pembs 22 D4
Mountbenger Borders 70 H2
Mountfield E Sus 12 D6
Mountgerald Highld 87 E8
Mountjoy Corn 3 C7
Mountnessing Essex 20 B3
Mounton Mon 15 B11
Mountsorrel Leics 36 D1
Mousehole Corn 2 G3
Mousen Northumb 71 G10
Mouswald Dumfries 60 F6
Mow Cop Ches E 44 G2
Mowhaugh Borders 62 A4
Mowsley Leics 36 G2
Moxley W Mid 34 F5
Moy Highld 80 E6
Moy Highld 87 H10
Moy Hall Highld 87 H10
Moy Ho. Moray 87 E13
Moy Lodge Highld 80 E6
Moyles Court Hants 9 D10
Moylgrove Pembs 22 B6
Muasdale Argyll 65 D7
Much Birch Hereford 26 E2
Much Cowarne Hereford 26 D3
Much Dewchurch Hereford 25 E11
Much Hadham Herts 29 G11
Much Hoole Lancs 49 G4
Much Marcle Hereford 26 E3
Much Wenlock Shrops 34 E2
Muchalls Aberds 83 D11
Muchelney Som 8 B3
Muchlarnick Corn 4 F3
Muchrachd Highld 86 H5
Muckernich Highld 87 F8
Mucking Thurrock 20 C3
Muckleford Dorset 8 E5
Mucklestone Staffs 34 B3
Muckleton Shrops 34 C1
Muckletown Aberds 83 A7
Muckley Corner Staffs 35 E6
Muckton Lincs 47 D7
Mudale Highld 93 F8
Muddiford Devon 6 C4
Mudeford Dorset 9 E10
Mudford Som 8 C4
Mudgley Som 15 G10
Mugdock Stirling 68 C4
Mugeary Highld 85 E9
Mugginton Derbys 35 A8
Muggleswick Durham 58 B1
Muie Highld 93 J9
Muir Aberds 82 E2
Muir of Fairburn Highld 86 F7
Muir of Fowlis Aberds 83 B7
Muir of Ord Highld 87 F8
Muir of Pert Angus 77 D7
Muirden Aberds 89 C7
Muirdrum Angus 77 D8
Muirhead Angus 76 D6
Muirhead Fife 76 G5
Muirhead N Lanark 68 D5
Muirhead S Ayrs 66 C6
Muirhouselaw Borders 70 H5
Muirhouses Falk 69 B9
Muirkirk E Ayrs 68 H5
Muirmill Stirling 68 B6
Muirshearlich Highld 80 E3
Muirskie Aberds 83 D10
Muirtack Aberds 89 E9
Muirton Highld 87 E10
Muirton Perth 76 E4
Muirton Perth 76 F2
Muirton Mains Highld 86 F7
Muirton of Ardblair Perth 76 C4
Muirton of Ballochy Angus 77 A9
Muiryfold Aberds 89 C7
Muker N Yorks 57 G11
Mulbarton Norf 39 E7
Mulben Moray 88 C3
Mulindry Argyll 64 C4
Mullardoch House Highld 86 H5
Mullion Corn 2 H5
Mullion Cove Corn 2 H5
Mumby Lincs 47 E9
Munderfield Row Hereford 26 C3
Munderfield Stocks Hereford 26 C3
Mundesley Norf 39 B9
Mundford Norf 38 F4
Mundham Norf 39 F9
Mundon Essex 20 A5
Mundurno Aberdeen 83 B11
Munerigie Highld 80 C4
Muness Shetland 96 C8
Mungasdale Highld 86 B2
Mungrisdale Cumb 56 C5
Munlochy Highld 87 F9
Munsley Hereford 26 D3
Munslow Shrops 33 G11
Murchington Devon 5 C7
Murcott Oxon 28 G2
Murkle Highld 94 D3
Murlaggan Highld 80 D2
Murlaggan Highld 80 E5
Murra Orkney 95 H3
Murrayfield Edin 69 C11
Murrow Cambs 37 E9
Mursley Bucks 28 F5
Murthill Angus 77 B7
Murthly Perth 76 D3
Murton Cumb 57 D9
Murton Durham 58 B4
Murton Northumb 71 F8
Murton York 52 D2
Musbury Devon 8 E1
Muscoates N Yorks 52 A2
Musdale Argyll 74 E2
Musselburgh E Loth 70 C2
Muston Leics 36 B4
Muston N Yorks 53 B6
Mustow Green Worcs 26 A5
Mutehill Dumfries 55 E9
Mutford Suff 39 G10
Muthill Perth 75 F11
Mutterton Devon 7 F9
Muxton Telford 34 D3
Mybster Highld 94 E3
Myddfai Carms 24 F4
Myddle Shrops 33 C10
Mydroilyn Ceredig 23 A9
Myerscough Lancs 49 F4
Mylor Bridge Corn 3 F7
Mynachlog-ddu Pembs 22 C6
Myndtown Shrops 33 G9
Mynydd Bach Ceredig 32 H3
Mynydd-bach Mon 15 B10
Mynydd Bodafon Anglesey 40 B6
Mynydd-isa Flint 42 F5
Mynyddygarreg Carms 23 F9
Mynytho Gwyn 40 G5
Myrebird Aberds 83 D9
Myrelandhorn Highld 94 E4
Myreside Perth 76 E5
Myrtle Hill Carms 24 E4
Mytchett Sur 18 F5
Mytholm W Yorks 50 G5
Mytholmroyd W Yorks 50 G6
Myton-on-Swale N Yorks 51 C10
Mytton Shrops 33 D10

N

Na Gearrannan W Isles 90 C6
Naast Highld 91 J13
Naburn York 52 E1
Nackington Kent 21 F8
Nacton Suff 31 D9
Nafferton E Yorks 53 D6
Nailbridge Glos 26 G3
Nailsbourne Som 7 D11
Nailsea N Som 15 D10
Nailstone Leics 35 E10
Nailsworth Glos 16 B5
Nairn Highld 87 F11
Nalderswood Sur 19 G9
Nancegollan Corn 2 F5
Nancledra Corn 2 F3
Nanhoron Gwyn 40 G4
Nannau Gwyn 32 C3
Nannerch Flint 42 F4
Nanpantan Leics 35 D11
Nanpean Corn 3 D8
Nanstallon Corn 3 C9
Nant-ddu Powys 25 G7
Nant-glas Powys 24 B6
Nant Peris Gwyn 41 E8
Nant Uchaf Denb 42 G3
Nant-y-Bai Carms 24 D4
Nant-y-cafn Neath 24 H5
Nant-y-derry Mon 25 H10
Nant-y-ffin Carms 23 C10
Nant-y-moel Bridgend 14 B5
Nant-y-pandy Conwy 41 C8
Nanternis Ceredig 23 A8
Nantgaredig Carms 23 D9
Nantgarw Rhondda 15 C7
Nantglyn Denb 42 F3
Nantgwyn Powys 32 H5
Nantlle Gwyn 41 E7
Nantmawr Shrops 33 C8
Nantmel Powys 25 B7
Nantmor Gwyn 41 F8
Nantwich Ches E 43 G9
Nantycaws Carms 23 E9
Nantyffyllon Bridgend 14 B4
Nantyglo Bl Gwent 25 G8
Naphill Bucks 18 B5
Nappa N Yorks 50 D4
Napton on the Hill Warks 27 B11
Narberth = Arberth Pembs 22 E6
Narborough Leics 35 F11
Narborough Norf 38 D3
Nasareth Gwyn 40 E6
Naseby Northants 36 H2
Nash Bucks 28 E4
Nash Hereford 25 B10
Nash Newport 15 C9
Nash Shrops 26 A3
Nash Lee Bucks 28 H5
Nassington Northants 37 F6
Nasty Herts 29 F10
Nateby Cumb 57 F9
Nateby Lancs 49 E4
Natland Cumb 57 H7
Naughton Suff 31 D7
Naunton Glos 27 F8
Naunton Worcs 26 E5
Naunton Beauchamp Worcs 26 C6
Navenby Lincs 46 G3
Navestock Heath Essex 20 B2
Navestock Side Essex 20 B2
Navidale Highld 93 H13
Nawton N Yorks 52 A2
Nayland Suff 30 E6
Nazeing Essex 29 H11
Neacroft Hants 9 E10
Neal's Green Warks 35 G9
Neap Shetland 96 H7
Near Sawrey Cumb 56 G5
Neasham Darl 58 E4
Neath = Castell-Nedd Neath 14 B3
Neath Abbey Neath 14 B3
Neatishead Norf 39 C9
Nebo Anglesey 40 A6
Nebo Ceredig 24 B2
Nebo Conwy 41 E10
Nebo Gwyn 40 E6
Necton Norf 38 E4
Nedd Highld 92 F4
Nedderton Northumb 63 E8
Nedging Tye Suff 31 D7
Needham Norf 39 G8
Needham Market Suff 31 C7
Needingworth Cambs 29 A10
Needwood Staffs 35 C7
Neen Savage Shrops 34 H2
Neen Sollars Shrops 26 A3
Neenton Shrops 34 G2
Nefyn Gwyn 40 F5
Neilston E Renf 68 E3
Neinthirion Powys 32 E5
Neithrop Oxon 27 D11
Nelly Andrews Green Powys 33 E8
Nelson Caerph 15 B7
Nelson Lancs 50 F4
Nelson Village Northumb 63 F8
Nemphlar S Lanark 69 F7
Nempnett Thrubwell N Som 15 E11
Nene Terrace Lincs 37 E8
Nenthall Cumb 57 B9
Nenthead Cumb 57 B9
Nenthorn Borders 70 G5
Nerabus Argyll 64 C3
Nercwys Flint 42 F5
Nerston S Lanark 68 E5
Nesbit Northumb 71 G8
Ness Ches W 42 E6
Nesscliffe Shrops 33 D9
Neston Ches W 42 E5
Neston Wilts 16 E5
Nether Alderley Ches E 44 E2
Nether Blainslie Borders 70 F4
Nether Booth Derbys 44 D5
Nether Broughton Leics 36 C2
Nether Burrow Lancs 50 B2
Nether Cerne Dorset 8 E5
Nether Compton Dorset 8 C4
Nether Crimond Aberds 89 F8
Nether Dalgliesh Borders 61 C8
Nether Dallachy Moray 88 B3
Nether Exe Devon 7 F8
Nether Glasslaw Aberds 89 C8
Nether Handwick Angus 76 C6
Nether Haugh S Yorks 45 C8
Nether Heage Derbys 45 G7
Nether Heyford Northants 28 C3
Nether Hindhope Borders 62 B3
Nether Howecleuch S Lanark 60 B6
Nether Kellet Lancs 49 C5
Nether Kinmundy Aberds 89 D10
Nether Langwith Notts 45 E9
Nether Leask Aberds 89 E10
Nether Lenshie Aberds 89 D6
Nether Monynut Borders 70 D6
Nether Padley Derbys 44 E6
Nether Park Aberds 89 C10
Nether Poppleton York 52 D1
Nether Silton N Yorks 58 G5
Nether Stowey Som 7 C10
Nether Urquhart Fife 76 G4
Nether Wallop Hants 17 H10
Nether Wasdale Cumb 56 F3
Nether Whitacre Warks 35 F8
Nether Worton Oxon 27 E11
Netheravon Wilts 17 G8
Netherbrae Aberds 89 C7
Netherbrough Orkney 95 G4
Netherburn S Lanark 69 F7
Netherbury Dorset 8 E3
Netherby Cumb 61 F9
Netherby N Yorks 51 E9
Nethercote Warks 28 B2
Nethercott Devon 6 C3
Netherend Glos 16 A2
Netherfield E Sus 12 E6
Netherhampton Wilts 9 B10
Netherlaw Dumfries 55 E10
Netherley Aberds 83 D10
Netherley Mers 43 D7
Nethermill Dumfries 60 E6
Nethermuir Aberds 89 D9
Netherplace E Renf 68 E4
Netherseal Derbys 35 D8
Netherthird E Ayrs 67 E8
Netherthong W Yorks 44 B5
Netherthorpe S Yorks 45 D9
Netherton Angus 77 B8
Netherton Devon 5 D9
Netherton Hants 17 F10
Netherton Mers 42 B6
Netherton Northumb 62 C5
Netherton Oxon 17 B11
Netherton Perth 76 B4
Netherton Stirling 68 C4
Netherton W Mid 34 G5
Netherton W Yorks 44 A5
Netherton W Yorks 51 H8
Netherton Worcs 26 D6
Nethertown Cumb 56 F1
Nethertown Highld 94 C5
Netherwitton Northumb 63 D7
Netherwood E Ayrs 68 H5
Nethy Bridge Highld 82 A2
Netley Hants 10 D3
Netley Marsh Hants 10 C2
Netteswell Essex 29 G11
Nettlebed Oxon 18 C4
Nettlebridge Som 16 G3
Nettlecombe Dorset 8 E4
Nettleden Herts 29 G7
Nettleham Lincs 46 E4
Nettlestead Kent 20 F3
Nettlestead Green Kent 20 F3
Nettlestone IoW 10 E5
Nettlesworth Durham 58 B3
Nettleton Lincs 46 B5
Nettleton Wilts 16 D5
Neuadd Carms 24 F3
Nevendon Essex 20 B4
Nevern Pembs 22 B5
New Abbey Dumfries 60 G5
New Aberdour Aberds 89 B8
New Addington London 19 E10
New Alresford Hants 10 A4
New Alyth Perth 76 C5
New Arley Warks 35 G8
New Ash Green Kent 20 E3
New Barn Kent 20 E3
New Barnetby N Lincs 46 A4
New Barton Northants 28 B5
New Bewick Northumb 62 A6
New-bigging Angus 76 C5
New Bilton Warks 35 H10
New Bolingbroke Lincs 47 G7
New Boultham Lincs 46 E3
New Bradwell M Keynes 28 D5
New Brancepeth Durham 58 B3
New Bridge Wrex 33 A8
New Brighton Flint 42 F5
New Brighton Mers 42 C6
New Brinsley Notts 45 G8
New Broughton Wrex 42 G6
New Buckenham Norf 39 F6
New Byth Aberds 89 C8
New Catton Norf 39 D8
New Cheriton Hants 10 B4
New Costessey Norf 39 D7
New Cowper Cumb 56 B3
New Cross Ceredig 32 H2
New Cross London 19 D10
New Cumnock E Ayrs 67 E9
New Deer Aberds 89 D8
New Delaval Northumb 63 F8
New Duston Northants 28 B4
New Earswick York 52 D2
New Edlington S Yorks 45 C9
New Elgin Moray 88 B2
New Ellerby E Yorks 53 F7
New Eltham London 19 D11
New End Worcs 27 C7
New Farnley W Yorks 51 F8
New Ferry Mers 42 D6
New Fryston W Yorks 51 G10
New Galloway Dumfries 55 B9
New Gilston Fife 77 G7
New Grimsby Scilly 2 C2
New Hainford Norf 39 D8
New Hartley Northumb 63 F9
New Haw Sur 19 E7
New Hedges Pembs 22 F6
New Herrington T&W 58 A4
New Hinksey Oxon 18 A2
New Holkham Norf 38 B4
New Holland N Lincs 53 G6
New Houghton Derbys 45 F8
New Houghton Norf 38 C3
New Houses N Yorks 50 B4
New Humberstone Leicester 36 E2
New Hutton Cumb 57 G7
New Hythe Kent 20 F4
New Inn Carms 23 C9
New Inn Mon 15 A10
New Inn Pembs 22 C5
New Inn Torf 15 B9
New Invention Shrops 33 H8
New Invention W Mid 34 E5
New Kelso Highld 86 G2
New Kingston Notts 35 C11
New Lanark S Lanark 69 F7
New Lane Lancs 43 A7
New Lane End Warr 43 C9
New Leake Lincs 47 G8
New Leeds Aberds 89 C9
New Longton Lancs 49 G5
New Luce Dumfries 54 C4
New Malden London 19 E9
New Marske Redcar 59 D7
New Marton Shrops 33 B9
New Micklefield W Yorks 51 F10
New Mill Aberds 83 E9
New Mill Herts 28 G6
New Mill W Yorks 44 B5
New Mill Wilts 17 E8
New Mills Ches E 43 D10
New Mills Corn 3 D7
New Mills Derbys 44 D3
New Mills Powys 33 E6
New Milton Hants 9 E11
New Moat Pembs 22 D5
New Ollerton Notts 45 F10
New Oscott W Mid 35 F6
New Park N Yorks 51 D8
New Pitsligo Aberds 89 C8
New Polzeath Corn 3 B8
New Quay = Ceinewydd Ceredig 23 A8
New Rackheath Norf 39 D8
New Radnor Powys 25 B9
New Rent Cumb 56 C6
New Ridley Northumb 62 H6
New Road Side N Yorks 50 E5
New Romney Kent 13 D9
New Rossington S Yorks 45 C10
New Row Ceredig 24 A4
New Row Lancs 50 F2
New Row N Yorks 59 E7
New Sarum Wilts 9 A10
New Silksworth T&W 58 A4
New Stevenston N Lanark 68 E6
New Street Staffs 44 G4
New Street Lane Shrops 34 B2
New Swanage Dorset 9 F9
New Totley S Yorks 45 E7
New Town E Loth 70 C3
New Tredegar = Tredegar Newydd Caerph 15 A7
New Trows S Lanark 69 G7
New Ulva Argyll 72 E6
New Walsoken Cambs 37 E10
New Waltham NE Lincs 46 B6
New Whittington Derbys 45 E7
New Wimpole Cambs 29 D10
New Winton E Loth 70 C3
New Yatt Oxon 27 G10
New York Lincs 46 G6
New York N Yorks 51 C7
Newall W Yorks 51 E7
Newark Orkney 95 D8
Newark Pboro 37 E8
Newark-on-Trent Notts 45 G11
Newarthill N Lanark 68 E6
Newbarns Cumb 49 B2
Newbattle Midloth 70 D2
Newbiggin Cumb 49 C2
Newbiggin Cumb 56 D6
Newbiggin Cumb 56 G2
Newbiggin Cumb 57 B7
Newbiggin Cumb 57 D8
Newbiggin Durham 57 D11
Newbiggin N Yorks 57 G11
Newbiggin N Yorks 57 H11
Newbiggin-by-the-Sea Northumb 63 E9
Newbiggin-on-Lune Cumb 57 F9
Newbigging Angus 77 D7
Newbigging Angus 77 D7
Newbigging S Lanark 69 F9
Newbold Derbys 45 E7
Newbold Leics 35 D10
Newbold on Avon Warks 35 H10
Newbold on Stour Warks 27 D9
Newbold Pacey Warks 27 C9
Newbold Verdon Leics 35 E10
Newborough Anglesey 40 D6
Newborough Pboro 37 E8
Newborough Staffs 35 C7
Newbottle Northants 28 E2
Newbottle T&W 58 A4
Newbourne Suff 31 D9
Newbridge Caerph 15 B8
Newbridge Ceredig 23 A10
Newbridge Corn 2 F3
Newbridge Corn 4 E4
Newbridge Dumfries 60 F5
Newbridge Edin 69 C10
Newbridge Hants 10 C1
Newbridge IoW 10 F3
Newbridge Pembs 22 C4
Newbridge Green Worcs 26 E5
Newbridge-on-Usk Mon 15 B9
Newbridge on Wye Powys 25 C7
Newbrough Northumb 62 G4
Newbuildings Devon 7 F6
Newburgh Aberds 89 C9
Newburgh Aberds 89 F9
Newburgh Borders 61 B9
Newburgh Fife 76 F5
Newburgh Lancs 43 A7
Newburn T&W 63 G7
Newbury W Berks 17 E11
Newbury Park London 19 C11
Newby Cumb 57 D7
Newby Lancs 50 E4
Newby N Yorks 50 B3
Newby N Yorks 58 E6
Newby N Yorks 59 G11
Newby Bridge Cumb 56 H5
Newby East Cumb 61 H10
Newby West Cumb 56 A5
Newby Wiske N Yorks 58 H4
Newcastle Mon 25 G11
Newcastle Shrops 33 G8
Newcastle Emlyn = Castell Newydd Emlyn Carms 23 B8
Newcastle-under-Lyme Staffs 44 H2
Newcastle Upon Tyne T&W 63 G8
Newcastleton or Copshaw Holm Borders 61 E10
Newchapel Pembs 23 C7
Newchapel Powys 32 G5
Newchapel Staffs 44 G2
Newchapel Sur 12 B2
Newchurch Carms 23 D8
Newchurch IoW 10 F4
Newchurch Kent 13 C9
Newchurch Lancs 50 F4
Newchurch Mon 15 B10
Newchurch Powys 25 C9
Newchurch Staffs 35 C7
Newcott Devon 7 F11
Newcraighall Edin 70 C2
Newdigate Sur 19 G8
Newell Green Brack 18 D5
Newenden Kent 13 D7
Newent Glos 26 F4
Newerne Glos 16 A3
Newfield Durham 58 C3
Newfield Highld 87 D10
Newford Scilly 2 C3
Newfound Hants 18 F2
Newgale Pembs 22 D3
Newgate Norf 39 A6
Newgate Street Herts 19 A10
Newhall Ches E 43 H9
Newhall Derbys 35 C8
Newhall House Highld 87 E9
Newhall Point Highld 87 E10
Newham Northumb 71 H10
Newham Hall Northumb 71 H10
Newhaven Derbys 44 G5
Newhaven E Sus 12 F3
Newhaven Edin 69 C11
Newhey Gtr Man 44 A3
Newholm N Yorks 59 E9
Newhouse N Lanark 68 D6
Newick E Sus 12 D3
Newingreen Kent 13 C10
Newington Kent 20 E5
Newington Kent 21 E10
Newington Kent 21 H8
Newington Notts 45 C10
Newington Oxon 18 B3
Newington Shrops 33 G10
Newland Glos 26 H2
Newland Hull 53 F6
Newland N Yorks 52 G2
Newland Worcs 26 D4
Newlandrig Midloth 70 D2
Newlands Borders 61 D11
Newlands Highld 87 G10
Newlands Moray 88 C3
Newlands Northumb 62 H6
Newland's Corner Sur 19 G7
Newlands of Geise Highld 94 D2
Newlands of Tynet Moray 88 B3
Newlands Park Anglesey 40 B4
Newlandsmuir S Lanark 68 E5
Newlot Orkney 95 G6
Newlyn Corn 2 G3
Newmachar Aberds 83 B10
Newmains N Lanark 69 E7
Newmarket Suff 30 B3
Newmarket W Isles 91 D9
Newmill Borders 61 B10
Newmill Corn 2 F3
Newmill Moray 88 C4
Newmill of Inshewan Angus 77 A7
Newmills of Boyne Aberds 88 C5
Newmiln Perth 76 D4
Newmilns E Ayrs 67 C8
Newnham Cambs 29 C11
Newnham Glos 26 G3
Newnham Hants 18 F4
Newnham Herts 29 E9
Newnham Kent 20 F6
Newnham Northants 28 C2
Newnham Bridge Worcs 26 B3
Newpark Fife 77 F7
Newport Devon 6 C4
Newport E Yorks 52 F4
Newport Essex 30 E2
Newport Highld 94 H3
Newport IoW 10 F4
Newport = Casnewydd Newport 15 C9
Newport Norf 39 D11
Newport = Trefdraeth Pembs 22 C5
Newport Telford 34 D3
Newport-on-Tay Fife 77 E7
Newport Pagnell M Keynes 28 D5
Newpound Common W Sus 11 B9
Newquay Corn 3 C7
Newsbank Ches E 44 F2
Newseat Aberds 89 D10
Newseat Aberds 89 E7
Newsham N Yorks 51 A9
Newsham N Yorks 58 E2
Newsham Northumb 63 F9
Newsholme E Yorks 52 G3
Newsholme Lancs 50 D4
Newsome W Yorks 44 A5
Newstead Borders 70 G4
Newstead Northumb 71 H10
Newstead Notts 45 G9
Newthorpe N Yorks 51 F10
Newton Argyll 73 D9
Newton Borders 62 A1
Newton Bridgend 14 D4
Newton Cambs 29 D11
Newton Cambs 37 D10
Newton Cardiff 15 D8
Newton Ches W 43 E8
Newton Ches W 43 F7
Newton Ches W 43 G8
Newton Cumb 49 B2
Newton Derbys 45 G8
Newton Dorset 9 C6
Newton Dumfries 61 D7
Newton Dumfries 61 F8
Newton Gtr Man 44 C3
Newton Hereford 25 E10
Newton Hereford 26 C2
Newton Highld 87 E10
Newton Highld 87 G10
Newton Highld 92 F5
Newton Highld 94 F5
Newton Lancs 49 F4
Newton Lancs 50 B1
Newton Lancs 50 D2
Newton Lincs 36 B6
Newton Moray 88 B1
Newton Norf 38 D4
Newton Northants 36 G4
Newton Northumb 62 G6
Newton Notts 36 A2
Newton Perth 75 D11
Newton S Lanark 68 D5
Newton S Lanark 69 G8
Newton S Yorks 45 B9
Newton Staffs 34 C6
Newton Suff 30 D6
Newton Swansea 14 C2
Newton W Loth 69 C9
Newton Warks 35 H11
Newton Wilts 9 B11
Newton Abbot Devon 5 D9
Newton Arlosh Cumb 61 H7
Newton Aycliffe Durham 58 D3
Newton Bewley Hrtlpl 58 D5
Newton Blossomville M Keynes 28 C6
Newton Bromswold Northants 28 B6
Newton Burgoland Leics 35 E9
Newton by Toft Lincs 46 D4
Newton Ferrers Devon 4 G6
Newton Flotman Norf 39 F8
Newton Hall Northumb 62 G6
Newton Harcourt Leics 36 F2
Newton Heath Gtr Man 44 B2
Newton Ho. Aberds 83 A8
Newton Kyme N Yorks 51 E10
Newton-le-Willows Mers 43 C8
Newton-le-Willows N Yorks 58 H3
Newton Longville Bucks 28 E5
Newton Mearns E Renf 68 E4
Newton Morrell N Yorks 58 F3
Newton Mulgrave N Yorks 59 E8
Newton of Ardtoe Highld 79 D9
Newton of Balcanquhal Perth 76 F4
Newton of Falkland Fife 76 G5
Newton on Ayr S Ayrs 66 D6
Newton on Ouse N Yorks 51 D11
Newton-on-Rawcliffe N Yorks 59 G9
Newton-on-the-Moor Northumb 63 C7
Newton on Trent Lincs 46 E2
Newton Park Argyll 73 G10
Newton Poppleford Devon 7 H9
Newton Purcell Oxon 28 E3
Newton Regis Warks 35 E8
Newton Reigny Cumb 57 C6
Newton St Cyres Devon 7 G7
Newton St Faith Norf 39 D8
Newton St Loe Bath 16 E4
Newton St Petrock Devon 6 E3
Newton Solney Derbys 35 C8
Newton Stacey Hants 17 G11
Newton Stewart Dumfries 55 C7
Newton Tony Wilts 17 G9
Newton Tracey Devon 6 D4
Newton under Roseberry Redcar 59 E6
Newton upon Derwent E Yorks 52 E3
Newton Valence Hants 10 A6
Newtonairds Dumfries 60 E4
Newtongrange Midloth 70 D2
Newtonhill Aberds 83 D11
Newtonhill Highld 87 G8
Newtonmill Angus 77 A9
Newtonmore Highld 81 D9
Newtown Argyll 73 C9
Newtown Ches W 43 E8
Newtown Corn 2 G6
Newtown Cumb 56 B2
Newtown Cumb 61 G11
Newtown Derbys 44 D3
Newtown Devon 7 D6
Newtown Glos 16 A3
Newtown Glos 26 E6
Newtown Hants 10 B2
Newtown Hants 10 C4
Newtown Hants 10 C1
Newtown Hants 10 C5
Newtown Hants 10 D3
Newtown Hants 17 E11
Newtown Hereford 26 D3
Newtown Highld 80 C5
Newtown IoM 48 E3
Newtown IoW 10 E3
Newtown Northumb 62 C6
Newtown Northumb 71 G8
Newtown Northumb 71 H9
Newtown Poole 9 E9
Newtown = Y Drenewydd Powys 33 F7
Newtown Shrops 33 B10
Newtown Staffs 44 F4
Newtown Staffs 44 F3
Newtown Wilts 9 B8
Newtown Linford Leics 35 E11
Newtown St Boswells Borders 70 G4
Newtown Unthank Leics 35 E10
Newtyle Angus 76 C5
Neyland Pembs 22 F4
Niarbyl IoM 48 E2
Nibley S Glos 16 C3
Nibley Green Glos 16 B4
Nibon Shetland 96 F5
Nicholashayne Devon 7 E10
Nicholaston Swansea 23 H10
Nidd N Yorks 51 C9
Nigg Aberdeen 83 C11
Nigg Highld 87 D11
Nigg Ferry Highld 87 E10
Nightcott Som 7 D7
Nilig Denb 42 G3
Nine Ashes Essex 20 A2
Nine Mile Burn Midloth 69 E10
Nine Wells Pembs 22 D2
Ninebanks Northumb 57 A9
Ninfield E Sus 12 E6
Ningwood IoW 10 F2
Nisbet Borders 70 H5
Nisthouse Orkney 95 G4
Nisthouse Shetland 96 G7
Niton IoW 10 G4
Nitshill Glasgow 68 D4
No Man's Heath Ches W 43 H8
No Man's Heath Warks 35 E8
Noak Hill London 20 B2
Noblethorpe S Yorks 44 B6
Nobottle Northants 28 B3
Nocton Lincs 46 F4
Noke Oxon 28 G2
Nolton Pembs 22 E3
Nolton Haven Pembs 22 E3
Nomansland Devon 7 E7
Nomansland Wilts 10 C1
Noneley Shrops 33 C10
Nonikiln Highld 87 D9
Nonington Kent 21 F9
Noonsbrough Shetland 96 H4
Norbreck Blackpool 49 E3
Norbridge Hereford 26 D4
Norbury Ches E 43 H8
Norbury Derbys 35 A7
Norbury Shrops 33 F9
Norbury Staffs 34 C3
Nordelph Norf 38 E1
Norden Gtr Man 44 A2
Norden Heath Dorset 9 F8
Nordley Shrops 34 F2
Norham Northumb 71 F8
Norley Ches W 43 E8
Norleywood Hants 10 E2
Norman Cross Cambs 37 F7
Normanby N Lincs 52 H4
Normanby N Yorks 52 A3
Normanby Redcar 59 E6
Normanby-by-Spital Lincs 46 D4
Normanby by Stow Lincs 46 D2
Normanby le Wold Lincs 46 C5
Normandy Sur 18 F6
Norman's Bay E Sus 12 F5
Norman's Green Devon 7 F9
Normanstone Suff 39 F11
Normanton Derby 35 B9
Normanton Leics 36 A4
Normanton Lincs 46 H3
Normanton Notts 45 G11
Normanton Rutland 36 E5
Normanton W Yorks 51 G9
Normanton le Heath Leics 35 D9
Normanton on Soar Notts 35 C11
Normanton-on-the-Wolds Notts 36 B2
Normanton on Trent Notts 45 F11
Normoss Lancs 49 F3
Norney Sur 18 G6
Norrington Common Wilts 16 E5
Norris Green Mers 43 C6
Norris Hill Leics 35 D9
North Anston S Yorks 45 D9
North Aston Oxon 27 F11
North Baddesley Hants 10 C2
North Ballachulish Highld 74 A3
North Barrow Som 8 B5
North Barsham Norf 38 B5
North Benfleet Essex 20 C4
North Bersted W Sus 11 D8
North Berwick E Loth 70 B4
North Boarhunt Hants 10 C5
North Bovey Devon 5 C8
North Bradley Wilts 16 F5
North Brentor Devon 4 C5
North Brewham Som 16 H4
North Buckland Devon 6 B3
North Burlingham Norf 39 D9
North Cadbury Som 8 B5
North Cairn Dumfries 54 B2
North Carlton Lincs 46 E3
North Carrine Argyll 65 H7
North Cave E Yorks 52 F4
North Cerney Glos 27 H7
North Charford Wilts 9 C10
North Charlton Northumb 63 A7
North Cheriton Som 8 B5
North Cliff E Yorks 53 E8
North Cliffe E Yorks 52 F4
North Clifton Notts 46 E2
North Cockerington Lincs 47 C7
North Coker Som 8 C4
North Collafirth Shetland 96 E5
North Common E Sus 12 D2
North Connel Argyll 74 D2
North Cornelly Bridgend 14 C4
North Cotes Lincs 47 B7
North Cove Suff 39 G10
North Cowton N Yorks 58 F3
North Crawley M Keynes 28 D6
North Cray London 19 D11
North Creake Norf 38 B4
North Curry Som 8 B2
North Dalton E Yorks 52 D5
North Dawn Orkney 95 H5
North Deighton N Yorks 51 D9
North Duffield N Yorks 52 F2
North Elkington Lincs 46 C6
North Elmham Norf 38 C5
North Elmshall W Yorks 45 A8
North End Bucks 28 F5
North End E Yorks 53 F8
North End Essex 30 G3
North End Hants 17 E11
North End Lincs 37 A8
North End N Som 15 E10
North End Ptsmth 10 D5
North End Som 8 B1
North End W Sus 11 D10
North Erradale Highld 91 J12
North Fambridge Essex 20 B5
North Fearns Highld 85 E10
North Featherstone W Yorks 51 G10
North Ferriby E Yorks 52 G5
North Frodingham E Yorks 53 D7
North Gluss Shetland 96 F5
North Gorley Hants 9 C10
North Green Norf 39 G8
North Green Suff 31 B10
North Greetwell Lincs 46 E4
North Grimston N Yorks 52 C4
North Halley Orkney 95 H6
North Halling Medway 20 E4
North Hayling Hants 10 D6
North Hazelrigg Northumb 71 G9
North Heasley Devon 7 C6
North Heath W Sus 11 B9
North Hill Cambs 37 H10
North Hill Corn 4 D3
North Hinksey Oxon 27 H11
North Holmwood Sur 19 G8
North Howden E Yorks 52 F3
North Huish Devon 5 F8
North Hykeham Lincs 46 F3
North Johnston Pembs 22 E4
North Kelsey Lincs 46 B4
North Kelsey Moor Lincs 46 B4
North Kessock Highld 87 G9
North Killingholme N Lincs 53 H7
North Kilvington N Yorks 58 H5
North Kilworth Leics 36 G2
North Kirkton Aberds 89 C11
North Kiscadale N Ayrs 66 D3
North Kyme Lincs 46 G5
North Lancing W Sus 11 D10
North Lee Bucks 28 H5
North Leigh Oxon 27 G10
North Leverton with Habblesthorpe Notts 45 D11
North Littleton Worcs 27 D7
North Lopham Norf 38 G6
North Luffenham Rutland 36 E5
North Marden W Sus 11 C7
North Marston Bucks 28 F4
North Middleton Midloth 70 E2
North Middleton Northumb 62 A6
North Molton Devon 7 D6
North Moreton Oxon 18 C2
North Mundham W Sus 11 D7
North Muskham Notts 45 G11
North Newbald E Yorks 52 F5
North Newington Oxon 27 E11
North Newnton Wilts 17 F8
North Newton Som 8 A1
North Nibley Glos 16 B4
North Oakley Hants 18 F2
North Ockendon London 20 C2
North Ormesby Mbro 58 D6
North Ormsby Lincs 46 C6
North Otterington N Yorks 58 H4
North Owersby Lincs 46 C4
North Perrott Som 8 D3
North Petherton Som 8 A1
North Petherwin Corn 4 C3
North Pickenham Norf 38 E4
North Piddle Worcs 26 C6
North Poorton Dorset 8 E4
North Port Argyll 74 E3
North Queensferry Fife 69 B10
North Radworthy Devon 7 C6
North Rauceby Lincs 46 H4
North Reston Lincs 47 D7
North Rigton N Yorks 51 E8
North Rode Ches E 44 F2
North Roe Shetland 96 E5
North Runcton Norf 38 D2
North Sandwick Shetland 96 D7
North Scale Cumb 49 C1
North Scarle Lincs 46 F2
North Seaton Northumb 63 E8
North Shian Argyll 74 C2
North Shields T&W 63 G9
North Shoebury Southend 20 C6
North Shore Blackpool 49 F3
North Side Cumb 56 D2
North Side Pboro 37 F8
North Skelton Redcar 59 E7
North Somercotes Lincs 47 C8
North Stainley N Yorks 51 B8
North Stainmore Cumb 57 E10
North Stifford Thurrock 20 C3
North Stoke Bath 16 E4
North Stoke Oxon 18 C3
North Stoke W Sus 11 C9
North Street Hants 10 A5
North Street Kent 21 F7
North Street Medway 20 D5
North Street W Berks 18 D3
North Sunderland Northumb 71 G11
North Tamerton Corn 6 G2
North Tawton Devon 6 F5
North Thoresby Lincs 46 C6
North Tidworth Wilts 17 G9
North Togston Northumb 63 C8
North Tuddenham Norf 38 D6
North Walbottle T&W 63 G7
North Walsham Norf 39 B8
North Waltham Hants 18 G2
North Warnborough Hants 18 F4
North Water Bridge Angus 83 G8
North Watten Highld 94 E4
North Weald Bassett Essex 19 A11
North Wheatley Notts 45 D11
North Whilborough Devon 5 E9
North Wick Bath 16 E2
North Willingham Lincs 46 D5
North Wingfield Derbys 45 F8
North Witham Lincs 36 C5
North Woolwich London 19 D11
North Wootton Dorset 8 C5
North Wootton Norf 38 C2
North Wootton Som 16 G2
North Wraxall Wilts 16 D5
North Wroughton Swindon 17 C8
Northacre Norf 38 F5
Northallerton N Yorks 58 G4
Northam Devon 6 D3
Northam Soton 10 C3
Northampton Northants 28 B4
Northaw Herts 19 A9
Northbeck Lincs 37 A6
Northborough Pboro 37 E7
Northbourne Kent 21 F10
Northbridge Street E Sus 12 D6
Northchapel W Sus 11 B8
Northchurch Herts 28 H6
Northcott Devon 6 G2
Northdown Kent 21 D10
Northdyke Orkney 95 F3
Northend Bath 16 E4
Northend Bucks 18 B4
Northend Warks 27 C10
Northenden Gtr Man 44 C2
Northfield Aberdeen 83 C11
Northfield Borders 71 D8
Northfield E Yorks 52 G6
Northfield W Mid 34 H6
Northfields Lincs 36 E6
Northfleet Kent 20 D3
Northgate Lincs 37 C7
Northhouse Borders 61 C10
Northiam E Sus 13 D7
Northill C Beds 29 D8
Northington Hants 18 H2
Northlands Lincs 47 G7
Northlea Durham 58 A5
Northleach Glos 27 G8
Northleigh Devon 7 G10
Northlew Devon 6 G4
Northmoor Oxon 17 A11
Northmoor Green or Moorland Som 8 A2
Northmuir Angus 76 B6
Northney Hants 10 D6
Northolt London 19 C8
Northop Flint 42 F5
Northop Hall Flint 42 F5
Northorpe Lincs 37 B8
Northorpe Lincs 37 D6
Northorpe Lincs 46 C2
Northover Som 8 B4
Northover Som 15 H10
Northowram W Yorks 51 G7
Northport Dorset 9 F8
Northpunds Shetland 96 L6
Northrepps Norf 39 B8
Northtown Orkney 95 J5
Northway Glos 26 E6
Northwich Ches W 43 E9
Northwick S Glos 16 C2
Northwold Norf 38 F3
Northwood Derbys 44 F6
Northwood IoW 10 E3
Northwood Kent 21 E10
Northwood London 19 B7
Northwood Shrops 33 B10
Northwood Green Glos 26 G4
Norton E Sus 12 F3
Norton Glos 26 F5
Norton Halton 43 D8
Norton Herts 29 E9
Norton IoW 10 F2
Norton Mon 25 G11
Norton Northants 28 B3
Norton Notts 45 E9
Norton Powys 25 B10
Norton S Yorks 51 H11
Norton Shrops 33 G10
Norton Shrops 34 E1
Norton Shrops 34 E3
Norton Stockton 58 D5
Norton Suff 30 B6
Norton W Sus 11 D8
Norton W Sus 11 E7
Norton Wilts 16 C5
Norton Worcs 26 C5
Norton Worcs 27 D7
Norton Bavant Wilts 16 G6
Norton Bridge Staffs 34 B4
Norton Canes Staffs 34 E6
Norton Canon Hereford 25 D10
Norton Corner Norf 39 C6
Norton Disney Lincs 46 G2
Norton East Staffs 34 E6
Norton Ferris Wilts 16 H4
Norton Fitzwarren Som 7 D10
Norton Green IoW 10 F2
Norton Hawkfield Bath 16 E2
Norton Heath Essex 20 A3
Norton in Hales Shrops 34 B3
Norton-in-the-Moors Stoke 44 G2
Norton-Juxta-Twycross Leics 35 E9
Norton-le-Clay N Yorks 51 B10
Norton Lindsey Warks 27 B9
Norton Malreward Bath 16 E3
Norton Mandeville Essex 20 A2
Norton-on-Derwent N Yorks 52 B3
Norton St Philip Som 16 F4
Norton sub Hamdon Som 8 C3
Norton Woodseats S Yorks 45 D7
Norwell Notts 45 F11
Norwell Woodhouse Notts 45 F11
Norwich Norf 39 E8
Norwick Shetland 96 B8
Norwood Derbys 45 D8
Norwood Hill Sur 19 G9
Norwoodside Cambs 37 F10
Noseley Leics 36 F3
Noss Shetland 96 M5
Noss Mayo Devon 4 G6
Nosterfield N Yorks 51 A8
Nostie Highld 85 F13
Notgrove Glos 27 F8
Nottage Bridgend 14 D4
Nottingham Nottingham 36 B1
Nottington Dorset 8 F5
Notton W Yorks 45 A7
Notton Wilts 16 E6
Nounsley Essex 30 G4
Noutard's Green Worcs 26 B4
Novar House Highld 87 E9
Nox Shrops 33 D10
Nuffield Oxon 18 C3
Nun Hills Lancs 50 G4
Nun Monkton N Yorks 51 D11
Nunburnholme E Yorks 52 E4
Nuncargate Notts 45 G9
Nuneaton Warks 35 F9
Nuneham Courtenay Oxon 18 B2
Nunney Som 16 G4
Nunnington N Yorks 52 B2
Nunnykirk Northumb 62 D6
Nunsthorpe NE Lincs 46 B6
Nunthorpe Mbro 59 E6
Nunthorpe York 52 D2
Nunton Wilts 9 B10
Nunwick N Yorks 51 B9
Nupend Glos 26 H4
Nursling Hants 10 C2
Nursted Hants 11 B6
Nutbourne W Sus 11 C9
Nutbourne W Sus 11 D6
Nutfield Sur 19 F10
Nuthall Notts 35 A11
Nuthampstead Herts 29 E11
Nuthurst W Sus 11 B10
Nutley E Sus 12 D3
Nutley Hants 18 G3
Nutwell S Yorks 45 B10
Nybster Highld 94 D5
Nyetimber W Sus 11 E7
Nyewood W Sus 11 B7
Nymet Rowland Devon 6 F6
Nymet Tracey Devon 7 F6
Nympsfield Glos 16 A5
Nynehead Som 7 D10
Nyton W Sus 11 D8

O

Oad Street Kent 20 E5
Oadby Leics 36 E2
Oak Cross Devon 6 G4
Oakamoor Staffs 35 A6
Oakbank W Loth 69 D9
Oakdale Caerph 15 B7
Oake Som 7 D10
Oaken Staffs 34 E4
Oakenclough Lancs 49 E5
Oakengates Telford 34 D3
Oakenholt Flint 42 E5
Oakenshaw Durham 58 C3
Oakenshaw W Yorks 51 G7
Oakerthorpe Derbys 45 G7
Oakes W Yorks 51 H7
Oakfield Torf 15 B9
Oakford Ceredig 23 A9
Oakford Devon 7 D8
Oakfordbridge Devon 7 D8
Oakgrove Ches E 44 F3
Oakham Rutland 36 E4
Oakhanger Hants 18 H4
Oakhill Som 16 G3
Oakhurst Kent 20 F2
Oakington Cambs 29 B11
Oaklands Herts 29 G9
Oaklands Powys 25 C7
Oakle Street Glos 26 G4
Oakley Bedford 29 C7
Oakley Bucks 28 G3
Oakley Fife 69 B9
Oakley Hants 18 F2
Oakley Oxon 18 A4
Oakley Poole 9 E9
Oakley Suff 39 H7
Oakley Green Windsor 18 D6
Oakley Park Powys 32 G5
Oakmere Ches W 43 F8
Oakridge Glos 16 A6
Oakridge Hants 18 F3
Oaks Shrops 33 E10
Oaks Green Derbys 35 B7
Oaksey Wilts 16 B6
Oakthorpe Leics 35 D9
Oakwoodhill Sur 19 H8
Oakworth W Yorks 50 F6
Oape Highld 92 J7
Oare Kent 21 E7
Oare Som 7 B7
Oare W Berks 18 D2
Oare Wilts 17 E8
Oasby Lincs 36 B6
Oathlaw Angus 77 B7
Oatlands N Yorks 51 D9
Oban Argyll 79 J11
Oban Highld 79 C11
Oborne Dorset 8 C5
Obthorpe Lincs 37 D6
Occlestone Green Ches W 43 F9
Occold Suff 31 A8
Ochiltree E Ayrs 67 D8
Ochtermuthill Perth 75 F11
Ochtertyre Perth 75 E11
Ockbrook Derbys 35 B10
Ockham Sur 19 F7
Ockle Highld 79 D8
Ockley Sur 19 H8
Ocle Pychard Hereford 26 D2
Octon E Yorks 52 C6
Octon Cross Roads E Yorks 52 C6
Odcombe Som 8 C4
Odd Down Bath 16 E4
Oddendale Cumb 57 E7
Odder Lincs 46 E3
Oddingley Worcs 26 C6
Oddington Glos 27 F9
Oddington Oxon 28 G2
Odell Bedford 28 C6
Odie Orkney 95 F7
Odiham Hants 18 F4
Odstock Wilts 9 B10
Odstone Leics 35 E9
Offchurch Warks 27 B10
Offenham Worcs 27 D7
Offham E Sus 12 E2
Offham Kent 20 F3
Offham W Sus 11 D9
Offord Cluny Cambs 29 B9
Offord Darcy Cambs 29 B9
Offton Suff 31 D7
Offwell Devon 7 G10
Ogbourne Maizey Wilts 17 D8
Ogbourne St Andrew Wilts 17 D8
Ogbourne St George Wilts 17 D9
Ogil Angus 77 A7
Ogle Northumb 63 F7
Ogmore V Glam 14 D4
Ogmore-by-Sea V Glam 14 D4
Ogmore Vale Bridgend 14 B5
Okeford Fitzpaine Dorset 9 C7
Okehampton Devon 6 G4
Okehampton Camp Devon 6 G4
Okraquoy Shetland 96 K6
Old Northants 28 A4
Old Aberdeen Aberdeen 83 C11
Old Alresford Hants 10 A4
Old Arley Warks 35 F8
Old Basford Nottingham 35 A11
Old Basing Hants 18 F3
Old Bewick Northumb 62 A6
Old Bolingbroke Lincs 47 F7
Old Bramhope W Yorks 51 E8
Old Brampton Derbys 45 E7
Old Bridge of Tilt Perth 81 G10
Old Bridge of Urr Dumfries 55 C10
Old Buckenham Norf 39 F6
Old Burghclere Hants 17 F11
Old Byland N Yorks 59 H6
Old Cassop Durham 58 C4
Old Castleton Borders 61 D11
Old Catton Norf 39 D8
Old Clee NE Lincs 46 B6
Old Cleeve Som 7 B9
Old Clipstone Notts 45 F10
Old Colwyn Conwy 41 C10
Old Coulsdon London 19 F10
Old Crombie Aberds 88 C5
Old Dailly S Ayrs 66 G5
Old Dalby Leics 36 C2
Old Deer Aberds 89 D9
Old Denaby S Yorks 45 C8
Old Edlington S Yorks 45 C9
Old Eldon Durham 58 D3
Old Ellerby E Yorks 53 F7
Old Felixstowe Suff 31 E10
Old Fletton Pboro 37 F7
Old Glossop Derbys 44 C4
Old Goole E Yorks 52 G3
Old Hall Powys 32 G5
Old Heath Essex 31 F7
Old Heathfield E Sus 12 D4
Old Hill W Mid 34 G5
Old Hunstanton Norf 38 A2
Old Hurst Cambs 37 H8
Old Hutton Cumb 57 H7
Old Kea Corn 3 E7
Old Kilpatrick W Dunb 68 C3
Old Kinnernie Aberds 83 C9
Old Knebworth Herts 29 F9
Old Langho Lancs 50 F3
Old Laxey IoM 48 D4
Old Leake Lincs 47 G8
Old Malton N Yorks 52 B3
Old Micklefield W Yorks 51 F10
Old Milton Hants 9 E11
Old Milverton Warks 27 B9
Old Monkland N Lanark 68 D6
Old Netley Hants 10 D3
Old Philpstoun W Loth 69 C9
Old Quarrington Durham 58 C4
Old Radnor Powys 25 C9
Old Rattray Aberds 89 C10
Old Rayne Aberds 83 A8
Old Romney Kent 13 D9
Old Sodbury S Glos 16 C4
Old Somerby Lincs 36 B5
Old Stratford Northants 28 D4
Old Thirsk N Yorks 51 A10
Old Town Cumb 50 A1
Old Town Cumb 57 B6
Old Town Northumb 62 D4
Old Town Scilly 2 C3
Old Trafford Gtr Man 44 C2
Old Tupton Derbys 45 F7
Old Warden C Beds 29 D8
Old Weston Cambs 37 H6
Old Whittington Derbys 45 E7
Old Wick Highld 94 E5
Old Windsor Windsor 18 D6
Old Wives Lees Kent 21 F7
Old Woking Sur 19 F7
Old Woodhall Lincs 46 F6
Oldany Highld 92 F4
Oldberrow Warks 27 B8
Oldborough Devon 7 F6
Oldbury Shrops 34 F3
Oldbury W Mid 34 G5
Oldbury Warks 35 F9
Oldbury-on-Severn S Glos 16 B3
Oldbury on the Hill Glos 16 C5
Oldcastle Bridgend 14 D5
Oldcastle Mon 25 F10
Oldcotes Notts 45 D9
Oldfallow Staffs 34 D5
Oldfield Worcs 26 B5
Oldford Som 16 F4
Oldham Gtr Man 44 B3
Oldhamstocks E Loth 70 C6
Oldland S Glos 16 D3
Oldmeldrum Aberds 89 F8
Oldshore Beg Highld 92 D4
Oldshoremore Highld 92 D5
Oldstead N Yorks 51 A11
Oldtown Aberds 83 A7
Oldtown of Ord Aberds 88 C6
Oldway Swansea 23 H10
Oldways End Devon 7 D7
Oldwhat Aberds 89 C8
Olgrinmore Highld 94 E2
Oliver's Battery Hants 10 B3
Ollaberry Shetland 96 E5
Ollerton Ches E 43 E10
Ollerton Notts 45 F10

Rho–Sly 149

Rhodiad Pembs 22 D2
Rhondda Rhondda 14 B5
Rhonehouse or Kelton Hill Dumfries 55 D10
Rhoose = Y Rhws V Glam 14 E6
Rhos-fawr Gwyn 40 G5
Rhos-goch Powys 25 D8
Rhos-hill Pembs 22 B6
Rhos-on-Sea Conwy 41 B10
Rhos-y-brithdir Powys 33 C7
Rhos-y-garth Ceredig 24 A3
Rhos-y-gwaliau Gwyn 32 B5
Rhos-y-llan Gwyn 40 G4
Rhos-y-Madoc Wrex 33 A9
Rhos-y-meirch Powys 25 B9
Rhosaman Carms 24 G4
Rhosbeirio Anglesey 40 A5
Rhoscefnhir Anglesey 41 C7
Rhoscolyn Anglesey 40 C4
Rhoscrowther Pembs 22 F4
Rhosesmor Flint 42 F5
Rhosgadfan Gwyn 41 E7
Rhosgoch Anglesey 40 B6
Rhoshirwaun Gwyn 40 H3
Rhoslan Gwyn 40 F6
Rhoslefain Gwyn 32 E1
Rhosllanerchrugog Wrex 42 H5
Rhosmaen Carms 24 F3
Rhosmeirch Anglesey 40 C6
Rhosneigr Anglesey 40 C5
Rhosnesni Wrex 42 G6
Rhosrobin Wrex 42 G6
Rhossili Swansea 23 H9
Rhosson Pembs 22 D2
Rhostryfan Gwyn 40 E6
Rhostyllen Wrex 42 H6
Rhosybol Anglesey 40 B6
Rhu Argyll 73 E11
Rhu Argyll 73 G7
Rhuallt Denb 42 E3
Rhuddall Heath Ches W 43 F8
Rhuddlan Ceredig 23 B9
Rhuddlan Denb 42 E3
Rhue Highld 86 B3
Rhulen Powys 25 D8
Rhunahaorine Argyll 65 D8
Rhuthun = Ruthin Denb 42 G4
Rhyd Gwyn 41 F8
Rhyd Powys 32 E5
Rhyd-Ddu Gwyn 41 E7
Rhyd-moel-ddu Powys 33 H6
Rhyd-Rosser Ceredig 24 B2
Rhyd-uchaf Gwyn 32 B5
Rhyd-wen Gwyn 32 D3
Rhyd-y-clafdy Gwyn 40 G5
Rhyd-y-fro Neath 24 H4
Rhyd-y-gwin Swansea 14 A2
Rhyd-y-meirch Mon 25 H10
Rhyd-y-meudwy Denb 42 G4
Rhyd-y-pandy Swansea 14 A2
Rhyd-y-sarn Gwyn 41 F8
Rhyd-yr-onen Gwyn 32 E2
Rhydaman = Ammanford Carms 24 G3
Rhydargaeau Carms 23 D9
Rhydcymerau Carms 23 C10
Rhydd Worcs 26 D5
Rhydding Neath 14 B3
Rhydfudr Ceredig 24 B2
Rhydlewis Ceredig 23 B8
Rhydlios Gwyn 40 G3
Rhydlydan Conwy 41 E10
Rhydness Powys 25 D8
Rhydowen Ceredig 23 B9
Rhydspence Hereford 25 D9
Rhydtalog Flint 42 G5
Rhydwyn Anglesey 40 B5
Rhydycroesau Powys 33 B8
Rhydyfelin Ceredig 32 H1
Rhydyfelin Rhondda 14 C6
Rhydymain Gwyn 32 C4
Rhydymwyn Flint 42 F5
Rhyl = Y Rhyl Denb 42 D3
Rhymney = Rhymni Caerph 25 H8
Rhymni = Rhymney Caerph 25 H8
Rhynd Fife 77 E7
Rhynd Perth 76 E4
Rhynie Aberds 82 A6
Rhynie Highld 87 D11
Ribbesford Worcs 26 A4
Ribblehead N Yorks 50 B3
Ribbleton Lancs 50 F1
Ribchester Lancs 50 F2
Ribigill Highld 93 D8
Riby Lincs 46 B5
Riby Cross Roads Lincs 46 B5
Riccall N Yorks 52 F2
Riccarton E Ayrs 67 C7
Richards Castle Hereford 25 B11
Richings Park Bucks 19 D7
Richmond London 19 D8
Richmond N Yorks 58 F2
Rickarton Aberds 83 E10
Rickinghall Suff 38 H6
Rickleton T&W 58 A3
Rickling Essex 29 E11
Rickmansworth Herts 19 B7
Riddings Cumb 61 F10
Riddings Derbys 45 G8
Riddlecombe Devon 6 E5
Riddlesden W Yorks 51 E6
Riddrie Glasgow 68 D5
Ridge Dorset 9 F8
Ridge Hants 10 C2
Ridge Wilts 9 A8
Ridge Green Sur 19 G10
Ridge Lane Warks 35 F8
Ridgebourne Powys 25 B7
Ridgehill N Som 15 E11
Ridgeway Cross Hereford 26 D4
Ridgewell Essex 30 D4
Ridgewood E Sus 12 E3
Ridgmont C Beds 28 E6
Riding Mill Northumb 62 G6
Ridleywood Wrex 43 G7
Ridlington Norf 39 B9
Ridlington Rutland 36 E4
Ridsdale Northumb 62 E5
Riechip Perth 76 C3
Riemore Perth 76 C3
Rienachait Highld 92 F3
Rievaulx N Yorks 59 H6
Rift House Hrtlpl 58 C5
Rigg Dumfries 61 G8
Riggend N Lanark 68 C6
Rigsby Lincs 47 E8
Rigside S Lanark 69 G7
Riley Green Lancs 50 G2
Rileyhill Staffs 35 D7
Rilla Mill Corn 4 D3
Rillington N Yorks 52 B4
Rimington Lancs 50 E4
Rimpton Som 8 B5
Rimswell E Yorks 53 G9
Rinaston Pembs 22 D4
Ringasta Shetland 96 M5
Ringford Dumfries 55 D9
Ringinglow S Yorks 44 D6
Ringland Norf 39 D7
Ringles Cross E Sus 12 D3
Ringmer E Sus 12 E3
Ringmore Devon 5 G7
Ringorm Moray 88 D2
Ring's End Cambs 37 E9
Ringsfield Suff 39 G10
Ringsfield Corner Suff 39 G10
Ringshall Herts 28 G6
Ringshall Suff 31 C7
Ringshall Stocks Suff 31 C7
Ringstead Norf 38 A3
Ringstead Northants 36 H5
Ringwood Hants 9 D10
Ringwould Kent 21 G10
Rinmore Aberds 82 B6
Rinnigill Orkney 95 J4
Rinsey Corn 2 G4
Riof W Isles 90 D6
Ripe E Sus 12 E4
Ripley Derbys 45 G7
Ripley Hants 9 E10
Ripley N Yorks 51 C8
Ripley Sur 19 F7
Riplingham E Yorks 52 F5
Ripon N Yorks 51 B9
Rippingale Lincs 37 C6
Ripple Kent 21 G10
Ripple Worcs 26 E5
Ripponden W Yorks 50 H6
Rireavach Highld 86 B3
Risabus Argyll 64 D4
Risbury Hereford 26 C2
Risby Suff 30 B4
Risca = Rhisga Caerph 15 B8
Rise E Yorks 53 E7
Riseden E Sus 12 C5
Risegate Lincs 37 C8
Riseholme Lincs 46 E3
Riseley Bedford 29 B7
Riseley Wokingham 18 E4
Rishangles Suff 31 B8
Rishton Lancs 50 F3
Rishworth W Yorks 50 H6
Rising Bridge Lancs 50 G3
Risley Derbys 35 B10
Risley Warr 43 C9
Risplith N Yorks 51 C8
Rispond Highld 92 C7
Rivar Wilts 17 E10
Rivenhall End Essex 30 G5
River Bank Cambs 30 B2
Riverhead Kent 20 F2
Rivington Lancs 43 A9
Roa Island Cumb 49 C2
Roachill Devon 7 D7
Road Green Norf 39 F8
Roade Northants 28 C4
Roadhead Cumb 61 F11
Roadmeetings S Lanark 69 F7
Roadside Highld 94 D3
Roadside of Catterline Aberds 83 F10
Roadside of Kinneff Aberds 83 F10
Roadwater Som 7 C9
Roag Highld 85 D7
Roath Cardiff 15 D7
Roberton Borders 61 B10
Roberton S Lanark 69 H8
Robertsbridge E Sus 12 D6
Roberttown W Yorks 51 G7
Robeston Cross Pembs 22 F3
Robeston Wathen Pembs 22 E5
Robin Hood W Yorks 51 G9
Robin Hood's Bay N Yorks 59 F10
Roborough Devon 4 E6
Roborough Devon 6 E4
Roby Mers 43 C7
Roby Mill Lancs 43 B8
Rocester Staffs 35 B7
Roch Pembs 22 D3
Roch Gate Pembs 22 D3
Rochdale Gtr Man 44 A2
Roche Corn 3 C8
Rochester Medway 20 E4
Rochester Northumb 62 D4
Rochford Essex 20 B5
Rock Corn 3 B8
Rock Northumb 63 A8
Rock W Sus 11 C10
Rock Worcs 26 A4
Rock Ferry Mers 42 D6
Rockbeare Devon 7 G9
Rockbourne Hants 9 C10
Rockcliffe Cumb 61 G9
Rockcliffe Dumfries 55 D11
Rockfield Highld 87 C12
Rockfield Mon 25 G11
Rockford Hants 9 D10
Rockhampton S Glos 16 B3
Rockingham Northants 36 F4
Rockland All Saints Norf 38 F5
Rockland St Mary Norf 39 E9
Rockland St Peter Norf 38 F5
Rockley Wilts 17 D8
Rockwell End Bucks 18 C4
Rockwell Green Som 7 D10
Rodborough Glos 16 A5
Rodbourne Swindon 17 C8
Rodbourne Wilts 16 C6
Rodbourne Cheney Swindon 17 C8
Rodd Hereford 25 B10
Roddam Northumb 62 A6
Rodden Dorset 8 F5
Rode Som 16 F5
Rode Heath Ches E 44 G2
Rodeheath Ches E 44 F2
Roden Telford 34 D1
Rodhuish Som 7 C9
Rodington Telford 34 D1
Rodley Glos 26 G4
Rodley W Yorks 51 F8
Rodmarton Glos 16 B6
Rodmell E Sus 12 F3
Rodmersham Kent 20 E6
Rodney Stoke Som 15 F10
Rodsley Derbys 35 A8
Rodway Som 15 H8
Rodwell Dorset 8 G5
Roe Green Herts 29 E10
Roecliffe N Yorks 51 C9
Roehampton London 19 D9
Roesound Shetland 96 G5
Roffey W Sus 11 A10
Rogart Highld 93 J10
Rogart Station Highld 93 J10
Rogate W Sus 11 B7
Rogerstone Newport 15 C8
Roghadal W Isles 90 J5
Rogiet Mon 15 C10
Rogue's Alley Cambs 37 E9
Roke Oxon 18 B3
Roker T&W 63 H10
Rollesby Norf 39 D10
Rolleston Leics 36 E3
Rolleston Notts 45 G11
Rolleston-on-Dove Staffs 35 C8
Rolston E Yorks 53 E8
Rolvenden Kent 13 C7
Rolvenden Layne Kent 13 C7
Romaldkirk Durham 57 D11
Romanby N Yorks 58 G4
Romannobridge Borders 69 F10
Romansleigh Devon 7 D6
Romford London 20 C2
Romiley Gtr Man 44 C3
Romsey Hants 10 B2
Romsey Town Cambs 29 C11
Romsley Shrops 34 G3
Romsley Worcs 34 H5
Ronague IoM 48 E2
Rookhope Durham 57 B11
Rookley IoW 10 F4
Rooks Bridge Som 15 F9
Roos E Yorks 53 F8
Roosebeck Cumb 49 C2
Rootham's Green Bedford 29 C8
Rootpark S Lanark 69 E8
Ropley Hants 10 A5
Ropley Dean Hants 10 A5
Ropsley Lincs 36 B5
Rora Aberds 89 C10
Rorandle Aberds 83 B8
Rorrington Shrops 33 E9
Roscroggan Corn 2 E5
Rose Corn 3 D6
Rose Ash Devon 7 D6
Rose Green W Sus 11 E8
Rose Grove Lancs 50 F4
Rose Hill E Sus 12 E3
Rose Hill Lancs 50 F4
Rose Hill Suff 31 D8
Roseacre Kent 20 F4
Roseacre Lancs 49 F4
Rosebank S Lanark 69 F7
Rosebrough Northumb 71 H10
Rosebush Pembs 22 D5
Rosecare Corn 4 B2
Rosedale Abbey N Yorks 59 G8
Roseden Northumb 62 A6
Rosefield Highld 87 F11
Rosehall Highld 92 J7
Rosehaugh Mains Highld 87 F9
Rosehearty Aberds 89 B9
Rosehill Shrops 34 B2
Roseisle Moray 88 B1
Roselands E Sus 12 F5
Rosemarket Pembs 22 F4
Rosemarkie Highld 87 F10
Rosemary Lane Devon 7 E10
Rosemount Perth 76 C4
Rosenannon Corn 3 C8
Rosewell Midloth 69 D11
Roseworth Stockton 58 D5
Roseworthy Corn 2 F5
Rosgill Cumb 57 E7
Roshven Highld 79 D10
Roskhill Highld 85 D7
Roskill House Highld 87 F9
Rosley Cumb 56 B5
Roslin Midloth 69 D11
Rosliston Derbys 35 D8
Rosneath Argyll 73 E11
Ross Dumfries 55 E9
Ross Northumb 71 G10
Ross Perth 75 E10
Ross-on-Wye Hereford 26 F3
Rossett Wrex 42 G6
Rossett Green N Yorks 51 D9
Rossie Ochill Perth 76 F3
Rossie Priory Perth 76 D5
Rossington S Yorks 45 C10
Rosskeen Highld 87 E9
Rossland Renfs 68 C3
Roster Highld 94 G4
Rostherne Ches E 43 D10
Rosthwaite Cumb 56 E4
Roston Derbys 35 A7
Rosyth Fife 69 B10
Rothbury Northumb 62 C6
Rotherby Leics 36 D2
Rotherfield E Sus 12 D4
Rotherfield Greys Oxon 18 C4
Rotherfield Peppard Oxon 18 C4
Rotherham S Yorks 45 C8
Rothersthorpe Northants 28 C4
Rotherwick Hants 18 F4
Rothes Moray 88 D2
Rothesay Argyll 73 G9
Rothiebrisbane Aberds 89 E7
Rothienorman Aberds 89 E7
Rothiesholm Orkney 95 F7
Rothley Leics 36 D1
Rothley Northumb 62 E6
Rothley Shield East Northumb 62 D6
Rothmaise Aberds 89 E6
Rothwell Lincs 46 C5
Rothwell Northants 36 G4
Rothwell W Yorks 51 G9
Rothwell Haigh W Yorks 51 G9
Rotsea E Yorks 53 D6
Rottal Angus 82 G5
Rotten End Suff 31 B10
Rottingdean Brighton 12 F2
Rottington Cumb 56 E1
Roud IoW 10 F4
Rough Close Staffs 34 B5
Rough Common Kent 21 F8
Rougham Norf 38 C4
Rougham Suff 30 B6
Rougham Green Suff 30 B6
Roughburn Highld 80 E5
Roughlee Lancs 50 E4
Roughley W Mid 35 F7
Roughsike Cumb 61 F11
Roughton Lincs 46 F6
Roughton Norf 39 B8
Roughton Shrops 34 F3
Roughton Moor Lincs 46 F6
Roundhay W Yorks 51 F9
Roundstonefoot Dumfries 61 C7
Roundstreet Common W Sus 11 B9
Roundway Wilts 17 E7
Rous Lench Worcs 27 C7
Rousdon Devon 8 E1
Routenburn N Ayrs 73 G10
Routh E Yorks 53 E6
Row Corn 4 D1
Row Cumb 56 H6
Row Heath Essex 31 G8
Rowanburn Dumfries 61 F10
Rowardennan Stirling 74 H6
Rowde Wilts 16 E6
Rowen Conwy 41 C9
Rowfoot Northumb 62 G2
Rowhedge Essex 31 F7
Rowhook W Sus 11 A10
Rowington Warks 27 B9
Rowland Derbys 44 E6
Rowlands Castle Hants 10 C6
Rowlands Gill T&W 63 H7
Rowledge Sur 18 G5
Rowlestone Hereford 25 F10
Rowley E Yorks 52 F5
Rowley Shrops 33 E9
Rowley Hill W Yorks 44 A5
Rowley Regis W Mid 34 G5
Rowly Sur 19 G7
Rowney Green Worcs 27 A7
Rownhams Hants 10 C2
Rowrah Cumb 56 E2
Rowsham Bucks 28 G5
Rowsley Derbys 44 F6
Rowstock Oxon 17 C11
Rowston Lincs 46 G4
Rowton Ches W 43 F7
Rowton Shrops 33 D9
Rowton Telford 34 D2
Roxburgh Borders 70 G6
Roxby N Lincs 52 H5
Roxby N Yorks 59 E8
Roxton Bedford 29 C8
Roxwell Essex 30 H3
Royal Leamington Spa Warks 27 B10
Royal Oak Darl 58 D3
Royal Oak Lancs 43 B7
Royal Tunbridge Wells Kent 12 C4
Royal Wootton Bassett Wilts 17 C7
Roybridge Highld 80 E4
Roydhouse W Yorks 44 A6
Roydon Essex 29 H11
Roydon Norf 38 C3
Roydon Norf 39 G6
Roydon Hamlet Essex 29 H11
Royston Herts 29 D10
Royston S Yorks 45 A7
Royton Gtr Man 44 B3
Rozel Jersey 11
Ruabon = Rhiwabon Wrex 33 A9
Ruaig Argyll 78 G3
Ruan Lanihorne Corn 3 E7
Ruan Minor Corn 2 H6
Ruarach Highld 80 A1
Ruardean Glos 26 G3
Ruardean Woodside Glos 26 G3
Rubery Worcs 34 H5
Ruckcroft Cumb 57 B7
Ruckhall Hereford 25 E11
Ruckinge Kent 13 C9
Ruckland Lincs 47 E7
Ruckley Shrops 33 E11
Rudbaxton Pembs 22 D4
Rudby N Yorks 58 F5
Ruddington Notts 36 B1
Rudford Glos 26 F4
Rudge Shrops 34 F4
Rudge Som 16 F5
Rudgeway S Glos 16 C3
Rudgwick W Sus 11 A9
Rudhall Hereford 26 F3
Rudheath Ches W 43 E9
Rudley Green Essex 20 A5
Rudry Caerph 15 C7
Rudston E Yorks 53 C6
Rudyard Staffs 44 G3
Rufford Lancs 49 H4
Rufforth York 51 D11
Rugby Warks 35 H11
Rugeley Staffs 34 D6
Ruglen S Ayrs 66 F5
Ruilick Highld 87 G8
Ruishton Som 8 B1
Ruisigearraidh W Isles 90 J4
Ruislip London 19 C7
Ruislip Common London 19 C7
Rumbling Bridge Perth 76 H3
Rumburgh Suff 39 G9
Rumford Corn 3 B7
Rumney Cardiff 15 D8
Runcorn Halton 43 D8
Runcton W Sus 11 D7
Runcton Holme Norf 38 E2
Rundlestone Devon 5 D6
Runfold Sur 18 G5
Runhall Norf 39 E6
Runham Norf 39 D10
Runham Norf 39 E11
Runnington Som 7 D10
Runsell Green Essex 30 H4
Runswick Bay N Yorks 59 E9
Runwell Essex 20 B4
Ruscombe Wokingham 18 D4
Rush Green London 20 C2
Rush-head Aberds 89 D8
Rushall Hereford 26 E3
Rushall Norf 39 G7
Rushall W Mid 34 E6
Rushall Wilts 17 F8
Rushbrooke Suff 30 B5
Rushbury Shrops 33 F11
Rushden Herts 29 E10
Rushden Northants 28 B6
Rushenden Kent 20 D6
Rushford Norf 38 G5
Rushlake Green E Sus 12 E5
Rushmere Suff 39 G10
Rushmere St Andrew Suff 31 D9
Rushmoor Sur 18 G5
Rushock Worcs 26 A5
Rusholme Gtr Man 44 C2
Rushton Ches W 43 F8
Rushton Northants 36 G4
Rushton Shrops 34 E2
Rushton Spencer Staffs 44 F3
Rushwick Worcs 26 C5
Rushyford Durham 58 D3
Ruskie Stirling 75 G9
Ruskington Lincs 46 G4
Rusland Cumb 56 H5
Rusper W Sus 19 H9
Ruspidge Glos 26 G3
Russell's Water Oxon 18 C4
Russel's Green Suff 31 A9
Rusthall Kent 12 C4
Rustington W Sus 11 D9
Ruston N Yorks 52 A5
Ruston Parva E Yorks 53 C6
Ruswarp N Yorks 59 F9
Rutherford Borders 70 G5
Rutherglen S Lanark 68 D5
Ruthernbridge Corn 3 C9
Ruthin = Rhuthun Denb 42 G4
Ruthrieston Aberdeen 83 C11
Ruthven Aberds 88 D5
Ruthven Angus 76 C5
Ruthven Highld 81 D9
Ruthven Highld 87 H11
Ruthven House Angus 76 C6
Ruthvoes Corn 3 C8
Ruthwell Dumfries 60 G6
Ruyton-XI-Towns Shrops 33 C9
Ryal Northumb 62 F6
Ryal Fold Blackburn 50 G2
Ryall Dorset 8 E3
Ryarsh Kent 20 F3
Rydal Cumb 56 F5
Ryde IoW 10 E4
Rye E Sus 13 D8
Rye Foreign E Sus 13 D7
Rye Harbour E Sus 13 E8
Rye Park Herts 29 G10
Rye Street Worcs 26 E4
Ryecroft Gate Staffs 44 F3
Ryehill E Yorks 53 G8
Ryhall Rutland 36 D6
Ryhill W Yorks 45 A7
Ryhope T&W 58 A5
Rylstone N Yorks 50 D5
Ryme Intrinseca Dorset 8 C4
Ryther N Yorks 52 F1
Ryton Glos 26 E4
Ryton N Yorks 52 B3
Ryton T&W 63 G7
Ryton-on-Dunsmore Warks 27 A10

S

Sabden Lancs 50 F3
Sacombe Herts 29 G10
Sacriston Durham 58 B3
Sadberge Darl 58 E4
Saddell Argyll 65 E8
Saddington Leics 36 F2
Saddle Bow Norf 38 D2
Saddlescombe W Sus 12 E1
Sadgill Cumb 57 F6
Saffron Walden Essex 30 E2
Sageston Pembs 22 F5
Saham Hills Norf 38 E5
Saham Toney Norf 38 E5
Saighdinis W Isles 84 B3
Saighton Ches W 43 F7
St Abbs Borders 71 D8
St Abb's Haven Borders 71 D8
St Agnes Corn 2 D6
St Agnes Scilly 2 D3
St Albans Herts 29 H8
St Allen Corn 3 D7
St Andrews Fife 77 F8
St Andrew's Major V Glam 15 D7
St Anne Ald 11
St Annes Lancs 49 G3
St Ann's Dumfries 60 D6
St Ann's Chapel Corn 4 D5
St Ann's Chapel Devon 5 G7
St Anthony-in-Meneage Corn 3 G6
St Anthony's Hill E Sus 12 F5
St Arvans Mon 15 B11
St Asaph = Llanelwy Denb 42 E3
St Athan V Glam 14 E6
St Aubin Jersey 11
St Austell Corn 3 D9
St Bees Cumb 56 E1
St Blazey Corn 4 F1
St Boswells Borders 70 G4
St Brelade Jersey 11
St Breock Corn 3 B8
St Breward Corn 4 D1
St Briavels Glos 16 A2
St Bride's Pembs 22 E3
St Brides Major V Glam 14 D4
St Bride's Netherwent Mon 15 C10
St Brides super Ely V Glam 14 D6
St Brides Wentlooge Newport 15 C8
St Budeaux Plym 4 F5
St Buryan Corn 2 G3
St Catherine Bath 16 D4
St Catherine's Argyll 73 C10
St Clears = Sanclêr Carms 23 E7
St Cleer Corn 4 E3
St Clement Corn 3 E7
St Clements Jersey 11
St Clether Corn 4 C3
St Colmac Argyll 73 G9
St Columb Major Corn 3 C8
St Columb Minor Corn 3 C7
St Columb Road Corn 3 D8
St Combs Aberds 89 B10
St Cross South Elmham Suff 39 G8
St Cyrus Aberds 77 A10
St David's Perth 76 E2
St David's = Tyddewi Pembs 22 D2
St Day Corn 2 E6
St Dennis Corn 3 D8
St Devereux Hereford 25 E11
St Dogmaels Pembs 22 B6
St Dogwells Pembs 22 D4
St Dominick Corn 4 E5
St Donat's V Glam 14 E5
St Edith's Wilts 16 E6
St Endellion Corn 3 B8
St Enoder Corn 3 D7
St Erme Corn 3 D7
St Erney Corn 4 F4
St Erth Corn 2 F4
St Ervan Corn 3 B7
St Eval Corn 3 C7
St Ewe Corn 3 E8
St Fagans Cardiff 15 D7
St Fergus Aberds 89 C10
St Fillans Perth 75 E9
St Florence Pembs 22 F5
St Genny's Corn 4 B2
St George Conwy 42 E2
St George's V Glam 14 D6
St Germans Corn 4 F4
St Giles Lincs 46 E3
St Giles in the Wood Devon 6 E4
St Giles on the Heath Devon 6 G2
St Harmon Powys 24 A6
St Helen Auckland Durham 58 D2
St Helena Warks 35 E8
St Helen's E Sus 13 E7
St Helens IoW 10 F5
St Helens Mers 43 C8
St Helier Jersey 11
St Helier London 19 E9
St Hilary Corn 2 F4
St Hilary V Glam 14 D6
Saint Hill W Sus 12 C2
St Illtyd Bl Gwent 15 A8
St Ippollytts Herts 29 F8
St Ishmael's Pembs 22 F3
St Issey Corn 3 B8
St Ive Corn 4 E4
St Ives Cambs 29 A10
St Ives Corn 2 E4
St Ives Dorset 9 D10
St James South Elmham Suff 39 G9
St Jidgey Corn 3 C8
St John Corn 4 F5
St John's IoM 48 D2
St John's Jersey 11
St John's Sur 18 F6
St John's Worcs 26 C5
St John's Chapel Durham 57 C10
St John's Fen End Norf 37 D11
St John's Highway Norf 37 D11
St John's Town of Dalry Dumfries 55 A9
St Judes IoM 48 C3
St Just in Roseland Corn 3 F7
St Just Corn 2 F2
St Katherine's Aberds 89 E7
St Keverne Corn 3 G6
St Kew Corn 3 B9
St Kew Highway Corn 3 B9
St Keyne Corn 4 E3
St Lawrence Corn 3 C9
St Lawrence Essex 20 A6
St Lawrence IoW 10 G4
St Leonard's Bucks 28 H6
St Leonards Dorset 9 D10
St Leonards E Sus 13 F6
Saint Leonards S Lanark 68 E5
St Levan Corn 2 G2
St Lythans V Glam 15 D7
St Mabyn Corn 3 B9
St Madoes Perth 76 E4
St Margaret South Elmham Suff 39 G9
St Margaret's Hereford 25 E10
St Margarets Herts 29 G10
St Margaret's at Cliffe Kent 21 G10
St. Margaret's Hope Orkney 95 J5
St Mark's IoM 48 E2
St Martin Corn 4 F3
St Martins Corn 2 G6
St Martin's Jersey 11
St Martins Perth 76 D4
St Martin's Shrops 33 B9
St Mary Bourne Hants 17 F11
St Mary Church V Glam 14 D6
St Mary Cray London 19 E11
St Mary Hill V Glam 14 D5
St Mary Hoo Medway 20 D5
St Mary in the Marsh Kent 13 D9
St Mary's Jersey 11
St Mary's Orkney 95 H5
St Mary's Bay Kent 13 D9
St Maughans Mon 25 G11
St Mawes Corn 3 F7
St Mawgan Corn 3 C7
St Mellion Corn 4 E4
St Mellons Cardiff 15 C8
St Merryn Corn 3 B7
St Mewan Corn 3 D8
St Michael Caerhays Corn 3 E8
St Michael Penkevil Corn 3 E7
St Michael South Elmham Suff 39 G9
St Michael's Kent 13 C7
St Michaels Worcs 26 B2
St Michael's on Wyre Lancs 49 E4
St Minver Corn 3 B8
St Monans Fife 77 G8
St Neot Corn 4 E2
St Neots Cambs 29 B8
St Newlyn East Corn 3 D7
St Nicholas Pembs 22 C3
St Nicholas V Glam 14 D6
St Nicholas at Wade Kent 21 E9
St Ninians Stirling 68 A6
St Osyth Essex 31 G8
St Osyth Heath Essex 31 G8
St Ouens Jersey 11
St Owens Cross Hereford 26 F2
St Paul's Cray London 19 E11
St Paul's Walden Herts 29 F8
St Peter Port Guern 11
St Peter's Jersey 11
St Peter's Kent 21 E10
St Petrox Pembs 22 G4
St Pinnock Corn 4 E3
St Quivox S Ayrs 67 D6
St Ruan Corn 2 H6
St Sampson Guern 11
St Stephen Corn 3 D8
St Stephen's Corn 4 C4
St Stephens Corn 4 F5
St Stephens Herts 29 H8
St Teath Corn 4 C1
St Thomas Devon 7 G8
St Tudy Corn 4 D1
St Twynnells Pembs 22 G4
St Veep Corn 4 F2
St Vigeans Angus 77 C9
St Wenn Corn 3 C8
St Weonards Hereford 25 F11
Saintbury Glos 27 E8
Salcombe Devon 5 H8
Salcombe Regis Devon 7 H10
Salcott Essex 30 G6
Sale Gtr Man 43 C10
Sale Green Worcs 26 C6
Saleby Lincs 47 E8
Salehurst E Sus 12 D6
Salem Carms 24 F3
Salem Ceredig 32 G2
Salen Argyll 79 G8
Salen Highld 79 E9
Salesbury Lancs 50 F2
Salford C Beds 28 E6
Salford Gtr Man 44 C2
Salford Oxon 27 F9
Salford Priors Warks 27 C7
Salfords Sur 19 G9
Salhouse Norf 39 D9
Saline Fife 69 A9
Salisbury Wilts 9 B10
Sallachan Highld 74 A2
Sallachy Highld 86 H2
Sallachy Highld 93 J8
Salle Norf 39 C7
Salmonby Lincs 47 E7
Salmond's Muir Angus 77 D8
Salperton Glos 27 F7
Salph End Bedford 29 C7
Salsburgh N Lanark 69 D7
Salt Staffs 34 C5
Salt End E Yorks 53 G7
Saltaire W Yorks 51 F7
Saltash Corn 4 F5
Saltburn Highld 87 E10
Saltburn-by-the-Sea Redcar 59 D7
Saltby Leics 36 C4
Saltcoats Cumb 56 G2
Saltcoats N Ayrs 66 B5
Saltdean Brighton 12 F2
Salter Lancs 50 C2
Salterforth Lancs 50 E4
Salterswall Ches W 43 F9
Saltfleet Lincs 47 C8
Saltfleetby All Saints Lincs 47 C8
Saltfleetby St Clements Lincs 47 C8
Saltfleetby St Peter Lincs 47 D8
Saltford Bath 16 E3
Salthouse Norf 39 A6
Saltmarshe E Yorks 52 G3
Saltney Flint 43 F6
Salton N Yorks 52 B3
Saltwick Northumb 63 F7
Saltwood Kent 21 H8
Salum Argyll 78 G3
Salvington W Sus 11 D10
Salwarpe Worcs 26 B5
Salwayash Dorset 8 E3
Sambourne Warks 27 B7
Sambrook Telford 34 C3
Samhla W Isles 84 B2
Samlesbury Lancs 50 F1
Samlesbury Bottoms Lancs 50 G2
Sampford Arundel Som 7 E10
Sampford Brett Som 7 B9
Sampford Courtenay Devon 6 F5
Sampford Peverell Devon 7 E9
Sampford Spiney Devon 4 D6
Sampool Bridge Cumb 56 H6
Samuelston E Loth 70 C3
Sanachan Highld 85 D13
Sanaigmore Argyll 64 A3
Sanclêr = St Clears Carms 23 E7
Sancreed Corn 2 G3
Sancton E Yorks 52 F5
Sand Highld 86 B2
Sand Shetland 96 J5
Sand Hole E Yorks 52 F4
Sand Hutton N Yorks 52 D2
Sandaig Highld 85 H12
Sandal Magna W Yorks 51 H9
Sandale Cumb 56 B4
Sandbach Ches E 43 F10
Sandbank Argyll 73 E10
Sandbanks Poole 9 F9
Sandend Aberds 88 B5
Sanderstead London 19 E10
Sandfields Glos 26 F6
Sandford Cumb 57 E9
Sandford Devon 7 F7
Sandford Dorset 9 F8
Sandford IoW 10 F4
Sandford N Som 15 F10
Sandford S Lanark 68 F6
Sandford Shrops 34 B1
Sandford on Thames Oxon 18 A2
Sandford Orcas Dorset 8 B5
Sandford St Martin Oxon 27 F11
Sandfordhill Aberds 89 D11
Sandgate Kent 21 H8
Sandgreen Dumfries 55 D8
Sandhaven Aberds 89 B9
Sandhead Dumfries 54 E3
Sandhills Sur 18 H6
Sandhoe Northumb 62 G5
Sandholme E Yorks 52 F4
Sandholme Lincs 37 B9
Sandhurst Brack 18 E5
Sandhurst Glos 26 F5
Sandhurst Kent 13 D6
Sandhurst Cross Kent 13 D6
Sandhutton N Yorks 51 A9
Sandiacre Derbys 35 B10
Sandilands Lincs 47 D9
Sandilands S Lanark 69 G7
Sandiway Ches W 43 E9
Sandleheath Hants 9 C10
Sandling Kent 20 F4
Sandlow Green Ches E 43 F10
Sandness Shetland 96 H3
Sandon Essex 20 A4
Sandon Herts 29 E10
Sandon Staffs 34 B5
Sandown IoW 10 F4
Sandplace Corn 4 F3
Sandridge Herts 29 G8
Sandridge Wilts 16 E6
Sandringham Norf 38 C2
Sandsend N Yorks 59 E9
Sandside Ho. Highld 93 C12
Sandsound Shetland 96 J5
Sandtoft N Lincs 45 B11
Sandway Kent 20 F5
Sandwell W Mid 34 G6
Sandwich Kent 21 F10
Sandwick Cumb 56 E6
Sandwick Orkney 95 K5
Sandwick Shetland 96 L6
Sandwith Cumb 56 E1
Sandy C Beds 29 D8
Sandy Carms 23 F9
Sandy Bank Lincs 46 G6
Sandy Haven Pembs 22 F3
Sandy Lane Wilts 16 E6
Sandy Lane Wrex 33 A9
Sandycroft Flint 42 F6
Sandyford Dumfries 61 D8
Sandyford Stoke 44 G2
Sandygate IoM 48 C3
Sandyhills Dumfries 55 D11
Sandylands Lancs 49 C4
Sandypark Devon 5 C8
Sandysike Cumb 61 G9
Sangobeg Highld 92 C7
Sangomore Highld 92 C7
Sanna Highld 78 E7
Sanndabhaig W Isles 84 D3
Sanndabhaig W Isles 91 D9
Sannox N Ayrs 66 B3
Sanquhar Dumfries 60 C3
Santon N Lincs 46 A3
Santon Bridge Cumb 56 F3
Santon Downham Suff 38 G4
Sapcote Leics 35 F10
Sapey Common Hereford 26 B4
Sapiston Suff 38 H5
Sapley Cambs 29 A9
Sapperton Glos 16 A6
Sapperton Lincs 36 B6
Saracen's Head Lincs 37 C9
Sarclet Highld 94 F5
Sardis Carms 23 F10
Sarn Bridgend 14 C5
Sarn Powys 33 F8
Sarn Bach Gwyn 40 H5
Sarn Meyllteyrn Gwyn 40 G4
Sarnau Carms 23 E8
Sarnau Ceredig 23 A8
Sarnau Gwyn 32 B5
Sarnau Powys 25 E7
Sarnau Powys 33 D8
Sarnesfield Hereford 25 C10
Saron Carms 23 C8
Saron Carms 24 G3
Saron Denb 42 F3
Saron Gwyn 40 E6
Saron Gwyn 41 D7
Sarratt Herts 19 B7
Sarre Kent 21 E9
Sarsden Oxon 27 F9
Sarsgrum Highld 92 C6
Satley Durham 58 B2
Satron N Yorks 57 G11
Satterleigh Devon 6 D5
Satterthwaite Cumb 56 G5
Satwell Oxon 18 C4
Sauchen Aberds 83 B8
Saucher Perth 76 D4
Sauchie Clack 69 A7
Sauchieburn Aberds 83 G8
Saughall Ches W 42 E6
Saughtree Borders 61 D11
Saul Glos 26 H4
Saundby Notts 45 D11
Saundersfoot Pembs 22 F6
Saunderton Bucks 18 A4
Saunton Devon 6 C3
Sausthorpe Lincs 47 F7
Saval Highld 93 J8
Savary Highld 79 G9
Savile Park W Yorks 51 G6
Sawbridge Warks 28 B2
Sawbridgeworth Herts 29 G11
Sawdon N Yorks 59 H10
Sawley Derbys 35 B10
Sawley Lancs 50 E3
Sawley N Yorks 51 C8
Sawston Cambs 29 D11
Sawtry Cambs 37 G7
Saxby Leics 36 D4
Saxby Lincs 46 D4
Saxby All Saints N Lincs 52 H5
Saxelbye Leics 36 C3
Saxham Street Suff 31 B7
Saxilby Lincs 46 E2
Saxlingham Norf 38 B6
Saxlingham Green Norf 39 F8
Saxlingham Nethergate Norf 39 F8
Saxlingham Thorpe Norf 39 F8
Saxmundham Suff 31 B10
Saxon Street Cambs 30 C3
Saxondale Notts 36 B2
Saxtead Suff 31 B9
Saxtead Green Suff 31 B9
Saxthorpe Norf 39 B7
Saxton N Yorks 51 F10
Sayers Common W Sus 12 E1
Scackleton N Yorks 52 B2
Scadabhagh W Isles 90 H6
Scaftworth Notts 45 C10
Scagglethorpe N Yorks 52 B4
Scaitcliffe Lancs 50 G3
Scalasaig Argyll 72 D2
Scalby E Yorks 52 G4
Scalby N Yorks 59 G11
Scaldwell Northants 28 A4
Scale Houses Cumb 57 B7
Scaleby Cumb 61 G10
Scaleby Hill Cumb 61 G10
Scales Cumb 49 B2
Scales Cumb 56 D5
Scales Lancs 49 F4
Scalford Leics 36 C3
Scaling Redcar 59 E8
Scallastle Argyll 79 H9
Scalloway Shetland 96 K6
Scalpay W Isles 90 H7
Scalpay Ho. Highld 85 F11
Scalpsie Argyll 73 H9
Scamadale Highld 79 B10
Scamblesby Lincs 46 E6
Scamodale Highld 79 D11
Scampston N Yorks 52 B4
Scampton Lincs 46 E3
Scapa Orkney 95 H5
Scapegoat Hill W Yorks 51 H6
Scar Orkney 95 D7
Scarborough N Yorks 59 H11
Scarcliffe Derbys 45 F8
Scarcroft W Yorks 51 E9
Scarcroft Hill W Yorks 51 E9
Scardroy Highld 86 F5
Scarff Shetland 96 E4
Scarfskerry Highld 94 C4
Scargill Durham 58 E1
Scarinish Argyll 78 G3
Scarisbrick Lancs 43 A6
Scarning Norf 38 D5
Scarrington Notts 36 A3
Scartho NE Lincs 46 B6
Scarwell Orkney 95 F3
Scatness Shetland 96 M5
Scatraig Highld 87 H10
Scawby N Lincs 46 B3
Scawsby S Yorks 45 B9
Scawton N Yorks 51 A11
Scayne's Hill W Sus 12 D2
Scethrog Powys 25 F8
Scholar Green Ches E 44 G2
Scholes W Yorks 44 B5
Scholes W Yorks 51 F9
Scholes W Yorks 51 G7
School Green Ches W 43 F9
Scleddau Pembs 22 C4
Sco Ruston Norf 39 C8
Scofton Notts 45 D10
Scole Norf 39 H7
Scolpaig W Isles 84 A2
Scone Perth 76 E4
Sconser Highld 85 E10
Scoonie Fife 76 G6
Scoor Argyll 78 K7
Scopwick Lincs 46 G4
Scoraig Highld 86 B3
Scorborough E Yorks 52 E6
Scorrier Corn 2 E6
Scorton Lancs 49 E5
Scorton N Yorks 58 F3
Scotbheinn W Isles 84 C3
Scotby Cumb 61 H10
Scotch Corner N Yorks 58 F3
Scotforth Lancs 49 D4
Scothern Lincs 46 E4
Scotland Gate Northumb 63 E8
Scotlandwell Perth 76 G4
Scots' Gap Northumb 62 E6
Scotsburn Highld 87 D10
Scotscalder Station Highld 94 E2
Scotscraig Fife 77 E7
Scotston Aberds 83 F9
Scotston Perth 76 C2
Scotstoun Glasgow 68 D4
Scotstown Highld 79 E11
Scotswood T&W 63 G7
Scottas Highld 85 H12
Scotter Lincs 46 B2
Scotterthorpe Lincs 46 B2
Scottlethorpe Lincs 37 C6
Scotton Lincs 46 C2
Scotton N Yorks 51 D9
Scotton N Yorks 58 G2
Scottow Norf 39 C8
Scoughall E Loth 70 B5
Scoulag Argyll 73 H10
Scoulton Norf 38 E5
Scourie Highld 92 E4
Scourie More Highld 92 E4
Scousburgh Shetland 96 M5
Scrabster Highld 94 C2
Scrafield Lincs 47 F7
Scrainwood Northumb 62 C5
Scrane End Lincs 37 A9
Scraptoft Leics 36 E2
Scratby Norf 39 D11
Scrayingham N Yorks 52 C3
Scredington Lincs 37 A6
Scremby Lincs 47 F8
Scremerston Northumb 71 F9
Screveton Notts 36 A3
Scrivelsby Lincs 46 F6
Scriven N Yorks 51 D9
Scrooby Notts 45 C10
Scropton Derbys 35 B7
Scrub Hill Lincs 46 G6
Scruton N Yorks 58 G3
Sculcoates Hull 53 F6
Sculthorpe Norf 38 B4
Scunthorpe N Lincs 46 A2
Scurlage Swansea 23 H9
Sea Palling Norf 39 C10
Seaborough Dorset 8 D3
Seacombe Mers 42 C6
Seacroft Lincs 47 F9
Seacroft W Yorks 51 F9
Seadyke Lincs 37 B9
Seafield S Ayrs 66 D6
Seafield W Loth 69 D9
Seaford E Sus 12 G3
Seaforth Mers 42 C6
Seagrave Leics 36 D2
Seaham Durham 58 B5
Seahouses Northumb 71 G11
Seal Kent 20 F2
Sealand Flint 42 F6
Seale Sur 18 G5
Seamer N Yorks 52 A6
Seamer N Yorks 58 E5
Seamill N Ayrs 66 B5
Searby Lincs 46 B4
Seasalter Kent 21 E7
Seascale Cumb 56 F2
Seathorne Lincs 47 F9
Seathwaite Cumb 56 E4
Seathwaite Cumb 56 G4
Seatoller Cumb 56 E4
Seaton Corn 4 F4
Seaton Cumb 56 C2
Seaton Devon 8 F1
Seaton Durham 58 A4
Seaton E Yorks 53 E7
Seaton Northumb 63 F9
Seaton Rutland 36 F5
Seaton Burn T&W 63 F8
Seaton Carew Hrtlpl 58 D6
Seaton Delaval Northumb 63 F9
Seaton Ross E Yorks 52 E3
Seaton Sluice Northumb 63 F9
Seatown Aberds 88 B5
Seatown Dorset 8 E3
Seave Green N Yorks 59 F6
Seaview IoW 10 E5
Seaville Cumb 56 A3
Seavington St Mary Som 8 C3
Seavington St Michael Som 8 C3
Sebergham Cumb 56 B5
Seckington Warks 35 E8
Second Coast Highld 86 B2
Sedbergh Cumb 57 G8
Sedbury Glos 15 B11
Sedbusk N Yorks 57 G10
Sedgeberrow Worcs 27 E7
Sedgebrook Lincs 36 B4
Sedgefield Durham 58 D4
Sedgeford Norf 38 B3
Sedgehill Wilts 9 B7
Sedgley W Mid 34 F5
Sedgwick Cumb 57 H7
Sedlescombe E Sus 13 E6
Sedlescombe Street E Sus 13 E6
Seend Wilts 16 E6
Seend Cleeve Wilts 16 E6
Seer Green Bucks 18 B6
Seething Norf 39 F9
Sefton Mers 42 B6
Seghill Northumb 63 F8
Seifton Shrops 33 G10
Seighford Staffs 34 C4
Seilebost W Isles 90 H5
Seion Gwyn 41 D7
Seisdon Staffs 34 F4
Seisiadar W Isles 91 D10
Selattyn Shrops 33 B8
Selborne Hants 10 A6
Selby N Yorks 52 F2
Selham W Sus 11 B8
Selhurst London 19 E10
Selkirk Borders 70 H3
Sellack Hereford 26 F2
Sellafirth Shetland 96 D7
Sellibister Orkney 95 D8
Sellindge Kent 13 C9
Sellindge Lees Kent 13 C10
Selling Kent 21 F7
Sells Green Wilts 16 E6
Selly Oak W Mid 34 G6
Selmeston E Sus 12 F4
Selsdon London 19 E10
Selsey W Sus 11 E7
Selsfield Common W Sus 12 C2
Selsted Kent 21 G9
Selston Notts 45 G8
Selworthy Som 7 B8
Semblister Shetland 96 H5
Semer Suff 30 D6
Semington Wilts 16 E5
Semley Wilts 9 B7
Send Sur 19 F7
Send Marsh Sur 19 F7
Senghenydd Caerph 15 B7
Sennen Corn 2 G2
Sennen Cove Corn 2 G2
Sennybridge = Pont Senni Powys 24 F6
Serlby Notts 45 D10
Sessay N Yorks 51 B10
Setchey Norf 38 D2
Setley Hants 10 D2
Setter Shetland 96 E6
Setter Shetland 96 H5
Setter Shetland 96 J7
Settiscarth Orkney 95 G4
Settle N Yorks 50 C4
Settrington N Yorks 52 B4
Seven Kings London 19 C11
Seven Sisters Neath 24 H5
Sevenhampton Glos 27 F7
Sevenoaks Kent 20 F2
Sevenoaks Weald Kent 20 F2
Severn Beach S Glos 15 C11
Severn Stoke Worcs 26 D5
Severnhampton Swindon 17 B9
Sevington Kent 13 B9
Sewards End Essex 30 E2
Sewardstone Essex 19 B10
Sewardstonebury Essex 19 B10
Sewerby E Yorks 53 C7
Seworgan Corn 2 F6
Sewstern Leics 36 C4
Sezincote Glos 27 E8
Sgarasta Mhor W Isles 90 H5
Sgiogarstaigh W Isles 91 A10
Shabbington Bucks 28 H3
Shackerstone Leics 35 E9
Shackleford Sur 18 G6
Shade W Yorks 50 G5
Shadforth Durham 58 B4
Shadingfield Suff 39 G10
Shadoxhurst Kent 13 C8
Shadsworth Blackburn 50 G3
Shadwell Norf 38 G5
Shadwell W Yorks 51 F9
Shaftesbury Dorset 9 B7
Shafton S Yorks 45 A7
Shalbourne Wilts 17 E10
Shalcombe IoW 10 F2
Shalden Hants 18 G3
Shaldon Devon 5 D10
Shalfleet IoW 10 F3
Shalford Essex 30 F4
Shalford Sur 19 G7
Shalford Green Essex 30 F4
Shallowford Devon 6 B6
Shalmsford Street Kent 21 F7
Shalstone Bucks 28 E3
Shamley Green Sur 19 G7
Shandon Argyll 73 E11
Shandwick Highld 87 D11
Shangton Leics 36 F3
Shankhouse Northumb 63 F8
Shanklin IoW 10 F4
Shanquhar Aberds 88 E5
Shanzie Perth 76 B5
Shap Cumb 57 E7
Shapwick Dorset 9 D8
Shapwick Som 15 H10
Shardlow Derbys 35 B10
Shareshill Staffs 34 E5
Sharlston W Yorks 51 H9
Sharlston Common W Yorks 51 H9
Sharnbrook Bedford 28 C6
Sharnford Leics 35 F10
Sharoe Green Lancs 49 F5
Sharow N Yorks 51 B9
Sharp Street Norf 39 C9
Sharpenhoe C Beds 29 E7
Sharperton Northumb 62 C5
Sharpness Glos 16 A3
Sharpthorne W Sus 12 C2
Sharrington Norf 38 B6
Shatterford Worcs 34 G3
Shaugh Prior Devon 4 E6
Shavington Ches E 43 G10
Shaw Gtr Man 44 B3
Shaw W Berks 17 E11
Shaw Wilts 16 E5
Shaw Green Lancs 49 H5
Shaw Mills N Yorks 51 C8
Shawbury Shrops 34 C1
Shawdon Hall Northumb 62 B6
Shawell Leics 35 G11
Shawford Hants 10 B3
Shawforth Lancs 50 G4
Shawhead Dumfries 60 F4
Shawhill Dumfries 61 G8
Shawton S Lanark 68 F5
Shawtonhill S Lanark 68 F5
Shear Cross Wilts 16 G5
Shearington Dumfries 60 G6
Shearsby Leics 36 F2
Shebbear Devon 6 F3
Shebdon Staffs 34 C3
Shebster Highld 93 C13
Sheddens E Renf 68 E4
Shedfield Hants 10 C4
Sheen Staffs 44 F5
Sheepscar W Yorks 51 F9
Sheepscombe Glos 26 G5
Sheepstor Devon 5 E6
Sheepwash Devon 6 F3
Sheepway N Som 15 D10
Sheepy Magna Leics 35 E9
Sheepy Parva Leics 35 E9
Sheering Essex 30 G2
Sheerness Kent 20 D6
Sheet Hants 11 B6
Sheffield S Yorks 45 D7
Sheffield Bottom W Berks 18 E3
Sheffield Green E Sus 12 D3
Shefford C Beds 29 E8
Shefford Woodlands W Berks 17 D10
Sheigra Highld 92 C4
Sheinton Shrops 34 E2
Shelderton Shrops 33 H10
Sheldon Derbys 44 F5
Sheldon Devon 7 F10
Sheldon W Mid 35 G7
Sheldwich Kent 21 F7
Shelf W Yorks 51 G7
Shelfanger Norf 39 G7
Shelfield W Mid 34 E6
Shelfield Warks 27 B8
Shelford Notts 36 A2
Shellacres Northumb 71 F7
Shelley Essex 20 A2
Shelley Suff 31 E7
Shelley W Yorks 44 A6
Shellingford Oxon 17 B10
Shellow Bowells Essex 30 H3
Shelsley Beauchamp Worcs 26 B4
Shelsley Walsh Worcs 26 B4
Shelthorpe Leics 35 D11
Shelton Bedford 29 B7
Shelton Norf 39 F8
Shelton Notts 36 A3
Shelton Shrops 33 D10
Shelton Green Norf 39 F8
Shelve Shrops 33 F9
Shelwick Hereford 26 D2
Shenfield Essex 20 B3
Shenington Oxon 27 D10
Shenley Herts 19 A8
Shenley Brook End M Keynes 28 E5
Shenley Church End M Keynes 28 E5
Shenleybury Herts 19 A8
Shenmore Hereford 25 E10
Shennanton Dumfries 54 C6
Shenstone Staffs 35 E7
Shenstone Worcs 26 A5
Shenton Leics 35 E9
Shenval Highld 80 A6
Shenval Moray 82 A4
Shepeau Stow Lincs 37 D9
Shephall Herts 29 F9
Shepherd's Green Oxon 18 C4
Shepherd's Port Norf 38 B2
Shepherdswell Kent 21 G9
Shepley W Yorks 44 B5
Shepperdine S Glos 16 B3
Shepperton Sur 19 E7
Shepreth Cambs 29 D10
Shepshed Leics 35 D10
Shepton Beauchamp Som 8 C3
Shepton Mallet Som 16 G3
Shepton Montague Som 8 A5
Shepway Kent 20 F4
Sheraton Durham 58 C5
Sherborne Dorset 8 C5
Sherborne Glos 27 G8
Sherborne St John Hants 18 F3
Sherbourne Warks 27 B9
Sherburn Durham 58 B4
Sherburn N Yorks 52 B5
Sherburn Hill Durham 58 B4
Sherburn in Elmet N Yorks 51 F10
Shere Sur 19 G7
Shereford Norf 38 C4
Sherfield English Hants 10 B1
Sherfield on Loddon Hants 18 F3
Sherford Devon 5 G8
Sheriff Hutton N Yorks 52 C2
Sheriffhales Shrops 34 D3
Sheringham Norf 39 A7
Sherington M Keynes 28 D5
Shernal Green Worcs 26 B6
Shernborne Norf 38 B3
Sherrington Wilts 16 H6
Sherston Wilts 16 C5
Sherwood Green Devon 6 D4
Shettleston Glasgow 68 D5
Shevington Gtr Man 43 B8
Shevington Moor Gtr Man 43 A8
Shevington Vale Gtr Man 43 B8
Sheviock Corn 4 F4
Shide IoW 10 F3
Shiel Bridge Highld 80 B1
Shieldaig Highld 85 A13
Shieldaig Highld 85 C13
Shieldhill Dumfries 60 E6
Shieldhill Falk 69 C7
Shieldhill S Lanark 69 F9
Shielfoot Highld 79 E9
Shielhill Angus 77 B7
Shielhill Invclyd 73 F11
Shifford Oxon 17 A10
Shifnal Shrops 34 E3
Shilbottle Northumb 63 C7
Shildon Durham 58 D3
Shillingford Devon 7 D8
Shillingford Oxon 18 B2
Shillingford St George Devon 5 C10
Shillingstone Dorset 9 C7
Shillington C Beds 29 E8
Shillmoor Northumb 62 C4
Shilton Oxon 27 H9
Shilton Warks 35 G10
Shilvington Northumb 63 E7
Shimpling Norf 39 G7
Shimpling Suff 30 C5
Shimpling Street Suff 30 C5
Shincliffe Durham 58 B3
Shiney Row T&W 58 A4
Shinfield Wokingham 18 E4
Shingham Norf 38 E3
Shingle Street Suff 31 D10
Shinner's Bridge Devon 5 E8
Shinness Highld 93 H8
Shipbourne Kent 20 F2
Shipdham Norf 38 E5
Shipham Som 15 F10
Shiphay Torbay 5 E9
Shiplake Oxon 18 D4
Shipley Derbys 35 A10
Shipley Northumb 63 B7
Shipley Shrops 34 F4
Shipley W Sus 11 B10
Shipley W Yorks 51 F7
Shipley Shiels Northumb 62 D3
Shipmeadow Suff 39 G9
Shippea Hill Sta. Cambs 38 G2
Shippon Oxon 17 B11
Shipston-on-Stour Warks 27 D9
Shipton Glos 27 G7
Shipton N Yorks 52 D1
Shipton Shrops 34 F1
Shipton Bellinger Hants 17 G9
Shipton Gorge Dorset 8 E3
Shipton Green W Sus 11 D7
Shipton Moyne Glos 16 C5
Shipton on Cherwell Oxon 27 G11
Shipton Solers Glos 27 G7
Shipton-under-Wychwood Oxon 27 G9
Shiptonthorpe E Yorks 52 E4
Shirburn Oxon 18 B3
Shirdley Hill Lancs 42 A6
Shirebrook Derbys 45 F9
Shiregreen S Yorks 45 C7
Shirehampton Bristol 15 D11
Shiremoor T&W 63 F9
Shirenewton Mon 15 B10
Shireoaks Notts 45 D9
Shirkoak Kent 13 C8
Shirl Heath Hereford 25 C11
Shirland Derbys 45 G7
Shirley Derbys 35 A8
Shirley London 19 E10
Shirley Soton 10 C3
Shirley W Mid 35 H7
Shirrell Heath Hants 10 C4
Shirwell Devon 6 C4
Shirwell Cross Devon 6 C4
Shiskine N Ayrs 66 D2
Shobdon Hereford 25 B11
Shobnall Staffs 35 C8
Shobrooke Devon 7 F7
Shoby Leics 36 D2
Shocklach Ches W 43 H7
Shoeburyness Southend 20 C6
Sholden Kent 21 F10
Sholing Soton 10 C3
Shoot Hill Shrops 33 D10
Shop Corn 3 B7
Shop Corn 6 E1
Shop Corner Suff 31 E9
Shore Mill Highld 87 E10
Shoreditch London 19 C10
Shoreham Kent 20 E2
Shoreham-By-Sea W Sus 11 D11
Shoresdean Northumb 71 F8
Shoreswood Northumb 71 F8
Shoreton Highld 87 E9
Shorncote Glos 17 B7
Shorne Kent 20 D3
Short Heath W Mid 34 E5
Shortacombe Devon 4 C6
Shortgate E Sus 12 E3
Shortlanesend Corn 3 E7
Shortlees E Ayrs 67 C7
Shortstown Bedford 29 D7
Shorwell IoW 10 F3
Shoscombe Bath 16 F4
Shotatton Shrops 33 C9
Shotesham Norf 39 F8
Shotgate Essex 20 B4
Shotley Suff 31 E9
Shotley Bridge Durham 58 A1
Shotley Gate Suff 31 E9
Shotleyfield Northumb 58 A1
Shottenden Kent 21 F7
Shottermill Sur 11 A7
Shottery Warks 27 C8
Shotteswell Warks 27 D11
Shottisham Suff 31 D10
Shottle Derbys 45 H7
Shottlegate Derbys 45 H7
Shotton Durham 58 C5
Shotton Flint 42 F6
Shotton Northumb 71 G7
Shotton Colliery Durham 58 B4
Shotts N Lanark 69 D7
Shotwick Ches W 42 E6
Shouldham Norf 38 E2
Shouldham Thorpe Norf 38 E2
Shoulton Worcs 26 C5
Shover's Green E Sus 12 C5
Shrawardine Shrops 33 D10
Shrawley Worcs 26 B5
Shrewley Common Warks 27 B9
Shrewsbury Shrops 33 D10
Shrewton Wilts 17 G7
Shripney W Sus 11 D8
Shrivenham Oxon 17 C9
Shropham Norf 38 F5
Shrub End Essex 30 F6
Shucknall Hereford 26 D2
Shudy Camps Cambs 30 D3
Shulishadermor Highld 85 D9
Shurdington Glos 26 G6
Shurlock Row Windsor 18 D5
Shurrery Highld 93 D13
Shurrery Lodge Highld 93 D13
Shurton Som 7 B11
Shustoke Warks 35 F8
Shute Devon 7 F7
Shute Devon 8 E1
Shutford Oxon 27 D10
Shuthonger Glos 26 E5
Shutlanger Northants 28 C4
Shuttington Warks 35 E8
Shuttlewood Derbys 45 E8
Siabost bho Dheas W Isles 90 C7
Siabost bho Thuath W Isles 90 C7
Siadar W Isles 91 B8
Siadar Iarach W Isles 91 B8
Siadar Uarach W Isles 91 B8
Sibbaldbie Dumfries 61 E7
Sibbertoft Northants 36 G2
Sibdon Carwood Shrops 33 G10
Sibford Ferris Oxon 27 E10
Sibford Gower Oxon 27 E10
Sible Hedingham Essex 30 E4
Sibsey Lincs 47 G7
Sibson Cambs 37 F6
Sibson Leics 35 E9
Sibthorpe Notts 45 H11
Sibton Suff 31 B10
Sibton Green Suff 31 A10
Sicklesmere Suff 30 B5
Sicklinghall N Yorks 51 E9
Sid Devon 7 H10
Sidbury Devon 7 G10
Sidbury Shrops 34 G2
Sidcot N Som 15 F10
Sidcup London 19 D11
Siddick Cumb 56 C2
Siddington Ches E 44 E2
Siddington Glos 17 B7
Sidemoor Worcs 26 A6
Sidestrand Norf 39 B8
Sidford Devon 7 G10
Sidlesham W Sus 11 E7
Sidley E Sus 12 F6
Sidlow Sur 19 G9
Sidmouth Devon 7 H10
Sigford Devon 5 D8
Sigglesthorne E Yorks 53 E7
Sighthill Edin 69 C10
Sigingstone V Glam 14 D5
Signet Oxon 27 G9
Silchester Hants 18 E3
Sildinis W Isles 91 F7
Sileby Leics 36 D1
Silecroft Cumb 49 A1
Silfield Norf 39 F7
Silian Ceredig 23 A10
Silk Willoughby Lincs 37 A6
Silkstone S Yorks 44 B6
Silkstone Common S Yorks 44 B6
Silloth Cumb 56 A3
Sills Northumb 62 C4
Sillyearn Moray 88 C5
Siloh Carms 24 E4
Silpho N Yorks 59 G10
Silsden W Yorks 50 E6
Silsoe C Beds 29 E7
Silver End Essex 30 G5
Silverburn Midloth 69 D11
Silverdale Lancs 49 B4
Silverdale Staffs 44 H2
Silvergate Norf 39 C7
Silverhill E Sus 13 E6
Silverley's Green Suff 39 H8
Silverstone Northants 28 D3
Silverton Devon 7 F8
Silvington Shrops 34 H2
Silwick Shetland 96 J4
Simmondley Derbys 44 C4
Simonburn Northumb 62 F4
Simonsbath Som 7 C6
Simonstone Lancs 50 F3
Simprim Borders 71 F7
Simpson M Keynes 28 E5
Simpson Cross Pembs 22 E3
Sinclair's Hill Borders 71 E7
Sinclairston E Ayrs 67 E7
Sinderby N Yorks 51 A9
Sinderhope Northumb 57 A10
Sindlesham Wokingham 18 E4
Singdean Borders 61 C11
Singleborough Bucks 28 E4
Singleton Lancs 49 F3
Singleton W Sus 11 C7
Singlewell Kent 20 D3
Sinkhurst Green Kent 13 B7
Sinnahard Aberds 82 B6
Sinnington N Yorks 59 H8
Sinton Green Worcs 26 B5
Sipson London 19 D7
Sirhowy Bl Gwent 25 G8
Sisland Norf 39 F9
Sissinghurst Kent 13 C6
Sisterpath Borders 70 F6
Siston S Glos 16 D3
Sithney Corn 2 G5
Sittingbourne Kent 20 E6
Six Ashes Staffs 34 G3
Six Hills Leics 36 C2
Six Mile Bottom Cambs 30 C2
Sixhills Lincs 46 D5
Sixpenny Handley Dorset 9 C8
Sizewell Suff 31 B11
Skail Highld 93 E10
Skaill Orkney 95 E5
Skaill Orkney 95 G3
Skaill Orkney 95 H6
Skares E Ayrs 67 E8
Skateraw E Loth 70 C6
Skaw Shetland 96 G7
Skeabost Highld 85 D9
Skeabrae Orkney 95 F3
Skeeby N Yorks 58 F3
Skeffington Leics 36 E3
Skeffling E Yorks 53 H9
Skegby Notts 45 F8
Skegness Lincs 47 F9
Skelberry Shetland 96 M5
Skelbo Highld 87 B10
Skelbrooke S Yorks 45 A9
Skeldyke Lincs 37 B9
Skellingthorpe Lincs 46 E3
Skellister Shetland 96 H6
Skellow S Yorks 45 A9
Skelmanthorpe W Yorks 44 A6
Skelmersdale Lancs 43 B7
Skelmonae Aberds 89 E8
Skelmorlie N Ayrs 73 G10
Skelmuir Aberds 89 D9
Skelpick Highld 93 D10
Skelton Cumb 56 C6
Skelton E Yorks 52 G3
Skelton N Yorks 58 F1
Skelton Redcar 59 E7
Skelton York 52 D1
Skelton-on-Ure N Yorks 51 C9
Skelwick Orkney 95 D5
Skelwith Bridge Cumb 56 F5
Skendleby Lincs 47 F8
Skene Ho. Aberds 83 C9
Skenfrith Mon 25 F11
Skerne E Yorks 52 D6
Skeroblingarry Argyll 65 F8
Skerray Highld 93 C9
Skerton Lancs 49 C4
Sketchley Leics 35 F10
Sketty Swansea 14 B2
Skewen Neath 14 B3
Skewsby N Yorks 52 B2
Skeyton Norf 39 C8
Skiag Bridge Highld 92 G5
Skibo Castle Highld 87 C10
Skidbrooke Lincs 47 C8
Skidbrooke North End Lincs 47 C8
Skidby E Yorks 52 F6
Skilgate Som 7 D8
Skillington Lincs 36 C4
Skinburness Cumb 61 H7
Skinflats Falk 69 B8
Skinidin Highld 84 D7
Skinnet Highld 93 C8
Skinningrove Redcar 59 D8
Skipness Argyll 73 H7
Skippool Lancs 49 E3
Skipsea E Yorks 53 D7
Skipsea Brough E Yorks 53 D7
Skipton N Yorks 50 D5
Skipton-on-Swale N Yorks 51 B9
Skipwith N Yorks 52 F2
Skirbeck Lincs 37 A9
Skirbeck Quarter Lincs 37 A9
Skirlaugh E Yorks 53 F7
Skirling Borders 69 G9
Skirmett Bucks 18 C4
Skirpenbeck E Yorks 52 D3
Skirwith Cumb 57 C8
Skirza Highld 94 D5
Skulamus Highld 85 F11
Skullomie Highld 93 C9
Skyborry Green Shrops 25 A9
Skye of Curr Highld 82 A1
Skyreholme N Yorks 51 C6
Slackhall Derbys 44 D4
Slackhead Moray 88 B4
Slad Glos 26 H5
Slade Devon 6 B4
Slade Pembs 22 E4
Slade Green London 20 D2
Slaggyford Northumb 57 A8
Slaidburn Lancs 50 D3
Slaithwaite W Yorks 44 A4
Slaley Northumb 62 H5
Slamannan Falk 69 C7
Slapton Bucks 28 F6
Slapton Devon 5 G9
Slapton Northants 28 D3
Slatepit Dale Derbys 45 F7
Slattocks Gtr Man 44 B2
Slaugham W Sus 12 D1
Slaughterford Wilts 16 D5
Slawston Leics 36 F3
Sleaford Hants 18 H5
Sleaford Lincs 46 H4
Sleagill Cumb 57 E7
Sleapford Telford 34 D2
Sledge Green Worcs 26 E5
Sledmere E Yorks 52 C5
Sleightholme Durham 57 E11
Sleights N Yorks 59 F9
Slepe Dorset 9 E8
Slickly Highld 94 D4
Sliddery N Ayrs 66 D2
Sligachan Hotel Highld 85 F9
Slimbridge Glos 16 A4
Slindon Staffs 34 B4
Slindon W Sus 11 D8
Slinfold W Sus 11 A10
Sling Gwyn 41 D8
Slingsby N Yorks 52 B2
Slioch Aberds 88 E5
Slip End C Beds 29 G7
Slip End Herts 29 E9
Slipton Northants 36 H5
Slitting Mill Staffs 34 D6
Slochd Highld 81 A10
Slockavullin Argyll 73 D7
Sloley Norf 39 C8
Sloothby Lincs 47 E8
Slough Slough 18 D6
Slough Green W Sus 12 D1
Sluggan Highld 81 A10
Slumbay Highld 85 E13
Slyfield Sur 18 F6

Place	Ref	Place	Ref	Place	Ref	Place	Ref
Slyne Lancs	49 C4	Southburgh Norf	38 E5	Stainburn Cumb	56 D2	Stapleford Herts	29 G10
Small Dole W Sus	11 C11	Southchurch		Stainburn N Yorks	51 E8	Stapleford Leics	36 D4
Small Hythe Kent	13 C7	Southcott	17 F8	Stainby Lincs	36 C5	Stapleford Lincs	46 G2
Smallbridge Gtr Man	50 H5	Southcourt Bucks	28 G5	Staincross S Yorks	45 A7	Stapleford Notts	35 B10
Smallburgh Norf	39 C9	Southdean Borders	62 C2	Staindrop Durham	58 D2	Stapleford Wilts	17 H7
Smallburn Aberds	89 D10	Southdene Mers	43 C7	Staines-upon-		Stapleford Abbotts	
Smallburn E Ayrs	68 H5	Southend Argyll	65 H7	Thames Sur	19 D7	Essex	20 B2
Smallholm Dumfries	61 F7	Southend W Berks	18 D2	Stainfield Lincs	37 C6	Stapleford Tawney	
Smannell Hants	17 G10	South End Bucks	28 F5	Stainfield Lincs	46 E5	Essex	20 B2

Thistleton Rutland 36 D5
Thistley Green Suff 38 H2
Thixendale N Yorks 52 C4
Thockrington Northumb 62 F5
Tholomas Drove Cambs 37 E9
Tholthorpe N Yorks 51 C10
Thomas Chapel Pembs 22 F6
Thomas Close Cumb 56 B6
Thomastown Aberds 88 E5
Thompson Norf 38 F5
Thomshill Moray 88 C2
Thong Kent 20 D3
Thongsbridge W Yorks 44 B5
Thoralby N Yorks 58 H1
Thoresway Lincs 46 C5
Thorganby Lincs 46 C6
Thorganby N Yorks 52 E2
Thorgill N Yorks 59 G8
Thorington Suff 31 A11
Thorington Street Suff 31 E7
Thorlby N Yorks 50 D5
Thorley Herts 29 G11
Thorley Street Herts 29 G11
Thorley Street IoW 10 F2
Thormanby N Yorks 51 B10
Thornaby-on-Tees Stockton 58 E5
Thornage Norf 38 B6
Thornborough Bucks 28 E4
Thornborough N Yorks 51 B8
Thornbury Devon 6 F3
Thornbury Hereford 26 C3
Thornbury S Glos 16 B3
Thornbury W Yorks 51 F7
Thornby Northants 36 H2
Thorncliffe Staffs 44 G4
Thorncombe Dorset 8 D2
Thorncombe Dorset 9 D7
Thorncombe Street Sur 19 G7
Thorncote Green C Beds 29 D8
Thorncross IoW 10 F3
Thorndon Suff 31 B8
Thorndon Cross Devon 6 G4
Thorne S Yorks 45 A10
Thorne St Margaret Som 7 D9
Thorner W Yorks 51 E9
Thorney Notts 46 E2
Thorney Pboro 37 E8
Thorney Crofts E Yorks 53 G8
Thorney Green Suff 31 B7
Thorney Hill Hants 9 E10
Thorney Toll Pboro 37 E9
Thornfalcon Som 8 B1
Thornford Dorset 8 C5
Thorngumbald E Yorks 53 G8
Thornham Norf 38 A3
Thornham Magna Suff 31 A8
Thornham Parva Suff 31 A8
Thornhaugh Pboro 37 E6
Thornhill Cardiff 15 C7
Thornhill Cumb 56 F2
Thornhill Derbys 44 D5
Thornhill Dumfries 60 D4
Thornhill Soton 10 C3
Thornhill Stirling 75 H9
Thornhill W Yorks 51 H8
Thornhill Edge W Yorks 51 H8
Thornhill Lees W Yorks 51 H8
Thornholme E Yorks 53 C7
Thornley Durham 58 C4
Thornley Durham 58 C2
Thornliebank E Renf 68 E4
Thorns Suff 30 C4
Thorns Green Ches E 43 D10
Thornsett Derbys 44 D4
Thornthwaite Cumb 56 D4
Thornthwaite N Yorks 51 D7
Thornton Angus 76 C6
Thornton Bucks 28 E4
Thornton E Yorks 52 E3
Thornton Fife 76 H5
Thornton Lancs 49 E3
Thornton Leics 35 E10
Thornton Lincs 46 F6
Thornton Mbro 58 E5
Thornton Mers 42 B6
Thornton Northumb 71 F8
Thornton Pembs 22 F4
Thornton W Yorks 51 F7
Thornton Curtis N Lincs 53 H6
Thornton Heath London 19 E10
Thornton Hough Mers 42 D6
Thornton in Craven N Yorks 50 E5
Thornton-le-Beans N Yorks 58 G4
Thornton-le-Clay N Yorks 52 C2
Thornton-le-Dale N Yorks 52 A4
Thornton le Moor Lincs 46 C4
Thornton-le-Moor N Yorks 58 H4
Thornton-le-Moors Ches W 43 E7
Thornton-le-Street N Yorks 58 H5
Thornton Rust N Yorks 57 H11
Thornton Steward N Yorks 58 H2
Thornton Watlass N Yorks 58 H3
Thorntonhall S Lanark 68 E4
Thorntonloch E Loth 70 C6
Thorntonpark Northumb 71 F8
Thornwood Common Essex 19 A11
Thornydykes Borders 70 F5
Thoroton Notts 36 A3
Thorp Arch W Yorks 51 E10
Thorpe Derbys 44 G5
Thorpe E Yorks 52 E5
Thorpe Lincs 47 D8
Thorpe N Yorks 50 C6
Thorpe Norf 39 F10
Thorpe Notts 45 H11
Thorpe Sur 19 E7
Thorpe Abbotts Norf 39 H7
Thorpe Acre Leics 35 C11
Thorpe Arnold Leics 36 C3
Thorpe Audlin W Yorks 51 H10
Thorpe Bassett N Yorks 52 B4
Thorpe Bay Southend 20 C6
Thorpe by Water Rutland 36 F4
Thorpe Common Suff 31 E9
Thorpe Constantine Staffs 35 E8
Thorpe Culvert Lincs 47 F8
Thorpe End Norf 39 D8
Thorpe Fendykes Lincs 47 F8
Thorpe Green Essex 31 F8
Thorpe Green Suff 30 C6
Thorpe Hesley S Yorks 45 C7
Thorpe in Balne S Yorks 45 A9
Thorpe in the Fallows Lincs 46 D3
Thorpe Langton Leics 36 F3
Thorpe Larches Durham 58 D4
Thorpe-le-Soken Essex 31 F8
Thorpe le Street E Yorks 52 E4
Thorpe Malsor Northants 36 H4
Thorpe Mandeville Northants 28 D2
Thorpe Market Norf 39 B8
Thorpe Marriot Norf 39 D7
Thorpe Morieux Suff 30 C6
Thorpe on the Hill Lincs 46 F3
Thorpe St Andrew Norf 39 E8
Thorpe St Peter Lincs 47 F8
Thorpe Salvin S Yorks 45 D9
Thorpe Satchville Leics 36 D3
Thorpe Thewles Stockton 58 D5
Thorpe Tilney Lincs 46 G5
Thorpe Underwood N Yorks 51 D10
Thorpe Waterville Northants 36 G6
Thorpe Willoughby N Yorks 52 F1
Thorpeness Suff 31 C11
Thorrington Essex 31 F7
Thorverton Devon 7 F8
Thrandeston Suff 39 H7
Thrapston Northants 36 H5
Thrashbush N Lanark 68 D6
Threapland Cumb 56 C3
Threapland N Yorks 50 C5
Threapwood Ches W 43 H7
Threapwood Staffs 34 A6
Three Ashes Hereford 26 F2
Three Bridges W Sus 12 C1
Three Burrows Corn 2 E6
Three Chimneys Kent 13 C7
Three Cocks Powys 25 E8
Three Crosses Swansea 23 G10
Three Cups Corner E Sus 12 D5
Three Holes Norf 37 E11
Three Leg Cross E Sus 12 C5
Three Legged Cross Dorset 9 D9
Three Oaks E Sus 13 E7
Threehammer Common Norf 39 D9
Threekingham Lincs 37 B6
Threemile Cross Wokingham 18 E4
Threemilestone Corn 3 E6
Threemiletown W Loth 69 C9
Threlkeld Cumb 56 D5
Threshfield N Yorks 50 C5
Thrigby Norf 39 D10
Thringarth Durham 57 D11
Thringstone Leics 35 D10
Thrintoft N Yorks 58 G4
Thriplow Cambs 29 D11
Throckenholt Lincs 37 E9
Throcking Herts 29 E10
Throckley T&W 63 G7
Throckmorton Worcs 26 D6
Throphill Northumb 63 E7
Thropton Northumb 62 C6
Throsk Stirling 69 A7
Throwleigh Devon 6 G5
Throwley Kent 20 F6
Thrumpton Notts 35 B11
Thrumster Highld 94 F5
Thrunton Northumb 62 B6
Thrupp Glos 16 A5
Thrupp Oxon 27 G11
Thrushelton Devon 4 C5
Thrussington Leics 36 D2
Thruxton Hants 17 G9
Thruxton Hereford 25 E11
Thrybergh S Yorks 45 C8
Thulston Derbys 35 B10
Thundergay N Ayrs 66 B1
Thundersley Essex 20 C4
Thundridge Herts 29 G10
Thurcaston Leics 36 D1
Thurcroft S Yorks 45 D8
Thurgarton Norf 39 B7
Thurgarton Notts 45 H10
Thurgoland S Yorks 44 B6
Thurlaston Leics 35 F11
Thurlaston Warks 27 A11
Thurlbear Som 8 B1
Thurlby Lincs 37 D7
Thurlby Lincs 46 F3
Thurleigh Bedford 29 C7
Thurlestone Devon 5 G7
Thurloxton Som 8 A1
Thurlstone S Yorks 44 B6
Thurlton Norf 39 F10
Thurlwood Ches E 44 G2
Thurmaston Leics 36 E2
Thurnby Leics 36 E2
Thurne Norf 39 D10
Thurnham Kent 20 F5
Thurnham Lancs 49 D4
Thurning Norf 39 C6
Thurning Northants 37 G6
Thurnscoe S Yorks 45 B8
Thurnscoe East S Yorks 45 B8
Thursby Cumb 56 A5
Thursford Norf 38 B5
Thursley Sur 18 H6
Thurso Highld 94 D3
Thurso East Highld 94 D3
Thurstaston Mers 42 D5
Thurston Suff 30 B6
Thurstonfield Cumb 61 H9
Thurstonland W Yorks 44 A5
Thurton Norf 39 E9
Thurvaston Derbys 35 B8
Thuxton Norf 38 E6
Thwaite N Yorks 57 G10
Thwaite Suff 31 B8
Thwaite St Mary Norf 39 F9
Thwaites W Yorks 51 E6
Thwaites Brow W Yorks 51 E6
Thwing E Yorks 53 B6
Tibbermore Perth 76 E3
Tibberton Glos 26 F4
Tibberton Telford 34 C2
Tibberton Worcs 26 C6
Tibenham Norf 39 G7
Tibshelf Derbys 45 F8
Tibthorpe E Yorks 52 D5
Ticehurst E Sus 12 C5
Tichborne Hants 10 A4
Tickencote Rutland 36 E5
Tickenham N Som 15 D10
Tickhill S Yorks 45 C9
Ticklerton Shrops 33 F10
Ticknall Derbys 35 C9
Tickton E Yorks 53 E6
Tidcombe Wilts 17 F9
Tiddington Oxon 18 A3
Tiddington Warks 27 C9
Tidebrook E Sus 12 D5
Tideford Corn 4 F4
Tideford Cross Corn 4 E4
Tidenham Glos 16 B2
Tideswell Derbys 44 E5
Tidmarsh W Berks 18 D3
Tidmington Warks 27 E9
Tidpit Hants 9 C9
Tidworth Wilts 17 G9
Tiers Cross Pembs 22 E4
Tiffield Northants 28 C3
Tifty Aberds 89 D7
Tigerton Angus 77 A8
Tigh-na-Blair Perth 75 F10
Tighnabruaich Argyll 73 F8
Tighnafiline Highld 91 J13
Tigley Devon 5 E8
Tilbrook Cambs 29 B7
Tilbury Thurrock 20 D3
Tilbury Juxta Clare Essex 30 D4
Tile Cross W Mid 35 G7
Tile Hill W Mid 35 H8
Tilehurst Reading 18 D3
Tilford Sur 18 G5
Tilgate W Sus 12 C1
Tilgate Forest Row W Sus 12 C1
Tillathrowie Aberds 88 E4
Tilley Shrops 33 C11
Tillicoultry Clack 76 H2
Tillingham Essex 20 A6
Tillington Hereford 25 D11
Tillington W Sus 11 B8
Tillington Common Hereford 25 D11
Tillyarblet Angus 83 G7
Tillybirloch Aberds 83 C8
Tillycorthie Aberds 89 F9
Tillydrine Aberds 83 D8
Tillyfour Aberds 83 B7
Tillyfourie Aberds 83 B8
Tillygarmond Aberds 83 D8
Tillygreig Aberds 89 F8
Tillykerrie Aberds 89 F8
Tilmanstone Kent 21 F10
Tilney All Saints Norf 38 D1
Tilney High End Norf 38 D1
Tilney St Lawrence Norf 37 D11
Tilshead Wilts 17 G7
Tilstock Shrops 33 B11
Tilston Ches W 43 G7
Tilstone Fearnall Ches W 43 F8
Tilsworth C Beds 28 F6
Tilton on the Hill Leics 36 E3
Timberland Lincs 46 G5
Timbersbrook Ches E 44 F2
Timberscombe Som 7 B8
Timble N Yorks 51 D7
Timperley Gtr Man 43 D10
Timsbury Bath 16 F3
Timsbury Hants 10 B2
Timsgearraidh W Isles 90 D5
Timworth Green Suff 30 B5
Tincleton Dorset 9 E6
Tindale Cumb 62 H2
Tingewick Bucks 28 E3
Tingley W Yorks 51 G8
Tingrith C Beds 29 E7
Tingwall Orkney 95 F4
Tinhay Devon 4 C4
Tinshill W Yorks 51 F8
Tinsley S Yorks 45 C8
Tintagel Corn 4 C1
Tintern Parva Mon 15 A11
Tintinhull Som 8 C4
Tintwistle Derbys 44 C4
Tinwald Dumfries 60 E6
Tinwell Rutland 36 E6
Tipperty Aberds 89 F9
Tipsend Norf 37 F11
Tipton W Mid 34 F5
Tipton St John Devon 7 G9
Tiptree Essex 30 G5
Tir-y-dail Carms 24 G3
Tirabad Powys 24 D5
Tiraghoil Argyll 78 J6
Tirley Glos 26 F5
Tirphil Caerph 15 A7
Tirril Cumb 57 D7
Tisbury Wilts 9 B8
Tisman's Common W Sus 11 A9
Tissington Derbys 44 G5
Titchberry Devon 6 D1
Titchfield Hants 10 D4
Titchmarsh Northants 36 H6
Titchwell Norf 38 A3
Tithby Notts 36 B2
Titley Hereford 25 B10
Titlington Northumb 63 B7
Titsey Sur 19 F11
Tittensor Staffs 34 B4
Tittleshall Norf 38 C4
Tiverton Ches W 43 F8
Tiverton Devon 7 E8
Tivetshall St Margaret Norf 39 G7
Tivetshall St Mary Norf 39 G7
Tividale W Mid 34 F5
Tivy Dale S Yorks 44 B6
Tixall Staffs 34 C5
Tixover Rutland 36 E5
Toab Orkney 95 H6
Toab Shetland 96 M5
Toadmoor Derbys 45 G7
Tobermory Argyll 79 F8
Toberonochy Argyll 72 C6
Tobha Mor W Isles 84 E2
Tobhtarol W Isles 90 D6
Tobson W Isles 90 D6
Tocher Aberds 89 E6
Tockenham Wilts 17 D7
Tockenham Wick Wilts 17 C7
Tockholes Blackburn 50 G2
Tockington S Glos 16 C3
Tockwith N Yorks 51 D10
Todber Dorset 9 B7
Todding Hereford 33 H10
Toddington C Beds 29 F7
Toddington Glos 27 E7
Todenham Glos 27 E9
Todhills Cumb 61 G9
Todlachie Aberds 83 B8
Todmorden W Yorks 50 G5
Todrig Borders 61 B10
Todwick S Yorks 45 D8
Toft Cambs 29 C10
Toft Lincs 37 D6
Toft Hill Durham 58 D2
Toft Hill Lincs 46 F6
Toft Monks Norf 39 F10
Toft next Newton Lincs 46 D4
Toftrees Norf 38 C4
Tofts Highld 94 D5
Toftwood Norf 38 D5
Togston Northumb 63 C8
Tokavaig Highld 85 G11
Tokers Green Oxon 18 D4
Tolastadh a Chaolais W Isles 90 D6
Tolastadh bho Thuath W Isles 91 C10
Toll Bar S Yorks 45 B9
Toll End W Mid 34 F5
Toll of Birness Aberds 89 E10
Tolland Som 7 C10
Tollard Royal Wilts 9 C8
Tollbar End W Mid 35 H9
Toller Fratrum Dorset 8 E4
Toller Porcorum Dorset 8 E4
Tollerton N Yorks 51 C11
Tollerton Notts 36 B2
Tollesbury Essex 30 G6
Tolleshunt D'Arcy Essex 30 G6
Tolleshunt Major Essex 30 G6
Tolm W Isles 91 D9
Tolpuddle Dorset 9 E6
Tolvah Highld 81 D10
Tolworth London 19 E8
Tomatin Highld 81 A10
Tombreck Highld 87 H9
Tomchrasky Highld 80 B4
Tomdoun Highld 80 C3
Tomich Highld 80 A5
Tomich Highld 87 D9
Tomich House Highld 87 G8
Tomintoul Aberds 82 D3
Tomintoul Moray 82 B3
Tomnaven Moray 88 E4
Tomnavoulin Moray 82 A4
Ton-Pentre Rhondda 14 B5
Tonbridge Kent 20 G2
Tondu Bridgend 14 C4
Tonfanau Gwyn 32 E1
Tong Shrops 34 E3
Tong W Yorks 51 F8
Tong Norton Shrops 34 E3
Tonge Leics 35 C10
Tongham Sur 18 G5
Tongland Dumfries 55 D9
Tongue Highld 93 D8
Tongue End Lincs 37 D7
Tongwynlais Cardiff 15 C7
Tonna Neath 14 B3
Tonwell Herts 29 G10
Tonypandy Rhondda 14 B5
Tonyrefail Rhondda 14 C6
Toot Baldon Oxon 18 A2
Toot Hill Essex 20 A2
Toothill Hants 10 C2
Top of Hebers Gtr Man 44 B2
Topcliffe N Yorks 51 B10
Topcroft Norf 39 F8
Topcroft Street Norf 39 F8
Toppesfield Essex 30 E4
Toppings Gtr Man 43 A10
Topsham Devon 5 C10
Torbay Torbay 5 F10
Torbeg N Ayrs 66 D2
Torboll Farm Highld 87 B10
Torbrex Stirling 68 A6
Torbryan Devon 5 E9
Torcross Devon 5 G9
Tore Highld 87 F9
Torinturk Argyll 73 G7
Torksey Lincs 46 E2
Torlum W Isles 84 C2
Torlundy Highld 80 F3
Tormarton S Glos 16 D4
Tormisdale Argyll 64 C2
Tormitchell S Ayrs 66 G5
Tormore N Ayrs 66 C1
Tornagrain Highld 87 G10
Tornahaish Aberds 82 C4
Tornaveen Aberds 83 C8
Torness Highld 81 A7
Toronto Durham 58 C2
Torpenhow Cumb 56 C4
Torphichen W Loth 69 C8
Torphins Aberds 83 C8
Torpoint Corn 4 F5
Torquay Torbay 5 E10
Torquhan Borders 70 F3
Torran Argyll 73 C7
Torran Highld 85 D10
Torran Highld 87 D10
Torrance E Dunb 68 C5
Torrans Argyll 78 J7
Torranyard N Ayrs 67 B6
Torre Torbay 5 E10
Torridon Highld 86 F2
Torridon Ho. Highld 85 C13
Torrin Highld 85 F10
Torrisdale Highld 93 C9
Torrisdale-Square Argyll 65 E8
Torrish Highld 93 H12
Torrisholme Lancs 49 C4
Torroble Highld 93 J8
Torry Aberdeen 83 C11
Torry Aberds 88 E4
Torryburn Fife 69 B9
Torterston Aberds 89 D10
Torthorwald Dumfries 60 F6
Tortington W Sus 11 D9
Tortworth S Glos 16 B4
Torvaig Highld 85 D9
Torver Cumb 56 G4
Torwood Falk 69 B7
Torworth Notts 45 D10
Tosberry Devon 6 D1
Toscaig Highld 85 E12
Toseland Cambs 29 B9
Tosside N Yorks 50 D3
Tostock Suff 30 B6
Totaig Highld 84 C7
Totaig Highld 85 F13
Tote Highld 85 D9
Totegan Highld 93 C11
Tothill Lincs 47 D8
Totland IoW 10 F2
Totnes Devon 5 E9
Toton Notts 35 B11
Totronald Argyll 78 F4
Totscore Highld 85 B8
Tottenham London 19 B10
Tottenhill Norf 38 D2
Tottenhill Row Norf 38 D2
Totteridge London 19 B9
Totternhoe C Beds 28 F6
Tottington Gtr Man 43 A10
Totton Hants 10 C2
Touchen End Windsor 18 D5
Tournaig Highld 91 J13
Toux Aberds 89 C9
Tovil Kent 20 F4
Tow Law Durham 58 C2
Toward Argyll 73 G10
Towcester Northants 28 D3
Towednack Corn 2 F3
Tower End Norf 38 D2
Towersey Oxon 28 H4
Towie Aberds 82 B6
Towie Aberds 89 B8
Towiemore Moray 88 D3
Town End Cambs 37 F10
Town End Cumb 49 A4
Town Row E Sus 12 C4
Town Yetholm Borders 71 H7
Townend W Dunb 68 C3
Towngate Lincs 37 D7
Townhead Cumb 57 C7
Townhead Dumfries 55 E9
Townhead S Ayrs 66 F5
Townhead S Yorks 44 B5
Townhead of Greenlaw Dumfries 55 C10
Townhill Fife 69 B10
Townsend Bucks 28 H4
Townsend Herts 29 H8
Townshend Corn 2 F4
Towthorpe York 52 D2
Towton N Yorks 51 F10
Towyn Conwy 42 E2
Toxteth Mers 42 D6
Toynton All Saints Lincs 47 F7
Toynton Fen Side Lincs 47 F7
Toynton St Peter Lincs 47 F8
Toy's Hill Kent 19 F11
Trabboch E Ayrs 67 D7
Traboe Corn 2 G6
Tradespark Highld 87 F11
Tradespark Orkney 95 H5
Trafford Park Gtr Man 43 C10
Trallong Powys 24 F6
Tranent E Loth 70 C3
Tranmere Mers 42 D6
Trantlebeg Highld 93 D11
Trantlemore Highld 93 D11
Tranwell Northumb 63 E7
Trapp Carms 24 G3
Traprain E Loth 70 C4
Traquair Borders 70 G2
Trawden Lancs 50 F5
Trawsfynydd Gwyn 41 G9
Tre-Gibbon Rhondda 24 H6
Tre-Taliesin Ceredig 32 F2
Tre-vaughan Carms 23 D8
Tre-wyn Mon 25 F10
Trealaw Rhondda 14 B6
Treales Lancs 49 F4
Trearddur Anglesey 40 C4
Treaslane Highld 85 C8
Trebanog Rhondda 14 B6
Trebanos Neath 14 A3
Trebartha Corn 4 D3
Trebarwith Corn 4 C1
Trebetherick Corn 3 B8
Treborough Som 7 C9
Trebudannon Corn 3 C7
Trebullett Corn 4 D4
Treburley Corn 4 D4
Trebyan Corn 4 E1
Trecastle Powys 24 F5
Trecenydd Caerph 15 C7
Trecwn Pembs 22 C4
Trecynon Rhondda 14 A5
Tredavoe Corn 2 G3
Treddiog Pembs 22 D3
Tredegar Bl Gwent 25 H8
Tredegar Newydd = New Tredegar Caerph 15 A7
Tredington Glos 26 F6
Tredington Warks 27 D9
Tredinnick Corn 3 B8
Tredomen Powys 25 E8
Tredunnock Mon 15 B9
Tredustan Powys 25 E8
Treen Corn 2 G2
Treeton S Yorks 45 D8
Tref-y-Clawdd = Knighton Powys 25 A9
Trefaldwyn = Montgomery Powys 33 F8
Trefasser Pembs 22 C3
Trefdraeth Anglesey 40 C6
Trefdraeth = Newport Pembs 22 C5
Trefecca Powys 25 E8
Trefechan Ceredig 32 G1
Trefeglwys Powys 32 F5
Trefenter Ceredig 24 B3
Treffgarne Pembs 22 D4
Treffynnon = Holywell Flint 42 E4
Treffynnon Pembs 22 D3
Trefgarn Owen Pembs 22 D3
Trefil Bl Gwent 25 G8
Trefilan Ceredig 23 A10
Trefin Pembs 22 C3
Treflach Shrops 33 C8
Trefnanney Powys 33 D8
Trefnant Denb 42 E3
Trefonen Shrops 33 C8
Trefor Anglesey 40 B5
Trefor Gwyn 40 F5
Treforest Rhondda 14 C6
Trefriw Conwy 41 D9
Trefynwy = Monmouth Mon 26 G2
Tregadillett Corn 4 C3
Tregaian Anglesey 40 C6
Tregare Mon 25 G11
Tregaron Ceredig 24 C3
Tregarth Gwyn 41 D8
Tregeare Corn 4 C3
Tregeiriog Wrex 33 B7
Tregele Anglesey 40 A5
Tregidden Corn 3 G6
Treglemais Pembs 22 D3
Tregole Corn 4 B2
Tregonetha Corn 3 C8
Tregony Corn 3 E8
Tregoss Corn 3 C8
Tregoyd Powys 25 E9
Tregroes Ceredig 23 B9
Tregurrian Corn 3 C7
Tregynon Powys 33 F6
Trehafod Rhondda 14 B6
Treharris M Tydf 14 B6
Treherbert Rhondda 14 B5
Trekenner Corn 4 D4
Treknow Corn 4 C1
Trelan Corn 2 H6
Trelash Corn 4 B2
Trelassick Corn 3 D7
Trelawnyd Flint 42 E3
Trelech Carms 23 C7
Treleddyd-fawr Pembs 22 D2
Trelewis M Tydf 15 B7
Treligga Corn 4 C1
Trelights Corn 3 B8
Trelill Corn 3 B9
Trelissick Corn 3 F7
Trellech Mon 26 H2
Trelleck Grange Mon 15 A10
Trelogan Flint 42 D4
Trelystan Powys 33 E8
Tremadog Gwyn 41 F7
Tremail Corn 4 C2
Tremain Ceredig 23 B7
Tremaine Corn 4 C3
Tremar Corn 4 E3
Trematon Corn 4 F4
Tremeirchion Denb 42 E3
Trenance Corn 3 C7
Trenarren Corn 3 E9
Trench Telford 34 D2
Treneglos Corn 4 C3
Trenewan Corn 4 F2
Trent Dorset 8 C4
Trent Vale Stoke 34 A4
Trentham Stoke 34 A4
Trentishoe Devon 6 B5
Treoes V Glam 14 D5
Treorchy = Treorci Rhondda 14 B5
Treorci = Treorchy Rhondda 14 B5
Tre'r-ddôl Ceredig 32 F2
Trerulefoot Corn 4 F4
Tresaith Ceredig 23 A7
Tresawle Corn 3 E7
Trescott Staffs 34 F4
Trescowe Corn 2 F4
Tresham Glos 16 B4
Tresillian Corn 3 E7
Tresinwen Pembs 22 B4
Treskinnick Cross Corn 4 B3
Tresmeer Corn 4 C3
Tresparrett Corn 4 B2
Tresparrett Posts Corn 4 B2
Tressait Perth 75 A11
Tresta Shetland 96 D8
Tresta Shetland 96 H5
Treswell Notts 45 E11
Trethosa Corn 3 D8
Trethurgy Corn 3 D9
Tretio Pembs 22 D2
Tretire Hereford 26 F2
Tretower Powys 25 F8
Treuddyn Flint 42 G5
Trevalga Corn 4 C1
Trevalyn Wrex 43 G6
Trevanson Corn 3 B8
Trevarren Corn 3 C8
Trevarrian Corn 3 C7
Trevarrick Corn 3 E8
Trevaughan Carms 22 E6
Treveighan Corn 4 D1
Trevellas Corn 2 D6
Treverva Corn 3 F6
Trevethin Torf 15 A8
Trevigro Corn 4 E4
Treviscoe Corn 3 D8
Trevone Corn 3 B7
Trewarmett Corn 4 C1
Trewassa Corn 4 C2
Trewellard Corn 2 F2
Trewen Corn 4 C3
Trewennack Corn 2 G5
Trewern Powys 33 D8
Trewethern Corn 3 B9
Trewidland Corn 4 F3
Trewint Corn 4 B2
Trewint Corn 4 C3
Trewithian Corn 3 F7
Trewoofe Corn 2 G3
Trewoon Corn 3 D8
Treworga Corn 3 E7
Treworlas Corn 3 F7
Treyarnon Corn 3 B7
Treyford W Sus 11 C7
Trezaise Corn 3 D8
Triangle W Yorks 50 G6
Triffleton Pembs 22 D4
Trimdon Durham 58 C4
Trimdon Colliery Durham 58 C4
Trimdon Grange Durham 58 C4
Trimingham Norf 39 B8
Trimley Lower Street Suff 31 E9
Trimley St Martin Suff 31 E9
Trimley St Mary Suff 31 E9
Trimpley Worcs 34 H3
Trimsaran Carms 23 F9
Trimstone Devon 6 B3
Trinafour Perth 75 A10
Trinant Caerph 15 A8
Tring Herts 28 G6
Tring Wharf Herts 28 G6
Trinity Angus 77 A9
Trinity Jersey 11
Trisant Ceredig 32 H3
Trislaig Highld 80 F2
Trispen Corn 3 D7
Tritlington Northumb 63 D8
Trochry Perth 76 C2
Trodigal Argyll 65 F7
Troed-rhiwdalar Powys 24 C6
Troedyraur Ceredig 23 B8
Troedyrhiw M Tydf 14 A6
Tromode IoM 48 E3
Trondavoe Shetland 96 F5
Troon Corn 2 F5
Troon S Ayrs 66 C6
Trosaraidh W Isles 84 G2
Trossachs Hotel Stirling 75 G8
Troston Suff 30 A5
Trottiscliffe Kent 20 E3
Trotton W Sus 11 B7
Troutbeck Cumb 56 D5
Troutbeck Cumb 56 F6
Troutbeck Bridge Cumb 56 F6
Trow Green Glos 26 H2
Trowbridge Wilts 16 F5
Trowell Notts 35 B10
Trowle Common Wilts 16 F5
Trowley Bottom Herts 29 G7
Trows Borders 70 G5
Trowse Newton Norf 39 E8
Trudoxhill Som 16 G4
Trull Som 7 D11
Trumaisgearraidh W Isles 84 A3
Trumpan Highld 84 B7
Trumpet Hereford 26 E3
Trumpington Cambs 29 C11
Trunch Norf 39 B8
Trunnah Lancs 49 E3
Truro Corn 3 E7
Trusham Devon 5 C9
Trusley Derbys 35 B8
Trusthorpe Lincs 47 D9
Trysull Staffs 34 F4
Tubney Oxon 17 B11
Tuckenhay Devon 5 F9
Tuckhill Shrops 34 G3
Tuckingmill Corn 2 E5
Tuddenham Suff 30 A4
Tuddenham St Martin Suff 31 D8
Tudeley Kent 20 G3
Tudhoe Durham 58 C3
Tudorville Hereford 26 F2
Tudweiliog Gwyn 40 G4
Tuesley Sur 18 G6
Tuffley Glos 26 G5
Tufton Hants 17 G11
Tufton Pembs 22 D5
Tugby Leics 36 E3
Tugford Shrops 34 G1
Tullibardine Perth 76 F2
Tullibody Clack 75 H11
Tullich Argyll 73 B9
Tullich Highld 81 A8
Tullich Muir Highld 87 D10
Tulliemet Perth 76 B2
Tulloch Aberds 83 F9
Tulloch Aberds 89 E8
Tulloch Perth 76 E3
Tulloch Castle Highld 87 E8
Tullochgorm Argyll 73 D8
Tulloes Angus 77 C8
Tullybannocher Perth 75 E10
Tullybelton Perth 76 D3
Tullyfergus Perth 76 C5
Tullymurdoch Perth 76 B4
Tullynessle Aberds 83 B7
Tumble Carms 23 E10
Tumby Woodside Lincs 46 G6
Tummel Bridge Perth 75 B10
Tunga W Isles 91 D9
Tunstall E Yorks 53 F9
Tunstall Kent 20 E5
Tunstall Lancs 50 B2
Tunstall N Yorks 58 G3
Tunstall Norf 39 E10
Tunstall Stoke 44 G2
Tunstall Suff 31 C10
Tunstall T&W 58 A4
Tunstead Derbys 44 E5
Tunstead Gtr Man 44 B4
Tunstead Norf 39 C8
Tunworth Hants 18 G3
Tupsley Hereford 26 D2
Tupton Derbys 45 F7
Tur Langton Leics 36 F3
Turgis Green Hants 18 F3
Turin Angus 77 B8
Turkdean Glos 27 G8
Turleigh Wilts 16 E5
Turn Lancs 50 H4
Turnastone Hereford 25 E10
Turnberry S Ayrs 66 F5
Turnditch Derbys 44 H6
Turners Hill W Sus 12 C2
Turners Puddle Dorset 9 E7
Turnford Herts 19 A10
Turnhouse Edin 69 C10
Turnworth Dorset 9 D7
Turriff Aberds 89 C7
Turton Bottoms Blackburn 50 H3
Turves Cambs 37 F9
Turvey Bedford 28 C6
Turville Bucks 18 B4
Turville Heath Bucks 18 B4
Turweston Bucks 28 E3
Tushielaw Borders 61 B9
Tutbury Staffs 35 C8
Tutnall Worcs 26 A6
Tutshill Glos 15 B11
Tuttington Norf 39 C8
Tutts Clump W Berks 18 D2
Tuxford Notts 45 E11
Twatt Orkney 95 F3
Twatt Shetland 96 H5
Twechar E Dunb 68 C6
Tweedmouth Northumb 71 E8
Tweedsmuir Borders 60 A6
Twelve Heads Corn 3 E6
Twemlow Green Ches E 43 F10
Twenty Lincs 37 C7
Twerton Bath 16 E4
Twickenham London 19 D8
Twigworth Glos 26 F5
Twineham W Sus 12 E1
Twinhoe Bath 16 F4
Twinstead Essex 30 E5
Twinstead Green Essex 30 E5
Twiss Green Warr 43 C9
Twiston Lancs 50 E4
Twitchen Devon 7 C6
Twitchen Shrops 33 H9
Two Bridges Devon 5 D7
Two Dales Derbys 44 F6
Two Mills Ches W 42 E6
Twycross Leics 35 E9
Twyford Bucks 28 F3
Twyford Derbys 35 C9
Twyford Hants 10 B3
Twyford Leics 36 D3
Twyford Lincs 36 C5
Twyford Norf 38 C6
Twyford Wokingham 18 D4
Twyford Common Hereford 26 E2
Twyn-y-Sheriff Mon 25 H11
Twynholm Dumfries 55 D9
Twyning Glos 26 E5
Twyning Green Glos 26 E6
Twynllanan Carms 24 F4
Twynmynydd Carms 24 G3
Twywell Northants 36 H5
Ty-draw Conwy 41 E10
Ty-hen Carms 23 D8
Ty-hen Gwyn 40 G3
Ty-mawr Anglesey 40 B6
Ty Mawr Carms 23 B10
Ty Mawr Cwm Conwy 42 H2
Ty-nant Conwy 32 A5
Ty-nant Gwyn 32 C5
Ty-uchaf Powys 32 C6
Tyberton Hereford 25 E10
Tyburn W Mid 35 F7
Tycroes Carms 24 G3
Tycrwyn Powys 33 D7
Tydd Gote Lincs 37 D10
Tydd St Giles Cambs 37 D10
Tydd St Mary Lincs 37 D10
Tyddewi = St David's Pembs 22 D2
Tyddyn-mawr Gwyn 41 F7
Tye Green Essex 29 H11
Tye Green Essex 30 E2
Tye Green Essex 30 F4
Tyldesley Gtr Man 43 B9
Tyler Hill Kent 21 E8
Tylers Green Bucks 18 B6
Tylorstown Rhondda 14 B6
Tylwch Powys 32 G5
Tyn-y-celyn Wrex 33 B7
Tyn-y-coed Shrops 33 C8
Tyn-y-fedwen Powys 33 B7
Tyn-y-ffridd Powys 33 B7
Tyn-y-graig Powys 25 C7
Ty'n-y-groes Conwy 41 C9
Ty'n-y-maes Gwyn 41 D8
Tyn-y-pwll Anglesey 40 B6
Ty'n-yr-eithin Ceredig 24 B3
Tyncelyn Ceredig 24 B3
Tyndrum Stirling 74 D6
Tyne Tunnel T&W 63 G9
Tyneham Dorset 9 F7
Tynehead Midloth 70 E2
Tynemouth T&W 63 G9
Tynewydd Rhondda 14 B5
Tyninghame E Loth 70 C5
Tynron Dumfries 60 D4
Tynygongl Anglesey 41 B7
Tynygraig Ceredig 24 B3
Tŷ'r-felin-isaf Conwy 41 D10
Tyrie Aberds 89 B9
Tyringham M Keynes 28 D5
Tythecott Devon 6 E3
Tythegston Bridgend 14 D4
Tytherington Ches E 44 E3
Tytherington S Glos 16 C3
Tytherington Som 16 G4
Tytherington Wilts 16 G6
Tytherleigh Devon 8 D2
Tywardreath Corn 4 F1
Tywyn Conwy 41 C9
Tywyn Gwyn 32 E1

U

Uachdar W Isles 84 C2
Uags Highld 85 E12
Ubbeston Green Suff 31 A10
Ubley Bath 15 F11
Uckerby N Yorks 58 F3
Uckfield E Sus 12 D3
Uckington Glos 26 F6
Uddingston S Lanark 68 D5
Uddington S Lanark 69 G7
Udimore E Sus 13 E7
Udny Green Aberds 89 F8
Udny Station Aberds 89 F9
Udston S Lanark 68 E5
Udstonhead S Lanark 68 F6
Uffcott Wilts 17 D8
Uffculme Devon 7 E9
Uffington Lincs 37 E6
Uffington Oxon 17 C10
Uffington Shrops 33 D11
Ufford Pboro 37 E6
Ufford Suff 31 C9
Ufton Warks 27 B10
Ufton Nervet W Berks 18 E3
Ugadale Argyll 65 F8
Ugborough Devon 5 F7
Uggeshall Suff 39 G10
Ugglebarnby N Yorks 59 F9
Ughill S Yorks 44 C6
Ugley Essex 30 F2
Ugley Green Essex 30 F2
Ugthorpe N Yorks 59 E8
Uidh W Isles 84 J1
Uig Argyll 73 E10
Uig Highld 84 C6
Uig Highld 85 B8
Uigen W Isles 90 D5
Uigshader Highld 85 D9
Uisken Argyll 78 K6
Ulbster Highld 94 F5
Ulceby Lincs 47 E8
Ulceby N Lincs 46 A5
Ulceby Skitter N Lincs 46 A5
Ulcombe Kent 20 G5
Uldale Cumb 56 C4
Uley Glos 16 B4
Ulgham Northumb 63 D8
Ullapool Highld 86 B4
Ullenhall Warks 27 B8
Ullenwood Glos 26 G6
Ulleskelf N Yorks 51 E11
Ullesthorpe Leics 35 G11
Ulley S Yorks 45 D8
Ullingswick Hereford 26 D2
Ullinish Highld 85 E8
Ullock Cumb 56 D2
Ulnes Walton Lancs 49 H5
Ulpha Cumb 56 G3
Ulrome E Yorks 53 D7
Ulsta Shetland 96 E6
Ulva House Argyll 78 H7
Ulverston Cumb 49 B2
Ulwell Dorset 9 F9
Umberleigh Devon 6 D5
Unapool Highld 92 F5
Unasary W Isles 84 F2
Underbarrow Cumb 56 G6
Undercliffe W Yorks 51 F7
Underhoull Shetland 96 C7
Underriver Kent 20 F2
Underwood Notts 45 G8
Undy Mon 15 C10
Unifirth Shetland 96 H4
Union Cottage Aberds 83 D10
Union Mills IoM 48 E3
Union Street E Sus 12 C6
Unstone Derbys 45 E7
Unstone Green Derbys 45 E7
Unthank Cumb 56 C6
Unthank Cumb 57 B8
Unthank End Cumb 56 C6
Up Cerne Dorset 8 D5
Up Exe Devon 7 F8
Up Hatherley Glos 26 F6
Up Holland Lancs 43 B8
Up Marden W Sus 11 C6
Up Nately Hants 18 F3
Up Somborne Hants 10 A2
Up Sydling Dorset 8 D5
Upavon Wilts 17 F8
Upchurch Kent 20 E5
Upcott Hereford 25 C10
Upend Cambs 30 C3
Upgate Norf 39 D7
Uphall W Loth 69 C9
Uphall Station W Loth 69 C9
Upham Devon 7 F7
Upham Hants 10 B4
Uphampton Worcs 26 B5
Uphill N Som 15 F9
Uplawmoor E Renf 68 E3
Upleadon Glos 26 F4
Upleatham Redcar 59 E7
Uplees Kent 20 E6
Uploders Dorset 8 E4
Uplowman Devon 7 E9
Uplyme Devon 8 E2
Upminster London 20 C2
Upnor Medway 20 D4
Upottery Devon 7 F11
Upper Affcot Shrops 33 G10
Upper Ardchronie Highld 87 C9
Upper Arley Worcs 34 G3
Upper Arncott Oxon 28 G3
Upper Astrop Northants 28 E2
Upper Badcall Highld 92 E4
Upper Basildon W Berks 18 D2
Upper Beeding W Sus 11 C10
Upper Benefield Northants 36 G5
Upper Bighouse Highld 93 D11
Upper Boddington Northants 27 C11
Upper Borth Ceredig 32 G2
Upper Boyndlie Aberds 89 B9
Upper Brailes Warks 27 E10
Upper Breakish Highld 85 F11
Upper Breinton Hereford 25 D11
Upper Broadheath Worcs 26 C5
Upper Broughton Notts 36 C2
Upper Bucklebury W Berks 18 E2
Upper Burnhaugh Aberds 83 D10
Upper Caldecote C Beds 29 D8
Upper Catesby Northants 28 C2
Upper Chapel Powys 25 D7
Upper Church Village Rhondda 14 C6
Upper Chute Wilts 17 F9
Upper Clatford Hants 17 G10
Upper Clynnog Gwyn 40 F6
Upper Cumberworth W Yorks 44 B6
Upper Cwm-twrch Powys 24 G4
Upper Cwmbran Torf 15 B8
Upper Dallachy Moray 88 B3
Upper Dean Bedford 29 B7
Upper Denby W Yorks 44 B6
Upper Denton Cumb 62 G2
Upper Derraid Highld 87 H13
Upper Dicker E Sus 12 F4
Upper Dovercourt Essex 31 E9
Upper Druimfin Argyll 79 F8
Upper Dunsforth N Yorks 51 C10
Upper Eathie Highld 87 E10
Upper Elkstone Staffs 44 G4
Upper End Derbys 44 E4
Upper Farringdon Hants 18 H4
Upper Framilode Glos 26 G4
Upper Glenfintaig Highld 80 E4
Upper Gornal W Mid 34 F5
Upper Gravenhurst C Beds 29 E8
Upper Green Mon 25 G10
Upper Green W Berks 17 E10
Upper Grove Common Hereford 26 F2
Upper Hackney Derbys 44 F6
Upper Hale Sur 18 G5
Upper Halistra Highld 84 C7
Upper Halling Medway 20 E3
Upper Hambleton Rutland 36 E5
Upper Hardres Court Kent 21 F8
Upper Hartfield E Sus 12 C3
Upper Haugh S Yorks 45 C8
Upper Heath Shrops 34 G1
Upper Hellesdon Norf 39 D8
Upper Helmsley N Yorks 52 D2
Upper Hergest Hereford 25 C9
Upper Heyford Northants 28 C3
Upper Heyford Oxon 27 F11
Upper Hill Hereford 25 C11
Upper Hopton W Yorks 51 H7
Upper Horsebridge E Sus 12 E4
Upper Hulme Staffs 44 F4
Upper Inglesham Swindon 17 B9
Upper Inverbrough Highld 87 H11
Upper Killay Swansea 23 G10
Upper Knockando Moray 88 D1
Upper Lambourn W Berks 17 C10
Upper Leigh Staffs 34 B6
Upper Lenie Highld 81 A7
Upper Lochton Aberds 83 D8
Upper Longdon Staffs 35 D6
Upper Lybster Highld 94 G4
Upper Lydbrook Glos 26 G3
Upper Maes-coed Hereford 25 E10
Upper Midway Derbys 35 C8
Upper Milovaig Highld 84 D6
Upper Minety Wilts 17 B7
Upper Mitton Worcs 26 A5
Upper North Dean Bucks 18 B5
Upper Obney Perth 76 D3
Upper Ollach Highld 85 E10
Upper Padley Derbys 44 E6
Upper Pollicott Bucks 28 G4
Upper Poppleton York 52 D1
Upper Quinton Warks 27 D8
Upper Ratley Hants 10 B2
Upper Rissington Glos 27 G9
Upper Rochford Worcs 26 B3
Upper Sandaig Highld 85 G12
Upper Sanday Orkney 95 H6
Upper Sapey Hereford 26 B3
Upper Saxondale Notts 36 B2
Upper Seagry Wilts 16 C6
Upper Shelton C Beds 28 D6
Upper Sheringham Norf 39 A7
Upper Skelmorlie N Ayrs 73 G11
Upper Slaughter Glos 27 F8
Upper Soudley Glos 26 G3
Upper Stondon C Beds 29 E8
Upper Stowe Northants 28 C3
Upper Stratton Swindon 17 C8
Upper Street Hants 9 C10
Upper Street Norf 39 D9
Upper Street Norf 39 D9
Upper Street Suff 31 E8
Upper Strensham Worcs 26 E6
Upper Sundon C Beds 29 F7
Upper Swell Glos 27 F8
Upper Tean Staffs 34 B6
Upper Tillyrie Perth 76 G4
Upper Tooting London 19 D9
Upper Tote Highld 85 C10
Upper Town N Som 15 E11
Upper Treverward Shrops 33 H8
Upper Tysoe Warks 27 D10
Upper Upham Wilts 17 D9
Upper Wardington Oxon 27 D11
Upper Weald M Keynes 28 E4
Upper Weedon Northants 28 C3
Upper Wield Hants 18 H3
Upper Winchendon Bucks 28 G4
Upper Witton W Mid 35 F6
Upper Woodend Aberds 83 B8
Upper Woodford Wilts 17 H8
Upper Wootton Hants 18 F2
Upper Wyche Hereford 26 D4
Upperby Cumb 56 A6
Uppermill Gtr Man 44 B3
Uppersound Shetland 96 J6
Upperthong W Yorks 44 B5
Upperthorpe N Lincs 45 B11
Upperton W Sus 11 B8
Uppertown Derbys 45 F7
Uppertown Highld 94 C5
Uppertown Orkney 95 J5
Uppingham Rutland 36 F4
Uppington Shrops 34 E2
Upsall N Yorks 58 H5
Upshire Essex 19 A11
Upstreet Kent 21 E9
Upthorpe Suff 30 A6
Upton Cambs 37 H7
Upton Ches W 43 F7
Upton Corn 6 F1
Upton Dorset 8 F6
Upton Dorset 9 E8
Upton Hants 10 C2
Upton Hants 17 F10
Upton Leics 35 F9
Upton Lincs 46 D2
Upton Mers 42 D5
Upton Norf 39 D9
Upton Northants 28 B4
Upton Notts 45 E11
Upton Notts 45 G11
Upton Oxon 18 C2
Upton Pboro 37 E7
Upton Slough 18 D6
Upton Som 7 D8
Upton W Yorks 45 A8
Upton Bishop Hereford 26 F3
Upton Cheyney S Glos 16 E3
Upton Cressett Shrops 34 F2
Upton Cross Corn 4 D3
Upton Grey Hants 18 G3
Upton Hellions Devon 7 F7
Upton Lovell Wilts 16 G6
Upton Magna Shrops 34 D1
Upton Noble Som 16 H4
Upton Pyne Devon 7 G8
Upton St Leonard's Glos 26 G5
Upton Scudamore Wilts 16 G5
Upton Snodsbury Worcs 26 C6
Upton upon Severn Worcs 26 D5
Upton Warren Worcs 26 B6
Upwaltham W Sus 11 C8
Upware Cambs 30 A2
Upwell Norf 37 E10
Upwey Dorset 8 F5
Upwood Cambs 37 G8
Uradale Shetland 96 K6
Urafirth Shetland 96 F5
Urchfont Wilts 17 F7
Urdimarsh Hereford 26 D2
Ure Shetland 96 F4
Ure Bank N Yorks 51 B9
Urgha W Isles 90 H6
Urishay Common Hereford 25 E10
Urlay Nook Stockton 58 E4
Urmston Gtr Man 43 C10
Urpeth Durham 58 A3
Urquhart Highld 87 F8
Urquhart Moray 88 B2
Urra N Yorks 59 F6
Urray Highld 87 F8
Ushaw Moor Durham 58 B3
Usk = Brynbuga Mon 15 A9
Usselby Lincs 46 C4
Usworth T&W 63 H9
Utkinton Ches W 43 F8
Utley W Yorks 50 E6
Uton Devon 7 G7
Utterby Lincs 47 C7
Uttoxeter Staffs 35 B6
Uwchmynydd Gwyn 40 H3
Uxbridge London 19 C7
Uyeasound Shetland 96 C7
Uzmaston Pembs 22 E4

V

Valley Anglesey 40 C4
Valley Truckle Corn 4 C1
Valleyfield Dumfries 55 D9
Valsgarth Shetland 96 B8
Valtos Highld 85 B10
Van Powys 32 G5
Vange Essex 20 C4
Varteg Torf 25 H9
Vatten Highld 85 D7
Vaul Argyll 78 G3
Vaynor M Tydf 25 G7
Veensgarth Shetland 96 J6
Velindre Powys 25 E8
Vellow Som 7 C9
Veness Orkney 95 F6
Venn Green Devon 6 E2
Venn Ottery Devon 7 G9
Vennington Shrops 33 E9
Venny Tedburn Devon 7 G7
Ventnor IoW 10 G4
Vernham Dean Hants 17 F10
Vernham Street Hants 17 F10
Vernolds Common Shrops 33 G10
Verwood Dorset 9 D9
Veryan Corn 3 F8
Vicarage Devon 7 H11
Vickerstown Cumb 49 C1
Victoria Corn 3 C8
Victoria S Yorks 44 B5
Vidlin Shetland 96 G6
Viewpark N Lanark 68 D6
Vigo Village Kent 20 E3
Vinehall Street E Sus 13 D6
Vine's Cross E Sus 12 E4
Viney Hill Glos 26 H3
Virginia Water Sur 18 E6
Virginstow Devon 6 G2
Vobster Som 16 G4
Voe Shetland 96 E5
Voe Shetland 96 G6
Vowchurch Hereford 25 E10
Voxter Shetland 96 F5
Voy Orkney 95 G3

W

Wackerfield Durham 58 D2
Wacton Norf 39 F7
Wadbister Shetland 96 J6
Wadborough Worcs 26 D6
Waddesdon Bucks 28 G4
Waddingham Lincs 46 C3
Waddington Lancs 50 E3
Waddington Lincs 46 F3
Wadebridge Corn 3 B8
Wadeford Som 8 C2
Wadenhoe Northants 36 G6
Wadesmill Herts 29 G10
Wadhurst E Sus 12 C5
Wadshelf Derbys 45 E7
Wadsley S Yorks 45 C7
Wadsley Bridge S Yorks 45 C7
Wadworth S Yorks 45 C9
Waen Denb 42 F4
Waen Denb 42 F2
Waen Fach Powys 33 D8
Waen Goleugoed Denb 42 E3
Wag Highld 93 G13
Wainfleet All Saints Lincs 47 G8
Wainfleet Bank Lincs 47 G8
Wainfleet St Mary Lincs 47 G9
Wainfleet Tofts Lincs 47 G8
Wainhouse Corner Corn 4 B2
Wainscott Medway 20 D4
Wainstalls W Yorks 50 G6
Waitby Cumb 57 F9
Waithe Lincs 46 B6
Wake Lady Green N Yorks 59 G7
Wakefield W Yorks 51 G9
Wakerley Northants 36 F5
Wakes Colne Essex 30 F5
Walberswick Suff 31 A11
Walberton W Sus 11 D8
Walbottle T&W 63 G7
Walcot Lincs 37 B6
Walcot N Lincs 52 G4
Walcot Shrops 33 G9
Walcot Swindon 17 C8
Walcot Telford 34 D1
Walcot Green Norf 39 G7
Walcote Leics 36 G1
Walcote Warks 27 C8
Walcott Lincs 46 G5
Walcott Norf 39 B9
Walden N Yorks 50 A6
Walden Head N Yorks 50 A5
Walden Stubbs N Yorks 52 H1
Waldersey Cambs 37 E10
Walderslade Medway 20 E4
Walderton W Sus 11 C6
Walditch Dorset 8 E3
Waldley Derbys 35 B7
Waldridge Durham 58 A3
Waldringfield Suff 31 D9
Waldringfield Heath Suff 31 D9
Waldron E Sus 12 E4
Wales S Yorks 45 D8
Walesby Lincs 46 C5
Walesby Notts 45 E10
Walford Hereford 25 A10
Walford Hereford 26 F2
Walford Shrops 33 C10
Walford Heath Shrops 33 D10
Walgherton Ches E 43 H9
Walgrave Northants 28 A5
Walhampton Hants 10 E2
Walk Mill Lancs 50 F4
Walkden Gtr Man 43 B10
Walker T&W 63 G8
Walker Barn Ches E 44 E3
Walker Fold Lancs 50 E2
Walkerburn Borders 70 G2
Walkeringham Notts 45 C11
Walkerith Lincs 45 C11
Walkern Herts 29 F9
Walker's Green Hereford 26 D2
Walkerville N Yorks 58 G3
Walkford Dorset 9 E11
Walkhampton Devon 4 E6
Walkington E Yorks 52 F5
Walkley S Yorks 45 D7
Wall Northumb 62 G5
Wall Staffs 35 E7
Wall Bank Shrops 33 F11
Wall Heath W Mid 34 G4
Wall under Heywood Shrops 33 F11
Wallaceton Dumfries 60 E4
Wallacetown S Ayrs 66 D6
Wallacetown S Ayrs 66 F5
Wallands Park E Sus 12 E3
Wallasey Mers 42 C6
Wallcrouch E Sus 12 C5
Wallingford Oxon 18 C3
Wallington Hants 10 D4
Wallington Herts 29 E9
Wallington London 19 E9
Wallis Pembs 22 D5
Walliswood Sur 19 H8
Walls Shetland 96 J4
Wallsend T&W 63 G8
Wallston V Glam 15 D7
Wallyford E Loth 70 C2
Walmer Kent 21 F10
Walmer Bridge Lancs 49 G4
Walmersley Gtr Man 44 A2
Walmley W Mid 35 F7
Walpole Suff 31 A10
Walpole Cross Keys Norf 37 D11
Walpole Highway Norf 37 D11
Walpole Marsh Norf 37 D10
Walpole St Andrew Norf 37 D11
Walpole St Peter Norf 37 D11
Walsall W Mid 34 F6
Walsall Wood W Mid 34 E6
Walsden W Yorks 50 G5
Walsgrave on Sowe W Mid 35 G9
Walsham le Willows Suff 30 A6
Walshaw Gtr Man 43 A10
Walshford N Yorks 51 D10
Walsoken Cambs 37 D10
Walston S Lanark 69 F9
Walsworth Herts 29 E9
Walters Ash Bucks 18 B5
Walterston V Glam 14 D6
Walterstone Hereford 25 F10
Waltham Kent 21 G8
Waltham NE Lincs 46 B6
Waltham Abbey Essex 19 A10
Waltham Chase Hants 10 C4
Waltham Cross Herts 19 A10
Waltham on the Wolds Leics 36 C4
Waltham St Lawrence Windsor 18 D5
Walthamstow London 19 C10
Walton Cumb 61 G11
Walton Derbys 45 F7
Walton Leics 36 G1
Walton M Keynes 28 E5
Walton Mers 42 C6
Walton Pboro 37 E7
Walton Powys 25 C9
Walton Som 15 H10
Walton Staffs 34 B4
Walton Suff 31 E9
Walton Telford 34 D1
Walton W Yorks 51 E10
Walton W Yorks 51 H9
Walton Warks 27 C9
Walton Cardiff Glos 26 E6
Walton East Pembs 22 D5
Walton-in-Gordano N Som 15 D10
Walton-le-Dale Lancs 50 G1
Walton-on-Thames Sur 19 E8
Walton on the Hill Staffs 34 C5
Walton on the Hill Sur 19 F9
Walton-on-the-Naze Essex 31 F9
Walton on the Wolds Leics 36 D1
Walton-on-Trent Derbys 35 D8
Walton West Pembs 22 E3
Walwen Flint 42 E5
Walwick Northumb 62 F5
Walworth Darl 58 E3
Walworth Gate Darl 58 D3
Walwyn's Castle Pembs 22 E3
Wambrook Som 8 D1
Wanborough Sur 18 G6
Wanborough Swindon 17 C9
Wandsworth London 19 D9
Wangford Suff 39 H10
Wanlockhead Dumfries 60 B4
Wansford E Yorks 53 D6
Wansford Pboro 37 F6
Wanstead London 19 C11
Wanstrow Som 16 G4
Wanswell Glos 16 A3
Wantage Oxon 17 C10
Wapley S Glos 16 D4
Wappenbury Warks 27 B10
Wappenham Northants 28 D3
Warbleton E Sus 12 E5
Warblington Hants 10 D6
Warborough Oxon 18 B2
Warboys Cambs 37 G9
Warbreck Blackpool 49 F3
Warbstow Corn 4 B3
Warburton Gtr Man 43 D10
Warcop Cumb 57 E9
Ward End W Mid 35 G7
Ward Green Suff 31 B7
Warden Kent 21 D7
Warden Northumb 62 G5
Wardhill Orkney 95 F7
Wardington Oxon 27 D11
Wardlaw Borders 61 B8
Wardle Ches E 43 G9
Wardle Gtr Man 50 H5
Wardley Rutland 36 E4
Wardlow Derbys 44 E5
Wardy Hill Cambs 37 G10
Ware Herts 29 G10
Ware Kent 21 E9
Wareham Dorset 9 F8
Warehorne Kent 13 C8
Waren Mill Northumb 71 G10
Warenford Northumb 71 H10
Warenton Northumb 71 G10
Wareside Herts 29 G10
Waresley Cambs 29 C9
Waresley Worcs 26 A5
Warfield Brack 18 D5
Warfleet Devon 5 F9
Wargrave Wokingham 18 D4
Warham Norf 38 A5
Warhill Gtr Man 44 C3
Wark Northumb 62 F4
Wark Northumb 71 G7
Warkleigh Devon 6 D5
Warkton Northants 36 H4
Warkworth Northants 27 D11
Warkworth Northumb 63 C8
Warlaby N Yorks 58 G4
Warland W Yorks 50 G5
Warleggan Corn 4 E2
Warlingham Sur 19 F10
Warmfield W Yorks 51 G9
Warmingham Ches E 43 F10
Warmington Northants 37 F6
Warmington Warks 27 D11
Warminster Wilts 16 G5
Warmlake Kent 20 F5
Warmley S Glos 16 D3
Warmley Tower S Glos 16 D3
Warmonds Hill Northants 28 B6
Warmsworth S Yorks 45 B9
Warmwell Dorset 9 F6
Warndon Worcs 26 C5
Warnford Hants 10 B5
Warnham W Sus 11 A10
Warninglid W Sus 11 B11
Warren Ches E 44 E2
Warren Pembs 22 G4
Warren Heath Suff 31 D9
Warren Row Windsor 18 C5
Warren Street Kent 20 F6
Warrington M Keynes 28 C5
Warrington Warr 43 D9
Warsash Hants 10 D3
Warslow Staffs 44 G4
Warter E Yorks 52 D4
Warthermarske N Yorks 51 B8
Warthill N Yorks 52 D2
Wartling E Sus 12 F5
Wartnaby Leics 36 C3
Warton Lancs 49 B4
Warton Lancs 49 G4
Warton Northumb 62 C6
Warton Warks 35 E8
Warwick Warks 27 B9
Warwick Bridge Cumb 61 H10
Warwick on Eden Cumb 61 H10
Wasbister Orkney 95 E4
Wasdale Head Cumb 56 F3
Wash Common W Berks 17 E11
Washaway Corn 3 C9
Washbourne Devon 5 F8
Washfield Devon 7 E8
Washfold N Yorks 58 F1
Washford Som 7 B9
Washford Pyne Devon 7 E7
Washingborough Lincs 46 E4
Washington T&W 63 H9
Washington W Sus 11 C10
Wasing W Berks 18 E2
Waskerley Durham 58 B1
Wasperton Warks 27 C9
Wasps Nest Lincs 46 F4
Wass N Yorks 52 B1
Watchet Som 7 B9
Watchfield Oxon 17 B9
Watchfield Som 15 G9
Watchgate Cumb 57 G7
Watchhill Cumb 56 B3
Watcombe Torbay 5 E10
Watendlath Cumb 56 E4
Water Devon 5 C8
Water Lancs 50 G4
Water End E Yorks 52 F3
Water End Herts 19 A9
Water End Herts 29 G7
Water Newton Cambs 37 F7
Water Orton Warks 35 F7
Water Stratford Bucks 28 E3
Water Yeat Cumb 56 H4
Waterbeach Cambs 29 B11
Waterbeck Dumfries 61 F8
Waterden Norf 38 B4
Waterfall Staffs 44 G4
Waterfoot E Renf 68 E4
Waterfoot Lancs 50 G4
Waterford Hants 10 E2
Waterford Herts 29 G10
Waterhead Cumb 56 F5
Waterhead Dumfries 61 D7
Waterheads Borders 69 E11
Waterhouses Durham 58 B2
Waterhouses Staffs 44 G4
Wateringbury Kent 20 F3
Waterloo Gtr Man 44 B3
Waterloo Highld 85 F11
Waterloo Mers 42 C6
Waterloo N Lanark 69 E7
Waterloo Norf 39 D8
Waterloo Perth 76 D3
Waterloo Poole 9 E9
Waterloo Shrops 33 B11
Waterloo Port Gwyn 40 D6
Waterlooville Hants 10 D5
Watermeetings S Lanark 60 B5
Watermillock Cumb 56 D6
Waterperry Oxon 28 H3
Waterrow Som 7 D9
Water's Nook Gtr Man 43 B9
Waters Upton Telford 34 D2
Watersfield W Sus 11 C9
Waterside Aberds 89 F10
Waterside Blackburn 50 G3
Waterside Cumb 56 B4
Waterside E Ayrs 67 B7
Waterside E Ayrs 67 F7
Waterside E Dunb 68 C5
Waterside E Renf 68 E4
Waterstock Oxon 28 H3
Waterston Pembs 22 F4
Watford Herts 19 B8
Watford Northants 28 B3
Watford Gap Staffs 35 E7
Wath N Yorks 51 B9
Wath N Yorks 51 C7
Wath N Yorks 52 B2
Wath Brow Cumb 56 E2
Wath upon Dearne S Yorks 45 B8
Watlington Norf 38 D2
Watlington Oxon 18 B3
Watnall Notts 45 H9
Watten Highld 94 E4
Wattisfield Suff 31 A7
Wattisham Suff 31 C7
Wattlesborough Heath Shrops 33 D9
Watton E Yorks 52 D6
Watton Norf 38 E5
Watton at Stone Herts 29 G10
Wattston N Lanark 68 C6
Wattstown Rhondda 14 B6
Wauchan Highld 80 E1
Waulkmill Lodge Orkney 95 H4
Waun Powys 32 E4
Waun-y-clyn Carms 23 F9
Waunarlwydd Swansea 14 B2
Waunclunda Carms 24 E3
Waunfawr Gwyn 41 E7
Waungron Swansea 23 F10
Waunlwyd Bl Gwent 25 H8
Wavendon M Keynes 28 E6
Waverbridge Cumb 56 B4
Waverton Ches W 43 F7
Waverton Cumb 56 B4
Wavertree Mers 43 D6
Wawne E Yorks 53 F6
Waxham Norf 39 C10
Waxholme E Yorks 53 G9
Way Kent 21 E10
Way Village Devon 7 E7
Wayfield Medway 20 E4
Wayford Som 8 D3
Waymills Shrops 34 A1
Wayne Green Mon 25 G11
Wdig = Goodwick Pembs 22 C4
Weachyburn Aberds 89 C6
Weald Oxon 17 A10
Wealdstone London 19 C8
Weardley W Yorks 51 E8
Weare Som 15 F10
Weare Giffard Devon 6 D3
Wearhead Durham 57 C10
Weasdale Cumb 57 F8
Weasenham All Saints Norf 38 C4
Weasenham St Peter Norf 38 C4
Weatherhill Sur 12 B2
Weaverham Ches W 43 E9
Weaverthorpe N Yorks 52 B5
Webheath Worcs 27 B7
Wedderlairs Aberds 89 E8
Wedderlie Borders 70 E5
Weddington Warks 35 F9
Wedhampton Wilts 17 F7
Wedmore Som 15 G10
Wednesbury W Mid 34 F5
Wednesfield W Mid 34 E5
Weedon Bucks 28 G5
Weedon Bec Northants 28 C3
Weedon Lois Northants 28 D3
Weeford Staffs 35 E7
Week Devon 7 E6
Week St Mary Corn 4 B3
Weeke Hants 10 A3
Weekley Northants 36 G4
Weel E Yorks 53 F6
Weeley Essex 31 F8
Weeley Heath Essex 31 F8
Weem Perth 75 C11
Weeping Cross Staffs 34 C5
Weethley Gate Warks 27 C7
Weeting Norf 38 G3
Weeton E Yorks 53 G9
Weeton Lancs 49 F3